MANAGERIAL ACCOUNTING

The Robert N. Anthony/Willard J. Graham Series in Accounting

MANAGERIAL ACCOUNTING

Calvin Engler, Ph.D., CPA, CCA

Professor of Accounting
Iona College

1987

IRWIN

Homewood, Illinois 60430

Materials from the Certificate in Management Accounting
Examinations, Copyright © 1972, 1973, 1974, 1975, 1976, 1977, 1978,
1979, 1980, 1981, 1982, 1983, and 1984 by the National Association
of Accountants are reprinted and/or adapted with permission.

Material from Uniform CPA Examination Questions and Unofficial
Answers, copyright © 1964, 1965, 1969, 1970, 1971, 1972, 1973, 1974,
1975, 1976, 1977, 1978, 1979, 1980, 1981, 1982, 1983, 1984, 1985 by
the American Institute of Certified Public Accountants, Inc., is
reprinted (or adapted) with permission.

ISBN 0-256-03318-8

Library of Congress Catalog Card No. 86–81610

Printed in the United States of America

1 2 3 4 5 6 7 8 9 0 V 4 3 2 1 0 9 8 7

To my parents and my wife, Phyllis

PREFACE

A knowledge of managerial accounting is essential for all aspiring accountants and managers of businesses and nonprofit entities. This text will help these individuals acquire the knowledge necessary to be successful in their chosen careers. It is presumed that students have already completed a course on the essentials of financial accounting.

Although this text was designed for a one-semester, undergraduate course, this text is sufficiently flexible that it can be used in a graduate course where no prior knowledge of managerial accounting is required. Also, the text may be used in those schools that follow a trimester or quarter system. The instructor's manual contains suggested course outlines for each of these programs.

Managers are concerned with the five major functions of management: (1) planning, (2) controlling, (3) organizing, (4) staffing, and (5) motivating. Since all of these functions deal with decision making, managers must have certain kinds of accounting information and then understand how to use this information. This book is designed to help aspiring managers acquire the knowledge needed to select and use the accounting information necessary for managerial decision making.

To provide students with a meaningful learning experience, the text is organized as follows:

1. At the beginning of each chapter the learning objectives of that chapter are stated to tell the students what they will learn.
2. Each topic is introduced by defining the key terms associated with that topic. All key terms in the chapter are printed in bold face type.
3. Each topic is discussed by first presenting the simplest aspects and then further developing the topic using a building block approach. Where necessary, the steps needed to prepare usable information are listed and discussed prior to the preparation of that information.
4. At the end of each chapter, there is a comprehensive summary of the chapter. Most of the key terms used in the chapter are discussed in the summary and are printed in bold face type.

5.   To give instructors latitude in selecting topical coverage, difficult and enriched topics are placed in appendixes at the end of the chapter. One example of an enrichment topic is "The Human Factors of Budgetary Planning and Control." All appendixes are independent of the chapter, and there is no interruption of the chapter's continuity if an instructor chooses not to use an appendix.

6.   In those chapters that require journal entries to illustrate a topic, these entries are minimal within the chapter. In general, an attempt has been made to defer journal entries to end-of-chapter Appendixes. The instructor then has the flexibility to decide whether to cover the journal entries without losing the continuity of the subject matter.

7.   Key concepts discussed in a chapter are tabulated at the end of that chapter. Also, the uses and applications of these concepts together with the kinds of information needed to reach a decision using the concept are shown.

8.   All key terms appear in a glossary at the end of each chapter. The definitions are similar to those found in the chapter. Over 350 key terms are defined in the glossaries.

9.   The end-of-chapter exercises and problems contain a rich variety of material ranging from simple to challenging. Many of these problems were specifically designed to accompany the text coverage. In addition, other problems were carefully selected from problems on professional examinations and are identified as AICPA or CMA adapted.

ORGANIZATION OF THE TEXT

The text is organized into three parts. Chapter 1 introduces these three major divisions. It also discusses the nature and objectives of management accounting. The first division, Part 1, discusses the essentials of managerial accounting and is subdivided into chapters that discuss: (1) cost definitions and concepts, (2) job order costing, (3) process costing, (4) cost behavior, and (5) cost, volume, and profit analysis and relationships. The second major division, Part 2, discusses planning and control and is subdivided into chapters that discuss: (1) the master budget, (2) standard costing and performance evaluation for direct materials and direct labor, (3) flexible budgeting and manufacturing overhead analysis, (4) the contribution approach to segment reporting, (5) relevant data for decision making, (6) capital budgeting, (7) income tax effects on capital budgeting decisions, and (8) decentralized operations and transfer pricing. The third major division discusses selected additional topics and is subdivided into chapters that discuss: (1) selected quantitative methods for managers that include linear programming, inventory planning and control (economic order quantity, lead time, and safety stock), expected value, and payoff tables, (2) the statement of changes in financial position, and (3) financial statement analysis.

TEACHING AIDS   Various teaching aids are available to adopters of the book. In addition to the Instructor's Manual, the following are available:

1. Overhead transparencies provide instructors with a visual representation of assorted topics.
2. The Study Guide, an integral part of the teaching package, is designed to help students move above the level of the average student in the course. The material for each chapter includes: an introduction to that chapter, a chapter outline, and approximately 30 questions. Depending on the chapter, these questions include True/False, Multiple Choice, short Exercises and some Matching questions.
3. The test bank has over 1,000 items arranged in three levels of difficulty. The first level of questions is similar to the examples in the text. The second level has more difficult questions while the third level has questions that are AICPA or CMA adapted.
4. A computerized software package increases the flexibility of the pedagogical approach to learning managerial accounting.
5. Check figures for the solution of textual material are available for instructors and students.

**ACKNOWLEDG-
MENTS**

There are many individuals who have contributed their expertise to improve the first draft of this book, and I am especially grateful to them. My first and foremost debt, however, is to University Distinguished Professor Emanuel Saxe. I was extremely privileged to have been his student and I am most fortunate to count him as one of my dearest friends. He painstakingly read this manuscript and made numerous suggestions for improving the initial draft. Only those individuals fortunate enough to have been exposed to his special analytical reviews can appreciate the impact of his contribution.

I am also grateful to one of my dearest friends and coauthor on another work, Leopold A. Bernstein, for his permission to rework portions of his book, Financial Statement Analysis, for use in Chapters 16 and 17 of this work. His analytical review of these resulting chapters is greatly appreciated.

Numerous other individuals have made contributions to this work. I am grateful to John G. Driscoll, President of Iona College, who generously gave his time during the incubation stage of this text and encouraged me to proceed with this project. Charles F. O'Donnell, Dean of the Hagan School of Business, provided me with moral support and was instrumental in securing my release time from teaching so that I could complete this project. Daniel K. Kast, the former chairperson of Iona's accounting department, also encouraged me to proceed with this project and was extremely cooperative during the writing phase of this book.

Of the many individuals who reviewed all or part of this book, I am especially grateful to Anthony P. Curatola of Louisiana State University and Kenneth P. Sinclair of Lehigh University. Their thorough and painstaking reviews provided me with valuable suggestions which were incorporated in the text. Anthony P. Curatola also deserves a special thanks for preparing the test bank and study guide that is available to users of this text.

Other reviewers who made valuable contributions to this work include Abdel Agami of Old Dominion University, David M. Buehlmann of the University of Nebraska at Omaha, J. Stephen Collins of Boston College, Paul Keat of IBM and Pace University, and my esteemed colleague at Iona College, Donald Moscato.

Students at Iona College who assisted me with the testing of the problem material and in the preparation of the solutions to the problems are Deborah Costello, Janet Lynch, and Geoffrey Shelton. The enormous typing task fell to Freda Strauss of Wordpro and she deserves many thanks for adhering to the typing schedule.

Permission has been received from the Institute of Management Accounting of the National Association of Accountants to use questions and/or unofficial answers from past CMA examinations.

No work of this magnitude can be completed without enormous sacrifices by the writer's family, and this is certainly true in my case. I am fortunate that my family fully understood the demands that the writing of this manuscript made on my leisure time. In addition, my wife, Phyllis, took time away from her own professional pursuits to provide me with invaluable editorial and proofreading assistance throughout the development of this book. My children, Linda and Mitchell, assisted me with proofreading various portions of the text and as college students, provided me with their reactions to the pedagogical treatment used in this book. I will always be grateful for the understanding and help my family has given me.

Of course, the work on a text is never truly complete. There is always room for polishing and revision. I welcome comments from adopters and others who can help me to improve this text in subsequent editions.

Calvin Engler

CONTENTS

PART 3 ADDITIONAL SELECTED TOPICS

MANAGERIAL ACCOUNTING

1

THE NATURE AND OBJECTIVES OF MANAGERIAL ACCOUNTING

LEARNING OBJECTIVES

After reading this chapter, you should be able to:

1 List the differences between financial accounting information and managerial accounting information.

2 Define the roles that planning, controlling, organizing, staffing, and motivating play in an organization.

3 Differentiate between quantitative information and qualitative information.

4 Construct a company organization chart.

5 Explain how lines of responsibility and delegation of authority affect an organization.

6 Differentiate between line and staff functions in organizations.

7 Construct an organization chart for the controller's function.

8 Explain the purposes of organizational goals and strategic planning.

9 Explain why feedback is necessary and how it contributes to the planning and control cycle.

10 Explain why decision making is the most important managerial function.

11 Identify the kinds of decisions managers make and the kinds of information managers need for decision-making purposes.

12 Differentiate between the CPA license and the CMA designation.

Accounting is the process of recording, classifying, summarizing, and reporting transactions and events of a financial nature, and interpreting the results. **Managerial accounting** is one area of accounting that specializes in providing information that the managers of an organization will find useful for the purposes of internal decision making. Thus, a firm's internal accounting information system should (1) enable managers to plan for the operations of their business, (2) include processes that enable managers to assess how effectively their plans are being implemented, (3) provide the data needed to control operations, and (4) provide the data needed for decision making. Of necessity, *some* information that managers need is historical in nature, but most of it is either very recent or future oriented.

FINANCIAL ACCOUNTING VERSUS MANAGERIAL ACCOUNTING

Financial Accounting

While managerial accounting serves a firm's internal needs by providing recent and future-oriented information, the focus of **financial accounting** is primarily on historical reports. The information that financial accountants compile is intended primarily for external use by investors, creditors, potential investors, employees and their unions, government agencies, and others. The information provided to these groups usually consists of the results of operations for a period of time (an income statement), the financial position of the organization at a specific point in time (a balance sheet), and a statement of changes in financial position for the period of operations under examination.

Financial accounting is regulated in an attempt to ensure that the resulting reports are understandable, reliable, and relatively consistent between comparable reporting periods. The principal regulatory body is the Securities and Exchange Commission (SEC). In addition, the American Institute of Certified Public Accountants (AICPA) sets ethical standards for the accounting profession, while the Financial Accounting Standards Board (FASB), an independent standard-setting body, sets procedural standards.

The FASB's pronouncements on accounting matters have come to be recognized as *generally accepted accounting principles (GAAP)*. As a result of the SEC's and the AICPA's efforts, all of a firm's financial statements must meet minimum standards of disclosure and show a degree of uniformity in the reporting of transactions that are the same or similar. Of necessity, the information must be summarized in the financial statements—rather than reported in full—because so many transactions occur during the course of a reporting period. However, user groups disagree on the amount and kind of information and disclosures that should be presented. To ensure adherence to GAAP, companies must hire public accounting firms to review their financial statements. The review procedure is conducted in a manner that meets generally accepted auditing standards (GAAS) as developed and codified by the AICPA.

The Nature of Managerial Accounting

Since managerial accounting serves internal purposes, it is not constrained by government regulations and generally accepted accounting principles. Instead, managerial accountants are free to generate any information that managers will find useful. To the extent possible, managerial accounting should provide information that will aid managers in carrying out their five basic duties:

1. **Planning**—Deciding what objectives to pursue during a future time period and what to do in order to achieve those objectives.

2. **Controlling**—Measuring performance against objectives, determining causes of deviations, and taking corrective action when necessary.

3. **Organizing**—Grouping activities, assigning activities, and providing the authority to carry out the activities.

4. **Staffing**—Determining human resource needs, recruiting, selecting, training, and developing human resources.

5. **Motivating**—Directing and channeling human behavior toward the accomplishment of objectives.[1]

These duties will be discussed in greater detail later in this chapter.

To be useful, managerial accounting information must be as reliable as possible, and when estimates are provided, they must be based on sound estimating practices. Thus, a management accountant must have some familiarity with statistical theory, probability theory, mathematics, and computer applications.

In addition to accounting information, managers use data provided by engineers, economists, mathematicians, sales and marketing specialists, psychologists, and others. The management accountant is but one member of a broad-based management team.

Illustration 1–1 summarizes and contrasts the differences and similarities between managerial and financial accounting.

INFORMATION FOR DECISION MAKERS

Sound **decision making**—the process of searching the environment for conditions that require attention, developing and analyzing possible responses, and selecting an appropriate course of action—is crucial to the success of any enterprise. Managers of businesses and not-for-profit organizations make many decisions in the course of their duties. These decisions run the gamut from how many units of a particular product to manufacture on a particular day to the kinds of products the company should produce in the coming decades and how to produce them. As a result, the information that managers require to make these decisions is varied. Much of the information is **quantitative**—that is, numerical in nature—and can be obtained either from the company's books and records or from industry statistics. Most kinds of quantitative information are estimated and may be based on statistical probability

---

[1] Leslie W. Rue and Lloyd L. Byars, *Management: Theory and Application,* 3d ed. (Homewood, Ill.: Richard D. Irwin, 1983), p. 11.

ILLUSTRATION 1–1   Differences and Similarities—Managerial and Financial Accounting

		Managerial Accounting	Financial Accounting
1.	Users of data.	Managers of the firm.	Outsiders—stockholders, investors, creditors, financial analysts, government, and employee unions.
2.	Record-keeping and reporting.	Not mandatory.	Mandatory—reporting to stockholders, regulatory commissions, and governmental agencies.
3.	Standards of reporting.	None.	Prescribed by the FASB, SEC, AICPA, and other regulatory agencies.
4.	Kind of information presented.	Recent actual data and estimated, future-oriented data.	Verifiable, typically historical data.
5.	Data's frame of reference.	Product lines, geographic territories, and production departments.	Company as a whole, with *some* segmented disclosure, but not in the same detail as in managerial accounting.
6.	Providers of information.	Managerial accountants, engineers, economists, mathematicians, sales and marketing specialists, and psychologists.	Financial accountants and independent auditors.
7.	Data format.	Any forms that managers find useful. No constraints.	Some flexibility within the constraints imposed by the SEC, FASB, and AICPA.

distributions or simulated models. In addition, information of a nonquantitative nature—or **qualitative information**—must also be factored into decision making. Because qualitative information is difficult to include with quantitative information, the decision-making process can become complicated.

Quantitative Information.   Most of the quantitative information that managers need can be provided by the management accountant. For example, a manager who is contemplating the remanufacture of a product that has not been made for a period of time will require two primary pieces of information: (1) the expected selling price of the product and (2) the expected cost of manufacturing the product. The management accountant, a member of the management team, would consult company records and report the cost of raw materials when the product was made previously, as well as past wages, required hours, and other *relevant* historical data. **Historical data** are numerical pieces of information based on past events. In addition, the management accountant would report the present wage rates for required labor, the present—actual or estimated—cost of raw materials, and other *relevant* current information. **Current data** are numerical bits of information applicable to the immediate future. Based on these data, the management accountant would be able to calculate the estimated current cost of manufacturing the product. In addition, the sales manager would be asked to provide estimates of the product's selling price based on competition and marketing strategies. A decision would then be made about whether to proceed with the manufacture of the product.

Other kinds of decisions that managers make and the kinds of quantitative information they require appear in Illustration 1–2. Although this list is not all inclusive, it illustrates that managers rely heavily on management accountants to supply the information they need to make decisions that will affect their company's financial success.

Qualitative Information.   Not all information needed for decision making is quantitative. Even though qualitative information cannot be reduced to numerical values, it can be very important. For example, if a manager is contemplating the installation of custom-made draperies in all executive offices, the cost can be measured quantitatively. But aside from the draperies' possible effect on the cost of heating, the benefits that the firm will derive

ILLUSTRATION 1–2   Kinds of Decisions and Related Quantitative Information Needed

Kinds of Decisions	Kinds of Quantitative Information Needed
1. Purchasing new equipment.	The cost of the new equipment; the costs saved by the new equipment.
2. Replacing old equipment.	The cost of the new equipment; the difference in operating costs between the old and the new equipment; the selling price of the old equipment.
3. Entering a new market.	Revenues and costs of entering the market.
4. Discontinuing a product.	Revenues lost and costs saved by discontinuing the product.
5. Making or buying component parts.	The costs of making the part; the cost of purchasing the part.
6. Expanding production of an existing product.	The additional revenues from expansion; the additional costs from expansion.
7. Decreasing production of an existing product.	The revenues lost and the costs saved by decreasing production.
8. Taking special orders at less than full cost.	Additional revenues and additional costs of the special order.
9. Product pricing.	Costs of producing the product.
10. Selling joint products at a split-off point or processing further.	Additional processing costs and additional revenues from further processing.
11. Purchasing an existing business.	Revenues generated and costs incurred as a result of the purchase.

from their installation are impossible to measure quantitatively. Assume, for instance, that based on a visit to an accounting firm's offices, a potential client decides to hire that firm. Measuring how much of the client's decision was based on the draperies and how much was based on discussions with the firm's partner is impossible. However, some value must be assigned to items such as draperies, carpeting, and impressive furniture. If not, there would be no purpose in incurring these costs when bare windows and floors and a simple desk and chair would accomplish the same result.

Other examples of qualitative information are:

1. The effect that the implementation of a nonunion negotiated pension plan has on employee productivity.

2. The effect that the automation of labor-intensive operations has on employee morale.

3. The effect that basing promotions on merit rather than on longevity has on employee morale.

4. The effect that keeping inventories low and allowing frequent stockouts to occur has on customer goodwill. (Note, however, that the lost profit on the lost sale can be measured quantitatively.)

5. The effect that the consideration of temporary layoffs has on employee morale.

6. The effect that busy telephone switchboards or asking customers to hold the line for long periods of time has on customer goodwill.

7. The effect that employees' rudeness to customers has on customer goodwill.

As the partial list suggests, managers must consider many kinds of qualitative information before making decisions.

ORGANIZATIONS AND THEIR STRUCTURE

A review of typical organizational structures can give some insight into the informational needs of management and the interrelationship of managers and management accountants. While basic organizational principles are usually thought of in terms of profit-oriented businesses, they are equally valid for not-for-profit entities such as hospitals, colleges, and community-service organizations.

Organization Charts

To ensure smooth operations, most firms are organized along specified lines of authority. In a very small firm, one leader can single-handedly run the company and make all necessary decisions. But as an organization grows, it becomes increasingly difficult for one individual to keep track of all pertinent information and make all decisions. As more people become involved in decision making, decentralization occurs. Most business experts agree that decisions should be made by the level of management that is closest to the situation. For example, if a decision must be made to allow some employees to work overtime on a particular day, the supervisor of that department should select the workers. The supervisor knows the affected individuals and would be best placed to select those with the required skills. The president of the company would rarely participate in such decisions. Instead, the president would usually focus on decisions that affect the company as a whole. Day-to-day decision making is usually delegated to lower level managers.

As companies become more decentralized, they often construct **organization charts** to define the structure of their organization, its breakdown into departments, and the resulting lines of authority. Illustration 1–3 depicts the organization chart for the Heart-Marks Corporation, a national retail chain. The chain has two major segments, the north region and the south region. Note that the board of directors is at the top of the hierarchy. They delegate authority—the responsibility for operating the corporation—to the president, who in turn delegates specific authorities to the vice presidents, and so on down the line. **Delegation of authority** includes (1) assigning duties

ILLUSTRATION 1–3   Organization Chart for Heart-Marks Corporation

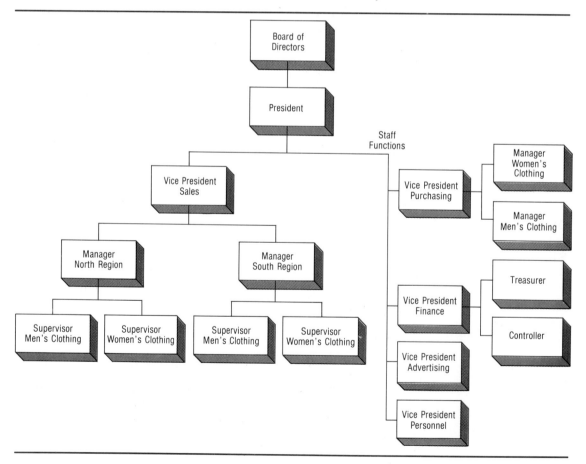

to immediate subordinates; (2) granting subordinates permission to make commitments, use resources, and take all actions necessary to perform the duties assigned; and (3) making the subordinate responsible for performing the duties in a satisfactory manner.[2]

The organization chart shown in Illustration 1–3 is relatively simple and merely represents one possible configuration. In contrast, an organization chart for a giant corporation may require hundreds of pages. One purpose of an organization chart is to indicate **lines of authority,** which are the paths responsibility takes as it is passed down from managers to subordinates. The following lines of authority can be seen in Illustration 1–3:

1. There are four supervisors of clothing. One supervisor of men's clothing and one supervisor of women's clothing report to the manager of the north region. The other two supervisors report to the manager of the south region.

2. Both the manager of the north region and the manager of the south region report to the vice president of sales.

3. Both the treasurer and the controller report to the vice president of finance.

4. All five vice presidents report to the president, who in turn reports to the board of directors.

The organization chart also clarifies line and staff functions.

Line Functions. Workers in **line functions** perform the primary business tasks for which the company was organized. For example, in a merchandising establishment, managers in line functions would perform jobs related to selling the organization's products. In a manufacturing company, managers in line functions would deal with the manufacture and sale of the organization's products.

Staff Functions. Workers in **staff functions** perform ancillary, or support, services for the people in line positions. Thus, in Illustration 1–3, purchasing, finance, advertising, and personnel are considered staff functions because they provide support services to the people involved in the actual selling of clothes. A staff function in one organization may be a line function in another organization. For example, the purchasing function is usually a staff function in most business organizations. But, in the garment industry, where there are buying offices whose business is to purchase clothing for a variety of retail stores, purchasing may be a line function. In effect, these buying offices sell their purchasing expertise. Thus, there would be no sales function for these organizations. In their organization charts, the purchasing function would be substi-

---

[2] William H. Newman, *Administrative Action,* 2d ed. (Englewood Cliffs, N.J.: Prentice-Hall, 1963), pp. 185–86.

tuted for the sales function shown in Illustration 1–3. Other examples of staff positions that may become line positions are managing attorneys in law firms, account executives in public accounting firms, and advertising executives in advertising agencies.

The table in Illustration 1–4 summarizes the distinctions between line and staff functions in retailing and manufacturing organizations.

For a company to operate effectively, interaction between line and staff functions is necessary. It would be highly unusual for a company's advertising department to decide which product lines to advertise without consulting the selling department. Similarly, when prices are not fixed by the market, sales managers would not set a product's selling price without consulting with the accounting department to determine the product's costs. Thus, interaction between departments is essential.

The Treasurer and the Controller. In most companies, the treasurer and the controller provide crucial—although different—financial services. The **treasurer** is an officer of the firm whose duties usually include (1) custodianship of the company's funds, (2) banking, (3) arranging for financing, (4) stockholder relations, (5) insurance coverage, and (6) extension of credit. On the other hand, the **controller** is typically responsible for (1) preparing budgets (planning), (2) operational reporting and interpreting (feedback), (3) evaluating differences between the budget and the operating results (variance analysis), (4) preparing tax returns and other governmental reports, and (5) establishing internal control procedures to safeguard the company's assets. For

ILLUSTRATION 1–4   **Examples of Line and Staff Functions**

Type of Firm	Line Functions	Staff Functions
1. Retailing.	Vice president of sales. Managers of all retail stores. Sales managers.	Warehousing. Advertising. Purchasing. Accounting. Finance. Legal. Personnel. Sanitation. Security.
2. Manufacturing.	Vice president of manufacturing. Vice president of sales. Manufacturing supervisors. Sales managers.	Repair and maintenance. Purchasing. Receiving. Stockroom. Factory cafeteria. Advertising. Accounting. Finance. Legal. Sanitation. Security.

example, internal control procedures established by the controller might require a cashier in the treasurer's office to take physical possession of the company's cash receipts and deposit them in the bank, while a bookkeeper in the controller's office would be responsible for recording the cash receipts. By ensuring that the cashier does not have access to the records and that the bookkeeper does not have access to the cash receipts, the controller makes it difficult for employees to appropriate company cash for their own use.

The controller is the firm's chief management accountant and a key staff member of the management team. He normally supplies significant portions of the data needed for decision making and, in addition, can interpret and analyze the data for his colleagues on the management team. In some organizations, the controller gets bogged down with everyday details, which can lessen his effectiveness. Ideally, the controller should delegate the details of running his office to subordinates so that he is free to actively participate in top-level decision making.

ILLUSTRATION 1–5   Organization Chart—Controller's Function

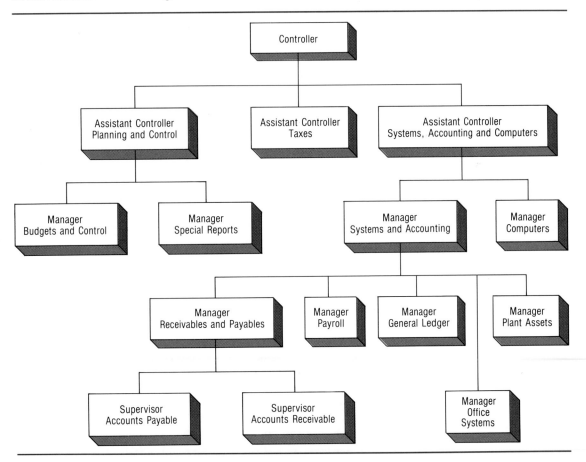

The Controller's Organization Chart.   An organization chart of the controller's office is shown in Illustration 1–5. The controller's function and its many responsibilities are the major focus of the study of managerial accounting. The chart shown in Illustration 1–5 would be a subset of the organization chart shown in Illustration 1–3.

GOAL SETTING AND DECISION MAKING

One of the most important responsibilities of top management is to set overall goals to guide the firm's activities. A **goal,** or objective, is a specific statement of the end toward which a company intends to direct its efforts. Goals, once set, tend to remain relatively constant in order to provide purpose and direction to managers and employees alike. Without clearly defined, well-understood goals, a company's activities would become unfocused and disorganized.

Most firms give high priority to the goal of profit maximization, tempered by legal and ethical constraints. In today's environment, however, this should not be an organization's only goal. Otherwise, the firm risks finding itself in conflict with employees' interests, environmental safety, and other forces that would limit its success. Thus, in addition to profit maximization, most organizations' goals address employee relations, pollution control, community involvement, charitable pursuits, and other social concerns. Although such goals may reduce short-term profits, they pay off in the long run. The amount of attention given to social responsibilities varies from organization to organization and is based on management's perception of the need for such action.

Another important goal pertains to the line of business that the company will pursue to earn its profits. For example, the Heart-Marks Corporation elected to operate a chain of retail stores specializing in both men's and women's clothing.

A company's goals form the basis for all subsequent decision making.

Strategic Planning—Long-Term Decision Making

Goal setting is the first step in the strategic planning process. **Strategic planning** is a long-term decision-making process that includes setting goals and selecting the means by which the goals will be attained. Goals can be pursued in many different ways, depending on management's perceptions and preferences. The methods used to pursue goals are called **strategies.** For example, one automaker's strategy might be to manufacture only one line of automobile, such as an ultraexpensive luxury car. Another automaker's strategy might be to manufacture many lines of automobiles, ranging from subcompacts to limousines. In another strategy decision, Company A may choose to manufacture the spark plugs used in its automobiles, while Company B may prefer to purchase them from another manufacturer.

The Heart-Marks Corporation's strategic decision regarding the kind of business it would operate is merely one of many that make up its master strategy. A **master strategy** addresses the "entire pattern of the company's basic mission, purpose, objectives, policies, and specific resource deployment."[3] Among the other examples of strategic decisions that Heart-Marks must make are:

1.   Should it manufacture its own line of clothing using its own label in addition to carrying other well-known designer labels?

2.   Should it carry a full line of merchandise from budget sportswear to custom tailored suits?

3.   Should it have its own tailoring and alteration department, or should alterations be subcontracted?

Strategic planning decisions usually have a long-range impact on organizations. Decisions about the line of business to enter and the image that the company wishes to project usually cannot be quickly reversed. For example, a business that was set up to manufacture clothing cannot quickly and easily shift to selling automobiles. Thus, strategic planning decisions must be carefully evaluated if far-reaching negative results are to be avoided.

Once the master strategy is completed, managers can turn to the activities involved in short-term decision making. These can be classified as (1) short-term planning, (2) controlling, (3) organizing, (4) staffing, and (5) motivating. The activities involved in each of these functions are listed in Illustration 1–6.

Short-Term Planning.   Short-term planning is similar to strategic planning except that it covers a shorter period of time—usually one year or less. Thus, **short-term planning** is a short-term decision-making process that includes setting objectives that are consistent with long-term goals and selecting the means by which the objectives will be attained. In the case of Heart-Marks, geographic areas and store locations must be decided on and the hours of operation must be delineated. These kinds of decisions should be periodically revaluated and changes should be made when needed.

Controlling.   **Controlling** is the process of ensuring that a firm's operating results are proceeding according to plan. The firm's actual results are compared with its predetermined plans, the sources of any deviations are identified, and, if necessary, action is taken to correct the deviations. The information obtained by comparing actual results to predetermined plans is called **feedback.** And good control is dependent on accurate feedback. This is where the management accounting system plays a crucial role. It must be structured to provide the data needed to evaluate performance and derive precise and reliable feedback.

An example from daily living will help to clarify the nature of control. When a heating thermostat is set at a temperature above the actual tempera-

---

[3] George A. Steiner and John B. Miner, *Management Policy and Strategy* (New York: Macmillan, 1977), p. 20.

ILLUSTRATION 1–6   **The Functions of Management**

Planning

1. Self audit—determining the present status of the organization.
2. Survey the environment.
3. Set objectives.
4. Forecast future situation.
5. State actions and resource requirements.
6. Evaluate proposed actions.
7. Revise and adjust the plan in light of control results and changing conditions.
8. Communicate throughout the planning process.

Controlling

1. Establish standards.
2. Monitor results and compare to standards.
3. Correct deviations.
4. Revise and adjust control methods in light of control results and changing conditions.
5. Communicate throughout the control process.

Organizing

1. Identify and define work to be performed.
2. Break work down into duties.
3. Group duties into positions.
4. Define position requirements.
5. Group positions into manageable and properly related units.
6. Assign work to be performed, accountability, and extent of authority.
7. Revise and adjust the organization in light of control results and changing conditions.
8. Communicate throughout the organizing process.

Staffing

1. Determine the human resource needs.
2. Recruit potential employees.
3. Select from the recruits.
4. Train and develop the human resources.
5. Revise and adjust the quantity and quality of the human resources in light of control results and changing conditions.
6. Communicate throughout the staffing process.

Motivating

1. Communicate and explain objectives to subordinates.
2. Assign performance standards.
3. Coach and guide subordinates to meet performance standards.
4. Reward subordinates based on performance.
5. Praise and censure fairly.
6. Provide a motivating environment by communicating the changing situation and its requirements.
7. Revise and adjust the methods of motivation in light of control results and changing conditions.
8. Communicate throughout the motivation process.

SOURCE: Leslie W. Rue and Lloyd L. Byars, *Management: Theory and Application*, 3d ed. (Homewood, Ill.: Richard D. Irwin). Copyright © 1983 by Richard D. Irwin, Inc. Reprinted by permission of the publisher.

ture in a room, it triggers a mechanism that activates the furnace and causes more heat to be produced. When the temperature of the room is approximately equal to the desired temperature, the furnace is deactivated and remains so until the room cools somewhat. Then the process is repeated. As long as the desired temperature is fairly evenly maintained, the thermostat and the heating system will not need further attention. But should the room become abnormally cool or hot, its occupant would become uncomfortable and investigate the problem to see if a repair is necessary.

In business, control operates similarly. The master strategy can be viewed as the desired temperature and feedback can be considered the actual temperature. If the feedback is fairly close to the desired result, no corrective action is required. But if comparison reveals widely disparate results, investigation by management becomes necessary. The approach to control in which a manager investigates only those differences between planned and actual results that are considered significant is called **management by exception.**

Organizing. Managers must also make many day-to-day operating decisions that can be classified as organizing—the combining and arranging of human and material resources in a system of activities that will attain established goals.[4] Organizing may include deciding selling prices, determining quantities of inventory, establishing credit policies, setting hours of operation, and dividing labor among departments. These decisions can be modified over relatively short periods of time—daily, and even hourly, if necessary. This does not mean that once managers start organizing they have stopped planning. In most business situations, both activities continue side by side. For example, two new stores might be in the strategic planning stage while six other stores require short-term planning and organizing.

Staffing. Staffing is the process of securing and developing personnel for the jobs that were created during the organizing process.[5] Employees must be hired, duties must be assigned, salary levels must be defined, fringe benefits must be selected, and other decisions of this type must be evaluated. Finally, a manager must motivate employees—that is, direct and channel workers' behavior to the accomplishment of company goals.

Motivating. The standards of work performance must be clearly explained and supervision must be provided to help employees meet those standards. In addition, a system of rewards should be established to encourage optimum performance. When employees are highly motivated, a manager will usually observe a substantial increase in performance and significant decrease in such problems as absenteeism, tardiness, turnover, and strikes.

---

[4] Benjamin M. Compaine and Robert F. Litro, *Business: An Introduction* (Chicago: The Dryden Press, 1984), p. 79.

[5] Rue and Byars, *Management: Theory and Application,* p. 231.

ILLUSTRATION 1–7   Planning and Control Cycle

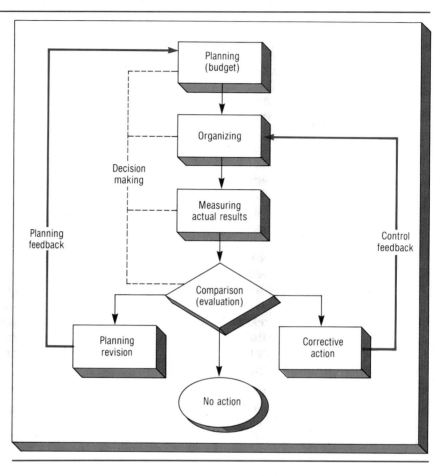

The Planning and Control Cycle

In a broad sense, everything that managers do involves decision making. But two managerial functions—planning and control—deserve special attention. Together they form the **planning and control cycle**—a continuous loop of planning, using feedback to evaluate results, taking corrective action if necessary, and returning to the planning stage. The actual results form the basis for any corrective action or revisions to the plan that may be needed. Thus, the plan provides the mechanism by which to evaluate performance, and the performance provides the mechanism by which the plan is revised, if necessary, for the next cycle.

The effect of decision making on the planning and control cycle can be demonstrated in a simple model, as shown in Illustration 1–7.

CAREERS IN MANAGEMENT ACCOUNTING

Four decades ago, all accounting students received the same training and preparation for careers as public accountants. Public accountants offer their professional services to the public for a fee, much like lawyers and doctors. Individuals and corporations most commonly call on public accountants for auditing of financial statements, accounting-related management advice, and tax services. But many accounting graduates never became public accountants. Instead, they entered private accounting, which meant working in the accounting department of a single enterprise. Such private accountants provided a variety of services to their companies' managers, including general accounting, cost accounting, budgeting, and internal auditing. As computerization advanced and became widespread, managers required more sophisticated information and reports. And it was natural that private accountants should become involved in supplying the necessary information. This led to the growth of the field of management accounting. Today, many colleges offer separate training for public accountants and management accountants.

Certificate in Management Accounting

In 1972, the National Association of Accountants (NAA) established the Institute of Management Accounting to recognize the accomplishments of management accountants. It established the **Certificate in Management Accounting (CMA)** as a means of designating management accountants who have fulfilled specified educational and experience requirements and have passed a rigorous series of examinations. The program is administered by the Institute of Management Accounting (IMA) and requires that candidates for the CMA pass an examination in:

1.   Economics and business finance.

2.   Organization and behavior, including ethical considerations.

3.   Public reporting standards, auditing, and taxes.

4.   Internal reporting and analysis.

5.   Decision analysis, including modeling and information systems.

The purposes and objectives of the CMA program are cited from the 1982–83 Announcement of the Institute of Management Accounting of the NAA:

> Significant changes have taken place in accounting and in the role of the accountant in business. The accountant is no longer simply a recorder of business history but now plays a dynamic role in making business decisions, in future planning, and in almost every aspect of business operations. The management accountant, who sits with top management, has key responsibilities for developing, producing, and analyzing information to help management make sound decisions. Many management accountants and financial managers earn their way into top management positions.
>
> In response to the needs of business and at the request of many in the academic community, the National Association of Accountants established a program to recognize professional competence and educational attainment in

this field—a program leading to the Certificate in Management Accounting.

The CMA program requires candidates to pass a series of uniform examinations and meet specific education and professional standards to qualify for and maintain the Certificate in Management Accounting. NAA has established the Institute of Management Accounting to administer the program, conduct the examinations, and grant certificates to those who qualify. The program is open to all interested persons, whether or not they are members of NAA.

The objectives of the program are threefold:

1. To establish management accounting as a recognized profession by identifying the role of the management accountant and financial manager and the underlying body of knowledge, and by outlining a course of study by which such knowledge can be acquired.

2. To foster higher educational standards in the field of management accounting.

3. To establish an objective measure of an individual's knowledge and competence in the field of management accounting.

Certified Public Accountant (CPA)

Another highly respected designation among accounting professionals is that of Certified Public Accountant. The legislative bodies of the individual states have established the procedures and requirements necessary to obtain a **Certified Public Accountant's license.** Although educational and experience requirements differ from state to state, the required examinations are uniform for all 50 of the states and are prepared and graded by the AICPA. There is reciprocity among most states to qualified CPAs who meet educational and experience requirements. A CPA is licensed to practice as an independent auditor.

Many people first obtain a CPA license and then become management accountants. Thus, many management accountants are CPAs, and many of them also possess the CMA. Management accountants who possess either the CMA or the CPA are recognized as having achieved a high level of professional competency.

SUMMARY

Managerial accounting is one area of accounting that specializes in providing financial information that managers will find useful for internal **decision making.** Such information may be either **quantitative** or **qualitative** and tends to be based on either **current** or future **data.** In contrast, **financial accounting** focuses on compiling financial information and reports for external users, such as investors, creditors, and government agencies. Financial accountants deal primarily with **historical information.** Within a company, the **controller** usually oversees managerial accounting activities while the **treasurer** is in charge of company funds, banking, financing, stockholder relations, insurance, and extension of credit. Financial accounting is controlled by a regulatory body, the SEC, and a professional organization, the AICPA, but managerial accounting faces no restrictions. Whatever information managers find useful is acceptable in managerial accounting.

To function optimally, a management accountant needs to understand organizations and their structure. An **organization chart** helps to define the **lines of authority, delegation of authority, line functions,** and **staff functions** within an organization. The controller, as a member of the management team, performs vital staff functions.

Organizational goals must be clearly defined if an organization is to be successful. Once the goals are defined, managers must select the **strategies** that are likely to move the organization toward achieving its goals. **Strategic planning** is concerned with long-range decision making, and its outcome— the **master plan**—is not usually reversible in the short run.

In addition, managers are constantly involved in **short-term planning** and decision making. The five key functions of management are usually defined as **planning, controlling, organizing, staffing,** and **motivating.** Two of these, planning and controlling, are often referred to as the **planning and control cycle,** an ongoing process that is essential to the success of any business. **Feedback** is a necessary ingredient of the planning and control cycle.

The **CMA** designation gives recognition to accountants who have met specific educational, experience, and testing requirements and confers a certain amount of status. The **CPA** license is primarily useful for professionals who practice as public accountants. Nonetheless, many management accountants also possess the CPA license and, as a result, enjoy greater distinction.

GLOSSARY OF KEY TERMS

Certificate in Management Accounting (CMA)   A designation granted by the Institute of Management Accounting to management accountants who have completed specific educational, experience, and testing requirements.

Certified Public Accountant (CPA) license   A license granted by State Boards of Accountancy, pursuant to statutory authority, generally upon the completion of certain educational, experience, and testing requirements.

Controller (comptroller)   The chief management accountant and key staff member of the management team whose duties include preparing budgets, operational reporting and interpreting, evaluating operating results and any differences from the plan, preparing income tax returns, and establishing internal control procedures to safeguard the company's assets.

Controlling   The process of ensuring that a firm's operating results are proceeding according to plan. The firm's actual results are compared with its predetermined plans, the sources of any deviations are identified, and, if necessary, action is taken to correct the deviations.

Current data   Numerical information applicable to the immediate future, such as present wage rates or expected costs of raw materials.

Decision making   The process of searching the environment for conditions requiring attention, developing and analyzing possible responses, and selecting an appropriate course of action.

Delegation of authority   Assigning duties to immediate subordinates; granting subordinates permission to make commitments, use resources, and to take all actions necessary to perform the duties assigned; and making the subordinate responsible for performing the duties in a satisfactory manner.

Feedback The information obtained by comparing actual results to predetemined plans.

Financial accounting Area of accounting concerned with compiling the information used to prepare financial statements on an historical cost basis. Financial accounting statements are intended for external users.

Goal A specific statement of the end toward which a company intends to direct its efforts.

Historical data Numerical information based on past events, such as former wage rates or past costs of raw materials.

Line function Any job related to the primary business tasks for which a company was organized.

Line of authority The path responsibility takes as it is passed down from managers to subordinates.

Management by exception An approach to control in which a manager investigates only those differences between planned and actual results that are considered significant.

Managerial accounting The area of accounting that specializes in providing information that managers find useful for internal decision making. Unlike financial accounting information, managerial accounting information is not regulated by outside agencies.

Master strategy The entire pattern of a company's basic mission, purpose, objectives, policies, and specific resource deployment.

Motivating Directing and channeling human behavior toward the accomplishment of company goals.

Organization chart A diagram defining the structure of an organization, its breakdown into departments, and the resulting lines of authority.

Organizing The combining and arranging of human and material resources in a system of activities that will attain desired goals.

Planning Deciding what objectives to pursue during a future time period and what to do in order to achieve those objectives.

Planning and control cycle A continuous loop of planning, using feedback to evaluate results, taking corrective action if necessary, and returning to the planning stage. The plan provides the mechanism by which to evaluate performance, and the performance provides the mechanism by which the plan is revised, if necessary, for the next cycle.

Qualitative information Data of a nonquantitative nature.

Quantitative information Data of a numerical nature.

Short-term planning A short-term decision-making process that includes setting objectives that are consistent with long-term goals and selecting the means by which the objectives will be attained.

Staff function Any job that provides ancillary, or support, services to line managers.

Staffing The process of securing and developing personnel for the jobs that were created during the organizing process.

Strategic planning A long-term decision-making process that includes setting goals and selecting the means by which the goals will be obtained.

Strategy The method used to pursue a goal.

Treasurer A financial officer of a firm whose duties include custodianship of the company's funds, banking, arranging for financing, stockholder relations, insurance coverage, and extension of credit.

QUESTIONS

1. Who are the users of financial accounting information and on what is it based?
2. Why does financial accounting have regulatory constraints? What are they?
3. Who are the users of managerial accounting information and on what is it based?
4. What is meant by a line function?
5. What is meant by a staff function?
6. What are the duties of a treasurer?
7. What are the duties of a controller?
8. What are organizational goals?
9. What is strategic planning?
10. What is a strategy?
11. What is a master strategy?
12. What is planning?
13. What is controlling?
14. What is organizing?
15. What is staffing?
16. What is motivation?
17. What is feedback?
18. What is the planning and control cycle?
19. What quantitative information is useful for decision making? Use an example to illustrate your answer.
20. What is qualitative information? Use an example to illustrate it.
21. What should information provided to managers do?
22. What types of decisions are managers called upon to make?
23. What is the CMA? How is it obtained and what are its objectives?
24. Assume that you are in the process of starting a business organized for profit. What organizational goals other than profit would you be likely to consider as being important?
25. Assume that you have been appointed the president of a newly formed private college. Discuss how you would implement each of the following:
    a. College goals.
    b. Strategic planning.
    c. Planning.
    d. Organizing.
    e. Control.

26. Does a charitable organization have a need for organizational goals, strategic planning, planning, organizing, and control? Explain.

27. Since controllership is a staff function, the controller's impact on the management function is advisory only. Thus, the controller is unimportant to the overall management process. Do you agree or disagree? Support your answer.

28. Qualitative data is nonnumerical in nature and is thus more difficult to evaluate than quantitative data. However, it is possible for the qualitative considerations affecting a decision to be more important than the quantitative considerations. Construct an example to illustrate such a case.

EXERCISES

1–1 Staff and Line Functions

The Interesting Toy Company is a manufacturer of toys. For each of the following, indicate which line manager or staff manager would be responsible for the costs incurred, and identify the manager as either line or staff.

1. Salaries of plastic molding employees.
2. Salaries of cafeteria employees.
3. Salaries of employees who repair and maintain the plastic molding machines.
4. Salaries of management accountants.
5. Salaries of night watchpersons.
6. Salaries of employees who package the toys.
7. Salaries of sales personnel.
8. Salaries of purchasing personnel.
9. Salaries of personnel who administer the collection and deposit of company funds.
10. Salaries of inspectors who inspect the toys prior to packaging.

1–2 Organization Chart

The Makemoney Merchandising Company is a retail establishment and has the following departments:

a. Furniture.
b. Linens.
c. Electronic home video equipment.
d. Small and major appliances.

Each department has a manager who is in charge of the sales personnel in his or her department. The managers report to a vice president who is in charge of sales.

There is a vice president in charge of purchasing who supervises four purchasing managers—one for each department.

There is also a vice president for finance to whom both the treasurer and the controller report.

There are also managers for advertising and sales personnel who report to the vice president of sales.

All vice presidents report to the president, who reports to the board of directors.

Required Prepare an organization chart for the Makemoney Merchandising Company.

PROBLEMS   **1–3   Line and Staff Authorities**

Special Alloys Corporation is a specialized production firm that manufacturers a variety of metal products for industrial use. Most of the revenues are generated by large contracts with companies which have government defense contracts. The company also develops and markets parts to the major automobile companies. The company employs many metallurgists and skilled technicians because most of its products are made from highly sophisticated alloys.

The company recently signed two large contracts; as a result, the workload of Wayne Washburn, the general manager, has become overwhelming. To relieve some of this overload, Mark Johnson was transferred from the research planning department to the general manager's office. Johnson, who had been a senior metallurgist and supervisor in the planning department, was given the title "assistant to the general manager."

Washburn assigned several responsibilities to Johnson in their first meeting. Johnson will oversee the testing of new alloys in the product planning department and be given the authority to make decisions as to the use of these alloys in product development; he will also be responsible for maintaining the production schedules for one of the new contracts. In addition to these duties, he will be required to meet with the supervisors of the production departments regularly to consult with them about production problems they may be experiencing. Washburn is expecting that he will be able to manage the company much more efficiently with Johnson's help.

Required a. Positions within organizations are often described as having (1) line authority or (2) staff authority. Describe what is meant by these two terms.

b. Of the responsibilities assigned to Mark Johnson as assistant to the general manager, which ones are considered line authority and which have staff authority?

b. Identify and discuss the conflicts Mark Johnson may experience in the production departments as a result of his new responsibilities.

(CMA adapted)

1–4   The Role of Line and Staff Management in Strategic Planning

One element necessary to the life of an organization is strategic planning. Strategic planning establishes an organization's long-range goals or objectives and the means to achieve the goals and objectives. Even before a company can begin operations, its managers must develop the plan or plans necessary to determine its future. For example, these include: What products or services will the organization provide? How will the organization be financed and structured? Where will the company and its distributors be located? How will its products or services be marketed?

Line and staff management play specific roles in strategic planning. They have different responsibilities and functions in an organization. In addition, the activities of these two management groups must be coordinated.

Required a In the formulation of an organization's strategic plans, describe the contribution to be made by:

(1) The line managers.

(2) The staff groups.

In your answer, identify the types of decisions these two groups of managers make as they participate in the formulation of strategic plans.

b. In the implementation of an organization's strategic plans:
   (1) State how the responsibilities of line management differ from those of staff groups.
   (2) Describe how line and staff interrelate in this process.

(CMA adapted)

1-5   Setting Long-Range Goals

Successful business organizations appear to be those which have clearly defined long-range goals and a well-planned strategy to reach the goals. These successful organizations understand the markets in which they do business as well as their internal strengths and weaknesses. These organizations take advantage of this knowledge to grow (through internal development or acquisitions) in a consistent and disciplined manner.

Required a. Discuss the need for long-range goals for business organizations.
   b. Discuss how long-range goals are set.
   c. Define the concepts of strategic planning and management control. Discuss how they relate to each other and contribute to the progress toward the attainment of long-range goals.

(CMA adapted)

1-6   Organizational Structures

The Hooper Company is considering a reorganization. The company's current organizational structure is represented by the chart shown below.

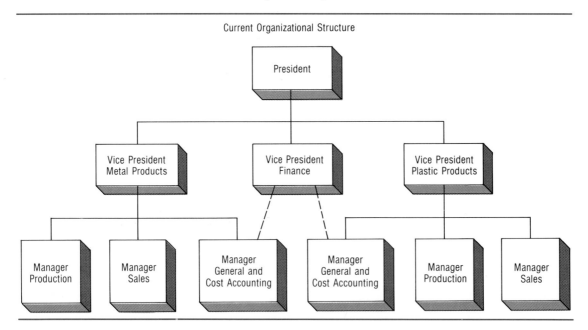

Current Organizational Structure

The company recently hired a new vice president for metal products. The new vice president for metal products has an extensive background in sales which complements the vice president for plastic products, whose background has been in production. The new vice president for metal products believes that Hooper Company would be more effective if it were reorganized according to the organizational chart presented as follows:

Proposed Organizational Structure

Required   *a.* Identify the two types of organizational structures depicted by the two charts.
   b. Compare the two organizational structures by discussing the advantages and disadvantages of each.
   c. Discuss the circumstances that would favor one form of organizational structure over the other.

(CMA adapted)

Part 1

ESSENTIALS OF MANAGERIAL ACCOUNTING

2

COST DEFINITIONS AND BEHAVIOR

LEARNING OBJECTIVES

After reading this chapter, you should be able to:

1 Distinguish between a cost and an expense.

2 Explain what product cost is for a manufacturing firm and identify the three elements that enter into a product's cost.

3 Classify costs of production according to the three elements of cost for a manufacturing firm.

4 Explain what product cost is for a merchandising establishment.

5 Describe the flow of costs for merchandising and manufacturing firms.

6 Explain how the financial statements of a merchandising establishment differ from those of a manufacturing establishment.

7 Describe the differences in behavior between fixed costs, variable costs, and mixed costs.

8 Explain the various cost classifications listed in the glossary at the end of this chapter.

For an accountant, the term *cost* can have many different definitions. At the most general level, a **cost** is the sacrifice made to acquire a good or service. Thus, in a simple transaction, the cost of an item such as an adding machine is the cash paid to acquire it, regardless of whether the cash is paid at the time of the purchase or at a later time.

Costs are extremely important to accountants and managers. They are used for a variety of purposes, including (1) pricing a product for sale to customers, (2) valuing inventories when preparing an income statement, (3) performance evaluation of groups of employees, (4) making decisions regarding alternative courses of action, and (5) budgeting for future operations. It is customary to describe costs with an adjective to signify their purpose.

For descriptive purposes, an accountant or manager may group costs in any of several ways: (1) as they relate to a specific product, (2) as they relate to a period of time rather than to a specific product, (3) by category based on behavior patterns, (4) into those that are needed to reach a managerial decision, and (5) into those needed for performance evaluation.

The nature of a business may also determine the way costs are described. While manufacturing, merchandising, and service industries may incur the same kind of costs, the description of the costs may differ in each industry.

While the measurement of costs is extremely important to all kinds of business entities, it is critical to the successful operation of a manufacturing firm.

COSTS AND EXPENSES

Costs may be subdivided into **unexpired costs,** which are sacrifices expected to benefit future accounting periods, and **expired costs,** which are sacrifices *not* expected to benefit future accounting periods. Unexpired costs are shown as assets on the balance sheet and consist of such items as inventories; unexpired insurance; and property, plant, and equipment. Expired costs, also called **expenses,** are shown as deductions from revenues and consist of such items as the current period's rent, telephone bill, advertising charges, administrative salaries, and electric bill. They are shown as expenses because no future benefit is expected from these items once the accounting period is ended.

The purchase of a machine that cost $5,000 would also entail an expense in the form of depreciation. If the machine had an estimated useful life of five years and no salvage value, its *expense* would be $1,000 a year if straight-line depreciation were used. This amount would be considered the *expired* portion of the original cost.

The distinction between costs and expenses is relevant when preparing financial statements for external use by stockholders, investors, financial analysts, and others. Managers are concerned with *costs* and how they affect a firm's operations. Thus, we will focus on costs throughout this book and refer to expenses only in relation to external reporting.

COSTS IN A MANUFACTURING FIRM

A manufacturing firm normally purchases raw materials and converts them into finished goods by combining and/or altering the raw materials. To accomplish this, a manufacturing firm usually utilizes both employees and machinery housed in some form of factory building. The resulting costs, which can be attributed specifically to products, are called **product costs** and fall into three categories: direct materials, direct labor, and manufacturing overhead.

Direct Costs

A **direct cost** is one that is directly related, or traceable, to a cost objective. A **cost objective** is any grouping to which costs are assigned, such as a unit of inventory, a department, a product line, a division, or the firm itself. A cost, such as a factory supervisor's salary, may be directly traceable to a firm's product line (i.e., television receivers), but it may *not* be directly traceable to a specific receiver or model. Thus, when speaking of a direct cost, the cost objective must be specified, or else the description will suffer from an imprecision that renders it meaningless.

Direct Materials. **Direct materials** include the cost of all raw materials that are necessary to produce a finished product for sale to customers. These costs can usually be calculated with a high degree of accuracy. In theory, direct materials would include every component of the finished product, including, for example, nails and glue. But in reality, most companies apply the cost/benefit rule, which states that a cost should not be incurred unless the corresponding benefit exceeds the cost. Consequently, the relatively high cost of maintaining bookkeeping records for items such as nails and glue results in these items being treated as *indirect materials*—an indirect cost, which we will discuss later. Direct materials, also known as *raw materials,* are *directly traceable to the finished product.*

A manufacturer's cost of direct materials includes:

1. The invoice price of the raw materials.
2. Shipping costs.
3. Import duties.
4. A reduction for any allowable discounts for prompt payment.

Other costs associated with raw materials, such as insurance during transit, receiving room costs, and stockroom costs, are difficult to assign to specific units and are thus treated as manufacturing overhead.

Direct Labor. **Direct labor** includes the wages paid to all employees who work directly on the transformation of raw materials into a finished product as well as the wages of inspectors who approve the product for sale to customers. Employees whose wages are not included as direct labor are: (1) the factory superintendent, (2) supervisory line employees who do not work directly on the product, (3) maintenance and repair employees, (4) security guards, (5) support personnel, and (6) cleaning staff. The efforts of these workers are considered to be indirect labor because it is impossible to trace their salaries and wages to any specific product. Indirect-labor costs are treated as manufacturing overhead.

For a manufacturer, the cost of raw materials used to manufacture a product and the cost of wages paid to employees who work on transforming raw materials into finished goods are easy to trace to a finished product.

Indirect Costs

Indirect costs (also called **common costs**) are costs that relate to more than one cost objective. If the cost objective is a particular product in a multi-product factory, all manufacturing costs other than direct materials and direct labor are considered indirect manufacturing costs and are called manufacturing overhead.

Manufacturing Overhead. A number of terms are used to describe manufacturing overhead, including **overhead pool, overhead, burden, factory burden, indirect manufacturing costs, factory expenses,** and **indirect factory expenses.** Whichever term is used, **manufacturing overhead** includes all *manufacturing* costs except direct materials and direct labor. The key point to remember is that *only manufacturing costs* are included in this category. For example, while factory rent is included in manufacturing overhead because the factory is essential to the production of a finished product, *office rent is excluded* because it is *not essential to production.* Other examples of indirect manufacturing costs are factory supervision, factory telephone, heat, light, power, factory bookkeeping salaries, insurance, depreciation of equipment and machinery, and all indirect materials and indirect labor, such as machinery lubricants, sweeping compound, salaries of cleaning staff, and salaries of security guards. These costs generally continue even when a specific product is discontinued as long as the factory continues to operate.

Although indirect costs cannot be traced directly to any single product, some method must be found to assign them to all products if proper dollar values are to be assigned to inventories on hand. **Assignable product costs,** usually referred to as **inventoriable costs,** include direct materials, direct labor, and all indirect manufacturing costs (overhead) necessary to produce a finished product ready for sale to customers. Once a product is in its normal salable condition at a specific location, no further costs are assignable to it.

Product Costs

To demonstrate what is included in product costs for a manufacturing firm, let us assume that during 19x1 the Mitchell Fabricating Corporation purchased raw materials for $500,000, incurred direct labor costs for $600,000, and incurred manufacturing overhead costs for $298,000. There are no beginning or ending inventories. The firm manufactures one product—bathroom scales—and 150,000 scales were manufactured during 19x1.

The *total product costs* for 19x1 may be summarized as follows:

Total product cost:
Direct materials	. . . .	$ 500,000
Direct labor	. . . .	600,000
Manufacturing overhead	. . . . .	298,000
Total	. . . .	$1,398,000

The **unit cost** per scale may be calculated by dividing the total product cost of $1,398,000 by the number of units produced, 150,000, as follows:

$$\text{Unit cost} = \frac{\$1,398,000}{150,000} = \$9.32 \text{ per scale}$$

In addition to product costs, firms incur other costs for marketing their products and administering day-to-day operations. These costs are referred to as period costs.

Period Costs

Period costs benefit a specific period of time and are *not related to production.* This distinguishes them from product costs, which are functions of production. An example of a period cost would be showroom rent cost. This would be classified as a marketing (or selling) cost and also as a period cost because the showroom does not benefit the product while it is being manufactured. In fact, all items classified as marketing and administrative costs would be considered period costs. Period costs are deducted from revenues earned during the period measured. Within each category of period costs, there are likely to exist the following subclassifications:

Type of Cost	Marketing	General and Administrative
1. Rent	Sales offices and selling showroom	General offices
2. Salaries	Sales managers and sales personnel	Corporate officers and office personnel
3. Telephone	Sales offices	General offices
4. Heat and light	Sales offices	General offices
5. Insurance	Sales offices	General offices
6. Depreciation	Sales equipment	Office equipment
7. Advertising	Sales promotion	—
8. Legal and accounting fees	—	Administrative costs

FINANCIAL STATEMENTS FOR A MANUFACTURING FIRM

Manufacturing firms generally have three classes of inventory: (1) raw materials, (2) work in process, and (3) finished goods. **Raw materials** are materials purchased for later use in the manufacturing cycle. The value of the **work in process** inventory represents the cost of raw materials placed into production plus the cost of labor and overhead expended up to the point in the

Inventory Classification

production cycle at which the value of the goods is measured. The goods in the work in process inventory are in unfinished condition. Most manufacturers have some unfinished goods at all times and thus must value this inventory at the end of an accounting period when an income statement is to be prepared. **Finished goods** are goods in finished condition awaiting sale to customers.

A Manufacturer's Balance Sheet

The major difference between a manufacturer's and a merchandiser's balance sheets is in how inventories are presented. A merchandiser has only one class of inventory, finished goods, and thus merely shows one amount for finished goods inventory in the current asset section of the balance sheet. A manufacturer shows a separate amount for each class of inventory.

The Mitchell Fabricating Corporation has inventories on December 31, 19x1, as follows:

Raw materials	$ 60,000
Work in process	130,000
Finished goods	300,000

The firm also has cash in bank of $100,000, accounts receivable (net of allowance for doubtful accounts) of $175,000, and prepaid expenses of $20,000. The current asset section of Mitchell's balance sheet appears in Illustration 2–1.

ILLUSTRATION 2–1

MITCHELL FABRICATING CORPORATION
Balance Sheet
December 31, 19x1

Current assets:		
Cash in bank		$100,000
Accounts receivable less allowance for doubtful accounts		175,000
Inventories:		
Raw materials	$ 60,000	
Work in process	130,000	
Finished goods	300,000	
Total inventories		490,000
Prepaid expenses		20,000
Total current assets		$785,000

A Manufacturer's Income Statement

As part of its management reporting system, a manufacturing firm prepares an income statement that includes both a statement of cost of goods sold and a statement of cost of goods manufactured. The income statement is normally prepared monthly, and it provides managers with the results of operations—net income or net loss—for the specified period of time. It is important for managers to monitor their firm's operating results frequently.

This will allow them *to alter operating strategies if the results are not satisfactory.* Managers who do not monitor their firm's operating results at frequent intervals, but instead wait for the firm's annual report to assess its operations, may be placed in the position of locking the stable door after the horse has escaped.

In order to prepare an income statement, it is necessary to ascertain both *beginning* and *ending* inventories for raw materials, work in process, and finished goods. Using the information previously provided for the Mitchell Fabricating Corporation, let us also assume that the beginning inventories are $80,000 for raw materials, $110,000 for work in process, and $250,000 for finished goods.

Four steps are needed to prepare an income statement for a manufacturing firm.

Step 1: The Schedule of Direct Materials Used in Production

Prepare a *schedule of direct materials used in production.* The cost of direct materials may be calculated using the following formula:

> **Raw materials used** = Beginning raw materials inventory + Raw materials purchased − Ending raw materials inventory

Considering Mitchell's beginning inventory of raw materials for $80,000, the purchases of $500,000, and the ending inventory of raw materials for $60,000, its schedule of direct materials used in production may be prepared as follows:

Beginning raw materials inventory	$ 80,000
Add: Raw materials purchased	
plus freight in	500,000
Raw materials available for use	580,000
Deduct: Ending raw materials inventory	60,000
Direct materials used in production	$520,000

This information may be presented as a separate schedule, or it may be incorporated into the statement of cost of goods manufactured. When used as a separate schedule, it must be labeled as such (i.e., Schedule 1) and should have a heading that includes the firm's name and the period of time covered. This author prefers to include it in the statement of cost of goods manufactured, provided that the statement does not become unwieldy as a result.

Step 2: The Statement of Cost of Goods Manufactured

Prepare a *statement of cost of goods manufactured* using the following formula:

> **Cost of goods manufactured** = Beginning work in process inventory + Raw materials used + Direct labor + Manufacturing overhead − Ending work in process inventory

Based on the data presented so far, and adding a detailed breakdown of manufacturing overhead costs, the Mitchell Fabricating Corporation's statement of cost of goods manufactured would appear as shown in Illustration 2–2.

It is customary to show the details of the manufacturing overhead incurred during the year. If the amount of detail makes the statement bulky, such information may be presented in a separate schedule, with only the total overhead ($298,000) shown in the cost of goods manufactured statement. The flow of costs that entered into the preparation of the statement of cost of goods manufactured is shown in Illustration 2–3. Note that Illustration 2–2 contains the cost inputs noted in Illustration 2–3, namely, direct materials, direct labor, and manufacturing overhead. However, in order to compute the cost of goods transferred to finished goods (cost of goods manufactured), it is necessary to add the beginning work in process inventory and deduct the ending work in process. The beginning work in process inventory must be included because the manufacturing costs expended during the current

ILLUSTRATION 2–2

MITCHELL FABRICATING CORPORATION
Statement of Cost of Goods Manufactured
For the Year Ended December 31, 19x1

Beginning work in process inventory			$ 110,000
Direct materials:			
Beginning raw materials inventory	$ 80,000		
Add: Purchases of raw materials			
plus freight in	500,000		
Raw materials available for use	580,000		
Deduct: Ending raw materials inventory	60,000		
Direct materials used in production		$520,000	
Direct labor		600,000	
Manufacturing overhead:			
Indirect materials	20,000		
Indirect labor	120,000		
Factory rent	60,000		
Heat, light, and power	30,000		
Factory telephone	10,000		
Factory insurance	8,000		
Depreciation of equipment	50,000		
Total overhead costs		298,000	
Total manufacturing costs incurred			
during the year			1,418,000
Total manufacturing goods in process			1,528,000
Deduct: Ending work in process inventory			130,000
Cost of goods manufactured			$1,398,000

ILLUSTRATION 2–3   Mitchell Fabricating Corporation: Cost Flow for the Statement of Cost of Goods Manufactured

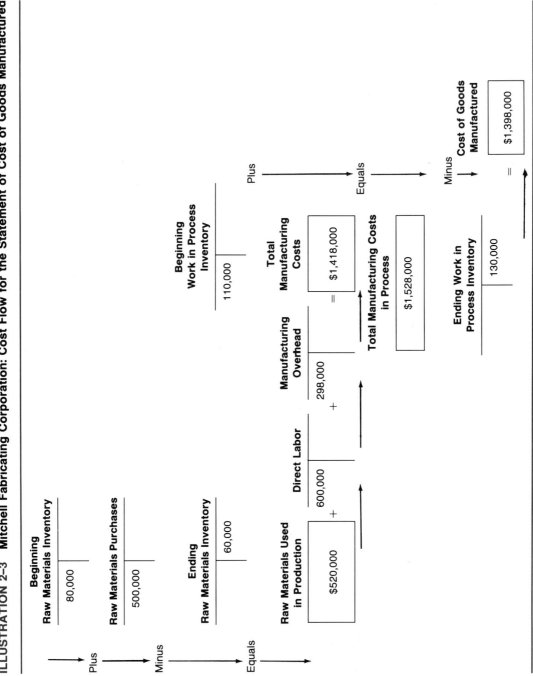

period do not include the costs expended in the prior period that are contained in the beginning work in process. By including these costs, the statement reflects all manufacturing costs expended in the current period as well as the costs expended in the prior period on *merchandise finished in the current period.* The beginning work in process becomes part of the finished goods in the current period, which must reflect both the costs expended in the prior period and the costs to finish them in the current period. Failure to include the beginning work in process costs in the statement would mean they would be unaccounted for.

The ending work in process costs must be subtracted if the statement is to reflect only the cost of goods completed. If the ending work in process inventory were not subtracted, the statement would contain both the cost of goods completed *and* the cost of the ending work in process inventory. Clearly, this would be undesirable if only the cost of goods completed is needed.

ILLUSTRATION 2–4   Mitchell Fabricating Corporation: Cost Flow for Cost of Goods Sold

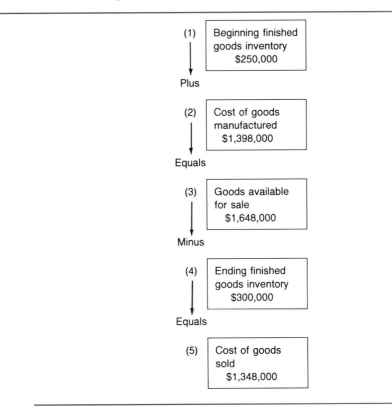

ILLUSTRATION 2–5

MITCHELL FABRICATING CORPORATION
Statement of Cost of Goods Sold
For the Year Ended December 31, 19x1

Cost of goods sold:		
Beginning finished goods inventory		$ 250,000
Add: Cost of goods manufactured		
(from Illustration 2–2)		1,398,000
Goods available for sale		1,648,000
Deduct: Ending finished goods inventory		300,000
Cost of goods sold		$1,348,000

Step 3: Statement of the Cost of Goods Sold

Prepare a *statement of cost of goods sold* based on the following formula:

Cost of goods sold = Beginning finished goods inventory + Cost of goods manufactured − Ending finished goods inventory

The flow of costs for the Mitchell Fabricating Corporation appears in Illustration 2–4. As shown in Illustration 2–3, work in process is the result of adding the costs of direct materials, direct labor, and manufacturing overhead. As the work is completed, these costs are transferred to finished goods and removed from work in process. When finished goods are sold, their cost is removed from finished goods and transferred to the *cost of goods sold* category. Continuing the example from Illustration 2–4, the cost of goods sold section of Mitchell's income statement would appear as in Illustration 2–5.

Step 4: The Income Statement

Using the statement of cost of goods sold, prepare an income statement by subtracting the cost of goods sold from sales revenue to arrive at the firm's **gross margin** (or **gross profit**). From the gross margin, deduct the marketing

ILLUSTRATION 2–6

MITCHELL FABRICATING CORPORATION
Income Statement
For the Year Ended December 31, 19x1

Sales revenue	$3,000,000
Deduct: Cost of goods sold (Illustration 2–5)	1,348,000
Gross margin	1,652,000
Deduct: Marketing and administrative costs	700,000
Operating profit before income taxes	952,000
Deduct: Income taxes (30 percent)	285,600
Net income	$ 666,400

---

and administrative costs. The result is the firm's **operating profit.** From this amount, a provision for income taxes may be deducted to arrive at **net income.**

For 19x1, the Mitchell Fabricating Corporation had sales revenues of $3 million, marketing costs of $300,000, administrative costs of $400,000, and an income tax rate of 30 percent. The firm's income statement for the year is shown in Illustration 2–6.

The Four Steps in Preparing a Manufacturer's Income Statement

Step 1:

Prepare a *schedule of direct materials used in production.* The cost of direct materials may be calculated using the following formula:

> **Raw materials used** = Beginning raw materials inventory + Raw materials purchased − Ending raw materials inventory

Step 2:

Prepare a *statement of cost of goods manufactured* using the following formula:

> **Cost of goods manufactured** = Beginning work in process inventory + Raw materials used + Direct labor + Manufacturing overhead − Ending work in process inventory

Step 3:

Prepare a *statement of cost of goods sold* based on the following formula:

> **Cost of goods sold** = Beginning finished goods inventory + Cost of goods manufactured − Ending finished goods inventory

Step 4:

Using the statement of cost of goods sold, prepare an income statement by subtracting the cost of goods sold from sales revenue to arrive at the firm's **gross margin** (or *gross profit*). From the gross margin, deduct the marketing and administrative costs. The result is the firm's **operating profit.** From this amount, a provision for income taxes may be deducted to arrive at **net income.**

Prime Costs and Conversion Costs

The term **prime cost** is used to denote the sum of direct material costs and direct labor costs—that is, the two kinds of costs that are directly traceable to the cost of a product. The term **conversion cost** refers to the sum of direct labor and manufacturing overhead. It stems from the notion that raw materials are *converted* into finished goods through the input of direct labor and manufacturing overhead. The interrelationships among prime cost, conversion cost, and the three elements of product cost are shown in Illustration 2–7.

ILLUSTRATION 2-7   **Interrelationship between Prime Costs, Conversion Costs, and Product Costs for a Manufacturing Firm**

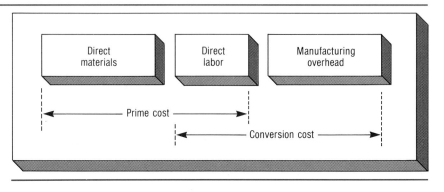

FINANCIAL STATEMENTS FOR A MERCHANDISING FIRM

Product Costs

For a merchandising establishment, product costs are usually easy to ascertain. Since merchandisers buy goods for resale, their product costs include the price paid for the goods purchased, shipping costs, insurance during transit, and import duties.

To demonstrate what is included in product cost for a merchandising firm, let us assume that the Sellmore Retail Outlet Company purchased and imported some television sets that involved the following costs:

1. Fifty television sets at $150 each with payment due in 30 days; a 2 percent discount would be allowed for payment within 10 days.

2. Freight and shipping costs of $300.

3. Insurance during transit costs of $150.

4. Import duties of $10 per set.

The total cost and unit cost of the television sets may be computed as follows:

Product costs	
Cost of sets—50 at $150	$7,500
Import duties—50 at $10	500
Shipping costs	300
Insurance in transit	150
Subtotal	8,450
Less: Purchase discount—2% × $7,500	150
Total cost	$8,300
Unit cost—$8,300 ÷ 50	$ 166

A Merchandiser's Balance Sheet

Merchandisers have only *one* classification of inventories—finished goods for sale to customers. Because of the single classification, merchandisers customarily use the simple label *Inventories* on their balance sheets.

ILLUSTRATION 2–8

CARSON PIRIE SCOTT & CO.
Consolidated Balance Sheet
January 31, 19x1

Assets

Current assets:	
Cash	$ 8,691,000
Receivables	88,325,000
Inventories	53,959,000
Supplies and prepaid expenses	2,747,000
Total current assets	$153,722,000

The current asset section of a merchandiser's balance sheet is shown in Illustration 2–8. Note that it has only one listing for inventories.

A Merchandiser's Income Statement

Except for the statement of cost of goods manufactured, which is not applicable to merchandisers, the income statements of manufacturers and merchansers are almost the same. The only difference between the two kinds of income statements occurs in the cost of goods sold section. For merchandisers, purchases of merchandise for resale are shown as purchases (plus freight in), while for manufacturers, the counterpart is shown as cost of goods manufactured. The statement of cost of goods sold for a merchandising firm is shown in Illustration 2–9.

The income statement for a merchandiser would take the same format as the income statement for a manufacturer, as shown in Illustration 2–6. You may want to review Illustration 2–6 at this time.

SERVICE BUSINESSES

Several decades ago, service firms paid little attention to costs. Their rationale was that since all their costs were period costs (they had no product costs

ILLUSTRATION 2–9

SELLMORE RETAIL OUTLET COMPANY
Statement of Cost of Goods Sold
For the Year Ended December 31, 19x2

Cost of goods sold:		
Beginning inventory		$150,000
Add: Purchases	$500,000	
Freight-in	6,000	506,000
Goods available for sale		656,000
Deduct: Ending inventory		140,000
Cost of goods sold		$516,000

because no products were sold), and since period costs varied little based on the amount of business activity, costs could be ignored. The objective of a service firm was to concentrate on attracting customers with the expectation that profits would thereby increase. Today, service industries are very mindful of costs and are now charging their customers and clients for many services that were provided free in the past. Examples of this are the charges that banks now make for certifying checks and cashing bearer-bond coupons and that attorneys now bill for telephone consultations.

The financial statements of service organizations are similar to those of merchandisers, except that their balance sheets do not normally contain inventories and their income statements do not contain cost of goods sold.

OTHER COST CONCEPTS

In Chapter 1, we noted that planning and controlling are important managerial duties. The cost data that managers need may not necessarily be classified in the same manner as the data used in the preparation of financial statements. For planning and control purposes, a manager is interested in how a cost behaves. **Cost behavior** is the manner in which a particular cost reacts to a change in business activity. At one end of the spectrum are variable costs, which fluctuate in relation to output. At the other end are fixed costs, which do not change within a given range of production. Between these extremes are mixed costs, which vary, but not in direct proportion to output. Mixed costs are discussed in Chapter 5.

Variable Costs

A **variable cost** varies *in total* directly with the number of units produced. When production is nil, the cost is nil, and when production doubles, the cost doubles. For example, if the raw materials cost of a table is $20, then the variable cost of raw materials is $20 if one table is produced, $40 if two tables are produced, and so forth. The total raw materials cost can be ascertained by multiplying the number of tables produced by $20.

In this definition of variable cost, *linearity* is assumed. Thus, we assume that the raw materials cost for *each table* remains $20 regardless of how many tables are produced. If a graph were constructed for the raw materials cost of the tables using a cost of $20 each, it would appear as in Illustration 2–10.

The graph shown in Illustration 2–10 may be summarized as follows:

Number of Units	Total Cost	Cost per Unit
10	$200	$20
20	400	20
30	600	20
40	800	20

ILLUSTRATION 2–10   Variable Cost Graph

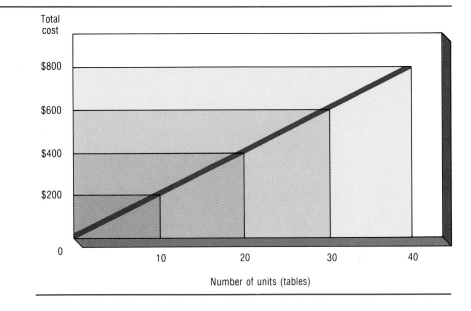

The important point to remember is that *a variable cost has a constant (fixed) cost per unit.* Other examples of variable costs are direct labor, electric power used to operate machinery, and commissions paid to salespeople.

Fixed Costs

Fixed costs are costs that remain constant for a particular range of production. If a firm rents a factory building in which to manufacture its products, the cost for rent is usually a fixed amount per month or year, so it is a fixed cost. Other costs that fall into this category are the factory superintendent's salary, insurance, and real estate property taxes.

It is important to recognize that a fixed cost remains fixed only for a particular range of production. For example, if the size of a factory building permits 400,000 units to be produced on any given day, its fixed cost has a range of 0 to 400,000 units per day. Whether 100,000 units or 350,000 units are produced, the cost for factory rent remains the same.

When a firm's output must be increased beyond its current capacity—in this case, beyond 400,000 units per day—several courses of action are available. A firm can: (1) utilize its present workers on an overtime basis, (2) hire a new staff and begin a two-shift operation, or (3) rent an additional factory building and employ an additional staff to operate two factories concurrently. The best course of action will depend on whether increased capacity is needed over a short or a long period. If the need is short term, the cost of operating a second shift should be compared with the cost of operating the existing staff on an overtime basis. If the need is long term, then the cost of constructing and operating an additional factory should be compared with the cost of a second shift and the cost of overtime. Other factors, such as expected productivity and employee morale, must also be considered. If the company decides to rent another factory with a capacity of 400,000 units per day, the total cost of factory rent and other fixed costs may be somewhat more or less than twice the current fixed costs, depending on the rent and other costs in the second factory. This illustrates that fixed costs remain the same only for a particular range of production. This range is usually called the **relevant range** of production. A firm has only one relevant range in a given time period and rarely, if ever, operates outside of its relevant range.

Illustration 2–11 shows a company's fixed costs within the range of 0 to 400,000 units of production.

Although constant in total, fixed costs are not constant on a per-unit basis. This is shown in Illustration 2–12, where it is assumed that fixed costs are $20,000 per month. As production increases, the cost per unit decreases. It is for this reason that managers prefer to operate their firms at or near full capacity, since the fixed cost per unit is minimized at this point.

Direct versus Indirect Costs

As noted earlier, a *direct cost* is one that can be traced exclusively to a particular *cost objective,* such as a product, a product line, a factory, a division, or a segment of a firm's operations. An *indirect* cost is one that is *common*

ILLUSTRATION 2–11   Fixed Cost Graph

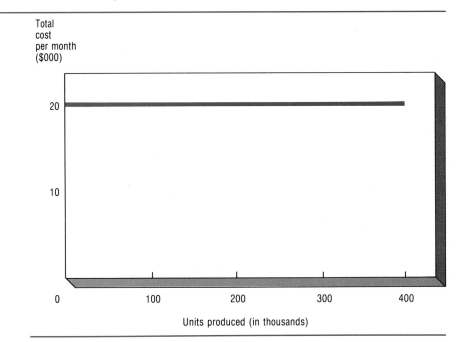

Total cost per month ($000)

20

10

0   100   200   300   400

Units produced (in thousands)

ILLUSTRATION 2–12   **Analysis of Rent per Unit**

Units Produced		Aggregate Cost per Month	Cost per Unit
1	. . . . . .	$20,000	$20,000.00
10,000	. . . . . .	20,000	2.00
100,000	. . . . . .	20,000	.20
400,000	. . . . . .	20,000	.05

to more than one cost objective and thus is *not* exclusive to any one product, product line, etc.

Direct costs are not limited to direct materials or direct labor. In fact, a cost can be direct in one instance and indirect in another. The *frame of reference* determines the nature of the cost. For example, a factory superintendent's salary, although classified as manufacturing overhead, can be a direct cost if a factory manufactures only one product and the cost objective is the product. On the other hand, it would be an indirect cost if the factory manufactured *several* products and the cost objective was *one* of the products. Another way of viewing this example is that in the first case, a decision to discontinue manufacturing the product would normally eliminate the need for the superintendent's services and thus eliminate his salary, while in the second case, the discontinuance of *one* product would not necessarily change the need for the superintendent's services or the need to pay his salary.

It should be noted that the direct/indirect classification is not limited to product costs. Marketing and administrative costs can also be classified as direct or indirect. For example, if the Chevrolet Motor Division of General Motors placed an advertisement for its Corvette, this would be considered a direct cost if the Corvette were the cost objective. If, however, General Motors placed an advertisement extolling the virtues of its efforts to manufacture pollution-free automobiles, the advertisement would be considered an indirect cost if the cost objective were still the Corvette.

Differential Costs

A **differential cost** is the difference between the costs of two alternative courses of action. This cost plays a crucial role in decision making.

When choosing among several courses of action, managers could consider either differential costs or aggregate costs. **Aggregate cost** is the total cost of a particular cost objective.

While it is possible to compute the aggregate cost for each alternative and then compare the two, this approach requires more effort than the differential cost approach. Proponents of the differential cost approach claim that considering only the *differences* between the two alternatives is clearer and more efficient.

If, for example, a firm is considering marketing a product called Delex at $20 per unit and it can manufacture Delex in two different ways, the costs can be calculated on an aggregate cost basis for each alternative or

ILLUSTRATION 2–13   Cost Analysis of Producing Delex

| Cost | Aggregate Cost Approach | | Differential Cost Approach |
	Process A	Process B	Increase (Decrease) in Cost of Process A over B
Direct materials	$ 6	$ 3	$3
Direct labor	4	5	(1)
Variable overhead	3	3	
Fixed overhead	2	2	
Totals	$15	$13	$2

on a differential cost basis. Each method is shown in Illustration 2–13. Columns 2 and 3 illustrate the aggregate cost approach, while the last column illustrates the differential cost approach. The final decision will be based on identical results—that is, process B is favored because it costs $2 less per unit. However, the differential cost computations are much simpler than those for the aggregate cost approach. The aggregate cost approach considers all costs, even if they are the same for both processes. But the differential approach ignores identical costs and considers only the differences in costs.

Opportunity Costs

An **opportunity cost** is the value of any opportunity one gives up in order to engage in an alternative activity. For example, a person who chooses to attend college full time instead of entering the employment market has an opportunity cost of going to college equal to the earnings forgone during the period of study. Although opportunity cost is not presently used in financial accounting, it is an extremely important element of the managerial decision-making process.

Let us assume that you have $100,000 in a savings account earning $10,000 of interest each year. You are offered an opportunity to invest the $100,000 in a business with almost no risk that will yield a yearly net income of $35,000. This business will require that you work there full time. You are presently employed full time and earning $30,000 annually for work that is similar to that required of you if you invest in the business. The opportunity costs of investing in this business may be summarized as follows:

Opportunity Costs	Amount
Employee's salary forgone	$30,000
Interest income forgone	10,000
Total opportunity costs	$40,000

By comparing the opportunity costs of $40,000 with the promised net income of $35,000, it would be to your financial advantage to keep the money in the bank and continue working as an employee.

Sunk Costs

A **sunk cost** is any cost that has already been incurred and cannot be reversed. Except for its impact on income taxes, a sunk cost is irrelevant for all decision-making purposes. For example, assume that an automobile manufacturer spent $10 million to set up an assembly line to manufacture 455-horsepower engines. Now, a month later, a gasoline shortage has developed, and the company is contemplating whether to continue manufacturing the 455-horse-power engines or produce smaller engines. The $10 million is a *sunk* cost and, as such, has no bearing on the decision except for the tax write-off that it would provide. The relevant information would be the cash costs of the new assembly line and the marketing benefits of producing a smaller, more fuel-efficient engine compared with the future costs and benefits of producing the larger, gas-guzzling engine.

Controllable and Noncontrollable Costs

In the long run, all costs are controllable at some level of management. For shorter intervals, many costs are controllable, while some are not. A **controllable cost** is one that can be altered at *a particular level of management,* while a **noncontrollable cost** is one that cannot be influenced or altered at *a particular level of management.* For example, factory rent might be a controllable cost at the vice presidential level. If the vice president of manufacturing can make the decision to rent particular premises, she should be held accountable for their cost. Similarly, a line foreman should be held accountable for the amount of direct labor cost expended on his assembly line. Since the foreman has the authority to decide which employees should be used for specific duties on his line, he has the ability to control the employees' performance levels and, thus, their cost. These costs would be considered controllable by the foreman.

A second factor in examining a cost's controllability is its time frame. Certain costs may be controllable in the long term and not in the short term. Consider the cost of constructing a factory building. The size of the building and the cost of construction materials are only controllable when the building is being constructed. Once the factory is constructed, its building cost (depreciation) would be noncontrollable until it is time to raze the old building and construct a new one—far into the future. Alternatively, the cost of truck maintenance—greasing and changing the oil—is controllable in the short run. The decision can be made to do the maintenance every 4,000 miles or every 2,000 miles.

For purposes of performance evaluation, a manager should be held accountable for only those costs that are controllable at his or her level. Noncontrollable costs at one level of management are normally controllable at a higher level. A reporting system in which a cost is charged to the lowest level of

ILLUSTRATION 2-14   Cost Classifications and Some of Their Uses

Cost Classification	Uses
Assignable product cost.	Inventory valuation and budget preparation.
Conversion cost.	Pricing, inventory valuation, and budget preparation.
Differential cost.	Compared with differential revenue to decide upon expansion or deletion of a particular product line.
Direct cost.	Sum of all direct costs of a product (line) compared with revenue from product (line) to determine if product (line) is profitable.
Expired cost.	Deducted from revenues of a stated period of time to compute net income for that period.
Fixed cost.	Computation of breakeven sales, long-term decisions, budget preparation, and cost-volume-profit decisions.
Opportunity cost.	Part of total cost to be considered for profitability decisions.
Period cost.	Matched against revenue to compute net income for a period of time.
Prime cost.	Inventory valuation, pricing, and budget preparation.
Sunk cost.	Computation of the tax consequences when purchasing replacement equipment.
Unexpired cost.	This cost, carried over into a subsequent accounting period, appears on the balance sheet at any given date.
Variable cost.	Pricing, inventory valuation, budget preparation, break-even sales, and cost-volume-profit decisions.

management that has responsibility for it is known as **responsibility accounting,** or **activity accounting.**

A summary of this chapter's cost classifications and some of their uses appears in Illustration 2–14.

SUMMARY

A cost is a sacrifice made to acquire a good or service. Costs can be classified in many different ways. The needs of managers and accountants govern the manner in which costs are classified.

Direct costs are costs that are directly traceable to a specific cost objective. **Indirect costs,** also called *common costs,* cannot be traced directly to a specific cost objective. Thus, they must be assigned on some rational basis to a specific **cost objective,** usually a specific product.

Costs that can be attributed to production are classified as **product costs,** in which case they are **assignable** or *inventoriable.* On the other hand, noninventoriable costs are called **period costs** and are usually classified according to their functional components, such as marketing costs and administrative costs. Period costs are usually **expired costs,** or *expenses.* **Unexpired costs** are assets.

The principal difference between the financial statements of merchandising firms and manufacturing firms is in how inventories are shown. Merchandisers have only one class of inventory, finished goods, which they show on their balance sheets as *Inventories.* Manufacturers, however, classify their inventories on their balance sheets into three classes: **raw materials, work in process, and finished goods.** In addition, manufacturers prepare a statement of **cost of goods manufactured,** which has no counterpart in a merchandiser's financial statements. Both merchandisers and manufacturers prepare income statements that show sales revenues, **costs of goods sold, gross margins, operating profits,** and **net incomes.**

Manufacturers break down their product costs into three components: **direct materials, direct labor,** and **manufacturering overhead.** Manufacturers also consider **prime costs** and **conversion costs.** Manufacturers place raw materials into production and by processing them with direct labor and overhead, transform them into work in process. When manufacturing is completed, the work in process becomes finished goods, which are then sold. At that time, the cost of the goods sold is aggregated. The **aggregate cost** of any cost objective is its *total cost.*

Cost behavior patterns are varied. At one end of the spectrum are **variable costs,** whose total varies proportionately with production. At the opposite end are **fixed costs,** which are constant within a **relevant range** of production. In between these extremes are mixed costs, which contain both fixed and variable elements.

Costs can also be classified as **controllable** or **noncontrollable.** This distinction is useful in **responsibility accounting** and for decision-making purposes. Other classifications, also useful for decision making, are **differential costs, opportunity costs,** and **sunk costs.** The use of these classified costs in the decision-making process forms the major focus of the remainder of this book.

GLOSSARY OF KEY TERMS

Activity accounting   See **responsibility accounting.**

Aggregate cost   The total cost of a particular cost objective.

Assignable product cost   Direct materials, direct labor, and all indirect manufacturing costs (overhead) necessary to produce a finished product ready for sale to customers.

Burden   See **manufacturing overhead.**

Common cost   See **indirect cost.**

Controllable cost   A cost that can be altered at a particular level of management.

Conversion cost   The sum of direct labor and manufacturing overhead.

Cost   A sacrifice made to acquire a good or service.

Cost behavior   The manner in which a cost reacts to a change in business activity.

Cost objective   A grouping to which costs are assigned, such as a unit of inventory, a department, a product line, a division, or the firm itself.

Cost of goods manufactured   Beginning work in process inventory + Raw materials used + Direct labor + Manufacturing overhead − Ending work in process inventory.

Cost of goods sold Beginning finished goods inventory + Cost of goods manufactured (for manufacturers) or cost of goods purchased (for merchandisers) − Ending finished goods inventory.

Differential cost The difference between the costs of two alternative courses of action.

Direct cost A cost that is directly related, or traceable, to a single cost objective.

Direct labor Wages paid to employees who work on transforming raw materials into a finished product as well as the wages of inspectors who approve the product for sale to customers.

Direct materials The cost of all raw materials that are necessary to produce a finished product for sale to customers.

Expense See **expired cost.**

Expired cost A sacrifice not expected to benefit future accounting periods. Also called an **expense.**

Factory burden See **manufacturing overhead.**

Factory expenses See **manufacturing overhead.**

Finished goods Goods in finished condition awaiting sale to customers.

Fixed cost A total cost that remains constant within a given range of activity and period of time. However, the *per-unit* cost decreases with increased output.

Gross margin (gross profit) On an income statement, sales revenue minus cost of goods sold.

Gross profit See **gross margin.**

Indirect cost A cost that relates to more than one cost objective.

Indirect factory expenses See **manufacturing overhead.**

Indirect manufacturing costs See **manufacturing overhead.**

Inventoriable costs See **assignable product cost.**

Manufacturing overhead Costs that are necessary to manufacture a finished product except for *direct materials* and *direct labor*. Manufacturing overhead is also called overhead, burden, factory burden, factory expenses, indirect factory expenses, indirect manufacturing costs, or overhead pool.

Net income Sales revenue minus cost of goods sold, marketing costs, administrative costs, and income taxes.

Noncontrollable cost A cost that cannot be influenced or altered at a particular level of management.

Operating profit Sales revenue minus cost of goods sold, marketing costs, and administrative costs.

Opportunity cost The value given up or the income that is forgone by employing a resource in an alternative use.

Overhead See **manufacturing overhead.**

Overhead pool See **manufacturing overhead.**

Period cost A cost that is related to a period of time and not to production. It is not a product cost and is classified as either a marketing cost or an administrative cost.

Prime cost The sum of direct material costs and direct labor.

Product cost   A cost that can be attributed specifically to products; direct materials, direct labor, and manufacturing overhead. Also called **inventoriable cost.**

Raw materials   Materials purchased for later use in the manufacturing cycle. Also, the cost of those materials. See **direct materials.**

Raw materials used   Beginning raw materials inventory + Raw materials purchased − Ending raw materials inventory.

Relevant range   The level of activity that a firm chooses for its operations. A firm normally operates within this range, although it may occasionally operate at a different level.

Responsibility accounting   A reporting system in which a cost is charged to the lowest level of management that has responsibility for it.

Sunk cost   A previously incurred cost that cannot be reversed. It is irrelevant for future decision making except for its tax consequences.

Unexpired cost   A sacrifice to acquire a good or service whose benefits will expire in a subsequent accounting period.

Unit cost   The total cost of a product divided by the number of units produced.

Variable cost   A total cost that varies proportionately with output. However, the *per-unit* cost is constant within a given range of production.

Work in process   Raw materials, direct labor, and manufacturing overhead expended on merchandise not yet in finished condition.

QUESTIONS

1. What is an expense?

2. What is a cost objective?

3. What is a direct cost?

4. What is an indirect cost?

5. What do direct materials consist of?

6. What is direct labor?

7. What is manufacturing overhead? Give some examples of what is included in manufacturing overhead.

8. What is a product cost for a manufacturing establishment?

9. How does cost of goods sold for a manufacturing business differ from that of a merchandising business?

10. How does a manufacturer's balance sheet differ from that of a merchandiser?

11. What is a product cost for a merchandising establishment?

12. What is prime cost?

13. What is conversion cost?

14. What is a period cost?

15. What is cost of goods sold for a merchandising business?

16. What is a variable cost? Give an example of a variable cost.

17. What is a fixed cost? Give an example of a fixed cost.

18. What is a mixed cost? Give an example of a mixed cost.

19. What is relevant range?

20. Is a cost always direct or indirect? Can it sometimes be one and at other times the other? Explain.

21. Contrast controllable and noncontrollable costs. Use examples to illustrate your discussion.

22. What is responsibility accounting?

23. What is meant by differential cost? Why is it used?

24. What is an opportunity cost? Why is it important for managers to use this cost concept?

25. What is a sunk cost? Is it relevant for decision making? Explain.

26. A statement was made to the effect that a fixed cost is a variable cost per unit and a variable cost is a fixed cost per unit. Do you agree? Explain your answer by using an example to prove your argument.

27. When a firm requires additional manufacturing capacity, there are several options available to the firm. What are they? How should the firm evaluate them to arrive at the optimum decision?

EXERCISES   **2–1**   **Cost Terms**

1. The term "incremental cost" refers to
   a. The difference in total costs which results from selecting one alternative instead of another.
   b. The profit forgone by selecting one alternative instead of another.
   c. A cost which does not entail any dollar outlay but which is relevant to the decision-making process.
   d. A cost which continues to be incurred even though there is no activity.
   e. A cost common to all alternatives in question and not clearly or practically allocable to any of the alternatives.

2. A sunk cost is
   a. A cost which may be saved by not adopting an alternative.
   b. A cost which may be shifted to the future with little or no effect on current operations.
   c. A cost which cannot be avoided because it has already been incurred.
   d. A cost which does not entail any dollar outlay but which is relevant to the decision-making process.
   e. A cost common to all alternatives in question and not clearly or practically allocable to any of the alternatives.

3. An opportunity cost is
   a. The difference in total costs which results from selecting one alternative instead of another.
   b. The profit forgone by selecting one alternative instead of another.
   c. A cost which may be saved by not adopting an alternative.
   d. A cost which may be shifted to the future with little or no effect on current operations.
   e. A cost which cannot be avoided because it has already been incurred.

4. Those costs referred to as "controllable costs" are
   a. Costs which management decides to incur in the current period to enable the company to achieve objectives other than the filling of orders placed by customers.
   b. Costs which are likely to respond to the amount of attention devoted to them by a specified manager.
   c. Costs which are governed mainly by past decisions that established the present levels of operating and organizational capacity and which only change slowly in response to small changes in capacity.
   d. Costs which fluctuate in total in response to small changes in the rate of utilization of capacity.
   e. Costs which will be unaffected by current managerial decisions.
5. The term "conversion costs" refers to
   a. Manufacturing costs incurred to produce units of output.
   b. All costs associated with manufacturing other than direct labor costs and raw material costs.
   c. Costs which are associated with marketing, shipping, warehousing, billing activities.
   d. The sum of direct labor costs and all factory overhead costs.
   e. The sum of raw material costs and direct labor costs.
6. The term "prime costs" refers to
   a. Manufacturing costs incurred to produce units of output.
   b. All costs associated with manufacturing other than direct labor costs and raw material costs.
   c. Costs which are predetermined and should be attained.
   d. The sum of direct labor costs and all factory overhead costs.
   e. The sum of raw material costs and direct labor costs.
7. Costs which are inventoriable are
   a. Manufacturing costs incurred to produce units of output.
   b. All costs associated with manufacturing other than direct labor costs and raw material costs.
   c. Costs which are associated with marketing, shipping, warehousing, billing activities.
   d. The sum of direct labor costs and all factory overhead costs.
   e. The sum of raw material costs and direct labor costs.
8. The term "variable costs" refers to
   a. All costs which are likely to respond to the amount of attention devoted to them by a specified manager.
   b. All costs which are associated with marketing, shipping, warehousing, billing activities.
   c. All costs which do not change in total for a given period of time and relevant range but become progressively smaller on a per-unit basis as volume increases.
   d. All manufacturing costs incurred to produce units of output.
   e. All costs which fluctuate in total in response to small changes in the rate of utilization of capacity.

(CMA adapted)

2–2 Cost Terms and Cost Behavior

Items 1 and 2 are based on the following data:

Roja Corporation makes aluminum fasteners. Among Roja's 19x1 manufacturing costs were the following:

Wages and salaries:	
Machine operators	$ 80,000
Factory foremen	30,000
Machine mechanics	20,000
Materials and supplies:	
Aluminum	$400,000
Machine parts	18,000
Lubricants for machines	5,000

1. Direct labor amounted to
    a. $ 80,000.
    b. $100,000.
    c. $110,000.
    d. $130,000.
2. Direct materials amounted to
    a. $400,000.
    b. $405,000.
    c. $418,000.
    d. $423,000.
3. Which of the following best describes an opportunity cost?
    a. It is usually relevant, but is not part of traditional accounting records.
    b. It is usually not relevant, but is part of traditional accounting records.
    c. It is usually relevant, and is part of traditional accounting records.
    d. It is usually not relevant, and is not part of traditional accounting records.
4. Information concerning Label Corporation's product A is as follows:

Sales	$300,000
Variable costs	$240,000
Fixed costs	$ 40,000

Assuming that Label increased sales of product A by 20 percent, what should the net income from product A be?
    a. $20,000.
    b. $24,000.
    c. $32,000.
    d. $80,000.

(AICPA adapted)

2–3 Cost Terms

Items 1 and 2 are based on the following data:

Morton Company's manufacturing costs for 19x1 were as follows:

Direct materials	$300,000
Direct labor	400,000

Factory overhead:
Variable   80,000
Fixed   50,000

1. Prime cost totaled
   a. $300,000.
   b. $380,000.
   c. $700,000.
   d. $830,000.
2. Conversion cost totaled
   a. $400,000.
   b. $480,000.
   c. $530,000.
   d. $830,000.
3. Gandy Company has 5,000 obsolete desk lamps that are carried in inventory at a manufacturing cost of $50,000. If the lamps are reworked for $20,000, they could be sold for $35,000. Alternatively, the lamps could be sold for $8,000 to a jobber located in a distant city. In a decision model analyzing these alternatives, the sunk cost would be
   a. $ 8,000.
   b. $15,000.
   c. $20,000.
   d. $50,000.

(AICPA adapted)

2–4 Cost Behavior and Cost Terms

The Ernie Company has provided information concerning its 19x9 projections as follows:

Net sales $10,000,000
Fixed manufacturing costs   1,000,000

1. Ernie projects variable manufacturing costs of 60 percent of net sales. Assuming no change in inventory, what will the projected cost of goods sold be?
   a. $5,000,000.
   b. $6,000,000.
   c. $7,000,000.
   d. $8,000,000.
2. Anthony Company has projected cost of goods sold of $4 million, including fixed costs of $800,000. Variable costs are expected to be 75 percent of net sales. What will be the projected net sales?
   a. $4,266,667.
   b. $4,800,000.
   c. $5,333,333.
   d. $6,400,000.
3. Keller Company is a manufacturer of rivets, and its 19x1 manufacturing costs were as follows:

Direct materials and direct labor $800,000
Depreciation of machines   100,000

Rent for factory building 60,000
Electricity to run machines 35,000

How much of these costs should be included as product cost?
a. $800,000.
b. $835,000.
c. $935,000.
d. $995,000.

(AICPA adapted)

2–5 Cost of Goods Manufactured and Sold

A partial trial balance of the Block Corporation as of December 31, 19x4, follows:

Raw materials inventory, January 1 . . . . $ 40,000
Work in process inventory, January 1 . . . 20,000
Finished goods inventory, January 1 100,000
Purchases of raw materials 150,000
Direct labor 200,000
Indirect labor 50,000
Factory rent 80,000
Office rent 30,000
Depreciation—machinery 40,000
Depreciation—office equipment 5,000
Insurance—factory 20,000
Salespersons' salaries 60,000
Repairs and maintenance—machinery . . 15,000
Miscellaneous factory costs 80,000
Miscellaneous office costs 25,000

The December 31 inventories are:

Raw materials . . . . $ 30,000
Work in process 25,000
Finished goods 90,000

Required a. Prepare a statement of cost of goods manufactured.
b. Prepare a statement of cost of goods sold.

2–6 Cost Classification

Classify the following costs as either (PR) product cost, or (PE) period cost:

1. Sweeping compound for the factory.
2. Light and heat for the factory.
3. Factory superintendent's salary.
4. Sales manager's travel costs.
5. Inspection salaries.
6. Receiving department salaries.
7. Salaries of stockroom personnel.
8. Salaries of finished goods warehouse personnel.
9. Payroll taxes on factory workers' salaries.
10. Night watchmen's salaries for factory building.

11. Telephone for factory.
12. Power.
13. Small tools—hammers, screwdrivers, etc.
14. Bookkeeping salaries to maintain customers' accounts receivable.
15. Computer rental to perform cost accounting function.
16. Computer rental to maintain finished goods inventory control system.
17. Travel cost for the vice president of manufacturing to a professional convention.
18. Salespersons' meeting cost to learn about the company's new product.

2–7   Cost Classification

Classify the following costs as either (V) variable; (F) fixed; (P) part fixed, part variable.

1. Sweeping compound for the factory.
2. Light and heat for the factory.
3. Factory superintendent's salary.
4. Factory line foremen—two lines per foreman.
5. Inspection salaries.
6. Receiving department salaries.
7. Salaries of stockroom personnel.
8. Salaries of finished goods warehouse personnel.
9. Payroll taxes on factory workers' salaries.
10. Night watchmen's salaries for factory building.
11. Telephone for factory.
12. Power.
13. Small tools—hammers, screwdrivers, etc.
14. Rental charges for machinery rented during busy periods.
15. Computer rental to perform cost accounting function.
16. Raw materials for product B—three products are produced; A, B, and C.
17. Repair and maintenance of factory machinery.
18. Photocopying machine rental. The monthly charge is $300 per month plus 3 cents per copy made.
19. Salaries of management accountants.

2–8   Cost Classification

Classify the following costs as either (D) direct or (I) indirect. The frame of reference is product B, and the company manufactures three products; A, B, and C.

1. Sweeping compound for the factory.
2. Light and heat for the factory.
3. *Factory superintendent's salary.
4. Factory line foreman—two lines, both producing product B.
5. Inspection salaries—inspectors work only on product B.
6. Receiving department salaries.
7. Salaries of stockroom personnel.
8. Shipping cartons—product B is not commingled with A or C.
9. Payroll taxes as a percentage of direct labor for product B.
10. Night watchmen's salaries for factory building.
11. Telephone for factory.
12. Power.
13. Small tools—hammers, screwdrivers, etc.

14. Rental charges for machinery rented during busy periods. The machinery is used on all products.
15. Computer rental to perform cost accounting function.
16. Raw materials for product B—three products are produced; A, B, and C.

2–9 Cost of Goods Manufactured and Sold

A partial trial balance of the Brett Corporation as of December 31, 19x4, follows:

Raw materials inventory, January 1	$ 60,000
Work in process inventory, January 1	25,000
Finished goods inventory, January 1	110,000
Purchases of raw materials	170,000
Direct labor	215,000
Indirect labor	45,000
Factory rent	72,000
Office rent	36,000
Depreciation—machinery	30,000
Depreciation—office equipment	10,000
Insurance—factory	15,000
Salespersons' salaries	66,000
Repairs and maintenance—machinery	10,000
Miscellaneous factory costs	90,000
Miscellaneous office costs	30,000

The December 31 inventories are:

Raw materials	$ 55,000
Work in process	30,000
Finished goods	95,000

Required a. Prepare a statement of cost of goods manufactured.
b. Prepare a statement of cost of goods sold.

2–10 Cost of Goods Manufactured and Sold

A partial trial balance of the Brown Corporation as of December 31, 19x4, follows:

Raw materials inventory, January 1	$ 45,000
Work in process inventory, January 1	30,000
Finished goods inventory, January 1	125,000
Purchases of raw materials	160,000
Direct labor	225,000
Indirect labor	40,000
Factory rent	84,000
Office rent	48,000
Depreciation—machinery	35,000
Depreciation—office equipment	8,000
Insurance—factory	18,000
Salespersons' salaries	72,000
Repairs and maintenance—machinery	12,000
Miscellaneous factory	100,000
Miscellaneous office	40,000

The December 31 inventories are:

Raw materials	$ 40,000
Work in process	35,000
Finished goods	110,000

Required   a.   Prepare a statement of cost of goods manufactured.
b.   Prepare a statement of cost of goods sold.

PROBLEMS   **2–11**   **Preparation of Statement of Cost of Goods Manufactured and Income Statement**

The president of the Baker Manufacturing Company has a son who just graduated from high school and does not plan to go to college. Mr. Baker offered his son a job in the accounting department of the firm, and the son accepted. Since the son had some bookkeeping in high school, he felt qualified to prepare the income statement for the six months ended June 30, 19x4. His prepared statement is as follows:

BAKER MANUFACTURING COMPANY
Income Statement
For the Six Months Ended June 30, 19x4

Sales		$900,000
Costs of goods sold:		
Beginning inventories:		
Raw materials	$ 60,000	
Work in process	20,000	
Finished goods	80,000	
Raw material purchases	200,000	
Direct labor	300,000	
Rent	90,000	
Light, heat, and power	30,000	
Telephone	10,000	
Depreciation	25,000	
Indirect labor	40,000	
Marketing and administrative salaries	60,000	
Insurance	5,000	
Miscellaneous manufacturing overhead	10,000	
Miscellaneous marketing and administrative costs . . .	12,000	
Total	942,000	
Less: Ending raw materials inventory	20,000	922,000
Net loss		$ 22,000

The following additional information is available:

1.   The ending inventory of work in process amounted to $30,000, and the ending inventory of finished goods amounted to $100,000.
2.   The following costs should be allocated:

	Manufacturing	Period
Rent	70%	30%
Light, heat, and power	80%	20%
Telephone	60%	40%
Insurance	70%	30%
Depreciation	90%	10%

Mr. Baker is concerned that his son's income statement shows a loss for the period. This is the first loss in the company's history.

Required
a. Prepare a statement of cost of goods manufactured in proper format. Make any corrections that are needed.

b. Prepare a corrected income statement using the statement from part *(a)*.

2–12 Matching of Cost Terms

The Prentiss Company manufactures children's clothing. A number of costs are listed in column A. A number of cost terms discussed in this chapter are listed in column B.

Column A		Column B	
a.	Fabric	1.	Variable cost
b.	Thread	2.	Fixed cost
c.	Factory superintendent's salary	3.	Product cost
d.	Night watchman's salary	4.	Period cost
e.	Direct labor	5.	Direct cost
f.	Factory power	6.	Indirect cost
g.	Factory rent	7.	Prime cost
h.	Heat for the office	8.	Conversion cost
i.	Salespersons' commissions.	9.	Opportunity cost
j.	Bookkeeping salaries	10.	Part variable, part fixed cost
k.	Depreciation of office equipment	11.	Marketing cost
l.	Salary of the sales manager	12.	Administrative cost
m.	The president's salary	13.	Manufacturing overhead
n.	Shipping cartons		
o.	Factory telephone		

Required
Match as many cost terms from column B to each cost listed in column A. The cost objective for a direct or indirect cost is a pair of denim boy's pants. The cost terms in column B may be used more than once, and each cost listed in column A may have more than one cost term assigned to it.

2–13 Cost of Goods Manufactured and Income Statement

Selected accounts from the trial balance of the Busch Corporation as of December 31, 19x2, appear below:

Administrative salaries	$ 70,000
Advertising	20,000
Depreciation, machinery	30,000
Depreciation, office equipment	5,000
Depreciation, shipping equipment	8,000
Direct labor	325,000
Factory supplies used	12,000
Factory bookkeeping	15,000
Freight on raw materials	5,000
Heat and power, factory	20,000
Indirect labor	55,000
Insurance, factory	14,000
Inventories:	
Raw materials, January 1	45,000
Raw materials, December 31	55,000
Work in process, January 1	20,000
Work in process, December 31	18,000
Finished goods, January 1	90,000
Finished goods, December 31	75,000
Miscellaneous factory	110,000
Office salaries	60,000
Raw material purchases	130,000
Rent, factory—75%; sales offices—15%;	
administrative—10%	120,000
Repairs to machinery	40,000
Sales	1,800,000
Sales discounts	25,000
Sales salaries	140,000
Superintendence, factory	60,000
Telephone, factory—40%; marketing—30%;	
administrative—30%	40,000

Required *a.* Prepare a statement of cost of goods manufactured.

           b. Prepare an income statement.

2–14   Cost of Goods Manufactured and Income Statement

Selected accounts from the trial balance of the Crush Corporation as of December 31, 19x2, appear below:

Administrative salaries	$ 65,000
Advertising	28,000
Depreciation, machinery	35,000
Depreciation, office equipment	4,000
Depreciation, shipping equipment	7,000
Direct labor	290,000
Factory supplies used	11,000
Factory bookkeeping	18,000
Freight on raw materials	3,000
Heat and power, factory	17,000
Indirect labor	70,000
Insurance, factory	15,000

Inventories:

Raw materials, January 1	50,000
Raw materials, December 31	45,000
Work in process, January 1	22,000
Work in process, December 31	24,000
Finished goods, January 1	95,000
Finished goods, December 31	85,000
Miscellaneous factory	120,000
Office salaries	65,000
Raw material purchases	140,000
Rent, factory—80%; sales offices—10%; administrative—10%	180,000
Repairs to machinery	35,000
Sales	1,900,000
Sales discounts	23,000
Sales salaries	150,000
Superintendence, factory	55,000
Telephone, factory—45%; marketing—35%; administrative—20%	50,000

Required
a. Prepare a statement of cost of goods manufactured.
b. Prepare an income statement.

2–15 Missing Data—Cost of Goods Manufactured and Sold

Supply the missing data for each company listed below:

		Companies		
	A	B	C	D
Sales	$100,000	$?	$130,000	$220,000
Raw materials inventory— beginning	9,000	10,000	7,000	?
Purchases of raw materials . .	14,000	15,000	16,000	21,000
Raw materials inventory— ending	?	8,000	9,000	8,000
Direct labor	25,000	?	17,000	35,000
Manufacturing overhead	20,000	18,000	25,500	31,500
Work in process—beginning . .	19,000	6,000	?	12,000
Work in process—ending	16,000	8,000	15,000	10,000
Finished goods—beginning . .	20,000	?	17,000	16,000
Finished goods—ending	23,000	11,000	?	18,000
Cost of goods manufactured . .	?	42,000	70,000	?
Cost of goods sold	?	44,000	?	100,000
Gross margin	43,000	48,000	54,000	?

2–16 Missing Data—Cost Behavior

Supply the missing data for each company listed below:

	Companies			
	A	**B**	**C**	**D**
Units produced	15,000	20,000	?	25,000
Total cost	$?	$70,000	$50,000	$?
Fixed cost	22,500	?	10,000	?
Fixed cost per unit . . .	?	2.00	2.00	?
Variable cost per unit . .	3.50	?	?	2.70
Total cost per unit . . .	?	?	?	4.10

2–17 **Cost of Goods Manufactured and Income Statement**

Selected accounts from the trial balance of the Laser Corporation as of December 31, 19x2, appear below:

Administrative salaries	$ 80,000
Advertising	25,000
Depreciation, machinery	20,000
Depreciation, office equipment	3,000
Depreciation, shipping equipment	5,000
Direct labor	300,000
Factory supplies used	10,000
Factory bookkeeping	12,000
Freight on raw materials	4,000
Heat and power, factory	14,000
Indirect labor	60,000
Insurance, factory	12,000
Inventories:	
Raw materials, January 1	40,000
Raw materials, December 31	50,000
Work in process, January 1	15,000
Work in process, December 31	13,000
Finished goods, January 1	80,000
Finished goods, December 31	90,000
Miscellaneous factory	100,000
Office salaries	40,000
Raw material purchases	120,000
Rent, factory—70%; sales offices—10%;	
administrative—20%	110,000
Repairs to machinery	18,000
Sales	1,600,000
Sales discounts	24,000
Sales salaries	160,000
Superintendence, factory	50,000
Telephone, factory—50%; marketing—20%;	
administrative—30%	30,000

Required   *a.*   Prepare a statement of cost of goods manufactured.

           b.   Prepare an income statement.

2–18   **Missing Data—Cost of Goods Manufactured and Sold**

Supply the missing data for each company listed below:

	Companies			
	A	**B**	**C**	**D**
Sales	$100,000	$120,000	$?	$180,000
Raw materials inventory—				
beginning	6,000	8,000	4,000	?
Purchases of raw materials . .	13,000	18,000	8,000	15,000
Raw materials inventory—				
ending	?	10,000	3,000	6,000
Direct labor	22,000	18,000	?	50,000
Manufacturing overhead	18,000	28,000	17,000	30,000
Work in process—beginning . .	16,000	?	8,000	10,000
Work in process—ending	14,000	14,000	7,000	9,000
Finished goods—beginning . .	15,000	18,000	?	15,000
Finished goods—ending	13,000	?	12,000	12,000
Cost of goods manufactured . .	?	65,000	38,000	?
Cost of goods sold	?	?	40,000	100,000
Gross margin	40,000	50,000	45,000	?

2–19 Missing Data—Cost Behavior

Supply the missing data for each company listed below:

	Companies			
	A	**B**	**C**	**D**
Units produced	10,000	5,000	?	8,000
Total cost	$?	$30,000	$20,000	$?
Fixed cost	5,000	?	6,000	?
Fixed cost per unit	?	1.50	3.00	?
Variable cost per unit	2.50	?	?	2.30
Total cost per unit	?	?	?	3.90

2–20 Cost Behavior Patterns

Given below are graphical representations of various cost behavior patterns. The vertical axis represents the total cost in dollars and the horizontal axis represents the volume—either units produced or units sold. In addition, various types of costs are listed, and for each cost it should be assumed that the cost behaves in its normal pattern.

A   B   C

1. Advertising.
2. Depreciation—units of production method.
3. Depreciation—straight-line method.
4. Direct materials used.
5. Direct labor.
6. Factory supplies used.
7. Freight on raw materials.
8. Heat and power, factory.
9. Rent.
10. Repairs to machinery.
11. Sales.
12. Sales salaries.
13. Superintendence, factory.

Required   Match each cost with a particular behavior pattern. Behavior patterns may be used more than once.

2–21   Cost Behavior Patterns

The management accountant for the Bern Corporation prepared cost estimates for the following levels of activity (in units):

	10,000 Units	15,000 Units
Raw materials	$28,400	$42,600
Direct labor	46,200	69,300
Factory rent	30,000	30,000
Indirect labor	18,000	24,000
Power	6,000	8,500
Superintendent's salary . . .	5,000	5,000
Payroll taxes	9,600	12,100

Required
a. Compute the unit cost for each cost at each level.
b. Indicate whether the cost is (V) variable; (F) fixed; (P) part variable, part fixed. Explain your reasoning for each designation using your computations from part (a).

2–22   Fixed Cost Behavior per Unit

Factory rent for the Brentwood Corporation is $100,000 per annum. The president of the corporation has asked you, as the company's management accountant, to analyze the effect of factory rent on the unit cost of the company's only product, Widget.

Required
a. Prepare a statement showing the unit cost of factory rent at 10,000 unit intervals starting with 10,000 and ending with 100,000 units.
b. Using your results in part (a), prepare a graph showing the average unit cost on the vertical axis and the units on the horizontal axis. Is it a straight line? Why?

2–23   Preparation of Income Statement and Statement of Cost of Goods Manufactured from Fragmented Information

The Recordless Manufacturing Company discovered that the company's bookkeeper failed to keep any records for the first six months of 19x3. However, the firm's independent auditors and the firm had certain information in their files which enabled the firm's management to provide you with the following:

1. Sales revenues for the first six months of 19x3—$800,000.
2. Inventories—January 1, 19x3:

Raw materials	$ 40,000
Work in process	30,000
Finished goods	100,000

3. The average percentage relationships for 19x1 and 19x2 are as follows:
   a. Gross margin as a percent of sales—40 percent.
   b. Direct labor is one third of conversion cost and 60 percent of prime cost.
4. For the first half of 19x2, marketing costs amounted to $80,000 and administrative costs amounted to $100,000. An increase of 10 percent is anticipated for period costs in 19x3.
5. A physical count of all inventories was made at June 30, 19x3. The estimated dollar amounts are:

Raw materials	$ 30,000
Work in process	25,000
Finished goods	120,000

Required

a. Prepare an estimated income statement for the six months ended June 30, 19x3.
b. Prepare an estimated statement of cost of goods manufactured for the six months ended June 30, 19x3.

   (Hint: (1) First, prepare the income statement using the available estimated information. Estimate the gross margin, the cost of goods sold, and finally, the cost of goods manufactured.

   (2) Second, after you have determined the cost of goods manufactured, use an algebraic equation to determine the amounts for raw materials used, direct labor, and manufacturing overhead.)

3

JOB ORDER COSTING

LEARNING OBJECTIVES	After reading this chapter you should be able to:
	1 Discuss why product cost information and a cost accounting system are needed.
	2 Differentiate between a process cost accounting system and a job order cost accounting system and identify the kinds of firms for which each would be appropriate.
	3 Trace the physical flow of production and the corresponding cost flow (the cost accounting cycle).
	4 Identify the different kinds of source documents and how they contribute to a job order cost system.
	5 Explain what book inventories are, how they are automatically generated in a job order cost system, and how they are used.
	6 Discuss why firms use estimated amounts rather than actual amounts to apply manufacturing overhead to production.
	7 Calculate predetermined overhead rates using five different bases and explain the circumstances under which each base is most effective.
	8 Dispose of underapplied and overapplied overhead at the end of the fiscal year.
	9 Describe two different ways of assigning payroll fringes to particular batches of production.

Learning Objectives *(concluded)*

10 Use the Raw Materials Inventory, Work in Process, and Finished Goods accounts to prepare the statements of cost of goods manufactured and cost of goods sold.

11 Determine when it may be necessary to prorate underapplied or overapplied overhead and explain how proration is accomplished.

12 Explain why it may be necessary to departmentalize manufacturing overhead and how to allocate service department overhead to producing departments.

Cost accounting is the subfield of accounting that records, measures, and reports information about costs. In a manufacturing setting, the cost accounting system usually focuses on product costs—that is, direct materials, direct labor, and manufacturing overhead—the costs that can be specifically attributed to products and are part of inventory. The resulting information plays a key role in such managerial activities as valuing inventory, pricing company products, preparing financial statements, planning and control, and decision making of all kinds.

The **cost accounting cycle**—the sequential recording and classifying of transactions that affect costs—usually corresponds to a firm's physical flow of operations. Based on this cycle, product costs are accumulated and assigned to units of product or departments. Because the way in which costs are accumulated and assigned can affect both the income statement and the balance sheet as well as many managerial decisions related to planning, control, and product pricing, it is crucial for managers to understand how their company's operations relate to its flow of costs and its cost accounting system.

In this chapter, we will examine **absorption costing**—also called **full costing**—a costing approach in which all manufacturing costs, both fixed and variable, are assigned to products and thus included in inventory. In Chapter 10, we will consider a different method of costing—variable costing—in which only variable manufacturing costs are inventoried.

The Uses of Product Cost Information

Inventory Valuation. Most managers and investors need financial information on a regular basis. Since inventory values are needed every time an interim or annual report is prepared, a physical count of all goods in stock—a costly and time-consuming process—would be required unless some other method could be found to calculate inventories. In addition, if the physical quantities are to be translated into dollars, some method must be found to calculate the unit cost of each item manufactured. An **integrated cost accounting system**—one that is an integral part of the firm's comprehensive record-keeping system—can provide the needed quantities and unit costs of inventories without the need for a physical count. These amounts, called

book inventories, enable a business to prepare interim financial statements as frequently as needed without taking a physical inventory count.

The book inventory does not replace the need for a physical inventory count, however. A physical inventory count is also necessary from time to time to determine that the quantities shown in the book inventory actually exist. It is not uncommon to find differences between the book inventory and the actual physical count. These differences may be due to theft, errors in record-keeping, or both. A company that relies only on a physical count or only on a book inventory is missing an important control device because one method acts as a check on the other.

Planning and Control.   A cost accounting system is extremely useful for providing the information needed to prepare a firm's budget for the next accounting period. As noted in Chapter 1, a firm must make plans for its operations in future accounting periods, and this is accomplished through the use of budgets.

Decision Making.   Cost accounting is indispensable for many decisions that managers must make on a routine basis. Here are some common managerial decisions and the cost accounting information they require:

Kinds of Decisions	Cost Accounting Information Required
1. Pricing a product	Costs of producing the product
2. Discontinuing a product	Costs saved
3. Making or buying component parts	Costs of making the part
4. Expanding production of an existing product	Additional costs due to expansion
5. Taking special orders at less than regular prices	Additional costs of the special order

Because cost accounting information is needed for (1) inventory pricing and valuation, (2) annual income statement and balance sheet preparation, (3) interim income statement and balance sheet preparation, (4) budget preparation, (5) planning and control, and (6) a variety of decisions that managers must make in carrying out their duties, a good cost accounting system is crucial to a company's success.

COST ACCOUNTING SYSTEMS

There are two basic kinds of cost accounting systems. In a **process cost accounting system,** product costs are accumulated for a specific period of time—a week or a month. The total of the accumulated costs is then divided by the number of units produced to arrive at an average unit cost for the period. This system is used primarily by firms that manufacture a relatively narrow range of products, such as paint manufacturers, petroleum refiners, and mining firms. Firms that use this system manufacture their products repetitively, and thus, their production is continuous. Process costing will be discussed further in Chapter 4.

The other system, a **job order cost accounting system,** accumulates costs for a particular batch of production, which is usually referred to as a **job.** A job has a definite starting point and completion point, as would, for example, the manufacture of 1,000 coffee tables. A furniture manufacturer may start and complete a batch of coffee tables and then not make coffee tables again for a six-month period. When the coffee tables are completed, a batch of sofas may follow, and when those are completed, a batch of dining room tables may be started, and so forth. This kind of production differs sharply from that of the paint manufacturer who produces paint on a continuous basis. In many cases, the paint manufacturer may have difficulty determining when one batch of paint ends and a new one begins, but the furniture manufacturer can clearly identify when the manufacture of each batch of products begins and ends. For manufacturers like the furniture maker, it is logical to relate manufacturing costs to the batch being manufactured. Among the firms that are likely to use job order systems are furniture manufacturers, clothing manufacturers, tool manufacturers, construction contractors, and ship and missile producers.

JOB ORDER COSTING

There is an interrelationship between (1) the physical flow of production, (2) source documents, and (3) the cost accounting cycle (cost accumulation). In a well-controlled system, a business form, or source document, known as a production order will be issued prior to the start of production to authorize the manufacture of a particular product. Additional source documents will be added as the production cycle progresses. In this way, source documents help the company keep track of its production process and form the basis of the journal entries that are part of its cost accounting system.

The Physical Flow of Production

The **physical flow of production** is the sequence of operating activity that begins with the decision to order raw materials and ends with a finished product ready for sale to customers. Although the intervening steps may vary from firm to firm, they share a common thread that allows one general example to be adapted to particular cases. A typical physical flow of production appears in Illustration 3–1. Each step in the flow is associated with a specific source document. The source documents explained in the next section are keyed to the numerical sequence shown in Illustration 3–1.

Source Documents

Source documents are business forms used to initiate or record a firm's accounting transactions. Although the specific forms may vary among organizations, certain kinds of information are common to them all. The source docu-

ILLUSTRATION 3–1   Sample Physical Flow of Production for a Manufacturing Firm

Step

1. A decision is made to order basic raw materials. (Specialized raw materials may be ordered as needed.)
2. Raw materials are ordered from vendors.
3. Raw materials are received and placed in the storeroom.
4. A decision is made to manufacture a specific product in a product line.
5. Raw materials are issued from the storeroom and placed into production.
6. Direct labor employees work on transforming the raw materials into work in process.
7. Other cost factors of production—the manufacturing overhead—are incurred in the process of transforming the raw materials into work in process.
8. The work in process is completed and becomes finished goods.
9. The finished goods are sold and become cost of goods sold.

ments presented here contain the essential information needed to maintain control of a firm's accounting system. In practice, a firm's source documents may contain additional information to satisfy the unique needs of its managers.

1. Purchase Requisition.   Most firms keep on hand a specified minimum stock of basic raw materials such as lumber, glue, nails, hardware, and the like. The purpose of maintaining such a minimum stock—called a **safety stock**—is to avoid the interruption of the production process that would occur if a crucial raw material were to go unexpectedly out of stock due to a delay in shipment or unusually heavy usage. A safety stock is usually maintained for all basic raw materials, but specialized raw materials may be ordered only as needed.

When the quantity of a raw material reaches the level at which it must be reordered, the storeroom clerk prepares a **purchase requisition,** a form requesting the purchase of the needed materials, and sends it to the purchasing department. The form usually includes:

1.   The date the form was prepared.

2.   A control number.

3.   A description of the desired raw material.

4.   The quantity needed.

5.   The date when the raw material is needed.

A sample purchase requisition is shown in Illustration 3–2. *No journal entry* is required when a purchase requisition is prepared.

2. Purchase Order. A purchase order, a document that authorizes a vendor to ship the desired merchandise ordered, is usually generated by the

ILLUSTRATION 3–2   **Sample Purchase Requisition**

Bettermade Furniture Company
1211 World Avenue
New York, N.Y. 10036
(212) 765-4321

Date *January 15, 19x2*

Requisition No. *432*

PURCHASE REQUISITION		
	Prepared by: L.A.B.	
Quantity	Description	Date Needed
10,000 ft.	*Clear Maple 1" x 6"*	*February 15, 19x2*
500 lbs	*4 penny finishing nails*	*March 1, 19x2*

purchasing department. It specifies the price and terms of the order and should contain:

1. The purchaser's name, billing address, and delivery address.

2. A purchase order number.

3. The date of the purchase order.

4. The requisition number.

5. The vendor's name and address.

6. The delivery date.

7. The quantity and description of the material.

8. The price and terms of payment.

9. Shipping instructions and terms.

ILLUSTRATION 3–3   Sample Purchase Order

Bettermade Furniture Company
1211 World Avenue
New York, N.Y. 10036
(212) 765-4321

Date *January 20, 1982*

Vendor	Ship To:	Purchase Order
Alco Lumber Co. *P.O. Box 17* *New York, N.Y. 10001*	*Factory* *14-24 Corona Ave.* *Long Island City* *New York*	No. *1344* (Please show this number on invoice, packing slip, and correspondence.)

F.O.B. Point	Ship Via	Terms	Delivery Date	Requisition No.
Factory-L.I.C., N.Y.	*RR or Truck*	*2/10, n/60*	*February 15, 1982*	*422*

Item No.	Quantity	Unit	Description	Unit Price	Extension
1	*10,000*	*Ft.*	*Clear maple 1" x 6"*	*$2.00 lineal foot*	*$20,000*

A sample purchase order appears in Illustration 3–3. *No journal entry* is required when raw materials are ordered.

3. Receiving Report. When the shipment arrives, the receiving department prepares a **receiving report,** which lists the descriptions and quantities of the goods received. A copy of this document is then sent to the storeroom along with the materials. The receiving report, together with a copy of the vendor's invoice, form the basis of an entry in the company's journals. If the Bettermade Furniture Company purchased lumber for $20,000, drawer hardware for $3,000, and lacquer for $4,000, the summary journal entry to record the purchases would be:

(a)

```
19x2
Feb. 15   Raw Materials Inventory  . . . . . . . . . . . . . . . . . .   27,000
              Accounts Payable  . . . . . . . . . . . . . . . . . .               27,000
                  To record the purchases of raw materials.
```

This entry requires posting to the general ledger account Raw Materials Inventory and to the raw materials ledger cards in the subsidiary ledger. A separate subsidiary ledger card is kept for each form of raw material. If Bettermade's beginning inventory balances were $12,500 for lumber, $3,500 for drawer hardware, and $3,000 for lacquer, and if they also had $600 of glue in beginning inventory, the general ledger account and the subsidiary ledger cards would appear as shown in Illustration 3–4.

A sample receiving report for the lumber purchased appears in Illustration 3–5. Receiving reports would also be prepared when the drawer hardware and the lacquer are delivered.

4. Production Order. While the use of a job order system may seem to imply that production begins only upon the receipt of an order from a customer, this is not the case. Production may begin with the receipt of a customer's order, but it may also start when a firm decides to produce finished goods for stock inventory to be sold at a later time. In either case, when a decision is made to produce a batch of goods, such as 200 desks, a **production order** is prepared and approved by the manager in charge. The production order authorizes the manufacture of a product and contains:

1.   A description of the product to be manufactured.
2.   The quantity required.
3.   A product model number.
4.   The estimated date of completion.
5.   A job order number.
6.   The date of the production order.
7.   The authorization signature.

No journal entries are required on the company's books when the production order is issued. A sample production order is presented in Illustration 3–6.

5. Materials Requisition. Once the production order is issued, a **materials requisition** form is prepared. This source document authorizes the transfer of the necessary materials from the storeroom to the production line to start

ILLUSTRATION 3–4   **Raw Materials Inventory Ledgers**

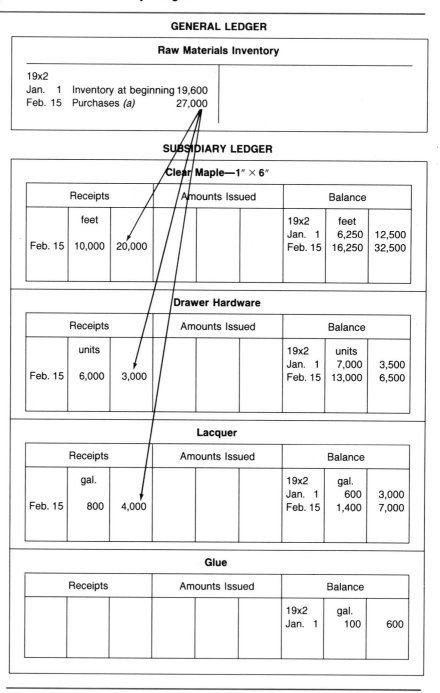

GENERAL LEDGER

Raw Materials Inventory

19x2		
Jan. 1	Inventory at beginning	19,600
Feb. 15	Purchases *(a)*	27,000

SUBSIDIARY LEDGER

Clear Maple—1″ × 6″

Receipts			Amounts Issued			Balance		
	feet					19x2	feet	
						Jan. 1	6,250	12,500
Feb. 15	10,000	20,000				Feb. 15	16,250	32,500

Drawer Hardware

Receipts			Amounts Issued			Balance		
	units					19x2	units	
						Jan. 1	7,000	3,500
Feb. 15	6,000	3,000				Feb. 15	13,000	6,500

Lacquer

Receipts			Amounts Issued			Balance		
	gal.					19x2	gal.	
						Jan. 1	600	3,000
Feb. 15	800	4,000				Feb. 15	1,400	7,000

Glue

Receipts			Amounts Issued			Balance		
						19x2	gal.	
						Jan. 1	100	600

ILLUSTRATION 3–5   Sample Receiving Report

Bettermade Furniture Company Receiving Report				
Received from: *Alea Lumber Company*			Receiving Report No. R 1842	
Freight: Ppd. ✔ Collect ☐			Purchase Order No. *1344*	
Date Received: *Feb. 15, 19X2*		Received by: *Leonard*		
Quantity	Description	Weight		
		Gross	Net	
10,006 lineal feet	*Clear maple 1" x 6"*			

manufacture. Thus far, we have used the term *raw materials* because it encompasses both *direct materials,* which are accounted for individually, and *indirect materials,* which are charged to manufacturing overhead and grouped with other indirect costs. The materials requisition should contain specific descriptions of the materials needed and distinguish between direct and indirect materials.

For control purposes, a storeroom clerk issues raw materials only upon

ILLUSTRATION 3–6   Sample Production Order

Bettermade Furniture Company
Production Order

Date: February 19, 19x2	Job No. 456

Manufactured for: Stock _____ Customer Smith's Dept. Store _____

Date needed: April 15, 19x2

Quantity	Model Number	Description
200	D 2051	Natural maple desks

Authorized by: _*Phyllis Tamara*_

---

receipt of a properly authorized materials requisition form. As shown in Illustration 3–7, a materials requisition form should contain places for:

1. The job number for which the materials are to be issued.
2. A description of the raw materials needed.
3. The quantity of each raw material needed.
4. The unit cost of each material.
5. The total cost.
6. Classification into direct materials and indirect materials.

When the materials are issued from the storeroom, the following entry is made in the company's journals:

(b)

19x2
Feb. 28 Work in Process   10,550
             Manufacturing Overhead*   30
                 Raw Materials Inventory   10,580
             To record the issuance of direct and indirect materials
             for Job No. 456.

  * As noted in Chapter 2, glue is treated as manufacturing overhead, even though it is really direct materials.

Journal entry *(b)* must be posted to the general ledger *and* to the subsidiary ledger cards for the raw materials inventory. After these postings, the ledgers for raw materials would appear as shown in Illustration 3–8. If a book inventory of raw materials is needed, the general ledger balance of $36,020 provides the information. This amount is supported by these individual balances in the subsidiary ledger:

Clear maple	$22,500
Drawer hardware	6,200
Lacquer	6,750
Glue	570
Total	$36,020

It is customary to *accumulate* the materials requisitions and *journalize* them as summary entries, either monthly or weekly depending on the frequency of the reporting system. However, *individual* materials requisitions are *posted* currently to the appropriate individual raw materials ledger cards.

ILLUSTRATION 3–7   Sample Materials Requisition Form

Materials Requisition Number 406		Date Feb. 28, 19x2		
Job Number to Be Charged 456				
Quantity	Description	Unit Cost	Total Cost	Classification
5,000 ft.	Clear maple 1″ × 6″	$2.00	$10,000	Direct
600	Drawer pulls	.50	300	Direct
50 gal.	Lacquer	5.00	250	Direct
5 gal.	Glue	6.00	30	Indirect
			$10,580	

L. Bern
Authorized signature

Direct materials	$10,550
Indirect materials	30

ILLUSTRATION 3–8   **Raw Materials Inventory Ledgers**

GENERAL LEDGER

Raw Materials Inventory

19x2				19x2		
Jan. 1	Inventory at beginning	19,600		Feb. 28	Issuances *(b)*	10,580
Feb. 28	Purchases *(a)*	27,000				
Bal.		*36,020*				

SUBSIDIARY LEDGER

Clear Maple—1″ × 6″

Receipts			Amounts Issued			Balance		
	feet			feet		19x2	feet	
						Jan. 1	6,250	12,500
Feb. 15	10,000	20,000				Feb. 15	16,250	32,500
			Feb. 28	5,000	10,000	28	11,250	22,500

Drawer Hardware

Receipts			Amounts Issued			Balance		
	units			units		19x2	units	
						Jan. 1	7,000	3,500
Feb. 15	6,000	3,000				Feb. 15	13,000	6,500
			Feb. 28	600	300	28	12,400	6,200

Lacquer

Receipts			Amounts Issued			Balance		
	gal.			gal.		19x2	gal.	
						Jan. 1	600	3,000
Feb. 15	800	4,000				Feb. 15	1,400	7,000
			Feb. 28	50	250	28	1,350	6,750

Glue

Receipts			Amounts Issued			Balance		
				gal.		19x2	gal.	
						Jan. 1	100	600
			Feb. 28	5	30	Feb. 28	95	570

Furthermore, while entry *(b)* summarizes cost information, it also corresponds to the physical flow of production. Thus, when the materials are transferred from the storeroom to the factory, they are no longer raw materials inventory; instead, they become *work in process.* The debit to Work in Process in entry *(b)* signifies that the direct materials are in the process of becoming finished goods.

Soon after the preparation of the production order, a **job cost sheet** is prepared. Its purpose is twofold. First, it is used to break down the job's costs into the components of direct materials, direct labor, and manufacturing overhead. The total costs are then divided by the number of units produced to arrive at the unit cost. Second, the job cost sheet acts as the subsidiary ledger to the Work in Process account in the general ledger. A separate sheet is kept for each job. Thus, the details of the work in process inventory at any point in time can be found by consulting the job cost sheets. The active file of job cost sheets contains only jobs that are still in process. When a job is *completed,* the cost summary at the bottom of the job cost sheet is filled in and the form is transferred to a file of completed jobs. The general ledger account for work in process and the related job cost sheet are shown in Illustration 3–9.

Let us assume that Jobs 457 and 458 are started on March 2, 19x2, and that the direct materials and indirect materials for these jobs are as shown in journal entry *(c):*

(c)

```
19x2
Mar. 31   Work in Process  . . . . . . . . . . . . . . . . . . . . . . . .   14,000
             Manufacturing Overhead  . . . . . . . . . . . . . . . . . .       900
                Raw Materials Inventory . . . . . . . . . . . . . . . .              14,900
             To record the issuance of materials for Jobs 457 and
             458 as follows:
```

	457	458
Direct materials	$6,000	$8,000
Indirect materials	400	500
Totals	$6,400	$8,500

The postings to the general ledger and job cost sheet would be similar to those shown for journal entry *(b).*

6. Job Time Ticket. If a cost accounting system is to operate properly, some method must be used to track the time that each employee spent on each job (batch) so that direct labor can be properly costed. Although tracking systems may vary from company to company, each depends on a **job time ticket,** a source document on which an employee records the amount of time he or she worked on a particular job. For example, time clocks may be located at each work station and an employee may have a supply of preprinted forms showing his or her employee number and job number. When a particular job is started, the employee inserts the form into the

ILLUSTRATION 3–9   Work in Process and Job Cost Sheet

GENERAL LEDGER

Work in Process

19x2	
Feb. 28 *(b)* 10,550	

SUBSIDIARY LEDGER

JOB COST SHEET

Job Number __456__   Date __Feb. 19, 19x2__

Date Completed _____

Units __200__

Item __D 2051 Desks__

For Stock _____

For Customer __Smith's Dept. Store__

Direct Materials			Direct Labor				Manufacturing Overhead			
Date	Req. No.	Amount	Date	Clock No.	Hours	Amount	Date	DLH	Rate	Amount
19x2 Feb. 28	406	$10,550								

Cost Summary	
Direct Materials	$
Direct Labor	$
Overhead	$
Total Cost	$
Unit Cost	$

clock and punches in. When going to another job, the employee punches out on the first form and punches a new form for the new job. These job time tickets are then costed using the employee's rate of pay. The total of an employee's job time tickets is compared to the employee's time card for the week, and any difference between them is considered idle time unless an obvious error exists. Illustration 3–10 presents an example of a job time ticket.

ILLUSTRATION 3–10   Job Time Ticket

JOB TIME TICKET	
Employee's Name A. Gucci	Date March 18, 19x2
Clock No. 613	Department Sanding
Operation Sanding	Time Finished 11:45 A.M.
Job No. 456	Time Started 10:15 A.M.

Hours	Rate of Pay	Direct Labor	Comments
1½	$10.00	$15.00	

Approved   *P. Block*

Another method of accomplishing the same result is to use prepunched cards that are processed by computer, which saves a considerable amount of time. Whichever method is used, a summary entry would be made, either monthly or weekly. At Bettermade, the total of March's job tickets amounted to $12,000, idle time was $500, and indirect labor was $4,000. An analysis of the month's job time tickets showed the following:

	Direct Labor
Job 456	$ 7,500.00
Job 457	2,500.00
Job 458	2,000.00
Total	$12,000.00

The journal entry to record the job time is:

(d)

19x2			
Mar. 31	Work in Process	12,000	
	Manufacturing Overhead—Idle Time	500	
	Manufacturing Overhead—Indirect Labor	4,000	
	Wages Payable		16,500
	To record the factory payroll for the month based on an analysis of job time tickets.		

Overtime Premium.   During a busy period, businesses may ask employees to work overtime. Most businesses are required to pay an **overtime premium**—or increased wage rate—for all hours over 40 that an employee works. The premium is usually equal to one half of the straight-time rate. If an employee's regular rate of pay is $8 per hour and she worked 46 hours in a particular week, she would receive the following as gross pay:

$$
\begin{array}{lr}
\text{40 hours at \$ 8} = & \$320 \\
\text{6 hours at 12} = & \underline{72} \\
\text{Total} & \$392
\end{array}
$$

Although it may seem that the overtime premium could be identified as belonging to the same product as the regular pay rate, some companies classify it differently. If a firm regularly produces many items, the product that required overtime work may be considered a random departure from the norm. In such a case, the cost of the product would be unduly burdened if the entire overtime premium were charged to it. When this occurs, it is customary to charge the overtime premium to manufacturing overhead and thereby spread the cost across all units produced during the year, much like factory rent. The treatment changes, however, if the firm is not in its busy season and if the overtime is worked because of a customer's rush order. Then the overtime premium should be charged to the specific job, since it can be said that the rush order caused the overtime. Another reason for charging the overtime to the specific job may be that the customer will be charged a premium for rush orders and, therefore, the premiums will be matched against each other.

Idle Time.   While most managers would prefer to avoid idle time, its total absence in a business environment would be the exception rather than the rule. **Idle time**—production time lost during a machine breakdown or when material shortages occur—occurs randomly, so its cost should be absorbed by all production rather than by a particular product. This is accomplished by charging the cost of idle time to overhead.

7. Manufacturing Overhead.   Factors of production other than direct materials and direct labor, such as rent, power, machinery, and the like, are necessary to transform direct materials into finished goods. Although such components of manufacturing overhead cannot be directly traced to a specific job because they are mostly fixed costs, they must be appropriately assigned to all jobs. This is not an easy task. If *actual* overhead were used, random fluctuations for items such as repairs might cause overhead costs in a particular month to be distorted. And to obtain actual costs, allocation would have to be deferred until the end of the fiscal year, when all overhead costs would be known. As a result, all job cost sheets would have to remain incomplete until the end of the year, despite the fact that most jobs would be physically complete. This approach would also prevent the firm from preparing interim financial statements, since without overhead figures, the total cost of goods manufactured and sold could not be computed. For these reasons, most firms use a *predetermined overhead rate* to *apply manufacturing overhead* to each job.

A **predetermined overhead rate** is based on estimates of overhead costs and the applicable activity base. Thus, to compute the predetermined overhead rate, a firm must first estimate its overhead for the coming year and project figures for a base, such as direct labor-hours. For example, if in 19x1, the Bettermade Furniture Company estimates that its 19x2 overhead will approximate $800,000 and its direct labor-hours (DLH) will approximate 40,000 hours, its predetermined overhead rate (POR) would be:

$$POR = \frac{\text{Estimated overhead}}{\text{Estimated direct labor-hours}} = \frac{\$800,000}{40,000} = \$20 \text{ per DLH}$$

Bettermade can then use the POR to apply manufacturing overhead to specific jobs. It would do this by multiplying the POR times the number of direct labor-hours (the base) that a particular job required. Thus, if a job required 100 direct labor-hours, its applied manufacturing overhead would be $2,000 (100 hours × $20 POR). Manufacturing overhead will be discussed in further detail later in this chapter.

An analysis of Bettermade's job time tickets for March 19x2 revealed the following:

Job Number	Direct Labor-Hours
456	750
457	250
458	200

The journal entry to apply overhead to production is as follows:

(e)

19x2		
Mar. 31 Work in Process 24,000		
Manufacturing Overhead Applied		24,000
To apply overhead to March's production		
as follows:		

Job 456 ($20 × 750 DLH) . . .	$15,000	
Job 457 ($20 × 250 DLH) . . .	5,000	
Job 458 ($20 × 200 DLH) . . .	4,000	
Total	$24,000	

After posting journal entries *(c), (d),* and *(e),* the Work in Process account and the job cost sheets would appear as shown in Illustration 3–11. Note that Job No. 457 is for 100 tables manufactured for stock and that Job No. 458 is for 400 chairs manufactured for stock. Jobs 456 and 457 are completed; thus, their cost summaries are filled in. But these two jobs have not yet been shipped to customers or transferred to the finished goods warehouse, so their total costs are still included in the Work in Process account

ILLUSTRATION 3–11   Work in Process and Job Cost Sheet

GENERAL LEDGER

Work in Process

19x2			
Feb. 28	(b)	10,550	
Mar. 31	(c)	14,000	
31	(d)	12,000	
31	(e)	24,000	
		60,550	

SUBSIDIARY LEDGER

JOB COST SHEET

Job Number 456   Date Feb. 19, 19x2
                                        Date Completed Mar. 31, 19x2
                                        Units 200

Item D 2051 Desks
For Stock
For Customer Smith's Dept. Store

Direct Materials			Direct Labor				Manufacturing Overhead			
Date	Req. No.	Amount	Date	Clock No.	Hours	Amount	Date	DLH	Rate	Amount
19x2 Feb. 28	406	$10,550	19x2 Mar. 31	613	190	$1,900	19x2 Mar. 31	750	$20	$15,000
				614	180	1,800				
				615	180	1,800				
				616	200	2,000				
		$10,550			750	$7,500				$15,000

Cost Summary

Direct Materials	$10,550
Direct Labor	$ 7,500
Overhead	$15,000
Total Cost	$33,050
Unit Cost	$165.25*

* $33,050 ÷ 200 = $165.25

Illustration 3–11 *(continued)*

JOB COST SHEET

Job Number 457   Date Mar. 5, 19x2
    Date Completed Mar. 31, 19x2
    Units 100

Item T 311 Tables
For Stock ✓
For Customer _____

Direct Materials			Direct Labor				Manufacturing Overhead			
Date	Req. No.	Amount	Date	Clock No.	Hours	Amount	Date	DLH	Rate	Amount
19x2 Mar. 5	407	$6,000	19x2 Mar. 31	617 618	130 120	$1,300 1,200	19x2 Mar. 31	250	$20	$5,000
		$6,000			250	$2,500				$5,000

Cost Summary	
Direct Materials	$ 6,000
Direct Labor	$ 2,500
Overhead	$ 5,000
Total Cost	$13,500
Unit Cost	$135.00*

* $13,500 ÷ 100 = $135.00

Illustration 3–11 (concluded)

JOB COST SHEET

Job Number 458

Date Mar. 5, 19x2

Date Completed _____

Units 400

Item CH 201 Chairs

For Stock ✓

For Customer _____

Direct Materials			Direct Labor				Manufacturing Overhead			
Date	Req. No.	Amount	Date	Clock No.	Hours	Amount	Date	DLH	Rate	Amount
19x2 Mar. 5	408	$8,000	19x2 Mar. 31	619 620	100 100	$1,000 1,000	19x2 Mar. 31	200	$20	$4,000

Cost Summary	
Direct Materials	$
Direct Labor	$
Overhead	$
Total Cost	$
Unit Cost	$

in the general ledger. This can be verified by totaling the costs expended on the three jobs:

Job Number	Total Costs
456	$33,050
457	13,500
458 ($8,000 + $2,000 + $4,000)	14,000
Total	$60,550

The total is then compared with the total of the general ledger account as shown in Illustration 3–11. The comparison generally proves that the journal entries posted to the Work in Process account in the general ledger have been correctly posted to the job cost sheets in the subsidiary ledger.

Although actual overhead costs are not assigned directly to jobs, they nevertheless are incurred and must be paid. Overhead entries are normally made as the costs are incurred. The following sample journal entry acts as a summary for the month of March 19x2:

(f)

```
19x2
Mar. 31  Manufacturing Overhead . . . . . . . . . . . . . . . . . .   22,000
             Accounts Payable . . . . . . . . . . . . . . . . . . .            22,000
         To record actual overhead incurred as follows:
```

Factory rent	.$10,000
Utilities	3,000
Other factory costs . . .	9,000
Total	.$22,000

8. Finished Goods Inventory Ledger Card. Similar to the raw materials inventory, a perpetual **finished goods inventory ledger**—one card for each different product—records all completed goods held for sale to customers. The structure of this finished goods inventory ledger card is similar to the raw materials inventory ledger card presented in Illustration 3–4. When work in process from Jobs 456 and 457 is completed and transferred to the finished goods warehouse, the following journal entry is made:

(g)

```
19x2
Mar. 31  Finished Goods . . . . . . . . . . . . . . . . . . . . . .   46,550
             Work in Process . . . . . . . . . . . . . . . . . . .            46,550
         To record the completion of Jobs 456 and 457 and their
         transfer to the finished goods warehouse as follows:
```

Job	Cost
456	$33,050
457	13,500
Total . . .	$46,550

After the posting of entry *(g),* the Work in Process account would appear as shown in Illustration 3–12. The balance of $14,000 reflects the amounts

ILLUSTRATION 3–12   Bettermade Furniture Company

GENERAL LEDGER

Work in Process

19x2			19x2		
Feb. 28	*(b)*	10,550	Mar. 31	*(g)*	46,550
Mar. 01	*(c)*	14,000			
31	*(d)*	12,000			
31	*(e)*	24,000			
		60,550			46,550
Balance		14,000			

ILLUSTRATION 3–13   **Finished Goods Inventory Ledgers**

GENERAL LEDGER

Finished Goods	
19x2 Mar. 31 *(g)* 46,550	

SUBSIDIARY LEDGER

Item D 2051 Desks   Location in Warehouse Rack T 10

Date	Manufactured			Sold			Balance		
	Units	Cost	Total	Units	Cost	Total	Units	Cost	Balance
19x2 Mar. 31	200	$165.25	$33,050				200	$165.25	$33,050

Item T 311 Tables   Location in warehouse Rack C 14

Date	Manufactured			Sold			Balance		
	Units	Cost	Total	Units	Cost	Total	Units	Cost	Balance
19x2 Mar. 31	100	$135.00	$13,500				100	$135.00	$13,500

shown on the job cost sheet for Job 458 (see Illustration 3–11), the only job that is still in process.

Note that Bettermade's cost accounting system shows that the firm has a book inventory of $14,000 of work in process at March 31, 19x2. Without this system, Bettermade would be obligated to take a physical inventory count each time it prepared interim income statements.

Entry *(g)* must also be posted to the Finished Goods account in the general ledger and to the finished goods inventory ledger cards in the subsidiary ledger. These postings and ledger cards appear in Illustration 3–13. The total of the finished goods inventory ledger cards corresponds to the Finished Goods account in the general ledger. This can be seen when the costs of the finished goods are added:

Description	Dollars
D 2051 Desks	$33,050
T 311 Tables	13,500
Total	$46,550

9. Cost of Goods Sold. Two more entries are necessary to complete the cost accounting cycle. These occur when Bettermade sells some of the furniture it has produced. One entry records the sale of the merchandise at its selling price and the other records Bettermade's cost of producing the merchandise.

On March 31, Bettermade shipped the following finished goods:

Date	Item	Quantity	Unit Selling Price	Sales Revenue
19x2				
March 31	D 2051 Desks	200	$300	$60,000
31	T 311 Tables	40	275	11,000
	Total			$71,000

To record the transactions, two journal entries were made:

(h)

19x2			
Mar. 31	Accounts Receivable	71,000	
	Sales Revenue		71,000
	As per schedule (above).		

ILLUSTRATION 3–14   Finished Goods Inventory Ledgers

GENERAL LEDGER

Finished Goods	
19x2	19x2
Mar. 31 *(f)* 46,550	Mar. 31 *(g)* 38,450
Balance 8,100	

SUBSIDIARY LEDGER

Item D 2051 Desks   Location in Warehouse Rack T 10

Date	Manufactured			Sold			Balance		
	Units	Cost	Total	Units	Cost	Total	Units	Cost	Balance
19x2									
Mar. 31	200	$165.25	$33,050				200	$165.25	$33,050
31				200	$165.25	$33,050	0	—	0

Item T 311 Tables   Location in Warehouse Rack C 14

Date	Manufactured			Sold			Balance		
	Units	Cost	Total	Units	Cost	Total	Units	Cost	Balance
19x2									
Mar. 31	100	$135.00	$13,500				100	$135.00	$13,500
31				40	$135.00	$5,400	60	135.00	8,100

(i)

19x2

Mar. 31   Cost of Goods Sold   38,450

                Finished Goods   38,450

            To record the cost of goods sold as follows

D 2051 Desks . . .	200 at $165.25 =	$33,050
T 311 Tables . . .	40 at $135.00 =	5,400
Total		$38,450

After the posting of entry *(i)*, the finished goods ledger would appear as shown in Illustration 3–14. The balance in the Finished Goods account is $8,100, which agrees with the balance shown on the finished goods ledger card for T 311 Tables, the only item of finished goods on hand.

Here, too, the cost accounting system provides a book inventory of finished goods without a physical count, and it also produces a dollar amount for cost of goods sold. Based on the book inventories and the cost of goods sold figure, the firm is able to prepare an interim income statement and balance sheet.

The complete cost accounting cycle is diagramed in Illustration 3–15. The arrows show the movement of costs from one T account to another. A careful study of this illustration should help you to understand the relationships among the T accounts that form the cost accounting cycle. The letter designations in parentheses correspond to the sample journal entries cited earlier.

The cost accounting cycle automatically yields book inventories as follows:

Raw materials	$21,120
Work in process	14,000
Finished goods	8,100

These results not only permit Bettermade to prepare financial statements (both interim and annual) without a physical count, but also act as a check on physical counts whenever they are taken. This check is a crucial part of the firm's control system because it will indicate if errors in record-keeping and/or thefts have occurred.

Automated Systems

While it is easier to understand the cost accounting cycle by studying manually prepared forms, most businesses have computerized their cost accounting system. In such cases, much of the data may be stored in the computer, and only certain source documents may actually be in printed form. For example, the materials requisition may be printed, while the raw materials inventory ledger, the job cost sheets (work in process inventory), and the finished goods inventory ledger are stored in the computer. The data in storage would be used for control purposes and to prepare interim or annual reports, but the detailed amounts shown in this chapter's illustrations would not be reproduced. Such details would be stored in computer memory and recalled only if necessary.

ILLUSTRATION 3–15   Cost Accounting Cycle

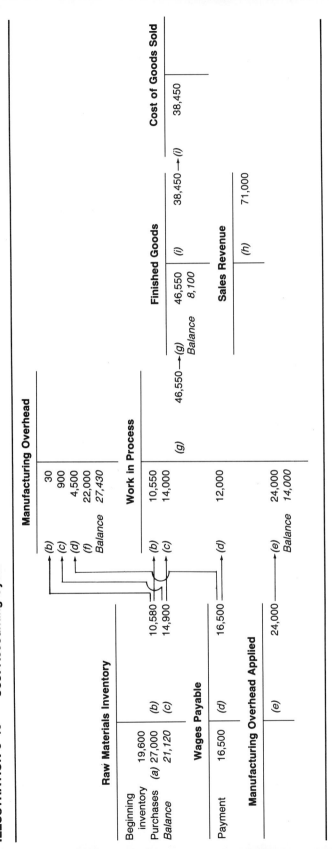

MANUFACTURING OVERHEAD

As noted in Chapter 2, **manufacturing overhead** encompasses all manufacturing costs other than direct materials and direct labor. It would be difficult, if not impossible, to attempt to charge each of these items to a particular product. Most manufacturing overhead items are common costs—costs that are shared by more than one product—and thus must be apportioned among products. Since the apportionment process used is based on predetermined estimates, it is less than exact, but its results are adequate provided that the allocation base is closely related to the nature of the firm's operations. An **allocation base** is a measurement used to assign manufacturing overhead to a cost objective (a product) in a logical manner based on the cause of the overhead and the benefits received by the product. Thus, a **labor-intensive firm**—a firm whose operations are performed manually and only incidentally by machines—should use a labor-oriented base, and a **machine-intensive firm**—a firm whose operations are highly automated—should use a machine-oriented base. The amount of estimated overhead assigned to jobs during a period of time through the use of an allocation base is called **applied manufacturing overhead.**

The Need for a Predetermined Rate

As noted earlier, if manufacturing overhead were assigned to a particular job on the basis of **actual** manufacturing overhead, it could only be done at the end of the fiscal year. This is highly unsatisfactory because a firm needs interim financial statements and must make timely decisions about pricing, profitability, and the like. Thus, some method must be found to assign manufacturing overhead to jobs as they progress and are completed. The most common practice is to use a predetermined rate calculation. Estimated manufacturing overhead for the coming year is used as the numerator of the calculation and the allocation base is used as the denominator:

$$POR = \frac{\text{Estimated overhead}}{\text{Allocation base}}$$

Allocation Bases

In practice, a company may use any one of several different allocation bases. The choice depends on the nature of the firm's manufacturing operations. The most commonly used bases are (1) direct labor cost, (2) direct labor-hours, (3) machine-hours, (4) materials cost, and (5) prime cost. The first three are used much more extensively than the last two.

For the purposes of our discussion, let us assume that the Mitchell Fabricating Corporation estimates the following information for the coming year, 19x3:

Direct materials cost	$300,000
Direct labor cost	$600,000
Direct labor-hours	120,000
Machine-hours	60,000
Manufacturing overhead	$900,000

Direct Labor Cost Base. When a **direct labor cost base** is used to assign manufacturing overhead, the estimated amount of direct labor cost to be incurred in the coming year appears as the denominator in the POR equation. Using this base, Mitchell's POR would be calculated as:

Estimated manufacturing overhead
Estimated direct labor cost

$$= \frac{\$900,000}{\$600,000} = 150 \text{ percent of direct labor cost}$$

This base is very popular because information about direct labor costs is readily available from the payroll records. It is most appropriate for labor-intensive manufacturing firms in which most employees *earn approximately the same hourly rates of pay.* On the other hand, it should be avoided when wage rates differ significantly because the resulting overhead assignments may be distorted for certain products.

For example, let us assume that a firm that uses direct labor costs as a base estimates that its factory rent is 10 percent of its estimated direct labor for the year. If employee A earns $5 per hour and employee B earns $10 per hour, and if each worked 40 hours on a product, the rent would be assigned as shown in Illustration 3–16. Note that even though both employees' work stations occupy the same amount of square footage, twice as much rent is charged to a job for employee B as for employee A. This would produce a questionable assignment of cost. To avoid this problem, when wage rates differ among employees, it is best to use a direct labor-hour base.

Direct Labor-Hours Base. When a **direct labor-hours base** is used to assign manufacturing overhead, the estimated amount of direct labor-hours to be worked by employees in the coming year appears as the denominator in the POR equation. Using this base, Mitchell's POR would be calculated as follows:

$$\frac{\text{Estimated manufacturing overhead}}{\text{Estimated direct labor-hours}} = \frac{\$900,000}{120,000} = \$7.50 \text{ per direct labor-hour}$$

Like the direct labor cost base, the direct labor-hours base is appropriate for labor-intensive manufacturers. Its advantage is that it can be used effectively *when hourly wage rates differ* as well as when hourly rates are uniform. However, because this base may have a slightly higher administrative cost, it is generally used only when the direct labor cost base is not appropriate.

When wage rates differ, the direct labor-hours base provides a better assignment of such overhead items as factory supervision and factory rent to all

ILLUSTRATION 3–16   **Assignment of Factory Rent to a Product's Cost**

	Employee A	Employee B
Salary for 40 hours	$200	$400
Factory rent—10 percent of direct labor cost	$ 20	$ 40

products. The cost of factory supervision is usually related to the number of hours worked rather than the dollar amount paid to an employee, and factory rent is related to the space occupied by an employee and not to his or her wages. Thus, since overhead should be assigned in a manner that correlates with its incurrence, direct labor cost is not a particularly useful overhead base for factory rent and factory supervision.

Using the data from Illustration 3–16 but substituting direct labor-hours (DLH) as the allocation base, the $60 of factory rent would be assigned to the product as follows:

	Employee A	Employee B
Number of hours worked	40	40
Factory rent—		
$60/80 DLH = $0.75 DLH	$30	$30

Thus, when direct labor-hours are used as a base, such factory overhead items as factory rent and factory supervision are not influenced by different wage rates, and their assignment to product costs is more closely related to the factors that cause the incurrence of those overhead items.

Machine-Hours Base. When a **machine-hours base** is used to assign manufacturing overhead, the denominator of the POR calculation is the estimated amount of factory activity as measured by the sum of all hours that each machine will be operated in the coming year. For example, if a factory has three machines, X, Y, and Z, and machines X and Y are each operated 40 hours per week and machine Z is operated 20 hours per week, the factory activity in machine-hours would be 100 (40 + 40 + 20) machine-hours per week and 5,000 hours per year for a 50-week year. If a particular job required machine time of 15 hours on machine X and 13 hours on machine Z, its machine-hours would be 28 hours. The computation of the Mitchell Fabricating Corporation's POR when this base is used would be:

$$\frac{\text{Estimated manufacturing overhead}}{\text{Estimated machine-hours}} = \frac{\$900,000}{60,000} = \$15 \text{ per machine-hour}$$

Machine-intensive firms are most apt to use a machine-hours base. Although figures on machine-hours may not be as readily available in a firm's accounting system as are figures on direct labor, the additional cost of using a machine-hours base is usually justified. In fact, using direct labor cost or direct labor-hours as a base for a machine-intensive firm may lead to inaccuracies in product costing and pricing decisions that would be more costly to the firm than would be the cost of administering a machine-hour base POR.

Materials Cost Base. When a **materials cost base** is used to assign manufacturing overhead, the estimated amount of direct materials to be used in the coming year appears as the denominator of the POR equation. If Mitchell used this base, the calculation of its POR would be:

$$\frac{\text{Estimated manufacturing overhead}}{\text{Estimated direct materials cost}} = \frac{\$900,000}{\$300,000}$$

$$= 300 \text{ percent of direct materials cost}$$

Few companies use materials cost as a base because very few manufacturing overhead costs are a function of materials cost. For example, a manufacturer of gold and silver rings should not use this base because the cost of gold far exceeds that of silver. If a materials cost base were used, the gold rings would absorb a much larger share of manufacturing overhead than would the silver rings, even though the overhead might be approximately the same for each.

The use of a materials cost base should be limited to firms whose direct material cost per unit of product is relatively uniform. For example, this method may be used effectively when raw materials of equal cost are fed into an automatic stamping machine at a uniform rate per hour, as in the manufacture of tokens for toll booths or subway turnstiles. Under such conditions, the direct materials cost is converted into a time basis that is compatible with the way in which overhead costs are generally incurred and allocated.

Prime Cost Base. When a **prime cost base** is used, the estimated amounts of direct materials and direct labor expected to be incurred in the coming year are used as the denominator in the POR computation. When this base is used, Mitchell's POR would be calculated as:

$$\frac{\text{Estimated manufacturing overhead}}{\text{Estimated prime cost}} = \frac{\$900,000}{\$900,000} = 100 \text{ percent of prime cost}$$

Prime cost consists of direct materials cost plus direct labor cost. Thus, a prime cost base suffers from the same weakness as a direct materials cost base. Because direct labor cost is included in a prime cost base, it is a compromise method, but it offers little, if any, advantage over a direct materials cost base.

The foregoing computations were provided only for illustrative purposes. In reality, a firm would select one of these predetermined rates based on the nature of its manufacturing operations and use it consistently year after year. A summary of allocation bases and their applicability appears in Illustration 3–17.

Seasonal and Other Fluctuations. Other reasons for using a predetermined rate include uneven cost occurrences and seasonal fluctuations. Under such circumstances, if the actual, uneven overhead were applied, the same product manufactured in two different batches could have widely divergent unit costs. For example, if there was a repair cost in January of $20,000, this amount would be factored into the cost of batch A. But batch B, manufactured in March, would escape this cost if no repairs were needed in that month. When a predetermined rate is used, the $20,000 repair is spread uniformly over all batches for the year, which is reasonable because the repair benefits the production process in other months besides January.

ILLUSTRATION 3–17   **Allocation Bases and Their Applicability**

Base	Applicability
1. Direct labor cost.	Labor-intensive firms where hourly wage rates are uniform. Minimal administrative costs.
2. Direct labor-hours.	Labor-intensive firms where hourly wage rates are not uniform. Slightly greater administrative costs than direct labor cost.
3. Machine-hours.	Machine-intensive firms. Greater administrative cost than labor-oriented base.
4. Materials cost.	Firms where direct materials cost is uniform per unit of production or where material is fed into automatic machines at a uniform rate per hour. Minimal administrative cost.
5. Prime cost.	Similar to materials cost.

Another problem with using actual costs stems from seasonal fluctuations. Assume that factory rent is $50,000 per month. If 20,000 units were manufactured in March and only 10,000 units were manufactured in April, the unit cost for rent in March would be $2.50, while the unit cost for April would be $5.00. All other manufacturing overhead items would similarly affect the unit costs for the two months.

If a company made pricing decisions based on such widely fluctuating monthly costs, its prices would also widely fluctuate. While seasonal price structures are appropriate for some service industries such as vacation hotels and restaurants, they are not practical for most businesses. Most customers expect the prices of the goods they buy to stay relatively stable from month to month. They would not trust a supplier whose prices constantly changed. Thus, to prevent short-term price variability, most firms use predetermined overhead rates based on long-term performance. These rates are also called normal overhead rates.

Normal Overhead Rates. A **normal overhead rate** is a predetermined overhead rate that is based on estimates for a complete business cycle—a period of three to five years—instead of for the coming year alone. Since it is an average rate for the entire business cycle, its results are more uniform from year to year than would be the case if a new POR were computed each year. Normalized overhead rates are discussed in greater detail in Chapter 9.

The use of a normal predetermined overhead rate does create one problem, however, which occurs at the end of the fiscal year: It is highly improbable that the dollar amounts of the actual overhead and the applied overhead will coincide, since the applied overhead is an estimated number. Thus, at the end of the year, there will usually be a difference between the two accounts. The difference is called **overapplied overhead** when the applied overhead is greater than the actual overhead. When the reverse is true—that is, when the actual overhead is greater than the applied overhead, the difference is referred to as **underapplied overhead.** The terms **overabsorbed overhead** and **underabsorbed overhead** are often used interchangeably with *overapplied overhead* and *underapplied overhead,* respectively.

Disposition of Overapplied or Underapplied Overhead.

Let us review the manufacturing overhead accounts shown in Illustration 3–15:

Manufacturing Overhead				Applied Manufacturing Overhead		
19x2				19x2		
Feb. 28	(b)	30		Mar. 31	(e)	24,000
Mar. 31	(c)	900				
31	(d)	4,500				
31	(f)	22,000				
Balance		27,430				

Note that the actual manufacturing overhead—the debit balance of $27,430—does not equal the applied overhead of $24,000. During interim periods, the difference of $3,430 would be shown in the balance sheet as a deferred debit.

Any underapplied or overapplied overhead that remained at the end of one fiscal year would not be carried forward to the next year. Instead, it would be closed to cost of goods sold as follows:

(j)

Applied Manufacturing Overhead	24,000	
Cost of Goods Sold	3,430	
Manufacturing Overhead		27,430

Such an entry is satisfatory for most business conditions if the amount of over- or underapplied overhead is relatively small. If the amount is large, however, another method may be used to achieve greater accuracy. This method is discussed in Appendix 3–A at the end of this chapter.

Payroll Fringes.

One component of overhead that requires further attention is **payroll fringes,** which generally include all payroll taxes, such as social security taxes and unemployment insurance taxes, vacation pay, holiday pay, union welfare contributions, hospitalization insurance, and other employee-related costs. Since these costs are significant—often in excess of 30 percent of the labor cost—some firms treat them differently from manufacturing overhead.

Most fringe-benefit costs are considered functions of labor cost and can thus be tacked on to direct labor. If, for example, payroll fringes amount to 30 percent of labor costs, a Payroll Fringe account can be established separately from the Overhead account, and payroll fringes can be assigned directly to direct labor at the rate of 30 percent. Then, if an employee who earns $6 per hour works for four hours on a particular job, the charge to that job would be:

Direct labor — 4 hours at $6.00 = . . . $24.00
Fringes at 30 percent 7.20
Total direct labor cost $31.20

Other firms may merely charge $24 to the job and charge all fringes to
manufacturing overhead to be applied to the job through the predetermined
overhead rate.

**STATEMENTS OF
COST OF GOODS
MANUFACTURED
AND COST OF
GOODS SOLD**

The Raw Materials Inventory, Work in Process, and Manufacturing Overhead
accounts provide the components for preparing the cost of goods manufactured statement. For your reference, these accounts from the Bettermade
Furniture Company are repeated in Illustration 3–18, while Bettermade's
statement of cost of goods manufactured for the three months ended March

ILLUSTRATION 3–18   Partial General Ledger

Raw Materials Inventory

19x2				19x2			
Jan. 1	Inventory at beginning	19,600		Feb. 28	Issuances	(b)	10,580
Feb. 28	Purchases (a)	27,000		Mar. 31	Issuances	(c)	14,900
Balance		21,120					

Work in Process

19x2			19x2		
Feb. 28	(b)	10,550	Mar. 31	(g)	46,550
Mar. 31	(c)	14,000			
31	(d)	12,000			
31	(e)	24,000			
		60,550			46,550
Balance		14,000			

Manufacturing Overhead

19x2		
Feb 28	(b)	30
Mar. 31	(c)	900
31	(d)	4,500
31	(f)	22,000
Balance		27,430

Applied Manufacturing Overhead

	19x2		
	Mar. 31	(e)	24,000

|

ILLUSTRATION 3–19

BETTERMADE FURNITURE COMPANY
Statement of Cost of Goods Manufactured
For the Three Months Ended March 31, 19x2

Direct materials		
Raw materials inventory, January 1	$19,600	
Add: Purchases of raw materials	27,000	
Total raw materials available	46,600	
Deduct: Raw materials inventory, March 31	21,120	
Raw materials issued	25,480	
Deduct: Indirect materials	930	
Direct materials used in production		$24,550
Direct labor		12,000
Manufacturing overhead:		
Indirect labor	$ 4,500	
Factory rent	10,000	
Utilities	3,000	
Indirect materials deducted above	930	
Miscellaneous factory costs	9,000	
Actual overhead costs	27,430	
Less: Underapplied overhead	3,430	
Overhead applied to work in process		24,000
Total manufacturing costs		60,550
Add: Beginning work in process inventory		–0–
Total manufacturing costs in process		60,550
Deduct: Ending work in process inventory		14,000
Cost of goods manufactured at normal costing		$46,550

Statement of Cost of Goods Manufactured

31, 19x2, is shown in Illustration 3–19. The beginning raw materials inventory, purchases, and ending raw materials inventory may be obtained from the Raw Materials Inventory account shown in Illustration 3–18. However, the *indirect materials* used must be deducted from the *raw materials* issued to arrive at the *direct materials* used in production. The $930 of indirect materials issued is shown as part of the actual overhead costs. The *total manufacturing*

ILLUSTRATION 3–20 **Finished Goods Inventory Ledger**

GENERAL LEDGER

Finished Goods		
19x2		19x2
Mar. 31 *(f)* 46,550		Mar. 31 *(g)* 38,450
Balance 8,100		

ILLUSTRATION 3–21

BETTERMADE FURNITURE COMPANY
Statement of Cost of Goods Sold
For the Three Months Ended March 31, 19x2

Beginning finished goods inventory	$ –0–
Add: Cost of goods manufactured at normal costing . .	46,550
Goods available for sale	46,550
Ending finished goods inventory	8,100
Cost of goods sold at normal costing	38,450
Add: Underapplied overhead	3,430
Cost of goods sold at actual costing	$41,880

costs in process ($60,550) should always agree with the debit side of the Work in Process account. After deducting the ending work in process inventory of $14,000, the cost of goods manufactured *at normal costing* should agree with the credit side of the Work in Process account. The practice of using *actual* direct materials, *actual* direct labor, and *applied* manufacturing overhead is known as **normal costing.**

The Manufacturing Overhead account provides the information for listing the actual overhead costs incurred. Normally, a subsidiary ledger contains the details. For this example, the details may be obtained by referring to journal entries *(b), (c), (d),* and *(f).* Adjusting the total actual overhead by the $3,430 of underapplied overhead reduces it to the $24,000 of overhead applied to production, which agrees with the credit balance shown in the Applied Manufacturing Overhead account.

Statement of Cost of Goods Sold

The Finished Goods account in Bettermade's general ledger is reproduced in Illustration 3–20. The information needed to prepare the statement of cost of goods sold is contained in this account.

Bettermade's statement of cost of goods sold for the three months ended March 31, 19x2, is shown in Illustration 3–21. For illustrative purposes, the underapplied overhead is shown on this statement. Usually, this is only done at the close of a company's fiscal year.

If there are no sales returns, the value of the goods available for sale should agree with the debit side of the Finished Goods account. If there was a beginning inventory of finished goods, the account and the statement would reflect it. The cost of goods sold at normal costing should agree with the credit side of the account.

SUMMARY

The purpose of **cost accounting** is to record, measure, and report information about costs. An **integrated cost accounting system** provides managers with the product costs they need for inventory valuations, pricing the company's products, preparation of interim financial statements, planning and control, and decision making.

Two systems of cost accounting are widely used. Firms that manufacture a few products on a repetitive basis use a **process cost system.** Firms that manufacture a variety of products, with each product manufactured in a separate batch, or job, use a **job order cost accounting system.**

Source documents are business forms that serve as the basis of the journal entries that record the **cost accounting cycle.** This flow of cost accumulation usually parallels the **physical flow** of production. A **purchase requisition** authorizes the purchasing department to issue a **purchase order** for the acquisition of raw materials. A **receiving report** records the receipt of the raw materials, which are then placed in the stockroom. The stockroom always maintains a **safety stock** of both direct and indirect materials to ensure that production will not be interrupted by delayed shipments or abnormally heavy usage. A **production order** is issued when a particular product is needed for either a specific customer or inventory in the finished goods warehouse. A **materials requisition** authorizes the stockroom to transfer raw materials to the production line.

At this point, a **job cost sheet** is started to keep track of the costs of the job. As they are incurred, all elements of cost—direct materials, direct labor, and manufacturing overhead—are recorded on the job cost sheet. Employees' **job time tickets** are used to arrive at the direct labor spent on the job. And through the use of a **predetermined overhead rate** based on estimated overhead for the year and an **allocation base,** such as direct labor cost or direct labor-hours, overhead is assigned. This method of costing, in which all manufacturing costs, both fixed and variable, are assigned to products and thus inventoried, is called **absorption costing.**

When a job is finished, the total on the job cost sheet is transferred to the **finished goods inventory ledger.** When goods are sold, their cost is deducted from the finished goods inventory ledger and transferred to cost of goods sold. The journal entries accompanying these events are the components of the cost accounting cycle. Subsidiary ledgers and controlling accounts provide managers with **book inventory** amounts that can be compared with periodic physical counts to control inventory and guard against errors and thefts.

The allocation base a company uses to apply manufacturing overhead to specific jobs depends on whether its operations are **labor intensive** or **machine intensive.**

The most commonly used allocation bases are **direct labor cost, direct labor-hours,** and **machine-hours.** Lesser used bases are **materials cost** and **prime cost.** Many firms use a **normal overhead rate,** which is an average rate for an entire business cycle, rather than a rate based on the coming year's activity alone. At the end of the firm's fiscal year, the difference between the actual overhead and the amount applied to production during the year is ordinarily closed to cost of goods sold. When **applied manufacturing overhead** exceeds actual overhead, the difference is called **overapplied overhead,** and when actual overhead exceeds applied overhead, the difference is called **underapplied overhead.**

The Raw Materials Inventory, Work in Process, and Manufacturing Overhead accounts provide the details needed to prepare the statement of cost of goods manufactured, which is usually prepared at **normal cost.** The overapplied or underapplied overhead usually appears as a separate item on the cost of goods sold statement.

GLOSSARY OF KEY TERMS

Absorption costing A method of assigning costs to a firm's products in which all fixed and variable manufacturing costs are inventoried.

Allocation base A measurement used to assign manufacturing overhead to a cost objective (a product) in a logical manner based on the cause of the overhead and the benefits received by the product.

Applied manufacturing overhead The amount of estimated overhead assigned to jobs during a period of time through the use of an allocation base.

Book inventory The dollar and quantity amounts generated by the records of a cost accounting system for raw materials, work in process, or finished goods, without taking a physical count.

Cost accounting A subfield of accounting that records, measures, and reports information about costs.

Cost accounting cycle The sequential recording and classifying of transactions that affect costs. The sequence usually corresponds to the firm's physical flow of operations.

Direct labor cost base A method of assigning overhead costs that uses the estimated amount of direct labor cost to be incurred in the coming year as the denominator in the POR equation.

Direct labor-hour base A method of assigning overhead costs that uses the estimated amount of direct labor-hours to be worked by employees in the coming year as the denominator in the POR equation.

Finished goods inventory ledger Perpetual inventory cards (or computer storage)—one card for each different product—that record all completed goods held for sale to customers.

Full costing See **absorption costing.**

Idle time Production time lost during a machine breakdown or when material shortages occur—manifests itself as the difference between the amount of hours shown on an employee's time card and the amount of time charged to specific jobs for that employee.

Integrated cost accounting system A cost accounting system that forms an integral part of a firm's books and reporting system.

Job A batch of production that has a definite starting point and completion point.

Job cost sheet A sheet for accumulating the cost of direct materials, direct labor, and applied manufacturing overhead during a firm's production cycle. A separate sheet is kept for each job, and the total of all costs on the uncompleted job cost sheets form the subsidiary ledger for the Work in Process account in the general ledger.

Job order cost accounting system A method of accumulating costs by batches of production.

Job time ticket   A source document on which an employee records the amount of time he or she worked on a particular job.

Labor-intensive firm (department)   A firm or department in which production operations are performed principally by manual labor and only incidentally by machinery.

Machine-hour base   A method of assigning overhead costs that uses the sum of all hours that each machine will be operated in the coming year as the denominator in the POR equation.

Machine-intensive firm (department)   A firm or department in which production operations are automated, with a concomitant reduction in direct labor costs.

Manufacturing overhead   All costs other than direct materials and direct labor that are necessary to manufacture a finished product.

Manufacturing overhead applied   See **applied manufacturing overhead.**

Materials cost base   A method of assigning overhead costs that uses the estimated amount of direct materials to be used in the coming year as the denominator in the POR equation.

Materials requisition   A source document authorizing the transfer of raw materials from the storeroom to the production line to start manufacture.

Normal costing   A cost accumulation system in which *actual* direct materials, *actual* direct labor, and *applied* manufacturing overhead are used for accounting and pricing purposes.

Normal overhead rate   A predetermined overhead rate based on estimates for a complete business cycle—usually three to five years; as a result, it is an *average* long-term rate.

Overabsorbed overhead   See **overapplied overhead.**

Overapplied overhead   The amount by which actual overhead for a period of time is less than estimated overhead that was allocated to specific jobs.

Overhead applied   See **applied manufacturing overhead.**

Overtime premium   An increased wage rate paid for all hours over 40 that an employee works—usually equal to one half of the straight-time rate.

Payroll fringes   Employee-related costs, such as social security taxes, unemployment insurance taxes, disability premiums, hospitalization insurance, vacation pay, holiday pay, and retirement benefit contributions.

Physical flow of production   The sequence of operating activity that begins with the purchase of raw materials and ends with a finished product ready for sale to customers.

Predetermined overhead rate (POR)   A method used to apply overhead to a job based on estimates of overhead costs and the applicable activity base.

Prime cost base   A method of assigning overhead costs that uses the estimated amounts of direct materials and direct labor expected to be incurred in the coming year as the denominator in the POR equation.

Process cost accounting system   A cost accounting method in which product costs are accumulated for a specific period of time and then the total cost is divided by the units produced to compute the unit cost for the period. This method is used by firms that produce relatively few products, with each product produced repetitively.

Production order   A source document issued prior to the start of production that authorizes the manufacture of a particular product.

Purchase order   A source document authorizing a vendor to ship the ordered goods (or services) at the specified price and terms.

Purchase requisition   A source document issued by the storeroom clerk requesting the firm's purchasing department to purchase needed raw materials.

Receiving report   A report prepared by a firm's receiving department listing the quantities and descriptions of merchandise received from vendors.

Safety stock   A specified minimum amount of raw materials inventory kept on hand at all times to provide a cushion against unusual delays in shipment and abnormally heavy usage.

Source document   Any original record or business form used by a firm to initiate or record any of its transactions. Such documents help a company keep track of its production process and form the basis of the journal entries that are part of its cost accounting system.

Underabsorbed overhead   See **underapplied overhead.**

Underapplied overhead   The amount by which the actual overhead for a period of time exceeds the estimated overhead allocated to specific jobs.

APPENDIX 3–A

THE PRORATION OF UNDERAPPLIED AND OVERAPPLIED MANUFACTURING OVERHEAD

As already noted, it is highly unlikely that actual manufacturing overhead will coincide with applied overhead for any given period. Thus, underapplied or overapplied overhead must be disposed of at the end of the fiscal year. During interim periods, it is preferable to carry forward any underapplied or overapplied overhead to the balance sheet as a deferred charge or a deferred credit, provided there is a reasonable expectation that the amount will be absorbed before the end of the fiscal year.

When the difference between the actual overhead and the applied overhead is small, most firms will expedite its disposition by closing it into cost of goods sold. However, when the amount of underapplied or overapplied overhead is large and if greater accuracy is desired, the amount may be prorated. Proration may be required for external reporting purposes and/or for income tax return preparation. The Internal Revenue Service accepts normal costing as long as the underapplied or overapplied overhead is small. When the amount is large, the IRS usually insists on proration. Independent auditors have similar requirements.

The Proration Procedure

The objective of **proration** is to convert any general ledger account balance that contains estimated (applied) overhead to reflect actual overhead. To do so, the amounts of applied overhead in the Work in Process, Finished Goods, and Cost of Goods Sold accounts must be ascertained, and the relationship that each amount bears to the yearly applied overhead must be determined. The resulting percentages are then used to apportion the under- or overapplied overhead among the accounts. After proration, the overhead in the accounts reflects actual amounts instead of estimated amounts.

Consider the following information as of December 31, 19x4:

1. The balance of the Work in Process account is:

Direct materials	$ 3,000
Direct labor	5,000
Manufacturing overhead . .	6,000
Total	$14,000

2. The balance in the Finished Goods inventory account consists of:

Direct materials	$15,000
Direct labor	30,000
Manufacturing overhead . .	36,000
Total	$81,000

3. The balance in the Cost of Goods Sold account consists of:

Direct materials	$125,000
Direct labor	215,000
Manufacturing overhead . .	258,000
Total	$598,000

4. The actual manufacturing overhead for 19x4 amounted to $340,000 and included expenditures that could not be anticipated prior to the last day of the year.

5. The applied overhead amounted to $300,000.

6. The underapplied overhead amounts to $40,000 ($340,000 actual minus the $300,000 applied).

To determine the appropriate prorations, the estimated overhead in each account is extracted and tabulated as shown in Illustration 3–22. First, the amount of overhead applied to each account is recorded in column 1. Note that the total of the first column equals the total amount of overhead applied for the year. The relationship that each account's applied overhead figure bears to the total yearly figure is then determined by dividing each account's overhead allocation by $300,000—the total amount of overhead applied. These percentages are entered in column 2. Finally, the prorated amount of underapplied overhead to be added to each account is calculated by multiplying $40,000—the total amount of underapplied overhead—by the corresponding percentage in column 2, and these figures are recorded in column 3.

ILLUSTRATION 3–22   **Proration of Underapplied Overhead**

	Applied	Percent	Underapplied Proration
Work in process	$ 6,000	2*	$ 800†
Finished goods inventory . .	36,000	12	4,800
Cost of goods sold	258,000	86	34,400
Total	$300,000	100	$40,000

* Six thousand dollars ÷ $300,000 = 2 percent.
† Two percent × $40,000 = $800.

The journal entry to close the underapplied overhead would be:

Work in Process	800	
Finished Goods Inventory	4,800	
Cost of Goods Sold	34,400	
Manufacturing Overhead Applied	300,000	
Manufacturing Overhead		340,000

After this entry is posted, we can verify that the estimated manufacturing overhead has been converted to actual overhead by totaling the applied figures plus the prorations to ensure that they equal the actual overhead figure. This proof is shown in Illustration 3–23.

ILLUSTRATION 3–23   **Proof of Conversion of Applied to Actual Overhead**

	Applied		Proration		Actual
Work in process	$ 6,000 +	$	800	= $	6,800
Finished goods inventory . .	36,000 +		4,800	=	40,800
Cost of goods sold	258,000 +		34,400	=	292,400
Total	$300,000 +	$40,000		= $340,000	

GLOSSARY OF KEY TERMS—APPENDIX 3–A

Proration A procedure used to convert estimated (applied) overhead, such as that found in the Work in Process, Finished Goods, and Cost of Goods Sold accounts, to reflect actual overhead.

APPENDIX 3–B

DEPARTMENTALIZING OVERHEAD AND ALLOCATING SERVICE DEPARTMENT OVERHEAD

If a firm has at least one labor-intensive department and one machine-intensive department, a factorywide overhead rate would produce distortions in the assignment of overhead to specific jobs and could possibly provide misleading information for pricing decisions. Although it is impossible to obtain completely accurate information, a firm that desires high accuracy will likely departmentalize its overhead application. In doing so, the firm must examine each item of manufacturing overhead and allocate it to all affected departments using a specific allocation mechanism. For example, if a firm has a machining department that is machine intensive and a finishing department that is labor intensive, the factory rent can be allocated on the basis of the square feet occupied by each department. A table of allocation bases for various forms of manufacturing overhead is presented in Illustration 3–24.

ILLUSTRATION 3–24   Allocation Bases for Departmentalizing Overhead

Factory Overhead	Basis for Allocation
Factory rent	Square feet occupied
Repairs to factory	Square feet occupied
Repairs to machinery	Direct to department
Depreciation—machinery	Direct to department
Superintendence	Number of employees
Heat	Square feet occupied
Light and power	Horsepower/kilowatt rating
Indirect labor	Direct to department
Insurance	Investment in equipment
Payroll fringes	Payroll cost
Factory cafeteria	Number of employees
Factory hospital	Number of employees
Cost accounting	Labor-hours
Maintenance	Direct to department

Overhead Departmentalization

A further refinement of departmentalization involves classification into producing departments and service departments. In a **producing department,** employees work on converting raw materials into finished goods, while in a **service department,** employees perform such ancillary functions as making repairs, operating the factory cafeteria, and maintaining personnel and payroll records.

In departmentalizing overhead, the first step is to prepare a factory survey, by department, of square feet occupied, number of employees, labor cost, and machinery horsepower ratings. Then, each item of overhead is allocated to a department using the bases suggested in Illustration 3–24. Next, the service departments' overhead is allocated to the producing departments. Since production passes only through *producing* departments, only *their* time is used to apply overhead to production. Finally, the total for each producing department is divided by an appropriate base to arrive at a predetermined rate for each producing department.

Illustrations 3–25 and 3–26 show a sample factory survey and the allocation of overhead to all departments. In addition:

1. The service log indicates that maintenance was done in accordance with the following schedule:

Producing department A . .	70 percent
Producing department B . .	20 percent
Factory cafeteria	5 percent
Factory hospital	5 percent

2. Producing department A is machine intensive and is estimated to operate at 40,000 machine-hours for the year.

3. Producing department B is labor intensive and is estimated to operate at 160,000 labor-hours for the year. The predetermined rate will be based on labor-hours.

ILLUSTRATION 3–25   Factory Survey

Department	Basis			
	Square Feet	No. of Employees	Payroll Cost	Horse-Power
Producing department A	16,000	20	$ 300,000	40,000
Producing department B	9,000	80	900,000	5,000
Maintenance service	5,000	10	120,000	3,500
Factory cafeteria	6,000	10	90,000	1,000
Factory hospital	4,000	5	90,000	500
Totals	40,000	125	$1,500,000	50,000

ILLUSTRATION 3–26   Departmental Overhead Allocation

Cost Item	Total	Producing Departments		Service Departments		
		A	B	Maintenance	Factory Cafeteria	Factory Hospital
Payroll fringes	$ 500,000	$100,000	$300,000	$ 40,000	$ 30,000	$ 30,000
Indirect labor	360,000	30,000	30,000	120,000	90,000	90,000
Superintendence	50,000	8,000	32,000	4,000	4,000	2,000
Factory rent	100,000	40,000	22,500	12,500	15,000	10,000
Light and power	75,000	60,000	7,500	5,250	1,500	750
Heat	20,000	8,000	4,500	2,500	3,000	2,000
Repairs to machinery	40,000	35,000	4,000	1,000	—	—
Depreciation of machinery	100,000	80,000	15,000	2,000	1,000	2,000
Totals	$1,245,000	$361,000	$415,500	$187,250	$144,500	$136,750

Allocation of Service Department Overhead to Producing Departments

There are many approaches to the allocation of service department overhead to producing departments. The most accurate is the mathematical approach, which uses complex equations that are best solved by computers or matrix inversion. Less sophisticated methods that yield approximate results make use of simple decision rules. Allocation problems arise when one service department renders service to another service department. It must then be determined which department's overhead should be allocated first, which should be allocated next, and so on.

Aside from a mathematical solution, one of three different approaches may be used: (1) the direct method, (2) the step-down method, and (3) the reciprocal, or redistribution, method.

The Direct Method. The simplest method to implement is the **direct method** because it ignores the services rendered between service departments and allocates all service department costs to producing departments only. It is also the least accurate of the three methods because it ignores the interdepartmental activities between service departments. Nonetheless, if the service departments' overhead is small in relation to the producing departments' overhead, the direct method may be used without causing wide distortions in overhead allocation. This method is shown in Illustration 3–27.

Although the maintenance log indicates that the factory cafeteria and the factory hospital each required 5 percent of the maintenance department's services, this aspect is *ignored* when the direct method is used, and the maintenance department's costs of $187,250 are assigned only to departments A and B in the ratio of 70:20 instead of 70:20:5:5, as noted in the service log. Similarly, while the maintenance department has 10 employees and the factory hospital has 5 employees, the two departments are ignored when allocating the factory cafeteria's costs of $144,500. These costs are allocated only to the producing departments in proportion to their number of employees (20:80). The factory hospital's costs are also allocated on the basis of the number of employees (20:80), and its services to the maintenance department and the factory cafeteria are ignored. Although the maintenance department allocation was completed first, the sequence of allocation is not relevant when the direct method is used. Any sequence of allocation would produce the same result.

When the allocations are completed, the predetermined rates are computed as follows:

Department A

$$\frac{\$562,889}{40,000 \text{ machine-hours}} = \$14.072 \text{ per machine-hour}$$

Department B

$$\frac{\$682,111}{160,000 \text{ labor-hours}} = \$ 4.263 \text{ per labor-hour}$$

ILLUSTRATION 3–27   Departmental Overhead Allocation: Direct Allocation Method

Cost Item	Total	Producing Departments		Service Departments		
		A	B	Maintenance	Factory Cafeteria	Factory Hospital
Payroll fringes	$ 500,000	$100,000	$300,000	$ 40,000	$ 30,000	$ 30,000
Indirect labor	360,000	30,000	30,000	120,000	90,000	90,000
Superintendence	50,000	8,000	32,000	4,000	4,000	2,000
Factory rent	100,000	40,000	22,500	12,500	15,000	10,000
Light and power	75,000	60,000	7,500	5,250	1,500	750
Heat	20,000	8,000	4,500	2,500	3,000	2,000
Repairs to machinery	40,000	35,000	4,000	1,000	—	—
Depreciation of machinery	100,000	80,000	15,000	2,000	1,000	2,000
Totals	$1,245,000	$361,000	$415,500	$187,250	$144,500	$136,750
Maintenance (7:2)*	–0–	145,639	41,611	(187,250)		
Factory cafeteria (2:8)†	–0–	28,900	115,600		(144,500)	
Factory hospital (2:8)†	–0–	27,350	109,400			(136,750)
Totals	$1,245,000	$562,889	$682,111	$ –0–	$ –0–	$ –0–
Basis		40,000 machine-hours				
Basis			160,000 labor-hours			
Predetermined rate		$14.072 per machine-hour	$4.263 per labor-hour			

* From the maintenance log, 70 percent and 20 percent.
† Based on the number of employees—department A, 20 employees, and department B, 80 employees.

The Step-Down Method. The **step-down method** is more sophisticated than the direct method and, therefore, produces a result that is more accurate. This approach recognizes services provided to other service departments and sequentially allocates overhead to each department. A popular set of decision rules for selecting the sequence of service department allocation is:

1. Begin with the department that services the largest number of other service departments. If it is impossible to select one department that meets this criterion, select the one with the largest dollar amount of overhead. The purpose is to distribute as much service department overhead as possible to other service departments before turning to the producing departments.

2. When rule 1 can no longer be applied, allocate the department that services the largest number of other departments including producing departments. When it is no longer possible to use this criterion, select the one with the largest dollar amount of overhead.

3. When all service department overhead accounts have been closed, the allocation procedure is complete.

When the step-down method is used, it is important to remember that *once a service department's overhead account is closed, it is not reopened.* The next service department is selected and the process is repeated until all service department accounts are closed. This method is shown in Illustration 3–28.

This example makes use of the basic step-down decision rules. Since all three service departments rendered services to the other two and were thus all tied for the first allocation, the one with the largest dollar amount of overhead—the maintenance department—was allocated first. This time, the ratio noted in the service log, 70:20:5:5, was used. The second allocation would be from the department that had the largest dollar amount of overhead *after* the allocation from the maintenance department. In this case, the dollar amount of overhead for the cafeteria was larger than that for the hospital *both before and after* the allocation from the maintenance department, but this need not be the case. The allocation ratio became 20:80:5 instead of 20:80:10:5 because the maintenance department's overhead account was closed once it was allocated. Finally, the factory hospital's Overhead is allocated using the ratio 20:80 because both the maintenance department and the factory cafeteria have been omitted.

When the allocations are completed, the predetermined rates are computed as follows:

Department A

$$\frac{\$552,070}{40,000 \text{ machine-hours}} = \$13.802 \text{ per machine-hour}$$

Department B

$$\frac{\$692,930}{160,000 \text{ labor-hours}} = \$4.331 \text{ per labor-hour}$$

Reciprocal (Redistribution) Method.   The **reciprocal method** is similar to the step-down method except that service department overhead accounts are reopened after each iteration, and the process is repeated until the amounts reallocated to a closed service department account are negligible (usually less than $100). Each round of closing and reopening produces succeedingly smaller numbers until the negligible amount is closed in the last iteration without reopening any service department account.

Illustration 3–29 shows the first and second cycles of the closing and

ILLUSTRATION 3–28   Departmental Overhead Allocation: Step-Down Allocation Method

Cost Item	Total	Producing Departments		Service Departments		
		A	B	Maintenance	Factory Cafeteria	Factory Hospital
Payroll fringes	$ 500,000	$100,000	$300,000	$ 40,000	$ 30,000	$ 30,000
Indirect labor	360,000	30,000	30,000	120,000	90,000	90,000
Superintendence	50,000	8,000	32,000	4,000	4,000	2,000
Factory rent	100,000	40,000	22,500	12,500	15,000	10,000
Light and power	75,000	60,000	7,500	5,250	1,500	750
Heat	20,000	8,000	4,500	2,500	3,000	2,000
Repairs to machinery	40,000	35,000	4,000	1,000	—	—
Depreciation of machinery	100,000	80,000	15,000	2,000	1,000	2,000
Totals	$1,245,000	$361,000	$415,500	$187,250	$144,500	$136,750
Maintenance (70:20:5:5)*	–0–	131,075	37,450	(187,250)	9,363	9,362
Factory cafeteria (20:80:5)† . . .	–0–	29,307	117,229		(153,863)	7,327
Factory hospital (20:80)‡	–0–	30,688	122,751			(153,439)
Totals	$1,245,000	$552,070	$692,930	$ –0–	$ –0–	$ –0–

Basis	40,000 machine-hours	

Basis		160,000 labor-hours

Predetermined rate	$13.802 per machine-hour	$4.331 per labor-hour

* From the maintenance log.
† Number of employees.
‡ Number of employees.

reopening process. For the maintenance department, the first cycle closing amounted to $187,250, and after the reopening, $26,112 was reallocated from the factory cafeteria and the factory hospital. In the second cycle, the $26,112 was again closed, and after the reopening, $1,381 remained. After several more cycles, the reopened balance was closed without any further reopenings.

It is interesting to note that the predetermined overhead rates in Illustration 3–29 ($14.160 and $4.241) are closer to those calculated with the direct method (Illustration 3–27) than they are to those calculated with the step-down method. This need not be the usual case.

ILLUSTRATION 3–29   Departmental Overhead Allocation: Reciprocal (Redistribution) Method

Cost Item	Total	Producing Departments		Service Departments		
		A	B	Maintenance	Factory Cafeteria	Factory Hospital
Payroll fringes	$ 500,000	$100,000	$300,000	$ 40,000	$ 30,000	$ 30,000
Indirect labor	360,000	30,000	30,000	120,000	90,000	90,000
Superintendence	50,000	8,000	32,000	4,000	4,000	2,000
Factory rent	100,000	40,000	22,500	12,500	15,000	10,000
Light and power	75,000	60,000	7,500	5,250	1,500	750
Heat	20,000	8,000	4,500	2,500	3,000	2,000
Repairs to machinery	40,000	35,000	4,000	1,000	—	—
Depreciation	100,000	80,000	15,000	2,000	1,000	2,000
Totals	$1,245,000	$361,000	$415,500	$187,250	$144,500	$136,750
Maintenance (70:20:5:5)	–0–	131,075	37,450	(187,250)	9,363	9,362
Factory cafeteria (20:80:10:5)	–0–	26,759	107,035	13,379	(153,863)	6,690
Factory hospital (20:80:10:10)	–0–	25,467	101,868	12,733	12,734	(152,802)
Subtotal, first cycle	$1,245,000	$544,301	$661,853	$ 26,112	$ 12,734	–0–
Second cycle:						
Maintenance (70:20:5:5)	–0–	18,278	5,222	(26,112)	1,306	1,306
Factory cafeteria (20:80:10:5)	–0–	2,442	9,767	1,221	(14,040)	610
Factory hospital (20:80:10:10)	–0–	319	1,277	160	160	(1,916)
Subtotal, second cycle	$1,245,000	$565,340	$678,119	$ 1,381	$ 160	$ –0–
Totals	$1,245,000	$566,381	$678,619	$ –0–	$ –0–	$ –0–
Basis		40,000 machine-hours				
Basis			160,000 labor-hours			
Predetermined rate		$14.160 per machine-hour	$4.241 per labor-hour			

Mathematical Approach. When the greatest degree of accuracy in allocating service department costs is desired, a **mathematical approach** must be used. In this approach, the information is set into mathematical equations that are solved either simultaneously or by substitution.

For example, assume that a firm has two producing departments, departments A and B, and two service departments, departments C and D. Their allocated overheads are:

$$
\begin{array}{lr}
\text{Department A} \ldots . & \$100{,}000 \\
\text{Department B} \ldots . & 200{,}000 \\
\text{Department C} \ldots . & 80{,}000 \\
\text{Department D} \ldots . & \underline{50{,}000} \\
\text{Total} \ldots \ldots . . & \underline{\underline{\$430{,}000}}
\end{array}
$$

Departments C and D render the following services:

$$
\begin{array}{ll}
\text{Department C} \ldots . . & \text{30 percent to A} \\
& \text{50 percent to B} \\
& \text{20 percent to D} \\
\text{Department D} \ldots . . & \text{60 percent to A} \\
& \text{30 percent to B} \\
& \text{10 percent to C}
\end{array}
$$

The equations can be solved by substitution and would be set up as:

$$A = \$100{,}000 + .3C + .6D$$
$$B = \$200{,}000 + .5C + .3D$$
$$C = \$\ \ 80{,}000 + \quad\quad .1D$$
$$D = \$\ \ 50{,}000 + .2C$$

The solution can start with equation C and substitute for D, or it can start with equation D and substitute for C. Starting with equation C, the solution proceeds as follows:

$$C = \$80{,}000 + .1D$$

By substitution:

$$C = \$80{,}000 + .1(\$50{,}000 + .2C)$$
$$C = \$80{,}000 + \$5{,}000 + .02C$$
$$C = \$85{,}000 + .02C$$
$$.98C = \$85{,}000$$
$$C = \$86{,}735$$

Therefore:

$$D = \$50{,}000 + .2C$$
$$D = \$50{,}000 + .2(\$86{,}735)$$
$$D = \$50{,}000 + \$17{,}347$$
$$D = \$67{,}347$$

And:

$$A = \$100{,}000 + .3C + .6D$$
$$A = \$100{,}000 + .3(\$86{,}735) + .6(\$67{,}347)$$
$$A = \$100{,}000 + \$26{,}020 + \$40{,}408$$
$$A = \$166{,}428$$

And:

$$B = \$200,000 + .5C + .3D$$
$$B = \$200,000 + .5(\$86,735) + .3(\$67,347)$$
$$B = \$200,000 + \$43,368 + \$20,204$$
$$B = \$263,572$$

The proof of the above calculations would be:

Total overhead	$430,000
Department A	$166,428
Department B	263,572
Total	$430,000

The results of the mathematical solution, which are technically accurate, can be compared with the results obtained by the step-down method shown in Illustration 3–30.

ILLUSTRATION 3–30   **Step-Down Overhead Allocation Method**

	Total	Producing Departments		Service Departments	
		A	B	C	D
Allocated overhead	$430,000	$100,000	$200,000	$80,000	$50,000
Department C—3:5:2	–0–	24,000	40,000	(80,000)	16,000
Department D—6:3	–0–	44,000	22,000		(66,000)
Totals	$430,000	$168,000	$262,000	$ –0–	$ –0–

While the difference in results between the mathematical solution and the step-down method is not large in this case, the results can be materially different, especially when increasingly more departments are involved. As the number of departments increases, the mathematical approach becomes unwieldy to perform manually and the use of a computer becomes preferable.

GLOSSARY OF KEY TERMS—APPENDIX 3–B

Direct method   A procedure for allocating service department overhead to producing departments only by ignoring the services rendered to other service departments.

Mathematical approach   A highly accurate method of assigning service department costs to producing departments, which makes use of mathematical equations that may be solved simultaneously, by substitution, or by computer.

Producing department   A segment of a manufacturing firm whose employees actually work on transforming raw materials into finished goods.

Reciprocal (redistribution) method A sequential allocation procedure used to assign service department costs to producing departments, which recognizes services provided to other service departments. The interservice department allocations are continued in each iteration until they are relatively small (usually less than $100), at which time they are allocated expeditiously.

Service department A segment of a manufacturing firm whose employees provide support services to a producing department.

Step-down method A sequential approach used to assign service department costs to producing departments, which recognizes services provided to other service departments. Once a service department's overhead account is closed, it is not reopened for an allocation of interservice department services.

QUESTIONS

1. Why is product cost information needed in connection with inventories?

2. For what purposes other than inventories is product cost information useful?

3. Explain how a process cost system differs from a job order system.

4. What is physical production flow? Is there usually a relationship between the physical flow and the cost accounting cycle? Explain.

5. What are source documents?

6. What is a purchase requisition? What basic information should it contain?

7. What is a purchase order? What basic information should it contain?

8. What is a receiving report? What information should it contain as a minimum? Should the *quantities ordered* be shown on the receiving report or should it be omitted? Present the arguments for their inclusion and omission.

9. What is a production order? Why is it used?

10. What should a materials requisition form contain and how is it used for control purposes?

11. What should a raw materials inventory ledger card contain and how is it used?

12. What is a job time ticket and how is it used?

13. What is a job cost sheet and what purpose does it serve?

14. What is a finished goods inventory ledger card and what purpose does it serve?

15. Is it usually possible to charge manufacturing overhead directly to a particular job? Why?

16. Why is it necessary to apply overhead to production through the use of a predetermined rate?

17. What allocation bases of applying overhead are usually found in practice? Are some used more than others? If so, which are they?

18. Does the use of direct labor cost as a base for applying overhead to production sometimes cause a misapplication? If so, use an example to illustrate the type of distortion. Does the use of direct labor-hours cure the distortion? Explain.

19. When should a machine-hour base be used for applying overhead? Does it cost more to use this base? Explain.

20. Is material cost widely used as a base for applying overhead? Explain.

21. How is a predetermined overhead rate computed? Use an example to demonstrate the procedure.

22. Do seasonal fluctuations and uneven cost flows impact on the use of actual overhead? Does the use of a predetermined overhead rate minimize the impact? Explain.

23. Does the use of a normal overhead rate serve any other purpose than smoothing seasonal fluctuations and uneven cost flows? Explain.

24. What are payroll fringes? Is there more than one way of treating them? Explain.

25. How is underapplied or overapplied overhead normally treated in interim reports? Are they usually treated differently in annual reports? Explain.

For Appendix 3–A

26. When is proration of under/overapplied overhead used? What does proration of overhead accomplish?

For Appendix 3–B

27. Why would a firm want to departmentalize its overhead?

28. What is the difference between a producing department and a service department?

29. What steps are necessary to departmentalize overhead?

30. What methods are in general usage for allocating service department overhead to producing departments?

31. What is the direct method of allocating service department overhead to producing departments and when should it be used?

32. What is the step-down method of allocating service department overhead to producing departments? Are there any problems with using this method? Explain.

33. What is the reciprocal (redistribution) method of allocating service department overhead to producing departments? Is it an efficient method to achieve accuracy? Explain.

EXERCISES

3–1 Journal Entries for the Job Order Cost Accounting Cycle

The following information and transactions are assumed to have occurred during the year 19x3 for the Juniper Company:

a. Purchases of raw materials amounted to $400,000.
b. Issuances of raw materials amounted to $385,000 for direct materials and $2,500 for indirect materials.
c. Payroll for the year 19x3 amounted to $340,000 for direct labor and $90,000 for indirect labor.
d. Manufacturing overhead is applied to production at 80 percent of direct labor cost.
e. Other manufacturing overhead for the year 19x3 amounted to $195,000. (Credit Sundry Credits.)
f. Finished goods for the year amounted to $985,000.
g. Sales on account for the year were $1.5 million.
h. The cost of these sales amounted to $960,000.

Required Journalize the transactions for the year.

3–2 Job Order Cost Concepts

Items 1 and 2 are based on the following information:

Hamilton Company uses job order costing. Factory overhead is applied to production at a predetermined rate of 150 percent of direct labor cost. Any over- or underapplied factory overhead is closed to the cost of goods sold account at the end of each month. Additional information is available as follows:

a. Job 101 was the only job in process at January 31, 19x2, with accumulated costs as follows:

Direct materials	$4,000
Direct labor	2,000
Applied factory overhead	3,000
Total	$9,000

b. Jobs 102, 103, and 104 were started during February.
c. Direct materials requisitions for February totaled $26,000.
d. Direct labor cost of $20,000 was incurred for February.
e. Actual factory overhead was $32,000 for February.
f. The only job still in process at February 28, 19x2, was Job 104, with costs of $2,800 for direct materials and $1,800 for direct labor.

1. The cost of goods manufactured for February 19x2 was
   a. $77,700.
   b. $78,000.
   c. $79,700.
   d. $85,000.
2. Over- or underapplied factory overhead should be closed to the cost of goods sold account at February 28, 19x2, in the amount of
   a. $ 700 overapplied.
   b. $1,000 overapplied.
   c. $1,700 underapplied.
   d. $2,000 underapplied.

(AICPA adapted)

3–3 Job Order Cost Concepts

1. Peters Company uses a flexible budget system and prepared the following information for 19x0:

Percent of Capacity	80%	90%
Direct labor hours	24,000	27,000
Variable factory overhead	$ 48,000	$ 54,000
Fixed factory overhead	$100,000	$100,000
Total factory overhead rate		
per direct labor-hour	$6.50	$6.00

Peters operated at 80 percent of capacity during 19x0 but applied factory overhead based on the 90 percent capacity level. Assuming that actual factory overhead was equal to the budgeted amount for the attained capacity, what is the amount of overhead variance for the year?

a. $ 6,000 overabsorbed.
b. $ 6,000 underabsorbed.
c. $12,000 overabsorbed.
d. $12,000 underabsorbed.

2. Worrell Corporation has a job order cost system. The following debits (credits) appeared in the general ledger account Work in Process for the month of March 19x2:

March 1, balance	$ 12,000
March 31, direct materials	40,000
March 31, direct labor	30,000
March 31, factory overhead	27,000
March 31, to finished goods	(100,000)

Worrell applies overhead to production at a predetermined rate of 90 percent based on the direct labor cost. Job No. 232, the only job still in process at the end of March 19x2, has been charged with factory overhead of $2,250. What was the amount of direct materials charged to Job No. 232?

a. $2,250.
b. $2,500.
c. $4,250.
d. $9,000.

3. Cannon Cannery, Inc., estimated its factory overhead at $510,000 for 19x1, based on a normal capacity of 100,000 direct labor-hours. Direct labor-hours for the year totaled 105,000, while the factory overhead account at the end of the year showed a balance of $540,000. How much was the underapplied factory overhead for 19x1?

a. $0.
b. $ 4,500.
c. $27,000.
d. $30,000.

(AICPA adapted)

3–4 Job Order Cost Concepts

The following data apply to items 1 through 4.

Department 203—work in process—beginning of period:

Job No.	Material	Labor	Overhead	Total
1376	$17,500	$22,000	$33,000	$ 72,500

Department 203 costs for 19x7:

Incurred by Jobs	Material	Labor	Other	Total
1376	$ 1,000	$ 7,000	—	$ 8,000
1377	26,000	53,000	—	79,000
1378	12,000	9,000	—	21,000
1379	4,000	1,000	—	5,000
Not Incurred by Jobs				
Indirect materials and supplies	15,000	—	—	15,000
Indirect labor	—	53,000	—	53,000
Employee benefits	—	—	$23,000	23,000
Depreciation	—	—	12,000	12,000
Supervision	—	20,000	—	20,000
Total	$58,000	$143,000	$35,000	$236,000

Department 203 overhead rate for 19x7:

Budgeted overhead:

Variable—Indirect materials	$ 16,000
Indirect labor	56,000
Employee benefits	24,000
Fixed—Supervision	20,000
Depreciation	12,000
Total	$128,000
Budgeted direct labor dollars	$ 80,000
Rate per direct labor dollar ($128,000 ÷ 80,000)	160%

1. The actual overhead for Department 203 for 19x7 was
   a. $156,000.
   b. $123,000.
   c. $70,000.
   d. $112,000.
   e. Not shown above.
2. Department 203 overhead for 19x7 was
   a. $11,000 underapplied.
   b. $11,000 overapplied.
   c. $44,000 underapplied.
   d. $44,000 overapplied.
   e. Not shown above.
3. Job No. 1376 was the only job completed and sold in 19x7. What amount was included in cost of goods sold for this job?
   a. $72,500.
   b. $91,700.
   c. $80,500.
   d. $19,200.
   e. Not shown above.

4. The value of work in process inventory at the end of 19x7 was
    a. $105,000.
    b. $180,600.
    c. $228,000.
    d. $205,800.
    e. Not shown above.

(CMA adapted)

3–5 Job Order Cost Concepts

The following data apply to items 1 through 4.

Selected data concerning the past fiscal year's operations of the Televans Manufacturing Company are presented below (in thousands):

	Inventories	
	Beginning	**Ending**
Raw materials	$75	$ 85
Work in process	80	30
Finished goods	90	110

Other data:	
Raw materials used	$326
Total manufacturing costs charged to production during the year (includes raw materials, direct labor, and factory overhead applied at a rate of 60 percent of direct labor cost)	686
Cost of goods available for sale	826
Marketing and administrative costs . . .	25

1. The cost of raw materials purchased during the year amounted to
    a. $411.
    b. $360.
    c. $316.
    d. $336.
    e. Some amount other than those shown above.
2. Direct labor costs charged to production during the year amounted to
    a. $135.
    b. $225.
    c. $360.
    d. $216.
    e. Some amount other than those shown above.
3. The cost of goods manufactured during the year was
    a. $636.
    b. $766.
    c. $736.
    d. $716.
    e. Some amount other than those shown above.

4. The cost of goods sold during the year was
   a. $736.
   b. $716.
   c. $691.
   d. $801.
   e. Some amount other than those shown above.

(CMA adapted)

3–6 Job Order Cost Concepts

The following data apply to items 1 through 6.

Baehr Company is a manufacturing company with a fiscal year that runs from July 1 to June 30. The company uses a job order accounting system for its production costs.

A predetermined overhead rate based upon direct labor-hours is used to apply overhead to individual jobs. A budget of overhead costs was prepared for the 19x7–x8 fiscal year as shown below.

Direct labor-hours	120,000
Variable overhead costs	$390,000
Fixed overhead costs	216,000
Total overhead	$606,000

The information presented below is for November 19x7. Jobs 77–50 and 77–51 were completed during November.

Inventories November 1, 19x7:	
Raw materials and supplies	$ 10,500
Work in process (Job 77–50)	54,000
Finished goods	112,500
Purchases of raw materials and supplies:	
Raw materials	$135,000
Supplies	15,000
Materials and supplies requisitioned for production:	
Job 77–50	$ 45,000
Job 77–51	37,500
Job 77–52	25,500
Supplies	12,000
Total	$120,000
Factory direct labor-hours:	
Job 77–50	3,500 DLH
Job 77–51	3,000 DLH
Job 77–52	2,000 DLH
Labor costs:	
Direct labor wages	$ 51,000
Indirect labor wages (4,000 hours) . .	15,000
Supervisory salaries	6,000

Building occupancy costs
(heat, light, depreciation, etc.):

Factory facilities	. . . .	$ 6,500
Sales offices	. . . .	1,500
Administrative offices	. . . .	1,000
Total	. . . .	$ 9,000

Factory equipment costs:

Power	. . . .	$ 4,000
Repairs and maintenance	. . . .	1,500
Depreciation	. . . .	1,500
Other	. . . .	1,000
Total	. . . .	$ 8,000

1. The predetermined overhead rate to be used to apply overhead to individual jobs during the 19x7–x8 fiscal year is
   a. $3.25 per DLH.
   b. $4.69 per DLH.
   c. $5.05 per DLH.
   d. $5.41 per DLH.
   e. Some rate other than those shown above.

   Note: Without prejudice to your answer to item 1, assume the predetermined overhead rate is $4.50 per direct labor-hour. Use this amount in answering items 2 through 6.

2. The total cost of job 77–50 is
   a. $81,750.
   b. $135,750.
   c. $142,750.
   d. $146,750.
   e. Some amount other than those shown above.
3. The factory overhead costs applied to job 77–52 during November were
   a. $9,000.
   b. $47,500.
   c. $46,500.
   d. $8,000.
   e. Some amount other than those shown above.
4. The total amount of overhead applied to jobs during November was
   a. $29,250.
   b. $38,250.
   c. $47,250.
   d. $56,250.
   e. Some amount other than those shown above.
5. Actual factory overhead incurred during November 19x7 was
   a. $38,000.
   b. $41,500.
   c. $47,500.
   d. $50,500.
   e. Some amount other than those shown above.
6. At the end of the last fiscal year (June 30, 19x7), Baehr Company had the following account balances:

Overapplied overhead . . . . . . $	1,000
Cost of goods sold	980,000
Work in process inventory	38,000
Finished goods inventory	82,000

The most common treatment of the overapplied overhead would be to

a. Prorate it between work in process inventory and finished goods inventory.

b. Prorate it between work in process inventory, finished goods inventory, and cost of goods sold.

c. Carry it as a deferred credit on the balance sheet.

d. Carry it as miscellaneous operating revenue on the income statement.

e. Credit it to cost of goods sold.

(CMA adapted)

3-7 Preparation of Statement of Cost of Goods Manufactured

The Helper Corporation manufactures one product and accounts for costs by a job order cost system. You have obtained the following information for the year ended December 31, 19x3, from the corporation's books and records:

1. Total manufacturing cost added during 19x3 (sometimes called cost to manufacture) was $1 million based on actual direct material, actual direct labor, and applied factory overhead on actual direct labor dollars.

2. Cost of goods manufactured was $970,000, also based on actual direct material, actual direct labor, and applied factory overhead.

3. Factory overhead was applied to work in process at 75 percent of direct labor dollars. Applied factory overhead for the year was 27 percent of the total manufacturing cost.

4. Beginning work in process inventory, January 1, was 80 percent of ending work in process inventory, December 31.

Required Prepare a formal statement of cost of goods manufactured for the year ended December 31, 19x3, for Helper Corporation. Use actual direct material used, actual direct labor, and applied factory overhead. Show supporting computations in good form.

(AICPA adapted)

3-8 Preparation of Statement of Cost of Goods Manufactured

The Rebecca Corporation is a manufacturer that produces special machines made to customer specifications. All production costs are accumulated by means of a job order costing system. The following information is available at the beginning of the month of October 19x0.

Direct materials inventory, October 1	$16,200
Work in process, October 1	3,600

A review of the job order cost sheets revealed the composition of the work in process inventory on October 1 as follows:

Direct materials	$1,320
Direct labor (300 hours)	1,500
Factory overhead applied	780
Total	$3,600

Activity during the month of October was as follows:

> Direct materials costing $20,000 were pur-
> chased.
> Direct labor for job orders totaled 3,300 hours
> at $5 per hour.
> Factory overhead was applied to production at
> the rate of $2.60 per direct labor-hour.

On October 31, inventories consisted of the following components:

Direct materials inventory	$17,000
Work in process inventory:	
Direct materials	$ 4,320
Direct labor (500 hours)	2,500
Factory overhead applied	1,300
Total	$ 8,120

Required Prepare in good form a detailed statement of the cost of goods manufactured for the month of October.

(AICPA adapted)

3-9 Job Cost Sheet and Unit Cost

The Herald Company manufactures clothing. Job No. 476 was started on February 14, 19x3, and completed on February 28, 19x3, and consisted of 1,000 raincoats. The following data is available:

	Week of February 14	Week of February 21
Materials purchased	$10,000	$ 1,000
Materials used—Job No. 476	$ 8,000	$ 1,500
Direct labor used	$20,000	$10,000
Actual overhead incurred	$15,000	$16,000

Factory overhead is applied at a rate of 80 percent of direct labor cost.

Required
a. Prepare a job cost sheet and compute the unit cost for Job 476.
b. What should the unit sales price be if Herald wants to earn 90 percent of cost as gross profit?

3-10 Journal Entries for Cost Accounting Cycle

The following transactions were completed during the month of March 19x4:

1. Materials in the amount of $80,000 were purchased on account.
2. Requisitions representing issues of direct material amounted to $65,000. Indirect materials in the amount of $1,000 were issued.
3. The factory payroll for March consisted of:

Direct labor $40,000
Indirect labor 15,000

4. Factory overhead is applied to production on the basis of 90 percent of direct labor cost.
5. Overhead costs in addition to those listed above amounted to $18,000.
6. Goods worth $100,000 were completed and transferred to the stockroom.
7. Sales to customers amounted to $150,000; the cost of these goods was $75,000.

Required a. Prepare journal entries to record the above information.
b. Compute the work in process at March 31, 19x4.

3–11 Computation and Use of Predetermined Overhead Rates

The Uniprojector Company manufactures photographic slide projectors. The firm operates in a seasonal market where 60 percent of the firm's annual sales occur during the months of October and November. The factory operates on a cyclical basis. Production for the year amounts to 300,000 units. The firm's manufacturing overhead mainly consists of fixed costs and usually amounts to $720,000 yearly.

The firm's cost accountant prepares monthly cost figures which are based on actual costs including actual overhead for the month. His cost calculations for the most recent three months are as follows:

	July	August	September
Direct materials	$ 50,000	$100,000	$ 400,000
Direct labor	75,000	150,000	600,000
Overhead	62,000	66,000	76,000
Total costs	$187,000	$316,000	$1,076,000
Units produced	5,000	10,000	40,000
Unit cost	$37.40	$31.60	$26.90

After reviewing these cost figures, the president of the company expressed concern about the widely fluctuating unit costs. He has heard somewhere that some firms use normal costing. The firm's direct labor for the year is estimated to be $4.5 million.

Required Redo the cost calculations using normal costing. Use direct labor cost as the base for applying overhead to production.

3–12 Computation of Predetermined Overhead Rate and Closing of Manufacturing Overhead Account

The Mayfair Company estimates that its direct labor cost for 19x3 will amount to $600,000, while its overhead for the year is expected to amount to $420,000. During the year, its actual direct labor cost amounted to $570,000 and its actual overhead amounted to $406,000. The company uses an Applied Manufacturing Overhead account when it applies overhead to production.

Required a. Compute the predetermined overhead rate that Mayfair should use for 19x3 using a direct labor cost base.

b. Prepare the summary journal entry for 19x3 showing the application of overhead for the year.

c. Close the Overhead and Applied Manufacturing Overhead accounts to Cost of Goods Sold.

3-13 Computation of Predetermined Overhead Rate and Completion of Job Cost Sheet

The Moveover Company estimates that its direct labor cost for 19x4 will amount to $800,000, while its overhead is expected to amount to $520,000 for the year. At the end of June 19x4, the debits in the Work in Process account consisted of the following:

Direct materials	$ 300,000
Direct labor	450,000
Overhead	292,500
Total debits	$1,042,500

Transfers to finished goods for the six months ended June 30, 19x4, amounted to $962,500. Only one job, Job No. 266, was still in process on June 30. The direct labor for Job No. 266 amounted to $26,000 at June 30.

Required a. Compute the predetermined overhead rate for Moveover using direct labor cost as the base.

b. Prepare the breakdown of direct materials, direct labor, and overhead that would appear on the job cost sheet for Job No. 266.

3-14 Computation of Predetermined Overhead Rate and Closing of Manufacturing Overhead Account

The Sawyer Company estimates that its direct labor cost for 19x3 will amount to $500,000, while its overhead for the year is expected to amount to $575,000. During the year, its actual direct labor cost amounted to $460,000 and its actual overhead amounted to $537,500. The company uses an Applied Manufacturing Overhead account when it applies overhead to production.

Required a. Compute the predetermined overhead rate that Sawyer should use for 19x3 using a direct labor cost base.

b. Prepare the summary journal entry for 19x3 showing the application of overhead for the year.

c. Close the Overhead and Applied Manufacturing Overhead accounts to Cost of Goods Sold.

3-15 (Appendix A): Disposition of Underapplied or Overapplied Overhead

This exercise is based on the data provided in Exercise 3-4.

Job No. 1376 was the only job completed and sold in 19x7. Assume that overhead was underapplied in the amount of $14,000 for department 203. If underapplied overhead was distributed between cost of goods sold and inventory, how much of the underapplied overhead was charged to the year-end work in process inventory?

a. $9,685.

b. $4,315.

c. $12,600.

d. $1,400.

e. The amount is not shown above.

(CMA adapted)

3–16 (Appendix A): Disposition of Underapplied or Overapplied Manufacturing Overhead

1. The balance of the Work in Process account on December 31, 19x4, is:

Direct materials	$15,000
Direct labor	30,000
Manufacturing overhead	30,600
Total	$75,600

2. The balance in the Finished Goods Inventory account on December 31, 19x4, consists of:

Direct materials	$10,000
Direct labor	20,000
Manufacturing overhead	20,400
Total	$50,400

3. The balance in the Cost of Goods Sold account on December 31, 19x4, consists of:

Direct materials	$140,000
Direct labor	283,333
Manufacturing overhead	289,000
Total	$712,333

4. The actual manufacturing overhead for 19x4 amounted to $304,000 and included expenditures which could not be anticipated prior to December 31, 19x4.

5. The applied overhead amounted to $340,000.

Required

a. Prepare a schedule to prorate the under/overapplied manufacturing overhead.

b. Prepare the journal entry to close the under/overapplied overhead as prorated in *(a)* above.

c. Prepare the journal entry to close the under/overapplied overhead if it is *not* prorated.

3–17 (Appendix B): Departmental Overhead Allocation

1. Tillman Corporation uses a job order cost system and has two production departments, M and A. Budgeted manufacturing costs for 19x0 are as follows:

	Department M	Department A
Direct materials	$700,000	$100,000
Direct labor	200,000	800,000
Manufacturing overhead	600,000	400,000

The actual material and labor costs charged to Job No. 432 during 19x0 were as follows:

Direct material			$25,000
Direct labor:			
Department M	$ 8,000		
Department A	12,000	20,000	

Tillman applies manufacturing overhead to production orders on the basis of direct labor cost using departmental rates predetermined at the beginning of the year based on the annual budget. The total manufacturing cost associated with Job No. 432 for 19x0 should be

a. $50,000.
b. $55,000.
c. $65,000.
d. $75,000.

2. Hartwell Company distributes the service department overhead costs directly to producing departments without allocation to the other service department. Information for the month of January 19x2 is as follows:

	Service Departments	
	Maintenance	Utilities
Overhead costs incurred	$18,700	$9,000
Service provided to:		
Maintenance department	—	10%
Utilities department	20%	—
Producing department A	40%	30%
Producing department B	40%	60%
Total	100%	100%

The amount of utilities department costs distributed to producing department B for January 19x2 should be

a. $3,600.
b. $4,500.
c. $5,400.
d. $6,000.

3–18   (Appendix B): Calculation of Departmental Overhead Rates

The Samuel Company uses a job order cost accounting system. They plan to use a normalized predetermined overhead rate on a departmentalized basis. For department A they plan to use a direct labor-hour basis and for department B they plan to use a machine-hour basis. Prior to 19x5, the company estimated the following for 19x5:

	Department A	Department B
Direct labor-hours	100,000	20,000
Machine-hours	10,000	80,000
Manufacturing overhead cost	$200,000	$72,000

In addition, assume that the job cost sheet for Job 152 contains the following:

	Department A	Department B
Materials requisitioned	$ 50,000	$20,000
Direct labor cost	$100,000	$20,000
Direct labor-hours	20,000	4,000
Machine-hours	1,000	15,000

Required
a. Compute the predetermined overhead rate to be used in each department.
b. Compute the total cost of Job 152 and compute the unit cost if 100,000 units were produced.

PROBLEMS 3–19 **Journal Entries for Cost Accounting Cycle and Preparation of Statement of Cost of Goods Sold**

The following information and transactions are assumed to have occurred during the year 19x3 for the Humbart Company:

1. The beginning inventory of raw materials amounted to $152,000.
2. Purchases of raw materials amounted to $467,000.
3. Issuances of raw materials amounted to $483,000 for direct materials and $2,500 for indirect materials.
4. The beginning inventories for work in process and finished goods were:

Work in process $46,000
Finished goods 98,000

5. Payroll for the year 19x3 amounted to $322,000 for direct labor and $90,000 for indirect labor.
6. Manufacturing overhead is applied to production at 80 percent of direct labor cost.
7. Other manufacturing overhead for the year 19x3 amounted to $208,500. (Credit Sundry Credits.)
8. Finished goods for the year amounted to $1,032,000.
9. Sales on account for the year were $1,684,000. The cost of these sales amounted to $995,000.
10. The company's policy is to close any underapplied or overapplied manufacturing overhead to cost of goods sold.

Required
a. Journalize the transactions for the year.
b. Open T accounts for the beginning inventory balances and post the journalized entries from (a) above.

c. Prepare a statement of cost of goods manufactured and a statement of cost of goods sold.

3–20   T Account Entries for Cost Accounting Cycle and Preparation of Statement of Cost of Goods Sold

The following information and transactions are assumed to have occurred during the year 19x3 for the Altosax Company:

1. The beginning inventory of raw materials amounted to $132,000.
2. Purchases of raw materials amounted to $427,000.
3. Issuances of raw materials amounted to $433,000 for direct materials and $2,000 for indirect materials.
4. The beginning inventories for work in process and finished goods were:

Work in process $56,000
Finished goods 88,000

5. Payroll for the year 19x3 amounted to $312,000 for direct labor and $80,000 for indirect labor.
6. Manufacturing overhead is applied to production at 80 percent of direct labor cost.
7. Other manufacturing overhead for the year 19x3 amounted to $158,000. (Credit Sundry Credits.)
8. Finished goods for the year amounted to $992,000.
9. Sales on account for the year were $1,624,000. The cost of these sales amounted to $965,000.
10. The company's policy is to close any under/overapplied manufacturing overhead to cost of goods sold.

Required *a.* Open T accounts for the beginning inventory balances and post the above transactions directly to the necessary T accounts.

b. Prepare a statement of cost of goods manufactured and a statement of cost of goods sold.

3–21   Cost Accounting Cycle from Fragmentary Data

The bookkeeper of the Harold Company found that a large backlog of work existed and he decided that he would take some work home to his farm for the weekend. After tending to the chickens and goats, the bookkeeper started working on the company's books while sitting on the outdoor porch. After about an hour's work, he got drowsy and dozed off. Hearing a noise, he awakened to see a goat enjoying her lunch of the company's records. Fortunately, there were some scraps left and the bookkeeper assembled the scraps to the extent possible and found the following:

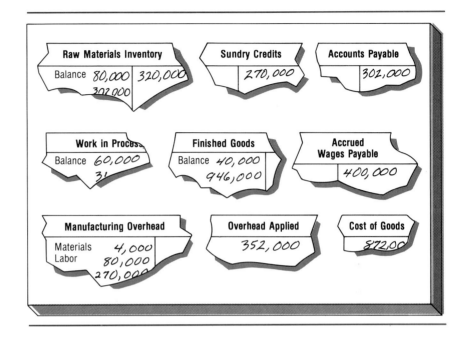

The bookkeeper seeks your advice to assist him in reconstructing the company's records. Assume that the records are for the year 19x6.

Required *a.* Prepare the journal entries that can be reconstructed from the above. (Any under/overapplied overhead is to be closed to cost of goods sold.)

b. Compute the ending inventories for:
1. Raw materials.
2. Work in process.
3. Finished goods.

c. Compute the predetermined overhead rate if direct labor cost was used as the base.

3–22 **Cost Accounting Cycle Prepared from Statement of Cost of Goods Manufactured and Sold**

ROBERT COMPANY
Statement of Cost of Goods Manufactured
For the Year Ended December 31, 19x3

Direct materials:

Raw materials inventory, January 1	$112,000	
Add: Purchases of raw materials	244,000	
Total raw materials available	356,000	
Deduct: Raw materials inventory, December 31	91,500	
Raw materials used	264,500	
Deduct: Indirect materials used	1,500	
Direct materials used in production		$263,000
Direct labor		330,000

Manufacturing overhead:

Indirect materials	1,500	
Indirect labor	65,000	
Miscellaneous factory costs	234,500	
Actual manufacturing overhead costs	301,000	
Less: Underapplied overhead	4,000	
Overhead applied to work in process		297,000
Total manufacturing costs		890,000
Add: Work in process, January 1		40,000
		930,000
Deduct: Work in process, December 31		35,000
Cost of goods manufactured at normal		$895,000

ROBERT COMPANY
Statement of Cost of Goods Sold
For the Year Ended December 31, 19x3

Finished goods inventory, January 1	$ 85,000
Cost of goods manufactured at normal	895,000
Goods available for sale	980,000
Finished goods inventory, December 31	70,000
Cost of goods sold at normal	910,000
Add: Underapplied manufacturing overhead	4,000
Cost of goods sold at actual	$914,000

The company closes its under/overapplied overhead to cost of goods sold.

Required *a.* From the above statements, you are asked to prepare all entries implicit in the cost accounting cycle that can be prepared.

b. The company uses direct labor cost as its base for applying overhead. Compute the company's predetermined overhead rate.

3-23 Individual Job Costs and the Cost Accounting Cycle

The following information and transactions are assumed to have occurred during the month of January 19x5 for the Charles Nailtop Company:

1. The beginning inventory of raw materials consisted of:

Material A	$ 6,000
Material B	5,000
Material C	8,000
Total	$19,000

2. Purchases of raw materials consisted of:

Material A	$20,000
Material B	25,000
Material C	40,000
Total	$85,000

3. Issuances of raw materials consisted of:

Material A	$18,000
Material B	26,000
Material C	39,000
Total	$83,000

The materials are to be charged to:

Job 101	$27,000
Job 102	23,000
Job 103	33,000
Total	$83,000

4. The beginning work in process inventory consisted of:

Job 101	$13,000
Job 102	15,000
Job 103	12,000
Total	$40,000

The beginning finished goods inventory consisted of:

30 desks at $150	$4,500
40 chairs at $70	2,800
Total	$7,300

5. Payroll for the month is:

Direct labor	$60,000
Indirect labor	15,000
Total	$75,000

The direct labor is chargeable 40 percent to Job 101, 25 percent to Job 102, and 35 percent to Job 103.

6. Manufacturing overhead is applied to production at 70 percent of direct labor cost.
7. Other manufacturing overhead for the month amounted to $30,000.
8. Jobs 101 and 102 are completed. Job 103 is not completed.
9. Job 101 was for 1,130 chairs and Job 102 was for 500 desks. Job 103 is for 600 tables.
10. Sales for the month were as follows:
    a. 1,000 chairs at $130.
    b. 400 desks at $300.
    The company uses the first-in, first-out method to account for all inventories.

Required   a. Prepare all of the necessary journal entries to record the above information.
              b. Prepare either job cost sheets for each job or a tabular summary of costs by job. (Do not forget to include beginning inventories.)
              c. Compute the unit costs for Job 101 and Job 102.
              d. Compute the following inventories at January 31, 19x5:
                   (1) Raw materials.
                   (2) Work in process.
                   (3) Finished goods.
              e. Prepare T accounts for raw materials inventory, work in process, and finished goods and compare your answers with your computations in part (d) above.

3–24 Journal Entries for Cost Accounting Cycle and Preparation of Statement of Cost of Goods Sold

The following information and transactions are assumed to have occurred during the year 19x3 for the Maxwell Company:

1. The beginning inventory of raw materials amounted to $140,600.
2. Purchases of raw materials amounted to $432,000.
3. Issuances of raw materials amounted to $446,800 for direct materials and $2,300 for indirect materials.
4. The beginning inventories for work in process and finished goods were:

> Work in process $42,500
> Finished goods   90,600

5. Payroll for the year 19x3 amounted to $298,000 for direct labor and $83,000 for indirect labor.
6. Manufacturing overhead is applied to production at 75 percent of direct labor cost.
7. Other manufacturing overhead for the year 19x3 amounted to $143,000. (Credit Sundry Credits.)
8. Finished goods for the year amounted to $954,600.
9. Sales on account for the year were $1,557,000. The cost of these sales amounted to $920,000.
10. The company's policy is to close any underapplied or overapplied manufacturing overhead to cost of goods sold.

Required   a. Journalize the transactions for the year.
              b. Open T accounts for the beginning inventory balances and post the journalized entries from (a) above.
              c. Prepare a statement of cost of goods manufactured and a statement of cost of goods sold.

3–25 T Account Entries for Cost Accounting Cycle and Preparation of Statement of Cost of Goods Sold

The following information and transactions are assumed to have occurred during the year 19x3 for the Garret Company:

1. The beginning inventory of raw materials amounted to $122,100.
2. Purchases of raw materials amounted to $395,000.
3. Issuances of raw materials amounted to $400,500 for direct materials and $1,800 for indirect materials.

4. The beginning inventories for work in process and finished goods were:

Work in process $52,000
Finished goods   81,400

5. Payroll for the year 19x3 amounted to $288,000 for direct labor and $74,000 for indirect labor.
6. Manufacturing overhead is applied to production at 75 percent of direct labor cost.
7. Other manufacturing overhead for the year 19x3 amounted to $146,000. (Credit Sundry Credits.)
8. Finished goods for the year amounted to $917,600.
9. Sales on account for the year were $1,502,000. The cost of these sales amounted to $892,600.
10. The company's policy is to close any under/overapplied manufacturing overhead to cost of goods sold.

Required   *a.* Open T accounts for the beginning inventory balances and post the above transactions directly to the necessary T accounts.

b. Prepare a statement of cost of goods manufactured and a statement of cost of goods sold.

3–26   Cost Accounting Cycle Prepared from Statement of Cost of Goods Manufactured and Sold

CALVERT COMPANY
Statement of Cost of Goods Manufactured
For the Year Ended December 31, 19x3

Direct materials:		
Raw materials inventory, January 1	$ 95,000	
Add: Purchases of raw materials	307,000	
Total raw materials available	402,000	
Deduct: Raw materials inventory, December 31	72,500	
Raw materials used	329,500	
Deduct: Indirect materials used	1,500	
Direct materials used in production		$328,000
Direct labor		224,000
Manufacturing overhead:		
Indirect materials	1,500	
Indirect labor	57,000	
Miscellaneous factory costs	114,500	
Actual manufacturing overhead costs	173,000	
Less: Underapplied overhead	5,000	
Overhead applied to work in process		168,000
Total manufacturing costs		720,000
Add: Work in process, January 1		40,000
		760,000
Deduct: Work in process, December 31		46,000
Cost of goods manufactured at normal		$714,000

CALVERT COMPANY
Statement of Cost of Goods Sold
For the Year Ended December 31, 19x3

Finished goods inventory, January 1	$ 63,000
Cost of goods manufactured at normal	714,000
Goods available for sale	777,000
Finished goods inventory, December 31	82,000
Cost of goods sold at normal	695,000
Add: Underapplied manufacturing overhead	5,000
Cost of goods sold at actual	$700,000

The company closes its under/overapplied overhead to cost of goods sold.

Required
a. From the above statements, you are asked to prepare all entries implicit in the cost accounting cycle that can be prepared.

b. The company uses direct labor cost as its base for applying overhead. Compute the company's predetermined overhead rate.

3–27 Individual Job Costs and the Cost Accounting Cycle

The following information and transactions are assumed to have occurred during the month of January 19x5 for the Seneca Company:

1. The beginning inventory of raw materials consisted of:

Material A	. . . .	$ 6,720
Material B	. . . .	5,700
Material C	. . . .	8,900
Total	. . . . . .	$21,320

2. Purchases of raw materials consisted of:

Material A	. . . .	$22,400
Material B	. . . .	28,000
Material C	. . . .	45,000
Total	. . . . . .	$95,400

3. Issuances of raw materials consisted of:

Material A	. . . .	$20,100
Material B	. . . .	29,100
Material C	. . . .	43,700
Total	. . . . . .	$92,900

The materials are to be charged to:

Job 101	. . . . .	$30,200
Job 102	. . . . .	25,700
Job 103	. . . . .	37,000
Total	. . . . .	$92,900

4. The beginning work in process inventory consisted of:

Job 101	. . . . .	$14,500
Job 102	. . . . .	16,800
Job 103	. . . . .	13,400
Total	. . . . .	$44,700

The beginning finished goods inventory consisted of:

30 desks at $170	. . . .	$5,100
40 chairs at $80	. . . . .	3,200
Total	. . . .	$8,300

5. Payroll for the month is:

Direct labor	. . . . .	$67,000
Indirect labor	. . . .	16,800
Total	. . . . . .	$83,800

The direct labor is chargeable 40 percent to Job 101, 25 percent to Job 102, and 35 percent to Job 103.

6. Manufacturing overhead is applied to production at 70 percent of direct labor cost.

7. Other manufacturing overhead for the month amounted to $33,000.

8. Jobs 101 and 102 are completed. Job 103 is not completed.

9. Job 101 was for 1,130 chairs and Job 102 was for 500 desks. Job 103 is for 600 tables.

10. Sales for the month were as follows:
    a. 1,000 chairs at $145.
    b. 400 desks at $340.
    The company uses the first-in, first-out method to account for all inventories.

Required
a. Prepare all of the necessary journal entries to record the above information.
b. Prepare either job cost sheets for each job or prepare a tabular summary of costs by job. (Do not forget to include beginning inventories.)
c. Compute the unit costs for Job 101 and Job 102.
d. Compute the following inventories at January 31, 19x5:
   1. Raw materials.
   2. Work in process.
   3. Finished goods.

e. Prepare T accounts for raw materials inventory, work in process, and finished goods and compare your answers with your computations in part *(d)* above.

3–28 T Account Entries for Cost Accounting Cycle and Preparation of Statement of Cost of Goods Sold

The following information and transactions are assumed to have occurred during the year 19x3 for the Practical Company:

1. The beginning inventory of raw materials amounted to $67,000.
2. Purchases of raw materials amounted to $217,000.
3. Issuances of raw materials amounted to $220,000 for direct materials and $1,200 for indirect materials.
4. The beginning inventories for work in process and finished goods were:

Work in process $28,000
Finished goods   41,000

5. Payroll for the year 19x3 amounted to $161,000 for direct labor and $41,000 for indirect labor.
6. Manufacturing overhead is applied to production at 70 percent of direct labor cost.
7. Other manufacturing overhead for the year 19x3 amounted to $72,000. (Credit Sundry Credits.)
8. Finished goods for the year amounted to $492,000.
9. Sales on account for the year were $834,000. The cost of these sales amounted to $487,000.
10. The company's policy is to close any under/overapplied manufacturing overhead to cost of goods sold.

Required   a. Open T accounts for the beginning inventory balances and post the above transactions directly to the necessary T accounts.

b. Prepare a statement of cost of goods manufactured and a statement of cost of goods sold.

3–29 (Appendix A): Disposition of Underapplied or Overapplied Manufacturing Overhead

1. The balance of the Work in Process account on December 31, 19x4, is:

Direct materials $18,000
Direct labor   40,000
Manufacturing overhead   24,000
Total $82,000

2. The balance in the Finished Goods Inventory account on December 31, 19x4, consists of:

Direct materials . . . . $ 20,000
Direct labor   80,000
Manufacturing overhead   48,000
Total $148,000

3. The balance in the Cost of Goods Sold account on December 31, 19x4, consists of:

Direct materials	$160,000
Direct labor	380,000
Manufacturing overhead	228,000
Total	$768,000

4. The actual manufacturing overhead for 19x4 amounted to $306,000 and included expenditures which could not be anticipated prior to December 31, 19x4.
5. The applied overhead amounted to $300,000.

Required
  a. Prepare a schedule to prorate the under/overapplied manufacturing overhead.
  b. Prepare a schedule to verify that the applied overhead would be converted to actual overhead if the proration from *(a)* above is journalized.
  c. Journalize the proration from *(a)* above.

3–30   **(Appendix B): Allocation of Service Department Overhead to Producing Departments**

Items 1 through 4 are based on the following information:

The Parker Manufacturing Company has two production departments (fabrication and assembly) and three service departments (general factory administration, factory maintenance, and factory cafeteria). A summary of costs and other data for each department prior to allocation of service department costs for the year ended June 30, 19x3, appears below items 1 through 4.

The costs of the general factory administration department, factory maintenance department, and factory cafeteria are allocated on the basis of direct labor-hours, square footage occupied, and number of employees, respectively.

Round all final calculations to the nearest dollar.

1. Assuming that Parker elects to distribute service department costs directly to production departments without interservice department cost allocation, the amount of factory maintenance department costs which would be allocated to the fabrication department would be
  a. $0.
  b. $111,760
  c. $106,091.
  d. $91,440.
2. Assuming the same method of allocation as in item 1, the amount of general factory administration department costs which would be allocated to the assembly department would be
  a. $0.
  b. $63,636.
  c. $70,000.
  d. $90,000.
3. Assuming that Parker elects to distribute service department costs to other service departments (starting with the service department with the greatest total costs) as well as the production departments, the amount of factory cafeteria department costs which would be allocated to the factory maintenance department would

be (Note: Once a service department's costs have been reallocated, no subsequent service department costs are recirculated back to it.)

    a. $0.

    b. $96,000.

    c. $3,840.

    d. $6,124.

4. Assuming the same method of allocation as in item 3, the amount of factory maintenance department costs which would be allocated to the factory cafeteria would be

    a. $0.

    b. $5,787.

    c. $5,856.

    d. $148,910.

	Fabrication	Assembly	General Factory Administration	Factory Maintenance	Factory Cafeteria
Direct labor costs	$1,950,000	$2,050,000	$90,000	$82,100	$87,000
Direct material costs	$3,130,000	$ 950,000	—	$65,000	$91,000
Manufacturing overhead costs	$1,650,000	$1,850,000	$70,000	$56,100	$62,000
Direct labor-hours	562,500	437,500	31,000	27,000	42,000
Number of employees	280	200	12	8	20
Square footage occupied	88,000	72,000	1,750	2,000	4,800

(AICPA adapted)

4

PROCESS COSTING

As noted in Chapter 3, cost information is useful for purposes of planning and control, inventory valuation, and decision making. Because the flow of costs parallels the flow of operations, a firm's production processes will influence its choice of a cost accounting system. Companies that manufacture discrete batches of different products usually prefer a job order cost accounting system, while firms that repetitively manufacture a single product or a few products generally find that a process cost accounting system better suits their needs. While a job order system accumulates costs by job, a **process cost accounting system** *accumulates costs by departments* for a period of time, usually a week or two, but no longer than a month. A department's total costs are then divided by the number of units produced to compute the unit cost for the period. This chapter focuses on the kinds of firms that use a process cost accounting system and the accounting procedures that such a system entails.

Firms that Use Process Cost Systems

When a firm manufactures a single product repetitively, a job order cost accounting system would be unnecessarily expensive. Since each job would consist of the same (or very similar) products, there would be no advantage to maintaining individual job cost sheets. The aggregate cost and the unit cost of a batch may be computed without a job cost sheet, thereby saving the costs associated with producing such records. Among the firms that find the process cost accounting system useful are (1) paint manufacturers, (2) oil refineries, (3) sugar refineries, (4) salt producers, and (5) public utilities. A company's decision to use process costing is based on the number of different products, the length of the production cycle, the amount of work in process at the end of an accounting period, and the number of departments involved in the production process.

Cost Accumulation Methods in Process Costing

Either of two cost-flow assumptions may be used to account for inventories and unit cost computations in a process cost accounting system. The **average cost assumption** (sometimes referred to as *moving average*) is the more commonly used in practice. It combines any costs assigned to the beginning work in process with the costs expended in the current period to arrive at the average costs assignable to the output in the current period. This eliminates the need to compute separate unit costs for the work in process and the current production costs because the two are combined for purposes of unit cost computations. This procedure is demonstrated in detail later.

The other cost-flow assumption, occasionally used in practice and regularly included on professional licensing examinations, is the **first-in, first-out (FIFO) method.** In this approach, the costs expended in a current period are unitized separately from the costs assigned to the beginning work in process inventory. The merchandise completed and transferred is accounted for in batches, and costs are assigned to the batches according to the sequence of processing. A discussion of this method appears in Appendix 4–A at the end of this chapter.

ILLUSTRATION 4–1   **Sequential Processing (salt manufacturing)**

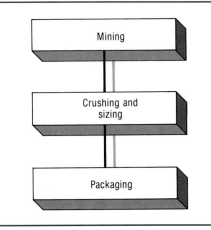

ILLUSTRATION 4–2   **Parallel Processing (meat processing)**

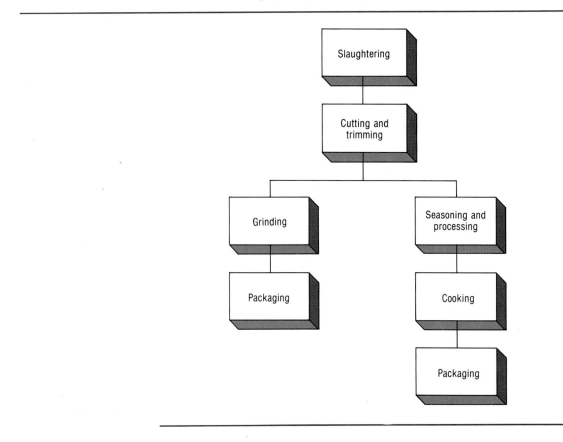

The Physical Flow of Processing

The flow of processing may follow several different patterns. In a **sequential process,** all basic raw materials pass through *all processing centers.* For example, note in Illustration 4–1 that all raw materials go through the same three phases of production—(1) mining, (2) crushing and sizing, and (3) packaging.

In a **parallel process,** common raw materials pass through some processing centers, but *not all* of them. For example, the physical flow of processing in a meat-packing plant might appear as in Illustration 4–2. Note that in this case, after cutting and trimming, some of the meat goes to the grinding department while other meat is sent to be seasoned and processed. Many variations of parallel processing are possible.

COST ACCUMULATION IN A PROCESS SYSTEM

In process costing, the components of manufacturing costs—direct materials, direct labor, and manufacturing overhead—are accumulated in much the same way as when job order costing is used. But they are accumulated by departments for a specific time period instead of by job. The period of time is flexible and depends on the information needs of the company. Cost accumulation is much simpler for a process cost system than for a job order system.

Direct Materials. In process costing as in job order costing, materials requisitions form the basis for issuing materials to production, but far fewer requisitions are usually required. A firm that uses a process costing system may have only one product or a few products in process at any one time, and thus may have just a few requisitions per month. The number of requisitions would depend on how often a batch of product is started.

The entry to record the issuance of materials for process costing is similar to the entry used for job order costing. However, since costs are accumulated by departments for a period of time, it is customary to departmentalize the work in process account.

The Jones Manufacturing Corporation has two departments—cutting and finishing. During the month of January 19x3, the corporation issued raw materials for production as follows:

Cutting department $144,000
Finishing department 9,000

The entry to record the issuance of raw materials would be:

(a)

Work in Process—Cutting 144,000
Work in Process—Finishing 9,000
Raw Materials Inventory 153,000

Direct Labor. As with direct materials, the cost accumulation of direct labor in a process cost system is much simpler than that for job order costing. Payroll costs are accumulated by department for a specified period of time, and the departmental payroll costs can usually be taken directly from the payroll records without much additional effort. It is not necessary to have employees punch in and out every time they work on a particular job, and it is not necessary to cost out separate job time tickets. This can mean a significant amount of savings in record-keeping costs. However, if employees perform work for more than one department, they will need to keep records of the time they spend in each department.

For the month of January 19x3, the Jones Manufacturing Corporation incurred the following direct labor costs:

Cutting department	$72,000
Finishing department	63,700

The entry to record direct labor is:

(b)

Work in Process—Cutting	72,000	
Work in Process—Finishing	63,700	
Accrued Wages Payable		135,700

Manufacturing Overhead. A normal predetermined overhead rate, as discussed in Chapter 3, is also needed when a process cost accounting system is used. An appropriate base—direct labor cost, direct labor-hours, machine-hours—would be selected in the same manner as in job order costing, and any underapplied or overapplied overhead would be disposed of as discussed in Chapter 3.

The Jones Manufacturing Corporation uses direct labor cost (DLC) as the base for applying manufacturing overhead to production, and the rates are 80 percent of DLC for the cutting department and 110 percent of DLC for the finishing department. The entry to record overhead for January 19x3 is:

(c)

Work in Process—Cutting	57,600	
Work in Process—Finishing	70,070	
Manufacturing Overhead Applied		127,670
To apply manufacturing overhead as follows:		
80% × $72,000 DLC = $57,600		
110% × 63,700 DLC = 70,070		

Unit Costs—No Work in Process

The computation of unit costs is relatively simple when there are no work in process inventories. A cost-flow assumption—average or FIFO—is not necessary when there are no inventories. For example, unit costs for a month would be computed as follows, assuming no work in process inventories, 40,000 units of production, direct materials costs of $120,000, direct labor costs of $80,000, and overhead of $48,000:

Direct materials	$120,000 ÷ 40,000 units =	$3.00 per unit
Direct labor	80,000 ÷ 40,000 =	2.00
Overhead applied	48,000 ÷ 40,000 =	1.20
Totals	$248,000	$6.20 per unit

Equivalent Production

When a firm uses a process costing system, it usually manufactures one or a few items repetitively and would thus be highly likely to have work in process inventory at the end of an accounting period. Therefore, the simple calculations shown above are not likely to be applicable. When work in process does exist, a cost-flow assumption must be made, and a method must be found to convert units that are partially complete into the equivalent of completed units. For example, if the 40,000 units shown above were only 60 percent complete, it would be impossible to compute unit costs for the month without further adjustments. The direct materials cost of $120,000 could not be unitized by dividing up 40,000 units, and the $3 unit cost for direct materials is relevant only if the 40,000 units are completed. When production figures are adjusted to include partially completed units that have been converted into an equivalent number of completed units, the result is known as equivalent production, or *equivalent units.*

Computing Equivalent Production. **Equivalent production** is calculated by multiplying the number of partially completed units produced by the percentage of completion. Thus, 100 units that are 30 percent complete are equivalent to 30 units that are fully complete. In other words, the total costs are the same to produce either 100 units that are 30 percent complete or 30 units that are complete. The adjusted figure for partial units is then added to the number of completed units to arrive at equivalent production. To compute the equivalent units at Jones Manufacturing Corporation, we need the following additional information for the month of January 19x3:

Number of units started	30,000
Number of units completed in the cutting department and	
transferred to the finishing department	20,000
Number of units partially complete (work in process)	10,000

All raw materials were added at the *beginning* of the process. Thus, the use of materials is 100 percent complete. But only 40 percent of the labor and applied overhead needed to finish the 10,000 units has been used.

Unit production information is often summarized in a quantity of production report. A **quantity of production report** summarizes unit productivity for a period of time, and it is usually included as part of the production report, discussed later. Jones's quantity of production report for the month of January 19x3 appears in Illustration 4–3.

To compute equivalent production (EP) for an *average cost* assumption, the following equation is used:

EP_{av} = (number of units completed) + [(Percentage of completion)
$\times$ (Ending work in process units)]

where

EP = Equivalent production
av = Average cost-flow assumption

ILLUSTRATION 4–3

JONES MANUFACTURING CORPORATION
Quantity of Production Report—Cutting Department
For the Month of January 19x3

To be accounted for:

Work in process, beginning	–0–
Started this period	30,000
Total to be accounted for	30,000

Accounted for as follows:

Completed and transferred to finishing		
department	20,000	
Work in process, ending	10,000	(100% materials; 40% labor and overhead)
Total accounted for	30,000	

Therefore, equivalent production for January would be:

$$EP_{av} \text{ (Materials)} = 20,000 + 100\% \ (10,000) = 30,000 \text{ units}$$

$$EP_{av} \text{ (Labor and applied overhead)} = 20,000 + 40\% \ (10,000) = 24,000 \text{ units}$$

The calculation for labor and overhead reflects the fact that 10,000 units that are 40 percent complete would have the same direct labor cost as 4,000 units that were 100 percent complete. Using this calculation, it is now possible to compute unit costs because the output can be measured as equivalent to 24,000 completed units.

THE PRODUCTION REPORT

A **production report,** a periodic report that summarizes unit costs and costs of inventories, usually consists of three sections—a quantity of production report, a cost of production report, and a cost recapitulation. The quantity of production report, as mentioned earlier, summarizes unit production for the period. The **cost of production report** summarizes and combines cost information for the purpose of calculating unit costs and costs of inventories of partially completed and finished goods. And the **cost recapitulation section** proves that all costs have been accounted for, forms the basis of journal entries, and provides beginning inventory figures for the next production report. Customarily, a production report is prepared each month for every department in a firm.

Production Report—Initial Department

The Jones Manufacturing Corporation production report for the cutting department for the month of January 19x3 is presented in Illustration 4–4. It is based on the production quantities provided in Illustration 4–3 and the cost data shown in journal entries *(a)*, *(b)*, and *(c)*.

ILLUSTRATION 4–4

JONES MANUFACTURING CORPORATION
Production Report—Cutting Department
For the Month of January 19x3

Step 1.   **Quantity of Production**

Quantity to be accounted for:
   Work in process, beginning . . . .   –0–
   Started or transferred in   30,000
      Total to be accounted for   30,000

Accounted for as follows:
   Completed and transferred   20,000
   Work in process, ending   10,000   (100% materials; 40%
                                      labor and overhead)

      Total accounted for   30,000

Cost of Production

Step 3.   Cost in this department:

	Work in Process +	Costs this Period =	Total Cost	Unit Cost
Direct materials	$–0–	$144,000	$144,000	$ 4.80[a]
Direct labor	–0–	72,000	72,000	3.00[b]
Overhead	–0–	57,600	57,600	2.40[c]
Totals	$–0–	$273,600	273,600	10.20
Total cost to be accounted for			$273,600	$10.20

Cost Recapitulation

Step 5.   Accounted for as follows:
      Completed and transferred . . 20,000 × $10.20 $204,000

      Work in process:
Step 6a.   Direct materials . . . . 10,000 × 100% × $4.80   48,000
Step 6b.   Direct labor . . . . 10,000 × 40% × 3.00   12,000
Step 6c.   Overhead . . . . 10,000 × 40% × 2.40   9,600
         Total   69,600
Step 7.   Total accounted for $273,600

Step 2.   Equivalent production:
      Materials = 30,000 units. Labor and overhead = 24,000 units.

Step 4.   *a.* $144,000 ÷ 30,000 = $4.80.
           b. $ 72,000 ÷ 24,000 = $3.00.
           c. $ 57,600 ÷ 24,000 = $2.40.

The steps used to prepare the production report are:

1.   Prepare the quantity of production section.

2.   Calculate the equivalent production for materials and labor and overhead.

3.   Insert the costs previously expended for the opening balance of the

work in process (in this case, zero), as well as the costs newly incurred in the current month, and add them to arrive at the figures in the total column. Sum the total column to compute the total cost to be accounted for.

4. Compute the unit costs of direct materials, direct labor, and applied overhead by dividing each component's total costs by the applicable equivalent production. (See footnotes *a, b,* and *c* at the bottom of the production report.) Sum the unit cost column to arrive at the *total* unit cost for the month.

5. Multiply the number of completed units by the *total* unit cost for the month to arrive at the total cost of units transferred to the next department.

6. Compute the ending work in process inventory by:
   a. Multiplying the number of units in the ending inventory by the stage of completion of *direct materials* by the unit cost of *direct materials* to arrive at the direct materials cost in the ending inventory.
   b. Repeat step 6*a,* substituting the state of completion and the unit cost of *direct labor* for the direct materials amounts.
   c. Repeat step 6*a,* substituting the stage of completion and the unit cost of applied *overhead* for the direct materials amounts.
   Sum the three calculations to arrive at the total work in process inventory at the end of the month.

7. Add the amounts computed in steps 5 and 6 and compare the total to the total cost to be accounted for as computed in step 3. The amounts should be the same.

In Illustration 4–4, note that:

1. The quantity of production report is identical to the information provided in Illustration 4–3.

2. Since there is no beginning inventory of work in process, there are no costs in that column.

3. The costs in the current period are taken from journal entries *(a), (b),* and *(c).*

4. The recapitulation section, showing the completed and transferred work of $204,000 and the ending work in process of $69,600, is a key element of the report. In addition to proving that all costs ($273,600) have been accounted for, these computations form the basis of journal entry *(d),* shown below, and provide the beginning inventory figures for the February 19x3 report.

After the report is prepared, it is possible to journalize the cost of units transferred by the cutting department to the finishing department. The amount—$204,000—is obtained from the recapitulation portion of the report. The needed journal entry would be:

(d)

Work in Process—Finishing	204,000	
Work in Process—Cutting		204,000

Production Report— Subsequent Department

It is now possible to prepare a production report for the *finishing department* using the information provided in journal entries *(a)*, *(b)*, *(c)*, and *(d)* together with the following production information:

	Units
Work in process, beginning	–0–
Transferred in from cutting department	20,000
Completed and transferred to finished goods	14,000
Work in process, ending (All materials are added at the beginning of the process. Thus, materials are 100 percent complete. Labor and overhead—conversion costs—are only 70 percent complete.)	6,000

The steps used to prepare the production report for the finishing department are similar to the ones used to prepare the production report for the cutting department, except that:

1. A new section is added in the cost of production section entitled "Cost in Preceding Department." This section is reserved for the cost of units transferred in from a preceding department, in this case $204,000. **Transferred-in cost** is the dollar value assigned to the units transferred into a department from a preceding department. **Transferred-out cost** is the dollar value assigned to the units transferred from a department to a subsequent department or to the finished goods warehouse. In this case, the *transferred-out costs* of the cutting department *become the transferred-in costs* of the finishing department.

2. The transferred-in costs are included in the *total cost to be accounted for*.

3. The ending work in process now includes another calculation for cost in preceding department.

The production report for the finishing department is presented in Illustration 4–5. The quantity of production report for the department appears at

ILLUSTRATION 4–5

JONES MANUFACTURING CORPORATION
Production Report—Finishing Department
For the Month of January 19x3
Quantity of Production

Quantity to be accounted for:
Work in process, beginning . . . .   –0–
Started or transferred in   20,000
   Total to be accounted for   20,000

Accounted for as follows:
Completed and transferred   14,000
Work in process, ending   6,000   (100% materials; 70% conversion costs)
   Total accounted for   20,000

Cost of Production

	Total Cost	Unit Cost
Cost in preceding department:		
Work in process, beginning	$ –0–	$
Transferred in during the period	204,000	10.20
Totals	204,000	10.20[a]

Cost in this department:

	Work in Process +	Costs this Period =		
Direct materials	$–0–	$ 9,000	9,000	0.45[b]
Direct labor	–0–	63,700	63,700	3.50[c]
Overhead	–0–	70,070	70,070	3.85[d]
Totals	$–0–	$142,770	142,770	7.80
Total cost to be accounted for			$346,770	$18.00

Cost Recapitulation

Accounted for as follows:
Completed and transferred . . . .   14,000 × $18.00 $252,000

Work in process:
Cost in preceding department .   6,000 × $10.20   61,200
Direct materials . . . .   6,000 × 100% × $0.45   2,700
Direct labor . . . .   6,000 × 70% × 3.50   14,700
Overhead . . . .   6,000 × 70% × 3.85   16,170
   Total   94,770
Total accounted for $346,770

Equivalent production:
Materials = 20,000 units. Labor and overhead = 18,200.

These costs appear in journal entries *(a)*, *(b)*, and *(c)*.

   a. $204,000 ÷ 20,000 units = $10.20.
   b. $ 9,000 ÷ 20,000 units = $ 0.45.
   c. $ 63,700 ÷ 18,200 units = $ 3.50.
   d. $ 70,070 ÷ 18,200 units = $ 3.85.

the top. Based on its figures, the equivalent production may be computed as follows:

	Units
Materials:	
Completed and transferred	14,000
Work in process—6,000 × 100%	6,000
Equivalent production	20,000
Labor and overhead:	
Completed and transferred	14,000
Work in process—6,000 × 70%	4,200
Equivalent production	18,200

The recapitulation section of the report shows the cost of the finished goods as $252,000. This forms the basis of the following journal entry:

(e)

Finished Goods	252,000	
Work in Process—Finishing Department		252,000

From Illustration 4–5, it can be seen that:

1. Since there was no work in process inventory at the beginning of the period, the spaces for these amounts show zero balances.

2. The recapitulation section of the report accounts for all costs, including the $204,000 of transferred-in costs from the cutting department.

3. The total unit cost of the finished goods is $18.00, which includes the $10.20 unit cost in the cutting department and the $7.80 unit cost in the finishing department.

Thus far, the illustrations have not included any work in process at the beginning of the period. If journal entries *(a)* through *(e)* were to be posted, the work in process and finished goods T accounts would appear as in Illustration 4–6 at the end of January 19x3. These balances become the beginning balances for February 19x3. Thus, beginning work in process balances would be present in the February 19x3 production reports.

The balances in the Work in Process accounts shown in Illustration 4–6 should be compared with the recapitulation sections of Illustrations 4–4 and 4–5 to verify that the work in process amounts shown in the production reports agree with the balances shown in the T accounts. A similar comparison can be made between the finished goods balance in Illustration 4–6 and the recapitulation section of Illustration 4–5.

ILLUSTRATION 4–6

JONES MANUFACTURING CORPORATION
Partial General Ledger
January 31, 19x3

Work in Process—Cutting				Work in Process—Finishing			
(1)	144,000	(4)	204,000	(1)	9,000	(5)	252,000
(2)	72,000			(2)	63,700		
(3)	57,600			(3)	70,070		
				(4)	204,000		
Balance	69,600			Balance	94,770		

Finished Goods			
(5)	252,000		
Balance	252,000		

Production Report—Beginning Work in Process Inventory

During the month of February 19x3, the Jones Manufacturing Corporation incurred direct material costs of $146,000 and direct labor costs of $102,080 in the cutting department. Manufacturing overhead was applied at 80 percent of direct labor cost ($81,664). The beginning inventory of work in process in the cutting department was 10,000 units (the same as the ending work in process inventory for January). In addition, 30,000 new units were started. Of the total 40,000 units in production, 32,000 units were completed and transferred to the finishing department. The remaining 8,000 units were 100 percent completed for direct materials and 60 percent completed for labor and applied overhead.

The steps needed to prepare the production report for the cutting department are similar to those used previously except for the beginning work in process column, which must now be filled in. The amounts of $48,000 for direct materials, $12,000 for direct labor, and $9,600 for applied overhead are obtained from the recapitulation section of the January production report for the cutting department.

The equivalent production computations are prepared using the equation approach and are shown at the bottom of the February production report presented in Illustration 4–7.

Illustration 4–7 reveals that:

1. The quantity of production report is easily prepared by adding the beginning work in process inventory of 10,000 units to the new units started—30,000. The completed and transferred units of 32,000 combined with the 8,000 units of ending work in process comprise the bottom portion of this section.

2. The cost in preceding department section is always zero in the first

ILLUSTRATION 4–7

JONES MANUFACTURING CORPORATION
Production Report—Cutting Department
For the Month of February 19x3
Quantity of Production

Quantity to be accounted for:
Work in process, beginning	10,000
Started or transferred in	30,000
Total to be accounted for	40,000

Accounted for as follows:
Completed and transferred	32,000	
Work in process, ending	8,000	(100% materials; 60% labor and overhead)
Total accounted for	40,000	

Cost of Production

Cost in this department:

	Work in Process	+	Costs this Period	=	Total Cost	Unit Cost
Direct materials	$48,000		$146,000		$194,000	$ 4.85[a]
Direct labor	12,000		102,080		114,080	3.10[b]
Overhead	9,600		81,664		91,264	2.48[c]
Totals	$69,600		$329,744		399,344	10.43
Total cost to be accounted for					$399,344	$10.43

Cost Recapitulation

Accounted for as follows:
Completed and transferred . .	32,000 × $10.43	$333,760

Work in process:
Direct materials	8,000 × 100% × $4.85	38,800
Direct labor	8,000 × 60% × 3.10	14,880
Overhead	8,000 × 60% × 2.48	11,904
Total		65,584
Total accounted for		$399,344

Equivalent production:
EP_{av} (Materials = 32,000 + 100% (8,000) = 40,000 units.
EP_{av} (Labor and applied overhead) = 32,000 + 60% (8,000) = 36,800 units.

---

a. $194,000 ÷ 40,000 units = $4.85.
b. $114,080 ÷ 36,800 units = $3.10.
c. $ 91,264 ÷ 36,800 units = $2.48.

department of the production cycle and is, therefore, omitted from this production report.

3. The work in process column contains the information obtained from the recapitulation section of the January production report for the cutting department (Illustration 4–4).

4. The recapitulation section contains the calculations of the cost of goods

completed and transferred and the work in process inventory. The total of these two equals the total cost to be accounted for.

Also during the month of February, the Jones Manufacturing Corporation incurred direct material costs of $16,300 and direct labor costs of $115,230 in the finishing department. Overhead of $126,753 was applied at the predetermined rate of 110 percent of direct labor cost. The beginning work in process inventory amounted to 6,000 units, and 32,000 units were transferred in from the cutting department. The finishing department completed 31,000 units and transferred them to the finished goods warehouse. In addition, 7,000 units were still in process at the end of February. These units are 100 percent completed for direct materials and 80 percent completed for conversion costs.

The steps needed to prepare the February production report for the finishing department are the same as those discussed previously, except that the cost in preceding department consists of two amounts—$61,200 assigned to work in process at the end of January (see recapitulation section of Illustration 4–5) and $333,760 of transferred-in costs from the cutting department (see Illustration 4–7). Since an average cost flow is assumed, the individual unit costs of these amounts are *not* shown on the production report; instead, the average unit cost of the total of these amounts ($394,960) is used. The unitizing may be calculated as $394,960 ÷ 38,000 units (total accounted for) = $10.3937.

This result can be seen in Illustration 4–8, the production report for the finishing department for the month of February 19x3.

In Illustration 4–8, note that:

1. The work in process column of cost in this department contains the breakdown shown in the proof section of the January 19x3 report for the finishing department—Illustration 4–5.

2. The recapitulation section contains a rounding difference of 60 cents. This is not unusual when the number of decimal places is carried to only four places. It is rarely worth the effort to carry the unit cost calculations beyond four places. The use of fewer decimal places usually increases the rounding difference. The number of decimal places in calculations depends on the needs of the company.

3. In any department after the first, ending work in process includes costs from the preceding department. In this example, the four elements of the ending inventory have a total unit cost of $18.3487. A check on the proper pickup of unit costs in the proof can be made by adding $10.3937 + $0.50 + $3.55 + $3.905 to arrive at the $18.3487 used to compute the cost of the completed and transferred units.

4. The ending work in process inventory of $94,770, shown in the recapitulation section of Illustration 4–5, is divided into two sections—$61,200 is shown in the cost in preceding department section; and $2,700, $14,700, and $16,170 (total $33,570) are shown in the cost in this department section.

ILLUSTRATION 4–8

JONES MANUFACTURING CORPORATION
Production Report—Finishing Department
For the Month of February 19x3

Quantity of Production

Quantity to be accounted for:
Work in process, beginning   6,000
Started or transferred in   32,000
Total to be accounted for   38,000

Accounted for as follows:
Completed and transferred   31,000
Work in process, ending   7,000   (100% materials; 80%
                                                              labor and overhead)

Total accounted for   38,000

Cost of Production

	Total Cost	Unit Cost
Cost in preceding department:		
Work in process, beginning	$ 61,200	$
Transferred in during the period	333,760	
Total	394,960	10.3937[a]

Cost in this department:

	Work in Process +	Costs this Period =		
Direct materials	$ 2,700	$ 16,300	19,000	0.5000[b]
Direct labor	14,700	115,230	129,930	3.5500[c]
Overhead	16,170	126,753	142,923	3.9050[d]
Totals	$33,570	$258,283	291,853	7.9550
Total cost to be accounted for			$686,813	$18.3487

Cost Recapitulation

Accounted for as follows:
Completed and transferred . . . . .   31,000 × $18.3487 $568,809.70

Work in process:
Cost in preceding department . .   7,000 × $10.3937   72,755.90
Direct materials . . . .   7,000 × 100% × $0.5000   3,500.00
Direct labor . . . .   7,000 × 80% × 3.5500   19,880.00
Overhead . . . .   7,000 × 80% × 3.9050   21,868.00
                                                                        118,003.90

Total accounted for . . . . $686,813.60[e]

Equivalent production:
EP_{av} (Transferred-in) = 6,000 + 32,000 = 38,000 units.
EP_{av} (Materials) = 31,000 + 100% (7,000) = 38,000 units.
EP_{av} (Conversion) = 31,000 + 80% (7,000) = 36,600 units.

a. $394,960 ÷ 38,000 units = $10.3937.
b. $ 19,000 ÷ 38,000 units =   0.5000.
c. $129,930 ÷ 36,600 units =   3.5500.
d. $142,923 ÷ 36,600 units =   3.9050.
e. There is a rounding difference of $0.60.

Lost Units, Normal Spoilage, and Abnormal Spoilage

Many manufacturing firms find that some of their raw materials evaporate during processing. This commonly happens among chemical, paint, and gasoline manufacturers. Other firms find that some of their products are spoiled during the manufacturing process. The spoilage may be usual for the process, in which case it would be considered normal spoilage, or it may be unusual, in which case it would be abnormal spoilage. Accounting for lost and spoiled units is discussed in Appendix 4–B.

SUMMARY

When a firm manufactures one or a few products repetitively, its use of a job order cost accounting system would lead to excessive bookkeeping costs. In such cases, whether the flow of processing is **sequential** or **parallel,** a **process cost accounting system** is more efficient. Instead of accumulating costs by jobs, a process cost accounting system accumulates costs by department for a specified period of time. This eliminates the need for job cost sheets and job time tickets. It also requires fewer materials requisitions.

Since costs are accumulated for a period of time, a method of measuring the output for that period must be found if unit costs are to be computed. Completed units are easily counted. However, work in process is another matter. Any uncompleted units on hand at the end of the cost-accumulation period must be converted into an equivalent number of completed units and added to the completed units to determine the **equivalent production** for the period. Unit costs for direct materials, direct labor, and overhead may then be computed. The sum of these figures equals the total unit cost for the period.

Although two cost-flow assumptions may be found in practice—**average** and **FIFO**—the average method is used most often. In such cases, the costs assigned to the beginning work in process inventory are merged with the costs expended in the current period. This results in an average of the two costs.

Most firms prepare a **production report** for each department for a specified period of time, usually a month. The report contains three sections—a **quantity of production report,** a **cost of production report,** and a **cost recapitulation section.** The production report must account for all **transferred-in costs** and all **transferred-out costs.**

The production report provides part of the information needed to record the journal entries that comprise the cost accounting cycle. The remaining information is obtained from the firm's material requisitions and payroll records.

GLOSSARY OF KEY TERMS

Average cost assumption   A method of accounting for inventories and unit cost computations in process cost accounting in which costs assigned to the beginning work in process are merged with the costs expended in the current period in order to compute average costs assignable to the output in the current period.

Cost of production report The part of a production report that summarizes and combines cost information for the purpose of calculating unit costs and costs of inventories of partially completed and finished goods.

Cost recapitulation section The part of a production report that proves that all costs have been accounted for, forms the basis of journal entries, and provides beginning inventory figures for the next production report.

Equivalent production A production figure that has been adjusted to include partially completed units that have been converted into an equivalent number of finished units. The number of partially completed units is multiplied by the percentage of completion and combined with the number of units started and finished in the period for the purpose of computing unit costs.

Equivalent units See **equivalent production.**

First-in, first-out (FIFO) cost assumption A method of accounting for inventories and unit cost computations in process cost accounting in which the costs expended in a current period are unitized separately from the costs assigned to the beginning work in process inventory. The merchandise completed and transferred is accounted for in batches, and costs are assigned to the batches according to the sequence of processing.

Parallel production process A sequence of production in which common raw materials pass through some of the same processing centers, but not all of them.

Process cost accounting system A cost accounting method in which product costs are accumulated by department for a specific period of time, usually a week or two, but no longer than a month. A department's total costs are then divided by the equivalent units produced to compute the unit cost for the period.

Production report A process cost accounting report that summarizes unit costs and costs of inventories. The report is usually prepared monthly and contains three sections—a quantity of production report, a cost of production report, and a cost recapitulation.

Quantity of production report A report that summarizes unit productivity for a period of time, usually included as part of the production report.

Sequential production process A sequence of production in which all raw materials pass through all processing centers.

Transferred-in cost The dollar value assigned to units transferred into a department from a preceding department.

Transferred-out cost The dollar value assigned to units transferred from a department to a subsequent department or to the finished goods warehouse.

APPENDIX 4–A   **PROCESS COST ACCUMULATION—THE FIFO METHOD**

A production report that uses the first-in, first-out (FIFO) method in place of average costing will produce different figures for equivalent production and unit cost *only when beginning work in process inventory is present.* If there is no beginning work in process inventory, the production reports for both methods will be exactly the same.

Reasons for Selecting Cost-Flow Assumption

Managers base their cost-flow assumptions on their perceptions of company objectives. During a period of significant price changes, FIFO costing retains the individual price changes from month to month, and these price changes are highlighted in comparative reports. On the other hand, average costing tends to lessen the effect of these price changes in comparative reports. For example, assume that 1,000 units of raw materials in beginning inventory were purchased at a cost of $5 each and that an additional 1,000 were purchased at $7 each. If the 2,000 units were used (or sold) during the month, the usage would be reported as:

FIFO:
1,000 units at $5 . . .	$ 5,000
1,000 units at $7 . . .	7,000
Total	$12,000

Average:
2,000 units at $6 . . .	$12,000

If only 1,500 units were used (or sold), they would be reported as:

FIFO:
1,000 units at $5 . . .	$5,000
500 units at $7 . . .	3,500
Total	$8,500

Average:
1,500 units at $6 . . .	$9,000

Thus, it can be seen that when all units are not used, different costs of usage prevail. Even when all of the units are used and the total costs are the same, the details of the costs may be significant. For these reasons, some firms prefer to use FIFO costing.

FIFO Equivalent Production

The principal difference between FIFO and average costing occurs in the computations of equivalent production and unit costs. Two different methods are used to compute FIFO equivalent production, and if both methods are used, one can act as a check on the other.

In one method, FIFO equivalent production is computed in the same way as average equivalent production except that the equivalent units in the beginning work in process inventory are subtracted. The result would be the equivalent work done in the period under consideration. The equation for this approach is:

$$EP_{FIFO} = \text{(Units completed)} + [\text{(Percentage of completion)} \times \text{(Ending work in process units)}] - [\text{(Percentage of completion)} \times \text{(Beginning work in process units)}]$$

where

$$EP = \text{Equivalent production}$$
$$FIFO = \text{First-in, first-out cost assumption}$$

If the Jones Manufacturing Corporation were to use FIFO costing instead of average costing, its production reports for January 19x3 would be *identical* to the average costing ones shown in Illustrations 4–4 and 4–5. This would occur because there were *no* beginning work in process inventories in either department. Since there are no beginning work in process units to subtract, the equation for EP_{FIFO} is equal to EP_{av}. However, for February, the equations are not equal to each other, and thus the production reports are different.

The quantity of production section from Illustration 4–7 is repeated in Illustration 4–9, except that the stages of completion of the beginning inventory have been inserted. The stages were obtained from the quantity of production section of the January report (see Illustration 4–4).

From Illustration 4–9, it is now possible to compute the FIFO equivalent production as follows:

$$EP_{FIFO} \text{ (Materials)} = 32,000 + 100\% \, (8,000) - 100\% \, (10,000) = 30,000 \text{ units}$$
$$EP_{FIFO} \text{ (Labor and Overhead)} = 32,000 + 60\% \, (8,000) - 40\% \, (10,000)$$
$$= 32,800 \text{ units}$$

In essence, these calculations indicate the number of equivalent units produced during the month of February by *excluding* the portion of the equivalent units *produced during January* and completed in February, but *including* the portion of equivalent units *produced during February* on the units started in January.

The second method of determining equivalent production under a FIFO cost assumption is to compute the amount of equivalent work needed to complete the beginning work in process inventory and to add the amount

ILLUSTRATION 4–9

JONES MANUFACTURING CORPORATION
Quantity Production Report—Cutting Department
For the Month of February 19x3

Quantity to be accounted for:		
Work in process, beginning	10,000	(100% materials; 40% labor and overhead)
Started or transferred in	30,000	
Total to be accounted for	40,000	
Accounted for as follows:		
Completed and transferred	32,000	
Work in process, ending	8,000	(100% materials; 60% labor and overhead)
Total accounted for	40,000	

ILLUSTRATION 4–10

JONES MANUFACTURING CORPORATION
Calculation of Equivalent Production—Cutting Department
For the Month of February 19x3

Materials

Completed and transferred:
  10,000—First batch:
      Beginning work in process—to complete—10,000 ×
      (100% − 100%) . . . .   –0–
  22,000—Second batch:
      Started new—22,000 × 100% 22,000
  32,000 Total completed and transferred 22,000
Ending work in process—8,000 × 100% 8,000
FIFO equivalent production 30,000

Conversion

Completed and transferred:
  10,000—First batch:
      Beginning work in process—to complete—10,000 ×
      (100% − 40%) 6,000
  22,000—Second batch:
      Started new—22,000 × 100% 22,000
  32,000 Total completed and transferred 28,000
Ending work in process—8,000 × 60% 4,800
FIFO equivalent production 32,800

---

of *new* equivalent work done in the period under consideration. The computation is based on a separation of the completed and transferred units into two batches—one batch equal to the beginning work in process inventory and the remainder coming from the new units started and completed in February. The calculations are shown in Illustration 4–10. This approach and the equation approach produce identical results.

FIFO Production Report

To prepare a FIFO production report, consider that:

1. When a beginning work in process inventory is present and FIFO costing is used, it is best to arrange the departmental cost in a vertical format instead of the format used for average costing because the beginning work in process costs are not used to compute unit costs for the current period. (See Illustration 4–11.)

2. The quantity of production section includes the stage of completion for *both* the beginning and ending work in process inventories, since they are needed to compute equivalent production.

3. The beginning work in process costs are included in the total cost to be accounted for even though they are not used to compute unit costs for the month.

4. In the cost recapitulation section of the production report, the cost of the completed and transferred units are calculated in batches. The first batch consists of the units in the beginning work in process inventory. The total cost of these units consists of the beginning inventory costs carried forward from the preceding production report and the costs expended in the current month to complete the units. The sum of these costs represents the total cost of the first batch. The cost of the second batch of completed and transferred goods is merely the remainder of the units completed and transferred multiplied by the *total* unit cost for the current month.

5. The ending work in process inventory is computed in the same way as it is in average costing.

The Jones Manufacturing Corporation's February production report for the cutting department appears in Illustration 4–11. Note that:

1. Only the current period costs are unitized. No unit costs are shown for the beginning work in process. Since these costs were incurred in the prior month, they do not affect unit costs for February. However, these costs enter into the recapitulation calculation of the completed and transferred units.

2. In the recapitulation section, the cost of the first batch of the completed and transferred units includes the $69,600 of costs assigned to the beginning inventory plus $0 for direct materials, $18,673 for direct labor, and $14,938 for overhead. Since direct materials in the beginning inventory were 100 percent complete, no additional materials were added in February. For direct labor and overhead, the beginning inventory

ILLUSTRATION 4–11

JONES MANUFACTURING CORPORATION
FIFO Production Report—Cutting Department
For the Month of February 19x3

Quantity Production

Quantity to be accounted for:		
Work in process, beginning	10,000	(100% materials; 40% labor and overhead)
Started or transferred in	30,000	
Total to be accounted for	40,000	
Accounted for as follows:		
Completed and transferred	32,000	
Work in process, ending	8,000	(100% materials; 60% labor and overhead)
Total accounted for	40,000	

ILLUSTRATION 4–11 *(concluded)*

Cost of Production	Total Cost	Unit Cost
Cost in this department:		
Work in process, beginning:		
Direct materials	$ 48,000	
Direct labor	12,000	
Overhead	9,600	
Current period costs:		
Direct materials	146,000	$ 4.8667[a]
Direct labor	102,080	3.1122[b]
Overhead	81,664	2.4897[c]
Total costs in this department	399,344	10.4686
Total cost to be accounted for	$399,344	$10.4686

Cost Recapitulation		
Accounted for as follows:		
Completed and transferred:		
First batch:		
Prior period costs	$ 69,600	
Costs to complete:		
Direct materials—10,000 × 0%	–0–	
Direct labor—10,000 × 60% × $3.1122	18,673	
Overhead—10,000 × 60% × 2.4897	14,938	
Total first batch	103,211	
Second batch:		
22,000 × $10.4686	230,309	
Total completed and transferred		$333,520
Work in process, ending:		
Direct materials—8,000 × 100% × $4.8667	38,934	
Direct labor—8,000 × 60% × $3.1122	14,939	
Overhead—8,000 × 60% × $2.4897	11,951	
Total work in process		65,824
Total accounted for		$399,344

Equivalent production:
EP_{FIFO} (Materials) = 32,000 + 100% (8,000) − 100% (10,000) = 30,000 units.
EP_{FIFO} (Labor and overhead) = 32,000 + 60% (8,000) − 40% (10,000) = 32,800 units.

---

a. $146,000 ÷ 30,000 units = $4.8667.
b. $102,080 ÷ 32,800 units = $3.1122.
c. $ 81,664 ÷ 32,800 units = $2.4897.

was only 40 percent complete. Thus, an additional 60 percent was needed to complete these units, and the $18,673 of additional direct labor and $14,938 of additional overhead reflect these additions of 60 percent.

Illustration 4–11 is based on the same information that was used to prepare the average costing production report shown in Illustration 4–7. A comparison of the two illustrations reveals that:

1. Unit cost differences between the two methods are less than $0.02 each for direct materials, direct labor, and overhead.

2. The difference in aggregate unit cost is less than $0.04—that is, $10.4686 versus $10.43.

3. The difference between the completed and transferred costs is $240, a difference of .06 percent of the total cost to be accounted for. The same $240 difference also exists for the ending work in process.

The difference in costing between average and FIFO is negligible in most cases, and thus the additional effort required for FIFO costing is usually not justified from a cost/benefit standpoint. However, it is possible for the differences to be larger, in which case the additional effort may be justified.

The procedures used to prepare the February production report for the cutting department apply equally to the preparation of the production report for the finishing department, except that:

1. The cost in preceding department section of the production report should reflect each batch separately, with a separate unit cost for each batch. The unit costs are not averaged as they are in average costing.

2. In the recapitulation section, the cost of the completed and transferred units should reflect a batch treatment, as demonstrated in Illustration 4–11, but it should also include the cost from the preceding department. Thus, the first batch of completed and transferred costs would include not only $2,700 for direct materials, $14,700 for direct labor, and $16,170 of overhead (see Illustration 4–8), but also $61,200 for costs from the preceding department. It would also include the costs expended in the finishing department during February to finish the beginning work in process of 6,000 units. The next batch of completed and transferred costs would be limited to costs incurred entirely in February, but the batch must include a transferred-in cost plus the costs for direct materials, direct labor, and overhead.

3. The ending work in process inventory would also include the cost from the preceding department in addition to the costs for direct materials, direct labor, and overhead. The cost in preceding department portion would come from the most recent transferred-in costs.

APPENDIX 4–B   **LOST UNITS AND SPOILED UNITS**

Lost units should be distinguished from defective units and spoiled units. **Lost units** are goods that disappear due to evaporation, breakage, or some other function of the production process. **Defective units** are goods of inferior quality that can be repaired at an additional cost and sold as first-quality merchandise. **Spoiled units,** however, are goods of inferior quality that cannot be repaired and sold as regular quality goods; they must be sold as seconds or scrap. An example of a spoiled unit would be a shirt with a permanent oil stain on its sleeve.

Lost Units

When a certain number of lost units is inherent in a firm's production process, it is customary to spread their cost over the remaining good units. One way of doing this is through the **method of neglect,** in which equivalent production is computed in *exactly* the same way as if there were no lost units. In essence, the lost units are ignored and the unit cost of usable units thereby includes the cost of the lost units.

Assume, for example, that:

1. The Kenyon Company incurred $140,000 of material costs for the month of January.

2. The company put into production 40,000 units of input and got 35,000 units of output. It is customary for the company to lose 12½ percent of its input in the production process.

3. The company would like to compute its unit cost for materials for the month using both the method of neglect and a method showing the separate cost for lost units.

The computation for the method of neglect would simply be:

$$\$140,000 \div 35,000 = \$4 \text{ per unit}$$

The computations showing a separate lost unit cost would be:

Input cost:
$140,000 ÷ 40,000 = $3.50 per unit

Lost unit cost:
5,000 × $3.50 = $17,500
$17,500 ÷ 35,000 units = $0.50 per unit

Total unit cost:
Input cost	$3.50
Lost unit cost	0.50
Total unit cost	$4.00

Thus, it can be seen that the input cost of $3.50 must be adjusted for the cost of the lost units ($17,500), and the cost of lost units must be spread over the output of 35,000 usable units. This amounts to $0.50 per unit, which brings the total cost of each usable unit to $4.00. Although the method-of-neglect computation is much simpler, it does not reveal the $0.50 per unit cost of the lost units. It merely distributes the total cost over usable output without regard to units of input.

When the method of neglect is used, the computation of equivalent production is *exactly the same* as demonstrated previously. The production report is also the same except for the quantity of production section. The lost units are shown as a separate item as follows:

Quantity of Production Report

Quantity to be accounted for:

Work in process, beginning	8,000
Started or transferred in	44,000
Total to be accounted for	52,000

Accounted for as follows:

Completed and transferred	36,000
Work in process, ending	12,000 (100% materials; 60% conversion costs)
Lost units	4,000
Total accounted for	52,000

EP_{av} (Materials) $= 36,000 + 100\%(12,000) = 48,000$ units
EP_{av} (Conversion costs) $= 36,000 + 60\%(12,000) = 43,200$ units

Spoiled Units

When the number of units that cannot be repaired and sold as first-quality units falls within an acceptable range of production, the amount is considered **normal spoilage.** On the production report, such units are treated in the same way as lost units. Unlike lost units, however, spoiled units can usually be sold for small amounts that are treated as miscellaneous revenue. When both lost units and spoiled units occur within an acceptable range, they are usually shown separately in the quantity of production section of the production report even though the method of neglect may be used for both.

Abnormal Lost or Spoiled Units

In most production processes, a certain amount of spoilage is considered normal. However, when spoilage exceeds the normal range due to poorly trained personnel, sabotage, or other reasons, it is considered **abnormal spoilage.** When this occurs, the cost of lost or spoiled units that is considered excessive should *not* be spread over the usable units; instead, it should be charged to income as a period cost. This procedure is preferred because abnormal spoilage is unexpected and rare and, therefore, should not be built into the pricing system or inventoried. Abnormal lost or spoiled units should be treated as a loss rather than a cost of manufacturing.

GLOSSARY OF KEY TERMS—APPENDIX 4–B

Abnormal spoilage An amount of scrap or second-quality merchandise that exceeds an acceptable (normal) range of production. The cost assigned to these units should be charged as a loss to income in the period of the loss.

Defective units Merchandise of inferior quality that can be repaired at an additional cost and then sold as first-quality merchandise.

Lost units Goods that disappear through evaporation, breakage, or some other function of the production process. If the loss is within an acceptable range—not due to sabotage or negligence—the cost of these units should be absorbed by the remaining usable units.

Method of neglect An approach used to spread the cost of lost units over the remaining usable units by treating the lost units as if they never existed and using only the usable units to compute unit costs.

Normal spoilage A number of units that cannot be repaired or sold as first-quality units and that fall within an acceptable range of production. These units are treated in the same manner as lost units except for any salvage value, which is usually handled expeditiously—treated as miscellaneous revenue. (See **method of neglect.**)

Spoiled units Goods of inferior quality that cannot be repaired and sold as regular finished goods. They must either be scrapped or sold as seconds.

QUESTIONS

1. What types of firms use a process cost system? Why?

2. There are two methods generally used to account for inventories and unit costs when process costing is used. Discuss each method.

3. There are generally two sequential physical flows of manufacturing processes. Discuss and illustrate each one.

4. How are costs accumulated for firms that use a process cost accounting system? How does this differ from cost accumulation under a job order cost accounting system?

5. Is it possible to compute unit costs of production when work in process exists at the end or beginning of an accounting period? How is this accomplished? Use an example to illustrate the procedure involved for average costing.

6. Is it appropriate to use a predetermined overhead rate for applying overhead to production when a process cost accounting system is used? Under what circumstances would it be acceptable to use actual overhead instead of applied overhead? When should applied overhead be used?

7. Assume that a firm has two departments, cutting and finishing. Prepare sample journal entries to illustrate the cost accounting cycle for direct materials, direct labor, and applied manufacturing overhead.

8. What are the components of a cost of production report? What is the purpose of each section?

    For Appendix 4–A

9. When is there a difference between the cost of production reports for average costing and FIFO costing?

10. There are two different ways to compute FIFO equivalent production. What are they and how are they computed?

    For Appendix 4–B

11. What is the difference between lost units, defective units, and spoiled units?

12. There are two methods of treating normal lost units. What are they? What is true regarding the end result on unit costs when each method is used?

13. How should abnormal spoilage or abnormal lost units be treated? Why should they be treated in this manner?

EXERCISES

4–1 Computation of Average Equivalent Units

Items 1 through 3 are based on the following information:

The Jorcano Manufacturing Company uses a process cost system to account for the costs of its only product, product D. Production begins in the fabrication department where units of raw material are molded into various connecting parts. After fabrication is complete, the units are transferred to the assembly department. There is no material added in the assembly department. After assembly is complete, the units are transferred to a packaging department where packing material is placed around the units. After the units are ready for shipping, they are sent to a shipping area.

At year-end June 30, 19x3, the following inventory of product D is on hand:

a. No unused raw material or packing material.
b. Fabrication department: 300 units, ⅓ complete as to raw material and ½ complete as to direct labor.
c. Assembly department: 1,000 units, ⅖ complete as to direct labor.
d. Packaging department: 100 units, ¾ complete as to packing material and ¼ complete as to direct labor.
e. Shipping area: 400 units.

1. The number of equivalent units of raw material in all inventories at June 30, 19x3, is
   a. 300.
   b. 100.
   c. 1,600.
   d. 925.
2. The number of equivalent units of fabrication department direct labor in all inventories at June 30, 19x3, is
   a. 1,650.
   b. 150.
   c. 300.
   d. 975.
3. The number of equivalent units of packing material in all inventories at June 30, 19x3, is
   a. 75.
   b. 475.
   c. 100.
   d. 425.

(AICPA adapted)

4–2 Computation of Average Equivalent Units

The Felix Manufacturing Company uses a process cost system to account for the costs of its only product, known as "Nino." Production begins in the fabrication department where units of raw material are molded into various connecting parts. After fabrication is complete, the units are transferred to the assembly department. There is no material added in the assembly department. After assembly is complete, the units are transferred to the packaging department where the units are packaged for shipment. At the completion of this process, the units are complete and they are transferred to the shipping department.

At year-end December 31, 19x7, the following inventory of Ninos is on hand:

1. No unused raw material or packing material.
2. Fabrication department: 6,000 units, 25 percent complete as to raw material and 40 percent complete as to direct labor.
3. Assembly department: 10,000 units, 75 percent complete as to direct labor.

4. Packaging department: 3,000 units, 60 percent complete as to packing material and 75 percent complete as to direct labor.
5. Shipping department: 8,000 units.

Required Prepare in proper form schedules showing the following at December 31, 19x7:

a. The number of equivalent units of raw material in all inventories.
b. The number of equivalent units of fabrication department direct labor in all inventories.
c. Number of equivalent units of packaging department material and direct labor in the packaging department inventory.

(AICPA adapted)

4-3 Average Costing Equivalent Units and Quantity Started

1. Sussex Corporation's production cycle starts in the mixing department. The following information is available for the month of April 19x0:

	Units
Work in process, April 1 (50% complete) . .	40,000
Started in April	240,000
Work in process, April 30 (60% complete) . .	25,000

Materials are added in the beginning of the process in the mixing department. Using the weighted-average method, what are the equivalent units of production for the month of April 19x0?

	Materials	Conversion
a.	240,000	250,000
b.	255,000	255,000
c.	270,000	280,000
d.	280,000	270,000

Items 2 and 3 are based on the following information:

Bronson Company had 6,000 units in work in process at January 1, 19x2, which were 60 percent complete as to conversion costs. During January, 20,000 units were completed. At January 31, 19x2, 8,000 units remained in work in process that were 40 percent complete as to conversion costs. Materials are added at the beginning of the process.

2. Using the weighted-average method, the equivalent units for January for conversion costs were
   a. 19,600.
   b. 22,400.
   c. 23,200.
   d. 25,600.
3. How many units were started during January?
   a. 18,000
   b. 19,600
   c. 20,000
   d. 22,000

(AICPA adapted)

4-4 Average Costing for a First Department

1. Maurice Company adds materials at the beginning of the process in the forming department, which is the first of two stages of its production cycle. Information concerning the materials used in the forming department in April 19x9 is as follows:

	Units	Materials Costs
Work in process at April 1, 19x9 . . .	12,000	$ 6,000
Units started during April	100,000	$51,120
Units completed and transferred to next department during April	88,000	

Using the weighted-average method, what was the materials cost of the work in process at April 30, 19x9?

  a. $ 6,120.
  b. $11,040.
  c. $12,000.
  d. $12,240.

2. Information for the month of January 19x2 concerning department A, the first stage of Ogden Corporation's production cycle, is as follows:

	Materials	Conversion
Work in process, beginning .	$ 8,000	$ 6,000
Current costs	40,000	32,000
Total costs	$ 48,000	$38,000
Equivalent units using weighted-average method .	100,000	95,000
Average unit costs	$ 0.48	$ 0.40
Goods completed		90,000 units
Work in process, end		10,000 units

Materials are added at the beginning of the process. The ending work in process is 50 percent complete as to conversion costs. How would the total costs accounted for be distributed, using the weighted-average method?

	Goods Completed	Work in Process, End
a.	$79,200	$6,800
b.	$79,200	$8,800
c.	$86,000	$ –0–
d.	$88,000	$6,800

(AICPA adapted)

4–5 Average Costing for a First Department

1. Information for the month of May concerning department A, the first stage of Wit Corporation's production cycle, is as follows:

	Materials	Conversion Costs
Work in process, beginning	$ 4,000	$ 3,000
Current costs	20,000	16,000
Total costs	$ 24,000	$19,000
Equivalent units based on weighted-average method . . .	100,000	95,000
Average unit costs	$ 0.24	$ 0.20
Goods completed		90,000 units
Work in process, end		10,000 units

Material costs are added at the beginning of the process. The ending work in process is 50 percent complete as to conversion costs. How would the total costs accounted for be distributed, using the weighted-average method?

	Goods Completed	Work in Process, End
a.	$39,600	$3,400
b.	$39,600	$4,400
c.	$43,000	$ –0–
d.	$44,000	$3,400

2. Information concerning department A of Stover Company for the month of June is as follows:

	Units	Materials Costs
Work in process, beginning . .	17,000	$12,800
Started in June	82,000	69,700
Units completed	85,000	
Work in process, end	14,000	

All materials are added at the beginning of the process. Using the weighted-average method, the cost per equivalent unit for materials costs is
a. $0.83.
b. $0.85.
c. $0.97.
d. $1.01.

3. Lucas Company adds materials in the beginning of the process in the forming department, which is the first of two stages of its production cycle. Information concerning the materials used in the forming department in October 19x8 is as follows:

	Units	Materials Costs
Work in process at October 1, 19x8 . .	6,000	$ 3,000
Units started during October	50,000	25,560
Units completed and transferred to next department during October .	44,000	

Using the weighted-average method, what was the materials cost of work in process at October 31, 19x8?

a. $3,060.
b. $5,520.
c. $6,000.
d. $6,120.

(AICPA adapted)

4–6   **Average Costing for a Second Department**

Items 1 and 2 are based on the following information:

On April 1, 19x7, the Collins Company had 6,000 units of work in process in department B, the second and last stage of their production cycle. The costs attached to these 6,000 units were $12,000 of costs transferred in from department A, $2,500 of material costs added in department B, and $2,000 of conversion costs added in department B. Materials are added in the beginning of the process in department B. Conversion was 50 percent complete on April 1, 19x7. During April, 14,000 units were transferred in from department A at a cost of $27,000; and material costs of $3,500 and conversion costs of $3,000 were added in department B. On April 30, 19x7, department B had 5,000 units of work in process 60 percent complete as to conversion costs. The costs attached to these 5,000 units were $10,500 of costs transferred in from department A, $1,800 of material costs added in department B, and $800 of conversion costs added in department B.

1. Using the weighted-average method, what were the equivalent units for the month of April?

	Transferred in from Department A	Materials	Conversion
a.	15,000	15,000	15,000
b.	19,000	19,000	20,000
c.	20,000	20,000	18,000
d.	25,000	25,000	20,000

2. Using the weighted-average method, what was the cost per equivalent unit for conversion costs?

a. $4,200 ÷ 15,000.
b. $5,800 ÷ 18,000.
c. $5,800 ÷ 20,000.
d. $5,000 ÷ 18,000.

3. Roy Company manufactures product X in a two-stage production cycle in departments A and B. Materials are added at the beginning of the process in department B. Roy uses the weighted-average method. Conversion costs for department B were 50 percent complete as to the 6,000 units in the beginning work in process and 75 percent complete as to the 8,000 units in the ending work in process. Twelve thousand units were completed and transferred out of department B during February 19x0. An analysis of the costs relating to work in process (WIP) and production activity in department B for February 19x0 is as follows:

	Costs		
	Transferred In	Materials	Conversion
WIP, February 1:			
Costs attached . . .	$12,000	$2,500	$1,000
February activity:			
Costs added	29,000	5,500	5,000

The total cost per equivalent unit transferred out for February 19x0 of product X, rounded to the nearest penny, was

a. $2.75.
b. $2.78.
c. $2.82.
d. $2.85.

(AICPA adapted)

4–7 Average Costing for a Second Department

Items 1 and 2 are based on the following information:

Information concerning department B of the Toby Company is as follows:

	Units	Costs
Beginning work in process	5,000	$ 6,300
Units transferred in	35,000	58,000
	40,000	$64,300
Units completed	37,000	
Ending work in process	3,000	

	Costs			
	Trans- ferred In	Materials	Conversion	Total Costs
Beginning work in process .	$ 2,900	$ —	$ 3,400	$ 6,300
Units transferred in	17,500	25,500	15,000	58,000
Total	$20,400	$25,500	$18,400	$64,300

Conversion costs were 20 percent complete as to the beginning work in process and 40 percent complete as to the ending work in process. All materials are added at the end of the process. Toby uses the weighted-average method.

1. The cost per equivalent unit for conversion costs, rounded to the nearest penny, is
   a. $0.44.
   b. $0.46.
   c. $0.48.
   d. $0.50.
2. The portion of the total cost of ending work in process attributable to transferred-in cost is
   a. $0.
   b. $1,500.
   c. $1,530.
   d. $1,650.

(AICPA adapted)

4–8   **(Appendix 4–A):   Computation of FIFO Equivalent Units**

1. On November 1, 19x7, Yankee Company had 20,000 units of work in process in department 1 which were 100 percent complete as to material costs and 20 percent complete as to conversion costs. During November, 160,000 units were started in department 1 and 170,000 units were completed and transferred to department 2. The work in process on November 30, 19x7, was 100 percent complete as to material costs and 40 percent complete as to conversion costs. By what amount would the equivalent units for conversion costs for the month of November differ if the first-in, first-out method were used instead of the weighted-average method?
   a. 20,000 decrease.
   b. 16,000 decrease.
   c. 8,000 decrease.
   d. 4,000 decrease.
2. A company uses the first-in, first-out method of costing in a process costing system. Material is added at the beginning of the process in department A, and conversion costs are incurred uniformly throughout the process. Beginning work in process inventory on April 1 in department A consisted of 50,000 units estimated to be 30 percent complete. During April, 150,000 units were started in department A, and 160,000 units were completed and transferred to department B. Ending work in process inventory on April 30 in department A was estimated to be 20 percent complete. What were the total equivalent units in department A for April for materials and conversion costs, respectively?
   a. 150,000 and 133,000.
   b. 150,000 and 153,000.
   c. 200,000 and 133,000.
   d. 200,000 and 153,000.
3. Department 1 is the first stage of Drucker Company's production cycle. The following information is available for conversion costs for the month of April:

	Units
Work in process, beginning	
(40 percent complete)	40,000
Started in April	320,000
Completed in April and transferred	
to department 2	340,000
Work in process, end (60 percent complete) . .	20,000

Using the FIFO method, the equivalent units for the conversion cost calculation are

a. 320,000.
b. 336,000.
c. 352,000.
d. 360,000.

(AICPA adapted)

4–9 (Appendix 4–A): Computation of FIFO Equivalent Units

1. Walton, Incorporated, had 8,000 units of work in process in department A on October 1, 19x8. These units were 60 percent complete as to conversion costs. Materials are added in the beginning of the process. During the month of October, 34,000 units were started and 36,000 units completed. Walton had 6,000 units of work in process on October 31, 19x8. These units were 80 percent complete as to conversion costs. By how much did the equivalent units for the month of October using the weighted-average method exceed the equivalent units for the month of October using the first-in, first-out method?

	Materials	Conversion Costs
a.	–0–	3,200
b.	–0–	4,800
c.	8,000	3,200
d.	8,000	4,800

2. Richardson Company computed the flow of physical units completed for department M for the month of March 19x2 as follows:

Units completed:	
From work in process on March 1, 19x2	15,000
From March production	45,000
Total	60,000

Materials are added at the beginning of the process. The 12,000 units of work in process at March 31, 19x2, were 80 percent complete as to conversion costs. The work in process at March 1, 19x2, was 60 percent complete as to conversion

costs. Using the FIFO method, the equivalent units for March conversion costs
were

   a. 55,200.
   b. 57,000.
   c. 60,600.
   d. 63,600.

3. The Ace Company had computed the physical flow (of physical units) for department A for the month of April 19x9 as follows:

Units completed:	
From work in process on April 1, 19x9	10,000
From April production	30,000
Total	40,000

Materials are added at the beginning of the process. Units of work in process at April 30, 19x9, were 8,000. The work in process at April 1, 19x9, was 80 percent complete as to conversion costs and the work in process at April 30, 19x9, was 60 percent complete as to conversion costs. What are the equivalent units of production for the month of April 19x9 using the FIFO method?

	Materials	Conversion Costs
a.	38,000	36,800
b.	38,000	38,000
c.	48,000	44,800
d.	48,000	48,000

(AICPA adapted)

4–10 (Appendix 4–A): FIFO Costing for a First Department

The cutting department is the first stage of Mark Company's production cycle. Conversion costs for this department were 80 percent complete as to the beginning work in process and 50 percent complete as to the ending work in process. Information as to conversion costs in the cutting department for January 19x0 is as follows:

	Units	Conversion Costs
Work in process at January 1, 19x0 .	25,000	$ 22,000
Units started and costs incurred during January	135,000	$143,000
Units completed and transferred to next department during January . .	100,000	

Using the FIFO method, what was the conversion cost of the work in process in the cutting department at January 31, 19x0?

a. $33,000.
b. $38,100.
c. $39,000.
d. $45,000.

(AICPA adapted)

4–11 **(Appendix 4–B): Equivalent Units with Lost and Spoiled Units—Average Costing**

1. *Materials are added at the start of the process* in Cedar Company's blending department, the first stage of the production cycle. The following information is available for the month of July 19x1:

	Units
Work in process, July 1 (60 percent complete as to conversion costs)	60,000
Started in July	150,000
Transferred to the next department	110,000
Lost in production	30,000
Work in process, July 31 (50 percent complete as to conversion costs)	70,000

Under Cedar's cost accounting system, the costs incurred on the lost units are absorbed by the remaining good units. Using the weighted-average method, what are the equivalent units for the materials unit cost calculation?

a. 120,000.
b. 145,000.
c. 180,000
d. 210,000.

2. Tooker Company adds materials at the *beginning* of the process in department A. Information concerning the materials used in April 19x2 production is as follows:

	Units
Work in process at April 1	10,000
Started during April	50,000
Completed and transferred to next department during April	36,000
Normal spoilage incurred	3,000
Abnormal spoilage incurred	5,000
Work in process at April 30	16,000

Under Tooker's cost accounting system, costs of normal spoilage are treated as a part of the costs of the good units produced. However, the costs of abnormal spoilage are charged to a loss account. Using the weighted-average method, what are the equivalent units for the materials unit cost calculation for the month of April?

- a. 47,000.
- b. 52,000.
- c. 55,000.
- d. 57,000.

3. Milton, Inc., had 8,000 units of work in process in its department M on March 1, 19x0, which were 50 percent complete as to conversion costs. Materials are introduced at the beginning of the process. During March, 17,000 units were started, 18,000 units were completed, and there were 2,000 units of normal spoilage. Milton had 5,000 units of work in process at March 31, 19x0, which were 60 percent complete as to conversion costs. Under Milton's cost accounting system, spoiled units reduce the number of units over which total costs can be spread. Using the weighted-average method, the equivalent units for March for conversion costs were

- a. 17,000.
- b. 19,000.
- c. 21,000.
- d. 23,000.

4. Read, Inc., instituted a new process in October 19x7. During October, 10,000 units were started in department A. Of the units started, 1,000 were lost in the process, 7,000 were transferred to department B, and 2,000 remained in work in process at October 31, 19x7. The work in process at October 31, 19x7, was 100 percent complete as to material costs and 50 percent complete as to conversion costs. Material costs of $27,000 and conversion costs of $40,000 were charged to department A in October. What were the total costs transferred to department B?

- a. $46,900.
- b. $53,600.
- c. $56,000.
- d. $57,120.

(AICPA adapted)

4–12   (Appendix 4–B): Average Costing for a Third Department

The following data apply to items 1 through 5:

JC Company employs a process cost system. A unit of product passes through three departments—molding, assembly, and finishing—before it is completed.

The following activity took place in the finishing department during May:

	Units
Work in process inventory, May 1	1,400
Units transferred in from the assembly department	14,000
Units spoiled	700
Units transferred out to finished goods inventory . .	11,200

Raw material is added at the beginning of the processing in the finishing department without changing the number of units being processed. The work in process inventory was 70 percent complete as to conversion on May 1 and 40 percent complete as to conversion on May 31. All spoilage was discovered at final inspection before the units were transferred to finished goods; 560 of the units spoiled were within the limit considered normal.

JC Company employs the weighted-average costing method. The equivalent units and the current costs per equivalent unit of production for each cost factor are as follows:

	Equivalent Units	Current Costs per Equivalent Unit
Cost of prior departments . . .	15,400	$5
Raw materials	15,400	1
Conversion cost	13,300	3
Total		$9

1. The cost of production transferred to the finished goods inventory is
   a. $100,800.
   b. $105,840.
   c. $107,100.
   d. $102,060.
   e. Some amount other than those given above.
2. The cost assigned to the work in process inventory on May 31 is
   a. $28,000.
   b. $31,000.
   c. $25,200.
   d. $30,240.
   e. Some amount other than those given above.
3. If the total costs of prior departments included in the work in process inventory of the finishing department on May 1 amounted to $6,300, the total cost transferred in from the assembly department to the finishing department during May is
   a. $70,000.
   b. $62,300.
   c. $70,700.
   d. $63,700.
   e. Some amount other than those given above.
4. The cost associated with the abnormal spoilage is
   a. $6,300.
   b. $1,260.
   c. $560.
   d. $840.
   e. Some amount other than those given above.
5. The cost associated with abnormal spoilage ordinarily would be
   a. Charged to inventory.
   b. Charged to a material variance account.
   c. Charged to retained earnings.
   d. Charged to manufacturing overhead.
   e. Charged to a special loss account.

(CMA adapted)

PROBLEMS   4–13   **Average Production Report for a First Department—
No Beginning Inventory**

The Lumbar Company had the following transactions for the month of January 19x1 in its only processing department:

Costs incurred:	
Materials	$124,000
Direct labor	142,800
Overhead	157,080
Total	$423,880
Production:	
Started new	40,000
Completed and transferred	30,000
Ending work in process	
(100 percent materials; 40 percent labor and overhead) . .	10,000

Required   *a.*   Prepare a production report.
              b.   Prepare the journal entries to record the issuance of materials, direct labor, applied overhead, and finished goods.

4–14   **Average Production Report for Two Departments—
No Beginning Inventory**

The Miramar Company had the following transactions for the month of January 19x2 in its two departments:

	Cutting	Finishing
Costs incurred:		
Materials	$135,000	$ 16,400
Direct labor	126,500	55,680
Overhead	101,200	50,112
Totals	$362,700	$122,192
Production:		
Started new	50,000	
Completed and transferred	40,000	32,000
Ending work in process:		
(100% materials; 60% labor and overhead) . .	10,000	
(100% materials; 80% conversion)		8,000

Required   *a.*   Prepare a production report.
              b.   Prepare all of the implicit journal entries for both departments assuming that overhead is applied to production on the basis of direct labor cost.

**4–15 Average Production Report for the First Department—
Beginning Inventory**

The Necknar Company's production process is limited to one department. For the month of March 19x4, the company incurred the following costs:

Direct materials	$146,350
Direct labor	157,880
Overhead	173,668
Total	$477,898

The beginning inventory on March 1, 19x4, amounted to:

Direct materials	$ 19,250
Direct labor	16,000
Overhead	17,600
Total	$ 52,850

The quantity production statistics for the month of March 19x4 are as follows:

Beginning inventory	7,000
Started new	53,000
Transferred out	45,000
Ending inventory (100% materials; 60% conversion) . .	15,000

Required *a.* Prepare production report using average costing. (Combine labor and overhead into conversion cost.)

b. Prepare all journal entries to record:
   (1) The issuance of direct materials.
   (2) The direct labor.
   (3) The applied overhead.
   (4) Finished goods.

**4–16 Average Production Report for a First Department—
No Beginning Inventory**

The Sunny Company had the following transactions for the month of January 19x1 in its only processing department:

Costs incurred:	
Materials	$ 61,250
Direct labor	82,800
Overhead	57,960
Total	$202,010
Production;	
Started new	25,000
Completed and transferred	20,000
Ending work in process	
(100% materials; 60% labor and overhead) . .	5,000

Required *a.* Prepare a production report.

b. Prepare the journal entries to record the issuance of materials, direct labor, applied overhead, and finished goods.

4–17 Average Production Report for a First Department— No Beginning Inventory

The Briggs Company had the following transactions for the month of January 19x1 in its only processing department:

Costs incurred:	
Materials	$121,500
Direct labor	149,800
Overhead	119,840
Total	$391,140
Production:	
Started new	75,000
Completed and transferred	55,000
Ending work in process	
(100% materials; 75% labor and overhead) ..	20,000

Required *a.* Prepare a production report.

b. Prepare the journal entries to record the issuance of materials, direct labor, applied overhead, and finished goods.

4–18 Average Production Report for Two Departments— No Beginning Inventory

The Vodar Company had the following transactions for the month of January 19x2 in its two departments:

	Cutting	Finishing
Costs incurred:		
Materials	$ 46,400	$ 18,880
Direct labor	84,480	72,220
Overhead	50,688	64,998
Totals	$181,568	$156,098
Production:		
Started new	40,000	
Completed and transferred	32,000	30,000
Ending work in process:		
(100% materials; 40% labor and overhead) ..	8,000	
(100% materials; 70% conversion)		2,000

Required *a.* Prepare a production report.

b. Prepare all of the implicit journal entries for both departments assuming that overhead is applied to production on the basis of direct labor cost.

**4-19 Average Production Report for the First Department—
Beginning Inventory**

The Byrd Company's production process is limited to one department. For the month of March 19x4, the company incurred the following costs:

Direct materials	$ 88,460
Direct labor	99,540
Overhead	79,632
Total	$267,632

The beginning inventory on March 1, 19x4, amounted to:

Direct materials	$ 16,540
Direct labor	22,500
Overhead	18,000
Total	$ 57,040

The quantity production statistics for the month of March 19x4 are as follows:

Beginning inventory	8,000
Started new	42,000
Transferred out	34,000
Ending inventory (100% materials; 70% conversion)	16,000

Required *a.* Prepare a production report using average costing. (Combine labor and overhead into conversion cost.)

b. Prepare all journal entries to record:
   (1) The issuance of direct materials.
   (2) The direct labor.
   (3) The applied overhead.
   (4) Finished goods.

**4-20 Average Production Report for Two Departments—No
Beginning Inventory**

The Greene Company had the following transactions for the month of January 19x2 in its two departments:

	Cutting	Finishing
Costs incurred:		
Materials	$ 67,500	$ 63,900
Direct labor	72,240	97,980
Overhead	65,010	68,586
Totals	$204,750	$230,466
Production:		
Started new	18,000	
Completed and transferred	15,000	11,000
Ending work in process:		
(100% materials; 60% labor and overhead)	3,000	
(100% materials; 80% conversion)		4,000

Required   *a.*   Prepare a production report.

    b.   Prepare all of the implicit journal entries for both departments assuming that overhead is applied to production on the basis of direct labor cost.

4–21   Average Production Report for Two Departments— Beginning Inventory

The Oar Company has two departments, mixing and coloring. For the month of March 19x4, the company incurred the following costs:

	Mixing	Coloring
Direct materials	$ 73,175	$ 12,500
Direct labor	78,940	142,600
Overhead	94,728	114,080
Totals	$246,843	$269,180

The beginning inventory on March 1, 19x4, amounted to:

	Mixing	Coloring
Cost in preceding department	$ –0–	$39,000
Direct materials	7,825	2,060
Direct labor	5,540	3,720
Overhead	6,648	2,976
Totals	$20,013	$47,756

The quantity production statistics for the month of March 19x4 are as follows:

	Mixing	Coloring
Beginning inventory	3,000	4,000
Started new	27,000	–0–
Transferred in	–0–	22,000
Transferred out	22,000	20,000
Ending inventory:		
(100% materials; 60% conversion)	8,000	
(100% materials; 40% conversion)		6,000

Required   *a.*   Prepare a production report using average costing. (Combine labor and overhead into conversion cost.)

    b.   Prepare all journal entries to record:
    (1)   The issuance of direct materials.
    (2)   The direct labor.
    (3)   The applied overhead.
    (4)   Finished goods.

**4-22   Average Production Report for a Second Department—
Beginning Inventory**

Lakeview Corporation is a manufacturer that uses the weighted-average process cost method to account for costs of production. Lakeview manufactures a product that is produced in three separate departments: molding, assembling, and finishing. The following information was obtained for the assembling department for the month of June 19x0.

Work in process, June 1—2,000 units composed of the following:

	Amount	Degree of Completion
Transferred in from the molding department	$32,000	100%
Costs added by the assembling department:		
Direct materials	$20,000	100%
Direct labor	7,200	60%
Factory overhead applied	5,500	50%
	32,700	
Work in process, June 1	$64,700	

The following activity occurred during the month of June:

1. 10,000 units were transferred in from the molding department at a cost of $160,000.
2. $150,000 of costs were added by the assembling department:

Direct materials	$ 96,000
Direct labor	36,000
Factory overhead applied	18,000
	$150,000

3. 8,000 units were completed and transferred to the finishing department.

At June 30, 4,000 units were still in work in process. The degree of completion of work in process at June 30 was as follows:

Direct materials	90%
Direct labor	70%
Factory overhead applied	35%

Required   Prepare in good form a production report for the assembling department for the month of June. Show supporting computations in good form. The report should include:

a. Equivalent units of production.
b. Total manufacturing costs.
c. Cost per equivalent unit.
d. Dollar amount of ending work in process.
e. Dollar amount of inventory cost transferred out.

(AICPA adapted)

4-23 Average Production Report for a Single Department—Compared to Book Inventory

You are engaged in the audit of the December 31, 19x8, financial statements of Spirit Corporation, a manufacturer of a digital watch. You are attempting to verify the costing of the ending inventory of work in process and finished goods which were recorded on Spirit's books as follows:

	Units	Cost
Work in process (50% complete as to labor and overhead)	300,000	$ 660,960
Finished goods	200,000	$1,009,800

Materials are added to production at the beginning of the manufacturing process, and overhead is applied to each product at the rate of 60 percent of direct labor costs. There was no finished goods inventory on January 1, 19x8. A review of Spirit's inventory cost records disclosed the following information:

	Units	Costs Materials	Labor	_OH._
Work in process January 1, 19x8 (80% complete as to labor and overhead)	200,000	$ 200,000	$ 315,000	189,800
Units started in production:	1,000,000			
Material costs		$1,300,000		
Labor costs			$1,995,000	
Units completed	900,000			

Required   a. Prepare schedules as of December 31, 19x8, to compute the following:
1. Equivalent units of production using the weighted-average method.
2. Unit costs of production of materials, labor, and overhead.
3. Costing of the finished goods inventory and work in process inventory.

b. Prepare the necessary journal entry to correctly state the inventory of finished goods and work in process, assuming the books have not been closed.

(AICPA adapted)

4-24 (Appendix 4-A): FIFO Production Report for a First Department

The Rosar Company has a single-stage production process. You are the company's cost accountant, and you are provided with the following information for the purpose of preparing a cost of production report.

Costs for the month of April 19x5 were:

Direct materials	$146,280
Direct labor	156,740
Overhead	172,414
Total	$475,434

The costs of the beginning inventory are:

Direct materials	$ 19,250
Direct labor	16,000
Overhead	17,600
Total	$ 52,850

The production statistics for April 19x5 were:

Beginning work in process:
   Materials—7,000 units 100% complete
   Conversion—7,000 units 70% complete

Started new—53,000 units

Ending work in process:
   Materials—15,000 units 100% complete
   Conversion—15,000 units 40% complete

There were no lost units or increased units.

Required   *a.* Prepare a production report using FIFO costing. (Combine labor and overhead into conversion cost.)

     b. Prepare all journal entries to record:
      (1) The issuance of direct materials.
      (2) The direct labor.
      (3) The applied overhead.
      (4) Finished goods.

4–25 **(Appendix 4–A): FIFO Production Report for One Department**

The Oar Company has one department. For the month of March 19x4, the company incurred the following costs:

Direct materials	$ 73,175
Direct labor	78,940
Overhead	94,728
Total	$246,843

The beginning inventory on March 1, 19x4, amounted to:

Direct materials	$ 7,825
Direct labor	5,540
Overhead	6,648
Total	$ 20,013

The quantity production statistics for the month of March 19x4 are as follows:

Beginning inventory (100% material; 40% conversion) . .	3,000
Started new	27,000
Transferred out	22,000
Ending inventory (100% materials; 60% conversion) . . .	8,000

Required   *a.*   Prepare a production report.

         b.   Prepare all journal entries to record:

             (1)   The issuance of direct materials.

             (2)   The direct labor.

             (3)   The applied overhead.

             (4)   The transfer to finished goods.

4–26   (Appendix 4–A):   FIFO Production Report for a Second Department

The Peer Company has two departments, a stripping department and a finishing department. For the month of March 19x4, the finishing department incurred the following costs:

Transferred-in cost	$196,000
Direct materials	48,000
Direct labor	84,840
Overhead	67,872
Total	$396,712

The beginning inventory on March 1, 19x4, amounted to:

Cost in preceding department	$48,000
Direct materials	11,800
Direct labor	12,900
Overhead	10,320
Total	$83,020

The quantity production statistics for the month of March 19x4 are as follows:

Beginning inventory (100% material; 60% conversion)	10,000
Transferred in	40,000
Transferred out	38,000
Ending inventory (100% materials; 70% conversion)	12,000

Required   *a.*   Prepare a production report.

         b.   Prepare all journal entries to record:

             (1)   The issuance of direct materials.

             (2)   The direct labor.

             (3)   The applied overhead.

             (4)   The transfer to finished goods.

4–27   (Appendix 4–B):   Average Production Report—Normal Spoilage and Lost Units

The Pillar Company operates a single-process manufacturing firm. For the month of March 19x4, the company incurred the following costs:

Direct materials	$ 32,300
Direct labor	73,200
Overhead	109,800
Total	$215,300

The beginning inventory on March 1, 19x4, amounted to:

Direct materials	$ 4,500
Direct labor	6,000
Overhead	9,000
Total	$19,500

The quantity production statistics for the month of March 19x4 are as follows:

Beginning inventory	10,000
Started new	75,000
Transferred out	60,000
Ending inventory (100% materials; 30% conversion)	20,000
Lost units—normal	?

The lost units—all considered normal—occur evenly throughout the production cycle. The company uses the method of neglect to account for them.

Required
  a. Prepare a production report using average costing.
  b. Prepare journal entries to record the issuance of materials, direct labor, applied overhead, and the transfer to finished goods.

4–28 (Appendix 4–B): Average Production Report for a Second Department— Normal Spoilage

Quasar Company has two departments, mixing and coloring. For the month of March 19x4, the company incurred the following costs:

	Coloring
Direct materials	$ 80,000
Direct labor	160,000
Overhead	176,000
Total	$416,000

The beginning inventory on March 1, 19x4, amounted to:

	Coloring
Cost in preceding department	$22,500
Direct materials	9,800
Direct labor	16,000
Overhead	17,600
Total	$65,900

The quantity production statistics for the month of March 19x4 are as follows:

	Coloring
Beginning inventory	10,000
Transferred in	70,000
Transferred out	60,000
Ending inventory (100% materials, 60% conversion)	16,000
Lost units—all normal	?

The mixing department costs for the 70,000 units transferred in amounted to $155,000.

The company uses the method of neglect to account for normal spoilage.

Required   Prepare a production report using average costing. (Combine labor and overhead into conversion cost.)

4-29   **(Appendix 4-B): Average Production Report for a First Department— with Spoilage**

West Corporation is a divisionalized manufacturing company. A product called Aggregate is manufactured in one department of the California division. Aggregate is transferred upon completion to the Utah division at a predetermined price where it is used in the manufacture of other products.

The raw material is added at the beginning of the process. Labor and overhead are added continuously throughout the process. Shrinkage of 10 to 14 percent, all occurring at the beginning of the process, is considered normal. In the California division, all departmental overhead is charged to the departments and divisional overhead is allocated to the departments on the basis of direct labor-hours. The divisional overhead rate for 19x9 is $2 per direct labor-hour.

The following information relates to production during November 19x9:

Work in process, November 1, (4,000 pounds—75% complete):	
Raw material	$22,800
Direct labor at $5 per hour	$24,650
Departmental overhead	$12,000
Divisional overhead	$ 9,860
Raw material:	
Inventory, November 1, 2,000 pounds	$10,000
Purchases, November 3, 10,000 pounds	$51,000
Purchases, November 18, 10,000 pounds	$51,500
Released to production during November, 16,000 pounds	
Direct labor costs at $5 per hour, $103,350	
Direct departmental overhead costs, $52,000	
Transferred to Utah division, 15,000 pounds	
Work in process, November 30, 3,000 pounds, 33⅓% complete.	

The FIFO method is used for materials inventory valuation and the weighted-average method is used for work in process inventories.

Required   Prepare a production report for the department of California division producing Aggregate for November 19x9 which presents:

1. The equivalent units of production by cost factor of Aggregate (e.g., raw material, direct labor, and overhead).
2. The equivalent unit costs for each cost factor of Aggregate.
3. The cost of Aggregate transferred to the Utah division.
4. The cost of abnormal shrinkage, if any.
5. The cost of the work in process inventory at November 30, 19x9.

(CMA adapted)

5

COST BEHAVIOR AND COST ESTIMATION

LEARNING OBJECTIVES

After reading this chapter, you should be able to:

1 Explain why decision makers must understand cost behavior.

2 Define the three basic patterns of cost behavior: variable costs, fixed costs, and mixed costs.

3 Distinguish between semivariable costs and step-variable costs.

4 Explain why mixed costs must be separated into their fixed and variable components.

5 Use account analysis, engineering cost analysis, and the high-low method to analyze mixed costs and separate them into their fixed and variable components.

6 Explain why a contribution margin income statement is more useful to managers than a traditional income statement.

7 Prepare a contribution margin income statement and use it to project future-oriented data for decision making.

8 Compute a firm's contribution margin ratio and a product's contribution margin per unit and use them to project changes in net income.

Fixed, variable, and mixed costs were first discussed in Chapter 2. These costs are explored further in this chapter because their behavior patterns affect many managerial decisions, including setting of selling prices, entering into new markets, introducing new products, eliminating existing products, investing in additional and/or replacement plant facilities, curtailing activity, and reaching make-or-buy decisions.

Cost behavior is the way in which a cost reacts to a change in business activity. It is essential for managers to understand cost behavior patterns if they are to accurately predict how a cost will react to a contemplated change in business activity. The failure to project cost effects when making a decision—or incorrect projections—may have serious consequences for a firm. Of course, as with any prediction, a certain amount of error is to be expected. But fortunately, cost-estimation techniques such as those that we will study in this chapter provide managers with reasonably accurate data for use in decision making.

COST BEHAVIOR

Curvilinear Cost Behavior

According to economic theory, **marginal cost**—the cost to produce one additional unit—does not increase in proportion to production or in a straight line when plotted on a graph. Rather, it increases disproportionately or as a curve on a graph. For example, consider the case of a furniture maker that is too small to afford automated equipment. If the company has only one employee, it is more than likely that he would perform some of the cutting, planing, and sandpapering by hand. If another employee is hired and the factory is large enough to accommodate both workers, output would be doubled but costs would be less than doubled, since such costs as factory rent, heat, and light would not increase. Thus, as production increases, output increases faster than costs—a curvilinear relationship.

If the firm reaches its optimal size and the factory is fully utilized, operations that were formerly performed manually can now be performed on machinery that was unaffordable when the firm was of suboptimal size. Changes in output affect only variable costs, while fixed costs remain constant. At the optimal level of production, output increases almost proportionately with costs—an approximately linear relationship. Once the optimal size is reached, further increases in production require that employees be paid an overtime premium. In addition, employee fatigue may result in less than normal pro-

ILLUSTRATION 5–1   Economist's Total Cost Behavior Curve

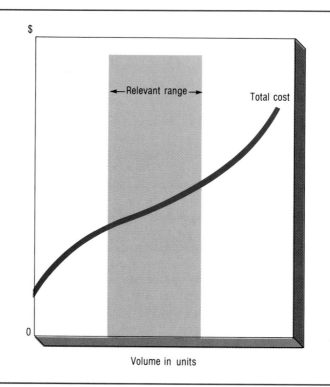

Volume in units

ductivity during the overtime hours. When this occurs, output increases more slowly than the rise in costs—a curvilinear relationship. Most firms choose to operate at their optimal level of production. Of course, it is not always possible to operate at exactly the same level. Thus, a firm will choose a span of activity levels near its optimal level called the **relevant range.** A firm usually operates within its relevant range, although production may occasionally vary from this norm.

Illustration 5–1 presents an example of the economist's curvilinear cost relationship. Note, however, that the relevant range reflects an approximately *linear* cost relationship. Thus, for many business analysis problems, it is possible to assume linear cost behavior. Because management accountants regularly make this assumption, we will limit our discussion to linear cost behavior problems and solutions.

Variable Costs

In Chapter 2, we defined **variable costs** as total costs that vary in direct proportion to output, although the per-unit cost is constant within a given range of production. A key aspect of the definition of variable cost is the fact that a change in a variable cost always corresponds to a change in a related item or event. An item or event that has a cause-and-effect relationship with the incurrence of a variable cost is called an **activity base.** The variable cost may then be measured in terms of its activity base. For example, in this chapter we will assume that a variable cost changes in direct proportion to sales volume. Therfore, if sales volume is expected to increase by 10 percent in a given period, a corresponding increase of 10 percent in variable cost is also expected. Another common activity base is units of production. Thus, if a company expects to produce 8 percent more hand-held calculators in August, it can expect its August cost for microchips to increase by 8 percent.

The most common activity bases are sales volume and units of production, but there are also many others. For example, the variable cost of gasoline used in a delivery truck may be measured in terms of the number of miles driven. Other examples of variable costs and related activity bases are: (1) clerical salaries in a college registrar's office measured by the number of students enrolled at the college, (2) nurses' salaries in a hospital measured by the number of patients treated, and (3) billing department salaries measured by the number of lines typed on sales invoices.

Managers must be familiar with activity bases and how they affect cost behavior. For example, managers who are considering the expansion of their firm's business not only must consider the increased revenues and product costs, but also must calculate the increased cost in the billing department that will result from the need to type additional invoices.

Fixed Costs

A **fixed cost** is a total cost that remains constant within a given range of activity and period of time. Within the limits of the activity range, per-unit fixed costs decrease with increased output. A fixed cost normally does not affect short-term decision making. If a manager must decide whether to accept a rush order that would cause employees to work overtime, her decision should be based on the increased revenue compared with the additional costs of raw materials, direct labor including the overtime premium, and variable overhead. Fixed costs such as factory rent should not influence the decision because they remain unchanged whether the rush order is accepted or rejected. When setting price policies, however, fixed costs must be included if the firm is to operate profitably in the long run.

Committed Costs. Fixed costs that continue for long periods of time are called **committed costs.** Once made, these costs are not reversible in the short term. An example of a committed cost would be the cost of constructing a factory building. A long-term lease for an office building would also be a committed cost, as would the construction of a computerized extruding mill. However, if instead of constructing a factory, an equipped factory is leased for one year at a time, the rent would be a discretionary cost rather than a committed cost.

Discretionary Costs. **Discretionary costs** are also fixed costs, but they differ from committed costs in that they are reversible after short periods of time. Advertising would be a discretionary cost because it is usually contracted for over short periods of time. Other examples of discretionary costs include supervisory salaries and security guards' salaries. When evaluating whether to invest in expensive labor-saving equipment—a committed cost— or to perform the tasks using direct labor, the distinction between committed and discretionary costs becomes important. At present, there is a trend toward converting labor-intensive tasks to machine-intensive tasks. Such a decision may impose huge losses on a business if it must be reversed. A sudden change in consumer demand, as occurs in the automobile and steel industries, may cause a firm to have huge committed costs and idle capacity that cannot be reversed in the short term. But discretionary costs such as direct labor can be reversed in the short term by laying off unnecessary employees.

Mixed Costs

Many costs cannot be neatly classified as either fixed or variable because they show characteristics of both. Such costs, because they contain both fixed and variable elements, are called **mixed costs.** Mixed costs may be subdivided into two categories—semivariable costs and step-variable costs.

Semivariable Costs. A **semivariable cost** is closely related to a variable cost. It consists of two components—a basic fixed charge (usually a monthly fee) and a variable charge based on the level of activity. This two-part structure often results from the way a supplier charges for its services. Among the more common semivariable costs are charges for telephone, power and lighting, photocopying, and auto and truck rentals when there is a basic charge plus a separate charge per mile.

Even when a firm purchases its own equipment, certain costs related to maintenance and repairs are semivariable costs. Some forms of maintenance are fixed costs because they must be done periodically regardless of usage. For example, the battery in a delivery truck may need to be changed every three years regardless of how many miles the truck is driven. Other maintenance activities, such as changing the oil and replacing the spark plugs, may depend directly on mileage. Thus, the total cost of the truck's repair and maintenance is a mixed cost made up of some fixed costs and some variable costs.

If the rental agreement for a truck requires a yearly charge of $3,000 plus 10 cents per mile, a graph of the annual cost would appear as shown in Illustration 5–2. Note that if 5,000 miles are driven, the total cost is $3,500 ($3,000 + $.10 × 5,000 miles); if 10,000 miles are driven, the total cost is $4,000 ($3,000 + $.10 × 10,000 miles), and so forth.

Step-Variable Costs. A **step-variable cost** consists of a series of fixed cost increments over short ranges of production within the relevant range. Thus, a step-variable cost increases in discrete jumps instead of in the continuous pattern of semivariable costs. Examples of this kind of cost are the salaries of foremen and maintenance workers. For example, assume that a plant has 10 assembly lines, that 6 lines are currently operating, and that 1 foreman can supervise 2 lines. Under such circumstances, 3 foremen would be em-

ILLUSTRATION 5–2   **Graph of the Semivariable Cost of Truck Rental**

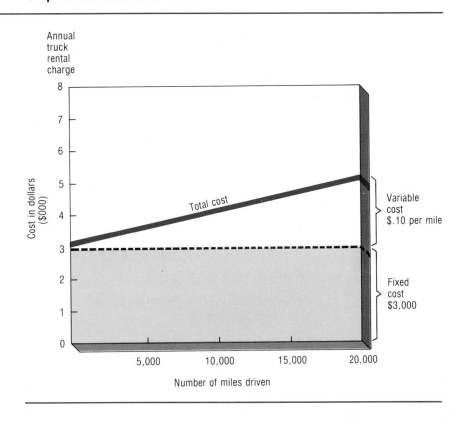

ployed. But if it becomes necessary to open a seventh line, another foreman would have to be hired at full salary, since it is impossible to hire a fraction of a foreman. The same is true for maintenance workers. This is quite different from direct labor, when employees can be added in small increments, on a daily or even on an hourly basis.

A graph of the step-variable cost of hiring foremen is shown in Illustration 5–3. Note that the foremen's salaries hold constant over entire ranges of production—from 0 to 5,000 units, then from 5,001 to 10,000 units, and so forth.

ANALYZING MIXED COSTS

All mixed costs should be separated into their fixed and variable elements and analyzed, even if the only gain is familiarity with the related account. A number of methods may be used to separate the elements of mixed costs. Among the most common are: (1) account analysis, (2) engineering cost analysis, (3) the high-low method, (4) the scattergraph method, and (5) the least squares method. The scattergraph and least squares methods are discussed in Appendix 5–A at the end of this chapter.

ILLUSTRATION 5–3   **Graph of the Step-Variable Cost of Foremen's Salaries**

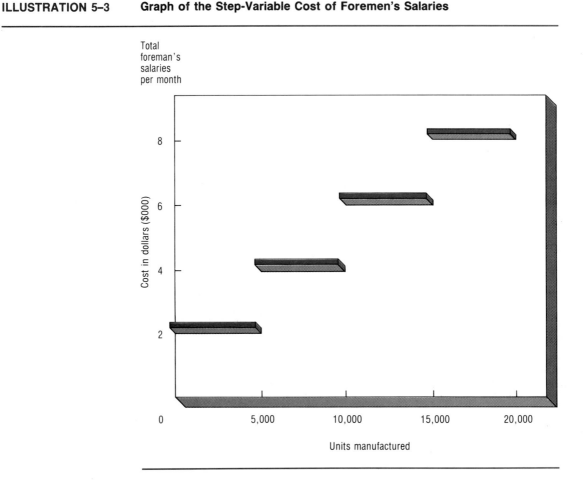

Total foreman's salaries per month

Cost in dollars ($000)

8

6

4

2

0   5,000   10,000   15,000   20,000

Units manufactured

Account Analysis

Account analysis consists of examining the composition of the balance in a general ledger account to determine if its fixed and variable portions can be identified. For example, if a power company charges a fixed amount per month regardless of usage plus a specific amount for each kilowatt-hour used, the fixed and variable components of power costs are easily obtained by analyzing the account. However, not all mixed costs fit neatly into this pattern. Such mixed costs as repairs and maintenance usually cannot be analyzed in this way, and any attempt to do so is likely to produce highly subjective, and therefore useless, results. Consequently, another method must be used in conjunction with account analysis to segregate mixed costs into their fixed and variable components.

Engineering Cost Analysis

In an **engineering cost analysis,** engineers carefully study a production process to determine what its costs should be. As a result, the cost analysis may be more objective, but a new problem may be introduced. Because engineering cost analyses focus on what cost *should be,* their findings may differ from what costs *actually are.* In theory, the two should be the same, but this is not always the case.

In light of this potential discrepancy, managers should be selective in their use and interpretation of engineering cost analyses. Such an approach can be usefully applied to direct materials, when an engineer can prepare a bill of materials and cost it out to determine how much should be spent. Similarly, an engineer can perform time and motion studies to estimate what direct labor costs should be. Engineering cost analysis may also be useful for calculating manufacturing overhead, although not to the same extent as for direct materials and direct labor.

By focusing on what costs ought to be, managers may find areas where increased efficiency may be obtained. However, for other kinds of management decisions such as product pricing, adding new product lines, and eliminating existing product lines, managers must consider costs as they are rather than costs as they ought to be.

The High-Low Method of Analyzing Mixed Costs

The High-Low Formula. The **high-low method** of analyzing mixed costs is based on a calculation that considers *only two* observations out of a series of time periods, normally the highest and lowest costs. The *difference in cost* between the two periods is then compared to the *difference in activity* to derive the variable portion of the cost. A key element of the high-low approach to mixed-cost analysis is that it uses information from the past. Thus, when the high-low method is used to predict future cost behavior, it is based on historical cost behavior.

To demonstrate the high-low method, assume the following maintenance costs for the Sonar Company:

Month	Machine-Hours	Monthly Cost
January	2,500	$ 5,000
February	2,800	5,200
March	3,000	5,300
April	3,400	5,700
May	4,000	6,100
June	5,000	7,100
July	7,000	8,500
August	9,000	10,100
September	10,000	11,000
October	6,000	7,800
November	3,000	5,300
December	2,600	5,100

The lowest month is January, with machine-hour activity of 2,500 hours, and the highest month is September, with machine-hour activity of 10,000 hours. These two months are selected and compared as shown in Illustration

ILLUSTRATION 5–4   Sonar Company: Segregation of Fixed and Variable Costs

	Month	Machine-Hours	Monthly Cost
High	September	10,000	$11,000
Low	January	2,500	5,000
	Differences	7,500	$ 6,000

Variable rate per hour:

$$\frac{\$6,000}{7,500} = \$.80 \text{ per machine-hour}$$

Calculation of the fixed cost:

Fixed cost (FC) = Total cost (TC) − Variable cost (VC)

September:
FC = $11,000 − (10,000 × $.80)
FC = $11,000 − $8,000
FC = $3,000

January:
FC = $5,000 − (2,500 × $.80)
FC = $5,000 − $2,000
FC = $3,000

The cost formula can be stated as:
Total cost = $3,000 + $.80 per machine-hour.

5–4 to determine the variable and fixed portions of the maintenance cost. Note that:

1. The difference in cost is divided by the difference in machine-hours to arrive at the variable rate per hour.

2. The fixed cost can be determined by subtracting the variable cost from the total cost.

3. The fixed cost can be obtained by using either month. Of course, if rates for both months are computed, one can act as a check on the other.

4. The variable cost is computed by multiplying the appropriate machine-hours by the variable rate of 80 cents per hour.

The cost formula may be formally stated as:

$$Y = a + bX$$

where

Y = Total cost
a = Fixed cost
b = Variable cost per unit of activity
X = Number of units of activity

One weakness of this method is that only 2 months out of 12 are used to calculate fixed costs. The other 10 months are usually ignored. However, if either the lowest or the highest point appears to be extreme, the second lowest or highest point should be selected instead. Whether the first or second points are selected, the procedure to calculate the variable rate and fixed cost remains the same.

Another weakness of this method is that if the computed variable cost per unit of activity is applied to any of the ignored months, the resulting fixed costs are unlikely to be the same. This can be seen by arbitrarily selecting the month of May for testing. Using the 80 cents variable rate, the calculation would be:

$$FC = \$6,100 - (4,000 \times \$.80)$$
$$= \$6,100 - \$3,200$$
$$= \$2,900$$

Of all the months other than January and September, only October results in a fixed cost of $3,000 when the variable rate of 80 cents per machine-hour is used. This could be considered a random event.

The High-Low Graph. A variation on the high-low method of analyzing mixed costs is the high-low graph. A high-low graph, as shown in Illustration 5–5, is constructed as follows:

1. Plot the high point at 10,000 hours/$11,000.

2. Plot the low point at 2,500 hours/$5,000.

3. Connect the points.

4. Continue the line (extrapolate) to the maintenance cost axis. The point at which the line intersects the axis represents the fixed portion of maintenance costs, or, in this case, $3,000.

Because only two points are used to make the calculation, the result is only an approximation. Nevertheless, it is satisfactory for many cost applications.

The analysis of mixed costs is continued until all costs are classified as either fixed or variable. Based on this grouping, a manager can begin to assess a cost's behavior and its effect on a decision to be made.

CONTRIBUTION FORMAT INCOME STATEMENTS

While it is crucial to know whether a cost is fixed or variable, such information alone will not suffice for most decision-making situations. Managers must also consider costs in terms of a larger context—that of the income statement. However, under such circumstances, a standard income statement will not suffice either. When an income statement is prepared in the traditional format, costs are grouped by functional classification—such as production, marketing, and administration—and since both fixed and variable costs appear in each category, the resulting summary may not be particularly helpful. The question is how to combine cost-behavior information with income statement informa-

ILLUSTRATION 5–5   **Sonar Company: Graphical Segregation of Fixed and Variable Costs within the Relevant Range**

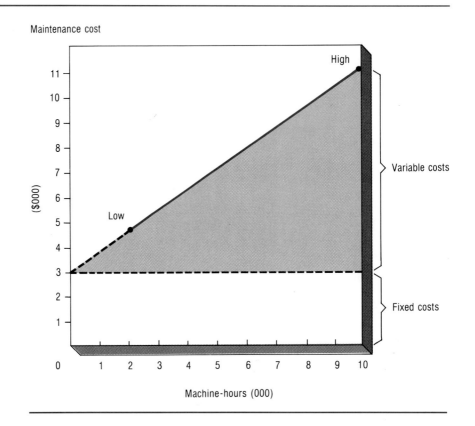

Maintenance cost

tion. The solution is a **contribution format income statement**—an income statement for managerial use that is classified into fixed and variable cost categories instead of into the functional categories of a traditional income statement.

Contribution Margin   The focus of a contribution format income statement is **contribution margin,** which is net sales minus variable costs (manufacturing, marketing, and administrative). In contrast, a standard income statement yields **gross margin,** which is net sales minus manufacturing cost of goods sold (both variable and fixed). Gross margin is not particularly useful for internal decision making because it reflects a deduction for fixed manufacturing costs, which may not change as a result of a contemplated decision, although variable manufacturing costs will change. Relying on a traditional income statement may create similar problems with marketing and administrative costs because they will not be broken down into fixed and variable portions either. A contribution format income statement is thus more suitable for internal decision making because it segregates fixed and variable costs, enabling managers to clearly assess net income changes when cost and/or volume changes occur.

The Contribution Margin Approach to Decision Making

Temar Company had sales volume in 19x2 of $900,000. Its cost of sales for the year amounted to $360,000 and consisted of $100,000 for direct materials, $160,000 for direct labor, $55,000 for variable overhead, and $45,000 for fixed overhead. Marketing costs of $100,000 for the year were also incurred, of which $18,000 were variable and $82,000 were fixed. Administrative costs—all fixed—amounted to $150,000. A traditional income statement was prepared for 19x2 and appears in Illustration 5–6.

If a manager wishes to project the effect on net income of an anticipated 20 percent increase in sales volume with no change in selling prices, a correct assessment would be impossible based on the income statement in Illustration 5–6. If the manager attempts to increase sales, cost of sales, and gross margin each by 20 percent while holding the marketing and administrative costs constant, the effect on net income would be incorrect because the manufacturing overhead of $100,000 includes $45,000 of fixed costs that are not expected to change in 19x3 and, therefore, should not be increased. In addition, the marketing costs of $100,000 include $18,000 of variable costs, and these should be increased. When the income statement is prepared in the contribution format, however, these costs are easily projected.

Preparing a Contribution Format Income Statement. As mentioned earlier, a contribution format income statement is classified into fixed and variable cost categories instead of into the functional categories used in traditional income statements. Although a contribution format income statement is not acceptable for external reporting to stockholders and other users, it is an extremely valuable management tool. As shown in Illustration 5–7, it

ILLUSTRATION 5–6

TEMAR COMPANY
Income Statement
For the Year Ended December 31, 19x2

			Percent
Sales		$900,000	100
Cost of sales:			
Direct materials	$100,000		
Direct labor	160,000		
Manufacturing overhead . . .	100,000	360,000	40
Gross margin		540,000	60
Marketing and administrative:			
Marketing costs	100,000		
Administrative costs	150,000	250,000	
Net income		$290,000	

ILLUSTRATION 5–7

TEMAR COMPANY
Income Statement—Contribution Format
For the Year Ended December 31, 19x2

			Percent
Sales		$900,000	100
Cost of sales:			
Direct materials	$100,000		
Direct labor	160,000		
Variable overhead	55,000	315,000	35
Variable manufacturing margin		585,000	65
Less: Variable marketing costs		18,000	2
Contribution margin		567,000	63
Fixed costs:			
Manufacturing	45,000		
Marketing	82,000		
Administrative	150,000	277,000	
Net income		$290,000	

---

begins with sales revenues, from which variable costs are deducted to arrive at contribution margin. Fixed costs are then deducted to arrive at net income. Occasionally, variable marketing costs are segregated from variable manufacturing costs, and an intermediate margin called variable manufacturing margin is shown.

If a manager wishes to assess the impact of a 20 percent increase in volume on net income and uses a contribution margin income statement, the analysis might appear as in Illustration 5–8. But in fact, once a contribution format

ILLUSTRATION 5–8

TEMAR COMPANY
Projected Increase in Net Income
Using Contribution Margin Income Statement
For the Year Ended December 31, 19x3

Sales ($900,000 × 120%)	$1,080,000
Less: Variable manufacturing costs ($315,000 × 120%)	378,000
Variable manufacturing margin	702,000
Less: Variable marketing costs ($18,000 × 120%)	21,600
Contribution margin	680,400
Less: Fixed costs	277,000
Projected net income	403,400
Less: 19x2 net income	290,000
Projected increase in net income	$ 113,400

---

income statement is prepared as in Illustration 5–7, the projected increase in net income may be determined through the following simple calculation:

Projected increase in net income for 19x3:

$$\text{19x2 contribution margin} = \$567,000 \times 20\% = \$113,400$$

This simplified calculation can be made only if the income statement is prepared in the contribution format.

Contribution Margin Ratio. A useful adjunct of the contribution margin format is the **contribution margin ratio (CMR),** which is the contribution margin divided by sales revenue. In Illustration 5–7, the contribution margin ratio is 63 percent:

$$\text{CMR} = \frac{\$567,000}{\$900,000} = .63 = 63\%$$

It may also be computed as follows:

$$\text{CMR} = 1 - \frac{\text{Variable cost}}{\text{Sales}} = 1 - \frac{\$333,000}{\$900,000} = 1 - .37 = .63, \text{ or } 63\%$$

If managers anticipate an increase in sales volume of $180,000 ($900,000 × 20 percent) for the following year, and if they know the CMR is 63 percent, they may compute the impact on net income as follows:

$$\$180,000 \times 63\% = \$113,400$$

When the CMR is known, it is possible to rapidly solve problems of this type without preparing a contribution income statement.

Contribution Margin per Unit. If the Temar Company manufactured only one product and sold 50,000 units in 19x2 (see Illustration 5–6), it could also calculate the **contribution margin per unit (CMPU).** This figure is found by dividing the contribution margin by the number of units sold:

$$\text{CMPU} = \frac{\$567,000}{50,000 \text{ units}} = \$11.34 \text{ per unit}$$

Thus, on each unit sold, Temar Company initially earns $11.34 toward the recovery of its fixed cost, and once the fixed costs are recovered, each additional unit sold produces $11.34 of profit. The evolution of contribution margin stems from the fact that it initially contributes to the recovery of fixed costs, and once these are recovered, it contributes to profit.

If the Temar Company anticipates a 20 percent increase in sales for 19x3, the computation of the increase in annual net income (provided the company had a net income in 19x2) is easily calculated as:

$$
\begin{aligned}
\text{Increase in net income} &= \text{Increased sales in units} \times \text{CMPU} \\
&= 50,000 \text{ units} \times 20\% = 10,000 \times \$11.34 \\
&= \$113,400
\end{aligned}
$$

Cost Structure   The relationship between a firm's fixed and variable costs is its **cost structure.** Managers constantly face trade-offs between fixed and variable costs during the decision-making process. A common example is the trade-off between a labor-intensive process (a low fixed cost structure) versus a machine-intensive process (a high fixed cost structure) that can be seen in the automobile manufacturing industry. Anyone who visited an auto assembly plant 10 or more years ago would have concluded that it was very machine intensive. Nevertheless, welding and many assembly operations were performed manually. Even when Japanese auto manufacturers began using robots to perform these functions, American auto manufacturers continued to perform them manually. One can ask why United States auto manufacturers have lagged behind the Japanese in robotics. The answer is complex. Some of the considerations relate to scarcity of capital, the state of robotic technology, union contracts, and cost structure.

Cost structure, assuming that capital is available, is extremely important to most managers. At one extreme is a completely labor-intensive process in which all operations are performed manually. Clearly, sewing a business suit of clothes entirely by hand would be more costly than sewing part or all of it by machine. The advantage of a labor-intensive structure is the degree of flexibility. If there is no work due to seasonal fluctuations or economic conditions, workers can be laid off, and most costs associated with labor cease.

At the other extreme is a completely machine-intensive operation that depends on computers and robots and requires few employees. Assuming that such an operation were possible and more cost efficient than using human labor, the bulk of the firm's costs would be fixed. In such cases, the cost of machines continues even during slack periods. Thus, for seasonal businesses, a completely machine-intensive operation may be more costly than a labor-intensive one. Most firms operate somewhere between the two extremes.

The choice of cost structure may have a profound effect on a firm's contribution margin and thus on its net income. A comparison of two firms with the same net income and different cost structures will illustrate the concept. Compu Company performs computer services for other firms. It owns a computer and employs two individuals. The bulk of its costs are rent expense and straight-line depreciation of the computer. The firm is considered machine intensive. For the year just ended, Compu Company had $500,000 of service revenues, $100,000 of variable costs, and $300,000 of fixed costs. Its net income amounted to $100,000.

The Made-to-Order Suit Company manufactures custom-made men's suits. Some sewing is done by machine, but the bulk of the manufacturing is performed by hand. Thus, the firm is considered to be labor intensive. For the year just ended, its revenues were also $500,000. However, its variable costs were $300,000 and its fixed costs were $100,000. Thus, its net income also amounted to $100,000. The different cost structures are shown in Illustration 5–9.

Although both firms have the same sales and net income, they differ opera-

ILLUSTRATION 5–9   **Compu Company and Made-to-Order Suit Company: Comparative Cost Structures**

	Compu Company		Made-to-Order Suit Company	
	Dollars	Percent	Dollars	Percent
Sales	$500,000	100	$500,000	100
Variable costs	100,000	20	300,000	60
Contribution margin . .	400,000	80	200,000	40
Fixed costs	300,000		100,000	
Net income	$100,000		$100,000	

tionally. In periods of increased activity, Compu Company will increase its profits by 80 cents for each additional dollar of sales, assuming no changes in selling prices, unit variable costs, and fixed costs. Made-to-Order Suit Company, however, will increase its profits by only 40 cents for each dollar of increased sales. Thus, in periods of increased activity, Compu Company's cost structure would be preferable.

In periods of diminished activity, Compu Company would lose 80 cents of profit for each dollar of diminished sales activity. Made-to-Order Suit Company, on the other hand, would lose only 40 cents of profit. Thus, you can see how a firm's cost structure can have significant effects on its profitability during periods of increased and diminished activity.

SUMMARY

Managers must understand **cost-behavior** patterns and cost-estimation techniques to effectively administer the affairs of their firms. In many cases, actual cost data may not be available for decision making, and estimated data must be used instead.

According to economic theory, **marginal cost** changes disproportionately to changes in production and is thus a curve when plotted on a graph. However, within the **relevant range**—the span of activity level in which a firm operates—the curve approximates a straight line. For this reason, most management accountants use a linear approach to solving business problems that require the computation of changes in costs when a contemplated change in an **activity base,** such as production, is considered.

Managers use **variable costs** and **fixed costs** in different ways. In evaluating proposals, managers sometimes use only variable costs, sometimes only fixed costs which may be subdivided into **committed costs** and **discretionary costs,** and sometimes both. When considering different strategies, managers must be able to project the changes in costs that are likely to occur. Variable and fixed costs are more easily projected than are **mixed costs** which contain some variable and some fixed costs. The fixed and variable portions of a mixed cost must be segregated if managers are to make effective decisions when projections of only one kind of cost or the other are needed. Mixed costs may be classified as either **semivariable costs** or **step-variable costs.**

A semivariable cost is composed of a basic fee, usually charged per month, plus a variable charge based on activity. In contrast, a step-variable cost holds constant for a certain level of activity and then increases in discrete jumps rather than in a continuous fashion.

Three common methods of dividing mixed costs into their fixed and variable components are **account analysis, engineering cost analysis,** and the **high-low method.** The high-low method uses the highest and lowest cost figures from a series of observations. The difference in these two costs is compared to the difference in their corresponding activity levels, and a variable cost inference is made. The fixed cost per period is then calculated.

Traditional income statements are of limited utility to managers because they are not usually classified according to fixed and variable costs. Instead, managers prefer an income statement that is prepared using a **contribution margin format.** The statement starts with net sales, from which variable costs are deducted to arrive at **contribution margin.** Fixed costs are then deducted to arrive at net income. Contribution margin plays a useful role in a variety of management decisions. Other helpful figures for decision making are the **contribution margin ratio** and the **contribution margin per unit.**

Managers often must decide whether to perform certain operations manually or to automate them. While the long-run average cost of automated operations may be less than that of the manual operations, the decision has a profound impact on a firm's **cost structure.** Automated firms have a high proportion of fixed costs to variable costs, while the reverse is true for firms that rely more on manual labor. During periods of increased activity, automated firms have a greater proportion of contribution to profit per increased sales dollar than do labor-intensive firms. During periods of decreased activity, however, automated firms have a greater diminution of contribution to profit per decreased sales dollar than do labor-intensive firms.

GLOSSARY OF KEY TERMS

Account analysis Examining the composition of the balance in a general ledger account to determine if its fixed and variable portions can be identified.

Activity base An item or event that has a cause-and-effect relationship with the incurrence of a variable cost. A variable cost may be measured in terms of its activity base.

Committed cost A fixed cost that continues for a long period of time and is not reversible in the short term.

Contribution format income statement An income statement for managerial use that is classified into fixed and variable cost categories instead of into the functional categories of a traditional income statement.

Contribution margin Sales revenues minus variable costs.

Contribution margin per unit (CMPU) Contribution margin divided by the number of units sold.

Contribution margin ratio (CMR) Contribution margin divided by sales revenue.

Cost behavior   The way in which a cost reacts to a change in business activity.

Cost structure   The relationship between a firm's fixed and variable costs.

Discretionary cost   Fixed costs that are reversible after short periods of time.

Engineering analysis   An engineer's detailed study of a production process to determine what its costs should be.

Fixed cost   A total cost that remains constant within a given range of activity and period of time. However, the *per-unit* cost decreases with increased output.

Gross margin   Net sales revenue minus manufacturing cost of goods sold.

High-low method   A method of analyzing mixed costs that considers only two observations out of a series of time periods, normally the highest and lowest costs. The difference in cost between the two periods is then compared to the difference in activity to derive the variable portion of the cost.

Marginal cost   The cost to produce one additional unit.

Mixed cost   A cost containing both fixed and variable elements.

Relevant range   The span of activity levels near its optimum level that a firm chooses for its operations. A firm usually operates within this range, although production may occasionally vary from this norm.

Semivariable cost   A mixed cost consisting of two components—a basic fixed charge and a variable charge based on the level of activity.

Step-variable cost   A mixed cost consisting of a series of fixed cost increments over short ranges of production within the relevant range.

Variable cost   A total cost that varies proportionately with output. However, the *per-unit* cost is constant within a given range of production.

APPENDIX 5–A   **MIXED COST ANALYSIS—SCATTER DIAGRAMS AND THE LEAST SQUARES METHOD**

When a firm wishes to analyze mixed costs into their fixed and variable portions based on *all* observations for a period of time instead of merely using the highest and lowest costs, it may use either the least squares method or a scatter diagram (scattergraph). The **least squares method** is a *statistical analytic technique* used to separate mixed costs into their fixed and variable components. All observations are used to fit a regression line so that the squared deviations from the line of each of the observations cancel out and are equal to zero. The **regression line** represents the average of all of the observations. A **scatter diagram** is a graph on which an entire series of observations are plotted and then *visually* fit with a regression line. The vertical distances of the points on either side of the line cancel each other out.

Mixed Cost Analysis—Scatter Diagram

A scatter diagram is an attempt to construct a regression line by plotting all observations on a graph and visually estimating a line that is representative of all the points plotted. It is not an attempt to connect any two observations, as is done in the high-low method. For example, here are the maintenance costs of the Sonar Company:

Month	Machine-Hours	Monthly Cost
January	2,500	$ 5,000
February	2,800	5,200
March	3,000	5,300
April	3,400	5,700
May	4,000	6,100
June	5,000	7,100
July	7,000	8,500
August	9,000	10,100
September	10,000	11,000
October	6,000	7,800
November	3,000	5,300
December	2,600	5,100

The 12 points reflecting the Sonar Company's machine-hours and monthly costs are plotted in Illustration 5–10. (Only 11 points actually appear because March and November are the same.) The solid sloping line is the fitted line that best approximates the regression line. Once the regression line is fitted, it is extrapolated to the Y intercept (vertical axis). The fixed cost can then be ascertained in the same way as in the high-low graphical solution. It is the solid horizontal line in Illustration 5–10. The variable cost for any month can be obtained by subtracting the fixed cost from the month's total cost. The fixed portion of the maintenance costs can be estimated at $2,900 per month. This solution differs somewhat from the $3,000 figure that was obtained using the high-low method, even though the same data were used. Such a discrepancy is to be expected.

The regression line in a scatter diagram may show some inaccuracy because it is visually fitted. However, the degree of inaccuracy may not be significant and the results may be satisfactory for many business applications. There are two principal advantages to this technique. First, it is based on all observations rather than on only the highest and lowest costs, and second, it allows the fixed cost to be easily calculated.

Least Squares Method

Some management accountants object to the use of scatter diagrams because of the imprecision of the visual-fit approach. Instead, they employ the least squares method to analyze mixed costs. The procedure requires the simultaneous solution of two linear equations so that the squared deviations from the regression line of each of the plotted points cancel out (are equal to zero). Least squares analysis measures the average change in a variable (in our example, maintenance cost) in relation to a unit of activity (here, machine-hours).

Most businesses use some form of computer processing and, accordingly, are apt to employ a more sophisticated technique to segregate mixed costs than the high-low method. The conceptual basis of the computer-applied approach is based on least squares analysis. Even firms that do not have

ILLUSTRATION 5–10   **Sonar Company: Scatter Diagram—Maintenance Costs**

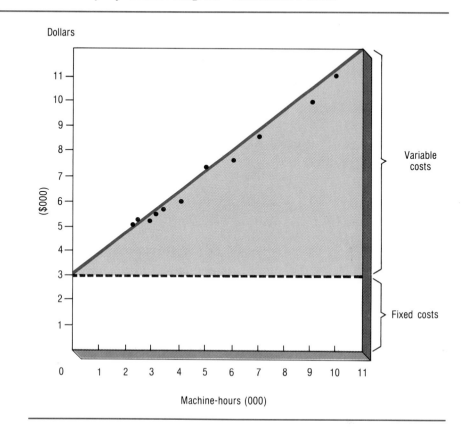

computer capability may wish to use the more sophisticated least squares method by performing the operations manually.

The equation for a linear function (straight line) with one independent variable is:

$$Y = a + bX$$

where

Y = The dependent variable
a = The constant
b = The slope of the line
X = the independent variable

The **dependent variable** is the total cost *(Y)* after performing the mathematical operations dictated by the equation $Y = a + bX$. The **independent variable** is the variable (unit of activity) that can take on any nonnegative value and affects the outcome of the dependent variable (the value of X in the equation $Y = a + bX$).

When an analysis is based on this equation, it is called **simple regression** because the dependent variable is based on *one* independent variable. When regression analysis has more than one independent variable, it is called **multiple regression**, which is considerably more complex. Multiple regression applications can be found in advanced cost and managerial accounting textbooks and in statistics textbooks.

The equations needed to perform the least squares analysis are:

$$\Sigma XY = a\,\Sigma X + b\,\Sigma X^2 \tag{1}$$
$$\Sigma Y = na + b\,\Sigma X \tag{2}$$

where

$a = $ Fixed cost
$b = $ Variable cost
$n = $ Number of observations
$X = $ Activity measure (hours, etc.)
$Y = $ Total mixed cost

The solution to these equations, based on the same data used for the scatter diagram, is:

Month	Machine-Hours	Monthly Cost	(000)	(000)
	X	Y	XY	X²
January	2,500	$ 5,000	$ 12,500	6,250
February	2,800	5,200	14,560	7,840
March	3,000	5,300	15,900	9,000
April	3,400	5,700	19,380	11,560
May	4,000	6,100	24,400	16,000
June	5,000	7,100	35,500	25,000
July	7,000	8,500	59,500	49,000
August	9,000	10,100	90,900	81,000
September ...	10,000	11,000	110,000	100,000
October	6,000	7,800	46,800	36,000
November ...	3,000	5,300	15,900	9,000
December ...	2,600	5,100	13,260	6,760
Totals	58,300	$82,200	$458,600	357,410

Substituting in the equations, we obtain:

$$\$458,600,000 = 58,300a + 357,410,000b \tag{1}$$
$$\$82,200 = \quad 12a + \quad\quad 58,300b \tag{2}$$

Dividing equation 1 by 1,000, we obtain:

$$\$458,600 = 58.3a + 357,410b \tag{3}$$
$$\$82,200 = \quad 12a + 58,300b \tag{2}$$

To solve the equations simultaneously, equation 3 is multiplied by 12 and equation 2 is multiplied by 58.3. The results after subtracting equation 5 from equation 4 are:

$$[12 \times (3)] \; \$5,503,200 = 699.6a + 4,288,920b \qquad \textbf{(4)}$$
$$[58.3 \times (2)] \; \$4,792,260 = 699.6a + 3,398,890b \qquad \textbf{(5)}$$
$$\$ \; 710,940 = \qquad\qquad 890,030b$$
$$\$.7988 = b$$

The variable portion of maintenance costs is $.7988 per machine-hour. The fixed portion is now calculated by substituting the value of b in either equation 1 or equation 2. Equation 2 is selected because it produces smaller numbers to work with. The substituted equation 2 becomes:

$$\$82,200 = 12a + 58,300(\$.7988)$$
$$\$82,200 = 12a + \$46,570$$
$$\$82,200 - \$46,570 = 12a$$
$$\$35,630 = 12a$$
$$\$2,969 = a$$

The fixed portion of the mixed cost is thus $2,969 per month. A comparison of this amount with the amount computed using the high-low method earlier in the chapter shows that the computation of $3,000 per month for fixed costs is a good approximation of the least squares approach. The variable rate of $.7988 per machine-hour as computed by least squares is also close to the $.80 per machine-hour computed using the high-low method. In fact, in this case, the results obtained by high-low appear to make the least squares approach unnecessary from a cost/benefit point of view. However, the results of the two methods may not always be so similar, and when this is the case, the least squares method can be justified.

Short-Cut Method of Least Squares. When performed manually, the least squares method can become burdensome because of the large numbers involved in the multiplication operations. Fortunately, there is a **short-cut method** based on the statistical concept of subtracting the mean $(\overline{X})$ of all the observations from each observation before proceeding with the solution to the problem. Since all observations are reduced by $\overline{X}$, the relationship of each observation to all observations remains unchanged, and all the numbers are smaller.

Using the same data from the Sonar Company, let us employ the short-cut method to determine fixed and variable costs. The first step is to compute the $\overline{X}$ of X and the $\overline{Y}$ of Y. From the least squares computations, the sum of $X = 58,300$ and the sum of $Y = \$82,200$. Dividing both of these sums by 12 (n) observations, the means are:

$$\overline{X} = 58,300 \div 12 = 4,858$$
$$\overline{Y} = \$82,200 \div 12 = \$6,850$$

ILLUSTRATION 5–11   Short-Cut Approach to Least Squares Method

Month	(1) Machine-Hours X $\bar{X}=4{,}858$	(2) Maintenance Cost Y $\bar{Y}=\$6{,}850$	(3) X'	(4) Y'	(5) (000) X'Y'	(6) (000) X'²
January	2,500	$ 5,000	−2,358	−1,850	$ 4,362	5,560
February	2,800	5,200	−2,058	−1,650	3,396	4,235
March	3,000	5,300	−1,858	−1,550	2,880	3,452
April	3,400	5,700	−1,458	−1,150	1,677	2,126
May	4,000	6,100	− 858	− 750	644	736
June	5,000	7,100	142	250	35	20
July	7,000	8,500	2,142	1,650	3,534	4,588
August	9,000	10,100	4,142	3,250	13,462	17,156
September	10,000	11,000	5,142	4,150	21,339	26,440
October	6,000	7,800	1,142	950	1,085	1,304
November	3,000	5,300	−1,858	−1,550	2,880	3,452
December	2,600	5,100	−2,258	−1,750	3,951	5,099
Totals	58,300	$82,200	4*	–0–	$59,245	74,168

$$\text{Variable cost} = \frac{X'Y'}{X'^2} = \frac{\$59{,}245}{74{,}168} = \$.7988 \text{ per machine-hour,}$$

and the fixed cost is computed as:

$$\bar{Y} = a + b\bar{X}$$
$$\$6{,}850 = a + \$.7988(4{,}858)$$
$$\$6{,}850 = a + \$3{,}881$$
$$\$2{,}969 = a$$

The equation for maintenance cost can be expressed as:

$$Y = \$2{,}969 + \$.7988X$$

---

* Rounding difference.

The solution using the short-cut approach appears in Illustration 5–11. It follows these steps:

1. Subtract the mean from each observation and record the difference as X' and Y'. The sum of X' should always equal zero, as should the sum of Y'. The sum of all deviations from a population mean must equal zero.

2. Multiply each X' by Y' and sum the results.

3. Multiply X' by itself (obtaining X'^2) and sum the results.

4. Divide the result obtained in step 2 by the result obtained in step 3. This produces the variable portion of the cost.

5. Using the equation $\bar{Y} = a + b\bar{X}$, substitute the variable portion b and solve for the fixed cost.

Note that the short-cut method produces the same result as the regular method of least squares.

ILLUSTRATION 5–12   Sonar Company: Computer Solution to Least Squares Regression

```
DO YOU WISH TO PRINT THE DATA JUST READ IN *
?
YES
   2500.000    5000.000
   2800.000    5200.000
   3000.000    5300.000
   3400.000    5700.000
   4000.000    6100.000
   5000.000    7100.000
   7000.000    8500.000
   9000.000   10100.000
  10000.000   11000.000
   6000.000    7800.000
   3000.000    5300.000
   2600.000    5100.000
DO YOU WISH TO CHANGE SOME VALUES
?
NO

SPECIFY THE COLUMN NUMBER OF THE DEPENDENT VARIABLE
?
2

SPECIFY THE COLUMN NUMBER OF THE INDEPENDENT VARIABLE
?
1

DO YOU WISH THE REGRESSION LINE TO PASS THROUGH THE ORIGIN
?
NO

INTERCEPT  . . . . . . . . . . .    2969.25220
REGRESSION COEFFICIENT . . . .        0.79878
```

As mentioned earlier, much time can be saved by performing regressions on a computer. A regression solution for the Sonar Company data, prepared on a computer, is shown in Illustration 5–12. The *intercept* corresponds to the fixed cost per month, and the *regression coefficient* corresponds to the variable cost per machine-hour.

**GLOSSARY
OF KEY TERMS—
APPENDIX 5–A**

Dependent variable The total cost *(Y)* after performing the mathematical operations dictated by the equation $Y = a + bX$.

Independent variable The variable (a unit of activity) that can take on any nonnegative value and affects the outcome of the dependent variable (the value of X in the equation $Y = a + bX$).

Least squares method An analytic technique used to separate mixed costs into their fixed and variable components. All observations are used in such a manner that the squared deviations from the regression line of each of the observations cancel out and are equal to zero. (See **regression line.**)

Multiple regression   A method for analyzing mixed costs into their fixed and variable components that uses two or more independent variables to arrive at the dependent variable.

Regression line   A line that is fitted to a series of observations plotted on a graph so that it represents the average of all the observations.

Scatter diagram   A graph on which an entire series of observations are plotted and then visually fit with a regression line. The vertical distances of the points on either side of the line cancel each other out.

Scattergraph   See **scatter diagram.**

Short-cut method of least squares   A variation of the least squares method in which smaller numbers are used by subtracting the mean of a series of variables from each observation. The results are identical to that produced by the least squares method.

Simple regression   A method of analyzing mixed costs into their fixed and variable components that uses only one independent variable to arrive at the dependent variable and is based on the equation of $Y = a + bX$.

QUESTIONS

1. Is the economist's total cost behavior pattern linear or curvilinear? Why is that so? What does the economist's cost graph look like?

2. What is the relevant range? What is its significance?

3. Why do accountants use a linear cost assumption for solving business problems?

4. What is a mixed cost? Give an example of one and explain why it is mixed.

5. Is there more than one method used to analyze mixed costs into their fixed and variable components? Name the method(s).

6. What is meant by account analysis of mixed costs? Is it useful in all cases? Explain.

7. What is meant by engineering cost analysis of mixed costs? Is it an effective technique for analyzing mixed costs? Explain.

8. What is meant by high-low analysis of mixed costs? Describe the technique.

9. What is (are) the principal weakness(es) of the high-low method?

10. Why are traditional income statements generally not useful for decision making? What statement format is better than the income statement?

11. If a change in sales revenue is expected without a change in selling price or cost, and the contribution margin is known, how can this be used to project the effect of the sales revenue change on net income?

12. What is the contribution margin ratio? How is it used?

13. What is the contribution margin per unit? How is it used?

14. What is meant by "cost structure" and why is it important? Use an example to demonstrate its application.

For Appendix 5–A

15. The least squares method is a linear method and is based on what equation? Explain each term in the equation.

16. What is the difference between simple regression and multiple regression?

17. What is a scatter diagram? How is it constructed?

18. What are the linear equations used to solve a least squares problem? Explain what each symbol means.

19. Is there a short-cut method for solving a least squares problem? On what theory is it based? Does it produce an identical answer to the regular least squares method?

20. How is the short-cut least squares method computed?

EXERCISES

5-1 High-Low Method

Items 1 and 2 are based on the following information:

Maintenance costs of a company are to be analyzed for purposes of constructing a budget. Examination of past records disclosed the following costs and volume measures:

	Highest	Lowest
Cost per month	$39,200	$32,000
Machine-hours	24,000	15,000

1. Using the high-low point method of analysis, the estimated variable cost per machine-hour is
   a. $1.25.
   b. $12.50.
   c. $0.80.
   d. $0.08.

2. Using the high-low technique, the estimated annual fixed cost for maintenance expenditures is
   a. $447,360.
   b. $240,000.
   c. $230,400.
   d. $384,000.

(AICPA adapted)

5-2 High-Low Method

Departmental overhead for the repair department of the X Company at the following levels of activity are as follows:

	40,000 Machine-Hours	60,000 Machine-Hours
Total overhead	$48,000	$60,000

The breakdown of the overhead at the 40,000-hour level is as follows:

Rent (fixed)	$20,000
Repair parts (variable)	8,000
Salaries (mixed)	20,000
Total	$48,000

Required a. Compute the estimated cost of repair parts at the 60,000-hour level.
  b. Compute the estimated salaries cost at the 60,000-hour level.
  c. Compute the fixed cost for the repair department.
  d. Prepare a cost formula for the repair department.
  e. Prepare an estimate of overhead costs for the repair department at the 50,000-hour level.

5–3 High-Low Method

1. Paine Corporation wishes to determine the fixed portion of its electricity cost (a semivariable cost), as measured against direct labor-hours, for the first three months of 19x7. Information for the first three months of 19x7 is as follows:

	Direct Labor-Hours	Electricity Cost
January 19x7	34,000	$610
February 19x7	31,000	585
March 19x7	34,000	610

What is the fixed portion of Paine's electricity cost, rounded to the nearest dollar?
  a. $283.
  b. $327.
  c. $372.
  d. $408.

2. Total production costs for Gallop, Inc., are budgeted at $230,000 for 50,000 units of budgeted output and at $280,000 for 60,000 units of budgeted output. Because of the need for additional facilities, budgeted fixed costs for 60,000 units are 25 percent more than budgeted fixed costs for 50,000 units. How much is Gallop's budgeted variable cost per unit of output?
  a. $1.60.
  b. $1.67.
  c. $3.00.
  d. $5.00.
(Hint: Set up two equations and solve them simultaneously.)

(AICPA adapted)

5–4 High-Low Method

The Bonar Company incurred the following inspection costs for the first six months of 19x4:

Month	Units Produced	Inspection Costs
January	3,500	$4,900
February	4,000	5,400
March	2,000	3,000
April	2,500	3,600
May	5,000	6,600
June	4,500	6,100

The above cost behavior is representative of the full year.

Required   *a.*   Using the high-low method, compute the fixed cost per month and the variable cost per unit.

           b.   Prepare the cost formula for inspection costs.

           c.   If the Bonar Company had an activity level of 3,000 units for the month of July 19x4, what would the expected costs be for the month?

5–5   Preparation of Contribution Format Income Statement

The Conar Company had the following income statement prepared for the year 19x5:

CONAR COMPANY
Income Statement
For the Year Ended December 31, 19x5

Sales	$1,000,000
Cost of goods sold	750,000
Gross margin	250,000
Marketing and administrative costs	150,000
Net income	$ 100,000

Included in the cost of goods sold are $200,000 of fixed manufacturing costs. The marketing and administrative costs include salespersons' commissions and other variable costs to the extent of $50,000. The balance of the marketing and administrative costs are fixed.

Conar Company manufactures and sells only one product at a selling price of $20 per unit.

Required   *a.*   Recast the income statement into a contribution format statement.

           b.   Compute the contribution margin ratio for the company.

           c.   Compute the contribution margin per unit for the company.

5–6   Cost Behavior Pattern Using the High-Low Method

The Donar Company had the following costs incurred for the months of June and July 19x6:

	June	July
Direct materials	$ 50,000	$ 75,000
Direct labor	75,000	112,500
Overhead	140,000	160,000
Total costs	$265,000	$347,500
Units produced	50,000	75,000

Required   *a.*   Compute the unit costs for the months of June and July showing the breakdown for each month analyzed into direct materials, direct labor, and overhead.

           b.   Compute the amount of fixed cost per month and the amount of variable cost per unit.

c. Prepare the cost formula for the company.

d. What should the costs incurred be for August if the anticipated production is 60,000 units?

5-7 Make-or-Buy Decision Requiring Fixed and Variable Cost Analysis

The Xyon Company has purchased 80,000 pumps annually from Kobec, Inc. The price has increased each year and reached $68 per unit last year. Because the purchase price has increased significantly, Xyon management has asked that an estimate be made of the cost to manufacture it in its own facilities. Xyon's products consist of stamping and castings. The company has little experience with products requiring assembly.

The engineering, manufacturing, and accounting departments have prepared a report for management which included the estimate shown below for an assembly run of 10,000 units. Additional production employees would be hired to manufacture the subassembly. However, no additional equipment, space, or supervision would be needed.

The report states that total costs for 10,000 units are estimated at $957,000 or $95.70 a unit. The current purchase price is $68 a unit, so the report recommends a continued purchase of the product.

Components (outside purchases)	$120,000
Assembly labor[1]	300,000
Factory overhead[2]	450,000
General and administrative overhead[3] . .	87,000
Total costs	$957,000
Fixed overhead	50% of direct labor dollars
Variable overhead	100% of direct labor dollars
Factory overhead rate	150% of direct labor dollars

[1] Assembly labor consists of hourly production workers.
[2] Factory overhead is applied to products on a direct labor dollar basis. Variable overhead costs vary closely with direct labor dollars.
[3] General and administrative overhead is applied at 10 percent of the total cost of material (or components), assembly labor, and factory overhead.

Required Was the analysis prepared by the engineering, manufacturing, and accounting departments of Xyon Company and the recommendation to continue purchasing the pumps which followed from the analysis correct? Explain your answer and include any supportive calculations you consider necessary.

(CMA adapted)

5-8 (Appendix 5-A): Least Squares Method

The controller of the Connecticut Electronics Company believes that the identification of the variable and fixed components of the firm's costs will enable the firm to make better planning and control decisions. Among the costs the controller is concerned about is the behavior of indirect supplies cost. He believes there is some correlation between the machine-hours worked and the amount of indirect supplies used.

A member of the controller's staff has suggested that a simple linear regression model be used to determine the cost behavior of the indirect supplies. The regression equation shown below was developed from 40 pairs of observations using the least squares method of regression. The regression equation and related measures are as follows:

$$S = \$200 + \$4H$$

where:

$$S = \text{Total monthly costs of indirect supplies}$$
$$H = \text{Machine-hours per month}$$

Required *a.* When a simple linear regression model is used to make inferences about a population relationship from sample data, what assumptions must be made before the inferences can be accepted as valid?

b. Assume the assumptions identified in requirement *a* are satisfied for the indirect supplies cost of Connecticut Electronics Company.
   (1) Explain the meaning of "200" and "4" in the regression equation $S = \$200 + \$4H$.
   (2) Calculate the estimated cost of indirect supplies if 900 machine-hours are to be used during a month.

(CMA adapted)

5–9 **(Appendix 5–A): Least Squares Method Cost Analysis (Regular Equation Approach)**

The Kent Company provides you with the following activity levels and monthly costs for the first six months of 19x4:

| | | (in thousands) |
Month	Units	Product Cost
January	30	$370
February	35	420
March	40	460
April	45	520
May	54	620
June	60	670

Required *a.* Compute the fixed cost per month and the variable cost per unit using the *regular least squares method.*

b. Prepare the equation for analyzing mixed costs for the Kent Company. (Use the form of $Y = a + bX$.)

c. Compute the estimated costs for August if the company is expected to produce 38,000 units during the month.

5–10 **(Appendix 5–A): Least Squares Method Cost Analysis (Short-Cut Approach)**

The Kent Company provides you with the following activity levels and monthly costs for the first six months of 19x4:

Month	Units	(in thousands) Product Cost
January	30	$370
February	35	420
March	40	460
April	45	520
May	54	620
June	60	670

Required

a. Compute the fixed cost per month and the variable cost per unit using the *short-cut least squares method.*

b. Prepare the equation for analyzing mixed costs for the Kent Company. (Use the form of $Y = a + bX$.)

c. Compute the estimated costs for August if the company is expected to produce 38,000 units during the month.

5–11 (Appendix 5–A): Least Squares Method

Labor-hours and production costs for the last four months of 19x9, which you believe are representative for the year, were as follows:

Month	Labor- Hours	Total Production Costs
September	2,500	$ 20,000
October	3,500	25,000
November	4,500	30,000
December	3,500	25,000
Total	14,000	$100,000

Based upon the above information and using the least squares method of computation with the letters listed below, select the best answer for each of questions 1 through 5.

Let a = Fixed production costs per month
b = Variable production costs per labor-hour
n = Number of months
x = Labor hours per month
y = Total monthly production costs
Σ = Summation

1. The equation(s) required for applying the least squares method of computation of fixed and variable production costs could be expressed
   a. $\Sigma xy = a\Sigma x + b\Sigma x^2$.
   b. $\Sigma y = na + b\Sigma x$.
   c. $y = a + bx^2$.
       $\Sigma y = na + b\Sigma x$.
   d. $\Sigma xy = a\Sigma x + b\Sigma x^2$.
       $\Sigma y = na + b\Sigma x$.
2. The cost function derived by the least squares method
   a. Would be linear.

    b. Must be tested for minima and maxima.

    c. Would be parabolic.

    d. Would indicate maximum costs at the point of the function's point of inflection.

3. Monthly production costs could be expressed

    a. $y = ax + b$.

    b. $y = a + bx$.

    c. $y = b + ax$.

    d. $y = \Sigma a + bx$.

4. Using the least squares method of computation, the fixed monthly production cost of trivets is approximately

    a. $10,000.

    b. $9,500.

    c. $7,500.

    d. $5,000.

5. Using the least squares method of computation, the variable production cost per labor-hour is

    a. $6.

    b. $5.

    c. $3.

    c. $2.

(AICPA adapted)

5–12 **(Appendix 5–A): Least Squares Method**

Armer Company is accumulating data to be used in preparing its annual profit plan for the coming year. The cost behavior pattern of the maintenance costs must be determined. The accounting staff has suggested that linear regression be employed to derive an equation in the form of $y = a + bx$ for maintenance costs. Data regarding the maintenance hours and costs for last year and the results of the regression analysis are as follows:

	Hours of Activity	Maintenance Costs
January	480	$ 4,200
February	320	3,000
March	400	3,600
April	300	2,820
May	500	4,350
June	310	2,960
July	320	3,030
August	520	4,470
September	490	4,260
October	470	4,050
November	350	3,300
December	340	3,160
Sum	4,800	43,200
Average	400	3,600
Average cost per hour (43,200 ÷ 4,800) = $9		
a coefficient		684.65
b coefficient		7.2884

1. In the standard regression equation of $y = a + bx$, the letter b is best described as the
   a. Independent variable.
   b. Dependent variable.
   c. Constant coefficient.
   d. Variable coefficient.
   e. Coefficient of determination.

2. The letter y in the standard regression equation is best described as the
   a. Independent variable.
   b. Dependent variable.
   c. Constant coefficient.
   d. Variable coefficient.
   e. Coefficient of determination.

3. The letter x in the standard regression equation is best described as the
   a. Independent variable.
   b. Dependent variable.
   c. Constant coefficient.
   d. Variable coefficient.
   e. Coefficient of determination.

4. If Armer Company uses the high-low method of analysis, the equation for the relationship between hours of activity and maintenance cost would be
   a. $y = 400 + 9.0x$.
   b. $y = 570 + 7.5x$.
   c. $y = 3,600 + 400x$.
   d. $y = 570 + 9.0x$.
   e. Some equation other than those given above.

5. Based upon the data derived from the regression analysis, 420 maintenance-hours in a month would mean the maintenance costs would be budgeted at
   a. $3,780.
   b. $3,461.
   c. $3,797.
   d. $3,746.
   e. Some amount other than those given above.

(CMA adapted)

PROBLEMS   **5–13**   **Preparation of Contribution Format Statement Using High-Low Analysis**

The Honar Company wishes to prepare a budgeted income statement for 19x6. It has available its income statements for the two prior years. However, the company wishes to experiment with an income statement prepared using the contribution format that it plans to use for various types of decision strategies contemplated for 19x6.

The income statements for 19x5 and 19x4 are as follows:

HONAR COMPANY
Income Statement
For the Years Ended December 31

	19x5	19x4
Sales	$1,500,000	$1,200,000
Cost of sales:		
Direct materials	150,000	120,000
Direct labor	225,000	180,000
Manufacturing overhead	430,000	400,000
Total cost of sales	805,000	700,000
Gross margin	695,000	500,000
Less: Marketing and administrative costs	315,000	300,000
Net income	$ 380,000	$ 200,000

Sales for both years were at $50 per unit. Manufacturing overhead consisted of:

	19x5	19x4
Factory rent	$180,000	$180,000
Indirect labor	40,500	35,400
Utilities	50,000	41,000
Miscellaneous overhead	159,500	143,600
Totals	$430,000	$400,000

Marketing and administrative costs include commissions to salespersons of 5 percent of sales. The balance of the marketing and administrative costs are fixed.

There were no beginning or ending inventories and none are expected for 19x6. All costs and selling prices are expected not to change for the year 19x6.

Required   *a.*   For each item of overhead, identify if it is (F) fixed, (V) variable, or (M) mixed.

         b.   Segregate each mixed cost into its fixed and variable components using the high-low method.

         c.   Prepare a cost formula for each mixed cost.

         d.   Prepare an income statement using the contribution format for 19x6. The projected sales volume is 26,000 units.

5–14   **Preparation of Contribution Format Income Statement and Changes in Sales Volume**

The Shure Company had the following income statement prepared for the year 19x5:

SHURE COMPANY
Income Statement
For the Year Ended December 31, 19x5

Sales	$1,000,000
Cost of goods sold	750,000
Gross margin	250,000
Marketing and administrative costs	150,000
Net income	$ 100,000

Included in the cost of goods sold are $490,000 of fixed manufacturing costs. The marketing and administrative costs include salespersons' commissions and other variable costs to the extent of $40,000. The balance of the marketing and administrative costs are fixed.

Shure Company manufactures and sells only one product at a selling price of $40 per unit.

Required   *a.* Recast the income statement into a contribution format statement.
   b. Compute the contribution margin ratio for the company.
   c. Compute the contribution margin per unit for the company.
   d. During 19x5, the economy was very sluggish. For 19x6, the president of the company either expects sales to increase 20 percent or decrease 30 percent depending on who wins the national presidential election. In either case, the company's president does not expect to change selling prices. Compute the expected change in net income for both possibilities. (You may wish to compute the expected changes using one method and check your calculations using another method.)

5–15   Preparation of Traditional and Contribution Income Statements Using the High-Low Method

The Adnil Company had the following costs incurred for the months of June and July 19x6:

	June	July
Direct materials	$ 50,000	$ 80,000
Direct labor	75,000	120,000
Overhead	140,000	170,000
Total costs	$265,000	$370,000
Units produced	50,000	80,000
Marketing costs	$ 80,000	$ 92,000
Administrative costs	90,000	96,000

There were no opening or closing inventories for either month. The selling price of the company's single product is $12 per unit.

Required   *a.* Compute the unit costs for the months of June and July showing the breakdown for each month analyzed into direct materials, direct labor, and overhead.

b. Compute the amount of fixed cost per month and the amount of variable cost per unit separately for:
   (1) Overhead.
   (2) Marketing costs.
   (3) Administrative costs.
c. Prepare cost formulas for the following:
   (1) Overhead.
   (2) Marketing costs.
   (3) Administrative costs.
d. The sales manager predicts that 60,000 units will be sold during August. You are asked to prepare projected income statements using:
   (1) The traditional format.
   (2) The contribution format.

5–16 Preparation of Estimated Traditional and Contribution Income Statements Using High-Low Cost Analysis Coupled with Price Changes

The Mountain Company closed for vacation on June 30, 19x3, and on July 4, 19x3, a fire totally destroyed the company's premises including all of its books and records. Fortunately, the firm's independent auditors had copies of the firm's annual reports. Condensed income statements of the firm appear below.

	19x2	19x1
MOUNTAIN COMPANY **Income Statements** **For the Years Ended December 31, 19x2, and 19x1**		
Sales revenue	$1,200,000	$1,000,000
Cost of sales:		
Direct materials	120,000	100,000
Direct labor	240,000	200,000
Manufacturing overhead—actual	296,000	280,000
Cost of sales	656,000	580,000
Gross margin	544,000	420,000
Other costs:		
Marketing	138,000	130,000
Administrative	172,000	160,000
Total	310,000	290,000
Net income	$ 234,000	$ 130,000

After conferring with the president and sales manager of the company, it was ascertained that:

1. The company manufactures only one product and previously sold it for $10 per unit. Effective January 1, 19x3, the price was increased by 10 percent.
2. Effective January 1, 19x3, the price of raw materials increased by 5 percent. There were no price increases in 19x1 or 19x2.
3. All of the variable marketing costs are due to salespersons' commissions. Effective January 1, 19x3, salespersons' commissions were increased by 10 percent.

4. The number of units sold for the six-month period ended June 30, 19x3, was 40,000.
5. The company had no inventories on June 30, 19x3, and December 31, 19x2.
6. Other than the information provided above, all fixed and variable costs during 19x3 were incurred in the same pattern as for 19x1 and 19x2.

Required a. Prepare an estimated traditional income statement for the six months ended June 30, 19x3.

b. Recast your income statement from (a) above into the contribution format.

5–17   Identification of Cost Behavior Patterns

On a lined sheet of paper, number the first 10 lines from 1 through 10. Select the graph which matches the numbered factory cost or period cost data and write the letter identifying the graph on the appropriate numbered line.

The vertical axes of the graphs represent *total* dollars of cost, and the horizontal axes represent production. In each case, the zero point is at the intersection of the two axes. The graphs may be used more than once.

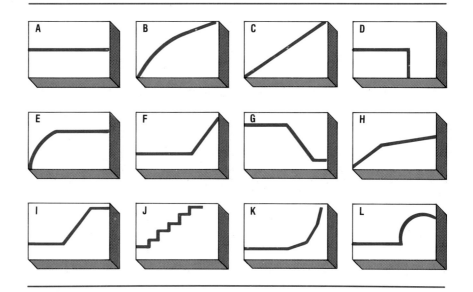

1. Depreciation of equipment, where the amount of depreciation charged is computed by the machine-hours method.
2. Electricity bill—a flat fixed charge, plus a variable cost after a certain number of kilowatt-hours are used.
3. City water bill, which is computed as follows:

First 1 million gallons or less	$1,000 flat fee
Next 10,000 gallons	0.003 per gallon used
Next 10,000 gallons	0.006 per gallon used
Next 10,000 gallons	0.009 per gallon used
Etc.	

4. Cost of lubricant for machines, where cost per unit decreases with each pound of lubricant used (for example, if one pound is used, the cost is $10.00; if two pounds are used, the cost is $19.98; if three pounds are used, the cost is $29.94; with a minimum cost per pound of $9.25).

5. Depreciation of equipment, where the amount is computed by the straight-line method. When the depreciation rate was established, it was anticipated that the obsolescence factor would be greater than the wear-and-tear factor.

6. Rent on a factory building donated by the city, where the agreement calls for a fixed-fee payment unless 200,000 man-hours are worked, in which case no rent need be paid.

7. Salaries of repairmen, where one repairman is needed for every 1,000 hours of machine-hours or less (that is, 0 to 1,000 hours requires one repairman, 1,001 to 2,000 hours requires two repairmen, etc.).

8. Federal unemployment compensation taxes for the year, where the labor force is constant in number throughout year (average annual salary is $12,000 per worker).

9. Cost of raw material used.

10. Rent on a factory building donated by county, where agreement calls for rent of $100,000 less $1 for each direct labor-hour worked in excess of 200,000 hours, but minimum rental payment of $20,000 must be paid.

(AICPA adapted)

5-18 Cost Structure

William and Mary Smith are brother and sister. Each operates the same type of business, but in two different cities. They both employ the same CPA, and there is a free exchange of information and business results between brother and sister.

Although they operate the same type of business, William prefers to have a great deal of flexibility in running his business. Thus, all employees are compensated on an hourly basis and all salespersons are compensated on a commission basis. Alternatively, Mary believes in running her business making maximum use of the latest automation. She employs very few employees, but she has a very large investment in machinery and equipment. Her employees are compensated on an annual basis and her salespeople are paid annual salaries with no commissions.

For 19x5, their condensed income statements were as follows:

	William's	Mary's
Sales revenues	$600,000	$600,000
Costs	510,000	510,000
Net income	$ 90,000	$ 90,000

Their CPA provided each of them with both income statements, and they were pleased to see that they each had the same net income. The CPA also informed them of the following:

William's fixed costs were $ 60,000.
Mary's fixed costs were $390,000.

William notified the CPA that he expects a 40 percent increase in sales volume for 19x6, with no expected changes in selling prices or fixed costs. Mary also notified the CPA that she expects only a 20 percent increase in sales volume, and she too does not expect any changes in selling prices or fixed costs. The CPA was asked to prepare forecasted income statements for 19x6 for both businesses. Condensed versions of his forecasts for 19x6 are as follows:

	William's	Mary's
Sales revenues	$840,000	$720,000
Costs	690,000	534,000
Net income	$150,000	$186,000

After reviewing the results, William had difficulty in understanding why Mary has a projected net income that is $36,000 higher than his projected net income when he anticipates a 40 percent increase in sales volume, while Mary only expects a 20 percent increase in volume.

Required

a. Recast the 19x5 income statements into the contribution format.

b. Do the same for the 19x6 projections.

c. Write an explanation for the apparent inconsistency for William. You may refer to your calculations in (a) and (b) above.

d. Mary is delighted with her projected income statement for 19x6. However, she is concerned with the economic outlook for 19x7. She expects that a 20 percent decline in her 19x5 sales for 19x7 is a real possibility. William also expects a 20 percent decline in his 19x7 sales volume from that of 19x5. Prepare projected income statements for them for 19x7, assuming that each will experience a 20 percent decline from 19x5 sales volume with no changes in selling prices or fixed costs. If the projection for Mary is different from the one prepared for William, explain the difference. (The 19x7 projected income statements should be in the contribution format.)

5–19 (Appendix 5–A): Least Squares Method Cost Analysis (Regular Equation Approach)

The Jonar Company provides you with the following activity levels and monthly costs for the year 19x3:

Month	(in thousands) Units	Product Cost
January	30	$370
February	35	420
March	40	460
April	45	520
May	55	620
June	60	680
July	25	310
August	30	380
September	50	550
October	80	860
November	70	740
December	56	630

Required   a. Construct a scatter diagram to determine the fixed cost per month.

b. Compute the fixed cost per month and the variable cost per unit using the *regular least squares method.*

c. Prepare the equation for analyzing mixed costs for the Jonar Company. (Use the form of $Y = a + bX$.)

5-20   (Appendix 5-A): Least Squares Method Cost Analysis (Short-Cut Approach)

The Jonar Company provides you with the following activity levels and monthly costs for the year 19x3:

		(in thousands)
Month	**Units**	**Product Cost**
January	30	$370
February	35	420
March	40	460
April	45	520
May	55	620
June	60	680
July	25	310
August	30	380
September	50	550
October	80	860
November	70	740
December	56	630

Required   a. Construct a scatter diagram to determine the fixed cost per month.

b. Compute the fixed cost per month and the variable cost per unit using the *short-cut least squares method.*

c. Prepare the equation for analyzing mixed costs for the Jonar Company. (Use the form of $Y = a + bX$.)

5-21   (Appendix 5-A): Mixed Cost Analysis Using Least Squares, Scattergraph, and High-Low Methods

The Ramon Company manufactures a wide range of products at several different plant locations. The Franklin plant, which manufactures electrical components, has been experiencing some difficulties with fluctuating monthly overhead costs. The fluctuations have made it difficult to estimate the level of overhead that will be incurred for any one month.

Management wants to be able to estimate overhead costs accurately in order to plan its operation and financial needs better. A trade association publication to which Ramon Company subscribes indicates that, for companies manufacturing electrical components, overhead tends to vary with direct labor-hours.

One member of the accounting staff has proposed that the cost behavior pattern of the overhead costs be determined. The overhead costs could be predicted from the budgeted direct labor-hours.

Another member of the accounting staff suggested that a good starting place for determining the cost behavior pattern of overhead costs would be an analysis of historical data. The historical cost behavior pattern would provide a basis for estimating future overhead costs. The methods proposed for determining the cost behavior pattern included the high-low method, the scattergraph method, simple linear regression, and multiple regression. Of these methods, Ramon Company decided to employ the high-low method, the scattergraph method, and simple linear regression. Data on direct labor-hours and the respective overhead costs incurred were collected for the past two years. The raw data are as follows:

	Direct Labor-Hours	Overhead Costs
19x3:		
January	20,000	$84,000
February	25,000	99,000
March	22,000	89,500
April	23,000	90,000
May	20,000	81,500
June	19,000	75,500
July	14,000	70,500
August	10,000	64,500
September	12,000	69,000
October	17,000	75,000
November	16,000	71,500
December	19,000	78,000
19x4:		
January	21,000	86,000
February	24,000	93,000
March	23,000	93,000
April	22,000	87,000
May	20,000	80,000
June	18,000	76,500
July	12,000	67,500
August	13,000	71,000
September	15,000	73,500
October	17,000	72,500
November	15,000	71,000
December	18,000	75,000

Required

a. Using the high-low method, determine the cost behavior pattern of the overhead costs for the Franklin plant.

b. Using all 24 observations, determine the cost formula for the Franklin plant using the short-cut least squares method.

c. Prepare a scattergraph for the 24 observations shown above. Fit a regression line to your plotted points. It is not necessary to prepare the cost formula.

d. Calculate the estimate of overhead costs for 22,500 direct labor-hours using:
   (1) The high-low formula.
   (2) The least squares formula.
   (3) The scattergraph. Read the amount directly from your graph.

e. Of the three proposed methods (high-low, scattergraph, linear regression), which one should Ramon Company employ to determine the historical cost behavior pattern of Franklin plant's overhead costs? Explain your answer completely, indicating the reasons why the other methods should not be used.

(CMA adapted)

5–22 **(Appendix 5–A): Preparation of Contribution Income Statement Using Least Squares Cost Analysis (Regular Equation Approach)**

The Kast Company had the following costs incurred and units sold for the months indicated:

	Manufacturing Overhead	Marketing Costs	Units Produced and Sold
19x7:			
January	$160,000	$90,000	75,000
February	140,000	80,000	50,000
March	170,000	92,000	80,000
April	150,000	85,000	60,000
May	155,000	88,000	65,000
June	143,000	81,000	54,000

The company has no inventories at the end of any month, that is, all units produced are sold in the month produced. The following additional information is available:

Direct materials cost . . . . $1.00 per unit
Direct labor cost . . . . $1.50 per unit
Administrative costs per month,
    all fixed . . . . $90,000 per month
Selling price . . . . $10.00 per unit

The company manufactures only one product. For July 19x7, the company estimates that it will sell 70,000 units.

Required *a.* Prepare the cost formulas for manufacturing overhead and marketing costs using the *regular equation approach* of the least squares method.

b. Prepare an estimated income statement for the month of July 19x7 using the contribution format.

5–23 **(Appendix 5–A): Preparation of Contribution Income Statement Using Least Squares Cost Analysis (Short-Cut Approach)**

The Kast Company had the following costs incurred and units sold for the months indicated:

	Manufacturing Overhead	Marketing Costs	Units Produced and Sold
19x7:			
January	$160,000	$90,000	75,000
February	140,000	80,000	50,000
March	170,000	92,000	80,000
April	150,000	85,000	60,000
May	155,000	88,000	65,000
June	143,000	81,000	54,000

The company has no inventories at the end of any month, that is, all units produced are sold in the month produced. The following additional information is available:

Direct materials cost	$1.00 per unit
Direct labor cost	$1.50 per unit
Administrative costs per month,	
all fixed	$90,000 per month
Selling price	$10.00 per unit

The company manufactures only one product. For July 19x7, the company estimates that it will sell 70,000 units.

Required

a. Prepare the cost formulas for manufacturing overhead and marketing costs using the *short-cut approach* of the least squares method.

b. Prepare an estimated income statement for the month of July 19x7 using the contribution format.

5–24 (Appendix 5–A): Least Squares Method Cost Analysis (Regular Equation Approach)

The Konar Company provides you with the following activity levels and monthly costs for the year 19x3:

		(in thousands)
Month	**Units**	**Product Cost**
January	45	$ 400
February	60	520
March	70	600
April	75	640
May	80	700
June	90	770
July	40	370
August	40	370
September	100	860
October	120	1,030
November	95	810
December	85	730

Required

a. Construct a scatter diagram to determine the fixed cost per month.

b. Compute the fixed cost per month and the variable cost per unit using the *regular least squares method*.

c. Prepare the equation for analyzing mixed costs for the Konar Company. (Use the form of $Y = a + bX$.)

5–25 (Appendix 5–A): Least Squares Method Cost Analysis (Short-Cut Approach)

The Konar Company provides you with the following activity levels and monthly costs for the year 19x3:

		(in thousands)
Month	**Units**	**Product Cost**
January	45	$ 400
February	60	520
March	70	600
April	75	640
May	80	700
June	90	770
July	40	370
August	40	370
September	100	860
October	120	1,030
November	95	810
December	85	730

Required

a. Construct a scatter diagram to determine the fixed cost per month.

b. Compute the fixed cost per month and the variable cost per unit using the *short-cut least squares method.*

c. Prepare the equation for analyzing mixed costs for the Konar Company. (Use the form of $Y = a + bX$.)

6

COST, VOLUME, AND PROFIT— ANALYSIS AND RELATIONSHIPS

LEARNING OBJECTIVES	After reading this chapter, you should be able to:

After reading this chapter, you should be able to:

1. Define breakeven sales in both dollars and units and discuss breakeven's uses and limitations.

2. Compute breakeven sales using an algebraic equation, the contribution margin ratio, and the contribution margin per unit.

3. Plot a breakeven graph and describe how it is used.

4. Compute the sales needed to produce a target income.

5. Plot and interpret a profit-volume graph.

6. Compute the margin of safety and explain its significance.

7. Explain what operating leverage is and how it affects profits.

8. Discuss how changes in selling price, cost, and volume affect profits.

9. Use comparative income statements, differential analysis, and the contribution margin approach to compute the effects that changes in selling price, cost, and volume will have on profit.

10. Compute breakeven sales and target income for a multiproduct firm and explain the role of sales mix in those computations.

As noted in Chapter 5, managers use contribution margin in making a variety of decisions. Many managerial decisions require the evaluation of alternative strategies involving costs, profit, and volume. These three factors are interrelated, so a change in one or more of them may well affect the others. When evaluating a particular strategy, a manager usually uses either the contribution margin ratio (CMR) or the contribution margin per unit (CMPU) to assess the effect on profit. Thus, in this chapter we will examine how the CMR and the CMPU are used in different kinds of strategic decisions. In particular, we will focus on **cost-volume-profit (CVP) analysis,** which measures the effects that changes in selling prices, costs, sales volume, and sales mix have on profits.

A special case of CVP is known as breakeven analysis. Because this technique is so widely used, we will examine it first.

BREAKEVEN ANALYSIS

When managers contemplate entering a new market or starting a new product line, they often ask, "What volume of sales do we need to break even?" **Breakeven sales** are the amount of sales revenue that equals total costs, or a zero profit. The amount may be stated in dollars or in units, and it may be ascertained algebraically, arithmetically, or from a breakeven graph. Breakeven sales may be expressed algebraically as:

$$BES = FC + VC$$

where

$$BES = \text{Breakeven sales}$$
$$FC = \text{Fixed costs}$$
$$VC = \text{Variable costs}$$

As an example, assume that:

1. Unar Company's fixed costs for 19x1 are expected to be $180,000.

2. The company's variable costs are 40 percent of sales. This figure, determined by dividing variable costs by sales revenue, is sometimes referred to as the **variable cost ratio (VCR).**

Inserting this information into the breakeven sales equation leads to:

$$BES = \$180,000 + .40BES$$

Transposing, the new equation and its solution are:

$$BES - .40BES = \$180,000$$
$$.60BES = \$180,000$$
$$BES = \frac{\$180,000}{.60}$$
$$BES = \$300,000$$

The proof of this solution would be:

		Percent
Sales	$300,000	100
Variable costs at 40 percent	120,000	40
Contribution margin	180,000	60
Fixed costs	180,000	
Net income	$ –0–	

The Contribution per Unit Approach.   Recall that the Unar Company's fixed costs are $180,000, its selling price per unit is $20, and its variable cost ratio is 40 percent. Therefore, the variable cost per unit is $8 and the contribution margin per unit (CMPU) is $12. **Breakeven units (BEU)**—the number of units that must be sold to equal total costs or yield a zero profit— may be ascertained algebraically as follows:

$$\text{Let } X = \text{Breakeven units}$$
$$FC = \text{Fixed costs}$$
$$VC = \text{Variable costs}$$
$$BES = \$20X$$
$$VC = \$\ 8X$$

Recalling the BES equation of:

$$BES = FC + VC$$

it is possible to substitute for BES and VC to arrive at:

$$\$20X = FC + \$8X$$

Inserting the fixed costs into the equation leads to:

$$\$20X = \$180,000 + \$8X$$

Solving the equation produces:

$$\$20X = \$180,000 + \$8X$$
$$\$20X - \$8X = \$180,000$$
$$\$12X = \$180,000$$
$$X = \frac{\$180,000}{\$12} = 15,000 \text{ units}$$

This solution eliminates the intermediate step of computing BES and then converting that dollar amount into units. It should be noted that the solution contains the following:

$$X = \frac{\$180,000}{\$12}$$

This can be restated as the **contribution margin per unit (CMPU) approach to breakeven**, or:

$$BEU = \frac{FC}{CMPU} = \frac{\$180,000}{\$12} = 15,000 \text{ units}$$

In this approach, BEU is computed simply by dividing fixed costs by CMPU. Because of its simplicity, the CMPU approach is used in this text whenever the BEU is to be computed directly.

The Contribution Margin Ratio Approach to Breakeven. In the algebraic approach to BES, note that the following is found just prior to solving the BES equation:

$$\text{BES} = \frac{\$180,000}{.60}$$

This means that breakeven sales equals fixed costs divided by the contribution margin ratio. Thus, the computation of breakeven sales can be simplified into the **contribution margin ratio (CMR) approach to breakeven,** or:

$$\text{BES} = \frac{\text{FC}}{\text{CMR}}$$

Since the CMR approach to breakeven is much simpler than the algebraic approach, this book will use the CMR in all computations that require breakeven sales in dollars.

When the CMR approach is used to determine BES in dollars, BEU may then be computed as follows:

$$\frac{\text{BES}}{\text{Selling price}} = \frac{\$300,000}{\$20} = 15,000 \text{ units}$$

It is important to note that:

$$\text{BEU} = \frac{\$\text{Fixed costs}}{\$\text{Contribution margin } per \ unit}$$

and

$$\text{BES} = \frac{\$\text{Fixed costs}}{\text{Contribution margin } ratio}$$

Breakeven Graph

In a **breakeven graph,** two lines—the total cost line and the total revenue line—are plotted, and their intersection indicates the breakeven point. For most managerial purposes, we can assume that both the cost line and the revenue line will be linear within the relevant range.

Constructing a Breakeven Graph. To construct a breakeven graph, let us assume that:

1. One product is sold at $20 per unit.

2. The variable cost ratio is 40 percent, and the variable cost per unit is $8.

3. Fixed costs amount to $180,000 annually.

Four steps are necessary to construct a breakeven graph:

1. To locate the slope of the variable cost line, as in Illustration 6–1, select any two random, but realistic, sales volume figures and multiply them by $8, the variable cost per unit. For example, 6,000 units multiplied by $8 equals $48,000 and 21,000 units multiplied by $8 equals $168,000 may be selected as the two points. Then locate the point of 6,000 units on the horizontal axis (volume) that coincides with $48,000 on the vertical axis (dollars) and indicate that point with a dot. Use the same procedure to locate the point where 21,000 units coincides with $168,000. Connect and extend a straight line between the two points. If done properly, the lower extension of the line will intersect the zero point (apex). If a point other than zero is reached, one or both of the dots is misplaced. This line represents the variable costs incurred by the firm at any level of volume.

2. Locate the fixed costs, $180,000, on the vertical ($) axis. Using that point, draw a line parallel to the variable cost line drawn in step 1.

ILLUSTRATION 6–1   Partially Completed Breakeven Graph

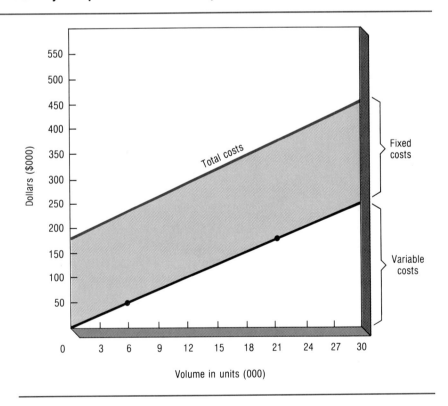

The *partial area below this line and above the variable cost line* represents the firm's fixed costs of $180,000. The *total area below the line* includes both fixed costs and variable costs. Thus, this line is labeled *total cost.* This can also be seen in Illustration 6–1.

3. Again, select any two realistic sales volume figures and multiply them by $20, the selling price per unit. If the figures from step 1 are used, the results would be $120,000 for 6,000 units and $420,000 for 21,000 units. Plot the points and connect them as in step 1. When extended, the line should also intersect at the zero point. This is the sales revenue line, which can be seen in Illustration 6–2.

4. The breakeven point falls where the *revenue line intersects the total cost line,* since at this point total revenues equal total costs. If a perpendicular line is dropped from the breakeven point to the horizontal axis, the breakeven sales in *units* may be obtained from the horizontal axis. In Illustration 6–2, it can be seen that BEU equals 15,000 units. This amount agrees with the algebraic and CMPU calculations. A horizontal

ILLUSTRATION 6–2   Breakeven Graph

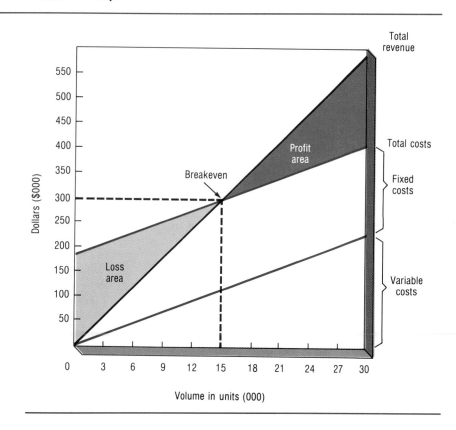

ILLUSTRATION 6–3   **Profit Calculation from Breakeven Graph**

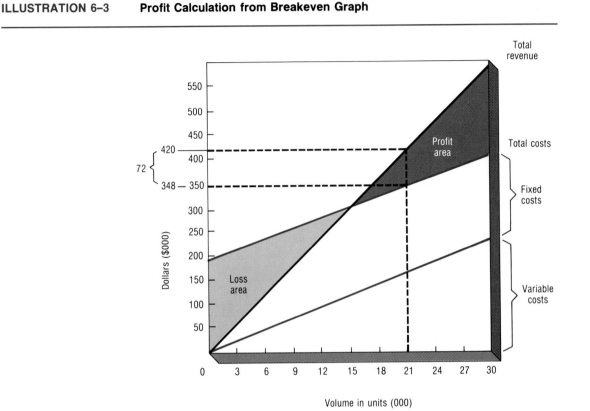

line drawn from the breakeven point to the vertical axis enables a reader of the graph to ascertain the breakeven sales in dollars. In Illustration 6–2, the amount is $300,000, which agrees with the BES calculation using the CMR approach.

Other Uses for Breakeven Graphs.   Breakeven graphs can also be used to calculate profits or losses at different levels of sales volume. For example, to estimate the profit that would be realized at a volume of 21,000 units, a perpendicular is erected at that volume level. The distance between the total revenue line and the total cost line would be the profit earned. This can be seen in Illustration 6–3. The perpendicular intersects the total revenue line at $420,000 and intersects the total cost line at $348,000. The difference between the two, $72,000, represents the profit earned at a volume of 21,000 units.

The amount can also be determined by using the CMPU approach. The computations are:

	Per Unit
Sales price	$20
Variable cost	8
Contribution margin	$12
Contribution margin earned (21,000 × $12)	$252,000
Less: Fixed costs	180,000
Net income	$ 72,000

Targeted Income

A firm's **targeted income** is the amount of income that it wishes to earn. The amount may be designated as *pre-tax operating income* or *after-tax operating income.* After-tax targeted income is discussed in Appendix 6–A at the end of this chapter. Thus, our discussion here is limited to pre-tax targeted operating income.

Many managers use a targeted income as the starting point in deciding which marketing and pricing strategies to use. The formula to determine a specific targeted income is an extension of the breakeven formula. The equation for targeted income is:

$$TI = S - VC - FC$$

where

$$S = \text{Sales revenue}$$
$$VC = \text{Variable costs}$$
$$FC = \text{Fixed costs}$$
$$TI = \text{Targeted income}$$

Since most firms know the value of the targeted income they hope to obtain, the real problem is to determine the sales revenue necessary to produce the targeted income. When sales revenue is the *unknown,* the equation is usually stated as:

$$S = VC + FC + TI$$

ILLUSTRATION 6–4

WEIMAR COMPANY
Income Statement—Contribution Format
For the Year Ended December 31, 19x2

		Percent
Sales (60,000 units at $10)	$600,000	100
Variable costs (60,000 at $4)	240,000	40
Contribution margin	360,000	60
Fixed costs	240,000	
Net income	$120,000	

Let us consider the income statement of the Weimar Company shown in Illustration 6–4. If the Weimar Company wishes to earn a targeted income of $180,000 for 19x3 based on its 19x2 operating results as shown in the illustration, the calculation of total needed sales revenue would be:

$$S = .4S + \$240,000 + \$180,000$$

Transposing .4S, the equation becomes:

$$S - .4S = \$240,000 + \$180,000$$
$$.6S = \$420,000$$

Dividing both sides of the equation by .6S, the result is:

$$S = \frac{\$420,000}{.6}$$

$$S = \$700,000$$

This solution assumes that there will be no change in fixed costs and that the CMR will remain at 60 percent for 19x3. The proof of the solution is:

		Percent
Sales	$700,000	100
Variable costs	280,000	40
Contribution margin	420,000	60
Fixed costs	240,000	
Net income	$180,000	

Note that the next-to-the-last line of the solution is:

$$S = \frac{\$420,000}{.6}$$

This may also be viewed as:

$$\frac{FC + TI}{CMR} = \frac{\$240,000 + \$180,000}{.6} = \frac{\$420,000}{.6}$$

Thus, a simplified approach to the calculation of the sales revenue necessary to produce a targeted income is merely to add targeted income to fixed costs and divide the total by the contribution margin ratio, as was done to compute breakeven sales.

If the answer is desired in units instead of in sales revenue, the same procedure would be used, but the division would be by the contribution margin per unit instead of by the CMR. For Weimar, the unit sales necessary to reach the target income of $180,000 would be:

$$\frac{FC + TI}{CMPU} = \frac{\$240,000 + \$180,000}{\$6} = \frac{\$420,000}{\$6} = 70,000 \text{ units}$$

ILLUSTRATION 6-5   Profit-Volume Graph

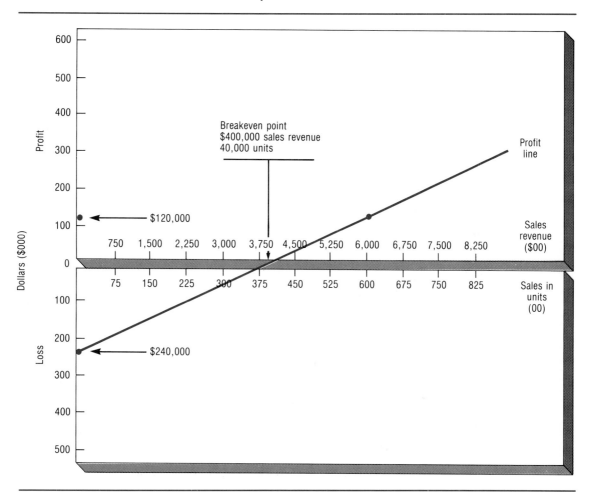

Profit-Volume Graph

A **profit-volume graph** shows a profit and loss line for various levels of sales volume, which enables managers to examine in series the sales (revenue and/or units) required to attain different levels of targeted income. The steps needed to prepare a profit-volume graph, as shown in Illustration 6–5, are:

1. Draw a vertical line at the left of the graph.

2. Place zero profit at the center of the vertical line.

3. Plot a point below the center of the vertical line equal to the fixed costs. This shows that at a zero volume the loss is equal to the fixed costs.

4. Draw a horizontal line at the zero point of the vertical line to the right of the vertical line. This line represents sales (revenues and units).

5. If the breakeven sales are known, indicate that point on the horizontal line and connect that point with the fixed costs point located in step 3. Extend the line above the horizontal line. If the breakeven sales are not known, any profit point that is known may be used instead.

Illustration 6–5 presents a profit-volume graph based on the information in Illustration 6–4. For step 3, $240,000 was used to locate the fixed cost loss point. The Weimar Company makes a profit of $120,000 at the $600,000 sales level, so this point was used. The breakeven sales of $400,000 could also have been used.

Note that the amounts above the horizontal line represent profits while the amounts below the line indicate losses. The horizontal line represents different levels of sales from which a profit or a loss may be deduced. Thus, for sales levels below $400,000 (40,000 units), a loss will occur, while for sales levels above $400,000 (40,000 units), a profit will occur.

For any given level of sales, the profit or loss may be obtained by (1) drawing a vertical line from the pertinent sales level to the profit line and (2) drawing a horizontal line from the intersection on the profit line to the left axis and obtaining the profit or loss from that axis. For any given level of profit or loss, the process is reversed—that is, a horizontal line is drawn from the left axis to the profit line and a vertical line is drawn from that intersection to the sales line. The required sales can then be obtained from the horizontal axis.

For example, assume that a manager wanted to use this profit-volume graph to determine the sales level necessary to increase income by 75 percent. The ramifications of raising the targeted income to $210,000 ($120,000 $\times$ 175 percent) are shown by the dotted lines in Illustration 6–6. The sales revenues would have to rise to $750,000 and the required units would be 75,000.

The main advantage of a profit-volume graph is that any targeted income and its related sales figure can easily be ascertained (within the range included on the graph) without performing separate calculations for each case.

The Margin of Safety

The **margin of safety** is the amount by which a firm's actual sales revenue exceeds its breakeven sales. This is the amount of sales revenue that could be lost before the company's profits would be reduced to zero. The formula for the margin of safety is:

Sales revenue $-$ Breakeven sales $=$ Margin of safety (MS)

Based on Illustration 6–4, Weimar's breakeven sales in dollars and margin of safety can be computed as:

$$\text{BES} = \frac{\text{FC}}{\text{CMR}} = \frac{\$240,000}{.6} = \$400,000$$

$$\text{MS} = \$600,000 - \$400,000 = \$200,000$$

Thus, sales revenue would have to decrease by more than $200,000 before the company would suffer a loss.

ILLUSTRATION 6–6   Profit-Volume Graph

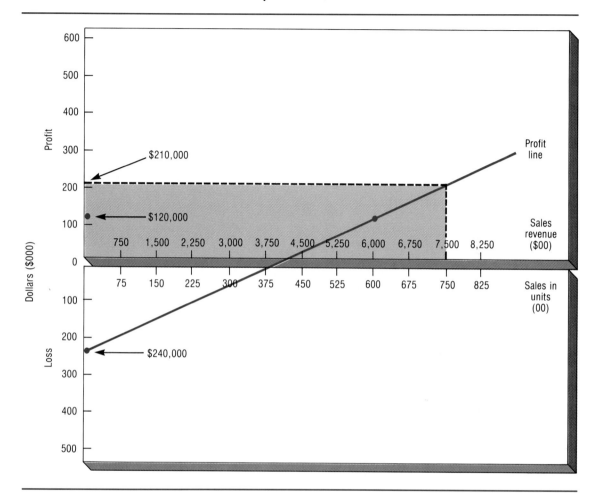

Limiting Assumptions of Breakeven Analysis

To avoid drawing invalid conclusions, managers must understand the assumptions on which breakeven analysis is based. In every breakeven analysis, it is assumed that:

1. All costs are classifiable as either fixed or variable.
2. Variable costs are proportional to sales volume.
3. Fixed costs are constant within the relevant range.
4. The selling price per unit will remain constant.
5. All functions—that is, sales, variable costs, and fixed costs—are linear.
6. The analysis is for either one product or a sales mix that remains constant.

7. The beginning and ending inventory levels are not significantly different.

8. There are no significant fluctuations in the efficiency of the firm's operations.

9. The only factor affecting costs is sales volume.

10. The prices of the cost factors will not change.

11. The general price level will remain relatively constant.

OPERATING LEVERAGE

Operating leverage is the use of fixed costs to increase profits at a faster rate than could be achieved through a corresponding increase in sales. Recall from Chapter 5 that a firm's cost structure depends on the extent of its labor intensiveness versus machine intensiveness. Thus, a firm that is labor intensive and has a low percentage of fixed costs to total costs uses less operating leverage than a machine-intensive firm that has a high percentage of fixed costs to total costs. Since fixed costs are constant within the relevant range, a machine-intensive company that has a 10 percent increase in sales volume will have a larger increase in profit than will a labor-intensive company with a corresponding increase in sales volume.

The **degree of operating leverage** is the measure of how a percentage change in sales volume at a *given level of sales activity* will affect profits. When a firm is operating at or near its breakeven point, the degree of operating leverage is greatest. As profitable operations move further away from the breakeven point, the degree of operating leverage is lessened. Degree of operating leverage is computed by dividing contribution margin by net income.

$$\text{Degree of operating leverage} = \frac{\text{Contribution margin}}{\text{Net income}}$$

Let us analyze the use of operating leverage at the Compu Company and the Made-to-Order Suit Company, first discussed in Chapter 5. Based

ILLUSTRATION 6–7

COMPU COMPANY AND MADE-TO-ORDER SUIT COMPANY
Comparative Cost Structures

	Compu Company		Made-to-Order Suit Company	
	Dollars	Percent	Dollars	Percent
Sales	$500,000	100	$500,000	100
Variable costs	100,000	20	300,000	60
Contribution margin . .	400,000	80	200,000	40
Fixed costs	300,000		100,000	
Net income	$100,000		$100,000	

on their cost structures as reproduced in Illustration 6–7, their degrees of operating leverage are:

$$\text{Compu Company:} \quad \frac{\$400,000}{\$100,000} = 4$$

$$\text{Made-to-Order Company} \quad : \quad \frac{\$200,000}{\$100,000} = 2$$

The degree of operating leverage can then be used to determine what effect a change in sales will have on profits. For example, if each company is expected to experience a 20 percent increase in sales volume, the effect on profits may be calculated as:

Compu Company: $100,000 × 20% × 4 = $80,000
Made-to-Order
Company   : $100,000 × 20% × 2 = $40,000

This can be verified by preparing projected income statements incorporating the 20 percent increase in sales volume, as shown in Illustration 6–8. Note

ILLUSTRATION 6–8

COMPU COMPANY AND MADE-TO-ORDER SUIT COMPANY
Projected Income Statements

	Compu Company		Made-to-Order Suit Company	
	Dollars	Percent	Dollars	Percent
Sales	$600,000	100	$600,000	100
Variable costs	120,000	20	360,000	60
Contribution margin . .	480,000	80	240,000	40
Fixed costs	300,000		100,000	
Net income	$180,000		$140,000	

that the projected income statements show that Compu Company's net income will increase by $80,000 ($180,000 − $100,000) and Made-to-Order Company's profits will increase by $40,000 ($140,000 − $100,000)—the same results obtained by using the degree of operating leverage.

It is important to remember that the degree of operating leverage varies at different levels of sales activity. It is highest near the breakeven sales and lessens with increased sales volume. This pattern can be clearly seen at the Compu Company. The firm's breakeven sales are:

$$\text{BES} = \frac{\text{Fixed costs}}{\text{CMR}} = \frac{\$300,000}{.80} = \$375,000$$

And its degrees of operating leverage at different levels of sales activity are:

Sales	$400,000	$450,000	$500,000	$600,000
Variable costs	80,000	90,000	100,000	120,000
Contribution margin (A)	320,000	360,000	400,000	480,000
Fixed costs	300,000	300,000	300,000	300,000
Net income (B)	$ 20,000	$ 60,000	$100,000	$180,000
Operating leverage (A) ÷ (B)	16	6	4	2.67

Operating leverage figures enable managers to quickly assess the impact on profits when either an increase or a reduction in sales activity is anticipated. For example, assume that the Compu Company is presently operating at a sales level of $500,000 with a degree of operating leverage of 4. If a reduction of 20 percent in sales activity is expected, the effect on profits may be calculated as:

$$\text{Effect on profits} = \text{Net income} \times \text{Increase or decrease in sales} \times \text{Degree of operating leverage}$$

$$\text{Effect on profits} = \$100,000 \times -20\% \times 4 = -\$80,000$$

Thus, net income will be reduced by $80,000, resulting in a $20,000 profit. For verification, this result may be compared with the $20,000 of net income computed for the sales level of $400,000.

COST-VOLUME-PROFIT ANALYSIS

The effects that changes in cost, volume, or selling price will have on net income can be measured by:

1. Preparing an income statement without the contemplated changes and comparing it with an income statement modified to reflect the changes.

2. Preparing a partial income statement that includes only those items that will change and examining the differences that would result.

3. Comparing the present contribution margin with a new contribution margin modified by the contemplated changes. The difference in contribution margins is then adjusted for any changes in fixed costs to produce the net effect that the contemplated changes would have on profits.

One manager may consistently rely on only one of these three methods, while another manager may prefer to use several, with one method acting as a check on another. Regardless of individual preferences, all three methods produce the same result.

Volume Changes Only

A change in the number of units sold without a change in the unit's selling price or manufacturing cost is the simplest situation to evaluate. Since neither the unit's contribution margin ratio nor its contribution margin per unit changes, both figures can be used without adjustment.

If the Weimar Company sold 60,000 units at $10 per unit in 19x2 and

ILLUSTRATION 6–9

WEIMAR COMPANY
Income Statement—Contribution Format
For the Year Ended December 31, 19x2

		Percent
Sales (60,000 units at $10)	$600,000	100
Variable costs (60,000 at $4)	240,000	40
Contribution margin	360,000	60
Fixed costs	240,000	
Net income	$120,000	

its variable costs were $4 per unit while its fixed costs were $240,000 per annum, its contribution income statement would appear as shown in Illustration 6–9. For 19x3, the company is considering a onetime, direct-mail sales campaign. The cost of the mailers and postage will be $5,000, and management estimates that sales volume will increase by 10 percent. At that volume, an additional foreman will be needed at an annual salary of $35,000. All other costs are expected to behave in their normal pattern without any increases. Based on these data, the company's management accountant must prepare an analysis to aid management in deciding whether to undertake the mailing campaign. There are at least three different ways to solve this problem, and all lead to the same conclusion.

The Comparative Income Statement Approach. One method of analyzing this decision problem is the **comparative income statement approach,** in which an income statement modified by the contemplated changes is compared to the unmodified income statement. It requires the following steps:

1. Prepare a contribution income statement without giving effect to any of the proposed changes.

2. Prepare a contribution income statement giving effect to all proposed changes. In this example, the following items must be adjusted:
    a. Sales revenue must be increased by 10 percent. Thus, sales revenue would be $600,000 × 110 percent = $660,000.
    b. Variable costs must be increased by 10 percent because of the increased volume. Variable costs should be $240,000 × 110 percent = $264,000. This amount may also be obtained by multiplying the projected sales revenue by the CMR shown in Illustration 6–9 ($660,000 × 40 percent = $264,000).
    c. Fixed costs must be increased by the additional $5,000 for advertising and $35,000 for the new foreman's salary.

3. Compare the two income statements and select the one that is more advantageous to the firm—generally, the one with the higher net income.

ILLUSTRATION 6–10

WEIMAR COMPANY
Actual and Projected Income Statements—Contribution Format
For the Year Ended December 31

	19x2	Percent	Projected 19x3
Sales	$600,000	100	$660,000*
Variable costs	240,000	40	264,000†
Contribution margin	360,000	60	396,000‡
Fixed costs	240,000		280,000
Net income	$120,000		$116,000

* $600,000 × 110% = $660,000.
† $240,000 × 110% = $264,000, or $660,000 × 40% = $264,000.
‡ $240,000 + $5,000 + $35,000 = $280,000.

The comparative contribution income statements for the Weimar Company are shown in Illustration 6–10.

This method has the advantage of showing both present income and projected income after additional expenditures. Based on this analysis, management should reject the mailing campaign because it will reduce net income by $4,000.

Differential (Incremental) Analysis. This problem could also be solved by considering *only* the proposed changes to determine their net effect. When this approach is used, only the following items are considered:

1. A sales revenue increase of $60,000 ($600,000 × 10 percent).

2. The variable cost increase of $24,000 ($60,000 × 40 percent CMR).

3. The increase in fixed costs of $40,000 ($5,000 + $35,000).

This method is usually referred to as **differential (or incremental) analysis** because only the differences (or increments) are used to arrive at the decision.

The differential analysis for the Weimar Company is summarized in Illustration 6–11. Note that, unlike the comparative income statement approach, differential analysis does not require the reader to compare data. Instead, the net loss of $4,000 is arrived at directly. Differential analysis is direct and succinct and allows the manager to focus on the effects of a proposal without being distracted by normal operating data. Nonetheless, some managers prefer the comparative income statement method because it enables them to better assess the relative size of the proposed changes.

The Contribution Margin Approach. A third way to analyze the impact that the direct-mail campaign would have on Weimar's income is the **contribution margin approach.** This method requires that a new total contribution margin be computed giving effect to the contemplated changes. The difference

ILLUSTRATION 6–11

WEIMAR COMPANY
Projected Differential Income for 19x3

Increase in sales volume ($600,000 × 10 percent) . .		$60,000
Less: Increase in variable costs		
($60,000 × 40 percent CMR)		24,000
Increase in contribution margin		36,000
Less: Increase in printing and mailing	$ 5,000	
Increase in foreman's salary	35,000	40,000
Net (loss)		$ (4,000)

between the new total contribution margin and the current total contribution margin reflects the expected change in that figure. The change in fixed costs is then taken into account to arrive at the net effect of the proposal. The solution using this approach is shown in Illustration 6–12.

Many managers find that the contribution margin approach is the easiest to compute and prefer it because it highlights the immediate effects of the decision to be made. They find that this approach is especially useful in complex problem-solving situations. In any event, all three methods indicate the same result, namely, a loss of $4,000; and in practice, individual preferences often dictate the form in which information is presented to managers.

Changes in Selling Prices and Sales Volume

When a change in selling price is contemplated, an additional step is required to compute its effect on net income. The contribution margin ratio and contribution margin per unit no longer apply, and a new CMR and a new CMPU must be computed. They are also needed for new breakeven computations because the previous ones are invalid.

ILLUSTRATION 6–12

WEIMAR COMPANY
Effects of Contemplated Mailing Campaign

		Per Unit
Selling price ($600,000 ÷ 60,000)		$10
Variable costs at 40 percent		4
Contribution margin		$ 6
Estimated contribution margin ($6 × 66,000) . .		$396,000
Present contribution margin ($6 × 60,000) . . .		360,000
Increase in contribution margin		36,000
Less: Printing and mailing costs	$ 5,000	
Additional foreman	35,000	40,000
Net (loss)		$ (4,000)

Referring to the contribution income statement presented in Illustration 6–9, assume that:

1. Weimar is contemplating raising the selling price by 5 percent to $10.50 per unit.

2. The company expects that its sales volume will decrease by 10 percent to 54,000 units.

3. All costs—fixed and variable—are expected to have the same behavior pattern they had in 19x2.

Any one of the three approaches discussed previously may be used to solve the problem.

The Comparative Income Statement Approach. The solution to the problem using the comparative income statement approach requires the following steps:

1. Adjust sales revenues for two factors—a change in selling price and a change in sales volume. Thus, the $600,000 of sales revenue must be reduced by the volume change of 10 percent ($60,000) and the result ($540,000) increased by the selling price change of 5 percent ($27,000) for an adjusted amount of $567,000.

2. Reduce variable costs of $240,000 by 10 percent ($24,000) to $216,000 because of the reduction in sales volume.

3. Leave fixed costs unchanged.

After giving effect to the proposed changes, the comparative income statements would appear as shown in Illustration 6–13. The results indicate that Weimar should not raise its prices for 19x3 because to do so would decrease net income by $9,000. This occurs despite the increase in Weimar's contribution margin ratio from 60 percent to 62 percent and the increase in its contribu-

ILLUSTRATION 6–13

WEIMAR COMPANY
Actual and Projected Income Statements—Contribution Format
For the Year Ended December 31

	19x2	Percent	Projected 19x3	Percent
Sales	$600,000	100	$567,000*	100
Variable costs	240,000	40	216,000†	38
Contribution margin . .	360,000	60	351,000	62
Fixed costs	240,000		240,000	
Net income	$120,000		$111,000	

* 54,000 × $10.50 = $567,000.
† 54,000 × $ 4.00 = $216,000.

tion margin per unit from $6.00 to $6.50 ($10.50 − $4.00). If the company could decrease some of its fixed costs in response to the 10 percent reduction in volume, the results might be different. This is an example of the kind of decisions that managers routinely face.

Differential (Incremental) Analysis. If differential analysis were used, it would require the following steps:

1. Calculate the decrease in sales revenue due to the decrease in sales volume. This may be calculated as 10 percent × $600,000 = $60,000, *or* 60,000 units × 10 percent = 6,000 units × $10 per unit = $60,000.

2. Calculate the increase in sales revenue due to the increase in selling price. The new sales volume (54,000 units) is multiplied by the increase in selling price (50 cents) to arrive at the desired amount of $27,000.

3. Calculate the decrease in variable cost by multiplying the decrease in sales volume (6,000 units) by the unit cost of $4 to arrive at $24,000. The amount may also be calculated by multiplying the present variable cost of $240,000 by 10 percent, or $24,000.

4. Since fixed costs are unchanged, no calculation for them is necessary.

5. Prepare a summary of the changes.

A summary of the differential analysis approach to solving the problem appears in Illustration 6–14. The advantages of this solution are that it is simpler to compute than the comparative income statement approach and it focuses only on the changes that are expected to occur.

The Contribution Margin Approach. The contribution margin method is usually the simplest to compute. When this approach is used, the following steps are helpful:

1. Calculate the present total contribution margin by multiplying the present sales volume (60,000 units) by the existing contribution margin per unit ($6), which yields $360,000.

2. Calculate the proposed contribution margin by multiplying the proposed sales volume (54,000 units) by the new contribution margin per unit ($6.50), which yields $351,000.

ILLUSTRATION 6–14

WEIMAR COMPANY	
Projected Differential Income for 19x3	
Increase in selling price (54,000 × $.50)	$ 27,000
Decrease in volume (6,000 × $10)	(60,000)
Net decrease in sales revenue	(33,000)
Decrease in variable cost (6,000 × $4)	24,000
Net decrease in net income	$ (9,000)

ILLUSTRATION 6–15

WEIMAR COMPANY
Effects of Contemplated Price Reduction

	Per Unit
Selling price contemplated	$10.50
Variable cost	4.00
Contribution margin	$ 6.50

Effects of price reduction:

Estimated contribution margin ($6.50 × 54,000)	$351,000
Present contribution margin ($6.00 × 60,000)	360,000
Loss on proposed price increase	$ (9,000)

3. Ignore fixed costs because they are unaffected by the proposal.

4. Compare the results.

Illustration 6–15 presents the comparison of the two contribution margins and the effect of the proposal on net income. Note that the $9,000 loss indicated by this method coincides with the amounts reached by the other two methods.

The main advantage of the contribution margin approach is its simplicity. However, some managers may find the information shown in Illustration 6–15 too skimpy. For this reason, familiarity with all three methods is desirable.

Changes in Variable Unit Costs

Whenever a change in variable unit cost is contemplated, the present contribution margin ratio and contribution margin per unit must be adjusted to reflect the cost change. An exception would occur if a compensating change in the selling price were made in order to maintain the existing contribution margin ratio. Nonetheless, in such a case, the contribution margin per unit would still change. On the other hand, if the contribution margin per unit were maintained, the contribution margin ratio would change.

For example, assume that a company's present sales are 10,000 units at $10 per unit, with variable costs of $4 per unit. The cost of the product is expected to rise 10 percent to $4.40, but the company wishes to maintain its existing contribution margin ratio. What should the product's new selling price be? Since the present variable cost ratio is 40 percent ($4.00 ÷ $10.00 = 40%), the new selling price would be $11.00 ($4.40 ÷ .40 = $11). However, the new CMPU would be $6.60, while the existing CMPU is $6.00 ($10.00 − $4.00). To maintain the CMPU at $6.00, the new selling price would have to be $10.40, and the new CMR would drop to 57.69 percent. It is important to remember these changes to avoid making errors in CVP analysis.

The Weimar Company's contribution format income statement for 19x2

ILLUSTRATION 6–16

WEIMAR COMPANY
Income Statement—Contribution Format
For the Year Ended December 31, 19x2

		Percent
Sales (60,000 units at $10)	$600,000	100
Variable costs (60,000 at $4)	240,000	40
Contribution margin	360,000	60
Fixed costs	240,000	
Net income	$120,000	

is reproduced in Illustration 6–16. The company wishes its management accountant to evaluate the following proposal:

1. The company would like to upgrade the quality of its only product. By using more expensive raw materials and making a slight design change, the company believes that it can sell the revised product at $15 per unit. However, at this price the company estimates that it will only sell 54,000 units annually.

2. The increased variable costs will amount to $3.50 per unit for a total variable unit cost of $7.50 per unit.

3. A quality control inspector will have to be employed to make sure that the employees maintain the higher standard of quality. The inspector will earn an annual salary of $25,000.

The contribution margin analysis for this situation is presented in Illustration 6–17. It indicates that the company should go ahead with the change

ILLUSTRATION 6–17

WEIMAR COMPANY
Effects of Contemplated Upgrade in Quality

	Per Unit	Percent
Selling price contemplated	$ 15.00	100
Variable cost contemplated	7.50	50
Contribution margin	$ 7.50	50
Effects of change:		
Estimated contribution margin ($7.50 × 54,000)	$405,000	
Present contribution margin (Illustration 6–16)	360,000	
Increase in contribution margin	45,000	
Less: Increase in fixed costs	25,000	
Increase in net income from expected change	$ 20,000	

in quality because net income will be increased by $20,000 if the estimates prove to be accurate. The same result can be obtained through the use of the comparative income statement approach or the differential analysis approach.

Whenever there is a change in selling price, variable unit cost, or fixed cost, a new breakeven sales in dollars and units must be computed when needed. The new CMR and/or CMPU is used with the new fixed costs.

SALES MIX

Most firms manufacture and sell more than one product. Thus, they must consider sales mix in their breakeven and CVP analyses. A firm's **sales mix** is its complete set of products classified by the relative amount that each product contributes to total sales revenue.

For example, the Yonar Company manufactures and sells three products—almond cookies, breadsticks, and croutons (hereafter referred to as A, B, and C). They are sold in the ratio of $3:1:4$—that is, three cases of almond cookies are sold for each case of breadsticks and four cases of croutons are sold for each case of breadsticks. Selling prices and variable costs per case of the three products are:

	A	B	C
Selling prices	$20	$20	$10
Variable costs	13	9	6
Contribution margin	$ 7	$11	$ 4

The contribution margins of A, B, and C cannot be used in this raw form. Instead, they must be weighted by the number of cases of each product expected to be sold. The combined total of the products' adjusted contribution margins is referred to as the **weighted contribution margin per mix (WCMPM).** This figure, once computed, is used in the same way as the contribution margin per unit would be in a single-product firm. To compute the weighted contribution margin per mix:

1. Multiply each product's contribution margin by its unit sales to arrive at its contribution margin per mix.

2. Sum the individual contribution margins per mix.

For example, as shown in Illustration 6–18, the contribution margin of product A is $7 per case and three cases of almond cookies are sold per mix. Thus, the contribution margin per mix of product A is $21. Following the same procedure, the contribution margin per mix of product B is $11 and the contribution margin per mix for product C is $16. We then sum these three figures to arrive at the WCMPM of $48.

ILLUSTRATION 6–18

YONAR COMPANY
Sales Mix and Weighted Contribution Margin per Mix

	Product A	B	C	Totals
Selling price	$20	$20	$10	
Variable costs	13	9	6	
Contribution margin	$ 7	$11	$ 4	
Units sold per mix	3	1	4	
Contribution margin per mix	$21	$11	$16	$ 48
Sales revenue per mix	$60	$20	$40	$120

Next, based on the WCMPM, the **contribution margin ratio per mix (CMRM)** can be derived. The contribution margin ratio of the mix is a combined weighted-average contribution margin ratio that, like the WCMPM, includes all of a firm's products. And it is used by multiproduct firms in place of the contribution margin ratio. The contribution margin ratio of the mix is determined by dividing the WCMPM by the total sales revenue per mix. Based on Illustration 6–18, we see that Yonar's total sales revenue per mix is $120. Thus:

$$\text{CMRM} = \frac{\$48}{\$120} = 40\%$$

Sales Mix Breakeven Analysis

Although the breakeven sales calculations for a multiproduct firm are similar to those for a single-product firm, they are valid only for a particular sales mix.

Yonar Company would like to know what its breakeven sales would be in dollars and units if its estimated fixed costs are $480,000 per annum. In this case, the breakeven calculations would be the same as for a single-product firm. They are:

$$\text{BES} = \frac{\text{FC}}{\text{CMRM}} = \frac{\$480,000}{.40} = \$1,200,000$$

and:

$$\text{BEU} = \frac{\text{FC}}{\text{WCMPM}} = \frac{\$480,000}{\$48} = 10,000 \text{ mixes}$$

The proof of the calculations is:

	Product			
	A	**B**	**C**	**Total**
Sales	$600,000*	$200,000†	$400,000‡	$1,200,000
Variable costs	390,000§	90,000‖	240,000 #	720,000
Contribution margin	$210,000	$110,000	$160,000	480,000
Fixed costs				480,000
Net income				$ –0–

* 10,000 × 3 × $20.
† 10,000 × 1 × $20.
‡ 10,000 × 4 × $10.
§ 10,000 × 3 × $13.
‖ 10,000 × 1 × $ 9.
10,000 × 4 × $ 6.

The breakeven sales in units are:

$$\text{Product A} = 10,000 \times 3 = 30,000 \text{ units}$$
$$\text{B} = 10,000 \times 1 = 10,000 \text{ units}$$
$$\text{C} = 10,000 \times 4 = 40,000 \text{ units}$$

Changes in Mix and CVP Analysis

The preceding calculations are valid only if a change in sales mix is not contemplated. However, changes in mix do occur due to variations in consumer demand, changes in costs, selling prices, and volume, and many other reasons. Any change in sales mix requires new computations for the contribution margin ratio per mix and the weighted contribution margin per mix. This is true even if the total sales revenue or number of mixes remains unchanged.

Yonar Company has reason to believe that its customers are becoming very conscious of diet and are eating more salads. The company expects to sell only one third of its present sales of almond cookies and to double its sales of croutons. Breadstick sales are expected to remain unchanged. Cost behavior patterns are expected to remain the same.

The president of Yonar Company asked the firm's management accountant to prepare calculations showing how many cases of each product must be sold and the sales revenue needed to:

1. Produce a targeted income of $240,000 if the sales mix remains unchanged.

2. Break even if the expected change in sales mix materializes.

3. Produce a targeted income of $240,000 if the change in sales mix materializes.

The targeted income calculations for requirement 1 are:

$$\text{Sales revenue} = \frac{FC + TI}{CMRM} = \frac{\$480,000 + \$240,000}{.40} = \$1,800,000$$

$$\text{Sales mixes} = \frac{FC + TI}{WCMPM} = \frac{\$480,000 + \$240,000}{\$48} = 15,000 \text{ mixes}$$

Sales in Units:

$$\text{Product } A = 15,000 \times 3 = 45,000 \text{ units}$$
$$B = 15,000 \times 1 = 15,000 \text{ units}$$
$$C = 15,000 \times 4 = 60,000 \text{ units}$$

ILLUSTRATION 6–19

YONAR COMPANY
Sales Mix and Weighted Contribution Margin per Mix

	Product A	B	C	Totals
Selling price	$20	$20	$10	
Variable costs	13	9	6	
Contribution margin	$ 7	$11	$ 4	
Units sold per mix	1	1	8	
Contribution margin per mix	$ 7	$11	$32	$ 50
Sales mix	$20	$20	$80	$120

For requirement 2, a new weighted contribution margin per mix and a new contribution margin ratio per mix are needed. Illustration 6–19 shows the calculations for the WCMPM ($50). With the CMRM equal to $41\frac{2}{3}$ percent ($50 ÷ $120), the new breakeven sales and breakeven units may be computed as:

$$\text{BES} = \frac{\text{FC}}{\text{CMRM}} = \frac{\$480,000}{.4167} = \$1,152,000$$

$$\text{BEU} = \frac{\text{FC}}{\text{WCMPM}} = \frac{\$480,000}{\$50} = 9,600 \text{ mixes}$$

The proof of the calculation is:

	Product A	B	C	Total
Sales	$192,000*	$192,000†	$768,000‡	$1,152,000
Variable costs	124,800§	86,400‖	460,800 #	672,000
Contribution margin	$ 67,200	$105,600	$307,200	480,000
Fixed costs				480,000
Net income				$ –0–

* 9,600 × 1 × $20.
† 9,600 × 1 × $20.
‡ 9,600 × 8 × $10.
§ 9,600 × 1 × $13.
‖ 9,600 × 1 × $ 9.
9,600 × 8 × $ 6.

The breakeven sales in units are:

$$
\begin{aligned}
\text{Product A} &= 9{,}600 \times 1 = 9{,}600 \\
\text{B} &= 9{,}600 \times 1 = 9{,}600 \\
\text{C} &= 9{,}600 \times 8 = 76{,}800
\end{aligned}
$$

Note that in this case, the sales revenue per sales mix remains unchanged at $120. Nevertheless, because of the change in sales mix, the weighted contribution margin per mix changed from $48 to $50 and the contribution margin ratio per mix increased from 40 percent to $41\frac{2}{3}$ percent. Thus, the change caused by the shift in the sales mix from the less profitable cookies to the more profitable croutons may be favorable to Yonar Company because WCMPM increased by $2, and the BES decreased from $1,200,000 to $1,152,000. If the number of units (mixes) actually sold remains unchanged, then a favorable condition exists. Profits will increase by $2 multiplied by the number of mixes sold.

Generally, less profitable merchandise is easier to sell than more profitable merchandise. Thus, when a change in sales mix is contemplated, the shift should emphasize the more profitable merchandise to the greatest extent possible. A change in sales mix may increase a firm's profits when this strategy is practiced. However, a change in sales mix may also decrease profits when a firm is unable to implement this strategy due to market factors.

The solution to requirement 3 for a targeted income of $240,000 is:

$$
\text{Sales revenue} = \frac{\text{FC} + \text{TI}}{\text{CMRM}} = \frac{\$480{,}000 + \$240{,}000}{.4167} = \$1{,}728{,}000
$$

$$
\text{Sales mixes} = \frac{\text{FC} + \text{TI}}{\text{WCMPM}} = \frac{\$480{,}000 + \$240{,}000}{\$50} = 14{,}400 \text{ mixes}
$$

Sales in Units:

$$
\begin{aligned}
\text{Product A} &= 14{,}400 \times 1 = 14{,}400 \text{ units} \\
\text{B} &= 14{,}400 \times 1 = 14{,}400 \text{ units} \\
\text{C} &= 14{,}400 \times 8 = 115{,}200 \text{ units}
\end{aligned}
$$

It is interesting to note that the number of mixes needed to produce the same targeted income of $240,000 decreases from 15,000 under the present mix to 14,400 under the expected mix. If Yonar Company can maintain a volume of 15,000 mixes after the change in mix occurs, profits will be $30,000 (15,000 × $2) higher than if the change did not occur.

A summary of the formulas and approaches used to solve CVP applications in this chapter appears in Illustration 6–20.

ILLUSTRATION 6–20   **Formulas and Methods for Use in Solving CVP Applictions**

Formula or Method	Use
1. BES = FC + VC	Breakeven sales in dollars
2. BES = $\dfrac{FC}{CMR}$	Breakeven sales in dollars
3. $S = FC + $VC	Breakeven sales in units
4. BEU = $\dfrac{FC}{CMPU}$	Breakeven sales in units
5. S = VC + FC + TI	Sales necessary to produce a desired income
6. S = $\dfrac{FC + TI}{CMR}$	Sales dollars necessary to produce a desired income
7. S = $\dfrac{FC + TI}{CMPU}$	Sales in units necessary to produce a desired income
8. MS = S − BES	Margin of safety—the amount of sales that could be lost before a loss would result
9. $\dfrac{\text{Contribution margin}}{\text{Net income}}$	Operating leverage—the use of fixed costs to increase profits at a faster rate than sales revenue
10. Comparative income statement approach	Comparing the results of operations from two alternative CVP decisions by preparing an income statement for each alternative
11. Differential (incremental) analysis	Considering only the items that differ between two alternative CVP decisions
12. Contribution margin approach	Comparing the new contribution margin and any change in fixed costs with the existing contribution margin and fixed costs for a CVP decision

SUMMARY

A question that managers often ask when they are about to enter a new market or make a new product is, "What volume of sales do we need to break even?" This information is helpful in assessing the risk involved in new market and new product decisions. The calculation of **breakeven sales** (in dollars and in units) may be calculated (1) algebraically, (2) by using the **contribution margin ratio,** and (3) by using the **contribution margin per unit.** Regardless of the method used, a firm's costs must be classified into two categories—fixed and variable. The variable cost per unit divided by the unit's selling price is the unit's **variable cost ratio.** Breakeven sales in dollars may be calculated by dividing a firm's fixed costs by its contribution margin ratio. Breakeven sales in units may be calculated by dividing a firm's fixed costs by its contribution margin per unit.

A valuable management tool is the **breakeven graph.** Managers can determine their firm's breakeven sales in dollars and in units directly from such a graph without making arithmetic calculations.

Breakeven sales calculations may also be used to determine the sales needed to produce a **targeted income.** To do so, fixed costs are added to the targeted income and the total is then divided either by the firm's contribution margin ratio to arrive at targeted-income sales revenue or by its contribution margin per unit to produce targeted-income sales in units. A breakeven graph may also be used to determine the sales needed to produce a targeted income. The advantage of using a breakeven graph for this purpose is that any number of targeted-income sales figures, within the range of the graph, may be determined without separate mathematical calculations. A breakeven graph may also be used to determine a firm's income for any given sales level.

A **profit-volume graph** enables managers to assess the effects that changes in sales volume will have on profits or losses. In a profit-volume graph, the profit line is plotted to intersect the sales line. Thus, it differs from a breakeven graph, in which the total cost line intersects the sales line.

The **margin of safety** provides managers with a measure of how much sales can decrease before the firm will operate at a loss. It is computed by subtracting the product's breakeven sales from the current sales level.

The use of **operating leverage** can enable a firm to increase profits at a faster rate than could be achieved through a corresponding increase in sales. The **degree of operating leverage** provides managers with a quick method of calculating the effect on profits of a contemplated change in sales revenue. It is calculated by dividing contribution margin by net income.

Through **cost-volume-profit analysis,** managers can assess the effects that contemplated changes in marketing strategy will have on their firm's net income. The three most common forms of CVP analysis are: (1) **comparative income statements,** in which current data are compared to data that reflect the contemplated changes; (2) **differential (incremental) analysis,** which considers only the items affected by the changes; and (3) the **contribution margin approach,** which compares the existing contribution margin with the contemplated contribution margin and adjusts the difference for any changes in fixed costs.

Most firms manufacture and/or sell a variety of products. In attempting to assess the effects that changes in cost, volume, and selling price will have on profits, managers of multiproduct firms must understand the concept of **sales mix** and the role it plays in computing **contribution margin ratio per mix** and **weighted contribution margin per mix.** A change in sales mix, with or without a change in total sales volume, may have a significant effect on a firm's profit or loss. An increase in the sales volume of one product, with a corresponding decrease in the sales volume of another product, may lead to greater profits if the product with increased volume has a higher contribution margin per unit than the product with decreased volume. Conversely, profits will decrease if the shift in sales volume favors the product with the smaller contribution margin per unit.

When calculating breakeven sales or targeted income for a change in sales mix, a new contribution margin ratio per mix and a new weighted contribution margin per mix must be computed.

GLOSSARY OF KEY TERMS

Breakeven graph A graph in which two lines—the total cost line and the total revenue line—are plotted, and their intersection indicates the breakeven point.

Breakeven sales (BES) The amount of sales equal to total costs, or a zero profit. The amount may be stated in dollars or in units, and it may be ascertained algebraically, arithmetically, or from a breakeven graph.

Breakeven units (BEU) The number of units that must be sold to equal total costs or yield a zero profit.

Comparative income statement approach to CVP analysis A method of assessing the effect on profit of contemplated changes in selling prices and/or costs and/or volume in which an income statement modified by the contemplated changes is compared to the unmodified income statement.

Contribution margin approach to CVP analysis A method of assessing the effect on profit of contemplated changes in selling prices, costs, or volume in which a new total contribution margin is computed giving effect to the contemplated changes. The difference between the new total contribution margin and the current total contribution margin reflects the expected change in that figure. The change in fixed costs is then taken into account to arrive at the net effect of the proposal.

Contribution margin per unit (CMPU) approach to breakeven Fixed costs are divided by the contribution margin per unit to arrive at breakeven sales in units.

Contribution margin ratio (CMR) approach to breakeven Fixed costs are divided by the contribution margin ratio to arrive at breakeven sales in dollars.

Contribution margin ratio per mix (CMRM) A combined, weighted-average contribution margin ratio that includes all of a firm's products and is used by multi-product firms in the same way that the contribution margin ratio is used by single-product firms.

Cost-volume-profit (CVP) analysis The measurement of the effects that changes in selling prices, costs, volume of sales activity, and sales mix have on profits.

Degree of operating leverage A measure of how a percentage change in sales volume at a given level of sales activity will affect profits. It is computed by dividing contribution margin by net income.

Differential (incremental) approach to CVP analysis A method of assessing the effect on profit of contemplated changes in selling prices and/or costs and/or volume in which only those items that are expected to change and the differences they would create are considered.

Margin of safety The amount by which a firm's actual sales revenue exceeds its breakeven sales. This is the amount of sales revenue that could be lost before the company's profits would be reduced to zero.

Operating leverage The use of fixed costs to increase profits at a faster rate than could be achieved through a corresponding increase in sales.

Profit-volume graph A graph showing a profit and loss line for various levels of sales volume, which enables managers to examine in series the sales (revenue and/or units) required to attain different levels of targeted income.

Sales mix   A firm's complete set of products classified by the relative amount that each product contributes to total sales revenue.

Targeted income (targeted-income sales)   The amount of income that a firm wishes to earn, designated as either pre-tax operating income or after-tax operating income.

Variable cost ratio (VCR)   The relationship of variable costs to sales revenue, computed by dividing variable costs by sales revenue.

Weighted contribution margin per mix (WCMPM)   A combined weighted-average contribution margin that includes all of a firm's products and is used by multi-product firms in the same way that the contribution margin per unit is used by single-product firms.

APPENDIX 6–A   **ADDITIONAL TOPICS FOR CVP ANALYSIS**

Targeted-income decision problems sometimes contain complexities that prohibit the use of the contribution revenue margin and contribution margin per unit approaches to cost-volume-profit analysis. Such complexities may occur, for example, when commissions on sales in excess of a specific volume are payable to salespersons, or when targeted income is based on after-tax income rather than on gross income. This kind of targeted income is usually referred to as *targeted net income* to clarify that it is the income that remains *after* the deduction of income taxes.

Special Problem— Commissions

The Zonar Company sells portable radios at the price of $20 per unit. Its variable cost per unit is $12, and its fixed cost per annum is $400,000. In 19x4, the Zonar Company wishes to earn a net income of $210,000; to achieve that end, it intends to offer its sales manager an incentive of $1 per unit on sales in excess of breakeven sales. The president of the company wishes to know how many units must be sold to earn a net income of $210,000. The problem can be solved as follows:

$$\text{Let BES} = \text{Breakeven sales in units (50,000)}$$
$$\text{TI} = \text{Targeted income}$$
$$\text{VC} = \text{Variable costs}$$
$$\text{FC} = \text{Fixed costs}$$
$$\text{C} = \text{Commission}$$
$$\text{X} = \text{Sales in units}$$

$$X = VC + FC + TI + C$$

$$(\$20)X = (\$12)X + \$400,000 + \$210,000 + (\$1)(X - 50,000)$$
$$(\$20)X = (\$12)X + \$400,000 + \$210,000 + (\$1)X - \$50,000$$
$$(\$7)X = \$560,000$$
$$X = 80,000 \text{ units}$$

The proof of the calculation is:

Sales (80,000 × $20)	$1,600,000
Variable cost (80,000 × $12)	960,000
Subtotal	640,000
Fixed cost	400,000
Subtotal	240,000
Commission (80,000 − 50,000) × $1	30,000
Net income	$ 210,000

A nonalgebraic solution would be to use the contribution margin per unit approach for those units above the breakeven sales. The contribution margin per unit for sales above the breakeven mark would be $7 ($8 less the commission of $1), and the computations would be:

$$\text{Above BES} = \frac{\text{TI}}{\text{New CMPU}} = \frac{\$210,000}{\$7} = 30,000 \text{ units}$$

Add: Breakeven sales   50,000 units
Required sales   80,000 units

After-Tax Net Income

Thus far, all targeted income problems considered only income before taxes. Since profitable companies usually pay income taxes, managers may prefer CVP analysis on an after-tax basis. The amount of income a company retains after taxes can be expressed as:

$$\text{NI} = 1 - t$$

where

$$\text{NI} = \text{After-tax net income}$$
$$t = \text{The average tax rate}$$

Using the same information as before—namely, a selling price of $20 per unit, a variable cost of $12 per unit, and fixed costs of $400,000 per annum—the Zonar Company would like to earn $210,000 on an after-tax basis. Its income tax rate is 30 percent of before-tax income.

Let X = Sales in units
FC = Fixed costs
VC = Variable costs
t = Tax rate
NI = After-tax net income

$$X = FC + VC + \frac{NI}{(1-t)}$$

$$(\$20)X = \$400,000 + (\$12)X + \frac{\$210,000}{(1-t)}$$

$$(\$20)X - (\$12)X = \$400,000 + \frac{\$210,000}{.7}$$

$$(\$8)X = \$400,000 + \$300,000$$
$$(\$8)X = \$700,000$$
$$X = 87,500 \text{ units}$$

The proof of the above calculation is:

Sales (87,500 × $20)	$1,750,000
Variable cost (87,500 × $12)	1,050,000
Contribution margin	700,000
Fixed costs	400,000
Income before income taxes	300,000
Income taxes at 30 percent	90,000
Net income	$ 210,000

QUESTIONS

1. Breakeven sales may be computed algebraically. Describe two different approaches to the algebraic solutions and the nature of the answers.

2. Why do some management accountants prefer the contribution margin ratio approach to breakeven analysis? How is it used? Use an example to demonstrate its use.

3. If a firm sells its only product for $20 per unit and its variable costs are 40 percent, construct the algebraic equation that is required for an answer of breakeven sales in dollars if its fixed costs are $360,000 per annum. Solve the equation.

4. How is a targeted income calculated?

5. What is a profit-volume graph and how is it constructed?

6. What is the "margin of safety"?

7. Are there any limiting assumptions to breakeven analysis? If so, what are they?

8. What is operating leverage?

9. What is the degree of operating leverage? How is it computed? Is it the same at all levels of sales activity within the relevant range? Explain.

10. A company's variable cost ratio is 40 percent, and its fixed costs are $600,000 per annum. What are its breakeven sales? Is the answer in dollars or units?

11. A firm's variable cost ratio is 30 percent, its fixed costs are $350,000, and it wishes to earn a targeted income of $140,000. Do you have enough information to compute the required sales in dollars? If so, how much sales revenue is needed to earn the targeted income? If not, what additional information is needed?

12. A firm's variable cost ratio is 35 percent, its fixed costs are $260,000 per annum, and it wishes to earn a targeted income of $130,000. Do you have enough information to compute the number of units that must be sold to earn the targeted income? If so, compute the required sales in units. If not, what additional information is needed?

13. If a firm sells its only product for $40 per unit and its variable costs are 40 percent, construct the algebraic equation that is required for an answer of breakeven sales in units if its fixed costs are $480,000 per annum. Solve the equation.

14. Three approaches have been advanced for solving CVP problems. Briefly explain each approach.

15. When there is a contemplated change in sales volume with no change in selling price or cost, what is true about the CMR and the CMPU after the change?

16. When there is a change in selling price or a change in variable cost, what is true about the CMR and the CMPU?

17. A firm has sales of $800,000 per annum. Its variable cost ratio is 40 percent and its fixed costs are $300,000 per annum. It is contemplating increasing its selling price by 10 percent, which could result in a 12½ percent reduction in volume. Would you recommend the price increase? Why?

18. What is sales mix?

19. How are sales-mix breakeven sales computed?

20. If there is a change in the sales mix, does the CMRM normally remain unchanged? Explain.

EXERCISES **6–1** **Breakeven Analysis**

The Bluebell Company manufactures one product, men's jeans. Last year it had sales of $4.5 million, variable costs of $2.7 million, and fixed costs of $1.2 million.

Required a. Compute the amount of sales dollars needed to break even.

b. The company is contemplating opening another factory to manufacture men's shirts. It plans to sell the shirts for $15 per unit. Variable costs are expected to be $9 per unit, and the fixed costs attributable to the new factory are expected to be $300,000 per year. Compute the amount of sales dollars needed to break even.

c. As an alternative to manufacturing men's shirts, the new factory can be used to manufacture ladies' blouses. As a result of a market survey, the company is certain that it can sell 100,000 blouses for $10 each. Variable costs per blouse would be $6. At this level of sales, the company would break even on the blouse manufacturing. What would the fixed costs be at the new factory opened for this purpose?

6–2 Breakeven Analysis

1. The Oliver Company plans to market a new product. Based on its market studies, Oliver estimates that it can sell 5,500 units in 19x6. The selling price will be $2 per unit. Variable costs are estimated to be 40 percent of the selling price. Fixed costs are estimated to be $6,000. What is the breakeven point?
   a. 3,750 units.
   b. 5,000 units.
   c. 5,500 units.
   d. 7,500 units.

2. At a breakeven point of 400 units sold, the variable costs were $400 and the fixed costs were $200. What will the 401st unit sold contribute to profit before income taxes?
   a. $0.
   b. $0.50.
   c. $1.00.
   d. $1.50.

3. In planning its operations for 19x1 based on a sales forecast of $6 million, Wallace, Inc., prepared the following estimated data:

	Costs	
	Variable	**Fixed**
Direct materials	$1,600,000	
Direct labor	1,400,000	
Factory overhead	600,000	$ 900,000
Marketing costs	240,000	360,000
Administrative costs	60,000	140,000
Total	$3,900,000	$1,400,000

What would be the amount of sales dollars at the breakeven point?
a. $2,250,000.
b. $3,500,000.
c. $4,000,000.
d. $5,300,000.

(AICPA adapted)

6-3 Breakeven Analysis

The following data apply to items 1 and 2.

The statement of income for Davann Company presented below represents the operating results for the fiscal year just ended. Davann had sales of 1,800 tons of product during the current year. The manufacturing capacity of Davann's facilities is 3,000 tons of product.

DAVANN COMPANY
Statement of Income
For the Year Ended December 31, 19x0

Sales	$900,000
Variable costs:	
Manufacturing	315,000
Marketing costs	180,000
Total variable costs	495,000
Contribution margin	405,000
Fixed costs:	
Manufacturing	90,000
Marketing	112,500
Administration	45,000
Total fixed costs	247,500
Net income before income taxes	157,500
Income taxes (40%)	63,000
Net income after income taxes	$ 94,500

1. The breakeven volume in tons of product for 19x0 is
    a.   420 tons.
    b.   1,100 tons.
    c.   495 tons.
    d.   550 tons.
    e.   Some amount other than those shown above.
2. Davann is considering replacing a highly labor-intensive process with an automatic
    machine. This would result in an increase of $58,500 annually in manufacturing
    fixed costs. The variable manufacturing costs would decrease $25 per ton. The
    new breakeven volume in tons would be
    a.   990 tons.
    b.   1,224 tons.
    c.   1,854 tons.
    d.   612 tons.
    e.   Some amount other than those shown above.

                                                                    (CMA adapted)

6-4 **Breakeven Graph**

A breakeven chart, as illustrated below, is a useful technique for showing relationships
between costs, volume, and profits.

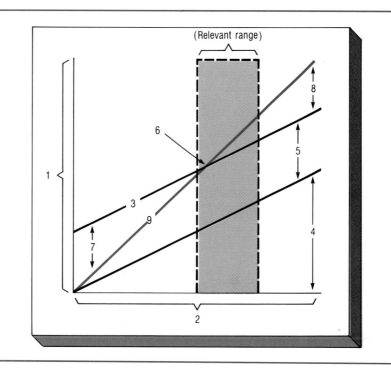

Required   a. Identify the numbered components of the breakeven chart.
           b. Discuss the significance of the concept of the "relevant range" to breakeven
               analysis.

                                                                    (AICPA adapted)

6-5 Construction of a Breakeven Graph

The Elnar Company manufactures one product that it sells for $5 per unit. Variable costs amount to $2 per unit, and fixed costs amount to $150,000 per year.

Required a. Construct a breakeven graph at intervals of 10,000 units on a scale of 10,000 units to 100,000 units.

b. What is the breakeven point in units and sales dollars?

6-6 Construction of a Profit-Volume Graph

Using the information provided in Exercise 6–5, you are asked to:

a. Construct a profit-volume graph.

b. Compute the profit or loss at the following levels of activity:
   (1) 30,000 units.
   (2) 50,000 units.
   (3) 80,000 units.

6-7 Breakeven and CVP Analysis

The Mystic Tie Company manufactures men's ties. Although the firm manufactures different patterns of fabric into ties, they all sell for $8 each and they all have the same raw materials cost.

Fixed costs amount to $240,000 per annum. Breakeven sales for 19x3 amounted to $600,000.

Required a. Compute the firm's contribution margin ratio and contribution margin per unit.

b. For 19x2, actual sales amounted to $800,000. What was the firm's net income for 19x2?

c. For 19x3, the firm is contemplating the use of a more expensive fabric which will increase its variable costs by 60 cents per tie.
   (1) What selling price would be required to maintain the same contribution margin ratio? What would the contribution margin per unit be at this selling price?
   (2) As noted above, the firm plans to upgrade its fabric at a cost of 60 cents per tie, and it also plans to increase its price to $10 each. What would its breakeven sales be for 19x3 if it plans to spend an additional $13,000 for advertising the new ties? Would you recommend the proposal if 65,000 ties can be sold at this price? Why?

6-8 Breakeven and CVP Analysis

The following data apply to items 1 through 3.

The Maxwell Company manufactures and sells a single product. Price and cost data regarding Maxwell's product and operations are as follows:

Selling price per unit	$25.00
Variable costs per unit:	
Raw materials	$11.00
Direct labor	5.00
Manufacturing overhead	2.50
Marketing	1.30
Total variable costs per unit	$19.80
Annual fixed costs:	
Manufacturing overhead	$192,000
Marketing and administrative	276,000
Total fixed costs	$468,000
Forecasted annual sales volume (120,000 units)	$3,000,000

1. Maxwell's breakeven point in units is
   a. 76,667.
   b. 90,000.
   c. 130,000.
   d. 72,000.
   e. Some amount other than those shown above.
2. Maxwell Company estimates that its direct labor costs will increase 8 percent next year. How many units will Maxwell have to sell next year to reach breakeven?
   a. 97,500 units.
   b. 101,740 units.
   c. 83,572 units.
   d. 86,250 units.
   e. None of the above responses is correct.
3. If Maxwell Company's direct labor costs do increase 8 percent, what selling price per unit of product must it charge to maintain the same contribution margin ratio?
   a. $25.51.
   b. $27.00.
   c. $25.40.
   d. $26.64.
   e. None of the above responses is correct.

(CMA adapted)

6-9 Breakeven and CVP Analysis

The following data apply to items 1 through 5.

Siberian Ski Company recently expanded its manufacturing capacity which will allow it to produce up to 15,000 pairs of cross country skis of the mountaineering model or the touring model. The sales department assures management that it can sell between 9,000 and 13,000 of either product this year. Because the models are very similar, Siberian Ski will produce only one of the two models.

The following information was compiled by the accounting department.

	Model	
	Mountaineering	**Touring**
Selling price per unit	$88.00	$80.00
Variable costs per unit	$52.80	$52.80

Fixed costs will total $369,600 if the mountaineering model is produced but will be only $316,800 if the touring model is produced. Siberian Ski Company is subject to a 40 percent income tax rate.

1. The contribution margin rate of the touring model is
   a. 40.0 percent.
   b. 66.0 percent.
   c. 51.5 percent.
   d. 34.0 percent.
   e. Some amount other than those given above.
2. If the Siberian Ski Company sales department could guarantee the annual sale of 12,000 skis of either model, Siberian would
   a. Produce touring skis because they have a lower fixed cost.
   b. Be indifferent as to which model is sold because each model has the same variable cost per unit.
   c. Produce mountaineering skis because they have a lower breakeven point.
   d. Be indifferent as to which model is sold because both are profitable.
   e. Produce mountaineering skis because they are more profitable.
3. How much would the variable cost per unit of the touring model have to change before it had the same breakeven point in units as the mountaineering model?
   a. $2.68/pair increase.
   b. $4.53/pair increase.
   c. $5.03/pair decrease.
   d. $2.97/pair decrease.
   e. Some amount other than those given above.
4. If the variable cost per unit of touring skis decreases by 10 percent, and the total fixed cost of touring skis increases by 10 percent, the new breakeven point will be
   a. Unchanged from 11,648 pairs because the cost changes are equal and offsetting.
   b. 10,730 pairs.
   c. 13,007 pairs.
   d. 12,812 pairs.
   e. Some amount other than those given above.
5. Which one of the following statements is *not* an assumption made when employing a cost-volume-profit study for decision analysis?
   a. Volume is the only relevant factor affecting costs.
   b. Changes in beginning and ending inventory levels are insignificant in amount.
   c. Sales mix is variable as total volume changes.

d. Fixed costs are constant over the relevant volume range.

e. Efficiency and productivity are unchanged.

(CMA adapted)

6–10 Breakeven and CVP Analysis

The Belair Company provides you with the following:

Fixed costs per annum . . .	$ 360,000
Breakeven sales	$1,200,000
Annual sales in units	40,000
Net income	$ 210,000

Required   a. Compute the variable cost ratio.

b. Compute the firm's sales for the year.

c. Compute the firm's variable costs for the year.

d. What is the firm's selling price per unit?

e. If the firm were able to change its variable cost ratio to 60 percent, would the breakeven sales change? If so, what would the new breakeven sales be?

f. If the firm were able to increase its sales volume by 5 percent without a change in its selling price, variable costs, or fixed costs, would this change the breakeven point? If so, by how much? If not, why not?

6–11 Breakeven and CVP Analysis

1. Cost-volume-profit analysis is a technique available to management to understand better the interrelationships of several factors which affect a firm's profit. As with many such techniques, the accountant oversimplifies the real world by making assumptions. Which of the following is *not* a major assumption underlying cost-volume-profit analysis:

a. All costs incurred by a firm can be separated into their fixed and variable components.

b. The product selling price per unit is constant at all volume levels.

c. Operating efficiency and employee productivity are constant at all volume levels.

d. For multiproduct situations, the sales mix can vary at all volume levels.

e. Costs vary only with changes in volume.

The following data apply to items 2 through 4.

Laraby Company produces a single product. It sold 25,000 units last year with the following results:

Sales		$625,000
Variable costs	$375,000	
Fixed costs	150,000	525,000
Net income before taxes		$100,000
Income taxes (45 percent) . . .		45,000
Net income		$ 55,000

In an attempt to improve its product, Laraby is considering replacing a component part in its product that has a cost of $2.50 with a new and better part costing $4.50 per unit in the coming year. A new machine would also be needed to increase plant capacity. The machine would cost $18,000 with a useful life of six years and no salvage value. The company uses straight-line depreciation on all plant assets.

2. What was Laraby Company's breakeven point in number of units last year?
   a. 6,000.
   b. 15,000.
   c. 21,000.
   d. 18,000
   e. None of the above responses is correct.

3. If Laraby Company holds the sales price constant and makes the suggested changes, how many units of product must be sold in the coming year to break even?
   a. 15,300.
   b. 18,750.
   c. 19,125.
   d. 21,000.
   e. None of the above responses is correct.

4. If Laraby Company wishes to maintain the same contribution margin ratio, what selling price per unit of product must it charge next year to cover the increased material costs?
   a. $27.00.
   b. $25.00.
   c. $32.50.
   d. $28.33.
   e. None of the above responses is correct.

(CMA adapted)

6–12 Breakeven and CVP Analysis

The Piper Bear Company manufactures industrial bearings that sell for $10 each. Variable costs are $6 per unit. Fixed costs for the year just ended amounted to $126,000. Sales for the year amounted to 40,000 units.

Required
a. Compute the company's breakeven sales in dollars.
b. What was the company's net income last year?
c. For next year, variable costs are expected to increase by 10 percent. Compute to the nearest dollar:
   (1) The new breakeven sales.
   (2) The expected net income for the coming year if the company can sell 50,000 units and the fixed costs remain unchanged.
d. If the variable costs do increase by 10 percent, what selling price would produce the same contribution margin ratio?

6–13 Breakeven and CVP Analysis

Items 1, 2, and 3 are based on the following information:

FULL TON COMPANY
Financial Projection for Product USA
For the Year Ended December 31, 19x7

Sales (100 units at $100 a unit)		$10,000
Manufacturing cost of goods sold:		
Direct labor	$1,500	
Direct materials used	1,400	
Variable factory overhead	1,000	
Fixed factory overhead	500	
Total manufacturing cost of goods sold		4,400
Gross profit		5,600
Marketing costs:		
Variable	600	
Fixed	1,000	
Administrative costs:		
Variable	500	
Fixed	1,000	
Total marketing and administrative costs		3,100
Operating income		$ 2,500

1. How many units of product USA would have to be sold to break even?
   a. 50.
   b. 58.
   c. 68.
   d. 75.
2. What would the operating income be if sales increase by 25 percent?
   a. $3,125.
   b. $3,750.
   c. $4,000.
   d. $5,000.
3. What would be the sales at the breakeven point if fixed factory overhead increases by $1,700?
   a. $6,700.
   b. $8,400.
   c. $8,666.
   d. $9,200.

(AICPA adapted)

6–14   CVP Analysis

1. Pitt Company is considering a proposal to replace existing machinery used for the manufacture of product A. The new machines are expected to cause increased annual fixed costs of $120,000; however, variable costs should decrease by 20 percent due to a reduction in direct labor-hours and more efficient usage of direct materials. Before this change was under consideration, Pitt had budgeted product A sales and costs for 19x1 as follows:

Sales	$2,000,000
Variable costs	70% of sales
Fixed costs	$ 400,000

Assuming that Pitt implemented the above proposal by January 1, 19x1, what would be the increase in budgeted operating profit for product A for 19x1?

   a. $160,000.
   b. $280,000.
   c. $360,000.
   d. $480,000.

2. Birney Company is planning its advertising campaign for 19x1 and has prepared the following budget data based on a zero advertising expenditure:

Normal plant capacity	200,000 units
Sales	150,000 units
Selling price	$25 per unit
Variable manufacturing costs	$15 per unit
Fixed costs:	
Manufacturing	$800,000
Marketing and administrative	$700,000

An advertising agency claims that an aggressive advertising campaign would enable Birney to increase its unit sales by 20 percent. What is the maximum amount that Birney can pay for advertising and obtain an operating profit of $200,000?

   a. $100,000.
   b. $200,000.
   c. $300,000.
   d. $550,000.

3. Kern Company prepared the following tentative forecast concerning product A for 19x2:

Sales	$500,000
Selling price per unit	$ 5
Variable costs	$300,000
Fixed costs	$150,000

A study made by the sales manager disclosed that the unit selling price could be increased by 20 percent, with an expected volume decrease of only 10 percent. Assuming that Kern incorporates these changes in its 19x2 forecast, what should be the operating income from product A?

   a. $ 66,000.
   b. $ 90,000.
   c. $120,000.
   d. $145,000.

(AICPA adapted)

6–15   CVP Analysis

The High Flyer Company manufactures lures for sport fishing. For 19x2, the company provides the following:

Selling price per unit	$5
Units sold	100,000
Variable costs	$300,000
Fixed costs	$150,000

A market research study indicates that the company could increase its selling price by 20 percent and its sales volume by 10 percent if it spends an additional $50,000 on advertising.

Required a. What is the company's net income for 19x2?

b. What will the company's net income be for 19x3 if it spends the $50,000 for advertising? (Use the differential approach.) Would you recommend the increased advertising cost? Why?

c. As an alternative to the proposal for spending an additional $50,000 for advertising, the firm's sales manager believes that a $25,000 increase in advertising would cause the sales volume to increase by 30 percent if there was no sales price increase. What would the firm's 19x3 income be if this proposal were adopted? (Use the contribution margin approach.) Would you recommend the $25,000 or the $50,000 advertising increase? Why?

6-16 CVP Analysis

The Corvair Company provides you with the following:

Fixed costs per annum ..	$300,000
Sales for the year	$900,000
Selling price per unit	$ 10
Variable cost ratio	40%

Required a. Compute the company's breakeven sales in dollars and units using the contribution margin approaches.

b. The company is planning to reduce the selling price of its only product from $10 to $9. A market survey indicates that volume will increase by 20 percent at that price. At that level of production, fixed costs will increase $10,000. Prepare an analysis of the proposal using the comparative income statement approach in the contribution format. Should the company proceed with the change? Why?

c. The company expects an increase in variable costs (direct materials and direct labor) for the following year. The increase is expected to amount to 60 cents per unit. Compute the new selling price needed to:
1. Maintain the same contribution margin per unit.
2. Maintain the same contribution margin ratio.

6-17 CVP Analysis and Targeted Income

1. Moon Company sells product Q at $6 a unit. In 19x0, fixed costs are expected to be $200,000 and variable costs are estimated at $4 a unit. How many units of product Q must Moon sell to generate operating income of $40,000?
   a. 50,000.
   b. 60,000.
   c. 100,000.
   d. 120,000.
2. Tice Company is a medium-sized manufacturer of lamps. During the year, a new line called "Horolin" was made available to Tice's customers. The breakeven point for sales of Horolin is $200,000 with a contribution margin of 40 percent. Assuming that the profit for the Horolin line during the year amounted to $100,000, total sales during the year would have amounted to
   a. $300,000.
   b. $420,000.
   c. $450,000.
   d. $475,000.

3. Purvis Company manufactures a product that has a variable cost of $50 per unit. Fixed costs total $1 million, allocated on the basis of the number of units produced. Selling price is computed by adding a 10 percent markup to full cost. How much should the selling price be per unit for 100,000 units?
   a. $55.
   b. $60.
   c. $61.
   d. $66.

4. Bert Company has projected cost of goods sold of $2 million including fixed costs of $400,000, and variable costs are expected to be 75 percent of net sales. What will be the projected net sales?
   a. $2,133,333.
   b. $2,400,000.
   c. $2,666,667.
   d. $3,200,000.

5. Warfield Company is planning to sell 100,000 units of product T for $12 a unit. The fixed costs are $280,000. In order to realize a profit of $200,000, what would the variable costs be?
   a. $480,000.
   b. $720,000.
   c. $900,000.
   d. $920,000.

(AICPA adapted)

6-18　CVP Analysis and Targeted Income

1. During March 19x2, Adams Company had sales of $5 million, variable costs of $3 million, and fixed costs of $1.5 million for product M. Assume that cost behavior and unit selling price remain unchanged during April. In order for Adams to realize operating income of $300,000 for product M for April, sales would have to be
   a. $3,750,000.
   b. $4,050,000.
   c. $4,500,000.
   d. $4,800,000.

2. Day Company is a medium-sized manufacturer of lamps. During 19x9, a new line called "Twilight" was made available to Day's customers. The breakeven point for sales of Twilight is $400,000, with a contribution margin of 40 percent. Assuming that the operating profit for the Twilight line for 19x9 amounted to $200,000, total sales for 19x9 amounted to
   a. $600,000.
   b. $840,000.
   c. $900,000.
   d. $950,000.

3. Lindsay Company reported the following results from sales of 5,000 units of product A for the month of June 19x1:

Sales	$200,000
Variable costs	120,000
Fixed costs	60,000
Operating income	20,000

Assume that Lindsay increases the selling price of product A by 10 percent on July 1, 19x1. How many units of product A would have to be sold in July 19x1 in order to generate an operating income of $20,000?

    a.   4,000.

    b.   4,300.

    c.   4,500.

    d.   5,000.

4. Dallas Corporation wishes to market a new product for $1.50 a unit. Fixed costs to manufacture this product are $100,000 for less than 500,000 units and $150,000 for 500,000 or more units. The contribution margin is 20 percent. How many units must be sold to realize net income from this product of $100,000?

    a.   333,333.

    b.   500,000.

    c.   666,667.

    d.   833,333.

5. The Seahawk Company is planning to sell 200,000 units of product B. The fixed costs are $400,000, and the variable costs are 60 percent of the selling price. In order to realize a profit of $100,000, the selling price per unit would have to be

    a. $3.75.

    b. $4.17.

    c. $5.00.

    d. $6.25.

(AICPA adapted)

6–19   CVP Analysis and Margin of Safety

1. A book publisher sells a textbook for $7. The variable cost per book is $5 at the current annual sales volume of 200,000 books; at this volume the publisher is just breaking even. What are the fixed costs?

    a. $200,000.

    b. $1,000,000.

    c. $400,000.

    d. $1,400,000.

    e.   Some amount other than those given above.

2. The Black Company manufactures and sells a specialty perfume. The company budgets a margin of safety of 20 percent for 19x8. Fixed costs are budgeted at $270,000 annually. Variable costs are $6.60 per ounce. If the sales price per ounce is $12, the budgeted level of sales revenue for 19x8 is

    a. $589,330.

    b. $720,000.

    c. $480,000.

    d. $750,000.

    e.   Not shown above.

3. Region Company sells a product for $35 per unit and the variable production and sales costs are $21 per unit. If Region Company adopts a 40 percent increase in selling price of its product, how much can unit sales decline before total profits decline?

    a.   40 percent.

    b.   50 percent.

    c.   57 percent.

d. 100 percent.

e. None of the above responses is correct.

(CMA adapted)

6–20   Breakeven Graph and Profit-Volume Graph

The Decair Company provides you with the following:

Fixed costs per annum . . .	$300,000
Sales for the year	$900,000
Selling price per unit	$10
Variable cost per unit	$4

Required

a. Construct a breakeven graph using 10,000 intervals for units and $100,000 intervals for dollars, from 0 to 100,000 units.

b. Construct a profit-volume graph using the same intervals as in (a).

c. Compute the profit or loss from *each* graph for:

(1) 30,000 units.

(2) 80,000 units

6–21   Profit-Volume Graph

The following data apply to items 1 through 5.

The SAB Company uses a profit-volume graph similar to the one shown below to represent the cost-volume-profit relationships of its operations. The vertical (Y-axis) is the profit in dollars and the horizontal (X-axis) is the volume in units. The diagonal line is the contribution margin line.

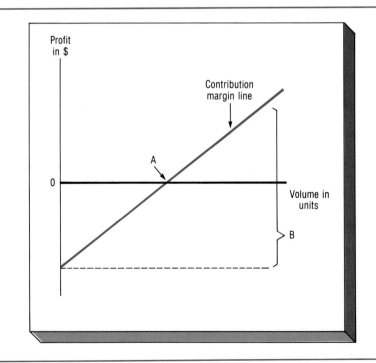

1. Point A on the profit-volume graph represents
    a. The point where fixed costs equal sales.
    b. The point where fixed costs equal variable costs.
    c. A volume level of zero units.
    d. The point where total costs equals total sales.
    e. The point where the rate of contribution margin increases.
2. The vertical distance from the dotted line to the contribution margin line denoted as B on the profit-volume graph represents
    a. The total contribution margin.
    b. The contribution margin per unit.
    c. The contribution margin rate.
    d. Total sales.
    e. The sum of the variable and fixed costs.
3. If SAB Company's fixed cost were to increase,
    a. The contribution margin line would shift upward parallel to the present line.
    b. The contribution margin line would shift downward parallel to the present line.
    c. The slope of the contribution margin line would be more pronounced (steeper).
    d. The slope of the contribution margin line would be less pronounced (flatter).
    e. The contribution margin line would coincide with the present contribution margin line.
4. If SAB Company's variable costs per unit were to increase but its unit selling price stays constant,
    a. The contribution margin line would shift upward parallel to the present line.
    b. The contribution margin line would shift downward parallel to the present line.
    c. The slope of the contribution margin line would be more pronounced (steeper).
    d. The slope of the contribution margin line would be less pronounced (flatter).
    e. The slope of the contribution margin line probably would change but how it would change is not determinable.
5. If SAB Company decided to increase its unit selling price to offset exactly the increase in the variable cost per unit,
    a. The contribution margin line would shift upward parallel to the present line.
    b. The contribution margin line would shift downward parallel to the present line.
    c. The slope of the contribution margin line would be more pronounced (steeper).
    d. The slope of the contribution margin line would be less pronounced (flatter).
    e. The contribution margin line would coincide with the present contribution margin line.

(CMA adapted)

6-22   Preparation of Contribution Format Income Statement and Use of Operating Leverage

The Conar Company had the following income statement prepared for the year 19x5:

CONAR COMPANY
Income Statement
For the Year Ended December 31, 19x5

Sales	$1,000,000
Cost of goods sold	750,000
Gross margin	250,000
Marketing and administrative costs	150,000
Net income	$ 100,000

Included in the cost of goods sold are $200,000 of fixed manufacturing costs. The marketing and administrative costs include salespersons' commissions and other variable costs to the extent of $50,000. The balance of the marketing and administrative costs are fixed.

Conar Company manufactures and sells only one product at a selling price of $20 per unit.

Required   a. Recast the income statement into a contribution format statement.
b. Compute the degree of operating leverage.
c. For 19x6, the company expects sales to increase by 30 percent. Using the operating leverage you computed in (b), compute the projected net income for 19x6.

6-23   Sales-Mix Breakeven and Targeted Income

The Baby Face Doll Company manufactures a doll that is sold with one set of clothing. It also sells a kit of clothing that permits the doll's clothing to be changed into different outfits. Dolls account for 60 percent of the firm's sales and the kits account for the remainder. The variable cost ratio for the dolls is 40 percent and for the kits is 65 percent. For 19x3, the fixed costs amounted to $200,000.

Required   a. What were the breakeven sales in dollars for the year?
b. If the company's sales for the year were $600,000, what net income did the company earn?
c. If the company's fixed costs are expected to increase to $250,000 for 19x4 and the company wishes to earn the same net income as it earned in 19x3, what sales revenue would be required to accomplish this?

6-24   Sales Mix and Breakeven Sales

The Dooley Company manufactures two products, baubles and trinkets. The following are projections for the coming year.

	Baubles		Trinkets		
	Units	Amount	Units	Amount	Totals
Sales	10,000	$10,000	7,500	$10,000	$20,000
Costs:					
Fixed		2,000		5,600	7,600
Variable		6,000		3,000	9,000
		8,000		8,600	16,600
Income before taxes		$ 2,000		$ 1,400	$ 3,400

1. Assuming that the facilities are not jointly used, the breakeven output (in units) for baubles would be
   a. 8,000.
   b. 7,000.
   c. 6,000.
   d. 5,000.
2. The breakeven volume (dollars) for trinkets would be
   a. $8,000.
   b. $7,000.
   c. $6,000.
   d. $5,000.
3. Assuming that consumers purchase composite units of four baubles and three trinkets, the composite unit contribution margin would be
   a. $4.40.
   b. $4.00.
   c. $1.33.
   d. $1.10.
4. If consumers purchase composite units of four baubles and three trinkets, the breakeven output for the two products would be
   a. 6,909 baubles; 6,909 trinkets.
   b. 6,909 baubles; 5,182 trinkets.
   c. 5,000 baubles; 8,000 trinkets.
   d. 5,000 baubles; 6,000 trinkets.
5. If baubles and trinkets become one-to-one complements and there is no change in The Dooley Company's cost function, the breakeven volume would be
   a. $22,500.
   b. $15,750.
   c. $13,300.
   d. $10,858.
6. If a composite unit is defined as one bauble and one trinket, the composite contribution margin ratio would be
   a. $7/10$.
   b. $4/7$.
   c. $2/5$.
   d. $19/50$.

(AICPA adapted)

6-25 **Sales Mix and Targeted Income**

1. The Insulation Corporation sells two products, D and W. Insulation sells these products at a rate of 2 units of D to 3 units of W. The contribution margin is $4 per unit for D and $2 per unit for W. Insulation has fixed costs of $420,000. What would be the total units sold at the breakeven point?
   a. 140,000.
   b. 150,000.
   c. 168,000.
   d. 180,000.
2. Jarvis Company has fixed costs of $200,000. It has two products that it can sell, Tetra and Min. Jarvis sells these products at a rate of 2 units of Tetra to 1 unit of Min. The contribution margin is $1 per unit for Tetra and $2 per unit for Min. How many units of Min would be sold at the breakeven point?

a. 44,444.
b. 50,000.
c. 88,888.
d. 100,000.

3. The Ship Company is planning to produce two products, Alt and Tude. Ship is planning to sell 100,000 units of Alt at $4 a unit and 200,000 units of Tude at $3 a unit. Variable costs are 70 percent of sales for Alt and 80 percent of sales for Tude. In order to realize a total profit of $160,000, what must the total fixed costs be?
    a. $ 80,000.
    b. $ 90,000.
    c. $240,000.
    d. $600,000.

(AICPA adapted)

6-26   **(Appendix 6–A): Net-of-Tax CVP Analysis**

1. Pawnee Company operated at normal capacity during the current year producing 50,000 units of its single product. Sales totaled 40,000 units at an average price of $20 per unit. Variable manufacturing costs were $8 per unit, and variable marketing costs were $4 per unit sold. Fixed costs were incurred uniformly throughout the year and amounted to $188,000 for manufacturing and $64,000 for marketing. There was no year-end work in process inventory.

    If Pawnee is subject to an income tax rate of 30 percent, the number of units required to be sold in the current year to earn an after-tax net income of $126,000 is
    a. 47,250
    b. 54,000.
    c. 67,500.
    d. 84,000.
    e. Some amount other than those given above.

2. This question is based on the information provided in Exercise 6–9.

    If Siberian Ski Company desires an after-tax net income of $24,000, how many pairs of touring model skis will the company have to sell?
    a. 13,118.
    b. 12,529.
    c. 13,853.
    d. 4,460.
    e. Some amount other than those given above.

3. This question is based on the information provided in Exercise 6–8. Maxwell's income tax rate is 40 percent.

    How many units would Maxwell Company have to sell in order to earn $156,000 after taxes?
    a. 120,000 units.
    b. 165,000 units.
    c. 140,000 units.
    d. 148,889 units.
    e. None of the above responses is correct.

(CMA adapted)

6-27 (Appendix 6-A): Net-of-Tax CVP Analysis

The following data apply to items 1 through 3.

The statement of income for Davann Company presented below represents the operating results for the fiscal year just ended. Davann had sales of 1,800 tons of product during the current year. The manufacturing capacity of Davann's facilities is 3,000 tons of product.

DAVANN COMPANY
Statement of Income
For the Year Ended December 31, 19x0

Sales	$900,000
Variable costs:	
Manufacturing	315,000
Marketing	180,000
Total variable costs	495,000
Contribution margin	405,000
Fixed costs:	
Manufacturing	90,000
Marketing	112,500
Administration	45,000
Total fixed costs	247,500
Net income before income taxes . .	157,500
Income taxes (40 percent)	63,000
Net income after income taxes	$ 94,500

---

1. If the sales volume is estimated to be 2,100 tons in the next year, and if the prices and costs stay at the same levels and amounts next year, the after-tax net income that Davann can expect for 19x1 is
   a. $135,000.
   b. $110,250.
   c. $283,500.
   d. $184,500.
   e. Some amount other than those shown above.

2. Davann plans to market its product in a new territory. Davann estimates that an advertising and promotion program costing $61,500 annually would need to be undertaken for the next two or three years. In addition, a $25 per ton sales commission over and above the current commission to the sales force in the new territory would be required. How many tons would have to be sold in the new territory to maintain Davann's current after-tax income of $94,500?
   a. 307.5 tons.
   b. 1,095.0 tons.
   c. 273.333 tons.
   d. 1,545.0 tons.
   e. Some amount other than those shown above.

3. Assume that Davann estimates that the per-ton selling price would decline 10 percent next year. Variable costs would increase $40 per ton and the fixed costs would not change. What sales volume in dollars would be required to earn an after-tax net income of $94,500 next year?

    a. $1,140,000.
    b. $825,000.
    c. $1,500,000.
    d. $1,350,000.
    e. Some amount other than those shown above.

(CMA adapted)

6–28   **(Appendix 6–A): Net-of-Tax CVP Analysis**

The Garsombke Company manufactures and sells one product. Its income statement for 19x5 is as follows:

Sales (20,000 units)		$600,000
Less: Variable costs	$360,000	
Fixed costs	120,000	480,000
Income before income taxes		120,000
Income taxes (40 percent)		48,000
Net income		$ 72,000

Required

a. The company is considering a new raw material which is more durable than the one presently used. This material would cost $3 more per unit. All other costs would remain unchanged. How many units would have to be sold in 19x6 to earn a net income (after taxes) of $90,000?

b. The company is also considering a move to a more convenient location. The move would increase fixed costs by $60,000 per year. If the company goes forward with the durable raw material and the move to a new location, how many units would have to be sold in 19x6 to earn the same net income as that for 19x5?

c. If the firm has a choice of continuing with its 19x5 costs and sales of 20,000 units or implementing its raw material change for 19x6 with sales of 25,000 units, which one would you recommend? Why?

6–29   **(Appendix 6–A): Net-of-Tax CVP Analysis**

All-Day Candy Company is a wholesale distributor of candy. The company services grocery, convenience, and drug stores in a large metropolitan area.

Small but steady growth in sales has been achieved by the All-Day Candy Company over the past few years while candy prices have been increasing. The company is formulating its plans for the coming fiscal year. Presented below are the data used to project the current year's after-tax net income of $110,400.

Average selling price	$4.00 per box
Average variable costs:	
Cost of candy	$2.00 per box
Marketing	0.40 per box
Total	$2.40 per box
Annual fixed costs:	
Marketing	$160,000
Administrative	280,000
Total	$440,000
Expected annual sales volume (390,000 boxes)	$1,560,000
Tax rate	40%

Manufacturers of candy have announced that they will increase prices of their products an average of 15 percent in the coming year due to increases in raw material (sugar, cocoa, peanuts, etc.) and labor costs. All-Day Candy Company expects that all other costs will remain at the same rates or levels as the current year.

Required

a. What is All-Day Candy Company's breakeven point in boxes of candy for the current year?

b. What selling price per box must All-Day Candy Company charge to cover the 15 percent increase in the cost of candy and still maintain the current contribution margin ratio?

c. What volume of sales in dollars must the All-Day Candy Company achieve in the coming year to maintain the same net income after taxes as projected for the current year if the selling price of candy remains at $4 per box and the cost of candy increases 15 percent?

(CMA adapted)

6–30 (Appendix 6–A): Algebraic Solutions

1. The following data apply to Frelm Corporation for a given period:

Total variable cost per unit	$3.50
Contribution margin ÷ sales	30%
Breakeven sales (present volume)	$1,000,000

Frelm wants to sell an additional 50,000 units at the same selling price and contribution margin. By how much can fixed costs increase to generate a gross margin equal to 10 percent of the sales value of the additional 50,000 units to be sold?

a. $50,000.
b. $57,500.
c. $67,500.
d. $125,000.

2. The Breiden Company sells rodaks for $6 per unit. Variable costs are $2 per

unit. Fixed costs are $37,500. How many rodaks must be sold to realize a profit before income taxes of 15 percent of sales?

    a. 9,375 units.
    b. 9,740 units.
    c. 11,029 units.
    d. 12,097 units.

3. Singer, Inc., sells product R for $5 per unit. The fixed costs are $210,000 and the variable costs are 60 percent of the selling price. What would be the amount of sales if Singer is to realize a profit of 10 percent of sales?

    a. $700,000.
    b. $525,000.
    c. $472,500.
    d. $420,000.

(AICPA adapted)

PROBLEMS

6–31 Breakeven and CVP Analysis

The Felnar Company manufactures and sells one product at a price of $30 per unit. Its variable cost is $12 per unit, and its fixed costs for the year amount to $360,000.

Required

a. Calculate the breakeven sales in dollars and in units.

b. The company's sales for 19x3 were 30,000 units. What profit was earned at that level of activity?

c. For 19x4, the company is contemplating an increase in selling price by 20 percent. This is expected to cause a reduction in sales volume of 30 percent. No change is expected in the fixed costs or in the variable cost per unit. What would be the effect of the price change on net income? Would you recommend the price change?

d. What would the new breakeven sales in units and dollars be if the change in (c) above were implemented? Does a lowering of the breakeven point always warrant its implementation? Why?

e. As an alternative to the strategy in (c) above, the company is considering improving the quality of the product, which would raise the variable cost per unit to $15. In addition, advertising of the product would be required at a cost of $20,000. This amount is in addition to the fixed costs of $360,000. The selling price would be increased to $40 per unit. At this price, it is expected that sales volume would be reduced by 20 percent. What would the effect on the company's income be of the proposed changes? Prepare your analysis using three different methods.

f. Compute the breakeven sales in dollars and in units of the strategy in (e) above.

g. What is the margin of safety for the company in 19x3? What would it be if the strategy in (e) were implemented?

6–32 Breakeven and CVP Analysis

The Estar Company manufactures and sells one product at a price of $40 per unit. Its variable cost is $10 per unit, and its fixed costs for the year amount to $210,000.

Required

a. Calculate the breakeven sales in dollars and in units.

b. The company's sales for 19x3 were 10,000 units. What profit was earned at that level of activity?

c. For 19x4, the company is contemplating a decrease in selling price by 5 percent. This is expected to cause an increase in sales volume of 15 percent. No change is expected in the fixed costs or in the variable cost per unit. What would be the effect of the price change on net income? Would you recommend the price change?

d.   What would be the new breakeven sales in units and in dollars if the change in *(c)* above were implemented?

e.   As an alternative to the strategy in *(c)* above, the company is considering improving the quality of the product, which would raise the variable cost per unit to $15. In addition, advertising of the product would be required at a cost of $14,000. This amount is in addition to the fixed costs of $210,000. The selling price would be increased to $50 per unit. At this price, it is expected that sales volume would be reduced by 15 percent. What would be the effect of the proposed changes on the company's income? Prepare your analysis using three different methods.

f.   Compute the breakeven sales in dollars and in units of the strategy in *(e)* above.

g.   What is the margin of safety for the company in 19x3? What would it be if the strategy in *(e)* were implemented?

6–33   CVP Analysis

The Helcair Company manufactures an electronic instrument that measures pulse and blood pressure for joggers. The instrument has a sleeve that joggers wear, and the dials are attached to the jogger's clothing. A contribution income statement for 19x4 appears below:

HELCAIR COMPANY
Contribution Format Income Statement
For the Year Ended December 31, 19x4

Sales revenue (12,000 units)	$600,000
Variable costs	240,000
Contribution margin	360,000
Fixed costs	180,000
Net income	$180,000

The director of marketing believes that sales can be increased substantially by increasing the advertising budget for 19x5. She believes that sales could increase as much as 25 percent.

Required   a.   The president of the company is willing to increase the advertising budget provided net income can be increased by 30 percent. What is the maximum amount of additional advertising that should be spent to achieve the president's goal assuming that the 25 percent increase in volume will occur? (Use the differential approach or the contribution margin approach.)

b.   Instead of increasing the advertising budget by the amount you computed in *(a)*, the president decided to increase the budget by $10,000. To his surprise, sales volume in 19x5 increased by 25 percent and net income increased by 30 percent. Having met his goal for the net income increase, he is planning to call the management team together to applaud their efforts during 19x5 and to consider some form of incentive reward. You are asked to analyze the results for 19x5 assuming that the contribution margin ratio for 19x5 is the same as that in 19x4. Would you recommend the incentive award for *both* the sales staff and the manufacturing staff? If not, indicate who should get the award and explain your reasons for giving or denying an award. (Hint: Prepare a comparative contribution income statement for 19x5 to determine where the inconsistent operating results are present, if any. There were no changes in fixed administrative costs, and the only change in fixed marketing costs is the increase in advertising cost of $10,000.)

6-34   Breakeven Graph and Profit-Volume Graph

The Gonar Company manufactures and sells one product at a selling price of $40 per unit. Its variable cost is $24 per unit and its fixed costs are $320,000 per annum.

Required

a. Prepare a breakeven graph using 5,000-unit intervals from 0 to 50,000 units.
b. Prepare a profit-volume graph using the same intervals as in *(a)* above.
c. What is the breakeven point in units and in dollars?
d. Compute the profit or loss from the profit-volume graph at the following levels of sales in units:
   (1) 10,000.
   (2) 30,000.
   (3) 40,000.

6-35   Preparation of Contribution Format Income Statement and Use of Operating Leverage

The Shure Company had the following income statement prepared for the year 19x5:

SHURE COMPANY
Income Statement
For the Year Ended December 31, 19x5

Sales	$1,000,000
Cost of goods sold	750,000
Gross margin	250,000
Marketing and administrative costs	150,000
Net income	$ 100,000

Included in the cost of goods sold are $490,000 of fixed manufacturing costs. The marketing and administrative costs include salespersons' commissions and other variable costs to the extent of $40,000. The balance of the marketing and administrative costs are fixed.

Shure Company manufactures and sells only one product at a selling price of $40 per unit.

Required

a. Recast the income statement into a contribution format statement.
b. Compute the company's degree of operating leverage.
c. During 19x5, the economy was very sluggish. For 19x6, the president of the company either expects sales to increase 20 percent or decrease 30 percent depending on who wins the national presidential election. In either case, the company's president does not expect to change selling prices. Compute the expected change in net income for both possibilities, using the operating leverage computed in part *(b)*.

6–36   **CVP Analysis**

The management of the Southern Cottonseed Company has engaged you to assist in the development of information to be used for managerial decisions.

The company has the capacity to process 20,000 tons of cottonseed per year. The yield of a ton of cottonseed is as follows:

Product	Average Yield per Ton of Cottonseed	Average Selling Price per Trade Unit
Oil	300 pounds	$ 0.15 per pound
Meal	600 pounds	50.00 per ton
Hulls	800 pounds	20.00 per ton
Lint	100 pounds	3.00 per cwt.
Waste	200 pounds	

A special marketing study revealed that the company can expect to sell its entire output for the coming year at the listed average selling prices.

You have determined the company's costs to be as follows:

Processing costs:
  Variable: $9 per ton of cottonseed put into process.
  Fixed: $108,000 per year.

Marketing costs:
  All variable: $20 per ton sold.

Administrative costs:
  All fixed: $90,000 per year.

From the above information, you prepared and submitted to management a detailed report on the company's breakeven point. In view of conditions in the cottonseed market, management told you that they would also like to know the average maximum amount that the company can afford to pay for a ton of cottonseed.

Management has defined the average maximum amount that the company can afford to pay for a ton of cottonseed as the amount that would result in the company's having losses no greater when operating than when closed down under the existing cost and revenue structure. Management states that you are to assume that the fixed costs shown in your breakeven point report will continue unchanged even when the operations are shut down.

Required   Compute the average maximum amount that the company can afford to pay for a ton of cottonseed.

(AICPA adapted)

6–37   **CVP Analysis**

The president of Beth Corporation, which manufactures tape decks and sells them to producers of sound reproduction systems, anticipates a 10 percent wage increase on January 1 of next year to the manufacturing employees (variable labor). He expects no other changes in costs. Overhead will not change as a result of the wage increase. The president has asked you to assist him in developing the information he needs to formulate a reasonable product strategy for next year.

You are satisfied by cost analysis that volume is the primary factor affecting costs and have separated the semivariable costs into their fixed and variable segments. You also observe that the beginning and ending inventories are never materially different.

Below are the current year data assembled for your analysis:

Current selling price per unit	$ 80.00
Variable cost per unit:	
Material	$ 30.00
Labor	12.00
Overhead	6.00
Total	$ 48.00
Annual volume of sales	5,000 units
Fixed costs	$51,000

Required Provide the following information for the president using cost-volume-profit analysis:

a. What increase in the selling price is necessary to cover the 10 percent wage increase and still maintain the current profit-volume-cost ratio?

b. How many tape decks must be sold to maintain the current net income if the sales price remains at $80 and the 10 percent wage increase goes into effect?

c. The president believes that an additional $190,000 of machinery (to be depreciated at 10 percent annually) will increase present capacity (5,300 units) by 30 percent. If all tape decks produced can be sold at the present price and the wage increase goes into effect, how would the estimated net income before capacity is increased compare with the estimated net income after capacity is increased? Prepare computations of estimated net income *before* and *after* the expansion.

(AICPA adapted)

6–38 Sales Mix

The Ionar Company manufactures and sells two products. The selling prices and variable costs of the products are as follows:

	Blujets	Penjets
Selling prices	$20	$40
Variable costs	8	24

The sales for 19x2 were in the ratio of 3 Blujets to 1 Penjet. Sales volume for 19x2 was $1 million. Fixed costs for 19x2 amounted to $390,000.

Required a. Compute the number of units sold in 19x2 for each product.

b. Compute the breakeven sales in dollars and in units.

c. If the sales mix was to change to 2 units of Blujets to 1 unit of Penjet, would this have any effect on the breakeven sales? If so, what would be the new breakeven sales in dollars and in units?

d. Assuming that the sales volume would remain at $1 million, what net income would be generated using the sales mix in part *(c)* above? What income was generated for 19x2?

e. If the firm wishes to generate a net income of $286,000, what sales revenue in dollars would be required to generate this income if the original mix of 3:1 prevailed? How many units of each product would be required to generate that net income?

6-39   (Appendix 6-A): Algebraic Solution to CVP Analysis—Before Income Tax

The Konar Company wishes to evaluate alternate strategies for the purpose of increasing sales volume. It presently manufactures and sells one product, and the sales and cost information is as follows:

Selling price	$40 per unit
Variable cost . . .	$16 per unit
Fixed costs	$360,000 per annum
Sales volume . . .	20,000 units per annum

Several proposals have been advanced for the purpose of increasing sales volume. Each proposal is independent of the others. The algebraic solution is to be used to solve all parts of the problem except for part *(a)*.

Required

a. Compute the company's present net income.

b. The company is contemplating an advertising campaign that would cost $60,000 per annum in excess of the amount included in the $360,000 of fixed costs. In addition, a 10 percent commission is to be offered to salespersons for sales in excess of breakeven sales under this proposal. The company requires an income before taxes of 15 percent of sales. What sales volume (in dollars and in units) would be required for the company to implement this proposal? Assuming that this volume is attainable, would you recommend this strategy instead of remaining with the present volume? Why?

c. As an alternate strategy to *(b)* above, the company would implement all of the conditions in *(b)* except that instead of giving salespersons a 10 percent commission on sales above breakeven sales, a 5 percent commission on sales above present sales would be given. What sales volume (in dollars and units) would be required for the company to implement this proposal? Assuming that this volume is attainable, would you recommend this strategy instead of remaining with the present volume? Why? Would you recommend this strategy over the strategy in *(b)* above? Why?

6-40   (Appendix 6-A): Algebraic Solution of Targeted Net Income (Net of Tax)

The Lenar Company would like to alter its strategy for the following year. For 19x5, the present year, the following information is available:

Selling price	$60 per unit
Variable cost	$27 per unit
Fixed costs	$495,000 per annum
Sales volume	20,000 units per annum
Income tax rate	40 percent

Required

a. What is the company's present net income (after income tax)?

b. What is the company's breakeven sales (in dollars and in units)?

c. The company would like to increase its present net income by 15 percent. What amount of sales (in dollars and in units) would be required to accomplish this? Use an algebraic solution to arrive at your answer.

6–41 **(Appendix 6–A): Breakeven Analysis, Change in Sales Mix, and Income Taxes**

Hewtex Electronics manufactures two products—tape recorders and electronic calculators—and sells them nationally to wholesalers and retailers. The Hewtex management is very pleased with the company's performance for the current fiscal year. Projected sales through December 31, 19x7, indicate that 70,000 tape recorders and 140,000 electronic calculators will be sold this year. The projected earnings statement, which appears below, shows that Hewtex will exceed its earnings goal of 9 percent on sales after taxes.

HEWTEX ELECTRONICS
Projected Earnings Statement
For the Year Ended December 31, 19x7
(dollars in thousands except per-unit amounts)

	Tape Recorders Total Amount	Tape Recorders Per Unit	Electronic Calculators Total Amount	Electronic Calculators Per Unit	Total
Sales	$1,050	$15.00	$3,150	$22.50	$4,200.0
Production costs:					
Materials	280	4.00	630	4.50	910.0
Direct labor	140	2.00	420	3.00	560.0
Variable overhead	140	2.00	280	2.00	420.0
Fixed overhead	70	1.00	210	1.50	280.0
Total production costs	630	9.00	1,540	11.00	2,170.0
Gross margin	$ 420	$ 6.00	$1,610	$11.50	2,030.0
Fixed marketing and administrative costs					1,040.0
Net income before income taxes					990.0
Income taxes (55 percent)					544.5
Net income					$ 445.5

The tape recorder business has been fairly stable the last few years, and the company does not intend to change the tape recorder price. However, the competition among manufacturers of electronic calculators has been increasing. Hewtex's calculators have been very popular with consumers. In order to sustain this interest in its calculators and to meet the price reductions expected from competitors, management has decided to reduce the wholesale price of its calculator from $22.50 to $20.00 per unit effective January 1, 19x8. At the same time, the company plans to spend an additional $57,000 on advertising during fiscal year 19x8. As a consequence of these actions, management estimates that 80 percent of its total revenue will be derived from calculator sales, as compared to 75 percent in 19x7. As in prior years, the sales mix is assumed to be the same at all volume levels.

The total fixed overhead costs will not change in 19x8, nor will the variable overhead cost rates (applied on a direct labor-hour base). However, the cost of materials and direct labor is expected to change. The cost of solid-state electronic components will be cheaper in 19x8. Hewtex estimates that material costs will drop 10 percent for the tape recorders and 20 percent for the calculators in 19x8. However, direct labor costs for both products will increase 10 percent in the coming year.

Required   *a.*   How many tape recorder and electronic calculator units did Hewtex Electronics have to sell in 19x7 to break even?

       b.   What volume of sales is required if Hewtex Electronics is to earn a profit in 19x8 equal to 9 percent on sales after taxes?

       c.   How many tape recorder and electronic calculator units will Hewtex have to sell in 19x8 to break even?

(CMA adapted)

Part

PLANNING AND CONTROL

7

THE MASTER BUDGET

LEARNING OBJECTIVES

After reading this chapter, you should be able to:

1 Explain why budgets are needed and how they are used.

2 Describe the difference between long-term and short-term planning.

3 Identify the duties of the budget committee and list its members.

4 Discuss what role the management accountant plays in budget preparation.

5 Explain the structure of the master budget and the nature of its subunits.

6 Describe how a sales forecast is derived and its role in the preparation of a sales budget.

7 Prepare a production budget, a raw materials budget, a direct labor budget, a manufacturing overhead budget, and an ending inventories budget.

8 Prepare a marketing cost budget and an administrative cost budget.

9 Explain the importance of good cash management and prepare a cash budget.

10 Prepare a budgeted income statement and a budgeted balance sheet.

11 Explain the difference between incremental budgeting and zero-base budgeting.

At the root of any firm's financial success is careful planning. **Planning** is the process of deciding what objectives to pursue during a future time period and what to do in order to achieve those objectives. **Profit planning** is the preparation of budgets to achieve the objectives that have been set. The budgeting process serves several purposes. First, it provides a financial blueprint that enables a firm to coordinate all its activities. Using budgets, managers can project outcomes and adjust strategies, where needed, before operations begin, thus avoiding costly errors. Second, the budgeting process forces managers to reexamine past performance, which may enable them to discover and correct inefficient, outmoded methods of operation. Third, budgets enable managers to implement the *planning and control* function discussed in Chapter 1. In **controlling,** managers measure their firm's performance against established objectives, determine the causes of deviations, and take corrective action where necessary. Without a budget, controlling would be extremely difficult because managers would lack a plan against which to measure performance.

THE ASPECTS OF BUDGETING

Definition of Budget

A **budget** is a financial plan that sets forth the resources necessary to carry out activities and meet financial goals for a future period of time. A **master budget** presents a company's overall financial plan for the coming year or other planning period. Among a master budget's usual components are an operating budget and a cash budget. The **operating budget,** which summarizes the firm's operating plans for the period, consists of a sales budget, a production budget, a raw materials budget, an ending inventories budget, a direct labor budget, a manufacturing overhead budget, a marketing cost budget, and an administrative cost budget. The **cash budget** is a summary of projected cash balances based on expected cash receipts from operations, cash payments for operations, and cash receipts and payments from financing and investing activities. The master budget also contains a complete set of projected financial statements for the ensuing period. Thus, it is future oriented and composed of estimated data rather than historical data, although the estimates may be based on past operating results.

The Need for Budgeting

Almost everyone uses some form of budgeting to handle personal finances. Whether it be a written plan for how much to spend for rent, food, clothing, entertainment, travel, and the like, or a mental plan for what to do on a Saturday night date, most individuals use some form of financial planning. Only rare individuals *consistently* buy everything they need on impulse.

Businesses must also plan ahead. Random business behavior is a rarity. Managers set many different goals for their businesses, but a common goal for almost every business is a planned profit. To ensure that its goals are attained, a firm must set limits on what is to be spent and what is to be considered acceptable operating performance. These limits are set forth in the master budget and compared with actual results as the year progresses. Without a budget, such comparison would be impossible, and a firm might suddenly find that its costs have far exceeded acceptable levels and that its sales have fallen far below the amount needed to remain profitable. Using a budget for frequent comparisons between planned and actual performance, a firm is able to isolate deviations from the budget soon after their occurrence and take appropriate corrective action.

The frequency of comparison varies from firm to firm. Usual comparison periods vary from one week to one month and, in many cases, are dictated by the availability of the data. With present-day computer capabilities, very frequent comparisons are possible at a negligible incremental cost. The author was associated with a steel fabricating firm where comparisons between budgeted and actual data were made daily.

The preparation of formal budgets is time consuming and expensive, but the cost of not budgeting may be far greater and may ultimately lead to a company's failure. In planning for profits, managers must consider two time horizons, the short term and the long term.

The Budget Time Frame

Short-Term Planning. **Short-term planning** is the process of deciding what objectives to pursue during a short, near-future period, usually one year, and what to do in order to achieve those objectives. For example, a firm must decide which units and what quantities to produce and sell during the next year. These decisions cannot be left to chance. Thus, a short-term plan must be compiled to give employees instructions for carrying out the firm's goals.

The typical short-term budget covers one year and is broken down into monthly or quarterly units. When quarterly units are used, the first quarter's budget is further subdivided into monthly segments. Then toward the end of each succeeding quarter, the next quarter's budget is also divided into months. Postponing the division of quarters into months leads to more accurate results because more recent data are available by the time the monthly figures are prepared.

Another method frequently used to prepare a short-term budget is the **continuous budget.** This kind of budget starts with an annual budget broken down into 12 monthly units. As each month arrives, it is dropped from the plan and replaced by a new month so that at any given time, the next 12 months are always shown. Thus, in a budgetary period covering January through December 19x4, when January 19x4 arrives, it would be dropped from the plan and replaced by January 19x5, so that a new budgetary period covering February 19x4 through January 19x5 would be created. Using this technique, a firm always has guidance for the full following year. When a continuous budget is not used, a firm will have guidance for only a month or two as it approaches the end of its budgetary period.

Long-Term Planning. **Long-term planning,** also known as *strategic planning,* is the process of setting long-term goals and determining the means by which they will be attained. While short-term planning is concerned with operating details for the next accounting period, long-term planning addresses broader issues, such as new product development, plant and equipment replacement, and other matters that require years of advance planning. For example, short-term planning in the automotive industry would be concerned with which and how many of the current year's models to manufacture, while long-range planning would focus on new model development and major design changes, as well as equipment replacements and modifications. The time frame for long-range planning may extend as far as 20 years in the future, but its usual range is from 2 to 10 years. An important part of long-term planning is the preparation of the **capital budget,** which details plans for the acquisition and replacement of major portions of property, plant, and equipment.

The Budget Committee

Responsibility for preparing the budget is usually assigned to several high-level managers. In most large firms, this group is referred to as the **budget committee.** The committee then calls on managers throughout the company for help in the budgeting process. Budgeting is a collective effort rather than the responsibility of one individual because if a budget is to be an effective tool of control, it must be accepted by the people who are responsible for its implementation. When managers and employees are given a voice in the preparation of the budget, they feel a greater stake in its success. Thus, budget preparation should be delegated to the lowest possible level of authority, subject to review and adjustment by superiors.

The budget committee generally consists of representatives from:

1. The president's office.
2. The executive vice president's office.
3. Sales and marketing.
4. Production and manufacturing.
5. Purchasing.
6. The controller's office.

Members of the budget committee are usually assistants, but they keep superiors up-to-date on their deliberations and actively involve the senior executives when upper-level decisions are needed.

Duties of the Budget Committee.

The budget committee's duties usually consist of:

1. Selecting budget policies compatible with organizational goals and objectives.
2. Reviewing budget estimates submitted by section heads.
3. Revising budget estimates when necessary.
4. Approving budget estimates.
5. Analyzing budget reports and recommending changes.

The Role of the Management Accountant. The controller occupies a special place on the budget committee. While the sales, production, and purchasing managers provide input regarding how much can be sold, how much can be manufactured, and how much production will cost, the controller's office usually bears responsibility for collecting such data and transforming them into coherent financial statements with appropriate supporting schedules. In effect, the management accountant—the representative from the controller's office—provides support to the production and sales functions by transforming their data into reports that will be useful for both planning and *control.*

Human factors play an important role in the budgeting process. These factors are discussed in Appendix 7–A, which appears at the end of this chapter.

BUDGET PREPARATION

The Master Budget

The master budget is an operational, short-term financial plan. In reality, it is an amalgamation of smaller specialized budgets, each based on information provided by the appropriate manager. For example, the information for the sales budget would come from the sales department's manager and related support personnel, such as management accountants and economists. Similarly, the purchasing department's manager would supply estimated costs for raw materials.

The subunits of the master budget may be classified as:

A. The operating budget.
    1. Sales budget.
    2. Production budget.
        a. Raw materials.
        b. Ending inventories
        c. Direct labor.
        d. Manufacturing overhead.
    3. Marketing cost budget.
    4. Administrative cost budget.
    5. Budgeted income statement.
B. The financial budget.
    1. Capital budget.
    2. Cash budget.
    3. Budgeted balance sheet.
    4. Budgeted statement of changes in financial position.*

* Chapter 16 is devoted to the preparation of this statement.

Some subunits of the master budget are interdependent. For example, the sales forecast is influenced by the amount spent for advertising and promotion, and these expenditures are, in turn, dependent on the sales forecast. The interrelationships of the elements of the master budget are shown in Illustration 7–1.

ILLUSTRATION 7–1   Master Budget Relationships

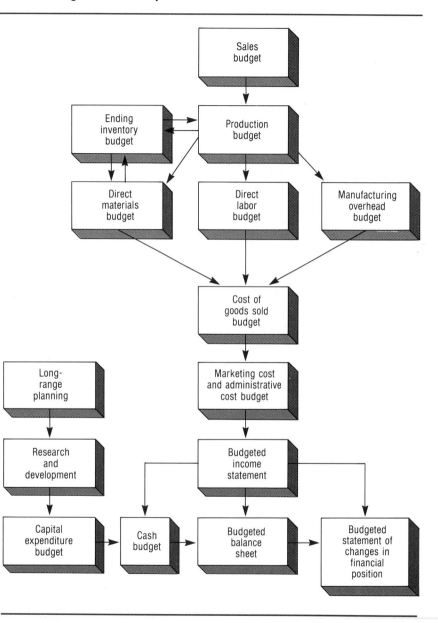

The Sales Budget

The preparation of the master budget must begin with the sales budget. A **sales budget** is a formal plan that sets forth a firm's anticipated sales—in quantities and in dollars—for the coming year based on the sales forecast. A **sales forecast** is a formal prediction of the quantities expected to be sold in the coming year based on such factors as past sales, economic and seasonal conditions, pricing policies, market research studies, and the like. Without forecasts of expected sales for the planning period, a firm would not know how many units to produce and could easily manufacture too many units or too few. Besides leading to overstocks or lost sales, the lack of reliable sales projections can lead to costly mistakes in purchasing materials and hiring employees. Thus, the sales budget and its forecasts provide a crucial foundation on which the preparation of all other components of the master budget depends.

Sales forecasting techniques can vary from simple estimates based on past experience to sophisticated statistical approaches and computer models. Whichever method is used, some prediction must be made regarding how many of each product can be sold in the forthcoming year and at what prices they can be sold.

The elements that enter into the preparation of the sales forecast are:

1. The prior periods' sales broken down by product line, types of customers, territories, and seasonal variations.

2. Present market share modified by future expectations.

3. Pricing policies modified by CVP adjustments.

4. General economic conditions.

5. Economic conditions of the particular industry.

6. Disposable income of consumers.

7. Advertising and promotion.

8. New product entries.

9. Market research studies.

10. Competition and the likely entry of new producers.

11. Backlog of unfilled orders.

ILLUSTRATION 7–2

FIBER COMPANY
Sales Forecast
For the Year Ended December 31, 19x2

Quarter	Number of Units	Price
19x2:		
First	10,000	$12
Second	12,000	12
Third	18,000	12
Fourth	30,000	13
19x3:		
First	12,000	13
Second	15,000	13

ILLUSTRATION 7–3

FIBER COMPANY
Sales Budget
For the Year Ended December 31, 19x2

Quarter	Number of Units	× Price	= Budgeted Sales Revenue
19x2:			
First	10,000	$12	$120,000
Second	12,000	12	144,000
Third	18,000	12	216,000
Fourth	30,000	13	390,000
Total			$870,000

Once estimates of unit sales and selling prices have been derived, the sales budget is well on its way. The actual figures are computed by multiplying the expected unit sales for each product by its selling price and then aggregating the results.

To demonstrate, let us assume that the Fiber Company manufactures a single product, powdered hand soap. The Fiber Company's sales forecast for 19x2 and the first two quarters of 19x3 appears in Illustration 7–2, while its sales budget is presented in Illustration 7–3. Note how estimates of unit sales and prices are multiplied and totaled to arrive at budgeted sales revenue.

The Production Budget

Once the sales forecast and the sales budget are completed, the next phase, the production budget, can be started. A **production budget** is a formal plan quantifying in units the required production for the coming year based on budgeted sales and the budgeted inventories of finished goods. Without the guidance of a production budget, a firm might not manufacture enough to meet sales requirements, or it might produce goods that are not needed. A firm must budget both required production and desired ending inventory. To do so, it must take into account the goods on hand from the beginning inventory. The production budget in units may be calculated as follows:

Expected sales + Desired ending finished goods inventory
    − Beginning finished goods inventory

= Required production

At Fiber Company the manufacture of a carton of powdered hand soap requires two pounds of tetraborate, which is expected to cost 20 cents per pound, and one pound of sodium soap at 15 cents per pound. The beginning inventories at January 1, 19x2, are estimated as:

Finished goods:
    Powdered soap .... 3,000 units at $5.30 per unit
Raw materials:
    Tetraborate ...... 6,000 pounds at $0.20 per pound
    Sodium soap ..... 3,000 pounds at $0.15 per pound

ILLUSTRATION 7–4

FIBER COMPANY
Production Budget in Units
For the Year Ended December 31, 19x2

	First Quarter	Second Quarter	Third Quarter	Fourth Quarter	Yearly Total
Sales	10,000	12,000	18,000	30,000	70,000
Add: Ending inventory	3,600	5,400	9,000	3,600	3,600*
Subtotal	13,600	17,400	27,000	33,600	73,600
Less: Beginning inventory . .	3,000	3,600	5,400	9,000	3,000
Required production	10,600	13,800	21,600	24,600	70,600

*30% × 12,000 units from the first quarter, 19x3.

The company's policy is to maintain inventories equal to 30 percent of its needs for the following quarter. This applies to both raw materials and finished goods. The company has no work in process inventories.

The steps necessary to prepare the production budget are:

Step 1 Compute the ending inventory for the first quarter by taking 30 percent of the second quarter's sales (12,000 units × 30 percent = 3,600).

Step 2 Add the amount from step 1 to the sales for the first quarter (10,000 units) for a subtotal of 13,600. Subtract the beginning inventory of 3,000 units (given information) to arrive at the required production of 10,600 units.

Step 3 Repeat steps 1 and 2 for the remaining three quarters. Note that the beginning inventory for any quarter after the first is the ending inventory for the preceding quarter. This relationship can be seen by the arrows shown in Illustration 7–4.

Step 4 Add the sales for the four quarters to arrive at the yearly sales total. Use the ending inventory for the *fourth quarter* as the ending inventory for the year, and add the two for a subtotal. Use the beginning inventory from the *first quarter* as the beginning inventory for the year and subtract it from the subtotal. The result is the required production for the year. This amount should agree with the sum of the required production for the four quarters.

The Fiber Company's production budget appears as Illustration 7–4.

The Raw Materials Budget. The **raw materials budget** is a formal plan indicating the quantities and dollar amounts of raw material purchases for the coming year based on required production and the budgeted raw materials inventories. Without the guidance of a raw materials budget, a firm may have to shut down production due to insufficient quantities of raw materials or may carry a larger inventory of raw materials than it actually needs. In either case, the failure to plan properly for the purchase of raw materials

7–5 and the beginning inventory is deducted from that subtotal to arrive at the required purchases of raw materials.

2. The ending inventory for any quarter is 30 percent of the production in pounds. This can be seen by examining the arrow relationships. The *ending inventory for the year* must be computed by first computing the required production in pounds for the first quarter of 19x3 and then multiplying this amount by 30 percent. This calculation is shown in the footnotes at the end of the illustration.

3. The beginning inventory of one period is merely the ending inventory of the preceding period. This is demonstrated by the arrows in the illustration.

Direct Labor Budget. A **direct labor budget** is a quantitative calculation and listing of planned expenditures for direct labor costs for the coming budget period. Like the raw (direct) material budget, the direct labor budget is based on the required production. To ease the complexities of computing this portion of the budget when multiple wage rates exist, a uniform wage rate is assumed. At the Fiber Company, the budgeted uniform rate, based on previous experience is $8 per hour, and the required time per unit, based on previous experience, is 15 minutes per unit.

Preparation of the direct labor budget starts with the required production as computed in Illustration 7–4. This figure is then multiplied by the required time per unit, which yields the required time in hours. This amount is then multiplied by the hourly rate to arrive at the direct labor amount in dollars. The direct labor budget for the Fiber Company appears as Illustration 7–6.

The direct labor budget provides management with an approximate schedule of its labor needs and helps the company plan for seasonal fluctuations in direct labor requirements. From Illustration 7–6, it can be seen that the third and fourth quarters of 19x2 will require a significant amount of additional direct labor over that needed for the first two quarters.

ILLUSTRATION 7–6

FIBER COMPANY
Direct Labor Budget
For the Year Ended December 31, 19x2

	First Quarter	Second Quarter	Third Quarter	Fourth Quarter	Yearly Total
Required production*	10,600	13,800	21,600	24,600	70,600
Required direct labor time in hours per unit	× ¼	× ¼	× ¼	× ¼	× ¼
Total direct labor in hours . . .	2,650	3,450	5,400	6,150	17,650
Hourly rate	× $8	× $8	× $8	× $8	× $8
Budgeted direct labor cost . . .	$21,200	$27,600	$43,200	$49,200	$141,200

* From Illustration 7–4.

Manufacturing Overhead Budget. A **manufacturing overhead budget** is a quantitative listing of each type of planned cost classified as manufacturing overhead, such as factory rent, factory supervision, and repairs, segregated into fixed and variable categories. Fixed costs are estimated by using last year's costs and modifying them by any expected changes. Variable costs are estimated by multiplying the rate per unit by the required production. Mixed costs are estimated by using the cost formula $Y = a + bX$ as discussed in Chapter 5. A predetermined overhead rate is then computed that will be used to apply overhead to production during the budget period. This procedure is demonstrated in Chapter 3.

The manufacturing overhead budget enables a firm to prepare the budgeted cost of goods manufactured and sold, which is needed for the budgeted income statement. In addition, the overhead budget provides needed information for the firm's cash budget, since the items in the overhead budget require an outlay of cash. Although depreciation of machinery and factory equipment are needed to compute the predetermined overhead rate, it must be remembered that depreciation does not require a cash outlay and should not be used when preparing the cash budget.

The Fiber Company's manufacturing overhead budget is shown in Illustra-

ILLUSTRATION 7–7

FIBER COMPANY
Manufacturing Overhead Budget
For the Year Ended December 31, 19x2

	First Quarter	Second Quarter	Third Quarter	Fourth Quarter	Yearly Total
Budgeted direct labor cost . . .	$21,200	$27,600	$43,200	$49,200	$141,200
Ⓐ Variable overhead at 80% of above	$16,960	$22,080	$34,560	$39,360	$112,960
Fixed overhead	20,000	20,000	20,000	20,000	80,000
Totals	$36,960	$42,080	$54,560	$59,360	$192,960

Schedule of Overhead

	Fixed	Variable	Total
Superintendence	$30,000		$ 30,000
Indirect labor	10,000	$ 20,000	30,000
Rent	24,000		24,000
Repairs	2,000	12,000	14,000
Light and power	1,000	15,000	16,000
Maintenance	3,000	3,000	6,000
Payroll fringes		42,360	42,360
Miscellaneous	1,000	20,600	21,600
Depreciation of machinery	9,000		9,000
Totals	$80,000	$112,960	$192,960

Ⓐ Variable rate per direct labor cost:
$112,960 ÷ $141,200 = 80% per direct labor dollar

tion 7–7. All information it presents is assumed, except for the direct labor cost, which is based on Illustration 7–6.

Ending Inventory Budget. Inventory planning and control is a very important part of a manager's responsibility because it can save a company from costly errors. A company that practices good inventory planning and control orders sufficient quantities of raw materials at the best prices available without carrying excessive quantities, and has sufficient quantities available to meet production requirements. It also carries sufficient quantities of finished goods to meet customers' demands but avoids maintaining a wasteful excess. Without careful planning and control, firms would accumulate inventories on a haphazard basis. This could result in an overinvestment in inventories as well as increased costs for storage, interest on invested capital, and insurance. In addition, obsolete merchandise would be more likely to accumulate, causing losses at the time of its disposal. Poor inventory planning and control can also cause shortages of raw materials that would lead to assembly-line shutdowns and lost sales for lack of finished goods. Thus, managers recognize the crucial importance of budgeting for ending inventories. (Inventory planning and control is discussed more fully in Chapter 15 of this book.)

ILLUSTRATION 7–8

FIBER COMPANY
Ending Finished Goods Inventory Budget
For the Year Ended December 31, 19x2

Powdered Hand Soap

Cost per unit:
Raw materials:
  Tetraborate—2 pounds at $.20* . . . . $ .40
  Sodium soap—1 pound at .15* 15
Direct labor:
  ¼ hour at $8 (from Illustration 7–6) 2.00
Overhead:
  Variable—80% of direct labor cost (from
  Illustration 7–7) 1.60
Fixed—$80,000 ÷ $141,200 = 56.66% of
  direct labor cost (from Illustration 7–7) 1.13
    Total cost per unit $5.28

Ending finished goods inventory:
Hand soap—3,600 units† × $5.28 = $19,008

---

* From Illustration 7–5.
† From Illustration 7–4.
Note: There is a rounding difference on the fixed overhead as follows:

  Powdered hand soap:
    Production of 70,600 × $1.13 = $79,778
    Budgeted fixed costs 80,000
      Rounding difference . . . . . .$ 222

An **ending inventory budget** is a quantitative calculation, in units and dollars, of the coming year's planned ending inventories for raw materials, work in process, and finished goods. Illustration 7–8 contains the Fiber Company's ending inventory budget for finished goods. Without this budget, it would be impossible to prepare a budgeted income statement.

The Marketing Cost Budget

A **marketing cost budget** is a quantitative listing of each planned marketing cost for the coming year, such as salespersons' salaries, commissions, and the like. A significant portion of this budget is dictated by the sales budget; thus, the two are usually prepared in conjunction with each other.

Like all other budgets, the marketing cost budget is useful for control purposes. A comparison between this budget and the actual costs at the end of an accounting period is likely to disclose differences, and if the differences are significant, managers should investigate the reasons for them and take the necessary corrective action. In addition, this budget is needed to prepare a budgeted income statement and a cash budget.

Illustration 7–9 presents the Fiber Company's marketing cost budget. All dollar amounts are assumed except the salespersons' commissions, which are based on the information provided in the sales budget in Illustration 7–3.

Administrative Cost Budget

An **administrative cost budget** is a quantitative listing of each planned administrative cost for the coming year, such as office rent, office salaries, and the like. The budget is constructed in the same way as the marketing cost budget and is useful for the same control purposes. Also like the marketing cost budget, the information provided by the administrative cost budget is needed to prepare the budgeted income statement and cash budget.

A sample administrative cost budget appears in Illustration 7–10. All dollar amounts are assumed.

ILLUSTRATION 7–9

FIBER COMPANY
Marketing Cost Budget
For the Year Ended December 31, 19x2

	First Quarter	Second Quarter	Third Quarter	Fourth Quarter	Yearly Total
Sales salaries	$ 5,000	$ 5,000	$ 5,000	$ 5,000	$20,000
Sales commissions*	3,600	4,320	6,480	11,700	26,100
Advertising	2,000	2,000	3,000	4,000	11,000
Travel	2,000	2,000	2,000	2,000	8,000
Rent	1,500	1,500	1,500	1,500	6,000
Utilities	1,000	1,000	1,000	1,000	4,000
Miscellaneous	2,000	2,000	2,000	2,000	8,000
Totals	$17,100	$17,820	$20,980	$27,200	$83,100

* 3% of sales per Illustration 7–3.

ILLUSTRATION 7–10

FIBER COMPANY
Administrative Cost Budget
For the Year Ended December 31, 19x2

	First Quarter	Second Quarter	Third Quarter	Fourth Quarter	Yearly Total
Administrative salaries	$20,000	$20,000	$20,000	$20,000	$ 80,000
Rent	2,000	2,000	2,000	2,000	8,000
Utilities	1,000	1,000	1,000	1,000	4,000
Insurance	1,500	1,500	1,500	1,500	6,000
Professional fees	2,000	2,000	2,000	2,000	8,000
Bad debts cost*	1,200	1,440	2,160	3,900	8,700
Payroll fringes	6,000	6,000	6,000	6,000	24,000
Miscellaneous	5,000	5,000	5,000	5,000	20,000
Totals	$38,700	$38,940	$39,660	$41,400	$158,700

* 1% of sales in Illustration 7–3.

Cash Management and Cash Budgeting

The cash budget is an extremely important cash management tool because it enables a firm to plan ahead for its day-to-day cash needs. Without a cash budget, a firm could suddenly find itself strapped for cash and scrambling to pay its bills. Lack of cash can lead to the loss of purchase discounts, poor credit ratings, and many lost opportunities.

Cash Management. Several decades ago, when interest rates hovered in the range of 2 percent to 4 percent, little attention was paid to cash management. But today, when interest rates are in double figures, cash management and the cash budget have become crucial parts of a firm's planning process. The goal of **cash management** is to plan a firm's cash position so that cash is available when it is needed and all available idle cash is invested to provide maximum income, taking into account the amount of risk the firm is willing to assume.

For example, to make sure that customers' payments are put to work as quickly as possible, many firms collect their bills through lockboxes. In such cases, customers send their payments directly to the firm's bank, where the checks are immediately entered as deposits. The bank then transmits a list of the deposited checks to the firm for the updating of its accounts receivable. Without a lockbox system, a firm would have to do the bookkeeping first and then deposit the funds. Such delays in depositing funds can be very costly when interest rates are in double digits.

To ensure that all available funds are optimally invested, some firms, in cooperation with their banks, maintain a zero balance in their bank accounts and fully invest all cash in government securities or money market funds. Each day that a firm's deposits exceed its cleared checks, the bank invests the excess in approved securities. And when cleared checks exceed deposits, the bank sells securities to cover the shortfall. As a result, on any given day all available cash is fully invested and earning interest. This procedure may still be used when a bank requires a firm to maintain a minimum balance by substituting the minimum balance for the zero balance.

The Cash Budget.   The cash budget is broken down into sections showing (1) cash receipts, (2) cash disbursements, (3) cash surplus or deficiency, and (4) financing activities—bank loans, other borrowings, and repayments. This system enables a firm to plan and time such discretionary payouts as dividend payments and equipment purchases. It also facilitates the arrangement of financing activities, such as bank borrowing, well in advance of actual need, thus avoiding the costs and inefficiencies of crisis financing.

The cash budget for the Fiber Company is based on all previously discussed elements of the master budget plus the following additional information:

1. Past experience has shown that the company collects its accounts receivable as follows:

    During the quarter of the sale . . . . 80 percent
    In the quarter following the
        quarter of the sale . . . . 19 percent
    Not collected . . . .   1 percent

2. Salaries and wages are paid in the current quarter.

3. All purchases of raw materials are paid 80 percent in the current quarter and 20 percent in the quarter following their incurrence. Overhead, period costs, and equipment purchases are paid currently.

4. Income taxes are estimated at $60,000 for the year, with 25 percent of this total being paid each quarter.

5. The company has a line of credit with its bank through which it can borrow at the beginning of any quarter at the simple interest rate of 12 percent per annum. The bank computes interest at the rate of 1 percent per month.

6. The company's policy is to maintain a minimum cash balance of $30,000. At the beginning of each quarter, the company will borrow a sufficient amount to maintain that balance and will repay any loans on the last day of a quarter whenever the balance exceeds $30,000.

7. Equipment is to be purchased as follows:

    First quarter . . . . . . $ 10,000
    Second quarter   30,000
    Third quarter   100,000
    Fourth quarter   20,000

Payment for the equipment is in accordance with the payment schedule in item 3 above.

8. Dividends are to be paid in the amount of $2,000 per quarter.

9. During the first quarter of 19x2, the company collected $75,000 of accounts receivable from the prior year. The balance of the opening accounts receivable as shown in Illustration 7–11 is not considered collectible and will be written off.

10. The entire balance of accounts payable on December 31, 19x1 (see Illustration 7–11) is to be paid in the first quarter of 19x2.

Some of the information required to prepare the cash budget is taken from the Fiber Company's estimated balance sheet as of the beginning of the year, January 1, 19x2, which appears in Illustration 7–11.

ILLUSTRATION 7–11

FIBER COMPANY
Budgeted Balance Sheet
January 1, 19x2

Assets

Current assets:			
Cash		$ 40,000	
Accounts receivable	$77,000		
Less: Allowance for uncollectibles	2,500	74,500	
Inventories:			
Raw materials	1,650		
Finished goods	15,900	17,550	
Total current assets			$132,050
Plant assets:			
Equipment		50,000	
Less: Accumulated depreciation		20,000	30,000
Total assets			$162,050

Liabilities and Stockholders' Equity

Current liabilities:			
Accounts payable		$ 5,000	
Total current liabilities			$ 5,000
Stockholders' equity:			
Common stock		100,000	
Retained earnings		57,050	
Total stockholders' equity			157,050
Total liabilities and stockholders' equity			$162,050

The steps used to prepare a cash budget, as shown in Illustration 7–12, are:

Step 1 Prepare a quarterly schedule of cash receipts from accounts receivable by calculating 80 percent of each quarter's sales and 19 percent of the prior quarter's sales. For the first quarter, the amount of $75,000 is used in place of the 19 percent of the prior quarter's sales, as instructed in item 9. (See Schedule A of Illustration 7–12.)

Step 2 Enter the beginning cash balance ($40,000 from Illustration 7–11) in the first quarter column of the cash budget.

Step 3 Enter the cash receipts computed in step 1 for each quarter. The yearly column may also be completed, both for the yearly cash collections and for the beginning cash balance of $40,000.

Step 4 Prepare a schedule of cash payments for materials by taking 80 percent of the current quarter's purchases and 20 percent of the prior quarter's purchases (purchases are found in Illustration 7–5). For the first quarter, $5,000 (the opening

ILLUSTRATION 7–12

FIBER COMPANY
Cash Budget
For the Year Ended December 31, 19x2

	See Illustration or Schedule	First Quarter	Second Quarter	Third Quarter	Fourth Quarter	Yearly Total
Cash balance, beginning		$ 40,000	$ 63,324	$ 30,000	$ 30,000	$ 40,000
Add receipts:						
From customers	(A)	171,000	138,000	200,160	353,040	862,200
Subtotal		211,000	201,324	230,160	383,040	902,200
Deduct disbursements:						
Raw materials	(B)	10,166	8,393	11,675	11,755	41,989
Direct labor	(7–6)	21,200	27,600	43,200	49,200	141,200
Manufacturing overhead	(7–7)	34,710*	39,830	52,310	57,110	183,960
Marketing	(7–9)	17,100	17,820	20,980	27,200	83,100
Administrative	(7–10)	37,500†	37,500	37,500	37,500	150,000
Equipment		10,000	30,000	100,000	20,000	160,000
Dividends		2,000	2,000	2,000	2,000	8,000
Income taxes		15,000	15,000	15,000	15,000	60,000
Subtotal		147,676	178,143	282,665	219,765	828,249
Excess (deficiency) of cash . . .		63,324	23,181	(52,505)	163,275	73,951
Financing:						
Borrowing			7,030	85,274		92,304
Repayment					(92,304)	(92,304)
Interest			(211)	(2,769)	(2,769)	(5,749)
Total financing		–0–	6,819	82,505	(95,073)	(5,749)
Cash balance, ending		$ 63,324	$ 30,000	$ 30,000	$ 68,202	$ 68,202

* Since depreciation does not require any cash outflow, each quarter's overhead was reduced by the depreciation per quarter ($9,000 ÷ 4 = $2,250).

† Bad debts is deducted each quarter since no cash is disbursed.

ILLUSTRATION 7–12 (*concluded*)

FIBER COMPANY
Supporting Schedules
to Illustration 7–12

Schedule A—Cash Receipts from Accounts Receivable

	First Quarter	Second Quarter	Third Quarter	Fourth Quarter
19x2:				
Balance from accounts receivable, 1/1/x2	$ 75,000			
Sales from first quarter*:				
80% × $120,000	96,000			
19% × $120,000		$ 22,800		
Sales from second quarter*:				
80% × $144,000		115,200		
19% × $144,000			$ 27,360	
Sales from third quarter*:				
80% × $216,000			172,800	
19% × $216,000				$ 41,040
Sales from fourth quarter*:				
80% × $390,000				312,000
Cash collections	$171,000	$138,000	$200,160	$353,040

Schedule B—Cash Payments for Materials

	First Quarter	Second Quarter	Third Quarter	Fourth Quarter
19x2:				
Balance from accounts payable, 1/1/x2	$ 5,000			
Payments from first quarter†:				
80% × ($4,696 + $1,761)	5,166			
20% × ($4,696 + $1,761)		$1,291		
Payments from second quarter†:				
80% × ($6,456 + $2,421)		7,102		
20% × (same)			$ 1,775	
Payments from third quarter†:				
80% × ($9,000 + $3,375)			9,900	
20% × (same)				$ 2,475
Payments from fourth quarter†:				
80% × ($8,436 + $3,164)				9,280
Cash payments	$10,166	$8,393	$11,675	$11,755

* From Illustration 7–3.
† From Illustration 7–5.

balance of the accounts payable) is used in accordance with item 10. (See Schedule B of Illustration 7–12.)

Step 5 Enter the payments for raw materials in the disbursements section. Enter the amounts for direct labor, manufacturing overhead, marketing costs, and administrative costs from Illustrations 7–6, 7–7, 7–9, and 7–10. However, the amounts for manufacturing overhead must be reduced by the depreciation and the administrative costs must be reduced by the bad debts because depreciation and bad debts do not require any cash payments. They are costs created by bookkeeping entries rather than by cash outflows.

Step 6 Enter the disbursements for equipment purchases, dividend payments, and estimated income tax payments. Add the totals of the disbursements for each quarter and for the year. For the first quarter, calculate the excess (or deficiency) of cash.

Step 7 Whenever the excess cash is greater than $30,000 (as in the first quarter), enter the ending cash balance as the beginning cash balance of the next quarter. When the excess cash is less than $30,000, or when a deficiency is present, calculate the deficiency from $30,000 and divide the result by 97 percent to allow for three months' interest (1 percent × 3 months), since any needed borrowings are to be made at the *beginning of the quarter.* For the second quarter, the borrowing may be calculated as $30,000 minus the excess cash of $23,181 = $6,819 ÷ .97 = $7,030. The interest for the second quarter would then be $7,030 × .03 = $211, and a cash balance of $30,000 would be maintained. The same procedure is used for the third quarter, except that the $211 of interest must be added to the cash deficiency. Thus, the calculation would be $52,505 deficiency + $30,000 cash balance + $211 of second quarter interest that must be paid for in the third quarter = $82,716 ÷ .97 = $85,274. The interest for the third quarter is calculated as 3 percent of the second and third quarter loans, or ($85,274 + $7,030 = $92,304 × .03 = $2,769). For the fourth quarter, there is sufficient cash to liquidate the loans and pay the interest of $2,769, which is the same as in the third quarter, since the loan is paid at the *end* of the quarter.

A review of Illustration 7–12 reveals that:

1. The cash balance at the beginning of the first quarter is $40,000, which is the amount shown in Illustration 7–11, the beginning balance sheet.

2. The cash receipts from accounts receivable are computed in the supporting schedules (Schedule A).

3. The cash disbursements are either computed in the supporting schedules or in the previously discussed subsidiary budgets, except for the equipment payments, dividends, and income taxes, which are given in items 4, 7, and 8.

4. Since the estimated cash balance at the end of the first quarter exceeds the minimum balance of $30,000, no borrowing is necessary. However, borrowings are required in the second and third quarters.

5. The computations for interest are shown in step 7 following the cash budget.

6. The cash budget enables the firm to plan for needed borrowing in the second and third quarters and repayment in the fourth quarter. A cash budget would also indicate if borrowing were needed but repayment were impossible in the current year. Under such circumstances, the company might consider alternative forms of long-term borrowing.

The Budgeted Income Statement

It is now possible to prepare the **budgeted income statement,** which is a projected income statement based on the various units of the operating budget. This statement is extremely important because it indicates how profitable the firm is expected to be. Each segment of the operating budget enhances planning and control, but it is the budgeted income statement that informs managers, *in advance,* whether the firm's operations for the coming year are expected to be profitable and how much the profit or loss is expected to be. If the projected operations are not satisfactory to management, altered strategies may be adopted to try to improve the results. Without a budgeted income statement, managers would discover unsatisfactory results after they had occurred, when it would be too late to make necessary adjustments. In addition, managers can compare the budgeted income statement to the actual income statement to determine if significant variances exist and whether corrective action is warranted.

The only additional information that is needed to prepare the budgeted income statement is the income tax rate. In our example, the Fiber Company pays income taxes at an average rate of 23.75 percent of pre-tax income.

ILLUSTRATION 7–13

FIBER COMPANY
Budgeted Income Statement
For the Year Ended December 31, 19x2

	From Illustration	
Sales	7–3	$870,000
Cost of goods sold*		369,882
Gross margin		500,118
Marketing and administrative costs:		
Marketing costs	7–9	83,100
Administrative costs	7–10	158,700
Total marketing and administrative . . .		241,800
Operating income before income taxes . . .		258,318
Less: Interest cost	7–12	5,749
Income before income taxes		252,569
Income taxes at 23.75 percent		59,985
Net income		$192,584

* Cost of goods sold:			
Beginning inventories:			
Finished goods (3,000 × $5.30)	7–11		$ 15,900
Raw materials	7–11		1,650
Purchases of raw materials	7–5		39,309
Direct labor	7–6		141,200
Manufacturing overhead	7–7		192,960
Subtotal			391,019
Less: Ending inventories:			
Finished goods	7–8	$19,008	
Raw materials—Tetraborate (7,740 × $.20)	7–5	1,548	
—Sodium soap (3,870 × $.15) . . .	7–5	581	21,137
Cost of goods sold			$369,882

The steps needed to prepare a budgeted income statement, as shown in Illustration 7–13, are:

Step 1 Use the sales from the sales budget (Illustration 7–3).

Step 2 Compute the cost of goods sold using the inventories of finished goods and raw materials from the budgeted balance sheet (Illustration 7–11). To these inventories, add the raw material purchases from the raw materials budget (Illustration 7–5), the direct labor from the direct labor budget (Illustration 7–6), and the manufacturing overhead from the manufacturing overhead budget (Illustration 7–7). Add them for a subtotal and then deduct the closing inventories from the ending finished goods inventory budget and the raw materials budget (Illustrations 7–8 and 7–5) to arrive at the cost of goods sold. The calculation may be seen at the bottom of the budgeted income statement shown in Illustration 7–13. Deduct the cost of goods sold from the sales to compute the gross margin for the year.

Step 3 Deduct the marketing costs shown in the marketing cost budget (Illustration 7–9) and the administrative costs shown in the administrative cost budget (Illustration 7–10) from the gross margin to arrive at operating income before income taxes. Next, deduct the interest cost shown on the cash budget (Illustration 7–12) to derive income before income taxes. Finally, multiply this amount by 23.75 percent, which is the Fiber Company's income tax, and deduct the result to arrive at the net income for the year.

The Budgeted Balance Sheet

A **budgeted balance sheet** is a projected statement of financial position that reflects the expected balances in the accounts at the end of the planning period. It is prepared by starting with the firm's balance sheet at the beginning of a year and adjusting each figure for all of the expected transactions shown in the operating and cash budgets. The budgeted balance sheet provides managers with the firm's expected financial position at the end of an accounting period. Based on this information, management may be able to predict poten-

ILLUSTRATION 7–14

FIBER COMPANY
Budgeted Balance Sheet
December 31, 19x2

Assets

Current assets:		
Cash		$ 68,202[a]
Accounts receivable	$82,800[b]	
Less: Allowance for uncollectibles	9,200[c]	73,600
Inventories:		
Raw materials	2,129[d]	
Finished goods	19,008[e]	21,137
Prepaid income taxes		15
Total current assets		$162,954
Plant assets:		
Equipment	210,000[f]	
Less: Accumulated depreciation	29,000[g]	181,000
Total assets		$343,954

ILLUSTRATION 7–14 (*concluded*)

Liabilities and Stockholders' Equity

Current liabilities:		
Accounts payable	$ 2,320[h]	
Total current liabilities		$ 2,320
Stockholders' equity:		
Common stock	100,000	
Retained earnings	241,634[i]	
Total stockholders' equity		341,634
Total liabilities and stockholders' equity		$343,954

a. Per cash budget, Illustration 7–12

b. Beginning balance, Illustration 7–11	$ 77,000	
Add: Sales, Illustration 7–3	870,000	
Less: Collections, Illustration 7–12	(862,200)	
Less: Bad debts written off	(2,000)	
Ending balance	$ 82,800	
c. Beginning balance, Illustration 7–11	$ 2,500	
Add: Bad debts provision (1% × $870,000),		
Illustration 7–10	8,700	
Less: Bad debts written off	(2,000)	
Ending balance	$ 9,200	
d. Tetraborate, (illustration 7–13, footnote)	$ 1,548	
Sodium soap, (Illustration 7–13, footnote)	581	
Total	$ 2,129	
e. From Illustration 7–8.		
f. Beginning balance, Illustration 7–11	$ 50,000	
Add: Purchases, Illustration 7–12	160,000	
Ending balance	$ 210,000	
g. Beginning balance, Illustration 7–11	$ 20,000	
Add: Depreciation, Illustration 7–7	9,000	
Ending balance	$ 29,000	
h. Beginning balance, Illustration 7–11	$ 5,000	
Add: Purchases, Illustration 7–5	39,309	
Less: Payments for materials, Illustration 7–12	(41,989)	
Ending balance	$ 2,320	
i. Beginning balance, Illustration 7–11	$ 57,050	
Add: Net income, Illustration 7–13	192,584	
Less: Dividends paid, Illustration 7–12	(8,000)	
Ending balance	$ 241,634	

tial trouble spots in liquidity and/or operating efficiency and take corrective action to prevent their occurrence.

The Fiber Company's budgeted balance sheet is presented in Illustration 7–14. The calculations of the individual amounts are detailed in the notes that accompany the illustration.

Budget Uses

Performance Reports. So far we have emphasized the use of a master budget to plan and guide a firm's operations for the coming year. But a master budget also serves another important function: it provides a basis of comparison against which actual results can be measured to determine if

ILLUSTRATION 7–15

FIBER COMPANY
Manufacturing Overhead Performance Report
For the Year Ended December 31, 19x2

	Budgeted Amounts	Actual Amounts	Over (Under) Budget	Explanation
Superintendence	$ 30,000	$ 30,000	$ –0–	
Indirect labor	30,000	32,000	2,000	Salary increase
Rent	24,000	24,000	–0–	
Repairs	14,000	26,000	12,000	Unexpected
Light and power	16,000	20,000	4,000	Rate increase
Maintenance	6,000	5,500	(500)	
Payroll fringes	42,360	42,960	600	
Miscellaneous	21,600	19,600	(2,000)	
Depreciation of machinery	9,000	10,000	1,000	New equipment
Totals	$192,960	$210,060	$17,100	

---

an organization is in control of its operations. A firm should monitor its actual results and compare them with its planned results to determine if there are any unusual variations that warrant investigation. This can be accomplished by preparing a **performance report** that contains four columns: one column for budgeted data, one for actual data, one showing the difference between budget and actual and whether the difference is over or under budget, and one for explanations of the differences. It is the differences that are of primary interest. Illustration 7–15 contains a sample performance report for the Fiber Company. The unexpected repairs of $12,000 merit investigation. Performance reports are discussed more fully in Chapters 8 and 9 of this book.

Budgeting in Not-for-Profit Organizations

Not-for-profit organizations, such as governments, hospitals, welfare organizations, schools, and colleges, make extensive use of budgets. In fact, budgets are usually required of these organizations by such regulatory authorities as legislatures, boards of trustees, and administrative agencies. While not-for-profit organizations rarely manufacture products and therefore do not start with a sales forecast as profit-oriented businesses do, they do provide services to their users. Consequently, they must prepare a forecast of the services to be rendered during the planning period (usually one year) to provide a starting point for the rest of the master budget.

Incremental Budgeting.　Many organizations make use of the incremental approach when preparing budgets. When **incremental budgeting** is used, *the previous period's budget is accepted as a base,* and those figures are either increased or decreased depending on whether the organization wishes to increase or decrease its output during the coming period.

The major advantage of using this approach is that the preparer starts with a budget—albeit last year's—already prepared, and merely has to add or subtract to arrive at the next year's budget. Thus, the work is greatly simplified.

The greatest disadvantage of using this approach is that the prior years' inefficiencies are automatically perpetuated and included in the current year's budget. In addition, the effectiveness of the programs remains unchallenged and perpetuated. Thus, programs continue in force through inertia.

Zero-Base Budgeting.   Zero-base budgeting has recently attracted increasing attention. Unlike incremental budgeting, which begins with the previous period's figures as a base, **zero-base budgeting** starts with a base of zero. Each program and its cost is then ranked, starting with the one that is most vital to the organization. In this manner, managers can choose to fund programs on the basis of merit, without preconceived notions about what must be included.

The major advantage of zero-base budgeting is that every year, every program and its cost must be justified before it can be included in the budget. In the process, weak programs and inefficiencies tend to be weeded out. Zero-base budgeting requires a great deal more effort than incremental budgeting, but in the long run it may be more efficient.

Applications to Businesses.   In most cases, a business's master budget starts with a sales forecast, which is based, in part, on the previous year's sales. Thus, incremental budgeting is used for products that the firm is already producing and selling. But when a firm brings out a new product, it uses zero-base budgeting because the product lacks a sales history. Even with existing products, a firm uses zero-base budgeting when evaluating whether to continue making them. Thus, businesses make use of both incremental and zero-base budgeting. Although several budgeting experts have written books advocating the extensive use of zero-base budgeting in business, few firms have put their ideas into practice. Nevertheless, the concept is a useful one.

SUMMARY

To ensure coherence and continuity, businesses must plan their operations and profit goals. During the **planning** process, a company sets goals, chooses strategies for attaining them, and quantifies its decisions. The result is a **master budget,** which provides an overall plan of operations for future periods.

Profit planning is best accomplished with a formalized master budget. A master budget presents a company's overall financial plan for the coming period, usually one year. A master budget falls within the realm of **short-term planning.** As part of their planning processes, an increasing number of firms are using **continuous budgeting** which starts with a full year's budget broken down into 12 monthly units. As each month arrives, it is dropped from the plan and replaced with a new month so that at any given time the next 12 months are always shown. **Long-term planning,** also known as strategic planning, is concerned with long-term goals, such as new product development, plant and equipment replacement, and other matters that require years of advance planning. An important part of long-term planning is the preparation of the **capital budget.** The prime responsibility for coordinating the master budget's preparation is given to the **budget committee,** which is made up of representatives from various high-level managers' offices. The master budget usually includes an **operating budget,** a cash budget, and projected financial statements.

The foundation of the master budget is the **sales forecast,** which is based on such factors as the firm's market share, economic and seasonal conditions, competitive factors, and prices. From the sales forecast, the **sales budget** can be constructed. It is then possible to prepare a **production budget,** which contains as subunits a **raw materials budget,** a **direct labor budget,** a **manufacturing overhead budget,** and an **ending inventories budget.** In addition, the master budget contains a **marketing cost budget,** an **administrative cost budget,** and a **cash budget.** These budgets in turn provide the information necessary to prepare budgeted financial statements—a **budgeted income statement,** a **budgeted balance sheet,** and a budgeted statement of changes in financial position.

With interest rates in double figures, cash management has become an increasingly important part of a financial manager's duties. **Cash management** is the planning of a firm's cash position so that cash is available when it is needed and all available idle cash is invested to provide maximum income, taking into account the amount of risk the firm is willing to assume. The cash budget plays a key role in cash management because it enables a firm to plan and time financing activities and discretionary payouts.

There are two basic approaches to budgeting. When the **incremental approach** is used, the previous year's budget is taken as the starting point and adjusted upward or downward to reflect anticipated changes for the coming year. With **zero-base budgeting,** each year a new budget is started from zero and all programs must be justified as if they were entirely new. This approach requires more effort than incremental budgeting, but its proponents claim that the effort is justified from a cost-benefit viewpoint.

Planning is the predecessor to the **control** function. As part of the control function, **performance reports** are used to compare the actual results of operations to the planned results to determine if there are any significant variations from the plan and, if so, whether further investigation is necessary.

Not-for-profit organizations must budget as carefully as for-profit organizations since they are normally subject to control by legislatures, boards of directors, and other regulatory bodies.

GLOSSARY OF KEY TERMS

Administrative cost budget   A quantitative listing of each planned administrative cost for the coming year, such as office rent, office salaries, and the like.

Budget A financial plan that sets forth the resources necessary to carry out activities and meet financial goals for a future period of time.

Budgeted balance sheet A projected statement of financial position that reflects the expected balances in the accounts at the end of the planning period. It is prepared by starting with a firm's balance sheet at the beginning of a year and adjusting each figure for all of the expected transactions shown in the operating and cash budgets.

Budget committee Representatives from various high-level managers' offices who have the primary responsibility for, and participate in, the preparation of the budget.

Budgeted income statement A projected income statement based on the various units of the operating budget that informs managers in advance whether the firm's operations are expected to be profitable and how much the profit or loss is expected to be.

Capital budget The planned amounts to be spent for the acquisition and replacement of major portions of property, plant, and equipment.

Cash budget A summary of projected cash balances based on expected cash receipts from operations, cash payments for operations, and cash receipts and payments from financing and investing activities.

Cash management The planning of a firm's cash position so that cash is available when it is needed and all available idle cash is invested to provide maximum income, taking into account the amount of risk the firm is willing to assume.

Continuous budget An annual budget broken down into 12 monthly units. As each month arrives, it is dropped from the plan and replaced by a new month so that at any given time, the next 12 months are always shown.

Controlling The process of measuring performance against the firm's objectives, determining the causes of deviations, and taking corrective action where necessary.

Direct labor budget A quantitative calculation and listing of planned expenditures for direct labor costs for the coming budget period.

Ending inventory budget A quantitative calculation, in units and dollars, of the coming year's planned ending inventories for raw materials, work in process, and finished goods.

Incremental budgeting A planning system that starts with the previous period's budget as a base and either increases or decreases those figures depending on whether the organization wishes to increase or decrease its output during the coming period.

Long-term planning The process of setting long-term goals and determining the means by which they will be attained. The time frame for long-range planning may extend as far as 20 years into the future, but its usual range is from 2 to 10 years.

Manufacturing overhead budget A quantitative listing of each type of planned cost classified as manufacturing overhead, such as factory rent, factory supervision, and repairs, segregated into fixed and variable categories.

Marketing cost budget A quantitative listing of each planned marketing cost for the coming year, such as salespersons' salaries, commissions, and the like.

Master budget A company's overall financial plan for the coming year or other planning period, which usually includes an operating budget, a cash budget, and projected financial statements.

Operating budget A firm's operating plans for the coming year consisting of a sales budget, a production budget, a raw materials budget, an ending inventories budget, a direct labor budget, a manufacturing overhead budget, a marketing cost budget, and an administrative cost budget.

Performance report   A report that compares actual results to planned results using four columns: one column for budgeted data, one for actual data, one showing the difference between budget and actual and whether the difference is over or under budget, and one for explanations of the difference.

Planning   The process of deciding what objectives to pursue during a future time period and what to do in order to achieve those objectives.

Production budget   A formal plan quantifying in units the required production for the coming year based on the budgeted sales and the budgeted inventories of finished goods.

Profit planning   The preparation of budgets to achieve the objectives that have been set.

Raw materials budget   A formal plan indicating the quantities and dollar amounts of raw material purchases for the coming year based on required production and the budgeted raw materials inventories.

Sales budget   A formal plan setting forth a firm's anticipated sales—in quantities and in dollars—for the coming year based on the sales forecast.

Sales forecast   A formal prediction of the quantities expected to be sold in the coming year based on such factors as past sales, economic and seasonal conditions, pricing policies, market research studies, etc.

Short-term planning   The process of deciding what objectives to pursue during a short, near-future period, usually one year, and what to do in order to achieve those objectives.

Zero-base budgeting   A method of budgeting that starts with a base of zero and ranks each program and its cost, starting with the one that is most vital to the organization. In this manner, managers can choose to fund programs on the basis of merit, without preconceived notions about what must be included.

APPENDIX 7–A   HUMAN FACTORS IN BUDGETARY PLANNING AND CONTROL

In a tight budget, maximum revenues and minimum costs are combined to produce an ideal budget. While this type of budget could theoretically be achieved, it does not allow for the human factors that normally prevent the achievement of perfection. While some individuals attempt to work at optimal levels, most people do not; thus, a very tight budget is considered unattainable. For this reason, such a budget is not considered an effective device for motivating employees. When employees realize that a budget is unattainable and that, as a result, they cannot possibly achieve any rewards for attainment, they will tend to rationalize, saying to themselves, "If we are going to miss the target, we might as well miss it by a mile as by an inch since the penalty and/or reward is the same for either one." Thus, they reject the budget.

On the other hand, a lax budget is equally unacceptable as a control device. When a sales budget is set so low that anyone can attain the required sales, or a production budget is set so low that employees can attain the required output with a minimum of effort, the result is a reward system that encourages unacceptable performance. Conscientious employees are likely to resent this type of budget because they receive the same rewards as employees who exert a minimum amount of effort. Consequently, too lax a budget may make a firm cost-inefficient in the long run and possibly even spell its demise.

Ultimately, the desired goal should be a budget that is fair to both the firm and its employees. A certain amount of lost efficiency due to human factors, such as illness, personal problems, and reasonable coffee breaks, is to be expected and should be built into the budgeting process. A budget that is reasonable to both employees and the firm can operate as an effective control mechanism that rewards exemplary performance and identifies mediocre performance.

Budget Slack

Budget slack occurs when an employee or manager deliberately causes a firm's sales revenues to be less than they could have been, causes actual costs to be more than they should have been, or both. For example, a sales representative may have reached her quota of budgeted sales for the year in the early part of December but may not have spent all her budgeted traveling costs for the year. Since she has met her budgeted sales, she may decide to cancel a scheduled 200-mile trip to Minnesota to meet with a new customer waiting to place an order and instead make a trip of 1,800 miles to Florida, where she may hope to meet some potential customers on the sun-filled golf courses. If she gains no customers in Florida and if the Minnesota customer decides to buy from a competitor, sales revenues will be less than they could have been and traveling costs will be more than they should have been. On the other hand, if the budget were set so tight that the salesperson had to go to Minnesota to keep her job, such slack would not be possible.

Much has been written in organizational behavior and management journals about the existence of slack in business organizations. One authority maintains that managers want to satisfy both their own goals and those of their firm. Since in many cases the two sets of goals are not perfectly congruent, a slack environment provides the best opportunity for satisfying both.[1] This is especially true at the lower levels of management. Upper-level managers enjoy great freedom in carrying out their duties and receive many perquisites—stock options, chauffeured limousines, corporate jets, etc.—while lower-level managers are usually less privileged. Thus, like the sales representative who traveled to Florida, lower-level managers often use budget slack as one means of satisfying personal goals.

---

[1] O. E. Williamson, *The Economics of Discretionary Behavior: Managerial Objectives in a Theory of the Firm* (Englewood Cliffs, N.J.: Prentice-Hall, 1964), pp. 28–37.

Other authorities have found that managers tend to satisfy personal goals by using slack in good years and converting slack into profits in bad years.[2] In effect, they keep the wolf away from the door by using the slack to satisfy the firm's goals when times are bad, but they use the slack for themselves once the firm's goals have been satisfied. This approach also ensures that the firm will not increase its expectations in future years. If the manager continued to use the slack to benefit the firm once its goals were satisfied, the firm would raise its goals for subsequent years, thereby taking control of the slack away from the manager.

Schiff and Lewin maintain that in a *decentralized company, slack is concentrated at the divisional level,* while in *a centralized company, slack extends throughout the entire company.*[3] They estimate that slack may comprise as much as 25 percent of a division's operating cost budget.[4]

Managers should recognize that slack is an ever-present problem in budget construction. While it is probably impossible to eliminate all slack, managers should attempt to determine an acceptable level and try to control its abuse. This can be accomplished to some extent through the use of engineering estimates that are adjusted for an acceptable amount of slack.

QUESTIONS

1. What is the difference between planning and profit planning?

2. Why are budgets needed for control purposes?

3. What is a master budget?

4. What is the difference between short-term planning and long-term planning?

5. What is a continuous budget? What are its advantages?

6. What is a budget committee? Evaluate the statement, "An effective budget committee dictates the budget policies of the firm and prepares the ensuing budget with as little help from nonmembers as is possible."

7. What role does the management accountant play in the development of the master budget? Use examples to explain your discussion.

8. What are the subunits of a master budget?

9. What factors enter into the preparation of the sales budget?

10. What is sales forecasting?

11. What is a production budget? What is required production?

12. Is it important to budget for ending inventories? Why?

13. How is the manufacturing overhead budget prepared?

14. What is the difference between cash management and cash budgeting?

---

[2] Michael Schiff and Arie Y. Lewin, "Where Traditional Budgeting Fails," *Financial Executive,* 36, (May 1968), pp. 50–52, 55–56, 61–62.

[3] Michael Schiff and Arie Y. Lewin, "The Impact of People on Budgets," *The Accounting Review,* 55, no. 2, (April 1970), p. 264.

[4] Ibid., p. 263.

15. What purpose does a budgeted income statement serve?

16. What is performance report? How is it used?

17. What is incremental budgeting? Why is it used?

18. What is zero-base budgeting? What are its advantages? Disadvantages?

For Appendix 7–A

19. Do human factors enter into the preparation of a budget? Explain.

20. What is budget slack? Is it usually present in budgets? Explain.

EXERCISES   **7–1**   **Budgeted Cash Collections, Operating Income, and Accounts Payable**

The January 31, 19x6, balance sheet of Shelpat Corporation follows:

Assets	
Cash	$ 8,000
Accounts receivable (net of allowance for	
uncollectible accounts of $2,000)	38,000
Inventory	16,000
Property, plant, and equipment (net of	
allowance for accumulated depreciation	
of $60,000)	40,000
Total assets	$102,000

Liabilities and Stockholders' Equity	
Accounts payable	$ 82,500
Common stock	50,000
Retained earnings (deficit)	(30,500)
Total liabilities and stockholders' equity	$102,000

Additional information:

a. Sales are budgeted as follows:

February $110,000
March $120,000

b. Collections are expected to be 60 percent in the month of sale, 38 percent the next month, and 2 percent uncollectible.

c. The gross margin is 25 percent of sales. Purchases each month are 75 percent of the next month's projected sales. The purchases are paid in full the following month.

d. Other costs for each month, paid in cash, are expected to be $16,500. Depreciation each month is $5,000.

1. What are the budgeted cash collections for February 19x6?
   a. $63,800.
   b. $66,000.

  c. $101,800.
  d. $104,000.
2. What is the budgeted income (loss) before income taxes for February 19x6?
  a. ($3,700).
  b. ($1,500).
  c. $3,800.
  d. $6,000.
3. What is the projected balance in accounts payable on February 29, 19x6?
  a. $82,500.
  b. $86,250.
  c. $90,000.
  d. $106,500.

(AICPA adapted)

7–2 Production Budget

The Eastern Hat Company manufactures ladies' hats and is preparing its production budget for the first three months of 19x2. The sales budget in units is as follows:

Month	Units
January	4,000
February	3,000
March	8,000
April	20,000
May	6,000

The December 31, 19x1, inventory is estimated as 800 units. The company normally maintains an inventory at the end of each month equal to 20 percent of the following month's sales. However, due to the surge of sales in April, the company normally maintains an inventory on March 31 equal to 40 percent of the anticipated sales for April.

The company's capacity is limited to 12,000 hats per month. If the production requirement exceeds this amount, the production is scheduled in the next preceding month when production capacity is available. Thus, if the required production for April cannot be met, it is produced in March if production is available, and if not, it is produced in February.

Required Prepare the production requirements for the months of January, February, and March. Also, use a total column to indicate the production requirement for the first quarter of 19x2.

7–3 Raw Materials Budget

The Western Desk Company manufactures desks. Each desk manufactured requires an average of 30 board feet of lumber. Normally, the company maintains an inventory of 15 percent of its needs for the following quarter. The firm's production budget is as follows:

Quarter		Units
19x3	First	5,000
	Second . . .	6,000
	Third	4,000
	Fourth	7,000
19x4	First	5,500

The projected beginning inventory on January 1, 19x3, is 23,000 board feet of lumber. The price of lumber is expected to be relatively stable for 19x3 at an average price of 80 cents per board foot.

Required *a.* Prepare a purchases budget for the company's lumber needs in board feet for each quarter and for the year.

b. Translate the board feet requirements into dollar purchases for each quarter and for the year.

7–4 Budgeted Cash Disbursements

1. Mapes Corporation has estimated its activity for January 19x1. Selected data from these estimated amounts are as follows:

Sales	$1,400,000
Gross profit (based on sales)	30%
Increase in trade accounts receivable during month	$ 40,000
Change in accounts payable during month	$ –0–
Increase in inventory during month	$ 20,000

Variable marketing and administrative costs (M&A) include a charge for uncollectible accounts of 1 percent of sales.

Total M&A is $142,000 per month plus 15 percent of sales.

Depreciation of $80,000 per month is included in fixed M&A.

What are the estimated cash disbursements for January 19x1?
a. $1,238,000.
b. $1,252,000.
c. $1,258,000.
d. $1,272,000.

2. Walsh, Inc., is preparing its cash budget for the month of November. The following information is available concerning its inventories:

Inventories at beginning of November	$180,000
Estimated cost of goods sold for November	900,000
Estimated inventories at end of November	160,000
Estimated payments in November for purchases prior to November	210,000
Estimated payments in November for purchases in November	80%

What are the estimated cash disbursements for inventories in November?
a. $720,000.
b. $914,000.
c. $930,000.
d. $1,042,000

3. Juniper Company is preparing its cash budget for the month of August 19x1. Projections for the month include the following:

Sales		$400,000
Gross profit (based on sales)		25%
Increase in inventories		$ 30,000
Decrease in trade accounts payable		$ 12,000

What are the estimated cash disbursements for inventories in August 19x1?

a. $142,000.
b. $312,000.
c. $318,000.
d. $342,000.

(AICPA adapted)

7-5 Budgeted Cash Receipts

1. Reid Company is developing a forecast of March 19x0 cash receipts from credit sales. Credit sales for March 19x0 are estimated to be $320,000. The accounts receivable balance at February 29, 19x0, is $300,000; one quarter of the balance represents January credit sales and the remainder is from February sales. All accounts receivable from months prior to January 19x0 have been collected or written off. Reid's history of accounts receivable collections is as follows:

In the month of sale	20%
In the first month after month of sale	50%
In the second month after month of sale	25%
Written off as uncollectible at the end of the second month after month of sale	5%

Based on the above information, Reid is forecasting March 19x0 cash receipts from credit sales of

a. $176,500.
b. $195,250.
c. $253,769.
d. $267,125.

2. The Fresh Company is preparing its cash budget for the month of May. The following information is available concerning its accounts receivable:

Estimated credit sales for May	$200,000
Actual credit sales for April	$150,000
Estimated collections in May for credit sales in May	20%
Estimated collections in May for credit sales in April	70%
Estimated collections in May for credit sales prior to April	$ 12,000
Estimated write-offs in May for uncollectible credit sales	$ 8,000
Estimated provision for bad debts in May for credit sales in May	$ 7,000

What are the estimated cash receipts from accounts receivable collections in May?
   a. $142,000.
   b. $149,000.
   c. $150,000.
   d. $157,000.

3. Pratt Company is preparing its cash budget for the month ending November 30, 19x2. The following information pertains to Pratt's past collection experience from its credit sales:

	Percent
Current month's sales	12
Prior month's sales	75
Sales two months prior to current month	6
Sales three months prior to current month	4
Cash discounts (2/30, net 90)	2
Doubtful accounts	1
Credit sales:	
November, estimated	$200,000
October	180,000
September	160,000
August	190,000

How much is the estimated credit to accounts receivable as a result of collections expected during November?
   a. $170,200.
   b. $174,200.
   c. $176,200.
   d. $180,200.

(AICPA adapted)

7-6 Cash Receipts Budget

The Epoxy Hardware Company sells hardware at the wholesale and retail levels. Its retail sales are for cash, and its wholesale sales are on credit.

The budgeted sales for the first quarter of 19x4 are as follows:

Month	Wholesale	Retail	Total
January	$100,000	$20,000	$120,000
February	80,000	18,000	98,000
March	120,000	25,000	145,000
Total	$300,000	$63,000	$363,000

Credit sales are normally collected as follows:

	Percent
In the month of sale	70
The month following the sale	10
The second month following the	
month of the sale	18
Bad debts, not collected	2

The firm's beginning balance of accounts receivable is $100,000 and is composed of the following:

From December 19x3 sales	$ 60,000
From November 19x3 sales	30,000
From prior sales	10,000
Total	$100,000

The company offers a 2 percent cash discount to its wholesale customers who pay their bills within the month of sale.

Required a. Compute the amount of sales for November and December.
b. Prepare a cash budget of cash collections for each month of the first quarter of 19x4 and a total for the quarter.
c. Calculate the balance of accounts receivable at March 31, 19x4.
d. Calculate the cash discounts taken during the first quarter of 19x4.

7-7 Cash Payments Budget

The All-Natural Bakery Company bakes a variety of bread and rolls for sale to retail food stores. The budgeted raw material purchases for the first quarter of 19x5 are:

Month	Purchases
January	$20,000
February	25,000
March	30,000
Total	$75,000

Budgeted direct labor for the months of January, February, and March are $100,000, $110,000, and $125,000, respectively. Manufacturing overhead for the same three months are budgeted at $90,000, $99,000, and $112,500, respectively.

Budgeted marketing costs for the quarter are $60,000 and administrative costs are budgeted at $90,000 for the quarter. Both occur uniformly on a monthly basis.

Equipment costing $50,000 is expected to arrive at the company's factory in February. The payment for the equipment is due 30 days, net, after its delivery.

Dividends of $10,000 per quarter are paid on the last day of the quarter.

The company takes advantage of all cash discounts offered. Past experience shows that 80 percent of the firm's vendors of raw materials offer a 2 percent cash discount if paid in the month of purchase. The remaining 20 percent of the purchases are paid in the month following the purchase. The beginning balance of accounts payable on January 1, 19x5, is expected to be $6,000.

Straight-line depreciation for the year is expected to be $120,000. This amount is allocated 85 percent to manufacturing overhead, 5 percent to marketing costs, and 10 percent to administrative costs, and these amounts are included in the respective amounts provided above for each category.

Bad debts for the quarter are expected to be negligible.

The first payment for estimated income taxes is due April 15, 19x5, and amounts to $20,000.

Required Prepare a cash payments budget for each month and for the quarter using a separate column for each month and a total column for the quarter.

7–8 Production Budget and Budgeted Raw Materials Purchases

1. Betz Company's sales budget shows the following projections for the year ending December 31, 19x3:

Quarter	Units
First	60,000
Second . . .	80,000
Third	45,000
Fourth	55,000
Total . . .	240,000

Inventory at December 31, 19x2, was budgeted at 18,000 units. The quantity of finished goods inventory at the end of each quarter is to equal 30 percent of the next quarter's budgeted sales of units. How much should the production budget show for units to be produced during the first quarter?

a. 24,000.
b. 48,000.
c. 66,000.
d. 72,000.

2. Reid Company is budgeting sales of 100,000 units of product R for the month of September 19x2. Production of one unit of product R requires two units of material A and three units of material B. Actual inventory units at September 1 and budgeted inventory units at September 30 are as follows:

	Actual Inventory at September 1	Budgeted Inventory at September 30
Product R	20,000	10,000
Material A	25,000	18,000
Material B	22,000	24,000

How many units of material B is Reid planning to purchase during September 19x2?
a. 328,000.
b. 302,000.
c. 298,000.
d. 272,000.

(AICPA adapted)

7-9 Projected Cash and Accounts Receivable Balances

1. Fields Corporation projects the following transactions for 19x1, its first year of operations:

Proceeds from issuance of common stock	$1,000,000
Sales on account	2,200,000
Collections of accounts receivable	1,800,000
Cost of goods sold	1,400,000
Disbursements for purchases of	
merchandise and other costs	1,200,000
Disbursements for income taxes	250,000
Disbursements for purchase of	
fixed assets	800,000
Depreciation on fixed assets	150,000
Proceeds from borrowings	700,000
Payments on borrowings	80,000

The projected cash balance at December 31, 19x1, is
a. $1,170,000.
b. $1,220,000.
c. $1,370,000.
d. $1,820,000.

2. In preparing its budget for July 19x2, Robinson Company has the following accounts receivable information available:

Accounts receivable at June 30, 19x2	$350,000
Estimated credit sales for July	400,000
Estimated collections in July for credit	
sales in July and prior months	320,000
Estimated write-offs in July for	
uncollectible credit sales	16,000
Estimated provision for doubtful	
accounts for credit sales in July	12,000

What is the projected balance of accounts receivable at July 31, 19x2?
a. $402,000.
b. $414,000.
c. $426,000.
d. $430,000.

(AICPA adapted)

7–10   Budgeted Cash Payments, Collections, and Inventory

Tomlinson Retail seeks your assistance to develop cash and other budget information for May, June, and July 19x3. At April 30, 19x3, the company had cash of $5,500, accounts receivable of $437,000, inventories of $309,400, and accounts payable of $133,055.

The budget is to be based on the following assumptions:

---

1. Sales
    a. Each month's sales are billed on the last day of the month.
    b. Customers are allowed a 3 percent discount if payment is made within 10 days after the billing date. Receivables are booked gross.
    c. Sixty percent of the billings are collected within the discount period, 25 percent are collected by the end of the month, 9 percent are collected by the end of the second month, and 6 percent prove uncollectible.

2. Purchases
    a. Fifty-four percent of all purchases of material and marketing and administrative costs are paid in the month purchased and the remainder in the following month.
    b. Each month's units of ending inventory is equal to 130 percent of the next month's units of sales.
    c. The cost of each unit of inventory is $20.
    d. Marketing and administrative costs, of which $2,000 is depreciation, are equal to 15 percent of the current month's sales.

Actual and projected sales are as follows:

19x3	Dollars	Units
March	$354,000	11,800
April	363,000	12,100
May	357,000	11,900
June	342,000	11,400
July	360,000	12,000
August	366,000	12,200

1. Budgeted cash disbursements during the month of June 19x3 are
    a. $292,900.
    b. $287,379.
    c. $294,900.
    d. $285,379.
2. Budgeted cash collections during the month of May 19x3 are
    a. $333,876.
    b. $355,116.
    c. $340,410.
    d. $355,656.
3. The budgeted number of units of inventory to be purchased during July 19x3 is

a. 15,860.
b. 12,260.
c. 12,000.
d. 15,600.

(AICPA adapted)

7–11   **Budgeted Cash Collections, Inventory, Purchases, and Payments for Merchandise**

The Russon Corporation is a retailer whose sales are all made on credit. Sales are billed twice monthly, on the 10th of the month for the last half of the prior month's sales and on the 20th of the month for the first half of the current month's sales. The terms of all sales are 2/10, net 30. Based upon past experience, the collection experience of accounts receivable is as follows:

Within the discount period 80%
On the 30th day 18%
Uncollectible 2%

The sales value of shipments for May 19x0 and the forecast for the next four months are:

May (actual) . . . $500,000
June   600,000
July   700,000
August   700,000
September   400,000

Russon's average markup on its products is 20 percent of the sales price.

Russon purchases merchandise for resale to meet the current month's sales demand and to maintain a desired monthly ending inventory of 25 percent of the next month's sales. All purchases are on credit with terms of net 30. Russon pays for one half of a month's purchases in the month of purchase and the other half in the month following the purchase.

All sales and purchases occur uniformly throughout the month.

1. How much cash can Russon Corporation plan to collect from accounts receivable collections during July 19x0?
    a. $574,000.
    b. $662,600.
    c. $619,000.
    d. $608,600.
    e. None of the above answers is correct.
2. How much cash can Russon plan to collect in September from sales made in August 19x0?
    a. $337,400.
    b. $343,000.
    c. $400,400.
    d. $280,000.
    e. None of the above answers is correct.

3. The budgeted dollar value of Russon's inventory on August 31, 19x0, will be
   a. $110,000.
   b. $80,000.
   c. $112,000.
   d. $100,000.
   e. Some amount other than those given above.
4. How much merchandise should Russon plan to purchase during June 19x0?
   a. $520,000.
   b. $460,000.
   c. $500,000.
   d. $580,000.
   e. None of the above answers is correct.
5. The amount Russon should budget in August 19x0 for the payment of merchandise is
   a. $560,000.
   b. $500,000.
   c. $667,000.
   d. $600,000.
   e. None of the above answers is correct.

Note: 2/10, net 30 means that a cash discount of 2 percent is allowed if paid within 10 days. The full amount is payable within 30 days.

(CMA adapted)

7–12 **Budgeted Purchases, Inventory, Payments for Purchases, Sales Discounts, and Cash Collections**

The Dilly Company marks up all merchandise at 25 percent of gross purchase price. All purchases are made on account with terms of 1/10, net 60. Purchase discounts, which are recorded as miscellaneous income, are always taken. Normally, 60 percent of each month's purchases are paid for in the month of purchase while the other 40 percent are paid during the first 10 days of the first month after purchase. Inventories of merchandise at the end of each month are kept at 30 percent of the next month's projected cost of goods sold.

Terms for sales on account are 2/10, net 30. Cash sales are not subject to discount. Fifty percent of each month's sales on account are collected during the month of sale, 45 percent are collected in the succeeding month, and the remainder are usually uncollectible. Seventy percent of the collections in the month of sale are subject to discount while 10 percent of the collections in the succeeding month are subject to discount.

Projected sales data for selected months follow:

	Sales on Account—Gross	Cash Sales
December	$1,900,000	$400,000
January	1,500,000	250,000
February	1,700,000	350,000
March	1,600,000	300,000

1. Projected gross purchases for January are
    a. $1,400,000.
    b. $1,470,000.
    c. $1,472,000.
    d. $1,248,000.
    e. None of the above.
2. Projected inventory at the end of December is
    a. $420,000.
    b. $441,600.
    c. $552,000.
    d. $393,750.
    e. None of the above.
3. Projected payments to suppliers during February are
    a. $1,551,200.
    b. $1,535,688.
    c. $1,528,560.
    d. $1,509,552.
    e. None of the above.
4. Projected sales discounts to be taken by customers making remittances during February are
    a. $5,250.
    b. $15,925.
    c. $30,500.
    d. $11,900.
    e. None of the above.
5. Projected total collections from customers during February are
    a. $1,875,000.
    b. $1,861,750.
    c. $1,511,750.
    d. $1,188,100.
    e. None of the above.

Note: 2/10, net 30 means that a cash discount of 2 percent is allowed if paid within 10 days. The full amount is payable within 30 days. 1/10, net 60 is treated in a similar manner.

(AICPA adapted)

7–13   Production and Raw Materials Purchases Budgets

The Seymour Picture Frame Company manufactures wooden picture frames. Its sales budget in units for part of 19x6 is as follows:

Month	Budgeted Sales in Units
January	10,000
February	12,000
March	9,000
April	15,000
May	8,000

Each picture frame requires three lineal feet of wood molding which costs 30 cents per foot. Glue and nails are ordered in bulk quantities and may be ignored.

It is the firm's policy to maintain a finished goods inventory equal to 30 percent of the following month's sales, and to maintain an inventory of raw materials equal to 40 percent of the production requirements for the following month.

The beginning inventories of finished goods and lumber are expected to be equal to the 30 percent and 40 percent respective requirements.

Required a. Prepare a production budget for each of the months in the first quarter and in total for the quarter.
b. Prepare a raw materials purchases budget, in lineal feet and in dollars, for the quarter in total and for each month of the quarter.

7–14 Production and Raw Materials Budgets from Missing Data

The Sealess Picture Frame Company manufactures wooden picture frames. Each picture frame requires one board foot of wood which costs 80 cents per board foot. Glue and nails are negligible and may be ignored.

It is the firm's policy to maintain a finished goods inventory equal to 20 percent of the following month's sales, and to maintain an inventory of raw materials equal to 30 percent of the production requirements for the following month.

The company's incomplete budgets, in units, are as follows for the first quarter of 19x6:

SEALESS PICTURE FRAME COMPANY
Partial Raw Materials Purchases and Production Budgets
For the First Quarter of 19x6

	January	February	March	Total
Raw materials purchases (in board feet):				
Production	?	?	?	?
Add: Ending inventory	?	?	?	?
Subtotal	27,240	30,120	29,980	?
Less: Beginning inventory	6,120	6,840	7,320	?
Required purchases	21,120	23,280	22,660	?
Production budget (in units):				
Budgeted sales	?	?	?	?
Add: Ending inventory	?	?	?	?
Subtotal	?	?	?	?
Less: Beginning inventory	4,000	4,400	5,200	?
Required production	?	?	?	?

Required a. Supply the missing data and complete the raw materials purchases budget and the production budget. (Hint: Complete the raw materials purchases budget first.)
b. Compute the budgeted sales for April and May.

7–15 Zero-Based Budgeting

There has been much recent publicity about a budgeting system called "zero-based" budgeting. The system can be applied in governmental, not-for-profit, and profit-making organizations. Its proponents believe that it represents a significant change in the budgeting process for most types of organizations and, thus, leads to more effective use of limited resources.

Required

a. Describe the "zero-based" budgeting system.

b. Explain how the proponents of "zero-based" budgeting say it differs from the traditional budgeting process.

c. Identify the advantages and disadvantages of the "zero-based" budgeting system.

(CMA adapted)

7–16 Budgeted Cash Collections, Cash Payments, and Cash Balance

The following information was available from Montero Corporation's books:

19x2	Purchases	Sales
January	$42,000	$72,000
February	48,000	66,000
March	36,000	60,000
April	54,000	78,000

Collections from customers are normally 70 percent in the month of sale, 20 percent in the month following the sale, and 9 percent in the second month following the sale. The balance is expected to be uncollectible. Montero takes full advantage of the 2 percent discount allowed on purchases paid for by the 10th of the following month. Purchases for May are budgeted at $60,000, while sales for May are forecasted at $66,000. Cash disbursements for costs are expected to be $14,400 for the month of May. Montero's cash balance at May 1 was $22,000.

Required Prepare the following schedules:

a. Expected cash collections during May.

b. Expected cash disbursements during May.

c. Expected cash balance at May 31.

(AICPA adapted)

PROBLEMS   7–17 Preparation of Operating Budget

The Scarborough Corporation manufactures and sells two products, Thingone and Thingtwo. In July 19x7, Scarborough's budget department gathered the following data in order to project sales and budget requirements for 19x8.

	19x8 Projected Sales	
Product	Units	Price
Thingone	60,000	$ 70
Thingtwo	40,000	$100

	19x8 Inventories (in units)	
	Expected	Desired
Product	January 1, 19x8	December 31, 19x8
Thingone	20,000	25,000
Thingtwo	8,000	9,000

In order to produce one unit of Thingone and Thingtwo, the following raw materials are used:

Raw Material	Unit	Amount Used per Unit	
		Thingone	Thingtwo
A	pounds	4	5
B	pounds	2	3
C	each		1

Projected data for 19x8 with respect to raw materials is as follows:

Raw Material	Anticipated Purchase Price	Expected Inventories January 1, 19x8	Desired Inventories December 31, 19x8
A	$8	32,000 pounds	36,000 pounds
B	$5	29,000 pounds	32,000 pounds
C	$3	6,000 each	7,000 each

Projected direct labor requirements for 19x8 and rates are as follows:

Product	Hours per Unit	Rate per Hour
Thingone	2	$3
Thingtwo	3	$4

Overhead is applied at the rate of $2 per direct labor-hour.

Required Based upon the above projections and budget requirements for 19x8 for Thingone and Thingtwo, prepare the following budgets for 19x8:

a. Sales budget (in dollars).
b. Production budget (in units).
c. Raw materials purchase budget (in quantities).
d. Raw materials purchase budget (in dollars).
e. Direct labor budget (in dollars).
f. Budgeted finished goods inventory at December 31, 19x8 (in dollars).

(AICPA adapted)

7–18   Procedures Used to Develop the Annual Budget

Arment Company has sales in the range of $25 to $30 million, has one manufacturing plant, employs 700 people, including 15 national account salesmen and 80 traveling sales representatives. The home office and plant is in Philadelphia, and the product is distributed east of the Mississippi River. The product is a line of pumps and related fittings used at construction sites, in homes, and in processing plants. The company has total assets equal to 80 percent of sales. Its capitalization is: accruals and current liabilities 30 percent, long-term debt 15 percent, and shareholders' equity 55 percent. In the last two years, sales have increased 7 percent each year, and income after tax has amounted to 5 percent of sales.

Required

a. Strategic decisions by top management on a number of important topics serve as a basis for the annual profit plan. What are these topics, and why are they important?

b. What specific procedures will be followed each year in developing the annual profit plan?

(CMA adapted)

7-19 Production Budget, Direct Materials Budget, and Direct Labor Budget

The Wyoming division of Reid Corporation produces an intricate component part used in Reid's major product line. The division manager has been concerned recently by a lack of coordination between purchasing and production personnel and believes that a monthly budgeting system would be better than the present system.

Wyoming's division manager has decided to develop budget information for the third quarter of the current year as a trial before the budget system is implemented for an entire fiscal year. In response to the division manager's request for data which could be used to develop budget information, the division controller accumulated the following data.

Sales

Sales through June 30, 19x7, the first six months of the current year, are 24,000 units. Actual sales in units for May and June and estimated unit sales for the next four months are detailed as follows:

May (actual)	4,000
June (actual)	4,000
July (estimated)	5,000
August (estimated)	6,000
September (estimated)	7,000
October (estimated)	7,000

Wyoming Division expects to sell 60,000 units during the year ending December 31, 19x7.

Direct Material

Data regarding the materials used in the component are shown in the schedule below. The desired monthly ending inventory for all direct materials is to have sufficient materials on hand to produce the next month's estimated sales.

Direct Material	Units of Direct Materials per Finished Component	Cost per Unit	Inventory Level 6/30/x7
#101	6	$2.40	35,000 units
#211	4	3.60	30,000 units
#242	2	1.20	14,000 units

Direct Labor

Each component must pass through three different processes to be completed. Data regarding the direct labor is presented below.

Process	Direct Labor-Hours per Finished Component	Cost per Direct Labor-Hour
Forming	.80	$8.00
Assembly	2.00	5.50
Finishing	.25	6.00

Finished Goods Inventory

The desired monthly ending inventory in units of completed components is 80 percent of the next month's estimated sales. There are 5,000 finished units in the inventory on June 30, 19x7.

Required
a. Prepare a production budget in units for the Wyoming division for the third quarter ending September 30, 19x7.

b. Without prejudice to your answer in requirement a, assume the Wyoming division plans to produce 18,000 units during the third quarter ending September 30, 19x7, and 60,000 units for the year ending December 31, 19x7.

(1) Prepare a direct materials purchase budget in units and dollars for the third quarter ending September 30, 19x7.

(2) Prepare a direct labor budget in hours and dollars for the third quarter ending September 30, 19x7.

(CMA adapted)

7-20 Preparation of a Cash Budget

The Ace Corporation ends its fiscal year on December 31. You have been requested early in January 19x3, to assist in making a cash budget or forecast. The following information is available from the company's records and interviews:

1. Management feels that the sales pattern for 19x2 is a reasonable basis for budgeting the sales for 19x3. Sales for 19x2 were as follows:

January	$ 360,000
February	420,000
March	600,000
April	540,000
May	480,000
June	400,000
July	350,000
August	550,000
September . . .	500,000
October	400,000
November . . .	600,000
December . . .	800,000
Total	$6,000,000

2. The accounts receivable December 31, 19x2, totaled $380,000. Sales collections are generally made as follows:

	Percent
During month of sale	60
In first subsequent month	30
In second subsequent month	9
Uncollectible	1

3. Cost of goods purchased averages 60 percent of the selling price. The cost of the inventory on hand December 31, 19x2, is $840,000, of which $30,000 is obsolete. Arrangements have been made to sell the obsolete inventory in January at half its normal selling price on a COD basis.

    The company wishes to maintain the inventory as of the first of each month at a level of three months' sales as determined by the sales forecast for the next three months. All purchases are paid for on the 10th of the following month. Accounts payable December 31, 19x2, were $370,000.

4. Recurring fixed costs amount to $120,000 *per month*, of which $20,000 is for depreciation. For accounting purposes, the company apportions the recurring fixed costs to the various months in the same proportion as the month's estimated sales bears to the total estimated annual sales. Variable costs amount to 10 percent of the sales. Payments are made as follows:

	During Month Incurred	Following Month
Fixed costs	55 percent	45 percent
Variable costs	70	30

5. Annual property taxes amount to $50,000 and are paid in two equal installments on December 31 and March 31. These taxes are in addition to the costs in item 4.
6. It is anticipated that a cash dividend of $20,000 will be paid on the 15th day of the third month in each quarter.
7. In addition to the costs indicated in 4 above, unusual advertising will require cash payments in February of $10,000 and in March of $15,000.
8. Equipment replacements are made at the rate of $3,000 per month. The equipment has an average estimated life of six years.
9. At December 31, 19x2, the company had a bank loan with an unpaid balance of $280,000. The loan requires a principal payment of $20,000 on the last day of each month, plus interest at ½ percent per month on the unpaid balance at the first of the month. The entire balance is due March 31, 19x3.
10. The cash balance December 31, 19x2, is $100,000.

Required   Prepare a cash budget for each month of the first three months of 19x3. The budget should show the amount of cash on hand (or deficiency of cash) at the end of each month. (Include a total column for the quarter.)

(AICPA adapted)

7–21   Preparation of Operating Budget and Budgeted Income Statement

The Realistic Company manufactures one product, Destro. The sales forecast for 19x3 and expected selling prices of Destro are as follows:

Quarter	Number of Units	Price
19x3:		
First	20,000	$8.00
Second	25,000	8.00
Third	30,000	8.00
Fourth	40,000	8.50
19x4:		
First	15,000	8.50
Second	20,000	8.50

Destro requires two pounds of Prest at 15 cents per pound and one pound of Sisal at 30 cents per pound. The beginning inventories at January 1, 19x3, are estimated as follows:

Prest	13,000 pounds at $.15 per pound
Sisal	6,300 pounds at $.30 per pound
Destro	6,000 units at $3.20 per unit

The company's policy is to carry as inventories 30 percent of its needs for the following quarter. This applies to both raw materials and finished goods. The company has no work in process inventories. Thus, the required beginning inventory of Destro is 30 percent of the first quarter's expected sales of 20,000 units or 6,000 (30% × 20,000) units. The ending inventories of each item are computed in this manner.

Destro requires an average of 10 minutes ($\frac{1}{6}$ of an hour) of direct labor to manufacture. Wage rates are fixed at $9 per hour.

Manufacturing overhead is applied to production at 80 percent of direct labor cost.

The information needed to prepare the marketing and administrative cost budgets is as follows:

REALISTIC COMPANY
Partial Marketing Cost Budget
For the Year Ended December 31, 19x3

	First Quarter	Second Quarter	Third Quarter	Fourth Quarter	Yearly Total
Sales salaries	$ 5,000	$ 5,000	$ 5,000	$ 5,000	$20,000
Sales commissions*	?	?	?	?	28?200
Advertising	2,000	2,000	3,000	4,000	11,000
Travel	2,000	2,000	2,000	2,000	8,000
Rent	1,500	1,500	1,500	1,500	6,000
Utilities	1,000	1,000	1,000	1,000	4,000
Miscellaneous	2,000	2,000	2,000	2,000	8,000
Totals	$?	$?	$?	$?	$?

* 3% of sales.

REALISTIC COMPANY
Partial Administrative Cost Budget
For the Year Ended December 31, 19x3

	First Quarter	Second Quarter	Third Quarter	Fourth Quarter	Yearly Total
Administrative					
salaries	$20,000	$20,000	$20,000	$20,000	$80,000
Rent	2,000	2,000	2,000	2,000	8,000
Utilities	1,000	1,000	1,000	1,000	4,000
Insurance	1,500	1,500	1,500	1,500	6,000
Professional fees	2,000	2,000	2,000	2,000	8,000
Bad debts cost*	?	?	?	?	9?00
Payroll fringes	6,000	6,000	6,000	6,000	24,000
Miscellaneous	5,000	5,000	5,000	5,000	20,000
Totals	$?	$?	$?	$?	$?

* 1% of sales.

Income taxes are expected to average 30 percent for the year.

Required a. Prepare quarterly budgets with a total column for the year for:
(1) Sales in dollars.
(2) Production in units.
(3) Raw material purchases in units and in dollars.
(4) Marketing costs.
(5) Administrative costs.
b. Prepare year-end inventories budgets for raw materials and finished goods.
c. Prepare a budgeted income statement.

7-22 Preparation of Cash Budget

The Surrey Company has prepared its operating budget for 19x4 and wishes to have a cash budget prepared. The following budgeted information is available (all in dollars):

	First Quarter	Second Quarter	Third Quarter	Fourth Quarter	Total
Sales	$150,000	$200,000	$240,000	$300,000	$890,000
Raw materials					
purchases	15,000	20,000	24,000	30,000	89,000
Direct labor	30,000	40,000	48,000	60,000	178,000
Manufacturing					
overhead	36,000	38,000	45,000	47,000	166,000
Marketing costs	23,000	24,000	24,800	26,000	97,800
Administrative					
costs	31,500	32,000	32,400	33,000	128,900
Estimated income					
taxes	20,000	20,000	20,000	20,000	80,000

Accounts receivable are collected as follows:

	Percent
During the quarter of sale	90
The subsequent quarter	9
Uncollectible	˙1

Payments are made as follows:

Raw materials purchases—80 percent in the quarter purchased, 20 percent in the following quarter.

Direct labor—100 percent in the quarter incurred.

Manufacturing overhead—75 percent in the quarter incurred, 25 percent in the following quarter.

Marketing and administrative costs—100 percent in the quarter incurred.

Accounts receivable on January 1, 19x4, is expected to contain the following:

From sales made in the fourth quarter, 19x3	$30,000
From sales made prior to the fourth	
quarter, 19x3	10,000
Total	$40,000

The accounts payable on January 1, 19x4, is expected to amount to $16,000. This includes $6,000 for raw materials purchases and $10,000 for manufacturing overhead.

Manufacturing overhead includes $10,000 per quarter for depreciation.

Administrative costs include a provision for bad debts equal to 1 percent of sales. The balance of administrative costs are fixed costs.

Equipment is to be purchased and paid for as follows:

Quarter	**Amount**
First	$ 5,000
Second	50,000
Third	10,000
Fourth	–0–

Dividends of $10,000 are paid on the last day of each quarter.

The cash balance on January 1, 19x4, is expected to be $50,000, and the company wishes to maintain a minimum cash balance of $40,000 at the end of each quarter.

The company has an arrangement with its bank to borrow money at a 12 percent interest rate. Borrowings, if needed, are made on the last day of the quarter, and maximum repayments are made on the last day of the quarter when the cash balance exceeds $40,000.

Required   Prepare a cash budget for each quarter of 19x4 and include a total column for the year.

7–23   Preparation of Budgeted Balance Sheet

The Fringe Company has prepared its budgeted income statement and its cash budget, which are presented below. Its budgeted balance sheet at January 1, 19x3, is also presented below.

FRINGE COMPANY
Budgeted Income Statement
For the Year Ended December 31, 19x3

Sales	$800,000
Cost of goods sold	360,000
Gross margin	440,000
Marketing and administrative costs:	
Marketing costs	90,000
Administrative costs	110,000
Total marketing and administrative costs	200,000
Operating income before income taxes	240,000
Income taxes	96,000
Net income	$144,000

FRINGE COMPANY
Cash Budget
For the Year Ended December 31, 19x3

Cash balance, beginning	$ 30,000
Add receipts:	
From customers	802,000
Subtotal	832,000
Deduct disbursements:	
Raw materials	85,000
Direct labor	145,000
Manufacturing overhead	112,000
Marketing	90,000
Administrative	102,000
Equipment	70,000
Dividends	60,000
Income taxes	96,000
Subtotal	760,000
Excess (deficiency) of cash	72,000
Financing:	
Borrowing	–0–
Repayment	–0–
Interest	–0–
Total financing	–0–
Cash balance, ending	$ 72,000

FRINGE COMPANY
Budgeted Balance Sheet
January 1, 19x3

Assets

Current assets:

Cash			$ 30,000
Accounts receivable	$35,000		
Less: Allowance for uncollectibles	2,500		32,500
Inventories:			
Raw materials	4,000		
Finished goods	18,000		22,000
Total current assets			$ 84,500
Plant assets:			
Equipment		100,000	
Less: Accumulated depreciation		25,000	75,000
Total assets			$159,500

Liabilities and Stockholders' Equity

Current liabilities:

Accounts payable		$ 6,000	
Total current liabilities			$ 6,000
Stockholders' equity:			
Common stock		50,000	
Retained earnings		103,500	
Total stockholders' equity			153,500
Total liabilities and stockholders' equity			$159,500

The following additional information is available:

1. The company provides for bad debts at 1 percent of sales.
2. During the year, $3,000 of accounts receivable were written off against the allowance for uncollectibles.
3. Depreciation for the year amounted to $20,000.
4. Inventories at December 31, 19x3, are expected to consist of:

> Raw materials . . . . $ 3,000
> Finished goods $21,000

Required Prepare a budgeted balance sheet at December 31, 19x3. (Show all computations.)

7–24 Preparation of Master Budget

The Foremost Company manufactures one product, Bestro. The sales forecast for 19x3 and expected selling prices of Bestro are as follows:

	Number of	
Quarter	Units	Price
19x3:		
First	28,000	$12.00
Second	26,000	12.00
Third	36,000	12.50
Fourth	40,000	13.00
19x4:		
First	25,000	13.50
Second	30,000	13.50

Bestro requires two pounds of Durest at 60 cents per pound. The beginning inventories at January 1, 19x3, are estimated as follows:

Bestro . . . . 5,600 units at $5.25 each
Durest . . . . 11,040 pounds at $0.60 per pound

The company's policy is to carry as inventories 20 percent of its needs for the following quarter. This applies to both raw materials and finished goods. The company has no work in process inventories.

Bestro requires an average of 15 minutes (¼ of an hour) of direct labor to manufacture. Wage rates are fixed at $9 per hour.

Manufacturing overhead is applied to production at 80 percent of direct labor cost and consists of the following:

	Fixed	Variable	Total
Superintendence	$ 50,000		$ 50,000
Indirect labor	20,000	$ 30,000	50,000
Rent	20,000		20,000
Repairs and maintenance	2,000	16,000	18,000
Light and power	1,000	19,000	20,000
Payroll fringes	7,000	41,460	48,460
Miscellaneous	1,460	10,000	11,460
Depreciation of machinery	15,000		15,000
Totals	$116,460	$116,460	$232,920

Overhead rate per direct labor cost:
$232,920 ÷ $291,150 = 80% per direct labor dollar

The information needed to prepare the marketing and administrative cost budgets is as follows:

FOREMOST COMPANY
Partial Marketing Cost Budget
For the Year Ended December 31, 19x3

	First Quarter	Second Quarter	Third Quarter	Fourth Quarter	Yearly Total
Sales salaries	$ 8,000	$ 8,000	$ 8,000	$ 8,000	$ 32,000
Sales commissions*	?	?	?	?	?
Advertising	3,000	3,000	4,000	4,000	14,000
Travel	2,000	2,000	2,000	2,000	8,000
Rent	2,500	2,500	2,500	2,500	10,000
Utilities	1,000	1,000	1,000	1,000	4,000
Miscellaneous	2,000	2,000	2,000	2,000	8,000
Totals	$?	$?	$?	$?	$?

* 3% of sales.

FOREMOST COMPANY
Partial Administrative Cost Budget
For the Year Ended December 31, 19x3

	First Quarter	Second Quarter	Third Quarter	Fourth Quarter	Yearly Total
Administrative					
salaries	$40,000	$40,000	$40,000	$40,000	$160,000
Rent	5,000	5,000	5,000	5,000	20,000
Utilities	1,000	1,000	1,000	1,000	4,000
Insurance	1,500	1,500	1,500	1,500	6,000
Professional fees	3,000	3,000	3,000	3,000	12,000
Bad debts cost*	?	?	?	?	?
Payroll fringes	12,000	12,000	12,000	12,000	48,000
Miscellaneous	5,000	5,000	5,000	5,000	20,000
Totals	$?	$?	$?	$?	$?

* 1% of sales.

Income taxes are expected to average 30 percent for the year, and estimated income taxes are $160,000, payable $40,000 each quarter. Any difference between the estimated taxes of $160,000 and the provision required on the income statement is to be shown on the balance sheet as either a current liability or a current asset, depending on whether the difference is debit or credit.

Accounts receivable are collected as follows:

	Percent
During the quarter of sale	90
The subsequent quarter	9
Uncollectible	1

Payments are made as follows

Raw materials purchases—80 percent in the quarter purchased, 20 percent in the following quarter.

Direct labor—100 percent in the quarter incurred.

Manufacturing overhead—90 percent in the quarter incurred, 10 percent in the following quarter.

Marketing and administrative costs—100 percent in the quarter incurred.

Accounts receivable on January 1, 19x3, is expected to contain the following:

From sales made in the fourth quarter, 19x2	$52,000
From sales made prior to the fourth quarter, 19x2	9,000
Total	$61,000

The accounts payable on January 1, 19x3, is expected to amount to $16,200. This includes $9,600 for raw materials purchases and $6,600 for manufacturing overhead.

Administrative costs include a provision for bad debts equal to 1 percent of sales. The balance of administrative costs are fixed costs.

Equipment is to be purchased and paid for as follows:

Quarter	Amount
First	$15,000
Second	80,000
Third	20,000
Fourth	10,000

Dividends of $20,000 are paid on the last day of each quarter.

The cash balance on January 1, 19x3, is expected to be $50,000, and the company wishes to maintain a minimum cash balance of $50,000 at the end of each quarter.

The company has an arrangement with its bank to borrow money at a 12 percent interest rate. Borrowings, if needed, are made on the last day of the quarter, and maximum repayments are made on the last day of the quarter when the cash balance exceeds $50,000.

During the year, $8,000 of accounts receivable were written off against the allowance for uncollectibles.

The company's budgeted balance sheet at January 1, 19x3, is as follows:

FOREMOST COMPANY
Budgeted Balance Sheet
January 1, 19x3
Assets

Current assets:

Cash		$ 50,000	
Accounts receivable	$61,000		
Less: Allowance for uncollectibles . . .	6,000	55,000	
Inventories:			
Raw materials	6,624		
Finished goods	29,400	36,024	
Total current assets			$141,024
Plant assets:			
Equipment		150,000	
Less: Accumulated depreciation		60,000	90,000
Total assets			$231,024

Liabilities and Stockholders' Equity

Current liabilities:

Accounts payable		$ 16,200	
Total current liabilities			$ 16,200
Stockholders' equity:			
Common stock		100,000	
Retained earnings		114,824	
Total stockholders' equity			214,824
Total liabilities and stockholders' equity			$231,024

Required

a. Prepare quarterly budgets with a total column for the year for
   (1) Sales in dollars.
   (2) Production in units.
   (3) Raw material purchases in units and in dollars.
   (4) Marketing costs.
   (5) Administrative costs.

b. Prepare year-end inventories budgets for raw materials and finished goods.

c. Prepare a budgeted income statement.

d. Prepare a cash budget for each quarter of 19x3 and include a total column for the year.

e. Prepare a budgeted balance sheet at December 31, 19x3. (Show all computations.)

7–25   Preparation of a Budgeted Statement of Financial Position (Balance Sheet) for a Not-for-Profit Organization

The Breckenridge Institute is a not-for-profit foundation that undertakes scientific research on a contract basis. The institute regularly does research for federal, state, and local governments as well as for business firms.

The statement of financial position for the institute at April 30, 19x6, is presented below. The statement of operations showing the actual results for the year ended April 30, 19x6, and the budgeted amount for the coming year ending April 30, 19x7, appears on the next page. The statement of cash receipts and disbursements presenting actual results and budgeted figures for the years ending April 30, 19x6, and 19x7, respectively, also appears below:

BRECKENRIDGE INSTITUTE
Statement of Financial Position
April 30, 19x6
(in thousands)

Assets

Current assets:			
Cash			$ 110
Marketable securities			80
Accounts receivable:			
Government contracts		$ 230	
Private contracts	$150		
Less: Allowance for uncollectibles	10	140	370
Materials and supplies			64
Prepaid insurance			6
Total current assets . . .			630
Plant and equipment (net of depreciation)			1,200
Total assets			$1,830

Equities

Current liabilities:			
Accounts payable			$ 120
Accrued payroll, payroll taxes, and benefits			46
Due to outside consultants			20
Interest payable			16
Current portion of long-term debt			60
Total current liabilities . . .			262
Long-term debt			240
Total liabilities			502
Original capital		$1,000	
Accumulated excess of revenues over expenditures		328	1,328
Total equities			$1,830

BRECKENRIDGE INSTITUTE
Statement of Operations
(in thousands)

	Actual Results for the Year Ended 4/30/x6	Budget for the Year Ended 4/30/x7
Revenues from operations:		
Federal government	$1,500	$1,650
State and local government	224	250
Private (less provision for		
bad debts of $19 and $25)	1,216	1,335
Interest	4	2
Total revenues	2,944	3,237
Operating costs:		
Personnel:		
Salaries	1,390	1,300
Wages	175	200
Employee benefits and		
payroll taxes	273	300
Consultants	35	250
Employee training	20	35
Material and supplies	548	600
Utilities	60	60
Insurance	20	20
Depreciation	160	165
Other costs	117	123
Interest charges	16	14
Total operating costs	2,814	3,067
Excess of revenues over costs	$ 130	$ 170

BRECKENRIDGE INSTITUTE
Cash Receipts and Disbursements
(in thousands)

	Actual Results for the Year Ended 4/30/x6	Budget for the Year Ended 4/30/x7
Receipts:		
Contracts		
Federal, state, and local governments	$1,700	$1,820
Private	1,200	1,300
	2,900	3,120
Interest	4	2
Sales of marketable securities	–0–	50
Total receipts	2,904	3,172
Disbursements:		
Salaries and wages	1,560	1,510
Employee benefits	260	300
Consultant fees	15	230
Employee training programs	20	35
Materials and supplies	540	575
Utilities	55	65
Insurance	20	22
Other costs	117	123
Interest	18	16
Retirement of debt	60	60
Purchases of capital equipment	80	315
Total disbursements	2,745	3,251
Increase (decrease) in cash	$ 159	$ (79)

During the construction of the budget, the following additional information was developed:

1. Purchases of materials and supplies were budgeted at $610,000
2. Write-offs of specific accounts receivable are estimated as follows:
   a. $8,000 of the accounts receivable balance at 4/30/x6.
   b. Uncollectible accounts of $12,000 from fiscal 19x7 sales to be written off in fiscal 19x7.
3. The unusually large budgeted expenditure for capital equipment is part of a three-year program begun in 19x6 to enable the institute to enter new areas of scientific research. Similar amounts will be spent in the next two years for additional equipment. Increased revenues from the new capabilities will not be significant until 19x9.

Required   In addition to the two budgeted statements already prepared for the coming fiscal year, prepare a budgeted statement of financial position as of April 30, 19x7, for presentation to the board of trustees.

(CMA adapted)

7-26   **Preparation of a Cash Budget for a Not-for-Profit Organization**

United Business Education, Inc., (UBE) is a nonprofit organization which sponsors a wide variety of management seminars throughout the United States. In addition, it is heavily involved in research into improved methods of educating and motivating business executives. The seminar activity is largely supported by fees and the research program from member dues.

UBE operates on a calendar year basis and is in the process of finalizing the budget for 19x1. The following information has been taken from approved plans which are still tentative at this time.

Seminar Program

Revenue—The scheduled number of programs should produce $12 million of revenue for the year. Each program is budgeted to produce the same amount of revenue. The revenue is collected during the month the program is offered. The programs are scheduled so that 12 percent of the revenue is collected in each of the first five months of the year. The remaining programs, accounting for the remaining 40 percent of the revenue, are distributed evenly through the months of September, October, and November. No programs are offered in the other four months of the year.

Direct costs—The seminar costs are made up of three segments:

1. Instructors' fees are paid at the rate of 70 percent of the seminar revenue in the month following the seminar. The instructors are considered independent contractors and are not eligible for UBE employee benefits.
2. Facilities fees total $5.6 million for the year. They are the same for each program and are paid in the month the program is given.
3. Annual promotional costs of $1 million are spent equally in all months except June and July when there is no promotional effort.

Research Program

Research grants—The research program has a large number of projects nearing completion. The other main research activity this year includes the feasibility studies for new projects to be started in 19x2. As a result, the total grant of $3 million for 19x1 is expected to be paid out at the rate of $500,000 per month during the first six months of the year.

Salaries and Other UBE Costs

Office lease—Annual amount of $240,000 paid monthly at the beginning of each month.

General administrative costs (telephone, supplies, postage, etc.)—$1.5 million annually or $125,000 a month.

Depreciation—$240,000 a year.

General UBE promotion—Annual cost of $600,000, paid monthly.

Salaries and benefits—

Number of Employees	Annual Salary Paid Monthly	Total Annual Salaries
1	$50,000	$ 50,000
3	40,000	120,000
4	30,000	120,000
15	25,000	375,000
5	15,000	75,000
22	10,000	220,000
50		$960,000

Employee benefits amount to $240,000 or 25 percent of annual salaries. Except for the pension contribution, the benefits are paid as salaries are paid. The annual pension payment of $24,000, based on 2.5 percent of salaries (included in the total benefits and the 25 percent rate), is due April 15, 19x1.

Other Information

Membership income—UBE has 100,000 members each of whom pays an annual fee of $100. The fee for the calendar year is invoiced in late June. The collection schedule is as follows.

	Percent
July	60
August	30
September	5
October	5
Total	100

Capital expenditures—The capital expenditures program calls for a total of $510,000 in cash payments to be spread evenly over the first five months of 19x1.

Cash and temporary investments at January 1, 19x1, are estimated at $750,000.

Required
a. Prepare a budget of the annual cash receipts and disbursements for UBE, Inc., for 19x1.
b. Prepare a cash budget for UBE, Inc., for January 19x1.
c. Using the information you developed in requirement *a* and *b,* identify two important operating problems of UBE, Inc.

(CMA adapted)

8

STANDARD COSTS AND PERFORMANCE EVALUATION

LEARNING OBJECTIVES

After reading this chapter, you should be able to:

1 Discuss why businesses need standard costs.

2 Explain the difference between effectiveness and efficiency.

3 Explain the difference between standard costs, budgeted costs, and actual costs.

4 List who the members of the standards committee are and discuss how standards are set.

5 List and discuss the uses of standard costs.

6 Differentiate between ideal standards and practical standards.

7 Compute standard costs for direct materials and direct labor.

8 Analyze a variance between actual and total standard costs to determine the price variance and the quantity variance.

9 Prepare a diagrammatic solution to variance analysis.

10 Prepare a performance report.

11 List the criteria used to select variances for investigation.

12 Prepare the journal entries needed when standard costs are part of a firm's cost accounting system (Appendix 8–A).

Standards, the expected levels of performance, play an important part in our daily lives. When attending high school or college, a student must perform at a certain level of scholarship in order to graduate and earn a diploma or a degree. When dining in a restaurant, a patron expects a certain level of quality in the food served, and when purchasing a product, a consumer demands a certain level of dependability and service. Thus, standards prevade all areas of human activity, including, as we shall see, the field of management, where it is vital that clear and quantitative standards be used to measure performance.

A firm is usually concerned with producing its product at the lowest possible cost consistent with the quality it wishes to maintain. Thus, the firm will monitor the prices that it pays for its raw materials, direct labor, and manufacturing overhead. Not only must it monitor these items, it must also control the quantities of these factors that it uses in its production process. Because of the volume of transactions that a firm has in an accounting period, such as one month, it is extremely impractical and costly to monitor every single transaction during the period. Thus, firms group large numbers of similar transactions and then compare the grouping to a norm that is set in advance of the actual occurrence of the transactions. The setting of norms to be used for the controlling of costs is known as standard costing. This chapter is concerned with the setting of predetermined (standard) costs and their use in a firm's accounting system, the identification of the differences between a firm's actual costs and standard costs, the analysis of these differences, and their interpretation.

Actual costs vary from predetermined costs for two reasons: the actual price paid for a good or service may differ from its estimated price and the quantity consumed may differ from the amount predicted. These differences may be classified as favorable when the price paid or the quantity consumed is less than expected, or they may be classified as unfavorable when the reverse is true. For cost control purposes, managers need timely performance reports showing the differences between standard costs and actual costs with analyses showing the causes of the differences and whether the differences are favorable or unfavorable.

Performance Evaluation

Everyone at one time or another is evaluated on his or her performance. Often, terms such as *effective* and *efficient* are used to rate favorable performance, while *ineffective* and *inefficient* are used to rate unfavorable performance. **Effectiveness** relates to whether an objective is achieved. **Efficiency,** on the other hand, is a measure of the means by which an objective is achieved—that is, whether it is achieved with the least amount of effort and the least possible cost. For example, if a sales representative is required to make a trip from New York to Florida to attend a sales convention, she may choose a direct flight from New York to Florida, which would be both efficient and effective. Alternatively, she could take a flight from New York to California and then take another flight from California to Florida. Although this route would be effective—the objective is to attend a sales convention in Florida—the means by which it is achieved is inefficient. Evaluating the effectiveness and efficiency of an employee's performance requires the setting of expected levels of performance, or standards.

STANDARDS

A standard is an established criterion used to measure the quality of performance. Unless a firm develops standards for measuring employee performance, a manager's evaluations are likely to be biased, subjective, and ineffective. Moreover, if employees are not told what level of performance is expected, they cannot be expected to take their manager's evaluations seriously. On the other hand, when an appropriate level of performance is clearly defined and when that level is reasonable and fair to both the employer and the employee, employees should expect rewards for superior performance and penalties for inferior performance. Thus, it is important that managers clearly define the levels of performance they expect of employees. These levels should be relatively free from bias and scientifically determined, when possible.

Standards may be developed to measure both effectiveness and efficiency. If a firm's factory is capable of producing 10,000 units of product per month and the firm's objective is to produce the full 10,000 units, this would be a standard of effectiveness. If 10,000 units are actually produced, then production is effective. In only 9,500 are produced, then production is ineffective. An efficiency standard relates to the *cost* of the units produced. If a particular task should take five hours of direct labor to perform and the rate of pay is $8 per hour, the cost of this task for direct labor is expected to be $40. However, if an employee works at a slower than normal pace and takes seven hours to complete the task, the cost for direct labor is $56 (7 hours × $8) and performance is inefficient. In effect, seven hours of direct labor were put into production and only five hours of output were received, leading to a waste of two hours at a cost of $8 per hour, or $16 of inefficiency. Efficiency standards are usually referred to as standard costs.

Standard Costs

A standard cost is a carefully predetermined cost used in evaluating performance. Since budgeted costs are also predetermined costs, one may ask, "What is the difference between standard costs and budgeted costs?" The answer is relatively simple. Standard cost applies to *one unit of output* efficiently produced, while budgeted cost relates to *total output* for a period of time. If the standard cost for one unit of production is multiplied by the expected number of units to be produced during a period of time, the result is the **budgeted cost** for the period.

Since the setting of standards tends to extend beyond the scope of any one individual, companies usually have a committee to set standards in accordance with the firm's goals and objectives.

The Standards Committee. A company's **standards committee** normally includes its controller, industrial engineer, purchasing manager, management accountants, factory superintendent, and line supervisors (foremen). Each member provides needed information within his or her area of expertise. The committee is directly responsible for the setting of standards.

Setting Standards. Standard costs are determined for direct materials, direct labor, and manufacturing overhead (discussed in Chapter 9). For standard costs to be an effective control mechanism, they must reflect what *future* costs should be and *not* what *past* costs were. Past costs may contain inefficiencies, and if they are automatically used as a starting point for the current year, the inefficiencies will be perpetuated. Furthermore, standard costs must be kept current. Even if the previous year's standard costs contain little or no inefficiencies, they may still be useless for the current year if there have been changes in prices, product quality, or operating practices and procedures.

When setting the standard cost for direct materials, the committee must consider both the *quantity* of each direct material and its price. The quantities of direct materials needed for one unit may be determined by having the firm's engineering staff prepare a bill of materials. A **bill of materials** is a detailed listing, right down to the smallest bolt and nut, of every item and quantity of direct material needed to manufacture one unit of finished product. The bill of materials is then priced out by asking the firm's purchasing department to quote the best prices available for each item, multiplying the quantities by the prices, and summarizing the results to obtain the total standard cost for direct materials.

A similar procedure may be used to obtain the standard cost for direct labor. However, while the quantities of direct labor may be obtained from engineering estimates, line supervisors can corroborate the estimates by observing and timing employees performing the task. The company's wage rates are then used to price out the standard direct labor cost for a unit of product.

Many firms now construct computer models of the operations to be performed, and through simulation studies, the standards committee can obtain additional corroboration of what standard costs should be.

Once standard costs are determined by the standards committee, managers and employees responsible for operating efficiency usually accept them as reasonable.

Uses of Standard Costs. Managers are able to utilize standard costs in a variety of ways. Among the most important uses are:

1. Control through performance reports.
2. Critical cost analysis when setting standards.
3. Pricing.
4. Inventory valuation.
5. Budget preparation.
6. Simplified record-keeping.

1. Control through Performance Reports. By comparing actual performance results with planned operations, managers are able to monitor subordinates' results. When employees know that their performance is being monitored, they are more likely to recognize the importance of meeting specified standards. When performance reports are prepared fairly and humanely, they should not be offensive to employees who understand the need for control.

2. Critical Cost Analysis when Setting Standards.   When setting or updating standards each year, the standards committee reexamines prior costs, which should lead to increased efficiencies.

3. Pricing.   Many firms believe that setting a long-run, stable selling price based on what costs should be (normal costs) is superior to constantly adjusting prices to reflect fluctuations in actual costs. Proponents of this strategy believe that customers prefer to purchase their goods knowing that in the foreseeable future the price will remain unchanged and that they will not obtain a better price by waiting. General Motors and other automobile manufacturers have been practicing this strategy for many years. Occasionally, the automobile manufacturers have been known to offer rebates on certain slow-selling models, but their overall policy has been to price their products using long-run standard costs rather than actual costs.

4. Inventory Valuation.   If a firm does not use standard costs, it must price its inventories at actual costs. This necessitates the use of a cost-flow assumption, such as FIFO, LIFO, or average, and the maintenance of a record-keeping system for inventories and cost of goods sold that is unnecessarily complex. With standard costs, all inventories (with the possible exception of raw materials) and cost of goods sold are priced at standard, and thus all units of the same kind are priced the same regardless of their actual costs. As a result, the need for a cost flow assumption is obviated and the record-keeping for inventories and cost of goods sold is simplified.

5. Budget Preparation.   When standard costs are used as part of a firm's accounting system, standard costs are also used for budget preparation. Instead of basing the coming year's budget on the preceding year's costs, standard costs for the expected level of activity are used. In this manner, the budget is based on *what costs should be* rather than on *what they were in the past.* From a control standpoint, comparing actual costs to standard costs is superior to comparing actual costs to estimated costs based on a previous year's actual results because as noted earlier, built-in inefficiencies tend to be weeded out when standard costs are used.

6. Simplified Record-Keeping.   When actual costs are used, records such as materials requisitions must be priced out using a cost-flow assumption. This entails using the actual purchase prices, which differ over time, on material requisitions for the same item. Clearly, a different cost for raw materials will be used whenever the price of a raw material changes and the firm uses FIFO, LIFO, or average unit costs for its raw materials prices on material requisitions. When standard costs are used, only one price—the standard unit price—is used even if the materials are issued from two batches purchased at different prices. In fact, the materials requisitions may have the prices preprinted on them, since only one price is used until a new standard price is adopted.

Ideal Standards versus Practical Standards.   Standard costs may be used to motivate employees to achieve organizational goals. However, when standards are selected, great care must be given to evaluating their attainability. If standards are too tight, they will discourage employee performance. If they are too loose, they will lead to inefficient operations. An **ideal standard** is a measurement for evaluating performance that is theoretically possible but impractical to attain because it does not allow for machine breakdowns, rest periods, and the like, and requires employees to work at a constant rate of peak performance without any interruptions. In contrast, **practical (attainable) standards** are set high enough to motivate employees and low enough to allow for normal interruptions.

Some firms mistakenly use ideal standards so that employees will always have something to strive for. However, when employees realize that it is impossible to reach the ideal, they usually lose both faith and interest in the system. Instead of being motivated, they become cynical and disgruntled. Consequently, most firms use practical standards that set realistic demands and reward employees for desired levels of performance.

After the standards committee has decided the question of attainability, it can turn to setting specific standards.

Standards for Direct Materials

Each amount of material listed in the bill of materials prepared by the engineering department must be adjusted to take into account normal spoilage, waste, shrinkage, and the like. For example, if a firm is manufacturing wooden bookcases, each piece of lumber must be adjusted to account for saw cuts, triming of ends, and random defects such as knots, planing, and sanding. The deduction of all such adjustments for each direct material yields the **standard quantity of direct materials.**

When the prices of direct materials are obtained from the purchasing department, they must be adjusted for such items as freight-in, insurance while in transit, cash discounts allowed, and import duties. After adjustment, the prices yield the **standard price of direct materials.**

The **standard cost of direct materials** may be expressed as:

Standard quantity of direct material
$\times$ Standard price per unit of direct material
$=$ Standard cost of direct material

If a bookcase requires 30 board feet (bd. ft.) of clear pine lumber and the lumber's standard cost is $1 per board foot, the standard cost for direct materials is $30 (30 feet $\times$ $1).

ILLUSTRATION 8–1

FOREMOST FURNITURE COMPANY
Standard Cost of Direct Materials and Direct Labor

Product: Pine unfinished bookcase

Description	Quantity	Price or Rate	Total
Direct materials—1″ clear pine*	30 board feet	$1	$30
Direct labor	1 hour	$8	8
Total			$38

---

* Although glue is also used, it is not listed here because it is considered an indirect material.

Normally, a tabulation is prepared listing the quantity, price, and total cost of the required direct materials, as shown in Illustration 8–1.

Standards for Direct Labor

The estimates of required direct labor-hours obtained from engineers and factory supervisors must be adjusted for reasonable personal needs, coffee breaks, machine breakdowns and maintenance, and the like. If the required time to manufacture a bookcase is 55 minutes and the adjustment for personal needs and the like is 40 minutes per 8-hour day, the **standard quantity of direct labor** is 60 minutes ($55 + {}^{40}\!/_8 = 60$ minutes).

If an employee who works on bookcases earns $8 per hour, the standard direct labor rate is $8 per hour. A **standard direct labor rate** is the normal rate of pay per hour paid to employees for a particular kind of work. The **standard cost of direct labor** may be expressed as:

Standard quantity of direct labor
$\times$ Standard direct labor rate
$=$ Standard cost of direct labor

Using the one-hour quantity and the $8 rate, the standard cost of direct labor at Foremost Furniture would be $8 (1 hour $\times$ $8), as summarized in Illustration 8–1.

We will discuss the determination of standard overhead in the next chapter.

Once the standard cost per unit is decided upon, work may proceed toward the construction of a budget.

Standard Quantity Allowed

As noted previously, a standard cost refers to only *one unit* of product. Since firms usually manufacture their products in batches, the standard cost per unit must be converted into budgeted data. This is accomplished by multiplying the expected number of units to be produced in an accounting period by the standard cost per unit. For example, the standard cost of direct materials for the Foremost Furniture Company's bookcase is $30 per unit. If the company expects to manufacture 100 bookcases for the month of January 19x1, its budgeted cost for direct materials is $3,000 (100 units

$\times$ \$30). A budgeted cost may be computed by multiplying the *estimated* production by the standard cost per unit:

$$\text{Budgeted cost} = \text{Estimated units} \times \text{Standard cost per unit} \qquad (1)$$

The budgeted cost for direct materials is useful for planning purposes. It provides a measure of the expected activity and how much direct materials will be needed for the month. However, it may not be useful for controlling purposes. In this case, if exactly 100 bookcases are produced in January, then the \$3,000 budgeted amount is useful for comparing the actual materials cost with the estimated cost to determine if the actual cost is higher than it should be (an unfavorable event) or lower than it should be (a favorable event). For example, if the actual direct materials cost for the bookcases during January is \$3,200 and 100 bookcases were manufactured, then the actual cost is \$200 greater than it should be—an unfavorable event. But if 110 bookcases were *actually* produced and the direct materials cost amounted to \$3,200, a manager's conclusion that the additional cost of \$200 is unfavorable might be erroneous. Before a conclusion can be reached about the \$3,200 actual cost, it is necessary to adjust the budgeted cost of \$3,000 to reflect the *actual* number of units produced. The means by which this is accomplished is to compute the **standard quantity allowed** using the formula:

$$\begin{aligned} \text{Standard quantity allowed} &= \text{Standard quantity of one unit} \qquad (2) \\ &\quad \times \text{Actual number of units produced} \end{aligned}$$

If 110 bookcases were manufactured, the standard quantity allowed for materials would be 3,300 board feet (110 units $\times$ 30 board feet per unit).

The standard quantity allowed is then used to compute the total standard cost. The formula to find the **total standard cost** for direct materials is:

$$\begin{aligned} \text{Total standard cost}_{dm} &= \text{Standard quantity allowed} \qquad (3) \\ &\quad \times \text{Standard unit price of direct material} \end{aligned}$$

Since Foremost normally pays \$1 per board foot of lumber, its total standard cost for direct materials would be \$3,300 (3,300 board feet $\times$ \$1). The same result may be achieved by multiplying the number of units produced by the standard cost per unit (110 units $\times$ \$30 = \$3,300). Although this calculation of the total standard cost is simpler to compute than the standard-quantity-allowed approach, we will see later that the standard quantity allowed provides some useful information for control purposes that is not found in this simpler calculation. However, the simpler calculation may be used as a check on the standard-quantity-allowed calculations.

It is now possible to make a valid comparison between the actual cost of \$3,200 for direct materials and the total standard cost of \$3,300. This comparison indicates that a favorable cost difference exists, instead of the unfavorable one indicated by the comparison of the budgeted cost with the actual cost. Thus, whenever actual production differs from estimated production, it is necessary to first compute the total standard cost for comparison with the actual cost. The budgeted cost should only be used for comparison when actual production coincides with estimated production.

Similar equations are used for analyzing direct labor, except that direct labor is substituted for direct materials. Therefore, equation 3 for direct labor becomes:

$$\text{Total standard cost}_{dl} = \text{Standard quantity allowed} \times \text{Standard rate per direct labor-hour} \qquad (4)$$

Using equation 2 for direct labor, the standard quantity allowed is 110 hours (110 units × 1 hour) and the total standard cost, using equation 4, is $880 (110 hours × $8 per hour). This amount should be used for comparison with the actual cost to determine if a favorable or unfavorable condition occurred during January 19x1.

When comparing actual costs with total standard costs, it is important for managers to recognize that a difference between the two costs is really composed of two factors, a quantity-used factor and a price factor. The individuals responsible for each factor are normally different, and thus it is necessary to analyze these factors to attribute the cause of a difference to the individual(s) responsible for it.

Input and Output

Input is a quantity of goods or services entered into production that is expected to yield a certain quantity of finished goods, while **output** is all completed units (or equivalent completed units) of product. Suppose that at Foremost, the input of 4,000 board feet of lumber and 130 direct labor-hours were used to produce the output of 110 bookcases. Based on standard quantity allowed, the 4,000 board feet of lumber should have produced 133 bookcases (4,000 board feet ÷ 30 board feet). Thus, the fact that only 110 bookcases were produced indicates that management should investigate the reason(s) for the difference. Similarly, 130 hours of direct labor should produce 130 units of output (130 hours ÷ 1 hour), so this difference, too, requires investigation.

VARIANCE ANALYSIS

In **variance analysis,** the difference between an actual cost and its budgeted, or standard, counterpart is segregated into price and quantity components. As noted before, these components are needed to properly assess responsibility. For example, responsibility for a direct materials price variance should rest with the manager of the purchasing department, while responsibility for a direct labor quantity variance, sometimes called an efficiency variance, should lie with the line supervisor whose employees created the variance. A **favorable variance** occurs when *output exceeds input* or when the price paid for a good or service is less than expected. An **unfavorable variance** arises when *output is less than input* or when the price paid for a good or service is greater than expected.

If your roommates went to the supermarket to buy two cans of tuna fish that normally cost $1.25 each, you would expect them to spend $2.50. If you discover that they spent $3.00 on tuna fish, you might conclude that this was an unfavorable transaction, since an extra $0.50 was actually expended. Your mental analysis would be:

Actual cost	$3.00
Planned (budgeted) cost	2.50
Unfavorable	$0.50

However, upon questioning your roommates you may learn that the tuna fish was on sale for $0.75 per can and that they bought four cans instead of the two you requested. Having completed a course in managerial accounting, your roommates then explain how important it is to analyze a seemingly unfavorable result before rushing to a conclusion that may be wrong. To help you understand the results, they present the following analysis:

Price difference:
4 cans at $0.50 ($1.25 − $0.75) . . . . $2.00 favorable

Quantity difference:
2 additional cans at $1.25 . . . . 2.50 unfavorable
Net difference expended . . . . . . $ .50 unfavorable

However, while the net difference in the amount spent is unfavorable, a proper analysis shows that there was a savings of 50 cents per can on the two originally requested and that you actually received two additional cans at a unit cost savings of 50 cents.

A manager who compares only actual and total standard costs without segregating them into their quantity and price components may also come to a wrong conclusion. Therefore, formulas have been developed to compare the components of actual and total standard costs so that managers can determine if a variance is detrimental or beneficial to their firm.

Direct Materials Variance Analysis

The Foremost Furniture Company's budgeted costs, total standard costs, and actual costs for direct materials and direct labor for the bookcases are summarized in Illustration 8–2. The actual data are assumed and 110 units are produced. Under these circumstances, the total standard cost for direct materials amounts to $3,300 ($30 × 110 bookcases). Now let us assume that the actual cost of direct materials is $3,200 (4,000 board feet at 80 cents per board foot). A comparison of the actual with the total standard cost indicates a savings of $100, an apparently favorable condition. However, this figure does not provide Foremost's managers with all the information they need to control their firm's operations. To be optimally helpful, the **total variance**—the difference between the actual cost and the total standard cost—needs to be broken down into price and quantity segments. A **price variance** is the actual quantity of a good or service used multiplied by the

ILLUSTRATION 8–2   **Foremost Furniture Company**

Budgeted Data

Direct materials—100 units × 30 board feet × $1.00 = $3,000
Direct labor   —100 units × 1 hour   × 8.00 =   800
   Total $3,800

Total Standard Cost

Direct materials—110 units × 30 board feet × $1.00 = $3,300
Direct labor   —110 units × 1 hour   × 8.00 =   880
   Total $4,180

Actual Cost

Direct materials—4,000 board feet   × $0.80 = $3,200
Direct labor   — 130 hours   × 8.10 = 1,053
   Total $4,253

---

difference between the actual and standard prices. For direct materials, the price variance may be stated as:

$$\text{Price variance}_{dm} = \text{Actual quantity of direct material} \tag{5}$$
$$\times (\text{Actual price per unit} - \text{Standard price per unit})$$

A **quantity variance** is the difference between the input quantity of a good or service and the corresponding output quantity (standard quantity allowed) multiplied by the standard price per unit of input. For direct materials, the quantity variance may be stated as:

$$\text{Quantity variance}_{dm} = \text{Standard price} \tag{6}$$
$$\times (\text{Actual quantity} - \text{Standard quantity allowed})$$

Inserting Foremost's numbers, the results are:

Direct materials price variance:
   4,000 board feet × ($0.80 − $1.00) . . . . $800 favorable

Direct materials quantity variance:
   $1.00 × (4,000 board feet − 3,300 board feet) . . . .   700 unfavorable
      Net variance . . . . $100 favorable

The combined $100 favorable variance assumes new importance when it is analyzed into price and quantity components. Upon investigation, Foremost's general manager found that the purchasing agent bought a lower grade of lumber at 20 cents per board foot below the clear-pine price. Because this grade of lumber has occasional knots, significant amounts of lumber were wasted to avoid flaws in the finished shelves.

The Diagrammatic Approach

Another format for analyzing variances into price and quantity components is shown in Illustration 8–3. Referred to as the diagrammatic approach, it is extremely useful for analyzing variances from fragmentary data. The **diagrammatic approach** shows the actual cost at the extreme left arrow, the

ILLUSTRATION 8-3   **Analysis of Direct Materials Variances**

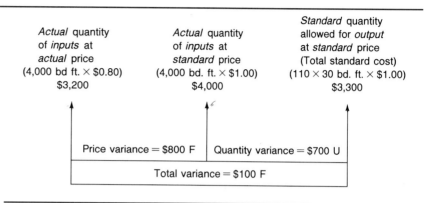

total standard cost at the extreme right arrow, and the actual quantity of inputs at the standard price per input in the center. The price variance is computed by subtracting the actual cost of inputs from the dollar amount above the center arrow. If the actual cost is less than the center amount, the price variance is favorable; otherwise, it is unfavorable. A similar subtraction is made between the total standard cost and the amount above the center arrow. If the total standard cost is less than the center amount, the variance is unfavorable; otherwise, it is favorable.

Under certain conditions, a firm may wish to analyze its direct materials variance into three components, which includes a joint price-quantity variance. This approach is discussed in Appendix 8-B at the end of this chapter.

Direct Labor Variance Analysis

When analyzing direct labor variances into their price and quantity components, most accountants, including this author, prefer to use the terms *rate variance* in place of *price variance* and *efficiency variance* in place of *quantity variance*. The reason for this is that employees earn a *rate* of pay and are either *efficient* or inefficient. The **direct labor rate variance** is computed in the same way as the material price variance and may be stated as:

$$\text{Rate variance}_{dl} = \text{Actual number of direct labor-hours} \times (\text{Actual rate per hour} - \text{Standard rate per hour}) \qquad (7)$$

The **direct labor efficiency variance** is the standard rate of pay per direct labor-hour multiplied by the difference between the input number of direct labor-hours and the corresponding output (standard quantity allowed). It may be stated as follows:

$$\text{Efficiency variance}_{dl} = \text{Standard rate per hour} \times (\text{Actual number of hours} - \text{Standard quantity allowed}) \qquad (8)$$

Using the information provided in Illustration 8-2, the direct labor rate and efficiency variances for the Foremost Furniture Company are:

Direct labor rate variance:
130 hours × ($8.10 − $8.00) . . . . $ 13 unfavorable

Direct labor efficiency variance:
$8.00 × (130 hours − 110 standard allowed hours) . . . . 160 unfavorable
      Total labor variance . . . . $173 unfavorable

While the variances themselves do not provide specific information, they do indicate when and where to investigate further. In this case, the rate variance of $13 would not require investigation or action because it is too small to warrant further attention. On the other hand, the $160 efficiency variance would be considered worthy of investigation because it represents an 18 percent deviation ($160 ÷ $880) from the total standard direct labor cost.

Upon investigation, Foremost found that the additional 20 hours of direct labor were spent on screening the lumber for knots and deciding where saw cuts should be made to minimize materials waste. Also, since 700 extra board feet of lumber were used because of the knots, additional cutting was needed to complete the 110 bookcases.

Based on the results of his investigation, the general manager concluded that the $800 that was saved by purchasing lower grade lumber was not beneficial to the company as a whole since there was $700 of wasted material and $160 of wasted direct labor, or a total of $860 of additional costs, attributable to the attempt to save on direct materials. Moreover, the extra 20 hours of direct labor would normally require that additional variable manufacturing overhead costs be incurred. What may have at first seemed a smart move by the purchasing agent turned out to be an added cost for the firm as a whole.

The diagrammatic approach to isolating direct labor rate and efficiency variances appears in Illustration 8–4. Note that it is similar to Illustration 8–3 except that direct labor costs are substituted for direct materials costs.

ILLUSTRATION 8–4   **Analysis of Direct Labor Variances**

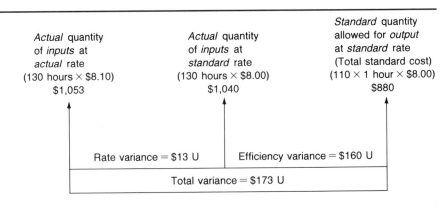

Actual quantity of *inputs* at *actual* rate
(130 hours × $8.10)
$1,053

Actual quantity of *inputs* at standard rate
(130 hours × $8.00)
$1,040

Standard quantity allowed for *output* at *standard* rate
(Total standard cost)
(110 × 1 hour × $8.00)
$880

Rate variance = $13 U   Efficiency variance = $160 U

Total variance = $173 U

Performance Reports

A **performance report** is a detailed comparison of *budgeted,* or *total standard,* costs with *actual costs.* Variances between the two are segregated into price and quantity components, and when a variance is significant, its source is explained. Although performance reports may differ in format from firm to firm, their purpose remains the same. They provide information and, when possible, explanations to assist managers in deciding what, if any, remedial action is needed when a significant unfavorable variance occurs. The remedial action should be taken as soon as possible after the triggering event. Otherwise, the negative situation is likely to continue and grow more costly. Furthermore, as time passes, people may forget details about the problem, making a solution more difficult to formulate.

As shown in Illustration 8–5, a performance report typically contains standard cost data, actual data, the difference between the two segregated into price and quantity components, and explanations of the variances, if they are available. The steps needed to prepare a performance report are:

Step 1 Compute the standard quantity allowed for direct materials and direct labor. Insert these amounts in the first column.

Step 2 Enter the actual quantities for direct materials and direct labor in the second column and place the respective standard prices in the third column.

Step 3 Determine the actual price for direct materials and the actual rate of pay for direct labor and insert these amounts in column 4.

Step 4 Compute the direct materials price variance using equation 5, the direct materials quantity variance using equation 6, the direct labor rate variance using equation 7, and the direct labor efficiency variance using equation 8. (The variances may

ILLUSTRATION 8–5

FOREMOST FURNITURE COMPANY
Performance Report
For the Month of January 19x1

Description	Standard Quantity Allowed	Actual Quantity	Standard Price	Actual Price	Variance F—Favorable U—Unfavorable	Explanation
Direct materials:						
Quantity variance	3300 bd. ft.	4,000 bd. ft.	$1.00		$700 U	Inferior materials— waste
Price variance		4,000	$1.00	$0.80	800 F	Cheaper grade of material
Total direct materials variance					$100 F	
Direct labor:						
Efficiency variance	110 hours	130 hours	$8.00		$160 U	Inferior materials— extra cutting
Rate variance		130 hours	$8.00	$8.10	13 U	
Total direct labor variance ..					$173 U	

also be computed using the diagrammatic approach instead of the equations.) Insert the variances in the fifth column and label each (F) if favorable or (U) if unfavorable.

Step 5 Investigate the reasons for the significant variances and report the findings in the final column.

Management by Exception

Once the performance report is prepared, managers must then decide which variances are worthy of investigation. When management chooses to investigate and take action on only those variances that depart significantly from prescribed standards, their approach is called **management by exception.** The crticial aspect of management by exception lies in the choice of variances to investigate.

Selecting Variances for Investigation

It is highly unlikely that an actual cost or revenue will coincide with its budgeted counterpart. Differences between actual and budgeted amounts can range in size from infinitesimal to extremely large, and investigation of each is not justifiable. Thus, each firm must develop decision rules for selecting which variances to investigate. Although practices vary from firm to firm, the following factors should be considered:

1. Size of variance.
2. Frequency of occurrence.
3. Kind of item.
4. Kind of variance (unfavorable versus favorable).

1. Size of Variance. When assessing the significance of the size of a variance, two measures are usually used—a specified dollar amount and a specified percentage of standard (or budgeted) cost. For example, if total standard cost is $50 and a $10 unfavorable variance occurs, the difference would amount to 20 percent of standard. While 20 percent is a significant variation, $10 is not a significant amount of money, so investigation would not be justified. To avoid such unjustifiable investigations, a percentage cutoff point is usually used in conjunction with a dollar value. Let us assume, for example, that a variance must exceed both 2 percent and $300. Then, if the total standard cost of an item is $50,000 and the variance is $1,100 (that is, 2.2 percent) the variance should be investigated. On the other hand, if the variance is $500 (1 percent), the item should not be investigated. In practice, many firms prefer to investigate any dollar variance greater than a set amount, regardless of its percentage of total standard cost. In such cases, the decision rule would be to investigate any variance that is at least $300 *or* at least 2 percent of total standard cost, whichever is smaller. This decision rule may be illustrated as follows:

Case 1: Total standard cost is $10,000 and variance is $150. *Action:* Do not investigate. The rationale for this decision might be that a variance of 1½ percent is a normal variance—one that is expected and due to random events. The manager's conclusion might be that there is nothing wrong and that $150 is too small an amount to worry about.

Case 2: Total standard cost is $20,000 and variance is $350. *Action:* Investigate. The rationale for this decision might be that although the variance, at 1¾ percent, is below the 2 percent threshold, $350 is a significant amount of money and justifies a manager's time to investigate. Through further study, the manager might find a control mechanism that would prevent the recurrence of this kind of unfavorable variance in the future.

Case 3: Total standard cost is $5,000 and variance is $150. *Action:* Investigate. Here the manager might decide that although $150 is not a significant amount of money because it amounts to 3 percent of total standard cost, the deviation might not be normal or random. In such a case, a manager should take corrective action before the condition becomes more serious and a significant amount of money is lost.

2. Frequency of Occurrence. This author was associated with a steel fabricating firm where daily performance reports were prepared by computer. One particular foreman's performance report was an ongoing concern for the firm's accountants. The report consistently showed an unfavorable direct labor efficiency variance, but the amount was always lower than the firm's investigative cut-off point. When such a condition exists, management may wish to investigate and take corrective action even though the variances are below the specified cut-off point. The fact that the variances are always unfavorable may be symptomatic of leadership problems or wasteful practices. The cumulative effect of consistently small unfavorable variances may be just as damaging to a firm's cost efficiency as an occasional large one. The foreman in this steel fabricating firm was ultimately replaced when it became clear that the unfavorable variances were likely to continue despite his attempts to correct them.

3. Kind of Item. Some variances require closer surveillance than others. For example, a foreman may have an unfavorable variance due to unexpected repairs to machinery and may attempt to compensate for it by foregoing required maintenance. While this tactic may temporarily negate the unfavorable variance, the foregone maintenance may cause more expensive repairs in the future that could have been avoided. Thus, favorable repair variances in one time period may lead to unfavorable repair variances in a subsequent period.

Another critical variance is light and power. If an unfavorable variance is due to a utility company's rate increase, it is uncontrollable and must be accepted. However, if the variance is due to an unreasonable number of kilowatt-hours having been consumed, it is possible that machines were left running when not in use. Other variances that require close surveillance are (1) the direct materials price variance, (2) the direct materials quantity variance, and (3) the direct labor efficiency variance.

4. Kind of Variance. Obviously, significant unfavorable variances require a manager's attention, but favorable variances should not be ignored. Significant favorable variances, on investigation, may reveal outdated standards, inferior raw materials, inferior workmanship, neglected maintenance or research and development, or exemplary performance. Thus, both favorable and unfavorable variances should be investigated when indicated by size, frequency of occurrence, and kind of item.

Once managers determine which variances are significant and warrant investigation, they must decide which variances require action and what kind of action to take.

Management Action

Based on the performance report shown in Illustration 8–5, the manager in charge of the purchasing department should investigate the reasons for the purchase of lower grade lumber. The purchasing agent might have erroneously believed that the $800 savings in price would more than compensate for the waste of $700 and that the firm would receive $100 in overall savings. If so, he should be made aware of the additional $160 in labor-hours that was spent. Another possibility is that clear pine lumber was not available from the firm's suppliers at the time of purchase. The manager should determine if the reasons are excusable. If they are, the variances are not charged to anyone. If the variances are due to errors in judgment by the purchasing agent, the resulting efficiency variance for direct labor should be charged to the purchasing department and *not* to the line supervisors in charge of direct labor.

JOURNAL ENTRIES

The journal entries associated with standard costs appear in Appendix 8–A at the end of this chapter.

SUMMARY

Estimated costs are useful for planning purposes. However, they are based on historical costs and thus may contain inefficiencies based on past performance. For this reason, they may not be useful for controlling costs. In contrast, **standard costs** are carefully predetermined to reflect what costs *ought to be* rather than what they were in prior periods. Since the setting of standards extends beyond any one department, standard costs are determined by a **standards committee** composed of engineers, management accountants, and various managers who base their decisions on **bills of materials,** prices of raw materials, time and motion studies, and direct labor wage rates.

Using standard costs, a firm can evaluate the efficiency of each segment's operations. **Efficiency** is a measure of whether an objective was accomplished with a minimum amount of effort and cost. Standard costs are especially suited for measuring efficiency, but they may also help in measuring **effectiveness**—that is, whether or not an objective was actually achieved.

Standard costs are used for (1) controlling through the use of performance reports, (2) critical cost analysis when the standards are set, (3) pricing, (4) inventory valuation, (5) budget preparation, and (6) simplified record-keeping.

In setting standards, managers must consider both **ideal standards,** which are theoretically possible but impractical to attain because they fail to allow for machine breakdowns, rest periods, and the like, and **practical standards,** which are set high enough to motivate employees and low enough to allow for normal, predictable interruptions and rest periods. If standards are to be useful, they must be both current and practical.

The **standard quantity of direct material** must allow for normal amounts of waste and scrap while the **standard price of direct material** includes the cash price paid for the material plus the cost of freight-in, insurance during transit, and import duties. The **standard cost of direct material** is equal to the standard quantity of direct materials multiplied by the standard price of direct materials.

The **standard quantity of direct labor** is the required time to manufacture one unit of product adjusted for normal interruptions, while the **standard direct labor rate** is the normal hourly rate paid to employees for a particular kind of work. The **standard cost of direct labor** is obtained by multiplying the standard quantity of direct labor by the standard direct labor rate.

A standard cost refers to the cost of one unit of product. In contrast, a **budgeted cost** is the estimated number of units to be produced multiplied by the standard cost. Budgeted costs are useful for planning, but they are only useful for controlling when the actual production is exactly as anticipated. When actual production differs from anticipated production, the **standard quantity allowed** must be used instead. The standard quantity allowed is the standard quantity for one unit multiplied by the actual number of units produced. This figure must then be converted to the **total standard cost,** which is the standard quantity allowed multiplied by the standard unit price of direct material or direct labor.

Efficiency may be measured by comparing an **input,** which is a commodity put into production, with its **output,** which is the completed units of product.

Comparing an actual cost for direct materials or direct labor with its total standard cost merely indicates that a **variance** exists. It does not explain why the variance arose or where its source might lie. Through **variance analysis,** a **total variance** is segmented into its **price (rate)** and **quantity (efficiency)** components, which when classified as either **favorable** or **unfavorable** can provide the additional information managers need to decide where potential problems may lie and what action may be needed. Variance analysis may be performed using either equations or the **diagrammatic approach.** Based on their variance analyses and related studies, management accountants usually prepare a **performance report** for use by managers. The report presents the total standard costs, the actual costs, the variances analyzed into their components, and explanations for significant variances.

For control purposes, managers employ the principle of **management by exception,** which means that they investigate only significant variances of actual costs compared with standard (or budgeted) costs. The factors that influence a manager's decision to investigate a variance are the size of the variance, the frequency of its occurrence, the kind of item creating the variance, and the kind of variance. Some items, such as machine maintenance, require more scrutiny than others such as direct labor, which may vary only slightly due to union contracts and/or employment policies.

GLOSSARY OF KEY TERMS

Bill of materials   A detailed listing of every item and quantity of direct material needed to manufacture one unit of finished product.

Budgeted cost   The estimated production multiplied by the standard cost per unit.

Diagrammatic approach   A method of analyzing variances in which the actual cost is shown at the extreme left, the total standard cost is shown at the extreme right, and the actual quantity of inputs at the standard price per input is shown in the center. The price and quantity variances are found by subtracting each end figure from the center figure.

Direct labor efficiency variance   The standard rate of pay per direct labor-hour multiplied by the difference between the input number of direct labor-hours and the corresponding output (standard quantity allowed).

Direct labor rate variance   The actual number of direct labor-hours multiplied by the difference between the actual rate of pay per hour and the standard rate of pay per hour.

Effectiveness   A measure of whether an objective is achieved.

Efficiency   A measure of the means by which an objective is achieved—that is, whether it is achieved with the least amount of effort and the least possible cost.

Favorable variance   A case in which output exceeds input or the price paid for a good or service is less than expected.

Ideal standard   A measurement for evaluating performance that is theoretically possible but impractical to attain because it does not allow for machine breakdowns, rest periods, and the like, and requires employees to work at a constant rate of peak performance without interruptions.

Input   A quantity of goods or services entered into production that is expected to yield a certain quantity of manufactured finished goods.

Management by exception   An approach in which management chooses to investigate and take action on only those variances that depart significantly from prescribed standards.

Output   All completed units (or equivalent completed units) of product.

Performance report   A detailed comparison of budgeted, or total standard, costs with actual costs. Variances between the two are segregated into price and quantity components, and when a variance is significant, its source is explained.

Practical standard   A measurement for evaluating performance that is set high enough to motivate employees and low enough to allow for normal machine breakdowns, rest periods, and the like.

Price variance   The actual quantity of a good or service used multiplied by the difference between the actual and standard prices.

Quantity variance   The difference between the input quantity of direct materials and the corresponding output quantity (standard quantity allowed) multiplied by the standard price per unit of input.

Standard cost   A carefully predetermined cost, usually per unit, used to evaluate performance.

Standard cost of direct labor The standard quantity of direct labor multiplied by the standard direct labor rate.

Standard cost of direct materials The standard quantity of direct materials multiplied by the standard price per unit of direct materials.

Standard direct labor rate The normal rate of pay per hour paid to employees for a particular kind of work.

Standard quantity allowed The standard quantity of one unit multiplied by the actual number of units produced.

Standard quantity of direct labor The estimated required direct labor-hours provided by engineers and factory supervisors adjusted for reasonable personal needs, coffee breaks, machine breakdowns, and the like.

Standard quantity of direct materials The required direct material listed in the bill of materials adjusted for normal spoilage, waste, shrinkage, and the like.

Standard price of direct materials The price of a direct material quoted by the purchasing department and adjusted for such items as freight-in, insurance during transit, cash discounts allowed, and import duties.

Standards committee A committee directly responsible for the setting of standards, composed of the company's controller, industrial engineer, purchasing manager, management accountants, factory superintendent, and line supervisors.

Total standard cost The standard quantity allowed multiplied by the standard price of direct material or direct labor.

Total variance The difference between the actual cost and the total standard cost.

Unfavorable variance A case in which output is less than input or the price paid for a good or service is greater than expected.

Variance analysis Segregating the difference between an actual cost and its budgeted counterpart into price (rate) and quantity (efficiency) components.

APPENDIX 8–A

JOURNAL ENTRIES TO RECORD STANDARD COSTS FOR DIRECT MATERIALS AND DIRECT LABOR

The use of standard costs is not a cost accounting system in and of itself; rather, standard costs are used in conjunction with job order costs, discussed in Chapter 3, or process costs, discussed in Chapter 4.

Direct Materials

Management accountants use two different methods to record direct materials price variances. Some record the price variance when the materials are issued, while others record the price variance at the time of purchase.

Variances Recorded at the Time of Use. When variances are recorded at the time that direct materials are issued for use, no variances are entered at the date of purchase and the Raw Materials Inventory account indicates *actual cost.* Thus, if the Foremost Furniture Company purchased 10,000 board feet of pine lumber at 80 cents per board foot, the entry to record the purchase would be:

(1a)

Raw Materials Inventory 8,000
    Accounts Payable 8,000
(10,000 board feet at 80 cents)

As long as this material remains in the stockroom, the price variance remains hidden in this account. Furthermore, if only part of the materials are used, only the portion of the price variance on the quantity used finds its way into the reporting system. At the Foremost Furniture Company, where the standard cost is $1 per board foot and 4,000 board feet of pine lumber were issued to the factory for manufacture into 110 bookcases, the standard quantity per bookcase is 30 board feet. The entry to record the price and quantity variances is:

(2a)

Work in Process (110 × 30 board feet × $1.00) 3,300
Materials Quantity Variance (4,000 board feet
  − 3,300 board feet = 700 board feet × $1.00) 700
  Materials Price Variance ($1.00 − $0.80
    = $0.20 × 4,000 board feet) 800
  Raw Materials Inventory (4,000 board feet ×
    $0.80 actual price) 3,200

Note the following:

1. The debit to Work in Process is always at the standard quantity allowed (110 × 30 = 3,300 board feet) multiplied by the standard price. *The Work in Process account is always stated at standard (budgeted) cost.*

2. The materials quantity variance is the difference between the actual quantity (4,000 board feet) and the standard quantity allowed (3,300 board feet) multiplied by the standard price ($1). Since the quantity variance is *unfavorable,* the variance appears as a *debit.*

3. The materials price variance is the quantity *used* (4,000 board feet) multiplied by the difference between the standard price and the actual price ($1.00 − $0.80 = $0.20). *Favorable variances appear as credits.*

4. The credit to the Raw Materials Inventory account is made at the actual quantity issued at the *actual* price paid.

The main disadvantage of using this approach is that only $800 of the variance is reported and, if a performance report is prepared at this time, only this portion is shown. The additional $1,200 (10,000 board feet × $0.20 = $2,000 − $800) remains in the Raw Materials Inventory account until subsequent issuances of the material to the factory. Thus, the $2,000 price variance is reflected on performance reports in a piecemeal fashion and often at a time much after its occurrence.

Variance Recorded at the Time of Purchase. Price variances may also be recorded at the time of purchase. When this approach is used, the Raw Materials Inventory account is carried at *standard cost* and all issuances are at that price. This is compatible with the use of standard costs since the work in process inventory, the finished goods inventory, and cost of goods sold are all carried at standard cost regardless of which method is used to reflect the price variance. Thus, when the price variance is recorded at the time of purchase, all inventory accounts are carried at standard cost.

An additional advantage of this method is that the entire price variance is reported currently regardless of when the direct materials are used. This is highly desirable for the purpose of controlling large variances and for reporting the variances quickly to the managers who can take appropriate remedial action.

The journal entries to record the purchase and issuance of direct materials are:

(1b)

Raw Materials Inventory (10,000 board feet × $1.00)	10,000	
Materials Price Variance (10,000 board feet × $0.20)		2,000
Accounts Payable (10,000 board feet × $0.80)		8,000

(2b)

Work in Process (110 × 30 board feet × $1.00)	3,300	
Materials Quantity Variance [same as in entry (2a)]	700	
Raw Materials Inventory (4,000 board feet × $1.00 standard cost)		4,000

A comparison of entries (1b) and (2b) with entries (1a) and (2a) indicates that:

1. The accounts payable, the materials quantity variance, and the work in process are the same for both methods.

2. The material price variance and the raw materials inventory accounts

ILLUSTRATION 8–6   **Partial General Ledger**

(a) (Price variance recorded when materials are *used*)				(b) (Price variance recorded when materials are *purchased*)		
Raw Materials Inventory				**Raw Materials Inventory**		
(1)	8,000	(2)	3,200	(1)	10,000	(2)	4,000
Balance	4,800			Balance	6,000		
Materials Price Variance				**Materials Price Variance**		
		(2)	800			(1)	2,000

are different. The price variance under *(a)* is based on materials *used,* while under *(b)* it is based on materials *purchased.* Raw materials inventory is carried at *actual* cost under *(a)* and at *standard* cost under *(b).* These differences appear in the corresponding ledger accounts shown in Illustration 8–6.

Direct Labor

Recall that the Foremost Furniture Company incurred $1,053 (130 hours × $8.10) of direct labor costs, while the budgeted cost for 110 bookcases is $880 (110 × 1 hour × $8.00). The entry to record the direct labor costs, based on the variance analysis shown in Illustration 8–4, is:

(3)

Work in Process (110 × $8.00)	880	
Labor Rate Variance (130 hours × $0.10)	13	
Labor Efficiency Variance (20 hours × $8.00)	160	
Wages Payable (130 hours × $8.10)		1,053

From entry (3) it can be seen that:

1. The debit to Work in Process is at standard cost.

2. Both the rate variance and the efficiency variance are unfavorable and hence are debits.

3. Wages payable are always the actual hours worked at the actual rate per hour.

APPENDIX 8–B   **JOINT PRICE AND QUANTITY VARIANCE**

When responsibility is assigned for unfavorable variances, the analysis of a variance into its price and quantity components may sometimes cause dissension among managers.

Let us assume, for example, that the Foremost Furniture Company manufactured a batch of 200 unfinished pine bookcases in February 19x1. The purchasing agent is no longer interested in buying inferior lumber. In fact, he is now extra careful to insist on premium grade clear pine and had to pay $1.05 per board foot. However, the line supervisor experienced some employee turnover, and as a result, a less experienced employee wasted lumber. The purchasing agent originally bought 6,000 board feet of clear pine for this batch, but had to purchase an extra 800 board feet because there was not enough lumber to finish the 200 bookcases. Thus, the actual direct materials cost amounted to $7,140 (6,800 board feet × $1.05), while the total standard cost is $6,000 (200 units × 30 board feet × $1.00). The resulting total variance amounted to $1,140 ($7,140 − $6,000) unfavorable, and the usual analysis would produce the following:

Price variance:
6,800 board feet × ($1.05 − $1.00) . . . . $ 340 unfavorable

Quantity variance:

$1.00 × (6,800 board feet − 6,000 board feet) . . . .   800 unfavorable

Total variance . . . . $1,140 unfavorable

Based on this analysis, the purchasing agent would be held responsible for $340 and the line supervisor would be held responsible for $800. The purchasing agent objects to this analysis, however, and as evidence of his position offers the analysis shown in Illustration 8–7. The agent maintains that the $40 shown in the joint price-quantity variance should also be charged to the line supervisor because he hired the inexperienced person who caused

ILLUSTRATION 8–7   Graphical Analysis of Direct Materials Variances

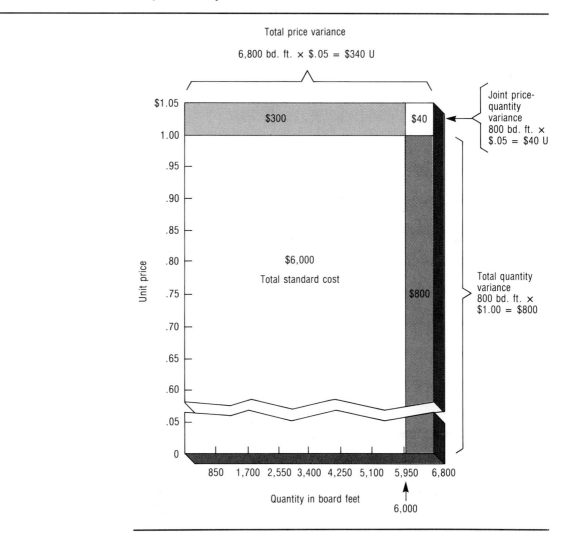

the extra lumber to be used. Thus, the purchasing agent believes that only $300 (6,000 board feet × $0.05) should be charged to him and that $840 should be charged to the line supervisor. Due to such potential problems, some firms prefer to analyze variances as shown in Illustration 8–7. The joint price-quantity portion of the price variance is then assigned only after the general manager reaches a conclusion about who is responsible for it.

QUESTIONS

1. What is the difference between effectiveness and efficiency? Use an example to demonstrate each.

2. What standards are used by businesses?

3. What is a standard for efficiency? Use an example to illustrate its use.

4. What is a standards committee and why do firms generally use one?

5. What are some of the uses of standard costs? Explain each one.

6. Explain the difference between ideal standards and practical standards. Which one would you use? Why?

7. What is the difference between a budgeted cost and a standard cost?

8. What is the standard quantity allowed? How is it used?

9. Differentiate input and output. Use an example to illustrate its use.

10. What is a quantity (efficiency) variance? How is it computed? Is it important? Why?

11. What is a price (rate) variance? How is it computed? Is it important? Why?

12. What is a performance report? What purpose does it serve?

13. Are all variances investigated? If not, how do managers select those variances that are to be selected for investigation?

14. What is management by exception?

For Appendix 8–A

15. There are two different approaches for recording material price variances. What are they? Explain the essential differences between them.

For Appendix 8–B

16. What is the joint price and quantity variance? Is it usually shown alone? If not, where is it usually shown? Why? Describe the circumstances when it might be important to compute the joint price-quantity variance.

EXERCISES   8–1   **Computations of Variances**

1. Buckler Company manufactures desks with vinyl tops. The standard material cost for the vinyl used per model S desk is $27.00 based on 12 square feet of vinyl at a cost of $2.25 per square foot. A production run of 1,000 desks in March 19x2 resulted in usage of 12,600 square feet of vinyl at a cost of $2 per square foot, a total cost of $25,200. The usage variance resulting from the above production run was
   a. $1,200 unfavorable.
   b. $1,350 unfavorable.

    c. $1,800 favorable.

    d. $3,150 favorable.

2. Information on Barber Company's direct labor costs for the month of January 19x1 is as follows:

Actual direct labor-hours	34,500
Standard direct labor-hours	35,000
Total direct labor payroll	$241,500
Direct labor efficiency variance—favorable	$ 3,200

What is Barber's direct labor rate variance?

    a. $17,250 unfavorable.

    b. $20,700 unfavorable.

    c. $21,000 unfavorable.

    d. $21,000 favorable.

3. Lion Company's direct labor costs for the month of January 19x0 were as follows:

Actual direct labor-hours	20,000
Standard direct labor-hours	21,000
Direct labor rate variance—unfavorable	$ 3,000
Total payroll	$126,000

What was Lion's direct labor efficiency variance?

    a. $6,000 favorable.

    b. $6,150 favorable.

    c. $6,300 favorable.

    d. $6,450 favorable.

4. Matt Company uses a standard cost system. Information for raw materials for product RBI for the month of October is as follows:

Standard unit price	$1.60
Actual purchase price per unit	$1.55
Actual quantity purchased	2,000 units
Actual quantity used	1,900 units
Standard quantity allowed for actual production	1,800 units

What is the materials purchase price variance?

    a. $90 favorable.

    b. $90 unfavorable.

    c. $100 favorable.

    d. $100 unfavorable.

(AICPA adapted)

8–2 Standard Costs, Computations of Variances, and Computations from Variances Supplied

1. Which one of the following is true concerning standard costs?

    a. Standard costs are estimates of costs attainable only under the most ideal conditions, but rarely practicable.

    b. Standard costs are difficult to use with a process costing system.

    c. If properly used, standards can help motivate employees.

d. Unfavorable variances, material in amount, should be investigated, but large favorable variances need *not* be investigated.

2. During March 19x1, Younger Company's direct material costs for the manufacture of product T were as follows:

Actual unit purchase price $6.50
Standard quantity allowed for actual production 2,100
Quantity purchased and used for actual production 2,300
Standard unit price $6.25

Younger's material quantity variance for March 19x1 was
a. $1,250 unfavorable.
b. $1,250 favorable.
c. $1,300 unfavorable.
d. $1,300 favorable.

3. Durable Company installs shingle roofs on residential houses. The standard material cost for a type R house is $1,250 based on 1,000 units at a cost of $1.25 each. During April 19x0, Durable installed roofs on 20 type R houses, using 22,000 units of material at a cost of $1.20 per unit, and a total cost of $26,400. Durable's material price variance for April 19x0 is
a. $1,000 favorable.
b. $1,100 favorable.
c. $1,400 unfavorable.
d. $2,500 unfavorable.

4. Information on Westcott Company's direct labor costs is as follows:

Standard direct labor rate . . . . $ 3.75
Actual direct labor rate . . . . $ 3.50
Standard direct labor hours 10,000
Direct labor usage (efficiency) variance—unfavorable . . . . . $ 4,200

What were the actual hours worked, rounded to the nearest hour?
a. 10,714.
b. 11,120.
c. 11,200.
d. 11,914.

5. Information on Hanley's direct labor costs for the month of January 19x2 is as follows:

Actual direct labor rate . . . . $ 7.50
Standard direct labor-hours allowed 11,000
Actual direct labor-hours 10,000
Direct labor rate variance—favorable . . . . . $ 5,500

What was the standard direct labor rate in effect for the month of January 19x2?
a. $6.95.
b. $7.00.
c. $8.00.
d. $8.05.

(AICPA adapted)

8-3   **Standard Process Costs with Equivalent Production**

The following data apply to items 1 through 6.

Dash Company adopted a standard cost system several years ago. The standard costs for the prime costs of its single product are as follows:

Material 8 kilograms at $5.00 per kilogram $40.00
Labor 6 hours at $8.20 per hour $49.20

The following operating data was taken from the records for November:

In-process beginning inventory—none.
In-process ending inventory—800 units, 75 percent complete as to labor; material is issued at the beginning of processing.
Units completed—5,600 units.
Budgeted output—6,000 units.
Purchases of materials—50,000 kilograms.
Total actual labor costs—$300,760.
Actual hours of labor—36,500 hours.
Material usage variance—$1,500 unfavorable.
Total material variance—$750 unfavorable.

1. The labor rate variance for November is
    a. $1,460 U.
    b. $1,460 F.
    c. $4,120 U.
    d. $4,120 F.
    e.   Some amount other than those shown above.
2. The labor efficiency variance for November is
    a. $4,100 U.
    b. $5,740 F.
    c. $15,580 F.
    d. $23,780 U.
    e.   Some amount other than those shown above.
3. The actual kilograms of material used in the production process during November is
    a.   45,100 kg.
    b.   49,900 kg.
    c.   50,000 kg.
    d.   51,500 kg.
    e.   Some amount other than those shown above.
4. The actual price paid per kilogram of material during November is
    a. $4,495.
    b. $4,985.
    c. $5,015.
    d. $5,135.
    e.   Some amount other than those shown above.
5. The total amounts of material and labor cost transferred to the finished goods account for November is
    a. $499,520.
    b. $535,200.
    c. $550,010.

    d. $561,040.

    e. Some amount other than those shown above.

6. The total amount of material and labor cost in the ending balance of work in process inventory at the end of November is

    a. $0.

    b. $9,840.

    c. $61,520.

    d. $71,360.

    e. Some amount other than those shown above.

(CMA adapted)

8–4   Computation of Price and Quantity Variances

The Mercer Company manufactures redwood window boxes. Each box requires the following direct materials and direct labor:

	Standard Quantity	Price (Rate)	Standard Cost
1″ clear redwood	5 board feet	$1.50 per board foot	$7.50
Direct labor	.5 hour	$9.00 per hour	4.50

During January 19x2, the following transactions occurred:

1. Purchases of lumber amounted to $37,700. The price paid was $1.45 per board foot. There was no raw materials inventory at the beginning or end of the month.
2. The direct labor cost was $21,840. The hourly rate of pay was $9.10.
3. There was no work in process inventory on January 31, 19x2, and 5,000 window boxes were manufactured.

Required   Using *both* the formula and diagrammatic approaches, compute the appropriate price (rate) and quantity (efficiency) variances and indicate if they are favorable or unfavorable.

8–5   Computation of Data from Variances

The Broome Company manufactures redwood flowerpots. Each flowerpot requires the following direct materials and direct labor:

	Standard Quantity	Price (Rate)	Standard Cost
1″ clear redwood	4 board feet	$1.50 per board feet	$6.00
Direct labor	.4 hour	$9.00 per hour	3.60

During March 19x2, the following was determined:

1. There was no work in process or raw materials inventory at the beginning or end of March, and 6,000 flowerpots were manufactured.
2. The total direct materials variance was $1,560 favorable, and the materials quantity variance was $900 unfavorable.
3. The direct labor cost for the month amounted to $22,540, and the direct labor rate variance was $490 unfavorable.

Required   *a.*   How many board feet of lumber were purchased?

                b.   What was the price paid per board foot?

                c.   What was the actual cost of the raw materials purchased?

                d.   How many hours were actually worked?

                e.   What was the hourly rate of pay?

8–6   Computation of Standard Cost per Unit from Variances and Actual Data

The Prince Company manufactures redwood outdoor furniture sets. The direct material consists of one item, 2″ × 4″ redwood. Screws and bolts may be ignored.

     The following information is available for the month of April 19x3:

1. The number of sets of furniture produced was 2,000. There are no beginning or ending inventories.
2. The actual cost of lumber purchased amounted to $163,620 for 202,000 board feet of redwood. The materials price variance amounted to $2,020 unfavorable, and the materials quantity variance amounted to $1,600 unfavorable.
3. The direct labor payroll for the month amounted to $96,760, and the labor rate variance was $2,360 unfavorable. The labor efficiency variance was $1,600 favorable. The actual hours worked was 11,800 hours.

Required   Compute the following:

     a.   The standard cost of one board foot of lumber.

     b.   The standard quantity of board feet per one set of furniture.

     c.   The actual cost per board foot.

     d.   The standard rate per hour of direct labor.

     e.   The standard quantity of hours needed per one set of furniture.

     f.   The actual labor rate per hour.

8–7   Computations of Variances and Information from Variances

1. Home Company manufactures tables with vinyl tops. The standard material cost for the vinyl used per type R table is $7.80 based on six square feet of vinyl at a cost of $1.30 per square foot. A production run of 1,000 tables in January 19x0 resulted in usage of 6,400 square feet of vinyl at a cost of $1.20 per square foot, a total cost of $7,680. The quantity variance resulting from the above production run was
    a. $120 favorable.
    b. $480 unfavorable.
    c. $520 unfavorable.
    d. $640 favorable.

     Items 2 and 3 are based on the following information:

     Data on Goodman Company's direct labor costs are given below:

Standard direct labor-hours	30,000
Actual direct labor-hours	29,000
Direct labor usage (efficiency) variance—favorable	$ 4,000
Direct labor rate variance—favorable	$ 5,800
Total payroll	$110,200

2. What was Goodman's actual direct labor rate?
    a. $3.60.
    b. $3.80.

    c. $4.00.

    d. $5.80.

3. What was Goodman's standard direct labor rate?

    a. $3.54.

    b. $3.80.

    c. $4.00.

    d. $5.80.

4. Perkins Company, which has a standard cost system, had 500 units of raw material X in its inventory at June 1, 19x2, purchased in May for $1.20 per unit and carried at a standard cost of $1.00. The following information pertains to raw material X for the month of June 19x2:

Actual number of units purchased	1,400
Actual number of units used	1,500
Standard number of units allowed for actual production	1,300
Standard cost per unit	$1.00
Actual cost per unit	$1.10

    The unfavorable materials purchase price variance for raw material X for June was

    a. $0.

    b. $130.

    c. $140.

    d. $150.

5. Information on Kennedy Company's direct material costs is as follows:

Standard unit price	$ 3.60
Actual quantity purchased	1,600
Standard quantity allowed for actual production	1,450
Materials purchase price variance—favorable	$ 240

    What was the actual purchase price per unit, rounded to the nearest penny?

    a. $3.06.

    b. $3.11.

    c. $3.45.

    d. $3.75.

(AICPA adapted)

8–8 Computation of Variances and Information from Variances

1. The following information pertains to Bates Company's direct labor for March 19x2:

Standard direct labor-hours	21,000
Actual direct labor-hours	20,000
Favorable direct labor rate variance	$ 8,400
Standard direct labor rate per hour	$ 6.30

    What was Bates's total actual direct labor cost for March 19x2?

    a. $117,600.

    b. $118,000.

    c. $134,000.

    d. $134,400.

2. Throop Company had budgeted 50,000 units of output using 50,000 units of raw materials at a total material cost of $100,000. Actual output was 50,000 units of product requiring 45,000 units of raw materials at a cost of $2.10 per unit. The direct material price variance and usage variance were

	Price	Quantity (Usage)
a.	$ 4,500 unfavorable	$10,000 favorable
b.	$ 5,000 favorable	$10,500 unfavorable
c.	$ 5,000 unfavorable	$10,500 favorable
d.	$10,000 favorable	$ 4,500 unfavorable

3. Lab Corporation uses a standard cost system. Direct labor information for product CER for the month of October is as follows:

Standard rate	$6.00 per hour
Actual rate paid	$6.10 per hour
Standard hours allowed for actual production	1,500 hours
Labor efficiency variance	$600 unfavorable

What are the actual hours worked?

    a. 1,400.

    b. 1,402.

    c. 1,598.

    d. 1,600.

(AICPA adapted)

8–9 Computation of Price and Quantity Variances

The Marder Company manufactures shoeshine boxes. Each box requires the following direct materials and direct labor:

	Standard Quantity	Price (Rate)	Standard Cost
1" clear oak	2.5 board feet	$1.00 per board foot	$2.50
Direct labor	.3 hour	$9.00 per hour	2.70

During January 19x2, the following transactions occurred:

1. Purchases of lumber amounted to $10,815. The price paid was $1.03 per board foot. There was no raw materials inventory at the beginning or end of the month.
2. The direct labor cost was $11,125. The hourly rate of pay was $8.50.
3. There was no work in process inventory on January 31, 19x2, and 4,000 shoeshine boxes were manufactured.

Required Using *both* the formula and diagrammatic approaches, compute the appropriate price (rate) and quantity (efficiency) variances and indicate if they are favorable or unfavorable.

8–10 Computation of Variances with Possible Explanations for Their Occurrence

The Saxonel Company manufactures draperies with the following standard costs:

Direct materials	20 yards at $1.20 per yard	$24.00
Direct labor	4 hours at $8.00 per hour	32.00

The following transactions occurred during the month of July 19x2:

1. Production of finished goods amounted to 5,000 pairs.
2. There were no beginning or ending inventories of raw materials or work in process.
3. Purchases of raw materials were 115,000 yards at $1 per yard.
4. The direct labor cost was for 22,000 hours at $7.50 per hour.

Required
a. Compute the materials price and quantity variances and indicate if they are favorable or unfavorable.
b. Compute the labor rate and efficiency variances, and indicate if they are favorable or unfavorable.
c. Write a brief explanation for the possible reason(s) that the labor efficiency variance is unfavorable.

8–11 Computation of Data from Variances

The Brisk Company manufactures redwood picnic tables. Each table requires the following direct materials and direct labor:

	Standard Quantity	Price (Rate)	Standard Cost
2" clear redwood	12 board feet	$1.10 per board foot	$13.20
Direct labor	.75 hour	$8.00 per hour	6.00

During March 19x2, the following was determined:

1. There was no work in process or raw materials inventory at the beginning or end of March, and 8,000 tables were manufactured.
2. The total direct materials variance was $2,136 favorable, and the materials quantity variance was $220 favorable.
3. The direct labor cost for the month amounted to $49,815, and the direct rate variance was $615 unfavorable.
4. Bolts and screws are considered indirect materials.

Required
a. How many board feet of lumber were purchased?
b. What was the price paid per board foot?
c. What was the actual cost of the raw materials purchased?
d. How many hours were actually worked?
e. What was the hourly rate of pay?

8–12 Computation of Variances with Possible Explanations for Their Occurrence

The Chambers Company manufactures a product with the following standard costs:

Direct materials	20 yards at $1 per yard	$20
Direct labor	2 hours at $8 per hour	16

The following transactions occurred during the month of July 19x2:

1. Production of finished goods amounted to 3,000 units.
2. There were no beginning or ending inventories of raw materials or work in process.
3. Purchases of raw materials were 68,000 yards at 80 cents per yard.
4. The direct labor cost was for 8,500 hours at $7 per hour.

Required

a. Compute the materials price and quantity variances and indicate if they are favorable or unfavorable.
b. Compute the labor rate and efficiency variances and indicate if they are favorable or unfavorable.
c. Write a brief explanation for the possible reason(s) that the labor efficiency variance is unfavorable.

8–13 Setting Standards for Direct Materials

Danson Company is a chemical manufacturer that supplies industrial users. The company plans to introduce a new chemical solution and needs to develop a standard product cost for this new solution.

The new chemical solution is made by combining a chemical compound (nyclyn) and a solution (salex), boiling the mixture, adding a second compound (protet), and bottling the resulting solution in 10-liter containers. The initial mix, which is 10 liters in volume, consists of 12 kilograms of nyclyn and 9.6 liters of salex. A 20 percent reduction in volume occurs during the boiling process. The solution is then cooled slightly before 5 kilograms of protet are added; the addition of protet does not affect the total liquid volume.

The purchase prices of the raw materials used in the manufacture of this new chemical solution are as follows.

Nyclyn	$1.30 per kilogram
Salex	1.80 per liter
Protet	2.40 per kilogram

Required

Determine the standard quantity for each of the raw materials needed to produce a 10-liter container of Danson Company's new chemical solution and the standard materials cost of a 10-liter container of the new product.

(CMA adapted)

8–14 Computations of Variances

The following information pertains to the month of July 19x1:

Direct materials purchased—18,000 yards at $1.38 per yard	$24,840
Direct materials used—9,500 yards	
Direct labor—2,100 hours at $9.15 per hour	19,215

Armando Corporation manufactures a product with the following standard costs:

Direct materials—20 yards at $1.35 per yard	$27
Direct labor—4 hours at $9.00 per hour	36

Five hundred units of the product were actually produced in July 19x1.

Required Prepare the following schedules for the month of July 19x1, indicating whether each variance is favorable or unfavorable:

  a. Materials price·variance (based on purchases).
  b. Materials usage variance.
  c. Labor rate variance.
  d. Labor efficiency variance.

(AICPA adapted)

8–15 Computation of Variances

The Carberg Corporation manufactures and sells a single product. The cost system used by the company is a standard cost system. The standard cost per unit of product is shown below:

Material—one pound plastic at $2.00	$2.00	
Direct labor 1.6 hours at $4.00	6.40	

The charges to the manufacturing department for November, when 5,000 units were produced, are given below:

Material	5,300 pounds at $2.00	$10,600.00
Direct labor	8,200 hours at $4.10	33,620.00

The purchasing department normally buys about the same quantity as is used in production during a month. In November, 5,200 pounds were purchased at a price of $2.10 per pound.

Required a. Calculate the following variances from standard costs for the data given:

  (1) Materials purchase price.
  (2) Materials quantity.
  (3) Direct labor wage rate.
  (4) Direct labor efficiency.

  b. The company has divided its responsibilities such that the purchasing department is responsible for the price at which materials and supplies are purchased. The manufacturing department is responsible for the quantities of materials used. Does this division of responsibilities solve the conflict between price and quantity variances? Explain your answer.

(CMA adapted)

8–16 Computation of Variances with Two Direct Materials

Eastern Company manufactures special electrical equipment and parts. Eastern employs a standard cost accounting system with separate standards established for each product.

A special transformer is manufactured in the transformer department. Production volume is measured by direct labor-hours in this department.

Standard costs for the special transformer are determined annually in September for the coming year. The standard cost of a transformer for 19x7 was computed as shown below.

Direct materials:		
Iron	5 sheets at $2	$10
Copper	3 spools at $3	9
Direct labor	4 hours at $7	28

During October 19x7, 800 transformers were produced. This was below expectations because a work stoppage occurred during contract negotiations with the labor force. Once the contract was settled, the department scheduled overtime in an attempt to catch up to expected production levels.

The following costs were incurred in October 19x7:

Direct Material	Direct Materials Purchased	Materials Used
Iron	5,000 sheets at $2.00 per sheet	3,900 sheets
Copper	2,200 spools at $3.10 per spool	2,600 spools

Direct labor
Regular time: 2,000 hours at $7.00
1,400 hours at $7.20
Overtime: 600 of the 1,400 hours were subject to overtime premium. The total overtime premium of $2,160 is included in variable overhead in accordance with company accounting practices.

Answer the following items:

1. The total material quantity variation is
    a. $200 favorable.
    b. $400 favorable.
    c. $600 favorable.
    d. $400 unfavorable.
    e. Some amount other than those shown above.
2. The labor rate (price) variation is
    a. $280 unfavorable.
    b. $340 unfavorable.
    c. $1,680 unfavorable.
    d. $2,440 unfavorable.
    e. None of the above responses is correct.

(CMA adapted)

8–17 (Appendix 8–A): Journal Entries for Standard Costs

Tolbert Manufacturing Company uses a standard cost system in accounting for the cost of production of its only product, product A. The standards for the production of one unit of product A are as follows:

Direct materials: 10 feet of item 1 at $0.75 per foot and 3 feet of item 2 at $1.00 per foot.
Direct labor: 4 hours at $3.50 per hour.

There was no inventory on hand at July 1, 19x2. Following is a summary of costs and related data for the production of product A during the year ended June 30, 19x3.

100,000 feet of item 1 were purchased at $0.78 per foot.
30,000 feet of item 2 were purchased at $0.90 per foot.

8,000 units of product A were produced which required 78,000 feet of item 1, 26,000 feet of item 2, and 31,000 hours of direct labor at $3.60 per hour.

6,000 units of product A were sold.

At June 30, 19x3, there are 22,000 feet of item 1, 4,000 feet of item 2, and 2,000 completed units of product A on hand. All purchases and transfers are "charged in" at standard.

1. For the year ended June 30, 19x3, the total debits to the Raw Materials account for the purchase of item 1 would be
   a. $75,000.
   b. $78,000.
   c. $58,500.
   d. $60,000.
2. For the year ended June 30, 19x3, the total debits to the Work in Process account for direct labor would be
   a. $111,600.
   b. $108,500.
   c. $112,000.
   d. $115,100.
3. The balance in the Material-Quantity-Variance account for item 2 was
   a. $1,000 credit.
   b. $2,600 debit.
   c. $600 debit.
   d. $2,000 debit.

(AICPA adapted)

8–18   (Appendix 8–A): Journal Entries for Standard Costs

The Canal Company manufactures wooden umbrella stands. Each stand requires the following direct materials and direct labor:

	Standard Quantity	Price (Rate)	Standard Cost
1″ clear oak	4 board feet	$1.00	$4.00
Direct labor	.5 hour	$5.00	$2.50
Glue and nails may be ignored.			

During January 19x5, the following transactions occurred:

1. Purchases of lumber amounted to $84,000. The price paid was $1.05 per board foot.
2. The direct labor cost was $23,460. The hourly wage rate was $4.60.
3. There was no work in process inventory at the beginning or end of the month.
4. The January 31, 19x5, inventory of raw materials consisted of 39,500 board feet of lumber.
5. Production amounted to 10,000 units.

Required   a. Prepare the journal entries to record the above transactions. Assume that the firm records material price variances at the time of purchase.

b. Redo the direct materials journal entries assuming that the firm keeps its raw materials inventory at actual cost.

8–19 **(Appendix 8–A): Reconstruction of Journal Entries from Missing Data**

The Clinton Company's bookkeeper was working on the company's general ledger. Disliking working on the pages in a binder, he left them loose on his desk which was near an open window. Since it was a warm day and he was thirsty, the bookkeeper went to the water fountain for a drink of water, and the person sitting at the desk near the bookkeeper's turned on the room's oscillating fan. When the bookkeeper returned, he was surprised to find his desk clear of all papers. Wondering what happened to the firm's general ledger, he looked out into the street and saw it scrambled on the pavement. He hastily retrieved the loose sheets, but to his chagrin, he found some sheets missing.

Some of the available T accounts are reproduced as follows:

Raw Materials Inventory				Accounts Payable	
19x1		19x1		19x1	
Jan. 31	30,000	Jan. 31	19,500	Jan. 31	32,000

Work in Process—Materials			Wages Payable	
19x1			19x1	
Jan. 31	18,750		Jan. 31	39,600

Work in Process—Direct Labor			Labor Rate Variance	
19x1			19x1	
Jan. 31	36,750		Jan. 31	1,100

Required

a. Prepare all of the journal entries, in journal entry form, that must have been prepared for direct materials and direct labor. The company uses a standard cost, job order system, and material price variances are recorded at the time of purchase. There are no beginning inventories.

b. If the company uses only one raw material in pounds, and the standard cost per pound is 75 cents, compute the following:
   (1) The number of pounds purchased.
   (2) The number of pounds put into production (input).
   (3) The standard quantity allowed in pounds (output).
   (4) The actual price paid per pound.

8–20 **(Appendix 8–A): Journal Entries for Standard Costs**

The Hall Company manufactures wooden telephone stands. Each stand requires the following direct materials and direct labor:

	Standard Quantity	Price (Rate)	Standard Cost
1″ clear pine	3 board feet	$0.80	$2.40
Direct labor	.8 hour	$6.00	$4.80
Glue and nails may be ignored.			

During January 19x5, the following transactions occurred:

1. Purchases of lumber amounted to $30,000. The price paid was 75 cents per board foot.
2. The direct labor cost was $40,300. The hourly wage rate was $6.20.
3. There was no work in process inventory at the beginning or end of the month.
4. The January 31, 19x5, inventory of raw materials consisted of 15,500 board feet of lumber.
5. Production amounted to 8,000 units.

Required   a. Prepare the journal entries to record the above transactions. Assume that the firm records material price variances at the time of purchase.

b. Redo the direct materials journal entries assuming that the firm keeps its raw materials inventory at actual cost.

PROBLEMS   8-21   Computation of Variances with Equivalent Production

The Lafayette Company manufactures one quality of men's jeans. The standard costs of direct materials and direct labor are:

Direct materials	36 yards at $1	$36
Direct labor . . : . . .	6 hours at $5	30

Thread, zippers, and labels may be ignored.

During the month of September 19x4, the company started two batches of 1,000 jeans each. One batch, lot 404, is completed. The other batch, lot 405, is 100 percent complete as to materials and 70 percent complete as to direct labor. There was no work in process inventory at the beginning of the month.

On September 1, 19x4, the company's direct materials inventory consisted of 10,000 years of fabric. Material price variances are recorded at the time of purchase.

The following transactions occurred during September:

1. Two batches of fabric were purchased as follows:

    40,000 yards at $1.20
    50,000 yards at $0.85

2. The quantities of fabric used were as follows:

    Lot 404 . . . .   10,000 yards from the beginning inventory,
                      26,600 yards from the first batch
                      purchased
    Lot 405 . . . .   13,400 yards from the first batch and
                      26,000 yards from the second batch

3. Direct labor was incurred as follows:

    Lot 404 . . . .   5,900 hours at $5.05 per hour
    Lot 405 . . . .   4,800 hours at $4.80 per hour

Required   a.   Compute each of the following variances separately for each lot and in total
                for both lots:
                (1) Materials quantity variance.
                (2) Labor rate variance.
                (3) Labor efficiency variance.
           b.   Compute the materials price variance separately for each purchase and in total
                for the month.
           c.   When preparing performance reports, would you recommend that one report
                be prepared for the entire month, or would you recommend that separate reports
                be prepared for each lot? Why?
           d.   Write a brief explanation of the possible reasons for the wide disparity in the
                price of fabric between the first and second purchases. Are there any other possible
                side effects that may have occurred as a result of this disparity? Explain.

8–22   Computation of Variances and Preparation of Performance Report

The Fulton Company manufactures one quality of men's dress shirts. The standard
costs of direct materials and direct labor are:

>   Direct materials . . . .   30 yards at $1 $30
>   Direct labor . . . . . .   4 hours at $5   20
>   Thread, buttons, and labels may be ignored.

During the month of September 19x5, the company started and completed one
batch of 2,000 shirts.

There was no raw materials or work in process inventory at the beginning or
end of the month.

The following transactions occurred during September:

1. Two batches of fabric were purchased as follows:

>   20,000 yards at $1.20
>   42,000 yards at $0.90

2. Direct labor was incurred as follows:

>   8,300 hours at $4.50 per hour

Required   a.   Compute each of the following variances:
                (1) Materials price variance.
                (2) Materials quantity variance.
                (3) Labor rate variance.
                (4) Labor efficiency variance.
           b.   Prepare a performance report showing the materials price variance separately
                for each purchase. Where possible, indicate explanations for any variance that
                is, in your opinion, significant.

8–23   Setting Direct Labor Standards

The Alton Company is going to expand its punch press department. It is about to
purchase three new punch presses from Equipment Manufacturers, Inc. Equipment
Manufacturers' engineers report that their mechanical studies indicate that for Alton's

intended use, the output rate for one press should be 1,000 pieces per hour. Alton has very similar presses now in operation. At the present time, production from these presses averages 600 pieces per hour.

A study of the Alton experience shows the average is derived from the following individual outputs.

Worker	Daily Output
L. Jones	750
J. Green	750
R. Smith	600
H. Brown	500
R. Alters	550
G. Hoag	450
Total	3,600
Average	600

Alton management also plans to institute a standard cost accounting system in the very near future. The company engineers are supporting a standard based upon 1,000 pieces per hour, the accounting department is arguing for 750 pieces per hour, and the department foreman is arguing for 600 pieces per hour.

Required
a. What arguments would each proponent be likely to use to support his case?
b. Which alternative best reconciles the needs of cost control and the motivation of improved performance? Explain why you made that choice.

(CMA adapted)

8–24 Computation of Variances with Equivalent Production

Vogue Fashions, Inc., manufactures ladies' blouses of one quality, produced in lots to fill each special order from its customers, comprised of department stores located in various cities. Vogue sews the particular stores' labels on the blouses. The standard costs for a dozen blouses are:

Direct materials	24 yards at $1.10	$26.40
Direct labor	3 hours at $4.90	14.70

During June 19x0, Vogue worked on three orders, for which the month's job cost records disclose the following:

Lot No.	Units in Lot (dozens)	Material Used (yards)	Hours Worked
22	1,000	24,100	2,980
23	1,700	40,440	5,130
24	1,200	28,825	2,890

The following information is also available:

1. Vogue purchased 95,000 yards of material during June at a cost of $106,400.

The materials price variance is recorded when goods are purchased. All inventories are carried at standard cost.

2. Direct labor during June amounted to $55,000. According to payroll records, production employees were paid $5 per hour.

3. There was no work in process at June 1. During June, lots 22 and 23 were completed. All material was issued for lot 24, which was 80 percent completed as to direct labor.

Required   a. Prepare a schedule showing the computation of the standard cost of lots 22, 23, and 24 for June 19x0.

b. Prepare a schedule showing the computation of the materials price variance for June 19x0. Indicate whether the variance is favorable or unfavorable.

c. Prepare a schedule showing, for each lot produced during June 19x0, computations of the
   (1) Materials quantity variance in yards.
   (2) Labor efficiency variance in hours.
   (3) Labor rate variance in dollars.
Indicate whether each variance is favorable or unfavorable.

(AICPA adapted)

8–25   Computation of Variances with Equivalent Production

The Lombard Company manufactures one quality of men's pants. The standard costs of direct materials and direct labor are:

Direct materials	36 yards at $2.50	$90.00
Direct labor	6 hours at $5.00	30.00
Thread, zippers, and labels may be ignored.		

During the month of September 19x4, the company started two batches of 1,000 pants each. One batch, lot 201, is completed. The other batch, lot 202, is 100 percent complete as to materials and 60 percent complete as to direct labor. There was no work in process inventory at the beginning of the month.

On September 1, 19x4, the company's direct materials inventory consisted of 20,000 yards of fabric. Material price variances are recorded at the time of purchase.

The following transactions occurred during September:

1. Two batches of fabric were purchased as follows:

          20,000 yards at $2.60
          50,000 yards at $2.46

2. The quantities of fabric used were as follows:

    Lot 201 . . . .   20,000 yards from the beginning inventory, 16,100 yards from the first batch purchased
    Lot 202 . . . .   3,900 yards from the first batch and 35,000 yards from the second batch

3. Direct labor was incurred as follows:

    Lot 201 . . . .   6,300 hours at $5.10 per hour
    Lot 202 . . . .   3,300 hours at $5.05 per hour

Required   a. Compute each of the following variances separately for each lot and in total for both lots:
   (1)   Materials quantity variance.
   (2)   Labor rate variance.
   (3)   Labor efficiency variance.

   b. Compute the materials price variance separately for each purchase and in total for the month.

   c. When preparing performance reports, would you recommend that one report be prepared for the entire month, or would you recommend that separate reports be prepared for each lot? Why?

8–26   Computations from Variances

On May 1, 19x5, Bovar Company began the manufacture of a new mechanial device known as "Dandy." The company installed a standard cost system in accounting for manufacturing costs. The standard costs for a unit of Dandy are as follows:

Raw materials	6 pounds at $1 per pound	$6
Direct labor	1 hour at $4 per hour	4

The following data were obtained from Bovar's records for the month of May:

	Units
Actual production of Dandy	4,000
Units sold of Dandy	2,500

	Debit	Credit
Sales		$50,000
Purchases (26,000 pounds)	$27,300	
Material price variance	1,300*	
Material quantlty variance	1,000	
Direct labor rate variance	760	
Direct labor efficiency variance		800

The amount shown above for material price variance is applicable to raw material purchased during May.

Required   Compute each of the following items for Bovar for the month of May.

   a. Standard quantity of raw materials allowed (in pounds).
   b. Actual quantity of raw materials used (in pounds).
   c. Standard hours allowed.
   d. Actual hours worked.
   e. Actual direct labor rate.
      * (Debits are unfavorable and credits are favorable.)

(AICPA adapted)

8–27   Computation of Variances

The Terry Company manufactures a commercial solvent that is used for industrial maintenance. This solvent is sold by the drum and generally has a stable selling price. Due to a decrease in demand for this product, Terry produced and sold 60,000 drums in December 19x6, which is 50 percent of normal capacity.

The following information is available regarding Terry's operations for the month of December 19x6:

1. Standard costs per drum of product manufactured were as follows:

Materials:		
	10 gallons of raw material	$20
	1 empty drum	1
	Total materials	$21
Direct labor:		
	1 hour	$ 7

2. Costs incurred during December 19x6 were as follows:

Raw materials:
    600,000 gallons were purchased at a
       cost of $1,150,000
    700,000 gallons were used

Empty drums:
    85,000 drums were purchased at a
       cost of $85,000
    60,000 drums were used

Direct labor:
    65,000 hours were worked at a
       cost of $470,000

Required Prepare a schedule computing the following variances for the month of December 19x6:

a. Materials price variance (computed at time of purchase).
b. Materials quantity variance.
c. Labor rate variance.
d. Labor usage (efficiency) variance.

Indicate whether each variance was favorable or unfavorable.

(AICPA adapted)

8–28 **Computation of Standard Cost per Unit from Variances and Actual Data, and Preparation of Performance Report**

The Worth Company manufactures redwood outdoor furniture sets. The direct material consists of one item, 2″ × 4″ redwood. Screws and bolts may be ignored.

The following information is available for the month of April 19x3:

1. The number of sets of furniture produced was 3,000. There are no beginning or ending inventories.

2. The actual cost of lumber purchased amounted to $116,250 for 155,000 board

feet of redwood. The materials price variance amounted to $7,750 favorable, and the materials quantity variance amounted to $4,000 unfavorable.

3. The direct labor payroll for the month amounted to $92,225, and the labor rate variance was $775 favorable. The labor efficiency variance was $3,000 unfavorable. The actual hours worked was 15,500 hours.

Required *a.* Compute the following:
- (1) The standard cost of one board foot of lumber.
- (2) The standard quantity of board feet per one set of furniture.
- (3) The actual cost per board foot.
- (4) The standard rate per hour of direct labor.
- (5) The standard quantity of hours needed per one set of furniture.
- (6) The actual labor rate per hour.

b. Prepare a performance report and insert any possible explanations for the variances that seem reasonable.

8–29   **(Appendix 8–A): Journal Entries and Computations from Fragmentary Data**

The Exchange Company manufactures one grade of ladies' slacks. The firm's bookkeeper was working on the general ledger when he decided to have a cup of coffee. As luck would have it, he stumbled over a tear in the carpeting near his desk and the coffee was spilled over the general ledger, obliterating parts of it.

The legible portion of selected T accounts appears as follows:

Raw Materials Inventory				Accounts Payable		
19x3		19x3			19x3	
Jan. 1 Bal. 8,000		Jan. 31 ,200			Jan. 1 Bal. 6,000	
					31 41,000	

Work in Process—Materials		Material Quantity Variance	
19x3		19x3	
Jan. 31 28,800		Jan. 31 00	

Work in Process—Direct Labor		Labor Rate Variance	
19x3		19x3	
Jan. 31 21,600		Jan. 31 40	

Labor Efficiency Variance		Wages Payable	
	19x3		19x3
	Jan. 31 00		Jan. 31 20,740

The following additional information is available:

1. The standard direct materials cost for one dozen slacks is 30 yards at 80 cents per yard.
2. The standard time of direct labor is three hours per dozen.
3. The purchase of direct materials was made at 2 cents above the standard price.

4. The material quantity variance is partially obliterated. However, the bookkeeper remembers that it was less than $500.

5. The labor rate variance was at the rate of 10 cents per hour.

Required   *a.* Compute the following:

(1) The price paid per yard of material.

(2) The quantity of yards purchased in January.

(3) The number of slacks manufactured in January in dozens.

(4) The actual quantity of yards used.

(5) The standard direct labor rate per hour.

(6) The actual direct labor rate per hour.

(7) The actual number of hours worked.

(8) The standard quantity of direct labor-hours allowed.

b. Reconstruct the journal entries made by the bookkeeper as of January 31, 19x3.

8–30   **(Appendix 8–B): Graphical Solution for Joint Price-Quantity Variance**

The Ideal Frame Company manufactures wood picture frames for sale to specialty stores. For the month of January 19x2, a batch of 1,000 frames were manufactured. All of the frames were the same size, 8″ × 10″, and are made from oak wood. The standard cost for one frame is:

Direct materials:
    3.1 lineal feet of oak molding at $0.60 ln. ft. = $1.86
Direct labor:
    .2 hours at $6.00 per direct labor-hour   = 1.20
    Total $3.06

The purchasing agent was unable to secure the oak molding from the firm's normal source of supply and she was required to purchase the molding elsewhere at a price of 70 cents per lineal foot. She purchased 3,100 lineal feet on January 2, 19x2. On January 6, she learned that the employee who was cutting the 45 degree miter had cut the molding for 200 frames before he found that the miter saw was set at 60 degrees instead of 45 degrees. The molding for the 200 frames will be recut next month for use in making 5″ × 7″ frames. However, the purchasing agent was instructed to purchase an additional 620 lineal feet of oak molding, which she did at 70 cents per lineal foot.

Required   *a.* Prepare a graphical solution for the price and quantity variances showing the joint price-quantity variance.

b. How much of the price variance should be charged to the purchasing agent? Explain your answer.

9

FLEXIBLE BUDGETING AND MANUFACTURING OVERHEAD ANALYSIS

LEARNING OBJECTIVES

After reading this chapter, you should be able to:

1 Explain the difference between a flexible budget and a static budget.

2 Prepare a flexible budget for manufacturing overhead.

3 Explain why certain activity bases are preferable to others when applying overhead to production.

4 Analyze and interpret variable and fixed overhead variances.

5 Discuss why some of the efficiency variance in variable overhead may be included in the variable overhead spending variance.

6 Prepare performance reports that include variance analyses.

7 Apply overhead to production when separate predetermined rates are used for variable and fixed overhead.

8 Prepare the closing entries for actual and applied manufacturing overhead and set up the overhead variances on a firm's books and records.

9 Prepare an income statement for management's use when standard cost variances are separately disclosed.

10 Explain how to treat standard cost variances in financial statements prepared for external use.

11 Select one of four capacity levels that is most consistent with a firm's objective when applying fixed overhead to production.

The control of manufacturing overhead is not as straightforward as the control of direct materials and direct labor. In Chapter 8, we discussed only the variable costs associated with direct materials and direct labor, and it was a relatively simple matter to compute the standard quantity allowed and total standard cost for such items. Also, by analyzing variances, it was usually simple to assign responsibility for the components of the variances associated with these costs. Manufacturing overhead does not fit into such neat compartments, however.

Manufacturing overhead has some variable costs, but it also has fixed costs and mixed costs. As a result, the analysis of variable overhead is similar to the method introduced in Chapter 8, but the assignment of responsibility for the variances may require further analysis than has been demonstrated thus far. Furthermore, the analysis of fixed overhead variances differs from that of variable costs. Fixed manufacturing overhead is made up of many different kinds of costs, such as factory rent, machinery repairs, factory telephone, and the like. Thus, instead of a few managers being responsible for large chunks of costs, as is the case for direct materials and direct labor, many managers are responsible for many different costs. These factors compound the problems of the general manager when it is time to assign responsibility for unfavorable variances from manufacturing overhead.

The starting point for controlling overhead costs is the firm's budget. The expected overhead stated in the budget provides a measure against which the actual overhead can be compared.

STATIC BUDGETS

A **static budget** is a budget prepared for a single level of activity. As such, it is useful for planning purposes because, in effect, it provides the firm with a road map of where to travel during the next accounting period. However, if the firm's actual results differ much from the expected level, the static budget may not be useful for control. In fact, a static budget's usefulness in control is limited only to cases in which the *actual level* of operations *coincides with the planned (budgeted) level.*

For example, assume that you were planning a 200-mile round trip by automobile and that you started your trip with a full tank of gasoline. In order to evaluate your automobile's efficiency, you intended to fill the tank again when you returned and then compute the rate of miles per gallon for the entire trip. However, after you drove 25 miles, there was a sudden change in the weather and you decided to return home. You stopped to fill the tank again and found that the tank took only two gallons of gasoline. Obviously, the miles per gallon for the shortened trip is 25 (50 miles ÷ 2 gallons) and not 100 (200 miles ÷ 2 gallons). While the original plan to drive 200 miles was useful in preparing for the trip and would have been used for evaluation if the trip had been completed, once the trip was shortened, the actual miles driven (50 miles) had to be used in your calculations. Using the planned mileage of 200 miles and arriving at a figure of 100 miles per gallon would yield false information about your car's efficiency.

Similarly, while performance reports based on the expected results presented in budgets can provide managers with much needed information, a manager would get a false idea of a firm's efficiency if performance reports were based solely on static budgets.

FLEXIBLE BUDGETS

A **flexible budget** is a series of static budgets for different levels of activity within a firm's relevant range. For example, if a factory has a relevant range of 70,000 units to 100,000 units per month and it expects to produce an average of 90,000 units per month, its accountants might prepare budgets for 80,000, 85,000, 90,000, and 95,000 units. Although flexible budgeting applies to all components of the budgeted income statement, we will focus only on manufacturing overhead. Nonetheless, the reader should bear in mind that the limitations of a static budget and the importance of a flexible budget carry over to all components of the statement.

The Importance of a Flexible Budget

The Block Manufacturing Company prepared a budget for manufacturing overhead at a level of 90,000 units, as shown in Illustration 9–1. At the end of the month, it was determined that only 80,000 units were produced. Using the static budget shown in Illustration 9–1 as the basis for comparison, the Block Manufacturing Company prepared the performance report shown in Illustration 9–2.

In evaluating this performance report, managers would first compare the actual production to the budgeted production to determine if there is a differ-

ILLUSTRATION 9–1

BLOCK MANUFACTURING COMPANY
Manufacturing Overhead Static Budget
For the Month of January 19x2

Production in units	90,000
Variable overhead:	
Power	$ 2,700
Repairs	4,500
Payroll fringes	63,000
Miscellaneous	9,000
Total variable overhead	79,200
Fixed overhead:	
Superintendence	8,000
Factory rent	10,000
Maintenance	3,000
Indirect labor	5,000
Depreciation of equipment	12,000
Miscellaneous	4,000
Total fixed overhead	42,000
Total overhead	$121,200

ILLUSTRATION 9–2

BLOCK MANUFACTURING COMPANY
Manufacturing Overhead Performance Report
For the Month of January 19x2

	Budget	Actual	Variance
Units	90,000	80,000	10,000
Variable overhead:			
Power	$ 2,700	$ 2,500	$ 200 F
Repairs	4,500	4,200	300 F
Payroll fringes	63,000	56,800	6,200 F
Miscellaneous	9,000	8,500	500 F
Total variable overhead . .	79,200	72,000	7,200 F
Fixed overhead:			
Superintendence	8,000	8,500	500 U
Factory rent	10,000	10,000	–0–
Maintenance	3,000	2,500	500 F
Indirect labor	5,000	5,200	200 U
Depreciation of equipment . .	12,000	12,000	–0–
Miscellaneous	4,000	4,300	300 U
Total fixed overhead	42,000	42,500	500 U
Total overhead	$121,200	$114,500	$6,700 F

F = Favorable.
U = Unfavorable.

ence and, if so, why the difference occurred. During January, the company produced 10,000 fewer units than anticipated. This might have been a planned reduction due to an unexpected reduction in sales, or it might have been a production shortfall due to problems in the factory. If the former is the case, no management action is required; if the latter occurred, management action may be indicated because of the failure in *effectiveness.*

Next, management would want to examine cost control, or *efficiency.* Unfortunately, this performance report would be useless for this purpose. Problems arise because even though the variable overhead variances are all favorable, they do not necessarily imply efficiency. Erroneous conclusions may be drawn because the actual results of 80,000 units are compared with the budget for 90,000 units. This comparison is analogous to the earlier example of computing miles per gallon by using the *actual* gallons used (2 gallons) and the budgeted mileage (200 miles). A proper comparison must be made with a budget of 80,000 units and not 90,000 units. Illustration 9–3 contains the proper performance report based on a budget for 80,000 units.

From Illustration 9–3, it can be seen that the variances for variable overhead are really unfavorable, although Illustration 9–2 indicated that they were favorable. A performance report based on a static budget that is not adjusted to the actual level of production is worse than no report, since managers may draw incorrect conclusions from it.

ILLUSTRATION 9–3

BLOCK MANUFACTURING COMPANY
Manufacturing Overhead Performance Report
For the Month of January 19x2

	Budgeted Costs per Unit	Budget	Actual	Variance
Units		80,000	80,000	–0–
Variable overhead:				
Power	$.03	$ 2,400	$ 2,500	$ 100 U
Repairs	.05	4,000	4,200	200 U
Payroll fringes	.70	56,000	56,800	800 U
Miscellaneous	.10	8,000	8,500	500 U
Total variable overhead . . .		70,400	72,000	1,600 U
Fixed overhead:				
Superintendence		8,000	8,500	500 U
Factory rent		10,000	10,000	–0–
Maintenance		3,000	2,500	500 F
Indirect labor		5,000	5,200	200 U
Depreciation of equipment . .		12,000	12,000	–0–
Miscellaneous		4,000	4,300	300 U
Total fixed overhead		42,000	42,500	500 U
Total overhead		$112,400	$114,500	$2,100 U

It is highly unlikely that, for any given time period, actual production will coincide exactly with budgeted production. Thus, a single static budget is usually useful only for planning but not for controlling. In anticipation of this, some firms find that constructing a series of budgets at budget-preparation time is easier than waiting to construct a new budget every time a performance report must be prepared. Other firms prefer to wait until the level of production is known and then prepare a flexible budget for that level.

Preparing a Flexible Budget

The steps to construct a flexible budget are:

1. Analyze the firm's costs into fixed, mixed, and variable categories.

2. Separate the fixed and variable portions of mixed costs, as discussed in Chapter 5.

3. Prepare cost formulas $(Y = a + bX)$ for all mixed costs.

4. Ascertain the firm's relevant operating range.

5. Determine the firm's most likely level of operation during each period (month or quarter) for which a performance report is to be prepared. (The production budget, as discussed in Chapter 7, provides the needed information.)

6. If the firm prepares a flexible budget in advance, then prepare a static budget for each level computed in step 5 above and for other levels below and above the expected level of operation. If the firm prepares the flexible budget after the level of production is known, then prepare *one* flexible budget for the actual level of operation.

Extending Illustration 9–3, the following is assumed:

1. The relevant range of operations for the Block Manufacturing Company is from 70,000 to 100,000 units per month.

2. Based on the firm's production budget, the most likely operating levels are 80,000 and 90,000 units per month.

3. Management decided to prepare a flexible budget using operating levels of 75,000, 80,000, 85,000, 90,000, and 95,000 units per month.

Block's flexible budget appears in Illustration 9–4. It was prepared using the budgeted variable costs per unit shown in the first column of Illustration 9–3.

Returning to Illustration 9–3, it can be seen that the budgeted activity level of 80,000 units agrees with that level of activity disclosed in the flexible budget shown in Illustration 9–4. Had the actual production been 75,000,

ILLUSTRATION 9–4

BLOCK MANUFACTURING COMPANY
Manufacturing Overhead Flexible Budget
For the Month of January 19x2

	Budgeted Costs per Unit	Level of Activity Units				
Units		75,000	80,000	85,000	90,000	95,000
Variable overhead:						
Power	$.03	$ 2,250	$ 2,400	$ 2,550	$ 2,700	$ 2,850
Repairs	.05	3,750	4,000	4,250	4,500	4,750
Payroll fringes	.70	52,500	56,000	59,500	63,000	66,500
Miscellaneous	.10	7,500	8,000	8,500	9,000	9,500
Total variable overhead	$.88	66,000	70,400	74,800	79,200	83,600
Fixed overhead:						
Superintendence		8,000	8,000	8,000	8,000	8,000
Factory rent		10,000	10,000	10,000	10,000	10,000
Maintenance		3,000	3,000	3,000	3,000	3,000
Indirect labor		5,000	5,000	5,000	5,000	5,000
Depreciation of equipment		12,000	12,000	12,000	12,000	12,000
Miscellaneous		4,000	4,000	4,000	4,000	4,000
Total fixed overhead . . .		42,000	42,000	42,000	42,000	42,000
Total overhead		$108,000	$112,400	$116,800	$121,200	$125,600

85,000, 90,000, or 95,000 units, that level of activity would have been extracted from Illustration 9–4 and a performance report similar to the one shown in Illustration 9–3 would have been prepared.

Once the flexible budget is prepared and compared with the actual results, the total variance for each item of overhead is computed. It is then possible for managers to further analyze the variances for variable manufacturing overhead. However, care must be exercised in selecting a proper overhead application base if the analysis is to be meaningful.

VARIABLE MANUFACTURING OVERHEAD

Selecting the Overhead Base

An **overhead application base** is a measure of activity, such as direct labor cost, direct labor-hours, and machine-hours, used in the calculation of a predetermined overhead rate. When selecting a base for use in the application and analysis of overhead, managers should select the one that has the strongest cause-and-effect relationship with overhead cost behavior. Thus, in a labor-intensive firm or department, the base should be direct labor, while in a machine-intensive firm or department, the base should be machine-hours. Although either direct labor cost or direct labor-hours may be used as a direct labor base, direct labor-hours usually produce a more accurate application and analysis of overhead.

Applying Variable Overhead to Production

Manufacturing overhead is rarely applied to production on a per-unit basis; instead, one of the bases noted above is usually used. Thus far, we have presented variable overhead on a per-unit basis, as shown in Illustration 9–4. But if the Block Manufacturing Company uses direct labor-hours to apply overhead to production, and if each unit requires one fourth of an hour of direct labor, the variable overhead per unit from Illustration 9–4 may be restated in direct labor-hours as shown in Illustration 9–5. Thus, the predetermined variable overhead rate is $3.52 per direct labor-hour.

ILLUSTRATION 9–5

BLOCK MANUFACTURING COMPANY
Budgeted Variable Manufacturing Overhead per Unit
and per Direct Labor-Hour

Overhead Cost	(1) Budgeted Cost per Unit	(2) Direct Labor-Hours per Unit	(3) Budgeted Cost per DLH (1) ÷ (2)
Power	$.03	.25	$ .12
Repairs	.05	.25	.20
Payroll fringes*	.70	.25	2.80
Miscellaneous	.10	.25	.40
Total	$.88		$3.52

* The company has uniform wage rates. Thus, payroll fringes per direct labor-hour do not distort this example.

Let us assume that 22,500 direct labor-hours (DLH) were budgeted for January 19x2. This means that 90,000 units (22,500 DLH ÷ .25 = 90,000 units) should have been produced. If only 80,000 units of ouput were produced, the standard hours allowed are 20,000 (80,000 units × .25 DLH).

Before proceeding with the analysis for controlling variable overhead, it is necessary to compute the total standard cost for variable overhead. The **total standard variable overhead cost** is the standard hours allowed multiplied by the variable overhead rate. In equation format, it may be stated as:

Total standard variable overhead cost
$$= \text{Standard hours allowed} \times \text{Variable overhead rate} \quad (1)$$

The total standard variable overhead cost for the Block Manufacturing Company for January is $70,400 (20,000 standard hours allowed × $3.52). This is also the amount of variable overhead applied to production. It is now possible to consider the controlling of variable overhead costs through the analysis of the variable overhead variance.

Analyzing Variable Overhead Variances

In Chapter 8, a direct labor variance was analyzed into its rate and efficiency components. The analysis of a variable overhead variance is very similar except that the portion that corresponds to a *rate* variance is usually called a *spending* variance instead.

The **variable overhead spending variance** is the actual number of hours of activity used in production multiplied by the difference between the actual and the standard rates of variable overhead per hour. The amount is derived using the equation:

Variable overhead spending variance
$$= \text{Actual hours} \times (\text{Actual rate per hour} - \text{Standard rate per hour}) \quad (2)$$

The variable overhead efficiency variance is also very similar to its counterpart in direct labor. The **variable overhead efficiency variance** is the standard variable overhead rate per hour multiplied by the difference between the actual hours worked and the standard hours allowed. It may be derived from the following equation:

Variable overhead efficiency variance
$$= \text{Standard rate per hour} \times (\text{Actual hours} - \text{Standard hours allowed}) \quad (3)$$

Firms usually find that calculations of the total spending variance and the total efficiency variance do not provide adequate information for control purposes. They need a more detailed analysis because variable overhead consists of many items, and a favorable variance of one item, such as power, may mask an unfavorable variance of another item, such as repairs. Therefore,

ILLUSTRATION 9–6

BLOCK MANUFACTURING COMPANY
Calculation of Actual Variable Overhead Rates
For January 19x2

Overhead Cost	Actual Cost	Actual DLH Worked	Rate per DLH
Power	$ 2,500	20,500	$ .12195
Repairs	4,200	20,500	.20488
Payroll fringes	56,800	20,500	2.77073
Miscellaneous	8,500	20,500	.41463
Total	$72,000		$3.51219

it is customary to prepare a variance report similar to the one shown in Illustration 9–3, except that the variances are further segregated into their spending and efficiency components. To do this, a starting point is to compute the *actual rate per direct labor-hour* for each item of variable overhead. Assuming that the actual number of hours (inputs) is 20,500 and using the actual variable overhead costs shown in Illustration 9–3, it is possible to compute the actual rates per direct labor-hour for each item as shown in Illustration 9–6.

Preparing Performance Reports that Include Variance Analyses

Using the budgeted costs per direct labor-hour hour, it is now possible to prepare a performance report suitable for segregating variances into their spending and efficiency components. Each cost must be analyzed separately using either the equation or the diagrammatic approach. The calculation of the spending and efficiency variances is shown in Illustration 9–7, while the performance report based on the variances computed in Illustration 9–7 is presented in Illustration 9–8.

ILLUSTRATION 9–7   **Analysis of Variable Overhead Variances**

Power

Actual quantity of *inputs* at actual rate (20,500 × $.12195) $2,500	*Actual* quantity of *inputs* at standard rate (20,500 × $.12) $2,460	*Standard* quantity allowed for *output* at *standard* rate (20,000 × $.12) $2,400

Spending variance = $40 U | Efficiency variance = $60 U

Total variance = $100 U

ILLUSTRATION 9–7   (*concluded*)

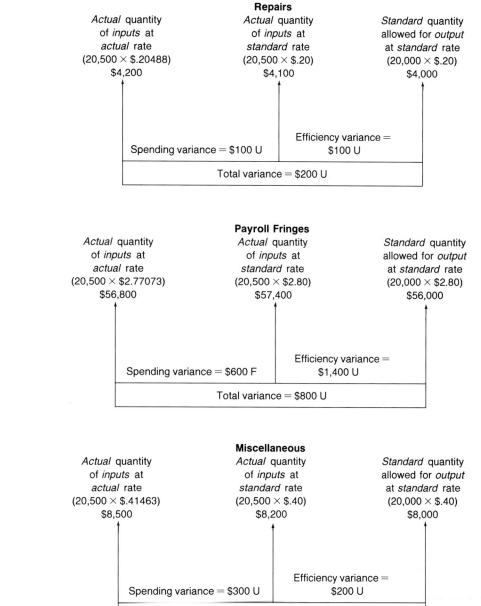

ILLUSTRATION 9–8

BLOCK MANUFACTURING COMPANY
Variable Manufacturing Overhead Performance Report
For the Month of January 19x2

Direct labor-hours:
Actual 20,500
Standard allowed 20,000
Variance—efficiency . . . . 500 U

Units produced 80,000
Units budgeted 90,000
Variance—effectiveness . . . . 10,000 U

Variable overhead:	Budgeted Cost per DLH	Total Standard Costs	Actual Costs	Total Variance	Spending Variance	Efficiency Variance
Power	$0.12	$ 2,400	$ 2,500	$ 100 U	$ 40 U	$ 60 U
Repairs	0.20	4,000	4,200	200 U	100 U	100 U
Payroll fringes	2.80	56,000	56,800	800 U	600 F	1,400 U
Miscellaneous	0.40	8,000	8,500	500 U	300 U	200 U
Total	$3.52	$70,400	$72,000	$1,600 U	$160 F	$1,760 U

Preparing Performance Reports in an Alternative Format

It is possible to avoid the use of the equation and diagrammatic approaches to analyze variances by inserting another column in the performance report for *budgeted costs* at the *actual* number of hours. The spending variance is then computed by subtracting the budgeted cost at the actual hours from the actual cost, and the efficiency variance is computed by subtracting the total standard cost from the budgeted cost at the actual number of hours.

Based on the information for power usage shown in Illustration 9–8, the total variance of $100 unfavorable may be analyzed as follows:

Actual cost $2,500
Total standard cost 2,400
Total variance . . . . $ 100 U

Budgeted cost at the actual number
of hours—20,500 hours × $.12 . . . $2,460
Total standard cost 2,400
Efficiency variance . . . . $ 60 U

Actual cost $2,500
Budgeted cost at actual hours 2,460
Spending variance . . . . $ 40 U

The performance report using this approach is shown in Illustration 9–9.

ILLUSTRATION 9–9

BLOCK MANUFACTURING COMPANY
Variable Manufacturing Overhead Performance Report
For the Month of January 19x2

Direct labor-hours:
Actual	20,500
Standard allowed	20,000
Variance	500 U

Units produced	80,000
Units budgeted	90,000
Variance	10,000 U

	(1) Budgeted Cost per DLH	(2) Total Standard Costs	Actual Costs	(3) Budgeted Costs at Actual Hours	Total Variance (2) − (1)	Spending Variance (2) − (3)	Efficiency Variance (3) − (1)
Variable overhead:							
Power	$0.12	$ 2,400	$ 2,500	$ 2,460	$ 100 U	$ 40 U	$ 60 U
Repairs	0.20	4,000	4,200	4,100	200 U	100 U	100 U
Payroll fringes	2.80	56,000	56,800	57,400	800 U	600 F	1,400 U
Miscel- laneous	0.40	8,000	8,500	8,200	500 U	300 U	200 U
Total	$3.52	$70,400	$72,000	$72,160	$1,600 U	$160 F	$1,760 U

Interpreting Variable Overhead Variances

Spending Variance. Illustration 9–8 provides a great deal more information about the composition of the variable overhead variances than does Illustration 9–3, where the spending component is not shown. Normally, a spending variance is composed of price changes exclusively, as in the cases of direct materials and direct labor. However, when it comes to variable overhead, it is possible for portions of an efficiency variance to find their way into the spending variance. This may occur because the efficiency variance computation for variable overhead is based on *direct labor or machine-hours* and *not* on a base that is part of overhead. To illustrate the problem, let us assume that each hour of direct labor used by the Block Manufacturing Company consumes one kilowatt-hour (kwhr) of power and that the *budgeted cost of power is 12 cents per kilowatt-hour.* Using the analysis of variances for power shown in Illustration 9–7 and the assumption that the *actual cost* of power for January 19x2 was 20,833 kilowatt-hours *at 12 cents* per kilowatt-hour for a total of $2,500, a different analysis may appear, as shown in Illustration 9–10.

The analysis presented in Illustration 9–10 should not be surprising since the *budgeted and actual prices of kilowatt-hours are the same* and, theoretically, no spending (price) variance should be expected. The analysis in Illustra-

ILLUSTRATION 9–10

BLOCK MANUFACTURING COMPANY
Analysis of Power Costs
For the Month of January 19x2

Total variance	$100 U
Efficiency variances:	
500 extra direct labor-hours at 12 cents . .	$ 60 U
333 extra kilowatt-hours at 12 cents	40 U
Total efficiency variance	$100 U

---

tion 9–7 is faulty because the cost of the extra usage of 333 kilowatt-hours has found its way into the spending variance, but only the portion that is based on direct labor-hours is labeled as the efficiency variance. Although this condition may occur for other variable overhead costs, the problem is not usually burdensome. When the spending variance merits management investigation, it is usually a simple matter to analyze items, such as kilowatt-hours used or indirect materials used, and reach the proper conclusions about spending versus efficiency variances.

Efficiency Variance. The variable overhead efficiency variance has little to do with the efficient utilization of overhead. Rather, it results from the efficient or inefficient use of direct labor-hours or machine-hours. It represents the amount of variable overhead costs saved or wasted because of saved or wasted direct labor. In theory, the variable overhead efficiency variance should be grouped with the direct labor efficiency variance, but in practice its use as a separate variance is deeply ingrained. Consequently, managers must understand how it is used. As noted in the discussion of the interpretation of the spending variance, portions of the efficiency variance for overhead costs are often included as part of the spending variance. Thus, when managers evaluate a direct labor efficiency variance, they should also consider the variable overhead efficiency caused by direct labor. They should also analyze significant spending variances to determine how much of these are caused by price factors and how much are caused by efficiency factors, as demonstrated in the analysis of power costs for the Block Manufacturing Company.

FIXED MANUFACTURING OVERHEAD

The analysis of fixed overhead variances differs substantially from the analysis of variable overhead variances. The differences arise because although the base used to apply overhead to production is the same for both, the behavior of fixed costs is markedly different from that of variable costs. For variable costs, there is a cause-and-effect relationship between the base and the incurrence of costs. But for fixed costs within the relevant range, there is no cause-and-effect relationship between the base and the incurrence of costs. Fixed costs are constant within the relevant range regardless of how many machine-hours or direct labor-hours are worked, yet fixed costs are applied to production at a fixed amount per direct labor-hour (or machine-hour), as is done for variable costs. Thus, in a sense, fixed costs are treated as variable costs when they are applied to production, but they must be analyzed differently if the variances are to be useful to managers. To properly analyze fixed overhead variances, a manager must understand how the predetermined fixed overhead rate is computed and how fixed overhead is applied to production.

Computing Predetermined Overhead Rates

Chapter 3 explained the computation of a single predetermined overhead rate with no distinction between variable and fixed costs. The procedure used to compute a single rate may be extended to compute separate rates, as follows:

$$\text{Predetermined variable overhead rate} = \frac{\text{Estimated variable overhead}}{\substack{\text{Direct labor-hours} \\ \text{(or machine-hours)}}}$$

$$\text{Predetermined fixed overhead rate} = \frac{\text{Estimated fixed overhead}}{\substack{\text{Direct labor-hours} \\ \text{(or machine-hours)}}}$$

If for 19x2 the Block Manufacturing Company estimated that its variable overhead would be $788,480, its fixed overhead would be $504,000, and its direct labor-hours would be 224,000, its predetermined overhead rates would be calculated as:

$$\text{Predetermined variable overhead rate} = \frac{\$788,480}{224,000 \text{ DLH}} = \$3.52 \text{ per DLH}$$

$$\text{Predetermined fixed overhead rate} = \frac{\$504,000}{224,000 \text{ DLH}} = \$2.25 \text{ per DLH}$$

Although Block could use the combined predetermined overhead rate of $5.77 ($3.52 + $2.25) if it did not wish to segregate overhead variances—and did not mind sacrificing some control—most firms prefer to segregate overhead variances, and thus use separate predetermined overhead rates for fixed and variable costs.

Applying Fixed and Variable Overhead to Production

In Chapter 8, we considered standard cost applications for direct materials and direct labor, but overhead must also be included to arrive at a firm's total standard cost for a unit of finished product. At the Block Manufacturing Company, the total standard cost of manufacturing one tie rack is as shown in Illustration 9–11.

ILLUSTRATION 9–11

BLOCK MANUFACTURING COMPANY.
Standard Cost Sheet

Product ___Oak tie racks___

Description	Quantity	Price or Rate	Total
Direct materials—			
1" clear oak	2 board feet	$1.00	$2.0000
Direct labor	¼ hour	$8.00	2.0000
Variable overhead . . .	¼ hour	$3.52	.8800
Fixed overhead	¼ hour	$2.25	.5625
Total			$5.4425

If 80,000 units are manufactured during the month of January 19x2, the journal entry to apply manufacturing overhead to production would be:

(a)

```
19x2
Jan. 31   Work in Process  . . . . . . . . . . . . . . . . . . . . . . .  115,400
                    Applied Manufacturing Overhead—Variable  . . . . .        70,400
                    Applied Manufacturing Overhead—Fixed  . . . . . .         45,000
              To apply overhead to production:
              Variable—80,000 × ¼ hour = 20,000 DLH × $3.52 = $70,400
              Fixed    —80,000 × ¼ hour = 20,000 DLH ×  2.25 =  45,000
```

Throughout the year, similar entries would be made. In addition, these entries would be posted to the job cost sheets, if a job order cost accounting system is used.

The Relationship between the Overhead Base and Fixed Costs

Ideally, a firm's overhead base should be strongly related to variable overhead costs, but such a relationship does not exist between the base and fixed costs. Nevertheless, the same base is used to apply fixed overhead to production as in journal entry *(a)*. This base is usually referred to as the **denominator activity** because it is the denominator when the predetermined fixed overhead rate is calculated. The base is also referred to as the **volume** or **capacity,** all of which refer to the firm's expected level of activity. Recall from Chapter 3 that the *base* is used to calculate the predetermined overhead rate. Applied overhead, however, is a function of the *standard hours allowed for actual production.*

Fixed Overhead Variance Analysis

To demonstrate the analysis of fixed overhead variances, we will assume that the Block Manufacturing Company uses the capacity of 224,000 direct labor-hours to compute its predetermined fixed overhead rate of $2.25 per direct labor-hour, as shown earlier. Block's flexible budget for 19x2's fixed costs is shown in Illustration 9–12, while its actual fixed overhead for January 19x2 is shown in Illustration 9–13.

ILLUSTRATION 9–12

BLOCK MANUFACTURING COMPANY
Flexible Budget for Fixed Manufacturing Overhead
For the Year Ended December 31, 19x2

Fixed overhead:

Superintendence	$ 96,000
Factory rent	120,000
Maintenance	36,000
Indirect labor	60,000
Depreciation of equipment	144,000
Miscellaneous	48,000
Total fixed overhead	$504,000

ILLUSTRATION 9–13

BLOCK MANUFACTURING COMPANY
Actual Fixed Manufacturing Overhead
For the Month of January 19x2

Fixed overhead:

Superintendence	$ 8,500
Factory rent	10,000
Maintenance	2,500
Indirect labor	5,200
Depreciation of equipment	12,000
Miscellaneous	4,300
Total fixed overhead	$42,500

Variance Computations. The total fixed overhead variance for the month of January 19x2 amounts to $2,500 favorable, calculated as follows:

Actual fixed overhead (Illustration 9–13)	$42,500
Applied fixed overhead [journal entry *(a)*] . . .	45,000
Total fixed overhead variance	$ 2,500 F

This total variance is usually segregated into two components, the spending variance and the volume variance. The **fixed overhead spending variance,** sometimes referred to as the *budget variance,* is the difference between the budgeted fixed overhead and the actual fixed overhead. The **fixed overhead volume variance,** also called the **capacity variance** or **denominator variance,** is the difference between the budgeted fixed overhead and the applied fixed overhead.

The equations for calculating these variances are:

Fixed overhead spending variance = Actual overhead
— Budgeted fixed overhead **(4)**

Fixed overhead volume variance = Budgeted fixed overhead   (5)
$-$ (Standard hours allowed $\times$ Fixed overhead rate)[1]

The calculations of the variances at Block Manufacturing are:

Fixed overhead spending variance:
Actual overhead (Illustration 9–13) $42,500
Flexible budget (Illustration 9–4)*   42,000
Spending variance . . . . $ 500 U

Fixed overhead volume variance:
Flexible budget (Illustration 9–4) $42,000
Applied fixed overhead (20,000 DLH $\times$ $2.25)   45,000
Volume variance . . . . $ 3,000 F

* Also, $504,000 (Illustration 9–12) ÷ 12 months = $42,000.

The fixed overhead volume variance may be verified by another calculation, as follows:

Budgeted hours at normal capacity:
224,000 DLH ÷ 12 months . . . .   18,666⅔ DLH
Standard hours allowed (80,000 units $\times$ ¼ DLH)   20,000   DLH
DLH worked in excess of budget . . . .   1,333⅓ DLH
Fixed overhead rate . . . . $\times$ $2.25
Favorable volume variance . . . . $ 3,000

The volume variance is favorable because the number of direct labor-hours worked was greater than anticipated. Thus, the fixed costs are spread over a greater number of units than expected, a favorable condition. When the reverse is true, that is, when the fixed costs must be spread over fewer units, the variance is unfavorable.

The total variance, $2,500 favorable, may also be segregated into its components through the use of the diagramatic approach. This method is shown in Illustration 9–14.

Illustration 9–14 demonstrates the analysis of variances for the *total* fixed overhead. In practice, however, this kind of analysis is applied to *each item* of fixed overhead, as was demonstrated for variable overhead in Illustration 9–7. Otherwise, a variance in one item, such as factory supervision, may mask a variance in another item, such as maintenance. In addition, the performance report for fixed overhead should be prepared using a format similar to that used in Illustration 9–8. The performance report for fixed overhead is usually shown in the same report used for variable overhead.

Once the fixed overhead variances have been analyzed, managers must discover why they occurred.

---

[1] This is the applied fixed overhead.

ILLUSTRATION 9-14   **Analysis of Fixed Overhead Variances**

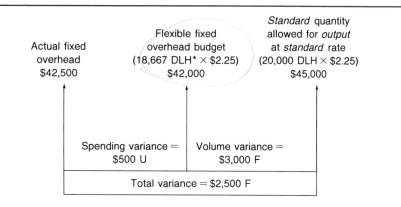

Actual fixed
overhead
$42,500

Flexible fixed
overhead budget
(18,667 DLH* × $2.25)
$42,000

Standard quantity
allowed for *output*
at *standard* rate
(20,000 DLH × $2.25)
$45,000

Spending variance =
$500 U

Volume variance =
$3,000 F

Total variance = $2,500 F

* Normal capacity of 224,000 DLH ÷ 12 months = 18,666⅔ DLH.

Interpreting Fixed Overhead Variances

Spending Variance. The spending variance usually results from price changes in the items included in fixed overhead. For example, there may have been a personnel change in the indirect labor category and the new employee may be paid at a different rate from that of the former employee. Variances may also stem from other personnel-related price changes, such as bonuses in profitable times and voluntary salary reductions during difficult times, both of which occurred in the automobile industry in the early 1980s. Other unexpected price changes may occur in real estate taxes on the factory building, heating fuel, and the like.

The spending variance may also reflect changed costs due to changed quantities. While this does not usually occur when production approximates the projected quantity, a sudden significant change may require the hiring of an additional foreman or the laying off of a foreman included in the budget. Thus, the spending variance may contain both a change in price and a change in quantity. Care must be exercised to disclose the makeup of the individual items in the spending variance. The variance should be further analyzed between price and quantity changes and separately disclosed in the performance report for fixed overhead.

Volume (Denominator) Variance. Conclusions should never be based on only one month's or several months' volume variance. Seasonal fluctuations may cause distortions in the volume variance for a particular month that will be averaged out over the course of the year.

It should be remembered that although Block Manufacturing charges fixed overhead to production at the rate of $2.25 per direct labor-hour, the fixed overhead is not incurred in this manner. The factory rent is $120,000 per year regardless of how many units are produced (or direct labor-hours worked). Thus, when fewer direct labor-hours are worked than anticipated, less overhead is charged to production and an unfavorable volume variance occurs. While this provides a measure of the underutilization of the factory compared to the planned amount, it may not necessarily be unfavorable for the firm as a whole. To continue to produce merchandise as planned when a sudden downward shift in the demand for a product occurs may later cause the firm to lose money due to high warehouse costs and/or selling below cost. Curtailing production, with a concomitant unfavorable volume variance, may be preferable if it produces smaller losses (or greater profits) for the firm than would the production of merchandise as planned.

The Graphical Solution to Fixed Overhead Variances

Further insight into fixed overhead variances may be gained through graphs. The graphical solution to fixed overhead variances at Block Manufacturing is shown in Illustration 9–15. This illustration indicates that:

1. The applied overhead of $45,000 is based on 20,000 standard hours allowed at $2.25 per direct labor-hour.

2. The budgeted overhead of $42,000 is based on the budgeted normal capacity of 18,667 direct labor-hours.

ILLUSTRATION 9–15

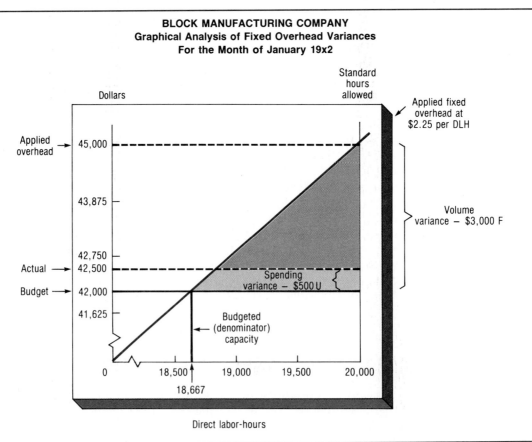

BLOCK MANUFACTURING COMPANY
Graphical Analysis of Fixed Overhead Variances
For the Month of January 19x2

3. The difference between the applied overhead and the budgeted overhead gives rise to the volume variance, in this case, favorable. Had applied and budgeted overhead coincided, one line would have been superimposed on the other and no volume variance would have been created.

An alternative form of graph, shown in Illustration 9–16, helps to clarify why a volume variance arises. Here, the fixed overhead is plotted as a horizon-

ILLUSTRATION 9–16

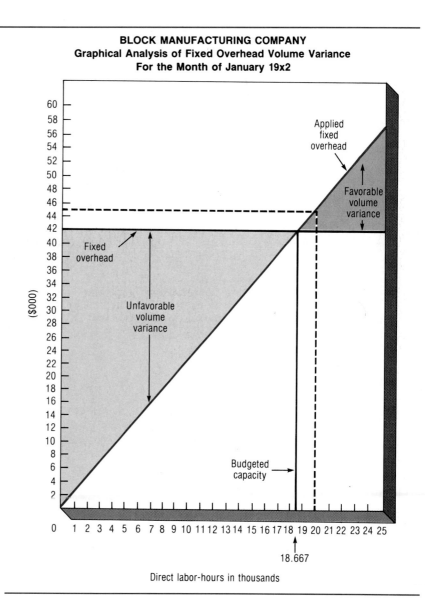

BLOCK MANUFACTURING COMPANY
Graphical Analysis of Fixed Overhead Volume Variance
For the Month of January 19x2

tal line while the applied overhead is plotted as a function of activity (direct labor-hours). The lines intersect at the firm's budgeted denominator capacity, 18,667 direct labor-hours (224,000 direct labor-hours ÷ 12 months). The area to the left of the intersection and beneath the fixed cost line, $42,000, represents the area of unfavorable volume variances, while the area to the right of the intersection and above the fixed cost line represents the area of favorable volume variances. The size of the variance may be obtained by (1) erecting a perpendicular line from the number of direct labor-hours worked to the applied overhead line and then drawing a horizontal line from that point to the left scale, and (2) subtracting the budgeted fixed overhead from the dollar amount indicated by the scale.

Journal Entries and Overhead Variances

The actual manufacturing overhead and applied manufacturing overhead accounts for the Block Manufacturing Company for the month of January 19x2 are shown in Illustration 9–17. These accounts are based on the data presented in Illustrations 9–8 and 9–14.

The actual and applied overhead accounts are *not normally* closed at the end of each month. Instead, they are carried forward, as they appear in Illustration 9–17, with additional amounts posted for each month until the end of the firm's fiscal year, at which time they are closed to cost of goods sold. For the sake of demonstration, however, let us assume that the Block Manufacturing Company wishes to close the accounts and record the variances at the end of January 19x2. The entries are:

(b)

Applied Variable Overhead	70,400	
Variable Overhead Efficiency Variance	1,760	
Variable Overhead Spending Variance		160
Variable Manufacturing Overhead		72,000

As per variance analysis in Illustrations 9–7 and 9–8.

ILLUSTRATION 9–17

BLOCK MANUFACTURING COMPANY
Selected T Account Balances
January 31, 19x2

Variable Manufacturing Overhead		Fixed Manufacturing Overhead	
72,000		42,500	

Applied Variable Overhead		Applied Fixed Overhead	
	70,400		45,000

(c)

Applied Fixed Overhead	45,000	
Fixed Overhead Spending Variance	500	
Fixed Overhead Volume Variance		3,000
Fixed Manufacturing Overhead		42,500

As per variance analysis in Illustration 9–14.

Presenting Variances on Income Statements for Managers

Although these variances are usually closed to cost of goods sold at the end of a firm's fiscal year, they are shown separate and apart from cost of goods sold on income statements prepared for managerial use. For example, for the month of January 19x2, the Block Manufacturing Company's books and records reflect the following variances for direct materials and direct labor:

Direct materials price variance	$2,000 U
Direct materials quantity variance	800 U
Direct labor rate variance	1,000 U
Direct labor efficiency variance	4,000 U

The following items have also been recorded:

Sales (80,000 × $10.00)	$800,000
Standard cost of goods sold (80,000 × $5.4425) (see Illustration 9–11)	435,400
Marketing and administrative costs	180,000
Income taxes	80,000

An income statement for managerial use is somewhat different from one issued to stockholders and other external users. The statement for managers contains a section for standard cost of goods sold. The **standard cost of goods sold** is the number of units sold in an accounting period multiplied by the standard cost per unit. The managerial income statement also contains a **standard gross margin,** which is the sales revenue in an accounting period minus the standard cost of goods sold for the period. An income statement prepared for external use contains *only* the *actual* cost of goods sold and the *actual* gross margin.

The variances noted above for direct materials and direct labor, together with the overhead variances shown in Illustrations 9–8 and 9–14, are deducted or added to adjust the standard cost of goods sold to actual cost of goods sold. The remainder of the income statement is prepared in the same format as that used for external reporting and discussed in Chapter 2.

The Block Manufacturing Company's income statement prepared for managerial use appears in Illustration 9–18.

The Treatment of Variances in Income Statements Prepared for External Use

When income statements are prepared for external use, it is customary to combine all variances with cost of goods sold and show cost of goods sold as a single amount, net of variances. An exception to this approach may pertain to the fixed overhead volume variance. If this variance is due to a seasonal fluctuation that will probably be countered by a future variance, it

ILLUSTRATION 9–18

BLOCK MANUFACTURING COMPANY
Income Statement for Managerial Use
For the Month of January 19x2

Sales (80,000 at $10.00)		$800,000
Standard cost of goods sold		
(80,000 at $5.4425)		435,400
Standard gross margin		364,600
Less: Variances from standard cost		
Direct materials price variance	$2,000 U	
Direct materials quantity variance	800 U	
Direct labor rate variance	1,000 U	
Direct labor efficiency variance	4,000 U	
Variable overhead spending variance	(160) F	
Variable overhead efficiency variance	1,760 U	
Fixed overhead spending variance	500 U	
Fixed overhead volume variance	(3,000) F	
Total variances from standard		6,900 U
Actual gross margin		357,700
Marketing and administrative costs		180,000
Operating income before income taxes		177,700
Provision for income taxes		80,000
Net income		$ 97,700

---

may be carried forward on the balance sheet and not offset against cost of goods sold.

If the Block Manufacturing Company were to prepare an income statement for external use based on Illustration 9–18 and the volume variance is *not* due to a seasonal fluctuation, it might appear as shown in Illustration 9–19.

If the fixed overhead volume variance were due to a seasonal variation that is expected to be countered in subsequent months, cost of goods sold

ILLUSTRATION 9–19

BLOCK MANUFACTURING COMPANY
Income Statement
For the Month of January 19x2

Sales	$800,000
Cost of goods sold	442,300
Gross margin	357,700
Marketing and administrative costs	180,000
Operating income before income taxes . . .	177,700
Provision for income taxes	80,000
Net income	$ 97,700

---

would be $3,000 higher and gross margin, operating income before income taxes, and net income would each be $3,000 lower. The balance sheet would reflect a *deferred credit* of $3,000 between liabilities and stockholders' equity.

STANDARD COSTING AND THE COST ACCOUNTING CYCLE

Appendix 9–A reviews the material covered in both Chapters 8 and 9 by showing the journal entries used to record the standard costing of direct materials, direct labor, and manufacturing overhead.

SELECTING A CAPACITY LEVEL FOR APPLYING OVERHEAD

In order to calculate the predetermined overhead rate, managers must normally select a capacity level. Depending on the objectives of their firm, they may choose an ideal capacity, a practical capacity, a normal capacity, or an expected capacity. The factors that influence management's decision when selecting a capacity level are discussed in Appendix 9–B.

SUMMARY

A budget prepared for a single level of activity, a **static budget,** is useful for planning purposes but cannot usually be used for controlling operations because, in most cases, a firm will not actually operate at an exact planned level. For comparison and control purposes, the actual level of operations must be compared to a budget prepared for that specific level. Many firms, therefore, prepare a **flexible budget** consisting of a series of static budgets within the firm's relevant range. Other firms wait until the level of production is known and then prepare a flexible budget for that level.

A firm's **overhead application base** should reflect a strong cause-and-effect relationship with variable overhead cost behavior. Thus, for a labor-intensive firm, the base should be direct labor, preferably direct labor-hours, and for a machine-intensive firm, the base should be machine-hours.

Each *element* of variable overhead should be analyzed separately into **spending** and **efficiency variances.** The spending variance usually measures the changes in the prices of the costs classified as variable overhead while the efficiency variance measures the quantity of variable overhead input that differs from the amount of input expected. Analyzing *total* variable overhead variances would yield unreliable results because an unfavorable variance in one element, such as indirect labor, could be masked by a favorable variance in another element, such as maintenance.

Each element of fixed overhead should also be analyzed into two components, which are usually called the **spending (budget) variance** and the **volume (capacity) variance.** The volume variance measures the difference between a firm's budgeted plant capacity and its actual level of operations, while the spending variance measures the changes in the prices of the inputs classified as fixed overhead from the prices budgeted for these items.

Income statements prepared for management's use separately disclose each variance for direct materials, direct labor, variable overhead, and fixed overhead. When income statements are prepared for external use, these variances are not disclosed separately, but are netted against cost of goods sold. The other principal difference is that an income statement prepared for a manager's use contains a section for **standard cost of goods sold** and **standard gross margin,** while an income statement for external use contains only actual cost of goods sold and actual gross margin.

GLOSSARY OF KEY TERMS

Capacity level   The volume of activity, expressed in direct labor-hours, machine-hours, or units, that a firm is capable of producing.

Denominator activity   See **capacity level.**

Fixed overhead capacity variance   See **fixed overhead volume variance.**

Fixed overhead denominator variance   See **fixed overhead volume variance.**

Fixed overhead spending variance   The difference between the budgeted fixed overhead and the actual fixed overhead.

Fixed overhead volume variance   The difference between the budgeted fixed overhead and the applied fixed overhead.

Flexible budget   A series of static budgets for different levels of activity within a firm's relevant range.

Overhead application base   A measure of activity, such as direct labor-hours or machine-hours, used in the calculation of a predetermined overhead rate.

Standard cost of goods sold   The number of units sold in an accounting period multiplied by the standard cost per unit.

Standard gross margin   Sales revenue in an accounting period minus the standard cost of goods sold for the period.

Static budget   A budget prepared for a single level of activity.

Total standard variable overhead cost   The standard hours allowed multiplied by the variable overhead rate.

Variable overhead efficiency variance   The standard variable overhead rate per hour multiplied by the difference between the actual hours worked and the standard hours allowed.

Variable overhead spending variance   The actual number of hours of activity used in production multiplied by the difference between the actual and the standard rates of variable overhead per hour.

APPENDIX 9–A   STANDARD COSTING AND THE COST ACCOUNTING CYCLE

To see how standard costing is reflected throughout the cost accounting cycle, let us assume that the Mentor Company manufactures butcher block tables. Each table requires the following direct materials, direct labor, and overhead:

	Standard Quantity	Price (Rate)	Standard Cost
2" clear maple	12 board feet	$1.00 per board foot	$12.00
Direct labor	2 hours	$9.00 per hour	18.00
Variable overhead	2 hours	$2.50 per hour	5.00
Fixed overhead	2 hours	$2.00 per hour	4.00
Total			$39.00

During January 19x2, the following transactions occurred:

1. Purchases of lumber amounted to $63,525. The price paid was $1.05 per board foot. There was no raw materials inventory at the beginning or end of the month. (The price variance is recorded at the time of purchase.)

2. The direct labor cost was $96,075. The hourly rate of pay was $9.15.

3. There was no work in process inventory on January 31, 19x2, and 5,000 tables were manufactured.

4. The actual overhead incurred amounted to:

    Variable $27,000
    Fixed 24,500

The budgeted capacity *for the year* is 72,000 units, or 144,000 direct labor-hours (72,000 units × 2 direct labor-hours = 144,000 direct labor-hours). It is the company's policy to record all variances and close them to cost of goods sold at the end of each month.

Sales for the month were 4,500 tables at a price of $100 per table. All sales are made on account.

The journal entries to record all transactions at the Mentor Company for January 19x2 would be:

19x2   (a)

Jan. 31 Raw Materials Inventory   60,500
        Materials Price Variance[1]   3,025
            Accounts Payable   63,525
        To record the purchase of raw materials—$63,525 ÷
        $1.05 = 60,500 board feet—60,500 board feet × $1.00
        = $60,500 standard cost.

                                        (b)

        Work in Process   60,000
        Materials Quantity Variance[2]   500
            Raw Materials Inventory   60,500
        To record the issuance of raw materials to
        production—5,000 units × 12 board feet × $1 =
        $60,000 total standard cost.

(c)

Work in Process	90,000	
Labor Rate Variance[3]	1,575	
Labor Efficiency Variance[4]	4,500	
Wages Payable		96,075

To record monthly payroll—5,000 units × 2 hours ×
$9 = $90,000 total standard cost.

(d)

Work in Process	45,000	
Applied Overhead—Variable		25,000
Applied Overhead—Fixed		20,000

Variable—5,000 units × 2 hours × $2.50 = $25,000.
Fixed   —5,000 units × 2 hours × $2.00 = $20,000.

(e)

Manufacturing Overhead Control—Variable	27,000	
Manufacturing Overhead Control—Fixed	24,500	
Accounts Payable, Cash, etc.		51,500

To record the actual overhead incurred.

(f)

Finished Goods	195,000	
Work in Process		195,000

To record completed goods—5,000 units × $39 =
$195,000.

(g)

Accounts Receivable	450,000	
Sales Revenue		450,000

To record sales—4,500 units × $100 = $450,000.

(h)

Cost of Goods Sold	175,500	
Finished Goods		175,500

To record the cost of units sold at standard cost—
4,500 units × $39 = $175,500.

(i)

Applied Overhead—Variable	25,000	
Variable Overhead Spending Variance[5]	750	
Variable Overhead Efficiency Variance[6]	1,250	
Manufacturing Overhead Control—Variable		27,000

To record variances for variable overhead.

(j)

Applied Overhead—Fixed	20,000	
Fixed Overhead Volume Variance[7]	4,000	
Fixed Overhead Spending Variance[8]	500	
Manufacturing Overhead Control—Fixed		24,500

To record variances for fixed overhead.

(k)

Cost of Goods Sold	16,100	
Materials Price Variance		3,025
Materials Quantity Variance		500
Labor Rate Variance		1,575
Labor Efficiency Variance		4,500
Variable Overhead Spending Variance		750
Variable Overhead Efficiency Variance		1,250
Fixed Overhead Volume Variance		4,000
Fixed Overhead Spending Variance		500

To close variances to cost of goods sold.

[1] 60,500 board feet $\times$ ($1.05 $-$ $1.00) = $3,025.
[2] (60,500 board feet $-$ 60,000 board feet) $\times$ $1 = $500.
[3] 10,500 direct labor-hours $\times$ ($9.15 $-$ $9.00) = $1,575.
[4] $9.00 $\times$ (10,500 direct labor-hours $-$ 10,000 direct labor-hours) = $4,500.
[5] $27,000 $-$ (10,500 direct labor-hours $\times$ $2.50) = $750.
[6] 10,500 direct labor-hours $-$ 10,000 direct labor-hours = 500 direct labor-hours $\times$ $2.50 = $1,250.
[7] Monthly budget = $24,000 (72,000 units $\times$ 2 hours $\times$ $2 = $288,000 $\div$ 12 months = $24,000). Budget $-$ Applied overhead = $24,000 $-$ $20,000 = $4,000.
[8] $24,500 actual $-$ $24,000 budget = $500.

The ending inventory of 500 tables is valued at the standard cost of $19,500 (500 units $\times$ $39). This is also the balance in the Finished Goods account, which may be computed by subtracting entry *(h)* from entry *(f)* ($195,000 $-$ $175,500 = $19,500).

APPENDIX 9-B   **SELECTING A CAPACITY LEVEL FOR APPLYING OVERHEAD**

In Chapter 8, two levels of standards were discussed—ideal standards and practical standards. These levels also apply to the amount of activity that is used in calculating the predetermined fixed overhead rate. Two other activity levels are also used in practice. Thus, the four possible activity levels are (1) ideal capacity, (2) practical capacity, (3) normal capacity, and (4) expected capacity. In choosing one of these activity levels as the basis for applying overhead, managers must consider the objectives of their firm.

1. Ideal Capacity   As noted in Chapter 8, ideal standards are of limited usefulness. Since an **ideal capacity level** does not allow for machine breakdowns, rest periods, and personal needs, it is attainable in only the rarest circumstances. When ideal capacity is used to calculate predetermined overhead rates, the applied overhead will invariably be less than the actual overhead, and underapplied overhead will be common. This is a questionable control mechanism, since standard costs and budgeted costs will be less than they should be and incorrect management decisions may result. To illustrate the problems that may arise, let us assume that the Block Manufacturing Company's ideal capacity

ILLUSTRATION 9–20

BLOCK MANUFACTURING COMPANY
Projected Results of Activity Levels
For the Year Ended December 31, 19x2

		$2.00 Rate	$2.25 Rate
Direct labor-hours worked	(a)	224,000	224,000
Overhead rate	(b)	$2.00	$2.25
Applied fixed overhead—(a) × (b) . . .		$448,000	$504,000
Actual fixed overhead		504,000	504,000
Underapplied fixed overhead		$ 56,000	$ –0–

is 252,000 direct labor-hours and that its estimated fixed overhead is $504,000. Its fixed predetermined overhead rate (POR) would therefore be:

$$\text{Predetermined fixed overhead rate} = \frac{\$504,000}{252,000 \text{ DLH}} = \$2 \text{ per DLH}$$

This rate should be compared with the previously computed rate of $2.25. At the $2.00 rate, each unit will have a cost of $0.25 less than it should have, and if the firm actually operates at 224,000 direct labor-hours, an under-applied overhead of $56,000 will result. This can be seen in Illustration 9–20.

Because this base almost always produces an unfavorable volume variance, it is not often used. When it is used, it is with the understanding that an unfavorable volume variance is expected.

2. Practical Capacity

As noted in Chapter 8, practical standards allow for machine breakdowns, rest periods, and personal needs. **Practical capacity** is similar in that in essence, it is ideal capacity minus an allowance for predictable interruptions. This capacity level presumes that a firm can sell all of its output, although in reality few firms sell 100 percent of their practical-capacity production over long periods of time. In fact, most industries in the United States have some idle capacity at various phases of our business and economic cycles. For example, this is especially true for firms in the steel, automobile, and farm machinery industries. When practical capacity is used to compute predeter-mined overhead rates, it is extremely likely that underapplied overhead will prevail during periods of idle capacity. Nevertheless, some firms find this level useful, since the underapplied overhead provides some indication that the plant is being underutilized.

3. Normal Capacity

Manufacturing firms often use normal capacity in computing POR. It is the average number of units that a firm expects to sell annually over the course of a complete business cycle, usually three to six years. Normal capacity is superior to practical capacity because it *spreads idle capacity fixed costs* over all units produced during the cycle. In contrast, when practical capacity is used, costs are charged off to cost of goods sold in the period they occur. To demonstrate, let us assume that Block's expected and actual fixed costs are $504,000 per year, its practical capacity is 240,000 direct labor-hours, and its normal capacity is 224,000 direct labor-hours. Normal capacity is the average of the expected annual production for each year during a projected business cycle. Thus, at Block, the normal capacity of 224,000 direct labor-hours is based on an assumed three-year cycle of 224,000 direct labor-hours for 19x2, 240,000 direct labor-hours for 19x3, and 208,000 direct labor-hours for 19x4. The projected results of the two capacities are shown in Illustration 9–21. The data indicate that:

ILLUSTRATION 9–21

BLOCK MANUFACTURING COMPANY
Projected Results of Activity Levels
For the Years Ended December 31, 19x2, 19x3, and 19x4

Calculation of predetermined fixed overhead rate:

$$\text{Practical capacity rate} = \frac{\$504{,}000}{240{,}000 \text{ DLH}} = \$2.10 \text{ per DLH}$$

$$\text{Normal capacity rate} = \frac{\$504{,}000}{224{,}000 \text{ DLH}} = \$2.25 \text{ per DLH}$$

		Normal Capacity	Practical Capacity
19x2:			
Actual DLH worked	(a)	224,000	224,000
Overhead rate	(b)	$2.25	$2.10
Applied fixed overhead—(a) × (b)		$504,000	$470,400
Actual fixed overhead		504,000	504,000
Charged off to cost of goods sold (underapplied overhead)		$ –0–	$ 33,600
19x3:			
Actual DLH worked	(c)	240,000	240,000
Overhead rate	(d)	$2.25	$2.10
Applied fixed cverhead—(c) × (d)		$540,000	$504,000
Actual fixed overhead		504,000	504,000
Credited to cost of goods sold (overapplied overhead)		$ 36,000	$ –0–
19x4:			
Actual DLH worked	(e)	208,000	208,000
Overhead rate	(f)	$2.25	$2.10
Applied fixed overhead—(e) × (f)		$468,000	$436,800
Actual fixed overhead		504,000	504,000
Charged to cost of goods sold (underapplied overhead)		$ 36,000	$ 67,200

1. The company operated at 100 percent of the practical capacity (240,000 direct labor-hours) in only one year, 19x3.

2. The amount of fixed overhead charged to production is $2.25 per unit when normal capacity is used and $2.10 per unit when practical capacity is used. Thus, if the practical-capacity cost of $2.10 is used for inventory valuation and pricing decisions, the cost per unit will be $0.15 less than if normal capacity is used.

3. When the $2.25 fixed cost per unit is used, there is no underapplied overhead in 19x2, there is an overapplied overhead of $36,000 in 19x3, and there is an underapplied overhead of $36,000 in 19x4. For the three-year cycle, overapplied and underapplied overhead cancel each other, and *all overhead* for the three years is charged to production. Thus, at a cost of $2.25 per unit, the entire fixed overhead for the three years is averaged over all units produced during those three years.

4. When the $2.10 fixed cost per unit is used, there is an underapplied overhead of $33,600 in 19x2, none in 19x3, and an underapplied overhead of $67,200 in 19x4, for a total underapplied overhead of $100,800 for the three-year period. Each amount is charged off in the year it is incurred. Thus, these amounts are *not* applied to the units produced in the three-year period but are written off without being inventoried.

Since it is not economically feasible to reduce the firm's plant capacity below 240,000 direct labor-hours—the capacity is needed in some years—it is difficult to justify the concept of "wasted plant capacity," which is normally written off as a loss. Rather, the 240,000 direct labor-hours is needed capacity in some years and *benefits all years* within the complete business cycle. Thus, the cost of the benefit should be allocated to all years benefited—that is, the complete cycle. The normal capacity is the one that accomplishes this objective.

When normal capacity is used, the same predetermined rate is maintained for the duration of the business cycle unless there is a change in the factors used in its calculation. Therefore, unless the firm's fixed costs or anticipated direct labor-hours change, the same rate would remain in use until the business cycle is completed. Shortly before that time, a new predetermined rate would be computed using the best estimates available at that time.

4. Expected Capacity

Expected capacity is the level of activity at which a firm expects to operate for the coming year. Since this capacity is concerned with the coming year only, a new predetermined rate is computed for each year in a business cycle. Using the same data for the three years in Illustration 9–21, Block's predetermined rates using expected capacity would be:

$$19x2 = \frac{\$504,000}{224,000 \text{ DLH}} = \$2.25 \text{ per DLH}$$

$$19x3 = \frac{\$504,000}{240,000 \text{ DLH}} = \$2.10 \text{ per DLH}$$

$$19x4 = \frac{\$504,000}{208,000 \text{ DLH}} = \$2.42 \text{ per DLH}$$

When expected capacity is used, the objective is to assign a given year's fixed overhead only to the units produced in that year. No attempt is made to allocate idle-capacity fixed costs to any year other than the current one. The use of this method produces different inventoriable costs in each year of Block's three-year cycle even though each year's total fixed costs are the same. When the actual direct labor-hours in any year equals the anticipated direct labor-hours, there is no underapplied or overapplied overhead.

Many firms believe that a change in unit costs should be made only when total costs change, and that when there is no change in total costs, unit costs should not be changed. The use of expected capacity is not compatible with this view. In a sense, when expected capacity is used, part of a unit's cost is determined by the number of units produced even though there is no change in the total fixed overhead during the three-year cycle. That is, when 224,000 direct labor-hours are worked, inventory values include $2.25 per unit for fixed overhead; when 208,000 direct labor-hours are worked, inventory values include $2.42 per unit for fixed overhead; and when 240,000 direct labor-hours are worked, inventory values include $2.10 per unit for fixed overhead. Many managers find this objectionable.

GLOSSARY OF KEY TERMS— APPENDIX 9–B

Expected capacity The level of activity at which a firm expects to operate for the coming year.

Ideal capacity A theoretical level of activity that does not allow for machine breakdowns, rest periods, employees' personal needs, and the like. It is attainable only in the rarest circumstances.

Normal capacity A level of activity that consists of the average number of units that a firm expects to sell annually over the course of a complete business cycle, usually three to six years.

Practical capacity A level of activity that allows for machine breakdowns, rest periods, employees' personal needs, etc., and assumes that a firm can sell all of the output it is capable of producing.

QUESTIONS

1. What is a static budget? Is it useful for planning? Controlling? Explain.

2. What is a flexible budget? Is it more useful than a static budget? Why?

3. How is a flexible budget prepared?

4. If you were given a static budget, the level of activity for the budget, and no other information, would it be possible to prepare a flexible budget from the information given? Explain why or why not.

5. Is it important to use care in selecting the overhead base for applying overhead to production? Why?

6. What variances are computed for variable overhead? Explain what each one normally contains.

7. Should the variances for variable overhead be computed only for the total variable overhead? Why or why not?

8. Spending (rate) variances for direct labor consist of the difference between the actual and standard rates of pay per hour multiplied by the number of hours worked. Is the same always true for the spending variance for variable overhead? Explain.

9. Fixed costs are incurred in large indivisible amounts, while variable costs are incurred in proportion to the number of units produced. When applying overhead to production, is fixed overhead applied differently from variable overhead? Why?

10. What variances are computed for fixed overhead? What do the variances contain?

11. When preparing a performance report for fixed overhead, should separate variances be computed for each item? Why?

12. What is a denominator variance? Why is it referred to in this manner?

13. When a significant unfavorable volume variance exists after one or a few months of a firm's fiscal year, is it always cause for concern? Discuss.

14. How should variances be treated in interim income statements prepared for management's use? Would the treatment be different if the income statement was for a full 12 months? Why?

15. How should variances be treated in interim income statements prepared for external use? Does this treatment differ from that used for internal use? Why?

16. When a significant volume variance exists, how should it be treated in interim income statements prepared for external use? Would your answer be different for annual income statements prepared for external use? Discuss.

For Appendix 9–B

17. When computing a predetermined overhead rate, one of four different activity levels must be selected for the computation. What are the four levels? For each level, discuss the factors that may influence your selection of the activity level.

EXERCISES   **9–1**   **Flexible Budgeting**

1. A static budget
   a. Drops the current month or quarter and adds a future month or a future quarter as the current month or quarter is completed.
   b. Presents a statement of expectations for a period of time but does not present a firm commitment.
   c. Presents the plan for only one level of activity and does not adjust to changes in the level of activity.
   d. Presents the plan for a range of activity so that the plan can be adjusted for changes in activity levels.
   e. Divides the activities of individual responsibility centers into a series of packages which are ranked ordinally.
2. A flexible budget
   a. Classifies budget requests by activity and estimates the benefits arising from each activity.

    b. Presents a statement of expectations for a period of time but does not present a firm commitment.

    c. Presents the plan for only one level of activity and does not adjust to changes in the level of activity.

    d. Presents the plan for a range of activity so that the plan can be adjusted for changes in activity levels.

    e. Divides the activities of individual responsibility centers into a series of packages which are ranked ordinally.

(CMA adapted)

3. Dean Company is preparing a flexible budget for 19x2, and the following maximum capacity estimates for department M are available:

	At Maximum Capacity
Direct labor-hours	60,000
Variable factory overhead	$150,000
Fixed factory overhead	$240,000

Assume that Dean's normal capacity is 80 percent of maximum capacity. What would be the total factory overhead rate, based on direct labor-hours, in a flexible budget at normal capacity?

    a. $6.00.

    b. $6.50.

    c. $7.50.

    d. $8.13.

(AICPA adapted)

9–2 Flexible Budgeting and Computation of the Differences between Actual Costs and the Flexible Budget

The Melcher Company produces farm equipment at several plants. The business is seasonal and cyclical in nature. The company has attempted to use budgeting for planning and controlling activities, but the variable nature of the business has caused some company officials to be skeptical about the usefulness of budgeting to the company. The accountant for the Adrian plant has been using a system he calls "flexible budgeting" to help his plant management control operations.

The company president asks him to explain what the term means, how he applies the system at the Adrian plant, and how it can be applied to the company as a whole. The accountant presents the following data as part of his explanation.

Budget data for 19x3:
Normal monthly capacity of the
plant in direct labor-hours . . . . 10,000 hours
Material costs . . . .   6 pounds at $1.50 $9.00 per unit
Labor costs . . . . .   2 hours at $3.00 $6.00 per unit

Overhead estimate at normal monthly capacity:
Variable (controllable):

Indirect labor	$ 6,650
Indirect materials	600
Repairs	750
Total variable	8,000

Fixed (noncontrollable):

Depreciation	3,250
Supervision	3,000
Total fixed	6,250
Total fixed and variable	$14,250

Planned units for January 19x3	4,000
Planned units for February 19x3	6,000

Actual data for January 19x3:

Hours worked	8,400
Units produced	3,800

Costs incurred:

Material (24,000 pounds)	$36,000
Direct labor	25,200
Indirect labor	6,000
Indirect materials	600
Repairs	1,800
Depreciation	3,250
Supervision	3,000
Total	$75,850

Required   a. Prepare a budget for January.

b. Prepare a report for January comparing actual and budgeted costs for the actual activity for the month.

c. Can flexible budgeting be applied to the nonmanufacturing activities of the company? Explain your answer.

(AICPA adapted)

9–3   Calculation of Predetermined Overhead Rate Using the High-Low Method, and How It May Be Used by Managers

Tastee-Treat Company prepares, packages, and distributes six frozen vegetables in two different-size containers. The different vegetables and different sizes are prepared in large batches. The company employs an actual cost job order costing system. Manufacturing overhead is assigned to batches by a predetermined rate on the basis of direct labor-hours. The manufacturing overhead costs incurred by the company during two recent years (adjusted for changes using current prices and wage rates) are presented below.

	Year 1	Year 2
Direct labor-hours worked	2,760,000	2,160,000
Manufacturing overhead costs incurred (adjusted for changes in current prices and wage rates):		
Indirect labor	$11,040,000	$ 8,640,000
Employee benefits	4,140,000	3,240,000
Supplies	2,760,000	2,160,000
Power	2,208,000	1,728,000
Heat and light	552,000	552,000
Supervision	2,865,000	2,625,000
Depreciation	7,930,000	7,930,000
Property taxes and insurance	3,005,000	3,005,000
Total overhead costs	$34,500,000	$29,880,000

Required   *a.*   Tastee-Treat Company expects to operate at a 2.3 million direct labor-hour level of activity in 19x1. Using the data from two recent years, calculate the rate Tastee-Treat should employ to assign manufacturing overhead to its products.

      b.   Explain how the company can use the information it developed for calculating the overhead rate for:

        (1)   Evaluation of product pricing decisions.

        (2)   Cost control evaluation.

        (3)   Development of budgets.

(CMA adapted)

9–4   Preparation of a Flexible Budget for Overhead

The Aberle Company presents you with the following information:

	Activity Levels	
	60,000 DLH	100,000 DLH
Indirect materials	$ 7,000	$11,000
Indirect labor	17,000	25,000
Power	3,000	5,000
Repairs	6,800	10,800
Maintenance	4,200	5,000
Depreciation of factory equipment	8,000	8,000
Miscellaneous	10,000	15,000
Total	$56,000	$79,800

Required   Prepare a flexible budget for activity levels of 70,000 direct labor-hours, 80,000 direct labor-hours, and 90,000 direct labor-hours. Segregate the budget into variable overhead and fixed overhead with subtotals for each. Label your first column *variable cost per unit.* (Note: Each item above may appear in both the variable and fixed categories.)

9-5 Preparation of a Flexible Budget from a Static Budget

The Shelton Company presents you with the following budget:

Activity level	40,000 DLH
Variable overhead:	
Indirect materials	$ 8,000
Indirect labor	4,400
Power	12,000
Repairs	2,600
Miscellaneous	7,800
Total	34,800
Fixed overhead:	
Indirect labor	8,000
Maintenance	5,000
Depreciation of factory equipment	11,000
Superintendence	5,000
Miscellaneous	3,000
Total	32,000
Total overhead	$66,800

Required   Prepare a flexible budget for activity levels of 50,000 direct labor-hours, 55,000 direct labor-hours, and 60,000 direct labor-hours. Label your first column *variable cost per unit.*

9-6 Comparison of Actual Data with Budgeted Data Prepared from Flexible Budget

The Newton Company provides you with the following:

	Activity Levels	
	30,000 DLH	**50,000 DLH**
Indirect materials	$ 2,100	$ 3,500
Indirect labor	14,400	18,000
Power	6,600	11,000
Repairs and maintenance	8,200	11,000
Depreciation of factory equipment	6,000	6,000
Factory rent	10,000	10,000
Miscellaneous	10,700	14,500
Total	$58,000	$74,000

Actual overhead for the period when 41,000 direct labor-hours were worked is:

Indirect materials	$ 3,000
Indirect labor	16,420
Power	9,100
Repairs and maintenance	9,620
Depreciation of factory equipment	6,000
Factory rent	10,000
Miscellaneous	12,190
Total	$66,330

Actual fixed overhead costs were the same as budgeted fixed overhead costs except for the following:

1. A factory line foreman left the employ of the company and a replacement earns $500 less.
2. One maintenance employee was furloughed for two weeks. His salary for that period of time was $600.

Required   a. Prepare a budget for 41,000 direct labor-hours. Segregate the variable overhead from the fixed overhead and use subtotals for each category. (Note: Each item of overhead may appear in both categories.)

b. Alongside the budget for 41,000 direct labor-hours, insert the actual amounts, by category, and indicate the amounts of the differences labeled favorable or unfavorable.

9–7   Computation of Predetermined Overhead Rates and Preparation of Standard Costs from a Flexible Budget

The Rutan Company manufactures only one product and provides you with the following:

	Activity Levels	
	30,000 DLH	**50,000 DLH**
Variable overhead	$42,000	$59,600
Fixed overhead	38,000	38,000
Total	$80,000	$97,600

The company's normal capacity is 40,000 direct labor-hours.

Each unit of product requires three pounds of Tigrin at a standard price of $0.40 per pound, and two hours of direct labor at a standard rate of $7 per hour.

Required   a. Compute predetermined overhead rates per direct labor-hour for variable overhead and fixed overhead.

b. Prepare a standard cost sheet for one unit of product.

9–8   Preparation of a Flexible Budget for Overhead

The Hendrix Company presents you with the following information:

	Activity Levels	
	30,000 DLH	40,000 DLH
Indirect materials	$ 3,800	$ 4,400
Indirect labor	10,000	11,200
Power	3,900	5,200
Repairs	6,200	7,600
Maintenance	3,600	3,800
Depreciation of factory equipment	12,000	16,000
Miscellaneous	9,000	11,000
Total	$48,500	$59,200

Required   Prepare a flexible budget for activity levels of 32,000 direct labor-hours, 34,000 direct labor-hours, 36,000 direct labor-hours, and 38,000 direct labor-hours. Segregate the budget into variable overhead and fixed overhead with subtotals for each. Label your first column *variable cost per unit*. (Note: Each item above may appear in both the variable and fixed categories.)

9-9   Preparation of a Flexible Budget from a Static Budget

The Brown Company presents you with the following budget:

Activity level	30,000 DLH
Variable overhead:	
Indirect materials	$ 1,800
Indirect labor	6,000
Depreciation of factory equipment	9,000
Power	2,100
Repairs	3,900
Miscellaneous	4,500
Total	27,300
Fixed overhead:	
Indirect labor	8,000
Maintenance	5,000
Superintendence	6,000
Miscellaneous	4,000
Total	23,000
Total overhead	$50,300

Required   Prepare a flexible budget for activity levels of 32,000 direct labor-hours, 34,000 direct labor-hours, and 36,000 direct labor-hours. Label your first column *variable cost per unit*.

9-10   Comparison of Actual Data with Budgeted Data Prepared from Flexible Budget

The Newton Company provides you with the following:

	Activity Levels	
	20,000 DLH	30,000 DLH
Indirect materials	$ 2,000	$ 2,600
Indirect labor	6,000	8,000
Power	2,200	3,300
Repairs and maintenance	5,000	6,000
Depreciation of factory equipment	7,000	10,500
Factory rent	12,000	12,000
Miscellaneous	9,000	11,500
Total	$43,200	$53,900

Actual overhead for the period when 26,000 direct labor-hours were worked is:

Indirect materials	$ 2,300
Indirect labor	7,100
Power	3,000
Repairs and maintenance	6,500
Depreciation of factory equipment	9,100
Factory rent	12,000
Miscellaneous	10,200
Total	$50,200

Actual fixed costs were the same as budgeted fixed costs except for the following:

1. A factory line foreman left the employ of the company and a replacement earns $300 more.
2. An independent repair consultant was hired at a fee of $600 to determine the cause of an unusual machine breakdown.

Required *a.* Prepare a budget for 26,000 direct labor-hours. Segregate the variable overhead from the fixed overhead and use subtotals for each category. (Note: Each item of overhead may appear in both categories.)

b. Alongside the budget for 26,000 direct labor-hours, insert the actual amounts, by category, and indicate the amounts of the differences labeled favorable or unfavorable.

9–11 Computation and Analysis of Variances

Items 1 and 2 are based on the following information:

The following information relates to a given department of Herman Company for the fourth quarter 19x4:

Actual total overhead (fixed plus variable)	$178,500
Budget formula	$110,000 plus $0.50 per hour
Total overhead application rate	$1.50 per hour

Spending variance—variable only	$8,000 unfavorable
Volume variance	$5,000 favorable
Spending variance—fixed	none

The total overhead variance is divided into three variances—spending, efficiency, and volume.

1. What were the actual hours worked in this department during the quarter?
   a. 110,000.
   b. 121,000.
   c. 137,000.
   d. 153,000.

2. What were the standard hours allowed for good output in this department during the quarter?
   a. 105,000.
   b. 106,667.
   c. 110,000.
   d. 115,000.

3. Information on Ripley Company's overhead costs for the January 19x0 production activity is as follows:

Budgeted fixed overhead	$75,000
Standard fixed overhead rate	
per direct labor-hour	$3
Standard variable overhead rate	
per direct labor-hour	$6
Standard direct labor-hours allowed	
for actual production	24,000
Actual total overhead incurred	$220,000

The volume (denominator) variance for January 19x0 is
   a. $3,000 unfavorable.
   b. $3,000 favorable.
   c. $4,000 unfavorable.
   d. $4,000 favorable.

4. Information on Fire Company's overhead costs is as follows:

Actual variable overhead	$73,000
Actual fixed overhead	$17,000
Standard hours allowed for	
actual production	32,000
Standard variable overhead rate	
per direct labor-hour	$2.50
Standard fixed overhead rate	
per direct labor-hour	$0.50

What is the total overhead variance?
   a. $1,000 unfavorable.
   b. $6,000 favorable.
   c. $6,000 unfavorable.
   d. $7,000 favorable.

(AICPA adapted)

9-12   Computation and Analysis of Variances

King Company estimates that it will operate its manufacturing facilities at 800,000 direct labor-hours for the year. The estimate for total budgeted overhead is $2 million. The standard variable overhead rate is estimated to be $2 per direct labor-hour or $6 per unit. The actual data for the year are presented below:

Actual finished units	250,000
Actual direct labor-hours	764,000
Actual variable overhead	$1,610,000
Actual fixed overhead	$ 392,000

1. The variable overhead spending variance for the year is
    a. $2,000 F.
    b. $10,000 U.
    c. $82,000 U.
    d. $110,000 U.
    e. Some amount other than those shown above.
2. The variable overhead efficiency variance for the year is
    a. $28,000 U.
    b. $100,000 U.
    c. $110,000 U.
    d. Determined from information other than that given above.
    e. Some response other than those shown above.
3. The fixed overhead spending variance for the year is
    a. $8,000 F.
    b. $10,000 U.
    c. $17,000 U.
    d. $74,000 U.
    e. Some amount other than those shown above.
4. The fixed overhead volume variance for the year is
    a. $7,000 U.
    b. $25,000 U.
    c. $41,667 U.
    d. $18,000 F.
    e. Some amount other than those shown above.

(CMA adapted)

9-13   Computation and Analysis of Variances

The Menton Company manufactures one product and provides you with the following information for the year 19x2:

Normal direct labor-hours	100,000
Standard variable overhead rate	$3
Standard variable overhead cost per unit	$6
Units manufactured—actual	48,000
Actual direct labor-hours	97,000
Actual overhead:	
Variable	$297,000
Fixed	$202,000
Total budgeted overhead	$500,000

Required *a.* Compute the variable overhead spending and efficiency variances.

b. Compute the fixed overhead spending and volume variances.

c. For each variance, indicate whether it is favorable or unfavorable.

9–14 Computation of Data from Given Variances

The Horlick Company provides you with the following information for the year 19x3:

Standard variable overhead rate . . . .$2 per DLH	
Actual variable overhead $202,500	
Actual fixed overhead $153,300	

	(F) Favorable (U) Unfavorable
Variances:	
Variable spending	$ 500 U
Variable efficiency	600 F
Fixed spending	300 U
Fixed volume	1,050 U

Required Compute the following:

a. Standard hours allowed.

b. Actual direct labor-hours.

c. Fixed overhead rate.

d. Budgeted fixed overhead.

e. Normal activity in direct labor-hours.

f. Applied overhead to production.

(Hint: Use the diagrammatic approach.)

9–15 Computation of Selected Data and Variances

The Winter Company provides you with the following information for the year 19x4:

Standard combined overhead rate . . . . . .$5 per DLH	
Applied fixed overhead $412,500	
Standard hours allowed 150,000	
Variable overhead efficiency variance . . . . .$ 1,125 U	
Actual variable overhead $340,000	
Budgeted fixed overhead $440,000	
Fixed overhead spending variance . . . . . .$ 2,000 U	

Required Compute the following:

a. Standard fixed overhead rate.

b. Standard variable overhead rate.

c. Applied variable overhead.

d. Actual direct labor-hours.

e. Normal activity in direct labor-hours.

f. Variable overhead spending variance. (Indicate whether it is favorable or unfavorable.)

g. Actual fixed overhead.

h. Fixed overhead volume variance. (Indicate whether it is favorable or unfavorable.) (Hint: Use the diagrammatic approach.)

PROBLEMS   **9–16**   **Flexible Budgeting and Comparison Report**

The University of Boyne offers an extensive continuing education program in many cities throughout the state. For the convenience of its faculty and administrative staff and also to save costs, the university operates a motor pool. Until February, the motor pool operated with 20 vehicles. However, an additional automobile was acquired in February this year, increasing the total to 21 vehicles. The motor pool furnishes gasoline, oil, and other supplies for the cars, and hires one mechanic who does routine maintenance and minor repairs. Major repairs are done at a nearby commercial garage. A supervisor manages the operations.

Each year, the supervisor prepares an operating budget for the motor pool. The budget informs university management of the funds needed to operate the pool. Depreciation on the automobiles is recorded in the budget in order to determine the costs per mile.

The schedule below presents the annual budget approved by the university. The actual costs for March are compared to one twelfth of the annual budget.

UNIVERSITY MOTOR POOL
Budget Report
For March 19x6

	Annual Budget	One Month Budget	March Actual	Over* Under
Gasoline	$24,000	$2,000	$2,800	$800*
Oil, minor repairs, parts, and supplies	3,600	300	380	80*
Outside repairs	2,700	225	50	175
Insurance	6,000	500	525	25*
Salaries and benefits	30,000	2,500	2,500	—
Depreciation	26,400	2,200	2,310	110*
	$92,700	$7,725	$8,565	$840*
Total miles	600,000	50,000	63,000	
Cost per mile	$0.1545	$0.1545	$0.1359	
Number of automobiles	20	20	21	

USE THIS FIGURE AS miLES TRAVELLED/moNTH [handwritten annotation]

The annual budget was constructed upon the following assumptions:

1. 20 automobiles in the pool.
2. 30,000 miles per year per automobile.
3. 15 miles per gallon per automobile.
4. $0.60 per gallon of gas.

5. $0.006 per mile for oil, minor repairs, parts, and supplies.
6. $135 per automobile in outside repairs.

The supervisor is unhappy with the monthly report comparing budget and actual costs for March. He claims it presents unfairly his performance for March. His previous employer used flexible budgeting to compare actual costs to budgeted amounts.

Required

a. Employing flexible budgeting techniques, prepare a report which shows budgeted amounts, actual costs, and monthly variation for March.

b. Explain briefly the basis of your budget figure for outside repairs.

(CMA adapted)

9-17 Flexible Budget and Performance Report with Analyzed Variances

The Martin Company provides you with the following information for the month of January 19x5:

	Activity Levels	
	60,000 DLH	70,000 DLH
Indirect materials	$ 4,400	$ 4,800
Indirect labor	16,000	17,000
Power	12,000	14,000
Repairs and maintenance	12,000	13,500
Depreciation of factory equipment	14,500	14,500
Factory rent	18,000	18,000
Miscellaneous	13,700	15,400
Total	$90,600	$97,200

Actual overhead for the period when 64,000 direct labor-hours were worked is:

	Variable	Fixed
Indirect materials	$ 2,600	$ 2,000
Indirect labor	6,500	11,000
Power	13,400	—
Repairs and maintenance	9,000	2,500
Depreciation of factory equipment	—	14,500
Factory rent	—	18,000
Miscellaneous	11,200	4,000
Total	$42,700	$52,000

The following additional information is available:

Normal activity . . . . 85,000 DLH per month
Units produced 31,500
Standard hours per unit 2

Required   *a.* Prepare a budget for 63,000 direct labor-hours. Segregate the variable overhead from the fixed overhead and use subtotals for each category. (Note: Each item of overhead may appear in both categories.)

       b. Prepare a performance report for the month of January 19x5. Each item of overhead (both variable and fixed) should be analyzed into appropriate variances labeled (F) or (U) for favorable or unfavorable.

       c. The total of all variances for variable overhead is substantially different from the total of all variances for fixed overhead. Explain why this is so. What reasons can you give for the significant volume variances?

9–18   **Variance Analysis and Performance Report for Direct Materials, Direct Labor, and Manufacturing Overhead**

The Rotor Company manufactures one product and presents you with the following for 19x6:

Standard cost sheet:		
Direct material	2 pounds at $1.10	$ 2.20
Direct labor	1 hour at $6.00	6.00
Variable overhead	1 hour at $2.50	2.50
Fixed overhead	1 hour at $2.00	2.00
Total		$12.70

The following information is also available:

Budgeted total overhead at normal activity	$675,000
Units produced	140,000
Materials purchased and used in production—	
285,000 pounds at $1.15 per pound	$327,750
Direct labor—142,000 hours at $6.20	$880,400
Actual overhead:	
Variable	$360,000
Fixed	315,000

Required   *a.* Calculate all appropriate variances for direct materials, direct labor, variable overhead, and fixed overhead.

       b. Prepare a performance report for the year using the following columnar headings:
         (1) Cost per unit.
         (2) Budget for 140,000 units.
         (3) Actual costs for 140,000 units.
         (4) Total variance.
         (5) Price (rate) (spending) variance.
         (6) Quantity (efficiency) variance.
         (7) Volume variance.

       c. For all variances shown in the performance report, indicate (F) for favorable variances and (U) for unfavorable variances.

9–19   Variance Analysis for Direct Materials, Direct Labor, and Overhead

The Terry Company manufactures a commercial solvent that is used for industrial maintenance. This solvent is sold by the drum and generally has a stable selling price. Due to a decrease in demand for this product, Terry produced and sold 60,000 drums in December 19x6, which is 50 percent of normal capacity.

The following information is available regarding Terry's operations for the month of December 19x6:

1. Standard costs per drum of product manufactured were as follows:

Materials:	
10 gallons of raw material	$20
1 empty drum	1
Total materials	$21
Direct labor:	
1 hour	$ 7
Factory overhead (fixed):	
Per direct labor-hour	$ 4
Factory overhead (variable):	
Per direct labor-hour	$ 6

2. Costs incurred during December 19x6 were as follows:

Raw materials:	
600,000 gallons were purchased at a cost of $1,150,000	
700,000 gallons were used	
Empty drums:	
85,000 drums were purchased at a cost of $85,000	
60,000 drums were used	
Direct labor:	
65,000 hours were worked at a cost of $470,000	
Factory overhead:	
Depreciation of building and machinery (fixed)	$230,000
Supervision and indirect labor (semivariable)	360,000
Other factory overhead (variable)	76,500
Total factory overhead	$666,500

3. The fixed overhead budget for the December level of production was $275,000.
4. In November 19x6, at normal capacity of 120,000 drums, supervision and indirect labor costs were $680,000. All cost functions are linear.

Required Prepare a schedule computing the following variances for the month of December 19x6:

- *a.* Materials price variance (computed at time of purchase).
- *b.* Materials usage variance.
- *c.* Labor rate variance.
- *d.* Labor usage (efficiency) variance.
- *e.* Factory overhead using a four-variance method. Each of the four variances should be appropriately titled.

Indicate whether each variance was favorable or unfavorable.

(AICPA adapted)

9–20 Analysis of Overhead Variances

The Jason plant of Cast Corporation has been in operation for 15 months. Jason employs a standard cost system for its manufacturing operations. The first six months performance was affected by the usual problems associated with a new operation. Since that time, the operations have been running smoothly. Unfortunately, however, the plant has not been able to produce profits on a consistent basis. As the production requirements to meet sales demand have increased, the profit performance has deteriorated.

The plant production manager commented at a staff meeting in which the plant general manager, the corporate controller, and the corporate budget director were in attendance, that the changing production requirements make it more difficult to control manufacturing costs. He further noted that the budget for the plant, included in the company's annual profit plan, was not useful for judging the plant's performance because of the changes in the operating levels. The meeting resulted in a decision to prepare a report which would compare the plant's actual manufacturing cost performance with a budget of manufacturing cost based on actual direct labor-hours in the plant.

The plant production manager and the plant accountant studied the cost patterns for recent months, and volume and cost data from other Cast plants. Then they prepared the following flexible budget schedule for a month with 200,000 planned production-hours which at standard would result in 50,000 units of output. The corporate controller reviewed and approved the flexible budget.

	Amount	Per Direct Labor-Hour
Manufacturing costs:		
Variable:		
Indirect labor	$160,000	$ .80
Supplies	26,000	.13
Power	14,000	.07
		$1.00
Fixed:		
Supervisory labor . . .	64,000	
Heat and light	15,000	
Property taxes	5,000	
	$284,000	

The manufacturing cost reports prepared for the first three months after the flexible budget program was approved were pleasing to the plant production manager. They showed that manufacturing costs were in line with the flexible budget allowance. This was also reflected by the report prepared for November, which is presented below, when 50,500 units were manufactured. However, the plant was still not producing an adequate profit because the variances from standard costs were quite large.

JASON PLANT
Manufacturing Costs
November 19x9
(220,000 actual direct labor production-hours)

	Actual Costs	Allowed Costs	(Over) Under Budget
Variable:			
Indirect labor	$177,000	$176,000	$(1,000)
Supplies	27,400	28,600	1,200
Power	16,000	15,400	(600)
Fixed:			
Supervisory labor	65,000	64,000	(1,000)
Heat and light	15,500	15,000	(500)
Property taxes	5,000	5,000	–0–
	$305,900	$304,000	$(1,900)

Required

a. Explain the advantages of flexible budgeting over fixed budgeting for cost control purposes.

b. Calculate the excess amount over standard spent on manufacturing cost items during November 19x9. Analyze this excess amount into those variances due to:
   (1) Efficiency.
   (2) Spending.

c. Explain what the management of Jason plant should do to reduce:
   (1) The efficiency variance.
   (2) The spending variance.

(CMA adapted)

9–21 Calculation of Variances and Preparation of a Performance Report

The Melon Company hired a new factory superintendent at the beginning of 19x2. Under the terms of their employment agreement, the superintendent is to receive a year-end bonus of 20 percent of his annual salary if his performance report for the year shows that costs under his control are equal to, or less than, the standard costs allowed for the year. The superintendent provides you with the following performance report to support his claim that he is entitled to receive the year-end bonus:

Activity	60,000 units	
	Budget	**Actual**
Sales	$900,000	$900,000
Cost of goods sold at		
standard cost ($6)	360,000	360,000
Gross margin—standard cost	540,000	540,000
Total variance from standard		
cost—favorable	—	12,000
Gross margin—actual cost	540,000	552,000
Marketing and administrative costs	200,000	205,000
Operating income before income taxes . .	340,000	347,000
Provision for income taxes	136,000	138,800
Net income	$204,000	$208,200

In order to evaluate the superintendent's claim, you are able to ascertain the following:

1. The company manufactures only one product, and its standard cost sheet consists of the following:

Direct materials, two pounds at $0.10	$0.20
Direct labor, ¼ hour at $8.00 per hour	2.00
Variable overhead, ¼ hour at $6.80 per hour	1.70
Fixed overhead, ¼ hour at $8.40 per hour	2.10
Standard cost per unit	$6.00

2. The normal activity for applying overhead to production is 12,500 direct labor-hours.
3. Actual costs for the year are:

Direct materials, 130,000 pounds at $0.11	$ 14,300
Direct labor, 15,300 hours at $8.10	123,930
Variable overhead	104,499
Fixed overhead	105,271

Required   a. Calculate the spending (price, rate) variances and efficiency (quantity) or volume variances for:
   (1) Direct materials.
   (2) Direct labor.
   (3) Variable overhead.
   (4) Fixed overhead.
   b. Recast the performance report to the format used in the chapter showing each of the variances you have calculated. Limit your report to costs only, i.e., exclude sales, gross margin, marketing and administrative costs, provision for income taxes, and net income.

c. Write a brief report to the president of the company explaining your position regarding the superintendent's claim that he is entitled to the bonus.

9–22   Calculation of Variances from Incomplete Data

Your friend registered for a correspondence course in managerial accounting and he is required to submit a completed solution to lesson 15. However, in reviewing the information provided by the school for lesson 15, your friend finds that he has misplaced one sheet of data for this lesson. If your friend writes to the school for the missing sheet, his answer will be delayed and points are deducted for late answers to lessons. Knowing that you are studying managerial accounting in college, your friend asks you to assist him in solving the problem for lesson 15.

The following information is available:

POLY COMPANY
Partial Trial Balance
January 31, 19x3

	Debits	Credits
Accounts payable		$44,100
Wages payable—direct labor		64,896
Manufacturing overhead control—variable	$22,500	
Manufacturing overhead control—fixed	51,000	

The company manufactures a solvent for use in manufacturing operations by the firm's customers. The company's standard cost for one container of solvent is:

2 gallons of raw materials at $2 per gallon . . .	$ 4.00
1 hour of direct labor at $6 per hour	6.00
1 hour of overhead at $6 per hour	6.00
Total	$16.00

All of the company's accounts payable are paid currently, and the amount shown in the partial trial balance consists of one invoice for raw materials used in production in January 19x3. No other raw materials were used in January and there were no raw materials inventories at the beginning or ending of January 19x3. Wages are paid on the first day of the month following the period when the direct labor is incurred. All other salaries are paid on the last day of the month in which the salaries are incurred.

The company's purchasing agent had difficulty in securing the raw materials from its normal source of supply. Consequently, the agent was forced to pay 5 percent more than the standard price per gallon. On January 15, 19x3, the company signed a new labor agreement with the union for the company's employees. The employees were granted a 4 percent wage increase retroactive to January 1, 19x3. This wage increase is reflected in the January payroll but not in the standard cost per hour.

Your friend remembers two items from the missing sheet. They are: an unfavorable labor efficiency variance of $2,400 for the month of January, and the annual capacity of 150,000 containers per year.

The firm charges its customers a $10 deposit for each container, which is refunded when the containers are returned to the company. Thus, the reusable shipping containers are not included as part of the standard cost per unit, since the containers are used over again.

The standard cost per unit for overhead has a composition of ⅓ variable costs and ⅔ fixed costs.

Required   Your friend asks you to help him compute the following:

a. The labor rate variance.
b. The number of direct labor-hours worked.
c. The standard hours allowed.
d. The number of units produced.
e. The materials price variance.
f. The materials quantity variance.
g. The variable overhead spending variance.
h. The variable overhead efficiency variance.
i. The fixed overhead spending variance.
j. The fixed overhead volume (denominator) variance.

9–23   Calculation of Variances and Preparation of a Performance Report

The Lotar Company hired a new factory superintendent at the beginning of 19x2. Under the terms of their employment agreement, the superintendent is to receive a year-end bonus of 20 percent of his annual salary if his performance report for the year shows that costs under his control are equal to, or less than, the standard costs allowed for the year. The superintendent was given the performance report shown below, and he believes that something is wrong. He is sure that he was very careful in monitoring all costs under his control, and he believes that his report should be a favorable one. He believes that he should get the bonus, despite the unfavorable variance shown in the following report.

Activity	20,000 units	
	Budget	**Actual**
Sales	$800,000	$800,000
Cost of goods sold at standard cost ($22)	440,000	440,000
Gross margin—standard cost	360,000	360,000
Total variance from standard cost—unfavorable	—	30,000
Gross margin—actual cost	360,000	330,000
Marketing and administrative costs	100,000	102,000
Operating income before income taxes	260,000	228,000
Provision for income taxes	91,000	80,000
Net income	$169,000	$148,000

The president of the company asks you to reevaluate the superintendent's claim, and in the process, you are able to ascertain the following:

1. The company manufactures only one product, and its standard cost sheet consists of the following:

Direct materials, three pounds at $0.30 . . . . $ 0.90
Direct labor, one hour at $10.00 . . . . 10.00
Variable overhead, one hour at $5.10 . . . . . 5.10
Fixed overhead, one hour at $6.00 . . . . 6.00
Standard cost per unit $22.00

2. The normal activity for applying overhead to production is 30,000 direct labor-hours.
3. Actual costs for the year are:

Direct materials, 59,800 pounds at $0.29 . . . . $ 17,342
Direct labor, 19,000 hours at $9.80 186,200
Variable overhead 96,458
Fixed overhead 170,000

Required a. Calculate the spending (price, rate) variances and efficiency (quantity) or volume variances for:
   (1) Direct materials.
   (2) Direct labor.
   (3) Variable overhead.
   (4) Fixed overhead.
b. Recast the performance report to the format used in the chapter showing each of the variances you have calculated. Limit your report to costs only, i.e., exclude sales, gross margin, marketing and administrative costs, provision for income taxes, and net income.
c. Write a brief report to the president of the company explaining your position regarding the superintendent's claim that he is entitled to the bonus.

9-24 (Appendix 9-A): Journal Entries for Recording Standard Costs and Variances

Use the information provided in problem 9-21 and assume that 130,000 units were sold at $20 per unit.

Required a. Prepare summary journal entries to record all transactions during the year 19x6. Where needed, credit Wages Payable or Accounts Payable, etc.
b. Prepare the entries to close the applied overhead accounts and set up overhead variances.
c. Prepare the closing entry(s) to close all variances at year-end.

9-25 (Appendix 9-A): Journal Entries for Recording Standard Costs and Variances

The Dryer Company manufactures one product and presents you with the following for 19x6:

Standard cost sheet:

Direct material	2 pounds at $3		$ 6
Direct labor	1 hour	at 7	7
Variable overhead	1 hour	at 2	2
Fixed overhead	1 hour	at 6	6
Total			$21

The following information is also available:

Budgeted total overhead at normal activity	$ 288,000
Units produced	38,000
Materials purchased and used in production—	
76,500 pounds at $2.95 per pound	$ 225,675
Direct labor—38,300 hours at $7.10	$ 271,930
Actual overhead:	
Variable	$ 78,515
Fixed	$ 220,000
Sales—35,000 units at $50.00	$1,750,000

Required *a.* Prepare summary journal entries to record all transactions during the year 19x6. Where needed, credit Wages Payable or Accounts Payable, etc.

b. Prepare the entries to close the applied overhead accounts and set up overhead variances.

c. Prepare the closing entry(s) to close all variances at year-end.

9–26 **(Appendix 9–B): Preparation of Standard Costs Using Alternative Capacity Levels**

The standards committee of the Robert Company is in the process of preparing standards for a new product. All of the needed information is now available; however, there is a difference of opinion regarding which capacity level to use. Some members prefer the normal capacity while other members prefer the expected capacity to compute the predetermined overhead rate used to apply overhead to production. You have been asked to assist the committee in reaching a decision as to which capacity level should be used.

The committee provides you with the following:

1. The estimated production for the ensuing business cycle is:

	Units
19x3	60,000
19x4	50,000
19x5	40,000

2. Estimates for materials, labor, and overhead are:

Direct materials	3 yards at $4 per yard
Direct labor	1 hour at $10 per hour

Variable overhead . . . . . 1 hour at \$3 per DLH
Fixed overhead . . . . . . \$240,000 per annum

3. The company uses direct labor-hours to apply overhead to production.
4. The company wishes to price the product to yield a profit before income taxes of 50 percent of cost, exclusive of marketing and administrative costs. The fixed costs of \$240,000 are incremental costs and pertain entirely to the new product.

Required

a. Prepare a standard cost sheet using the normal capacity level and compute the selling price per unit at this level.

b. Prepare a standard cost sheet using the expected capacity level for 19x3 and compute the selling price per unit at this level.

c. Draft a memorandum to the standards committee explaining the differences between (a) and (b). Indicate the advantages and disadvantages of each level and your preference for one level, if you have one.

10

CONTRIBUTION APPROACH TO SEGMENT REPORTING

LEARNING OBJECTIVES

After reading this chapter, you should be able to:

1 Differentiate between absorption costing and variable costing.

2 Explain why variable costing is superior to absorption costing for management reporting purposes.

3 Prepare an income statement using the variable-costing approach.

4 Reconcile the difference in net income between absorption costing and variable costing when there is an inventory buildup or an inventory liquidation.

5 Prepare a segmented income statement using either absorption costing or variable costing.

6 Explain the difference between direct fixed costs and common fixed costs and how a direct fixed cost for a particular segment may become a common fixed cost when that segment is further disaggregated.

7 Discuss the problems associated with allocating common costs, including why segmented reports may lead to incorrect decision making.

8 Explain how segmented income statements are used.

Traditional costing for external reporting purposes, known as **absorption costing** or *full costing,* is a method of assigning manufacturing costs to production so that *both* variable and fixed manufacturing costs are included in inventories and cost of goods sold. While this type of costing is also required for income tax reporting, it is rarely relevant for managerial decision making and can lead to incorrect decisions. In contrast, **variable costing,** also known as **direct costing** or **marginal costing,** is a method of assigning manufacturing costs to production so that *only* variable manufacturing costs are included in inventories and cost of goods sold. Variable costing provides useful information for a variety of managerial decisions, such as

1. Entering a new market.

2. Discontinuing a product.

3. Making or buying component parts.

4. Expanding or contracting production of an existing product.

5. Taking special orders at less than full cost.

Its data also enhance cost-volume-profit analysis and breakeven analysis. Because variable costing plays such a vital role in decision making, managers need to know how it differs from absorption costing and how it is used to prepare financial statements and reports.

Variable costing is also useful in the preparation of segmented reports. When a firm has multiple product lines and/or operates in different geographic territories, a companywide income statement may mask some serious problems. For example, the profits from a successful product may mask the losses from an unsuccessful product, or the profits from one geographic area may mask the losses of another. Segmented income statements that show profits and losses separately for each product or geographic location provide managers with the more detailed information they need to evaluate, monitor, and reach appropriate decisions about an individual segment's operations.

Segmented income statements should be prepared using variable costing. Absorption-costing income statements, prepared for each segment, may not provide managers with all the information they need.

VARIABLE COSTING VERSUS ABSORPTION COSTING

A business firm often faces a dilemma when making decisions about its record-keeping requirements. On the one hand, it may prefer to keep its records on an absorption-costing basis in order to generate the information needed for external reporting and income tax preparation. When this approach is used, however, the data generated by the firm's management information system will require conversion to the variable-costing approach before they will be useful to managers. On the other hand, if the firm decides to keep its records on a variable-costing basis so that managers can use its reports without adjustment, the variable-costing data will have to be converted to absorption costing when information is needed for external reporting or income tax preparation.

In this author's opinion, the variable-costing method is preferable, since the need to convert variable cost data to absorption costing may occur only quarterly, when reports must be issued to stockholders. On the other hand, reports for managers are usually prepared monthly or, in many cases, weekly. Thus, based on frequency alone, it seems preferable for a firm to keep its books and records on a variable-costing basis.

Variable Costing— No Beginning or Ending Inventories

The term direct costing is firmly ingrained in accounting literature despite the fact that it is a misnomer. When used to mean variable costing, it is used incorrectly because some fixed costs are also direct costs. At the same time, variable overhead costs are not always direct costs to a product, yet variable overhead is included as a product cost when variable costing is used. In Chapter 2, we noted that a **direct cost** is any cost that is traceable to a single cost objective, and many fixed costs, in addition to variable costs, fall into this category. Despite this incongruity, accountants refer to variable costing as direct costing and are likely to continue this practice in the foreseeable future. Hence, managers should be familiar with both the correct terminology and the terminology used in everyday practice.

When variable costing is used, inventoriable costs consist of direct materials, direct labor, and *variable* manufacturing overhead. Fixed overhead is *not* inventoried; instead, it is charged to income as a period cost, as are marketing and administrative costs.

Variable costing may be used in conjunction with standard costing, as is the case for most large firms. Alternatively, it may also be used with normal costing—actual direct materials, actual direct labor, and estimated overhead.

To illustrate the concept, assume that the Charles River Company manufactures one product and that its standard cost sheet for the product is:

Direct materials	3 yards at $2.40 per yard	$ 7.20
Direct labor	1 hour at $8.00 per hour	8.00
Variable overhead	1 hour at $3.80 per hour	3.80
Fixed overhead	1 hour at $5.00 per hour	5.00
Total standard cost per unit .		$24.00

For the year 19x2, we will assume the following:

Normal activity	20,000 units
Selling price per unit	$40 per unit
Salespersons' commissions	4% of sales
Fixed marketing costs	$ 80,000
Administrative costs—all fixed	$100,000

ILLUSTRATION 10–1 Income and Cost Flow for Variable Costing

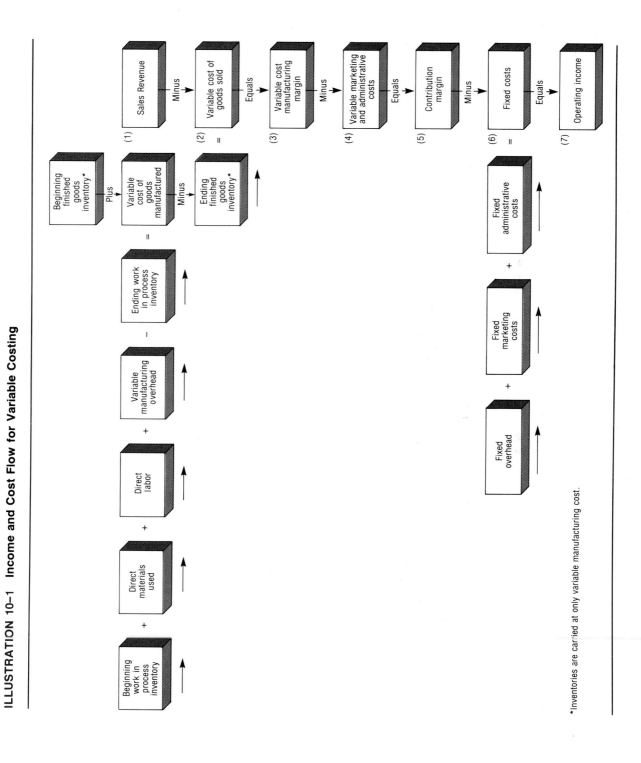

*Inventories are carried at only variable manufacturing cost.

To simplify our presentation, we will also assume that there are no variances from standard—that is, all actual costs are the same as the applied costs for overhead and the standard costs allowed for direct materials and direct labor. Hence, actual production equals 20,000 units (normal activity), sales are also 20,000 units, and there is no beginning or ending inventory of finished goods or work in process.

The data generated by variable costing can be easily incorporated into a contribution format income statement. **A contribution format income statement** is prepared for managerial use and is classified into fixed and variable cost categories instead of into the functional categories of a traditional income statement. Instead of including fixed manufacturing overhead in cost of goods manufactured, it is shown as a period cost *after* contribution margin. The variable marketing costs (such as commissions) are shown *before* contribution margin but after variable cost of goods sold. This flow of costs may be diagramed as shown in Illustration 10–1. The Charles River Company's income statement using variable costing is presented in Illustration 10–2.

To illustrate the significance of variable costing, we will compare the results achieved by this method to the results achieved by absorption costing.

ILLUSTRATION 10–2

CHARLES RIVER COMPANY
Contribution Format Income Statement
For the Year Ended December 31, 19x2

Sales (20,000 units × $40)		$800,000
Variable cost of goods sold:		
Beginning inventory, finished goods	$ –0–	
Direct materials (20,000 units × $7.20)	144,000	
Direct labor (20,000 units × $8)	160,000	
Variable manufacturing overhead		
(20,000 × $3.80)	76,000	
Variable cost of goods manufactured	380,000	
Less: Ending inventory, finished goods	–0–	
Variable cost of goods sold		380,000
Variable cost manufacturing margin		420,000
Salespersons' commissions (4% × $800,000)		32,000
Contribution margin		388,000
Less: Fixed costs:		
Fixed manufacturing overhead		
(20,000 units × $5)	100,000	
Fixed marketing costs	80,000	
Fixed administrative costs	100,000	
Total fixed costs		280,000
Operating income before income taxes		$108,000

ILLUSTRATION 10–3   Income and Cost Flow for Absorption Costing

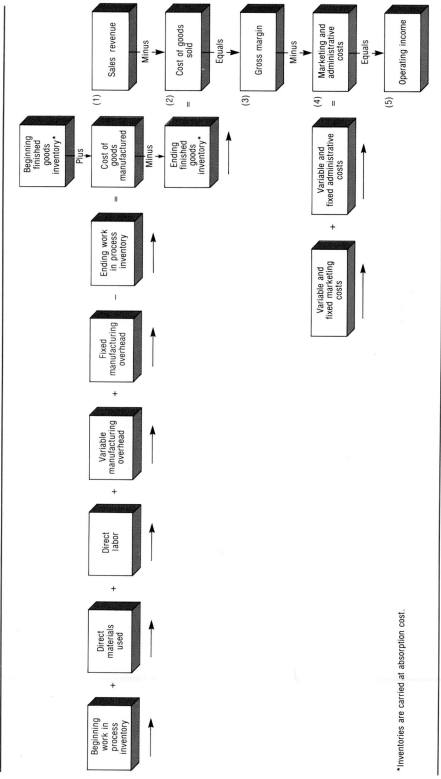

*Inventories are carried at absorption cost.

Absorption Costing—No Beginning or Ending Inventories

When absorption costing is used to prepare a traditional income statement, both fixed and variable manufacturing costs are included in the cost of goods manufactured. The cost and income flows for absorption costing may be diagramed as shown in Illustration 10–3.

To contrast the preparation of variable-costing statements with absorption-costing statements, the data from Illustration 10–2 were used to prepare the income statement using absorption costing shown in Illustration 10–4.

A comparison of Illustrations 10–2 and 10–4 discloses that:

1. The operating income of $108,000 is the same for both variable costing and absorption costing.

2. The cost of goods manufactured differs by $100,000, the amount of the fixed manufacturing overhead.

3. The variable salespersons' commissions are deducted from the variable cost manufacturing margin in Illustration 10–2 to arrive at the contribution margin, while in Illustration 10–4 the commissions are deducted as a period cost, *after* the gross margin is derived.

ILLUSTRATION 10–4

CHARLES RIVER COMPANY
Income Statement Using Absorption Costing
For the Year Ended December 31, 19x2

Sales (20,000 units × $40)		$800,000
Cost of goods sold:		
Beginning inventory, finished goods	$ –0–	
Direct materials (20,000 units × $7.20)	144,000	
Direct labor (20,000 units × $8)	160,000	
Variable manufacturing overhead (20,000 × $3.80)	76,000	
Fixed manufacturing overhead (20,000 × $5.00)	100,000	
Cost of goods manufactured	480,000	
Less: Ending inventory, finished goods	–0–	
Cost of goods sold		480,000
Gross margin		320,000
Marketing and administrative costs:		
Marketing costs	112,000*	
Administrative costs	100,000	212,000
Operating income before income taxes		$108,000

* Variable + fixed = $32,000 + $80,000 = $112,000.

4.   The fixed manufacturing overhead is shown as a period cost in Illustration 10–2, while this cost is shown as a manufacturing cost in Illustration 10–4.

Although the operating income is the same in both illustrations, this is not always the case. This occurred because Charles River's beginning and ending finished goods inventories for 19x2 were identical. Whenever there is a difference between a firm's beginning and ending finished goods inventories (which reflects the difference between the number of units produced and the number sold), variable and absorption costing will produce different net incomes. This case is now considered.

Variable Costing versus Absorption Costing—Beginning and Ending Inventories of Finished Goods

Inventory buildup occurs when a firm's ending inventory is greater than its beginning inventory for any accounting period. The reverse condition, **inventory liquidation,** occurs when a firm's ending inventory is less than its beginning inventory for any accounting period. Under either of these conditions, the net incomes produced by variable costing and absorption costing will differ by the amount of fixed overhead included in the inventories of the absorption-costing income statement.

Let us expand the information for the Charles River Company to include the following:

	19x3	19x4	19x5
Beginning inventory in units	–0–	10,000	10,000
Units manufactured	20,000	30,000	10,000*
Available for sale	20,000	40,000	20,000
Ending inventory in units	10,000	10,000	–0–
Units sold	10,000	30,000	20,000

* The normal activity is assumed to be 20,000 units (20,000 + 30,000 + 10,000 = 60,000 ÷ 3 years = 20,000 units. See Chapter 9 for a discussion of normal activity.)

For each of the three years, actual costs are equal to budgeted costs. Thus, the only variance present is a volume variance when actual production is different from the normal capacity of 20,000 units.

The income statements for the three years using variable costing appear in Illustration 10–5, while the income statements using absorption costing appear in Illustration 10–6.

ILLUSTRATION 10–5

CHARLES RIVER COMPANY
Income Statements Using Variable Costing
For the Years Ended December 31

	19x3	19x4	19x5
Sales (10,000 units, 30,000 units, and 20,000 units at $40)	$400,000	$1,200,000	$800,000
Variable cost of goods sold:			
Beginning inventory, finished goods	–0–	190,000	190,000
Direct materials (20,000 units, 30,000 units, and 10,000 units at $7.20)	144,000	216,000	72,000
Direct labor (at $8.00)	160,000	240,000	80,000
Variable overhead (at $3.80)	76,000	114,000	38,000
Cost of goods manufactured	380,000	760,000	380,000
Less: Ending finished goods inventory (10,000 units, 10,000 units, and 0 units at $19)	190,000	190,000	–0–
Variable cost of goods sold	190,000	570,000	380,000
Variable cost manufacturing margin	210,000	630,000	420,000
Salespersons' commissions (4% of sales)	16,000	48,000	32,000
Contribution margin	194,000	582,000	388,000
Less: Fixed costs:			
Fixed manufacturing overhead	100,000	100,000	100,000
Fixed marketing costs	80,000	80,000	80,000
Fixed administrative costs	100,000	100,000	100,000
Total fixed costs	280,000	280,000	280,000
Operating income (loss) before income taxes	$ (86,000)	$ 302,000	$108,000

In comparing Illustrations 10–5 and 10–6, note that:

1. Sales in units, gross margin, and contribution margin for the three years are tabulated as follows:

		Gross Margin		Contribution Margin	
Year	Sales in Units	Total	Per Unit	Total	Per Unit
19x3	10,000	$160,000	$16.00	$194,000	$19.40
19x4	30,000	530,000	17.67	582,000	19.40
19x5	20,000	270,000	13.50	388,000	19.40

ILLUSTRATION 10–6

CHARLES RIVER COMPANY
Income Statements Using Absorption Costing
For the Years Ended December 31

	19x3	19x4	19x5
Sales (10,000 units, 30,000 units, and 20,000 units at $40)	$400,000	$1,200,000	$800,000
Cost of goods sold:			
Beginning inventory, finished goods	–0–	240,000	240,000
Direct materials (20,000 units, 30,000 units, and 10,000 units at $7.20)	144,000	216,000	72,000
Direct labor (at $8.00)	160,000	240,000	80,000
Variable overhead (at $3.80)	76,000	114,000	38,000
Fixed overhead (at $5.00)	100,000	150,000	50,000
Cost of goods manufactured— at standard cost	480,000	960,000	480,000
Less: Ending finished goods inventory (10,000 units, 10,000 units, and 0 units at $24)	240,000	240,000	–0–
Cost of goods sold— at standard cost	240,000	720,000	480,000
Add (deduct) volume variance [0 units, (10,000 units), 10,000 units at $5]	–0–	(50,000)	50,000
Cost of goods sold— at actual cost	240,000	670,000	530,000
Gross margin—at actual cost	160,000	530,000	270,000
Marketing and administrative costs:			
Marketing costs*	96,000	128,000	112,000
Administrative costs	100,000	100,000	100,000
Total marketing and administrative costs	196,000	228,000	212,000
Operating income (loss) before income taxes	$ (36,000)	$ 302,000	$ 58,000

* $80,000 + 4% of sales.

When there is no change in selling price and costs, a manager can expect that profit margin will be a function of units sold. Contribution margin meets this objective, as can be seen from the following:

Year	Sales in Units	Contribution Margin
19x3	10,000	$194,000
19x4	3 × 10,000 = 30,000	3 × $194,000 = $582,000
19x5	2 × 10,000 = 20,000	2 × $194,000 = $388,000

The same analysis is not true for gross margin. This can be observed from the following:

Year	Sales in Units	Projected Gross margin Based on Linear Relationship	Actual Gross Margin	Difference More (Less)
19x3	10,000	$160,000	$160,000	$ –0–
19x4	3 × 10,000	3 × $160,000 = $480,000	530,000	50,000
19x5	2 × 10,000	2 × $160,000 = $320,000	270,000	(50,000)

Thus, when a firm's information system uses absorption costing, the reports generated must first be converted to variable costing in order to be used in CVP analysis as discussed in Chapter 6. Also, information based on absorption costing may lead to wrong conclusions when used in the decision-making situations noted at the beginning of this chapter. For example, consider the following results of operations for the Hudson River Company for the year 19x3:

HUDSON RIVER COMPANY
Income Statement Using Absorption Costing
For the Year Ended December 31, 19x3

Sales (50,000 units at $10)	$500,000
Cost of goods sold (50,000 at $6)	300,000
Gross margin	200,000
Marketing and administrative	
costs—all fixed	160,000
Operating income	$ 40,000

The cost of goods sold includes $4 of variable costs and $2 of fixed costs per unit. For 19x4, the company expects sales volume to decrease by 20 percent and all cost behavior patterns to remain unchanged. Given the forecasted falling demand for their product, Hudson River's board of directors has announced that unless the company will operate at the breakeven point or at a profit in the coming year, they will cease operations. Accurate CVP analysis is thus important. Using the absorption costing data as submitted, a manager might compute the reduction in profit as 20 percent multiplied by the gross margin of $200,000, or $40,000. This would indicate that the company would reach its breakeven point and that operations should continue.

Such as analysis is faulty, however, because it assumes a 20 percent reduction in fixed overhead, which is at odds with the given information. The correct analysis would be an expected loss of $20,000. This amount may be readily obtained from an income statement prepared using the contribution margin format, as follows:

HUDSON RIVER COMPANY
Income Statement Using the Contribution Margin Format
For the Year Ended December 31, 19x3

Sales (50,000 at $10)		$500,000
Variable cost of goods sold		
(50,000 at $4)		200,000
Contribution margin		300,000
Marketing and administrative		
costs—all fixed	$160,000	
Fixed overhead	100,000	
Total fixed costs		260,000
Operating income		$ 40,000

To consider the effect of the anticipated decrease in sales, a manager would multiply the contribution margin by the expected 20 percent decline. The resulting $60,000 reduction in operating income (.20 × $300,000) would produce a loss of $20,000, indicating that the firm should cease operations under the given conditions.

2. The differences in operating incomes for the three years may be analyzed as follows:

	Operating Income (Loss)		Difference
Year	Variable Costing	Absorption Costing	VC higher (AC higher)
19x3	$ (86,000)	$ (36,000)	$(50,000)
19x4	302,000	302,000	–0–
19x5	108,000	58,000	50,000
Total for three years	$324,000	$324,000	$ –0–

For 19x3, 20,000 units were manufactured and only 10,000 units were sold, resulting in an *inventory buildup* of 10,000 units. Thus, at a standard fixed overhead cost of $5 per unit, the difference between variable costing and absorption costing amounts to $50,000 for the year. When there is an inventory buildup, absorption costing produces a higher operating income because the fixed overhead in the closing inventory (10,000 units × $5 per unit, or $50,000) is deferred and shifted into the next accounting period as part of that beginning inventory. This can be seen by looking at the closing inventories for 19x3 in Illustrations 10–5 and 10–6 (AC = $240,000 and VC = $190,000), which become the opening inventories for 19x4. Thus, for absorption costing, an extra $50,000 of inventory valuation is shifted to 19x4 and becomes part of cost of goods sold in that year.

For 19x4, there is no inventory buildup or liquidation—that is, the beginning and ending inventories are the same. Hence, there is no difference in the operating incomes of $302,000 shown in the two income statements.

For 19x5, there is an *inventory liquidation* of 10,000 units, so at a standard fixed overhead cost of $5 per unit, the difference between variable costing and absorption costing amounts to $50,000 for the year. When there is an inventory liquidation, variable costing produces the higher operating income.

3. For the three years together, there is neither inventory buildup nor inventory liquidation, since the beginning inventory for 19x3 and the ending inventory for 19x5 are both zero. Consequently, it is not surprising that the total operating income for the three-year period, $324,000, is the same for both methods.

If a firm wishes to prepare its income statement using one method (either variable or absorption costing) but also wishes to determine its operating income under the other method, it does not need to prepare a second income statement. Instead, it can compute the operating income using the following generalized formulas:

Inventory Buildup (Absorption-Costing Income is Higher)

Inventory buildup = (Number of units in ending inventory)
             − (Number of units in beginning inventory)

$$ACOI = VCOI + (Inventory\ buildup \times Fixed\ overhead\ per\ unit)\quad \textbf{(1)}^*$$

or

$$VCOI = ACOI − (Inventory\ buildup \times Fixed\ overhead\ per\ unit)\quad \textbf{(2)}^*$$

where

$$ACOI = Absorption\text{-}costing\ operating\ income$$

$$VCOI = Variable\text{-}costing\ operating\ income$$

Inventory Liquidation (Variable-Costing Income is Higher)

Inventory liquidation = (Number of units in beginning inventory)
                − (Number of units in ending inventory)

$$ACOI = VCOI − (Inventory\ liquidation \times Fixed\ overhead\ per\ unit)\quad \textbf{(3)}^*$$

or

$$VCOI = ACOI + (Inventory\ liquidation \times Fixed\ overhead\ per\ unit)\ \textbf{(4)}^*$$

* Equations 1, 2, 3, and 4 can be used only with standard or normal costing. When actual costing is used, the fixed overhead per unit will usually fluctuate between the beginning and ending inventories, so each unit cost would have to be considered separately.

For 19x3, the Charles River Company's operating income using variable costing is a *loss* of $86,000 (see Illustration 10–5). Instead of preparing an income statement as shown in Illustration 10–6, a manager could compute the firm's operating income under absorption costing by using equation 1, as follows:

$$ACOI = \$(86,000) + (10,000 \text{ units} \times \$5 \text{ per unit})$$
$$ACOI = \$(86,000) + \$50,000$$
$$ACOI = \$(36,000)$$

When there is an inventory liquidation as in 19x5, the Charles River Company could use equation 3 to compute its ACOI from Illustration 10–5, as follows:

$$ACOI = \$108,000 - (10,000 \text{ units} \times \$5 \text{ per unit})$$
$$ACOI = \$108,000 - \$50,000$$
$$ACOI = \$58,000$$

There is considerable controversy regarding the difference in net income between absorption costing and variable costing. Some accountants believe that variable costing should be accepted for external reporting and income tax purposes in addition to being used for internal reporting. But the Internal Revenue Service, with rare exceptions, offers no hope for its acceptance in the near future, and independent auditors doubt that change is likely. Thus, despite its limited use in decision making, managers should understand absorption costing because of its importance in financial reporting to shareholders and its effect on the amount of income tax that a firm pays.

Management accounting should be based on the information that will be most useful to managers and, in such cases, variable costing is clearly superior. When a firm keeps its books and records on this basis, it can open T accounts such as the following to convert its books for external reporting and income tax preparation:

Fixed Overhead in Inventory		Income Summary	
19x3 *(a)* 50,000			19x3 *(a)* 50,000

Each year, the Fixed Overhead in Inventory account is adjusted in accordance with the generalized formulas for inventory buildup or inventory liquidation. When a firm has both finished goods and work in process inventories, it is customary to use separate T accounts for each.

SEGMENT REPORTING

A companywide income statement does not provide individual managers with the information they need to effectively plan, coordinate, and control their operations because it merely indicates whether the company as a whole showed a profit or a loss during an accounting period. It does not indicate which product lines, sales territories, and divisions contributed profits or losses to the firm's overall operations. It is quite conceivable that a particular product, division, or sales territory may be suffering an undetected loss that is masked

ILLUSTRATION 10–7   Analysis of Income Statement Data into Segments Based on Product Lines

ILLUSTRATION 10–8   Analysis of Income Statement Data into Segments Based on Sales Territories

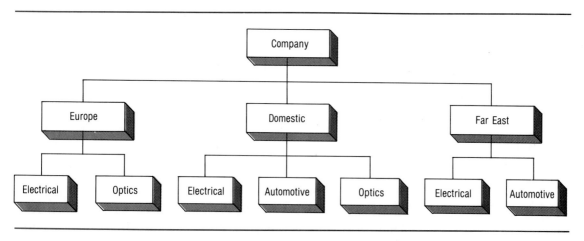

by the profits of another product, division, or territory. To ferret out the needed information, it is necessary to use a **segmented reporting system** that breaks the companywide income statement into segments starting with the largest sections, such as divisions, and continuing with smaller and smaller units, such as product lines and then particular products. Two possible methods of segmentation are diagramed in Illustrations 10–7 and 10–8. The configurations and degrees of segmentation vary among firms and are based on managers' needs for specific kinds of information.

The Format of Segmented Income Statements

The format of a firm's segmented income statements depends on whether it uses absorption costing or variable costing in its information system.

Absorption Costing. When a firm uses absorption costing, its segmented income statement follows the format of its traditional external reporting counterpart. For example, the Conglomerate Company may prepare its segmented income statement as shown in Illustration 10–9.

Only one product is manufactured in each line of business, and sales (in units) are 40,000, 10,000, and 40,000, respectively, for electrical, automotive, and optics. All marketing and administrative costs are fixed. Information about the Conglomerate Company's unit costs is presented in Illustration 10–10.

If a Conglomerate manager decided to eliminate the optics division based on the income statement shown in Illustration 10–9, the decision most probably would be faulty. The reason for the error would be that although the

ILLUSTRATION 10–9

CONGLOMERATE COMPANY
Income Statement—Absorption Costing
For the Year Ended December 31, 19x3

	Total	Electrical	Automotive	Optics
Sales	$1,000,000	$400,000	$300,000	$300,000
Cost of goods sold:				
Direct materials	100,000	40,000	20,000	40,000
Direct labor	200,000	80,000	40,000	80,000
Manufacturing overhead	200,000	60,000	60,000	80,000
Cost of goods sold	500,000	180,000	120,000	200,000
Gross margin	500,000	220,000	180,000	100,000
Marketing and administrative costs:				
Marketing costs	100,000	40,000	30,000	30,000
Administrative costs	200,000	60,000	60,000	80,000
Total marketing and administrative costs	300,000	100,000	90,000	110,000
Operating income (loss) before income taxes	$ 200,000	$120,000	$ 90,000	$ (10,000)

ILLUSTRATION 10–10

CONGLOMERATE COMPANY
Supplementary Data per Unit

Per Unit	Electrical	Automotive	Optics
Selling price	$10.00	$30.00	$7.50
Direct materials	$ 1.00	$ 2.00	$1.00
Direct labor	$ 2.00	$ 4.00	$2.00
Variable overhead	$ 0.50	$ 4.00	$1.00
Fixed overhead	$ 1.00*	$ 2.00†	$1.00‡

* $40,000 ÷ 40,000 units = $1 per unit.
† $20,000 ÷ 10,000 units = $2 per unit.
‡ $40,000 ÷ 40,000 units = $1 per unit.

optics division shows an operating loss of $10,000 before income taxes, the loss arises after the deduction of fixed overhead, marketing, and administrative costs. It is highly probable that some of these fixed costs would continue, and if they exceeded $10,000 for 19x3 then the optics division contributed to the overall profitability of the company, and its elimination would cause company operating income to fall below the current $200,000. The fixed costs not eliminated by the discontinuance of the optics division must be absorbed by the two remaining lines of business, thereby decreasing their operating income. Thus, when an absorption-costing income statement is used to decide whether to discontinue a product, product line, or division, fixed costs must be analyzed to determine which will be eliminated and which will continue. Those that are eliminated when a particular cost objective is discontinued or eliminated are called **avoidable costs.** All fixed costs other than avoidable costs must be absorbed by the remaining segments.

For example, if all fixed costs for the optics division are classified as direct and indirect, the analysis might appear as shown in Illustration 10–11.

ILLUSTRATION 10–11

CONGLOMERATE COMPANY
Analysis of Fixed Costs for Optics Division
For the Year Ended December 31, 19x3

	Total	Direct (Avoidable)	Indirect
Fixed manufacturing overhead			
($1 × 40,000 units)	$ 40,000	$ 30,000	$ 10,000
Marketing costs	30,000	25,000	5,000
Administrative costs	80,000	10,000	70,000
Total	$150,000	$ 65,000	$ 85,000

A decision to eliminate the optics division would result in a decrease in operating income before income taxes from $200,000 to $125,000, as the following analysis shows:

Electrical operating income (from Illustration 10–9)	$120,000
Automotive operating income	90,000
Subtotal	210,000
Less: Indirect fixed overhead and other costs from optics division to be absorbed by the remaining divisions	85,000
Overall company operating income	$125,000

The same result may also be achieved by the following calculation:

Present company operating income	$200,000
Less: Common costs which must be absorbed by the remaining segments . .	85,000
Subtotal	115,000
Add: Elimination of Optics' loss	10,000
Projected overall company operating income	$125,000

Hence, it is obvious that the elimination of the optics business would cause a $75,000 diminution of the company's operating income before taxes, a result not evident from the absorption income statement shown in Illustration 10–9.

Instead of using the format shown in Illustration 10–9, it is possible to use a contribution margin format that shows a segment margin for each line of business. When this kind of income statement is used, there is no need to adjust operating income as there is with absorption costing. The information needed to decide whether or not to discontinue a segment is readily available on the contribution margin income statement.

Segment Margin. **Segment margin,** an important managerial concept, is a segment's sales revenue minus its direct variable and direct fixed costs. Stated differently, it is the sales revenue minus the directly traceable costs of a cost objective. Thus, segment margin is the amount of profit that a line of business contributes to the overall profitability of a company. When this measure of margin is used, a manager is able to directly assess a segment's profitability from a segment margin income statement.

Segment Margin Income Statement. A **segment margin income statement** is a contribution format income statement that breaks down total operating results by reportable segment such as a division, product line, or sales territory. Each segment's direct fixed costs are deducted from its contribution margin to arrive at the segment margin. **Common costs**—costs that cannot be traced to a single cost objective but may be allocated through the use of a logical allocation base—are usually not allocated in a segment margin income statement. Instead, they are deducted only in the total column to arrive at operating income before income taxes. Using the data given for the Conglomerate Company in Illustrations 10–9, 10–10, and 10–11, a seg-

ILLUSTRATION 10–12

CONGLOMERATE COMPANY
Segment Margin Income Statement—Contribution Format
For the Year Ended December 31, 19x3

	Total	Electrical	Automotive	Optics
Sales	$1,000,000	$400,000	$300,000	$300,000
Variable cost of goods sold:				
Direct materials	100,000	40,000	20,000	40,000
Direct labor	200,000	80,000	40,000	80,000
Variable overhead*	100,000	20,000	40,000	40,000
Variable cost of goods sold	400,000	140,000	100,000	160,000
Contribution margin	600,000	260,000	200,000	140,000
Less: *Direct* fixed overhead and other costs:				
Fixed overhead	70,000	25,000	15,000	30,000
Marketing costs	55,000	20,000	10,000	25,000
Administrative costs	35,000	15,000	10,000	10,000
Total direct fixed costs	160,000	60,000	35,000	65,000
Segment margin	440,000	$200,000	$165,000	$ 75,000
Less: *Indirect* fixed overhead and other costs (common costs):				
Fixed overhead	30,000	(i.e., $200,000 − $100,000 − $70,000)		
Marketing costs	45,000	(i.e., $100,000 − $55,000)		
Administrative costs	165,000	(i.e., $200,000 − $35,000)		
Total common costs	240,000			
Operating income before income taxes	$ 200,000			

* Electrical—40,000 units at $0.50 per unit = $20,000.
 Automotive—10,000 units at $4.00 per unit = $40,000.
 Optics—40,000 units at $1.00 per unit = $40,000.

ment margin income statement may be prepared as shown in Illustration 10–12. The direct and indirect fixed overhead and other costs for the electrical and automotive businesses are assumed.

In studying Illustration 10–12, note that:

1. Only the fixed costs that are *directly traceable* to a segment are deducted to arrive at segment margin.

2. The fixed costs that are common to more than one segment appear only in the total (companywide) column. Allocating these costs to particular segments is based on arbitrary assumptions and may provide misleading information to managers.

3. The contribution and segment margins provide useful information to managers. For example, the optics division shows a segment margin (or profitability) of $75,000. This amount agrees with the earlier analysis which indicated that overall company operating income would be

$125,000 without the optics business and $200,000 (as shown in Illustration 10–9) with it. The $10,000 operating loss for the optics division shown in Illustration 10–9 is faulty for this kind of decision making because it is based on arbitrary allocations of common fixed costs. This does not mean that common fixed costs should be ignored.

In the long run, a firm must recover all costs—variable, direct fixed, and common fixed. Despite the need to earn sufficient profits in the long run to recover all costs including common costs, the allocation of common costs for decision making could lead to wrong decisions, and the practice is avoided by many firms.

Differentiation between Direct Fixed Costs and Common Costs

Direct fixed costs are usually easily identified. For example, line foremen who work exclusively for the Conglomerate Company's optics division are not likely to be retained if that segment ceases to operate. It is also unlikely that these people supervise workers in more than one segment, such as in both the optics and the automotive divisions. Thus, the costs of maintaining the optics division's foremen are relatively easy to classify as direct fixed.

Another easily classified fixed cost is advertising. An advertisement for one of the firm's optical products is not likely to be combined with an advertisement for an automotive or electrical product. Thus, such an ad would be a direct fixed cost. On the other hand, an advertisement extolling the company's programs to promote environmental protection that was placed for the purpose of enhancing the general corporate image would be classified as a common cost.

Most common costs are also easily classified. While the salaries of line personnel are not apt to be considered a common cost, the manufacturing vice president's salary would be. Certainly most, if not all, staff functions (as discussed in Chapter 1) would be considered common costs.

Common Costs and the Allocation Problem

Any allocation of a common cost to a particular segment is based on somewhat arbitrary assumptions. Even when the chosen assumptions appear to be quite logical, a difference of opinion regarding their use is possible. For example, occupancy costs (rent, real estate taxes, and the like) are usually allocated to segments on the basis of square feet occupied, an apparently logical base. Yet, if a retail department store occupies a 10-story building, with its perfumes and toiletries department occupying the entire 1st floor and its furniture department occupying the entire 10th floor, may accountants and managers might question the appropriateness of allocating equal amounts of rent to the two departments. Many might argue that the perfumes and toiletries department should bear a larger share of occupancy costs, since all customers must pass through it and thus possibly be tempted to do some impulse purchasing on the way to a department on another floor.

Similar debates may arise over any base used to allocate common costs. As a solution, some accountants suggest that the sales revenues provided by each segment may provide an equitable base. Others maintain that contribution margin is a superior base to sales revenue, since one of a firm's objectives is to maximize contribution margin rather than sales revenue. When the contribution margin ratios of two segments are the same, the maximization of sales revenue in each segment also maximizes contribution margin and vice versa.

The use of sales revenue as an allocation base can lead to distortions in the analysis of a division's operating results. For example, if a firm has two divisions, division A and division B, with the same sales revenues and contribution margins, and if they occupy the same square footage of space, then the cost of rent would be allocated 50 percent to each division. The operating results of the two divisions might appear as follows:

	Division A	Division B	Total
Sales	$100,000	$100,000	$200,000
Variable costs	40,000	40,000	80,000
Contribution margin	60,000	60,000	120,000
Rent and other common			
fixed costs	40,000	40,000	80,000
Operating income	$ 20,000	$ 20,000	$ 40,000

Now let us assume that in the following year, all cost patterns remain unchanged and that division A manages to increase its sales revenue to $400,000. If common costs are again allocated on the basis of sales revenue, the operating results for that year would appear as follows:

	Division A	Division B	Total
Sales	$400,000	$100,000	$500,000
Variable costs	160,000*	40,000	200,000
Contribution margin	240,000	60,000	300,000
Rent and other common			
fixed costs	64,000†	16,000‡	80,000
Operating income	$176,000	$ 44,000	$220,000

* $400,000 × 40% = $160,000.
† $400,000/$500,000 × $80,000 = $64,000.
‡ $100,000/$500,000 × $80,000 = $16,000.

Note that division B's operating income automatically grew from $20,000 to $44,000—not because division B increased its sales, but because division A increased its sales. And due to its improved sales volume, division A was also charged with an additional $24,000 of common fixed costs. These results can lead to problems.

First, the manager of division A might resent the increased charge to her division and the windfall to division B. Second, the two divisions' performances may be misinterpreted by people who do not understand the pitfalls of using sales revenue as the base for allocating common fixed costs.

Although some common costs may be allocated with somewhat realistic results, other common costs present stubborn allocation problems that are not easily solved. Since allocated common costs can produce arbitrary allocated net incomes, many firms prefer not to allocate common costs to individual segments in internal reports. Instead, they deduct the total common costs from the total segment margins, as shown in Illustration 10–12. This approach is used throughout the remainder of this chapter.

Preparing Segmented Income Statements

The segmentation of a firm's income statement may be accomplished in different ways. Illustrations 10–7 and 10–8 indicate some of the possibilities. The segmented report may begin with product lines, with each product line subdivided into products and ultimately into models. Alternatively, the income statement may be segregated by sales territories. The disaggregation may also start with divisions followed by product lines and then by sales territories, a blending of Illustrations 10–7 and 10–8. Essentially, the segmentation may take whatever form a firm finds useful.

The Multyproduct Company has two divisions—automotive and electron-

ILLUSTRATION 10–13

MULTYPRODUCT COMPANY
Income Statement Segmented by Division—Contribution Format
For the Year Ended December 31, 19x3
(in thousands of dollars)

	Total	Automotive	Electronics
Sales	$945,000	$400,000	$545,000
Variable cost of goods sold	416,000	160,000	256,000
Variable cost manufacturing margin	529,000	240,000	289,000
Variable marketing costs	28,350	12,000	16,350
Contribution margin	500,650	228,000	272,650
Less: *Direct* fixed overhead and other costs:			
Fixed overhead	130,000	50,000	80,000
Marketing costs	40,000	20,000	20,000
Administrative costs	40,000	20,000	20,000
Total direct fixed costs	210,000	90,000	120,000
Divisional segment margin	290,650	$138,000	$152,650
Less: *Indirect* fixed overhead and other costs (common costs)			(see Illustration 10–14)
Fixed overhead	40,000		
Marketing costs	30,000		
Administrative costs	50,000		
Total common costs	120,000		
Operating income before income taxes	$170,650		

ics. The automotive division manufactures spark plugs, electronic ignition modules, and various relay switches, while the electronics division manufactures automobile radios and digital clock radios. The firm's segmented income statement by divisions for the year 19x3 appears in Illustration 10–13.

The steps needed to prepare segmented statements reflecting segment margins by divisions, products, models, and territories may be summarized as follows:

Step 1

Prepare the income statement for the firm as a whole and analyze all income statement data between divisions, excluding common costs that can only be assigned to a division using an allocation formula. The analysis should include all variable costs and direct fixed costs (see Illustration 10–13).

ILLUSTRATION 10–14

MULTYPRODUCT COMPANY
Electronics Division Income Statement Segmented by Product—
Contribution Format
For the Year Ended December 31,19x3
(in thousands of dollars)

		Electronics	
	Total	Auto Radios	Clock Radios
Sales	$545,000	$310,000	$235,000
Variable cost of goods sold	256,000	136,000	120,000
Variable cost manufacturing margin	289,000	174,000	115,000
Variable marketing costs	16,350	9,300	7,050
Contribution margin	272,650	164,700	107,950
Less: *Direct* fixed overhead and other costs:			
Fixed overhead	60,000	20,000	40,000
Marketing costs	18,000	3,000	15,000
Administrative costs	10,000	2,000	8,000
Total direct fixed costs	88,000	25,000	63,000
Product segment margin	184,650	$139,700	$ 44,950
Less: *Indirect* fixed overhead and other costs (common costs):			(see Illustration 10–15)
Fixed overhead	20,000		
Marketing costs	2,000		
Administrative costs	10,000		
Total common costs	32,000 (i.e., $120,000 − $88,000)		
Divisional segment margin	$152,650		

Step 2

Repeat step 1 *for each division,* analyzing the data by product (see Illustration 10–14).

Step 3

Repeat step 1 for each product, analyzing the data by model (see Illustration 10–15).

Step 4

Repeat step 1 for each model, analyzing the data by sales territory (see Illustration 10–16).

ILLUSTRATION 10–15

MULTYPRODUCT COMPANY
Clock Radio Income Statement Segmented by Model—
Contribution Format
For the Year Ended December 31, 19x3
(in thousands of dollars)

		Clock Radios	
			Model
	Total	Deluxe	Regular
Sales	$235,000	$160,000	$75,000
Variable costs of goods sold	120,000	72,000	48,000
Variable cost manufacturing			
margin	115,000	88,000	27,000
Variable marketing costs	7,050	4,800	2,250
Contribution margin	107,950	83,200	24,750
Less: *Direct* fixed overhead			
and other costs:			
Fixed overhead	30,000	15,000	15,000
Marketing costs	14,000	2,000	12,000
Administrative costs	6,000	2,500	3,500
Total direct fixed costs	50,000	19,500	30,500
Model segment margin (loss)	57,950	$ 63,700	$ (5,750)
Less: *Indirect* fixed over-			(see
head and other costs			Illustration
(common costs):			10–16)
Fixed overhead	10,000		
Marketing costs	1,000		
Administrative costs	2,000		
Total common costs	13,000	(i.e., $63,000 − $50,000)	
Product segment margin	$ 44,950		

ILLUSTRATION 10–16

MULTYPRODUCT COMPANY
Regular Clock Radio Income Statement Segmented by Territory—
Contribution Format
For the Year Ended December 31, 19x3
(in thousands of dollars)

	Regular Clock Radios		
	Total	Domestic	Foreign
Sales	$75,000	$50,000	$25,000
Variable cost of goods sold	48,000	32,000	16,000
Variable cost manufacturing			
margin	27,000	18,000	9,000
Variable marketing costs	2,250	1,500	750
Contribution margin	24,750	16,500	8,250
Less: *Direct* fixed overhead			
and other costs:			
Fixed overhead	13,000	8,000	5,000
Marketing costs	11,500	2,500	9,000
Administrative costs	2,500	1,000	1,500
Total direct fixed costs	27,000	11,500	15,500
Territorial segment margin (loss)	(2,250)	$ 5,000	$ (7,250)
Less: *Indirect* fixed over-			
head and other costs			
(common costs):			
Fixed overhead	2,000		
Marketing costs	500		
Administrative costs	1,000		
Total common costs	3,500 (i.e., $30,500 − $27,000)		
Model segment margin (loss)	$ (5,750)		

Analysis of Common Costs. Different levels of segmentation have different direct costs, as indicated in Illustrations 10–13 through 10–16. Some examples that explain the differences are:

1. The president's salary is a common administrative cost in Illustration 10–13, while the divisional managers' salaries are direct fixed administrative costs to the respective divisions.

2. The divisional manager's salary is a common administrative cost in Illustration 10–14 (electronics division), while the product foremen's salaries are direct fixed overhead costs to the respective products.

3. The product foreman's salary is a common fixed overhead cost in Illustration 10–15 (models), while the line foremen's salaries are direct fixed overhead costs to the respective models.

A similar case can be made for machinery and equipment. The depreciation for equipment used by the electronics division would be a direct fixed cost (if the straight-line method is used) to the division in Illustration 10–13, while it would be a common fixed cost in Illustration 10–14, if the equipment were used for both automobile radios and clock radios.

In interpreting Illustrations 10–13 through 10–16, one might conclude that:

1. The company as a whole is profitable, as are the automotive and electronics divisions (see Illustration 10–13).

2. Auto radios and clock radios are both profitable (see Illustration 10–14).

3. Deluxe clock radios are profitable, while regular clock radios appear to be unprofitable. Sales revenues of regular clock radios are sufficient to cover variable costs but not direct fixed costs. If a managerial analysis of regular clock radios were based on Illustration 10–15 alone, a decision might be made to eliminate the manufacture of regular clock radios.

4. Regular clock radios sold in the United States are profitable, while foreign sales are unprofitable (see Illustration 10–16). The sales revenues of regular clock radios are sufficient to cover their variable costs. The problem appears to be in the direct fixed marketing costs. Upon investigation, a manager may determine that the foreign sales representative may be compensated partially on a fixed salary, or that advertising costs may be disproportionate to the amount of sales expected from the advertising, or a combination of both. In any event, Illustration 10–16 points to a problem that might remain undetected if segmented reports are not prepared.

5. Although the deluxe clock radio appears profitable (see Illustration 10–15), a statement segmented by territory may reveal a similar condition to that of the regular clock radio. Thus, regardless of whether a segment is profitable or unprofitable, additional segmentation (for example, by territory) may reveal an unprofitable condition or a potential trouble spot.

In addition to revealing trouble spots and unprofitable conditions, contribution segmented reports may be extremely useful for CVP analysis. They may point out products or territories where additional sales efforts, such as advertising and other forms of sales promotion, may yield the greatest contribution to profit.

USES OF SEGMENT DATA Firms vary widely in their use of segment data. An important consideration in the preparation of segment data is the cost-benefit rule. Obviously, the benefit derived from the use of segment data should exceed the cost of obtaining them. Thus, a firm that has a substantial amount of foreign sales would probably want a statement segmented by geographic areas, while a firm that has mostly localized sales might not prepare such a statement.

Among the more important uses of segmented reports are:

1. Detecting segments operating at a loss.

2. Pinpointing the source of a loss, such as the failure to cover variable costs or the coverage of variable costs but the failure to cover direct fixed costs.

3. Deciding whether to continue operating a particular segment.

4. Analyzing CVP relationships—altering a segment's selling price, cost, and volume for the purpose of increasing its contribution to profit.

5. Analyzing the potential results of altering marketing strategies, such as advertising, salespersons' visits to customers, and brochure mailings, to increase contribution to profit.

6. Evaluating managerial performance and implementing or amending incentive compensation plans, such as rewarding managers with a profit percentage of a segment's margin.

1. Detecting Segments Operating at a Loss. In many cases, a profitable firm may have one or more segments that produce a loss for the firm. Sometimes the segment producing a loss is obvious; other times, the loss is masked when the segment's operations are combined with a similar segment that operates at a profit. Unmasking a losing segment may occasionally be a tricky process. A particular product, or even one model of a product, may show profits despite the fact that a particular sales territory where it is sold produces losses. A careful choice of levels of segmentation should reveal all actual or potential loss producers.

The mere fact that a product or territory produces a loss does not mean that it should be eliminated. First, the loss may be an isolated or temporary event. In this case, the trend of the loss producer should be monitored, possibly for a period of one or two years, before a conclusion is reached that the loss will continue. Second, a trend analysis of any item contributing to the loss condition should be made to establish if the problem can be corrected. Third, marketing strategies should be examined to determine if a change in strategies might cure the condition. Only when it becomes clear that the loss condition is likely to be permanent, and corrective action is not likely to cure it, should a decision be made to abandon a loss producer.

2. Pinpointing the Source of a Loss. Even when it is obvious that a segment is operating at a loss, the contribution format segmented statement provides useful information not found in absorption-income statements. A segment's contribution margin indicates whether its sales revenues are sufficient to cover its variable costs. A case in which sales revenues are insufficient to cover variable costs is much more serious than a case in which revenues fail to cover direct fixed costs. When variable costs are not covered by sales revenue, *every additional sale increases the amount of the loss* and, thus, additional sales volume will only exacerbate the loss. The only solutions to the problem are either an increase in selling price without a loss in sales volume or a reduction in the variable cost per unit.

On the other hand, a segment may be covering its variable costs but not its direct fixed costs. The remedies for this condition might include:

a. Raising selling prices, if possible, without a significant loss of sales volume (CVP analysis would be used here).

b. Reducing the variable cost per unit without a significant loss in volume (CVP analysis would be used here too).

c. Reducing direct fixed costs, if possible.

d. Implementing an aggressive marketing campaign to increase sales volume and produce an increase in contribution margin that is greater than the cost of the marketing campaign (once again, CVP analysis would be used).

3. Continuing the Operations of a Segment. In addition to helping to detect and analyze segments operating at a loss, a segmented report may assist managers in assessing whether to continue operating profitable segments. Profitability does not automatically justify a segment's continued existence. A profitable segment must continually demonstrate that its profits compare favorably with a target return based on the firm's investment of assets in that segment. Since a firm is always faced with scarce resources, it must channel them into those segments that produce the greatest profit in accordance with overall objectives. Thus, it is quite conceivable that a firm may choose to discontinue a profitable segment in favor of another segment that may produce a greater profit. Segmented statements provide the information needed to make these kinds of decisions.

4. Cost-Volume-Profit Analysis. For a multiproduct firm, reliable CVP analysis can be accomplished only with segmented data. As noted in Chapter 6, CVP analysis for two products produces an average contribution margin and is valid only if the product mix remains unchanged. If a change in mix occurs, the contribution margin must be recomputed. Thus, an average may be used for very limited cases, usually two or three products. A diversified firm would have to use segmented data for CVP analysis, since figures based on a product mix of spark plugs, automotive radios, and household clock radios would be meaningless. A product mix of deluxe clock radios and regular clock radios might be used for CVP analysis, but even in this case, more informative results would probably be obtained through separate analyses for each radio.

5. Altering Marketing Strategies. The same problems that affect multiproduct CVP analyses arise when a company considers changing its strategies. Changes in marketing strategies can be effective only when a manager knows which products require a change and why they are not adequately profitable. Segmented statements highlight problem areas and provide managers with the information they need to make proper decisions.

6. Evaluating and Rewarding Managerial Performance. Studies in organizational behavior have shown that incentive compensation motivates most managers in a fashion that maximizes their income while maximizing the firm's income. On the other hand, when compensation is fixed and based on time worked, employees' goals may conflict with company goals. Thus, by instituting an incentive compensation program that gives employees a percentage of profits, a company may be able to lessen goal conflict.

Sales revenue, despite its widespread use in the computation of salespeople's commissions, is not an effective base for incentive compensation. Its deficiency stems from the fact that increases in sales volume do not necessarily guarantee maximum contribution margins. As a result, it is possible for a salesperson to maximize sales revenue by selling low-profit merchandise and thereby maximize her incentive compensation without maximizing profit to the firm.

Contribution margin makes a better base for profit sharing than does sales revenue, but it suffers from some of the same drawbacks. As shown in Illustration 10–16, a segment may simultaneously have a positive contribution margin and a negative segment margin. Thus, when profit sharing is based on contribution margin, a manager may receive incentive pay even though his segment is contributing a loss to overall company profitability.

Segment margin makes the best base for evaluating a manager's performance for a number of reasons. First, a maximization of segment margin generally maximizes a firm's overall profitability. Thus, if employees wish to maximize their incentive compensation when this base is used, their goal and the firm's goal will coincide. Second, since only direct costs are deducted to arrive at segment margin, the inequities of common cost allocations are avoided. Third, managers usually feel that segment margin is a fair base, since all costs deducted to arrive at segment margin are theoretically under their control and they can accept responsibility for the costs' incurrence.

SUMMARY

For external reporting and the preparation of income tax returns, firms must use **absorption costing.** When this method of costing is used, both fixed and variable manufacturing overhead are assigned to production and thus included in finished goods inventories. Despite its widespread use, absorption costing is not particularly suited to managerial decision making.

In contrast, with **variable costing,** also known as **direct costing** and **marginal costing,** only variable manufacturing costs are assigned to production and inventoried. Fixed manufacturing overhead is charged to income, as are marketing and administrative costs. The difference between the two methods of costing is that fixed manufacturing overhead is included in inventories with absorption costing and omitted from inventories with variable costing.

Because the results are "purer," managers prefer to base their decisions on variable-costing data.

When the beginning and ending finished goods inventories are the same in any year, operating income is the same for both variable and absorption costing. Operating income under the two approaches will differ, however, when there is either an **inventory buildup** or an **inventory liquidation.** The difference in operating income between the two methods may be computed by multiplying the number of units built up—or liquidated—by the fixed cost per unit.

Segment reporting is an extremely important component of a management reporting system when used in conjunction with **contribution format income statements. A segment margin income statement** is prepared by showing the contribution margin for each reportable segment, such as a division, product line, or sales territory, and then deducting each segment's **direct fixed costs** to arrive at **segment margin.** In essence, all **avoidable costs** for a segment are deducted from its sales to produce its margin. **Common costs** should not be allocated to each segment; instead, they should be deducted from the total of all segment margins to arrive at operating income.

Segmented income statements are extremely useful because they can reveal segments that are contributing losses to a firm's overall profitability. In income statements that report companywide results, one segment's losses may be masked by another segment's profits, so that loss-producing segments may go undetected for long periods of time.

In addition to unmasking loss-producing segments, segmented reports are useful for determining the possible reasons of the losses, deciding whether to continue operating both loss-producing and profitable segments, analyzing CVP relationships, altering market strategies, and the implementing or amending of incentive compensation plans.

GLOSSARY OF KEY TERMS

Absorption costing (full costing) A method of assigning manufacturing costs to production so that *both* variable and fixed manufacturing costs are included in inventories and cost of goods sold.

Avoidable cost Those costs that are eliminated when a particular cost objective is discontinued or altered.

Common cost A cost that cannot be traced to a single cost objective but may be allocated through the use of a logical allocation base.

Contribution format income statement An income statement classified into fixed and variable cost categories instead of into the functional categories of a traditional income statement. Instead of including fixed manufacturing overhead in cost of goods manufactured, it is shown as a period cost after contribution margin.

Direct cost A cost that can be traced to a single cost objective.

Direct costing See **variable costing.**

Inventory buildup The excess that occurs when a firm's ending finished goods inventories are greater than its beginning inventories for any accounting period.

Inventory liquidation The decrease that occurs when a firm's ending inventories are less than its beginning inventories for any accounting period.

Marginal costing See **variable costing.**

Segment margin Sales revenue minus variable and fixed costs that would not be incurred (that is, avoidable costs) if the line of business ceased to operate. It is the amount of profit that a line of business contributes to the overall profitability of a company.

Segment margin income statement A contribution format income statement that breaks down total operating results by reportable segment, such as division, product line, or sales territory. Each segment's direct fixed costs are deducted from its contribution margin to arrive at the segment margin. Common costs are then deducted in the total column to determine operating income before taxes.

Segmented reporting system A management reporting system that breaks companywide income statements into segments starting with the largest sections, such as divisions, and continuing with smaller and smaller units, such as product lines and then particular products.

Variable costing A method of assigning manufacturing costs to production so that *only* variable manufacturing costs are included in inventories and cost of goods sold.

QUESTIONS

1. How does absorption costing differ from variable costing?

2. Explain why variable costing is superior to absorption costing in making managerial decisions. In which kinds of decisions is variable costing especially useful?

3. Are variable marketing costs inventoriable when variable costing is used? Why?

4. Are variable marketing costs deducted to arrive at contribution margin? Why?

5. What is inventory buildup? Inventory liquidation? Do they play any role in the amount of reported net income when absorption costing is used? Explain.

6. When the number of units sold equals the number of units manufactured, does absorption costing or variable costing produce the higher net income? Explain.

7. How is fixed manufacturing overhead shifted into a subsequent accounting period when absorption accounting is used? Use an example to demonstrate the concept.

8. Is it possible to increase net income under absorption costing without increasing sales volume? Explain.

9. Is it possible for a firm to keep its reporting system on a variable-costing basis and still satisfy the firm's independent auditors and the Internal Revenue Service? Explain.

10. What is a segment? Use examples of segments in your answer.

11. Is is possible to prepare a segmented income statement using absorption costing? If so, what are the limitations of using such a statement for managerial decision making?

12. What are avoidable costs? How should they be used?

13. What is segment margin? How is a contribution format segmented margin income statement used?

14. What is a common cost? Give some examples of common costs.

15. Is a contribution format segmented income statement preferable to one prepared using absorption costing? Why?

16. What is the difference between contribution margin and segment margin?

17. Should common costs be allocated to segments? Why?

18. Is it possible for the same cost to be a direct cost in one segmented income statement and a common cost in another segmented income statement? Explain.

EXERCISES   **10–1**   **Variable-Costing and Absorption-Costing Calculations**

The following data apply to items 1 through 4.

Denham Company began operations on January 3, 19x3. Standard costs were established in early January assuming a normal production volume of 160,000 units. However, Denham produced only 140,000 units of product and sold 100,000 units at a selling price of $180 per unit during 19x3. Variable costs totaled $7 million of which 60 percent were manufacturing and 40 percent were marketing. Fixed costs totaled $11.2 million of which 50 percent were manufacturing and 50 percent were marketing. Denham had no raw materials or work in process inventories at December 31, 19x3. Actual input prices per unit of product and actual input quantities per unit of product were equal to standard.

1. Denham's cost of goods sold at standard cost for 19x3 using full absorption costing is
   a. $8.2 million.
   b. $7.2 million.
   c. $6.5 million.
   d. $7 million.
   e. Some amount other than those given above.

2. The value assigned to Denham's December 31, 19x3, inventory using variable (direct) costing is
   a. $2.8 million.
   b. $1.2 million.
   c. $2 million.
   d. $3 million.
   e. Some amount other than those given above.

3. Denham's manufacturing overhead volume variance in 19x3 using full absorption costing is
   a. $800,000 unfavorable.
   b. $800,000 favorable.
   c. $700,000 unfavorable.
   d. $700,000 favorable.
   e. Some amount other than those given above.

4. Denham's 19x3 income from operations using variable (direct) costing is
   a. $3.4 million.
   b. $1.8 million.
   c. $2.6 million.
   d. $1 million.
   e. Some amount other than those given above.

(CMA adapted)

10–2 Variable-Costing and Absorption-Costing Calculations

The Penney Corporation produces and sells one item. The following information on the company for 19x6 is available:

Direct materials	$ 90,000
Direct labor	105,000
Variable overhead	60,000
Fixed overhead	75,000
Units produced	15,000 units
Units sold	12,500 units
Units in beginning inventory	–0–
Salespersons' commissions	$ 37,500
Fixed marketing costs	$ 42,000
Fixed administrative costs	$ 35,000

There are no work in process inventories.

Required

a. Compute the ending finished goods inventory using absorption costing.
b. Compute the ending finished goods inventory using variable costing.
c. Does absorption costing or variable costing show a higher operating income for 19x6? By how much?

10–3 Absorption-Costing Income Statement Converted to Variable-Costing Income Statement

The Praline Company provides you with the following income statement:

PRALINE COMPANY
Income Statement Using Absorption Costing
For the Year Ended December 31, 19x2

Sales		$600,000
Cost of goods sold:		
Beginning inventory—finished goods	$ –0–	
Direct materials	100,000	
Direct labor	175,000	
Manufacturing overhead	200,000	
Cost of goods manufactured	475,000	
Less: Ending inventory—finished goods	95,000	
Cost of goods sold		380,000
Gross margin		220,000
Marketing and administrative costs:		
Marketing	80,000	
Administrative	100,000	180,000
Operating income before income taxes		$ 40,000

During 19x2, the company manufactured only one product. The number of units produced was 50,000, and there are no work in process inventories.

The variable overhead is $1.50 per unit. Variable marketing costs amount to $24,000. The administrative costs are all fixed.

Required   a.   How many units are there in the ending finished goods inventory?

               b.   How much is the fixed overhead per unit?

               c.   How much fixed overhead is there in the ending finished goods inventory?

               d.   Prepare an income statement using the variable-costing format.

               e.   Explain the difference between your operating income before income taxes and the $40,000 shown in the above income statement.

10-4   Variable-Costing Income Statement Converted to Absorption-Costing Income Statement

The Polly Company manufactures only one product, and during 19x2 it manufactured 40,000 units.

There were no work in process inventories at the beginning and ending of 19x2. The company's variable-costing income statement for 19x2 appears below:

THE POLLY COMPANY
Income Statement Using Variable Costing
For the Year Ended December 31, 19x2

Sales		$720,000
Variable cost of goods sold:		
Beginning inventory—finished goods	$ –0–	
Direct materials	120,000	
Direct labor	160,000	
Variable manufacturing overhead	80,000	
Variable cost of goods manufactured	360,000	
Less: Ending inventory—finished goods	36,000	
Variable cost of goods sold		324,000
Variable cost manufacturing margin		396,000
Salespersons' commissions		30,000
Contribution margin		366,000
Less: Fixed costs:		
Fixed manufacturing overhead	160,000	
Fixed marketing costs	60,000	
Fixed administrative costs	100,000	
Total fixed costs		320,000
Operating income before income taxes		$ 46,000

Required   a.   Prepare an absorption-costing income statement for 19x2.

               b.   Reconcile your operating income before income taxes with the $46,000 shown above.

10-5   Preparation of Absorption-Costing and Variable-Costing Income Statements

The Real Corporation manufactures and sells packaged, custom-designed decks of playing cards. The following information on the company is available for 19x3.

Units produced	12,000 units
Units sold	10,000 units
Selling price per unit	$16.00

Variable costs per unit:

Direct materials	2.40
Direct labor	1.20
Variable manufacturing overhead	3.60
Variable marketing costs	3.20

Fixed costs:

Manufacturing overhead	$12,000
Marketing costs	14,000
Administrative costs	6,000
Beginning inventory	–0–

There are no work in process inventories.
There are no variable administrative costs.

Required

a. What is the cost of a unit of product using absorption costing? Using variable costing?

b. Prepare income statements for 19x3 using absorption costing and then variable costing.

c. Reconcile the difference between the two income statements.

10–6 **Preparation of a Variable-Costing Income Statement from an Absorption-Costing Income Statement**

Dublin, Inc., was organized on January 1, 19x5. The absorption-costing income statement for the year ending December 31, 19x5, is shown below.

DUBLIN, INC.
Income Statement—Absorption Costing
For the Year Ending December 31, 19x5

Sales (4,000 units × $130)		$520,000
Cost of goods sold:		
Beginning inventory	$ –0–	
Direct materials (5,000 units × $30)	150,000	
Direct labor (5,000 units × $20)	100,000	
Variable manufacturing overhead		
(5,000 units × $10)	50,000	
Fixed manufacturing overhead		
(5,000 units × $40)	200,000	
Goods available for sale	500,000	
Less: Ending inventory—finished		
goods (1,000 units × $100)	100,000	
Cost of goods sold		400,000
Gross margin		120,000
Marketing and administrative costs:		
Marketing	35,000	
Administrative	45,000	80,000
Operating income before income taxes		$ 40,000

There are no work in process inventories.

The total marketing costs of $35,000 consist of variable marketing costs of $24,000 and fixed marketing costs of $11,000. There are no variable administrative costs.

Required *a.* Prepare another income statement for Dublin, Inc., this time using variable costing.

b. Is there a difference in operating income between the absorption-costing and variable-costing income statements? Explain any difference.

10–7 Computation of Variable-Costing Operating Income from Selected Data with an Inventory Buildup and an Inventory Liquidation

The Progress Company manufactures one product. Selected data for 19x1 and 19x2 are as follows:

	19x1	19x2
Absorption-costing operating income .	$100,000	$ 80,000
Fixed manufacturing overhead	$200,000	$210,000
Units manufactured	50,000	35,000
Units sold	40,000	40,000
Beginning finished goods inventory—		
in units	5,000	?
Fixed overhead costs in beginning		
inventory	$ 22,000	?

There are no work in process inventories and the company uses a FIFO cost flow. Marketing and administrative costs are all fixed costs.

Required *a.* How many units are there in ending finished goods inventory for 19x1? For 19x2?

b. How much fixed overhead is there in the ending finished goods inventory for 19x1? For 19x2?

c. How much is the variable-costing operating income for 19x1? For 19x2?

10–8 Computation of Absorption-Costing Operating Income from Selected Data with an Inventory Buildup and an Inventory Liquidation

The Regress Company manufactures one product. Selected data for 19x1 and 19x2 are as follows:

	19x1	19x2
Variable-costing operating income . . .	$160,000	$180,000
Fixed manufacturing overhead	$300,000	$340,000
Units manufactured	60,000	40,000
Units sold	50,000	58,000
Beginning finished goods inventory—		
in units	10,000	?
Fixed overhead costs in absorption-		
costing beginning inventory	$ 45,000	?

There are no work in process inventories and the company uses a FIFO cost flow. Marketing and administrative costs are all fixed costs.

Required *a.* How many units are there in ending finished goods inventory for 19x1? For 19x2?

b. How much fixed overhead is there in the absorption-costing ending finished goods inventory for 19x1? For 19x2?

c. How much is the absorption-costing operating income for 19x1? For 19x2?

10–9 Reasons for Using Variable Costing for Internal Reporting

Grisp Company, a manufacturer with heavy investments in property, plant, and equipment, is presently using absorption costing for both its external and internal reporting. The management of Grisp Company is considering using the variable-costing method for internal reporting only.

Required *a.* What would be the rationale for using the variable-costing method for internal reporting?

b. Assuming that the quantity of ending inventory is higher than the quantity of beginning inventory, would operating income using variable costing be different from operating income using absorption costing? If so, specify if it would be higher or lower. Discuss the rationale for your answer.

(AICPA adapted)

10–10 Absorption Costing and Variable Costing from Partial Information

The Compact Company prepared condensed comparative income statements for 19x1 and 19x2. During the two years, there were *no changes* in costs or selling price of the company's single product, and the company does not have any work in process inventories. The condensed income statements are as follows:

	19x2	19x1
Sales	$600,000	$400,000
Cost of goods sold	360,000	240,000
_____?_____ margin	240,000	160,000
Other costs	120,000	120,000
Operating income before income taxes .	$120,000	$ 40,000

Marketing and administrative costs are all fixed. Fixed overhead for each year amounted to $60,000.

The company began operating on January 1, 19x1, and during 19x1, it produced 30,000 units. Sales for 19x1 amounted to 20,000 units. There was no finished goods inventory on December 31, 19x2.

Required *a.* Are the above income statements prepared in accordance with absorption costing? Explain your reasons for your conclusion.

b. Recast the condensed income statements into condensed income statements of the other format, i.e., variable costing if they are absorption costing or absorption costing if they are variable costing.

10–11 Strategy Changes and the Preparation of a Segmented Income Statement

The Relaxation Company manufactures Aspirin and Relaxaid. A segmented income statement for 19x3 is as follows:

	Total	Aspirin	Relaxaid
Sales	$900,000	$400,000	$500,000
Variable costs	400,000	200,000	200,000
Contribution margin	500,000	200,000	300,000
Direct fixed costs	180,000	80,000	100,000
Product segment margin	320,000	$120,000	$200,000
Common costs	120,000		
Operating income before income taxes	$200,000		

Cost behavior patterns are not expected to change during 19x4.

Required   *a.*   A $12,000 advertisement for either product is expected to produce a 5 percent increase in sales volume. Would you recommend the advertisement for Aspirin? For Relaxaid? Why?

           b.   Prepare a projected segmented income statement for 19x4 if the sales of Aspirin are expected to increase by 10 percent and the sales of Relaxaid are expected to increase by 20 percent. Fixed costs are expected to increase by 10 percent.

10–12   **Segmented Income Statement**

The Burns Company has two divisions—clothing and jewelry. The firm's segmented income statement by divisions for the year 19x5 appears below:

BURNS COMPANY
Segmented Income Statement—Contribution Format
For the Year Ended December 31, 19x5

	Total	Clothing	Jewelry
Sales	$460,000	$320,000	$140,000
Variable cost of goods sold	131,000	96,000	35,000
Variable cost manufacturing margin	329,000	224,000	105,000
Variable marketing costs	32,950	25,600	7,350
Contribution margin	296,050	198,400	97,650
Less: Direct fixed overhead and other costs:			
Fixed overhead	71,000	45,000	26,000
Marketing costs	13,000	8,000	5,000
Administrative costs	7,250	3,750	3,500
Total direct fixed costs	91,250	56,750	34,500
Divisional segment margin	204,800	$141,650	$ 63,150
Less: Indirect fixed overhead and costs (common costs):			
Fixed overhead	30,000		
Marketing costs	43,850		
Administrative costs	82,150		
Total common costs	156,000		
Operating income before income taxes	$ 48,800		

Required
a. Compute the change in operating income if the clothing division increases sales by 12 percent.

b. Compute the change in operating income if the jewelry division increases sales by 12 percent.

c. If you had a choice of increasing sales by 12 percent in the clothing division or by 12 percent in the jewelry division, which would you prefer? Why? What is the contribution margin ratio of each division? Did you select the one with the higher ratio? Explain.

10–13 Preparation of a Segmented Income Statement

The Fairway Company manufactures two products, automobile heater hose and hose clamps. During 19x3, the company sold 400,000 feet of hose and 150,000 clamps. The selling price of hose is 60 cents per foot while clamps sell for 40 cents each.

The costs during the year were as follows:

	Hose	Clamps
Variable costs	24 cents per foot	10 cents each
Direct fixed costs	$50,000	$30,000

Common fixed costs amounted to $50,000.

Required Prepare an income statement segmented by product using the contribution format.

10–14 Cost-Volume-Profit Strategies for Segments

The Collins Company manufactures two products—blankets and pillows. The firm's segmented income statement by products for the year 19x4 appears below:

COLLINS COMPANY
Segmented Income Statement—Contribution Format
For the Year Ended December 31, 19x4

	Total	Blankets	Pillows
Sales	$380,000	$180,000	$200,000
Variable cost of goods sold	134,000	54,000	80,000
Variable cost manufacturing margin	246,000	126,000	120,000
Variable marketing costs	44,000	36,000	8,000
Contribution margin	202,000	90,000	112,000
Less: Direct fixed overhead and other costs:			
Fixed overhead	48,000	22,000	26,000
Marketing costs	19,850	11,500	8,350
Administrative costs	17,250	3,750	13,500
Total direct fixed costs	85,100	37,250	47,850
Product segment margin	116,900	$ 52,750	$ 64,150
Less: Indirect fixed overhead and costs (common costs)	54,100		
Operating income before income taxes	$ 62,800		

The Collins Company intends to spend $5,000 in a direct-mail campaign for either the blankets or the pillows. If the $5,000 is spent on either product, sales of that product will increase by $50,000. Cost behavior patterns will be unchanged by the direct-mail cost.

Required a. For which of the two products should the Collins Company spend the $5,000 direct-mail campaign funds? Show the computations you made to arrive at your decision.

b. Instead of a direct-mail campaign, the Collins Company may spend the $5,000 on direct advertising for either the blankets or the pillows. If it is spent on the pillows, sales of pillows will increase by $20,000, while if the $5,000 is spent on the blankets, sales of blankets will increase by $30,000. Should the Collins Company spend the $5,000 in direct advertising on the pillows or blankets? Show the computations you made to arrive at your decision.

10–15 Preparation of a Segmented Income Statement

The condensed income statement as shown below demonstrates a loss for the Palmar Company for 19x2:

Sales		$850,000
Variable costs*		470,000
Contribution margin . .		380,000
Fixed costs:		
Fixed overhead . . .	$183,000	
Marketing	90,000	
Administrative	122,000	
Total fixed costs .		395,000
Net income (loss) . . .		$ (15,000)

* There are no variable marketing costs.

The Palmar Company produces greeting cards, posters, and stationery. A manager of the company has ordered a segmented income statement by product to trace the loss. Given the following data:

	Greeting Cards	Posters	Stationery
Sales	$400,000	$250,000	$200,000
Contribution margin ratio	65%	20%	35%
Direct fixed overhead and other costs:			
Fixed overhead	$ 17,000	$ 37,000	$ 13,000
Marketing	18,000	19,000	28,000
Administrative	10,000	29,000	14,000
Total direct fixed costs	$ 45,000	$ 85,000	$ 55,000

Required a. Prepare a segmented income statement showing segmented margin by product.

b. The manager believes that the sales of posters would increase by 40 percent if the direct-mail campaign funds were increased by $25,000. Would you advise an increased direct-mail campaign? Show the computations you made to arrive at your answer.

10–16   Strategy Changes and the Preparation of a Segmented Income Statement

The Clark Company manufactures two products, product A and product B. A segmented income statement for 19x3 is as follows:

	Total	Product A	Product B
Sales	$800,000	$600,000	$200,000
Variable costs	480,000	400,000	80,000
Contribution margin	320,000	200,000	120,000
Direct fixed costs	260,000	100,000	160,000
Product segment margin	60,000	$100,000	$ (40,000)
Common costs	80,000		
Operating loss before			
income taxes	$ (20,000)		

Cost behavior patterns are not expected to change during 19x4.

Required
- *a.*   If the company expects no change in volume for 19x4, should the company cease to operate? Explain your reasons for your conclusions.
- *b.*   The company believes that spending $25,000 for advertising product A could increase its sales by 10 percent *or* spending $15,000 for advertising product B could increase its sales by 50 percent. Which course of action would you recommend? Explain.
- *c.*   Prepare a segmented income statement using your recommendation from *(b)*.

10–17   Segmented Income Statement

The Crum Company has two divisions—division C and division D. The firm's segmented income statement by divisions for the year 19x5 appears below:

CRUM COMPANY
Segmented Income Statement—Contribution Format
For the Year Ended December 31, 19x5

	Total	Division C	Division D
Sales	$1,000,000	$400,000	$600,000
Variable cost of goods sold	340,000	100,000	240,000
Variable cost manufacturing margin	660,000	300,000	360,000
Variable marketing costs	110,000	80,000	30,000
Contribution margin	550,000	220,000	330,000
Fixed costs	500,000	250,000	250,000
Operating income (loss)			
before income taxes	$ 50,000	$ (30,000)	$ 80,000

The president of the company is considering whether to cease operating division C. She asks you to analyze the fixed costs and prepare a segmented income statement suitable for reaching a conclusion regarding the future operations of division C.

An analysis of the company's fixed costs provides you with the following:

	Total	Division C	Division D
Direct fixed costs . . .	$300,000	$100,000	$200,000
Common fixed costs .	200,000		
Total	$500,000		

For 19x6, the company anticipates that sales volume for division C will increase by 5 percent while its direct fixed costs will increase by 20 percent. Division D's sales volume is expected to increase by 10 percent while its direct fixed costs are expected to increase by 30 percent. Common fixed costs are expected to increase by 10 percent.

Required Prepare a projected segmented income statement showing segment margin for 19x6 suitable for decision making.

10–18 **Preparation of a Segmented Income Statement**

The condensed income statement as shown below demonstrates a loss for the Poma Company for 19x2:

Sales		$1,400,000
Variable costs*		710,000
Contribution margin . . .		690,000
Fixed costs:		
Fixed overhead	$350,000	
Marketing	200,000	
Administrative	190,000	
Total fixed costs . .		740,000
Net income (loss)		$ (50,000)

* There are no variable marketing costs.

The Poma Company produces two products—product G and product H. A manager of the company has ordered a segmented income statement by product to trace the loss. Given the following data:

	Product G	Product H
Sales	$800,000	$600,000
Contribution margin ratio	60%	35%
Direct fixed overhead and other costs:		
Fixed overhead	$130,000	$150,000
Marketing	90,000	50,000
Administrative	80,000	60,000
Total direct fixed costs . .	$300,000	$260,000

Required   a.   Prepare a segmented income statement showing segment margin by product.
           b.   The manager believes that the sales of product H would increase by 30 percent if the direct-mail campaign funds were increased by $35,000. Would you advise an increased direct-mail campaign? Show the computations you used to arrive at your conclusion.

PROBLEMS   **10–19**   **Preparation of Absorption-Costing and Variable-Costing Income Statements**

The Lafayette Company was organized on January 1, 19x4. The company produces and sells one product. The cost data for that product are as follows:

Manufacturing costs:	
Variable cost per unit	$26
Direct materials	15
Direct labor	5
Variable overhead	6
Fixed overhead costs	$45,000
Marketing and administrative costs:	
Salespersons' commissions . . .	8%
Fixed marketing costs	$220,000
Fixed administrative costs	$270,000

Production and sales data for 19x4 and 19x5 are as follows:

	Units Produced	Units Sold
19x4	50,000	45,000
19x5	50,000	55,000

The selling price is $50.

Required   a.   Prepare income statements for 19x4 and 19x5 using the absorption-costing approach.
           b.   Prepare income statements for 19x4 and 19x5 using the variable-costing method.
           c.   Reconcile the variable-costing and absorption-costing figures for operating income.
           d.   Compute the cost of a single unit of the product under absorption costing and under variable costing.

10–20   **Preparation of Variable-Costing Income Statements and Reconciliation with Absorption-Costing Income Statements**

The Midland Corporation manufactures and sells a single product. The absorption-costing income statements for the Midland Corporation for 19x7 and 19x8 are shown below:

MIDLAND CORPORATION
Income Statement—Absorption Costing
For the Years Ending December 31, 19x7, and December 31, 19x8

	19x7	19x8
Sales	$120,000	$120,000
Less: Cost of goods sold	66,000	63,000
Gross margin	54,000	57,000
Marketing and administrative costs	51,600	51,600
Operating income before income taxes . .	$ 2,400	$ 5,400

Sales and production data are as follows:

	19x7	19x8
Units sold	3,000	3,000
Units produced	3,000	4,000

Fixed overhead is allocated to production on the number of units produced. Variable and fixed production costs are:

	19x7	19x8
Variable production cost per unit .	$18	$18
Fixed manufacturing overhead . .	$12,000	$12,000

Marketing and administrative costs:

Variable marketing costs	8% of sales
Fixed marketing costs	$10,800
Fixed administrative costs	31,200

Variable production cost per unit:

Direct materials	$6
Direct labor	9
Variable manufacturing overhead	3

Required

a. Determine the cost of a single unit of product under absorption costing and variable costing for both 19x7 and 19x8.

b. Prepare variable-costing income statements for the Midland Corporation for both 19x7 and 19x8.

c. Reconcile the absorption-costing and variable-costing operating income figures for 19x8.

d. Explain why the operating income for 19x8 is higher than the operating income for 19x7 although the number of units sold in each year is the same.

10–21   Preparation of Variable-Costing and Absorption-Costing Income Statements

The cost and revenue data for the Reincort Company for 19x6 are as follows:

$$
\begin{array}{lr}
\text{Beginning inventory} & \text{--0--} \\
\text{Production in units} & 6,000 \\
\text{Sales in units} & 4,200 \\
\text{Sales price per unit} & \$20
\end{array}
$$

Marketing and administrative costs:

$$
\begin{array}{lr}
\text{Salesperson's commissions} & 8\% \text{ of sales} \\
\text{Fixed marketing costs} & \$5,400 \\
\text{Fixed administrative costs} & 9,080
\end{array}
$$

Production costs per unit:

$$
\begin{array}{lr}
\text{Direct materials} & \$2 \\
\text{Direct labor} & 5 \\
\text{Variable overhead} & 4 \\
\text{Fixed overhead} & 3
\end{array}
$$

Required

a. Prepare an income statement for the Reincort Company for 19x6 using absorption costing. Compute the cost per unit of product.

b. Prepare an income statement for 19x6 using variable costing. Compute the cost per unit of product.

c. Compute the value of the ending inventory using absorption costing and variable costing.

d. Explain any difference in the ending inventory under the two costing approaches. Explain any difference in operating income between the two approaches.

10–22 Preparation of Variable-Costing Income Statements and Comparison with Absorption-Costing Income Statements

The absorption-costing income statements for the Royale Company's first two years of operation for its only product are shown below:

	19x2	19x3
Sales	$150,000	$350,000
Cost of goods sold:		
Opening inventory	--0--	52,000
Cost of goods manufactured (at $13)	130,000	130,000
Goods available for sale	130,000	182,000
Less: Ending inventory (at $13)	52,000	--0--
Cost of goods sold	78,000	182,000
Gross margin	72,000	168,000
Marketing and administrative costs	39,500	49,500
Operating income before income taxes	$ 32,500	$118,500

The cost of goods manufactured per unit of product is computed as follows:

Direct materials	$ 5	
Direct labor	3	
Variable manufacturing overhead	2	
Fixed manufacturing overhead	3	
Total cost per unit	$13	

Production and sales data are as follows:

	19x2	19x3
Units produced	10,000	10,000
Units sold	6,000	14,000

Marketing and administrative costs:

	19x2	19x3
Variable marketing costs	$ 7,500	$17,500
Fixed marketing costs	15,000	15,000
Fixed administrative costs	17,000	17,000
Total	$39,500	$49,500

There are no work in process inventories.

Required *a.* Prepare income statements for the Royale company for each year using the variable-costing method.

b. Reconcile the absorption-costing and variable-costing operating incomes for each year.

c. Which income statement format is more suitable for managerial decision making? Discuss your position by incorporating in your discussion the income statements you prepared.

10–23 Preparation of Variable-Costing Income Statements

The absorption-costing income statements for the Marlin Company's first two years of operation for its only product are shown below.

	19x5	19x6
Sales	$360,000	$720,000
Cost of goods sold:		
Opening inventory	–0–	100,000
Cost of goods manufactured	400,000	450,000
Goods available for sale	400,000	550,000
Less: Ending inventory	100,000	–0–
Cost of goods sold	300,000	550,000
Gross margin	60,000	170,000
Marketing and administrative costs	60,000	90,000
Operating income before income taxes	$ –0–	$ 80,000

The cost of goods manufactured per unit of product is computed as follows for 19x5:

Direct materials	$ 2
Direct labor	2
Variable manufacturing overhead	1
Fixed manufacturing overhead	5
Total cost per unit	$10

The total dollar amount of fixed overhead costs for 19x5 is unchanged for 19x6. Variable manufacturing costs per unit and the selling price of the company's product are also unchanged for 19x6. Production and sales data are as follows:

	19x5	19x6
Units produced	40,000	50,000
Units sold	30,000	60,000

Marketing and administrative costs:

	19x5	19x6
Variable marketing costs . .	$30,000	$60,000
Fixed marketing costs . . .	10,000	10,000
Fixed administrative costs .	20,000	20,000
Total	$60,000	$90,000

There are no work in process inventories.

Required a. Prepare income statements for the company for each year using the variable-costing method.
b. Reconcile the absorption-costing and variable-costing operating incomes for each year.
c. The company's management accountant calculated Marlin's breakeven sales as:

$$\frac{\$230,000}{\$12 - \$5} = 32,857 \text{ units} \times \$12 = \$394,284$$

For 19x5, the income statement provided above shows sales of $360,000 and a breakeven ($0 operating income). Is the $394,284 breakeven wrong? Explain.

10–24 Preparation of Variable-Costing and Absorption-Costing Income Statements: Comparisons with Breakeven Sales

Julian, Inc., was organized on January 1, 19x1. Sales and production data are as follows:

Units produced	6,000
Units sold	3,800
Selling price per unit	$26

Production costs:

Direct materials per unit	$6
Direct labor per unit	$8
Variable overhead per unit	$2
Fixed overhead per annum . . .	$18,000

Marketing and administrative costs:

Variable marketing costs	$9,600
Fixed marketing costs	$6,400
Fixed administrative costs	$6,600

Required *a.* Determine the cost of a single unit of product under absorption costing and variable costing.

b. Prepare income statements for 19x1 using absorption costing and variable costing.

c. Reconcile the absorption-costing and variable-costing figures for operating income.

d. Compute the company's breakeven sales in dollars. How does your calculation of breakeven sales compare with your income statement prepared under absorption costing? Explain your comparison.

10–25 Preparation of Variable-Costing Income Statements and Analysis of Income Statement Differences

The Kircus Company was organized on January 1, 19x7. The absorption-costing income statements for the first three years are given below:

	19x7	19x8	19x9
Sales	$750,000	$600,000	$750,000
Less: Cost of goods sold:			
Beginning inventory	–0–	–0–	200,000
Cost of goods produced	525,000	600,000	450,000
Goods available for sale	525,000	600,000	650,000
Less: Ending inventory	–0–	200,000	112,500
Cost of goods sold	525,000	400,000	537,500
Gross margin	225,000	200,000	212,500
Marketing and administrative			
costs	140,000	128,000	140,000
Operating income (loss)			
before income taxes	$ 85,000	$ 72,000	$ 72,500

Sales and production data are as follows:

	19x7	19x8	19x9
Units sold	25,000	20,000	25,000
Units produced	25,000	30,000	20,000

Marketing and administrative costs:

Variable marketing costs	8% of sales
Fixed marketing costs	$35,000
Fixed administrative costs	$45,000

Fixed overhead is charged to production on the basis of *each year's production.* The company uses FIFO in valuing its inventories.

Required

a. Prepare income statements for each of the three years using the variable-costing approach.

b. Reconcile the absorption-costing and variable-costing figures for operating income for each year. (Hint: Use the high-low method to determine the fixed overhead.)

c. Explain why the 19x9 operating income under absorption costing is different from the 19x7 operating income although the same number of units were sold in both years, and fixed costs for the the two years were unchanged while variable costs per unit were also unchanged.

d. Given that the fixed costs for the three years are the same and the variable cost per unit is also the same in each of the three years, why is the operating income in 19x9 only $500 more than the operating income in 19x8 despite an increase in sales of 25 percent?

10-26 Preparation of Variable-Costing Income Statements

The absorption-costing income statements for the Maxim Company's first two years of operation for its only product are shown below:

	19x5	19x6
Sales	$400,000	$600,000
Cost of goods sold:		
Opening inventory	–0–	112,000
Cost of goods manufactured	336,000	312,000
Goods available for sale	336,000	424,000
Less: Ending inventory	112,000	72,000
Cost of goods sold	224,000	352,000
Gross margin	176,000	248,000
Marketing and administrative costs	60,000	70,000
Operating income before income taxes	$116,000	$178,000

The cost of goods manufactured per unit of product is computed as follows for 19x5:

Direct materials	$ 3.00
Direct labor	2.00
Variable manufacturing overhead	1.00
Fixed manufacturing overhead	5.20
Total cost per unit	$11.20

The total dollar amount of fixed overhead costs for 19x5 is unchanged for 19x6. Variable manufacturing costs per unit and the selling price of the company's product are also unchanged for 19x6. Production and sales data are as follows:

	19x5	19x6
Units produced	30,000	26,000
Units sold	20,000	30,000

Marketing and administrative costs:

	19x5	19x6
Variable marketing costs	$20,000	$30,000
Fixed marketing costs	10,000	10,000
Fixed administrative costs	30,000	30,000
Total	$60,000	$70,000

There are no work in process inventories.

Required   *a.*   Prepare income statements for the company for each year using the variable-costing method.

b.   Reconcile the absorption-costing and variable-costing operating incomes for each year.

c.   The president of the company notes that sales revenue in 19x6 increased by 50 percent while the gross margin for 19x6 using absorption costing only increased by 40.9 percent. How do you explain this?

10–27   Cost-Volume-Profit Decision Making for Product Lines

The officers of Bradshaw Company are reviewing the profitability of the company's four products and the potential effect of several proposals for varying the product mix. An excerpt from the income statement and other data follow:

	Totals	Product P	Product Q	Product R	Product S
Sales	$62,600	$10,000	$18,000	$12,600	$22,000
Cost of goods sold	44,274	4,750	7,056	13,968	18,500
Gross profit	18,326	5,250	10,944	(1,368)	3,500
Operating costs	12,012	1,990	2,976	2,826	4,220
Income before income taxes	$ 6,314	$ 3,260	$ 7,968	$ (4,194)	$ (720)
Units sold		1,000	1,200	1,800	2,000
Sales price per unit		$10.00	$15.00	$7.00	$11.00
Variable cost of goods sold per unit		$2.50	$3.00	$6.50	$6.00
Variable operating costs per unit		$1.17	$1.25	$1.00	$1.20

Each of the following proposals is to be considered independently of the other proposals. Consider only the product changes stated in each proposal; the activity of other products remains stable. Ignore income taxes.

Required   *a.*   If product R is discontinued, the effect on income will be
   (1) $900 increase.
   (2) $4,194 increase.
   (3) $12,600 decrease.
   (4) $1,368 increase.
   (5)   None of the above.

b. If product R is discontinued and a consequent loss of customers causes a decrease of 200 units in sales of Q, the total effect on income will be
    (1) $15,600 decrease.
    (2) $2,866 increase.
    (3) $2,044 increase.
    (4) $1,250 decrease.
    (5) None of the above.

c. If the sales price of R is increased to $8 with a decrease in the number of units sold to 1,500, the effect on income will be
    (1) $2,199 decrease.
    (2) $600 decrease.
    (3) $750 increase.
    (4) $2,199 increase.
    (5) None of the above.

d. The plant in which R is produced can be utilized to produce a new product, T. The total variable costs per unit of T are $8.05, and 1,600 units can be sold at $9.50 each. If T is introduced and R is discontinued, the total effect on income will be
    (1) $2,600 increase.
    (2) $2,320 increase.
    (3) $3,220 increase.
    (4) $1,420 increase.
    (5) None of the above.

e. Part of the plant in which P is produced can easily be adapted to the production of S, but changes in quantities may make changes in sales prices advisable. If production of P is reduced to 500 units (to be sold at $12 each) and production of S is increased to 2,500 units (to be sold at $10.50 each), the total effect on income will be
    (1) $1,765 decrease.
    (2) $250 increase.
    (3) $2,060 decrease.
    (4) $1,515 decrease.
    (5) None of the above.

f. Production of P can be doubled by adding a second shift, but higher wages must be paid, increasing variable cost of goods sold to $3.50 for each of the additional units. If the 1,000 additional units of P can be sold at $10 each, the total effect on income will be
    (1) $10,000 increase.
    (2) $5,330 increase.
    (3) $6,500 increase.
    (4) $2,260 increase.
    (5) None of the above.

(AICPA adapted)

10-28 Preparation of Segmented Income Statements and Analysis of Results

The Summar Company manufactures two products—televisions and clock radios. They are sold in two markets—European and Asian. The condensed income statement for the Summar Company is shown below:

SUMMAR COMPANY
Income Statement—Contribution Format
For the Year Ended December 31, 19x5

Sales		$720,000
Variable manufacturing costs		180,000
Contribution margin		540,000
Fixed costs:		
Fixed overhead	$197,150	
Marketing costs	135,100	
Administrative costs	97,500	
Total fixed costs		429,750
Operating income before		
income taxes		$110,250

There are no variable marketing costs.

A sales manager is convinced that there is a problem in the Asian territory and has instructed you to find it. You are provided with the following information:

1. Two thirds of the Summar Company's sales are from the European territory. Fifty percent of the variable manufacturing costs are traceable to each territory.
2. The fixed costs are traced to each territory as follows:
   a. Fixed overhead of $73,375 and $55,500 to the European and Asian territories, respectively.
   b. Marketing costs of $68,500 and $32,375 to the European and Asian territories, respectively.
   c. Administrative costs of $42,150 and $27,125 to the European and Asian territories, respectively.
3. Seventy-five percent of the Asian territory's sales are attributable to televisions. The contribution margin ratio is 70 percent for televisions and 40 percent for clock radios.
4. The fixed costs for each product within the Asian territory are as follows:
   a. Fixed overhead is $17,500 for televisions and $14,500 for clock radios.
   b. Marketing costs are $4,500 and $13,500 for the televisions and clock radios, respectively.
   c. Administrative costs are $20,625 for televisions and $3,375 for clock radios.

Required
a. You are to prepare segmented income statements first by territory and then by product within the Asian sales territory.
b. Describe the problem in the Asian sales territory and how you would advise solving it.

10–29 **Preparation of a Segmented Income Statement and Analysis of Results**

An absorption-costing income statement for 19x7 is shown below for the Garrin Drug Company. The Garrin Drug Company sells aspirin and cough syrup in two sales territories—northwest and northeast.

GARRIN DRUG COMPANY
Absorption-Costing Income Statement
For the Year Ended December 31, 19x7

	Total	North-west	North-east
Sales	$470,000	$240,000	$230,000
Cost of goods sold	320,270	171,135	149,135
Gross margin	149,730	68,865	80,865
Marketing and administrative			
costs	146,630	76,765	69,865
Operating income (loss) before			
income taxes	$ 3,100	$ (7,900)	$ 11,000

A company manager notices the loss in the northwest territory and orders an investigation of that territory to determine whether it should be eliminated. You are provided with the following information:

1. Sales by product and variable costs:

	Aspirin	Cough Syrup
Sales	$320,000	$150,000
Ratio of variable manufacturing		
costs to sales	45%	64%
Ratio of variable marketing		
costs to sales	8%	3%

2. Sales of product by region:

Product	Northwest	Northeast
Aspirin	$140,000	$180,000
Cough syrup	100,000	50,000
Total	$240,000	$230,000

3. The total fixed manufacturing overhead amounts to $80,270 of which $37,210 is direct to the northwest region, $29,210 is direct to the northeast region, and the balance is common and allocated 50 percent to each region.

4. The total fixed marketing costs amount to $58,580 of which $22,040 is direct to the northwest region, $24,290 is direct to the northeast region, and the balance is common and allocated 50 percent to each region.

5. The total fixed administrative costs amount to $57,950 of which $30,025 is direct to the northwest region, $19,175 is direct to the northeast region, and the balance is common and allocated 50 percent to each region.

Required

a. Prepare a segmented contribution income statement showing segment margin by territory for the Garrin Drug Company.

b. Do you recommend eliminating the northwest territory which is operating under a loss? Support your conclusion.

10–30   **Preparation of Segmented Income Statement and Analysis of Results**

The Bobbin Company's segmented income statement by territory for 19x5 is shown below.

BOBBIN COMPANY
Segmented Income Statement—Contribution Format
For the Year Ended December 31, 19x5

	Total	European	Domestic
Sales	$450,000	$157,500	$292,500
Variable cost of goods sold	202,500	70,850	131,650
Contribution margin	247,500	86,650	160,850
Less: Direct fixed overhead and other costs:			
Fixed overhead	70,000	40,000	30,000
Marketing costs	66,000	23,000	43,000
Administrative costs	50,000	37,500	12,500
Total direct fixed costs	186,000	100,500	85,500
Territorial segment margin	61,500	$ (13,850)	$ 75,350
Less: Indirect fixed overhead and other costs (common costs):			
Fixed overhead	15,000		
Marketing costs	12,000		
Administrative costs	17,000		
Total common costs	44,000		
Operating income before income taxes	$ 17,500		

The Bobbin Company produces two items—sewing machines and calculators. The company's president wants to study the loss incurred by the European sales territory. An investigation of company records reveals the following:

1. In the European territory, $100,000 of total sales are traceable to calculators. The contribution margin ratios are:

    Calculators 51%
    Sewing machines 62%

2. In the European territory, $35,000 of the total fixed overhead is traceable to direct fixed overhead and the remainder to common fixed overhead. Of the $35,000 direct fixed overhead, $19,000 is traceable to sewing machines and the remainder to calculators. In addition, $20,500 of the total fixed marketing costs are direct fixed costs and $15,500 of these are traceable to sewing machines. Finally, $34,000 of the total administrative costs are direct costs and $26,500 of these are traceable to sewing machines.

Required   *a.* Prepare a segmented income statement by product within the European territory for the company president.

b. Discuss any problems that you find in the European territory. Make recommendations to the company's president that you feel would be useful in correcting the existing problems.

10–31   Preparation of Segmented Income Statements

The Justa Corporation produces and sells three products. The three products, A, B, and C, are sold in a local market and in a regional market. At the end of the first quarter of the current year, the following income statement has been prepared:

	Total	Local	Regional
Sales	$1,300,000	$1,000,000	$300,000
Cost of goods sold	1,010,000	775,000	235,000
Gross margin	290,000	225,000	65,000
Marketing costs	105,000	60,000	45,000
Administrative costs	52,000	40,000	12,000
	157,000	100,000	57,000
Net income	$ 133,000	$ 125,000	$ 8,000

Management has expressed special concern with the regional market because of the extremely poor return on sales. This market was entered a year ago because of excess capacity. It was originally believed that the return on sales would improve with time, but after a year no noticeable improvement can be seen from the results as reported in the above quarterly statement.

In attempting to decide whether to eliminate the regional market, the following information has been gathered:

	Products		
	A	B	C
Sales	$500,000	$400,000	$400,000
Variable manufacturing costs as a percentage of sales	60%	70%	60%
Variable marketing costs as a percentage of sales	3%	2%	2%

Sales by Markets

Product	Local	Regional
A	$400,000	$100,000
B	300,000	100,000
C	300,000	100,000

All administrative costs and fixed manufacturing costs are common to the three products, and the two markets and are fixed for the period. Remaining marketing costs are fixed for the period and separable by market. All fixed costs are based upon a prorated yearly amount.

Required

a. Prepare the quarterly income statement showing contribution margins by markets.

b. Assuming there are no alternative uses for the Justa Corporation's present capacity, would you recommend dropping the regional market? Why or why not?

c. Prepare the quarterly income statement showing contribution margins by products.

(CMA adapted)

10–32   Preparation of Segmented Income Statement

Pralina Products Company is a regional firm which has three major product lines—cereals, breakfast bars, and dog food. The income statement for the year ended April 30, 19x8, is shown below; the statement was prepared by product line using absorption (full) costing.

PRALINA PRODUCTS COMPANY
Income Statement
For the Year Ended April 30, 19x8
(in thousands)

	Cereals	Breakfast Bars	Dog Food	Total
Sales in pounds	2,000	500	500	3,000
Revenue from sales	$1,000	$400	$200	$1,600
Cost of sales:				
Raw materials	330	160	100	590
Direct labor	90	40	20	150
Factory overhead	108	48	24	180
Total cost of sales	528	248	144	920
Gross margin	472	152	56	680
Operating costs:				
Marketing costs:				
Advertising	50	30	20	100
Commissions	50	40	20	110
Salaries and related benefits	30	20	10	60
Total marketing costs	130	90	50	270
General and administrative costs:				
Licenses	50	20	15	85
Salaries and related benefits	60	25	15	100
Total general and administrative costs	110	45	30	185
Total operating costs	240	135	80	455
Operating income before taxes	$ 232	$ 17	$ (24)	$ 225

Other Data

1. *Cost of sales.* The company's inventories of raw materials and finished products do not vary significantly from year to year. The inventories at April 30, 19x8, were essentially identical to those at April 30, 19x7.

   Factory overhead was applied to products at 120 percent of direct labor dollars. The factory overhead costs for the 19x7–x8 fiscal year were as follows:

Variable indirect labor and supplies	$ 15,000
Variable employee benefits on factory labor	30,000
Supervisory salaries and related benefits	35,000
Plant occupancy costs	100,000
	$180,000

   There was no overapplied or underapplied overhead at year-end.

2. *Advertising.* The company has been unable to determine any direct causal relationship between the level of sales volume and the level of advertising expenditures. However, because management believes advertising is necessary, an annual advertising program is implemented for each product line. Each product line is advertised independently of the others.

3. *Commissions.* Sales commissions are paid to the sales force at the rates of 5 percent on the cereals and 10 percent on the breakfast bars and dog food.

4. *Licenses.* Various licenses are required for each product line. These are renewed annually for each product line.

5. *Salaries and related benefits.* Sales and general and administrative personnel devote time and effort to all product lines. Their salaries and wages are allocated on the basis of management's estimates of time spent on each product line.

Required   The president of the company is concerned about the loss shown by the dog food product line. She is wondering whether or not to discontinue the product line. The controller of Pralina Products Company has recommended that the company do a cost-volume-profit (CVP) analysis of its operations. As a first step, the controller has requested that you prepare a revised income statement for Pralina Products Company that employs a product contribution margin format which will be useful in CVP analysis. The statement should show the profit contribution for each product line and the income before taxes for the company as a whole.

   Should the product line be discontinued? Explain.

   (CMA adapted)

10–33   Preparation of Segmented Income Statement and Discussion of the Results

The Nanuet Publishing Company is concerned about its poor profit performance. In an attempt to pinpoint problem areas, the company's president asked the firm's CPA to prepare a territorial segmented income statement. A copy of the statement appears below.

NANUET PUBLISHING COMPANY
Segmented Income Statement—Absorption Costing
For the Year Ended December 31, 19x3

	Total	Northeast	Southeast	West
Sales	$900,000	$300,000	$200,000	$400,000
Cost of goods sold	180,000	60,000	40,000	80,000
Gross margin	720,000	240,000	160,000	320,000
Marketing and administrative costs:				
Commissions	45,000	15,000	10,000	20,000
Salaries	120,000	50,000	30,000	40,000
Utilities	13,000	5,000	4,000	4,000
Occupancy	55,000	20,000	15,000	20,000
Advertising	150,000	50,000	40,000	60,000
Administrative	300,000	120,000	120,000	60,000
Total marketing and administrative costs	683,000	260,000	219,000	204,000
Operating income before income taxes	$ 37,000	$ (20,000)	$ (59,000)	$116,000

After reviewing the segmented income statement, the president is concerned about the losses shown in the northeast and southeast territories. His son is taking a managerial accounting course in college and just studied contribution format income statements. The father showed the segmented income statement to his son and the son suggested that a contribution format income statement be prepared before a decision is reached regarding the territories showing losses.

The company engages contractors for the production of its books. Typesetting, printing, and binding are considered variable costs and the costs of goods sold are all variable.

The following information is also available:

1. Commissions, salaries, utilities, and occupancy costs are all direct territorial costs.
2. Advertising costs consist of the following:

	Northeast	Southeast	West
Direct cost	$35,000	$30,000	$40,000
General advertising—allocated	15,000	10,000	20,000
Total	$50,000	$40,000	$60,000

3. Administrative costs consist of the following:

	Northeast	Southeast	West
Direct cost	$ 90,000	$ 90,000	$30,000
Allocated cost	30,000	30,000	30,000
Total	$120,000	$120,000	$60,000

Required   *a.* Prepare a segmented income statement using the contribution format showing segment margins.
b. Should the northeast territory be discontinued? Explain.
c. Should the southeast territory be discontinued? Explain.
d. Discuss the usefulness of segmented income statements which contain common costs allocated to individual segments.

10–34   Preparation of Segmented Income Statements

The Klug Corporation produces and sells three products. The three products, A, B, and C, are sold in two markets—east and west. At the end of the first year, the following income statement has been prepared:

	Total	East	West
Sales	$1,750,000	$1,300,000	$450,000
Cost of goods sold	1,075,000	760,000	315,000
Gross margin	675,000	540,000	135,000
Marketing costs	128,500	80,000	48,500
Administrative costs	270,000	150,000	120,000
Total marketing and administrative costs	398,500	230,000	168,500
Operating income (loss) before taxes	$ 276,500	$ 310,000	$ (33,500)

Management has expressed concern with the west market because of the loss of $33,500.

In attempting to decide whether to eliminate the west market, the following information has been gathered:

	Products		
	A	B	C
Sales	$800,000	$650,000	$300,000
Variable manufacturing costs as a percentage of sales	40%	50%	60%
Variable marketing costs as a percentage of sales	5%	3%	4%

Sales by Markets

Product	East	West
A	$600,000	$200,000
B	500,000	150,000
C	200,000	100,000

All administrative costs and fixed manufacturing costs are common to the three products and the two markets and are fixed for the period. The fixed marketing costs are direct costs and separable by market. All fixed costs are based upon a prorated yearly amount.

Required

a. Prepare an income statement showing contribution margins and segment margins by markets.

b. Assuming there are no alternative uses for the corporation's present capacity, would you recommend dropping the west market? Why or why not?

c. Prepare an income statement showing contribution margins and segment margins by products.

10–35 Preparation of Segmented Income Statements

The Krew Corporation produces and sells three products. The three products, A, B, and C, are sold in two markets—east and west. At the end of the first year, the following income statement has been prepared:

	Total	East	West
Sales	$2,400,000	$900,000	$1,500,000
Cost of goods sold	1,460,000	540,000	920,000
Gross margin	940,000	360,000	580,000
Marketing costs	324,000	178,000	146,000
Administrative costs	450,000	200,000	250,000
Total marketing and administrative	774,000	378,000	396,000
Operating income (loss) before taxes	$ 166,000	$ (18,000)	$ 184,000

Management has expressed concern with the east market because of the loss of $18,000.

In attempting to decide whether to eliminate the east market, the following information has been gathered:

	Products		
	A	B	C
Sales	$800,000	$600,000	$1,000,000
Variable manufacturing costs as a percentage of sales	50%	35%	30%
Variable marketing costs as a percentage of sales	4%	2%	3%

Sales by Markets

Product	East	West
A	$300,000	$500,000
B	200,000	400,000
C	400,000	600,000

Direct fixed costs by market are:

	East	West
Manufacturing . . .	$140,000	$180,000
Marketing	100,000	60,000
Administrative	150,000	175,000

Administrative costs are all fixed costs.

Required *a.* Prepare an income statement showing contribution margins and segment margins by markets.

b. Assuming there are no alternative uses for the corporation's present capacity, would you recommend dropping the east market? Why or why not?

c. Prepare an income statement showing contribution margins and segment margins by products.

11

SELECTING RELEVANT DATA FOR DECISION MAKING

A significant portion of a manager's time is spent on decision making. When a firm has a sophisticated management information system, the amount of information available to its managers is almost infinite. Thus, managers must be selective in requesting specific kinds of information if they wish to avoid being inundated in a sea of data. The key to limiting the flow of data is to request only relevant information.

Different decisions require different types of data. An important part of any decision is its cost. Most of us are constantly faced with decisions about items and their costs that run the gamut from what to purchase in a supermarket to which brand of automobile to buy. Managers are often faced with a variety of decisions that rely on cost data, such as whether to (1) purchase new equipment, (2) replace existing equipment, (3) enter a market with a new product, (4) take special orders at less than full cost, (5) make or buy component parts, and (6) sell multiple products from a common raw material at the split-off point or process them further. In addition, cost information is needed for (7) product-pricing decisions and (8) the allocation of scarce resources to particular products. To arrive at correct decisions, managers need certain cost and revenue information referred to as relevant costs and relevant revenues.

RELEVANT DATA

In the decision-making process, any cost that differs among alternatives and will influence the outcome is a **relevant cost.** Similarly, a **relevant revenue** is any revenue that differs among alternatives and will influence the final outcome. Since a decision applies to future actions, relevant costs are *future costs* rather than *historical costs.* Of course, historical costs may be used to estimate future costs, but the pertinent costs are still future costs even if they are the same as last year's historical costs. (Note: In Chapter 2, we discussed a variety of basic cost concepts and terms. Because many of those terms and concepts are used in this chapter, readers may wish to refer to Chapter 2 to refresh their memories.)

Irrelevant Costs

Before proceeding to the selection and identification of relevant costs, it is useful to identify the **irrelevant costs** that will not affect the decision. They fall into two main groups:

1. Sunk costs.
2. Costs that are the same for each alternative.

Sunk Costs. A **sunk cost** is a cost that has already been incurred and that cannot be changed by any future action. Thus, except for its effect on the amount of income taxes that a firm will pay, a sunk cost cannot affect the decision-making process. For example, if a firm purchases a special-purpose machine for $50,000, this is a sunk cost that will not affect any future decisions regarding the machine. If the machine has a 10-year useful life and after one year of use a new, more efficient machine is available at a cost of $60,000, the decision of whether or not to purchase the newer machine should be based on the cost savings of the newer machine compared to its net cost ($60,000 minus the sales proceeds from selling the older machine). Both the original cost of the machine ($50,000) and its current book value (the original cost of the machine minus any depreciation) are sunk costs and will not affect the decision except for any tax savings that a tax-deductible loss may bring.

Future Costs that Are the Same for Each Alternative.   When deciding among two alternatives, the difference in their costs must be considered. However, if the costs are the same, they may be ignored *provided that it has already been decided that one of the alternatives will be selected.* For example, if a decision *has already been made* to purchase one of two new cars and their costs are the same, the choice will be based on each car's reputation, features, styling, etc., and *not on its price.* However, if a decision is to be made about whether or not to purchase a new car, then price will obviously play an important role.

Using Costs in Decision Making

As noted in Chapter 6, two different approaches may be used to solve problems for decision-making purposes. The comprehensive comparative income approach includes both relevant and irrelevant costs, while the simpler differential analysis includes only relevant costs. When the **comparative income approach** is used, the net operating income for each alternative is computed and compared. All revenues and costs are considered—even those that are the same for each alternative. On the other hand, in **differential analysis,** only revenues and costs that differ among the alternatives are considered. The end result—a correct decision—will be the same regardless of which method is used.

Sentimentality and financial accounting conventions should never be allowed to cloud the reasoning behind a decision. Many of us have heard someone state that while his shares of X Corporation stock have declined in market value, he has not incurred a loss because he has not sold the shares. Managers should not use this type of reasoning. The cost of the shares is a *sunk cost,* and while the failure to sell an investment may postpone the recognition of a loss on a firm's financial statements (a bookkeeping convention), the decision to retain an investment must be based on what *the market value is today* and what the future cash inflows are likely to be. If a larger profit can be made by holding the investment instead of selling it and reinvesting the proceeds, then retention is indicated.

Another way of viewing this decision is to realize that whenever a manager decides not to sell an investment, a decision is really being made to reinvest in the same investment. Thus, the criterion for retention should be the same as overt investment—a comparison of current cost (not the sunk cost) with the expected future cash inflows. Too often managers are concerned with the book value of an existing investment in a product, machine, etc., and its effects on the firm's income statement when a loss must be recognized for financial accounting purposes. Instead, managers should recognize that it may be to the firm's advantage—and eventually to the manager's advantage—to bite the bullet now in favor of a new product, machine, etc., that will enhance future profits more than will the immediate write-off of book values. Book values should not color a manager's thinking or decision making despite their use in calculating gains and losses for financial accounting purposes.

Once a manager recognizes which costs are not relevant for decision-making purposes, he or she is ready to begin analyzing data.

IDENTIFYING RELEVANT DATA FOR SPECIFIC DECISIONS

The selection of relevant data—revenues and costs—will depend on the kind of decision to be made. Although all eight kinds of decisions mentioned at the beginning of this chapter have a common thread, the data needed to arrive at the correct decision for each varies to some degree. We will now examine these decisions one by one, focusing on the information that is relevant to each. To simplify our discussion, we will defer income tax considerations to Chapter 13 and the time value of money (interest) to Chapters 12 and 13.

Purchasing New Equipment

The data that are relevant to the purchase of new equipment that will not replace existing equipment are simpler to identify than the relevant data for other kinds of decisions. The process entails identifying the *net cash inflows* and the *net cash outflows* for the useful life of the equipment and then comparing the two. The net cash outflows may be grouped and referred to as the *net investment,* which consists of (1) the cash purchase price of the machine, (2) the cost of insurance during shipment from the vendor, and (3) freight in.

The cash inflows are grouped together and referred to as the cash operating advantage. The **cash operating advantage** is the cash effect of the difference in revenues minus the cash effect of the difference in cash operating costs as a result of a contemplated change in a firm's operations. In this case, the change in operations is the purchase of a new machine. The decision of whether or not to purchase the machine is then based on a comparison of the net investment with the cash operating advantage for the useful life of the machine.

The Automated Manufacturing Company is contemplating the purchase of a piece of sophisticated machinery. The following information is available:

| Purchase price of new machine . . . . | $90,000 |
| Useful life of machine . . . . | 5 years |
| Salvage value at the end |
| of five years . . . . | $ 5,000 |

Annual Operating Information

	With New Machine	Without New Machine
Sales	$500,000	$500,000
Direct materials cost	95,000	100,000
Direct labor	46,000	60,000
Variable overhead	32,200	42,000
Fixed overhead	100,000	100,000
Depreciation	17,000	–0–

The differential analysis of the relevant data may be organized as shown in Illustration 11–1.

Ignoring income taxes and the time value of money, the purchase of the new machine appears to be a favorable investment. A net cash outflow of $85,000 will result in a cash inflow of $144,000 over the five-year period. The fixed overhead of $100,000 was ignored in this calculation because it would be unchanged by the decision and is thus an irrelevant cost.

The depreciation of $17,000 is also ignored because the recording of *depreci-*

ILLUSTRATION 11–1

AUTOMATED MANUFACTURING COMPANY
Calculation of Net Investment and Cash Operating Advantage
For the Purchase of a New Machine
Differential Income Approach

Net investment:	
Purchase price of machine	$ 90,000
Less: Salvage value	5,000
Net investment	$ 85,000
Cash operating advantage:	
Savings in direct materials cost	
($100,000 − $95,000)	$ 5,000
Savings in direct labor cost	
($60,000 − $46,000)	14,000
Savings in variable overhead	
($42,000 − $32,200)	9,800
Cash operating advantage—	
one year	28,800
Useful life of machine	× 5
Cash operating advantage—	
five years	$144,000

ation is a bookkeeping convention that *has no effect on cash* when taxes are ignored, as can be seen from the following entry:

Depreciation 17,000
    Accumulated Depreciation 17,000
    ($90,000 − $5,000 salvage = $85,000 ÷ 5 years).

The investment decision should be based on the cash effects of the decision over the estimated life of the machine. The cash effects over the five years may be summarized as follows:

	Cash Inflow (Outflow)
Savings in variable costs ($28,800 × 5)—also the cash operating advantage	$144,000
Cost of machine	(90,000)
Salvage value at the end of five years	5,000
Net cash inflow for five years	$ 59,000

When differential analysis is used, as above, depreciation is ignored because the focus is on *cash flows.* The investment decision is based on the difference between the net cash inflows and the net cash outflows.

The decision of whether to replace an existing machine with a newer, more efficient machine is similar to the decision of whether to purchase a new machine except that additional relevant data must be considered.

Replacing Existing Equipment

The relevant data needed for a decision to replace existing equipment is similar to that for purchasing a new machine except that the sales value of the old machine must be considered. Although the sales value of the old equipment is a cash inflow, it is customarily shown as a reduction of the investment to arrive at the net investment.

The Mature Products Company is contemplating the replacement of one of its present machines with a faster machine. The older machine is nearing the end of its economic useful life, but its life can be extended by a major overhaul. The available information is shown in Illustration 11–2.

Care must be taken to select only the data that are relevant to the decision. As noted for the purchase of new equipment, depreciation is not relevant. And when considering replacement, the book value of the old equipment is not relevant either. This can be seen by comparing Illustration 11–3, which indicates the net income for each alternative (old machine versus new machine), with Illustration 11–4, which is prepared on a net cash flow basis.

ILLUSTRATION 11–2

MATURE PRODUCTS COMPANY
Machine Replacement Data

Original cost of the present machine . . . . $ 40,000
    Less: Accumulated depreciation   30,000
Book value . . . . $ 10,000

Purchase price of new machine $100,000
Useful life of new machine . . . . 5 years
Remaining useful life of old machine . . . . 2 years
Overhaul of old machine extending its
    useful life to a total of five years . . . . $ 10,000
Salvage value of new machine . . . . –0–
Market value of old machine, if sold . . . . . $ 4,000

	Old Machine	New Machine
Annual operating information:		
Sales	$400,000	$400,000
Direct materials cost	90,000	90,000
Direct labor cost	80,000	60,000
Variable overhead	48,000	36,000
Fixed overhead exclusive of		
depreciation	100,000	100,000
Depreciation:		
Old machine—2 years at		
$5,000 per year	10,000	
New machine—5 years at		
$20,000 per year		100,000

After comparing Illustration 11–3 with Illustration 11–4 you should conclude that the following items are not relevant when the differential analysis is used:

1. *Sales revenue* because it is the same for both alternatives.

2. *Direct materials* because it is the same for both alternatives.

3. *Fixed overhead* because it is the same for both alternatives.

4. *Depreciation of the old machine* because it is a sunk cost that has no effect on cash flow.

From Illustration 11–4, it can be seen that only the following items are relevant:

1. *The purchase price of the new machine* because it is a cash outflow.

2. *The sales proceeds from the sale of the old machine* because it is a cash inflow.

3. *The savings in direct labor costs and variable overhead* because these costs would differ if the new machine were purchased.

ILLUSTRATION 11-3

MATURE PRODUCTS COMPANY
Comparative Income Statements for
Retaining Old Machine or Purchasing New Machine
For the Five-Year Useful Life of the New Machine

	Keep Old Machine	Purchase New Machine	Effect on Net Income— Increase (Decrease)
Sales revenue (5 × $400,000)	$2,000,000	$2,000,000	$ –0–
Costs:			
Direct materials			
(5 × $90,000)	450,000	450,000	–0–
Direct labor			
(5 × $80,000; 5 × $60,000)	400,000	300,000	100,000
Variable overhead			
(5 × $48,000; 5 × $36,000) . . .	240,000	180,000	60,000
Fixed overhead			
(5 × $100,000)	500,000	500,000	–0–
Depreciation: Old machine (2 ×			
$5,000); new machine (5 × $20,000)	10,000	100,000	(90,000)
Overhaul of old machine	10,000	–0–	10,000
Total costs	1,610,000	1,530,000	
Operating income	390,000	470,000	
Other income or (loss):			
Sales proceeds from			
old machine		4,000	4,000
Book value of old machine		(10,000)	(10,000)
Loss on sale of old			
machine		(6,000)	
Income before income tax	$ 390,000	$ 464,000	$ 74,000

ILLUSTRATION 11-4

MATURE PRODUCTS COMPANY
Analysis of Decision to Retain
Old Machine or Replace with New Machine
For the Five-Year Useful Life of the New Machine
Differential Income Approach

Net investment:		
Purchase price of new machine		$100,000
Less: Sales proceeds from		
old machine		4,000
Net investment		96,000
Cash operating advantage:		
Direct labor savings	$100,000	
Variable overhead savings	60,000	
Old machine overhaul		
savings	10,000	170,000
Net cash advantage in favor		
of replacing old machine		$ 74,000

4.   *The cost of overhauling the old machine* because this represents the avoidance of a cash outflow (equivalent to a cash inflow).

Entering a Market with a New Product

When deciding whether to introduce a new product, a firm must consider several other relevant costs in addition to those already discussed. These usually include advertising, incremental marketing costs, salespersons' commissions, and incremental administrative costs. Furthermore, the company must consider the amount of working capital that will be tied up in inventories and accounts receivable since this cash will not be available for other uses until the end of the product's life, perhaps in the far distant future. Even when the end of a product's life is foreseeable, the working capital released at its termination may differ from that invested due to losses on obsolete merchandise or the bargain sale of merchandise remaining on hand.

The Physico Company plans to enter the physical fitness market with a treadmill for gymnasium and home use. Based on a market survey and cost estimates provided by the firm's engineering and accounting departments, Physico's accounting department compiled the information shown in Illustration 11–5.

The analysis of the relevant data for deciding whether to enter the new market may be organized as shown in Illustration 11–6.

Ignoring income taxes and the time value of money, the decision favors entering the new market because a net investment of $930,000 should bring

ILLUSTRATION 11–5

PHYSICO COMPANY
Data for Entering a New Market

Sales: 10,000 at $250 each	$2,500,000
Incremental costs:	
Direct materials (10,000 at $60)	$ 600,000
Direct labor (10,000 at $50)	$ 500,000
Variable overhead (10,000 at $38)	$ 380,000
Fixed overhead exclusive of new	
machinery noted below	$ 400,000
Salespersons' commissions	5% of sales
Fixed marketing and administrative	
costs	$ 200,000
Purchase of machinery needed for	
manufacturing this product	$ 900,000
Useful life of machinery	10 years
Salvage value of machinery	$ 20,000
Working capital needed at inception	$ 400,000
Working capital returned at end of 10	
years when the demand for this	
product is expected to be nil	$ 350,000
Depreciation of machinery	
($1,000,000 − $20,000 =	
$980,000 × 10%) = ...	$ 98,000

ILLUSTRATION 11–6

PHYSICO COMPANY
Calculation of Cash Outflows and Cash Inflows
For Entering a New Market for the
10-Year Useful Life of the Product
Differential Income Approach

	Inflow (Outflow)
Net investment:	
Purchase price of the machinery	$ (900,000)
Salvage value of machine	20,000
Working capital at inception	(400,000)
Release of working capital at the	
end of 10 years	350,000
Net investment	$ (930,000)
Cash operating advantage:	
Sales per annum	$2,500,000
Variable costs per annum:	
Direct materials	(600,000)
Direct labor	(500,000)
Variable overhead	(380,000)
Commissions (5% × $2.5 million)	(125,000)
Fixed costs per annum:	
Manufacturing overhead	(400,000)
Marketing and administrative costs	(200,000)
Cash operating advantage per annum	295,000
Life of product	× 10
Cash operating advantage for 10 years	$2,950,000

a 10-year net cash operating inflow of $2,950,000. The depreciation of the new machine is not factored into the calculations because, as mentioned previously, it stems from a bookkeeping convention that has no effect on cash flow.

The numerous kinds of decisions a manager must make always have some relevant data in common, but each decision usually involves some relevant costs that pertain to it alone. For example, when deciding whether to accept special orders at less than full cost, managers must base their decision on some data that are not relevant when deciding whether to introduce a new product.

Accepting Special Orders at Less than Full Cost

At first glance, it may appear that accepting a special order at less than full cost can only contribute a loss to a firm's overall profitability. This is not necessarily the case. Under certain conditions, a special order at less than full cost may, in fact, increase a firm's overall profitability. The necessary conditions are:

1. The firm has some unused capacity, usually of a seasonal or temporary nature.

2. The special order is for a *segmented market that does not compete with the firm's regular sales.* The special order may be packaged under a private label that does not compete with the firm's brand name or it may be sold in a foreign market where the firm's product is not sold.

3. Although the price offered may be less than the firm's total cost per unit (including fixed costs), the price must be high enough to cover the firm's variable costs, any special costs associated with producing and shipping the special order, and some contribution margin.

The Glossy Soap Company manufactures liquid soap and markets it under its brand name. Although the firm is profitable and its product enjoys a good reputation, it is only operating at 80 percent of capacity. Glossy plans to expand into foreign markets in the future, but the unused capacity of 20 percent will not be used during the remainder of 19x3. A soap wholesaler in Mexico wishes to expand its business by marketing liquid soap, which it presently does not sell. The Mexican wholesaler has approached the Glossy Soap Company with an offer to purchase 10,000 cases of soap at a price of $20 per case.

The condensed income statement for the Glossy Soap Company appears in Illustration 11–7. The variable costs for this special order will be the same as those for the firm's normal operations. In addition, Glossy Soap will be required to ship the merchandise FOB destination at a freight charge of $1,400. The sales manager would like to assess the effects on net income of accepting the order at $20 per case even though the company's cost per case is $27 ($5 + $6 + $6 + $10).

The company's income statement with and without the special order is shown in Illustration 11–8. Note that the special order would add $20,020 of net income to the company's overall profitability, provided it does not

ILLUSTRATION 11–7

GLOSSY SOAP COMPANY
Income Statement
For the Six Months Ended June 30, 19x3

Sales (80,000 cases at $50)		$4,000,000
Cost of goods sold:		
Direct materials (80,000 cases at $5)	400,000	
Direct labor (80,000 cases at $6)	480,000	
Variable overhead (80,000 cases at $6)	480,000	
Fixed overhead (80,000 cases at $10)	800,000	2,160,000
Gross margin		1,840,000
Marketing and administrative costs—all fixed		800,000
Operating income before income taxes		1,040,000
Provision for income taxes at 30 percent		312,000
Net income		$ 728,000

ILLUSTRATION 11–8

GLOSSY SOAP COMPANY
Income Statements
Without and With a Special Order
For the Six Months Ended June 30, 19x3

	Without Order	With Order	Difference
Sales	$4,000,000	$4,200,000	$200,000[a]
Cost of goods sold:			
Direct materials	400,000	450,000	50,000[b]
Direct labor	480,000	540,000	60,000[c]
Variable overhead	480,000	540,000	60,000[d]
Fixed overhead	800,000	800,000	–0–
Total cost of goods sold	2,160,000	2,330,000	170,000
Gross margin	1,840,000	1,870,000	30,000
Marketing and administrative			
costs—all fixed	800,000	800,000	–0–
Freight out	–0–	1,400	1,400
Total marketing and			
administrative costs	800,000	801,400	1,400
Operating income before			
income taxes	1,040,000	1,068,600	28,600
Provision for income taxes			
at 30 percent	312,000	320,580	8,580
Net income	$ 728,000	$ 748,020	$ 20,020

[a] 10,000 units at $20 per unit.
[b] 10,000 units at $5 per unit.
[c] 10,000 units at $6 per unit.
[d] 10,000 units at $6 per unit.

intrude on regular sales. If the special order could compete with the firm's normal sales and if normal sales decreased by 10,000 cases, the firm's profitability would decrease by $210,980 instead of increase by $20,020. This can be seen from the following:

Normal sales (10,000 × $50)	$500,000
Special order (10,000 × $20)	200,000
Net decrease in sales revenue	300,000
Add freight out*	1,400
	301,400
Income tax at 30 percent	90,420
Decrease in net income	$210,980

* Other variable and fixed costs are unaffected since the same number of units (80,000 cases) will be produced both with and without the order.

Because of the potential danger of competition, a firm must be certain that a special order will not undermine its regular sales. If Glossy is uncertain of the effects of the special order it should probably forgo the additional net income of $20,020 and not risk the alternative of a $210,980 decrease in net income.

It is not necessary to compare full income statements to determine the effects of a special order. In fact, by recognizing and using only those revenues and costs that are relevant, it is possible to achieve the desired result much more efficiently. The relevant costs and revenues are those that change. Thus, the fixed overhead and the fixed marketing and administrative costs may be ignored. The analysis may be prepared as shown in Illustration 11–9.

ILLUSTRATION 11–9

GLOSSY SOAP COMPANY
Analysis of Relevant Costs and Revenues for Special Order
Differential Income Approach

Revenue (10,000 × $20)		$200,000
Less: Incremental costs:		
Direct materials (10,000 × $5)	$50,000	
Direct labor (10,000 × $6)	60,000	
Variable overhead (10,000 × $6)	60,000	
Freight out	1,400	171,400
Increase in operating income before income tax		28,600
Income tax at 30 percent		8,580
Increase in net income		$ 20,020

By concentrating only on relevant costs, Glossy's managers can focus more sharply on the items involved in the decision. The inclusion of items that have no effect on the decision may confuse the issue, especially if the original offer of $20 per case can be renegotiated or if the relevant costs (variable costs and freight out) can be altered.

Another decision that managers must often make is whether to purchase component parts from other firms or manufacture them internally. While the selection of the relevant data for taking a special order at less than full cost is very similar to the selection of relevant data for the make-or-buy decision, some additional concepts must be introduced.

Making or Buying Component Parts

The make-or-buy decision cannot be reduced to mere quantitative factors. While quantitative considerations are important and may be the deciding factor, a manager would be remiss if he or she failed to also weigh the relevant qualitative factors. Among the qualitative considerations that must be evaluated are:

1. The supplier's reliability. An interruption in the delivery of a component part may totally shut down a firm's operations.

2. The supplier's quality control. A defective component part may damage the reputation and reliability of the firm's product.

3. The supplier's labor-management relations. Frequent or wildcat strikes may produce an erratic delivery schedule.

4. Whether a supplier's low price (an order for less than full cost) is stable. A low price may be available only for the period of a supplier's idle capacity and prices may increase at a later date. A contract for a long period of time (one to two years) may help to avoid this problem.

5. How long it would take to start manufacturing the part again if the supplier fails to deliver as promised. Retraining and rehiring of personnel may be an important consideration.

The quantitative relevant costs are the purchase price versus the component part's variable and direct fixed costs. However, it may also be necessary to consider the opportunity cost of any plant capacity that can be converted to an alternative use if it is released from manufacturing the component part. For example, freed plant capacity may be used to manufacture a new product or expand production of an existing product, or it may be sublet to another firm. In any case, the income that could be earned from any of these alternatives is an opportunity cost and must be factored into the quantitative analysis.

The Electric Motor Company manufactures electric motors for use in machinery. Although it currently manufactures its own armatures, it is considering purchasing them from a vendor. The armatures can be purchased from a reliable vendor for a two-year period at a price of $20 each. The firm's standard cost sheet for the armature is:

Direct materials	$ 6
Direct labor	5
Variable overhead	4
Fixed overhead	10
Total	$25

An analysis of the fixed overhead indicates that $3 is direct fixed overhead and $7 is common fixed overhead. The company uses 30,000 armatures per annum. If it decides to purchase the armatures, it can sublet the part of its plant where the armatures are now manufactured for $30,000 a year.

The cost analysis may be organized as follows:

Avoidable Costs	Cost per Unit	Annual Usage	Total
Direct materials	$6	30,000	$180,000
Direct labor	5	30,000	150,000
Variable overhead	4	30,000	120,000
Direct fixed overhead	3	30,000	90,000
Out-of-pocket costs to make			540,000
Add opportunity cost:			
Rental income forgone when armatures are manufactured			30,000
Total costs to make			570,000
Deduct: Purchase of part (30,000 × $20)			600,000
Advantage of making the part			$ 30,000

If the company can use the vacated premises for another purpose, the decision may differ. For example, if a new product can be manufactured in place of the armature and if the firm is able to earn a segment margin of $100,000 a year on the new product, the decision would be in favor of buying:

Out-of-pocket costs to make	$540,000
Add opportunity cost:	
Segment margin on new product forgone when armatures are manufactured	100,000
Total cost to make	640,000
Deduct: Purchase of part (30,000 × $20)	600,000
Advantage of buying the part	$ 40,000

Therefore, it can be seen how important it is that a manager understand how to select all the costs that are relevant to a decision about whether to make or buy component parts. These relevant costs are usually all of the variable costs, the direct fixed costs, and any opportunity costs that can be identified, using the greatest amount of forgone income from the alternatives available. Common fixed costs that continue when the part is purchased are ignored.

Thus far, we have seen that there is much overlapping of relevant costs and revenues among the kinds of decisions that managers must make. The decision of whether to sell a product from a common raw material at its split-off point or to process it further is no exception. However, when making this kind of decision, an additional concept of relevance must be examined.

Joint Product Decisions

Often a firm manufactures several different products from the same raw material. For example, an oil refinery may process crude petroleum into

ILLUSTRATION 11–10   Relationships between Joint Products and Their Costs

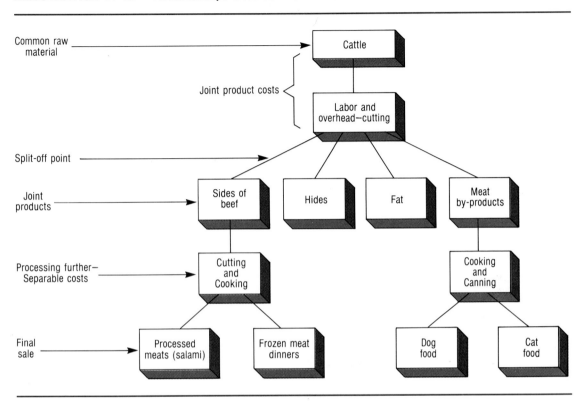

gasoline and petrolatum. Such products, produced from a common input and a common production process, are called **joint products.** The point in the production process at which the joint products are separated is known as the **split-off point.** At the split-off point, a product may either be sold or be treated to further processing. The costs of acquiring and processing a common raw material up to the split-off point are **joint product costs,** while the costs of further processing after the split-off point are **separable costs.** The relationships among joint products and their costs at a beef-processing plant are shown in Illustration 11–10.

At the split-off point, management must often decide whether it is more advantageous to sell the joint products as is or process them further. When such a choice is available, managers must be familiar with the relevant cost and revenue data in order to reach a correct conclusion.

Allocated Costs and Decision Making.   Income statements and balance sheets cannot be prepared without valuing inventories at a dollar amount. Thus, when joint products are on hand at the end of an accounting period, some value must be assigned to them. To do so, joint product costs must be allocated to specific units of inventory.

The use of allocated costs for inventory valuation should not be confused with their use for decision making, however. For example, if a furniture manufacturer cuts lumber into the parts used in its production process, it is bound to have ends and other pieces of wood left over. These leftover pieces can be further processed into sawdust for use as sweeping compound. Let us assume that the cost of such further processing is $4 per bag and that the compound can be sold for $10 per bag. The accountants for the firm determine that the allocated cost of the leftover lumber, using a cost per board foot basis, amounts to $7 per bag. If the total of the allocated cost per bag plus the additional processing cost per bag—or $11—were used for decision making, management would elect to throw the leftover pieces away because a loss per bag would be predicted as follows:

		Per Bag
Selling price		$10
Costs:		
Allocated cost	$7	
Additional processing	4	11
Loss		$ (1)

Such a decision process would be faulty, however, because the allocated cost of the leftovers is a sunk cost and is thus irrelevant. The proper analysis, using relevant data, is:

	Per Bag
Selling price	$10
Less: Additional processing cost	4
Profit	$ 6

Sell at Split-Off Point or Process Further. The relevant data for a sell-at-split-off-point-or-process-further decision are the additional revenue earned by further processing and the separable costs.

For example, the Rink Company uses a common raw material R that has a joint product cost of $16,000 and yields 6,000 pounds of product X selling for $3.00 per pound and 4,000 pounds of product Y selling for $3.50 per pound. Product X can be processed further at an additional cost of $8,000, and product Y can be processed further at an additional cost of $6,000. The new products, XP and YP, can then be sold for $4 and $6 per pound, respectively. The relevant data needed for the decision may be summarized and analyzed as follows:

Product XP:

Sales revenue (6,000 × $4.00)	$24,000
Less: Sales value at split-off point	
(6,000 × $3.00)	18,000
Additional sales revenue	6,000
Less: Separable costs	8,000
(Loss) on processing further	$ (2,000)

Product YP:

Sales revenue (4,000 × $6.00)	$24,000
Less: Sales value at split-off point	
(4,000 × $3.50)	14,000
Additional sales revenue	10,000
Less: Separable costs	6,000
Advantage of processing further . . .	$ 4,000

From this analysis, a manager would correctly conclude that product X should be sold at the split-off point and product Y should be processed into product YP. The joint product cost of $16,000 should not be used to reach this decision. Rather, the analysis should be limited to the difference between the incremental revenue and the incremental (separable) cost.

Pricing Decisions

Another important decision is the determination of the best price for a product. While a pricing decision must include consideration of competitive market factors, it must also be based on future relevant costs to avoid long-run profitability and survival problems.

In some industries, firms must price their products to compete with the prices already established by others in the market. Examples are the agriculture industry, in which farmers either price their products at the established market prices or they do not produce, and the automobile industry, in which a price leader sets the price and others must follow if they wish to participate in the market. Members of such industries must concentrate on their costs to be sure they can earn a reasonable profit, or else they must leave the market.

In contrast, firms that have some control over the prices they can charge may use various strategies and pricing policies. While firms vary considerably in their pricing techniques, some of the more popular approaches are (1) skimming, (2) market penetration, (3) markup pricing, (4) target-return pricing, (5) demand-related pricing, and (6) competition-based pricing.

1. Skimming. Certain kinds of products such as new electric appliances, toys, games, and home computers lend themselves to a pricing strategy known as **skimming the market.** When a firm decides to skim the market, it initially sets the price of a new product quite high so that it will attract only a small number of consumers. The company then gradually lowers the price to eventually capture more and more of the market. This pricing strategy provides manufacturers with a cushion against high risk when introducing a new product. By setting a higher than normal initial price, they can more quickly recover a greater portion of their start-up costs. Then, if the product is successful and they want to expand production, they systematically lower the price to attract more consumers. As a result, the firm will earn a higher revenue for the same number of units sold while limiting demand to match its production capabilities.

A skimming strategy is most effective when it is difficult for competitors to enter the market—as when a company holds the patent on some crucial technology. But when it is easy to enter the market, competitors will be attracted by the potential profits, and the higher than normal price will be difficult to maintain.

Skimming the market has been used many times. For example, consider the *original* prices of instant cameras, calculators, electronic typewriters, and videocassette recorders and compare them to their prices today.

2. Market Penetration. When it is very easy to enter a market, a firm may prefer to penetrate the market rather than skim it. In **market-penetration** pricing, a company sets the initial price of a new product low enough to immediately capture a large share of the market. A firm may also prefer penetration pricing when it believes that entering a market at $4 and lowering the price to $2 a month or two later may not enhance the firm's image in the marketplace. In such a case, the firm may wish to penetrate the market with the $2 price per unit at the outset. This might be especially true for firms that have a very high fixed cost with a low variable cost. If the company can penetrate the market with a high volume and a low price, the fixed cost per unit will decrease rapidly, and overall profitability will increase *because of the large sales volume.* Of course, it should be remembered that fixed costs are constant and are therefore not relevant. The larger sales volume, however, is relevant.

3. Markup Pricing. In **markup pricing,** a predetermined percentage is included in a product's cost to cover the seller's operating costs, income taxes, and a reasonable profit. For example, a women's clothing store may set a 100 percent markup on the dresses it sells. Thus, if the shop pays $60 for a dress, it will resell it for $120, with the $60 markup going to cover operating costs, income taxes, and profit. The amount added is usually a percentage of either the item's cost to the seller or its final selling price. This is referred to as the *markup percentage.* When using this approach, managers must be careful to specify whether the markup percentage is based on cost or selling price, since the results are quite different. A markup percentage based on cost is simple to compute. For example, if a dress shop owner wishes to use a markup of 75 percent based on cost, the calculation would be:

```
Cost of dress  . . . . . . . . . . . .   $ 60
Markup on cost—75 percent  . . . .      45
Selling price  . . . . . . . . . . .   $105
```

On the other hand, if the markup of 75 percent is based on selling price, the calculation is:

```
Selling price . . . .  100%
Markup   . . . . . .    75%
Cost  . . . . . . .     25%
```

Therefore:

$$\frac{\$60 \text{ cost}}{.25} = \$240$$

or

$$\$60 \times 4 = \$240$$

Proof:

		Percent
Selling price	$240	100
Cost	60	25
Markup (gross margin)	$180	75

Most retailers use a markup percentage based on cost—a method known as **cost-plus pricing.** The term *cost-plus pricing* is used to distinguish markup pricing based on cost from markup pricing based on selling price.

Manufacturers who wish to use markup pricing face an additional problem. Before the markup percentage can be computed, the base cost must be determined. Some firms use absorption, or full, costing while others use variable costing.

Absorption Costing. When a manufacturing firm uses markup pricing, managers must clearly understand which costs are included in the cost base and which costs are to be recovered in the markup percentage. If a firm uses absorption costing, then direct materials, direct labor, variable overhead, and fixed overhead are included in the cost base, and the markup percentage should include amounts for variable and fixed marketing and administrative costs, income taxes, and profit.

The Morson Company plans to manufacture cabinets for which it wishes to establish a selling price. The standard cost sheet for the product is:

```
Direct materials  —10 board feet of oak at $0.95 per board foot . . . . . . . . .   $ 9.50
Direct labor      —4 hours at $7.00 per hour  . . . . . . . . . . . . . . . . . . . .    28.00
Variable overhead—4 hours at $4.00 per hour  . . . . . . . . . . . . . . . . . . .    16.00
Fixed overhead    —4 hours at $6.00 per hour  . . . . . . . . . . . . . . . . . . . .    24.00
   Total standard cost . . . . . . . . . . . . . . . . . . . . . . . . . . . . . . . . . .   $77.50
```

The fixed overhead of $24 is based on an annual volume of 10,000 units, or 40,000 hours of direct labor. In addition, variable marketing costs are 5 percent of sales, fixed marketing costs are $100,000, administrative costs are $150,000, income taxes are 40 percent of operating income before income taxes, and a profit after income taxes of $240,000 is desired. The markup percentage on cost may be computed as follows:

Step 1

Convert the desired profit after income taxes to a before-tax amount:

$$\$240,000 \div (1 - \text{Tax rate}) =$$
$$\$240,000 \div (1 - .4) \quad =$$
$$\$240,000 \div .6 \quad\quad = \$400,000$$

Step 2

Add all the fixed costs plus the before-tax profit to the total product costs for the year:

Fixed marketing costs	$ 100,000
Fixed administrative costs	150,000
Profit before income taxes	400,000
Subtotal	650,000
Product costs (10,000 × $77.50)	775,000
Total	$1,425,000

Step 3

Compute the sales volume by dividing the total in step 2 by (1 − Variable marketing cost percentage):

$$\$1,425,000 \div (1 - .05) =$$
$$\$1,425,000 \div .95 \quad = \$1,500,000$$

Step 4

Compute the unit selling price:

$$\$1,500,000 \div 10,000 \text{ units} = \$150 \text{ per unit}$$

Step 5

Compute the markup percentage on cost:

$$\$150.00 - \$77.50 = \$72.50 \text{ markup}$$

$$\text{Markup percentage} = \frac{\$\text{Markup}}{\$\text{Product cost}} = \frac{\$72.50}{\$77.50} = .9355 = 93.55\% \text{ rounded}$$

The percentage may be used as follows:

Standard product cost	$ 77.50
Markup (93.55% × $77.50)	72.50
Selling price	$150.00

The proof of the selling price would be:

Sales (10,000 at $150)	$1,500,000
Cost of goods sold (10,000 × $77.50)	775,000
Gross margin	725,000
Marketing and administrative costs:	
Variable marketing (5% × $1,500,000)	75,000
Fixed marketing	100,000
Fixed administrative	150,000
Total marketing and administrative costs	325,000
Operating income before income taxes	400,000
Income taxes at 40 percent	160,000
Net income	$ 240,000

Variable Costing. If the Morson Company used variable costing instead of absorption costing, the procedure for computing a markup percentage would be:

Step 1

Compute the firm's variable manufacturing costs:

Direct materials	$ 9.50 × 10,000 =	$ 95,000
Direct labor	28.00 × 10,000 =	280,000
Variable overhead	16.00 × 10,000 =	160,000
Total	$53.50	$535,000

Step 2

Compute the firm's fixed costs:

Manufacturing overhead (10,000 × $24)	$240,000
Marketing costs	100,000
Administrative costs	150,000
Total fixed costs	$490,000

Step 3

Convert the after-tax desired net income of $240,000 to before-tax operating income:

(See step 1 for absorption costing)	$400,000

Step 4

Combine the amounts computed in steps 1, 2, and 3:

($535,000 + $490,000 + $400,000)	$1,425,000

Step 5

Compute the selling price per unit:

(See steps 3 and 4 for absorption costing) . . . . . $150 per unit

Step 6

Compute the markup percentage:

$$\$150.00 - \$53.50 = \$96.50 \text{ markup}$$

$$\text{Markup percentage} = \frac{\$96.50}{\$53.50} = 1.8037 = 180.37\%$$

The proof of the percentage and its use is:

Variable manufacturing costs	$ 53.50
Markup (180.37% × $53.50)	96.50
Selling price	$150.00

Although the selling price is the same for both accounting systems, the markup percentages are different because the starting points—product costs—are different.

A close relative of markup pricing is target-return pricing.

4. Target-Return Pricing.   **Target-return pricing** bases price on a specified return on investment (ROI) in place of the desired dollar profit used in markup pricing. Thus, in place of the $240,000 of net income used in the previous example, a predetermined ROI is employed. A problem arises with the term *investment,* however. Investment may be either *net* assets (assets minus liabilities) or *total* assets (without deductions for liabilities). In practice, each firm chooses its preferred definition, but the definition must be clearly stated if ROI-based pricing is to be used effectively.

If the Morson Company requires a 12 percent after-tax ROI instead of the $240,000 profit after taxes stated earlier, and if the ROI is to be based on net assets of $2 million, the computations would be:

Step 1

Convert the after-tax ROI to a before-tax rate:

$$\text{Before-tax ROI} = \frac{\text{After-tax ROI}}{(1 - \text{Tax rate})} = \frac{12\%}{(1 - .40)} = 20\%$$

Step 2

Multiply the before-tax rate by the assets (total or net, as indicated) employed:

$2,000,000 \times 20\% = \$400,000$ targeted income before income taxes

The remaining steps are the same as those noted for markup pricing.

Some firms apply target-return pricing to short intervals and adjust their prices often to reflect changes in costs and net assets. Others, like General Motors, use long-term pricing and attempt to keep their prices stable for long periods, such as a year or more. When long-term target pricing is used, the firm focuses on the average long-term ROI, even while the short-term ROIs may not reflect the desired returns.

5. Demand-Oriented Pricing. Firms such as restaurants and hotels may charge different prices for the same item in response to changes in demand. For example, a hotel usually charges more for rooms and meals during its busy season than it does during its off-season. Similarly, the same restaurant meal may cost more at dinner than it does at lunch. The practice of pricing a firm's product by using a higher price when the demand is high and a lower price when demand is low is known as **demand-oriented pricing.**

Manufacturers who use this form of pricing must be careful not to violate the Robinson-Patman Act, however. The act prohibits price discrimination among *the same class of customers* (all lunch-time diners, all wholesalers, all retailers) unless it can be justified by cost differentials. Cost differentials must be found among the marketing and administrative costs and *not* in manufacturing costs. Thus, a manufacturer cannot charge one customer for full manufacturing costs including overhead and charge another customer *in the same class* for only direct materials and labor.

6. Competition-Based Pricing. When a firm uses a **competition-based pricing** strategy, it prices a product to compete with a competitor's price and then assesses whether or not the product can be manufactured at a cost that will yield a satisfactory profit. The price may be the same as the competitor's or it might be slightly higher or lower. When competition-based pricing is used, a firm may not be able to realize its normal markup or target-return percentage. In such a case, the firm must decide if it is preferable (1) not to enter the market, (2) to cut the cost of the product, if possible, so that the normal percentage may be realized, or (3) to settle for less than the normal percentage with a view toward later revaluating its decision to enter the market.

The Starlight Company would like to enter the market with a solid brass lamp that other companies sell for $90. For competitive purposes, Starlight also wants to price the lamp at $90. Marketing and administrative costs are each expected to amount to $100,000 at a volume of 15,000 per year, and the company would like a 20 percent before-tax ROI on its investment in net assets amounting to $2 million. The calculations to assess the amount available for manufacturing costs are:

Estimated sales (15,000 × $90)		$1,350,000
Less:		
Marketing and administrative costs		
($100,000 + $100,000)	$200,000	
ROI (20% × $2 million)	400,000	600,000
Amount available for manufacturing costs		$ 750,000

Per unit amount = $750,000 ÷ 15,000 units = $50 per unit

The engineering, accounting, and purchasing departments must now determine if the product can be made for $50 per unit. If not, the firm must decide whether to forgo entering the market, cut the cost of manufacturing, or accept a lower ROI.

In many cases, managers face pricing decisions without constraints. In other cases, there may be alternative products competing for scarce resources such as capital, material, and labor. Then, in addition to pricing, managers must decide how to allocate scarce resources to particular products in ways that maximize the company's objectives.

Allocating Scarce Resources

Sometimes due to scarce resources, a firm must select one product or several products to emphasize while downplaying other products. When one of the firm's goals is to maximize profits, linear programming or mathematical models may be used to reach an optimal solution. However, when it is simply a matter of choosing the best way to allocate resources, the decision maker may use a less complex technique based on the contribution margin per limiting factor. The **contribution margin per limiting factor** is the contribution margin per unit of a firm's product expressed in terms of a production-limiting factor, such as available machine-hours or direct labor-hours. With this approach, management determines the contribution margin per limiting factor for each of their products and selects the product(s) with the highest contribution margin as the one(s) to produce.

The Shamrin Company manufactures two products. Their selling prices and variable costs are:

		Product A		Product B
Selling price per unit		$20		$10
Variable costs:				
Direct materials	$2		$2	
Direct labor	4		1	
Variable overhead	3		2	
Variable marketing costs	1	10	1	6
Contribution margin		$10		$ 4

If the firm has no production-limiting factors, the firm should produce *both A and B* to the extent that they *can be sold* in the marketplace.

On the other hand, if the number of units that can be produced is limited, managers must decide which product(s) to produce and in what amount(s). Production limitations may relate to (1) labor-hours of capacity for a labor-intensive product, (2) machine-hours of capacity for a machine-intensive product, or (3) units of raw materials available from suppliers. These limiting factors are referred to as **constraints.** It is possible for production to be limited by more than one constraint.

If product A requires 1 hour of direct labor and product B requires ¼ hour of direct labor, and the Shamrin Company has only 100,000 hours of direct labor capacity available, management must decide how many of each product to produce. The firm estimates that it can sell 100,000 units of product A and 200,000 units of product B for the coming year without changing their selling prices.

Normally, a firm should choose to emphasize the product with the largest contribution margin. In this case, at $10 per unit, product A has the larger contribution margin. However, a manager should compute the contribution margin per limiting factor, in this case direct labor-hours, in order to make the appropriate decision. The computations are:

	Product A	Product B
Contribution margin per unit	$10	$ 4
Contribution margin per direct labor-hour:		
Product A ($10 ÷ 1 hour)	$10	
Product B ($ 4 ÷ ¼ hour)		$16

The results indicate that it is possible to produce four units of product B for every unit of product A. Thus, product B can earn $16 in the same amount of direct labor time as product A earns $10. For this reason, product B should be emphasized over product A. The capacities of production may be calculated as follows:

Capacity of product A:

100,000 ÷ 1 direct labor-hour = 100,000 units

Capacity of product B:

100,000 ÷ ¼ direct labor-hour = 400,000 units

The contribution margins at the limits of production and sales are:

Produce and sell at product A's limit:	
Production and market limitation of 100,000 units at $10 contribution margin	$1,000,000
Produce and sell at product B's limit:	
Market limitation of 200,000 units at $4 contribution margin	$ 800,000

Balance of production capacity assigned to product A:

Total direct labor-hour capacity	100,000 hours
Less: Used by product B (200,000 × ¼ hour)	50,000 hours
Balance available	50,000 hours

Sales or product A:

50,000 hours ÷ 1 hour = 50,000 units × $10 contribution margin	500,000
Total contribution margin	$1,300,000

From this analysis, it can be seen that producing 200,000 units of product B and 50,000 units of product A will cause the firm's contribution margin to be $300,000 ($1,300,000 − $1,000,000) greater than if the firm produced only 100,000 units of product A.

RECAPITULATION

A recapitulation of the kinds of decisions managers make and the relevant data needed to arrive at correct conclusions appears in Illustration 11–11.

ILLUSTRATION 11–11   Managerial Decisions and Corresponding Relevant Data

Kind of Decision	Relevant Data Needed
1. Purchasing new labor-saving equipment.	Cost of equipment; salvage value; useful life of machine; *changes in* sales, direct material costs, direct labor costs, variable overhead, fixed overhead; and cost of repairs to new machine.
2. Replacing old equipment with newer equipment.	Cost of new equipment; useful life of new equipment; remaining life of old equipment; salvage value of new equipment; present resale value of old equipment; needed repairs to old equipment; repairs to new equipment; *changes in* sales, direct material costs, direct labor costs, variable overhead, and fixed overhead.
3. Entering a new market with a new product.	Cost of equipment; salvage value, useful life of project; investment of working capital; release of working capital; anticipated sales revenue, direct material costs, direct labor costs, variable overhead, fixed overhead, marketing, and administrative costs.

ILLUSTRATION 11–11   (*continued*)

Kind of Decision	Relevant Data Needed
4. Taking an order at less than full cost.	The effect on the company's regular sales volume, the price offered, the variable costs of producing the order, the incremental costs incurred as a result of taking the order.
5. Making or buying component parts.	Qualitative considerations such as supplier's reliability, supplier's quality control, supplier's labor problems, supplier's price stability, and start-up costs to renew making the component. Quantitative considerations, including cost per unit to manufacture for direct materials, direct labor, variable overhead, total direct fixed overhead, the purchase price from the vendor, the annual usage, and the opportunity cost of the resources used to manufacture the component.
6. Selling products from a common raw material at the split-off point or processing further.	The difference in revenue between selling the product at the split-off point and at the end of additional processing compared with the costs of additional processing.
7. Pricing: *a.* Skimming.	The variable cost to manufacture the product, the elasticity of the product's demand function.
b. Market penetration.	Same as for skimming.
c. Markup pricing.	For merchandisers—the cost of a product and its markup percentage. For manufacturers—either the variable cost to manufacture or the full, absorption cost to manufacture and the respective markup percentages for each.
d. Target-return pricing.	The desired return on investment, whether to use net assets or total assets, and the firm's tax rate. The remainder of the information needed is the same as for markup pricing.
e. Demand-oriented pricing.	Demand patterns over time periods, such as seasons, special hours, or special days (weekend or weekdays); elasticity of demand functions for each pattern; variable cost of product or service.
f. Competition-based pricing.	The competitor's price, the desired profit, marketing and administrative costs, and costs to manufacture.
8. Allocating scarce resources to particular products.	A limiting factor, such as direct labor-hours, machine-hours, or direct materials; contribution margin per unit; and contribution margin per limiting factor.

ILLUSTRATION 11–11   (*concluded*)

Kind of Decision	Relevant Data Needed
9. Cost-volume-profit.	Present variable costs, fixed costs, sales revenues and proposed variable costs, fixed costs, and sales revenues. (See Chapter 6.)
10. Discontinuing a product or segment.	The product's or segment's sales revenues, variable costs, direct fixed costs, and allocated common costs. (See Chapter 10.)

SUMMARY

As part of their decision-making responsibilities, managers have access to large amounts of data. To simplify the decision-making process, managers must decide which data are relevant. **Relevant costs** and **relevant revenues** are those costs and revenues that differ among alternatives and will influence the outcome of the decision-making process. Since decision making is future oriented, relevant data consist of future costs and revenues. Past costs, called **sunk costs,** do not affect the outcomes of decisions to be made and are therefore **irrelevant costs,** as are all other costs and revenues that will remain unchanged among the alternatives being considered.

Different decisions require different relevant data. Thus, managers must be familiar with the most common kinds of business decisions and the specific data needed for each. The required data depend on whether the decision maker will use (1) **differential analysis,** in which only the differences in cash flows among the alternatives are considered, or (2) the **comprehensive comparative income approach,** in which all costs and revenues are considered.

The decisions most often made by managers are (1) whether to purchase new labor-saving equipment, (2) whether to replace existing equipment with newer equipment, (3) whether to introduce a new product, (4) whether to take a special order at less than full cost, (5) whether to make or buy component parts, (6) whether to sell joint products at the split-off point or to process them further, (7) what prices to charge for the firm's products, and (8) how to allocate scarce resources to particular products. The selection of the relevant data needed for each of these decisions is the key to reaching a correct conclusion.

A manager most often examines **cash operating advantage** when deciding whether to purchase a new machine, replace an existing machine, or introduce a new product. When considering the acceptance of a special order at less than full cost, a manager must analyze overall profitability both with the order and without. The decision of whether to make or buy component parts hinges on the price at which the parts can be made compared to the costs that can be avoided by purchasing them. The opportunity cost of the space used to make the parts must also be factored into the calculation.

Managers must often decide whether to sell **joint products** at their **split-off point** or process them further. The costs of the common raw material and processing up to the split-off point are **joint product costs,** while the costs of additional processing after the split-off point are **separable costs.** To decide whether further processing is desirable, the decision maker must compare the product's separable costs with the increased revenue that will result from additional processing.

Businesses use a variety of pricing strategies. Among the most common are **skimming, market-penetration pricing, markup pricing** (one form of which is **cost-plus pricing**), **target-return pricing, demand-oriented pricing,** and **competition-based pricing.** When pricing a product, decision makers must consider competitive market factors as well as future relevant costs to avoid long-run profitability and survival problems.

When a firm has limited capacity or materials, it should allocate its resources to yield the optimum contribution margin. One means of accomplishing this is to emphasize those products which have the highest **contribution margin per limiting factor.** A limiting factor is called a **constraint.**

GLOSSARY OF KEY TERMS

Cash operating advantage The cash effect of the difference in revenues minus the cash effect of the difference in cash operating costs as a result of a contemplated change in a firm's operations.

Comparative income approach A method of assessing the effect on profit of a contemplated change in operations in which the net operating income for each alternative is computed and compared. All revenues and costs are considered—even those that are the same for each alternative.

Competition-based pricing Pricing a product to compete with a competitor's price and then assessing whether or not the product can be manufactured at a cost that will yield a satisfactory profit.

Constraint A limiting factor, such as available machine-hours, available direct labor-hours, or available materials, that limits the amount of production.

Contribution margin per limiting factor The contribution margin per unit of a firm's product expressed in terms of a production-limiting factor, such as available machine-hours or available direct labor-hours.

Cost-plus pricing A form of markup pricing in which a predetermined percentage of a product's cost is included in its selling price to cover the seller's operating costs, income taxes, and a reasonable profit.

Demand-oriented pricing Pricing a product by using a higher price when demand is high and a lower price when the demand is low.

Differential analysis A method of assessing the effect on profit of a contemplated change in operations. Only revenues and costs that differ among the alternatives are considered.

Irrelevant costs Costs that do not affect a decision to be made, such as sunk costs and costs that are the same for each alternative under consideration.

Joint product Two or more products produced from a common raw material and a common production process.

Joint product costs   The costs of acquiring and processing a single raw material up to the split-off point of the joint products.

Market-penetration pricing   Setting the initial price of a new product low enough to immediately capture a large share of the market.

Markup pricing   The inclusion of a predetermined percentage in a product's price to cover the seller's operating costs, income taxes, and a reasonable profit. The markup percentage may be based on either the item's cost or its final selling price.

Relevant cost   Any cost that differs among alternatives and will influence the outcome of the decision-making process.

Relevant revenue   Any revenue that differs among alternatives and will influence the outcome of the decision-making process.

Separable costs   The costs of the further processing of joint products after the split-off point.

Skimming the market   Setting the price of a product high enough to get a small share of the market initially, and then lowering the price to attract more consumers for a larger share of the market.

Split-off point   The stage in the production process at which joint products are separated.

Sunk cost   A previously incurred cost that cannot be changed by any future action.

Target-return pricing   Setting the price of a product so that a predetermined amount will be earned as a return on the investment.

QUESTIONS

1. What are relevant costs in the decision-making process? Use examples to illustrate them.

2. What are irrelevant costs in the decision-making process? Use examples to illustrate them.

3. What is the differential income approach to decision making? What are its advantages?

4. What is the comparative income approach to decision making? What are its advantages and disadvantages?

5. Are variable costs always relevant costs? Explain.

6. Are fixed costs always irrelevant costs? Explain.

7. Identify the relevant costs needed to reach a decision regarding the purchase of new equipment.

8. What is the cash operating advantage? How is it used?

9. Identify the relevant costs needed to reach a decision on whether to replace existing equipment. Is the needed information the same as that needed for purchasing new equipment? Explain.

10. Name the relevant costs for entering a new market.

11. Is it possible for a firm to increase its net income by sometimes accepting an order at a price less than its full cost? Explain.

12. What does the make-or-buy decision consist of? What are the relevant costs for this kind of decision?

13. What is an opportunity cost? For what kinds of decisions is it relevant? Explain.

14. What is a common raw material? A joint product cost?

15. Are allocated joint product costs useful? If so, for what purposes? If not, explain.

16. What information is needed for the process-further-or-sell-at-split-off-point decision? Are allocated joint product costs useful for this decision? Explain.

17. Firms often use different pricing strategies. Name some of these pricing strategies and indicate the relevant information needed to implement them.

18. Linear programming is often used to solve complex scarce resource allocation problems. However, simpler allocation problems may be solved without using linear programming. How may this be accomplished? Under what conditions may this method be used?

EXERCISES **11–1** **Purchasing a New Machine and Replacing an Existing Machine**

The Montana Corporation is presently using a machine, M–1, in its production process. It is contemplating the purchase of a newer, more efficient machine, M–2. The following information is available:

	M–1	M–2
Purchase price	$500,000	$1,000,000
Useful life	15 years	10 years
Salvage value	$ 50,000	$ 80,000
Accumulated depreciation ($450,000 ÷ 15 years =		
$30,000); $30,000 × 5 years =	$150,000	–0–
Depreciation per annum	$ 30,000	$ 92,000
Sales revenue	$500,000	$ 600,000
Direct materials cost	90,000	108,000
Direct labor	150,000	130,000
Variable overhead	90,000	78,000
Fixed overhead	70,000	90,000

Income taxes and the time value of money are to be ignored.

Required *a.* Assume that the Montana Corporation is contemplating the purchase of M–2 and intends to keep M–1 also. There is a sufficient market for the firm's output from both machines. Prepare schedules to compute:
   (1) The net investment of M–2.
   (2) The cash operating advantage of M–2 for the 10-year life of the machine.
   (3) The net cash flow for the 10-year period.

b. Assume that market conditions are such that the corporation can sell the output from M–2 or M–1, but not both. Thus, if M–2 is purchased, M–1 will be sold for $100,000. Using differential analysis, prepare schedules to compute:
   (1) The net investment of M–2.
   (2) The cash operating advantage of M–2 for the 10-year life of the machine.
   (3) The net cash flow for the 10-year period. Should M–2 be purchased?

11-2 Replacement of Equipment

The Nebraska Corporation is presently using a machine, K–1, in its production process. It is contemplating the purchase of a newer, more efficient machine, K–9. The following information is available:

	K–1	K–9
Purchase price	$65,000	$100,000
Useful life	12 years	8 years
Salavage value	$ 5,000	$ 4,000
Accumulated depreciation ($60,000 ÷ 12 years = $5,000);		
$5,000 × 8 years =	$40,000	–0–
Depreciation per annum	$ 5,000	$ 12,000
Sales revenue	$50,000	$ 60,000
Direct materials cost	10,000	12,000
Direct labor	12,000	9,000
Variable overhead	6,000	4,500
Fixed overhead	10,000	11,000
Cost to overhaul K–1 to extend its remaining life by		
four years for a total of eight years	15,000	–0–

The time value of money and income taxes are to be ignored.

Required a. Using the comparative income approach, compute the following:
  (1) The net investment of purchasing K–9.
  (2) The cash operating advantage of K–9 for the eight-year period.
  (3) The net cash flow for the eight-year period.
 b. Assume that K–1 can be sold for $30,000. Compute the following for K–1:
  (1) The net investment of K–1. (Hint: Use opportunity cost.)
  (2) The cash operating advantage of K–1 for the eight-year life of the machine.
  (3) The net cash flow for the eight-year period.
 c. Should K–9 be purchased? Why?

11-3 Entering a New Market

The Aromatic Company, which produces inexpensive automatic coffeemakers, is thinking of introducing a new line of expensive automatic coffeemakers which will both grind the coffee beans and then brew the coffee. A market survey indicates that because of its high cost, there is only a limited market for this product and estimates that after five years there will be no market at all.

The following annual information about the new product is available to you:

Estimated sales (15,000 × $50)	$750,000
Cost of direct materials and direct labor	250,000
Variable overhead	70,000
Variable marketing costs	37,500
Fixed overhead, marketing, and administrative costs	150,000

Additional information is as follows:

Price of new machinery	$750,000
Salvage value at the end of five years	10,000
Working capital needed at inception	70,000
Working capital returned at the end of five years	65,000
Depreciation of new machinery per annum	48,000

Required

a. Which of the above data is relevant to you in recommending whether it is advantageous for Aromatic to enter this new market?

b. Using relevant data only, determine if it is advantageous for Aromatic to enter this new market.

11-4 Accepting a Special Order at Less than Full Price

1. Spencer Company's regular selling price for its product is $10 per unt. Variable costs are $6 per unit. Fixed costs total $1 per unit based on 100,000 units and remain unchanged within the relevant range of 50,000 units to total capacity of 200,000 units. After sales of 80,000 units were projected for 1982, a special order was received for an additional 10,000 units. To increase its operating income by $10,000, what price per unit should Spencer charge for this special order?

   a. $ 7.
   b. $ 8.
   c. $10.
   d. $11.

2. Boyer Company manufactures basketballs. The forecasted income statement for the year before any special orders is as follows:

	Amount	Per Unit
Sales	$4,000,000	$10.00
Manufacturing cost of		
goods sold	3,200,000	8.00
Gross profit	800,000	2.00
Marketing costs	300,000	0.75
Operating income	$ 500,000	$ 1.25

Fixed costs included in the above forecasted income statement are $1.2 million in manufacturing cost of goods sold and $100,000 in marketing costs.

A special order offering to buy 50,000 basketballs for $7.50 each was made to Boyer. There will be no addditional marketing costs if the special order is accepted. Assuming Boyer has sufficient capacity to manufacture 50,000 more basketballs, by what amount would operating income be increased or decreased as a result of accepting the special order?

   a. $25,000 decrease.
   b. $62,500 decrease.
   c. $100,000 increase.
   d. $125,000 increase.

3. Argus Company, a manufacturer of lamps, budgeted sales of 400,000 lamps at $20 per unit for 19x0. Variable manufacturing costs were budgeted at $8 per unit and fixed manufacturing costs at $5 per unit. A special order offering to

buy 40,000 lamps for $11.50 each was received by Argus in April 19x0. Argus has sufficient plant capacity to manufacture the additional quantity of lamps; however, the production would have to be done by the present work force on an overtime basis at an estimated additional cost of $1.50 per lamp. Argus will not incur any marketing costs as a result of the special order. What would be the effect on operating income if the special order could be accepted without affecting normal sales?

a. $60,000 decrease.
b. $80,000 increase.
c. $120,000 decrease.
d. $140,000 increase.

(AICPA adapted)

11–5 Accepting a Special Order at Less than Full Price

1. Relay Corporation manufactures batons. Relay can manufacture 300,000 batons a year at a variable cost of $750,000 and a fixed cost of $450,000. Based on Relay's predictions, 240,000 batons will be sold at the regular price of $5 each. In addition, a special order was placed for 60,000 batons to be sold at a 40 percent discount off the regular price. By what amount would income before income taxes be increased or decreased as a result of the special order?

a. $60,000 decrease.
b. $30,000 increase.
c. $36,000 increase.
d. $180,000 increase.

2. Brike Company, which manufactures robes, has enough idle capacity available to accept a special order of 10,000 robes at $8 a robe. A predicted income statement for the year without this special order is as follows:

	Per Unit	Total
Sales	$12.50	$1,250,000
Manufacturing costs, variable	6.25	625,000
Manufacturing costs, fixed	1.75	175,000
Manufacturing costs, total	8.00	800,000
Gross profit	4.50	450,000
Marketing costs, variable	1.80	180,000
Marketing costs, fixed	1.45	145,000
Marketing costs, total	3.25	325,000
Operating income	$ 1.25	$ 125,000

Assuming no additional marketing costs, what would be the effect on operating income if the special order was accepted?

a. $8,000 increase.
b. $17,500 increase.
c. $32,500 decrease.
d. $40,000 increase.

3. Woody Company, which manufactures sneakers, has enough idle capacity available to accept a special order of 20,000 pairs of sneakers at $6 a pair. The normal

selling price is $10 a pair. Variable manufacturing costs are $4.50 a pair, and fixed manufacturing costs are $1.50 a pair. Woody will not incur any marketing costs as a result of the special order. What would the effect on operating income be if the special order could be accepted without affecting normal sales?

a. $0
b. $30,000 increase.
c. $90,000 increase.
d. $120,000 increase.

4. Wagner Company sells product A at a selling price of $21 per unit. Wagner's cost per unit based on the full capacity of 200,000 units is as follows:

Direct materials	$ 4
Direct labor	5
Overhead (two thirds of which is fixed)	6
Total	$15

A special order offering to buy 20,000 units was received from a foreign distributor. The only marketing costs that would be incurred on this order would be $3 per unit for shipping. Wagner has sufficient existing capacity to manufacture the additional units. In negotiating a price for the special order, Wagner should consider that the minimum selling price per unit should be

a. $14.
b. $15.
c. $16.
d. $18.

(AICPA adapted)

11–6 Accepting an Order at Less than Full Cost

The Fancy Cosmetics Company produces and sells in the United States an antichapping lip liner that also prevents lipstick from smearing. The demand for this product is much higher in the winter, and there are times that the company could produce more than it sells. An Icelandic Company has approached Fancy, offering to buy 15,000 cases of lip liners which it will sell under its own name. While Fancy sells its lip liners at $6 per case in the United States, the Icelandic Company has offered to pay $3 per case and has agreed to take shipment whenever Fancy has the unused capacity to produce the lip liners.

The following information is available to you:

Cost of direct materials	$ 50,000
Cost of direct labor	$ 75,000
Variable overhead	$ 45,000
Fixed overhead	$ 80,000
Fixed marketing and administrative costs	$100,000
Freight out to Iceland	$ 1,500
Annual sales in units	100,000

Required   a. In determining whether to recommend the acceptance of this order, which items would be relevant to your decision? Should the order be accepted? Why?

b. If instead of being sold to the Icelandic firm these lip liners were to be sold to a firm in the United States that would compete with Fancy, would the items considered relevant be different? Explain. Your answer should include consideration of qualitative matters, if they are appropriate for reaching this decision.

11-7 Accepting an Order at Less than Full Cost

The Mason Company manufactures one product—toolboxes—and is operating at 60 percent of its normal capacity. It sells the toolboxes at $10 each. An income statement for the first six months of 19x5 is as follows:

MASON COMPANY
Income Statement
For the Six Months Ended June 30, 19x5

Sales (60,000 at $10)		$600,000
Cost of goods sold:		
Direct materials (60,000 at $2.00)	$120,000	
Direct labor (60,000 at $3.00)	180,000	
Variable overhead (60,000 at $0.50)	30,000	
Fixed overhead (60,000 at $1.50)	90,000	420,000
Gross margin		180,000
Marketing and administrative costs—		
all fixed		80,000
Operating income before income taxes		$100,000

A major retailer has offered to purchase 40,000 toolboxes modified to the retailer's specifications. The toolboxes will be significantly different from Mason's design, and the retailer will market the toolboxes under its own private label. Thus, these toolboxes will not compete with Mason's regular toolboxes.

The retailer has offered Mason $5.50 per toolbox. Direct labor and overhead will be at the same unit cost as Mason's regular toolboxes. Direct materials will amount to $1.50 per unit. Shipping costs, to be borne by Mason will amount to 10 cents per unit.

Required a. Should Mason accept the order for the remainder of 19x5? Why?

b. Prepare a projected income statement for the remaining six months of 19x5 assuming that Mason accepts the order and that the sales and costs of the regular toolboxes are the same as for the first six months.

11-8 Make-or-Buy Decision

1. Buck Company manufactures Part No. 1700 for use in its production cycle. The costs per unit for 5,000 units of Part No. 1700 are as follows:

Direct materials	$ 2
Direct labor	12
Variable overhead	5
Fixed overhead applied	7
Total	$26

Hollow Company has offered to sell Buck 5,000 units of Part No. 1700 for $27 per unit. If Buck accepts the offer, some of the facilities presently used to manufacture Part No. 1700 could be used to help with the manufacture of Part No. 1211 and thus save $40,000 in relevant costs in the manufacture of Part No. 1211, and $3 per unit of the fixed overhead applied to Part No. 1700 would be totally eliminated. By what amount would net relevant costs be increased or decreased if Buck accepts Hollow's offer?

a. $35,000 decrease.
b. $20,000 decrease.
c. $15,000 decrease.
d. $5,000 increase.

2. Kingston Company needs 10,000 units of a certain part to be used in its production cycle. The following information is available:

Cost to Kingston to make the part:

Direct materials	$ 6
Direct labor	24
Variable overhead	12
Fixed overhead applied	15
Total	$57
Cost to buy the part from Utica Company	$53

If Kingston buys the part from Utica instead of making it, Kingston could not use the released facilities in another manufacturing activity. Sixty percent of the fixed overhead applied will continue regardless of what decision is made.

In deciding whether to make or buy the part, the total relevant costs to make the part are

a. $342,000.
b. $480,000.
c. $530,000.
d. $570,000.

3. Motor Company manufactures 10,000 units of Part M–1 for use in its production annually. The following costs are reported:

Direct materials	$ 20,000
Direct labor	55,000
Variable overhead	45,000
Fixed overhead	70,000
Total	$190,000

Valve Company has offered to sell Motor 10,000 units of Part M–1 for $18 per unit. If Motor accepts the offer, some of the facilities presently used to manufacture Part M–1 could be rented to a third party at an annual rental of $15,000. Additionally, $4 per unit of the fixed overhead applied to Part M–1 would be totally eliminated. Should Motor accept Valve's offer, and why?

a. No, because it would be $5,000 cheaper to make the part.
b. Yes, because it would be $10,000 cheaper to buy the part.
c. No, because it would be $15,000 cheaper to make the part.
d. Yes, because it would be $25,000 cheaper to buy the part.

(AICPA adapted)

11–9 Make-or-Buy Decision

1. Plainfield Company manufactures part G for use in its production cycle. The costs per unit for 10,000 units of part G are as follows:

Direct materials	$ 3
Direct labor	15
Variable overhead	6
Fixed overhead	8
Total	$32

Verona Company has offered to sell Plainfield 10,000 units of part G for $30 per unit. If Plainfield accepts Verona's offer, the released facilities could be used to save $45,000 in relevant costs in the manufacture of part H. In addition, $5 per unit of the fixed overhead applied to part G would be totally eliminated. What alternative is more desirable and by what amount is it more desirable?

	Alternative	Amount
a.	Manufacture	$10,000
b.	Manufacture	$15,000
c.	Buy	$35,000
d.	Buy	$65,000

2. Golden, Inc., has been manufacturing 5,000 units of part 10541 which is used in the manufacture of one of its products. At this level of production, the cost per unit of manufacturing part 10541 is as follows:

Direct materials	$ 2
Direct labor	8
Variable overhead	4
Fixed overhead applied	6
Total	$20

Brown Company has offered to sell Golden 5,000 units of part 10541 for $19 a unit. Golden has determined that it could use the facilities presently used to manufacture part 10541 to manufacture product RAC and generate an operating profit of $4,000. Golden has also determined that two thirds of the fixed overhead applied will continue even if part 10541 is purchased from Brown. To determine whether to accept Brown's offer, the net relevant costs to Golden are

a. $70,000.
b. $80,000.
c. $90,000.
d. $95,000.

3. The Reno Company manufactures Part No. 498 for use in its production cycle. The cost per unit for 20,000 units of Part No. 498 are as follows:

Direct materials	$ 6
Direct labor	30
Variable overhead	12
Fixed overhead applied	16
Total	$64

The Tray Company has offered to sell 20,000 units of Part No. 498 to Reno for $60 per unit. Reno will make the decision to buy the part from Tray if there is a savings of $25,000 for Reno. If Reno accepts Tray's offer, $9 per unit of the fixed overhead applied would be totally eliminated. Furthermore, Reno has determined that the released facilities could be used to save relevant costs in the manufacture of Part No. 575. In order to have a savings of $25,000, the amount of relevant costs that would be saved by using the released facilities in the manufacture of Part No. 575 would have to be

a. $ 80,000.
b. $ 85,000.
c. $125,000.
d. $140,000.

(AICPA adapted)

11–10   Make-or-Buy Decision

The management accountant of the Met Company prepared the following summary of costs for Part No. 170, used in the manufacture of an only product:

Direct materials	$ 40,000
Direct labor	160,000
Variable overhead	60,000
Direct fixed overhead:	
Supervisory salaries	40,000
Depreciation of equipment	30,000
Common fixed overhead—allocated	100,000
Total	$430,000

The firm uses 10,000 units of Part No. 170 each year. The Cascade Company offered to supply Part No. 170 to the Met Company at a cost of $33 per unit.

The depreciation of $30,000 per annum is on special-purpose equipment that cannot be used for any other purpose except to manufacture Part No. 170. The equipment has no resale value.

Required   a. Assume that the space used to manufacture Part No. 170 cannot be used for any other purpose, nor can it be sublet to another firm. Should the Met Company accept Cascade's offer? Why?

b. If the space could be sublet, would you recommend accepting Cascade's offer if the annual rental income is:
(1) $20,000.
(2) $30,000.
(3) $50,000.
For each answer, show your computations and give the reasons why you have taken the position you recommend.

11–11   Make-or-Buy Decision

The Distinctive Coat Company makes its own cloth-covered buttons for the coats and jackets it manufactures. It is considering purchasing these buttons from a very reliable manufacturer of buttons. If it does so, it can rent the part of the loft it would no longer need to a small dress manufacturer for $12,000 per annum. The company uses 120,000 buttons per annum. The following information is available from the standard cost sheet for the buttons:

	Per 100
Direct materials	$ 6
Direct labor	4
Variable overhead	3
Fixed overhead, direct	3
Fixed overhead, common	5
Total	$21

The button manufacturer has offered to make the buttons for $26 per 100 buttons, or 26 cents per button.

Required　*a.* Should the offer be accepted and why?

b. Instead of renting out the extra space, Distinctive may decide to manufacture skirts to coordinate with their jackets. These skirts would generate a segment margin of $20,000 per annum. Under these conditions, would you recommend that Distinctive stop making its own buttons? Why?

11-12 Sell at Split-Off Point or Process Further

1. Helen Corporation manufactures products W, X, Y, and Z from a joint process. Additional information is as follows:

			If Processed Further	
Product	Units Produced	Sales Value at Split-Off	Additional Costs	Sales Value
W	6,000	$ 80,000	$11,500	$ 90,000
X	5,000	60,000	6,000	70,000
Y	4,000	40,000	4,000	50,000
Z	3,000	20,000	12,500	30,000
	18,000	$200,000	$34,000	$240,000

Each product may be sold at the split-off point or processed further. The maximum amount that can be earned from further processing is:

a. $6,000.

b. $40,000.

c. $12,500.

d. $10,000.

2. Ashwood Company manufactures products F, G, and W from a joint process. Joint costs are allocated on the basis of relative sales value at split-off. Additional information for the June 19x1 production activity is as follows:

	Products			
	F	G	W	Total
Units produced	50,000	40,000	10,000	100,000
Joint costs	$252,000	$162,000	$36,000	$450,000
Sales value at split-off	$420,000	$270,000	$60,000	$750,000
Additional costs if processed further . .	$ 88,000	$ 30,000	$12,000	$130,000
Sales value if processed further	$538,000	$320,000	$78,000	$936,000

Assuming that the 10,000 units of W were processed further and sold for $78,000, what was Ashwood's gross profit on this sale?

a. $21,000.

b. $28,500.

c. $30,000.

d. $66,000.

3. Pendall Company manufactures products Dee and Eff from a joint process. Product Dee has been allocated $2,500 of total joint costs of $20,000 for the 1,000 units produced. Dee can be sold at the split-off point for $3 per unit, or it can be processed further with additional costs of $1,000 and sold for $5 per unit. If Dee is processed further and sold, the result would be

a. A break-even situation.

b. An additional gain of $1,000 from further processing.

c. An overall loss of $1,000.

d. An additional gain of $2,000 from further processing.

(AICPA adapted)

11–13   **Sell at Split-Off Point or Process Further**

Items 1 and 2 are based on the following information:

From a particular joint process, Watkins Company produces three products, X, Y, and Z. Each product may be sold at the point of split-off or processed further. Additional processing requires no special facilities, and production costs of further processing are entirely variable and traceable to the products involved. In 19x3, all three products were processed beyond split-off. Joint production costs for the year were $60,000. Sales values and costs needed to evaluate Watkins' 19x3 production policy follow:

			Additional Costs and Sales Values if Processed Further	
Product	Units Produced	Sales Values at Split-Off	Sales Values	Added Costs
X	6,000	$25,000	$42,000	$9,000
Y	4,000	41,000	45,000	7,000
Z	2,000	24,000	32,000	8,000

Joint costs are allocated to the products in proportion to the relative physical volume of output.

1. For units of Z, the unit production cost most relevant to a sell-or-process-further decision is
   a. $5.
   b. $12.
   c. $4.
   d. $9.
2. To maximize profits, Watkins should subject the following products to additional processing:
   a.   X only.
   b.   X, Y, and Z.
   c.   Y and Z only.
   d.   Z only.

(AICPA adapted)

11–14   Sell at Split-Off Point or Process Further

The Flavor Company produces three products, A, B, and C, from a joint process. Each product may be sold at the split-off point or processed further into a packaged health food. The cost of producing all three products is $56,000. The process produces 10,000 gallons each of A and B and 8,000 gallons of C. You must decide which products to sell at the split-off point and which to process further. The following information is available to you:

Product	Sales Value at Split-Off Point	Costs to Process Further	Sales Value after Processing
A	$40,000	$25,000	$80,000
B	35,000	20,000	50,000
C	25,000	15,000	45,000

Required   Which products would you recommend that Flavor sell at the split-off point and which should Flavor process further? Show your calculations.

11–15   Pricing Decision: Skimming versus Market Penetration

The Biltmore Electronics Company plans to market a new product. The firm's marketing research department completed a marketing survey and determined that the product's demand function is:

$$Q = 10 - P$$

where

$$Q = \text{The quantity demanded (in millions)}$$
$$P = \text{Price of the product}$$

In tabular form, the demand function may appear as follows:

Price	Quantity (in millions)	Total Revenue
$10	0	$ -0-
9	1	9,000,000
8	2	16,000,000
7	3	21,000,000
6	4	24,000,000
5	5	25,000,000
4	6	24,000,000
3	7	21,000,000

The variable cost of the product is $3 per unit, and there are no incremental fixed costs associated with the product.

The firm believes that the maximum number of units that can be sold is 7 million units.

Biltmore does not believe its image will be affected if it uses a skimming-the-market pricing policy. On the other hand, it is also considering a market penetration pricing policy.

Required   a.   If Biltmore wishes to penetrate the market, what price should it charge? Why?
           b.   If instead of penetrating the market the firm wishes to maximize its income by skimming the market, what strategy would you recommend? Show your computations to justify your solution.

11–16   Pricing and Markup Percentages

The Harlan Company is in the process of setting a selling price for one of its products. The accounting department provides you with the following:

	Per Unit
Direct materials	$2
Direct labor	4
Variable overhead	1
Fixed overhead ($300,000 ÷ 100,000 units)	3
Variable marketing costs	2
Fixed marketing and administrative costs ($400,000 ÷ 100,000 units)	4

The company computed a markup percentage based on absorption costing of 110 percent. This percentage is sufficient to cover marketing and administrative costs and income tax.

Required   a.   Compute the selling price if the markup percentage is to be based on absorption costing.
           b.   Compute the markup percentage if the firm wishes to base its selling price—computed in (a) above—on variable manufacturing costing.
           c.   Compute the markup percentage if the firm wishes to base its selling price—computed in (a) above—using the contribution approach. Is your answer the same as in (b) above? Why?

11-17   Computation of Markup Percentage for Pricing Products

The controller for the Sundam Corporation prepared the following standard cost sheet:

Direct materials	5 yards at $2.15 per yard	$10.75
Direct labor	3 hours at $8.00 per hour . . .	24.00
Variable overhead	3 hours at $2.00 per hour . . .	6.00
Fixed overhead	3 hours at $4.00 per hour . . .	12.00
Total		$52.75

The fixed overhead of $4 per hour is based on a volume of 120,000 hours per annum. Variable marketing costs are 3 percent of sales, while fixed marketing and administrative costs are $300,000 per annum. The firm's income tax rate is 35 percent.

Required   *a.*   Compute the markup percentage using absorption costing if Sundam is to earn a $325,00 net income (after income tax). What selling price would produce the desired net income?

b.   Compute the markup percentage using the variable manufacturing cost approach.

c.   Compute the markup percentage using the contribution margin approach.

11-18   Target-Return Pricing

The Welsh Company wishes to earn a target return on one of its product lines. The following information is available:

Variable manufacturing costs per unit		$20
Fixed manufacturing costs per unit		
($400,000 ÷ 80,000 units)		5
Total manufacturing costs		$25
Fixed marketing and administrative costs . . .		$320,000
Investment in assets for this product line		$1,200,000
Desired rate of return		18%
Income tax rate		40%

Required   *a.*   Compute the markup percentage assuming that the firm uses absorption costing as the basis for its markup.

b.   What is the selling price? Prove that it is correct.

11-19   Target-Return Pricing

The Griffin Company wishes to earn a target return on one of its product lines. The following information is available:

Variable manufacturing costs per unit	$24
Fixed manufacturing costs per unit	
($300,000 ÷ 30,000 units)	10
Total manufacturing costs	$34
Variable marketing costs	$90,000
Fixed marketing and administrative costs . . .	$300,000
Investment in assets for this product line	$1,500,000
Desired rate of return	18%
Income tax rate	25%

Required *a.* (1) Compute the markup percentage assuming that the firm uses variable manufacturing cost as the basis for its markup.

(2) What is the selling price? Prove that it is correct.

b. Repeat *a*(1) and *a*(2) assuming that the firm uses the contribution margin approach.

11–20 Target-Return Pricing

The Yates Company is introducing a new product and wishes to earn a target return on it. The following information is available:

Variable manufacturing costs per unit	$12
Variable marketing costs per unit	$2
Fixed manufacturing costs	$500,000
Fixed marketing and administrative costs	$200,000
Investment in assets for this product	$2,000,000
Desired rate of return	15%
Income tax rate	25%

The firm is uncertain how many units can be sold each year. However, the director of marketing believes that the number of units sold will depend on the selling price. Initially, the director would like to know what the selling price would be at different levels of projected sales volume.

The firm uses a markup percentage based on absorption costing.

Required *a.* Compute the selling prices for each of the following projected sales volumes:

(1) 40,000 units.

(2) 50,000 units.

(3) 80,000 units.

b. For each of the above sales volumes, compute the markup percentage based on absorption costing.

11–21 Optimum Allocation of Scarce Resources

The Good Health Baking Company produces a salt-free whole-grain bread (B) and a carob-chip cookie (C). The demand for B and C from health food stores is exceeding Good Health's production capacity. It only has 80,000 direct labor-hours available, and a case of B requires one direct labor-hour while a case of C requires one half direct labor-hour. The company estimates that it can sell 100,000 cases of B and 50,000 cases of C in the next year.

As the production manager, you must decide what quantities of B and C to produce. You have the following information available:

	B	C
Selling price per case	$60	$30
Variable costs per case:		
Direct materials	13	4
Direct labor	8	4
Variable overhead	2	1
Variable marketing costs	2	1

Required

a. What is the contribution margin per case and per direct labor-hour for B and C?

b. Calculate how many cases of B and C the corporation should produce in the next year to achieve the maximum total contribution margin.

11–22 **Allocating Scarce Machine-Hours to Manufacturing for Optimum Cost Savings**

Items 1 and 2 are based on the following information:

Standard costs and other data for two component parts used by Griffon Electronics are presented below:

	Part A4	Part B5
Direct material	$0.40	$ 8.00
Direct labor	1.00	4.70
Factory overhead	4.00	2.00
Unit standard cost	$5.40	$14.70
Units needed per year	6,000	8,000
Machine-hours per unit	4	2
Unit cost if purchased	$5.00	$15.00

In past years, Griffon has manufactured all of its required components; however, in 19x4, only 30,000 hours of otherwise idle machine time can be devoted to the production of components. Accordingly, some of the parts must be purchased from outside suppliers. In producing parts, factory overhead is applied at $1 per standard machine-hour. Fixed capacity costs, which will not be affected by any make-or-buy decision, represent 60 percent of the applied overhead.

1. The 30,000 hours of available machine time are to be scheduled such that Griffon realizes maximum potential cost savings. The relevant unit production costs which should be considered in the decision to schedule machine time are

    a. $5.40 for A4 and $14.70 for B5.
    b. $5.00 for A4 and $15.00 for B5.
    c. $1.40 for A4 and $12.70 for B5.
    d. $3.00 for A4 and $13.50 for B5.

2. If the allocation of machine time is based upon potential cost savings per machine-hour, then Griffon should produce
    a. 3,500 units of A4 and 8,000 units of B5.
    b. 6,000 units of A4 and 8,000 units of B5.
    c. 6,000 units of A4 and 3,000 units of B5.
    d. No units of A4 and 8,000 units of B5.

(AICPA adapted)

11–23 Taking a Special Order, Further Processing, Cost-Volume-Profit Analysis, and Allocating Scarce Resources

The following data applies to item 1.

The Bodine Company produces a single product that currently sells for $5. Fixed costs are expected to amount to $60,000 for the year and all variable manufacturing and administrative costs are expected to be incurred at a rate of $3 per unit. Bodine has two salesmen who are paid strictly on a commission basis. Their commission is 10 percent of the sales dollars they generate.

1. The Sorde Company has just approached Bodine to make a special onetime purchase of 10,000 units. These units would not be sold by the salesmen, and therefore, no commission would have to be paid. The price Bodine would have to charge per unit on this special order to earn additional profit of $20,000 before taxes is
    a. $4.50 per unit.
    b. $5.00 per unit.
    c. $2.50 per unit.
    d. $5.60 per unit.
    e. Some amount other than those given above.
2. The Cum-Clean Corporation produces a variety of cleaning compunds and solutions for both industrial and household use. While most of its products are processed independently, a few are related.

    Grit 337 is a coarse cleaning powder with many industrial uses. It costs $1.60 a pound to make and has a selling price of $2.00 a pound.

    A small portion of the annual production of this product is retained for further processing in the mixing department, where it is combined with several other ingredients to form a paste which is marketed as a silver polish selling for $4 per jar. This further processing requires one fourth of a pound of Grit 337 per jar. Other ingredients, labor, and variable overhead associated with this further processing cost $2.50 per jar. Variable marketing costs amount to 30 cents per jar. If the decision were made to cease production of the silver polish, $5,600 of fixed mixing department costs could be avoided.

    The minimum number of jars of silver polish that would have to be sold to justify further processing of Grit 337 is
    a. 5,600 jars.
    b. 4,667 jars.
    c. 7,000 jars.
    d. 8,000 jars.
    e. Some amount other than those given above.

The following data apply to items 3 through 5.

Moorehead Manufacturing Company produces two products for which the following data have been tabulated. Fixed manufacturing cost is applied at a rate of $1 per machine-hour.

Per Unit	XY–7	BD–4
Selling price	$4.00	$3.00
Variable manufacturing cost . .	2.00	1.50
Fixed manufacturing cost . . .	0.75	0.20
Variable marketing cost	1.00	1.00

The sales manager has had a $160,000 increase in his budget allotment for advertising and wants to apply the money on the most profitable product. The products are not substitutes for one another in the eyes of the company's customers.

3. Suppose the sales manager chose to devote the entire $160,000 to increased advertising for XY–7. The minimum increase in *sales units* of XY–7 required to offset the increased advertising would be
   a. 640,000 units.
   b. 160,000 units.
   c. 80,000 units.
   d. 128,000 units.
   e. Some amount other than those given above.
4. Suppose the sales manager chose to devote the entire $160,000 to increased advertising for BD–4. The minimum increase in *sales dollars* of BD–4 required to offset the increased advertising would be
   a. $160,000.
   b. $320,000.
   c. $960,000.
   d. $1,600,000.
   e. Some amount other than those given above.
5. Suppose Moorehead has only 100,000 machine-hours that can be made available to produce XY–7 and BD–4. If the potential increase in sales units for either product resulting from advertising is far in excess of these production capabilities, which product should be advertised and what is the estimated increase in contribution margin earned?
   a. Product XY–7 should be produced yielding a contribution margin of $75,000.
   b. Product XY–7 should be produced yielding a contribution margin of $133,333.
   c. Product BD–4 should be produced yielding a contribution margin of $250,000.
   d. Product BD–4 should be produced yielding a contribution margin of $187,500.
   e. Some answer other than those given above.

(CMA adapted)

PROBLEMS   **11–24**   **Purchasing a New Machine and Replacing an Existing Machine**

The Oregon Corporation is presently using two machines, K–1 and K–2, in its production process. It is contemplating the purchase of an automated, more efficient machine, K–5. The following information is available:

	K-1	K-2	K-5
Purchase price	$ 50,000	$ 70,000	$150,000
Useful life	10 years	7 years	5 years
Salvage value	$ 5,000	$ 7,000	$ 15,000
Accumulated depreciation:			
K-1 ($45,000 ÷ 10 years = $4,500			
per annum × 5 years)	22,500		
K-2 ($63,000 ÷ 7 years = $9,000 per			
annum × 2 years)		18,000	
Depreciation per annum	4,500	9,000	27,000
Sales revenue	400,000	400,000	400,000
Direct materials cost	80,000	80,000	80,000
Direct labor	100,000	100,000	60,000
Variable overhead	40,000	40,000	24,000
Fixed overhead	80,000	80,000	100,000

At present, the company uses the K-2 machine as its principal machine, while the K-1 machine is only used when the K-2 is down for repairs and maintenance. Occasionally, the K-1 machine is also used when the firm is very busy and must add a special shift of employees. The K-1 and K-2 machines are similar except that the K-1 is older and better constructed. Actually, the K-1 is in better condition in some respects. At the present time, they both have the same resale value of $30,000.

The factory supervisor of the department where the machines are used asked the accounting department to furnish him with the book values of K-1 and K-2. He then prepared the following:

	K-1	K-2
Original cost	$50,000	$ 70,000
Accumulated depreciation	22,500	18,000
Book value	27,500	52,000
Resale value	30,000	30,000
Gain (loss) on sale	$ 2,500	$(22,000)

Income taxes and the time value of money are to be ignored.

Required *a.* Assume that the Oregon Corporation is contemplating the purchase of K-5 and also intends to keep both K-1 and K-2. There is a sufficient market for the firm's output from all machines. Prepare schedules to compute:
   (1) The net investment of K-5.
   (2) The cash operating advantage of K-5 for the five-year life of the machine.
   (3) The net cash flow for the five-year period.

b. Assume that market conditions are such that the corporation can sell the output from K-5 or K-2 but not both. Thus, if K-5 is purchased, either K-1 or K-2 will be sold and the one not sold will be used as a spare for K-5. Using differential analysis, prepare schedules to compute:
   (1) The net investment of K-5.
   (2) The cash operating advantage of K-5 for the five-year life of the machine.

(3)   The net cash flow for the five-year period. Should K–5 be purchased?

c.   Assume that your answer in *b*(3) is that K–5 should be purchased. The factory supervisor informs you that although K–1 is in better condition than K–2, he intends to sell K–1 because it would show a gain of $2,500 on the sale while a sale of K–2 would show a loss of $22,000, and he does not want that loss to appear on his performance report. Draft a response to his argument.

11–25   **Relevant Costs; Purchase of a New Machine**

The Happiness Corporation purchased a machine three years ago at a cost of $80,000. It had a useful life of 10 years with no salvage value and is depreciated using the straight-line method. However, it can be overhauled at a cost of $20,000 which will increase its useful life by five years.

The president has heard about a new machine which performs the same work as this machine and costs $120,000. Because it uses newer technology, it would cut direct labor costs by $5,000 a year and variable overhead by $3,000 a year.

This new machine has a useful life of 12 years and a salvage value of $15,000. If the new machine is purchased, the old machine can be sold for $30,000.

The president has asked her son, who is working with the controller for the summer, to determine whether the new machine should be purchased or the old machine overhauled. The son has prepared the following analysis:

Savings using new machine ($8,000 × 12 years)		$ 96,000
Cost of new machine:		
Price	$120,000	
Loss on old machine (Cost — Resale value —		
Depreciation)	26,000	146,000
Net disadvantage of purchasing new machine		$ (50,000)

On the basis of his analysis, the son explained to his mother that the purchase of the new machine, which looked attractive because of the annual savings, would actually cause the business to incur a loss.

Variable overhead is $8,000 per year, direct materials is $8,000 per year, and direct labor costs are $12,000 per year. Sales are expected to remain at $60,000 per year.

Required   *a.*   Prepare comparative income statements for retaining the old machine and purchasing a new machine for the 12-year useful life of the new machine.

b.   Using only relevant costs, analyze whether it is desirable to purchase the new machine or whether you would agree with the president's son (differential income approach).

c.   Comment on the president's son's analysis.

11–26   **Entering a New Market, Competition Pricing, and Targeted Return on Investment (ROI)**

The Whole Person Company has learned of the success the Good Health Company is having with its bread and has decided to enter the market to compete with Good

Health's bread. The Good Health bread sells for $1 a loaf. Whole Person knows that in order to compete it must charge the same price. In addition, Whole Person's company policy is to have a 12 percent ROI on its investment of net assets amounting to $900,000. Whole Person's income tax rate is 40 percent.

The company estimates that it can sell 1 million loaves of bread annually and that its marketing and administrative costs will be $200,000. Of this amount, $40,000 is expected to be variable costs and the balance ($160,000) is expected to be fixed.

The investment of $900,000 consists of the following:

Working capital	$100,000
Machinery and equipment with a useful life of 10 years and no salvage value	800,000
Total	$900,000

The annual cost of the 1 million loaves of bread is expected to be:

Direct materials	$100,000
Direct labor	?
Variable overhead	100,000
Fixed overhead—in addition to the machinery and equipment . . .	200,000

The investment of $100,000 in working capital is expected to be released at the end of 10 years.

Required

a. Compute the amount that the firm can pay for direct labor.

b. Assume that the firm estimates that the direct labor needed can be obtained for $200,000 including all payroll fringes. Would you recommend that Whole Person go ahead with the project? Explain.

c. Compute the net investment.

d. Compute the cash operating advantage for the 10-year period.

11–27 **Expanding a Product Line**

Helene's, a high-fashion women's dress manufacturer, is planning to market a new cocktail dress for the coming season. Helene's supplies retailers in the east and mid-Atlantic states.

Four yards of material are required to lay out the dress pattern. Some material remains after cutting, which can be sold as remnants.

The leftover material could also be used to manufacture a matching cape and handbag. However, if the leftover material is to be used for the cape and handbag, more care will be required in the cutting, which will increase the cutting costs.

The company expected to sell 1,250 dresses if no matching cape or handbag were available. Helene's market research reveals that dress sales will be 20 percent higher if a matching cape and handbag are available. The market research indicates that the cape and/or handbag will not be sold individually but only as accessories with the dress. The various combinations of dresses, capes, and handbags which are expected to be sold by retailers are as follows:

	Percent of Total
Complete sets of dress, cape, and handbag	70%
Dress and cape	6
Dress and handbag . . . . : . . .	15
Dress only	9
Total	$100%

The material used in the dress costs $12.50 a yard or $50.00 for each dress. The cost of cutting the dress if the cape and handbag are not manufactured is estimated at $20 a dress, and the resulting remnants can be sold for $5 for each dress cut out. If the cape and handbag are to be manufactured, the cutting costs will be increased by $9 per dress. There will be no salable remnants if the capes and handbags are manufactured in the quantities estimated.

The selling prices and the costs to complete the three items once they are cut are presented below:

	Selling Price per Unit	Unit Cost to Complete (Excludes Cost of Material and Cutting Operation)
Dress	$200.00	$80.00
Cape	27.50	19.50
Handbag	9.50	6.50

Required
a. Calculate Helene's incremental profit or loss from manufacturing the capes and handbags in conjunction with the dresses.

b. Identify any nonquantitative factors that could influence Helene's management in its decision to manufacture the capes and handbags which match the dress.

(CMA adapted)

11–28 Accepting a Special Order at Less than Full Cost

The Burr Electronics Company normally produces 150,000 units of K–9 per year. Due to an economic downturn, the company has some idle capacity. K–9 sells for $15 per unit.

The firm's production, marketing, and administrative costs at its normal capacity are:

	Per Unit
Direct materials	$1.00
Direct labor	2.00
Variable overhead	1.50
Fixed overhead	
($450,000 ÷ 150,000 units)	3.00
Variable marketing costs	1.05
Fixed marketing and administrative	
costs ($210,000 ÷ 150,000 units) . . .	1.40
Total	$9.95

Required   *a.*   Compute the firm's operating income before income taxes if the firm sold 110,000 units in 19x4.

           b.   For 19x5, the firm expects to sell the same number of units as it sold in 19x4. However, in a trade newspaper, the firm noticed an invitation to bid on selling K–9 to a state government. There are no marketing costs associated with the order if Burr is awarded the contract. The company wishes to prepare a bid for 40,000 units at its full manufacturing cost plus 25 cents per unit. How much should they bid? If Burr is successful in getting the contract, what would be its effect on operating income?

           c.   Assume that the company is awarded the contract on January 2, 19x5, and that in addition, it also receives an order from a foreign vendor for 40,000 units at the regular price of $15 per unit. The foreign shipment will require the firm to incur its normal marketing costs. The government contract contains a 10-day escape clause, i.e., the firm can reject the contract within 10 days without any penalty. If the firm accepts the government contract, overtime pay at 1½ times the straight-time rate will be paid on the 40,000 units. In addition, fixed overhead will increase by $60,000 and variable overhead will behave in its normal pattern. Decide the following:

                (1)   Should the firm accept the foreign order? Show the effect on operating income of accepting the order.

                (2)   Assuming the foreign order is accepted, should the firm accept the government order? Show the effect on operating income of accepting the government order.

11–29   Relevant Costs for Accepting a Special Order

George Jackson operates a small machine shop. He manufactures one standard product available from many other similar businesses and he also manufactures products to customer order. His accountant prepared the annual income statement shown below:

	Custom Sales	Standard Sales	Total
Sales	$50,000	$25,000	$75,000
Costs:			
Material	10,000	8,000	18,000
Labor	20,000	9,000	29,000
Depreciation	6,300	3,600	9,900
Power	700	400	1,100
Rent	6,000	1,000	7,000
Heat and light	600	100	700
Other	400	900	1,300
Total costs	44,000	23,000	67,000
Net income	$ 6,000	$ 2,000	$ 8,000

The depreciation charges are for machines used in the respective product lines. The power charge is apportioned on the estimate of power consumed. The rent is for the building space which has been leased for 10 years at $7,000 per year. The rent and heat and light are apportioned to the product lines based on amount of floor space occupied. All other costs are current costs identified with the product line causing them.

A valued custom parts customer has asked Mr. Jackson if he would manufacture 5,000 special units for him. Mr. Jackson is working at capacity and would have to give up some other business in order to take this business. He cannot renege on custom orders already agreed to but he could reduce the output of his standard product by about one half for one year while producing the specially requested custom part. The customer is willing to pay $7 for each part. The material cost will be about $2.00 per unit and the labor will be $3.60 per unit. Mr. Jackson will have to spend $2,000 for a special device which will be discarded when the job is done.

Required   a.   Calculate and present the following costs related to the 5,000 unit custom order:
- (1)   The incremental cost of the order.
- (2)   The full cost of the order.
- (3)   The opportunity cost of taking the order.
- (4)   The sunk costs related to the order.

      b.   Should Mr. Jackson take the order? Explain your answer with computations supporting your position.

(CMA adapted)

11–30   **Make-or-Buy Decision**

The Good-4-U Salad Dressing Company produces four varieties of salad dressings. A major ingredient of each salad dressing is low-fat yogurt, which the company produces itself. A well-known, long-established dairy has offered to make this yogurt for Good-4-U and sell it to them at $15 a case.

You are asked to advise the president whether to accept this offer. It has been determined that Good-4-U would require 20,000 cases of yogurt per year. You have compiled the following information concerning the company's cost of making the yogurt:

Per Case	
Direct materials	$ 4.00
Direct labor	3.50
Variable overhead	3.00
Fixed overhead*	12.00

* Five dollars is direct fixed overhead and $7 is common fixed overhead.

Required   a.   Assume that the facilities now used to produce the yogurt can be used for storage instead of the warehouse for which the company is now paying $20,000 a year as rent. Would you recommend that the dairy's offer be accepted? Show your computations.

      b.   (1)   Aside from the calculations in (a), should any qualitative factors be considered in your decision? If so, discuss them.

            (2)   Would your recommendation in (a) be different if the president told you that he planned to keep the yogurt-producing premises intact in the event that the dairy is unable to deliver as promised? Show your computations.

      c.   Assume that if the company were no longer producing yogurt, it would use the facilities to produce a new line of diet salad dressings. It is estimated that the new product would generate a segment margin of $35,000. Should the offer be accepted? Show your calculations.

11-31   **Make-or-Buy Decision and Accepting a Special Order**

The Sonic Company manufactures electric pencil sharpeners. At present, the company fabricates and manufactures all of the parts required to produce the product. The sharpeners sell for $20 each, and the standard cost for a sharpener consists of:

Direct materials	$ 4.00
Direct labor	3.00
Manufacturing overhead:	
Variable	1.00
Fixed ($500,000 ÷ 200,000	
units = $2.50)	2.50
Total	$10.50

The company received an offer from an electric motor manufacturer to manufacture the motors used in the sharpeners for a price of $2 each. If the company accepts the offer, direct materials will decrease by 20 percent, direct labor and variable overhead will decrease by 15 percent, and fixed overhead will decrease by $60,000.

Required   *a.*   Should Sonic purchase the motors from an outside firm if the space occupied by the motor manufacturing department has no alternative use and the salvage value of the department's equipment is equal to the cost of dismantling the equipment? Show computations.

   b.   A foreign purchaser approached Sonic with an offer to purchase 50,000 sharpeners at a price of $10.50. Sonic has sufficient capacity to manufacture the additional 50,000 units except for the electric motors. Sonic is considering the following actions:

   (1)   Subcontracting the manufacture of all of the electric motors and accepting the foreign order.

   (2)   Subcontracting the manufacture of 50,000 motors at $2 each and accepting the foreign order.

   (3)   Rejecting the foreign order.

   For each alternative, calculate its effect on the company's operating income. Show all computations. Which alternative would you select? Why?

   c.   Would your answer in *(a)* above be any different if the firm could sublet the vacated space for $50,000 per annum? For $90,000 per annum? Explain.

   d.   What qualitative factors must also be considered before a firm buys components from another manufacturer?

11-32   **Sell or Process Further**

The Copper Mining Company produces copper, gold, and silver from its mines. The gold and silver are sold to jewelry fabricators while the copper is sold by the pound, but it can be manufactured into soft copper tubing by additional processing.

If the copper is sold by the pound, the firm's profit per pound is computed as follows:

Selling price	$0.60
Less: Allocated joint	
product cost	0.35
Profit per pound	$0.25

A roll of tubing sells for $8.00 and requires $2.50 of additional processing costs and eight pounds of copper.

a. Should the company process the copper into tubing? Show your computations.
b. What is the profit per pound of additional processing?
c. Assume that the price of copper increases to $0.70 per pound and the additional processing costs rise to $3.00. What price will the company require before it is willing to process copper into tubing?

11–33   Sell at Split-Off Point or Process Further

The Healthful Extract Company uses a common raw material, CG9, to produce three joint products, AX6, BJ7, and JT8. The cost of each batch of CG9 processed is:

100,000 pounds of CG9	$ 80,000
Direct labor	30,000
Overhead	30,000
Total per batch	$140,000

The yield per batch and the selling prices of each product are:

Product	Pounds	Selling Price per Pound
AX6	40,000	$2.50
BJ7	25,000	2.20
JT8	30,000	1.50

There is a loss of 5,000 pounds per batch in processing.

Each product can be sold in a market to other producers or it can be processed further into another product. The additional processing costs and the selling prices after additional processing are:

Product	Separable Costs per Batch	Selling Price per Pound after Additional Processing
AX6	$24,000	$3.00
BJ7	6,250	2.50
JT8	9,000	1.90

a. Would you recommend that any of the products be processed further? Show your computations to support your position.
b. Assume that the joint product cost of $140,000 is allocated to each product as follows:

AX6	$ 70,000
BJ7	38,500
JT8	31,500
Total	$140,000

(1) Prepare a schedule showing the gross profit for each product and the total for the batch assuming the three products are sold at the split-off point.

(2) Prepare a schedule showing the gross profit for each product and the total for the batch assuming the three products are sold as you recommended in (a).

11-34   Pricing Decision: Skimming versus Market Penetration

The Crescent Electronics Company plans to market a new product. The firm's marketing research department completed a marketing survey and determined that the product's demand function is:

$$Q = 30 - 2P$$

where

$$Q = \text{The quantity demanded (in millions)}$$
$$P = \text{Price of the product}$$

In tabular form, the demand function may appear as follows:

Price	Quantity (in millions)	Total Revenue
$15	0	$ –0–
14	2	28,000,000
13	4	52,000,000
12	6	72,000,000
11	8	88,000,000
10	10	100,000,000
9	12	108,000,000
8	14	112,000,000
7	16	112,000,000

The variable cost of the product is $4 per unit and there are no incremental fixed costs associated with the product.

The firm believes that the maximum number of units that can be sold is 16 million units.

Crescent does not believe its image will be affected if it uses a skimming-the-market pricing policy. On the other hand, it is also considering a market penetration pricing policy.

Required
a. If Crescent wishes to penetrate the market, what price should it charge? Why?
b. If instead of penetrating the market the firm wishes to maximize its income by skimming the market, what strategy would you recommend? Show your computations to justify your solution.
c. If instead of skimming the market the firm wishes to use a strategy of initially offering the product at one price and then penetrating the market, what should the initial price and the subsequent price be? Show your computatons.

11-35   Pricing and Markup Percentages

The Primer Company is in the process of setting a selling price for one of its products. The accounting department provides you with the following for 19x3:

	50,000 Units
Sales	$2,000,000
Cost of goods sold	800,000
Gross margin	1,200,000
Marketing and administrative costs	400,000
Operating income before income taxes	800,000
Income taxes	320,000
Net income	$ 480,000

Cost of goods sold includes $300,000 of fixed overhead, and the $400,000 of marketing and administrative costs consist of $100,000 of variable marketing costs with the remainder fixed.

For 19x4, the firm is contemplating the manufacture of a competing product marketed under a different label with some design modifications. However, costs and the selling price are expected to parallel this product. The firm wishes to earn the same net income in 19x4.

Required a. What should the selling price be?

  b. Compute the markup percentage if the firm wishes to base its selling price on absorption costing.

  c. Recast the 19x3 income statement into a variable-costing format.

  d. Compute the markup percentage if the firm wishes to base its selling price— computed in (a) above—on variable manufacturing costing.

  e. Compute the markup percentage if the firm wishes to base its selling price— computed in (a) above—using the contribution approach. Is your answer the same as in (d) above? Why?

11–36 Markup Pricing

E. Berg and Sons build custom-made pleasure boats which range in price from $10,000 to $250,000. For the past 30 years, Mr. Berg, Sr., has determined the selling price of each boat by estimating the costs of material, labor, a prorated portion of overhead, and adding 20 percent to these estimated costs.

For example, a recent price quotation was determined as follows:

Direct materials	$ 5,000
Direct labor	8,000
Overhead	2,000
	15,000
Plus 20 percent	3,000
Selling price	$18,000

The overhead figure was determined by estimating total overhead costs for the year and allocating them at 25 percent of direct labor.

If a customer rejected the price and business was slack, Mr. Berg, Sr., would often be willing to reduce his markup to as little as 5 percent over estimated costs. Thus, average markup for the year is estimated at 15 percent.

Mr. Ed Berg, Jr., has just completed a course on pricing and believes the firm could use some of the techniques discussed in the course. The course emphasized the contribution margin approach to pricing and Mr. Berg, Jr., feels such an approach would be helpful in determining the selling prices of their custom-made pleasure boats.

Total overhead, which includes marketing and administrative costs for the year, has been estimated at $150,000 of which $90,000 is fixed and the remainder is variable in direct proportion to direct labor.

Required   *a.* Assume the customer in the example rejected the $18,000 quotation and also rejected a $15,750 quotation (5 percent markup) during a slack period. The customer countered with a $15,000 offer.

    (1) What is the difference in net income for the year between accepting or rejecting the customer's offer?

    (2) What is the minimum selling price Mr. Berg, Jr., could have quoted without reducing or increasing net income?

  b. What advantages does the contribution margin approach to pricing have over the approach used by Mr. Berg, Sr.?

  c. What pitfalls are there, if any, to contribution margin pricing?

(CMA adapted)

11–37 **Markup Pricing and Accepting a Bid**

Jenco, Inc., manufactures a combination fertilizer/weed killer under the name Fertikil. This is the only product Jenco produces at the present time. Fertikil is sold nationwide through normal marketing channels to retail nurseries and garden stores.

Taylor Nursery plans to sell a similar fertilizer/weed killer compound through its regional nursery chain under its own private label. Taylor has asked Jenco to submit a bid for a 25,000-pound order of the private brand compound. While the chemical composition of the Taylor compound differs from Fertikil, the manufacturing process is very similar.

The Taylor compound would be produced in 1,000-pound lots. Each lot would require 60 direct labor-hours and the following chemicals:

Chemicals	Quantity in Pounds
CW–3	400
JX–6	300
MZ–8	200
BE–7	100

The first three chemicals (CW–3, JX–6, MZ–8) are all used in the production of Fertikil. BE–7 was used in a compound that Jenco has discontinued. This chemical was not sold or discarded because it does not deteriorate and there have been adequate storage facilities. Jenco could sell BE–7 at the prevailing market price less 10 cents per pound selling/handling costs.

Jenco also has on hand a chemical called CN–5 which was manufactured for use in another product that is no longer produced. CN–5, which cannot be used in Fertikil, can be substituted for CW–3 on a one-for-one basis without affecting the quality of the Taylor compound. The quantity of CN–5 in inventory has a salvage value of $500.

Inventory and cost data for the chemicals which can be used to produce the Taylor compound are as shown below.

Raw Material	Pounds in Inventory	Actual Price per Pound when Purchased	Current Market Price per Pound
CW–3	22,000	$ .80	$ .90
JX–6	5,000	$ .55	$ .60
MZ–8	8,000	$1.40	$1.60
BE–7	4,000	$ .60	$ .65
CN–5	5,500	$ .75	(salvage)

The current direct labor rate is $7 per hour. The manufacturing overhead rate is established at the beginning of the year and is applied consistently throughout the year using direct labor-hours (DLH) as the base. The predetermined overhead rate for the current year, based on a two-shift capacity of 400,000 total DLH with no overtime, is as follows:

Variable manufacturing overhead	$2.25 per DLH
Fixed manufacturing overhead	3.75 per DLH
Combined rate	$6.00 per DLH

Jenco's production manager reports that the present equipment and facilities are adequate to manufacture the Taylor compound. However, Jenco is within 800 hours of its two-shift capacity this month before it must schedule overtime. If need be, the Taylor compound could be produced on regular time by shifting a portion of Fertikil production to overtime. Jenco's rate for overtime hours is one-and-one-half the regular pay rate, or $10.50 per hour. There is no allowance for any overtime premium in the manufacturing overhead rate.

Jenco's standard markup policy for new products is 25 percent of full manufacturing cost.

Required a. Assume Jenco, Inc., has decided to submit a bid for a 25,000-pound order of Taylor's new compound. The order must be delivered by the end of the current month. Taylor has indicated that this is a onetime order which will not be repeated.

Calculate the lowest price Jenco should bid for the order and not reduce its net income.

b. Without prejudice to your answer to requirement (a), assume that Taylor Nursery plans to place regular orders for 25,000-pound lots of the new compound during the coming year. Jenco expects the demand for Fertikil to remain strong again in the coming year. Therefore, the recurring orders from Taylor will put Jenco over its two-shift capacity. However, production can be scheduled so that 60 percent of each Taylor order can be completed during regular hours or Fertikil production could be shifted temporarily to overtime so that the Taylor orders could be produced on regular time. Jenco's production manager has estimated that the prices of all chemicals will stabilize at the current market rates for the coming year and that all other manufacturing costs are expected to be maintained at the same rates or amounts.

Calculate the price Jenco, Inc., should quote Taylor Nursery for each 25,000-pound lot of the new compound assuming that there will be recurring orders during the coming year.

(CMA adapted)

11–38 Target-Return Pricing and Accepting a Special Order

The Roberts Company wishes to earn a target return on one of its product lines. The following information is available:

Variable manufacturing costs per unit	$25
Fixed manufacturing costs per unit	
($900,000 ÷ 60,000 units)	15
Total manufacturing costs	$40
Variable marketing costs	$30,000
Fixed marketing and administrative costs . . .	$270,000
Investment in assets for this product line . . .	$1,500,000
Desired rate of return	15%
Income tax rate	25%

Required

a. (1) Compute the markup percentage assuming that the firm uses absorption costing as the basis for its markup.
   (2) What is the selling price? Prove that it is correct.

b. (1) Compute the markup percentage assuming that the firm uses variable manufacturing cost as the basis for its markup.
   (2) What is the selling price? Prove that it is correct.

c. Repeat b(1) and b(2) assuming that the firm uses the contribution margin approach.

d. It appears that the firm will only sell 40,000 units next year. A foreign purchaser has offered to purchase 20,000 units at a price of $30 per unit. These units will not compete with the firm's regular sales. There will be no variable marketing costs associated with the order. Should the order be accepted? Why? What effect would the acceptance of this order have on the firm's operating income?

11–39 Target-Return Pricing

The Graybar Company is introducing a new product and wishes to earn a target return on it. The following information is available.

Variable manufacturing costs per unit	$10
Variable marketing costs per unit	$2
Fixed manufacturing costs	$400,000
Fixed marketing and administrative costs . . .	$300,000
Investment in assets for this product	$1,000,000
Desired rate of return	18%
Income tax rate	40%

The firm is uncertain how many units can be sold each year. However, the director of marketing believes that the number of units sold will depend on the selling price. Initially, the director would like to know what the selling price would be at different levels of projected sales volume.

Required

a. Compute the selling prices for each of the following projected sales volumes:
   (1) 40,000 units.
   (2) 50,000 units.
   (3) 80,000 units.
b. For each of the above sales volumes, compute the markup percentage based on absorption costing.
c. Repeat part (b) using a markup percentage based on variable manufacturing costs.
d. Repeat part (b) using a markup percentage based on the contribution margin approach.
e. Write a brief explanation stating why the selling prices and markup percentages are different at different operating levels.

11–40   Optimum Allocation of Scarce Resources

The Custom Jewelry Company manufactures selected designs of gold jewelry. The company's business has been expanding during the past few years. Previously, it was able to manufacture sufficient quantities to supply all of its customers, but the company is projecting that it will be unable to fill all of its orders for the coming year.

The company prepared the following estimated data for the next year:

Product	Estimated Demand in Units	Selling Price	Direct Materials	Direct Labor
Earrings	8,000	$ 15	$ 2	$ 3
Lockets	4,000	60	10	10
Pendants	12,000	80	12	8
Bracelets	10,000	200	30	28
Rings	15,000	150	20	22

The following information is also available:

1. Variable overhead is 40 percent of direct labor cost.
2. Fixed overhead is $800,000 per annum and fixed marketing and administrative costs are $600,000 annually. There are no variable marketing and administrative costs.
3. The direct labor rate is $10 per hour and the factory has a capacity of 60,000 hours. The company has no plans to operate a second shift or seek additional plant capacity.
4. Competition will prevent the firm from increasing its prices.

Required

a. Compute the contribution margin per unit for each product.
b. Compute the direct labor time required per unit for each product.
c. Compute the contribution margin per direct labor-hour for each product.
d. Compute the total amount of plant capacity needed to produce the estimated demand for the coming year.

e. Prepare a schedule showing how to allocate the 60,000 hours of plant capacity to produce optimum profits for the company.

f. Excluding plant expansion and a second shift, is there any way that additional capacity may be obtained? If so, how? What problems may be encountered if the additional capacity is obtained?

12

CAPITAL BUDGETING

Capital budgeting is concerned with the planning and financing of a firm's long-term investment decisions. The most frequent capital-budgeting decisions are (1) whether to purchase new labor-saving equipment to perform operations presently performed manually, a cost-reduction decision; (2) whether to replace existing equipment with more efficient, newer equipment, also a cost-reduction decision; and (3) whether to enter a new market by developing a new product or purchasing an existing business already in that market, a profit-expansion decision. These are long-term decisions that are likely to affect a firm's operations for many years to come, in contrast to short-term decisions, such as investments in small hand and power tools, which may affect the firm's operations for only one or two years.

All firms have limited amounts of available capital, and most firms have more investment opportunities than they can satisfy with their available resources. Thus, a firm must commonly decide which investment opportunities to reject and which to accept in order to satisfy its operational objectives.

The selection process of capital budgeting may be broken down into two phases. In the initial phase, **screening,** a specific cutoff criterion is used to eliminate unprofitable and/or high-risk investment proposals. Projects that fail to satisfy the screening criterion are rejected, and the remaining projects are subjected to further analysis. In the second phase, **preference selection,** the surviving projects are subjected to a ranking criterion, which results in the selection of the most favorable projects for any given amount of capital to be invested.

Not all firms use the same screening tests. However, most firms use one or more of the most popular ones, which are (1) the discounted cash flow model, (2) payback, and (3) the accounting rate of return (simple rate of return). The discounted cash flow model is conceptually superior to the other screening tests and, thus, is most widely used.

DISCOUNTED CASH FLOW MODELS

The discussion that follows presumes a knowledge of compound-interest and present value concepts. Students who are not already familiar with these topics or who would like some review should consult Appendix 12–A at the end of this chapter.

A **discounted cash flow model** is a technique used to evaluate investment projects that applies the time value of money to all cash inflows and outflows by discounting them to their present values. The two most commonly used discounted cash flow models are:

1. The net present value method (NPV).

2. The internal rate of return method (IRR), also called the *time-adjusted rate of return* (TARR).

Net Present Value Method

In the **net present value method** of evaluating investment projects, all future cash inflows and outflows are discounted to their present values using an appropriate interest rate. The total of the present values of the cash outflows is subtracted from the total of the present values of the cash inflows to arrive at the project's net present value. If the result is positive, the investment promises more than the interest rate used to evaluate the proposal. If the amount is negative, the reverse is true and the project should be rejected because the required rate of return will not be earned. The interest rate used to find the present value of a future cash flow is called the **discount rate.**

When making short-term investment decisions, a manager may ignore the time value of money without serious consequences to the firm, but this is not the case for long-term investments (those that span more than one year). In fact, the consequences of failing to recognize the time value of money become more serious as the life of an investment increases.

Consideration of the time value of money can materially alter the attractiveness of an investment opportunity. To illustrate the use of NPV in evaluating the purchase of a new labor-saving machine, we will use the example of the Automated Manufacturing Company first introduced in Chapter 11. The basic data given in Chapter 11 are reproduced below, while the analysis of relevant data using the differential income approach is reproduced in Illustration 12–1.

Purchase price of new machine	$ 90,000
Useful life of machine	5 years
Salvage value at the end of five years	$ 5,000

Annual Operating Information

	With New Machine	Without New Machine
Sales	$500,000	$500,000
Direct materials cost	95,000	100,000
Direct labor	46,000	60,000
Variable overhead	32,200	42,000
Fixed overhead	100,000	100,000

Net Present Value Using the Differential Income Approach. The steps needed to compute net present value when the differential income approach is used are:

Step 1

Prepare a tabulation of the net investment (cash outflows) as in Illustration 12–1.

Step 2

Prepare a tabulation of the cash operating advantage (cash inflows) as in Illustration 12–1.

ILLUSTRATION 12–1

AUTOMATED MANUFACTURING COMPANY
Calculation of Net Investment and Cash Operating Advantage
For the Purchase of a New Machine
Differential Analysis

Net investment:

Purchase price of machine	$ 90,000
Less: Salvage value	5,000
Net investment	$ 85,000

Cash operating advantage:

Savings in direct materials cost	
($100,000 − $95,000)	$ 5,000
Savings in direct labor cost	
($60,000 − $46,000)	14,000
Savings in variable overhead	
($42,000 − $32,200)	9,800
Cash operating advantage—	
one year	28,800
Using life of machine	× 5
Cash operating advantage—	
five years	$144,000

Step 3

Assign a present value factor of 1 to all cash flows *on the investment date.* Assign all other cash flows appropriate present value factors from Tables 2 and 4 in Appendix 12–B. Based on a desired discount rate of 20 percent, Automated Manufacturing's accountants would use the following present value factors:

	Factor
Purchase price of $90,000	1.00000
Salvage value of $5,000, from	
Table 2 for $n = 5$, $i = 20\%$	.40188
Cash operating advantage of	
$28,800, from Table 4 for	
$n = 5$, $i = 20\%$	2.99061

The cash flows and their corresponding present value factors are listed in Illustration 12–2.

Step 4

Perform the arithmetic operations of multiplication and summation. Thus, in Illustration 12–2, the cash inflow from operations of $28,800 is multiplied by the present value factor of 2.99061 for a present value of $86,130. The purchase price of $90,000 is multiplied by the present value factor of 1 for a present value of $90,000. And the salvage value of $5,000 is multiplied by the present value factor of .40188 for a present value of

ILLUSTRATION 12–2

AUTOMATED MANUFACTURING COMPANY
Calculation of Net Present Value
Purchase of New Equipment
Differential Income Approach

Item	Value in Present Dollars	Present Value Factor	Time Period 0	1	2	3	4	5
Cash operating advantage:								
Net cash inflow from operations	$ 86,130	2.99061*		$28,800	$28,800	$28,800	$28,800	$28,800
Total	$ 86,130							
Net investment:								
Purchase price . .	$(90,000)	1.00000	$(90,000)					
Salvage value . .	2,009	.40188†						5,000
Total	(87,991)							
Net present value	$ (1,861)							

* From Table 4 in Appendix 12–B, $n = 5$, $i = 20\%$.
† From Table 2 in Appendix 12–B, $n = 5$, $i = 20\%$.

$2,009. The present values are then added and subtracted as indicated to produce a cash-operating-advantage present value of $86,130 and a net-investment present value of $87,991. The net investment is then subtracted from the cash operating advantage. *If the result* (net present value) *is positive,* the *investment yields a rate greater than* the discount rate and is favorable. *If the result is negative,* the investment *yields a rate less than* the discount rate, which means that it is unfavorable and should be rejected. In this case, since the net present value is −$1,861, the project should be rejected.

Note how consideration of the time value of money affected the attractiveness of this investment opportunity. From Illustration 12–1, it appears that a net investment of $85,000 will return $144,000 in cost savings, a net return of $59,000. However, when the time value of money is factored into the calculations, the use of a discount rate of 20 percent converts what appeared to be a profitable investment into an unprofitable one, as shown in Illustration 12–2. The negative net present value means that the investment will earn *less than 20 percent,* which is inadequate to finance it. Thus, investment analysis for decision making should consider the time value of money to avoid incorrect conclusions.

It is important to remember that the net present value method of analyzing investment proposals provides for two things—a return on the net investment at the specified discount rate and the recovery of the investment itself over the life of the investment period.

Let us assume that an investment of $37,908 will provide a firm with an annual cash operating advantage of $10,000 each year for five years and that the required discount rate is 10 percent. The present value of the cash operating advantage may be computed as follows:

Cash operating advantage	$10,000
Present value factor*	× 3.79079
Present value in dollars	$37,908

* From Table 4, Appendix 12–B, $n = 5$, $i = 10\%$.

Since the net investment and the present value of the cash operating advantage are the same—$37,908—the net present value is zero. Thus, the investment will earn exactly 10 percent. An amortization table, as shown in Illustration 12–3, demonstrates that the investment will earn 10 percent and also recover the initial cash outflow of $37,908.

ILLUSTRATION 12–3   **Amortization Schedule: Investment at a 10 Percent Return**

End of Year	Annual Cash Inflow	Return on Investment at 10 Percent	Recovery of Investment	Balance of Investment
Initial date				$37,908
First	$10,000	$3,791*	$6,209†	31,699‡
Second	10,000	3,170	6,830	24,869
Third	10,000	2,487	7,513	17,356
Fourth	10,000	1,735	8,265	9,091
Fifth	10,000	909	9,091	–0–
Total	$50,000	$12,092	$37,908	

* $37,908 × 10% = $3,791.
† $10,000 − $3,791 = $6,209.
‡ $37,908 − $6,209 = $31,699.

Note that of the $50,000 of cash inflow for the five-year period, $12,092 represents the return *on* investment and $37,908 represents the return *of* investment. Since the cost of the investment is recovered, it is not necessary to consider depreciation when using discounted cash flow analysis.

The Cost of Capital Discount Rate. The discount rate used in computing NPV is usually either the firm's cost of capital or a rate based on its cost of capital. While the calculation of a firm's cost of capital is not an easy matter and is usually discussed in detail in finance courses, it is possible to take a simplified approach. In this book, we will say that the **cost of capital**

is the combined, weighted-average rate of cost that a firm incurs on its long-term debt, preferred stock, and common stock.

Assume that the Automated Manufacturing Company has the following forms, amounts, and after-tax costs of capital:

Form of Capital	Market Value	Assumed After-Tax Cost
Long-term debt	$1,500,000	10%
Preferred stock	1,000,000	15%
Common stock	2,500,000	18%
Total	$5,000,000	

Based on this information, Automated's weighted-average after-tax cost of capital would be computed as 15 percent, as shown in Illustration 12–4. The company may use this 15 percent cost-of-capital rate as its discount rate for capital-budgeting decisions, or it may adjust its rate upward to reflect such factors as risk and inflation. An important point to remember is that the discount rate should *not* be merely the cost of borrowing funds—in this case, 10 percent after taxes. Rather, the discount rate should include the cost of attracting *all* forms of capitalization that a firm uses.

All investment decisions should be based on after-tax figures. For ease of presentation, however, income tax considerations are deferred until the next chapter and income taxes are ignored for all present value investment decisions in this chapter.

Replacing Existing Equipment—The Differential Income Approach. When deciding whether to replace existing equipment, the NPV analysis is

ILLUSTRATION 12–4

AUTOMATED MANUFACTURING COMPANY
Calculation of Weighted-Average After-Tax Cost of Capital

Form of Capital	(1) Dollar Amount	(2) Percent of Total	(3) After-Tax Cost	(4) Weighted-Average After-Tax Cost (2) × (3)
Long-term debt	$1,500,000	30%	10%	3%
Preferred stock	1,000,000	20%	15%	3%
Common stock	2,500,000	50%	18%	9%
Total	$5,000,000	100%		15%

similar to that for purchasing a new machine except that additional factors must be considered. Among these are the proceeds from selling the old machine and the cost of overhauling the old machine.

We will use the example of the Mature Products Company from Chapter 11 to illustrate the use of NPV in analyzing the replacement of existing equipment. Recall that the company is contemplating the replacement of one of its present machines with a faster machine. The older machine is nearing the end of its economic useful life, but its life can be extended by a major overhaul. The following information is available:

Original cost of the present machine	$ 40,000
Less: Accumulated depreciation	30,000
Book value (undepreciated cost)	$ 10,000
Purchase price of new machine	$100,000
Useful life of new machine	5 years
Remaining useful life of old machine	2 years
Overhaul of old machine will extend its useful life by three years for a total of five years at a cost of	$ 10,000
Salvage value of new machine	–0–
Market value of old machine, if sold now	$ 4,000

	Old Machine	New Machine
Annual operating information:		
Sales	$400,000	$400,000
Direct materials cost	90,000	90,000
Direct labor cost	80,000	60,000
Variable overhead	48,000	36,000
Fixed overhead exclusive of depreciation	100,000	100,000

To simplify the solution to this problem, we will assume that all cash flows occur at the end of the year except for the purchase of the new machine and the sale of the old machine, which occur at the beginning of the year. The differential analysis of the relevant data appears in Illustration 12–5, while the computation of the net present value, using a discount rate of 20 percent, is shown in Illustration 12–6.

Illustration 12–6 indicates that the replacement of the old machine will yield a positive net present value of $6,643 and, thus, the 20 percent discount rate will be earned with a modest amount to spare. Note that the positive cash flow of $74,000 derived in Illustration 12–5 is reduced to only $6,643 once the time value of money is factored in.

ILLUSTRATION 12–5

MATURE PRODUCTS COMPANY
Differential Analysis of Decision to Retain Old Machine
or Replace with a New Machine
For the Five-Year Useful Life of the New Machine

Net investment:		
Purchase price of new machine		$100,000
Less: Sales proceeds for old machine		4,000
Net investment		96,000
Cash operating advantage:		
Direct labor savings	$100,000	
Variable overhead savings	60,000	
Old machine overhaul savings	10,000	170,000
Net cash advantage in favor		
of replacing old machine		$ 74,000

Replacing Existing Equipment—The Comparative Income Approach. The solution shown in Illustration 12–6 may also be obtained with the comparative income approach. Instead of using only the differences in cash flow between the old machine and the new machine, the cash flows of each alternative may be discounted to their respective present values and then compared for the purpose of selecting the most favorable outcome. The solution using the comparative income approach appears in Illustration 12–7.

While the comparative income and differential income approaches to capital budgeting produce the same result, the differential income approach requires less effort and is used more often.

Entering a New Market—The Differential Income Approach. When entering a new market, working capital is an important element of capital budgeting. As noted in Chapter 11, working capital is normally invested in accounts receivable and inventories for the entire time that the firm is in the new market. Because a long period of time is involved, the time value of money must be factored into the calculation for the investment and release of working capital, even when the investment and release are the same. During this period of investment, the firm incurs its cost of capital on the invested funds, so the cost must be earned back for the investment to be feasible. Failure to consider the time value of money on invested working capital may lead a manager to think an investment is profitable when in fact it is not.

As first mentioned in Chapter 11, the Physico Company plans to enter the physical fitness market with a treadmill for gymnasium and home use.

ILLUSTRATION 12–6

MATURE PRODUCTS COMPANY
Calculation of Net Present Value
Retaining Old Machine or Purchasing a New Machine
Differential Income Approach

Item	Present Value Dollars	Present Value Factor	0	Time Period 1	2	3	4	5
Cash operating advantage:								
Direct labor savings	$ 59,812	2.99061*		$20,000	$20,000	$20,000	$20,000	$20,000
Variable overhead savings	35,887	2.99061		12,000	12,000	12,000	12,000	12,000
Savings of old machine overhaul	6,944	.69444†			10,000			
Total	$ 102,643							
Net investment:								
Purchase price of new machine	$(100,000)	1.00000	$(100,000)					
Sales proceeds of old machine	4,000	1.00000	4,000					
Net investment	(96,000)							
Net present value	$ 6,643							

* From Table 4, $n = 5$, $i = 20\%$.
† From Table 2, $n = 2$, $i = 20\%$.

ILLUSTRATION 12–7

MATURE PRODUCTS COMPANY
Calculation of Net Present Value
Retaining Old Machine or Purchasing a New Machine
Comparative Income Approach

Calculation of Net Cash Inflow from Operations

	Keep Old Machine	Purchase New Machine
Sales revenue	$400,000	$400,000
Less:		
Direct materials	$ 90,000	$ 90,000
Direct labor	80,000	60,000
Variable overhead	48,000	36,000
Fixed overhead	100,000	100,000
	318,000	286,000
Net cash inflow from operations . .	$ 82,000	$114,000

	Present Value in Dollars	Present Value Factor	Time Period					
Item			0	1	2	3	4	5
Keep old machine:								
Net cash inflow from operations	$ 245,230	2.99061		$ 82,000	$ 82,000	$ 82,000	$ 82,000	$ 82,000
Opportunity cost of keeping old machine—market value proceeds forgone	(4,000)	1.00000	$ (4,000)					
Overhaul of old machine at the end of second year	(6,944)	.69444			(10,000)			
Net present value	$ 234,286							
Purchase new machine:								
Net cash inflow from operations	$ 340,929	2.99061		114,000	114,000	114,000	114,000	114,000
Purchase price of new machine	(100,000)	1.00000	(100,000)					
Net present value	$ 240,929							

Recapitulation

Net present value of purchasing new machine	$240,929
Net present value of keeping old machine	234,286
Net present value in favor of new machine	$ 6,643

Based on a market survey and cost estimates provided by the firm's engineering and accounting departments, the following information is available:

Sales (10,000 at $250 each)	$2,500,000
Incremental costs:	
Direct materials (10,000 at $60)	$ 600,000
Direct labor (10,000 at $50)	$ 500,000
Variable overhead (10,000 at $38)	$ 380,000
Fixed overhead exclusive of new machinery noted below	$ 400,000
Variable marketing costs	5% of sales
Fixed marketing and administrative costs	$ 200,000
Purchase of machinery needed for manufacturing this product	$ 900,000
Useful life of machinery	10 years
Salvage value of machinery	$ 20,000
Working capital needed at inception	$ 400,000
Working capital returned at end of 10 years when the demand for this product is expected to be nil	$ 350,000

ILLUSTRATION 12–8

PHYSICO COMPANY
Calculation of Cash Outflows and Cash Inflows
For Entering a New Market for the
10-Year Useful Life of the Product
Differential Income Approach

	Inflow (Outflow)
Net investment:	
Purchase price of the machinery	$ (900,000)
Salvage value of machine	20,000
Working capital at inception	(400,000)
Release of working capital at the end of 10 years	350,000
Net investment	$ (930,000)
Cash operating advantage:	
Sales per annum	$2,500,000
Variable costs per annum:	
Direct materials	(600,000)
Direct labor	(500,000)
Variable overhead	(380,000)
Commissions (5% × $2.5 million)	(125,000)
Fixed cost per annum:	
Manufacturing overhead	(400,000)
Marketing and administrative costs	(200,000)
Cash operating advantage per annum	295,000
Life of product	× 10
Cash operating advantage for 10 years	$2,950,000

The analysis of the relevant data for the decision of whether or not to enter the new market may be organized as shown in Illustration 12–8, and the tabulation for net present value analysis using a 20 percent discount rate appears in Illustration 12–9.

Illustration 12–9 indicates that this investment is not feasible since it will produce a negative net present value of $3,462 and the 20 percent discount rate will not be earned. This result should be compared to the outcome predicted in Illustration 12–8, where the investment of $930,000 yields a profit of $2,020,000 (cash operating advantage of $2,950,000 minus the invest-

ILLUSTRATION 12–9

PHYSICO COMPANY
Calculation of Net Present Value
Entering a New Market
Differential Income Approach

Calculation of Net Cash Inflow from Operations

Sales revenue		$2,500,000
Less:		
Direct materials	$600,000	
Direct labor	500,000	
Variable overhead	380,000	
Variable marketing costs . . .	125,000	
Fixed overhead	400,000	
Fixed marketing and		
administrative costs	200,000	2,205,000
Net cash inflow from operations		$ 295,000

Item	Present Value in Dollars	Present Value Factor	Time Period 0	1	2	. . .	10
Cash operating advantage:							
Net cash inflow from operations	$ 1,236,779	4.19247*		$295,000	$295,000	. . .	$295,000
Net investment:							
Purchase price of machine	$ (900,000)	1.00000	$(900,000)				
Salvage value of machine	3,230	.16151†					20,000
Investment of working capital	(400,000)	1.00000	(400,000)				
Release of working capital at end	56,529	.16151†					350,000
Net investment	$(1,240,241)						
Net present value	$ (3,462)						

* From Table 4 in Appendix 12–B, $n = 10$, $i = 20\%$.
† From Table 2 in Appendix 12–B, $n = 10$, $i = 20\%$.

ment of $930,000). The results change dramatically when the time value of money is factored into the calculations.

The importance of including both the investment and release of working capital in the calculation is highlighted by this example. What appears to be a $50,000 ($400,000 — $350,000) loss of working capital becomes a $343,471 ($400,000 — $56,529) loss once the time value of money is applied to both the investment and the release. Even if the full $400,000 of invested working capital would be released at the end of the project, it would only have a net present value of $64,604 ($400,000 × .16151), a dimunition in present value of $335,396.

The failure to include the investment and release of working capital in this investment's analysis might have led a manager to make an incorrect decision in favor of accepting the project when in fact it should have been rejected.

Internal Rate of Return

Many managers wish to know not only the net present value of a project but also the discounted cash flow percentage of return. The size of this percentage, called the internal rate of return, is important in helping managers to choose among projects once a proposal passes the screening phase of the capital-budgeting decision.

The **internal rate of return** (IRR), also known as the *time-adjusted rate of return,* is the rate of interest that produces a zero net present value when a project's discounted cash operating advantage is netted against its discounted net investment. Some managers prefer to use the IRR when screening competing investment projects. They first establish a **cutoff rate,** which is the minimum rate of return that an investment must promise before the firm will commit its resources. Only those projects whose IRRs exceed the cutoff rate (sometimes called the target rate or hurdle rate) receive further consideration. Managers then rank the surviving projects in descending order by their promised internal rates of return and select the projects with successively lower rates until the capital available for investment is exhausted.

Calculating the Internal Rate of Return. The IRR can be computed by dividing the net investment by the *annual* cash operating advantage to find the investment's present value factor. It is then necessary to turn to Table 4 and scan across the interest rate columns that correspond to the length of the investment until that present value factor (or its closest approximation) is reached. The IRR will be the percentage at the top of the column. For example, if the Belair Company is contemplating the purchase of a machine for $35,999 with no salvage value and if the annual cash operating advantage is $9,176 for the 10-year life of the machine, the IRR may be computed as follows:

$$\frac{\text{Net investment in project}}{\text{Annual cash operating advantage}} = \text{Present value factor}$$

$$\frac{\$35,999}{\$9,176} = 3.92317 = 22\%$$

Another manufacturer offers a more advanced machine for $53,999 that will produce a cash operating advantage of $12,880. Its IRR may be calculated as follows:

$$\frac{\$53,999}{\$12,880} = 4.19247 = 20\%$$

Even if the firm's cutoff rate is 18 percent, the $35,999 machine should still be purchased because it promises a higher IRR.

Linear Interpolation. When the present value factor falls between two figures shown in Table 4, a proportional (fractional) calculation called **linear interpolation** is made to estimate the internal rate of return. For example, if the incremental investment of the more advanced machine ($53,999 − $35,999 = $18,000) is compared to the annual incremental cash operating advantage ($12,880 − $9,176 = $3,704), the present value factor on the increments may be computed as usual:

$$\frac{\$18,000}{\$3,704} = 4.85961$$

Since this PV factor falls between the factors for 15 and 16 percent, linear interpolation is necessary as follows:

Rate	Present Value Factor	
15%	5.01877	
?	4.85961	5.01877 − 4.83323 = .18554
16%	4.83323	

Linear interpolation:

$$15\% + \frac{5.01877 - 4.85961}{.18554} \times (1\%) = 15.86\%$$

or

$$16\% - \frac{4.85961 - 4.83323}{.18554} \times (1\%) = 15.86\%$$

The incremental investment promises an IRR of only 15.86 percent, which is below the cutoff rate of 18 percent. Thus, the cheaper machine is the better investment, as indicated by the initial IRR calculation of 22 percent.

Uneven Cash Flows. For many capital-budgeting decisions, cash inflows and outflows vary. This is especially likely if both revenues and costs are involved, as when entering a new market. In such cases, and also when salvage value is expected at the end of the project's life, the internal rate of return is found through a trial-and-error approach using the NPV method.

The goal of this technique is to find the discount rate that will yield an NPV of zero. A discount rate is selected, such as 15 percent, and the net present value is computed. If the NPV is positive, a higher rate is selected that will produce a negative NPV. The two rates are then interpolated to see if that rate will yield a zero NPV. If the result is other than zero, other discount rates are tried until a zero NPV is derived. Most large firms use computers to calculate the IRR for investment decisions. A sufficient variety of IRR software packages is available to enable most firms to avoid using the manual trial-and-error approach.

Project Selection

When net present value is used to evaluate competing projects, it is often misleading to use the results to rank and select the most profitable choices. For this reason, managers normally use a profitability index instead.

The Profitability Index

When two or more competing projects have positive net present values, the project with the highest NPV may not necessarily be the best investment. To obtain further information, the amount of net present value should be examined in relation to the amount of the investment needed to produce it. One way to do this is by determining each project's **profitability index** (PI), which is computed by dividing an investment's discounted cash inflows (cash operating advantage) by the required net investment. The resulting ratios can then be used to rank the projects by profitability: the higher the profitability index, the more desirable the project.

The Markon Company is using a cutoff rate of 12 percent to evaluate two competing projects, both with five-year useful lives. The projects' net investments and cash inflows are summarized below:

	Project C	Project D
Investment	$90,000	$22,500
Annual cash operating advantage	$27,487	$ 7,857

The net present values of the projects may be calculated as follows:

		Project C	Project D
Annual cash operating advantage	(a)	$27,487	$ 7,857
Present value factor—			
$n = 5, i = 12\%$	(b)	3.60478	3.60478
Present value of cash operating			
advantage—(a) × (b)		$99,085	$28,323
Less: Net investment		90,000	22,500
Net present value		$ 9,085	$ 5,823

Although project C has a higher net present value than project D, it may not be the better choice. The analysis should include the calculation of the two projects' profitability indexes, as follows:

$$\text{Profitability index (PI)} = \frac{\text{Discounted cash inflows}}{\text{Net investment}}$$

Project C:

$$\text{PI} = \frac{\$99,085}{\$90,000} = 1.10$$

Project D:

$$\text{PI} = \frac{\$28,323}{\$22,500} = 1.26$$

If these projects are mutually exclusive (that is, if only one can be selected), on the basis of PI, a manager should select project D over project C.

The use of profitability indexes for preference decisions usually leads to the correct decision. However, one caveat should be observed: the difference in the projects' costs must be invested at a certain minimum rate. In our example, the \$67,500 (\$90,000 − \$22,500) not invested because project D is chosen over project C must be invested at an IRR of approximately 14 percent (the computation of this rate is complex and thus is not shown) or greater if project D is to be the preferable one. If the \$67,500 cannot be invested at 14 percent or greater, project C would be a better choice.

Profitability indexes are also useful for evaluating projects with unequal lives. If a manager is unsure of what investment opportunities will be available when the cash flows are released at the end of a shorter project's life, profitability indexes will lead to the correct decision while the NPV and IRR may not. For example, if project F promises an annual cash operating advantage of \$20,000 for *3 years* and requires a net investment of \$40,845, while project G promises an annual cash operating advantage of \$10,000 for *10 years* and requires a net investment of \$44,941, the analyses of the two projects using a 12 percent cost of capital may appear as shown in Illustration 12–10.

The results show that the IRR and the net present value approaches can send conflicting signals when competing projects have unequal lives. The profitability index points to the correct decision, however, and is preferable under these circumstances.

Thus far, we have assumed that all cash inflows and outflows could be accurately predicted. In the real world this is not the case, and managers must deal with data that are subject to varying degrees of uncertainty.

Dealing with Uncertainty

Most of the data used for capital-budgeting decisions are estimated. Some of the estimates may be categorized as "hard" data while others are considered "soft." **Hard data** consist of information that may be ascertained with a high degree of precision and for which uncertainty is either small or nonexistent, while **soft data** consist of information that is subject to a high degree of uncertainty. Examples of hard data are the cost of a new machine, freight

ILLUSTRATION 12–10   **Comparison of Projects with Unequal Lives Using Profitability Indexes and IRR**

Net Present Value

	Project F	Project G
Discounted cash inflow:		
Project F: $20,000 × 2.40183*	$48,037	
Project G: $10,000 × 5.65022†		$56,502
Less: Net investment	40,845	44,941
Net present value	$ 7,192	$11,561

Profitability Index

$$\text{Project F} = \frac{\$48,037}{\$40,845} = 1.176$$

$$\text{Project G} = \frac{\$56,502}{\$44,941} = 1.257$$

Internal Rate of Return

$$\text{Project F} = \frac{\$40,845}{\$20,000} = 2.04225 = 22\%$$

$$\text{Project G} = \frac{\$44,941}{\$10,000} = 4.49410 = 18\%$$

* From Table 4, $n = 3$, $i = 12\%$.
† From Table 4, $n = 10$, $i = 12\%$.

in, insurance during transit, investment of working capital, and direct labor cost savings in the earlier years of a project's life. Examples of soft data are repairs to machinery, savings on variable overhead, revenues when entering a new market (especially after the first year or two), and the rate of inflation during the life of the project.

Hard Data. Some capital-budgeting data qualify as hard data for two reasons. First, some of the data, such as the cost of a new machine, are fixed-price quotations. Second, some items, such as working capital invested, occur at the outset when it is possible to estimate them with a high degree of precision. In either case, hard data present few problems, if any, to managers concerned with capital budgeting.

Soft Data. Generally, soft data fall into two categories: (1) data from segment managers who deliberately overstate revenues and understate costs in the hope that their projects will be selected, and (2) data that require projection into the future, often 10 or more years, for which precise estimates are impossible.

Segment managers may be tempted to estimate data in ways that enhance the chance of having their projects accepted. A manager's worth to a firm and, therefore, his or her compensation usually correspond to the relative size of the segment managed. Thus, growth through capital-budgeting projects may be an important goal. For example, consider the following condensed income statement for a firm with two product lines:

	Automotive Division	Percent	Electronics Division	Percent
Sales revenue	$20,000,000	100	$1,000,000	100
Costs and income taxes	17,000,000	85	800,000	80
Net income	$ 3,000,000	15	$ 200,000	20

Although the electronics division earns 20 percent on its revenues while the automotive division earns only 15 percent, the automotive division is more valuable to the firm because its $3 million of net income accounts for the bulk (94 percent) of the firm's net income. Accordingly, the manager of the automotive division would have a much higher compensation package, and if the manager of the electronics division wishes similar compensation, she will try to expand her division.

Managers who evaluate capital-budgeting proposals should be aware of this tendency and carefully scrutinize all estimates of soft data. Segment managers who consistently distort soft data will ultimately be exposed when the actual results of their projects are compared to their original proposals. However, there may be a significant time lag before this occurs, and the firm may be harmed in the meantime.

In most cases, managers can compensate for the second kind of soft data—uncertain predictions—by using a probability distribution approach that yields expected values. This quantitative method of dealing with uncertainty is discussed in Chapter 15.

Another approach can be taken in coping with uncertainty about the effect of inflation on a capital-budgeting decision. The solution is to adjust *both* the estimated cash flows and the cutoff rate by the expected rate of inflation over the life of the project. Since both the cash flows and the cutoff rate are adjusted for the effects of inflation, the net effect of the adjustments on NPV is zero. Thus, many firms choose not to adjust for inflation. For an expanded discussion of the effects of inflation on capital-budgeting decisions, you may wish to consult Appendix 12–C at the end of this chapter.

Auditing Capital-Budgeting Decisions

Most management decisions should be subjected to follow-up evaluations to determine the effectiveness of the decision-making process. This is especially true for capital-budgeting decisions. In an **audit of capital-budgeting projects,** the actual results of an investment project are compared with its expected results. Such an audit is used both for control purposes and for decision making during the project when modifications can be made. Such a process enables management to (1) detect troublesome projects in their early stages, when they can be either altered or terminated to avoid large losses; (2) detect projects that are performing better than anticipated to see if increased investment will lead to even greater returns; (3) evaluate the investment proposal process to determine its effectiveness; and (4) deter segment managers who may be tempted to submit proposals that contain inflated returns.

If credibility is to be maintained, it is important that the audit use the same investment criteria that were employed to evaluate the investment proposal. Changing the rules in the middle of the game is unfair to the segment manager submitting the investment proposal.

OTHER CAPITAL-BUDGETING TECHNIQUES

Not all firms use the discounted cash flow (DCF) model for investment decisions. Some firms prefer a simpler method or one that is more compatible with the way they keep their accounting records. These simpler methods generally suffer from several conceptual defects, the principal one being the failure to consider the time value of money.

Managers who prefer capital-budgeting evaluation methods that are simpler than the discounted cash flow model most typically use two other techniques—the payback method and the accounting rate of return. Some firms use either or both of these methods in place of the DCF model, while others use either or both to supplement the DCF model. Although the payback method and the accounting rate of return are conceptually inferior to the DCF model, their wide usage makes it imperative that managers know how to compute and use them.

The Payback Method

Simply stated, **payback** is the period of time. ated in years, that it will take a firm to recoup its investment in a project. It is very simple to compute. When the cash flows are uniform and no salvage value or release of working capital is involved, the computation is:

$$\text{Payback} = \frac{\text{Net investment}}{\text{Cash inflow per annum}}$$
$$\text{(Cash operating advantage)}$$

For example, if the Automated Manufacturing Company is contemplating the purchase of a new machine for $90,000 with expected cash inflow of $28,800 per year for a period of five years, the calculation of the payback for this machine would be:

$$\frac{\$90,000}{\$28,800} = 3.125 \text{ years}$$

This machine will have its cash outlay returned to the firm in 3⅛ years.

Uses and Limitations of the Payback Method. The payback method suffers from two deficiencies—it fails to consider the time value of money and it provides no indication of whether or not the investment will be profitable. To determine profitability, further analysis is necessary, and at a minimum, the payback should be compared with the project's total life to make sure that the life is the greater of the two. Although such a comparison does not prove that a project is profitable, it should eliminate any project whose life is *shorter* than its payback.

ILLUSTRATION 12–11   **Cash Flows and Payback for Projects K and L**

		Years							
Project	Total	1	2	3	4	5	6	7	8
K	$200,000	$50,000	$50,000	$50,000	$50,000	—	—	—	—
L	200,000	25,000	25,000	25,000	$25,000	$25,000	$25,000	$25,000	$25,000

The payback for each project is:

$$\text{Project K} = \frac{\$100,000}{\$50,000} = 2 \text{ years}$$

$$\text{Project L} = \frac{\$100,000}{\$25,000} = 4 \text{ years}$$

Despite payback's shortcomings, managers use it extensively as an initial screening tool. Projects that have high paybacks tend to be less profitable than projects with shorter paybacks. For example, consider competing projects K and L. Each requires a net investment of $100,000, will return $200,000 over its useful life, and has cash inflows as shown in Illustration 12–11. Using a discount rate of 20 percent, the net present values for projects K and L are shown in Illustration 12–12.

The calculations show that project K, with a two-year payback, has a much higher net present value than project L, which has a four-year payback, despite the fact that the two projects' total cash inflows are the same. An interesting result in this case—although it is not true in all cases—is that project K has a significantly high net present value (a favorable project for a 20 percent cutoff rate), while project L has a negative net present value (an unacceptable project). Thus, a higher payback may indicate lower profitability on a present value basis.

Users of payback generally employ it to weed out projects that have high risk and low profitability. Thus, a payback cutoff point, such as six years, may be used to screen all incoming projects, with those that survive then subjected to the more rigorous discounted cash flow tests.

Uneven Cash Flows.   When a project's cash flows are uneven, the simple calculation approach to payback cannot be used. Instead, it becomes necessary

ILLUSTRATION 12–12   **Calculation of Net Present Value for Projects K and L**

Project K:

$50,000 × 2.58873* = $129,437 − $100,000 = $29,437

Project L:

$25,000 × 3.83716† = $95,929 − $100,000 = $(4,071)

* From Table 4, $n = 4$, $i = 20\%$.
† From Table 4, $n = 8$, $i = 20\%$.

ILLUSTRATION 12–13   **Computation of Payback for Investment Proposal**

	(1)	(2)	Unrecovered Investment
Year	Cash Outflow	Cash Inflow	(1) – (2)
Initial investment	$72,000		$72,000
1		$19,000	53,000
2		18,000	35,000
3		16,000	19,000
4	10,000	20,000	9,000
4.5*		9,000	–0–

* The fifth year's inflow of $18,000 is prorated by using the unrecovered investment balance as a percent of the total inflows for the year—i.e., $9,000 ÷ $18,000 = 50 percent. Hence, one half of a year is added to the 4 preceding years for a payback of 4.5 years.

to start with the unrecovered investment balance and deduct each year's cash inflow and add further outflows until the balance is zero. The amount of time necessary to reach the zero balance is the payback period.

The Lorton Company is considering the purchase of a machine for $72,000. The machine has an eight-year useful life and no salvage value. The estimated cash flows are:

End of Year	Inflows	Major Repair— Outflow
1	$19,000	
2	18,000	
3	16,000	
4	20,000	$10,000
5	18,000	
6	16,000	
7	18,000	
8	20,000	

The payback may be calculated as shown in Illustration 12–13. Lorton would use the results in the same manner discussed previously.

The Accounting Rate of Return

Another evalution method that managers often use, the **accounting rate of return** (ARR), also known as the *simple rate of return,* is computed by dividing accounting net income for a project (revenues minus costs *including depreciation* and income taxes) by the average net investment (ANI) in the project. If there are no revenues but a reduction in costs, the calculation becomes:

$$ARR_{ANI} = \frac{\text{Cost savings} - \text{Depreciation} - \text{Income taxes}}{\text{Average net investment}}$$

The accounting rate of return has two shortcomings that managers should be aware of. First, because it fails to consider the time value of money, the ARR treats the net income (or operating advantage) for each year during a project's life as having no interest cost. Thus, a net income of $10,000 in year 1 is considered to be equivalent to a net income of $10,000 in year 10. The second deficiency that managers should understand is that users of ARR disagree about the amount that should be used as the net investment in the denominator. Because the numerator is decreased by depreciation each year, the denominator should also be adjusted for the sake of consistency. The disagreement is over just how the adjustment in the denominator should be made. Two approaches are used: (1) the average net investment or (2) the original net investment (ONI).

The Landy Company has analyzed its expected cost savings from the use of a new machine it plans to purchase. The analysis indicates that (1) the cash savings before income taxes amount to $38,000 per annum, (2) the cost of the new machine is $90,000, (3) the company's income tax on this project is $2,000 annually, (4) there is no salvage value for the machine, and (5) the machine is expected to last five years. The numerator may be calculated as:

$$\$38,000 - \frac{\$90,000}{5 \text{ years}} - \$2,000 = \$18,000$$

Using the *average* net investment, the accounting rate of return is then computed as:

$$\text{ARR}_{\text{ANI}} = \frac{\$18,000}{(\$90,000 + \$0) \div 2} = \frac{\$18,000}{\$45,000} = .4 = 40\%$$

Using the *original* net investment, the ARR may also be calculated as:

$$\text{ARR}_{\text{ONI}} = \frac{\$18,000}{\$90,000} = .2 = 20\%$$

Note that the ARR_{ANI} of 40 percent is exactly twice the ARR_{ONI} of 20 percent. Despite this difference in results, both methods are commonly used. The choice depends on management's perception of which rate is more useful rather than on the formula's degree of sophistication. Once the ARR is computed, it is used for screening and preference in the same manner as the IRR.

Advocates of the accounting rate of return believe that it is useful because its calculation is compatible with the way accounting net income is calculated from the company's books and records. There is some truth in this thinking, but not a lot. In this author's opinion, ARR's shortcomings far outweigh its small advantage over the discounted cash flow methods.

RECAPITULATION

A recapitulation of the various methods and techniques managers use in reaching investment decisions appears in Illustration 12–14.

ILLUSTRATION 12–14   Methods and Techniques Used for Capital-Budgeting Decisions

Method or Technique	Principal Use	Required Data	Assumptions and Limitations
Discounted cash flow model:			
a. Net present value.	To screen investment proposals to determine their profitability.	Cash inflows, cash outflows, a hurdle or discount rate—either a firm's cost of capital or a modified rate based on cost of capital.	Cash inflows as they are released from a project *are reinvested at the discount rate used* to evaluate the project. Both profitability and the time value of money are considered.
b. Internal rate of return.	To screen investment proposals to determine their profitability, to rank the proposals for preferability.	Cash inflows, cash outflows, a hurdle or discount rate—either a firm's cost of capital or a modified rate based on cost of capital.	Cash inflows as they are released from a project *are reinvested at the computed internal rate of return.* Both profitability and the time value of money are considered.
Profitability index.	To convert the present values of competing projects to an index ranking for the purpose of making a preference selection. Especially useful for competing projects with unequal lives or unequal net investments.	The discounted net investment and discounted cash inflows for each competing investment.	When used for competing projects with unequal net investments, care must be exercised in selecting the project with the higher profitability index. In some cases, the project with the lower profitability index may be preferable if a suitable alternative investment is not available for the funds not invested when the project with the lower net investment is selected.
Payback.	To weed out high-risk, low-return proposals as an initial screening device to be followed by another evaluation method.	Cash inflows and net investment.	Its principal shortcomings are that it fails to consider the time value of money and gives no indication of whether or not the project is profitable.
Accounting rate of return.	To screen investment proposals to determine their profitability, to rank the proposals for profitability.	Incremental revenues minus incremental costs including depreciation, and net investment. For cost reduction projects, cost savings minus depreciation is used together with the net investment.	The concept is based on accounting net income. The time value of money is *not* considered. The investment base may be either the average investment or the original investment.

SUMMARY

Managers must often make **capital-budgeting** decisions about cost reductions, such as whether to invest in new labor-saving equipment or whether to replace an existing machine with a newer, more efficient model. They also must make decisions about expanding profits, such as whether to market a new product or whether to purchase an existing business. The capital-budgeting process usually consists of two phases—**screening** and **preference selection.** Evaluation techniques for screening range from the simplistic payback method, which merely indicates the amount of time it takes for a firm to recoup its investment, to the sophisticated **discounted cash flow models** known as the net present value method and the internal rate of return.

The **net present value method** requires that the cash inflows be discounted by an appropriate **discount rate,** usually the firm's **cost of capital** or a variant of it, and compared to the present value of the net investment. If the present value of the cash inflows exceeds the present value of the net investment— a positive net present value—the discount rate will be earned. If the reverse is true and the discounted net investment exceeds the discounted cash inflows, the net present value is negative, and the proposal should be rejected because the discount rate will not be earned.

The **internal rate of return** also makes use of present value concepts. It is the discount rate at which the present value of a project's cash inflows is equal to the present value of the net investment so that the project's net present value is zero. Most firms use computers to calculate the IRR of investment decisions, but when calculations are performed manually, **linear interpolation** is often necessary. The resulting internal rate of return is then compared to the firm's cost of capital or some other hurdle or **cutoff rate.** If the internal rate of return is greater than the cutoff rate, the project is favorable. Otherwise, the project should be rejected.

When projects must compete for scarce resources (capital), the internal rate of return can be used as a ranking tool. Competing projects evaluated by the net present value method may also be ranked by converting the present values of the cash inflows and the net investment to a **profitability index.** This index is especially suitable for competitive projects that have unequal lives or unequal net investments.

The data used in the discounted cash flow models are subject to a considerable amount of uncertainty. Much of the data are estimated amounts that can be classified as either **hard data,** which involve little or no uncertainty, or **soft data,** which involve estimates far into the future and are thus far less certain than hard data.

Capital-budgeting proposals are most often prepared by a firm's segment managers. An important control device to monitor a manager's effectiveness is the **audit of capital-budgeting projects.** In such an audit, the actual results of an investment project are compared with the estimates that were prepared by the manager responsible for the project's proposal.

Due to its simplicity, the **payback method** is a very popular screening tool among managers. Although payback falls to consider the time value of money (interest), it is an effective indicator of the time it will take for a firm to recover its investment in a project. A long payback may indicate a greater than normal risk. Many firms have a cutoff point for payback. Only those projects with paybacks that are lower than the cutoff point are given further consideration and then subjected to discounted cash flow analysis.

Another screening method that managers use is the **accounting rate of return.** Like payback, this method lacks the sophistication of the discounted cash flow model because it does not consider the time value of money. Managers also disagree over whether to use a project's average investment or gross investment when computing this rate. Despite the ARR's shortcomings, some managers prefer to use it because of its similarity to the way in which accounting net income is derived from the firm's books and records.

Regardless of their differences, all of these evaluation techniques share a common handicap: All are subject to considerable uncertainty when cash inflows and outflows must be estimated well into the future.

GLOSSARY OF KEY TERMS

Accounting rate of return A measure used to evaluate investment proposals that is computed by dividing accounting net income for a project (revenues minus costs, including depreciation and income taxes) by the average net investment in the project. Also called the *simple rate of return.*

Audit of capital-budgeting projects The follow-up practice of comparing the actual results of an investment project with its expected results. It is used for control purposes and for decision making during the project when modifications may be indicated.

Capital budgeting The planning and financing of long-term investments such as buying equipment and introducing new products.

Cost of capital The combined weighted-average rate of cost that a firm incurs on its long-term debt, preferred stock, and common stock.

Cutoff rate The minimum rate of return that an investment must promise before a firm will commit its resources to the investment. Also called the *hurdle rate* or *target rate of return.*

Discount rate The interest rate used to find the present value of a future cash flow.

Discounted cash flow model A technique used to evaluate investment projects that applies the time value of money to all cash inflows and outflows by discounting them to their present values. The two most commonly used discounted cash flow models are the net present value (NPV) method and the internal rate of return (IRR) method.

Hard data Information that may be ascertained with a high degree of precision and for which uncertainty is either small or nonexistent.

Internal rate of return The rate of interest that produces a zero net present value when a project's discounted cash operating advantage is netted against its discounted net investment.

Linear interpolation A proportional (fractional) calculation made to estimate a project's internal rate of return when the present value factor falls between two figures shown in the present value tables.

Net present value method The amount available after subtracting the discounted net investment from the discounted cash inflows. If the amount is positive, the investment promises more than the discount rate used to evaluate the proposal. If the amount is negative, the reverse is true and the project should be rejected.

Payback The amount of time, stated in years, that it will take a firm to recoup its investment in a project.

Preference selection The second phase of capital budgeting, in which investment projects that survive the screening process are subjected to a ranking criterion, which results in the selection of the most favorable projects for any given amount of capital to be invested.

Profitability index The ratio obtained by dividing an investment's discounted cash inflow by the required net investment. Competing projects may be ranked by their profitability indexes: the higher the profitability index, the more desirable the project.

Screening The initial phase of capital budgeting, in which a specific cutoff criterion is used to eliminate unprofitable and/or high-risk investment proposals.

Soft data Information that is subject to a high degree of uncertainty.

APPENDIX 12–A   COMPOUND INTEREST AND PRESENT VALUE

All of us have been exposed to the concept of interest at one time or another. From interest received on savings accounts to interest paid on credit card balances, installment loans, and home mortgages, our experiences have likely included both simple interest and compound interest.

There is general agreement that an individual or a business would prefer to have a dollar today rather than receive a dollar at a later date, such as one year from today. The reason is that the dollar received today can be invested to earn interest, say 10 percent. In one year, the value of that dollar would increase to $1.10 (the original dollar plus the interest of 10 percent of $1.00). In contrast, a dollar received one year from now would be worth only its face value—$1.

Uncertainty and inflation also influence the preference for collecting money today instead of in the future. Despite a debtor's promise to pay a dollar in the future, a creditor can never be sure that the debt will actually be paid. Furthermore, a dollar received in the future may have less purchasing power than a dollar received today. Thus, considering all factors, it is preferable to receive a dollar sooner rather than later.

Given that a dollar received today can be invested to earn interest, it is clear that time can affect the value of money. The **time value of money** is measured by the amount of interest that is (or can be) earned on an investment for a given period of time. The time value of money may be computed in two different ways. One method uses simple interest while the other uses compound interest.

Simple Interest

Simple interest is computed by multiplying the *principal (P),* also called the investment, by the *interest rate (R)* and the *time period (T).* The interest amount is computed only on the principal and *not* on the interest earned. The equation is usually shortened to:

$$\text{Interest} = P \times R \times T$$

Assume that Harry Jones borrowed $1,000 from his aunt for a period of three years at the simple-interest rate of 10 percent per annum. The maturity value of the loan may be computed as follows:

$$\text{Interest} = \$1,000 \times \frac{10}{100} \times \frac{3}{1} = \$300$$

$$\text{Maturity value} = \$1,000 + \$300 \text{ interest} = \$1,300$$

The computations needed for compound interest are somewhat more complex.

Compound Interest   Compound interest differs from simple interest in its calculation of maturity value—**compound interest** is calculated on both the principal and the previous interest earned. Thus, if Harry Jones were to pay his aunt compound interest, the time period of three years would be broken into shorter time periods, such as three one-year periods. The number of times compounding takes place within *one year* is referred to as the *frequency of compounding.* Thus, compounding that occurs once per year is considered *annual compounding.*

While the computation of maturity value using simple interest may be completed in one step, the computation of the maturity value using compound interest requires the same number of steps as the frequency of compounding. For example, for a three-year period with annual compounding, three separate steps would be required. Interest for the first compounding period is computed in the same way as simple interest. The next step is to compute the interest on the *principal plus the interest computed in the preceding step.* The process is repeated, each time adding on the previously computed interest, until the full period of time is reached—in this case, three years.

Future Value.   If Harry Jones's loan were compounded annually, its maturity value would be computed as follows:

First year:

$$\text{Interest} = \$1,000 \times \frac{10}{100} \times \frac{1}{1} = \$100$$

$$\text{Interim value} = \$1,000 + \$100 = \$1,100$$

Second year:

$$\text{Interest} = \$1,100 \times \frac{10}{100} \times \frac{1}{1} = \$110$$

$$\text{Interim value} = \$1,100 + \$110 = \$1,210$$

Third year:

$$\text{Interest} = \$1{,}210 \times \frac{10}{100} \times \frac{1}{1} = \$121$$

$$\text{Maturity value} = \$1{,}210 + \$121 = \$1{,}331$$

The total compound interest for the three-year period is $331 ($1,331 − $1,000), as compared to the $300 simple interest computed earlier.

The same result may be achieved by performing the following multiplication:

$$\$1{,}000[(1 + i) \times (1 + i) \times (1 + i)] = \$1{,}000(1 + i)^3$$

Inserting the 10 percent interest rate, it becomes:

$$\$1{,}000[(1 + .10) \times (1 + .10) \times (1 + .10)]$$
$$= \$1{,}000(1 + .10)^3 = \$1{,}000[1.331] = \$1{,}331$$

The loan's maturity value of $1,331 may also be referred to as its future value. **Future value** is the amount that a single payment invested at interest rate i will amount to at the end of the investment period, including interest accumulated for n periods. A generalized formula for the expression of the future value of $1 compounded for n periods at interest rate i may be expressed as:

$$f = (1 + i)^n$$

where

$$f = \text{Future value of } \$1$$
$$i = \text{Interest rate per period}$$
$$n = \text{Number of periods}$$

Fortunately, to save time, tables are available that present the future value factors for different interest rates and different periods of n. A sample is Table 1 in Appendix 12–B. Our previous calculation of 1.331 for $(1 + .10)^3$ can be verified by consulting Table 1 under the column for 10 percent and across the row for three periods ($n = 3$). The figure 1.33100 indicates the amount that $1 will amount to in three years at $i = 10$ percent. Thus, it is a simple matter to multiply this factor by the amount of Harry Jones's loan ($1,000) to arrive at the maturity value:

$$\$1{,}000 \, (1.33100) = \$1{,}331$$

When compounding occurs more than once a year, the compound-interest equation is adjusted by dividing i and multiplying n by the frequency of compounding. For example, if the Harry Jones loan provides for semiannual compounding, the equation would be adjusted as follows:

$$f = \left(1 + \frac{i}{2}\right)^{n \cdot 2} = \left(1 + \frac{.10}{2}\right)^{3 \cdot 2} = (1.05)^6$$

Referring again to Table 1, the needed factor is found under the column for 5 percent and across the row for six periods ($n = 6$)—1.34010. So the maturity value of the loan would be:

$$\$1,000 \ (1.34010) = \$1,340.10$$

The maturity value of the loan increases by \$9.10 (\$1,340.10 − \$1,331.00) as a result of the semiannual compounding. Tables with fractional interest rates may be obtained when the frequency of compounding necessitates their use.

Thus far, we have only considered the future value of an amount for n periods at interest rate i. For many kinds of business problems, however, the future value is already known, and there is a need to determine how much must be invested now in order to have that amount available when needed. This concept is known as present value.

Present Value. The concept of present value is closely related to future value. **Present value** is the estimated worth today of an amount to be received in the future. The amount to be received is adjusted by deducting interest at a rate of i for n interest periods. The present value is always *less than* the amount to be received in the future. Its formula is the reciprocal of the future value formula and is stated as:

$$p = (1 + i)^{-n} = \frac{1}{(1 + i)^n}$$

There are many uses for present value. For example, assume that a firm plans to give an employee a \$10,000 bonus five years from now, at the time of her retirement. In preparation, the company would like to immediately invest the required amount of money at 10 percent per annum compounded annually. How much must the company invest today in order to have \$10,000 five years from today? The amount can be determined using Table 2. The present value factor corresponding to $i = 10$ percent and $n = 5$ is multiplied by the desired future value to arrive at the present value:

$$\$10,000 \ (.62092) = \$6,209$$

Thus, if \$6,209 is deposited today at an interest of 10 percent compounded annually, it will amount to \$10,000 in five years. This can be proven by using the factor for $i = 10$ percent, $n = 5$, from Table 1 and multiplying it by \$6,209, as follows:

$$\$6,209 \ (1.61051) = \$10,000$$

The Future Value of an Annuity. Very often, a series of uniform payments are required in a transaction, such as an annual payment each year for a period of 10 years. A series of uniform payments for a specified period of time are called an **annuity.** When a series of uniform payments are deposited into a fund, it is possible to use Table 1 to compute the future value of each deposit.

For example, if John Fallon expects to deposit $2,000 into an individual retirement arrangement (IRA) for a period of 10 years and each deposit is made on the *last* day of each year, Table 1 may be used to compute the future value of each payment separately. The maturity values are then totaled to compute the balance in the fund. (Note: Only nine payments earn interest. The last payment earns no interest since it is deposited on the last day of the 10th year.)

However, this procedure may entail more arithmetic than necessary. The same results may be obtained using Table 3, which is constructed from Table 1. Table 3 is a table of cumulative values—an annuity—except that it assumes that the first payment is made on the *last* day of each year, while Table 1 assumes that the payments are made on the *first* day of the year. A series of uniform periodic payments made on the last day of each year (period) is called an **ordinary annuity.**

Returning to our IRA example, John Fallon is interested in knowing how much his fund will amount to at the end of 10 years assuming each $2,000 payment will earn 10 percent per annum compounded annually. Based on Table 3, the factor for $n = 10$, $i = 10$ is 15.93742, so the calculation would be:

$$\text{Future value} = \$2,000 \, (15.93742) = \$31,875$$

The accumulation of the future value of an annuity may be visualized as shown in Illustration 12–15.

Like the present value of a single payment, the present value of an annuity also has many business applications.

The Present Value of an Annuity.   The **present value of an annuity** is the estimated value today of a series of uniform periodic payments to be received in the future. The amounts to be received are adjusted by deducting interest at the rate of i for n periods. When a series of uniform payments are expected to be received for a certain number of years into the future, such as from a retirement pension, the recipient may be interested in knowing how much to accept as a lump-sum payment in lieu of the periodic payments. Table 4 provides the factors needed to compute the present value of an ordinary annuity.

James Stinton, at 70 years of age, is retiring form his job. He must choose between receiving $10,000 per annum for a guaranteed period of 15 years or accepting a lump-sum payment of $80,000. Mr. Stinton believes he can invest the $80,000 at a 10 percent return, compounded annually, and he will withdraw $10,000 each year for his personal use. Should he accept the lump sum of $80,000 or the annual payments of $10,000 for 15 years?

Table 4 provides the needed factor. Using the 10 percent column for $n = 15$, the factor is 7.60608, so:

$$\text{Present value} = \$10,000 \, (7.60608) = \$76,061$$

ILLUSTRATION 12–15   Future Value of an Ordinary Annuity at 10 Percent per Annum

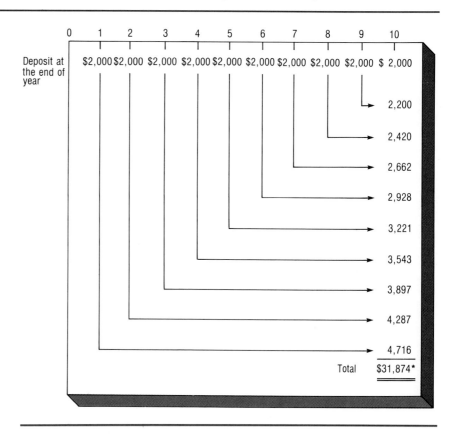

* Difference of $1 due to rounding.

If Mr. Stinton were offered $76,061 as a lump sum, he should be indifferent, since a periodic payment of $10,000 per annum for 15 years is the same as $76,061 today, when interest is 10 percent per annum compounded annually. He should accept the lump-sum payment of $80,000, however, since this amount is greater than $76,061. The present value of an ordinary annuity may be visualized as shown in Illustration 12–16.

When annual periodic payments are not uniform, the present value of the payments must be computed individually using Table 2.

Present value concepts can be applied to a variety of business situations. Businesses must frequenty budget for cash outlays that will bring in cash receipts for years after the outlays are made. In order to properly equate a current cash outlay with the cash receipts it will generate in the future, a firm must convert the expected receipts to their present value at the time

ILLUSTRATION 12–16   Present Value of an Ordinary Annuity at 10 Percent per Annum

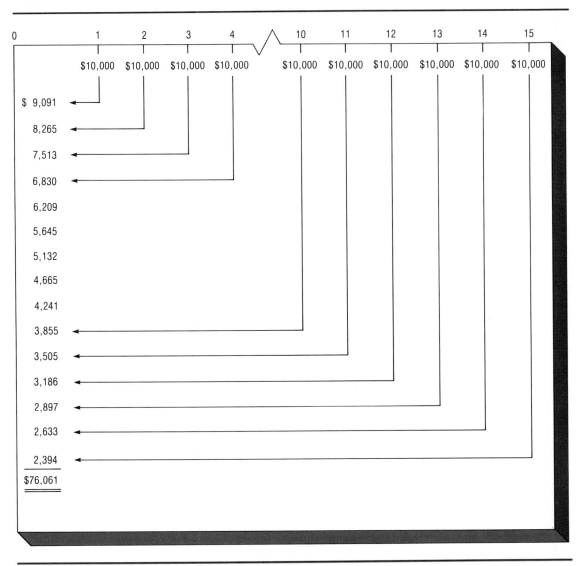

of the expenditure. The process of adjusting future cash receipts to reflect their present value is known as **discounting.** A firm will not normally invest in a project unless its expected discounted future cash receipts exceed the initial cash outlay. A variety of business problems that require the use of discounting are discussed in this chapter.

A summary of the four compound-interest tables appears in Illustration 12–17.

ILLUSTRATION 12–17   Summary of Compound-Interest Tables

Table Number	Use
1	Future value of a *single* payment at the *beginning* of the *first* year
2	Present value of a *single* payment at the *end* of the *nth* year
3	Future value of an annuity with each year's payment occurring at the *end* of *each* year
4	Present value of an annuity with each year's payment occurring at the *end* of *each* year

GLOSSARY OF KEY TERMS— APPENDIX 12–A

Annuity   A series of uniform payments for a specified period of time.

Compound interest   Interest calculated on both the principal amount and the previous interest earned.

Discounting   The process of adjusting future cash receipts to reflect their present value.

Future value   The amount that a single payment invested at interest rate i will amount to at the end of the investment period, including interest accumulated for n periods.

Ordinary annuity   A series of uniform periodic payments made on the last day of the period.

Present value   The estimated value today of an amount to be received in the future. The amount to be received is adjusted by deducting interest at a rate of i for n interest periods.

Present value of an annuity   The estimated value today of a series of uniform periodic payments to be received in the future. The amounts to be received are adjusted by deducting interest at the rate of i for n periods.

Simple interest   Computed by multiplying the principal (P), also called the investment, by the interest rate (R) and the time period (T). The interest amount is computed only on the principal and not on the interest earned.

Time value of money   The amount of interest that is (or can be) earned on an investment for a given period of time.

COMPOUND-INTEREST TABLES

TABLE 1

Future Value of 1, $f = (1 + i)^n$

Periods	2%	2½%	3%	4%	5%	6%	7%	8%	9%	10%
1	1.02000	1.02500	1.03000	1.04000	1.05000	1.06000	1.07000	1.08000	1.09000	1.10000
2	1.04040	1.05063	1.06090	1.08160	1.10250	1.12360	1.14490	1.16640	1.18810	1.21000
3	1.06121	1.07689	1.09273	1.12486	1.15763	1.19102	1.22504	1.25971	1.29503	1.33100
4	1.08243	1.10381	1.12551	1.16986	1.21551	1.26248	1.31080	1.36049	1.41158	1.46410
5	1.10408	1.13141	1.15927	1.21665	1.27628	1.33823	1.40255	1.46933	1.53862	1.61051
6	1.12616	1.15969	1.19405	1.26532	1.34010	1.41852	1.50073	1.58687	1.67710	1.77156
7	1.14869	1.18869	1.22987	1.31593	1.40710	1.50363	1.60578	1.71382	1.82804	1.94872
8	1.17166	1.21840	1.26677	1.36857	1.47746	1.59385	1.71819	1.85093	1.99256	2.14359
9	1.19509	1.24886	1.30477	1.42331	1.55133	1.68948	1.83846	1.99900	2.17189	2.35795
10	1.21899	1.28008	1.34392	1.48024	1.62889	1.79085	1.96715	2.15892	2.36736	2.59374
11	1.24337	1.31209	1.38423	1.53945	1.71034	1.89830	2.10485	2.33164	2.58043	2.85312
12	1.26824	1.34489	1.42576	1.60103	1.79586	2.01220	2.25219	2.51817	2.81266	3.13843
13	1.29361	1.37851	1.46853	1.66507	1.88565	2.13293	2.40985	2.71962	3.06580	3.45227
14	1.31948	1.41297	1.51259	1.73168	1.97993	2.26090	2.57853	2.93719	3.34173	3.79750
15	1.34587	1.44830	1.55797	1.80094	2.07893	2.39656	2.75903	3.17217	3.64248	4.17725
16	1.37279	1.48451	1.60471	1.87298	2.18287	2.54035	2.95216	3.42594	3.97031	4.59497
17	1.40024	1.52162	1.65285	1.94790	2.29202	2.69277	3.15882	3.70002	4.32763	5.05447
18	1.42825	1.55966	1.70243	2.02582	2.40662	2.85434	3.37993	3.99602	4.71712	5.55992
19	1.45681	1.59865	1.75351	2.10685	2.52695	3.02560	3.61653	4.31570	5.14166	6.11591
20	1.48595	1.63862	1.80611	2.19112	2.65330	3.20714	3.86968	4.66096	5.60441	6.72750
21	1.51567	1.67958	1.86029	2.27877	2.78596	3.39956	4.14056	5.03383	6.10881	7.40025
22	1.54598	1.72157	1.91610	2.36992	2.92526	3.60354	4.43040	5.43654	6.65860	8.14027
23	1.57690	1.76461	1.97359	2.46472	3.07152	3.81975	4.74053	5.87146	7.25787	8.95430
24	1.60844	1.80873	2.03279	2.56330	3.22510	4.04893	5.07237	6.34118	7.91108	9.84973
25	1.64061	1.85394	2.09378	2.66584	3.38635	4.29187	5.42743	6.84848	8.62308	10.83471

Periods	11%	12%	14%	15%	16%	18%	20%	22%	24%	25%
1	1.11000	1.12000	1.14000	1.15000	1.16000	1.18000	1.20000	1.22000	1.24000	1.25000
2	1.23210	1.25440	1.29960	1.32250	1.34560	1.39240	1.44000	1.48840	1.53760	1.56250
3	1.36763	1.40493	1.48154	1.52088	1.56090	1.64303	1.72800	1.81585	1.90662	1.95313
4	1.51807	1.57352	1.68896	1.74901	1.81064	1.93878	2.07360	2.21533	2.36421	2.44141
5	1.68506	1.76234	1.92541	2.01136	2.10034	2.28776	2.48832	2.70271	2.93163	3.05176
6	1.87041	1.97382	2.19497	2.31306	2.43640	2.69955	2.98598	3.29730	3.63522	3.81470
7	2.07616	2.21068	2.50227	2.66002	2.82622	3.18547	3.58318	4.02271	4.50767	4.76837
8	2.30454	2.47596	2.85259	3.05902	3.27841	3.75886	4.29982	4.90771	5.58951	5.96046
9	2.55804	2.77308	3.25195	3.51788	3.80296	4.43545	5.15978	5.98740	6.93099	7.45058
10	2.83942	3.10585	3.70722	4.04556	4.41144	5.23384	6.19174	7.30463	8.59443	9.31323
11	3.15176	3.47855	4.22623	4.65239	5.11726	6.17593	7.43008	8.91165	10.65709	11.64153
12	3.49845	3.89598	4.81790	5.35025	5.93603	7.28759	8.91610	10.87221	13.21479	14.55192
13	3.88328	4.36349	5.49241	6.15279	6.88579	8.59936	10.69932	13.26410	16.38634	18.18989
14	4.31044	4.88711	6.26135	7.07571	7.98752	10.14724	12.83918	16.18220	20.31906	22.73737
15	4.78459	5.47357	7.13794	8.13706	9.26552	11.97375	15.40702	19.74229	25.19563	28.42171
16	5.31089	6.13039	8.13725	9.35762	10.74800	14.12902	18.48843	24.08559	31.24259	35.52714
17	5.89509	6.86604	9.27646	10.76126	12.46768	16.67225	22.18611	29.38442	38.74081	44.40892
18	6.54355	7.68997	10.57517	12.37545	14.46251	19.67325	26.62333	35.84899	48.03860	55.51115
19	7.26334	8.61276	12.05569	14.23177	16.77652	23.21444	31.94800	43.73577	59.56786	69.38894
20	8.06231	9.64629	13.74349	16.36654	19.46076	27.39303	38.33760	53.35764	73.86415	86.73617
21	8.94917	10.80385	15.66758	18.82152	22.57448	32.32378	46.00512	65.09632	91.59155	108.42022
22	9.93357	12.10031	17.86104	21.64475	26.18640	38.14206	55.20614	79.41751	113.57352	135.52527
23	11.02627	13.55235	20.36158	24.89146	30.37622	45.00763	66.24737	96.88936	140.83116	169.40659
24	12.23916	15.17863	23.21221	28.62518	35.23642	53.10901	79.49685	118.20502	174.63064	211.75824
25	13.58546	17.00006	26.46192	32.91895	40.87424	62.66863	95.39622	144.21013	216.54199	264.69780

TABLE 2

Present Value of 1, $p = \dfrac{1}{(1+i)^n}$

Periods	2%	2½%	3%	4%	5%	6%	7%	8%	9%	10%
1	.98039	.97561	.97087	.96154	.95238	.94340	.93458	.92593	.91743	.90909
2	.96117	.95181	.94260	.92456	.90703	.89000	.87344	.85734	.84168	.82645
3	.94232	.92860	.91514	.88900	.86384	.83962	.81630	.79383	.77218	.75131
4	.92385	.90595	.88849	.85480	.82270	.79209	.76290	.73503	.70843	.68301
5	.90573	.88385	.86261	.82193	.78353	.74726	.71299	.68058	.64993	.62092
6	.88797	.86230	.83748	.79031	.74622	.70496	.66634	.63017	.59627	.56447
7	.87056	.84127	.81309	.75992	.71068	.66506	.62275	.58349	.54703	.51316
8	.85349	.82075	.78941	.73069	.67684	.62741	.58201	.54027	.50187	.46651
9	.83676	.80073	.76642	.70259	.64461	.59190	.54393	.50025	.46043	.42410
10	.82035	.78120	.74409	.67556	.61391	.55839	.50835	.46319	.42241	.38554
11	.80426	.76214	.72242	.64958	.58468	.52679	.47509	.42888	.38753	.35049
12	.78849	.74356	.70138	.62460	.55684	.49697	.44401	.39711	.35553	.31863
13	.77303	.72542	.68095	.60057	.53032	.46884	.41496	.36770	.32618	.28966
14	.75788	.70773	.66112	.57748	.50507	.44230	.38782	.34046	.29925	.26333
15	.74301	.69047	.64186	.55526	.48102	.41727	.36245	.31524	.27454	.23939
16	.72845	.67362	.62317	.53391	.45811	.39365	.33873	.29189	.25187	.21763
17	.71416	.65720	.60502	.51337	.43630	.37136	.31657	.27027	.23107	.19784
18	.70016	.64117	.58739	.49363	.41552	.35034	.29586	.25025	.21199	.17986
19	.68643	.62553	.57029	.47464	.39573	.33051	.27651	.23171	.19449	.16351
20	.67297	.61027	.55368	.45639	.37689	.31180	.25842	.21455	.17843	.14864
21	.65978	.59539	.53755	.43883	.35894	.29416	.24151	.19866	.16370	.13513
22	.64684	.58086	.52189	.42196	.34185	.27751	.22571	.18394	.15018	.12285
23	.63416	.56670	.50669	.40573	.32557	.26180	.21095	.17032	.13778	.11168
24	.62172	.55288	.49193	.39012	.31007	.24698	.19715	.15770	.12640	.10153
25	.60953	.53939	.47761	.37512	.29530	.23300	.18425	.14602	.11597	.09230

Periods	11%	12%	14%	15%	16%	18%	20%	22%	24%	25%
1	.90090	.89286	.87719	.86957	.86207	.84746	.83333	.81967	.80645	.80000
2	.81162	.79719	.76947	.75614	.74316	.71818	.69444	.67186	.65036	.64000
3	.73119	.71178	.67497	.65752	.64066	.60863	.57870	.55071	.52449	.51200
4	.65873	.63552	.59208	.57175	.55229	.51579	.48225	.45140	.42297	.40960
5	.59345	.56743	.51937	.49718	.47611	.43711	.40188	.37000	.34111	.32768
6	.53464	.50663	.45559	.43233	.41044	.37043	.33490	.30328	.27509	.26214
7	.48166	.45235	.39964	.37594	.35383	.31393	.27908	.24859	.22184	.20972
8	.43393	.40388	.35056	.32690	.30503	.26604	.23257	.20376	.17891	.16777
9	.39092	.36061	.30751	.28426	.26295	.22546	.19381	.16702	.14428	.13422
10	.35218	.32197	.26974	.24718	.22668	.19106	.16151	.13690	.11635	.10737
11	.31728	.28748	.23662	.21494	.19542	.16192	.13459	.11221	.09383	.08590
12	.28584	.25668	.20756	.18691	.16846	.13722	.11216	.09198	.07567	.06872
13	.25751	.22917	.18207	.16253	.14523	.11629	.09346	.07539	.06103	.05498
14	.23199	.20462	.15971	.14133	.12520	.09855	.07789	.06180	.04921	.04398
15	.20900	.18270	.14010	.12289	.10793	.08352	.06491	.05065	.03969	.03518
16	.18829	.16312	.12289	.10686	.09304	.07078	.05409	.04152	.03201	.02815
17	.16963	.14564	.10780	.09293	.08021	.05998	.04507	.03403	.02581	.02252
18	.15282	.13004	.09456	.08081	.06914	.05083	.03756	.02789	.02082	.01801
19	.13768	.11611	.08295	.07027	.05961	.04308	.03130	.02286	.01679	.01441
20	.12403	.10367	.07276	.06110	.05139	.03651	.02608	.01874	.01354	.01153
21	.11174	.09256	.06383	.05313	.04430	.03094	.02174	.01536	.01092	.00922
22	.10067	.08264	.05599	.04620	.03819	.02622	.01811	.01259	.00880	.00738
23	.09069	.07379	.04911	.04017	.03292	.02222	.01509	.01032	.00710	.00590
24	.08170	.06588	.04308	.03493	.02838	.01883	.01258	.00846	.00573	.00472
25	.07361	.05882	.03779	.03038	.02447	.01596	.01048	.00693	.00462	.00378

TABLE 3

Future Value of Annuity of n Rents of 1 Each (ordinary), $F_o = \dfrac{(1+i)^n - 1}{i}$

Periodic Rents (n)	2%	2½%	3%	4%	5%	6%	7%	8%	9%	10%
1	1.00000	1.00000	1.00000	1.00000	1.00000	1.00000	1.00000	1.00000	1.00000	1.00000
2	2.02000	2.02500	2.03000	2.04000	2.05000	2.06000	2.07000	2.08000	2.09000	2.10000
3	3.06040	3.07563	3.09090	3.12160	3.15250	3.18360	3.21490	3.24640	3.27810	3.31000
4	4.12161	4.15252	4.18363	4.24646	4.31013	4.37462	4.43994	4.50611	4.57313	4.64100
5	5.20404	5.25633	5.30914	5.41632	5.52563	5.63709	5.75074	5.86660	5.98471	6.10510
6	6.30812	6.38774	6.46841	6.63298	6.80191	6.97532	7.15329	7.33593	7.52333	7.71561
7	7.43428	7.54753	7.66246	7.89829	8.14201	8.39384	8.65402	8.92280	9.20043	9.48717
8	8.58297	8.73612	8.89234	9.21423	9.54911	9.89747	10.25980	10.63663	11.02847	11.43589
9	9.75463	9.95452	10.15911	10.58280	11.02656	11.49132	11.97799	12.48756	13.02104	13.57948
10	10.94972	11.20338	11.46388	12.00611	12.57789	13.18079	13.81645	14.48656	15.19293	15.93742
11	12.16872	12.48347	12.80780	13.48635	14.20679	14.97164	15.78360	16.64549	17.56029	18.53117
12	13.41209	13.79555	14.19203	15.02581	15.91713	16.86994	17.88845	18.97713	20.14072	21.38428
13	14.68033	15.14044	15.61779	16.62684	17.71298	18.88214	20.14064	21.49530	22.95338	24.52271
14	15.97394	16.51895	17.08632	18.29191	19.59863	21.01507	22.55049	24.21492	26.01919	27.97498
15	17.29342	17.93193	18.59891	20.02359	21.57856	23.27597	25.12902	27.15211	29.36092	31.77248
16	18.63929	19.38022	20.15688	21.82453	23.65749	25.67253	27.88805	30.32428	33.00340	35.94973
17	20.01207	20.86473	21.76159	23.69751	25.84037	28.21288	30.84022	33.75023	36.97370	40.54470
18	21.41231	22.38635	23.41444	25.64541	28.13238	30.90565	33.99903	37.45024	41.30134	45.59917
19	22.84056	23.94601	25.11687	27.67123	30.53900	33.75999	37.37896	41.44626	46.01846	51.15909
20	24.29737	25.54466	26.87037	29.77808	33.06595	36.78559	40.99549	45.76196	51.16012	57.27500
21	25.78332	27.18327	28.67649	31.96920	35.71925	39.99273	44.86518	50.42292	56.76453	64.00250
22	27.29898	28.86286	30.53678	34.24797	38.50521	43.39229	49.00574	55.45676	62.87334	71.40275
23	28.84496	30.58443	32.45288	36.61789	41.43048	46.99583	53.43614	60.89330	69.53194	79.54302
24	30.42186	32.34904	34.42647	39.08260	44.50200	50.81558	58.17667	66.76476	76.78981	88.49733
25	32.03030	34.15776	36.45926	41.64591	47.72710	54.86451	63.24904	73.10594	84.70090	98.34706

Periodic Rents (n)	11%	12%	14%	15%	16%	18%	20%	22%	24%	25%
1	1.00000	1.00000	1.00000	1.00000	1.00000	1.00000	1.00000	1.00000	1.00000	1.00000
2	2.11000	2.12000	2.14000	2.15000	2.16000	2.18000	2.20000	2.22000	2.24000	2.25000
3	3.34210	3.37440	3.43960	3.47250	3.50560	3.57240	3.64000	3.70840	3.77760	3.81250
4	4.70973	4.77933	4.92114	4.99338	5.06650	5.21543	5.36800	5.52425	5.68422	5.76563
5	6.22780	6.35285	6.61010	6.74238	6.87714	7.15421	7.44160	7.73958	8.04844	8.20703
6	7.91286	8.11519	8.53552	8.75374	8.97748	9.44197	9.92992	10.44229	10.98006	11.25879
7	9.78327	10.08901	10.73049	11.06680	11.41387	12.14152	12.91590	13.73959	14.61528	15.07349
8	11.85943	12.29969	13.23276	13.72682	14.24009	15.32700	16.49908	17.76231	19.12294	19.84186
9	14.16397	14.77566	16.08535	16.78584	17.51851	19.08585	20.79890	22.67001	24.71245	25.80232
10	16.72201	17.54874	19.33730	20.30372	21.32147	23.52131	25.95868	28.65742	31.64344	33.25290
11	19.56143	20.65458	23.04452	24.34928	25.73290	28.75514	32.15042	35.96205	40.23787	42.56613
12	22.71319	24.13313	27.27075	29.00167	30.85017	34.93107	39.58050	44.87370	50.89495	54.20766
13	26.21164	28.02911	32.08865	34.35192	36.78620	42.21866	48.49660	55.74591	64.10974	68.75958
14	30.09492	32.39260	37.58107	40.50471	43.67199	50.81802	59.19592	69.01001	80.49608	86.94947
15	34.40536	37.27971	43.84241	47.58041	51.65951	60.96527	72.03511	85.19221	100.81514	109.68684
16	39.18995	42.75328	50.98035	55.71747	60.92503	72.93901	87.44213	104.93450	126.01077	138.10855
17	44.50084	48.88367	59.11760	65.07509	71.67303	87.06804	105.93056	129.02009	157.25336	173.63568
18	50.39594	55.74971	68.39407	75.83636	84.14072	103.74028	128.11667	158.40451	195.99416	218.04460
19	56.93949	63.43968	78.96923	88.21181	98.60323	123.41353	154.74000	194.25350	244.03276	273.55576
20	64.20283	72.05244	91.02493	102.44358	115.37975	146.62797	186.68800	237.98927	303.60062	342.94470
21	72.26514	81.69874	104.76842	118.81012	134.84051	174.02100	225.02560	291.34691	377.46477	429.68087
22	81.21431	92.50258	120.43600	137.63164	157.41499	206.34479	271.03072	356.44323	469.05632	538.10109
23	91.14788	104.60289	138.29704	159.27638	183.60138	244.48685	326.23686	435.86075	582.62984	673.62636
24	102.17415	118.15524	158.65862	184.16784	213.97761	289.49448	392.48424	532.75011	723.46100	843.03295
25	114.41331	133.33387	181.87083	212.79302	249.21402	342.60349	471.98108	650.95513	898.09164	1054.79118

TABLE 4

Present Value of Annuity of n Rents of 1 Each (ordinary), $P_o = \dfrac{1 - \dfrac{1}{(1+i)^n}}{i}$

Periodic Rents (n)	2%	2½%	3%	4%	5%	6%	7%	8%	9%	10%
1	.98039	.97561	.97087	.96154	.95238	.94340	.93458	.92593	.91743	.90909
2	1.94156	1.92742	1.91347	1.88609	1.85941	1.83339	1.80802	1.78326	1.75911	1.73554
3	2.88388	2.85602	2.82861	2.77509	2.72325	2.67301	2.62432	2.57710	2.53129	2.48685
4	3.80773	3.76197	3.71710	3.62990	3.54595	3.46511	3.38721	3.31213	3.23972	3.16987
5	4.71346	4.64583	4.57971	4.45182	4.32948	4.21236	4.10020	3.99271	3.88965	3.79079
6	5.60143	5.50813	5.41719	5.24214	5.07569	4.91732	4.76654	4.62288	4.48592	4.35526
7	6.47199	6.34939	6.23028	6.00205	5.78637	5.58238	5.38929	5.20637	5.03295	4.86842
8	7.32548	7.17014	7.01969	6.73274	6.46321	6.20979	5.97130	5.74664	5.53482	5.33493
9	8.16224	7.97087	7.78611	7.43533	7.10782	6.80169	6.51523	6.24689	5.99525	5.75902
10	8.98259	8.75206	8.53020	8.11090	7.72173	7.36009	7.02358	6.71008	6.41766	6.14457
11	9.78685	9.51421	9.25262	8.76048	8.30641	7.88687	7.49867	7.13896	6.80519	6.49506
12	10.57534	10.25776	9.95400	9.38507	8.86325	8.38384	7.94269	7.53608	7.16073	6.81369
13	11.34837	10.98318	10.63496	9.98565	9.39357	8.85268	8.35765	7.90378	7.48690	7.10336
14	12.10625	11.69091	11.29607	10.56312	9.89864	9.29498	8.74547	8.24424	7.78615	7.36669
15	12.84926	12.38138	11.93794	11.11839	10.37966	9.71225	9.10791	8.55948	8.06069	7.60608
16	13.57771	13.05500	12.56110	11.65230	10.83777	10.10590	9.44665	8.85137	8.31256	7.82371
17	14.29187	13.71220	13.16612	12.16567	11.27407	10.47726	9.76322	9.12164	8.54363	8.02155
18	14.99203	14.35336	13.75351	12.65930	11.68959	10.82760	10.05909	9.37189	8.75563	8.20141
19	15.67846	14.97889	14.32380	13.13394	12.08532	11.15812	10.33560	9.60360	8.95011	8.36492
20	16.35143	15.58916	14.87747	13.59033	12.46221	11.46992	10.59401	9.81815	9.12855	8.51356
21	17.01121	16.18455	15.41502	14.02916	12.82115	11.76408	10.83553	10.01680	9.29224	8.64869
22	17.65805	16.76541	15.93692	14.45112	13.16300	12.04158	11.06124	10.20204	9.44243	8.77154
23	18.29220	17.33211	16.44361	14.85684	13.48857	12.30338	11.27219	10.37106	9.58021	8.88322
24	18.91393	17.88499	16.93554	15.24696	13.79864	12.55036	11.46933	10.52876	9.70661	8.98474
25	19.52346	18.42438	17.41315	15.62208	14.09394	12.78336	11.65358	10.67478	9.82258	9.07704

Periodic Rents (n)	11%	12%	14%	15%	16%	18%	20%	22%	24%	25%
1	.90090	.89286	.87719	.86957	.86207	.84746	.83333	.81967	.80645	.80000
2	1.71252	1.69005	1.64666	1.62571	1.60523	1.56564	1.52778	1.49153	1.45682	1.44000
3	2.44371	2.40183	2.32163	2.28323	2.24589	2.17427	2.10648	2.04224	1.98130	1.95200
4	3.10245	3.03735	2.91371	2.85498	2.79818	2.69006	2.58873	2.49364	2.40428	2.36160
5	3.69590	3.60478	3.43308	3.35216	3.27429	3.12717	2.99061	2.86364	2.74538	2.68928
6	4.23054	4.11141	3.88867	3.78448	3.68474	3.49760	3.32551	3.16692	3.02047	2.95142
7	4.71220	4.56376	4.28830	4.16042	4.03857	3.81153	3.60459	3.41551	3.24232	3.16114
8	5.14612	4.96764	4.63886	4.48732	4.34359	4.07757	3.83716	3.61927	3.42122	3.32891
9	5.53705	5.32825	4.94637	4.77158	4.60654	4.30302	4.03097	3.78628	3.56550	3.46313
10	5.88923	5.65022	5.21612	5.01877	4.83323	4.49409	4.19247	3.92318	3.68186	3.57050
11	6.20652	5.93770	5.45273	5.23371	5.02864	4.65601	4.32706	4.03540	3.77569	3.65640
12	6.49236	6.19437	5.66029	5.42062	5.19711	4.79322	4.43922	4.12737	3.85136	3.72512
13	6.74987	6.42355	5.84236	5.58315	5.34233	4.90951	4.53268	4.20277	3.91239	3.78010
14	6.98187	6.62817	6.00207	5.72448	5.46753	5.00806	4.61057	4.26456	3.96160	3.82408
15	7.19087	6.81086	6.14217	5.84737	5.57546	5.09158	4.67547	4.31522	4.00129	3.85926
16	7.37916	6.97399	6.26506	5.95423	5.66850	5.16235	4.72956	4.35673	4.03330	3.88741
17	7.54879	7.11963	6.37286	6.04716	5.74870	5.22233	4.77463	4.39077	4.05911	3.90993
18	7.70162	7.24967	6.46742	6.12797	5.81785	5.27316	4.81219	4.41866	4.07993	3.92794
19	7.83929	7.36578	6.55037	6.19823	5.87746	5.31624	4.84350	4.44152	4.09672	3.94235
20	7.96333	7.46944	6.62313	6.25933	5.92884	5.35275	4.86958	4.46027	4.11026	3.95388
21	8.07507	7.56200	6.68696	6.31246	5.97314	5.38368	4.89132	4.47563	4.12117	3.96311
22	8.17574	7.64465	6.74294	6.35866	6.01133	5.40990	4.90943	4.48822	4.12998	3.97049
23	8.26643	7.71843	6.79206	6.39884	6.04425	5.43212	4.92453	4.49854	4.13708	3.97639
24	8.34814	7.78432	6.83514	6.43377	6.07263	5.45095	4.93710	4.50700	4.14281	3.98111
25	8.42174	7.84314	6.87293	6.46415	6.09709	5.46691	4.94759	4.51393	4.14742	3.98489

APPENDIX 12–C   CAPITAL BUDGETING AND INFLATION

Logic might seem to dictate that the effects of inflation should be factored into any capital-budgeting decision. The effects of inflation are not as important to capital budgeting as it might appear, however, due to the nature of the adjustments that must be made. To account for inflationary effects, it is necessary to adjust both the expected cash inflows and outflows and the discount rate for the expected rates of inflation. As a result, the adjustments cancel each other and the net present value is the same as the unadjusted net present value.

Let us assume that the Eyecor Manufacturing Company is contemplating the purchase of a new machine at a cost of $25,000. The machine will not have any salvage value at the end of its three-year useful life and the firm expects a cash operating advantage of $15,000 during each year of the machine's operation. The firm's cutoff rate for this kind of decision is 12 percent. The unadjusted net present value would be:

Cash operating advantage	$15,000
Factor, Table 4, $i = 12\%$, $n = 3$	× 2.40183
Present value of cash receipts	36,027
Less: Net investment	25,000
Net present value	$11,027

Let us also assume that the inflation rate is expected to be 10 percent each year for the next three years. The necessary adjustment of the cash operating advantage would be:

First year, $15,000 × 110%	$16,500
Second year, $16,500 × 110%	18,150
Third year, $18,150 × 110%	19,965

The discount rate must be adjusted for two factors—the 10 percent of expected inflation and the combined effect of the inflation and the discount rate (12% × 10% = 1.2%). The adjusted discount rate would then be:

	Rate
Discount rate	12.0%
Inflation rate	10.0%
Combined effect	1.2%
Total adjusted rate	23.2%

The adjusted net present value would then be computed as:

Year	Adjusted Cash Operating Advantage	Adjusted Discount Rate	Present Value
1	$16,500	.8117*	$13,393
2	18,150	.6588†	11,957
3	19,965	.5348‡	10,677
Total present value			36,027
Less: Net investment			25,000
Net present value			$11,027

* 1/(1.232).
† 1/(1.232)².
‡ 1/(1/232)³.

Note that the adjusted and unadjusted net present values are the same. For this reason, many firms do not adjust for inflation in this manner.

Problems may arise, however, if no adjustment is made for inflation, because the post-audit comparisons may provide misleading results. For example, let us assume that the cash operating advantage in the first year is, in fact, the projected $16,500, which includes the actual inflation. When this amount is compared to the original $15,000 used in the budget proposal, the project may appear more favorable than it really is. A simple method to correct for this is to take the actual cash advantage of $16,500 and divide it by 110 percent (100% + 10% inflation) to arrive at the amount exclusive of inflation—$15,000 ($16,500 ÷ 110% = $15,000). The amount for the second year would also be $15,000. It would be computed using a 21 percent inflation rate [10% + (10% of 110%) = 21%] and would be calculated as $18,150 ÷ 121% = $15,000. This method has the advantage of using an actual rate of inflation for the audit comparison instead of the assumed rate of inflation used earlier.

QUESTIONS

1. What is capital budgeting?

2. What is the difference between the screening and preference-selection decisions associated with capital budgeting?

3. What is the discounted cash flow model?

4. What is the net present value approach to capital budgeting?

5. What is the internal rate of return approach to capital budgeting? How does it differ from the net present value approach?

6. What is a firm's cost of capital? How is it computed? How is it used?

7. What is a cutoff rate? How is it used?

8. When the net present value method is used, the answer may be positive, zero, or negative. Explain what each one means.

9. When a firm is contemplating the purchase of a piece of equipment and the vendor

offers the firm a financing rate of 12 percent, should the firm use this rate if it differs from its cost of capital rate? Why?

10. What is the underlying assumption of the net present value method?

11. What is the underlying assumption of the internal rate of return? How does it differ from that associated with the net present value method?

12. Explain how the profitability index is computed and used. Are there limitations associated with this method? Discuss.

13. When dealing with uncertainty, managers often must evaluate both hard data and soft data. Discuss.

14. Is it important to audit capital-budgeting results? Why?

15. What is the payback method? How is it computed? Does it have any severe limitations? If so, what are they?

16. The payback method is a very popular screening method. How do you explain its popularity?

17. What is the accounting rate of return method? How is it computed? Does it have any serious limitations? Discuss.

18. The accounting rate of return takes depreciation into account, while the discounted cash flow methods do not. Therefore, the discounted cash flow methods are inferior to the accounting rate of return method. Discuss.

EXERCISES   **12–1**   **Calculating the Present Value of a Machine Purchase**

The Mayfair Company purchased a machine that has an estimated useful life of six years and is expected to have a salvage value of $3,000 at the end of that time. Mayfair expects to save $4,000 in operating costs each year by using the new machine. The internal rate of return promised by the machine's vendor is 16 percent.

Required   *a.* Compute the cost of the machine.

b. Should the machine have been purchased if the firm's cost of capital is:
   (1) 14 percent? Why?
   (2) 16 percent? Why?
   (3) 18 percent? Why?

12–2   **Present Value Computations**

1. Tracy Corporation is planning to invest $80,000 in a three-year project. Tracy's expected rate of return is 10 percent. The present value of $1 at 10 percent for one year is .909, for two years is .826, and for three years is .751. The cash flow, net of income taxes, will be $30,000 for the first year (present value of $27,270) and $36,000 for the second year (present value of $29,736). Assuming the rate of return is exactly 10 percent, what will the cash flow, net of income taxes, be for the third year?
   a. $17,268.
   b. $22,000.
   c. $22,994.
   d. $30,618.

2. Hilldale Company purchased a machine for $480,000. The machine has a useful life of six years and no salvage value. Straight-line depreciation is to be used.

The machine is expected to generate cash flow from operations, net of income taxes, of $140,000 in each of the six years. Hillsdale's desired rate of return is 14 percent. Information on present value factors is as follows:

Period	Present Value of $1 at 14 Percent	Present Value of Ordinary Annuity of $1 at 14 Percent
1	.877	0.877
2	.769	1.647
3	.675	2.322
4	.592	2.914
5	.519	3.433
6	.456	3.889

What would be the net present value?
a. $63,840.
b. $64,460.
c. $218,880.
d. $233,340.

3. Hamilton Company invested in a two-year project having an internal rate of return of 12 percent. The project is expected to produce cash flow from operations, net of income taxes, of $60,000 in the first year and $70,000 in the second year. The present value of $1 for one period at 12 percent is 0.893 and for two periods at 12 percent is 0.797. How much will the project cost?
a. $103,610.
b. $109,370.
c. $116,090.
d. $122,510.

4. Kipling Company invested in an eight-year project. It is expected that the annual cash flow from the project, net of income taxes, will be $20,000. Information on present value factors is as follows:

Present value of $1 at 12% for eight periods 0.404
Present value of an ordinary annuity of $1 at 12%
   for eight periods 4.968

Assuming that Kipling based its investment decision on an internal rate of return of 12 percent, how much did the project cost?
a. $160,000.
b. $99,360.
c. $80,800.
d. $64,640.

5. Scott, Inc., is planning to invest $120,000 in a 10-year project. Scott estimates that the annual cash inflow, net of income taxes, from this project will be $20,000. Scott's desired rate of return on investments of this type is 10 percent. Information on present value factors is as follows:

	At 10 Percent	At 12 Percent
Present value of $1 for		
10 periods	0.386	0.322
Present value of an annuity		
of $1 for 10 periods	6.145	5.650

Scott's expected rate of return on this investment is
a. Less than 10 percent, but more than 0 percent.
b. 10 percent.
c. Less than 12 percent, but more than 10 percent.
d. 12 percent.

(AICPA adapted)

12–3 **Net Present Value Analysis for Competing Investments and Profitability Index**

Central State University has decided that in order to remain competitive with other local colleges and universities, it must expand and update its computer science department. State is convinced that in order to accomplish this, it must purchase a new central processing unit (CPU). Officials of the school have been negotiating with two mainframe manufacturers, JCN Corporation and C.N.R. Technologies. The representative of JCN Corporation has advised State that their model ZIPPY 1000 would be appropriate for the needs of the school. The cost of the machine would be $500,000. In 10 years, the machine would be obsolete, at which time it would have a disposal value of $50,000. After a detailed study, the representative has convinced State that additional student revenues and savings from administrative costs would provide a net cash inflow of $100,000 annually.

The representative of C.N.R. Technologies is offering State its model SPEEDY 250 at a cost of $750,000. The SPEEDY 250 would also be obsolete in 10 years but would have a disposal value of $125,000. Net cash inflow from this machine would be $125,000 per year.

Required a. Assuming Central State desires a 12 percent return on its investment, use the net present value concept to determine which machine the school should purchase.
b. Compute the profitability index for each investment. Is your answer the same as in part (a)? Is this always true? Explain.

12–4 **Net Present Value and Internal Rate of Return**

The Marlow Auto Repair Company is contemplating the purchase of electronic testing equipment which will enable the firm to perform emission control inspections. The equipment has a useful life of 10 years, no salvage value, and can be purchased at a cost of $20,962.

Marlow estimates that revenues from inspections will be $23,000 per annum and direct labor and variable overhead costs will be $18,000 per annum.

Required a. Compute the internal rate of return for this investment.
b. Compute the net present value for each of the following discount rates and indicate whether or not the investment should be made at that rate:
(1) 18 percent.
(2) 20 percent.
(3) 22 percent.

c. Reconsider the net present value computed in b(2) above. What is the significance of that net present value?

12-5 Competing Investments and Net Present Value

The Driscoll Company has $100,000 to invest. A suggestion made by the plant superintendent is to purchase a new, more efficient machine. On the other hand, the financial vice president would like the firm to purchase a competing firm's customer list that is for sale. The machine has a useful life of five years and the customer list is also expected to yield cash flows for a five-year period. Neither investment is expected to have any residual value.

The projected cash advantage per annum for each investment is:

Year	Machine	Customer List
19x1	$ 60,000	$ 20,000
19x2	50,000	40,000
19x3	40,000	50,000
19x4	30,000	60,000
19x5	20,000	70,000
Total	$200,000	$240,000

Required a. Using a cutoff rate of 22 percent, calculate the net present value of each investment. If only one investment can be made, which one would you choose? Why?

b. Redo *(a)* except that a cutoff rate of 18 percent is to be used. Is your answer different from *(a)?* Explain.

12-6 Net Present Value and Internal Rate of Return

The Building Corporation, a heavy construction business, is interested in replacing one of its backhoes with a new model. The cost of the new equipment is $125,000 and has an expected useful life of 10 years. At the end of its useful life, the equipment will have a salvage value of $7,500. Due to increased efficiency, the company expects to save 1,000 hours per year in labor costs. A backhoe operator earns $20 per hour including fringe benefits.

The manufacturer is offering a $15,000 trade-in allowance on the old equipment, which has a current book value of $75,000 and a zero disposal value at the end of its useful life in 10 years. Building Corporation considers a return of 14 percent on its investments as a minimum rate.

Required a. Using net present value analysis, determine whether or not Building Corporation should purchase the equipment.

b. Compute the internal rate of return for this investment, interpolating to the nearest two decimal places.

12-7 Computation of Cost of Capital

The Feder Company has the following capital structure:

	Market Value
Long-term debt	$ 5,000,000
Preferred stock	4,000,000
Common stock	16,000,000
Total	$25,000,000

The long-term debt also has a maturity (face) value of $5 million and pays interest at 15 percent per annum for a total of $750,000 per annum. The after-tax cost of this interest is $450,000.

The preferred stock has a par value of $4 million and pays dividends at 12 percent per annum. Preferred stock dividends are *not* deductible on the company's income tax return.

The after-tax cost of the common stock is 16 percent.

Required Compute the firm's after-tax cost of capital.

12–8 Simplified Internal Rate of Return

The Commerce Company is contemplating the purchase of two machines, X–1 and X–2. The cost of X–1 is $42,883, while the cost of X–2 is $102,600. Neither machine will have a salvage value, and the useful life of X–1 is 7 years, while the useful life of X–2 is 10 years. The cash operating advantages (cash inflows) are $10,000 per annum for X–1 and $22,000 per annum for X–2.

Interpolation should be carried to two decimal places.

Required a. Compute the internal rate of return for machine X–1 using the simplified method.
b. Compute the internal rate of return for machine X–2 using the simplified method.

12–9 Profitability Index

The Mandrin Company is considering four different projects. They are mutually exclusive, i.e., only one project will be selected. All four projects have the same useful life, eight years, and no salvage value. The investments and the promised cash inflows are:

	Project			
	G	**H**	**J**	**K**
Investment	$80,000	$60,000	$70,000	$90,000
Cash inflow per annum	21,500	14,000	18,000	24,000

The firm's cost of capital is 15 percent.

Required a. Calculate the net present value for each project and rank them. Which project would you select on the basis of this ranking?
b. Calculate the profitability index for each project and rank them. Which project would you select on the basis of this ranking? Is the answer the same as in part *(a)* above? If not, explain the reason for the difference.

12–10 Auditing Capital-Budgeting Results

Firms generally use capital-budgeting evaluation techniques for (1) purchasing new equipment, (2) replacing existing equipment, and (3) entering a new market. Failure to follow up a capital-budgeting project after its implementation may have negative short-run and long-run implications for a firm.

Required *a.* What benefits could a company derive from a postimplementation audit?

b. What difficulties are likely to be encountered in accumulating the data needed to conduct a postimplementation audit?

12–11 Payback and Net Present Value

The Patron Company is contemplating an investment in one of three possible projects. All three require the same amount of investment, $150,000, and none of the three has a salvage value. The useful life of five years is the same for all three projects.

The cash operating advantages (cash inflows) for the three projects are as follows:

	Project		
Year	L	M	N
19x1 . . .	$ 60,000	$ 20,000	$ (10,000)
19x2 . . .	60,000	40,000	50,000
19x3 . . .	60,000	60,000	90,000
19x4 . . .	60,000	150,000	200,000
19x5 . . .	60,000	100,000	60,000
Total .	$300,000	$370,000	$390,000

The firm's cost of capital is 18 percent.

Required *a.* Calculate the payback period for each project. Rank them using payback.

b. Calculate the net present value for each project. Rank them by using net present value.

c. Is there a relationship between payback and net present value for these three projects? Explain.

12–12 Payback and Net Present Value

Items 1 and 2 are based on the following information:

Fleming, Inc., is planning to acquire a new machine at a total cost of $36,000. The estimated life of the machine is six years with no salvage value.

Flemming estimates that the annual cash flow from operations, before income taxes, from using this machine will be $7,800. Assume that Flemming's cost of capital is 8 percent. The present value of $1 at 8 percent for six years is 0.630. The present value of an annuity of $1 in arrears at 8 percent for six years is 4.623.

1. What would the payback period be?
   a. 4.0 years.
   b. 4.6 years.
   c. 5.7 years.
   d. 6.7 years.

2. What would the net present value be?
   a. $59.
   b. $5,607.
   c. $10,800.
   d. $13,140.

3. The Polar Company is planning to purchase a new machine for $30,000. The payback period is expected to be five years. The new machine is expected to produce cash flow from operations, net of income taxes, of $7,000 a year in each of the next three years and $5,500 in the fourth year. Depreciation of $5,000 a year will be charged to income for each of the five years of the payback period. What is the amount of cash flow from operations, net of taxes, that the new machine is expected to produce in the last (fifth) year of the payback period?
   a. $1,000.
   b. $3,500.
   c. $5,000.
   d. $8,500.

4. Bernie Company purchased a new machine with an estimated useful life of five years with no salvage value for $45,000. The machine is expected to produce cash flow from operations, net of income taxes, as follows:

First year	$ 9,000
Second year	12,000
Third year	15,000
Fourth year	9,000
Fifth year	8,000

   What is the payback period?
   a. 2 years.
   b. 3 years.
   c. 4 years.
   d. 5 years.

5. Energy Company is planning to spend $84,000 for a new machine that it will depreciate on the straight-line basis over 10 years with no salvage value. The related cash flow from operations, net of income taxes, is expected to be $10,000 a year for each of the first six years and $12,000 for each of the next four years. What is the payback period?
   a. 4.4 years.
   b. 7.6 years.
   c. 7.8 years.
   d. 8.0 years.

6. Brunswick Company is planning to purchase a new machine. The payback period will be six years. The new machine is expected to produce cash flow from operations, net of income taxes, of $3,500 a year for each of the first three years of the payback period and $2,500 a year for each of the last three years of the payback period. Depreciation of $2,000 a year will be charged to income for each of the six years of the payback period. How much will the machine cost?
   a. $6,000.
   b. $12,000.
   c. $18,000.
   d. $21,000.

(AICPA adapted)

12–13 Accounting Rate of Return and Payback

1. The Herb Company acquired a new machine for $16,000 that it will depreciate on a straight-line basis over a 10-year period. A full year's depreciation was taken in the year of acquisition. The accounting (book value) rate of return is expected to be 12 percent on the initial increase in required investment. If we assume a uniform cash inflow, the annual cash flow from operations, net of income taxes, will be
   - a. $320.
   - b. $1,728.
   - c. $1,920.
   - d. $3,520.

2. The Fudge Company is planning to purchase a new machine that it will depreciate on a straight-line basis over a 10-year period with no salvage value and a full year's depreciation taken in the year of acquisition. The new machine is expected to produce cash flow from operations, net of income taxes, of $66,000 a year in each of the next 10 years. The accounting (book value) rate of return on the initial investment is expected to be 12 percent. How much will the new machine cost?
   - a. $300,000.
   - b. $550,000.
   - c. $660,000.
   - d. $792,000.

3. Saratoga Company is planning to purchase a new machine for $600,000. The new machine will be depreciated on the straight-line basis over a six-year period with no salvage, and a full year's depreciation will be taken in the year of acquisition. The new machine is expected to produce cash flow from operations, net of income taxes, of $150,000 a year in each of the next six years. The accounting (book value) rate of return on the initial investment is expected to be
   - a. 8.3 percent.
   - b. 12.0 percent.
   - c. 16.7 percent.
   - d. 25.0 percent.

(AICPA adapted)

12–14 Accounting Rate of Return

Boyle Industries uses the accounting rate of return to evaluate its investments in fixed assets. The following data regarding three alternative projects under consideration are available:

Project	Initial Investment	Annual Cash Inflow	Useful Life	Income Taxes
A	$35,000	$8,500	7 years	$1,400
B	32,000	7,250	8 years	1,300
C	36,000	9,000	6 years	1,200

Required Using the average investment, determine which project would yield the highest return.

12–15   (Appendix 12–A):   Using Future Value Compound-Interest Tables

1. James Martin borrowed $5,000 from his employer for a period of four years. Compute the maturity value of the loan if the interest rate is 12 percent and the frequency of compounding is:
    a. Annually.
    b. Semiannually.
    c. Quarterly.
2. Mitchell Lawrence plans to retire in 10 years. He plans to deposit $2,250 per annum into an IRA. How much will he have at retirement if he can earn 10 percent annually and the frequency of compounding is:
    a. Annually?
    b. Semiannually? (Assume that the deposit of $2,250 will be made in two installments of $1,125 each.)

12–16   (Appendix 12–A):   Using Present Value Compound-Interest Tables

1. Linda Brooke expects to retire in five years. At that time, she would like to take an extensive trip that is estimated to cost $10,000. She believes she can earn 12 percent interest during the five-year period. How much money should she deposit today to have the $10,000 available if interest is compounded:
    a. Annually?
    b. Semiannually?
    c. Quarterly?
2. Marshall Burton plans to retire in 10 years. At that time, he would like to purchase an annuity from an insurance company that will provide him with $30,000 annually for a period of 12 years. How much will he have to deposit 10 years from now if the interest rate allowed by the insurance company is 10 percent per annum and it is compounded:
    a. Annually?
    b. Semiannually? (Assume that the $30,000 will be paid twice per annum at $15,000 each.)

12–17   (Appendix 12–A):   Using Compound-Interest Tables

1. Charles Philip plans to retire in 10 years. At that time, he would like to have $100,000 available to purchase a home in a retirement community. How much should he deposit at the end of each year for the next 10 years in order to have the $100,000 if he can earn interest at 11 percent compounded annually?
2. Rita Sutton has a 10-year old daughter. The mother expects her daughter to attend college in eight years. It is estimated that college tuition will then be $15,000 per annum for the four years. How much should the mother deposit at the end of each year during the next eight years to provide for the college tuition if the fund can earn interest at the rate of 12 percent per annum compounded annually? (Hint: Consider the annual tuition of $15,000 as one part of the solution and the amount to contribute to the fund as the other part of the solution.)

12–18   (Appendix 12–A):   Using Compound-Interest Tables

1. Ronald Samuels entered a giveaway contest and won first prize. The winner can elect to receive the prize in one of four ways. They are:
    a. $250,000 in one sum today.
    b. $400,000 at the end of five years.

c. $65,000 at the end of each year for five years, the first payment commencing one year from now.

d. $40,000 at the end of each year for 10 years, the first payment commencing one year from now.

Assume that Samuels can earn 10 percent interest per annum compounded annually. Income tax considerations are to be ignored. Which option should Samuels take? Why?

Would your answer be different if the first payment in options (c) and (d) were to commence today? Why?

2. Gabriel Shane won a lottery. The lottery advertises a jackpot of $3.5 million. Payments are made at the rate of $175,000 per annum for 20 years. If money can be invested at 12 percent and the payments are made at the end of each year, how much did Shane really win?

12–19 (Appendix 12–A): Using Compound-Interest Tables

Ralph Hunter is contemplating the purchase of a $10,000 bond that matures in 15 years, i.e., the face value of $10,000 will be paid at maturity. The bond pays interest annually, at the end of each year. The amount of the interest paid is $800. Hunter wishes to earn 10 percent on his investment.

Required a. How much should Hunter pay for the bond in order to earn 10 percent?

b. Using the same procedure you used in (a), calculate the price Hunter should pay for the bond if he is willing to earn only 8 percent on his investment. How do you explain your answer?

PROBLEMS 12–20 Net Present Value Analysis for Purchasing a New Machine and Replacing an Existing Machine (Extension of Exercise 11–1)

The Montana Corporation is presently using a machine, M–1, in its production process. It is contemplating the purchase of a newer, more efficient machine, M–2. The following information is available:

	M–1	M–2
Purchase price	$500,000	$1,000,000
Useful life	15 years	10 years
Salvage value	$ 50,000	$ 80,000
Sales revenue	500,000	600,000
Direct materials cost	90,000	108,000
Direct labor	150,000	130,000
Variable overhead	90,000	78,000
Direct fixed overhead	70,000	90,000

Income taxes are to be ignored. The firm's cutoff rate for investments is 18 percent.

Required a. Assume that the Montana Corporation is contemplating the purchase of M–2 and intends to keep M–1 also. There is a sufficient market for the firm's output from both machines. Prepare schedules to compute:

(1) The net investment of M–2.

(2) The cash operating advantage of M–2.

(3) The net present value to determine if M–2 should be purchased. Should M–2 be purchased? Why?

b. Assume that market conditions are such that the corporation can sell the output from M–2 or M–1 but not both. Thus, if M–2 is purchased, M–1 will be sold for $100,000. Using differential analysis, prepare schedules to compute:

(1) The net investment of M–2.
(2) The cash operating advantage of M–2.
(3) The net present value to determine if M–1 should be replaced. Should M–1 be replaced? Why?

12–21 Net Present Value Analysis for Purchasing a New Machine and Replacing an Existing Machine

The Monterey Corporation is presently using a machine, R–1, in its production process. It is contemplating the purchase of a newer, more efficient machine, R–2. The following information is available:

	R-1	R-2
Purchase price	$ 80,000	$220,000
Useful life	8 years	6 years
Salvage value	$ 5,000	$ 12,000
Sales revenue	400,000	450,000
Direct materials cost	80,000	80,000
Direct labor	100,000	90,000
Variable overhead	60,000	54,000
Direct fixed overhead	120,000	140,000

Income taxes are to be ignored. The firm's cutoff rate for investments is 16 percent.

Required

a. Assume that the Monterey Corporation is contemplating the purchase of R–2 and intends to keep R–1 also. There is a sufficient market for the firm's output from both machines. Prepare schedules to compute:

(1) The net investment of R–2.
(2) The cash operating advantage of R–2.
(3) The net present value to determine if R–2 should be purchased. Should R–2 be purchased? Why?

b. Assume that market conditions are such that the corporation can sell the output from R–2 or R–1 but not both. Thus, if R–2 is purchased, R–1 will be sold for $50,000. Using differential analysis, prepare schedules to compute:

(1) The net investment of R–2.
(2) The cash operating advantage of R–2.
(3) The net present value to determine if R–1 should be replaced. Should R–1 be replaced? Why?

12–22 Net Present Value Analysis for Replacing Equipment (Extension of Exercise 11–2): Comparative Income Approach

The Nebraska Corporation is presently using a machine, K–1, in its production process. It is contemplating the purchase of a newer, more efficient machine, K–9. The following information is available:

	K–1	K–9
Purchase price	$65,000	$100,000
Useful life	12 years	8 years
Salvage value	$ 5,000	$ 4,000
Present resale value	30,000	
Sales revenue	50,000	60,000
Direct materials cost	10,000	12,000
Direct labor	12,000	9,000
Variable overhead	6,000	4,500
Direct fixed overhead	10,000	11,000
Cost to overhaul K–1 to extend		
its remaining life by four years		
for a total of eight years	15,000	

Income taxes are to be ignored. The firm's cutoff rate for investments is 14 percent.

Required a. Using the comparative income approach, compute the following:
   (1) The net investment of purchasing K–9.
   (2) The cash operating advantage of K–9.
   (3) The net present value to determine if K–9 should be purchased.
 b. Using the comparative income approach, compute the following:
   (1) The net investment of retaining K–1. (Hint: Use K–1's opportunity cost.)
   (2) The cash operating advantage of K–1.
   (3) The net present value to determine if K–1 should be retained.
 c. Should K–9 be purchased and K–1 sold? Why?

12–23 Net Present Value Analysis for Replacing Equipment (Extension of Exercise 11–2): Differential Income Approach

The Nebraska Corporation is presently using a machine, K–1, in its production process. It is contemplating the purchase of a newer, more efficient machine, K–9. The following information is available:

	K–1	K–9
Purchase price	65,000	$100,000
Useful life	12 years	8 years
Salvage value	$ 5,000	$ 4,000
Present resale value	30,000	
Sales revenue	50,000	60,000
Direct materials cost	10,000	12,000
Direct labor	12,000	9,000
Variable overhead	6,000	4,500
Direct fixed overhead	10,000	11,000
Cost to overhaul K–1 to extend		
its remaining life by four years		
for a total of eight years	15,000	

Income taxes are to be ignored. The firm's cutoff rate for investments is 14 percent.

Required a. Using the differential income approach, compute the following:
   (1) The net investment of replacing K–1.

(2) The cash operating advantage of replacing K–1.

b. Compute the net present value to determine if K–1 should be replaced. Should K–1 be replaced? Why?

12-24 Comparative Income and Differential Income Approaches to Net Present Value Analysis of Replacing a Machine

The management of Universal Technical Systems is contemplating the purchase of a new machine (at a cost of $100,000) that is capable of producing 192,000 units per year. This machine would replace a machine that is capable of producing 130,000 units per annum and that can be sold for $20,000. The contribution margin per unit from operating the new machine is $0.125, while it is $0.10 per unit from operating the old machine.

The useful life of the old machine was 10 years when it was purchased two years ago. The useful life of the new machine is eight years. The new machine has a salvage value of $20,000, while the old machine's salvage value is zero. The old machine will require an overhaul at the end of two years from today at a cost of $10,000. The new machine will require an overhaul at the end of the fourth year at a cost of $8,000.

The firm's cutoff rate for investment decisions is 10 percent. Income taxes are to be ignored.

Required a. Using the comparative income approach and net present value analysis, determine if the old machine should be replaced.

b. Redo (a) using the differential income approach to reach your decision.

12-25 Comparative Income and Differential Income Approaches to Net Present Value Analysis of Replacing a Machine

Carmel Company purchased a machine two years ago at a cost of $750,000. At that time, the equipment had a useful life of 12 years and a salvage value of $100,000. At the end of the fifth year (three years from now), the equipment is due for a $75,000 overhaul. Estimated cash inflow from the equipment is $35,000 per year. The company is considering the purchase of newer equipment as a replacement. The cost of the new equipment would be $1.4 million. The equipment manufacturer is offering a trade-in allowance of $250,000 for the old equipment. The new equipment represents state-of-the-art technology and the company expects productivity savings of $190,000 per year over the old equipment. The new equipment will have a useful life of 10 years and a disposal value of $250,000. The company considers a return of less than 12 percent on investments unacceptable.

Required a. Using the comparative income approach and net present value analysis, determine if the old machine should be replaced.

b. Redo (a) using the differential income approach to reach your decision.

12-26 Differential Income Approach and Net Present Value Analysis for Purchasing a New Machine and Replacing an Existing Machine (Extension of Problem 11–24)

The Oregon Corporation is presently using two machines, K–1 and K–2, in its production process. It is contemplating the purchase of an automated, more efficient machine, K–5. The following information is available:

	K-1	K-2	K-5
Purchase price	$ 50,000	$ 70,000	$150,000
Useful life	10 years	7 years	5 years
Salvage value	$ 5,000	$ 7,000	$ 15,000
Accumulated depreciation			
K-1 ($45,000 ÷ 10 years = $4,500 per			
annum × 5 years)	22,500		
K-2 ($63,000 ÷ 7 years = $9,000 per			
annum × 2 years)		18,000	
Depreciation per annum	4,500	9,000	27,000
Sales revenue	400,000	400,000	400,000
Direct materials cost	80,000	80,000	80,000
Direct labor	100,000	100,000	60,000
Variable overhead	40,000	40,000	24,000
Direct fixed overhead	80,000	80,000	100,000

At present, the company uses the K–2 machine as its principal machine, while the K–1 machine is only used when the K–2 is down for repairs and maintenance. Occasionally, the K–1 machine is also used when the firm is very busy and must add a special shift of employees. The K–1 and K–2 machines are similar except that the K–1 is older and better constructed. Actually, the K–1 is in better condition in some respects. At the present time, they both have the same resale value of $30,000.

Income taxes are to be ignored. The firm's cutoff rate on investments is 16 percent.

Required a. Assume that the Oregon Corporation is contemplating the purchase of K–5 and also intends to keep both K–1 and K–2. There is a sufficient market for the firm's output from all machines. Prepare schedules to compute:
(1) The net investment of K–5.
(2) The cash operating advantage of K–5.
(3) The net present value to determine if K–5 should be purchased. Should K–5 be purchased? Why?

b. Assume that market conditions are such that the corporation can sell the output from K–5 or K–2 but not both. Thus, if K–5 is purchased, either K–1 or K–2 will be sold and the one not sold will be used as a spare for K–5. Using the differential income approach, prepare schedules to compute:
(1) The net investment of K–5.
(2) The cash operating advantage of K–5.
(3) The net present value to determine if K–5 should be purchased and either K–1 or K–2 be sold. Should K–5 be purchased? Why?

12–27 Comparative Income and Differential Income Approaches to the Net Present Value Analysis of Replacing a Machine

The Canals Company is considering the purchase of a new piece of equipment (machine B) to use in its manufacturing process as a replacement for an old machine (machine A). Operating costs for machine A have been running at an average annual rate of $60,000. At the end of its useful life, five years from now, machine A will have a disposal value of $6,000. Three years from now, machine A will be due for a complete overhaul at a cost of $15,000. The book value of this machine is currently $36,000. It is being depreciated by the straight-line method and was purchased five years ago.

Machine B will cost the company $60,000 and have a disposal value of $4,500 at the end of its five-year useful life. The annual operating costs for this machine are estimated to be $40,000 annually.

Income taxes are to be ignored and the company uses a cutoff rate of 18 percent for this kind of investment.

Required

a. Using the comparative income approach, compute the net present value to determine if machine A should be replaced. Should machine A be replaced? Why?

b. Redo (a) using the differential income approach to reach your decision.

12–28 **Net Present Value Analysis for Entering a New Market (Extension of Exercise 11–3)**

The Aromatic Company, which produces inexpensive automatic coffeemakers, is thinking of introducing a new line of expensive automatic coffeemakers which will both grind the coffee beans and then brew the coffee. A market survey indicates that because of its high cost, there is only a limited market for this product and estimates that after five years there will be no market at all.

The following annual information about the new product is available to you:

Estimated sales (15,000 × $50)	$750,000
Cost of direct materials and direct labor	250,000
Variable overhead	70,000
Variable marketing costs	37,500
Direct fixed overhead, marketing, and administrative costs	150,000

Additional information:

Price of new machine	$750,000
Salvage value at the end of five years	10,000
Working capital needed at inception	70,000
Working capital returned at the end of five years . .	65,000
Depreciation of new machinery per annum	48,000

Income taxes are to be ignored. The firm's cutoff rate is 14 percent.

Required

a. Which of the above data is relevant to you in recommending whether it is advantageous for Aromatic to enter this new market?

b. Using net present value analysis, determine if it is advantageous for Aromatic to enter this new market.

12–29 **Purchasing an Existing Business, Net Present Value Analysis**

Sparky Little is working for a large corporation in its accounting department. It appears that Little's progress is blocked and he would like to try something else. Several evenings each week, Little visits a tavern called "Archer's Place." One evening when Little was feeling very discouraged, he learned that the tavern was for sale, and in the conversation that followed, Archer offered to sell the tavern to Little.

Archer has a 10-year assignable lease of the property. Little hired an engineering consultant to evaluate the equipment, and it was determined that the refrigeration unit would require an overhaul at a cost of $5,000 in five years.

Archer is asking $100,000 for the leasehold and equipment. The equipment should be worth about $20,000 at the end of the 10-year lease.

Little engaged the services of a CPA to review the tavern's records. The CPA is confident that the tavern will yield $20,000 in cash flow for the coming year. Little is equally confident that he can increase cash flow each year by 10 percent over the preceding year's cash flow. Working capital of $15,000 will be needed during the 10 years of operation and will be released at the end of the lease.

Income taxes are to be ignored. Little will only purchase the tavern if it yields a return of 18 percent or more.

Required Using net present value analysis at the 18 percent cutoff rate, determine if Little should purchase the tavern.

12–30 Simplified Calculation of Internal Rate of Return

The Berry Company is considering the purchase of one of two machines. The following information regarding each machine is available:

	Machine X	Machine Y
Cost	$150,000	$200,000
Useful life	15 years	20 years
Annual production	350,000 units	475,000 units
Contribution margin per unit	15 cents	16 cents
Direct annual fixed costs	$30,000	$45,000
Salvage value	–0–	–0–

The company is capable of selling all of the output produced by either machine. Income taxes are to be ignored.

Required a. Calculate the internal rate of return within two decimal places for each machine. Which machine should be purchased if the firm's cutoff rate is 12 percent?

b. The machines have different useful lives. What assumption is implicit when competing projects have unequal lives and the internal rate of return is used to evaluate the projects?

12–31 Profitability Index

The Booker Company is evaluating several investment projects. The following information is available:

	Project			
	N	O	P	Q
Net investment	$100,000	$120,000	$80,000	$150,000
Net present value	$ 49,227	$ 41,725	$32,605	$ 75,120
Life of project in years	8	10	7	12
Internal rate of return	25%	20%	24%	22%

The company's cutoff rate is 12 percent. The maximum amount that the company plans to invest is $150,000.

Required
a. Compute the profitability index for each project.
b. Rank the projects according to:
    (1) Net present value.
    (2) Internal rate of return.
    (3) Profitability index.
c. Explain why the rankings produce different preferences.
d. Which ranking is preferable? Why?

12–32 Lease or Purchase

The T&K Trucking Company's business is expanding and the firm's management decided that an additional truck is needed. The firm must decide whether to purchase or lease the truck.

Information regarding the purchase of the truck is as follows:

Purchase price	$30,000
Annual operating costs for maintenance, licenses, and fees	$ 2,000
Annual repairs:	
Year 1	$ 500
2	1,000
3	1,500
4	5,000
5	2,000
6	2,500
Useful life	6 years
Salvage value	$ 4,000

The truck can be leased for six years at an annual rental of $9,000 plus 10 cents per mile driven. The lessor will be responsible for repairs, maintenance, licenses, and fees. At the end of the lease term, the truck will be returned to the lessor.

The lessee is responsible for insurance and gasoline usage in either case. T&K normally uses the truck at the rate of 25,000 miles annually. Any damage to the truck is the responsibility of the lessee. The lessor requires a deposit of $4,000 which will be refunded at the end of the lease term if the truck is returned undamaged.

The cost of capital for T&K is 12 percent.

Required
(Ignore income taxes.)
a. Using present value analysis, compute the cost of purchasing the truck.
b. Using present value analysis, compute the cost of renting the truck for six years.
c. What choice do you recommend? Why?

12–33 Lease or Purchase

The Sellmore company hired an additional traveling salesman. Since it is the firm's policy to provide every salesperson with an automobile, Sellmore must decide whether to purchase or lease an automobile for the new salesman.

Information regarding the purchase of the auto is as follows:

Purchase price	$12,000
Annual operating costs for maintenance,	
licenses, and fees	$ 600
Annual repairs:	
Year 1	$ 300
2	1,000
3	1,500
4	2,000
Useful life	4 years
Salvage value	$ 3,000

The automobile can be leased for four years at an annual rental of $4,000 plus 10 cents per mile driven in excess of 60,000 miles. The lessor will be responsible for repairs, maintenance, licenses, and fees. At the end of the lease term, the auto will be returned to the lessor and the lessee will pay the excess mileage charge at that time.

The lessee is responsible for insurance and gasoline usage in either case. Sellmore expects its salesman to use the automobile at the rate of 20,000 miles annually. Any damage to the auto is the responsibility of the lessee. The lessor requires a deposit of $2,000 which will be refunded at the end of the lease term if the auto is returned undamaged.

The cost of capital for Sellmore is 12 percent.

Required

(Ignore income taxes.)

a. Using present value analysis, compute the cost of purchasing the automobile.

b. Using present value analysis, compute the cost of renting the automobile for four years.

c. What choice do you recommend? Why?

12–34 **Discontinuing a Segment of a Business and Net Present Value Analysis**

The Crum Company has two divisions—division C and division D. The firm's segmented income statement by divisions for the year 19x5 appears below:

CRUM COMPANY
Segmented Income Statement—Contribution Format
For the Year Ended December 31, 19x5

	Total	Division C	Division D
Sales	$1,000,000	$400,000	$600,000
Variable cost of goods sold	340,000	100,000	240,000
Variable cost manufacturing margin	660,000	300,000	360,000
Variable marketing costs	170,000	140,000	30,000
Contribution margin	490,000	160,000	330,000
Fixed costs	500,000	250,000	250,000
Operating income (loss) before income taxes	$ (10,000)	$ (90,000)	$ 80,000

The president of the company is considering whether to cease operating division C. She asks you to analyze the operations of the division so that she can reach a decision regarding the future operations of the division.

The following information is available for your analysis:

1. Division C's fixed costs consist of:

Direct fixed costs	$150,000
Common costs	70,000
Depreciation of machinery	30,000
Total	$250,000

2. If division C is discontinued, division D can be expanded. The marketing department is fairly certain that the sales of division D can be increased by 20 percent. Variable costs at this level are expected to maintain their existing relationship.
3. The machinery used by division C cannot be adapted to division D's production. Thus, it must be sold in the secondhand market. Its resale value is $30,000.
4. New equipment will be required by division D. Its cost is expected to amount to $340,000 with a useful life of 10 years. Salvage value at that time is projected at $30,000.
5. Division C has $40,000 of working capital which will be released to division D. An additional $10,000 of working capital will be required for a total of $50,000. This amount will be released at the end of this expansion phase 10 years hence.

Income taxes are to be ignored. The firm's cutoff rate for investments is 14 percent.

Required   *a.* Using the differential income approach, compute:
    (1) The net investment.
    (2) The cash operating advantage.
  b. Using net present value analysis, determine if division C should be discontinued.
  c. Compute the internal rate of return to within two decimal places.

12–35   **Payback, Net Present Value, Internal Rate of Return, Profitability Index, and Accounting Rate of Return**

The president of Carmel Company has asked you to evaluate an investment she is considering. Two machines, machine R and machine S, are under consideration. Only one machine will be purchased.

Information concerning the machines is as follows:

	Machine R	Machine S
Investment	$200,000	$180,000
Annual cash operating advantage	$ 50,000	$ 36,000
Useful life	10 years	15 years
Salvage value	–0–	–0–

Income taxes are to be ignored. The firm's cost of capital is 14 percent. The company uses straight-line depreciation.

Required a. For each machine, compute:
    (1) Payback.
    (2) The net present value.
    (3) The internal rate of return to two decimal places.
    (4) The profitability index.
    (5) The accounting rate of return using the gross investment as the base.
    b. For each calculation in *(a)*, indicate your preference. Are they all consistent? Do they have to be consistent? Explain.

12–36 Payback, Net Present Value, Internal Rate of Return, Profitability Index, and Accounting Rate of Return

The president of Camden Company has asked you to evaluate an investment he is considering. Two machines, machine T and machine V, are under consideration. Only one machine will be purchased.

Information concerning the machines is as follows:

	Machine T	Machine V
Investment	$400,000	$360,000
Annual cash operating advantage	$100,000	$ 70,000
Useful life	8 years	15 years
Salvage value	–0–	–0–

Income taxes are to be ignored. The firm's cost of capital is 14 percent. The company uses straight-line depreciation.

Required a. For each machine, compute:
    (1) Payback.
    (2) The net present value.
    (3) The internal rate of return to two decimal places.
    (4) The profitability index.
    (5) The accounting rate of return using the gross investment.
    b. For each calculation in *(a)*, indicate your preference. Are they all consistent? Do they have to be consistent? Why?

12–37 Payback, Accounting Rate of Return, and Internal Rate of Return

The Crest Service Station sells gasoline at the retail level and is contemplating the acquisition of an automatic car wash.

The following information is relevant to the acquisition of the car wash:

1. The cost of the car wash is $80,000.
2. The anticipated revenue from the car wash is $50,000 per annum.
3. The useful life of the car wash is 10 years.
4. Annual operating costs are expected to be:

Salaries	$15,000
Utilities	4,800
Water usage	2,200
Supplies	3,000
Repairs and maintenance	5,000

5. The firm uses straight-line depreciation.
6. The salvage value for the car wash is $0.
7. The company's cutoff points are as follows:

Payback . . . .   3 years
Accounting rate of return . . . . .   18 percent
Internal rate of return . . . .   18 percent

Ignore income taxes.

Required   *a.* Compute the cash operating advantage.
              b. Compute accounting operating income.
              c. Compute payback.
              d. Compute the accounting rate of return using the gross investment as the base.
              e. Compute the internal rate of return to the nearest two decimal places.
              f. Should the car wash be purchased? Explain your answer.

12–38   Payback, Accounting Rate of Return, and Internal Rate of Return

The operator of a self-service gasoline filling station is contemplating the addition of a convenience food store to the premises. The landlord has agreed to construct an addition to the building to house the food mart. The additional rent cost would amount to $24,000 per year.

Additional information is as follows:

1. Fixtures, refrigerators, and shelves would cost $125,000 with a useful life of eight years.
2. The expected sales are $500,000 per annum on which the contribution margin ratio is 30 percent.
3. Annual operating fixed costs are expected to be:

Salaries $30,000
Utilities   9,000
Supplies   10,000
Repairs and maintenance   6,000
Other costs   40,000

4. The salvage value of the fixtures is expected to be $0, and straight-line depreciation is used.
5. The operator of the food mart plans to retire at the end of eight years.
6. The company's cutoff points are as follows:

Payback . . . .   4 years
Accounting rate of return . . . . .   16 percent
Internal rate of return . . . .   16 percent

Ignore income taxes.

Required   *a.* Compute the cash operating advantage.
              b. Compute accounting operating income.
              c. Compute payback.
              d. Compute the accounting rate of return using the gross investment as the base.
              e. Compute the internal rate of return to the nearest two decimal places.
              f. Should the food mart be opened? Explain your answer.

13

INCOME TAX EFFECTS ON CAPITAL-BUDGETING DECISIONS

Assume that you won $1 million in a lottery, payable at $50,000 a year for a period of 20 years. It would certainly be exciting to learn that you had won $1 million. However, after the initial surprise, you would have to decide how much of each annual payment you would like to save, how much you would like to spend, and what items you would like to buy. In doing so, you would not base your decisions on the gross annual amount of $50,000 but rather on the amount that would remain after you paid the required income taxes. Thus, your decision would be based on your *after-tax* disposable income. The same concept applies to capital-budgeting decisions. For a capital-budgeting decision to be correct, it must be made on an *after-tax basis.*

DECISION MAKING AND INCOME TAXES

Income taxes affect all facets of decision making, and the failure to consider them may lead to incorrect decisions. For example, assume that a firm has some seasonally idle cash to invest and is considering investing $1 million in either U.S. government notes paying 10 percent and maturing in six months or municipal bonds of the same risk paying 8 percent and also maturing in six months. The interest received on the municipal bonds will be exempt from federal income taxation, and the firm's income tax rate is 40 percent. If the decision were based on the gross amount of interest received, the firm would favor the U.S. government securities, since it would receive $50,000

($1 million $\times \dfrac{10}{100} \times \dfrac{6}{12} =$ $50,000) from this investment and only $40,000

($1 million $\times \dfrac{8}{100} \times \dfrac{6}{12} =$ $40,000) from the municipal bonds. However, given the firm's 40 percent income tax rate, this decision would be incorrect. The analysis should be made as follows:

	U.S. Government Notes	Municipal Bonds
Interest income	$50,000	$40,000
Less: Income tax at 40 percent	20,000	–0–
Disposable income after income tax	$30,000	$40,000

By considering the income tax effect on income, the firm would reach the correct decision and purchase the municipal bonds instead of the U.S. government notes.

The analysis may be simplified considerably by converting the gross revenues directly into after-tax revenues. Any revenue or cost may be converted into its after-tax equivalent as follows:

$$\text{After-tax revenue or cost} = \text{Revenue (or cost)} \times (1 - \text{Tax rate}) \quad \textbf{(1)}$$

When the interest on the U.S. government note is inserted into equation (1), the result is:

$$\$50,000 \; (1 - .40) = \$30,000$$

The after-tax revenue of $30,000 may then be compared directly with other competing after-tax revenues for the purpose of selecting the largest.

The same procedure may be applied to compute an after-tax cost. For example, if a firm is contemplating a direct-mail campaign that is expected to cost $20,000, its after-tax cost, using a 40 percent tax rate, would be:

$$\text{After-tax cost} = \$20,000 \; (1 - .40) = \$12,000$$

An essential ingredient of capital-budgeting decisions is the present value of the cash operating advantage. Nonprofit hospitals, schools, and governmental units pay no income taxes; thus, their capital-budgeting decisions may be based on the analysis presented in Chapter 12. However, for-profit firms must pay income taxes, and the managers of these firms must use after-tax cash flows for present value analysis if their decisions are to be valid.

After-Tax Cash Flows for Capital-Budgeting Analysis

An **after-tax cash flow** is the value of a cash inflow or outflow after giving effect to income taxes. The computation of the after-tax cash operating advantage is very similar to the technique used to compute cash operating advantage in Chapter 12 except that the before-tax amount must be reduced by the amount of income tax to be paid.

Tax Shields.　A **tax shield** is any *deduction on a firm's income tax return* that does *not* require an outlay of cash in *that* period. Although depreciation is not a relevant cost for capital-budgeting decisions, *it is deductible for income tax purposes* and thus has an effect on the amount of income taxes that a firm pays. The same is true for the book value (the tax basis) of a machine that is to be sold at a loss or scrapped when newer equipment is bought to replace it. The most common tax shields are depreciation and losses on the disposal of assets. The computation of the tax saving resulting from a tax shield is:

$$\text{Tax saving} = \text{Tax shield} \times \text{Tax rate}$$

ILLUSTRATION 13–1

MAYFAIR COMPANY
Calculation of After-Tax Cash Operating Advantage

Annual direct labor cost savings	$40,000
Less: Depreciation ($90,000 ÷ 6 years)	15,000
Operating advantage before income tax	25,000
Less: Income tax at 40 percent	10,000
Net income	15,000
Add: Depreciation*	15,000
Cash operating advantage after income tax . .	$30,000

* Depreciation must be added back to net income to arrive at the cash inflow because it is *not a cash outflow* but is deductible on the firm's income tax return.

The Mayfair Company is planning to purchase a new machine for $90,000 and expects to save direct labor costs of $40,000 per annum for a period of six years, the useful life of the machine. Mayfair's income tax rate is 40 percent, and for ease of presentation, we will ignore salvage value. The after-tax cash operating advantage may be computed as shown in Illustration 13–1. It is important to note that depreciation is deducted to arrive at the amount of income subject to income tax but that the depreciation must be added back to the after-tax net income because it is *not a cash outflow* and does not affect cash. It merely affects the amount of income tax that the firm pays.

The results may be verified by the following:

Annual direct labor cost savings	$40,000
Less: Income tax	10,000
Cash operating advantage after income tax	$30,000

An alternate method of determining the after-tax cash operating advantage is to compute the after-tax direct labor cost savings and then add the tax savings of the depreciation to the result. Using its depreciation of $15,000, the Mayfair Company would compute its tax savings from depreciation as:

$$\text{Tax savings} = \$15,000 \times 40 \text{ percent} = \$6,000$$

Then its cash operating advantage after taxes could be computed as:

After-tax savings of direct labor = $40,000 (1 − .40) . .	$24,000
Add: Income tax savings from depreciation tax shield ($15,000 × .40)	6,000
Cash operating advantage after income tax	$30,000

Notice that the after-tax cash flow from the saving of direct labor is computed using 1 minus the tax rate (60 percent), while the saving from the depreciation tax shield is computed using the tax rate itself (40 percent). The 60 percent rate is applied to cash inflows because the objective is to compute how much is left for the firm after *paying* income tax on the cash inflow. The 40 percent rate is applied to tax shields because the objective is to compute how much income tax the firm is *not paying* as a result of using a tax shield. Since the objectives differ, the rates differ.

For tax purposes, the book value of old equipment that will be sold or scrapped if new equipment is purchased may also be a tax shield. Since a *loss* on the sale of old equipment is deductible on an income tax return and since no cash for the loss is disbursed (cash may, in fact, be *received*), a firm will have the equivalent of a cash receipt equal to the income tax saved. The calculation of the tax shield is similar to that for depreciation except that the book value of the old equipment must be reduced by the expected sales proceeds.

The Saybrook Company is contemplating the replacement of an existing machine with a newer, more efficient machine. The old machine has a book value of $20,000 and can be sold for $4,000. The tax shield would be $16,000 ($20,000 − $4,000), and the tax savings, using a 40 percent tax rate, would be:

$$\text{Tax savings} = \$16,000 \times 40 \text{ percent} = \$6,400$$

A tax shield can sometimes make the difference between a project that is profitable and not profitable. For example, the Taylor Company is considering two competing projects. The projects have the same useful life, the same net investment, the same cash operating advantage before income taxes, and the same income tax rates. The only difference is that the net investment in project A may be depreciated over its useful life for tax purposes, while the net investment in project B cannot be depreciated but must be carried at its original amount until the company is either sold or liquidated, at which time the original amount may be deducted in full on the firm's final tax return. An example of such an investment would be the goodwill acquired in a business merger. Here are the relevant data for the two projects:

	Project A	Project B
Net investment	$100,000	$100,000
Useful life	10 years	10 years
Annual cash operating advantage		
before income tax	$ 30,000	$ 30,000
Income tax rate	40%	40%
After-tax discount rate	14%	14%

Each project's cash operating advantage after income tax may be computed as follows:

Project A:		
Annual after-tax cash inflow: $30,000 (1 − .40)	$18,000
Add: Tax savings on depreciation tax shield	
($100,000 ÷ 10 years = $10,000 × 40%)	4,000
Cash operating advantage after income tax	$22,000
Project B:	
After-tax cash inflow: $30,000 (1 − .40) =	
$18,000 (also cash operating advantage	
after income tax)	$18,000

The net present value of each project would be:

Project A:
Present value of cash inflow
   ($22,000 × 5.21612*) $114,755
Less: Net investment at present value
   ($100,000 × 1.00000)   100,000
              Net present value . . . . $ 14,755

Project B:
Present value of cash inflow
   ($18,000 × 5.21612*) . . . . $ 93,890
Less: net investment at present value
   ($100,000 × 1.0000)   100,000
              Net present value . . . . $ (6,110)

* From Table 4, $n = 10$, $i = 14\%$.

This analysis indicates that project A passes the cutoff rate while project B does not. In effect, the depreciation tax shield may be the difference that makes a project acceptable. The present value of the tax shield for project B is ignored because the present value of its tax benefit is very small and thus would not alter the decision. For example, if it is anticipated that the company will be sold or liquidated more than 25 years into the future, the present value of the tax savings from the net investment in project B would be *less than $3,779,* computed as follows:

$$\text{Present value} = \$100,000 \times .03779^* = \$3,779$$

* From Table 2, $n = 25$, $i = 14\%$.

A longer time horizon, such as 50 years, would produce a present value of $100 ($100,000 × .001—from another table). In either case, the present value of the tax savings does not affect the outcome of the decision in this case, and for most other cases the decision might be unchanged as well.

Like the depreciation tax shield, the choice of depreciation method, when a choice is available, may also alter a capital-budgeting decision. Thus, managers must understand how different depreciation methods affect after-tax income.

Depreciation Methods and Their Effects on Capital-Budgeting Decisions

Prior to 1981, taxpayers could choose one of several depreciation methods: the straight-line, sum-of-the-years'-digits, declining-balance, and units-of-production methods. Since these methods may still be used under certain conditions, managers should be familiar with their computations, which are thoroughly discussed in most financial accounting textbooks.

By law, the choice of depreciation methods has been narrowed for years after 1980. Congress legislated a new approach, the accelerated cost recovery system (ACRS), and taxpayers must now use either the ACRS or the straight-line method in computing their taxes.

ILLUSTRATION 13–2 **Classification by Recovery Period of Property Used in a Trade or Business**

Recovery Period	Kind of Property
3-year	Automobiles, taxis, light-duty trucks, research and experimentation equipment, and special tools used in certain manufacturing industries
5-year	All other machinery and equipment not included in another class
10-year	Certain public utility property, such as railroad tank cars and coal-burning equipment, and certain real property, such as amusement parks and manufactured residential homes
15-year	All public utility property not included as 10-year property
18-year	Most real property not included as 10-year property

ILLUSTRATION 13–3 **Allowable ACRS Depreciation Deductions**

The applicable percentage for the class of property is:

If the Taxable Year is:	3-Year	5-Year	10-Year	15-Year Public Utility	18-Year Real Property*
1	25	15	8	5	9
2	38	22	14	10	9
3	37	21	12	9	8
4		21	10	8	7
5		21	10	7	7
6			10	7	6
7			9	6	5
8			9	6	5
9			9	6	5
10			9	6	5
11				6	5
12				6	5
13				6	4
14				6	4
15				6	4
16					4
17					4
18					4

* The amounts shown for 18-year real property are to be used only if the real property is acquired in January (or in the first month of a company's fiscal year). Different amounts must be used if the property is acquired in a different month. These amounts may be obtained by consulting Internal Revenue Service publications.

The Accelerated Cost Recovery System. Federal tax laws require taxpayers to use ACRS unless they elect the straight-line method of depreciation. The **accelerated cost recovery system** is a depreciation method used for income tax purposes that classifies property into one of five groupings without regard to the property's actual useful life. The percentage of depreciation that may be claimed in each year an asset is owned is specified for each category. Prior to ACRS, one taxpayer could estimate a delivery van's useful life at three years while another taxpayer could estimate it at five years, depending on the number of miles driven per year. This is no longer possible because ACRS requires that all taxpayers use the same useful life for similar property. The ACRS classifications of property are presented in Illustration 13–2, while the percentages of deductible depreciation for each year are shown in Illustration 13–3.

The purchase date of equipment does not affect the amount of depreciation allowed in any year, nor does salvage value. Thus, a full year's depreciation is taken in the first year regardless of whether the property is purchased in the first or second half of the taxable year.

Taypayers are not required to use ACRS. Instead, they may use straight-line depreciation. If a taxpayer elects straight-line depreciation, the investment property must still be classified using the ACRS categories in Illustration 13–2. However, the property may be depreciated over either the usual recovery period or a longer specified period. The recovery periods and the optional depreciation periods are as follows:

In the Case of:	The Taxpayer May Elect a Recovery Period of:
3-year property	3, 5, or 12 years
5-year property	5, 12, or 25 years
10-year property	10, 25, or 35 years
15-year public utility property	15, 35, or 45 years

Thus, a taxpayer may choose to depreciate an automobile over 3 years, 5 years, or 12 years, without regard to its estimated useful life. When the straight-line method is elected, it is subject to the half-year convention.

The Half-Year Convention. When straight-line depreciation is elected, the recovery periods noted in Illustration 13–2 apply to the property placed in service, but only one half of a full year's depreciation is claimed in the first year, regardless of the date the property was purchased. Similarly, a half year's depreciation is claimed in the last year of the recovery period. This treatment, known as the **half-year convention,** may be illustrated as follows for an asset with a five-year recovery period:

Year	Percent of Depreciation Allowed
1	10
2	20
3	20
4	20
5	20
6	10
Total	100

Salvage value is ignored for both approaches to depreciation, as discussed later.

Selecting a Depreciation Method. Whenever a choice exists, the objective of a capital-budgeting decision should be to accelerate as many cash inflows as possible to the earliest years of the project. In addition, an attempt should be made to have larger inflows in the earlier years and smaller inflows in the later years. Because the earlier years have higher present value factors than the later years, these strategies will result in a higher net present value for a project and make the project more favorable to the firm. A dollar received now is worth more than a dollar received five years from now, and a tax shield that can be accelerated is worth more than one of an equivalent amount that cannot be accelerated.

The Estar Company is contemplating the purchase of a new machine for $100,000. The machine is five-year property, Estar Company's income tax rate is 40 percent, and it wishes to use an after-tax discount rate of 15 percent. The present values of the income tax savings using both the ACRS table from Illustration 13–3 and the straight-line method are shown in Illustration 13–4.

The comparison demonstrates that when a choice exists, the ACRS rates are usually more advantageous than the straight-line method with the half-year convention because the straight-line method produces smaller present value tax savings.

Once the depreciation strategy is decided, it is possible to apply it to the kinds of decisions managers must make when investment proposals are received.

AFTER-TAX CAPITAL BUDGETING

The most common capital-budgeting decisions usually involve cost-reduction decisions—such as the purchase of new labor-saving equipment or the replacement of an existing machine with a newer, more efficient machine—or profit-expansion decisions—such as entering a new market or introducing a new product. Because most of the after-tax capital-budgeting computations are the same for both the purchase of a new machine and the replacement of

ILLUSTRATION 13–4

ESTAR COMPANY
Computation of Present Values of Income Tax Savings
Using Alternative Depreciation Methods

ACRS Five-Year Method

(1)	(2)	(3)	(4)	(5)
			Present	
		Income Tax	Value of	Present
		Savings	15 Percent—From	Value
Year	Depreciation	(2) × 40%	Table 2	(3) × (4)
1	$ 15,000*	$ 6,000	.86957	$ 5,217
2	22,000†	8,800	.75614	6,654
3	21,000‡	8,400	.65752	5,523
4	21,000	8,400	.57175	4,803
5	21,000	8,400	.49718	4,176
Total	$100,000	$40,000		$26,373

Straight-Line Method

(1)	(2)	(3)	(4)	(5)	(6)
				Present	
			Income Tax	Value of	Present
			Savings	15 Percent—From	Value
Year	Percent	Depreciation	(3) × 40%	Table 2	(4) × (5)
1	10	$ 10,000	$ 4,000	.86957	$ 3,478
2	20	20,000	8,000	.75614	6,049
3	20	20,000	8,000	.65752	5,260
4	20	20,000	8,000	.57175	4,574
5	20	20,000	8,000	.49718	3,977
6	10	10,000	4,000	.43233	1,729
Total	100	$100,000	$40,000		$25,067

* $100,000 × 15% = $15,000.
† $100,000 × 22% = $22,000.
‡ $100,000 × 21% = $21,000.

an existing machine, our discussion will focus on a single cost-reduction example—the replacement of an existing machine. We will then examine the after-tax capital-budgeting procedures used when entering a new market.

Purchasing New or Replacement Equipment— Additional Tax Considerations

In Chapter 11, we discussed how to calculate the before-tax *net investment* and *cash operating advantage* when purchasing equipment. To be more accurate, however, these calculations should be made on an *after-tax basis,* since income taxes affect these cash flows just as they affect any other cash inflow or outflow.

Salvage Value

When evaluating a project's profitability, in addition to the depreciation tax shield, a firm must consider the salvage value of the machine and its after-tax effect on the net investment. Under ACRS, salvage value is not taken into account when computing the annual deduction for depreciation, but when the property is fully depreciated for tax purposes, its *basis*—the amount used to calculate a taxable gain—is zero. Thus, the proceeds from the sale of fully depreciated property at the end of its useful life would be subject to income tax. The after-tax cash inflow of $5,000 from the sale of a fully depreciated machine using a 40 percent tax rate may be calculated as follows:

$$\text{After-tax cash inflow} = (\text{Sales proceeds} - \text{Basis}) \, (1 - t) \qquad (2)$$
$$\text{After-tax cash inflow} = (\$5,000 - \$0) \, (1 - .40) = \$3,000$$

The Book Value of an Existing Machine

In our previous discussion, we noted that book value is not relevant to the decision to replace an old machine with a newer machine if differential analysis is used. However, when the old machine will be sold if the new machine is purchased, the book value of the existing machine must be used to calculate the tax consequences of its sale.

If a *taxable gain* results from the old machine's sale, the income tax due is a *cash outflow.* If a *taxable loss* results from the sale, the income tax saved is a *cash inflow.* The income tax consequences may be calculated as follows if the book value of the old equipment is $10,000, the sales proceeds are $4,000, and the tax rate is 25 percent:

$$\text{Income tax savings} = (\text{Book value} - \text{Sales proceeds}) \times \text{Tax rate} \qquad (3)$$
$$\text{Income tax savings} = (\$10,000 - \$4,000) \times .25 = \$1,500$$

ILLUSTRATION 13–5

MATURE PRODUCTS COMPANY
Information for the Replacement of a Machine

Original cost of the present machine	$40,000
Less: Accumulated depreciation	30,000
Book value (remaining undepreciated cost)	$10,000
Purchase price of new machine	$95,000
Useful life of new machine	5 years
Remaining useful life of old machine	2 years
Overhaul of old machine will extend its two-year remaining useful life by three years for a total of five years at a cost of	$10,000*
Salvage value of new machine	$ 6,000
Market value of old machine, if sold	4,000

	Old Machine	New Machine
Annual operating information:		
Sales	$400,000	$400,000
Direct material cost	90,000	90,000
Direct labor cost	80,000	60,000
Variable overhead	48,000	36,000
Fixed overhead exclusive of depreciation	100,000	100,000

* This will be deducted on the tax return in full in the year paid.

If a gain is anticipated, the equation may be modified to:

$$\text{Income tax due} = (\text{Sales proceeds} - \text{Book value}) \times \text{Tax rate} \qquad \textbf{(4)}$$

Differences in Tax Shields.   Another factor that must be considered when replacing existing equipment is the *difference* in the depreciation tax shields between the old machine and the new machine. When *differential analysis* is used, the difference is arrived at by netting the two. When the *comparative income approach* is used, each depreciation tax shield is considered separately.

We will now expand our machine replacement example from Chapter 11 to include the salvage value for the new machine. Remember that the Mature Products Company may replace one of its old machines with a faster machine. The older machine is nearing the end of its economic useful life, but its life can be extended by a major overhaul. The information needed to evaluate the replacement decision is presented in Illustration 13–5.

In addition, the Mature Products Company estimates that its after-tax cost of capital is 14 percent and its income tax rate is 25 percent. The company uses its cost of capital as the cutoff rate for capital-budgeting decisions.

Differential Analysis.   The steps needed to analyze the relevant data for a capital-budgeting decision using differential analysis are:

Step 1

Convert the before-tax annual cash operating advantage items to an after-tax basis, using equation (1):

After-tax annual direct labor savings = \$20,000 (1 − .25) = \$15,000
After-tax annual variable overhead savings = \$12,000 (1 − .25) = \$9,000
After-tax old machine overhaul = \$10,000 (1 − .25) = \$7,500*

  * For tax purposes, the cost of the machine overhaul is fully deductible in the year of the expenditure.

Step 2

Convert the salvage value of the new machine to an after-tax basis:

$$\text{After-tax salvage value} = \$6,000 \ (1 - .25) = \$4,500$$

Step 3

Using equation (3), compute the income tax savings on the book loss created when the old machine is sold:

$$\text{Income tax savings} = (\$10,000 - \$4,000) \times .25 = \$1,500$$

Step 4

Compute the differences in the amounts of depreciation allowable for tax purposes between the old machine and the new machine and convert them to the amount of tax savings for each year. The old machine is being depreciated on the straight-line basis. This analysis and computation appear in Illustration 13–6.

ILLUSTRATION 13–6

MATURE PRODUCTS COMPANY
Computation of the Income Tax Savings Resulting
from the Difference between the Depreciation Tax Shields
of Two Machines

	Amount	×	Tax Rate	=	Income Tax Savings
New machine:					
Cost of five-year property	$95,000				
Depreciation allowable:					
First year (15% × $95,000)	$14,250	×	.25	=	$3,563
Second year (22% × $95,000) . . .	20,900	×	.25	=	5,225
Third year (21% × $95,000)	19,950	×	.25	=	4,988
Fourth year (21% × $95,000)	19,950	×	.25	=	4,988
Fifth year (21% × $95,000)	19,950	×	.25	=	4,988
Total depreciation	$95,000				
Old machine:					
First year (10,000 book value ÷ 2 years)	$ 5,000	×	.25	=	$1,250
Second year	5,000	×	.25	=	1,250
Third year	0	×	.25	=	0
Fourth year	0	×	.25	=	0
Fifth year	0	×	.25	=	0
Total depreciaiton	$10,000				

	Income Tax Savings		
	New Machine	**Old Machine**	**Differential Amount**
Comparison:			
First year	$3,563	$1,250	$2,313
Second year	5,225	1,250	3,975
Third year	4,988	0	4,988
Fourth year	4,988	0	4,988
Fifth year	4,988	0	4,988

Step 5

Using the amounts computed in steps 1 through 4 together with the sales proceeds from the old machine and the investment, prepare the present value analysis needed to reach an investment decision as shown in Illustration 13–7.

Note the following from Illustration 13–7:

1. The direct labor savings, variable overhead savings, and machine-over-haul savings are all used on an *after-tax* basis.

ILLUSTRATION 13–7

MATURE PRODUCTS COMPANY
Calculation of Net Present Value on an After-Tax Basis
Retaining Old Machine or Purchasing a New Machine
Differential Analysis

Item	Present Value in Dollars	Present Value Factor	Time Period					
			0	1	2	3	4	5
Cash operating advantage:								
Direct labor savings	$ 51,496‡	3.43308*		$15,000	$15,000	$15,000	$15,000	$15,000
Variable overhead savings . . .	30,898	3.43308		9,000	9,000	9,000	9,000	9,000
Savings of old machine								
overhaul	5,771	.76947†			7,500			
	2,029	.87719†		2,313				
Depreciation tax shield	3,059	.76947†			3,975			
	3,367	.67497†				4,988		
	2,953	.59208†					4,988	
	2,591	.51937†						4,988
Total	$ 102,164							
Net Investment:								
Purchase price of								
new machine	$(95,000)	1.00000	$(95,000)					
Sales proceeds of								
old machine	4,000	1.00000	4,000					
Tax shield from loss on								
sale of old machine . . .	1,500	1.00000	1,500					
Salvage value of								
new machine	2,337§	.51937†						4,500
Net investment	(87,163)							
Net present value	$ 15,001‖							

* From Table 4.
† From Table 2.
‡ $15,000 × 3.43308 = $51,496.
§ $ 4,500 × .51937 = $ 2,337.
‖ The present value of the cash operating advantage minus the present value of the net investment ($102,164 − $87,163).

2. The purchase price of the new machine is *not* adjusted for income taxes. The deduction for tax purposes of this cash outlay is recouped by the depreciation tax shield.

3. The sales proceeds from the old machine are *not* adjusted for income taxes, while the *loss on the sale of the old machine* is recouped as a tax savings on a net-tax basis. The rationale for this treatment is that the book value (tax basis) of $10,000 may be viewed as consisting of two parts. The first part is the $4,000 of cost that is recovered from the machine's sale and no tax effects should occur when something is sold for the exact amount of its cost. The second part is the remaining $6,000, which will not be recovered and is lost. This loss is deductible on the firm's tax return, and at a 25 percent tax rate, the firm will save $1,500 ($6,000 × .25) in taxes.

The Comparative Income Approach.   The comparative income approach can lead to the same results as differential analysis if present values are computed separately for each alternative—that is, keeping the old machine and purchasing the new machine. The steps needed to prepare the comparative income analysis are:

Step 1

Convert all revenues and costs to an after-tax basis for each alternative using equation (1).

For example, sales revenue may be converted as follows:

$$\text{After-tax sales revenue} = \$400,000 \, (1 - .25) = \$300,000$$

Step 2

Convert the salvage value of the new machine to an after-tax basis:

$$\text{After-tax salvage value} = \$6,000 \, (1 - .25) = \$4,500$$

Step 3

Using equation (3), compute the income tax savings on the book loss created when the old machine is sold:

$$\text{Income tax savings} = (\$10,000 - \$4,000) \times .25 = \$1,500$$

Step 4

Compute the amounts of depreciation allowable for tax purposes for the old machine and the new machine and convert them to the amounts of tax savings for each year. The old machine is being depreciated on the straight-line basis. This analysis and computation appear in Illustration 13–8.

Step 5

Using the amounts computed in steps 1 through 4 together with the sales proceeds from the old machine and the investment, prepare the present

ILLUSTRATION 13–8

MATURE PRODUCTS COMPANY
Computation of Income Tax Savings
Difference between the Depreciation Tax Shields of Two Machines

	Amount	Tax × Rate	=	Income Tax Savings
New machine:				
Cost of five-year property	$95,000			
Depreciation allowable:				
First year (15% × $95,000)	$14,250 ×	.25	=	$3,563
Second year (22% × $95,000) . . .	20,900 ×	.25	=	5,225
Third year (21% × $95,000)	19,950 ×	.25	=	4,988
Fourth year (21% × $95,000)	19,950 ×	.25	=	4,988
Fifth year (21% × $95,000)	19,950 ×	.25	=	4,988
Total depreciation	$95,000			
Old machine:				
First year ($10,000 book				
value ÷ 2 years)	$ 5,000 ×	.25	=	$1,250
Second year	5,000 ×	.25	=	1,250
Third year	0 ×	.25	=	0
Fourth year	0 ×	.25	=	0
Fifth year	0 ×	.25	=	0
Total depreciation	$10,000			

value analyses needed to reach an investment decision, as shown in Illustration 13–9.

Note the following about Illustration 13–9:

1. All inflows and outflows resulting in the net cash inflow from operations are computed on an *after-tax* basis.

2. If the old machine is retained, two items are given up: the sales proceeds from the sale of the old machine ($4,000) and the tax loss of $6,000 which is deductible on the firm's tax return. Both are opportunity costs that must be considered as costs of keeping the old machine. (To review why the $4,000 is not adjusted for tax effects while the $6,000 is, see point 3 of the discussion following Illustration 13–7.)

The analyses in Illustrations 13–7 and 13–9 both indicate that it would be favorable to replace the old machine with the new one. However, the comparative income approach (Illustration 13–9) requires much greater effort than does the differential analysis approach (Illustration 13–7). Of course, many firms have the computer capability to generate both analyses with

ILLUSTRATION 13-9

MATURE PRODUCTS COMPANY
Calculation of Net Present Value on an After-Tax Basis
Retaining Old Machine or Purchasing a New Machine
Comparative Income Approach

Item	Present Value in Dollars	Present Value Factor	0	1	2	3	4	5
					Time Period			
Keep old machine:								
Net cash inflow from operations	$211,134	3.43308*		$61,500‡	$61,500	$61,500	$61,500	$61,500
Depreciation tax shield	1,096	.87719†		1,250				
	962	.76947†			1,250			
Opportunity cost of forgoing tax loss on the sale of the old machine	(1,500)	1.00000	(1,500)					
Opportunity cost of keeping old machine—market value proceeds forgone	(4,000)	1.00000	(4,000)					
Overhaul of old machine at the end of second year	(5,771)	.76947†			(7,500)			
Net present value	$201,921							
Purchase new machine:								
Net cash inflow from operations	$293,528	3.43308*		$85,500§	$85,500	$85,500	$85,500	$85,500
Depreciation tax shield	3,125	.87719†		3,563				
	4,021	.76947†			5,225			
	3,367	.67497†				4,988		
	2,953	.59208†					4,988	
	2,591	.51937†						4,988
Salvage value	2,337	.51937†						4,500
Purchase price of new machine	(95,000)	1.00000	(95,000)					
Net present value	$216,922							

Recapitulation:

Net present value of purchasing new machine	$216,922
Net present value of keeping old machine	201,921
Net present value in favor of new machine	$ 15,001

* From Table 4.
† From Table 2.
‡ See Schedule 1.
§ See Schedule 2.

SCHEDULE 1
Keep Old Machine—
Net Cash Inflow from Operations

Sales revenue—$400,000 (1 − .25) . . .	$300,000
Direct materials—$90,000 (1 − .25) . . .	(67,500)
Direct labor—$80,000 (1 − .25)	(60,000)
Variable overhead—$48,000 (1 − .25) . . .	(36,000)
Fixed overhead—$100,000 (1 − .25) . . .	(75,000)
Net cash inflow from operations after income taxes	$ 61,500

SCHEDULE 2
Purchase New Machine—
Net Cash Inflow from Operations

Sales revenue—$400,000 (1 − .25) . . .	$300,000
Direct materials—$90,000 (1 − .25) . . .	(67,500)
Direct labor—$60,000 (1 − .25)	(45,000)
Variable overhead—$36,000 (1 − .25) . . .	(27,000)
Fixed overhead—$100,000 (1 − .25) . . .	(75,000)
Net cash inflow from operations after income taxes	$ 85,500

relative ease. Appendix 13–A includes an example of a computer-generated capital-budgeting printout.

Entering a new market or introducing a new product requires after-tax analyses similar to those for purchasing a new machine and replacing existing equipment. However, several additional after-tax concepts are needed.

Entering a New Market or Introducing a New Product— Additional Tax Considerations

Working Capital.   Entering a new market or introducing a new product requires that a firm invest working capital in accounts receivable and inventories. This working capital is then unavailable for other uses and must be treated like any other investment for capital-budgeting purposes. However, the investment in working capital *does not provide a tax shield* similar to that provided by depreciation when there is an investment in equipment. The difference occurs because an investment in equipment is partially consumed each year until the end of its useful life, when only salvage value remains, while an investment in working capital is usually maintained and returned at the end of the project. Thus, since there is no diminution of the working capital investment, there is no income tax deduction. In some cases, a portion of working capital may not be recovered because of obsolete inventory that has to be sold at a loss. This portion would be a tax shield at the time of the loss. Such an event is difficult to foresee and quantify, however, and it will probably occur so far into the future that it may safely be ignored because of its small present value factor.

The release of working capital at the end of a project also has no income tax effects. Since the investment of working capital is not deductible for tax purposes, its release should also be free from taxes, and this is the case.

ILLUSTRATION 13–10

PHYSICO COMPANY
Information for Entering the Treadmill Market

Sales (10,000 at $250 each)	$2,500,000
Incremental costs:	
Direct materials (10,000 at $60)	$ 600,000
Direct labor (10,000 at $50)	$ 500,000
Variable overhead (10,000 at $38)	$ 380,000
Fixed overhead exclusive of new machinery	
noted below	$ 400,000
Variable marketing costs	5% of sales
Fixed marketing and administrative costs	$ 200,000
Purchase of machinery needed for manufacturing	
this product	$ 950,000
Useful life of machinery	10 years
Salvage value of machinery	$ 20,000
Working capital needed at inception	$ 400,000
Working capital returned at end of 10	
years when the demand for this	
product is expected to be nil	$ 400,000

ILLUSTRATION 13–11

PHYSICO COMPANY
Calculation of Cash Outflows and Cash Inflows
For Entering a New Market
Differential Income Approach

	(Outflow) Inflow
Net investment:	
Purchase price of the machinery	$ (950,000)
Salvage value of machine	20,000
Working capital at inception	(400,000)
Release of working capital at the end of 10 years	400,000
Net investment	$ (930,000)
Cash operating advantage:	
Sales per annum	$2,500,000
Variable costs per annum:	
Direct materials	(600,000)
Direct labor	(500,000)
Variable overhead	(380,000)
Marketing costs (5% × $2.5 million)	(125,000)
Fixed costs per annum:	
Manufacturing overhead	(400,000)
Marketing and administrative costs	(200,000)
Cash operating advantage per annum	$ 295,000

Differential Analysis.   To illustrate the after-tax analysis for introducing a new product, we will continue with the example from Chapter 11 with one alteration. In this case, the release of working capital is the same as the amount invested. Recall that the Physico Company plans to enter the physical fitness market with a treadmill for gymnasium and home use. Based on a market survey and cost estimates provided by the firm's engineering and accounting departments, the information presented in Illustration 13–10 was derived.

The analysis of the relevant data for deciding whether or not to enter the new market may be organized on a *before-tax basis* as shown in Illustration 13–11.

In addition, the Physico Company estimates that its income tax rate will be 25 percent and its after-tax cost of capital is 14 percent. It wishes to use its cost of capital as the cutoff rate. The steps needed to compute the net present value on an *after-tax basis* are as follows:

Step 1

Convert the annual before-tax cash operating items to an after-tax basis by multiplying them by $(1 - t)$:

After-tax sales		= $2,500,000 (1 − .25) = $1,875,000
Less:		
After-tax direct materials	=	600,000 (1 − .25) = (450,000)
After-tax direct labor	=	500,000 (1 − .25) = (375,000)
After-tax variable overhead	=	380,000 (1 − .25) = (285,000)
After-tax variable marketing costs	=	125,000 (1 − .25) = (93,750)
After-tax fixed manufacturing overhead	=	400,000 (1 − .25) = (300,000)
After-tax fixed marketing and		
administrative costs	=	200,000 (1 − .25) = (150,000)
After-tax cash operating advantage		$ 221,250

Step 2

Convert the salvage value to an after-tax basis:

$$\text{After-tax salvage value} = \$20,000 \ (1 - .25) = \$15,000$$

Step 3

Translate the depreciation tax shield into the amounts of income tax saved each year. The computation appears in Illustration 13–12.

ILLUSTRATION 13–12

PHYSICO COMPANY
Calculation of Income Tax Savings from
the Depreciation Tax Shield

	Amount	× Tax Rate	= Income Tax Savings
Cost of five-year property	$950,000		
Depreciation allowable:			
First year (15% × $950,000)	$142,500 ×	.25	= $35,625
Second year (22% × $950,000)	209,000 ×	.25	= 52,250
Third year (21% × $950,000)	199,500 ×	.25	= 49,875
Fourth year (21% × $950,000)	199,500 ×	.25	= 49,875
Fifth year (21% × $950,000)	199,500 ×	.25	= 49,875
Total depreciation	$950,000		

Step 4

Using the information from steps 1, 2, and 3 together with the investment of $950,000, and the investment and release of the working capital of $400,000, prepare an after-tax net present value computation as shown in Illustration 13–13.

Based on this analysis, management could assume that the investment is favorable because the positive net present value of $76,562 indicates that the after-tax cutoff rate of 14 percent will be earned. Of course, if there are competing projects, this investment must be ranked for preference selection.

ILLUSTRATION 13–13

PHYSICO COMPANY
Calculation of After-Tax Net Present Value for Entering a New Market
Differential Analysis

| Item | Present Value in Dollars | Present Value Factor | Time Period | | | | | |
			0	1	2	3	4	5 . . . 10
Cash operating advantage:								
Net cash inflow from operations	$1,154,067	5.21612*		$221,250	221,250	221,250	221,250 . . .	221,250
Depreciation tax shield	31,250	.87719†		35,625				
	40,205	.76947			52,250			
	33,664	.67497				49,875		
	29,530	.59208					49,875	
	25,904	.51937						49,875
Total	$1,314,620							
Net investment:								
Purchase price of machine . . .	$ (950,000)	1.00000	(950,000)					
Salvage value of machine . . .	4,046	.26974†						15,000
Investment of working capital . .	(400,000)	1.00000	(400,000)					
Release of working capital at end	107,896	.26974†						400,000
Net investment	(1,238,058)							
Net present value	$ 76,562							

* From Table 4.
† From Table 2.

SUMMARY

Because income taxes affect all facets of business, a manager's failure to consider them when making decisions may have a serious impact on a firm's profitability. Decisions should therefore be made on an after-tax basis.

To be effective, capital-budgeting decisions must not only be based on **after-tax cash flows** but must also recognize the effects of **tax shields.** Two common tax shields are the realized loss on the sale of old equipment when new equipment is purchased and the amount of tax-deductible depreciation that will result from an investment decision.

The selection of a particular depreciation method can have a significant impact on an investment decision and may, in some cases, be the *determining factor that makes an investment decision profitable.* For tax purposes, generally only two depreciation methods may be used: the **accelerated cost recovery system (ACRS)** and straight-line. Because larger deductions in the earlier years of a project's life provide greater tax savings on a present value basis, *the ACRS method generally provides more favorable results than straight-line depreciation.* If the straight-line method is selected, only one half of a year's depreciation may be taken in the first year. This practice is known as the **half-year convention.**

The net present value analysis needed to make an investment decision should be prepared by converting cash inflows and outflows to an after-tax basis. This may be accomplished by multiplying each cash inflow or outflow by 1 minus the tax rate. Tax shields, such as depreciation, should be converted into tax savings by *multiplying the shield by the tax rate.* The NPV analysis is then prepared as discussed in Chapter 12.

GLOSSARY OF KEY TERMS

Accelerated cost recovery system (ACRS) A method of depreciation used for income tax purposes that classifies depreciable property into one of five groupings without regard to the property's actual useful life. The percentage of depreciation that may be claimed in each year an asset is owned is specified for each category.

After-tax cash flow The value of a cash inflow or outflow after giving effect to income taxes.

Half-year convention The method of claiming depreciation on income tax returns when straight-line depreciation is elected. The ACRS recovery periods apply to the property placed in service, but only one half of a full year's depreciation is claimed in the first year regardless of the date the property was purchased. Similarly, a half year's depreciation is claimed in the last year of the recovery period.

Tax shield Any deduction on a firm's income tax return that does not require an outlay of cash in that period.

APPENDIX 13–A   **COMPUTER-PREPARED INVESTMENT DECISION ANALYSES**

Using a computer to prepare the analysis needed to reach an investment decision can save considerable time and effort. Because more and more firms

ILLUSTRATION 13–14 **Investment Decision—Purchase Automobile or Pay Mileage (computerized input printout)**

```
AUTOMOBILE PROBLEM:  BUY OR PAY MILEAGE
A.  BUY
    1.  Purchase price of car—$9000
    2.  Estimated life—4 years
    3.  Three-year ACRS is to be used
    4.  Salvage value at end of four years—$1500
    5.  Estimated annual costs
        Gasoline              $800
        Licenses & insurance  $400
        Garaging              $300
        Maintenance & repairs $200 in first year
                              $300 in second year
                              $400 in third year
                              $500 in fourth year

B.  PAY MILEAGE
    1.  Pay at rate of $.205 per mile.
    2.  Salesman will drive 18000 miles per year for business.

C.  OTHER INFORMATION
    1.  Cost of capital—12%
    2.  Company's marginal tax rate—45%
```

have the required computer capability, this appendix presents an example of a computer-prepared investment analysis.

A firm is considering whether it would be more profitable to have an employee use his own automobile or a company automobile for business purposes. If the employee uses his own car, the company will reimburse him at the rate of 20½ cents per business mile. If the employee uses company-provided transportation, the firm must buy a new car and pay its operating costs. The cost of the new auto, the salvage value, the annual operating costs, the firm's cost of capital, and the firm's income tax rate were all entered into a computer and printed out, as shown in Illustration 13–14.

The tax shield and tax savings are computed as follows:

Year

First	$9,000 × 25% = $2,250 × 45% = $1,013
Second	$9,000 × 38% = $3,420 × 45% = $1,539
Third	$9,000 × 37% = $3,330 × 45% = $1,498

The after-tax salvage value would be:

Salvage value = $1,500 (1 − .45) = $825

The after-tax costs for gasoline, licenses and insurance, and garaging may be computed as follows:

$$\text{Gasoline} \qquad\qquad = \$800\,(1-.45) = \$440 \text{ per year}$$
$$\text{Licenses and insurance} = \$400\,(1-.45) = \$220 \text{ per year}$$
$$\text{Garaging} \qquad\qquad = \$300\,(1-.45) = \$165 \text{ per year}$$

The repairs and maintenance are similarly converted, except that each year is computed separately:

$$\text{First year} \quad = \$200\,(1-.45) = \$110$$
$$\text{Second year} = \$300\,(1-.45) = \$165$$
$$\text{Third year} \quad = \$400\,(1-.45) = \$220$$
$$\text{Fourth year} = \$500\,(1-.45) = \$275$$

The after-tax annual cost of mileage may be computed as:

$$18{,}000 \text{ miles} \times \$0.205 = \$3{,}690\,(1-.45) = \$2{,}030 \text{ per year}$$

The needed analysis, prepared manually, is shown in Illustration 13–15, while the computer-generated solution appears in Illustration 13–16.

ILLUSTRATION 13–15　Investment Decision—Buy Automobile or Pay Mileage

Item	Present Value in Dollars	Present Value Factor	Time Period 0	1	2	3	4
Purchase auto:							
Purchase price of automobile .	$(9,000)	1.00000	$(9,000)				
Gasoline	(1,336)	3.03735*		$ (440)	$ (440)	$ (440)	$ (440)
Licenses and insurance	(668)	3.03735*		(220)	(220)	(220)	(220)
Garaging	(501)	3.03735*		(165)	(165)	(165)	(165)
Repairs and maintenance . . .	(98)	.89286†		(110)			
	(132)	.79719‡			(165)		
	(157)	.71178§				(220)	
	(175)	.63552‖					(275)
Depreciation tax shield	904	.89286†		1,013			
	1,227	.79719‡			1,539		
	1,066	.71178§				1,498	
Salvage	524	.63552‖					825
Total	$(8,346)						
Pay mileage:							
Mileage at $0.205 per mile	$(6,165)	3.03735*		(2,030)	(2,030)	(2,030)	(2,030)

Recapitulation:

Present value cost of purchasing auto	$8,346
Present value cost of paying mileage allowance .	6,165
Savings in favor of paying mileage	$2,181

* From Table 4, $n = 4$, $i = 12\%$.
† From Table 2, $n = 1$, $i = 12\%$.
‡ From Table 2, $n = 2$, $i = 12\%$.
§ From Table 2, $n = 3$, $i = 12\%$.
‖ From Table 2, $n = 4$, $i = 12\%$.

ILLUSTRATION 13–16   Investment Decision—Purchase Automobile or Pay Mileage (computerized solution printout)

SOLUTION

		0	1	2	3	4
Purchase		9000				
Gasoline			800	800	800	800
Licenses & insurance			400	400	400	400
Garaging			300	300	300	300
Repairs & maintenance			200	300	400	500
Depreciation			2250	3420	3330	
Salvage						−1500
Totals		9000	3950	5220	5230	500
Income Tax	0.45		−1778	−2349	−2354	−225
Totals after tax		9000	2173	2871	2877	275
Depreciation			−2250	−3420	−3330	
After-tax cash flow		9000	−78	−549	−454	275
PV of annual cash flows	0.12	−655				
PV cost of purchase		8345				
Annual mileage	18000		3690	3690	3690	3690
Income Tax	0.205 / 0.45		−1661	−1661	−1661	−1661
After-tax cost			2030	2030	2030	2030
PV of mileage cost	0.12	6164				

Based on this analysis, management should pay mileage because the present value of purchasing the automobile is an outflow (cost) of $8,346, while the present value of paying mileage is an outflow (cost) of only $6,164.

QUESTIONS

1. Is it necessary to consider the effects of income taxes when making a capital-budgeting decision? Why?

2. What is an after-tax cost? How is it computed?

3. What is after-tax cash flow? How is it computed?

4. What is a tax shield? Why is it important for capital-budgeting decisions?

5. If an investment in a machine has an estimated useful life of eight years and it is five-year ACRS property, how is the difference between eight and five years treated in a capital-budgeting analysis?

6. What is the half-year convention?

7. If a firm has a choice between ACRS and straight-line depreciation, which method should the firm use on its income tax return if the firm is operating at a profit? Why?

8. Depreciation has no effect on cash flow. Discuss the validity of this statement if:
   a. Income taxes *are not* considered when making a capital-budgeting decision.
   b. Income taxes *are* considered when making a capital-budgeting decision.

9. The book value of a machine that is being replaced with a newer machine has no effect on a firm's cash flow. Discuss the validity of this statement if:
   a. Income taxes *are not* considered when making a capital-budgeting decision.
   b. Income taxes *are* considered when making a capital-budgeting decision.

10. When a firm sells an old machine at a taxable gain, it has both an inflow and an outflow, but if the machine is sold at a taxable loss, only cash inflows result. Explain.

11. A firm plans to spend $30,000 for an advertisement and its income tax bracket is 40 percent. What is the after-tax cost of the advertisement?

12. A firm plans to purchase a machine for $60,000. The machine is five-year ACRS property. Calculate the tax shield if the firm is in the 30 percent income tax bracket.

13. A firm is evaluating the purchase of a machine that has a cost of $90,000 and a useful life of six years. The firm plans to use straight-line depreciation and the machine has a zero salvage value. The machine is expected to earn revenues of $80,000 in the second year of its useful life and variable costs are expected to be $30,000 in that year. There are no direct fixed costs associated with the machine. The firm's income tax rate is 40 percent. Compute the firm's after-tax cash inflow from the machine in the second year of its useful life.

EXERCISES

13–1 Net Present Value—ACRS Depreciation

The Newton Auto Repair Company is contemplating the purchase of electronic testing equipment that will enable the firm to perform emission control inspections. The equipment has a useful life of 10 years, no salvage value, and can be purchased at a cost of $20,000.

Newton estimates that revenues from inspections will be $20,000 per annum and direct labor and variable overhead costs will be $15,000 per annum.

The property qualifies as five-year ACRS property. The company's income tax rate is 25 percent.

Required Compute the net present value for each of the following after-tax discount rates and indicate whether or not the investment should be made at that rate:

(1) 18 percent.
(2) 20 percent.
(3) 22 percent.

13-2 Net Present Value—Straight-Line Depreciation

The Newton Auto Repair Company is contemplating the purchase of electronic testing equipment that will enable the firm to perform emission control inspections. The equipment has a useful life of 10 years, no salvage value, and can be purchased at a cost of $20,000.

Newton estimates that revenues from inspections will be $20,000 per annum and direct labor and variable overhead costs will be $15,000 per annum.

The property is to be depreciated using the straight-line method over the shortest period possible for five-year property. The company's income tax rate is 25 percent.

Required Compute the net present value for each of the following after-tax discount rates and indicate whether or not the investment should be made at that rate:

(1) 18 percent.
(2) 20 percent.
(3) 22 percent.

13-3 Net Present Value Analysis for Competing Investments and Profitability Index—ACRS Depreciation

Brown Business School has decided that in order to remain competitive with other local business schools it must expand and update its computer science department. Brown is convinced that in order to accomplish this it must purchase a new central processing unit (CPU). Officials of the school have been negotiating with two mainframe manufacturers, JCN Corporation and C.N.R. Technologies. The representative of JCN Corporation has advised Brown that their model ZIPPY 1000 would be appropriate for the needs of the school. The cost of the machine would be $500,000. In 10 years, the machine would be obsolete, at which time it would have a disposal value of $50,000. After a detailed study, the representative has convinced Brown that additional student revenues and savings from administrative costs would provide a net cash inflow of $100,000 annually.

The representative of C.N.R. Technologies is offering Brown its model SPEEDY 250 at a cost of $750,000. The SPEEDY 250 would also be obsolete in 10 years but would have a disposal value of $125,000. Net cash inflow from this machine would be $125,000 per year.

The property qualifies as five-year ACRS property. The school's income tax rate is 25 percent.

Salvage value is not taken into account when computing ACRS depreciation.

Required *a.* Assuming the school desires a 12 percent after-tax return on its investment, use the net present value concept to determine which machine the school should purchase.

b. Compute the profitability index for each investment. Is your answer the same as in part *(a)*? Is this always true? Explain.

13-4 Net Present Value Analysis for Competing Investments and Profitability Index—Straight-Line Depreciation

Brown Business School has decided that in order to remain competitive with other local business schools it must expand and update its computer science department. Brown is convinced that in order to accomplish this it must purchase a new central processing unit (CPU). Officials of the school have been negotiating with two mainframe manufacturers, JCN Corporation and C.N.R. Technologies. The representative of JCN Corporation has advised Brown that their model ZIPPY 1000 would be appropriate for the needs of the school. The cost of the machine would be $500,000. In 10 years, the machine would be obsolete, at which time it would have a disposal value of $50,000. After a detailed study, the representative has convinced Brown that additional student revenues and savings from administrative costs would provide a net cash inflow of $100,000 annually.

The representative of C.N.R. Technologies is offering Brown its model SPEEDY 250 at a cost of $750,000. The SPEEDY 250 would also be obsolete in 10 years but would have a disposal value of $125,000. Net cash inflow from this machine would be $125,000 per year.

The school elects to take straight-line depreciation over the shortest period possible for five-year property. The school's income tax rate is 25 percent.

Required
a. Assuming the school desires a 12 percent after-tax return on its investment, use the net present value concept to determine which machine the school should purchase.
b. Compute the profitability index for each investment. Is your answer the same as in part *(a)*? Is this always true? Explain.

13-5 Competing Investments and Net Present Value

The Driscoll Company has $100,000 to invest. A suggestion made by the plant superintendent is to purchase a new, more efficient machine. On the other hand, the financial vice president would like the firm to purchase a competing firm's customer list that is for sale. The machine has a useful life of five years, and the customer list is also expected to yield cash flows for a five-year period. Neither investment is expected to have any residual value.

The projected cash advantage per annum for each investment is:

Year	Machine	Customer List
19x1	$ 80,000	$ 27,000
19x2	67,000	53,000
19x3	53,000	67,000
19x4	40,000	80,000
19x5	27,000	93,000
Total	$267,000	$320,000

The machine qualifies as five-year ACRS property. The company's income tax rate is 25 percent.

The customer list is not ACRS property. However, it will qualify for straight-line depreciation. The half-year convention does not apply to the customer list.

Required   *a.*   Using an after-tax cutoff rate of 22 percent, calculate the net present value of each investment. If only one investment can be made, which one would you choose? Why?

b.   Redo *(a)* except that an after-tax cutoff rate of 10 percent is to be used. Is your answer different from *(a)*? Explain.

13–6   Competing Investments and Net Present Value

The Burton Company has $250,000 to invest. A suggestion made by the plant superintendent is to purchase a new, more efficient machine. On the other hand, the financial vice president would like the firm to purchase a competing firm's customer list that is for sale. The machine has a useful life of five years, and the customer list is also expected to yield cash flows for a five-year period. Neither investment is expected to have any residual value.

The projected cash advantage per annum for each investment is:

Year	Machine	Customer List
19x1	$150,000	$ 67,000
19x2	117,000	100,000
19x3	100,000	167,000
19x4	83,000	150,000
19x5	100,000	150,000
Total	$550,000	$634,000

The machine qualifies as five-year ACRS property. The company's income tax rate is 40 percent.

The customer list is not ACRS property. However, it will qualify for straight-line depreciation. The half-year convention does not apply to the customer list.

Required   *a.*   Using an after-tax cutoff rate of 16 percent, calculate the net present value of each investment. If only one investment can be made, which one would you choose? Why?

b.   Redo *(a)* except that an after-tax cutoff rate of 10 percent is to be used. Is your answer different from *(a)*? Explain.

13–7   Net Present Value, After-Tax Payback, and After-Tax Accounting Rate of Return

Items 1 and 2 are based on the following information:

George Company is planning to acquire a new machine at a total cost of $30,600. The estimated life of the machine is six years, and estimated salvage value is $600. George Company estimates annual cash savings from using this machine will be $8,000. Assume the company's cost of capital is 8 percent and its income tax rate is 40 percent. The present value of $1 at 8 percent for six years is .630. The present value of an annuity of $1 in arrears at 8 percent for six years is 4.623.

1. What are the annual after-tax net cash benefits of this investment?
   a. $3,000.
   b. $4,800.
   c. $5,400.
   d. $6,800.
2. If the annual after-tax net cash benefits of this investment were $5,000, what would the net present value of this investment be?
   a. $7,485 negative.
   b. $7,107 negative.
   c. $7,107 positive.
   d. $7,485 positive.
3. Nelson Company is planning to purchase a new machine for $500,000. The new machine is expected to produce cash flow from operations, before income taxes, of $135,000 a year in each of the next five years. Depreciation of $100,000 a year will be charged to income for each of the next five years. Assume that the income tax rate is 40 percent. The payback period would be approximately
   a. 2.2 years.
   b. 3.4 years.
   c. 3.7 years.
   d. 4.1 years.
4. Hanley Company purchased a machine for $125,000 which will be depreciated on the straight-line basis over a five-year period with no salvage value. The related cash flow from operations, net of income taxes, is expected to be $45,000 a year. Assume that Hanley's effective income tax rate is 40 percent for all years.

   What is the accounting (book value) rate of return on the initial increase in required investment?
   a. 16 percent.
   b. 24 percent.
   c. 28 percent.
   d. 36 percent.

(AICPA adapted)

13–8   Net Present Value (Extension of Exercise 12–6)—ACRS Depreciation

The Building Corporation, a heavy construction business, is interested in replacing one of its backhoes with a new model. The cost of the new equipment is $125,000 and has an expected useful life of 10 years. At the end of its useful life, the equipment will have a salvage value of $7,500. Due to increased efficiency, the company expects to save 1,000 hours per year in labor costs. A backhoe operator earns $20 per hour including fringe benefits.

The old backhoe can be sold for $15,000 and it has a current book value of $75,000. Its disposal value at the end of its useful life in 10 years is zero. Building Corporation considers an after-tax return of 14 percent on its investments as a minimum rate.

The property qualifies as five-year ACRS property. The company's income tax rate is 25 percent.

Required   Using net present value analysis, determine whether or not Building Corporation should purchase the equipment.

13–9   Net Present Value (Extension of Exercise 12–6)—Straight-Line Depreciation

The Building Corporation, a heavy construction business, is interested in replacing one of its backhoes with a new model. The cost of the new equipment is $125,000 and has an expected useful life of 10 years. At the end of its useful life, the equipment will have a salvage value of $7,500. Due to increased efficiency, the company expects to save 1,000 hours per year in labor costs. A backhoe operator earns $20 per hour including fringe benefits.

The old backhoe can be sold for $15,000 and it has a current book value of $75,000. Its disposal value at the end of its useful life in 10 years is zero. Building Corporation considers an after-tax return of 14 percent on its investments as a minimum rate.

The company elects to take straight-line depreciation over the shortest period possible for five-year property. The company's income tax rate is 25 percent.

Required   Using net present value analysis, determine whether or not Building Corporation should purchase the equipment.

13–10   Net Present Value—Straight-Line Depreciation

The Boise Company, an electronics manufacturer, is interested in replacing one of its machines with a new model. The cost of the new equipment is $150,000 and has an expected useful life of 10 years. At the end of its useful life, the equipment will have a salvage value of $10,000. Due to increased efficiency, the company expects to save 5,000 hours per year in labor costs. A machine operator earns $10 per hour including fringe benefits.

The old machine can be sold for $20,000 and it has a current book value of $50,000. Its disposal value at the end of its useful life in 10 years is zero. Boise considers an after-tax return of 16 percent on its investments as a minimum rate.

The company elects to take straight-line depreciation over the shortest period possible for five-year property. The company's income tax rate is 30 percent.

Required   Using net present value analysis, determine whether or not Boise should purchase the equipment.

PROBLEMS   13–11   Net Present Value Analysis for Purchasing a New Machine and Replacing an Existing Machine (Extension of Problem 12–20)—Straight-Line Depreciation

The Montana Corporation is presently using a machine, M–1, in its production process. It is contemplating the purchase of a newer, more efficient machine, M–2. The following information is available:

	M-1	M-2
Purchase price	$500,000	$1,000,000
Useful life	15 years	10 years
Salvage value	$ 50,000	$ 80,000
Accumulated depreciation—($450,000 ÷ 15 years =		
$30,000); $30,000 × 5 years =	150,000	–0–
Depreciation per annum	30,000	95,000
Sales revenue	500,000	600,000
Direct materials cost	90,000	108,000
Direct labor	150,000	130,000
Variable overhead	90,000	78,000
Direct fixed overhead	70,000	90,000

The property is to be depreciated by the straight-line method over the shortest period possible for five-year property. The company's income tax rate is 25 percent. The after-tax cutoff rate for investments is 14 percent.

Required

a. Assume that the Montana Corporation is contemplating the purchase of M-2 and intends to keep M-1, also. There is a sufficient market for the firm's output from both machines. Prepare schedules to compute:
   (1) The net investment of M-2.
   (2) The cash operating advantage of M-2.
   (3) The net present value to determine if M-2 should be purchased. Should M-2 be purchased? Why?

b. Assume that market conditions are such that the corporation can sell the output from M-2 or M-1 but not both. Thus, if M-2 is purchased, M-1 will be sold for $100,000. Using differential analysis, prepare schedules to compute:
   (1) The net investment of M-2.
   (2) The cash operating advantage of M-2.
   (3) The net present value to determine if M-1 should be replaced. Should M-1 be replaced? Why?

13-12 Net Present Value Analysis for Purchasing a New Machine and Replacing an Existing Machine (Extension of Problem 12-20)—ACRS Depreciation

The Montana Corporation is presently using a machine, M-1, in its production process. It is contemplating the purchase of a newer, more efficient machine, M-2. The following information is available:

	M-1	M-2
Purchase price	$500,000	$1,000,000
Useful life	15 years	10 years
Salvage value	$ 50,000	$ 80,000
Accumulated depreciation—($450,000 ÷ 15 years =		
$30,000); $30,000 × 5 years =	150,000	–0–
Depreciation per annum	30,000	ACRS
Sales revenue	500,000	600,000
Direct materials cost	90,000	108,000
Direct labor	150,000	130,000
Variable overhead	90,000	78,000
Direct fixed overhead	70,000	90,000

The property qualifies as five-year ACRS property. The company's income tax rate is 25 percent.

The after-tax cutoff rate for investments is 14 percent.

Required a. Assume that the Montana Corporation is contemplating the purchase of M–2 and intends to keep M–1 also. There is a sufficient market for the firm's output from both machines. Prepare schedules to compute:
   (1) The net investment of M–2.
   (2) The cash operating advantage of M–2.
   (3) The net present value to determine if M–2 should be purchased. Should M–2 be purchased? Why?

b. Assume that market conditions are such that the corporation can sell the output from M–2 or M–1 but not both. Thus, if M–2 is purchased, M–1 will be sold for $100,000. Using differential analysis, prepare schedules to compute:
   (1) The net investment of M–2.
   (2) The cash operating advantage of M–2.
   (3) The net present value to determine if M–1 should be replaced. Should M–1 be replaced? Why?

13–13 Net Present Value Analysis for Replacing Equipment (Extension of Problem 12–22) Comparative Income Approach—ACRS Depreciation

The Nebraska Corporation is presently using a machine, K–1, in its production process. It is contemplating the purchase of a newer, more efficient machine, K–9. The following information is available:

	K–1	K–9
Purchase price	$65,000	$100,000
Useful life	12 years	8 years
Salvage value	$ 5,000	$ 4,000
Accumulated depreciation—($60,000 ÷ 12 years = $5,000);		
$5,000 × 8 years =	40,000	–0–
Present resale value	30,000	
Depreciation per annum	5,000	ACRS
Sales revenue	50,000	60,000
Direct materials cost	10,000	12,000
Direct labor	12,000	9,000
Variable overhead	6,000	4,500
Direct fixed overhead	10,000	11,000
Cost to overhaul K–1 to extend its remaining life by four years for a total of eight years	15,000	

The property qualifies as five-year ACRS property. The company's income tax rate is 25 percent.

The firm's after-tax cutoff rate for investments is 14 percent.

Required a. Using the comparative income approach, compute the following:
   (1) The net investment of purchasing K–9.
   (2) The cash operating advantage of K–9.
   (3) The net present value to determine if K–9 should be purchased.

    b. Using the comparative income approach, compute the following:
        (1) The net investment of retaining K–1. (Hint: Use K–1's opportunity cost.)
        (2) The cash operating advantage of K–1.
        (3) The net present value to determine if K–1 should be retained.
    c. Should K–9 be purchased and K–1 sold? Why?

13–14   **Net Present Value Analysis for Replacing Equipment (Extension of Problem 12–23)—Differential Income Approach; ACRS Depreciation**

The Nebraska Corporation is presently using a machine, K–1, in its production process. It is contemplating the purchase of a newer, more efficient machine, K–9. The following information is available:

	K–1	K–9
Purchase price	$65,000	$100,000
Useful life	12 years	8 years
Salvage value	$ 5,000	$ 4,000
Accumulated depreciation—($60,000 ÷ 12 years = $5,000);		
$5,000 × 8 years =	40,000	–0–
Present resale value	30,000	
Depreciation per annum	5,000	ACRS
Sales revenue	50,000	60,000
Direct materials cost	10,000	12,000
Direct labor	12,000	9,000
Variable overhead	6,000	4,500
Direct fixed overhead	10,000	11,000
Cost to overhaul K–1 to extend its remaining life by four years		
for a total of eight years	15,000	

The property qualifies as five-year ACRS property. The company's income tax rate is 25 percent.

The firm's after-tax cutoff rate for investments is 14 percent.

Required   Using the differential income approach, compute the following:
    (1) The net investment of replacing K–1.
    (2) The cash operating advantage of replacing K–1.
    (3) The net present value to determine if K–1 should be replaced. Should K–1 be replaced? Why?

13–15   **Payback, Accounting Rate of Return, Net Present Value, Profitability Index, and Internal Rate of Return—Straight-Line Depreciation**

Hazman Corporation plans to replace an old piece of equipment which is obsolete and is expected to be unreliable under the stress of daily operations. The equipment is fully depreciated, and no salvage value can be realized upon its disposal.

One piece of equipment being considered would provide annual cash savings of $7,000 before income taxes. The equipment would cost $18,000 and have an estimated useful life of five years. No salvage value would be used for depreciation purposes because the equipment is expected to have no value at the end of five years.

Hazman uses the straight-line depreciation method on all equipment for tax purposes. The company is subject to a 40 percent tax rate. Hazman has an after-tax cost of capital of 14 percent.

Required   *a.*   Calculate for Hazman Company's proposed investment in new equipment the after-tax:
  (1) Payback period.
  (2) Accounting rate of return.
  (3) Net present value.
  (4) Profitability (present value) index.
  (5) Internal rate of return.
  Assume all operating revenues and costs occur at the end of the year.

   b.   Identify and discuss the issues Hazman Company should consider when deciding which of the five decision models identified in requirement (*a*) it should employ to compare and evaluate alternative capital-investment projects.

(CMA adapted)

13–16 Comparative Income and Differential Income Approaches to Net Present Value Analysis of Replacing a Machine—ACRS Depreciation

The management of Yates Stamping Company is contemplating the purchase of a new machine, at a cost of $80,000, which is capable of producing 180,000 units per year. This machine would replace a machine which is capable of producing 130,000 units per annum and which can be sold for $20,000. The contribution margin per unit from operating the new machine is $0.125, while it is $0.10 per unit from operating the old machine.

The useful life of the old machine was 10 years when it was purchased 2 years ago. The useful life of the new machine is eight years. The new machine has a salvage value of $20,000 while the old machine's salvage value is zero. The old machine will require an overhaul at the end of two years from today at a cost of $10,000. The new machine will require an overhaul at the end of the fourth year at a cost of $8,000.

The firm's after-tax cutoff rate for investment decisions is 14 percent. The property qualifies as five-year ACRS property. Income taxes are at the rate of 20 percent.

Required   *a.*   Using the comparative income approach and net present value analysis, determine if the old machine should be replaced.

   b.   Redo (*a*) using the differential income approach to reach your decision.

13–17 Comparative Income and Differential Income Approaches to Net Present Value Analysis of Replacing a Machine (Extension of Problem 12–25)—Straight-Line Depreciation

Carmel Company purchased a machine two years ago at a cost of $750,000. At that time, the equipment had a useful life of 12 years and a salvage value of $100,000. At the end of the fifth year (three years from now), the equipment is due for a $75,000 overhaul. Estimated cash inflow from the equipment is $35,000 per year. The company is considering the purchase of newer equipment as a replacement. The cost of the new equipment would be $1.4 million. The equipment manufacturer is offering a trade-in allowance of $250,000 for the old equipment. The new equipment represents state-of-the-art technology, and the company expects productivity savings of $190,000 per year over the old equipment. The new equipment will have a useful life of 10 years and a disposal value of $250,000. The company elects straight-line depreciation on all assets of this type and considers an after-tax return of less than 12 percent on investments unacceptable.

Its income tax rate is 30 percent.

Required *a.* Using the comparative income approach and net present value analysis, determine if the old machine should be replaced.

b. Redo *(a)* using the differential income approach to reach your decision.

13–18 Comparative Income and Differential Income Approaches to the Net Present Value Analysis of Replacing a Machine (Extension of Problem 12–27)—ACRS Depreciation

The Canals Company is considering the purchase of a new piece of equipment (machine B) to use in its manufacturing process as a replacement for an old machine (machine A). Operating costs for machine A have been running at an average annual rate of $60,000. At the end of its useful life, five years from now, machine A will have a disposal value of $6,000. Three years from now, machine A will be due for a complete overhaul at a cost of $15,000. The book value of this machine is currently $36,000. It is being depreciated by the straight-line method and was purchased five years ago.

Machine B will cost the company $60,000 and have a disposal value of $4,500 at the end of its five-year useful life. The annual operating costs for this machine are estimated to be $40,000 annually.

The property qualifies as five-year ACRS property. The company's income tax rate is 25 percent.

The firm's after-tax cutoff rate for this kind of investment is 18 percent.

Required *a.* Using the comparative income approach, compute the net present value to determine if machine A should be replaced. Should machine A be replaced? Why?

b. Redo *(a)* using the differential income approach to reach your decision.

13–19 Net Present Value for Entering a New Market—Straight-Line Depreciation

The Gambel Company is considering whether to market a newly developed dishwashing compound. The following information is available:

1. A mixing and packaging machine would be required that would cost $500,000. The machine would have a useful life of 10 years. The company uses straight-line depreciation for tax purposes. At the end of 10 years, the machine would have a salvage value of $20,000.

2. At the end of the fifth year, the machine would require an overhaul at a cost of $80,000. This amount would be deductible on the company's income tax return in that year.

3. Working capital would be required at the beginning of the first year in the amount of $50,000. At the end of the third year, another $20,000 will be required. The full $70,000 will be released at the end of the 10-year period when the firm expects to drop this product and market a replacement product.

4. The firm will launch the marketing with an advertising blitz at a cost of $80,000. This will occur at the beginning of the first year, and is in addition to the regular recurring advertising.

5. The operating cash inflows before income taxes are expected to be:

Years	Amount
1 through 3	$125,000
4 through 6	180,000
7 through 10	120,000

The company's after-tax cutoff rate is 14 percent. Income taxes are 30 percent.

Required   *a.* Using net present value analysis, prepare schedules to compute the net present value of the project.

  b. Should the firm go ahead with the project? Why?

13-20 Net Present Value for Entering a New Market—ACRS Depreciation

The Gambel Company is considering whether to market a newly developed dishwashing compound. The following information is available:

1. A mixing and packaging machine would be required that would cost $500,000. The machine would have a useful life of 10 years. The company uses ACRS depreciation for tax purposes. At the end of 10 years, the machine would have a salvage value of $20,000.
2. At the end of the fifth year, the machine would require an overhaul at a cost of $80,000. This amount would be deductible on the company's income tax return in that year.
3. Working capital would be required at the beginning of the first year in the amount of $50,000. At the end of the third year, another $20,000 will be required. The full $70,000 will be released at the end of the 10-year period when the firm expects to drop this product and market a replacement product.
4. The firm will launch the marketing with an advertising blitz at a cost of $80,000. This will occur at the beginning of the first year and is in addition to the regular recurring advertising.
5. The operating cash inflows before income taxes are expected to be:

Years	Amount
1 through 3	$125,000
4 through 6	180,000
7 through 10	120,000

The company's after-tax cutoff rate is 14 percent. Income taxes are 30 percent.

Required   *a.* Using net present value analysis, prepare schedules to compute the net present value of the project.

  b. Should the firm go ahead with the project? Why?

13-21 Net Present Value Analysis for Entering a New Market (Extension of Problem 12–28)—ACRS Depreciation

The Aromatic Company, which produces inexpensive automatic coffemakers, is thinking of introducing a new line of expensive automatic coffeemakers which will both grind the coffee beans and then brew the coffee. A market survey indicates that because of its high cost, there is only a limited market for this product and estimates that after five years there will be no market at all.

The following annual information about the new product is available to you:

Estimated sales (15,000 × $50)	$750,000
Cost of direct materials and direct labor	250,000
Variable overhead	70,000
Variable marketing costs	37,500
Direct fixed overhead, marketing, and administrative costs	150,000

Additional information:

Price of new machine	$750,000
Salvage value at the end of five years	10,000
Working capital needed at inception	70,000
Working capital returned at the end of five years	65,000
Depreciation of new machinery	ACRS

The firm's after-tax cutoff rate for investments of this type is 14 percent. The property qualifies as five-year ACRS property. The company's income tax rate is 25 percent.

Required
a. Which of the above data is relevant to you in recommending whether it is advantageous for Aromatic to enter this new market?
b. Using net present value analysis, determine if it is advantageous for Aromatic to enter this new market.

13–22 Purchasing an Existing Business and Net Present Value Analysis (Extension of Problem 12–29)—Straight-line Amortization of Leasehold

Sparky Little is working for a large corporation in its accounting department. It appears that Little's progress is blocked and he would like to try something else. Several evenings each week, Little visits a tavern called "Archer's Place." One evening when Little was feeling very discouraged, he learned that the tavern was for sale, and in the conversation that followed, Archer offered to sell the tavern to Little.

Archer has a 10-year assignable lease of the property. Little hired an engineering consultant to evaluate the equipment, and it was determined that the refrigeration unit would require an overhaul at a cost of $5,000 in five years.

Archer is asking $100,000 for the leasehold and equipment. The equipment should be worth about $20,000 at the end of the 10-year lease. Of the $100,000, $60,000 is attributable to the equipment, which is to be depreciated by the straight-line method allowable by ACRS rules. The balance of $40,000 is attributable to the leasehold, which is to be amortized by the straight-line method over the remaining term of the lease. This amortization is also deductible on Little's tax return. Little's income tax rate is 30 percent.

Little engaged the services of a CPA to review the tavern's records. The CPA is confident that the tavern will yield $20,000 in cash flow for the coming year. Little is equally confident that he can increase cash flow each year by 10 percent over the preceding year's cash flow. Working capital of $15,000 will be needed during the 10 years of operation and will be released at the end of the lease.

Little will only purchase the tavern if it yields an after-tax return of 18 percent.

Required Using net present value analysis, determine if Little should purchase the tavern.

13–23 Lease or Purchase (Extension of Problem 12–32)—ACRS Depreciation

The T&K Trucking Company's business is expanding, and the firm's management decided that an additional truck is needed. The firm must decide whether to purchase or lease the truck.

Information regarding the purchase of the truck is as follows:

Purchase price	$30,000
Annual operational costs for maintenance, licenses, and fees	$ 2,000
Annual repairs:	
Year 1	$ 500
2	1,000
3	1,500
4	5,000
5	2,000
6	2,500
Useful life	6 years
Salvage value	$ 4,000

The truck can be leased for six years at an annual rental of $9,000 plus 10 cents per mile driven. The lessor will be responsible for repairs, maintenance, licenses, and fees. At the end of the lease term, the truck will be returned to the lessor.

The lessee is responsible for insurance and gasoline usage in either case. T&K normally uses the truck at the rate of 25,000 miles annually. Any damage to the truck is the responsibility of the lessee. The lessor requires a deposit of $4,000 which will be refunded at the end of the lease term if the truck is returned undamaged.

If the truck is purchased, it will qualify as three-year property for ACRS purposes, which will be used on the firm's income tax return. The firm's income tax rate is 30 percent.

The after-tax cost of capital for T&K is 12 percent.

Required a. Using present value analysis, compute the cost of purchasing the truck.

b. Using present value analysis, compute the cost of renting the truck for six years.

c. What choice do you recommend? Why?

13–24 Lease or Purchase (Extension of Problem 12–33)—ACRS Depreciation

The Sellmore company hired an additional traveling salesman. Since it is the firm's policy to provide every salesperson with an automobile, Sellmore must decide whether to purchase or lease an automobile for the new salesman.

Information regarding the purchase of the auto is as follows:

Purchase price	$12,000
Annual operating costs for maintenance, licenses, and fees	600
Annual repairs:	
Year 1	300
2	1,000
3	1,500
4	2,000
Useful life	4 years
Salvage value	$ 3,000

The automobile can be leased for four years at an annual rental of $4,000 plus 10 cents per mile driven in excess of 60,000 miles. The lessor will be responsible for repairs, maintenance, licenses, and fees. At the end of the lease term, the auto will be returned to the lessor and the lessee will pay the excess mileage charge at that time.

The lessee is responsible for insurance and gasoline usage in either case. Sellmore expects its salesman to use the automobile at the rate of 20,000 miles annually. Any damage to the auto is the responsiblity of the lessee. The lessor requires a deposit of $2,000 which will be refunded at the end of the lease term if the auto is returned undamaged.

If the automobile is purchased, it will qualify as three-year property for ACRS purposes, which will be used on the firm's income tax return. The firm's income tax rate is 30 percent.

The after-tax cost of capital for Sellmore is 12 percent.

Required

a. Using present value analysis, compute the cost of purchasing the automobile.
b. Using present value analysis, compute the cost of renting the automobile for four years.
c. What choice do you recommend? Why?

14

DECENTRALIZED OPERATIONS AND TRANSFER PRICING

Controlling a firm's operations is a vital part of a manager's duties. The management by exception principle, discussed in Chapter 8 in conjunction with standard costing and performance reporting, is but one aspect of the controlling function. A senior manager must also delegate authority and the responsibility for making decisions to others. The amount of authority that is delegated varies widely among companies.

To monitor managers to whom authority has been delegated, many firms incorporate responsibility accounting into their performance reporting system. As discussed in Chapter 2, *responsibility accounting* is a reporting system in which a cost is charged to the lowest level of management that has responsibility for it. In this chapter, this concept is expanded to include not only costs but, in certain cases, revenues. The reporting system begins with a performance report at the lowest level of management responsibility. This report is then included in the next level of management responsibility, and the process is repeated until the top-level of management is reached.

Different criteria are used to evaluate the performance of responsibility centers. The choice depends on the extent of authority delegation and a manager's preference for a particular criterion. The most commonly used criterion is return on investment (ROI), or a variation of it.

RESPONSIBILITY ACCOUNTING

In Chapter 1, the functions of management were discussed. One function, the delegation of authority, is often used in the largest companies, and these firms are referred to as *decentralized firms.* **Decentralization** is the delegation of a great deal of authority to the lowest level of management responsibility that can make important decisions. On the other hand, a **centralized organization** is one in which little authority is delegated to lower level managers.

When a firm is highly decentralized, it must have a control mechanism that effectively monitors and motivates employees to behave in ways that will help the firm to meet its objectives. While the bottom line—profit maximization—should be one of a firm's goals, other goals, and the manner in which they are achieved, are equally important. Thus, there may be different routes for achieving a specific objective and the route taken should be compatible with the company's image. To ensure control, the firm's objectives, which may include targeted profits, market leadership, excellent employee relations, social consciousness, and quality of products, should be clearly delineated together with the routes by which the goals are to be achieved. In addition, some form of incentive compensation is apt to motivate managers to behave in accordance with organizational goals. One way in which decentralized firms can delegate authority yet retain control and monitor managers' performance is to structure the organization into responsibility centers.

Responsibility Centers

A **responsibility center** is a segment of an organization that has the authority to incur and control costs, earn revenues, and invest funds in assets. A responsibility center may be responsible for all three functions or for only one function. A responsibility center may be a cost center, a revenue center, a profit center, or an investment center.

Cost Center. A **cost center** is a segment of an organization that has the authority to incur and control costs. An example of a cost center is a fabricating department in a manufacturing firm. The department would have no revenues if *all of its production is part of the production process.* However, the department's manager would be responsible for the department's variable costs and direct fixed costs.

Revenue Center. A **revenue center** is a segment of an organization that is responsible only for the *revenues* it earns. Typically, the manager of a revenue center is responsible for marketing a product or product line. However, a revenue center normally has some costs, even if they are only salaries and occupancy costs. Thus, a revenue center is responsible primarily for revenues and only incidentally for some costs, usually not product costs. In that way, a revenue center differs from a cost center, which has primary responsibility for product costs, and a profit center, which has primary responsibility for both revenues and product costs.

Profit Center. A **profit center** is a segment of an organization that has the authority to incur and control costs and to control the revenues it earns. A typical profit center would be a specific product line. The manager of a profit center has the ability to control the center's variable and direct fixed costs. In addition, he or she can decide how many units to produce and thus control the revenues earned. A profit center manager also has the ability to control some of the investments in assets, but not all. By controlling revenues and costs, the manager is also able to *control profits.*

Investment Center. An **investment center** is a segment of an organization that has the authority to incur and control costs, earn revenues, and control investments in assets. An investment center is an autonomous company except for its linkage to an overall corporate headquarters. An example of an investment center might be an automobile product line that is manufactured on its own premises and whose manager has complete autonomy as long as the operations are compatible with overall corporate objectives.

Most organizations have cost centers, while many have profit centers. The use of investment centers depends on the degree of decentralization desired, the preferences of top management, and the perceived benefits derived from decentralization.

Advantages and Disadvantages of Decentralization

The terms *decentralization* and *centralization* refer to two extremes. While most firms operate somewhere between these two extremes, the question of how much decentralization is optimal will depend on a company's individual circumstances.

The advantages of decentralization are that:

1.   Top-level managers are relieved of making routine decisions and can concentrate on making important and difficult decisions.

2.   Employee morale is higher because lower level managers become involved in the decision-making process instead of having a title with little or no authority.

3.   Lower level managers are better equipped for promotion to upper level positions because they gain valuable knowledge about the company's operations through their involvement in the decision-making process.

4.   Decision making becomes more effective because the person most familiar with the circumstances of the decision, the lower level manager, has the final say.

The disadvantages of decentralized operations are:

1.   Upper level managers lose some control.

2.   The lack of goal congruence between the firm and the employee may introduce dysfunctional consequences.

3.   There may be duplication of effort.

The amount of decentralization employed by a firm should be periodically reviewed for its effectiveness, and adjustments should be made when necessary.

Reporting System for Responsibility Accounting

As noted in Chapter 8 and 9, performance reports generally contain columns for budgeted and actual data, a variance column, and a space for explanations of variances. These performance reports are prepared for cost centers, profit centers, and investment centers starting at the lowest level. That report is then incorporated into the next level and so on until the president's report is prepared. To ensure the success of this process, it is extremely important that the levels of management responsibility be clearly delineated, a task that can be easily accomplished by an organization chart showing responsibility centers and lines of authority. An organization chart for the Universal Motor Car Company appears in Illustration 14–1. The company manufactures three product lines—the Yanker, the Metson, and the Cubby—and each product line manufactures different models.

Each responsibility center requires a performance report. Starting with the reports for the lowest level—that is, the cost centers of fabricating, assembling, and painting—the reports are incorporated into the next level's report—compact model—and so on until the president's report is prepared. Sample reports may be seen in Illustration 14–2.

By following the arrows in Illustration 14–2, you should see that the reporting system starts with the fabricating department's performance report, which shows an unfavorable variance of $1,780,000. The totals on this line are carried forward to the supervisor's report for the compact model. The totals of the compact model supervisor's report are then carried forward to the Metson vice president's report, and his totals are then carried forward

ILLUSTRATION 14–1 **Universal Motor Car Company: Organization Chart by Product Line**

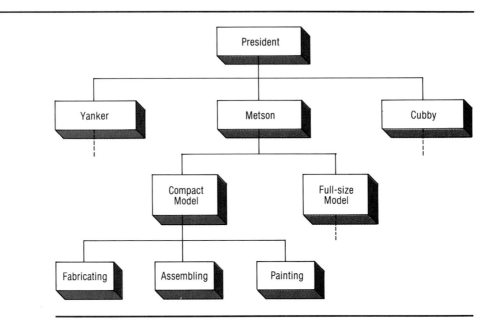

to the president's report. Note that each responsibility center has direct costs that are *not allocated* to a lower level manager's report.

The fabricating, assembling, and painting departments are cost centers. If the supervisor of the compact model has control of revenues (as shown in Illustration 14–2), the responsibility center would be a profit center. The responsibility center for the vice president of the Metson product line would be an investment center if the vice president controlled the investment in assets for Metson. If not, the center would be a profit center. Of course, the company as a whole would be an investment center.

Evaluating Performance Reports

Cost Centers.   Cost centers may be subdivided into **standard cost centers,** in which there is a clear relationship between standard inputs and standard outputs, and **discretionary cost centers,** in which costs are clearly specified but outcomes are not directly related to inputs. Typical standard cost centers would be the fabricating and assembling departments shown in Illustration 14–1. Typical discretionary cost centers would be the research and development department of a manufacturing firm and the administrative departments, such as marketing and accounting, in any company.

Cost centers are expected to perform within an area of targeted costs, usually budgeted or standard costs. A standard cost center's actual costs are compared to the standard costs allowed for a period of time and the variances between the two are computed and explained to the extent possible. Illustration 8–7 (in Chapter 8) shows a responsibility performance report

ILLUSTRATION 14–2

UNIVERSAL MOTOR CAR COMPANY
Sample Performance Reports
(in thousands of dollars)

	Budget	Actual	Variance
President's report:			
President's office	$(15,000)	$ (16,000)	$1,000(U)
Yanker vice president	310,000	315,000	5,000(F)
Metson vice president	203,000	205,420	2,420(F) ←
Cubby vice president	220,000	221,000	1,000(F)
Operating income before income taxes . .	$718,000	$725,420	$7,420(F)
Metson's vice president's report:			
Vice president's office	$(10,000)	$ (10,500)	$ 500(U)
Compact model	→133,000	134,420	1,420(F)
Full-size model	80,000	81,500	1,500(F)
Operating income before income taxes . .	$203,000	$205,420	$2,420(F) —
Supervisor's report for compact model:			
Revenue	$300,000	$305,000	$5,000(F)
Costs:			
Fabricating	72,000	73,780	1,780(U) ←
Assembling	60,000	61,000	1,000(U)
Painting	15,000	14,800	200(F)
Other direct costs	20,000	21,000	1,000(U)
Total costs	167,000	170,580	3,580(U)
Operating income before income taxes . .	$133,000	$134,420	$1,420(F)
Supervisor's report for fabricating department:			
Direct materials	$ 10,000	$ 10,500	$ 500(U)
Direct labor	20,000	20,800	800(U)
Variable overhead	12,000	12,480	480(U)
Direct fixed overhead	30,000	30,000	–0–
Total direct costs	$ 72,000	$ 73,780	$1,780(U) —

for a standard cost center. Discretionary cost centers are usually assigned a budgeted amount of costs for a period of time. The performance report should compare the center's actual costs with the budgeted amounts, and any unusual variances should be investigated by senior managers. Because there is little cause and effect between output and costs, managers of research and development discretionary cost centers must be evaluated using such criteria as patentable discoveries, process improvements, and new production designs.

Revenue Centers. A revenue center is normally responsible for generating a portion of a firm's sales revenue. As such, the performance report for a revenue center should contain the budgeted sales for the center segregated by products and analyzed as discussed in Chapter 10. The budgeted sales should be compared to the actual sales and any variances should be computed and analyzed. If the revenue center manager has the authority to set prices, she should be accountable for *price variances* and *volume variances* and the *standard contribution margin* resulting from those variances. Otherwise, her performance should be evaluated on the basis of volume variances only.

The Bobbie Company manufactures a variety of toys and has a revenue center for its doll division. The manager of the division has the authority to set prices. For 19x2, the center's *budget* is:

Dolls:
    500,000 units at $3.00 per unit $1,500,000
Clothing:
    1,000,000 units at $2.00 per unit 2,000,000
       Budgeted sales $3,500,000

Actual results for 19x2 are:

Dolls:
    600,000 units at $2.95 per unit $1,770,000
Clothing:
    1,100,000 units at $2.10 per unit 2,310,000
       Actual sales $4,080,000

The *standard variable costs* for manufacturing are $1.00 per unit for dolls and $0.80 per unit for clothing. Standard variable costs (or budgeted costs per unit) should be used in the evaluation of revenue centers rather than *actual* costs. The difference between actual and standard costs is chargeable to the cost center manufacturing the product.

A responsibility performance report may be prepared by isolating and analyzing the variances from budgeted sales as follows:

Step 1

Compare the budgeted units of a product with the actual sales in units and multiply the difference by the budgeted price per unit. The result is the *volume variance,* which may be expressed as:

Volume variance = (Actual units − Budgeted units) × Budgeted price

Step 2

Multiply the actual units sold by the difference in price between the budgeted price and the actual price. The result is the *price variance,* which may be expressed as:

Price variance = (Actual price − Budgeted price) × Actual units sold

Step 3

Compute the *standard contribution margin* effects from the variances computed in steps 1 and 2 and prepare the performance report.

ILLUSTRATION 14–3

BOBBIE COMPANY
Performance Report for the Doll Revenue Center

Sales

Product	Actual Sales	Budgeted Sales	Variance (F) = Favorable (U) = Unfavorable
Dolls	$1,770,000	$1,500,000	$270,000(F)
Clothing	2,310,000	2,000,000	310,000(F)
Total sales	$4,080,000	$3,500,000	$580,000(F)

Standard Variable Cost of Sales

	Actual	Budgeted	Variance
Dolls (600,000 × $1.00) and (500,000 × $1.00)	$ 600,000	$ 500,000	$100,000
Clothing (1.1 million × $0.80) and (1 million × $0.80)	880,000	800,000	80,000
Total standard costs	$1,480,000	$1,300,000	$180,000

Recapitulation

	Dolls	Clothing	Total
Increase in sales revenue	$270,000	$310,000	$580,000(F)
Increase in standard variable costs . .	100,000	80,000	180,000
Increase in standard contribution margin	$170,000	$230,000	$400,000(F)

Analysis of Variances

Volume:	
Increase in sales of dolls (600,000 units − 500,000 units) × $3 . . .	$300,000(F)
Increase in sales of clothing (1.1 million units − 1 million units) × $2	200,000(F)
Total volume variance	500,000(F)
Price:	
Decrease in the price of dolls ($2.95 − $3.00) × 600,000 units	30,000(U)
Increase in the price of clothing ($2.10 − $2.00) × 1 million units	110,000(F)
Total price variance	80,000(F)
Total sales revenue variance	$580,000(F)

The revenue center performance report for the Bobbie Company appears in Illustration 14–3.

In evaluating the revenue center's performance, note that:

1. Although the sales revenue from dolls increased by $270,000 ($1,770,000 − $1,500,000), there was a price reduction of 5 cents per unit. Thus,

for 600,000 units, a price reduction of $30,000 resulted. For this reason, it is important to look at the *increase in standard contribution margin* rather than the increase in sales revenue. It is usually possible to increase sales volume by reducing selling prices. In an extreme case, it is possible for *sales revenue to increase dramatically with a concomitant reduction in contribution margin.* If a manager received a reward for the increase in sales revenue in such a case, the reward would be improper because a penalty should have been invoked. Thus, in the Bobbie Company case, the manager should be evaluated on the basis of the $170,000 increase in the contribution margin for dolls and *not* on the $270,000 increase in doll sales revenue.

2. The manager's performance regarding clothing is positive for both volume and price, since both increased. This may be seen more clearly by comparing the sales revenue increases for dolls and clothing with their respective increases in contribution margins as follows:

	Dolls	Clothing	Clothing Increase
Increase in sales revenue (from recapitulation)	$270,000	$310,000	$40,000
Increase in contribution margin (from recapitulation)	$170,000	$230,000	$60,000

While the increase in clothing sales revenue exceeded that of dolls by $40,000, the contribution margin increase was $60,000. An increase in sales revenue *may* increase a firm's profitability, but it is the contribution margin that affects a firm's profitability when fixed costs remain unchanged. Thus, the performance of clothing is preferred to that of dolls. Nonetheless, rewards are indicated for the performance of both since both added to the contribution margin.

Profit Centers. For profit centers, performance evaluation hinges on segmented income statements as discussed in Chapter 10. The responsibility reporting system should provide management with: (1) budgeted income statements showing targeted segment margins by profit center, (2) actual income statements showing segment margins by profit center, and (3) any variances between the two. A manager of a profit center is usually rewarded when his center's segment margin is equal to or greater than his targeted segment margin. The reward system is usually a function of the amount by which the actual segment margin exceeds the targeted margin—that is, the greater the excess, the greater the reward. Conversely, sanctions are usually applied in cases where actual margins are less than targeted margins unless the condition was not controllable by the manager of the profit center.

Investment Centers. A performance report for an investment center contains data on its revenues and costs and on its assets employed to earn the center's segment margin. A common measurement used to evaluate the performance of an investment center is return on investment (ROI). **Return on investment** is a measure of profitability computed by dividing the amount of operating income earned by the average investment in operating assets required to earn the income. If an investor purchases a certificate of deposit for $100,000 and receives $12,000 annually as interest income, ROI may be computed as:

$$\text{ROI} = \frac{\text{Operating income}}{\text{Investment in average operating assets}}$$

$$\text{ROI} = \frac{\$12,000}{\$100,000} = .12 = 12\%$$

The ROI concept is very similar to the internal rate of return and the accounting rate of return discussed in Chapter 12.

EVALUATING A MANAGER'S PERFORMANCE USING THE ROI MODEL

Operating Income and Operating Assets

A clear understanding of the ROI model is needed if it is to be used effectively in evaluating an investment center's performance.

Chapters 12 and 13 discuss the evaluation techniques used when acquiring operating assets such as equipment and machinery. If the assets are acquired by borrowing the necessary funds, the firm will incur interest costs. On the other hand, if the firm uses cash or sells capital stock, no interest cost will appear on its income statement. Thus, interest costs are related to the means by which assets *are acquired* but not to how effectively assets *are used*. Since the ROI model measures how effectively assets are used to earn income, interest costs should not be included. Thus, the numerator of the ROI formula should exclude interest costs.

The income taxes that a firm pays are influenced by many factors. Among these are the depreciation method used (ACRS, straight-line, etc.), gains and losses on investments in stocks and bonds, foreign tax credits, and the results of sophisticated tax-planning techniques. Obviously, these factors should not influence how effectively assets are employed to earn income. Therefore, income taxes are normally excluded from the numerator of the ROI formula. However, some firms use income *after* income taxes when a manager is given the responsibility to make decisions that affect the amount of income taxes that a firm will pay.

The numerator of the ROI formula is sometimes referred to as EBIT (earnings before interest and taxes). In previous chapters, the term *operating income before income taxes* has been used. This term is now shortened to *operating income.*

Since the numerator is limited to income earned from operating activities, the denominator should also be limited to operating assets. Thus, if idle operating cash is invested in stocks, bonds, and real estate not used by the firm in its operations, these assets are excluded from the denominator. Hence, the denominator is referred to as *investment in average operating assets.* Since operating income is earned throughout a period of time, such as a year, it is necessary to use the *average* assets for the year rather than the assets on any particular day. If the period of time in which the operating income is earned is less than a year, the average assets for that period of time is used as the denominator. The term *investment in average operating assets* is now shortened to *average operating assets.* Average operating assets is usually an average of a firm's beginning and ending amounts for a particular year.

Analysis of the ROI Formula

It is important for managers to understand how ROI can be influenced. For example, an increase in the numerator (operating income) could increase ROI. However, a decrease in the denominator (average operating assets) could also increase ROI. If an investment center's operating income for 19x1 amounted to $100,000 and its average operating assets amounted to $1 million, its ROI would be:

$$\text{ROI} = \frac{\$100,000}{\$1,000,000} = .10 = 10\%$$

If in 19x2 its operating income increased to $125,000 while its average operating assets remained at $1 million, its ROI would be 12.5 percent. The calculation would be:

$$\text{ROI} = \frac{\$125,000}{\$1,000,000} = .125 = 12.5\%$$

This increase in ROI would be considered a favorable condition for the firm, provided that a 12.5 percent ROI is greater than the firm's cost of capital (discussed in Chapter 12).

It is also possible to increase ROI by lowering average operating assets. If in 19x2 operating income remained at $100,000 but average operating assets were reduced to $800,000, ROI would also be 12.5 percent:

$$\text{ROI} = \frac{\$100,000}{\$800,000} = .125 = 12.5\%$$

This condition may be favorable, but it may also be unfavorable. Further analysis is required before a manager could reach a conclusion. To aid in analysis, managers should break ROI into its two component parts: the operating margin percentage and asset turnover. This analysis was pioneered by the E. I. du Pont de Nemours Company (Du Pont).

Operating Margin Percentage. The **operating margin percentage** may be defined as operating income divided by sales revenue. If a firm has an investment center that has sales revenue of $10 million and an operating income of $1.5 million, its operating margin percentage (OMP) may be computed as:

$$\text{OMP} = \frac{\text{Operating income}}{\text{Sales revenue}} = \frac{\$1,500,000}{\$10,000,000} = .15 = 15\%$$

This measurement indicates the percentage of sales dollars available to cover interest costs, income taxes, and profit. Obviously, the higher the percentage, the greater the amount of profit per dollar of sales available to the firm. This measurement enables top managers to:

1. Compare an investment center's percentage over a period of years to determine whether it is constant, increasing, or decreasing. Managers usually become concerned if the percentage is decreasing. The percentage may be increased by increasing selling prices, reducing costs, or a combination of both.

2. Compare profit centers where margin percentages are low with other profit centers. A low-percentage profit center may require greater scrutiny by top-level managers to determine if the percentage can be increased.

3. Compare their percentage with competitors' percentages when available. The competitors' information may be available from published financial statements and financial reporting services such as Dun & Bradstreet and Financial Research Associates.

Asset Turnover.   **Asset turnover** may be defined as sales revenue divided by average operating assets. A simple example of the turnover concept would be the case of a firm selling one unit of a VCR and earning an operating income of $35. If the firm's investment in the VCR is $315 and the firm sells one VCR per year, its turnover is 1 and it will earn $35 on an investment of $315. On the other hand, if the firm sells two VCRs per year, it will earn $70 ($35 $\times$ 2) on the same investment of $315, and its turnover would be 2. Thus, the higher the turnover, the more the company will earn per dollar of investment in operating assets. Our discussion of the turnover concept in this chapter is limited to operating asset turnover. Asset turnovers for individual assets, such as accounts receivable and inventories, are also useful management tools, but in another context. These turnover concepts are discussed in Chapter 17.

If a firm has sales revenue of $10 million and its average operating assets are $5 million, its asset turnover may be computed as:

$$\text{Asset turnover} = \frac{\text{Sales revenue}}{\text{Operating assets}} = \frac{\$10,000,000}{\$5,000,000} = 2$$

We would expect that different investment centers would have different turnover ratios. For example, we all hope that a fresh fruit and vegetables market would have a very high turnover, possibly 150. Alternatively, heavy industrial equipment would have a much lower turnover, possibly 5 or less.

Asset turnover is also useful for evaluating an investment center. Depending on its pattern, asset turnover may indicate potential trouble or convey other useful information. For example:

1. A decreasing turnover trend may indicate that the center is carrying unneeded plant assets, experiencing increased collection time for receivables, carrying obsolete inventories, and/or experiencing diminished sales revenues. A decreasing turnover trend may also mean a diminished ROI and lower profits to the firm.

2. A higher turnover trend may signal a shift away from owning plant assets and toward leasing them. By leasing plant assets, the manager of an investment center is able to decrease the denominator and thereby increase asset turnover without necessarily increasing the effective utilization of plant assets. Since neither rental costs nor ownership costs associated with plant assets appear in the asset turnover ratio, it is possible to increase this ratio by renting equipment instead of purchasing it. While it is true that the operating margin percentage *may* be affected by rental costs if they exceed ownership costs, the increase in the turnover ratio may more than offset the decrease in the operating margin percentage.

ROI may be obtained by multiplying its component parts as follows:

$$\text{Operating margin percentage} \times \text{Asset turnover} = \text{ROI}$$

Therefore, using the previous calculations, ROI may be computed as:

$$\text{ROI} = 15\% \times 2 = 30\%$$

or:

$$\text{ROI} = \frac{\$1,500,000}{\$10,000,000} \times \frac{\$10,000,000}{\$5,000,000} = 30\%$$

Notice that the sales revenue appears in both fractions and that in fact, they cancel each other:

$$\frac{\$1,500,000}{\$\cancel{10,000,000}} \times \frac{\$\cancel{10,000,000}}{\$5,000,000} = \frac{\$1,500,000}{\$5,000,000} = 30\%$$

The final fraction after the cancellation of sales revenue is the basic ROI equation of:

$$\text{ROI} = \frac{\text{Operating income}}{\text{Operating assets}}$$

When ROI changes from one period to the next, it is important to know the cause. The change in the operating margin percentage and/or the change in the asset turnover ratio provide the answers.

Using ROI

ROI is a more effective evaluation tool than the mere comparison of an investment center's actual operating income with its targeted amount. Managers generally agree that the ROI concept is superior to many other measurements because it relates operating income to the assets employed to earn that income.

Investment center managers should be rewarded when their ROI performance warrants it. This reward should be correlated to the magnitude of the ROI improvement. Improvements in ROI can be achieved by:

1. Increasing sales revenue.

2. Reducing costs.

3. Reducing operating assets.

Consider the following information for the Pluto Investment Center for 19x2:

Sales revenue	$6,000,000
Operating income	720,000
Operating assets, January 1, 19x2	2,800,000
Operating assets, December 31, 19x2	3,200,000

The operating margin percentage for 19x2 would be:

$$\text{OMP} = \frac{\text{Operating income}}{\text{Sales revenue}} = \frac{\$720,000}{\$6,000,000} = .12 = 12\%$$

The asset turnover for 19x2 would be:

$$\text{Asset turnover} = \frac{\text{Sales revenue}}{\text{Average operating assets}}$$

$$= \frac{\$6,000,000}{\frac{1}{2}\ (\$2,800,000 + \$3,200,000)}$$

$$= \frac{\$6,000,000}{\$3,000,000} = 2$$

The ROI for 19x2 would be:

$$\text{OMP} \times \text{Asset turnover} = 12\% \times 2 = 24\%$$

Calculating ROI for an Increase in Sales.   The manager of Pluto believes that he can increase sales in 19x3 by 15 percent. The 19x2 variable cost ratio of 40 percent is expected to stay the same for 19x3. No increase in fixed costs for 19x3 is anticipated, and average operating assets for 19x3 are also expected to remain unchanged at $3 million. Recall that an increase in sales will affect both the operating margin percentage and the asset turnover. The calculation would be:

$$\text{ROI} = \frac{\$1,260,000^*}{\$6,900,000\dagger} \times \frac{\$6,900,000\dagger}{\$3,000,000}$$

$$\text{ROI} = \quad 18.26\% \quad \times \quad 2.3 \quad = 42\%$$

* $6,000,000 × 15% = $900,000 − (40% × $900,000)
= $540,000 + $720,000 = $1,260,000.
† $6,000,000 + 15% ($6,000,000) = $6,900,000.

Note how a 15 percent increase in sales caused the operating margin ratio to increase from 12 percent to 18.26 percent *and* it caused the asset turnover ratio to increase from 2 to 2.3. The net effect on ROI was an increase from 24 percent to 42 percent.

Calculating ROI for a Reduction in Costs. If instead of an expected increase in sales, the manager of Pluto concentrated on cost reduction, and the only change expected in 19x3 were a savings of fixed costs of $300,000, the ROI would be calculated as:

$$ROI = \frac{\$720,000 + \$300,000}{\$6,000,000} \times \frac{\$6,000,000}{\$3,000,000}$$

$$ROI = \quad 17\% \quad \times \quad 2 \quad = 34\%$$

The savings in fixed costs of $300,000 will cause the operating margin percentage to increase from 12 percent to 17 percent while the asset turnover ratio remains unchanged at 2. Thus, ROI will increase from 24 percent to 34 percent. Note how the separate components of ROI—the increase in operating margin percentage and the unchanged asset turnover—provide more information than would be available if only the change in ROI were shown.

Calculating ROI for a Reduction in Operating Assets. The third possibility for increasing ROI is to decrease the average investment in operating assets. Let us assume that the only change anticipated for 19x3 is a decrease in operating assets on December 31, 19x3, to $1.8 million. The calculation of ROI would be:

$$ROI = \frac{\$720,000}{\$6,000,000} \times \frac{\$6,000,000}{\$2,500,000*}$$

$$ROI = \quad 12\% \quad \times \quad 2.4 \quad = 28.8\%$$

* ($3,200,000 + $1,800,000) ÷ 2 = $2,500,000.

The increase in asset turnover caused the ROI to increase from 24 percent to 28.8 percent. Thus, it is important for the manager of an investment center to control asset turnover when trying to increase the ROI for his center.

Controlling Asset Turnover. While managers have always been aware of operating margins and tried to improve them with increased sales and cost reductions, they gave asset turnover scant attention when interest rates and cost of capital rates were relatively low. With the advent of double-digit interest rates, however, managers began to pay a great deal of attention to asset turnover. When working capital is needlessly invested in assets, a firm sacrifices a part of its ROI, which may place it at a competitive disadvantage.

As firms showed increased attention to asset turnover, they began to tighten lax collection policies for delinquent accounts receivable. Many firms also

ILLUSTRATION 14–4

BAGLEY COMPANY
Segmented Income Statements
For the Year Ended December 31, 19x3

	Division A	Division B
Sales	$4,000,000	$4,000,000
Variable costs	1,200,000	1,200,000
Contribution margin	2,800,000	2,800,000
Direct fixed costs	1,000,000	1,000,000
Segment margin	$1,800,000	$1,800,000

had their customers' payments delivered to a lockbox, with the firm's bank depositing the checks upon receipt and the firm doing the accounts receivable bookkeeping at a later date. Previously, the process was reversed, with a correspondingly greater investment in accounts receivable.

Similarly, little attention had been paid to excessive inventories. But sophisticated techniques are now used to minimize investment in inventories without interrupting production or sales practices. This subject is discussed more fully in Chapter 15.

Overzealous investment center managers may attempt to lower their investments in operating assets by leasing them instead of purchasing them. For example, consider the operating results of a firm's two divisions, as shown in Illustration 14–4. Presently, they both have an investment in average operating assets of $9 million. Their ROIs are the same and may be computed as:

$$\text{ROI} = \frac{\$1,800,000}{\$9,000,000} = .2 = 20\%$$

For 19x4, both divisions expect to replace equipment that originally cost $3 million with new equipment expected to cost $3 million. The new equipment is expected to last 10 years. Division A plans to purchase the equipment, while division B plans to lease the equipment for only five years. To simplify the ROI calculations, let us assume that the cost of leasing is approximately the same as owning the equipment. The results of operations for 19x5 are expected to be the same as that for 19x3. The projected ROIs for 19x5 are:

$$\text{Division A's ROI} = \frac{\$1,800,000}{\$9,000,000} = .2 = 20\%$$

$$\text{Division B's ROI} = \frac{\$1,800,000}{\$9,000,000 - \$3,000,000} = .3 = 30\%$$

Because division B plans to replace $3 million of equipment with leased equipment, its average operating assets will decrease by $3 million and its ROI will increase from 20 percent to 30 percent, while division A's ROI will remain at 20 percent. To prevent individuals from employing this device to the detriment of the company, investment center managers should be permitted the latitude of purchasing or leasing assets as long as the decision can be justified by net present value analysis, discussed in Chapters 12 and 13.

Allocated Common Costs

While it is true that an investment center is theoretically an autonomous business, this is not always the case. There may still be some centralized services that the investment center may use or benefit from. Examples are computer services, printing services, legal and accounting services, and management consulting. If these services were not available from corporate headquarters, the investment center would be obligated to acquire them from outsiders. Thus, it is reasonable to allocate their costs to the investment center. The allocation should be based on usage, possibly employing an hourly rate or a competitive rate charged by outsiders and not an arbitrary allocation formula. For this reason, operating income (after the allocated common costs) is used to evaluate investment centers instead of segment margin (before allocated common costs), which is used to evaluate profit centers.

Investment Center Performance Report

While comparisons using ROI can be useful, upper level managers should make their decisions based on more detailed and informative investment center performance reports. These reports should contain budgeted data, actual data, and a column showing the difference between the two. Such a report appears in Illustration 14–5.

ILLUSTRATION 14–5

LATUR COMPANY
Investment Center Performance Report
For the Year Ended December 31, 19x5
(in thousands of dollars)

	Budget	Actual	Variance
Sales	$5,000	$5,400	$400
Variable costs	1,500	1,600	100
Contribution margin	3,500	3,800	300
Direct fixed costs	1,200	1,250	50
Segment margin	2,300	2,550	250
Allocated common costs	800	825	25
Operating income	$1,500	$1,725	$225
Average operating assets:			
Cash	$ 300	$ 350	$ 50
Receivables	800	825	25
Inventories	900	925	25
Plant assets, net of accumulated depreciation	4,000	4,200	200
Total	$6,000	$6,300	$300
ROI	25%	27.38%	2.38%

Despite its popularity and superiority over a targeted segment margin for a profit center, ROI can be less than optimal as an evaluation technique for investment centers. Some firms prefer a variation of ROI called *residual income.*

RESIDUAL INCOME Just as ROI is related to the accounting rate of return and the internal rate of return discussed in Chapters 12 and 13, residual income is related to the net present value concept discussed in these same chapters. **Residual income** is the amount of investment center operating income left after deducting a desired rate of return on the average operating assets employed by the investment center. The minimum desired rate of return may be viewed as similar to the cutoff rate (cost of capital) used in net present value analysis.

For the Pluto Investment Center with its 19x2 operating income of $720,000 together with its average operating assets of $3 million, the residual income, using a minimum desired rate of return of 16 percent, would be calculated as:

Operating income	$720,000
Less: Desired return on average operating assets (16% × $3 million)	480,000
Residual income	$240,000

Incentive compensation for an investment center's manager would normally be a function of the amount of residual income. The residual income evaluation concept has certain advantages over the ROI method. In particular, it eliminates (1) false signals generated by using a rate of return and failing to consider dollar amounts, and (2) distortions that may result when a manager's objectives conflict with organizational objectives.

1. Eliminating False Signals. The importance of individual investment centers may be obscured by using ROI and failing to consider the dollar amounts involved. To demonstrate the concept, consider the information presented in Illustration 14–6 for two investment centers at the Mutak Company.

ILLUSTRATION 14–6

MUTAK COMPANY
Performance Report for Investment Centers—ROI

	Investment Center X		Investment Center Y	
	19x3	19x4	19x3	19x4
Operating income	$ 6,000,000	$ 7,200,000	$100,000	$125,000
Average operating assets . . .	$40,000,000	$40,000,000	$500,000	$500,000
ROI	15%	18%	20%	25%

ILLUSTRATION 14–7

MUTAK COMPANY
Performance Report for Investment Centers
Residual Income

	Investment Center X		Investment Center Y	
	19x3	19x4	19x3	19x4
Average operating assets . . .	$40,000,000	$40,000,000	$500,000	$500,000
Operating income	$ 6,000,000	$ 7,200,000	$100,000	$125,000
Less: Desired return (14% × Average operating assets) . . .	5,600,000	5,600,000	70,000	70,000
Residual income	$ 400,000	$ 1,600,000	$ 30,000	$ 55,000

If the evaluation of the investment centers is based solely on ROI, the conclusions reached might be as follows:

1. Investment center Y is more valuable to the firm because its ROI for 19x3 was 20 percent while investment center X's ROI was only 15 percent.

2. The manager of investment center Y should receive a greater reward than the manager of X because he increased his ROI from 20 percent to 25 percent, which is greater than X's increase from 15 percent to 18 percent.

Of course, by looking at dollar amounts, Y's increase in operating income from 19x3 to 19x4 is only $25,000, while X's increase is $1.2 million for the same period. Thus, residual income may enable an upper level manager to have a clearer picture of each center's performance. Using a desired rate of return of 14 percent, the analysis using residual income appears in Illustration 14–7.

Note how the signal given by residual income differs from that given by ROI. Each center's relative value to the firm is clearly evident in 19x3, as is the magnitude of each center's improvement in 19x4.

2. Eliminating Conflicting Objectives.   When ROI is used as the reward criterion, a manager's objective is usually to increase ROI and thereby to increase his or her reward. Normally, the firm benefits from an increased ROI and, therefore, the goals of the manager and the firm are congruent. However, this is not always the case. Reconsider investment center Y's performance for 19x3, shown in Illustration 14–6. For that year:

$$\text{ROI} = \frac{\$100,000}{\$500,000} = .2 = 20\%$$

Suppose that it is possible to expand the center by investing $300,000 in operating assets on which $48,000 of operating income can be earned. On this investment:

$$ROI = \frac{\$48,000}{\$300,000} = .16 = 16\%$$

The manager of Y would normally reject this project because it would lower his ROI. The computations are:

$$ROI = \frac{\$100,000 + \$48,000}{\$500,000 + \$300,000} = .185 = 18.5\%$$

However, this may not be the correct decision for the firm. Since the firm's desired rate of return is 14 percent, a 16 percent return would be favorable. Residual income would increase if the project were accepted. The calculation is shown in Illustration 14–8.

From this analysis, it is clear that the manager of an investment center is likely to reject a project that would lower his or her ROI even if the project will enhance the company's profitability. This condition does not exist when residual income is used to evaluate managerial performance.

Relying exclusively on residual income may also present an incorrect signal, however. When investment centers are different sizes, residual income, used by itself, may cause an investment center manager to be treated unfairly.

For example, assume that the Sunset Company has two investment centers, R and S, and that their operating results are as shown in Illustration 14–9. The firm uses residual income to evaluate the managers.

If residual income were to be used exclusively, then investment center S would be considered the winner and its manager would be rewarded more handsomely than R's manager. However, when the operating assets are factored into the calculations, S produced only $12,500 ($52,500 − $40,000) of additional residual income even though its investment in operating assets is three times that of R. Stated differently, a $500,000 investment in R produced $40,000 of residual income but an extra $1 million ($1,500,000 − $500,000) of investment in S produced only an extra $12,500 of residual income. Thus, top-level managers should be aware of this limitation of residual income, and when faced with a situation similar to that shown in Illustration

ILLUSTRATION 14–8

MUTAK COMPANY
Effect of Accepting an Expansion Project
for Investment Center Y

	19x3	Expansion Project	Combined
Operating assets	$500,000	$300,000	$800,000
Operating income	$100,000	$ 48,000	$148,000
Less: Desired return (14% × Operating assets)	70,000	42,000	112,000
Residual income	$ 30,000	$ 6,000	$ 36,000

ILLUSTRATION 14–9

SUNSET COMPANY
Performance Report for Investment Centers
Residual Income

	R	S
Average operating assets	$500,000	$1,500,000
Operating income	$110,000	$ 262,500
Less: Desired return (14% × Average operating		
assets)	70,000	210,000
Residual income	$ 40,000	$ 52,500

14–9, they should analyze the results by comparing the returns on operating assets.

TRANSFER PRICES   Many firms have responsibility centers that manufacture products that may be sold both to outsiders and to other responsibility centers within the firm. An example would be a center that produces spark plugs and transfers them to another center for use in the manufacture of automobiles and also sells them to retailers of automotive supplies. When a firm has these kinds of responsibility centers, special problems arise if ROI or residual income is used to evaluate a center's performance. An important issue is the **transfer price**—the price charged by one responsibility center for goods and services transferred to another responsibility center. Transfer prices can be especially problematical when the entire output of a center is "sold" to another responsibility center or when there is no market for an intermediate product that must be transferred to another center. The major oil companies, which are usually vertically integrated, in that they extract crude oil, refine it, wholesale it, and even retail it as gasoline and petroleum products, make great use of transfer prices.

The determination of an appropriate transfer price can be difficult. In many cases, manufacturers of intermediate products find that a well-defined market exists for their products and, thus, external market prices may be used to gauge transfer prices. In other cases, the markets may be thin, and although market prices are available, they may not be relevant for large purchases. In still other cases, there may be no market for the intermediate product, and hence no external market price.

The most commonly used transfer prices generally fall into five categories:

1.   Variable cost (incremental cost).
2.   Full cost (variable plus fixed costs).
3.   Cost plus a markup.
4.   External market price.
5.   Negotiated price (internal market price).

Variable Cost. In the context of transfer pricing, *variable cost* is generally used synonymously with *incremental cost.* Occasionally, it may be necessary to incur an additional fixed cost when manufacturing an intermediate product, and when this is the case, incremental cost should be used instead of variable cost.

Some problems are associated with the use of variable cost as a transfer price. First, if a responsibility center charges only its variable costs, it will not recover its fixed costs and, thus, not show a profit. The manager of such a responsibility center could not be evaluated using ROI or residual income and the responsibility center would be restricted to the role of cost center. Second, if costs could be passed on to another responsibility center without limit, the cost center manager would lack any incentive to control costs, which consequently might escalate. In addition, the purchasing center's manager would probably object to the cost center's inefficiencies being passed along as part of the variable costs billed to him. Therefore, in fairness to both parties, *standard* variable costs should be used as a transfer price in this situation.

Under certain conditions, variable cost should be used as a transfer price in order to maximize overall company profits. If a lamp manufacturer manufactures its own lamp sockets in its socket responsibility center and the socket center sells both to outsiders and to the company's assembly center, a condition may arise in which variable cost, or one slightly above it, may be the best transfer price. The preference for variable cost depends on whether the socket center can sell all of its output to outsiders or if it has idle capacity. The situation is analogous to accepting a special order at less than full cost, discussed in Chapter 11. Recall that a firm with idle capacity can increase contribution margin by accepting an order at less than full cost as long as the price exceeds variable (incremental) cost.

Consider the present operating results of the two responsibility centers

ILLUSTRATION 14–10

DECORATIVE LAMP COMPANY
Contribution Margin Statement
For the Year Ended December 31, 19x2

	Sockets (200,000 Units)	Assembling (100,000 Units)	Total
Sales (50 cents per socket and $25 per lamp)	$100,000	$2,500,000	$2,600,000
Variable costs:			
Sockets (20 cents and 35 cents, respectively)	40,000	35,000	75,000
Other parts ($10 each)		1,000,000	1,000,000
Total variable costs	40,000	1,035,000	1,075,000
Contribution margin	$ 60,000	$1,465,000	$1,525,000

shown in Illustration 14–10. In this case, the socket center is capable of selling all of its output to outsiders and the assembly center purchases its sockets at the special price of 35 cents each from an outsider.

Now let us assume that for 19x3, the socket center will be able to sell only 100,000 sockets to outsiders. Should the assembling center continue to purchase the sockets externally at 35 cents if the socket center insists on getting 50 cents for its sockets? When the only alternative is an internal transfer price of 50 cents, the answer is to purchase externally. However, this is not the best solution for the firm. Assume that all factors are expected to be the same for 19x3 except for the projected reduction in the sales volume of sockets. The budgeted contribution margin statement for 19x3 appears in Illustration 14–11.

To fully appreciate the impact of the decision to purchase the sockets externally, Illustration 14–11 should be compared with the results obtainable if the socket division were to sell its idle capacity output of 100,000 sockets at a transfer price of 20 cents, its variable cost. This budgeted statement appears in Illustration 14–12.

By comparing Illustration 14–12 to Illustration 14–11, we can see that the firm would gain $15,000 ($1,510,000 − $1,495,000) if the socket center were to sell to assembling. Note that the socket center has a contribution margin of $30,000 in either case and therefore should be willing to sell to assembling for the benefit of the firm. Of course, the manager of assembling could offer to pay a small amount above variable cost, say 25 cents. Therefore, both centers would be the beneficiaries, since sockets would earn a contribution margin of 5 cents per socket and assembling would still save 10 cents per socket over purchasing from outsiders. *The firm would be in the same position regardless of the transfer price as long as the sockets are purchased internally.* In fact, for external reporting purposes, the purchase and sale cancel each other and do not appear in the firm's published income statement.

ILLUSTRATION 14–11

DECORATIVE LAMP COMPANY
Budgeted Contribution Margin Statement
For the Year Ended December 31, 19x3

	Sockets (100,000 Units)	Assembling (100,000 Units)	Total
Sales (50 cents per socket and $25 per lamp)	$50,000	$2,500,000	$2,550,000
Variable costs:			
Sockets (20 cents and 35 cents, respectively)	20,000	35,000	55,000
Other parts ($10 each)		1,000,000	1,000,000
Total variable costs	20,000	1,035,000	1,055,000
Contribution margin	$30,000	$1,465,000	$1,495,000

ILLUSTRATION 14–12

DECORATIVE LAMP COMPANY
Budgeted Contribution Margin Statement
For the Year Ended December 31, 19x3

	Sockets (200,000 Units)	Assembling (100,000 Units)	Total
Sales:			
Sales to outsiders (100,000 at 50 cents and 100,000 at $25)	$50,000	$2,500,000	$2,550,000
Sales to assembling (100,000 at 20 cents)	20,000		20,000
Total sales	70,000	2,500,000	2,570,000
Variable costs:			
Sockets (20 cents)	40,000	20,000	60,000
Other parts ($10 each)		1,000,000	1,000,000
Total variable costs	40,000	1,020,000	1,060,000
Contribution margin	$30,000	$1,480,000	$1,510,000

Transfer prices higher than variable cost and lower than market price are discussed in the section about *negotiated price.*

Full cost. The problems associated with a transfer price at variable cost also apply to a transfer price at full cost. Thus, if full cost is used, it should also be at *standard* cost or normal cost rather than at actual cost. This transfer price is normally used by cost centers. Normal cost transfers were discussed in Chapter 3 for job order cost systems and in Chapter 4 for process cost systems. Standard cost transfers were discussed in Chapters 8 and 9.

Cost plus a Markup. When a transfer price will include a markup, standard cost should be used as the base. Such a transfer price permits a responsibility center to earn a profit, which is not the case when the transfer price is either variable cost or full cost. Therefore, when cost plus a markup is used, the selling responsibility center could be a profit center or an investment center which permits the use of ROI or residual income for evaluation purposes. The problem with using this transfer price is that it does not reflect the competitive spirit of the marketplace. And to the extent that the standard cost may be biased, the markup compounds the bias. Nevertheless, when there is no market for an intermediate product, cost plus a markup may be used effectively.

External Market Price. When a division manager has complete freedom to sell internally or externally, an external market price is the most effective transfer price between profit or investment centers. Such a price reflects the arm's-length nature of parties doing business as strangers. If a purchasing center is able to purchase externally at a specific price and the selling center has no idle capacity, each manager is free to conduct business with outsiders or insiders without detriment to the firm.

In some cases, a transfer price based on market price may require an adjustment for quantity discounts and/or cost savings that arise from selling internally. Among the costs that may be saved and thus should be considered are shipping costs, selling commissions, bookkeeping costs for customers' ledgers, and credit and collection costs. Although the selling center may not have a quantity discount policy, a discount may have to be factored into the transfer price. In most situations, if the buying center were an external customer, the selling center would offer a volume discount, so a similar discount should be offered as part of the transfer price. Thus, although the transfer price is based on the market price, the two may differ significantly.

The Eastern Electronics Company manufactures toaster ovens. One of its responsibility centers manufactures timers that can be used in the ovens. This center is presently operating at full capacity and selling its entire output to outsiders. Fifty percent of its output is sold to one customer at a price of $1.80, which is 10 percent less than its regular price of $2.00. The cost of shipping and sales commissions amount to 20 cents per unit on regular business and 18 cents per unit for its large customer. The operating results for 19x1, the first year of operations, appear in Illustration 14–13.

The contribution margin statement shown in Illustration 14–13 is suboptimal for the company since the toaster center paid $2.00 for timers while the timer center sold them at $1.80 in large quantities. Furthermore, the

ILLUSTRATION 14–13

EASTERN ELECTRONICS COMPANY
Contribution Margin Statement
For the Year Ended December 31, 19x1

	Timers (400,000 Units)	Toasters (200,000 Units)	Total
Sales:			
($ 2.00 × 200,000)	$400,000		$ 400,000
($ 1.80 × 200,000)	360,000		360,000
($20.00 × 200,000)		$4,000,000	4,000,000
Total sales	760,000	4,000,000	4,760,000
Variable costs:			
Timers ($0.88 × 200,000)	176,000		176,000
($0.90 × 200,000)	180,000		180,000
($2.00 × 200,000)		400,000	400,000
Other costs ($6 × 200,000)		1,200,000	1,200,000
Total variable costs	356,000	1,600,000	1,956,000
Contribution margin	$404,000	$2,400,000	$2,804,000

timer center incurred costs of 18 cents per timer that could have been avoided if the timers were sold to the toaster center.

Let us assume that for 19x2, the toaster center would like to purchase the timers internally because it encountered some minor quality and delivery problems during 19x1. What price would be fair to both centers? One approach would be to pay the timer center for its variable costs per unit plus the per-unit contribution margin it would lose by giving up its large customer. As a generalized equation, we might state:

$$\text{Transfer price} = \text{Variable cost per unit} + \text{Contribution margin per unit}$$
$$\text{lost on outside sales}$$

First, we would compute the contribution margin per unit:

	Per Unit
Selling price	$1.80
Less: Variable costs	0.88
Contribution margin	$0.92

Then, the out-of-pocket costs to produce the timers for sale to the toaster center is computed as:

	Per Unit
Total variable cost	$0.88
Less: Freight and commissions	0.18
Net variable cost	$0.70

So the price to be charged according to the generalized equation is:

$$\text{Transfer price} = \$0.70 + \$0.92 = \$1.62$$

For 19x2, the *only change* in operations anticipated is the internal purchase of timers. The budgeted contribution margin statement for 19x2 appears in Illustration 14–14.

The budgeted contribution margin statement shown in Illustration 14–14 is optimal from the company's perspective. In comparing Illustrations 14–13 and 14–14, note that:

1. The 19x2 contribution margin is $76,000 more than the 19x1 contribution margin ($2,880,000 − $2,804,000). This amount consists of:

Difference between the price paid by the toaster center and the price received by the timer center ($2.00 − $1.80 = $0.20 × 200,000 units	$40,000
Savings in freight and commissions ($0.18 × 200,000)	36,000
Total company savings	$76,000

ILLUSTRATION 14-14

EASTERN ELECTRONICS COMPANY
Budgeted Contribution Margin Statement
For the Year Ended December 31, 19x2

	Timers (400,000 Units)	Toasters (200,000 Units)	Total
Sales:			
($ 2.00 × 200,000)	$400,000		$ 400,000
($ 1.62 × 200,000)	324,000		324,000
($20.00 × 200,000)		$4,000,000	4,000,000
Total sales	724,000	4,000,000	4,724,000
Variable costs:			
Timers ($0.70 × 200,000) . . .	140,000		140,000
($0.90 × 200,000) . . .	180,000		180,000
($1.62 × 200,000)		324,000	324,000
Other costs ($6 × 200,000) . .		1,200,000	1,200,000
Total variable costs	320,000	1,524,000	1,844,000
Contribution margin	$404,000	$2,476,000	$2,880,000

---

2. The variable cost for timers sold to the toaster center is 70 cents.

3. The contribution margin shown by the timer center is $404,000 in both illustrations. Thus, the manager of the timer center will receive the same reward whether she sells to an outsider or to the toaster center.

4. The sale and purchase of timers in the amount of $324,000 could have been canceled in the companywide column.

This example highlights the value of managers being team players. As long as the manager of timers is not sacrificing any contribution margin, she should be willing to sell the timers to the toaster centers.

The generalized equation also applies to centers that have idle capacity. In the case of the Decorative Lamp Company (Illustrations 14-11 and 14-12) in which the socket center had idle capacity of 100,000 units, we concluded that the transfer price should be at variable cost. Using the generalized equation, the transfer price would be:

$$\text{Transfer price} = \text{Variable cost per unit} + \text{Contribution}$$
$$\text{margin lost on outside sales}$$
$$\text{Transfer price} = \$0.20 + \$0 = \$0.20$$

Thus, the generalized formula produces optimal results for the company by recommending a transfer price at variable cost when idle capacity is present.

Negotiated Price. Typically, a transfer price is negotiated when there is no market for an intermediate product manufactured by a responsibility center. An example would be a center that produces circuit boards for a radio manufacturer. Circuit boards are custom tailored to a manufacturer's specifications. Normally, a center that produced circuit boards for internal use only would be a cost center, and a transfer price would not be needed. However, suppose the center manufactures circuit boards for an external television manufacturer as well as for the internal radio center. In this case, the center would normally be a profit or investment center, and a negotiated transfer price would be needed because there is no external market for the radio circuit board.

The generalized equation may be used to set the negotiated transfer price. For example, the circuit board center devotes 40 percent of its capacity to manufacturing the television circuit boards. The television circuit boards are sold for $10 each and have a variable cost of $3 each. Sales for 19x2 amounted to 200,000 units. Because the radio circuit boards are smaller and simpler to make, the center is able to manufacture 600,000 circuit boards, as needed by the radio center. Variable costs are 80 cents each.

The circuit board center could sell its entire output to the television manufacturer if it did not make the circuit boards for the radio center. Thus, the opportunity cost of making radio circuit boards is the income given up by not making television circuit boards.

The negotiated transfer price may be set as follows:

	Per Unit
Contribution Margin Forgone:	
Selling price	$ 10
Variable cost	3
Contribution margin	$ 7

	Units
Number of units forgone:	
Factory capacity (200,000 ÷ .40)	500,000
Less: Units sold	200,000
Units forgone	300,000
Contribution margin forgone (300,000 × $7)	$2,100,000

The contribution margin needed is $3.50 ($2.1 million ÷ 600,000) per unit. Adding the $3.50 to the variable cost of $0.80 per unit produces a negotiated transfer price of $4.30 per unit. The proof of the calculation is:

Entire output sold externally:	
500,000 × $7.00 contribution margin	$3,500,000
Output sold internally and externally:	
200,000 × $7.00	$1,400,000
600,000 × $3.50	2,100,000
Total contribution margin	$3,500,000

ILLUSTRATION 14–15   Transfer-Pricing Diagram

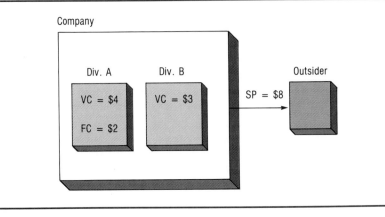

The transfer price of $4.20 is fair to both parties and should be accepted by both, provided they understand the managerial and cost concepts as just illustrated.

A negotiated transfer price may also be used in place of variable cost when a center has idle capacity. When variable cost is used, the selling center neither gains nor loses by selling at variable cost. On the other hand, the buying center acquires the product at a substantial amount below market price because fixed costs and profits are omitted from the transfer price. Under such circumstances, using a negotiated transfer price in place of variable cost would provide an incentive to the selling center, and the buying center would still pay less than it would to an outside supplier.

When a transfer-pricing problem is encountered that contains complex relationships, it is possible to diagram the problem to clarify the complexities. A sample diagram appears in Illustration 14–15.

Behavioral Aspects of Transfer Pricing

Ideally, managers of responsibility centers should be free to make decisions without fear of being vetoed by top management. Occasionally, a center manager, believing that he is acting in the best interest of both his center and the company, may make a decision that is detrimental to the company as a whole. And on rare occasions, a manager may stubbornly stick to a decision, knowing it is wrong for the company. Whatever the reason, if a manager's decision is overturned by top management, the firm is closer to centralization than to decentralization. To achieve the benefits of decentralization, top management must sit back and allow the consequences of the wrong decision to materialize. In the process, center managers will learn to trust the system and probably make fewer poor decisions.

The key to encouraging center managers to make correct decisions for the firm as a whole is education. Center managers should be encouraged to be team players. As a team player, a center manager should recognize that sometimes a decision must be made for the benefit of the company, such as when idle capacity exists, and that when needed, the center manager can expect reciprocity. Furthermore, all managers should have a thorough understanding of their center's cost behavior patterns and cost structure so that when it is necessary for them to sell at variable cost, they will understand that they are not being hurt. They should also understand that if they make many wrong decisions, they will be held accountable.

SUMMARY

Practically all large firms have some form of **decentralization.** A highly decentralized firm delegates a great deal of authority for making important decisions to lower level managers, while a **centralized organization** delegates little authority.

A decentralized firm is usually divided into **responsibility centers**—individual segments that have control over their own costs and/or revenues. A segment that controls only costs is a **cost center,** while a segment that controls only revenues is a **revenue center.** A segment that controls both costs and revenues but not investments in its assets is a **profit center,** while a segment that controls costs, revenues, and its investment in assets is an **investment center.** Regardless of its kind, a responsibility center's performance should be evaluated according to specified criteria. To accomplish this, most firms make use of responsibility accounting, which requires that performance reports be prepared for each segment, starting with the lowest level of authority. Each report is incorporated into the next level's report and builds to the president's report, which then includes the entire company's operating results.

Standard costs are used to evaluate the performance of cost centers. For this purpose, cost centers are normally divided into two categories. In **standard cost centers,** there is a high correlation between inputs and outputs, as there is in producing departments. In **discretionary cost centers,** only inputs can be controlled, as is the case in research and development centers.

Budgeted contribution margin is used to evaluate revenue centers, while budgeted segment margin is used to assess profit centers. Finally, investment centers are often judged by **return on investment (ROI),** which may be broken into its component parts of **operating margin percentage** multiplied by **asset turnover.** Since ROI may be increased in different ways, the component parts provide more information about an investment center than does ROI alone. In some cases, a manager may be tempted to use ROI to further his own goals, although it would be detrimental to the firm. For this reason, many firms, such as Du Pont, prefer to use a variant of ROI known as **residual income.** This evaluation technique requires that a charge for the assets used by a segment be deducted from its operating income to arrive at residual income.

Many firms transfer goods and services among segments. The price at which the goods are transferred is known as the **transfer price.** Depending on the circumstances, the transfer price may be based on variable cost, full cost, or cost plus a markup. As another alternative, many managers prefer to use the market price if a market for the product exists. If there is no market, then a negotiated transfer price may be used. The transfer price used depends on the degree of autonomy granted to the firm's segments and whether the selling segment is operating at full capacity or limited capacity.

GLOSSARY OF KEY TERMS

Asset turnover   Sales revenue divided by average operating assets.

Centralized organization   A firm in which little authority is delegated to lower level managers.

Cost center   A segment of an organization that has the authority to incur and control costs.

Decentralization   The delegation of a great deal of authority to the lowest level of management responsibility that is capable of making important decisions.

Discretionary cost center   A segment of a firm in which costs are clearly specified but outcomes are not clearly related to inputs, as in a research and development center.

Investment center   A segment of an organization that has the authority to incur and control costs, earn revenues, and control investments in assets.

Operating margin percentage   Operating income divided by sales revenue.

Profit center   A segment of an organization that has the authority to incur and control costs and to control the revenues it earns.

Residual income   The amount of investment center operating income left after deducting a desired rate of return on the average operating assets employed by the investment center.

Responsibility center   A segment of an organization that has the authority to incur and control costs, earn revenues, and invest funds in assets. It is possible for a responsibility center to be responsible for all three functions or for only one function.

Return on investment (ROI)   A measure of profitability computed by dividing the amount of operating income earned by the average investment in operating assets required to earn the income.

Revenue center   A segment of an organization that is responsible only for the revenues it earns.

Standard cost center   A segment of a firm in which there is a clear relationship between standard inputs and standard outputs, as in a producing department.

Transfer price   The price charged by one responsibility center for goods or services transferred to another responsibility center.

REVIEW PROBLEM

The Westman Company has a lens division that is operated as an investment center. The division is operating at only 60 percent of capacity. The results of operations for 19x3 are shown in Illustration 14–16.

ILLUSTRATION 14–16

WESTMAN COMPANY
Lens Division
Statement of Operating Income
For the Year Ended December 31, 19x3

Sales (120,000 × $10)	$1,200,000
Variable costs (at $4)	480,000
Contribution margin	720,000
Direct fixed costs	300,000
Segment margin	420,000
Invoiced common costs for services	
from other divisions	180,000
Operating income	$ 240,000
Operating assets—January 1, 19x3	$ 460,000
Operating assets—December 31, 19x3 . . .	$ 500,000

The company's minimum desired rate of return for residual income purposes is 15 percent.

Required

a. Compute:
   (1) The operating margin percentage.
   (2) Asset turnover.
   (3) ROI.

b. Compute residual income.

c. For 19x4, the lens division expects its operations to be unchanged from that of 19x3. However, it has an opportunity to accept a special order from an outsider for 80,000 lenses at a price of $6. The order will not affect its regular sales and will require an additional outlay of $100,000 for direct fixed costs. Additional operating assets will be needed at a cost of $150,000. Calculate the following for the *special order only:*
   (1) ROI.
   (2) Residual income.
   Would you expect the manager of the lens division to accept the order if the parameter used for evaluation is ROI? Why? Would your answer be different if the parameter used is residual income? Why?

d. The Westman Company is planning to market a new product, binoculars. The lenses manufactured by the lens division could be used in the binoculars. Assume that the offer in *(c)* was withdrawn by the offeror. Thus, the lens division will still have the idle capacity. The manager in charge of producing the binoculars learned that he could purchase externally the 80,000 lenses he needs for $9 each. What price should the lens division quote for the lenses assuming no increase in fixed costs and no additional investment will be needed by the lens division? Why?

e. Assume the same facts as in *(d)* except that the lens division has a customer who is willing to purchase the 80,000 lenses in 19x4 for $10 each. The lenses will not require any shipping costs or sales commissions. What price should the lens division now quote to the binocular division? What should the binocular manager's reaction be to the prices quoted? Why?

f. Assume the same facts as in *(e)* except that shipping costs and sales commissions amount to $2 per unit on the 80,000 lenses. What price should be quoted? What should the binocular manager do? Why?

g. Assume that the lens division can only sell 120,000 lenses in 19x4 and its budgeted statement of operating income for 19x4 is the same as Illustration 14–16. The binocular division expects to use 200,000 lenses and thus would require all of the output of the lens division. There are no shipping costs or sales commissions in Illustration 14–16. What price should be charged by the lens division? What should the binocular manager do if he can purchase the lenses externally at $8.50 per lens? Why?

SOLUTION TO REVIEW PROBLEM

a. (1)

$$OMP = \frac{\$240,000}{\$1,200,000} = .2 = 20\%$$

(2) Asset turnover $= \dfrac{\$1,200,000}{\frac{1}{2}\,(\$460,000 + \$500,000)} = \dfrac{\$1,200,000}{\$480,000} = 2.5$

(3) ROI $= 20\% \times 2.5 = 50\%$

b. Residual income:

Operating income	$240,000
Less: Desired return	
$\left(15\% \times \dfrac{\$460,000 + \$500,000}{2}\right)$	72,000
Residual income	$168,000

c. (1) Operating income:

Sales (80,000 × $6)	$480,000
Variable costs (at $4)	320,000
Contribution margin	160,000
Direct fixed costs	100,000
Operating income	$ 60,000
Average operating assets*	$150,000

* The $150,000 will be expended at the *beginning* of the year. Thus, the average is $150,000.

ROI:

$$ROI = \frac{\$60,000}{\$150,000} = .4 = 40\%$$

(2) Residual income:

Operating income	$ 60,000
Less: Desired return	
(15% × $150,000)	22,500
Residual income	$ 37,500

The manager of the lens division would probably reject the special order because it only produces an ROI of 40 percent, which will lower his present ROI of 50 percent.

The manager of the lens division would accept the special order if residual income is used to evaluate his performance because the order produces an additional $37,500 of residual income.

d. The minimum price in this case should be $4, the variable cost. Using the generalized formula, the price may be computed as:

$$\text{Transfer price} = \text{Variable cost per unit} \\ + \text{Lost contribution margin per unit}$$
$$\text{Transfer price} = \$4 + \$0 = \$4$$

The binocular manager may be willing to pay more than $4 but less than $9 so that the lens division would have an incentive to sell internally and the binocular division could still purchase the lenses for less than the external price.

e. Using the generalized formula, the price would be $10, computed as follows:

$$\text{Transfer price} = \$4 + \$6 = \$10$$

The binocular manager should purchase the lenses externally because $9 is less than the internal price of $10. If the lens division were to quote a $9 price, the firm would lose $80,000 (80,000 lenses $\times$ $1).

f. The contribution margin is:

		Per Unit
Selling price		$10
Less:		
Variable manufacturing cost	$4	
Shipping and sales commissions . . .	2	6
Contribution margin		$ 4

The transfer price should be $8 and may be computed, using the generalized formula, as follows:

$$\text{Transfer price} = \$4 + \$4 = \$8$$

The binocular manager should purchase internally because $8 is less than $9.

g. The contribution margin of $720,000 presently earned will be sacrificed, and thus it must be spread over the expected 200,000 lenses as follows:

$$\frac{\$720,000}{200,000} = \$3.60 \text{ per unit}$$

Using the generalized formula, the transfer price is $7.60, computed as follows:

$$\text{Transfer price} = \$4.00 + \$3.60 = \$7.60$$

The lenses should be purchased internally because $7.60 is less than $8.50.

QUESTIONS

1. What does decentralization mean? Which kinds of firms employ the concept? Why?

2. What is a responsibility center? Why is it important for decentralized firms to use responsibility centers?

3. Distinguish between a cost center, a revenue center, a profit center, and an investment center.

4. What are the advantages and disadvantages of decentralized operations?

5. Describe the operation of a reporting system for a decentralized firm that uses responsibility accounting.

6. What parameter is generally used to evaluate cost centers? What is the difference between a standard cost center and a discretionary cost center? Are they evaluated differently? Explain.

7. What parameter is used to evaluate a revenue center? Are actual costs or standard costs used in the evaluation process? Why? Is it possible for the sales revenue of a revenue center to increase and yet be considered a negative performance by the center's manager? Explain.

8. Are different parameters used to evaluate profit centers and investment centers? Explain.

9. Is ROI a superior measurement over a targeted operating income? Why?

10. Is there more than one way to compute ROI? If so, which one do you prefer? Why?

11. What is the operating margin percentage? Why is it important?

12. What is asset turnover? Why is it important?

13. Could the use of ROI result in a manager's performance that may be detrimental to the firm? Explain.

14. What is residual income? It has a certain advantage over ROI. Explain. There may be a disadvantage encountered when using residual income. Explain.

15. What is a transfer price? Why is it needed?

16. What are the three cost-based transfer prices? When should each be used?

17. Why is the external market price for an intermediate product preferred as a transfer price?

18. When should a negotiated transfer price be used?

19. Is it important for a responsibility center manager to be a team player? Explain.

EXERCISES

14-1 ROI and Residual Income

The Burns Company has two investment centers, clothing and jewelry. Selected information for each segment follows:

	Clothing	Jewelry
Sales	$960,000	$1,700,000
Operating income	172,800	357,000
Operating assets—January 1, 19x2	360,000	870,000
Operating assets—December 31, 19x2	440,000	1,018,888

The firm's minimum desired rate of return for investment center evaluation is 20 percent.

All calculations for percentages should be carried to one decimal place.

Required *a.* Calculate the following for each segment:
  (1) Operating margin percentage.
  (2) Asset turnover.
  (3) ROI.
  (4) Residual income.

b. Which segment appears to be performing better on the basis of:
  (1) ROI? Explain by examining the components of ROI.
  (2) Residual income? Explain.

14–2 ROI and Residual Income

The Collins Company has two investment centers, blankets and pillows. Selected information for each segment follows:

	Blankets	Pillows
Sales	$900,000	$1,500,000
Operating income	108,000	150,000
Operating assets—January 1, 19x3	430,000	460,000
Operating assets—December 31, 19x3	470,000	540,000

The firm's minimum desired rate of return for investment center evaluation is 18 percent.

Required *a.* Calculate the following for each segment:
  (1) Operating margin percentage.
  (2) Asset turnover.
  (3) ROI.
  (4) Residual income.

b. Which segment appears to be performing better on the basis of:
  (1) ROI? Explain by examining the components of ROI.
  (2) Residual income? Explain.

14–3 Responsibility Centers

1. A segment of an organization is referred to as a profit center if it has
   a. Authority to make decisions affecting the major determinants of profit, including the power to choose its markets and sources of supply.
   b. Authority to make decisions affecting the major determinants of profit, including the power to choose its market and sources of supply and significant control over the amount of invested capital.
   c. Authority to make decisions over the most significant costs of operations, including the power to choose the sources of supply.
   d. Authority to provide specialized support to other units within the organization.
   e. Responsibility for combining the raw materials, direct labor, and other factors of production into a final output.
2. A segment of an organization is referred to as an investment center if it has
   a. Authority to make decisions affecting the major determinants of profit, including the power to choose its markets and sources of supply.

b. Authority to make decisions affecting the major determinants of profit, including the power to choose its market and sources of supply and significant control over the amount of invested capital.

c. Authority to make decisions over the most significant costs of operations, including the power to choose the sources of supply.

d. Authority to provide specialized support to other units within the organization.

e. Responsibility for developing markets for and selling of the output of the organization.

3. A segment of an organization is referred to as a service center if it has

a. Responsibility for developing markets for and selling of the output of the organization.

b. Responsbility for combining the raw materials, direct labor, and other factors of production into a final output.

c. Authority to make decisions affecting the major determinants of profit, including the power to choose its markets and sources of supply.

d. Authority to provide specialized support to other units within the organization.

e. Authority to make decisions over the most significant costs of operations, including the power to choose the sources of supply.

4. A segment of an organization is referred to as a cost center if it has

a. Responsibility for developing markets for and selling of the output of the organization.

b. Authority to make decisions affecting the major determinants of profit, including the power to choose its markets and sources of supply.

c. Authority to make decisions over the most significant costs of operations, including the power to choose the sources of supply.

d. Authority to provide specialized support to other units within the organization.

e. Responsibility for combining the raw materials, direct labor, and other factors of production into a final output.

(CMA adapted)

14–4   Residual Income

1. The basic objective of the residual income approach of performance measurement and evaluation is to have a division maximize its

a. Return on investment rate.

b. Imputed interest rate charge.

c. Cash flows.

d. Cash flows in excess of a desired minimum amount.

e. Income in excess of a desired minimum return.

2. The imputed interest rate used in the residual income approach for performance measurement and evaluation can best be characterized as the

a. Historical weighted-average cost of capital for the company.

b. Marginal after-tax cost of new equity capital.

c. Average return on investment that has been earned by the company over a particular time period.

d. Target return on investment set by management.

e. Average prime lending rate for the year being evaluated.

3. Which one of the following items would most likely *not* be incorporated into the calculation of a division's investment base when using the residual income approach for performance measurement and evaluation?
   a. Fixed assets employed in divisional operations.
   b. Vacant land being held by the division as a potential site for a new plant.
   c. Divisional inventories when division management exercises control over the inventory levels.
   d. Divisional accounts payable when division management exercises control over the amount of short-term credit utilized.
   e. Divisional accounts receivable when division management exercises control over credit policy and credit terms.

   (CMA adapted)

14–5   ROI and Residual Income

Fill in the missing data in the following cases.

	Investment Center		
	A	B	C
Sales	$900,000	$?	$?
Operating income	?	240,000	210,000
Average operating assets	?	?	450,000
Operating margin percentage	?	?	14%
Asset turnover	2.5	4	?
ROI	35%	48%	?
Minimum desired rate of return percentage	20%	?	?
Residual income	?	150,000	115,500

14–6   ROI and Residual Income

Fill in the missing data in the following cases.

	Investment Center		
	D	E	F
Sales	$?	$800,000	$1,200,000
Operating income	?	?	?
Average operating assets	480,000	400,000	?
Operating margin percentage	?	11%	12.5%
Asset turnover	3.2	?	?
ROI	48%	?	40%
Minimum desired rate of return percentage	21%	?	?
Residual income	?	20,000	67,500

14–7 Costs for Investment Centers

For each item listed below, indicate whether the cost should be deducted on an investment center's income statement to arrive at operating income, and give a brief explanation of your position.

1. The cost of fuel pumps purchased from another investment center at the price sold in the intermediate market.
2. Computer services billed by the computer service center at a competitive hourly rate per hour used.
3. The corporate president's salary and other corporate costs at 2 percent of sales revenue.
4. Industrial psychology service cost which is billed by allocating the department's costs over the firm's number of employees.
5. The factory cafeteria's operating loss allocated over the number of factory employees employed.

14–8 Transfer Pricing

The Masterson Electric Company manufactures electric motors and electric hair dryers. The electric motors are sold for $8 each and have a variable cost of $3 each. Direct fixed costs are $2 each at a capacity of 200,000 motors. The hair dryer division uses 50,000 motors per annum which are purchased externally at $7 each. The motors used by the hair dryer division are similar to those manufactured by the electric motor division.

Required *a.* Assume that 200,000 electric motors are sold externally at $8. What transfer price should be quoted to the hair dryer division if the 50,000 motors are to be purchased internally? Will the internal purchase and sale take place? Explain.

b. Assume that for the following year, only 150,000 electric motors can be sold externally. What transfer price should be quoted to the hair dryer division for the 50,000 motors assuming no change in costs? Will the internal purchase and sale take place? Explain.

14–9 Transfer Pricing

The Fabric Manufacturing Company manufactures piece goods suitable for manufacture into men's and ladies' suits. The company also manufactures men's suits. The piece goods division sells a particular fabric for $15 per yard. For 19x3, the piece goods division operated at full capacity of 1 million yards, all sold externally. Variable costs amounted to $4 per yard and direct fixed costs amounted to $5 per yard, or $5 million annually.

The men's suits division purchased all of its fabric needs externally during 19x3. For 19x4, the suit division expects to enter a different men's suit market which will require 500,000 yards of fabric similar to that manufactured by the piece goods division. Checking with other piece goods manufacturers, the suit division was able to ascertain that it could purchase the needed fabric at $15 per yard less a quantity discount of 8 percent.

The piece goods division pays a commission of 4 percent of sales to its salespeople. In addition, it pays shipping costs which average 20 cents per yard. These two costs would not be incurred if the piece goods are sold to the suit division.

Required   *a.*   If the suit division wishes to purchase the piece goods internally, what transfer price should be quoted if the piece goods division expects to operate at full capacity in 19x4? Will the internal sale and purchase take place? Explain.

   b.   If the piece goods division expects to operate at 50 percent of capacity in 19x4, what transfer price should it quote to the suit division? Will the internal sale and purchase take place? Explain.

14–10   Transfer Pricing

The Brass Fabricating Company has a brass tubing division that manufactures brass tubing used in the manufacture of lamps. For 19x3, the division operated at 70 percent of capacity, which is expected to continue for 19x4. Its contribution margin income statement for 19x3 is as follows:

BRASS FABRICATING COMPANY
Brass Tubing Division
Contribution Margin Income Statement
For the Year Ended Decemer 31, 19x3

Sales (7 million feet at 40 cents per foot)	$2,800,000
Less: Variable costs (at 15 cents per foot)	1,050,000
Contribution margin	$1,750,000

The company plans to manufacture lamps during 19x4. The lamps will sell for $25 each and will have variable costs as follows:

Brass tubing—2 feet at 40 cents	$ 0.80
Other variable costs	9.20
Total variable costs	$10.00

The company believes it can sell 1 million lamps in 19x4. No change is expected in sales of brass tubing to outsiders in 19x4. Variable cost patterns are also expected to be unchanged.

Required   *a.*   Prepare a contribution margin income statement for each division assuming that the tubing is purchased internally at 40 cents per foot. Also prepare a combined contribution margin statement. Use three columns, labeled *Tubing, Lamps,* and *Combined.* (Show the internal purchase and sale separately in the individual and combined columns.)

   b.   Redo *(a)* using a transfer price of 15 cents per foot for tubing. What conclusion can you reach regarding the transfer price charged for internal sales when idle capacity exists in the selling division?

14–11   Transfer Pricing

   1.   The blade division of Dana Company produces hardened steel blades. One third of the blade division's output is sold to the lawn products division of Dana; the remainder is sold to outside customers. The blade division's estimated sales and standard cost data for the fiscal year ending June 30, 19x1, are as follows:

	Lawn Products	Outsiders
Sales	$15,000	$40,000
Variable costs	(10,000)	(20,000)
Fixed costs	(3,000)	(6,000)
Gross margin	$ 2,000	$14,000
Unit sales	10,000	20,000

The lawn products division has an opportunity to purchase 10,000 identical quality blades from an outside supplier at a cost of $1.25 per unit on a continuing basis. Assume that the blade division cannot sell any additional products to outside customers. Should Dana allow its lawn products division to purchase the blades from the outside supplier, and why?

a. Yes, because buying the blades would save Dana Company $500.
b. No, because making the blades would save Dana Company $1,500.
c. Yes, because buying the blades would save Dana Company $2,500.
d. No, because making the blades would save Dana Company $2,500.

2. Mar Company has two decentralized divisions, X and Y. Division X has always purchased certain units from division Y at $75 per unit. Because division Y plans to raise the price to $100 per unit, division X desires to purchase these units from outside suppliers for $75 per unit. Division Y's costs follow:

Y's variable costs per unit	$ 70
Y's annual fixed costs	$15,000
Y's annual production of these units for X	1,000 units

If division X buys from an outside supplier, the facilities division Y uses to manufacture these units would remain idle. What would be the result if Mar enforces a transfer price of $100 per unit between divisions X and Y?

a. It would be suboptimization for the company because X should buy from outside suppliers at $75 per unit.
b. It would provide lower overall company net income than a transfer price of $75 per unit.
c. It would provide higher overall company net income than a transfer price of $75 per unit.
d. It would be more profitable for the company than allowing X to buy from outside suppliers at $75 per unit.

(AICPA adapted)

PROBLEMS   14–12   **ROI and Residual Income**

The Heron Company has a motor division that manufactures small electric motors. The division is operated as an investment center and is operating at only 50 percent of capacity. The results of operations for 19x3 are shown below.

HERON COMPANY
Motor Division
Statement of Operating Income
For the Year Ended December 31, 19x3

Sales (100,000 × $6)	$600,000
Variable costs (at $2)	200,000
Contribution margin	400,000
Direct fixed costs	250,000
Segment margin	150,000
Billed common costs for services from	
other divisions	30,000
Operating income	$120,000
Operating assets, January 1, 19x3	$480,000
Operating assets, December 31, 19x3	$520,000

The Company's minimum desired rate of return to be used for residual income is 14 percent.

Required *a.* Compute:
  (1) The operating margin percentage.
  (2) Asset turnover.
  (3) ROI.
b. Compute residual income.
c. For 19x4, the division expects its operations to be unchanged from that of 19x3. However, it has an opportunity to accept a special order from a foreign manufacturer for 80,000 motors at a price of $3. The order will not affect its regular sales and will require an additional outlay of $40,000 for direct fixed costs. Additional operating assets will be needed at a cost of $200,000. Calculate the following for 19x4, if the special order is accepted (combine the special order with the regular operations):
  (1) The operating margin percentage.
  (2) Asset turnover.
  (3) ROI.
  (4) Residual income.
  Would you expect the manager of the motor division to accept the order if the parameter used for evaluation is ROI? Why? Would your answer be different if the parameter used is residual income? Why?

14–13   ROI, Residual Income, and CVP Analysis

The manager of an investment center presents you with her division's operating results for the year just completed, 19x4, as follows:

STONES INVESTMENT CENTER
Operating Income Statement
For the Year Ended December 31, 19x4

Sales (500,000 at $8)	$4,000,000
Variable costs (at $3)	1,500,000
Contribution margin	2,500,000
Direct fixed costs	2,020,000
Operating income	$ 480,000

Operating assets on January 1, 19x4, amounted to $2,000,000, while on December 31, 19x4, they amounted to $2,444,444.

The minimum desired rate of return for residual income is 16 percent.

Required *a.* Compute:

    (1) The operating margin percentage.

    (2) Asset turnover.

    (3) ROI.

    (4) Residual income.

  b. Each of the following is to be considered independently:

    (1) For 19x5, the manager would like the division to show an increase in the operating margin percentage to 15 percent. This can be accomplished by fixed cost savings. How much would operating income have to increase in order to reach this goal?

    (2) If in part *b*(1) the goal is to be achieved by an increase in sales instead of by cost savings, how much increased sales would be needed to reach the goal, assuming no increase in direct fixed costs and no change in the variable cost ratio? (Hint: Use an algebraic equation to solve the problem.)

    (3) For 19x5, the manager would like to increase the asset turnover to 2. By how much would operating assets have to decrease on December 31, 19x5, to accomplish this objective?

    (4) If in part *b*(3) the objective is to be achieved by an increase in sales instead of a reduction in operating assets, how much would sales have to increase in order to reach this objective? Assume that operating assets will remain unchanged during 19x5.

    (5) If the selling price were increased by 15 percent in 19x5, sales volume would decrease by 10 percent. Assuming no change in operating assets for 19x5, what effect would this action have on:

      (a) The operating margin percentage?

      (b) Asset turnover?

      (c) ROI?

      (d) Residual income?

14–14 ROI, Residual Income, and CVP Analysis

The manager of an investment center presents you with his division's operating results for the year just completed, 19x4, as follows:

SILVER INVESTMENT CENTER
Operating Income Statement
For the Year Ended December 31, 19x4

Sales (300,000 at $12)	$3,600,000
Variable costs (at $6)	1,800,000
Contribution margin	1,800,000
Direct fixed costs	1,404,000
Operating income	$ 396,000

Operating assets on January 1, 19x4, amounted to $2.1 million, while on December 31, 19x4, they amounted to $2.4 million.

The minimum desired rate of return for residual income is 14 percent.

Required

a. Compute:
  (1) The operating margin percentage.
  (2) Asset turnover.
  (3) ROI.
  (4) Residual income.

b. Each of the following is to be considered independently:
  (1) For 19x5, the manager would like the division to show an increase in the operating margin percentage to 14 percent. This can be accomplished by fixed cost savings. How much would operating income have to increase in order to reach this goal?
  (2) If in part b(1) the goal is to be achieved by an increase in sales instead of by cost savings, how much increased sales would be needed to reach the goal, assuming no increase in direct fixed costs and no change in the variable cost ratio? (Hint: Use an algebraic equation to solve the problem.)
  (3) For 19x5, the manager would like to increase the asset turnover to 1.8. By how much would operating assets have to decrease on December 31, 19x5, to accomplish this objective?
  (4) If in part b(3) the objective is to be achieved by an increase in sales instead of a reduction in operating assets, how much would sales have to increase in order to reach this objective? Assume that operating assets will remain unchanged during 19x5.
  (5) If the selling price were decreased by 10 percent in 19x5, sales volume would increase by 20 percent. Assuming no change in operating assets for 19x5, what effect would this action have on:
    (a) The operating margin percentage.
    (b) Asset turnover.
    (c) ROI.
    (d) Residual income.

14–15 Discussion of a Performance Evaluation Program

The ATCO Company purchased the Dexter Company three years ago. Prior to the acquisition, Dexter manufactured and sold plastic products to a wide variety of customers. Dexter has since become a division of ATCO and now only manufactures plastic components for products made by ATCO's Macon division. Macon sells its products to hardware wholesalers.

ATCO's corporate management gives the Dexter division management a considerable amount of authority in running the division's operations. However, corporate management retains authority for decisions regarding capital investments, price setting of all products, and the quantity of each product to be produced by the Dexter division.

ATCO has a formal performance evaluation program for the management of all of its divisions. The performance evaluation program relies heavily on each division's return on investment. The income statement of Dexter division presented below provides the basis for the evaluation of Dexter's divisional management.

The financial statements for the divisions are prepared by the corporate accounting staff. The corporate general services costs are allocated on the basis of sales dollars and the computer department's actual costs are apportioned among the divisions on the basis of use. The net division investment includes division fixed assets at net book value (cost less depreciation), division inventory, and corporate working capital apportioned to the divisions on the basis of sales dollars.

ATCO COMPANY
Dexter Division
Income Statement
For the Year Ended October 31, 19x0
(in thousands)

Sales		$4,000
Costs:		
Product costs:		
Direct materials	$ 500	
Direct labor	1,100	
Factory overhead	1,300	
Total	2,900	
Less: Increase in inventory	350	2,550
Engineering and research		120
Shipping and receiving		240
Division administration:		
Manager's office	210	
Cost accounting	40	
Personnel	82	332
Corporate costs:		
Computer	48	
General services	230	278
Total costs		3,520
Divisional operating income		$ 480
Net plant investment		$1,600
Return on investment		30%

Required

a. Discuss the financial reporting and performance evaluation program at ATCO Company as it relates to the responsibilities of the Dexter division.

b. Based upon your response to requirement (a), recommend appropriate revisions of the financial information and reports used to evaluate the performance of

Dexter's divisional management. If revisions are not necessary, explain why revisions are not needed.

(CMA adapted)

14–16 ROI and Residual Income

The Mango Company has three divisions that are operated as investment centers. For residual income calculations, the firm requires a mimimum desired rate of return of 16 percent.

Selected information for the three divisions follows:

	Division		
	X	Y	Z
Sales	$800,000	$600,000	$500,000
Operating income	88,000	60,000	60,000
Average operating assets	363,636	240,000	217,391

Required a. For each division, compute the following:
    (1) The operating margin percentage.
    (2) Asset turnover.
    (3) ROI.
    (4) Residual income.
  b. Select the division that is doing the best job for the company. Give the reasons for your choice and explain why you selected the division that is the best one and explain why you rejected the other two.
  c. Division Z has some idle capacity. It has the opportunity to earn an additional $20,000 of operating income which will require an additional investment of $80,000. Would you expect the division manager to accept the additional project if the evaluation parameter is ROI? Explain. Suppose that instead of ROI the company uses residual income to evaluate its managers. Would you expect the manager of division Z to accept the project? Explain.

14–17 Transfer Pricing

The Portable Electric Company has several divisions. One division manufactures small electric motors used in the manufacture of electric hand tools. The motors are sold for $8 each in the intermediate market. During 19x5, the division sold externally 500,000 motors, its full capacity. The variable cost per motor was $2 each, while the direct fixed costs amounted to $4 per motor at the 500,000 capacity.

For the coming year, 19x6, the company plans to market electric drills. The company estimates that it can market 200,000 drills annually at a price of $24 each. The expected costs to manufacture are:

Variable costs:		
Electric motor	. . . .	$ 7.20
Other costs	. . . .	4.00
Direct fixed costs	. . . . .	6.00
Total costs	. . . . . .	$17.20

Required   *a.* A price quote from an external electric motor manufacturer was received at a price of $8 less a quantity discount of 10 percent. If the motor division can sell its entire output (500,000 units) externally, what transfer price should be quoted to the drill division for the 200,000 motors? Will the internal sale and purchase take place? Explain. What is the difference in company income of purchasing internally?

b. If the motor division expects to sell only 300,000 motors in 19x6, what transfer price should be quoted to the drill division for the 200,000 motors? Will the internal sale and purchase take place? Explain. What is the difference in company income of purchasing internally?

c. If the motor division can sell its entire output externally but can save 60 cents per unit in shipping costs and sales commissions for units sold internally, what transfer price should be quoted? Will the internal sale and purchase take place? Explain. What is the difference in company income of purchasing internally?

d. If the motor division can only sell 400,000 motors in 19x6 and the drill division must purchase at least 200,000 motors to get the 10 percent quantity discount off the regular price of $8, what transfer price should be quoted? Will the internal sale and purchase take place? Explain. What is the difference in company income of purchasing internally?

14–18   Transfer Pricing

The Diversified Company has a chemical division that manufactures product A which is sold externally for $12 per pound. It has a variable cost of $3 per pound and a direct fixed cost of $1 per pound at its present maximum capacity of 1 million pounds per year.

The company also has a fertilizer division that uses product B in its formula. Product B has been purchased externally, but the fertilizer division received a notice that this manufacturer will be discontinuing the manufacture of product B. The company cannot locate another manufacturer of product B. However, the chemical division of the company can manufacture product B. The variable costs of manufacturing product B amount to $2 per pound. No change in direct fixed costs will occur if product B is manufactured.

The fertilizer division requires 500,000 pounds of product B per annum. If product B is manufactured by the chemical division, it will only be able to manufacture 600,000 pounds of product A.

The fertilizer division normally produces 10 million pounds of fertilizer per year at a sales price of 50 cents per pound. The costs for the fertilizer last year at the 10 million pound capacity level were:

	Per Hundred Pounds
Product B—4 pounds at $5 per pound	$20
Other ingredients	5
Direct fixed costs	1
Total per 100 pounds	$26
Cost per pound—$26 ÷ 100 pounds	$.26

Required   *a.* Prepare a contribution margin income statement for the preceding year for the chemical division, the fertilizer division, and combined for the two divisions, assuming sales at full capacity for both divisions.

b. What transfer price should the chemical division charge for product B assuming that there is a market for all of its output (1 million pounds) of product A? Using this transfer price for product B and assuming the transfer takes place, prepare a budgeted contribution margin income statement for the coming year using the same format you used in *(a)*. Compare your result for the chemical division with its result in *(a)*. Explain.

c. Prepare a contribution margin income statement for the preceding year for the chemical division, the fertilizer division, and combined for the two divisions, assuming sales of 600,000 pounds of product A and full capacity for the fertilizer division.

d. What transfer price should the chemical division charge for product B assuming that it can only sell 600,000 pounds of product A for the coming year? Using this transfer price for product B and assuming the transfer takes place, prepare a budgeted contribution margin income statement for the coming year using the same format you used in *(c)*. Compare your result for the chemical division with its result in *(c)*. Explain.

14–19   Profit Center Evaluation and Transfer Prices

A. R. Oma, Inc. manufactures a line of men's perfumes and after-shaving lotions. The manufacturing process is basically a series of mixing operations with the addition of certain aromatic and coloring ingredients; the finished product is packaged in a company-produced glass bottle and packed in cases containing six bottles.

A. R. Oma feels that the sale of its product is heavily influenced by the appearance and appeal of the bottle and has therefore devoted considerable managerial effort to the bottle production process. This has resulted in the development of certain unique bottle production processes in which management takes considerable pride.

The two areas (i.e., perfume production and bottle manufacture) have evolved over the years in an almost independent manner; in fact, a rivalry has developed between management personnel as to "which division is the more important" to A. R. Oma. This attitude is probably intensified because the bottle manufacturing plant was purchased intact 10 years ago and no real interchange of management personnel or ideas (except at the top corporate level) has taken place.

Since the acquisition, all bottle production has been absorbed by the perfume manufacturing plant. Each area is considered a separate profit center and evaluated as such. As the new corporate controller, you are responsible for the definition of a proper transfer value to use in crediting the bottle production profit center and in debiting the packaging profit center.

At your request, the bottle division general manager has asked certain other bottle manufacturers to quote a price for the quantity and sizes demanded by the perfume division. These competitive prices are:

Volume	Total Price	Price per Case
2 million equivalent cases*	$ 4 million	$2.00
4 million	$ 7 million	$1.75
6 million	$10 million	$1.67

* An "equivalent case" represents six bottles each.

A cost analysis of the internal bottle plant indicates that they can produce bottles at these costs.

Volume	Total Price	Cost per Case
2 million equivalent cases	$3.2 million	$1.60
4 million	$5.2 million	$1.30
6 million	$7.2 million	$1.20

(Your cost analysts point out that these costs represent fixed costs of $1.2 million and variable costs of $1 per equivalent case.)

These figures have given rise to considerable corporate discussion as to the proper value to use in the transfer of bottles to the perfume division. This interest is heightened because a significant portion of a division manager's income is an incentive bonus based on profit center results.

The perfume production division has the following costs in addition to the bottle costs:

Volume	Total Cost	Cost per Case
2 million cases	$16.4 million	$8.20
4 million	$32.4 million	$8.10
6 million	$48.4 million	$8.07

After considerable analysis, the marketing research department has furnished you with the following price-demand relationship for the finished product:

Sales Volume	Total Sales Revenue	Sales Price per Case
2 million cases	$25.0 million	$12.50
4 million	$45.6 million	$11.40
6 million	$63.9 million	$10.65

Required

a. The A. R. Oma Company has used market price transfer prices in the past. Using the current market prices and costs and assuming a volume of 6 million cases, calculate the income for
   (1) The bottle division.
   (2) The perfume division.
   (3) The corporation.

b. Is this production and sales level the most profitable volume for
   (1) The bottle division?
   (2) The perfume division?
   (3) The corporation?
   Explain your answer.

c. The A. R. Oma Company uses the profit center concept for divisional operation.
    (1) Define "profit center."
    (2) What conditions should exist for a profit center to be established?
    (3) Should the two divisions of the A. R. Oma Company be organized as profit
         centers?

(CMA adapted)

14–20   **Transfer Pricing**

The Southern Company has two divisions, S and T. Division S manufactures product
C, which is also used by Division T. Presently, division T is purchasing product C
externally for $12 per pound. The following information is available:

	Product C	Division T
Selling price per unit	$ 14	$50
Costs:		
Product C	$–0–	$12
Other variable costs	4	10
Direct fixed costs	3	6
Total costs	$ 7	$28
Capacity	60,000 pounds	40,000 pounds

Required   a. Assume that division S is selling its entire output (60,000 pounds) externally at
              $14 per pound. It pays its salespeople a commission of 5 percent of sales, which
              could be avoided by selling to division T. Shipping costs amount to 30 cents
              per pound. What transfer price should division S quote to division T? Would
              you expect the internal sale to take place? Explain.
          b. Division T would like to alter the formula of its product and use product D in
              place of product C. Product D is presently unavailable in the intermediate market.
              The variable cost of producing product D, exclusive of commissions and shipping
              costs, is $2 per pound. If division S produces 40,000 pounds of product D—the
              annual requirement by division T—it will still be able to produce 40,000 pounds
              of product C for sale externally. No change in direct fixed costs would be necessary
              if product D is produced. What transfer price should be quoted for product D?
              Explain.

14–21   **Transfer Pricing, ROI, and Residual Income**

The Northern Corporation has a switch division that is operated as an investment
center. The division is operating at only 80 percent of capacity. The result of operations
for 19x3 are shown below:

NORTHERN COMPANY
Switch Division
Statement of Operating Income
For the Year Ended December 31, 19x3

Sales (80,000 × $12)	$960,000
Variable costs (at $6)	480,000
Contribution margin	480,000
Direct fixed costs	360,000
Segment margin	120,000
Billed common costs for services from	
other divisions	33,600
Operating income	$ 86,400
Operating assets—January 1, 19x3	$510,000
Operating assets—December 31, 19x3	$556,666

The company's minimum desired rate of return to be used for residual income is 12 percent.

Required   a.   Compute:
  (1)   The operating margin percentage.
  (2)   Asset turnover.
  (3)   ROI.
 b.   Compute residual income.
 c.   For 19x4, the switch division expects its operations to be unchanged from that of 19x3. However, it has an opportunity to accept a special order from an outsider for 20,000 switches at a price of $8. The order will not affect its regular sales and will require an additional outlay of $20,000 for direct fixed costs. Additional operating assets will be needed at a cost of $145,000. Calculate the following for the combined operations assuming that the order is accepted:
  (1)   ROI.
  (2)   Residual income.
  Would you expect the manager of the switch division to accept the order if the parameter used for evaluation is ROI? Why? Would your answer be different if the parameter used is residual income? Why?
 d.   The Northern Company is planning to market a new product. The switches manufactured by the switch division could be used in the new product. Assume that the offer in (c) was withdrawn by the offeror. Thus, the switch division will still have the idle capacity. The manager in charge of producing the new product learned that he could purchase the 20,000 switches externally for $10 each. What price should the switch division quote for the switch assuming no increase in fixed costs and no additional investment will be needed by the switch division? Why?
 e.   Assume the same facts as in (d) except that the switch division has a customer who is willing to purchase the 20,000 switches in 19x4 for $11 each. The switches will not require any shipping costs or sales commissions. What price should the switch dvision now quote to the purchasing division? What should the purchasing manager's reaction be to the price quoted? Why?
 f.   Assume the same facts as in (e) except that shipping costs and sales commissions

amount to $2 per unit on the 20,000 switches. What price should be quoted? What should the purchasing manager do? Why?

g. Assume that the switch division can only sell 80,000 switches (80 percent of capacity) in 19x4 and its budgeted statement of operating income for 19x4 is the same as that shown for 19x3. The purchasing division expects to use 100,000 switches and thus would require all of the output of the switch division. There are no shipping costs or sales commissions in the income statement for 19x3. What price should be charged by the switch division? What should the purchasing manager do if he can purchase the switches externally at $10.50 per switch? Why?

14–22 Transfer Pricing

National Industries is a diversified corporation with separate and distinct operating divisions. Each division's performance is evaluated on the basis of total dollar profits and return on division investment.

The WindAir division manufactures and sells air conditioner units. The coming year's budgeted income statement, based upon a sales volume of 15,000 units, appears below.

NATIONAL INDUSTRIES
WindAir Division
Budgeted Income Statement
For the 19x8–x9 Fiscal Year

	Per Unit	Total (in thousands)
Sales revenue	$400	$6,000
Manufacturing costs:		
Compressor	70	1,050
Other raw materials	37	555
Direct labor	30	450
Variable overhead	45	675
Fixed overhead	32	480
Total manufacturing costs	214	3,210
Gross margin	186	2,790
Operating costs:		
Variable marketing	18	270
Fixed marketing	19	285
Fixed administrative	38	570
Total operating costs	75	1,125
Net income before taxes	$111	$1,665

WindAir's division manager believes sales can be increased if the unit selling price of the air conditioners is reduced. A market research study conducted by an independent firm at the request of the manager indicates that a 5 percent reduction in the selling price ($20) would increase sales volume 16 percent, or 2,400 units. WindAir has sufficient production capacity to manage this increased volume with no increase in fixed costs.

At the present time, WindAir uses in its units a compressor that it purchases from an outside supplier at a cost of $70 per compressor. The division manager of WindAir has approached the manager of the compressor division regarding the sale of a compressor unit to WindAir. The compressor division currently manufactures and sells a unit exclusively to outside firms which is similar to the unit used by WindAir. The specifications of the WindAir compressor are slightly different, which would reduce the compressor division's raw material cost by $1.50 per unit. In addition, the compressor division would not incur any variable marketing costs in the units sold to WindAir. The manager of WindAir wants all of the compressors it uses to come from one supplier and has offered to pay $50 for each compressor unit.

The compressor division has the capacity to produce 75,000 units. The coming year's budgeted income statement for the compressor division is shown below and is based upon a sales volume of 64,000 units without considering WindAir's proposal.

NATIONAL INDUSTRIES
Compressor Division
Budgeted Income Statement
For the 19x8–x9 Fiscal Year

	Per Unit	Total (in thousands)
Sales revenue	$100	$6,400
Manufacturing costs:		
Raw materials	12	768
Direct labor	8	512
Variable overhead	10	640
Fixed overhead	11	704
Total manufacturing costs	41	2,624
Gross margin	59	3,776
Operating costs:		
Variable marketing	6	384
Fixed marketing	4	256
Fixed administrative	7	448
Total operating costs	17	1,088
Net income before taxes	$ 42	$2,688

Required

a. Should WindAir division institute the 5 percent price reduction on its air conditioner units even if it cannot acquire the compressors internally for $50 each? Support your conclusion with appropriate calculations.

b. Without prejudice to your answer to requirement (a), assume WindAir needs 17,400 units. Should the compressor division be willing to supply the compressor units for $50 each? Support your conclusions with appropriate calculations.

c. Without prejudice to your answer to requirement (a), assume WindAir needs 17,400 units. Would it be in the best interest of National Industries for the compressor division to supply the compressor units at $50 each to the WindAir division? Support your conclusions with appropriate calculations.

(CMA adapted)

Part

ADDITIONAL SELECTED TOPICS

15

SELECTED QUANTITATIVE METHODS FOR MANAGERS

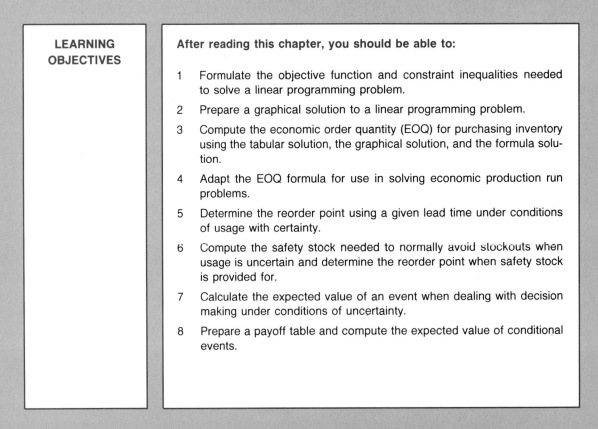

LEARNING OBJECTIVES

After reading this chapter, you should be able to:

1 Formulate the objective function and constraint inequalities needed to solve a linear programming problem.

2 Prepare a graphical solution to a linear programming problem.

3 Compute the economic order quantity (EOQ) for purchasing inventory using the tabular solution, the graphical solution, and the formula solution.

4 Adapt the EOQ formula for use in solving economic production run problems.

5 Determine the reorder point using a given lead time under conditions of usage with certainty.

6 Compute the safety stock needed to normally avoid stockouts when usage is uncertain and determine the reorder point when safety stock is provided for.

7 Calculate the expected value of an event when dealing with decision making under conditions of uncertainty.

8 Prepare a payoff table and compute the expected value of conditional events.

Management science is a field of study that attempts to solve complex managerial problems, often using mathematical and statistical solutions. While some large firms employ individuals who specialize in this field, most firms expect managers and management accountants to possess the math skills necessary to solve their own business problems. Therefore, it is important for managers to understand the principles and procedures used by management scientists.

One common problem that lends itself to a mathematical solution is the allocation of scarce resources—materials, direct labor, and machine capacity—in order to maximize profits. The mathematical approach that yields the optimal solution to this kind of problem is known as linear programming. Another frequent problem pertains to how much inventory to order and how much inventory to carry in order to minimize storage and ordering costs. In such situations, several different mathematical approaches may be used to determine the optimal economic order quantity (EOQ). Finally, managers must often make decisions regarding future events that cannot be predicted with accuracy. Thus, they must deal with the problem of uncertainty. By assigning a statistical probability to the likelihood of an event's occurrence, a manager can quantify his uncertainty. Then he can take the expected value of the event into consideration during the decision-making process.

LINEAR PROGRAMMING

Linear programming is a mathematical technique that shows managers how to allocate scarce resources in order to maximize profits or minimize costs. The maximization or minimization of some quantity is an important basic property of all linear programming problems. For example, a manager's goal may be to maximize the use of raw materials that can only be purchased in limited quantities. Or he may want to make maximum use of direct labor-hours or machine-hours that are limited due to the size of his firm's manufacturing facilities. Sometimes a linear programming problem is based on the number of units of a product that can be sold in the marketplace. This occurs when the number of units that *can be produced* exceeds the number of units that can be sold. All of these factors restrict a company from the unlimited pursuit of its goals. In linear programming, these factors are called constraints. A **constraint** is a limiting factor under which the firm must operate, such as a shortage of raw materials, limited plant capacity (labor-hours and/or machine-hours), and limited market demand for a product.

Linear programming is based on five assumptions:

1. The revenue functions and cost functions of a firm's products are linear; hence, a firm's contribution margin is a linear function.

2. A firm's time and material usage rates and limitations are linear.

3. Since negative production is impossible, it is not permissible in solutions to linear programming problems (although this may seem obvious).

4. Fractional units of production are permitted because units not finished

in one period can be finished in a succeeding period. (All functions are continuous.)

5.   All parameters are known with certainty.

Functional
Relationships

The solution to a linear programming problem requires that certain relationships be shown in functional format. The needed functions are (1) the objective function and (2) the constraint functions. The **objective function** is a relationship that sets the goal that is to be achieved by the linear programming solution, such as the maximization of contribution margin or the minimization of costs. The **constraint functions** are relationships that set the limitations under which the firm must operate, such as material shortages, limited labor-hours, limited machine-hours, and limited market demand for the product.

To see how linear programming works, we will study the Thaxton Company which produces two products, X and Y. Each product passes through two departments, cutting and finishing. Product X requires six hours of cutting and five hours of finishing, while product Y requires four hours of cutting and four hours of finishing. The cutting department has three machines that can operate 8 hours per day for a total of 24 hours per day. The finishing department also has three machines that operate a total of 24 hours per day, but the machines have to be stopped for cleaning, which reduces the capacity of the finishing department to 22 hours per day. Product X sells for $60 per unit and has a variable cost of $20 per unit, resulting in a contribution margin of $40 per unit. Product Y sells for $50 per unit and has a variable cost of $20 per unit, resulting in a contribution margin of $30 per unit. There are no material shortages and the company can sell all of its output.

Stating the Objective Function.   The objective function should set forth the goal that is to be achieved. In this example, a maximization problem, the goal is to produce a product mix that will produce the maximum contribution margin possible. This may be represented by the following equation:

$$\text{Max } Z = \$40X + \$30Y \tag{1}$$

where

Z = The total contribution margin
X = The number of units of X to be produced and sold
Y = The number of units of Y to be produced and sold

Stating the Constraint Functions.   The constraint functions should set the time requirement (in machine-hours) for each product in each department. Since the number of units to be produced is unknown and since it is possible that less than the maximum capacity may be utilized, it is necessary to use inequalities in place of equations. Recall that product X requires six hours of cutting and product Y requires four hours of cutting. Thus, the constraint inequality for the cutting department's 24 hours of capacity would be expressed as:

$$6X + 4Y \leq 24 \qquad (2)$$

Since product X requires 5 hours of finishing and product Y requires 4 hours of finishing, the constraint inequality for the finishing department's 22 hours of capacity may be expressed as:

$$5X + 4Y \leq 22 \qquad (3)$$

Although the following constraints are understood, because negative production is not possible, they are included for completeness.

$$X \geq 0 \qquad (4)$$
$$Y \geq 0 \qquad (5)$$

The Graphical Solution to a Maximization Problem

The graphical solution to a maximization problem requires the following steps:

1. Plot the constraint inequalities on a graph. (Note: Although the inequalities are technically not equations, in this case, they are treated as if they are equations. The mathematics needed to bridge this gap is *not* shown. Thus, = signs will be substituted for the ≤ signs.)

2. Determine the area of feasible (possible) solutions.

3. Locate the corner points of the area of feasible solutions. The optimal solution will be at one of these corner points.

4. For each solution at a corner point, insert the contribution margin per unit for each product in the candidate solution and sum the contribution margin. Select the solution with the highest total contribution margin.

1. Plot the Constraints. Starting with equation (2), first assume that only product X and no product Y will be manufactured. This produces the following:

$$
\begin{aligned}
6X + 4Y &\leq 24 \qquad (2) \\
6X + 4(0) &= 24 \\
6X &= 24 \\
X &= 4
\end{aligned}
$$

Then, assume that only product Y and no product X will be produced. This produces the following:

$$
\begin{aligned}
6X + 4Y &\leq 24 \qquad (2) \\
6(0) + 4Y &= 24 \\
4Y &= 24 \\
Y &= 6
\end{aligned}
$$

It is now possible to plot the constraint for the cutting department as $(X = 4, Y = 0)$ and $(X = 0, Y = 6)$ on the graph. This line serves as the boundary or limit for the finishing department. This may be seen in Illustration 15–1.

The same procedure is applied to equation (3). The results are:

$$5X + 4Y \leq 22 \tag{3}$$
$$5X + 4(0) = 22$$
$$5X \qquad = 22$$
$$X \qquad = 4\tfrac{2}{5}$$

and

$$5X + 4Y \leq 22 \tag{3}$$
$$5(0) + 4Y = 22$$
$$4Y = 22$$
$$Y = 5\tfrac{1}{2}$$

ILLUSTRATION 15–1   **Graphical Solution for Maximizing Contribution Margin—Two Constraints (area of feasible solutions)**

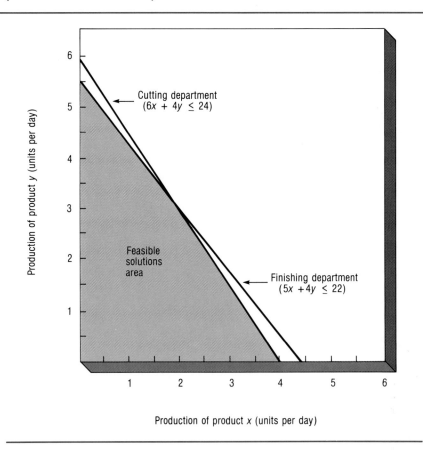

The constraint for the finishing department can now be plotted as ($X = 4\frac{2}{5}$, $Y = 0$) and ($X = 0$, $Y = 5\frac{1}{2}$). This line represents the limiting condition for the cutting constraint, and may be seen in Illustration 15–1.

2. Area of Feasible Solutions. The **area of feasible solutions** for a maximization problem is the area on a linear programming graph that lies beneath the boundaries of *all* of the constraint inequalities. This area is shaded in Illustration 15–1. Remember that *any point* within this area represents a *possible* production combination.

3. Locating the Corner Points. Since any point, including the origin ($X = 0$, $Y = 0$), within the feasible solutions area is a possible solution, the objective of the linear programming solution is to find the point furthest from the origin that will produce the greatest total contribution margin. For this reason, the optimal solution lies at one of the corner points of the

ILLUSTRATION 15–2   **Graphical Solution for Maximizing Contribution Margin—Two Constraints (corner points of the feasible solutions area)**

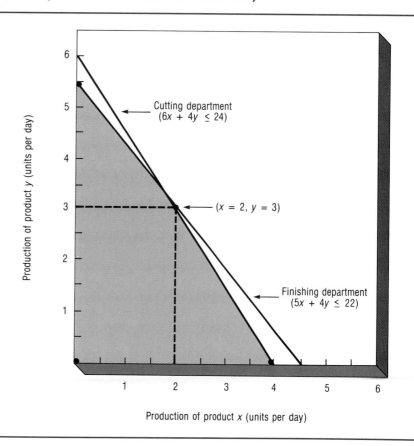

feasible solutions area other than the origin. In Illustration 15–2, the corner points are circled. The point of intersection of the cutting and finishing department constraints may be obtained by drawing a perpendicular line from the intersection and reading it from the x axis. In this case, it is $x = 2$, shown as a dotted line in Illustration 15–2. As shown in the same illustration, a horizontal line may also be drawn to obtain the value of $Y = 3$.

4. Insert Contribution Margins at the Corner Points. The contribution margin for each corner point may be obtained by performing the operations dictated by the objective function. Thus, for each corner point shown in Illustration 15–2, the quantities of products X and Y will be inserted into the objective function (Max $Z = \$40X + \$30Y$) to arrive at the total contribution margin as follows:

Corner Point X Y	Objective Function	Total Contribution Margin
0, 0	$40(0) + $30(0)	$ 0
4, 0	$40(4) + $30(0)	160
2, 3	$40(2) + $30(3)	170
0, 5½	$40(0) + $30(5½)	165

The optimal solution is to produce two units of product X and three units of product Y per day to produce a total contribution margin of $170 per day.

While this solution is relatively simple, linear programming problems may become quite complex, especially when more than two variables (products) are involved. A more rigorous solution to linear programming problems is the *simplex method,* which can be used to solve any linear programming problem, especially those with three or more variables (products). The procedure used to solve a simplex programming problem may be found in advanced managerial and linear programming texts. However, most firms that use linear programming to solve business problems use a computer.

Computer Solutions to Linear Programming Problems

The Thaxton Company problem can also be solved using a computer to achieve a direct optimal solution without having to test the corner points. The computer solution appears in Illustration 15–3.

Although the optimal solution to this problem lies where the constraints intersect ($X = 2$, $Y = 3$), it would be wrong to assume that this is always

ILLUSTRATION 15–3   **Computer Solution for Maximizing Contribution Margin Using Linear Programming**

```
* * * * * * * * * * * * * * * * * * * * * * * * *
*                                             *
*        LINEAR PROGRAMMING          *
*             ANALYSIS                    *
*                                             *
* * * * * * * * * * * * * * * * * * * * * * * * *
    * *          INFORMATION          * *
NUMBER OF CONSTRAINTS               2
NUMBER OF VARIABLES                 2
NUMBER OF <= CONSTRAINTS            2
NUMBER OF  = CONSTRAINTS            0
NUMBER OF >= CONSTRAINTS            0

MAXIMIZATION PROBLEM
     40 X 1          + 30 X 2

SUBJECT TO
      6 X 1        + 4 X 2           <=    24
      5 X 1        + 4 X 2           <=    22

    * * RESULTS * *

                  VARIABLE      ORIGINAL       COEFF.
VARIABLE           VALUE         COEFF.        SENS.
  X 1               2             40            0
  X 2               3             30            0

CONSTRAINT       ORIGINAL      SLACK OR       SHADOW
NUMBER             RHS         SURPLUS        PRICE
  1                24             0            2.5
  2                22             0            5.01

OBJECTIVE FUNCTION VALUE : 170

    * * END OF ANALYSIS * *
```

the case. Different contribution margins may cause the optimal solution to be a different corner point.

Alternative Contribution Margins in the Objective Function

Using the same constraint inequalities and thus the same corner points shown in Illustration 15–2, let us assume that the objective function is now changed to contribution margins of $10 for product X and $50 for product Y. The new objective function would be:

$$\text{Max } Z = \$10X + \$50Y \tag{6}$$

The total contribution margin using equation (6) may be computed as:

	Corner Point	Objective Function	Total Contribution Margin
	X Y		
	0, 0	$10(0) + $50(0) =	$ 0
	4, 0	$10(4) + $50(0) =	40
	2, 3	$10(2) + $50(3) =	170
	0, 5½	$10(0) + $50(5½) =	275

Note how the optimal solution is now $X = 0$, $Y = 5\frac{1}{2}$ because the contribution margin per unit of product Y is five times that of product X, while in equation (1), the contribution margin of product X was slightly more than that of product Y. If the objective function were to shift so that the contribution margin of product X became five times that of product Y, the optimal solution would be $X = 4$, $Y = 0$. (You may wish to verify this by using an objective function of Max $Z = \$50X + \$10Y$.)

Increased Constraints

The graphical solution may still be used effectively with three or even four constraints if the variables (products) are limited to two. Consider the following example:

$$\text{Max } Z = \$30X + \$70Y \tag{7}$$

Subject to

$$3X + 2Y \leq 15 \tag{8}$$
$$2X + 4Y \leq 18 \tag{9}$$

In addition, material shortages will prevent the production of more than 4 units of product X per day, while the market demand for product Y cannot exceed 3.5 units per day. Thus, there are now two additional constraints, as follows:

$$X \leq 4 \tag{10}$$
$$Y \leq 3.5 \tag{11}$$

The points for plotting inequality (8) may be obtained as follows:

$$3X + 2Y = 15 \tag{8}$$
$$3X + 2(0) = 15$$
$$X = 5$$

and

$$3(0) + 2Y = 15$$
$$Y = 7\frac{1}{2}$$

Therefore, the line ($X = 5$, $Y = 0$) and ($X = 0$, $Y = 7\frac{1}{2}$) can now be plotted on a graph. Using the same procedure for inequality (9), the points ($X = 9$, $Y = 0$) and ($X = 0$, $Y = 4\frac{1}{2}$) can also be plotted along with $X = 4$ for inequality (10) and $Y = 3.5$ for inequality (11). These lines all appear in Illustration 15–4 together with the feasible solutions area.

ILLUSTRATION 15–4 **Graphical Solution for Maximizing Contribution Margin—Four Constraints (area of feasible solutions)**

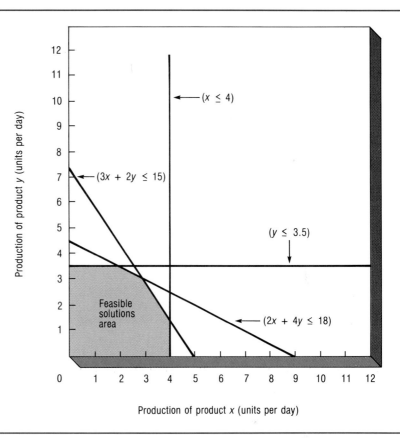

Production of product y (units per day)

Production of product x (units per day)

As before, the corner points may be ascertained by drawing perpendicular and horizontal lines as shown by the dotted lines in Illustration 15–5. The corner points and the computations of the contribution margins are:

Corner Points		Objective Function	Total Contribution Margin
X	Y		
0	0	$30(0) + $70(0) =	$ 0
0	3½	$30(0) + $70(3½) =	245
2	3½	$30(2) + $70(3½) =	305
3	3	$30(3) + $70(3) =	300
4	1½	$30(4) + $70(1½) =	225
4	0	$30(4) + $70(0) =	120

ILLUSTRATION 15–5 **Graphical Solution for Maximizing Contribution Margin—Four Constraints (corner points of the feasible solutions area)**

Production of product *y* (units per day)

Production of product *x* (units per day)

Note how the demand constraint of 3.5 units of product Y coincides with the optimal solution.

Minimization Problems

Thus far, we have seen that maximization problems are concerned with maximizing contribution magin. Minimization problems are similar to maximization problems except that instead of using contribution margin as the focal point, the emphasis is now on *minimizing costs.* Some typical minimization problems might involve achieving certain nutritional combinations in food at the least cost, blending ingredients in foods and candies at least cost, and combining ingredients in livestock feed at least cost.

The Besta Pasta Company uses two main ingredients in preparing its pasta. Ingredient A contains 36 units of protein and 12 units of carbohydrates per pound while ingredient B contains 12 units of protein and 24 units of carbohydrates per pound. Each carton of pasta must contain at least 108 units of protein and 96 units of carbohydrates. The cost of ingredient A is 18 cents per pound while the cost of ingredient B is 30 cents per pound.

The objective function for a minimization problem is similar to that of a maximization problem except that the coefficients of the variables *(A, B)* are costs instead of contribution margins. The objective of the firm is to minimize costs *(C)* given that the costs of ingredients A and B are 18 cents and 30 cents, respectively. The objective function may be stated as:

$$\text{Min } C = \$.18A + \$.30B \tag{12}$$

The constraint inequalities for a minimization problem are also similar to the constraints previously discussed except that instead of using *equal to or less than,* the inequalities are stated in terms of *equal to or greater than.*

For protein, the inequality is stated as:

$$36A + 12B \geq 108 \tag{13}$$

For carbohydrates, the inequality is stated as:

$$12A + 24B \geq 96 \tag{14}$$

The graphical solution can now proceed as before. Using inequality (13), the points of the line may be calculated as follows:

$$
\begin{aligned}
36A \;+\; 12B \;&\geq\; 108 \tag{13}\\
36(0) + 12B \;&=\; 108\\
12B \;&=\; 108\\
B \;&=\; 9
\end{aligned}
$$

and

$$
\begin{aligned}
36A \;+\; 12(0) &= 108\\
36A &= 108\\
A &= 3
\end{aligned}
$$

The points to locate inequality (14) may be calculated as:

$$
\begin{aligned}
12A \;+\; 24B \;&\geq\; 96 \tag{14}\\
12(0) + 24B \;&=\; 96\\
24B \;&=\; 96\\
B \;&=\; 4
\end{aligned}
$$

and

$$
\begin{aligned}
12A \;+\; 24(0) &= 96\\
12A &= 96\\
A &= 8
\end{aligned}
$$

The lines for these constraints are shown in Illustration 15–6 together with the feasible solutions area. Compare this feasible solutions area with

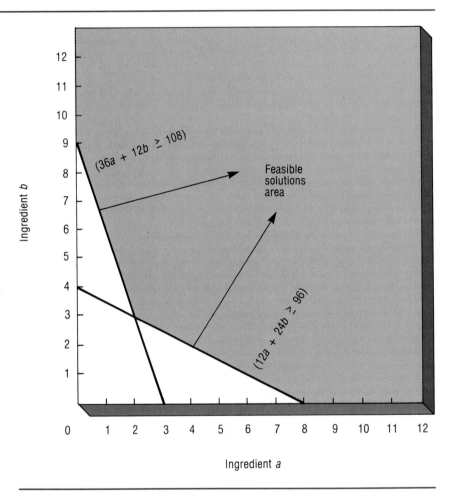

the one in Illustration 15–1. Note that because this problem is a minimization problem, the feasible solution area is *above* the intersecting lines, the exact opposite of a maximization problem.

Again, the optimal solution will lie at one of the corner points. Only this time, the task is to *get as close to the origin as possible* since the objective is to minimize costs within the constraints given. The corner points bounding the feasible solutions area are shown in Illustration 15–7.

The determination of the costs at each of the corner points is similar to that for a maximization problem. The calculation of costs is:

Corner Points		Objective Function	Total Cost
A	B		
0	9	$.18(0) + $.30(9) =	$2.70
2	3	$.18(2) + $.30(3) =	1.26
8	0	$.18(8) + $.30(0) =	1.44

ILLUSTRATION 15–7   **Graphical Solution for Minimizing Costs—Two Constraints (corner points of the feasible solutions area)**

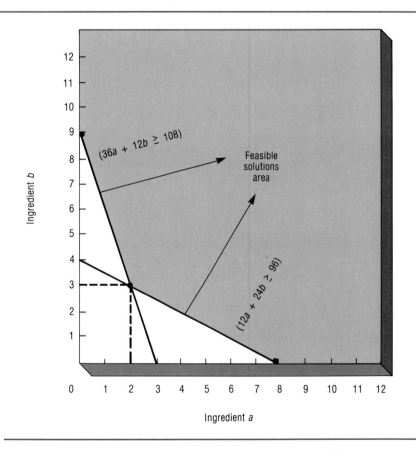

The optimal solution is to use two pounds of ingredient A and three pounds of ingredient B for each carton of pasta manufactured. It might be interesting to see how many units of protein and carbohydrates would be used at each corner point. This may be calculated as:

Corner Point		Units of Protein per Pound	Units of Carbohydrates per Pound	Total Protein	Total Carbohydrates
A	B				
0	9	. . . . . (B) 12	24	108*	216†
2	3	. . . . . (A) 36	12	108‡	96§
		(B) 12	24		
8	0	. . . . . (A) 36	12	288‖	96 #

* $9 \times 12 = 108$.
† $9 \times 24 = 216$.
‡ $(2 \times 36) + (3 \times 12) = 108$.
§ $(2 \times 12) + (3 \times 24) = 96$.
‖ $8 \times 36 = 288$.
\# $8 \times 12 = 96$.

Note that all three solutions equal or exceed the minimum requirements of 108 units of protein and 96 units of carbohydrates, but only the optimal solution meets the requirements exactly. This may not always be the case, however.

INVENTORY PLANNING AND CONTROL

In inventory planning and control, the two basic questions to be resolved are, "When should an order for inventory be placed?" and "How much should be ordered?" Through **inventory planning and control,** a firm attempts to ensure that an optimum level of inventory will be maintained so that the costs of carrying and ordering inventories will be minimized and sufficient quantities will be on hand to avoid production interruptions due to stockouts (not having a needed material on hand). **Inventory carrying costs** include storage costs, insurance, interest on funds invested in inventories, personal property taxes, and obsolescence and deterioration. **Inventory ordering costs** include the costs associated with placing a purchase order, transportation costs, and receiving and handling costs. Carrying costs and ordering costs conflict with each other. At one extreme, a firm could order a full year's supply of raw materials, which would require only one purchase order, one transportation cost, and one receiving report. As a result, ordering costs would be relatively small. However, carrying costs would be unnecessarily high because of the large inventory needed to accommodate a full year's production requirements. At the other extreme, a purchase order could be placed 250 times (50 weeks × 5 days) per year. This would result in insignificant carrying costs since inventories would be very small, but it would produce 250 purchase orders, 250 transportation costs, and 250 receiving reports. Somewhere between these two extremes lies an optimum ordering quantity at which the sum of carrying and ordering costs would be less than at any other ordering quantity.

Unfortunately, accounting systems do not normally provide the data needed to measure carrying and ordering costs per se. Interest on investment in inventories is an opportunity cost that is not reflected in accounting records. The cost to place an order is normally not detailed in a firm's accounting system, although purchasing department salaries are shown in total. Thus, cost studies are usually required to arrive at the appropriate amounts to use when considering the effects of carrying and ordering costs on inventory planning and control.

Economic Order Quantity (EOQ)

The **economic order quantity** is the amount of materials that should be ordered to minimize the total of the inventory carrying costs and the inventory ordering costs. EOQ is based on five assumptions. They are:

1. The demand (usage) rate is constant over a period of time, such as one year, and the rate is known with certainty.

2. The carrying costs are proportional to the number of units carried in inventory—a linear variable cost (a fixed cost per unit).

3. The order costs are fixed per order—a variable cost per unit.

4. The purchase price per unit of inventory is fixed.

5. Delivery is instantaneous.

There are three ways to calculate EOQ. One method is to prepare a tabulation of the total relevant costs at various order sizes until the order size with the lowest cost is reached. The other two methods, a graphical solution and a mathematical formula, arrive at the optimum solution directly.

Let us assume that the Martin Company uses 5,000 units of raw material Beta annually. Each unit of Beta costs $20 and the inventory carrying costs are 12 percent of the unit's cost, or $2.40 per unit. The inventory ordering costs are $24 per purchase order placed.

The EOQ Table

The steps needed to prepare a tabulation to determine the EOQ are:

Step 1

Select a series of approximately six order sizes that are likely to be near the EOQ. Since the EOQ is unknown, the selection of the order sizes is done through trial and error. A possible beginning is to take the annual demand (usage), in this case 5,000 units, and divide it by 10. Then use either 50-unit or 100-unit intervals below and above the 500 units (5,000 ÷ 10).

Step 2

For each order size selected in step 1, compute the average inventory by dividing the order size by 2. The reason for this computation is that the carrying costs are applied to the *average* amount of units carried in inventory and not to the order size. Since the total amount ordered is carried in inventory only at the beginning of the ordering cycle and since the inventory may be reduced by usage until it reaches zero, the average inventory may be computed as:

$$\text{Average inventory} = \frac{\text{Order size} + 0}{2}$$

Step 3

Compute the number of purchase orders per annum for each order size. This step may be computed as:

$$\text{Number of purchase orders} = \frac{\text{Annual usage}}{\text{Order size}}$$

Step 4

Compute the annual carrying costs for each order size by multiplying the average inventory in units by the carrying cost per unit.

$$\text{Annual carrying costs} = \text{Carrying cost per unit} \left(\frac{\text{Order size}}{2} \right)$$

Step 5

Compute the annual purchase ordering costs for each order size by multiplying the number of purchase orders computed in step 3 by the cost of placing a purchase order, in this case $24.

$$\text{Annual order costs} = \text{Cost per order} \left(\frac{\text{Annual usage}}{\text{Order size}} \right)$$

Step 6

Total the carrying and ordering costs to arrive at the total annual costs for each order size.

The tabulation is shown in Illustration 15–8. The order size that minimizes total annual costs is approximately 300 units; thus, the firm should order approximately 300 units each time it orders material Beta.

ILLUSTRATION 15–8

THE MARTIN COMPANY
Determining Economic Order Quantity
Tabulation of Total Relevant Costs for Ordering Inventory

Steps	Symbols*		250	300	400	500	600	1,000
Step 1		**Order Size in Units**	**250**	**300**	**400**	**500**	**600**	**1,000**
Step 2	OS/2	Average inventory in units . .	125	150	200	250	300	500
Step 3	A/OS	Number of purchase orders .	20	16⅔	12½	10	8⅓	5
Step 4	C(OS/2)	Annual carrying cost at $2.40 per unit	$300	$360	$480	$600	$720	$1,200
Step 5	P(A/OS)	Annual purchase-order cost at $24 per order	480	400	300	240	200	120
Step 6	TC	Total annual costs	$780	$760	$780	$840	$920	$1,320

* OS = Order size in units.
  A = Annual usage in units.
  C = Annual cost of carrying one unit in inventory.
  P = Cost of placing a purchase order.
  TC = Total cost.

ILLUSTRATION 15–9

THE MARTIN COMPANY
Tabulation of Selected Total Relevant Costs
for Ordering Inventory

Symbols	Order Size in Units	200	800
OS/2	Average inventory in units	100	400
A/OS	Number of purchase orders	25	6¼
C(OS/2)	Annual carrying cost of $2.40 per unit	$240	$ 960
P(A/OS)	Annual purchase-order cost at $24 per order	600	150
TC		$840	$1,110

The EOQ Graph

The graphical solution may be prepared from the tabular solution. If different order sizes are desired for the graphical solution, their total costs would be computed as shown in Illustration 15–8. The calculations for the additional order sizes of 200 and 800 units of Beta are shown in Illustration 15–9.

The annual carrying costs for order sizes of 200, 400, 600, 800, and 1,000 units of Beta are plotted on the graph in Illustration 15–10. Note that this line is a linear function. The annual purchase-order costs for these five different order sizes are similarly plotted in the same illustration. Note that this is a curvilinear function. The total costs for these same order sizes are also plotted, and this, too, is a curvilinear function. By dropping a perpendicular line from where the annual carrying costs intersect the annual purchase-order costs, the optimum solution may be obtained from the purchase-order axis. The solution indicates an amount slightly above 300 units. When the perpendicular is extended to the total cost function, as shown by the dotted line in Illustration 15–10, it hits the lowest point on the total cost line, thus indicating that total costs are at a minimum.

Although the optimum solution is slightly greater than 300 units, the firm would probably round its order size to 300 units because suppliers prefer to deal in round lots.

The EOQ Formula

The economic order quantity may also be determined by using a mathematical formula. This formula, derived by calculus, is:

$$EOQ = \sqrt{\frac{2\,A\,P}{C}}$$

where

EOQ = Economic order quantity
A = Annual usage in units
P = The cost of placing an order
C = The annual cost of carrying one unit in inventory

ILLUSTRATION 15–10   Graphical Solution to Determining Economic Order Quantity

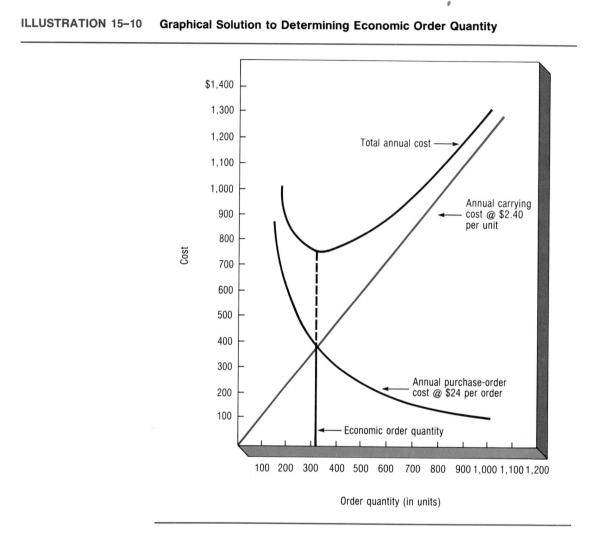

Order quantity (in units)

Using this formula and the information about the Martin Company's orders of Beta, the mathematical computation of EOQ would be:

$$EOQ = \sqrt{\frac{2(5000)(\$24)}{\$2.40}} = \sqrt{100,000} = 316$$

Although the mathematical solution is the simplest to compute, it does not provide as much information as the tabular and graphical solutions. Firms prefer to find a range that produces minimum costs rather than a single precise point. Ranges of costs for order sizes from 250 to 500 units can be obtained from either the table or the graph, but information about only a single order size—316 units—is obtained from the formula. The range provides greater flexibility in ordering.

Production Runs

The EOQ formula is also suitable for computing an optimum production run when a firm must change its machinery setup to accommodate a particular product's manufacturing requirements. The cost of setting up the machinery is used in place of the purchase-order cost, and the remainder of the items in the equation are treated the same as for ordering materials. An **economic production run in units** is the number of units to produce to minimize the total of inventory carrying costs and production setup costs.

The Brooke Company manufactures a variety of belt buckles. All of the buckles are made on a punch press, but the die (a form used to shape metal) must be changed for each style. The cost of carrying the western buckle in inventory is 25 cents per buckle per annum. Annual sales of this buckle are 60,000 units, while the cost of setting up the punch press for a production run is $300 per setup.

The mathematical formula for computing the optimal size production run is:

$$EPR = \sqrt{\frac{2\,A\,R}{C}}$$

where

EPR = Economic production run in units
A = Annual production in units
R = Setup cost for each change in production runs
C = The annual cost of carrying one unit in inventory

Inserting the information about the western buckle into the equation provides the following economic production run in units:

$$EPR = \sqrt{\frac{2(60,000)(\$300)}{\$.25}} = \sqrt{144,000,000} = 12,000 \text{ units}$$

The optimum production run is 12,000 units, or five production runs per year.

Reordering Point

Thus far, we have addressed the problem of *how much* to order. The remaining discussion of inventory planning and control is concerned with determining *when* to place the order. In making this determination, an essential ingredient is the lead time. **Lead time** is the interval of time between the placing of an order and the receipt of the ordered merchandise on the purchaser's premises. Another key ingredient is the usage rate. The amount used per period (daily or weekly) may be known with certainty, or it may fluctuate, in which case a firm may prefer to carry extra inventory to accommodate sudden spurts in demand for the material.

Reordering Point under Conditions of Certainty. The **reorder point** is the point in time when depleted inventory must be reordered. When the usage rate is known with certainty, it may be expressed as:

$$\text{Reorder point} = \text{Lead time} \times \text{Usage rate}$$

If the Martin Company uses 100 units of Beta per week (5,000 units per year ÷ 50 weeks) and the lead time is two weeks, the reorder point would be:

$$\text{Reorder point} = 2 \text{ weeks} \times 100 \text{ units} = 200 \text{ units}$$

Therefore, whenever the inventory of Beta falls to 200 units, the company will place an order for 300 units (computed earlier as EOQ). This calculation is shown graphically in Illustration 15–11.

Reordering Point under Conditions of Uncertainty.   While firms would like to be certain about their usage rates, it is usually not possible. In reality, most firms operate under conditions in which usage rates are likely to fluctuate. In such cases, ordering as shown in Illustration 15–11 is likely to produce a stockout whenever a sudden spurt in usage occurs. Therefore, firms are likely to provide for this contingency by carrying a safety stock. **Safety stock** is the amount of inventory carried to accommodate the difference between the maximum expected usage and the average usage of materials during the lead time.

ILLUSTRATION 15–11   **Determining the Reorder Point under Conditions of Certainty (graphical solution)**

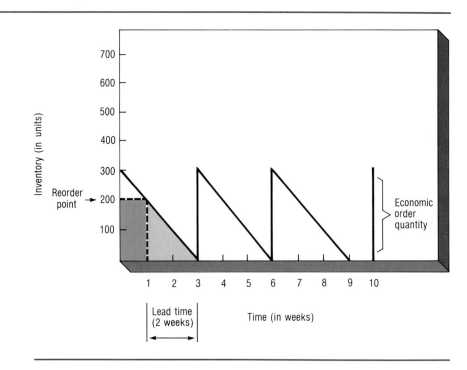

Recall the case of the Martin Company, which always uses 100 units of Beta per week and reorders 300 units (EOQ) with two weeks of lead time. Let us now assume that instead of always using 100 units per week, the company uses an average of 100 units per week with usage in some weeks reaching as high as 125 units. The highest amount, 125 units, is referred to as the *maximum usage*. To provide for reasonable maximum usage, firms normally provide for a safety stock that is calculated as follows:

	Units
Maximum usage per week	125
Average usage per week	100
Excess usage	25
Lead time	× 2 weeks
Safety stock	50

The equation to compute safety stock is:

Safety stock = Lead time × (Maximum usage − Average usage)

To calculate the reorder point when safety stock is needed, add the safety stock to the reorder point as computed under conditions of certainty. The

ILLUSTRATION 15–12 **Determining the Reorder Point under Conditions of Uncertainty (graphical solution)**

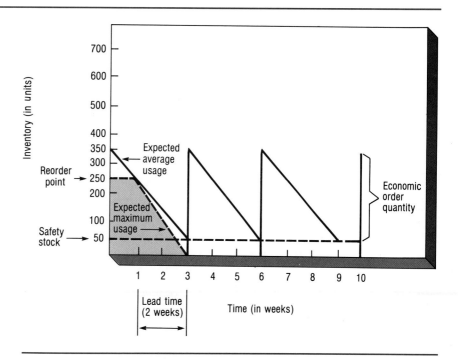

equation used to compute the reorder point under conditions of uncertainty may be stated as:

Reorder point = (Lead time × Average usage) + Safety stock

Inserting the data for the Martin Company into the equation, the result is:

Reorder point = (2 weeks × 100 units) + 50 units = 250 units

The graphical approach to computing the reorder point under conditions of uncertainty is shown in Illustration 15–12. Note how the *expected average usage* line descends to the safety stock of 50 units when the new shipment arrives and *only* the *expected maximum usage line* descends to zero when the new shipment arrives.

DECISION MAKING AND UNCERTAINTY

Managers must often make decisions without knowing their outcomes. For example, a manager must plan for his firm's operations for the coming year. However, his operating decisions will depend on the firm's expected sales volume which is unknown at the planning stage. To cope with such situations, managers may use several different methods devised by statisticians. One such method is to list all of the possible outcomes of an event and to assign a value to the likelihood of the event's occurrence, called a probability.

A **probability** is the long-run likelihood of an event's occurrence. Consider the probability of the toss of a perfectly balanced two-sided coin. In the long run, 50 percent of the tosses will be heads and 50 percent of the tosses will be tails. The percentages may be converted to probabilities by changing them to decimals, i.e., probabilities of .5 each. The sum of the probabilities are always 1 when all of the possibilities are considered. In the case of the coins, .5 + .5 = 1.

When a manager believes that the expected sales for the forthcoming year may be one of several different amounts but he is unsure which amount it will be, he may be able to compute the expected value of the sales by using the probabilities assigned to each of the possible sales figures.

Expected Value

When making decisions under conditions of uncertainty, managers often compute the expected value of the event under consideration. **Expected value** is the weighted average of the possible outcomes of an event's occurrence weighted by their respective probabilities.

The Herald Construction Company is in the process of projecting how many houses it can sell for the coming year. Because of the long lead time between the commencement of construction and the delivery of the houses, the firm must take certain steps now for next year's sales. The firm's sales

ILLUSTRATION 15–13

THE HERALD CONSTRUCTION COMPANY
Computation of Expected Value

Sales Values in Units	Probabilities	Expected Value in Units
600	.10	60
800	.60	480
1,000	.30	300
	1.00	840

are related to interest rates. When interest rates are low, the firm can sell 1,000 units. When interest rates are average (medium), it can sell 800 units, while when interest rates are high, it can only sell 600 units. After talking with an economic consultant, the firm was able to ascertain that there is a 30 percent chance that interest rates would be low, a 60 percent chance that interest rates would be medium, and a 10 percent chance that interest rates would be high. How many units should the firm plan for?

The solution to this problem may be arrived at by computing the expected value of the event as follows:

1. List the values for each occurrence.

2. Assign probabilities to each value.

3. Multiply each value by its probability.

4. Sum the results to obtain the expected value.

As shown in Illustration 15–13, the firm should plan to build 840 houses.

Payoff Tables

The expected value computation can be extended to assess possible decisions based on the expected profits and losses of specific actions. This step is done through the use of payoff tables.

A **payoff table** is a tabulation of the expected vlaues of various events taking into consideration their probabilities and their respective profits and/ or losses.

The Morosco Bakery bakes and sells cherry pies. The daily demand for the pies fluctuates. The normal selling price of a pie is $4.00, while the variable cost per pie is $1.50. At the end of each day, all remaining pies are sold to a thrift shop for $1 each.

The company would like to know how many pies to bake each day. As part of the decision-making process, they analyzed last year's daily sales. The results were:

Demand	Frequency of Occurrence in Percent
0	10
1	20
2	30
3	20
4	15
5	5
6 or more	0
	100

To reach the decision, Morosco could use a payoff table. The steps needed to construct the payoff table are:

Step 1

Determine the contribution margin for each pie sold at the retail level and the loss for each pie sold to the thrift store. The contribution margin is $2.50 per pie ($4.00 − $1.50), while the loss is $0.50 per pie ($1.50 − $1.00).

Step 2

For each action (pies baked), consider the financial consequences of each demand possibility—that is, 0, 1, 2, 3, 4, and 5. The calculations for all demand possibilities when three pies are baked are shown in column 2 of Illustration 15–14. The resulting conditional values are shown in column 3.

Step 3

Weight each conditional value computed in step 2 by the probability of the event and sum the results. This yields the *expected value* shown at the bottom of column 5 in Illustration 15–14.

ILLUSTRATION 15–14   Calculation of Expected Value for the Action of Baking Three Pies

Event (Demand)	Calculation	Conditional Value	Probability	Expected Value
0	3 × $−.50	$−1.50	.10	$−.15
1	(1 × $2.50) + (2 × $−.50)*	1.50	.20	.30
2	(2 × $2.50) + (1 × $−.50)†	4.50	.30	1.35
3	3 × $2.50	7.50	.20	1.50
4	3 × $2.50	7.50	.15	1.125
5	3 × $2.50	7.50	.05	.375
			1.00	$ 4.50

* Since three pies are baked and one is sold at the regular price, two pies are sold at a loss.
† Since three pies are baked and two are sold at the regular price, one pie is sold at a loss.

ILLUSTRATION 15–15

Payoff Table

Events (Demand)	Probability	Actions (Pies Baked)					
		0	1	2	3	4	5
0	.10	$0	$−.50	$−1.00	$−1.50	$−2.00	$−2.50
1	.20	0	2.50	2.00	1.50	1.00	.50
2	.30	0	2.50	5.00	4.50	4.00	3.50
3	.20	0	2.50	5.00	7.50	7.00	6.50
4	.15	0	2.50	5.00	7.50	10.00	9.50
5	.05	0	2.50	5.00	7.50	10.00	12.50
	1.00						
Expected value		$0	$ 2.20*	$ 3.80†	$ 4.50‡	$ 4.60§	$ 4.25‖

* .10($−.50) + .20($2.50) + .30($2.50) + .20($2.50) + .15($2.50) + .05($2.50) = $2.20.
† .10($−1.00) + .20($2.00) + .30($5.00) + .20($5.00) + .15($5.00) + .05($5.00) = $3.80.
‡ .10($−1.50) + .20($1.50) + .30($4.50) + .20($7.50) + .15($7.50) + .05($7.50) = $4.50.
§ .10($−2.00) + .20($1.00) + .30($4.00) + .20($7.00) + .15($10.00) + .05($10.00) = $4.60.
‖ .10($−2.50) + .20($.50) + .30($3.50) + .20($6.50) + .15($9.50) + .05($12.50) = $4.25.

The payoff table that summarizes the outcomes of all possible pie-baking variations and their probabilities at the Morosco Bakery is shown in Illustration 15–15. As you study the illustration, note that:

1. The optimal solution without any additional information is to bake four pies each day because the bakery will average a daily contribution margin of $4.60. This average is greater than the average for any other action.

2. Once the number of pies baked equals the demand, all subsequent conditional values for that number of pies baked are the same because the maximum sales for that action have been reached. For example, when two pies are baked, the maximum contribution is $5.00 (2 × $2.50) and all subsequent conditional values for the baking of two pies are also $5.00. Using the same focal point of $5.00, the baking of each additional pie reduces the contribution margin by $0.50—the loss on each additional pie that must be sold to the thrift shop. Thus, when two pies are demanded, producing three pies yields $4.50, producing four pies yields $4.00, and producing five pies yields $3.50. These figures are enclosed by broken lines in Illustration 15–15.

SUMMARY

Managers must use a variety of quantitative techniques to solve business problems. For example, when allocating resources, they may use **linear programming, inventory planning and control,** they may determine the **economic order quantity,** and for decision making under conditions of uncertainty, they may rely on the use of **probabilities.**

Linear programming is especially useful for maximization problems, when the objective is to allocate scarce resources or consider market limitations, called **constraints,** in order to maximize profit or contribution margin. It can also be used effectively for minimization problems, when the objective is to minimize costs subject to the applicable constraints. The first step in solving a linear programming problem is to formulate an **objective function** and the corresponding **constraint functions.** Then, the constraint functions are plotted as a graph. The area that lies under the constraint functions in a maximization problem (or above the constraint functions in a minimization problem) is the **area of feasible solutions.** The optimal solution to the problem usually lies at one of the corner points bounding this area and will depend on the slope of the objective function.

Inventory planning and control is used to answer two questions: How much to order? and when should the order be placed? How much to order is determined by first computing the **inventory ordering costs** and the **inventory carrying costs** for various order sizes. The optimum order size, or economic order quantity, may be ascertained using a table to determine the order size at which the total of the two costs is lowest. The EOQ may also be obtained by plotting a graph to discover the order size where the two costs intersect (are equal). While a mathematical EOQ formula may also be used, it does not provide a range of least cost as do the other two solutions. When an order should be placed depends on the **lead time** and the usage rate of the material. An important factor is whether the usage rate is known with certainty or whether it can vary due to unpredictable changes in demand. In the latter case, a firm will provide for a **safety stock** to minimize stockouts. The reorder point when safety stock is necessary will differ from the reorder point under conditions of certainty. Few firms have usage rates that can be predicted with certainty.

A **probability** is the long-run likelihood of an event's occurrence. Probabilities are stated in decimals, and when all possible outcomes are listed with their respective probabilities, the sum of the probabilities is equal to 1.

When making decisions under conditions of uncertainty, managers often calculate the **expected value** of the event under consideration. This is accomplished by listing all of the possible outcomes of an event's occurrence and multiplying each outcome by the probability of its occurrence. The results of the outcomes multiplied by their probabilities are then totaled to yield the expected value. The expected value tells a manager that in the long run, all of the occurrences of the event will average the amount computed as the expected value. In addition, profits and losses may be factored into the calculation of expected value through the use of a **payoff table.** The payoff table yields an optimum solution based on the available information.

GLOSSARY OF KEY TERMS

Area of feasible solutions　For a maximization linear programming problem, it is the area on a linear programming graph that lies beneath the boundaries of *all* of the constraint inequalities. For a minimization problem, it is the area that lies above the constraint inequalities.

Constraint A limiting factor under which a firm must operate, such as a shortage of raw materials, limited plant capacity (labor-hours and/or machine-hours), and limited market demand for a product.

Constraint function An equation that sets forth the limitations under which a firm must operate, such as material shortages, limited labor-hours, limited machine-hours, and limited market demand for the product.

Economic order quantity The amount of materials that should be ordered to minimize the total of inventory carrying costs and inventory ordering costs.

Economic production run in units The number of units to produce to minimize the total of inventory carrying costs and production setup costs.

Expected value The weighted average of the possible outcomes of an event's occurrence weighted by their respective probabilities.

Inventory carrying costs Storage costs, insurance, interest on funds invested in inventories, personal property taxes, and obsolescence and deterioration.

Inventory ordering costs Costs associated with placing a purchase order, transportation costs, and receiving and handling costs.

Inventory planning and control Techniques used to ensure that an optimum level of inventory will be maintained so that the costs of carrying and ordering inventories will be minimized and sufficient quantities will be on hand to avoid production interruptions due to stockouts (not having a needed material on hand).

Lead time The interval of time between the placing of an order and the receipt of the ordered merchandise on the purchaser's premises.

Linear programming A mathematical technique that shows managers how to allocate scarce resources in order to maximize profits or minimize costs.

Objective function An equation that sets forth the goal that is to be achieved by a linear programming solution, such as the maximization of contribution margin or the minimization of costs.

Payoff table A tabulation of the expected values of various events, taking into consideration their probabilities and their respective profits and/or losses.

Probability The long-run likelihood of an event's occurrence.

Reorder point The point in time when depleted inventory must be reordered. When the usage rate is known with certainty, it is computed by multiplying the lead time by the usage rate.

Safety stock The amount of inventory carried to accommodate the difference between the maximum expected usage and the average usage of materials during the lead time.

QUESTIONS

1. What kinds of business problems are especially suitable for linear programming solutions? Be specific.

2. What is an objective function? A constraint inequality?

3. What is the area of feasible solutions? Why is it important?

4. A firm has two constraints, both relating to machine capacity. The firm manufactures two products, product R and product S. The objective function is Max $Z = \$16\,R + \$18\,S$. There is no market limitation. For the coming year, the contribution

margin for product S is expected to be only $3. Would you expect the firm to continue its present product mix for the coming year? Why?

5. Your boss has a son who is studying linear programming in college. The son provides you with his formulation of a linear programming problem. Is it correct? If not, help him to correct it. His formulation is:

$$\text{Max } Z = 6X + 3Y$$

subject to:

$$\$3X + \$2Y \geq \$20$$
$$\$6X + \$2Y \geq \$26$$

6. What is inventory planning and control? Why is it important?

7. What are inventory carrying costs? Are they normally a linear function or a curvilinear function? Explain.

8. What are inventory purchasing costs? Are they normally a linear function or a curvilinear function? Explain.

9. Why do inventory carrying costs and inventory purchasing costs pull in opposite directions?

10. What is EOQ? Describe the different ways it can be computed.

11. What is lead time in relation to inventory purchasing? How is it used by managers?

12. What is safety stock? Why is it important?

13. What is expected value? Why is it important to managers?

14. What is a payoff table? How is it used by managers?

EXERCISES   **15–1**   **Linear Programming: Maximization Problem**

The Eden Company manufactures two products, X and Y. The contribution margins are $10 for product X and $12 for product Y. The products move through two departments, machining and polishing. The time requirements and limits for each department are as follows:

	Machining	Polishing
Product X	6	2
Product Y	4	4
Hours available	64	40

Required   *a.* Formulate the objective function and the constraint inequalities.

b. Use the graphical solution to determine the optimum number of X and Y to produce. Show your computations.

15–2   **Linear Programming: Maximization Problem**

The Garnet Company manufactures two products, X and Y. The contribution margins are $100 for product X and $125 for product Y. The products move through two departments, machining and polishing. The time requirements and limits for each department are as follows:

	Machining	Polishing
Product X	2	4
Product Y	4	4
Hours available	56	80

Required *a.* Formulate the objective function and the constraint inequalities.

b. Use the graphical solution to determine the optimum number of X and Y to produce. Show your computations.

15–3   Linear Programming: Maximization Problem

The Bruce Company manufactures two products S and T. Each product must pass through two departments, cutting and painting. The time requirements and limits of each department are as follows:

Department	Product		Daily Capacity Limit
	S	**T**	
Cutting	3	8	36
Painting	3	4	24

The contribution margin of S is $60 per unit while the contribution margin of T is $40 per unit.

Market demand will limit the sales of S to six units per day.

Required *a.* Formulate the objective function and the constraint inequalities.

b. Use the graphical solution to determine the optimum quantities of S and T to produce. Show all computations.

15–4   Linear Programming: Maximization Problem

The Gautner Company manufactures two products, X and Y. Each product must ᵽass through two departments, cutting and finishing. The time requirements and ᵐits of each department are as follows:

Department	Product		Daily Capacity Limit
	X	**Y**	
Cutting	8	5	120
Finishing	5	5	90

The contribution margin of X is $15 per unit, while the contribution margin of Y is $60 per unit.

Market demand will limit the sales of Y to 15 units per day.

Required *a.* Formulate the objective function and the constraint inequalities.

b. Use the graphical solution to determine the optimum quantities of X and Y to produce. Show all computations.

15–5 Linear Programming: Maximization Problems

1. Hayes Company manufactures two models, standard and deluxe. Each product must be processed in each of two departments, grinding and finishing. The standard model requires two hours of grinding and three hours of finishing. The deluxe model requires three hours of grinding and four hours of finishing. The contribution margin is $3.50 for the standard model and $5.00 for the deluxe model. Hayes has four grinding machines and five finishing machines which run 16 hours a day for 6 days a week. How would the restriction (constraint) for the finishing department be expressed?

   a. $3X + 4Y = 5$.
   b. $3X + 4Y \leqslant 480$.
   c. $\$3.50X + \$5.00Y = 5$.
   d. $\$3.50(3)X + \$5.00(4)Y \leqslant 480$.

2. Williamson Manufacturing intends to produce two products, X and Y. Product X requires 6 hours of time on machine 1 and 12 hours of time on machine 2. Product Y requires four hours of time on machine 1 and no time on machine 2. Both machines are available for 24 hours. Assuming that the objective function of the total contribution margin is $2X + $1Y, what product mix will produce the maximum profit?

   a. No units of product X and six units of product Y.
   b. One unit of product X and four units of product Y.
   c. Two units of product X and three units of product Y.
   d. Four units of product X and no units of product Y.

3. Milford Company manufactures two models, medium and large. The contribution margin expected is $12 for the medium model and $20 for the large model. The medium model is processed two hours in the machining department and four hours in the polishing department. The large model is processed three hours in the machining department and six hours in the polishing department. How would the formula for determining the maximization of total contribution margin be expressed?

   a. $\$5X + \$10Y$.
   b. $\$6X + \$9Y$.
   c. $\$12X + \$20Y$.
   d. $\$12X (2 + 4) + \$20Y (3 + 6)$.

(AICPA adapted)

15–6 Linear Programming: Maximization Problems

1. The Hale Company manufactures products A and B, each of which requires two processes, polishing and grinding. The contribution margin is $3 for product A and $4 for product B. The graph below shows the maximum number of units of each product that may be processed in the two departments.

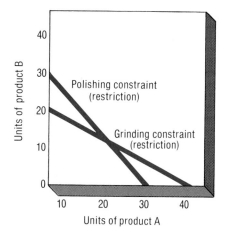

Considering the constraints (restrictions) on processing, which combination of products A and B maximizes the total contribution margin?

a. 0 units of A and 20 units of B.
b. 20 units of A and 10 units of B.
c. 30 units of A and 0 units of B.
d. 40 units of A and 0 units of B.

2. The Pauley Company plans to expand its sales force by opening several new branch offices. Pauley has $10.4 million in capital available for new branch offices. Pauley will consider opening only two types of branches: 20-person branches (type A) and 10-person branches (type B). Expected initial cash outlays are $1.3 million for a type A branch and $670,000 for a type B branch. Expected annual cash inflow, net of income taxes, is $92,000 for a type A branch and $36,000 for a type B branch. Pauley will hire no more than 200 employees for the new branch offices and will not open more than 20 branch offices. Linear programming will be used to help decide how many branch offices should be opened.

In a system of equations for a linear programming model, which of the following equations, would *not* represent a constraint (restriction)?

a. $A + B \leq 20$.
b. $20 A + 10 B \leq 200$.
c. $\$92,000 A + \$36,000 B \leq \$128,000$.
d. $\$1,300,000 A + \$670,000 B \leq \$10,400,000$.

(AICPA adapted)

15–7 Linear Programming: Minimization Problem

The Laurence Company manufactures one product which uses raw materials L and M. Material L costs $50 per pound while material M costs $75 per pound. Material L has four units of alloy and four units of precious metal. Material M has three units of alloy and eight units of precious metal. The minimum requirements in each unit of product is 30 units of alloy and 40 units of precious metal.

Required   a. Formulate the objective function and the constraint inequalities.
b. Use the graphical solution to determine the optimum quantities of L and M to use in manufacturing. Show all computations.

15–8 Linear Programming: Minimization Problem

The Monel Company manufactures one product which uses raw materials X and Y. Material X costs $40 per pound while Material Y costs $15 per pound. Material X has nine units of alloy and three units of precious metal. Material Y has three units of alloy and three units of precious metal. The minimum requirements in each unit of product is 45 units of alloy and 27 units of precious metal.

Required   *a.*   Formulate the objective function and the constraint inequalities.

           b.   Use the graphical solution to determine the optimum quantities of X and Y to use in manufacturing. Show all computations.

15–9 Economic Order Quantity (EOQ)

The Gender Company uses 10,000 units of LS–6 per annum. The cost of placing a purchase order and receiving the merchandise is $40 per order. The cost of insurance, property taxes, and interest on the investment in inventory is 40 cents per unit per annum.

Required   Compute the economic order quantity. Use the formula method.

15–10 Economic Order Quantity (EOQ)

The Marcus Company uses 15,000 units of MT–3 per annum. The costs of placing an order and carrying a unit in inventory annually consist of the following:

Interest on investment	$ 0.40 per unit
Receiving department costs	$ 6.00 per order
Purchasing department costs	$15.00 per order
Insurance	$ 0.20 per unit
Property taxes	$ 0.10 per unit

Required   Compute the economic order quantity. Use the formula method.

15–11 Economic Order Quantity (EOQ)

A firm computed its economic order quantity for Part No. 22 as 447.2136. Its purchase-order costs are $36 while its carrying costs are $3.60 per unit per annum.

Required   Compute the firm's annual usage for Part No. 22.

15–12 Economic Order Quantity (EOQ)

The Gemset Company uses 50,000 units of RH–5 per annum. The cost of placing an order is $30 per order and the annual carrying cost in inventory is $1 per unit.

Required   *a.*   Compute the economic order quantity. Use the formula method.

           b.   The firm has been purchasing RH–5 in 5,000 order size lots. How much will the firm save annually if the firm will now purchase in the order size you computed in *(a)?*

15–13 Optimal Production Run (EOQ)

1. Politan Company manufactures bookcases. Setup costs are $2. Politan manufactures 4,000 bookcases evenly throughout the year. Using the economic order quantity approach, the optimal production run would be 200 when the cost of carrying one bookcase in inventory for one year is

  a. $0.05.
  b. $0.10.
  c. $0.20.
  d. $0.40.

2. Pierce Incorporated has to manufacture 10,000 blades for its electric lawn mower division. The blades will be used evenly throughout the year. The setup cost every time a production run is made is $80, and the cost to carry a blade in inventory for the year is 40 cents. Pierce's objective is to produce the blades at the lowest cost possible. Assuming that each production run will be for the same number of blades, how many production runs should Pierce make?
  a. 3.
  b. 4.
  c. 5.
  d. 6.

3. The following information relates to the Gerald Company:

Optimal production run	500
Average inventory in units	250
Number of production runs	10
Cost per unit produced	$ 5
Desired annual return on inventory investment	10%
Setup costs per production run	$ 10

Assuming that the units will be required evenly throughout the year, what are the total annual relevant costs using the economic order quantity approach?
  a. $ 225.
  b. $ 350.
  c. $1,350.
  d. $2,625.

(AICPA adapted)

15–14 Economic Order Quantity (EOQ)

Items 1 and 2 are based on the following information:

Expected annual usage of a particular raw material is 2 million units, and the standard order size is 10,000 units. The invoice cost of each unit is $500, and the cost to place one purchase order is $80.

1. The average inventory is
  a. 1 million units.
  b. 5,000 units.
  c. 10,000 units.
  d. 7,500 units.

2. The estimated annual order cost is
  a. $16,000.
  b. $100,000.
  c. $32,000.
  d. $50,000.

3. The Aron Company requires 40,000 units of product Q for the year. The units will be required evenly throughout the year. It costs $60 to place an order. It

costs $10 to carry a unit in inventory for the year. What is the economic order quantity?

 a. 400.
 b. 490.
 c. 600.
 d. 693.

4. The following data refer to various annual costs relating to the inventory of a single-product company:

	Cost per Unit
Transportation-in on purchases	$0.20
Storage	0.12
Insurance	0.10

	Total per Year
Interest that could have been earned on alternate investment of funds	$ 800
Units required	10,000

What is the annual carrying cost per unit?

 a. $0.22.
 b. $0.30.
 c. $0.42.
 d. $0.50.

(AICPA adapted)

15–15 Optimal Production Run (EOQ)

The Surefire Fabricating Company sells 60,000 units of product W per annum. The product is formed on a hydraulic press using a forming die. The cost of setting up the die is $60 each time it is set up. The annual carrying costs of carrying one unit in inventory is $4.

Required Compute the optimal size production run.

15–16 Safety Stock and Reorder Point

The Ferret Company provides you with the following information:

Economic order quantity	500 units
Lead time	3 weeks
Average weekly usage	100 units
Maximum weekly usage	140 units

Required
 a. Compute the safety stock.
 b. Compute the reorder point using the safety stock computed in (a).
 c. Assume that the average weekly usage is known with certainty, i.e., there is no maximum weekly usage. Compute the reorder point.

15–17 Expected Value

1. Duguid Company is considering a proposal to introduce a new product, XPL. An outside marketing consultant prepared the following payoff probability distri-

bution describing the relative likelihood of monthly sales volume levels and related income (loss) for XPL:

Monthly Sales Volume	Probability	Income (Loss)
3,000	.10	$(35,000)
6,000	.20	5,000
9,000	.40	30,000
12,000	.20	50,000
15,000	.10	70,000

If Duguid decides to market XPL, the expected value of the added monthly income will be

a. $ 24,000.
b. $ 26,500.
c. $ 30,000.
d. $120,000.

2. Your client wants your advice on which of two alternatives he should choose. One alternative is to sell an investment now for $10,000. Another alternative is to hold the investment three days, after which he can sell it for a certain selling price based on the following probabilities:

Selling Price	Probability
$ 5,000	.4
$ 8,000	.2
$12,000	.3
$30,000	.1

Using probability theory, which of the following is the most reasonable statement?

a. Hold the investment three days because the expected value of holding exceeds the current selling price.
b. Hold the investment three days because of the chance of getting $30,000 for it.
c. Sell the investment now because the current selling price exceeds the expected value of holding.
d. Sell the investment now because there is a 60 percent chance that the selling price will fall in three days.

(AICPA adapted)

PROBLEMS 15–18 **Linear Programming: Maximization Problem**

The Elon Company manufactures two industrial products—X–10 which sells for $90 per unit and Y–12 which sells for $85 per unit. Each product is processed through both of the company's manufacturing departments. The limited availability of labor, material, and equipment capacity has restricted the ability of the firm to meet the demand for its products. The production department believes that linear programming can be used to routinize the production schedule for the two products.

The following data are available to the production department.

	Amount Required per Unit	
	X–10	Y–12
Direct material: Weekly supply is limited to 1,800 pounds at $12 per pound	4 pounds	2 pounds
Direct labor:		
Department 1—Weekly supply limited to 10 people at 40 hours each at an hourly cost of $6	⅔ hour	1 hour
Department 2—Weekly supply limited to 15 people at 40 hours each at an hourly rate of $8	1¼ hours	1 hour
Machine time:		
Department 1—Weekly capacity limited to 250 hours	½ hour	½ hour
Department 2—Weekly capacity limited to 300 hours	0 hours	1 hour

The overhead costs for Elon are accumulated on a plant-wide basis. The overhead is assigned to products on the basis of the number of direct labor-hours required to manufacture the product. This base is appropriate for overhead assignment because most of the variable overhead costs vary as a function of labor time. The estimated overhead cost per direct labor-hour is:

Variable overhead cost	$ 6
Fixed overhead cost	6
Total overhead cost per direct labor-hour	$12

The production department formulated the following equations for the linear programming statement of the problem.

$$A = \text{Number of units of X–10 to be produced}$$
$$B = \text{Number of units of Y–12 to be produced}$$

Objective function to minimize costs:
Minimize $Z = 85A + 62B$

Constraints:
Material:
4A + 2B ≤ 1,800 pounds

Department 1 labor:
$\frac{2}{3}$ A + 1B $\leq$ 400 hours
Department 2 labor:
$1\frac{1}{4}$ A + 1B $\leq$ 600 hours
Nonnegativity:
A $\geq$ O, B $\geq$ O.

Required   *a.*   The formulation of the linear programming equations as prepared by Elon Company's production department is incorrect. Explain what errors have been made in the formulation prepared by the production department.

       b.   Formulate and label the proper equations for the linear programming statement of Elon Company's production problem.

       c.   Explain how linear programming could help Elon Company determine how large a change in the price of direct materials would have to be to change the optimum production mix of X–10 and Y–12.

(CMA adapted)

15–19   **Economic Order Quantity, Safety Stock, and Reorder Point**

The Starry Company uses part U–Z in its production process. Annual usage amounts to 75,000 units per year. The company operates 250 days per year. The cost of placing an order is $25 per order, while the annual carrying costs are $2 per unit.

The delivery time from the vendor fluctuates from 10 days to 15 days. The probability distribution of delivery time is as follows:

Delivery Time in Days	Probability
9 days or less	.00
10	.40
11	.25
12	.15
13	.10
14	.05
15	.05
16 days or more	.00
	1.00

Required   *a.*   Compute the economic order quantity.

       b.   Compute the weighted average of the delivery time (expected value in days). Round your answer to the nearest whole number.

       c.   Compute the reorder point using the delivery time computed in *(b)*. What percent of the time will the company experience a stockout?

       d.   Compute the safety stock and reorder point assuming the company is willing to risk a stockout only 10 percent of the time.

       e.   Compute the safety stock and reorder point assuming the company is not willing to risk any stockout.

       f.   Compute the additional annual cost of carrying the additional units between your answers in *(d)* and *(e)*.

15-20   Tabular Computation of Economic Order Quantity

The Ashton Company uses 30,000 units of part B–12 per annum. At the present time, it only has storage space to accommodate 6,000 units. The minimum quantity that it can order is 500 units without paying a small-order surcharge. Ashton has been ordering in 6,000 order size lots.

The cost of placing a purchase order is $25 and the annual cost of carrying one unit in inventory is $1.

Required   *a.*   Using the tabular approach, compute the economic order quantity.
            b.   How much would the company save annually by ordering the EOQ amount instead of 6,000 units per order?

15-21   Economic Order Quantity (EOQ)

The Lear Company uses 40,000 units of part number 542 per annum. Purchase-order costs are $35.00 per order and annual carrying costs are $1.75 per unit.

Required   *a.*   Compute the economic order quantity.
            b.   If the purchase-order cost were to rise to $50 per order and all other data remain unchanged, what effect will this have on the EOQ? Explain why the change occurred.
            c.   Referring to the given data, assume that the only change will be the annual carrying costs that are expected to increase to $2.50 per unit. What effect will this have on the EOQ you computed in *(a)*? Explain why the change occurred.

15-22   Graphical Solution to Economic Order Quantity (Exercise 15–12)

Using the data provided in Exercise 15–12, prepare a graphical solution to compute the economic order quantity.

15-23   Economic Order Quantity and Reorder Point

SaPane Company is a regional distributor of automobile window glass. With the introduction of the new subcompact car models and the expected high level of consumer demand, management recognizes a need to determine the total inventory cost associated with maintaining an optimal supply of replacement windshields for the new subcompact cars introduced by each of the three major manufacturers. SaPane is expecting a daily demand for 36 windshields. The purchase price of each windshield is $50.

Other costs associated with ordering and maintaining an inventory of these windshields are as follows:

1.   The historical ordering costs incurred in the purchase-order department for placing and processing orders is shown below:

Year	Orders Placed and Processed	Total Ordering Costs
19x1	20	$12,300
19x2	55	12,475
19x3	100	12,700

Management expects the ordering costs to increase 16 percent over the amounts and rates experienced the last three years.

2. The windshield manufacturer charges SaPane a $75 shipping fee per order.
3. A clerk in the receiving department receives, inspects, and secures the windshields as they arrive from the manufacturer. This activity requires eight hours per order received. This clerk has no other responsibilities and is paid at the rate of $9 per hour. Related variable overhead costs in this department are applied at the rate of $2.50 per hour.
4. Additional warehouse space will have to be rented to store the new windshields. Space can be rented as needed in a public warehouse at an estimated cost of $2,500 per year plus $5.35 per windshield.
5. Breakage cost is estimated to be 6 percent of the average inventory value.
6. Taxes and fire insurance on the inventory are $1.15 per windshield.
7. The desired rate of return on the investment in inventory is 21 percent of the purchase price.

Six working days are required from the time the order is placed with the manufacturer until it is received. SaPane uses a 300-day work year when making economic order quantity computations.

Required
Calculate the following values for SaPane Company.
a. The value for ordering cost that should be used in the EOQ formula.
b. The value for storage cost that should be used in the EOQ formula.
c. The economic order quantity.
d. The minimum annual relevant cost at the economic order quantity point.
e. The reorder point in units.

(CMA adapted)

15–24 Economic Order Quantity, Safety Stock, and Reorder Point

You have been engaged to install an accounting system for the Kaufman Corporation. Among the inventory control features Kaufman desires as a part of the system are indicators of "how much" to order "when." The following information is furnished for one item, called a komtronic, which is carried in inventory:

1. Komtronics are sold by the gross (12 dozen) at a list price of $800 per gross FOB shipper. Kaufman receives a 40 percent trade discount off list price on purchases in gross lots.
2. Freight cost is $20 per gross from the shipping point to Kaufman's plant.
3. Kaufman uses about 5,000 komtronics during a 259-day production year and must purchase a total of 36 gross per year to allow for normal breakage. Minimum and maximum usages are 12 and 28 komtronics per day, respectively.
4. Normal delivery time to receive an order is 20 working days from the date a purchase request is initiated. A rush order in full gross lots can be received by air freight in five working days at an extra cost of $52 per gross. A stockout (complete exhaustion of the inventory) of komtronics would stop production, and Kaufman would purchase komtronics locally at list price rather than shut down.
5. The cost of placing an order is $10, the cost of receiving an order is $20.
6. Space storage cost is $12 per year per gross stored.
7. Insurance and taxes are approximately 12 percent of the net delivered cost of average inventory, and Kaufman expects a return of at least 8 percent on its average investment (ignore return on order and carrying cost for simplicity).

Required *a.* Prepare a schedule computing the total annual cost of komtronics based on uniform order lot sizes of one, two, three, four, five, and six gross of komtronics. (The schedule should show the total annual cost according to each lot size.) Indicate the economic order quantity (economic lot size to order).

b. Prepare a schedule computing the minimum stock reorder point for komtronics. The komtronics inventory should not fall below this point without reordering if the company is to guard against a stockout. Factors to be considered include average lead-period usage and safety stock requirements.

(AICPA adapted)

15–25   Expected Value

PART A

The Wing Manufacturing Corporation produces a chemical compound, product X, which deteriorates and must be discarded if it is not sold by the end of the month during which it is produced. The total variable cost of the manufactured compound, product X, is $50 per unit and its selling price is $80 per unit. Wing can purchase the same compound from a competing company at $80 per unit plus $10 freight per unit. Management has estimated that failure to fill orders would result in the loss of 80 percent of customers placing orders for the compound. Wing has manufactured and sold product X for the past 20 months. Demand for product X has been irregular and at present there is no consistent sales trend. During this period, monthly sales have been as follows:

Units Sold per Month	Number of Months
8,000	5
9,000	12
10,000	3

Required *a.* Compute the probability of sales of product X of 8,000, 9,000, or 10,000 units in any month.

b. Compute what the contribution margin would be if 9,000 units of product X were ordered and either 8,000, 9,000, or 10,000 units were manufactured in that same month (with additional units, if necessary, being purchased).

c. Compute the average monthly contribution margin that Wing can expect if 9,000 units of product X are manufactured every month and all sales orders are filled.

PART B

In the production of product X, Wing uses a primary ingredient, K–1. This ingredient is purchased from an outside supplier at a cost of $24 per unit of compound. It is estimated that there is a 70 percent chance that the supplier of K–1 may be shut down by a strike for an indefinite period. A substitute ingredient, K–2, is available at $36 per unit of compound, but Wing must contact this alternative source immediately to secure sufficient quantities. A firm purchase contract for either material must now be made for production of the primary ingredient next month. If an order were placed for K–1 and a strike occurred, Wing would be released from the contract and management would purchase the chemical compound from its competitor. Assume that 9,000 units are to be manufactured and all sales orders are to be filled.

Required

a. Compute the monthly contribution margin from sales of 8,000, 9,000, and 10,000 units if the substitute ingredient, K–2, is ordered.

b. Prepare a schedule computing the average monthly contribution margin that Wing should expect if the primary ingredient, K–1, is ordered with the existing probability of a strike at the supplier. Assume that the expected average monthly contribution margin from manufacturing will be $130,000 using the primary ingredient, and the expected average monthly loss from purchasing product X from the competitor (in case of a strike) will be $45,000.

(AICPA adapted)

15–26 **Payoff Table**

Jackston, Inc., manufactures and distributes a line of Christmas toys. The company had neglected to keep its dollhouse line current. As a result, sales have decreased to approximately 10,000 units per year from a previous high of 50,000 units. The dollhouse has been redesigned recently and is considered by company officials to be comparable to its competitors' models. The company plans to redesign the dollhouse each year in order to compete effectively. Joan Blocke, the sales manager, is not sure how many units can be sold next year, but she is willing to place probabilities on her estimates. Blocke's estimates of the number of units that can be sold during the next year and the related probabilities are as follows:

Estimated Sales in Units	Probability
20,000	.10
30,000	.40
40,000	.30
50,000	.20

The units would be sold for $20 each.

The inability to estimate the sales more precisely is a problem for Jackston. The number of units of this product is small enough to schedule the entire year's sales in one production run. If the demand is greater than the number of units manufactured, then sales will be lost. If demand is below supply, the extra units cannot be carried over to the next season and would be given away to various charitable organizations. The production and distribution cost estimates are listed below.

	Units Manufactured			
	20,000	**30,000**	**40,000**	**50,000**
Variable costs	$180,000	$270,000	$360,000	$450,000
Fixed costs	140,000	140,000	160,000	160,000
Total costs	$320,000	$410,000	$520,000	$610,000

The company intends to analyze the data to facilitate making a decision as to the proper size of the production run.

Required   Prepare a payoff table for the different sizes of production runs required to meet the four sales estimates prepared by Joan Blocke for Jackston, Inc. If Jackston, Inc., relied solely on the expected monetary value approach to make decisions, what size of production run would be selected?

(CMA adapted)

15–27   Probability and Payoff Table

Vendo, Inc., has been operating the concession stands at the university football stadium. The university has had successful football teams for many years; as a result, the stadium is always full. The university is located in an area that suffers no rain during the football season. From time to time, Vendo has found itself very short of hot dogs and at other times it has had many left. A review of the records of sales of the past five seasons revealed the following frequency of hot dogs sold.

	Total Games
10,000 hot dogs	5 times
20,000 hot dogs	10 times
30,000 hot dogs	20 times
40,000 hot dogs	15 times
	50 total games

Hot dogs sell for 50 cents each and cost Vendo 30 cents each. Unsold hot dogs are given to a local orphanage without charge.

Required   a. Assuming that only the four quantities listed were ever sold and that the occurrences were random events, prepare a payoff table (ignore income taxes) to represent the four possible strategies of ordering 10,000; 20,000; 30,000; or 40,000 hot dogs.

b. Using the expected value decision rule, determine the best strategy.

(CMA adapted)

16

STATEMENT OF CHANGES IN FINANCIAL POSITION

LEARNING OBJECTIVES

After reading this chapter, you should be able to:

1 Describe the significance and purpose of the statement of changes in financial position.

2 List the major sources and uses of working capital.

3 Discuss the major financing and investing transactions.

4 Analyze the changes in the components of working capital.

5 Prepare a statement of changes in financial position using a working capital focus.

6 Convert an accrual basis income statement to a cash basis.

7 Prepare a statement of changes in financial position using a cash focus.

Three statements are presented whenever a firm issues financial statements for external use. They are: (1) an income statement, (2) a balance sheet, and (3) a statement of changes in financial position. The last statement, mandated by *APB Opinion No. 19,* may be prepared using either the working capital basis or the cash basis.[1] **Working capital** is a firm's current assets minus its current liabilities. **Current assets** include cash and other assets that are expected to be converted into cash, or sold or consumed, within one year or within the firm's operating cycle, whichever is longer. **Current liabilities** are debts or other obligations that must be liquidated within one year or within the firm's operating cycle. A statement of changes in financial position prepared using the working capital basis is based on the inflows and outflows of working capital, while a statement prepared using the cash basis is based on the inflows and outflows of cash.[2]

SIGNIFICANCE AND PURPOSE

The cash and working capital of a business entity are important indicators of its financial health. The ability of an enterprise to meet its obligations on time and its ability to expand and grow depend on adequate levels of cash. The **statement of changes in financial position (SCFP)** provides information about the sources and uses of working capital or cash over a period of time as well as information about major financing and investment activities that do not involve sources and uses of working capital or cash.

While fragmentary information on sources and uses of funds can be obtained from comparative balance sheets and income statements, a comprehensive picture of this area of activity is learned only from a SCFP. This fact accounts for the growing importance and use of this statement which answers such questions as:

1. What use was made of funds provided by operations?

2. What was the source of funds invested in new plant and equipment?

3. What use was made of funds from a new bond issue or the sale of common stock?

4. How could the regular dividend continue if there was an operating loss?

5. How was the debt repaid or what was the source of the funds used to redeem the preferred stock?

6. How was the increase in working capital financed?

---

[1] AICPA, *APB Opinion No. 19,* "Reporting Changes in Financial Position" (New York, 1971), par. 7.

[2] The author is grateful to Professor Leopold A. Bernstein for permission to abstract portions of his book, *Financial Statement Analysis,* published by Richard D. Irwin, Inc., in 1983. Those who are interested in a definitive treatment of this subject matter should refer to Chapter 13 of the book.

7. Why, even though there were record profits, is the working capital position lower than last year?

TWO MAJOR CONCEPTS OF LIQUIDITY

There are many recognized indicators of liquidity, but the two most common are working capital and cash (including cash equivalents such as marketable securities). In this context, the term *funds* is equivalent to *working capital*, and these two terms are often used interchangeably. A **statement of sources and uses of working capital (funds)** explains the change in the level of working capital between two dates by listing the factors that caused its increase and those that caused its decrease. Similarly, a **statement of sources and uses of cash** explains the reasons for increases and decreases of this asset over a given period of time.

STATEMENT OF CHANGES IN FINANCIAL POSITION—A BROADER CONCEPT

The statement of sources and applications of working capital or of cash can omit important financing and investing transactions that do not involve either working capital or cash. Therefore, *APB Opinion No. 19* called for a broadening of both statements to include such transactions and recommended that it be called a statement of changes in financial position (SCFP). This statement is now a basic financial statement that must be provided whenever a profit-oriented business entity issues financial statements that present *both* financial position (balance sheet) *and* results of operations (statement of income and retained earnings).

The following items should be shown at the gross amount and not netted against each other unless one item is immaterial:

1. Acquisition and retirement of property, plant, and equipment.
2. New long-term borrowings and repayment of long-term debt. The effects of extraordinary items should be reported separately.

The intelligent analysis and use of any financial statement requires a thorough understanding of the principles and methods that underlie its preparation. Below we shall examine the principles underlying the preparation of the SCFP—working capital basis. The principles governing the preparation of the SCFP—cash basis will be discussed later in this chapter.

SOURCES AND USES OF WORKING CAPITAL

On a financial statement, the reasons for the change in working capital are necessary items. The principal reasons for changes in working capital are divided into: (1) sources of working capital and (2) uses of working capital.

Sources of Working Capital

The sources of working capital can be divided into two categories: (1) working capital provided by operations and (2) working capital provided by other sources.

1. Working Capital Provided by Operations. When operations are profitable, working capital normally increases, but not usually by the amount of net income shown on the income statement. Some charges and credits used in the income statement to arrive at net income do not affect working capital. Thus, some of them must be reversed on the SCFP when the statement uses net income (or income before extraordinary items) as the starting point. Consider the following entry for depreciation:

(a)

Depreciation xxx
    Accumulated Depreciation xxx

This depreciation entry reduces a firm's income, yet it does not reduce working capital. Since working capital is *not* reduced by depreciation, it must be added back to net income to arrive at the working capital provided by operations. Compare the above entry with the following entry for material costs:

(b)

Material Cost xxx
    Cash (or Accounts Payable) xxx

Note that material cost also reduces income, but it also affects working capital in entry *(b)*. Therefore, material cost is not added back to net income because *both income and working capital are reduced* by material cost.

Working capital may be provided by sources other than operations. However, a firm's long-term profitable operations provide it with the ability to continue its long-term existence.

2. Working Capital Provided by Other Sources. Working capital may be provided by sources other than operations. The principal sources are:

1. Long-term borrowings.
2. Sales of preferred stock.
3. Sales of common stock.
4. Sales of property, plant, and equipment.
5. Sales of investments.
6. Sales of treasury stock.

The sale of property, plant, and equipment occurs regularly as older equipment is replaced with new equipment. However, these sales are usually not a significant source of working capital unless a firm disposes of a significant portion of its plant assets as a result of a significant contraction of its operations.

Normally, funds from the sale of investments and investment income are not a significant source of working capital. However, recently, certain large corporations have been aggressive purchasers and sellers of large blocks of capital stock of other corporations. For these companies, the sale of a large *long-term* investment in another corporation will be a significant source of working capital.

Uses of Working Capital

The principal uses of working capital are:

1. Unprofitable operations.
2. Purchases of property, plant, and equipment.
3. Purchases of *long-term* investments.
4. Retirements of long-term indebtedness.
5. Payments of dividends.
6. Purchases of a firm's own stock (treasury stock), either for retirement or future resale.

1. Unprofitable Operations.   In some cases, unprofitable operations may result in a use of working capital. However, in many cases, the depreciation and amortization add-back to an operating loss are greater than the loss from operations and produces a source of working capital rather than a use of working capital. When this occurs, the *loss from operations is shown as a source of working capital from operations.*

Assume that the Shure company has an operating loss from operations of $300,000 for 19x3. During the same year, its depreciation amounted to $400,000. The operating loss would be shown as a source of working capital as follows:

Sources of funds:	
Funds provided by operations:	
Net loss	$(300,000)
Add back—charges not requiring funds in the current period:	
Depreciation	400,000
Total sources of funds from operations	$ 100,000

In cases where an operating loss exceeds the sum of all the add-backs, the *net* use of working capital—the operating loss minus the add-back—should be shown as a use of working capital.

2. Purchases of Property, Plant, and Equipment.   A significant part of a firm's uses of working capital is the replacement (and expansion) of its plant assets. This condition is ongoing if a firm is to remain operating. Because of inflation, improved technologies, and expansion, a firm may find that the trend of its purchases of plant assets exceeds the trend of its depreciation write-offs. In some years, it may be necessary to finance an unusually large purchase of plant assets by issuing long-term debt (or capital stock), but the bulk of plant asset purchases should come from profitable operations.

3. Purchases of Long-Term Investments. For many firms, this item is insignificant. For others, especially insurance companies, these purchases may be an ongoing activity, and thus, they would appear regularly on the SCFP as a use of working capital. Of course, the sale of long-term investments would be a source of working capital, as noted previously.

4. Retirement of Long-Term Indebtedness. From time to time, a firm may retire a portion of its long-term debt. A retirement alone is different from a refinancing of debt which consists of *both* a retirement of one issue and the issuance of another issue, usually at a lower interest rate. In either a refinancing or a retirement alone, the retirement of debt is shown as a use of working capital. A refinancing would also require the disclosure of the issuance of new long-term debt as a source of working capital.

5. Payment of Dividends. Most firms usually pay dividends in cash, but occasionally they may issue scrip—a long-term note—or property. The payment of dividends should not be confused with stock dividends—the distribution of a firm's own shares as a dividend—which is discussed later. The payment of cash dividends, scrip, or property dividends are a use of working capital.

6. Purchases of a Firm's Own Stock. Firms often purchase shares of their own common stock. The reasons for buying their stock are (1) to reissue it at a later date to employees as stock options, (2) to reissue it at a later date as part of a conversion of convertible bonds and/or convertible preferred stock into common stock, (3) to use it in acquiring an existing business (a business combination), (4) to use it for retirement when excess cash is available, and (5) to purchase the shares when they are selling at a relatively low market price for later reissuance at a higher price. A firm's purchase of its own shares requires the use of working capital—usually cash—and is therefore shown as a use of working capital.

All Significant Financing and Investing Activities

APB Opinion No. 19 mandates that a firm should disclose all of the important aspects of a firm's financing and investing activities.[3] This approach to preparing a SCFP is referred to as the all-resources concept. The **all-resources concept** requires that all of a firm's significant financing and investing activities, including exchanges that do not involve working capital (or cash), be reflected in its statement of changes in financial position. The two major financing and investing transactions that do not involve working capital (funds) are:

1. The issuance of securities (long-term bonds and/or capital stock) to acquire property or other long-term assets.

2. The conversion of long-term debt or preferred stock into common stock.

---

[3] AICPA, *APB Opinion No. 19*, par. 8.

These exchange transactions must be disclosed as both a source and use of working capital. If the first exchange transaction is a two-step transaction, i.e., the sale of securities and the use of these proceeds to purchase property or other long-term assets, both transactions would require disclosure in the SCFP. The fact that the two-step transaction occurred as a single exchange transaction does not alter the fact that a financing transaction *and* an investing transaction occurred. A similar analysis may be applied to the second exchange transaction. Therefore, *any* material exchange transaction that is of interest to the user of a SCFP should be disclosed as both a source and use of funds.

Stock Dividends. Recall that a stock dividend does not alter a firm's assets or liabilities; it is merely a bookkeeping entry that transfers a dollar amount from Retained Earnings to Common Stock (and possibly Additional Paid-In Capital). The firm does not disburse any assets, nor do the recipients of the stock dividend receive any assets. The recipients merely have more shares of the company, but their percentages of ownership of the firm remain unchanged. Since there are no financing or investing activities involved in a stock dividend, no disclosure of this item is required in the SCFP. The same treatment applies to stock splits, which are similar to stock dividends because the number of outstanding shares are increased. The difference between a stock dividend and a stock split is in bookkeeping; in substance they are the same.

Basis of Preparation

In order to focus on changes in working capital, we will discuss two condensed balance sheets. These balance sheets are divided into sections that disclose (1) current (or working capital) items and (2) all the other (noncurrent) accounts:

	End of Year 1	End of Year 2
Current items:		
Current assets	$12,000	$16,000
Current liabilities	8,000	10,000
Net current items (working capital)	4,000	6,000
Noncurrent items:		
Noncurrent assets	(6,000)	(8,000)
Long-term liabilities	3,000	5,000
Equity (capital) accounts	7,000	9,000
Net noncurrent items	$ 4,000	$ 6,000

Even though the above illustration is not the conventional form of a balance sheet, it provides a useful framework for understanding the interaction between changes in the current (i.e., working capital) section and changes in the noncurrent section. Thus, we can observe that the change in working capital from year-end 1 to year -end 2 ($2,000) is matched exactly, both in amount and direction, by the change in the net noncurrent items between these two year-ends ($2,000). This is true because assets always equal liabilities plus capital; so a change in one sector of the balance sheet must be matched by an equal change in the remaining accounts.

This relationship between the current and noncurrent sectors of the balance sheet provides a way to understand the basis underlying the preparation of the SCFP—working capital focus. Visualizing the two sections of the balance sheet as follows,

Current section:	Current assets	Current liabilities
Noncurrent section:	Fixed assets Other assets	Long-term liabilities Deferred credits Equity accounts

these generalizations may be made:

1. Net changes in the current section can be explained in terms of changes in the accounts of the noncurrent section. These are the *only* changes with which the SCFP is concerned.

2. Internal changes *within* the current section are not relevant here because the statement indicates the *net* change in working capital without regard to individual changes in the composition of the working capital accounts. For example, the purchase of inventory for cash or the payment of a current liability, while affecting the composition of the working capital, leaves no effect on its net amount. *APB Opinion No. 19* requires, however, a separate statement explaining the net changes in working capital components.

3. Similarly, internal changes *within* the noncurrent section have no effect on working capital. However, changes caused by transactions such as the conversion of debt into equity or the acquisition of fixed assets with long-term debt are significant financial transactions, and the SCFP would include these.

The best way to start the discussion of how the SCFP is prepared is to examine a simple illustration of the principles involved. Following is a pair of simplified and condensed comparative balance sheets at two consecutive year-ends:

ILLUSTRATION 16–1   Condensed Balance Sheets (in thousands)

	December 31		Changes during 19x2	
	19x1	19x2	Use of Funds	Source of Funds
1. Working capital	$320	$ 290		$ 30
2. Fixed assets	660	874	$214	
3. Accumulated depreciation	(200)	(244)		44
4. Intangible assets	150	100		50
Total assets	$930	$1,020		
5. Long-term debt	$420	$ 400	20	
6. Capital stock and paid-in capital	250	300		50
7. Retained earnings	260	320		60
Total equities	$930	$1,020		
Total			$234	$234

The extension columns showing the year-end to year-end changes in account balances do not represent a comprehensive SCFP because they can hide a considerable amount of significant detail. The following analysis of each change will make this clear:

1. The $30,000 change in working capital is the difference that should be explained because it is the change in funds (i.e., working capital) on which the statement focuses.

2. The net change in the fixed assets account of $214,000 has two elements as follows:

Purchase of new assets	$314,000
Less: Sale of old assets with an original cost of $100,000	100,000
Net change	$214,000

The net change in the accumulated depreciation account consists of the following:

Depreciation for the year	$64,000
Less: Accumulated depreciation on the assets sold during the year	20,000
Net change	$44,000

The book value and the selling price of the assets sold during the year are as follows:

Original cost	$100,000
Less: Accumulated depreciation	20,000
Book value	80,000
Selling price	80,000
Gain or loss on sale	$ –0–

3. The net increase in accumulated depreciation of $44,000 is after a charge to that account of $20,000 for accumulated depreciation on the assets sold [see (2) above]. Thus, the total addition to the accumulated depreciation account (with a contra charge to depreciation) was $64,000.

4. Without further data, the decline of $50,000 in the intangible assets can represent a sale of an intangible or the amortization of the intangible by a charge to income. Let us assume that the latter is true.

5. The reduction of $20,000 in the long-term debt represents a repayment of $20,000.

6. The increase in the capital stock and paid-in capital accounts is from the sale of stock of $50,000.

7. The change in the retained earnings balance almost always requires more data for proper analysis. The data provided here are as follows:

Balance of retained earnings, January 1, 19x2	$260,000
Net income for 19x2	180,000
	440,000
Less: Cash dividends paid	120,000
Balance of retained earnings, December 31, 19x2	$320,000

From the above discussion it is clear that the cash dividend represented a use of funds of $120,000 and that the net income of $180,000 provides the basis for the computing the sources of funds from operations. The reason that the $180,000 cannot be taken to be a source of funds arising from operations is that the income statement includes items of income and expired costs that do not provide or use funds (working capital items). The net income figure must be adjusted for such items. Let us now see how this is done.

Arriving at "Sources of Funds from Operations"

Normally, a detailed income statement is provided. In the present example, the income statement is shown in Illustration 16–2.

An examination of this income statement reveals that the individual items have the following usual (normal) effect on other balance sheet items:

	Items Affected	
	Working Capital	**Other**
Sales	Cash, accounts receivable	
Labor	Cash, accounts payable	
Material	Cash, accounts payable, and inventories	
Depreciation		Fixed assets
Other overhead	Cash, accounts payable, and prepaid costs	
Marketing and administrative costs . .	Cash, accounts payable, and prepaid costs	
Amortization of intangibles		Intangible assets
Income taxes (current)	Cash, accounts payable	

ILLUSTRATION 16-2

Income Statement
For the Year Ended December 31, 19x2

Sales		$900,000
Cost of sales:		
Labor	$200,000	
Material	120,000	
Depreciation	64,000	
Other overhead	76,000	460,000
Gross margin		440,000
Marketing and administrative costs (including $50,000 of intangible amortization)		85,000
Income before taxes		355,000
Income taxes—current		175,000
Net income		$180,000

In this example, depreciation and amortization of intangibles are costs that, unlike all others, do not require an outlay of current funds. In other words, they derive from the noncurrent section of the balance sheet, and since the income statement is included in the retained earnings account of the balance sheet, they are internal to the noncurrent section of the balance sheet and do not affect funds.

The required adjustment in our case is to start with the net income (or income before extraordinary items which is to be shown separately) of $180,000 and add back charges that did not require funds.

Net income		$180,000
Depreciation	$64,000	
Amortization of intangibles	50,000	114,000
Funds provided by operations		$294,000

This figure of $294,000 could also have been obtained by reconstructuring the income statement to include only those items that either provide or require funds (working capital).

The reason the net-income-adjustment method is almost always used in practice to arrive at the "funds provided by operations" figure is that it makes unnecessary the reciting of all the above detail that is to be found in the income statement anyway. Thus, the "net income" figure is a convenient starting point for arriving at the adjusted "funds provided by operations" figure. Moreover, this method provides a verifiable and reassuring link to the income statement.

In addition to depreciation and amortization of intangibles, the following are further examples of items that may appear in the income statement and that have no effect on funds (working capital).

Income Statement Item	Related to the Following Noncurrent Balance Sheet Item
Amortization of bond premium	Unamortized bond premium
Amortization of bond discount	Unamortized bond discount
Warranty costs	Provision for warranty costs (noncurrent)
Deferred income tax	Deferred taxes (noncurrent)

THE STATEMENT OF CHANGES IN FINANCIAL POSITION

We can now construct a SCFP that is more detailed and more comprehensive than one based solely on the changes that we could have developed from the comparative balance sheets above.

ILLUSTRATION 16–3

Statement of Changes in Financial Position
For the Year Ended December 31, 19x2

Sources of funds:			
Funds provided by operations:			
Net income		$180,000	
Add back charges not requiring funds in the current period:			
Depreciation	$64,000		
Amortization of intangibles	50,000	114,000	$294,000
Sale of fixed assets			80,000
Sale of capital stock			50,000
Total sources of funds			424,000
Uses of funds:			
Purchases of fixed assets			314,000
Payment of dividends			120,000
Repayment of long-term debt			20,000
Total uses of funds			454,000
Decrease in working capital			$ 30,000

ILLUSTRATION OF THE T-ACCOUNT TECHNIQUE FOR THE SCFP— WORKING CAPITAL FOCUS

The simple illustration above indicated some of the more common problems involved in the preparation of the SCFP. These, and others found in more complex examples, are:

1. The analysis of net changes based on further detail provided.

2. The reversal or elimination of transactions internal to the noncurrent accounts.

3. Regrouping and reconstruction of transactions in the noncurrent group that affect, and hence explain, the changes in the working capital sector.

The methods used to implement these adjustments vary from elaborate multicolumn worksheets to highly summarized adjustments that are performed mentally. One of the most direct and most flexible methods utilizes the reconstruction of summarized T accounts, developed by Professor W. J. Vatter.

The basic objective of the T-account method is to reconstruct in summary fashion, using T accounts for the noncurrent accounts, all the transactions that went through them during the period reported upon. If the reconstructed transaction reveals that it was a source or a use of funds, it is posted to the summary Working Capital T account. If the transaction has no effect on funds and is not of a significant investing or financing nature, it is reversed among the applicable noncurrent T accounts. The following is a summary of the steps involved in this method.

1. A T account is set up for each noncurrent account appearing in the change column of the comparative balance sheet. The opening and closing balance of the account is posted to the T account as follows:

Fixed Assets

B*	660
B†	874

* Signifies opening balance.
† Signifies closing balance.

2. A Working Capital T account, divided into an "Operations" and an "Other" section, as illustrated in the comprehensive example that follows, is also opened.

3. Based on information supplied and inferences drawn from the changes in the noncurrent account, the balance in the T account is reconstructed by:
   a. Debiting or crediting all revenue and cost items to the "Operations" section of the Working Capital account.
   b. Debiting or crediting all other items affecting working capital (funds) to the "Other" section of the Working Capital account.

4. When the process is completed, the Working Capital T account will contain the detail necessary for the preparation of the SCFP.

Illustration 16–4, which follows, provides a more comprehensive example of the steps required in the preparation of the SCFP.

The income statement for the year ending December 31, 19x2, of the Vatter Company is shown in Illustration 16–5.

The following additional information is available:

1. On March 1, 19x2, the company bought for cash of $510,000 fixed assets having a value of $450,000 and intangible assets having a value of $60,000.

ILLUSTRATION 16–4

THE VATTER COMPANY
Comparative Balance Sheets
As of December 31, 19x1 and 19x2

Assets	19x1	19x2	Increase (Decrease)
Current assets:			
Cash	$ 240,000	$ 120,000	$ (120,000)
Receivables	360,000	450,000	90,000
Inventories	750,000	1,053,000	303,000
Total current assets	1,350,000	1,623,000	273,000
Fixed assets	4,500,000	6,438,000	1,938,000
Less: Accumulated depreciation	(1,500,000)	(1,740,000)	(240,000)
Investments in marketable securities	1,000,000	1,050,000	50,000
Intangibles	950,000	980,000	30,000
Total assets	$6,300,000	$8,351,000	$2,051,000
Liabilities and Capital			
Accounts payable	$ 360,000	$ 590,000	$ 230,000
Bonds payable	300,000	700,000	400,000
Deferred income taxes	240,000	260,000	20,000
Common stock	2,400,000	3,200,000	800,000
Paid-in capital	900,000	1,300,000	400,000
Retained earnings	2,100,000	2,301,000	201,000
Total liabilities and capital	$6,300,000	$8,351,000	$2,051,000

ILLUSTRATION 16–5

THE VATTER COMPANY
Income Statement
For the Year Ended December 31, 19x2

Sales		$19,950,000
Cost of goods sold (includes $360,000 depreciation)		11,101,000
Gross profit		8,849,000
Marketing and administrative costs	$7,000,000	
Amortization of intangibles	30,000	7,030,000
		1,819,000
Investment income		50,000
Gain on sale of fixed assets		2,000
Income before taxes		1,871,000
Income taxes:		
Current	900,000	
Deferred	20,000	920,000
Net income		$ 951,000

2. Old machinery was sold for $18,000; it originally cost $36,000, and $20,000 of depreciation had been accumulated to date of sale.

3. In April, the company acquired $100,000 in fixed assets by issuing bonds with $100,000 par value.

4. In June, the company received $1 million in cash for a new issue of capital stock with a par value of $600,000. Two hundred thousand dollars of convertible bonds were converted into capital stock, par value $200,000. Long-term bonds were also sold for $500,000 (at par).

5. Fully depreciated assets of $100,000 were written off.

6. Dividends paid amounted to $750,000.

Based on the above financial statements and the additional data, we prepared a SCFP, working capital focus, using the T-account method.

ILLUSTRATION 16–6

THE VATTER COMPANY
T Accounts
(in thousands of dollars)

Working Capital

B		990*		

Operations

Net income	(m)	951	2	(b)	Gain on sale of fixed assets
Depreciation	(g)	360			
Deferred income taxes	(k)	20			
Intangible amortization	(o)	30			

Other

Sale of fixed assets	(b)	18	450	(a)	Acquisition of fixed assets
			60	(a)	Acquisition of intangibles
Bonds issued to acquire fixed assets	(d)	100	100	(c)	Fixed assets acquired with bonds
			1,524	(f)	Purchase of fixed assets
Bonds sold	(h)	500			
Stock issued in bond conversion	(j)	200	200	(i)	Bond conversion into stock
Sale of capital stock	(l)	1,000	750	(n)	Dividends paid
			50	(p)	Purchase of marketable securities
B		1,033†			

ILLUSTRATION 16–6 (*concluded*)

Fixed Assets				Accumulated Depreciation			
B	4,500					1,500	B
(a)	450			(b)	20	360	(g)
(c)	100	36	(b)	(e)	100		
(f)	1,524	100	(e)				
B	6,438					1,740	B

Investment in Marketable Securities				Intangibles			
B	1,000			B	950		
(p)	50			(a)	60		
						30	(o)
B	1,050			B	980		

Bonds Payable				Deferred Income Taxes			
		300	B			240	B
(i)	200	100	(d)			20	(k)
		500	(h)				
		700	B			260	B

Capital Stock				Paid-In Capital			
		2,400	B			900	B
		200	(g)			400	(l)
		600	(l)				
		3,200	B			1,300	B

Retained Earnings			
		2,100	B
(n)	750	951	(m)
		2,301	B

* CA − CL = $1,350,000 − $360,000.
† $1,623,000 − $590,000.

The *first* step is to set up T accounts for:

1. A Working Capital account subdivided into an "Operations" section and an "Other"section.

2. All noncurrent accounts in order to reconstruct the transactions affecting working capital (funds).

The *second* step is to enter the opening and closing balances in each T account and designate these as "B" for balance. The upper amount is the opening balance and the amount below the bottom line is the closing balance.

The *third* step is to reconstruct all the transactions for the year in the T accounts in summary fashion. It is best to start first with the supplementary information given.

Fixed Assets and Intangibles

The acquisition of the fixed assets and intangibles can be reconstructed as follows:

(a)

Fixed Assets	450,000	
Intangibles	60,000	
Working Capital—Other		450,000
Working Capital—Other		60,000

Since we are explaining here changes in working capital, we post the payment as a use of working capital.

We know that equipment costing $36,000 and having accumulated depreciation of $20,000 was sold for $18,000. Entry *(b)* reconstructs the transactions in summary fashion.

(b)

Working Capital—Other	18,000	
Accumulated Depreciation	20,000	
Fixed Assets		36,000
Working Capital—Operations		2,000

Working Capital—Other is debited for the cash received on the sale of the old machinery. By showing the entire proceeds of $18,000 as a source of working capital, we must remove from net income the $2,000 gain included there. In effect, we are combining the recovery of the book value of the equipment of $16,000 ($36,000 − $20,000) with the $2,000 gain to show the entire proceeds as a source of Working Capital—Other. The removal of the $2,000 gain on sale of equipment is achieved by crediting Working Capital—Operations. That credit *reduces* the amount of working capital provided by operations.

We know that $100,000 of fixed assets were acquired through issuance of bonds. This transaction does not affect working capital but must be shown in the statement because it represents a significant investing and financing transaction. It can be reconstructed as follows:

(c)

Fixed Assets	100,000	
Resources Used (Working Capital account)		100,000

(d)

Resources Obtained (Working Capital account)	100,000	
Bonds Payable		100,000

These types of transactions that do not affect working capital are self-balancing. For convenience of statement preparation, they are posted to the

Working Capital account where their net effect cancels out, thus confirming that they have no effect on working capital.

We also know that fully depreciated assets with a cost of $100,000 were written off. This bookkeeping entry does not represent an important investing or financing transaction so the entry that reconstructs this transaction cancels out and bypasses the Working Capital account since it does not affect items appearing in the SCFP.

(e)

Accumulated Depreciation	100,000	
Fixed Assets		100,000

Now that we have posted all known entries to the Fixed Asset T account, we still need a debit of $1,524,000 in order to balance the account. Without specific information, we assume, as we always do in this process, the most reasonable and plausible transaction, i.e., that this amount represents purchases of fixed assets during the year. The entry is as follows:

(f)

Fixed Assets	1,524,000	
Working Capital—Other		1,524,000

Accumulated Depreciation

We now have two debits posted to the account totaling $120,000. In order to balance the account, we need a credit of $360,000 that we know coincides with the total depreciation shown in the income statement. The entry is:

(g)

Working Capital—Operations	360,000	
Accumulated Depreciation		360,000

The charge to Working Capital—Operations represents an add-back of an item deducted in arriving at net income which does not require working capital.

Bonds Payable

The sale of bonds resulted in a source of funds that is reflected as follows:

(h)

Working Capital—Other	500,000	
Bonds Payable		500,000

The conversion of bonds into capital stock is not a transaction affecting working capital. It is, nevertheless, a significant financing transaction resulting in a change in capital structure and as such should be reflected in the SCFP. This is done as follows:

(i)

Bonds Payable	200,000	
Resources Used (Working Capital account)		200,000

(j)

Resources Obtained (Working Capital account)	200,000	
Capital Stock		200,000

Deferred Income Taxes

The charge for deferred income taxes increases a noncurrent deferred credit account and, like that for depreciation and intangible amortization, does not require current funds, and thus the adjustment is carried to Working Capital—Operations. It is an add-back to income for an item not requiring working capital.

(k)

Working Capital—Operations	20,000	
Deferred Income Taxes		20,000

Capital Stock and Paid-In Capital

The sale of stock is a source of funds and is reconstructed as follows:

(l)

Working Capital—Other	1,000,000	
Capital Stock		600,000
Paid-In Capital		400,000

Retained Earnings

Reconstruction of the Retained Earnings account change usually relies on supplementary detail provided or, as in this case, the income statement. Thus, net income amounted to $951,000, and this source of funds (*before* adjustment for nonfund items) is transferred to Operations Summary.

(m)

Working Capital—Operations	951,000	
Retained Earnings		951,000

The cash dividends amounted to $750,000, and this is a use of funds.

(n)

Retained Earnings	750,000	
Working Capital—Other		750,000

Intangible Amortization

From the income statement, we learn that $30,000 of intangibles was amortized in 19x2. Since this charge to income did not require funds (i.e., it drew a "noncurrent" account), we increase the operations summary by this amount, thus:

(o)

Working Capital—Operations	30,000	
Intangibles		30,000

Thus, the net change in the Intangibles account has been accounted for.

Investment in Marketable Securities

The entry to reconstruct the purchase of marketable securities is:

(p)

Investment in Marketable Securities	50,000	
Working Capital—Other		50,000

We have now accounted for the changes in all the noncurrent T accounts. The changes internal to the noncurrent group of T accounts do not affect working capital. However, most such changes, which represent significant financing and/or investing activities, must be included in the SCFP.

ILLUSTRATION 16–7

THE VATTER COMPANY
Statement of Changes in Financial Position
For the Year Ended December 31, 19x2

Sources of funds:			
Net income			$ 951,000
Add: Charges not requiring outlay of working			
capital in the current period:			
Depreciation of fixed assets	$360,000		
Amortization of intangibles	30,000		
Deferred income taxes	20,000	410,000	
Deduct: Income not providing working capital:			
Deduct gain on sale of fixed assets (included			
in proceeds from sale)		(2,000)	
Working capital provided by operations			$1,359,000
Sale of fixed assets		18,000	
Net proceeds of sale of bonds		500,000	
Issuance of bonds in exchange of fixed			
assets		100,000	
Issuance of stock for conversion of bonds .		200,000	
Sale of capital stock		1,000,000	1,818,000
Total resources provided			3,177,000
Uses of funds:			
Purchase of fixed assets*		1,974,000	
Purchase of goodwill		60,000	
Fixed assets acquired for bonds		100,000	
Purchase of marketable securities		50,000	
Retirement of debentures on conversion into			
capital stock		200,000	
Payment of dividends		750,000	
Total resources used			3,134,000
Increase in working capital			$ 43,000

* $450,000 + $1,524,000 = $1,974,000.

The Working Capital account now contains all the detail needed to prepare the SCFP shown in Illustration 16–7.

Analysis of Changes in Working Capital

APB Opinion No. 19 requires that a firm include an analysis of changes in working capital whenever it presents a SCFP using a working capital focus.[4] An **analysis of changes in working capital** is a schedule showing the increase or decrease effect on working capital for each component of working capital. The analysis of changes in working capital for the Vatter Company appears in Illustration 16–8.

[4] Ibid., par. 12.

ILLUSTRATION 16–8

THE VATTER COMPANY
Analysis of Changes in Working Capital
For the Year Ended December 31, 19x2

	19x1	19x2	Increase (Decrease) in Working Capital
Current assets:			
Cash	$ 240,000	$ 120,000	$(120,000)
Receivables	360,000	450,000	90,000
Inventories	750,000	1,053,000	303,000
Total current assets	1,350,000	1,623,000	273,000
Current liabilities:			
Accounts payable	360,000	590,000	(230,000)
Total current liabilities	360,000	590,000	(230,000)
Working capital	$ 990,000	$1,033,000	$ 43,000

STATEMENT OF CHANGES IN FINANCIAL POSITION—CASH FOCUS

While many published SCFP focus on explaining changes in working capital, in addition to other important investing and financing transactions, there are *increasing demands for these statements to focus on cash.* One such emphasis was expressed in *SFAC No. 1*[5] which concluded that the objectives of financial reporting indicate that users need information about cash inflows and outflows to help with assessments of future cash flows and to provide feedback about previous assessments.[6]

Moreover, cash flow information is needed by many decision makers, including a firm's managers, and particularly by lenders who are concerned with the inflows and outflows of the means of payment, i.e., cash. *Net income has never been a good surrogate for cash flow from operations in the short run,* and this is especially true in times of inflation when the gap between earnings and cash flow from operations widens. That gap is widened by an ever-increasing investment in receivables and inventories that is not fully offset by a corresponding increase in trade credit.

Because of the increasing importance of cash flow analysis, we shall discuss the technique of preparing the SCFP—cash focus. Since the statement user will often find statements prepared with a different focus (i.e., working capital) or in a format not useful for analysis, Appendix 16–A presents methods of converting such statements to the more useful cash flow statements.

---

[5] FASB, *Statement of Financial Accounting Concepts No. 1,* "Objectives of Financial Reporting by Business Enterprises" (Stamford, Conn., 1978).

[6] See also FASB, "Reporting Income, Cash Flows, and Financial Position of Business Enterprises," Exposure Draft, November 16, 1981.

Preparation of the Statement of Changes in Financial Position— Cash Focus

Let us first consider the impact that changes in the working capital accounts have on operations as distinguished from "other" effects.

Considering operations as the *earning related activities* of the enterprise, it is clear that changes in most working capital accounts would affect operations. In that case, the focus is not only on income and cost items but also on the inflows and outflows of funds that operations impose on the enterprise, e.g., extension of credit to customers, investment in inventories, and conversely obtaining credit from suppliers.

Consider the change in accounts receivable as an example. The amount increased by $90,000 during 19x2, so that on a net basis, the sales figure for the year is $90,000 higher than the collections of cash from sales. This can also be shown by a reconstruction of the *aggregate* entries in the Accounts Receivable account for 19x2.

Accounts Receivable
(in thousands of dollars)

B	360		
Sales	19,950	Cash collections	19,860
B	450		

Using a similar line of analytical reasoning, we can see that changes in the following working capital accounts would have effects as follows:

Account	Change: Dr. (debit) Cr. (credit)	Effect on Operations
Accounts Receivable	Increase (Dr.)	Sales not collected in cash
	Decrease (Cr.)	Collections exceed sales for the period, i.e., some prior period receivables collected
Inventories	Increase (Dr.)	Purchases exceed cost of goods sold
	Decrease (Cr.)	Some of the cost of goods sold represents a reduction in inventories, i.e., purchases are less than cost of goods sold
Prepaid Costs	Increase (Dr.)	Cash laid out for costs that are to be charged to future periods
	Decrease (Cr.)	Some costs in the income statement were paid for in prior years and did not require a current cash outlay
Trade Accounts or Notes Payable	Increase (Cr.)	Some purchases were not yet paid for in cash
	Decrease (Dr.)	Cash payments to suppliers exceed purchases for the period

A study of the above chart reveals that the use of the debit and credit designation for changes in the current accounts is a useful check on the effects of changes on sources and uses of cash. Thus, a credit change adds to cash from operations while a debit change reduces cash from operations.

Recall that in Illustration 16–6, the focus was on changes in working capital. The master T account will now be labeled Cash and we will record in it all the entries *(a)* through *(p)* which explained the changes in the noncurrent accounts. Next, we establish T accounts for all the other current accounts.

In order to distinguish clearly the entries that explain the changes in the current accounts from those relating to the noncurrent accounts, we will identify them in Illustration 16–9 with double letters starting with *(aa):*

ILLUSTRATION 16–9

THE VATTER COMPANY
T Accounts for Preparation of SCFP—Cash Focus
(in thousands of dollars)

Cash

B		240			

Operations

Net income	*(m)*	951	Gain on sale of fixed assets	*(b)*	2
Depreciation	*(g)*	360			
Deferred income taxes	*(k)*	20	Increase in receivables	*(aa)*	90
Intangibles amortization	*(o)*	30	Increase in inventories	*(bb)*	303
Increase in accounts payable	*(cc)*	230			

Other

Sale of fixed assets	*(b)*	18	Acquisition of fixed assets	*(a)*	450
			Acquisition of goodwill	*(a)*	60
Bonds issued to acquire fixed assets	*(d)*	100	Fixed assets acquired with bonds	*(c)*	100
Bonds sold	*(h)*	500	Purchase of fixed assets	*(f)*	1,524
Stock issued in bond conversion	*(j)*	200	Bond conversion into stock	*(i)*	200
Sale of capital stock	*(l)*	1,000	Dividends paid	*(n)*	750
			Purchase of marketable securities	*(p)*	50
B		120			

Receivables				**Inventories**			
B		360		B		750	
(aa)		90		*(bb)*		303	
B		450		B		1,053	

Accounts Payable		
	B	360
	(cc)	230
	B	590

ILLUSTRATION 16–9 (concluded)

(aa)*		
Receivables	90,000	
Cash—Operations		90,000
(bb)*		
Inventories	303,000	
Cash—Operations		303,000
(cc)*		
Cash—Operations	230,000	
Accounts Payable		230,000

* For an explanation of and the rationale for these entries, see the preceding discussion.

ILLUSTRATION 16–10

THE VATTER COMPANY
Statement of Changes in Financial Position
For the Year Ended December 31, 19x2

Sources of cash:			
Net income		$ 951,000	
Add: Charges not requiring cash:			
Depreciation of fixed assets	$360,000		
Amortization of intangibles	30,000		
Deferred income taxes	20,000		
Increase in accounts payable	230,000	640,000	
		1,591,000	
Deduct:			
Increase in receivables	90,000		
Increase in inventories	303,000		
Gain on sale of fixed assets (included			
in proceeds from sale)	2,000	395,000	
Cash provided by operations			$1,196,000
Sale of fixed assets		18,000	
Net proceeds of sale of bonds		500,000	
Issuance of bonds in exchange of fixed			
assets		100,000	
Issuance of stock for conversion			
of bonds		200,000	
Sale of capital stock		1,000,000	1,818,000
			3,014,000
Decrease in cash			120,000
			$3,134,000
Uses of cash:			
Purchase of fixed assets*		$1,974,000	
Purchase of intangibles		60,000	
Fixed assets acquired for bonds		100,000	
Purchase of marketable securities		50,000	
Retirement of debentures on conversion			
into capital stock		200,000	
Payment of dividends		750,000	$3,134,000

* $450,000 + $1,524,000.

With the posting of these additional entries, the change in the Cash T account, from opening balance of $240,000 to ending balance of $120,000, is now fully explained and we can use the detail in it to construct Illustration 16–10, which shows the SCFP—cash focus.

DEPRECIATION—A SOURCE OF FUNDS?

One major cause for the belief that depreciation is a source of funds is the manner in which it is presented in some SCFPs. Thus, the adding back of depreciation to net income is often not shown as an *adjustment* of net income in order to arrive at the desired figure of "funds provided by operations" but rather as if it is an independent source of funds similar to that stemming from borrowing of money or the sales of assets.

ILLUSTRATION 16–11

Misleading Presentation		Proper Presentation		
Sources of funds:		**Sources of funds:**		
Net income	$ 75,000	Net income	$75,000	
Depreciation	25,000	Add back * deprecia-		
Sale of bonds	60,000	tion charge	25,000	
Sale of machinery	40,000	Funds provided by		
		operations		$100,000
		Sale of bonds		60,000
		Sale of machinery		40,000
Total	$200,000	Total		$200,000

* Charge not requiring current outlay of funds.

It is easy to understand why the misleading presentation could lead people to believe that depreciation is a source of funds. Since it is shown in the same way as all sources of funds, it would seem to suggest that the act of increasing depreciation will increase the total sources of funds. This thinking overlooks the fact that depreciation acts to reduce net income, and thus the act of increasing depreciation can have no effect on funds. On the other hand, the act of increasing permitted depreciation charges for tax return purposes may temporarily conserve funds by reducing the current tax liability.

The thinking regarding depreciation as a source of funds is encouraged by articles in some financial publications. Thus, *Business Week* commented, "Since then the company has improved cash flow further by depreciating existing planes."[7] However, added depreciation (except that resulting in added tax write-offs) cannot be considered a source of cash.

The proper presentation brings out the essential fact that the reason depreci-

---

[7] Dated May 19, 1980, in an article entitled "Trans World Corporation—The Strategy Squeeze on the Airline."

ation (or similar charges or credits that do not affect current funds) is shown in the SCFP is to show the reader how the net income figure is converted to a "funds provided by operations" figure needed in the funds statement.

The essential fact is that aside from miscellaneous sources of income, the *basic* source of funds from operations in any enterprise is sales to customers. It is from sales that all costs are recovered and a profit, if any, is earned. If the sales price is sufficient to cover *all* costs, that is, those requiring and those not requiring current funds, then the process of sales will recover the depreciation costs in addition to other costs. If the sales price is not sufficiently high to cover all costs, depreciation will not be recovered or will not be fully recovered. Thus, the importance of revenues as *the* source of funds from operations should always be remembered.

SUMMARY

When a firm issues financial statements for external use, it must include a **statement of changes in financial position (SCFP).** The statement may be prepared using a working capital basis or a cash basis. In 1971, prior to the issuance of *APB Opinion No. 19,* a firm usually supplied a **statement of sources and uses of working capital** or a **statement of sources and uses of cash.** Although these two statements are similar to the SCFP, the former using a working capital basis and the latter using a cash basis, the two statements did not contain significant financing and investing activities which had no effect on working capital or cash. The broader based SCFP is now prepared using the **all-resources concept** which requires that all significant financing and investing activities be included even though they do not affect working capital or cash.

Working capital is derived by subtracting **current liabilities** from **current assets.** When the SCFP is prepared using the working capital basis, the statement consists of two parts. Part one, the **analysis of changes in working capital,** shows the net change in each component of working capital that occurred between the beginning and ending of the year or operating cycle. The net changes are then totaled to arrive at the net increase or decrease in working capital for the year, or within the operating cycle. Part two, the SCFP itself, explains the reasons for the net increase or decrease in working capital, such as working capital provided by operations, long-term borrowings, and sales of capital stock, together with the uses of working capital, such as the purchase of equipment and the payment of dividends. The net result, i.e., the increase or decrease in working capital, is the same for each part.

When the SCFP is prepared using the cash basis, it is similar to one prepared using a working capital basis except that the statement only consists of one part. Except for the change in cash, all of the other changes in the components of working capital shown in the analysis of changes in working capital schedule are shown in the SCFP. This practice obviates the need for a two-part statement.

GLOSSARY OF KEY TERMS

All-resources concept A SCFP that shows all the firm's significant financing and investing activities on the statement, including exchanges that do not involve working capital (or cash).

Analysis of changes in working capital A schedule showing the increase or decrease effect on working capital for each component of working capital. The schedule is a part of the SCFP.

Current assets Cash and other assets that are reasonably expected to be converted into cash, or sold or consumed, within one year or within the firm's operating cycle, whichever is longer.

Current liabilities Debts or other obligations that must be liquidated within one year or within the firm's operating cycle.

Statement of changes in financial position (SCFP) A statement providing information regarding the sources and uses of working capital or cash over a period of time as well as information about major financing and investing activities that do not involve sources and uses of working capital or cash.

Statement of sources and uses of cash A statement explaining the reasons for increases and decreases of cash over a given period of time.

Statement of sources and uses of working capital (funds) A statement explaining the change in the level of working capital between two dates by listing the factors that contributed to its increase and those that brought about its decrease.

Working capital A firm's current assets minus its current liabilities.

APPENDIX 16–A

STATEMENT CONVERSION FROM WORKING CAPITAL FOCUS TO CASH FOCUS

In this chapter, we discussed the importance of cash flows and particularly of cash from operations (CFO) as contrasted to working capital from operations (WCFO).

While the trend is rapidly moving in the direction of refocusing of the statement of changes in financial position (SCFP) *from working capital to cash,* many companies still focus on changes in working capital. Moreover, among the companies who focus on cash in preparing the SCFP, many present the conventional funds provided by operations format, which focuses on working capital. In addition, the format used in presenting WCFO or CFO is the net, or indirect, approach that starts with net income (which of course is a net figure that represents neither a source nor a use of any type of funds) rather than the more desirable inflow-outflow or direct format.[8]

The Inflow-Outflow Format

The most useful way to compute CFO is to show the elements of revenue that generate cash and the costs that use cash (the *inflow-outflow* format)

---

[8] AICPA's *Accounting Trends & Techniques* reported that in 1980, 517 of 600 companies surveyed used the net or indirect approach in presenting WCFO or CFO.

rather than to adjust net income for noncash affecting items (the *net* format).

The first step is to identify and list all elements of income and cost *that affect* working capital. The second step is to adjust these for changes in *working capital items* (other than cash) that are *assumed* to affect operations. Thus:

From cash inflows:
Starting with sales
  + Decrease (− increase) in accounts receivable
  = Cash collections on sales
  + Other revenues (+ or − adjustments for noncash items)
  = Total cash collections from operations

Deduct cash outflows:
Cost of goods sold* (e.g., *excluding* depreciation, amortization, etc.)
Operating costs*
  Other costs (including interest)
  + Increase (− decrease) in inventories
  + Decrease (− increase) in trade payables
  + Increase (− decrease) in prepaid costs
  + Decrease (− increase) in accrued liabilities
Income taxes* (e.g. excluding deferred taxes—noncurrent)
  + Decrease (− increase) in accrued taxes
  = Total cash outflows for operations
Result: Cash from or for operations (CFO)

* Excluding items which don't affect cash.

ILLUSTRATION 16–12

VATTER COMPANY
Direct Conversion of WCFO to CFO for 19x2
(in thousands)

Sales	$19,950	
Less: Increase in receivables	90	
Cash collections		$19,860
Cash outflows:		
Cost of goods sold	11,101	
Less: Depreciation	360	
	10,741	
Add: Increase in inventories	303	
	11,044	
Marketing and administrative costs	7,000	
Less: Increase in accounts payable	(230)	17,814
Income taxes—current		900
Total cash outflows		18,714
Cash from operations (CFO)		$ 1,146

Using the financial statements of the Vatter Company shown in Illustrations 16–4 and 16–5, the direct (or mental) form of preparation is shown in Illustration 16–12. The simplicity of these financial statements makes this approach appropriate.

For the sake of consistency with prior presentations, the $2,000 gain on sale of fixed assets was omitted from the CFO computation. The omission, as was noted before, is intended to link it with the proceeds from the sale of equipment as an "other" rather than "operating" source of cash.

The Net Format

The net format of converting WCFO to CFO is easier to compute. The approach is:

I. Start with working capital provided by operations.

II. *Add* the amount of *change* in working capital accounts (other than cash) that experienced a net *credit* change for the period. That is, reductions in current assets* (other than cash) or increases in current liabilities,* all of which increases the amount of available cash.

III. *Deduct* the amount of *change* in working capital accounts (other than cash) that experienced a net *debit* change during the period. That is, increases in current assets* (other than cash) and decreases in current liabilities,* all of which decreases the amount of available cash.

IV. The result is net cash flow from operations.

---

* Excluding nonoperating items such as changes in marketable securities, which are not cash equivalents, bank loans, and dividends payable.

The application of the above approach to the Vatter Company figures is as follows (in thousands):

Working capital provided by operation (WCFO) ..		$1,309
Add: Increase in accounts payable (net credit) . . .		230
		1,539
Deduct: Increase in receivables (net debit)	$ 90	
Increase in inventories (net debit)	303	393
Cash from operations (CFO)		$1,146

The "net format" should be used when only the CFO figure is desired and the detail of how it is obtained is not important to the user. It can also be used as a quick check on the CFO computation under the inflow-outflow format.

The above techniques can be used to convert an entire SCFP from a working capital basis to a cash basis. In such a conversion, those accounts (other than cash) that do not affect operations (e.g., loans payable, dividends payable) are used to adjust nonoperating sources and uses in order to arrive at their net cash effect.

ILLUSTRATION 16–13

THE VATTER COMPANY
Statement of Changes in Financial Position
For the Year Ended December 31, 19x2

Sources of cash:

From operations:

Cash collections from sales			$19,860,000
Less:			
Cash payments for cost of			
goods sold	$10,814,000		
Cash payments for marketing			
and administrative costs	7,000,000		
Current income taxes	900,000	18,714,000	
Cash provided by operations		1,146,000	
Sale of fixed assets		18,000	
Investment income		50,000	
Net proceeds of sale of bonds		500,000	
Issuance of bonds in exchange of			
fixed assets		100,000	
Issuance of stock for conversion			
of bonds		200,000	
Sale of capital stock		1,000,000	1,868,000
			3,014,000
Decrease in cash			120,000
			$ 3,134,000

Uses of cash:

Purchase of fixed assets*		$ 1,974,000	
Purchase of intangibles		60,000	
Fixed assets acquired for bonds		100,000	
Purchase of marketable securities		50,000	
Retirement of debentures on			
conversion into capital stock		200,000	
Payment of dividends		750,000	$ 3,134,000

* $450,000 + $1,524,000.

Once the CFO of $1,146,000 is reached, either by the direct method or the net method, the remainder of the SCFP—cash focus would appear as shown in Illustration 16–10. A completed SCFP—cash focus, using the direct method, appears in Illustration 16–13.

QUESTIONS

1. What information can the user of financial statements obtain from the SCFP?

2. Which are the two major concepts of liquidity commonly used in the preparation of the SCFP?

3. While the SCFP focuses normally on changes of working capital or cash, it also includes transactions that affect neither. Give two examples of such transactions.

4. In addition to depreciation, what are some other examples of costs not requiring the outlay of cash or working capital? What are examples of income items not bringing in cash or working capital?

5. Could the form in which revenues are received affect the SCFP?

6. *APB Opinion No. 19* states that stock dividends and split-ups are not required to be disclosed in the SCFP. What is the reason for this exception? Would the conversion of preferred stock into common be shown in the SCFP?

7. Why is there increasing interest in the cash focus in the preparation of the SCFP?

8. *a.* How can the technique of preparing the cash focus SCFP be viewed?
   b. What effect do changes in the working capital accounts have on operations?

9. Contrast the concept of income with those of working capital from operations and cash from operations.

10. A member of the board of directors of a company that faces a shortage of funds in the coming year is told that none of the sources of funds available in the preceding year can be increased. He thereupon suggests increasing the amount shown as "depreciation" in the "sources" section of the funds statement. Comment on his suggestion.

11. A prominent academician wrote some years ago: "Just as in the first half of this century we saw the income statement displace the balance sheet in importance, so we may now be deemphasising the income statement in favour of a statement of fund flows or cash flows. . . . My own guess is that, so far as the history of accounting is concerned, the next 25 years may subsequently be seen to have been the twilight of income measurement."
   Comment on this prediction.

Appendix 16–A

12. *a.* What are the underlying principles and assumptions in the conversion of WCFO to CFO?
    b. Contrast the inflow-outflow approach of conversion to the net approach under the direct conversion method.

EXERCISES

16–1 Preparation of an Analysis of Changes in Working Capital

Baxter Company's current asset and current liability sections of its balance sheets for the two preceding years are as follows:

	December 31	
	19x4	19x3
Current assets:		
Cash	$ 12,908	$ 13,506
Accounts receivable	211,714	219,868
Inventory	395,722	254,180
Prepaid costs	42,444	42,800
Total current assets	$662,788	$530,354
Current liabilities:		
Accounts payable	$234,108	$185,126
Wages payable	74,074	65,630
Income taxes payable	69,698	54,126
Total current liabilities	$377,880	$304,882

Required Prepare an analysis of changes in working capital.

16–2 Preparation of an Analysis of Changes in Working Capital

Conklin Company's account balances for selected accounts are as follows:

	December 31	
	19x6	19x5
Debits		
Accounts receivable	$ 310,986	$ 290,680
Cash	540,380	10,420
Inventory	307,520	362,849
Prepaid costs	39,670	38,540
Property, plant, and equipment	4,101,235	3,772,331
Credits		
Accounts payable	136,590	105,992
Accumulated depreciation	967,655	836,158
Allowance for doubtful accounts	15,032	12,232
Income taxes payable	48,968	4,476
Notes payable—current	–0–	120,000
Wages payable	90,272	88,820

Required Prepare an analysis of changes in working capital.

16–3 Preparation of SCFP—Working Capital Focus

The Doreen Company presents you with the following data:

	December 31	
	19x2	19x1
Debits		
Current assets	$ 600,000	$ 520,000
Property, plant, and equipment . . .	987,000	800,000
Intangibles	400,000	400,000
Total	$1,987,000	$1,720,000
Credits		
Accumulated depreciation—		
property, plant, and equipment . .	$ 230,000	$ 200,000
Accumulated amortization—		
intangibles	60,000	40,000
Current liabilities	280,000	300,000
Bonds payable	250,000	250,000
Premium on bonds payable	27,000	30,000
Preferred stock	200,000	200,000
Common stock	400,000	300,000
Additional paid-in capital—		
common stock	20,000	–0–
Retained earnings	520,000	400,000
Total	$1,987,000	$1,720,000

An analysis of the company's Retained Earnings account produced the following:

Retained earnings—January 1, 19x2	$400,000
Add: Net income	150,000
Subtotal	550,000
Less: Cash dividends	30,000
Retained earnings—December 31, 19x2 ..	$520,000

There were no sales, trade-ins, or disposals of any property, plant, and equipment.

Required *a.* Compute the net change in working capital for the year. (It is not necessary to prepare an analysis of changes in working capital.)

b. Prepare a SCFP using a working capital focus.

16–4 Preparation of SCFP—Working Capital Focus

The Edward Company presents you with the following data:

	December 31	
	19x3	**19x2**
Debits		
Current assets	$ 440,000	$ 300,000
Property, plant, and equipment . . .	1,160,000	1,080,000
Treasury stock	100,000	–0–
Total	$1,700,000	$1,380,000
Credits		
Accumulated depreciation	$ 290,000	$ 250,000
Current liabilities	180,000	160,000
Long-term notes payable	200,000	150,000
Common stock	450,000	400,000
Additional paid-in capital	200,000	120,000
Retained earnings	380,000	300,000
Total	$1,700,000	$1,380,000

An analysis of the company's Retained Earnings account produced the following:

Retained earnings—January 1, 19x3	$300,000
Add: Net income	170,000
Subtotal	470,000
Less: Cash dividends	90,000
Retained earnings—December 31, 19x3 . . .	$380,000

There were no sales, trade-ins, or disposals of any property, plant, and equipment.

Required   *a.*   Compute the net change in working capital for the year. (It is not necessary to prepare an analysis of changes in working capital.)

        b.   Prepare a SCFP using a working capital focus.

16–5   **Computations for Use in a SCFP—Working Capital Focus**

1.   Selected information from the 19x6 accounting records of the Soccer Company is as follows:

Working capital provided from operations	$ 2,000,000
Collection of short-term receivables	40,000,000
Payments of accounts payable	30,000,000
Capital expenditures	2,800,000
Proceeds from long-term borrowings	1,500,000
Payments on long-term borrowings	500,000
Dividends on common stock	900,000
Purchases of treasury stock	200,000
Sales of stock to officers and employees	100,000
Working capital at December 31, 19x5	18,000,000

Assuming funds are defined as working capital, what should be the working capital at December 31, 19x6, shown on Soccer's statement of changes in financial position for the year ended December 31, 19x6?

a. $17,200,000.
b. $17,300,000.
c. $18,200,000.
d. $27,200,000

2. The net income for the year ended December 31, 19x9, for Diamond Company was $2.5 million. Additional information is as follows:

Depreciation of fixed assets	$2,900,000
Dividends paid on preferred stock	200,000
Long-term debt:	
Bond discount amortization	50,000
Interest	800,000
Provision for deferred income taxes	250,000
Amortization of goodwill	90,000

What should be the working capital provided from operations in the statement of changes in financial position for the year ended December 31, 19x9?
a. $5,490,000.
b. $5,540,000.
c. $5,790,000.
d. $5,990,000.

3. The following information was taken from the accounting records of Oregon Corporation for 19x9:

Proceeds from issuance of preferred stock	$4,000,000
Dividends paid on preferred stock	400,000
Bonds payable converted to common stock	2,000,000
Purchases of treasury stock, common	500,000
Sale of plant building	1,200,000
2 percent stock dividend on common stock	300,000

Oregon's statement of changes in financial position for the year ended December 31, 19x9, should show the following sources and uses of funds, based on the information above

	Sources	Uses
a.	$5,200,000	$1,200,000
b.	$5,500,000	$1,200,000
c.	$7,200,000	$2,900,000
d.	$7,500,000	$3,200,000

(AICPA adapted)

16–6 Computations for Use in a SCFP—Working Capital Focus and Cash Focus

Aaron Corporation's comparative statement of financial position as of December 31, 19x3, and 19x2 is presented below. Additional information regarding Aaron's activities during 19x3 follows the statement.

AARON CORPORATION
Comparative Statement of Financial Position
December 31, 19x3, and 19x2

	19x3	19x2
Assets		
Cash	$ 130,000	$ 100,000
Accounts receivable	480,000	400,000
Inventory	600,000	600,000
Property, plant, and equipment	2,000,000	1,000,000
Less: Accumulated depreciation	(400,000)	(400,000)
Long-term investments	100,000	200,000
Intangibles	90,000	100,000
Total assets	$3,000,000	$2,000,000
Liabilities and Stockholders' Equity		
Accounts payable	$ 240,000	$ 200,000
Bonds payable	1,000,000	1,000,000
Less: Unamortized discount	(30,000)	(50,000)
Common stock	500,000	400,000
Retained earnings	1,290,000	450,000
Total liabilities and stockholders' equity	$3,000,000	$2,000,000

Additional Data

- Dividends of $250,000 were declared and paid in 19x3.
- Equipment that had cost $400,000 was sold in 19x3 for $150,000. The accumulated depreciation to the date of sale was $200,000.
- Long-term investments were sold in 19x3 for $120,000. There were no other transactions regarding long-term investments.

1. During 19x3, Aaron Corporation's working capital
   a. Increased $150,000.
   b. Decreased $70,000.
   c. Increased $70,000.
   d. Increased $110,000.
   e. Changed by some amount other than those given above.
2. The 19x3 net income (loss) for Aaron Corporation was
   a. $590,000.
   b. $1,090,000.
   c. $940,000.
   d. $840,000.
   e. Some amount other than those given above.
3. Working capital provided by operations during 19x3 was
   a. $1,120,000.
   b. $1,290,000.
   c. $1,320,000.
   d. $1,350,000.
   e. Some amount other than those given above.
4. Cash provided by operations during 19x3 was

    a. $30,000.
    b. $230,000.
    c. $1,310,000.
    d. $1,350,000.
    e. $1,270,000.

5. Working capital provided during 19x3 by sources other than operations was
    a. $370,000.
    b. $270,000.
    c. $250,000.
    d. $220,000.
    e. Some amount other than those given above.

6. Working capital applied during 19x3 totaled
    a. $1,670,000.
    b. $1,650,000.
    c. $1,400,000.
    d. $250,000.
    e. Some amount other than those given above.

(CMA adapted)

16–7 SCFP—Working Capital Focus

The statement of changes in financial position is normally a required basic financial statement for each period for which an earnings statement is presented. The reporting entity has flexibility in form, content, and terminology of this statement to meet the objectives of differing circumstances. For example, the concept of "funds" may be interpreted to mean, among other things, cash or working capital. However, the statement should be prepared based on the "all financial resources" concept.

Required
  a. What is the "all financial resources" concept?
  b. What are two types of financial transactions that would be disclosed under the all financial resources concept that would not be disclosed without this concept?
  c. What effect, if any, would each of the following seven items have upon the preparation of a statement of changes in financial position prepared in accordance with generally accepted accounting principles using the cash concept of funds?
    (1) Accounts receivable—trade.
    (2) Inventory.
    (3) Depreciation.
    (4) Deferred income tax credit from interperiod allocation.
    (5) Issuance of long-term debt in payment for a building.
    (6) Payoff of current portion of debt.
    (7) Sale of a fixed asset resulting in a loss.

(AICPA adapted)

16–8 SCFP—Working Capital Focus: Effects of Transactions

Chen Engineering Company is a young and growing producer of electronic measuring instruments and technical equipment. You have been retained by Chen to advise it in the preparation of a statement of changes in financial position. For the fiscal year ended October 31, 19x5, you have obtained the following information concerning certain events and transactions of Chen.

1. The amount of reported earnings for the fiscal year was $800,000, which included a deduction for an extraordinary loss of $93,000 (See item 5 below).
2. Depreciation of $240,000 was included in the earnings statement.

3. Uncollectible accounts receivable of $30,000 were written off against the allowance for uncollectible accounts. Also, $37,000 of bad debts was included in determining earnings for the fiscal year, and the same amount was added to the allowance for uncollectible accounts.

4. A gain of $4,700 was realized on the sale of a machine; it orginally cost $75,000 of which $25,000 was undepreciated on the date of sale.

5. On April 1, 19x5, a freak lightning storm caused an uninsured inventory loss of $93,000 ($180,000 loss, less reduction in income taxes of $87,000). This extraordinary loss was included in determining earnings as indicated in (1) above.

6. On July 3, 19x5, building and land were purchased for $600,000; Chen gave in payment $100,000 cash, $200,000 market value of its unissued common stock, and a $300,000 purchase-money mortgage.

7. On August 3, 19x5, $700,000 face value of Chen's 6 percent convertible debentures were converted into $140,000 par value of its common stock. The bonds were originally issued at face value.

8. The board of directors declared a $320,000 cash dividend on October 20, 19x5, payable on November 15, 19x5, to stockholders of record on November 5, 19x5.

Required For each of the eight numbered items above, explain whether each item is a source or use of working capital and explain how it should be disclosed in Chen's statement of changes in financial position for the fiscal year ended October 31, 19x5. If any item is neither a source nor a use of working capital, explain why it is *not* and indicate the disclosure, if any, that should be made of the item in Chen's statement of changes in financial position for the fiscal year ended October 31, 19x5.

(AICPA adapted)

16–9 Effects of Transactions

For each of the following transactions, use the all-resources concept to determine if it is a source of working capital (SW), a use of working capital (UW), a source of cash (SC), a use of cash (UC), or determine if it has no effect on working capital (NW), or no effect on cash (NC).

1. Purchased inventory on account for $100,000.
2. Purchased treasury stock for $150,000 cash.
3. Paid for the merchandise in (1).
4. Purchased equipment for $50,000 by issuing a one-year note payable.
5. Purchased land by issuing common stock in the amount of $200,000.
6. Collected $150,000 of accounts receivable.
7. Declared a cash dividend of $80,000, but did not pay it.
8. Declared a stock split by issuing to stockholders one additional share for each share held (a 2-for-1 split).
9. Paid the cash dividend in (7).
10. Amortized bond discount for $2,000.
11. Refinanced $1 million of bonds payable by issuing a like amount at a lower interest rate.
12. Sold equipment with a book value of $10,000 for $6,000 cash.
13. Interest cost of $40,000 was recorded as payable but not paid.
14. Recorded depreciation of $210,000.
15. Exchanged a piece of heavy-duty machinery for three delivery trucks.

Required For each number (1 through 15), insert a parenthetical designation. A transaction may require more than one designation.

16–10   Preparation of Working Capital Provided by Operations

The following is the income statement of NYC Corporation for the year ended December 31, 19x0.

NYC CORPORATION
Income Statement
For the Year Ended December 31, 19x0
(in thousands)

Revenues:
Sales	$2,690	
Gain on sale of machinery	20	
Gain on bond retirement	65	
Total revenues		$2,775

Costs and other deductions:
Cost of goods sold	1,350	
Marketing and administrative costs	757	
Depreciation	45	
Interest*	33	
Total deductions		2,185
Income before taxes		590

Income taxes:
Current	165	
Deferred	115	280
Net income		$ 310

In preparing its SCFP, NYC Corporation shows *total* proceeds from sales of fixed assets as sources of funds.
   * Interest includes bond discount amortization, $8,000.

Required   Compute working capital provided by operations during 19x0.

16–11   Effects of Transactions

The ability to visualize quickly the effect of a given transaction on the working capital (or cash) resources of an enterprise is a valuable skill. Such visualization requires an understanding of the reality behind the transaction as well as how it is accounted for. Expressing such accounting in journal entry form is the most helpful approach.

A simplified schematic statement of changes in financial position of a company for the year is shown below. The company closes its books once each year, on December 31.

Nine of the lines in the schematic shown below are given labels (letters). For each of the activities listed, identify which of these nine lines is affected and by *how much*. Use the labels (letters) shown below. Do not indicate the effect on any line not given a label. If a transaction has no effect, write *none*. In indicating effects for lines Y and WC, use a + to indicate an increase and a − to indicate a decrease. Be sure to show the amount!

Note: Every item with an effect affects at least two lines (Debits must equal credits.)

Schematic Statement of Changes in Financial Position of the Company for the Year

Sources of working capital:

(Y)   Net income .... _____(Y)

(YA) Additions or addbacks for cost, losses, etc.,
       not using working capital .... _____(YA)

(YS) Subtractions for revenues, gains, etc., not
       producing working capital .... _____(YS)

      Total sources from operations =
        $Y + YA - YS$ .... _____

(DE) Proceeds of debt and equity issues .... _____(DE)

(AD) Proceeds of long-term asset dispositions .... _____(AD)

      Total sources .... _____

Uses of working capital:

(ID) Income distributions .... _____(ID)

(R)   Retirements of debt and equity .... _____(R)

(AA) Long-term assets acquisitions .... _____(AA)

      Total uses .... _____

(WC) Increase (decrease) in working capital for year .... _____(WC)

Illustrations:

  0. Sales of $10,000 are made on account.

 00. Dividends of $4,000 are declared.

    Answers:

      0. +WC 10,000   +Y 10,000

     00.   ID   4,000 −WC 4,000

1. Inventories that originally cost $10,000 have been used by production departments in producing finished goods that have been sold for $15,000 in cash and $5,000 in accounts receivable.
2. Accounts receivable of $8,000 are written off. There is an allowance for doubtful accounts balance of $5,000 only.
3. The company acquired a long-lived asset for $100,000 in cash. Of that amount, the company decided to amortize $20,000 this year and to amortize $10,000 in the following eight consecutive years.
4. A machine that costs $15,000 and had an accumulated depreciation of $10,000 is sold for $8,000 in cash.
5. Treasury stock with a cost of $7,000 is retired and canceled.
6. The company has outstanding 50,000 shares of common stock with par value of $1. The company declared a 20 percent stock dividend at the end of the year when the stock was selling for $16 a share.
7. Inventory costing $12,000 has been destroyed by fire. The insurance company paid only $10,000 for that loss, although the market value of the inventory was $15,000.
8. The company bought a patent for $25,000 in cash. This amount will be amortized over five years—beginning next year.
9. Depreciation of $16,000 was charged to cost of goods sold.
10. A building was acquired by issuance of a long-term mortgage note for $100,000, the first payment of $10,000 being due 10 months from now.

Required   For each of the 10 transactions, analyze each one as shown in the illustration.

16–12 Preparation of SCFP—Working Capital Focus

The following financial statements and data relate to the Debbie Dress Shops, Inc.

DEBBIE DRESS SHOPS, INC.
Balance Sheets

	December 31	
	19x1	19x0
Assets		
Current assets:		
Cash	$ 300,000	$ 200,000
Accounts receivable—net	840,000	580,000
Merchandise inventory	660,000	420,000
Prepaid costs	100,000	50,000
Total current assets	1,900,000	1,250,000
Long-term investments	80,000	—
Land, buildings, and fixtures	1,130,000	600,000
Less: Accumulated depreciation	110,000	50,000
	1,020,000	550,000
Total assets	$3,000,000	$1,800,000
Equities		
Current liabilities:		
Accounts payable	$ 530,000	$ 440,000
Accrued liabilities	140,000	130,000
Dividends payable	70,000	—
Total current liabilities	740,000	570,000
Note payable—due 19x3	500,000	—
Stockholders' equity:		
Common stock	1,200,000	900,000
Retained earnings	560,000	330,000
	1,760,000	1,230,000
Total liabilities and stockholders' equity	$3,000,000	$1,800,000

DEBBIE DRESS SHOPS, INC.
Income Statements

	Year Ended December 31	
	19x1	19x0
Net credit sales	$6,400,000	$4,000,000
Cost of goods sold	5,000,000	3,200,000
Gross profit	1,400,000	800,000
Other costs (including income taxes)	1,000,000	520,000
Net income	$ 400,000	$ 280,000

Additional information available included the following:

1. All accounts receivable and accounts payable relate to trade merchandise. Accounts payable are recorded net and always are paid to take all of the discount allowed. The allowance for doubtful accounts at the end of 19x1 was the same as at the end of 19x0; no receivables were charged against the allowance during 19x1.
2. The proceeds from the note payable were used to finance a new store building. Capital stock was sold to provide additional working capital.

There were no sales, trade-ins, or exchanges of land, buildings, and fixtures, except for the note payable transaction noted above.

Required   *a.* Prepare an analysis of changes in working capital.
             b. Prepare a SCFP—working capital focus.

(AICPA adapted)

16–13   Preparation of SCFP—Cash Focus

Refer to the data contained in Exercise 16–12.

Required   Prepare a SCFP—cash focus.

16–14   Preparation of SCFP—Cash Focus

The Fredrick Company's balance sheets are shown below (in thousands of dollars).

	December 31	
	19x8	**19x7**
Assets		
Current assets:		
Cash	$ 14,522	$ 20,962
Accounts receivable	91,314	79,328
Inventory	73,632	67,622
Prepaid costs	7,680	6,954
Total current assets	187,148	174,866
Property, plant, and equipment:		
Land	3,698	3,698
Building	34,142	32,988
Machinery and equipment	66,808	57,952
Total	104,648	94,638
Less: Accumulated depreciation	44,210	37,828
Total property, plant, and equipment	60,438	56,810
Total assets	$247,586	$231,676

Liabilities and Stockholders' Equity

Current liabilities:

Accounts payable	$ 42,844	$ 40,490
Wages payable	4,651	3,787
Income taxes payable	7,198	4,596
Total current liabilities	54,693	48,873

Long-term liabilities:

Bonds payable	45,000	40,000
Premium on bonds payable	2,180	2,420
Total long-term liabilities	47,180	42,420

Stockholders' equity:

Common stock	37,500	32,500
Additional paid-in capital	50,800	44,600
Retained earnings	57,413	63,283
Total stockholders' equity	145,713	140,383
Total liabilities and stockholders' equity	$247,586	$231,676

An analysis of the company's Retained Earnings account produced the following:

Retained earnings—January 1, 19x8	$63,283
Add: Net income	2,130
Subtotal	65,413
Less: Cash dividends	8,000
Retained earnings—December 31, 19x8	$57,413

There were no sales, trade-ins, or disposals of any property, plant, and equipment. Bonds sold during the year were sold at par.

Required   Prepare a SCFP—cash focus.

16–15   **Preparation of SCFP—Cash Focus**

The Garrett Company presents you with the following data:

	December 31	
	19x5	**19x4**
Debits		
Accounts receivable—net	$ 240,000	$260,000
Cash	80,000	100,000
Inventory	130,000	110,000
Prepaid marketing and administrative costs	10,000	9,000
Property, plant, and equipment	520,000	480,000
Treasury stock	270,000	–0–
Total	$1,250,000	$959,000

Credits

Accumulated depreciation	$ 240,000	$210,000
Accounts payable	120,000	80,000
Long-term notes payable	175,000	100,000
Common stock	400,000	300,000
Additional paid-in capital	105,000	80,000
Retained earnings	210,000	189,000
Total	$1,250,000	$959,000

An analysis of the company's Retained Earnings account produced the following:

Retained earnings—January 1, 19x5	$189,000
Add: Net income	101,000
Subtotal	290,000
Less: Cash dividends	80,000
Retained earnings—December 31, 19x5	$210,000

There were no sales, trade-ins, or disposals of any property, plant, and equipment.

Required   Prepare a SCFP—cash focus.

16–16   **(Appendix 16–A): Preparation of SCFP—Cash Focus (Inflow-Outflow Approach)**

The Garrett Company's income statement for 19x5 is as follows:

GARRETT COMPANY
Income Statement
For the Year Ended December 31, 19x5

Sales	$1,500,000
Cost of goods sold	900,000
Gross margin	600,000
Marketing and administrative costs	450,000
Income before income taxes	150,000
Income taxes	49,000
Net income	$ 101,000

Required   Using the information provided in Exercise 16–15 together with the above income statement, prepare a SCFP—cash focus, using the inflow-outflow approach.

16–17   **(Appendix 16–A): Preparation of SCFP—Cash Focus (Inflow-Outflow Approach)**

The Harrod Company provides you with the following:

HARROD COMPANY
Income Statement
For the Year Ended December 31, 19x6

Sales	$2,000,000
Cost of goods sold	800,000
Gross margin	1,200,000
Marketing and administrative costs	600,000
Income before income taxes	600,000
Income taxes	240,000
Net income	$ 360,000

	December 31	
	19x6	**19x5**
Debits		
Accounts receivable—net	$ 210,000	$180,000
Cash	100,000	80,000
Inventory	120,000	110,000
Prepaid marketing and administrative costs	10,000	12,000
Property, plant, and equipment	580,000	480,000
Treasury stock	110,000	–0–
Total	$1,130,000	$862,000
Credits		
Accumulated depreciation	$ 300,000	$260,000
Accounts payable	110,000	80,000
Long-term notes payable	75,000	100,000
Common stock	360,000	300,000
Additional paid-in capital	85,000	50,000
Retained earnings	200,000	72,000
Total	$1,130,000	$862,000

An analysis of the company's Retained Earnings account produced the following:

Retained earnings—January 1, 19x6		$ 72,000
Add: Net income		360,000
Subtotal		432,000
Less:		
Cash dividends	$137,000	
Stock dividend	95,000	232,000
Retained earnings—December 31, 19x6		$200,000

There were no sales, trade-ins, or disposals of any property, plant, and equipment. There were no sales of common stock. The changes in the common stock and additional paid-in capital accounts stem from the stock dividend.

Required Prepare a SCFP—cash focus, using the inflow-outflow approach.

16–18 **(Appendix 16–A): Preparation of SCFP—Cash Focus (Inflow-Outflow Approach)**

Refer to the data contained in Exercise 16–12.

Required Prepare a SCFP—cash focus, using the inflow-outflow approach.

PROBLEMS 16–19 **Preparation of SCFP—Working Capital Focus**

The James Company provides you with the following:

JAMES COMPANY
Income Statement
For the Year Ended December 31, 19x6

Sales	$2,600,000
Cost of goods sold	1,000,000
Gross margin	1,600,000
Marketing and administrative costs	900,000
Income before income taxes	700,000
Income taxes	280,000
Net income	$ 420,000

	December 31	
	19x6	19x5
Debits		
Accounts receivable, net	$ 180,000	$ 250,000
Cash	75,000	225,000
Intangibles	290,000	300,000
Inventory	180,000	260,000
Investment in affiliate	650,000	–0–
Prepaid marketing and administrative costs	13,000	15,000
Property, plant, and equipment	1,367,000	700,000
Total	$2,755,000	$1,750,000
Credits		
Accumulated depreciation	$ 280,000	$ 200,000
Accounts payable	140,000	80,000
Deferred income tax	80,000	60,000
Long-term notes payable	25,000	100,000
Common stock	500,000	300,000
Additional paid-in capital	825,000	250,000
Retained earnings	905,000	660,000
Wages payable	–0–	100,000
Total	$2,755,000	$1,750,000

An analysis of the company's Retained Earnings account produced the following:

Retained earnings—January 1, 19x6		$ 660,000
Add: Net income		420,000
Subtotal		1,080,000
Less:		
Cash dividends	$ 50,000	
Stock dividend	125,000	175,000
Retained earnings—December 31, 19x6		$ 905,000

There were no sales, trade-ins, or disposals of any property, plant, and equipment.

The changes in the Common Stock and Additional Paid-In Capital accounts arose from the acquisition of shares of stock in an affiliate and the payment of the stock dividend. There were no sales of common stock.

The president of the company, Rita Duggan, is concerned about the decrease in cash to below $200,000 as well as an apparent decrease in working capital. She believes that the company had a satisfactory year from its operations, earning $420,000 after income taxes, and only paying a cash dividend of $50,000. Taking into account the depreciation charge to income that does not require working capital and the fact that the acquisition of the affiliate's shares did not affect the working capital, she would like an explanation of why working capital decreased during 19x6.

Required   *a.*   Prepare a SCFP—working capital focus. (Include an analysis of changes in working capital.)

b.   Write a brief report to the president explaining why working capital decreased.

16–20   Preparation of SCFP—Cash Focus

Refer to the data contained in Problem 16–19.

Required   Prepare a SCFP—cash focus.

16–21   Preparation of SCFP—Working Capital Focus

The Kenneth Company's accounts reflect the following:

KENNETH COMPANY
Balance Sheets
December 31, 19x3, and 19x2

	19x3	19x2
Assets		
Current assets:		
Cash	$ 200,000	$ 120,000
Accounts receivable, net	250,000	200,000
Inventory	280,000	260,000
Prepaid marketing and administrative costs	10,000	15,000
Total current assets	740,000	595,000
Investment in marketable securities	385,000	360,000
Property, plant, and equipment	950,000	920,000
Less: Accumulated depreciation	380,000	300,000
Net property, plant, and equipment	570,000	620,000
Patent	360,000	420,000
Total assets	$2,055,000	$1,995,000

Liabilities and Stockholders' Equity

Current liabilities:

Accounts payable	$ 210,000	$ 190,000
Notes payable	70,000	100,000
Accrued liabilities	85,000	80,000
Total current liabilities	365,000	370,000

Long-term liabilities:

Bonds payable	600,000	400,000
Premium on bonds payable	120,000	90,000
Total long-term liabilities	720,000	490,000

Stockholders' equity:

Preferred stock	100,000	–0–
Common stock	660,000	600,000
Additional paid-in capital	170,000	150,000
Retained earnings	40,000	385,000
Total stockholders' equity	970,000	1,135,000
Total liabilities and stockholders' equity	$2,055,000	$1,995,000

KENNETH COMPANY
Income Statement
For the Year Ended December 31, 19x3

Sales	$4,000,000
Cost of goods sold	2,200,000
Gross margin	1,800,000
Marketing and administrative costs	2,000,000
Operating loss	(200,000)
Add: Investment income	25,000
Net loss	$ (175,000)

An analysis of the company's Retained Earnings account produced the following:

Retained earnings—January 1, 19x3		$ 385,000
Net loss		(175,000)
Subtotal		210,000
Less:		
Cash dividend	$90,000	
Stock dividend	80,000	170,000
Retained earnings—December 31, 19x3		$ 40,000

There were no sales, trade-ins, or disposals of any property, plant, and equipment. There were no sales of common stock. The change in the Common Stock and Additional Paid-In Capital accounts stem from the stock dividend.

During the year, bonds payable with a face value of $200,000 were sold at a premium of $40,000 for a total of $240,000.

A relative of yours received a copy of the Kenneth Company's financial statements and wonders how a company that pays a cash dividend of $90,000 and has a net loss of $175,000 can show an increase in cash and an increase in working capital.

Required   *a.*   Prepare a SCFP—working capital focus. (Include an analysis of changes in working capital.)

         b.   Write a brief report for your relative explaining the increase in working capital.

16–22   Preparation of SCFP—Cash Focus

Refer to the data contained in Problem 16–21.

Required   Prepare a SCFP—cash focus.

16–23   Preparation of SCFP—Working Capital Focus

BEST CORPORATION
Balance Sheets
For the Years Ended December 31, 19x2, and 19x1

	19x2	19x1
Assets		
Current assets:		
Cash	$ 480,000	$ 220,000
Accounts receivable, net	840,000	560,000
Merchandise inventory	760,000	470,000
Total current assets	2,080,000	1,250,000
Land, buildings, and fixtures	1,330,000	800,000
Less: Accumulated depreciation	210,000	150,000
	1,120,000	650,000
Total assets	$3,200,000	$1,900,000
Liabilities and Stockholders' Equity		
Current liabilities:		
Accounts payable	$ 830,000	$ 440,000
Accrued liabilities	300,000	130,000
Dividends payable	40,000	—
Total current liabilities	1,170,000	570,000
Stockholders' equity:		
Common stock ($10 par value)	1,200,000	900,000
Additional paid-in capital	200,000	100,000
Retained earnings	630,000	330,000
Total stockholders' equity	2,030,000	1,330,000
Total liabilities and stockholders' equity	$3,200,000	$1,900,000

BEST CORPORATION
Income Statements
For the Years Ended December 31, 19x2, and 19x1

	19x2	19x1
Credit sales	$6,300,000	$4,000,000
Cost of goods sold	4,900,000	3,200,000
Gross profit	1,400,000	800,000
Other costs (including income taxes)	700,000	630,000
Net income	$ 700,000	$ 170,000

BEST CORPORATION
Changes in Stockholders' Equity
For the Years Ended December 31, 19x2, and 19x1

	19x2	19x1
Common stock:		
Balance, 1/1	$ 900,000	$ 900,000
Sold, 4/1/x2	100,000	—
20% stock dividend, 6/1/x2	200,000	—
Balance, 12/31	$1,200,000	$ 900,000
Additional paid-in capital:		
Balance, 1/1	$ 100,000	$ 100,000
Sold, 4/1/x2	25,000	—
20% stock dividend, 6/1/x2	75,000	—
Balance, 12/31	$ 200,000	$ 100,000
Retained earnings:		
Balance, 1/1	$ 330,000	$ 250,000
Net income	700,000	170,000
Cash dividends	(125,000)	(90,000)
Stock dividends	(275,000)	—
Balance, 12/31	$ 630,000	$ 330,000

Additional available information included the following:

1. Although Best will report all changes in financial position, management has adopted a format emphasizing the flow of working capital.

2. During 19x2, Best sold, at a $10,000 loss, fixtures with a book value of $30,000 ($100,000 cost minus $70,000 accumulated depreciation). This loss was included in the income statement. Depreciation for 19x2 was $130,000. Best purchased $630,000 of new fixtures during 19x2.

3. Common stock issued during 19x2 was as follows:

Date	Number of Shares
4/1/x2	10,000
6/1/x2	20,000

Required *a.* Prepare an analysis of changes in working capital.
    b. Prepare a SCFP—working capital focus.

(AICPA adapted)

16–24 Preparation of SCFP—Cash Focus

Refer to the data contained in Problem 16–23.

Required Prepare a SCFP—cash focus.

16–25 Preparation of SCFP—Working Capital Focus and Cash Focus

An investor concerned by the decline in both the cash and the working capital of the Fluid Corporation hands you the following data:

FLUID CORPORATION
Comparative Balance Sheets
As of December 31, 19x3, and 19x2
(in thousands)

	19x3	19x2
Assets		
Current assets:		
Cash	$ 50	$ 450
Accounts receivable	1,000	750
Inventories	500	450
Prepaid costs	300	350
Total current assets	1,850	2,000
Property, plant, and equipment	4,000	3,250
Less: Accumulated depreciation	(850)	(550)
Patents	200	300
Total assets	$5,200	$ 5,000
Liabilities and Stockholders' Equity		
Current liabilities:		
Accounts payable	$ 500	$ 400
Notes payable	250	250
Accrued liabilities	400	350
Total current liabilities	1,150	1,000
Bonds payable	1,000	1,400
Common stock	2,700	2,300
Retained earnings	350	300
Total liabilities and stockholders' equity	$5,200	$ 5,000

FLUID CORPORATION
Income Statement
For the Year Ended December 31, 19x3

Sales		$20,000
Cost of goods sold		15,000
Gross profit		5,000
Depreciation ($400) and patent amortization ($100)	$ 500	
Marketing and administrative costs	2,650	
Other costs	1,700	4,850
Income from operations		150
Add: Gain on sale of equipment ($200) net of loss on land		100
		250
Interest cost		150
Pretax income		100
Income taxes (50 percent)		50
Net income		$ 50

Additional information:

1. Equipment originally costing $500,000 was sold for $600,000.
2. Land with an original cost of $250,000 was sold for $150,000.

3. Convertible bonds in the amount of 400,000 were converted into $400,000 of common stock.

Required   a. Prepare a statement of changes in financial position (working capital focus) using the T-account method. Show full proceeds from sales of property as "other" sources.

b. Prepare a statement of changes in financial position (cash focus) using the T-account method and on the same basis as the SCFP in (a) above.

16-26   **Reconstruction of a Balance Sheet from a SCFP—Working Capital Focus**

While on an urgent assignment, you discover to your dismay that you have left behind the balance sheet of Zeta Corporation as of January 1, 19x0. You realize that you do have the following data on that company:

ZETA CORPORATION
Post-Closing Trial Balance
December 31, 19x0

Debit balances:

Current assets	$ 350,000
Property, plant, and equipment	550,000
Other noncurrent investments	200,000
Total	$1,100,000

Credit balances:

Current liabilities	$ 180,000
Accumulated depreciation	270,000
Long-term debt	200,000
Common stock	300,000
Retained earnings	150,000
Total	$1,100,000

ZETA CORPORATION
Statement of Changes in Financial Position
For the Year Ended December 31, 19x0

Sources of working capital:

From operations:

Net income		$150,000
Add: Charges and losses not using working capital:		
Depreciation	$85,000	
Loss on sale of equipment	5,000	90,000
		240,000
Deduct: Revenues and gains not producing working capital:		
Gains on sale of noncurrent investments		50,000
Working capital provided by operations		190,000
Other sources:		
From issuance of common stock		10,000
From issuance of long-term debt		15,000
From sale of equipment		10,000
From sale of investments		95,000
Total sources of working capital		320,000

Uses of working capital:

Cash dividends on common stocks	80,000
Purchase of plant and equipment	150,000
Total uses of working capital	230,000
Increase in working capital for the year	$ 90,000

Additional information:

1. The equipment which has been sold had accumulated depreciation of $50,000.
2. On January 1, 19x0, total current assets were $250,000.

Required Reconstruct the T accounts of Zeta Corporation by use of the above data and information. Use the T accounts to prepare the balance sheet of Zeta Corporation as of January 1, 19x0, which you so urgently need.

16–27 (Appendix 16–A): Preparation of SCFP—Cash Focus (Inflow-Outflow Approach)

Refer to the data contained in Problem 16–21.

Required Prepare a SCFP—cash focus, using the inflow-outflow approach.

16–28 (Appendix 16–A): Preparation of SCFP—Cash Focus (Inflow-Outflow Approach)

Refer to the data contained in Problem 16–23.

Required Prepare a SCFP—cash focus, using the inflow-outflow approach.

17

■ ANALYSIS OF FINANCIAL STATEMENTS

LEARNING OBJECTIVES	After reading this chapter, you should be able to:
	1 Explain how different groups of financial statement users depend on financial statement analysis.
	2 Discuss the principal tools used by analysts of financial statements.
	3 Prepare comparative financial statements showing year-to-year changes in absolute dollars and in percentages and indicate how these statements are used.
	4 Convert selected financial-statement data into an index-number trend series and interpret the results of the data.
	5 Transform absolute-dollar financial statements into common-size statements and explain how the results help financial statement users.
	6 Compute the ratios used to determine the status of a firm's short-term liquidity and explain their significance.
	7 Calculate the ratios that determine a firm's capital structure and long-term solvency and discuss how the ratios are used.
	8 Illustrate the ratios used for return on investment analysis.
	9 Compute various market ratios and measures and indicate their importance to users of financial statements.

Managers, stockholders, potential investors, creditors, financial analysts, employees, and their representatives are the major users of a firm's financial statements. Since financial statements are prepared using a historical cost framework, the statements represent a summary of past transactions. While external users may be interested in historical results to evaluate the company's past performance, their main focus is future oriented, i.e., how well the company will perform in the future. Management's concerns are also future oriented. Thus, statement users must use various analytical tools in order to make inferences from historical financial statements regarding a firm's future expected performance. The inferences are used to assist users in their decision making.

The principal analytical tools of financial statement analysis consist of comparisons of year-to-year changes, trend analysis, structural analysis, ratio analysis, and other specialized analyses.

REASONS FOR STATEMENT ANALYSIS

All user groups are concerned with the future course that a company will probably take. Managers are concerned with the firm's future operating results and its ability to attract capital. Satisfactory profits are needed to keep stockholders satisfied and to preserve their tenure as managers. Sufficient cash must be generated for the firm to continue operating and pay dividends. Stockholders are concerned with a firm's operating performance and its profits. Dividend payments and the stock market price of a firm's shares are usually a function of the firm's profit performance. Potential stockholders have similar concerns. Creditors are concerned that interest and principal payments will be paid when due. Normally, a sufficient cash flow must be generated to provide for these payments. Financial analysts provide advisory services to other users, and their recommendations are dependent on their ability to make satisfactory predictions regarding a firm's future operations and financial condition. Employees and their collective bargaining representatives are concerned with negotiating increases in wages and benefits without forcing the firm into bankruptcy. Essentially, a firm's employees are interested in securing a "fair share of the pie," so they need analysts to project what the size of the pie will be in the future. Thus, they must also project what the firm's future results of operations will probably be.

While financial statement analysis by itself cannot provide all the answers to the concerns of the decision makers noted above, it can assist them in their deliberations. Other factors that may assist the decision makers, such as forecasting techniques, are discussed in Chapter 7 in the section on budgeting.

THE PRINCIPAL TOOLS OF ANALYSIS

In the analysis of financial statements, a statement user has available a variety of tools from which she can choose those best suited to her specific purpose. The principal tools of analysis are:

1. Comparative financial statements.
   a. Year-to-year changes.

2. Index-number trend series.

3. Common-size financial statements.
   a. Structural analysis.

4. Ratio analysis.

5. Specialized analyses.
   a. Cash forecasts.
   b. Analysis of changes in financial position.
   c. Statement of variation in gross margin.
   d. Breakeven analysis.

Comparative Financial Statements

The comparison of financial statements is done by setting up balance sheets, income statements, or statements of changes in financial position (SCFP), side by side, and reviewing the changes that have occurred in individual categories from year to year and over the years.

The most important factor shown by comparative financial statements is trend. **Trend** is the general direction of financial data expressed in terms of a base period (usually one year). The comparison of financial statements over a number of years will also reveal the velocity of trend. The **velocity of trend** is the rate of movement of financial data in a general direction.[1]

Further analysis can be done to compare the trends in related items. For example, a year-to-year increase in sales of 10 percent accompanied by an increase in freight-out costs of 20 percent requires an investigation and explanation of the reasons for the difference. Similarly, an increase of accounts receivable of 15 percent during the same period would also warrant an investigation into the reasons for the difference in the rate of increase of sales as against that of receivables.

Year-to-Year Change. A comparison of financial statements over two to three years can be undertaken by computing the *year-to-year change* in absolute amounts and in terms of percentage changes. When a two- or three-year comparison is attempted, such presentations are manageable and can be understood by the reader. These comparisons present changes in terms of absolute dollar amounts as well as in percentages. Both have to be considered because the dollar size of the different bases on which percentage changes are computed may yield large percentage changes that are out of proportion to their real significance. For example, in the same financial statements, a 50 percent change from a base figure of $1,000 is less significant than the

---

[1] The author is grateful to Professor Leopold A. Bernstein for permission to abstract portions of his book, *Financial Statement Analysis,* published by Richard D. Irwin, Inc., in 1983. Those who are interested in a definitive treatment of this subject matter should refer to the third edition of his book.

same percentage change from a base of $100,000. Thus, reference to the dollar amounts involved is always necessary in order to retain the proper perspective and to reach valid conclusions regarding the relative significance of the changes disclosed by this type of analysis.

The computation of year-to-year changes is simple. However, a few clarifying rules should be remembered. When a negative amount appears in the base year and a positive amount in the following year, or vice versa, no percentage change can be computed. When an item has a value in a base year and none in the following period, the decrease is 100 percent. Where there is no figure for the base year, no percentage change can be computed. The following summary will illustrate this:

| Item | 19x1 | 19x2 | Change Increase (Decrease) | |
			Amount	Percent
Net income (loss)	$ (4,500)	$ 1,500	$ 6,000	—
Tax cost	2,000	(1,000)	(3,000)	—
Notes payable	—	8,000	8,000	—
Notes receivable	10,000	—	(10,000)	(100)

Comparative financial statements can also be presented so that the cumulative total for the period for each item under study and the average for that period are shown.

The value of comparing yearly amounts with an average covering a number of years is that unusual factors in any one year are highlighted. Averages smooth out erratic or unusual fluctuations in data.

An example of comparative balance sheets and income statements for the Freder Company showing the absolute and percentage changes is shown in Illustrations 17–1 and 17–2. These statements will also be used for further analysis throughout this chapter.

Comparative statements of retained earnings appear in Illustration 17–3.

Index-Number Trend Series

When a comparison of financial statements for more than three years is undertaken, the year-to-year method of comparison may become too cumbersome. The best way to effect such longer term trend comparisons is by means of index numbers. An **index number** is a measure used to indicate common qualities to a group of items. The computation of a series of index numbers requires the choice of a base year that will, for all items, have an index amount of 100. Since such a base year represents a frame of reference for all comparisons, it is best to choose a year that, in a business conditions sense, is as typical or normal as possible. If the earliest year in the series compared cannot fulfill this function, another year is chosen.

As is the case with the computation of year-to-year percentage changes, certain changes, such as those from negative to positive amounts, cannot

ILLUSTRATION 17–1

FREDER COMPANY
Comparative Balance Sheets
December 31, 19x7, and 19x8

	19x8	19x7	Change Increase (Decrease) Amount	Change Increase (Decrease) Percent
Assets				
Current assets:				
Cash	$ 14,522	$ 20,962	$ (6,440)	(30.7)
Accounts receivable	91,314	79,328	11,986	15.1
Inventory	73,632	67,622	6,010	8.9
Prepaid costs	7,680	6,954	726	10.4
Total current assets	187,148	174,866	12,282	7.0
Property, plant, and equipment:				
Land	3,698	3,698	–0–	–0–
Building	34,142	32,988	1,154	3.5
Machinery and equipment	66,808	57,952	8,856	15.3
Total	104,648	94,638	10,010	10.6
Less: Accumulated depreciation	44,210	37,828	6,382	16.9
Total property, plant, and equipment . . .	60,438	56,810	3,628	6.4
Total assets	$247,586	$231,676	$15,910	6.9
Liabilities and Stockholders' Equity				
Current liabilities:				
Accounts payable	$ 42,716	$ 40,490	$ 2,226	5.5
Wages payable	4,651	3,787	864	22.8
Income taxes payable	7,198	4,596	2,602	56.6
Total current liabilities	54,565	48,873	5,692	11.6
Long-term liabilities:				
Bonds payable	45,000	40,000	5,000	12.5
Premium on bonds payable	2,180	2,420	(240)	(9.9)
Total long-term liabilities	47,180	42,420	4,760	11.2
Total liabilities	101,745	91,293	10,452	11.4
Stockholders' equity:				
Preferred stock—$100 par, 10 percent	20,000	20,000	–0–	–0–
Common stock—$5 par	37,500	32,500	5,000	15.4
Additional paid-in capital	30,800	24,600	6,200	25.2
Retained earnings	57,541	63,283	(5,742)	(9.1)
Total stockholders' equity	145,841	140,383	5,458	3.9
Total liabilities and stockholders' equity	$247,586	$231,676	$15,910	6.9

ILLUSTRATION 17–2

FREDER COMPANY
Comparative Income Statements
For the Years Ended December 31, 19x7, and 19x8

	19x8	19x7	Change Increase (Decrease) Amount	Percent
Sales	$720,860	$676,080	$44,780	6.6
Cost of goods sold	453,178	414,554	38,624	9.3
Gross margin	267,682	261,526	6,156	2.4
Marketing and administrative:				
Marketing costs	129,939	124,382	5,557	4.5
Administrative costs	122,730	116,996	5,734	4.9
Total marketing and administrative . .	252,669	241,378	11,291	4.7
Operating income	15,013	20,148	(5,135)	(25.5)
Interest cost	5,000	4,500	500	11.1
Income before income taxes	10,013	15,648	(5,635)	(36.0)
Income tax provision (40 percent)	4,005	6,259	(2,254)	(36.0)
Net income	$ 6,008	$ 9,389	$ (3,381)	(36.0)

ILLUSTRATION 17–3

FREDER COMPANY
Retained Earnings Statements
For the Years Ended December 31, 19x7, and 19x8

	19x8	19x7
Retained earnings, January 1	$63,283	$64,344
Add: Net income	6,008	9,389
Subtotal	69,291	73,733
Deduct dividends:		
Preferred stock	2,000	2,000
Common stock	9,750	8,450
Total deductions	11,750	10,450
Retained earnings, December 31 . .	$57,541	$63,283

be expressed by means of index numbers. All index numbers are computed by reference to the base year.

Let us assume that in the base year at 12/31/19xA, there is a cash balance of $12,000. Based on an index number of 100 for 19xA, if the cash balance in the following year (at 12/31/19xB) is $18,000, then the index number will be

$$\frac{\$18,000}{\$12,000} \times 100 = 150$$

On 12/31/19xC, the cash balance is $9,000; the index will be 75, arrived at as follows:

$$\frac{\$9,000}{\$12,000} \times 100 \left(\frac{\text{Balance in current year}}{\text{Balance in base year}} \times 100 \right)$$

When using index numbers, percentage changes cannot be read off directly except by reference to the base year. Thus, the change of the cash balance between 19xA and 19xB is 50 percent (index 150 − index 100), which can be read off directly from the index numbers. The change from 19xB to 19xC, however, is not 75 percent (150 − 75), as a direct comparison may suggest, but rather 50 percent (i.e., $9,000/$18,000), which involves computing the 19xB to 19xC change by reference to the amount at 19xB. The percentage change can, however, be computed by use of the index numbers only, for example, 75/150 = .5, or a change of 50 percent.

In planning an index-number trend comparison, it is not necessary to include all the items in the financial statements. Only the most significant items need to be included in such a comparison.

Care should be exercised in the use of index-number trend comparisons because such comparisons have weaknesses as well as strengths. Thus, in trying to assess changes in the current financial condition, the analyst may use comparative statements of changes in financial position to advantage. On the other hand, the index-number trend comparison is well suited to a comparison of the changes in the *composition* of working capital items over the years.

Let us extend the Freder Company data to include the following:

	19x8	19x7	19x6	19x5	19x4
Sales	$720,860	$676,080	$592,290	$478,447	$465,895
Cost of goods sold	453,178	414,554	357,839	287,379	276,699
Gross margin	267,682	261,526	234,451	191,068	189,196
Marketing costs	129,939	124,382	108,945	90,470	89,520
Administrative costs	122,730	116,996	103,815	79,120	78,225
Net income	6,008	9,389	10,015	9,887	9,871

Note that sales, cost of goods sold, gross margin, marketing costs, and administrative costs all increased when compared to the respective item in the preceding year. However, net income increased in 19x5 and 19x6, while it decreased in 19x7 and 19x8. To assess the reasons for these results, a statement user would find it difficult to reach a conclusion if the absolute data are used as given. The reasons become readily apparent when the data are converted into an index-number trend series, as shown in Illustration 17–4.

Note in Illustration 17–4 that while sales increased each year, cost of goods sold increased at a faster rate, thus causing gross margin to increase at a slower rate. In addition, marketing costs and administrative costs generally increased at a more rapid rate than that for gross margin. Net income

ILLUSTRATION 17–4

FREDER COMPANY
Income Statement Data
Converted into an Index-Number Trend Series
For the Years Ended December 31

	19x8	19x7	19x6	19x5	19x4
Sales	158	145	127	103	100
Cost of goods sold	164	150	129	104	100
Gross margin	141	138	124	101	100
Marketing costs	145	139	122	101	100
Administrative costs	157	149	132	101	100
Net income	61	95	101	100	100

Common-Size Financial Statements

remained relatively static for 19x5, 19x6, and 19x7 and then declined at a rapid rate in 19x8. With this analysis, a manager can determine where the problem areas are and attempt to implement corrective action. Trend analysis is often referred to as **horizontal analysis.**

A **common-size statement** is one in which each component of the statement is shown as a percentage instead of in dollar amounts. In the analysis of financial statements, it is often helpful to find out the proportion that a single item represents of a total group or subgroup. In a balance sheet, the assets as well as the liabilities and capital are each expressed as 100 percent, and each item in these categories is expressed as a percentage of the respective totals. Similarly, in the income statement, net sales are set at 100 percent and every other item in the statement is expressed as a percent of net sales. Since the totals always equal 100 percent, these statements are referred to as "common size." Similarly, following the eye as it reviews the common-size statement is referred to as **vertical analysis.**

Structural Analysis. The analysis of common-size financial statements may be described as an analysis of the internal structure of the financial statements. In the analysis of a balance sheet, this structural analysis focuses on two major aspects:

1. The sources of capital of the enterprise, that is, the distribution of equities between current liabilities, long-term liabilities, and equity capital.

2. The amount of capital from all sources, the distribution of assets (current, fixed, and other) in which it is invested. Stated differently, the mix of assets with which the enterprise has chosen to conduct its operations.

The common-size balance sheet analysis can be carried further and extended to an examination of what proportion of a subgroup, rather than the total, an item is. Thus, in assessing the liquidity of current assets, it may be interesting to know not only what proportion of total assets is invested in inventories but also what proportion of current assets is represented by this asset.

With the income statement, common-size statement analysis is a useful tool that may even be more important than the analysis of the balance sheet. The income statement lends itself to an analysis because each item is related

ILLUSTRATION 17–5

FREDER COMPANY
Comparative Balance Sheets
December 31, 19x7, and 19x8

	19x8	19x7	Common-Size Percentages 19x8	19x7
Assets				
Current assets:				
Cash	$ 14,522	$ 20,962	5.9	9.0
Accounts receivable	91,314	79,328	36.9	34.3
Inventory	73,632	67,622	29.7	29.2
Prepaid costs	7,680	6,954	3.1	3.0
Total current assets	187,148	174,866	75.6	75.5
Property, plant, and equipment:				
Land	3,698	3,698	1.5	1.6
Building	34,142	32,988	13.8	14.2
Machinery and equipment	66,808	57,952	27.0	25.0
Total	104,648	94,638	42.3	40.8
Less: Accumulated depreciation	44,210	37,828	17.9	16.3
Total property, plant, and equipment	60,438	56,810	24.4	24.5
Total assets	$247,586	$231,676	100.0	100.0
Liabilities and Stockholders' Equity				
Current liabilities:				
Accounts payable	$ 42,716	$ 40,490	17.2	17.5
Wages payable	4,651	3,787	1.9	1.6
Income taxes payable	7,198	4,596	2.9	2.0
Total current liabilities	54,565	48,873	22.0	21.1
Long-term liabilities:				
Bonds payable	45,000	40,000	18.2	17.3
Premium on bonds payable	2,180	2,420	.9	1.0
Total long-term liabilities	47,180	42,420	19.1	18.3
Total liabilities	101,745	91,293	41.1	39.4
Stockholders' equity:				
Preferred stock—$100 par, 10 percent	20,000	20,000	8.1	8.7
Common stock—$5 par	37,500	32,500	15.2	14.0
Additional paid-in capital	30,800	24,600	12.4	10.6
Retained earnings	57,541	63,283	23.2	27.3
Total stockholders' equity	145,841	140,383	58.9	60.6
Total liabilities and stockholders' equity	$247,586	$231,676	100.0	100.0

to a central quantum, that is, sales. With some exceptions, the level of each cost item is affected by the level of sales, and thus it is helpful to know what proportion of the sales dollar is absorbed by the various costs incurred by the enterprise.

Comparisons of common-size statements of a single enterprise over the years are valuable because they show the changing proportions of components within groups of assets, liabilities, costs, and other financial statement categories. However, care must be exercised in interpreting such changes and the trend that they disclose. For example, the table below shows the amount of land and total assets of an enterprise over three years:

	19x3	19x2	19x1
Land	$ 50,000	$ 50,000	$ 50,000
Total assets	$1,000,000	$750,000	$500,000
Land as a percentage of total assets . .	5%	6.67%	10%

While the amount of land remained unchanged, the increase in total assets made this item a progressively smaller proportion of total assets. Since this proportion can change with either a change in the absolute amount of the item or a change in the total of the group of which it is a part, the interpretation of a common-size statement comparison requires an examination of the actual figures and the basis on which they are computed.

Comparative balance sheets and income statements for the Freder Company showing the common-size percentages are shown in Illustrations 17–5 and 17–6.

ILLUSTRATION 17–6

FREDER COMPANY
Comparative Income Statements
For the Years Ended December 31, 19x7, and 19x8

	19x8	19x7	Common-Size Percentages 19x8	Common-Size Percentages 19x7
Sales	$720,860	$676,080	100.0	100.0
Cost of goods sold	453,178	414,554	62.9	61.3
Gross margin	267,682	261,526	37.1	38.7
Marketing and administrative:				
Marketing costs	129,939	124,382	18.0	18.4
Administrative costs	122,730	116,996	17.0	17.3
Total marketing and administrative	252,669	241,378	35.0	35.7
Operating income	15,013	20,148	2.1	3.0
Interest cost	5,000	4,500	.7	.7
Income before income taxes	10,013	15,648	1.4	2.3
Income tax provision (40 percent)	4,005	6,259	.6	.9
Net income	$ 6,008	$ 9,389	.8	1.4

Following are observations about Illustrations 17–5 and 17–6:

1.   Although stockholders' equity increased in absolute dollars in 19x8, its common-size percentage decreased (see Illustration 17–5). Therefore, the firm is relying on a greater use of borrowed funds relative to equity funds. This concept is discussed in the section about debt-to-equity ratio.

2.   Illustration 17–2 shows that both sales and cost of goods sold in absolute dollars increased in 19x8. However, cost of goods sold increased at a faster rate in 19x8, and while gross margin increased in absolute dollars in 19x8, its common-size percentage decreased (see Illustration 17–6). This implies that either (1) increases in costs were *not* proportionately passed on to the firm's customers, or (2) the firm lowered its selling prices to increase its volume without a proportionate reduction in its costs, or (3) a combination of the two. In each case, the policy of the firm may partially explain the reduction in net income for 19x8. If this policy continues, the firm may operate at a loss in the future.

3.   Marketing costs and administrative costs (see Illustration 17–6) increased at a rate slightly less than that for sales. Normally, when sales increase, marketing and administrative costs also increase, but not proportionately to sales; these costs should increase at a significantly slower rate than sales because many marketing and administrative costs are fixed. In 19x8, these costs occupy about the same common-size percentage as in 19x7, which indicates that these costs may be a troublesome area that should be investigated by the managers who control them.

RATIOS

Ratio Analysis

Ratios are among the best known and most widely used tools of financial analysis. At the same time, their functions is often misunderstood, and consequently their significance may easily be overrated.

A **ratio** expresses the mathematical relationship between two quantities. The ratio of 200 to 100 is expressed as 2:1, or as 2. While the computation of a ratio involves a simple arithmetical operation, its interpretation is a more complex matter.

The ratio must express a relationship that has significance. Thus, there is a clear, direct, and understandable relationship between the sales price of an item and its cost. As a result, the ratio of cost of goods sold to sales is significant. On the other hand, there is no a priori or understandable relationship between freight costs incurred and the marketable securities held by an enterprise; and hence, a ratio of one to the other has no significance.

Ratios are tools of analysis that provide the analyst with clues and symptoms of underlying conditions. Ratios properly interpreted can also identify areas requiring further investigation and inquiry. The analysis of a ratio can disclose relationships as well as bases of comparison that reveal conditions and trends that cannot be detected by an inspection of the individual components of the ratio.

Interpretation of Ratios

Ratios should always be interpreted carefully since factors affecting the numerator may correlate with those affecting the denominator. Thus, it is possible to improve the ratio of operating costs to sales by reducing costs that act to stimulate sales. If the cost reduction results in a loss of sales or share of market, such a seeming improvement in profitability may, in fact, have an overall detrimental effect on the future prospects of the enterprise and must be interpreted accordingly. Also, many ratios have important variables in common with other ratios, so they can vary and be influenced by the same factors. Consequently, there is no need to use all available ratios in order to diagnose a given condition.

Ratios, like most other relationships in financial analysis, are not significant in themselves and can be interpreted only by comparison with (1) past ratios of the same enterprise or (2) some predetermined standard or (3) ratios of other companies in the industry. The range of a ratio over time is also significant as is the trend of a given ratio over time. Appendix 17–A contains sources of information on financial and operating ratios.

ILLUSTRATION OF RATIO COMPUTATIONS

Many ratios can be developed from the items included in an enterprises' financial statements. Some ratios have general application in financial analysis, while others have specific uses in certain circumstances or in specific industries. Discussed below are some of the more significant ratios that can be applied generally to business situations. They are grouped by major objectives of financial analysis.

SHORT-TERM LIQUIDITY

The short-term liquidity of an enterprise is measured by the degree to which it can meet its short-term obligations. Liquidity implies the ready ability to convert assets into cash or to obtain cash. The short term is conventionally viewed as a time span up to a year, although it is sometimes also identified with the normal operating cycle of a business, that is, the time span which is the buying-producing-selling and collecting cycle of an enterprise.

The importance of short-term liquidity can best be measured by examining the repercussions that stem from a lack of ability to meet short-term obligations.

A lack of liquidity may mean that the enterprise cannot take advantage of favorable discounts and profitable business opportunities as they arise. At this stage, a lack of liquidity implies a lack of freedom of choice as well as constraints on management's freedom of movement.

A more serious lack of liquidity means that the enterprise is unable to pay its current debts and obligations. This can cause the forced sale of long-term investments and assets and, in its most severe form, insolvency and bankruptcy.

One of the most widely used measures of liquidity is working capital. In addition to its importance as a pool of liquid assets that provides a safety cushion to creditors, net working capital is also important because it provides a liquid reserve with which to meet contingencies and the ever-present uncertainty regarding an enterprise's ability to balance the outflow of funds with an adequate inflow of funds.

Working Capital

Basically, **working capital** is the excess of current assets over current liabilities. That excess is sometimes referred to as *net working capital* because some businesses consider current assets as working capital. A working capital deficiency exists when current liabilities exceed current assets.

The most common categories of current assets are:

1. Cash.
2. Cash equivalents (i.e., temporary investments).
3. Accounts and notes receivable.
4. Inventories.
5. Prepaid costs.

Current liabilities are obligations that would, generally, require the use of current assets for their discharge or, alternatively, the creation of other current liabilities. The most common categories of current liabilities are:

1. Accounts payable.
2. Notes payable.
3. Short-term bank and other loans.
4. Tax and other accruals.
5. Current portion of long-term debt.

The absolute amount of working capital has significance only when related to other variables such as sales, total assets, and so forth. It has limited value for comparison purposes and for judging the adequacy of working capital. This can be illustrated as follows:

	Company A	Company B
Current assets	$300,000	$1,200,000
Current liabilities	100,000	1,000,000
Working capital	$200,000	$ 200,000

While both companies have an equal amount of working capital, a cursory comparison of the relationship of current assets to current liabilities suggests that company A's current condition is superior to that of company B. This example illustrates the need for further analysis, discussed later in the current-ratio section.

The working capital for the Freder Company may be computed as follows:

	19x8	19x7
Current assets	$187,148	$174,866
Current liabilities	54,565	48,873
Working capital	$132,583	$125,993

The analysis of working capital by itself is insufficient to reach a conclusion regarding a firm's short-term liquidity. Four ratios should be used in conjunction with working capital to reach an opinion about a firm's short-term liquidity position. These ratios are the: (1) current ratio, (2) acid-test ratio, (3) average-accounts-receivable-turnover ratio, and (4) inventory-turnover ratio.

Current Ratio

The **current ratio** is a firm's current assets divided by its current liabilities and is often expressed as:

$$\text{Current ratio} = \frac{\text{Current assets}}{\text{Current liabilities}} \tag{1}$$

The current ratios for the Freder Company for 19x8 and 19x7 are:

19x8	19x7
$\dfrac{\$187,148}{\$54,565} = 3.42$ to 1	$\dfrac{\$174,866}{\$48,873} = 3.58$ to 1

Note that the current ratio deteriorated to 3.42:1 in 19x8 from 3.58:1 despite an increase in working capital in 19x8 of $6,590 ($132,583 − $125,993). This highlights the importance of analyzing data in more than one approach (i.e., by using absolute dollars and relative relationships).

Some of the reasons for the widespread use of the current ratio as a measure of liquidity are:

1. It measures the degree to which current assets cover current liabilities. The higher the amount of current assets in relation to current liabilities, the greater the assurance that these liabilities can be paid out of such assets.

2. The excess of current assets over current liabilities provides a buffer against losses that may be incurred in the disposition or liquidation of the current assets other than cash. The more substantial such a buffer is, the better for creditors. Thus, the current ratio measures the margin of safety available to cover any possible shrinkage in the value of current assets.

3. It measures the reserve of liquid funds in excess of current obligations that is available as a margin of safety against uncertainty and the random shocks to which the flows of funds in an enterprise are subject. Random shocks, such as strikes, extraordinary losses, and other uncertainties, can temporarily and unexpectedly stop or reduce the inflow of funds.

ILLUSTRATION 17–7

$$\frac{\text{Current assets}}{\text{Current liabilities}} = \frac{\text{Cash and cash equivalents} + \text{Accounts receivable} + \text{Inventories}}{\text{Current liabilities}}$$

Limitations of the Current Ratio.   The first step in our examination of the current ratio as a tool of liquidity and short-term solvency analysis is to examine the components that are normally included in the ratio shown in Illustration 17–7.

Disregarding, for purposes of this evaluation, prepaid costs and similar unsubstantial items entering the computation of the current ratio, we have the above four major elements that comprise this ratio.

If we define liquidity as the ability to balance required cash outflows with adequate inflows, including an allowance for unexpected interruptions of inflows or increases in outflows, we must ask: Does the relationship of these four elements at a given point in time—

1.   Measure and predict the pattern of future fund flows?

2.   Measure the adequacy of future fund inflows in relation to outflows?

The answer to these questions is negative. The current ratio is a static or "stock" concept of what resources are available at a given time to meet obligations at that moment. The existing reservoir of net funds does not have a logical or causative relationship to the future funds that will flow through it. And yet, it is the future flows that are the subject of our greatest interest in the assessment of liquidity. These flows depend importantly on elements *not* included in the ratio itself, such as sales, profits, and changes in business conditions. To elaborate, let us examine more closely the four elements comprising the ratio.

Cash and Cash Equivalents.   The amount of cash held by a well-managed enterprise is a precautionary reserve, intended to take care of short-term imbalances in cash flows. In cases of a business downturn, sales may fall more rapidly than outlays for purchases and other costs. Since cash is a nonearning asset and cash equivalents are usually low-yielding securities, the investment in such assets is kept at a safe minimum. To consider this minimum balance as available for payment of current debts would require the dropping of the going-concern assumption underlying accounting statements. While the balance of cash has some relation to the existing level of activity, such a relationship is not strong nor does it contain predictive implications regarding the future. In fact, some enterprises may use cash substitutes such as open lines of credit that do not enter into the computation of the current ratio.

The important link between cash and solvency is due to the well-known fact that a shortage of cash, more than any other factor, is the element that can clinch the insolvency of an enterprise.

Accounts Receivable.   The major determinant of the level of accounts receivable is sales. The size of accounts receivable in relation to sales is governed by terms of trade and credit policy. Changes in receivables will correspond to changes in sales though not necessarily on a directly proportional basis.

When we look at accounts receivable as a source of cash, we must, except in the case of liquidation, recognize the revolving nature of the asset with the collection of one account replaced by the extension of fresh credit. Thus, the level of receivables is not an index to future net inflows of cash.

Inventories. As is the case with accounts receivable, the main determinant of the size of inventories is the level of sales, or expected sales, rather than the level of current liabilities. Given that the level of sales is a measure of the level of demand then, scientific methods of inventory management (economic order quantities, safe stock levels, and reorder points) generally establish that inventory increments vary not in proportion to demand but vary rather with the *square root* of demand.

The relationship of inventories to sales is further accented by the fact that sales is the one essential element that starts the conversion of inventories to cash. Moreover, the determination of future cash inflows through the sale of inventories is dependent on the profit margin that can be realized because inventories are generally stated at the lower of *cost* or market. The current ratio, while including inventories, does not recognize the sales level or profit margin, both of which are important elements entering into the determination of future cash inflows.

Current Liabilities. The level of current liabilities, the safety of which the current ratio is intended to measure, is also largely determined by the level of sales.

Current liabilities are a source of funds in the same sense that receivables and inventories tie up funds. Since purchases, which give rise to accounts payable, are a function of the level of activity (i.e., sales), these payables vary with sales. As long as sales remain constant or are rising, the payment of current liabilities is essentially a refunding operation. The components of the current ratio give little, if any, recognition to these elements and their effects on the future flow of funds. Nor do the current liabilities that enter into the computation of the current ratio include prospective outlays, such as commitments under construction contracts, loans, leases, or pensions, all of which affect the future outflow of funds.

The Use of Rules-of-Thumb Standards. A currently popular belief is that the current ratio can be evaluated by means of *rules of thumb*. Thus, if the current ratio is 2:1 (or 200 percent), it is sound; anything below that norm is bad, while the higher above that figure the current ratio is, the better.

The 2:1 standard means that there are $2 of current assets available for each dollar of current liabilities or that the value of current assets can, on liquidation, shrink by 50 percent before it will be inadequate to cover the current liabilities. A current ratio much higher than 2:1, while implying a superior coverage of current liabilities, may also mean a wasteful accumulation of liquid resources which do not "carry their weight" by earning an appropriate return for the enterprise.

The evaluation of the current ratio in terms of rules of thumb is a technique of dubious validity for two major reasons:

1. The quality of the current assets, as well as the composition of the current liabilities that make up this ratio, are the most important determinants in an evaluation of the quality of the current ratio. Thus, two companies that have identical current ratios may be in quite different current financial condition due to variations in the quality of the working capital components.

2. The need of an enterprise for working capital varies with industry conditions as well as with the length of its own particular *net trade cycle.*

The following assumed data concerning the Brace and Hall Companies illustrate two companies that have identical current ratios but have different positions of short-term liquidity.

	Brace Company	Hall Company
Current assets:		
Cash	$100,000	$ 10,000
Accounts receivable, net	80,000	30,000
Merchandise inventory	120,000	260,000
Total current assets	$300,000	$300,000
Current liabilities	$150,000	$150,000
Current ratio	2:1	2:1

The short-term liquidity of the Brace Company is preferable to that of the Hall Company notwithstanding the fact that they both have the same current ratio.

Another short-term liquidity measure, the acid-test ratio, helps users to differentiate preferable short-term liquidity in cases like this.

Acid-Test Ratio   The most liquid of current assets is cash, which is the standard of liquidity. A close second to cash is "temporary investments" that are usually highly marketable and relatively safe temporary repositories of cash. These are, in effect, considered "cash equivalents" and usually earn a modest return. Accounts receivable are only one step removed from cash and are normally converted into cash within a relatively short period of time (usually 30 to 60 days). Thus, accounts receivable is also considered a relatively liquid asset. Although inventories are current assets, they are not nearly as liquid as accounts receivable. They must first be sold before they become liquid assets in the form of accounts receivable. During periods of economic recession, inventories may not be immediately saleable in the normal course of business. Therefore, users of financial statements also use a more stringent test than the current ratio to evaluate a firm's liquidity. Prepaid costs and inventories are excluded from the numerator of this test because prepaid costs are not normally converted into cash and inventories must first be sold. The stringent test, the **acid-test ratio,** consists of a numerator composed of cash, short-term marketable securities, and accounts (and short-term notes) receivable divided by the denominator of current liabilities. The acid-test ratio, also known as the *quick ratio,* may be expressed as:

Acid-test ratio

$$= \frac{\text{Cash} + \text{Short-term marketable securities} + \text{Current receivables}}{\text{Current liabilities}} \quad (2)$$

As with the current ratio where a popular rule-of-thumb standard exists for that ratio, the acid-test ratio also has a standard. Although the standard has dubious validity, many users of financial statements feel that the acid-test ratio should be a minimum of $1:1$. While a ratio of $1:1$ implies that a sufficient amount of liquid assets is available to meet the demands of the firm's present current liabilities, the ratio does not imply that the condition is likely to continue in the future, nor does the ratio factor in different requirements for different industries.

The calculations of the ratio for the Freder Company for 19x8 and 19x7 are:

	19x8	19x7
Cash	$ 14,522	$ 20,962
Accounts receivable . .	91,314	79,328
Total quick assets	$105,836	$100,290
Current liabilities	$ 54,565	$ 48,873
Acid-test ratio	1.94:1	2.05:1

While the acid-test ratios for the Freder Company are in excess of the rule-of-thumb standard, it should be noted that the ratio decreased in 19x8. This may be a sign that the company's trend of short-term liquidity is weakening.

Average-Accounts-Receivable-Turnover Ratio

In most enterprises that sell on credit, accounts and notes receivable are a significant part of working capital. In assessing the quality of working capital and of the current ratio, it is important to get some measure of the quality and the liquidity of the receivables.

Both the quality and liquidity of accounts receivable are affected by their rate of turnover. Quality means the likelihood of collection without loss. An indicator of this likelihood is the degree to which receivables are within the terms of payment set by the enterprise. Experience has shown that the longer receivables remain outstanding beyond the date on which they are due, the lower is the probability of their collection in full. Turnover is an indicator of the age of the receivables, particularly when it is compared with an expected turnover rate that is determined by credit terms granted.

The measure of liquidity is concerned with the speed with which accounts receivables will, on average, be converted into cash. Here again, turnover is among the best measures to use.

The **accounts-receivable-turnover ratio** is computed by dividing net credit sales by the average accounts receivable. Average accounts receivable may be computed by adding the beginning and ending balances of accounts receivable and then dividing the sum by 2. The ratio may be expressed as:

$$\text{Accounts receivable turnover} = \frac{\text{Net sales on credit}}{\text{Average accounts receivable}} \qquad (3)$$

Notes receivable arising from normal sales should be included in the accounts receivable figure in computing the turnover ratio. Discounted notes receivable that are still outstanding should also be included in the accounts receivable total.

The sales figure used in computing the ratio should be that of credit sales only, because cash sales do not generate receivables. Since published financial statements rarely disclose the division between cash and credit sales, the external analyst may have to compute the ratio under the assumption that cash sales are insignificant. If they are not insignificant, then a degree of distortion may occur in the ratio. However, if the proportion of cash sales to total sales remains relatively constant, the year-to-year comparison of changes in the receivables-turnover ratio may nevertheless be validly based.

The average-receivables-turnover figure indicates how many *times,* on average, the receivables revolve, that is, are generated and collected during the year.

The accounts-receivable-turnover ratio for the Freder Company is:

$$\frac{\$720,860}{(\$79,328 + \$91,314) \div 2} = \frac{\$720,860}{\$85,321} = 8.4 \text{ times}$$

While the turnover figure furnishes a sense of the speed of collections and is valuable for comparison purposes, it is not directly comparable to the terms of trade that the enterprise normally extends. Such comparison is best made by converting the turnover into days of sales tied up in receivables.

Collection Period for Accounts Receivable

This measure, also known as *days' sales in accounts receivable,* measures the number of days it takes, on average, to collect accounts (and notes) receivable. The number of days can be obtained by dividing the average-accounts-receivable-turnover ratio discussed above into 360, the approximate round number of days in the year. Thus,

$$\text{Collection period} = \frac{360}{\text{Average accounts receivable turnover}} \qquad (4)$$

Using the figures of the preceding example, the collection period is:

$$\frac{360}{8.4} = 43 \text{ days}$$

Accounts-receivable-turnover rates or collection periods can be compared to industry averages (see Appendix 17–A) or to the credit terms granted by the enterprise.

When the collection period is compared with the terms of sale allowed by the enterprise, the degree to which customers are paying on time can be assessed. Thus, if the average terms of sale in the illustration used above are 30 days, then an average collection period of 43 days reflects either some or all of the following conditions:

1. A poor collection job.

2. Difficulty in obtaining prompt payment from customers in spite of diligent collection efforts.

3. Customers in financial difficulty.

The first conclusion calls for remedial managerial action, while the last two reflect on both the quality and the liquidity of the accounts receivable.

An *average* figure may not be representative of the receivables population it represents. Thus, it is possible that the 43-day average collection period does not represent an across-the-board payment tardiness on the part of customers but is rather caused by the excessive delinquency of one or two substantial customers.

The best way to investigate further an excessive collection period is to *age* the accounts receivable so that the distribution of each account by the number of days past due is clearly apparent. An aging schedule in a format such as given below will show whether the problem is widespread or concentrated:

Accounts Receivable Aging Schedule

	Current	Days Past Due			
		0–30	31–60	61–90	Over 90
Accounts receivable					

The age distribution of the receivables will, of course, lead to better informed conclusions regarding the quality and the liquidity of the receivables as well as the kind of action that is necessary to remedy the situation. Another dimension of receivables classification is by quality ratings of credit agencies such as Dun & Bradstreet.

Notes receivable also deserve scrutiny because while they are normally regarded as more negotiable than open accounts, they may be of poorer quality than regular receivables if they originated as an extension device for an unpaid account rather than at the inception of the original sale.

Inventory-Turnover Ratio

In many cases, inventories represent a substantial proportion of the current asset group. This fact has little effect on an enterprise's objective of maintaining adequate levels of liquid funds. Reserves of liquid funds are seldom kept in the form of inventories. Inventories represent investments made to obtain a return. The return is derived from the expected profits that may result from sales. In most businesses, a certain level of inventory must be kept in order to generate an adequate level of sales. If the inventory level is inadequate, the sales volume will fall below the level otherwise attainable. Excessive inventories, on the other hand, expose the enterprise to costs such as storage costs, insurance, and taxes, as well as to risks of loss of value through obsolescence and physical deterioration. Moreover, excessive inventories tie up funds that can be used more profitably elsewhere.

Due to the risk involved in holding invetories and the fact that inventories are one step further removed from cash than receivables (they have to be sold before they are converted into receivables), inventories are normally considered the least liquid component of the current assets group. However, this generalization is not always true. Certain staple items, such as commodities, raw materials, standard sizes of structural steel, etc., enjoy broad and ready markets and can usually be sold with little effort, cost, or loss. On the other hand, fashion merchandise, specialized components, or perishable items can lose their value rapidly unless they are sold on a timely basis.

The evaluation of the current ratio, which includes inventories in its computation, must include a thorough evaluation of the quality as well as the liquidity of these assets. Here again, measures of turnover are the best overall tools available for this purpose.

The **inventory-turnover ratio** measures the average rate of speed with which inventories move through and out of the enterprise, and is computed by dividing cost of goods sold by average inventory.

Computation. The computation of the average-inventory turnover is as follows:

$$\text{Inventory-turnover ratio} = \frac{\text{Cost of goods sold}}{\text{Average inventory}} \qquad (5)$$

The average inventory figure is most readily obtained as follows:

$$\frac{\text{Opening inventory} + \text{Closing inventory}}{2}$$

Further refinement in the averaging process can be achieved, where possible and necessary, by averaging quarterly or monthly inventory figures.

When an inventory-turnover ratio is computed in order to evaluate the *level* of inventory at a certain date, such as the year-end inventory, the inventory figure in the denominator should be the figure as of that date rather than an average-inventory figure.

The 19x8 inventory turnover for the Freder Company may be computed as follows:

$$\frac{\text{Cost of goods sold}}{\text{Average inventory}} = \frac{\$453{,}178}{(\$67{,}622 + \$73{,}632) \div 2} = \frac{\$453{,}178}{\$70{,}627} = 6.4 \text{ times}$$

Days to Sell Inventory

Another measure of inventory turnover that is also useful in assessing purchasing policy is the required number of days to sell inventory. The number of **days to sell inventory** measures the number of days it takes to sell the average inventory and is computed by dividing the number of days in a year (rounded to 360 days) by the average-inventory turnover. It may be presented as:

$$\text{Days to sell inventory} = \frac{360 \text{ days}}{\text{Average-inventory turnover}} \tag{6}$$

The Freder Company's days to sell inventory for 19x8 is computed as follows:

$$\frac{360}{6.4 \text{ times}} = 56\frac{1}{4} \text{ days}$$

Interpretation of Inventory-Turnover Ratios. The current ratio computation views its current asset components as sources of funds that can, as a means of last resort, be used to pay off the current liabilities. Viewed this way, the inventory-turnover ratios give us a measure of the quality as well as of the liquidity of the inventory component of the current assets.

In practice, a going concern cannot use its investment in inventory for the payment of current liabilities because any drastic reduction in normal inventory levels will cut into the sales volume.

A rate of turnover that is slower than that experienced historically, or that is below that normal in the industry, would lead to the preliminary conclusion that it includes items that are slow moving because they are obsolete, in weak demand, or otherwise unsalable. Such conditions do cast doubt on the feasibility of recovering the cost of such items.

CAPITAL STRUCTURE AND LONG-TERM SOLVENCY RATIOS

Long-term creditors have two main concerns. In the short run, they are concerned about receiving their annual interest payments; while in the long run, they are concerned about receiving the maturity value of their loans when they become due. While the ratios discussed below are important to the long-term creditors in assessing long-term solvency, the ability of a firm to meet its debts when due depends on *earnings.* If a firm is unprofitable in the long run, it will be unable to meet its obligations when they mature, nor will the company be able to refinance its debts. However, the trend of the ratios discussed below may highlight a deteriorating condition well in advance of a company's impending default on its long-term debt.

The basic ratio measurements of capital structure relate the various components of the capital structure to each other or to their total. Some of these ratios in common use are explained below.

Debt-to-Equity Ratio

The most comprehensive ratio in this area, the **debt-to-equity ratio,** measures the relationship between *total debt* (Current liabilities + Long-term liabilities) to total *stockholders' equity.* The ratio is total debt divided by total stockholders' equity and may be expressed as:

$$\text{Debt-to-equity ratio} = \frac{\text{Total liabilities}}{\text{Total stockholders' equity}} \qquad (7)$$

The computation of the debt-to-equity ratio for the years 19x8 and 19x7 for the Freder Company is as follows:

	19x8	19x7
Total current liabilities	$ 54,565	$ 48,873
Total long-term liabilities	47,180	42,420
Total liabilities	$101,745	$ 91,293 (A)
Total stockholders' equity	$145,841	$140,383 (B)
Debt-to-equity ratio (A) ÷ (B) . . .	.70	.65

This ratio means that Freder's total debt in 19x8 is 70 percent of its equity capital, or that the creditors advanced 70 cents for every dollar of the company's stockholders' equity. This ratio varies for different types of businesses. For example, traditionally, public utilities have a high debt-to-equity ratio in relation to manufacturing firms because the stability of their revenues allows them to carry more debt. Although a debt-to-equity ratio of .70 may be comfortable for the creditors of Freder, they may feel that the movement from .65 in 19x7 to .70 in 19x8 should be watched. The higher this ratio becomes, the more risk the creditors assume because the stockholders' equity acts as a buffer when operating losses occur. The operating losses are charged against stockholders' equity before any of the losses are assumed by the creditors, and the lower this ratio, the greater the buffer.

Times Interest Earned Ratio

An important measure of protection for the long-term creditor is the number of times interest is earned. The **times interest earned ratio** measures the likelihood that long-term creditors will continue to receive their interest when due and is computed by dividing the numerator consisting of net income, income taxes, and interest cost by the denominator consisting of the firm's interest cost. The ratio may be expressed as:

$$\frac{\text{Times interest}}{\text{earned}} = \frac{\text{Net income} + \text{Income taxes} + \text{Interest cost}}{\text{Interest cost}} \qquad (8)$$

For many firms, the numerator will be the same as their operating income. The operating income of the Freder Company (see Illustration 17–2) is $15,013 for 19x8, and this amount would be the numerator for this ratio. The computation for 19x8 is as follows:

$$\frac{\$6,008 + \$4,005 + \$5,000}{\$5,000} = \frac{\$15,013}{\$5,000} = 3 \text{ times}$$

Income taxes must be added back to the numerator because income taxes are only paid if profits exist, and interest must be deducted first before profits become subject to income taxes. Interest cost must also be added back to the numerator since this item is measured by the denominator.

Some users of this ratio believe that a rule-of-thumb ratio provides a measure of safety for the long-term creditor. More important than a single year's ratio, the trend of the ratio over a period of years provides the long-term creditor with the likelihood that interest payments will be met when due.

RETURN-ON-INVESTMENT RATIOS

There are many criteria by which performance can be measured. Changes in sales, in profits, or in various measures of output are among the criteria frequently used.

None of these measurements standing by itself is useful as a comprehensive measure of enterprise performance. The reasons for this are easy to grasp. Increases in sales are desirable only if they result in increased profits. The same is true of increases in volume of production. Increases in profits, on the other hand, must be related to the capital that is invested in order to attain these profits.

Return on Investment (ROI)

The relationship between net income and the capital invested in the generation of that income is one of the most valid and most widely recognized measures of enterprise performance. In relating income to invested capital, the ROI measure allows the analyst to compare it to alternative uses of capital as well as to the return realized by enterprises subject to similar degrees of risk. The investment of capital can always yield some return. If capital is invested in government bonds, the return will be low because of the small risk involved. Riskier investments require higher returns in order to make them worthwhile. The ROI measure relates income (reward) to the size of the capital that was needed to generate it.

Economic performance is the first purpose of business enterprise. It is the reason for its existence. The effectiveness of operating performance determines the ability of the enterprise to survive financially, to attract suppliers of funds, and to reward them adequately. ROI is the prime measure of economic performance. The analyst uses it as a tool in three areas of great importance:

1.   An indicator of managerial effectiveness.

2.   A measure of an enterprise's ability to earn a satisfactory return on investment.

3.   A method of projecting earnings.

An Indicator of Managerial Effectiveness.   The earning of an adequate or superior return on funds invested in an enterprise depends first on the resourcefulness, skill, ingenuity, and motivation of management. Thus, the longer term ROI has great interest and importance to the financial analyst because it offers a prime means of evaluating this indispensible criterion of business success: the quality of management.

A Measure of Enterprise Ability to Earn a Satisfactory ROI.   While related to managerial effectiveness, this measure is a far more reliable indicator of long-term financial health than is any measure of current financial strength based only on balance sheet relationships. For this reason, ROI has great importance and interest to longer term creditors as well as to equity investors.

A Method of Projecting Earnings.   A third important function of the ROI measure is that of a means of earnings projection. The advantage of this method of earnings projection is that it links the estimated amount of earnings that an enterprise will earn to the total invested capital. This adds discipline and realism to the projection process.

The rate of ROI method of earnings projection can be used by the analyst as either the primary method of earnings projection or as a supplementary check on estimates derived from other projection methods.

Basic Elements of ROI

The basic concept of ROI is simple to understand. However, care must be used in determining the elements for its computation because there are a variety of views, which reflect different objectives, of how these elements should be defined.

The basic formula for computing ROI is as follows:

$$\frac{\text{Income}}{\text{Investment}}$$

We shall now examine the various definitions of *investment* and of *income*.

There is no one generally accepted measure of capital investment on which the rate of return is computed. The different concepts of investment reflect different objectives. Since the term *return on investment (ROI)* covers a multitude of concepts of investment base and income, we need more specific terms to describe the actual investment base used.

Total Assets.   Return on total assets is perhaps the best measure of the *operating efficiency* of an enterprise. It measures the return obtained on *all* the assets entrusted to management. *By removing from this computation the effect of the method used in financing the assets,* the analyst can concentrate on the evaluation or projection of operating performance.

In the computation of ROI, the definition of return (income) depends on the definition of the investment base. If the investment base is defined as comprising total assets, then income *before* interest cost is used. The exclusion of interest from income deductions occurs because it is regarded as a payment for the use of money to the suppliers of debt capital in the same way that dividends are regarded as a reward to suppliers of equity capital.

The **return on the total assets** measures the effectiveness of asset utilization and is computed by dividing a numerator consisting of a firm's net income plus its after-tax cost of interest by a denominator consisting of the firm's average total assets. The ROI may be expressed as:

$$\frac{\text{Return on}}{\text{total assets}} = \frac{\text{Net income} + \text{Interest cost} \ (1 - \text{Tax rate})}{\text{Average total assets}} \qquad (9)$$

The calculation of this return for the Freder Company for 19x8 is as follows:

$$\frac{\$6,008 + \$5,000(1 - 40\%)}{(\$231,676 + \$247,586) \div 2} = \frac{\$9,008}{\$239,631} = .038 = 3.8\%$$

By most standards, a 3.8 percent return on total assets would be considered unsatisfactory. In addition to this year's performance, the trend as well as the level of this parameter must be evaluated.

Return on Common Stockholders' Equity. Although a corporation's objectives are varied, the main reason for its existence is to earn a satisfactory return for its common stockholders. The measure used to evaluate this performance is **return on common stockholders' equity** and is computed by dividing a numerator consisting of net income minus preferred dividends by a denominator of average common stockholder's equity. The formula may be expressed as:

$$\frac{\text{Return on common}}{\text{stockholders' equity}} = \frac{\text{Net income} - \text{Preferred dividends}}{\text{Average common stockholders' equity}} \qquad (10)$$

The return on common stockholders' equity for the Freder Company for 19x8 is as follows:

Net income	$ 6,008	
Less: Preferred dividends	2,000	
Net income available to common stockholders	$ 4,008	(A)
Stockholders' equity, January 1, 19x8	$140,383	
Stockholders' equity, December 31, 19x8	145,841	
Total	$286,224	
Average stockholders' equity ($286,224 ÷ 2)	$143,112	
Less: Average preferred stock	20,000*	
Average common stockholders' equity	$123,112	(B)
Return on common stockholders' equity (A) ÷ (B)	3.3%	

* $20,000 + $20,000 = $40,000 ÷ 2 = $20,000.

ILLUSTRATION 17–8

FREDER COMPANY
Analysis of the Cost of Liabilities and Preferred Stock
For the Year Ended December 31, 19x8

Interest cost, net of tax ($5,000 × .60)	$ 3,000	
Add: Preferred dividends	2,000	
Total cost of interest and preferred dividends	$ 5,000	(C)
Average liabilities and preferred stock:		
Average total assets—computed above		
in conjunction with formula (9)	$239,631	
Less: Average common stockholders' equity—		
computed above in conjunction with		
formula (10) (labeled B)	123,112	
Average liabilities and preferred stock	$116,519	(D)
Average cost of liabilities and preferred stock (C) ÷ (D)	4.3%	

Note that the return on common stockholders' equity decreased to 3.3 percent when compared to the return on total assets of 3.8 percent. The reason for this decrease is that the firm's interest cost of liabilities (net of income tax) plus the cost of the preferred stock is greater than the 3.8 percent return on total assets. This analysis is shown in Illustration 17–8.

When the return on total assets is less than the after-tax cost of liabilities and preferred stock, the return on common stockholders' equity is less than the return on total assets. On the other hand, when the after-tax interest cost of liabilities and the cost of preferred stock is less than the return on total assets, the return on common stockholders' equity will be greater than that for total assets. Incurring debt is known as employing financial leverage.

Financial Leverage. Using borrowed funds or funds acquired from the sale of preferred stock—both of which require fixed costs for the use of the funds—in place of funds acquired from the sale of common stock is known as **financial leverage.** Financial leverage, also called *trading on the equity,* is normally employed to increase the return to common stockholders, and when successful, the financial leverage is said to be positive. **Positive financial leverage** exists when the cost of borrowed funds (and/or the dividend cost of preferred stock) is less than the return on total assets, and the return on common stockholders' equity exceeds the return on total assets.

Let us assume that the Freder Company has an opportunity to enter a new market with an investment of $200,000 that will yield an operating income of $80,000 per year. The firm plans to borrow the $200,000 at an interest rate of 10 percent per annum. The simple return on this investment may be computed as follows:

Operating income	$80,000
Less: Interest cost ($200,000 × 10%)	20,000
Income before income taxes	60,000
Income taxes (40 percent)	24,000
Net income	$36,000

Return on this investment:

$$\frac{\$36,000}{\$200,000} = 18\%$$

We can now modify the previously given data of the Freder Company for 19x8 to see what effect this investment will have on the return on total assets and the return on common stockholders' equity.

Return on Total Assets

Modified net income:	
Net income as given	$ 6,008
Add: Net income from the project	36,000
Modified net income	$ 42,008
Modified total assets:	
Average net assets as given	
[See information for formula (9)]	$239,631
Add: Assets acquired for project	200,000
Modified total assets	$439,631

Using formula (9), the return on total assets would be:

$$\frac{\$42,008 + [\$5,000 + \$20,000 = \$25,000(1 - .40)]}{\$439,631} = \frac{\$57,008}{\$439,631} = 13\%$$

Return on common stockholders' equity

$$\frac{\text{Net income} - \text{Preferred dividends}}{\text{Average common stockholders' equity}} \qquad \textbf{(10)}$$

$$\frac{\$42,008 - \$2,000}{\$123,112^*} = \frac{\$40,008}{123,112} = 32.5\%$$

* This amount is unchanged since the project's funds would be all borrowed.

Note that the return on total assets increased from 3.8 percent to 13 percent as a result of factoring in the contemplated project; the return on common stockholders' equity increased more dramatically from 3.3 percent to 32.5 percent. Hence, positive financial leverage may have a profound effect on the return on common stockholders' equity. However, financial leverage may be negative, as in the original data presented for the Freder Company, and when this occurs, the opposite effect is encountered. **Negative financial leverage** exists when the cost of borrowing funds (and/or the dividend cost of preferred stock) is greater than the return on total assets, and the return on common stockholders' equity is less than the return on total assets.

Although borrowed funds and funds from the sale of preferred stock with a fixed yield are both sources of financial leverage, they have different effects on a firm's use of financial leverage.

Effects of Financial Leverage. Long-term debt, consisting mainly of bonds payable, notes payable, and lease obligations under capitalized leases, has a fixed interest cost, whether it is stated interest or imputed interest. Short-term debt may have some elements, such as notes payable, that have a fixed interest cost, but other elements, such as accounts payable and accrued wages payable, have no interest cost. Thus, when the return on common stockholders' equity is computed, debt without any interest cost benefits common stockholders.

Long-term notes payable and long-term bonds payable benefit common stockholders less than accounts payable but more than preferred stock, because the interest cost associated with long-term debt is deductible for income tax purposes while the dividends paid to preferred stockholders is not deductible.

To illustrate the different effects on the use of leverage, assume that a company's stockholders' equity and total assets are $300,000 and consist entirely of common stock. Its earnings before income taxes are $60,000 and its income tax rate is 40 percent. The firm can double its operating income to $120,000 by doubling its total assets to $600,000 by using one of three possible plans. These plans are: (1) issuing $300,000 of common stock, (2) issuing $300,000 of preferred stock with a 10 percent dividend, and (3) issuing $300,000 of 10 percent bonds payable. The effects of the three plans on the return on common stockholders' equity are shown in Illustration 17–9.

ILLUSTRATION 17–9   **Effects of Leverage Using Common Stock, Preferred Stock, and Bonds Payable**

	Common Stock	Preferred Stock	Bonds Payable
Operating income	$120,000	$120,000	$120,000
Less: Interest cost (10% × $300,000)	—	—	30,000
Income before income taxes	120,000	120,000	90,000
Income taxes at 40 percent	48,000	48,000	36,000
Net income	72,000	72,000	54,000
Less: Preferred dividends (10% × $300,000)	—	30,000	—
Net income available to common stockholders	$ 72,000	$ 42,000	$ 54,000 (A)
Common stockholders' equity	$600,000	$300,000	$300,000 (B)
Return on common stockholders' equity (A) ÷ (B)	12%	14%	18%

Illustration 17–9 indicates that when financial leverage is positive, the use of long-term debt has the greatest impact on the return on common stockholders' equity while the use of preferred stock has a lesser impact. Most firms use financial leverage, and the blend of long-term debt, preferred stock, and common stock is usually dictated by market forces and conditions.

Notice that for the Freder Company the cost of liabilities and preferred stock (see Illustration 17–8) is only 4.3 percent even though the pre-tax interest cost on the bonds payable is greater than 10 percent ($5,000 ÷ $47,180) (from Illustrations 17–1 and 17–2) and the preferred dividend cost is 10 percent (from Illustration 17–1). The reason for this is that current liabilities have a zero cost, while the weighted average after-tax cost of the bonds payable is 6.7 percent, computed as follows:

Bonds payable, January 1, 19x8	$42,420
Bonds payable, December 31, 19x8	47,180
Total	$89,600
Average ($89,600 ÷ 2)	$44,800
Net-of-tax interest = $5,000 (1 − .40)	$ 3,000
After-tax cost of bonds ($3,000 ÷ $44,800)	6.696%

The cost shown in Illustration 17–8 may also be computed as follows:

	(1) Weighted-Average Amount	(2) Percent of Total	(3) Rate Cost	(4) Weighted Rate Cost (2) × (3)
Current liabilities	$ 51,719	44.39	–0–	–0–
Bonds payable	44,800	38.45	6.7%	2.6%
Preferred stock	20,000	17.16	10.0%	1.7%
Total	$116,519	100.00		4.3%

EARNINGS PER SHARE (EPS)

Earnings per share is a statistic quoted by investment services, stock brokerage reports on specific companies, and various financial publications. Also, it is the single statistic most often relied on by investors as the measure of a company's operating performance. **Earnings per share** is computed by dividing the numerator of a firm's net income available to common stockholders by the denominator of the weighted-average number of common shares outstanding for the period. Earnings per share may be expressed as:

$$\frac{\text{Earnings}}{\text{per share}} = \frac{\text{Net income} - \text{Preferred dividends}}{\text{Weighted-average common shares outstanding}} \qquad (11)$$

The weighted-average common shares outstanding for the Freder Company is easily calculated. At the beginning of the year (see Illustration 17–1), there were 6,500 ($32,500 ÷ $5 par value) shares outstanding. At the end of the year, there were 7,500 ($37,500 ÷ $5 par value) shares outstanding. If the additional 1,000 shares were sold on April 1, 19x8, the weighted-average number of shares may be calculated as follows:

Date	Shares Outstanding	Months Unchanged	Product
19x8			
January 1	6,500	3	19,500
April 1	7,500	9	67,500
Total		12	87,000
Weighted average (87,000 ÷ 12)			7,250

The calculation of earnings per share for 19x8 for the Freder Company is:

$$\frac{\$6,008 - \$2,000}{7,250 \text{ shares}} = \frac{\$4,008}{7,250 \text{ shares}} = \$.55 \text{ per share}$$

While the earnings per share statistic is useful when used with the share's market price (discussed later), over a period of years this statistic's trend provides users with its greatest use. Remember that net income is derived from accounting practices that permit the selection of various alternatives, such as inventory valuations and depreciation methods. If a firm consistently uses the same accounting alternatives from year to year, then its trend of EPS is reliable. However, care must be exercised when comparisons between competing firms are made. It may be that these firms are using different accounting methods, such as for depreciation and inventory valuation. When this is the case, comparisons may still be made if the differences created by the accounting methods are factored into the comparisons.

Another problem in relying on a single EPS number is that a variety of potentially dilutive securities, such as options, warrants, convertible debt, and convertible preferred stock are not included in the EPS calculation. When a firm has these securities outstanding, the firm must present additional EPS statistics.

Primary and Fully Diluted Earnings per Share. During the past two decades, there has been an increased tendency for firms to issue bonds payable and preferred stock that can be converted into specific numbers of shares of common stock. When an investor exercises this conversion feature, the bond and/or the preferred stock is surrendered and common stock is received in its place. Because of the uncertainty regarding the ultimate outcome of conversion, a question arises regarding how these securities should be treated for EPS calculations. In 1970, the Accounting Principles Board of the American Institute of Certified Public Accountants determined that the best approach to disclosing the problems created by potentially dilutive securities is to present two EPS statistics, one similar to that discussed previously[2] and another giving effect to the possible full dilution (lower amount) of EPS. **Fully diluted earnings per share** is computed by dividing the net income available to common shareholders by the weighted-average common shares outstanding and then adjusting both the numerator and denominator for the assumed conversion of all potentially dilutive securities. Computing earnings per share can be quite complex, and of necessity, the discussion of this topic is limited to the simpler calculations.

Let us assume that the Freder Company's preferred stock and bonds payable shown in Illustration 17–1 are convertible into common stock. The preferred stock can be converted into 5,000 shares of common stock and the bonds can be converted into 10,000 shares of common stock.

The starting point of the calculation is the previously computed earnings per share fraction. An important point to remember is that fully diluted EPS *cannot be* greater than the original EPS of 55 cents per share for the Freder Company as a result of the adjustments for potentially dilutive securities. If this amount is greater, a condition known as *antidilution,* then the fully diluted EPS is *not* shown and the presentation is limited to a single presentation, 55 cents per share.

The denominator of the basic fraction is adjusted by the amount of common shares that would be issued for the conversion of the preferred stock and bonds payable. Since these adjustments assume that the preferred stock is no longer outstanding, the preferred dividend of $2,000 must be added back to the numerator because it would no longer be paid. The same is true for the $5,000 of interest cost for the bonds payable, except that it must be added back net of tax because interest is deductible on the firm's income statement to arrive at net income. The calculation would be as follows:

Fully diluted EPS

$$= \frac{\$4,008 + \$2,000 + \$5,000(1 - .40)}{7,250 + 5,000 + 10,000} = \frac{\$9,008}{22,250} = \$.40 \text{ per share}$$

Since fully diluted EPS is 40 cents per share and it is less than 55 cents per share (the original amount), both amounts are shown. The 55 cents per share amount is called *primary EPS.*

When a firm has extraordinary items on its income statement, EPS is computed separately for *income before extraordinary items, extraordinary items,* and *net income.* This is done for both primary EPS and fully diluted

---

[2] When certain dilutive securities called common stock equivalents are present in a firm's capital structure, the simple EPS figure is modified by these dilutive securities, and the new EPS figure is called *primary EPS.* This calculation is discussed in intermediate accounting texts.

EPS. Thus, six EPS numbers would be required when a firm has both extraordinary items and potentially dilutive securities outstanding.

MARKET MEASURES

Price-Earnings Ratio

Investors and potential investors relate a firm's EPS to the market price of its stock. The **price-earnings ratio** is computed by dividing the market price of a firm's share of common stock by the primary earnings per share. The price-earnings ratio (PE ratio) may also be expressed as:

$$\text{Price-earnings ratio} = \frac{\text{Market price per share}}{\text{Earnings per share}} \qquad (12)$$

Assuming a market price of $8 per share for the Freder Company, its PE ratio for 19x8 would be computed as follows:

$$\frac{\$8}{\$.55} = 14.5$$

This means that the firm's shares are selling at 14.5 times earnings.

While investors use PE ratios as a measure of a company's future prospects, the ratio also provides investors with a measurement by which to gauge competing investments in the same industry. PE ratios vary between firms in different industries and between growth companies and well-seasoned companies. The trend of a firm's PE ratio also provides useful information for investors and indicates whether a particular stock is cheap or expensive in relation to competing investments.

Dividend Payout and Yield Ratios

Different stockholders have different investment objectives. Investors who are taxed at relatively low income tax brackets may prefer a high current income in the form of dividends which are taxed at ordinary income tax rates. They are willing to accept this high current income with a concomitant low amount of capital appreciation. Other investors who are taxed at high income tax rates would probably prefer to invest in so-called *growth companies* that pay low dividends and reinvest their earnings for growth potential. These investors are willing to forgo current income in favor of capital appreciation of their stock which would be taxed at reduced capital-gains rates. The dividend payout ratio would help investors determine which company's stock would meet their objectives.

Dividend Payout Ratio. The **dividend payout ratio** is computed by dividing common stock dividends per share by primary earnings per share. This ratio may be shown as follows:

$$\frac{\text{Dividend}}{\text{payout ratio}} = \frac{\text{Common stock dividends per share}}{\text{Primary earnings per share}} \qquad (13)$$

Assume that the common stock dividends per share for the Freder Company are $1.34 for 19x8. The dividend payout ratio for the firm would be:

$$\frac{\$1.34}{\$0.55} = 2.436 = 243.6\%$$

While this ratio is extremely unusual, a company may occasionally pay more dividends than it earns when the reduction in earnings is temporary and the firm wishes to maintain its dividend paying record. If this payout ratio were maintained for any significant length of time, the company would be engaged in a partial liquidation.

Let us now assume that the Hall Company pays a common dividend per share of $1.00 and its primary earnings per share are $2.50. Its dividend payout ratio would be:

$$\frac{\$1.00}{\$2.50} = .40 = 40\%$$

This ratio would be considered average, but ratios fluctuate widely. As noted, growth companies with good investment opportunities would have dividend payout ratios considerably less than 40 percent, while firms with limited investment opportunities, such as some public utilities, have dividend payout ratios considerably in excess of 40 percent.

Dividend Yield Ratio. The dividend yield ratio is computed by dividing a firm's dividends per share by its market price per share, and may be shown as follows:

$$\text{Dividend yield ratio} = \frac{\text{Dividends per share}}{\text{Market price per share}} \qquad \textbf{(14)}$$

Using the assumed dividends per common share of $1.34 and the market price per share of $8.00 for the Freder Company, the common stock dividend yield ratio for 19x8 would be as follows:

$$\frac{\$1.34}{\$8.00} = .1675 = 16.75\%$$

When an investor makes this calculation, she should use the *current* market price and not the price she paid for the investment. By continuing to hold this stock, she gives up her right to receive $8 per share (her opportunity cost). The *current dividend* must be related to the *current cost* of purchasing the stock. Otherwise, a meaningless yield ratio may be the result.

Although EPS is an important statistic for investors, they rarely, if ever, actually receive a firm's EPS. Instead, they usually receive an amount each year in the form of dividends and hopefully some capital gains when the stock is sold. Therefore, when evaluating an investment (or potential investment), the investor must look to the yield received in the form of dividends.

A tabulation of all of the ratios previously discussed is provided in Illustration 17–10.

Appendix 17–A contains a listing of various sources of published financial

ILLUSTRATION 17–10   **Tabulation of Ratios**

Number	Ratio	Formula
(1)	Current ratio	$\dfrac{\text{Current assets}}{\text{Current liabilities}}$
(2)	Acid-test ratio (quick ratio)	$\dfrac{\text{Cash} + \text{Short-term marketable securities} + \text{Current receivables}}{\text{Current liabilities}}$
(3)	Accounts-receivable-turnover ratio	$\dfrac{\text{Net sales on credit}}{\text{Average accounts receivable}}$
(4)	Collection period of receivables	$\dfrac{360}{\text{Average-accounts-receivable-turnover ratio}}$
(5)	Inventory-turnover ratio	$\dfrac{\text{Cost of goods sold}}{\text{Average inventory}}$
(6)	Days to sell inventory	$\dfrac{360}{\text{Average inventory turnover}}$
(7)	Debt-to-equity ratio	$\dfrac{\text{Total liabilities}}{\text{Total stockholders' equity}}$
(8)	Times interest earned ratio	$\dfrac{\text{Net income} + \text{Income taxes} + \text{Interest cost}}{\text{Interest cost}}$
(9)	Return on total assets	$\dfrac{\text{Net income} + \text{Interest cost} (1 - \text{Tax rate})}{\text{Average total assets}}$
(10)	Return on common stockholders' equity	$\dfrac{\text{Net income} - \text{Preferred dividends}}{\text{Average common stockholders' equity}}$
(11)	Earnings per share	$\dfrac{\text{Net income} - \text{Preferred dividends}}{\text{Weighted-average common shares outstanding}}$
(12)	Price-earnings ratio	$\dfrac{\text{Market price per share}}{\text{Earnings per share}}$
(13)	Dividend payout ratio	$\dfrac{\text{Common stock dividends per share}}{\text{Primary earnings per share}}$
(14)	Dividend yield ratio	$\dfrac{\text{Dividends per share}}{\text{Market price per share}}$

and operating ratios classified by the type of source that collects and compiles them.

SUMMARY

Financial statements are prepared using a historical basis and thus are based on past transactions. While investors find this information useful from a stewardship viewpoint, managers and other external users of financial statements are more interested in the future course that a company is likely to take. Therefore, financial statements are used to assist users in making inferences about a company's future. Financial statement analysis provides users with the needed information.

The principal tools of financial statement analysis consist of (1) comparative financial statements showing year-to-year changes, (2) index-number trend series which show the relative changes of the subsequent periods' items compared to a base period, often called **horizontal analysis, (3) common-size statements** also called **vertical analysis,** where each component of a statement is shown as a percentage of the total instead of in absolute dollars, and (4) **ratio analysis,** where a numerical value is shown in relation to another value. An **index number** which is used to measure a quality that is common to a group of items has little useful value by itself. When an index number is used as part of a trend analysis, which indicates the general direction that the measured attribute is taking, then the index number achieves its greatest usefulness. The **velocity of the trend,** which measures the rate of movement in a general direction, is also extremely useful for predicting the future course of a business.

Ratios have various classifications. One group of ratios is the short-term liquidity classification which is related to **working capital** and includes the **current ratio,** the **acid-test (quick) ratio,** the **average-accounts-receivable-turnover ratio,** the **collection period for accounts receivable,** the **inventory-turnover ratio,** and the **days to sell inventory.**

Another group of ratios is the capital structure and long-term solvency ratios which include the **debt-to-equity ratio** and the **times interest earned ratio.**

A third ratio group is the return on investment classification, which include the **return on total assets ratio** and the **return on common stockholders' equity ratio.** Since a firm is operated primarily to benefit common stockholders, a major objective of most firms is to improve and maintain the return to common stockholders. One method of accomplishing this is to increase earnings. Another possible method is to make use of **financial leverage** which is borrowing funds, or selling preferred stock, in place of raising additional funds through the sale of common stock. When the fixed cost (in percentage terms) paid to lenders or to the preferred stockholders is less than the return on total assets, **positive financial leverage** is said to exist. When the reverse is true, **negative financial leverage** exists.

The most often quoted single statistic that relates to a firm's operating performance is **earnings per share.** This measure is used to indicate the amount of net income available to common stockholders on a per share basis. When a firm has potentially dilutive securities outstanding, such as options, warrants, convertible bonds payable, or convertible preferred stock, the effects of these securities' *assumed* conversion into common stock is factored into the original EPS and shown as an additional EPS statistic labeled **fully diluted earnings per share.** When this figure is shown, the original EPS is labeled primary earnings per share.

Still another grouping of ratios is the market measure ratios classification. This includes the **price-earnings ratio,** the **dividend payout ratio,** and the **dividend yield ratio.** The price-earnings ratio provides investors with a means of comparing competing investments to determine which ones are expensive or inexpensive. The dividend payout ratio and the dividend yield ratio provide investors with data that helps them achieve their investment objectives.

Ratios can be potent analytical tools if they are analyzed in conjunction with the trend of each ratio. While it is important to see a particular relationship at a point in time, it is more important to examine the trend of a ratio and the velocity of the trend for that ratio.

GLOSSARY OF KEY TERMS

Common-size statements   A financial statement where each component of the statement is shown as a percentage instead of as dollar amounts.

Financial leverage   Using borrowed funds or funds acquired from the sale of preferred stock—both of which require fixed costs for the use of the funds—in place of funds acquired from the sale of common stock.

Horizontal analysis   Trend analysis.

Index number   A measure used to indicate common qualities to a group of items.

Negative financial leverage   When the cost of borrowed funds (and/or the dividend cost of preferred stock) is greater than the return on total assets, and the return on common stockholders' equity is less than the return on total assets.

Positive financial leverage   When the cost of borrowed funds (and/or the dividend cost of preferred stock) is less than the return on total assets, and the return on common stockholders' equity exceeds the return on total assets.

Ratio   An expression of the mathematical relationship between one quantity and another.

Trend   The general direction of financial data expressed in terms of a base period (usually one year).

Velocity of trend   The rate of movement of financial data in a general direction.

Vertical analysis   Common-size statements.

Working capital   The excess of current assets over current liabilities.

GLOSSARY OF KEY RATIOS

Accounts-receivable-turnover ratio   Computed by dividing net credit sales by the average accounts receivable.

Acid-test ratio (quick ratio)   A numerator composed of cash, short-term marketable securities, and accounts (and short-term notes) receivable divided by a denominator of current liabilities.

Collection period for accounts receivable   A measure of the number of days it takes, on average, to collect accounts (and notes) receivable. It is obtained by dividing the average-accounts-receivable-turnover ratio into 360 days.

Current ratio   A firm's current assets divided by its current liabilities.

Days to sell inventory   A measure of the number of days it takes to sell the average inventory and is computed by dividing the number of days in a year by the average-inventory turnover.

Debt-to-equity ratio   A measure of the relationship between total debt (current liabilities + long-term liabilities) to total stockholders' equity, that is computed by dividing total debt by stockholders' equity.

Dividend payout ratio Computed by dividing common stock dividends per share by primary earnings per share.

Dividend yield ratio Computed by dividing a firm's dividends per share by its market price per share.

Earnings per share (primary earnings per share) Computed by dividing the numerator of a firm's net income available to common stockholders by the denominator of the weighted-average number of common shares outstanding for the period.

Fully diluted earnings per share Earnings per share adjusted for the assumed conversion of all potentially dilutive securities.

Inventory-turnover ratio A measurement of the average speed with which inventories move through and out of the enterprise and is computed by dividing cost of goods sold by average inventory.

Price-earnings ratio Computed by dividing the market price of a firm's share of stock by the primary earnings per share.

Return on common stockholders' equity Computed by dividing a numerator consisting of net income minus preferred dividends by a denominator of average common stockholders' equity.

Return on total assets A measure of the effectiveness of asset utilization computed by dividing a numerator consisting of a firm's net income plus its after-tax cost of interest by a denominator consisting of the firm's average assets.

Times interest earned ratio A measurement of the likelihood that long-term creditors will continue to receive their interest when due that is computed by dividing the numerator consisting of net income, income taxes, and interest cost by the denominator consisting of the firm's interest cost.

APPENDIX 17–A

SOURCES OF INFORMATION ON FINANCIAL AND OPERATING RATIOS

A good way to achieve familiarity with the wide variety of published financial and operating ratios available is to classify them by the type of source that collects or compiles them. The specific sources given under each category are intended to exemplify the type of material available. These are by no means complete lists:

Professional and Commerical Organizations

Dun & Bradstreet, Inc., Business Economics Division, New York, N.Y.
Key Business Ratios. Important operating and financial ratios in 190 lines.
Selected operating cost figures for many retailing, wholesaling, manufacturing lines, as well as for contract construction; service/transportation/communication; finance/insurance/real estate; agriculture/forestry/fishing; mining.
Cost-of-Doing-Business Series. Typical operating ratios for 185 lines of business, showing national averages. They represent a percentage of business receipts reported by a representative sample of the total of all federal tax returns.

Moody's Investor Service, New York, N.Y.

Moody's Manuals contain financial and operating ratios on individual companies covered.

National Cash Register Company. *Expenses in Retail Businesses.* Biennial.
Operating ratios for 35 lines of retail business, as taken from trade associations and other sources including many from *Barometer of Small Business.*

Robert Morris Associates. *Annual Statement Studies.*
Financial and operating ratios for about 300 lines of business—manufacturers, wholesalers, retailers, services, and contractors—based on information obtained from member banks of RMA. Data is broken down by company size.

Standard & Poor's Corporation
Industry Surveys in two parts: (1) Basic Analysis and (2) Current Analysis contains many industry and individual company ratios.
Analysts Handbook. "Composite corporate per share data—by industries," for over 90 industries. Statistics and percentages cover 13 components, including sales, operating profits, depreciation, earnings dividends, and the like.
Industry Surveys. Basic data on 36 important industries, with financial comparisons of the leading companies in each industry. Includes a "Basic Analysis" for each, revised annually. A "Current Analysis" is published quarterly for each industry. A monthly "Trends and Projections" includes tables of economic and industry indicators.

Almanac of Business and Industrial Financial Ratios by Leo Troy. Prentice-Hall, Englewood Cliffs, N.J.
A compilation of corporate performance ratios (operating and financial). The significance of these ratios is explained. All industries are covered in the study; each industry is subdivided by asset size.

The Federal Government

Small Business Administration
Publications containing industry statistics:
Small Marketers Aid.
Small Business Management Series.
Business Service Bulletins.

U.S. Department of Commerce
Census of Business—Wholesale Trade—Summary Statistics. Monthly Wholesale Trade Report. Ratio of operating costs to sales.

Department of The Treasury
Statistics of Income, Corporation Income Tax Returns. Operating Statistics based on income tax returns.

Federal Trade Commission—Securities and Exchange Commission
Quarterly Financial Report for Manufacturing, Mining, and Trade Corporations. Contains operating ratios and balance sheet ratios as well as the balance sheet in ratio format.

U.S. Internal Revenue Service
Source Book: Statistics of Income: Corporation Income Tax Returns. Washington, D.C. Annual. "Balance sheet, income statement, tax items by major and minor industries, broken down by size of total assets."
Statistics of Income: Corporation Income Tax Returns. Washington, D.C.: U.S. Government Printing Office. Annual. Balance sheet and income statement statistics from a sample of corporate returns. Includes tables by major industry, by asset size, and so on. Includes historical summaries.

QUESTIONS

1. Give four broad categories of analysis tools.

2. Is the trend of the past a good predictor of the future? Give reasons for your argument.

3. Which is the better indicator of significant change—the absolute amount of change or the change in percentage? Why?

4. What conditions would prevent the computation of a valid percentage change? Give an example.

5. What are some of the criteria to be used in picking out a base year in an index-number comparative analysis?

6. What information can be obtained from trend analysis?

7. What is a common-size financial statement? How do you prepare one?

8. What does a common-size financial statement tell about an enterprise?

9. Do all ratios have significance? Explain.

10. What are some of the limitations of ratio analysis?

11. Give three ratios that can be prepared by use of balance sheet figures only.

12. Give four ratios that require data from both the balance sheet and the income statement.

13. Why is short-term liquidity so significant? Explain from the viewpoint of various parties concerned.

14. The concept of working capital is simple, that is, the excess of current assets over current liabilities. What are some of the factors that make this simple computation complicated in practice?

15. What are cash equivalents? How should an analyst value them in his analysis?

16. Your careful computation of the working capitals of companies A and B reveals that both have the same amount of working capital. Are you ready to conclude that the liquidity position of both is the same? Explain.

17. What is the current ratio? What does it measure? What are the reasons for its widespread use?

18. What does the average-accounts-receivable-turnover ratio measure?

19. What is the collection period for accounts receivable? What does it measure?

20. A company's collection period is 60 days this year as compared to 40 days last year. Give three or more possible reasons for this change.

21. What is an accounts receivable aging schedule? What is its use in the analysis of financial statements?

22. What are the repercussions to an enterprise of (a) overinvestment or (b) underinvestment in inventories?

23. What is the rule of thumb governing the expected size of the current ratio? What dangers are there in using this rule of thumb mechanically?

24. What are the dangers for investors who rely on EPS?

25. What is financial leverage?

26. What is the difference between positive financial leverage and negative financial leverage?

27. Assume that you are considering the purchase of common stock in a particular firm. As an inducement to speed your contemplated purchase, your stockbroker states that the company has no long-term debt and has never borrowed any funds except in the ordinary course of purchasing its raw materials on account. Comment on your stockbroker's assertion that the company is so sound that it never had to borrow funds for any period longer than 30 days.

28. Different firms traditionally have different debt-to-equity ratios. Use examples to explain why this is so.

29. Is there a difference between the positive leverage obtained from long-term debt and preferred stock? Explain.

30. Different firms have different dividend payout ratios. Explain why.

31. Different investors have different investment objectives. Explain.

EXERCISES   **17–1**   **Preparation of Year-to-Year Changes for a Balance Sheet**

Given below are comparative balance sheets for Jem Stores, Inc.

JEM STORES, INC.
Comparative Condensed Balance Sheets
As of June 30, 19x4, and 19x3

	19x4	19x3
Assets		
Cash	$ 13,000	$ 15,000
Accounts receivable, net	78,000	58,000
Inventory	120,000	50,000
Other current assets	7,000	5,000
Plant and equipment (net)	70,000	60,000
Total assets	$288,000	$188,000
Liabilities and Equity		
Accounts payable	$ 70,000	$ 30,000
Federal income tax payable	14,000	20,000
Long-term liabilities	70,000	48,000
Common stock	90,000	70,000
Retained earnings	44,000	20,000
Total liabilities and equity	$288,000	$188,000

Required   a. Prepare comparative balance sheets showing the year-to-year changes in *both* dollars and percent. Use 19x3 as the base period.

b. Write a brief report highlighting the changes you consider important.

17–2   **Preparation of Year-to-Year Changes for an Income Statement**

Given below are comparative income statements for Jem Stores, Inc.

JEM STORES, INC.
Condensed Income Statements
For the Years Ended June 30, 19x4, and 19x3

	19x4	19x3
Net sales	$1,300,000	$1,000,000
Cost of goods sold	800,000	500,000
Gross margin on sales	500,000	500,000
Marketing and administrative costs	460,000	430,000
Income before federal income tax	40,000	70,000
Income tax	16,000	28,000
Net income	$ 24,000	$ 42,000

Required a. Prepare comparative income statements showing the year-to-year changes in *both* dollars and percent. Use 19x3 as the base period.

b. Write a brief report highlighting the changes you consider important.

17–3 Index-Number Trend Series

The Burrows Company provides you with the following selected data:

	19x8	19x7	19x6	19x5	19x4
Sales	$1,133,611	$952,614	$807,300	$690,000	$600,000
Cost of goods sold	547,822	421,402	339,840	283,200	240,000
Gross margin	585,789	531,212	467,460	406,800	360,000
Marketing costs	149,021	145,356	122,148	104,400	90,000
Administrative costs	190,418	165,581	147,840	132,000	120,000
Net income	147,810	132,165	118,483	102,240	90,000

Required a. Convert the data into an index-number trend series using 19x4 as the base period.

b. Write a brief explanation of the information revealed by the index-number trend series that is not readily apparent from the given data.

17–4 Preparation of Common-Size Balance Sheets

Refer to the balance sheets given in Exercise 17–1.

Required a. Prepare comparative common-size balance sheets for Jem Stores, Inc.

b. Write a brief report highlighting the changes in 19x4 from 19x3 that you consider important.

17–5 Preparation of Common-Size Income Statements

Refer to the income statements given in Exercise 17–2.

Required a. Prepare a comparative common-size income statements for Jem Stores, Inc.

b. Write a brief report highlighting the changes in 19x4 from 19x3 that you consider important.

17–6 Calculation of Ratios

The following data apply to items 1 through 7.

The statement of financial position and income statement for MND Corporation for the 19x0–x1 fiscal year are presented below:

MND CORPORATION
Statement of Financial Position
May 31, 19x1
(in thousands)

Assets

Cash		$ 8,000
Accounts receivable		12,000
Inventory		9,000
Property, plant, and equipment	$48,400	
Less: Allowance for depreciation	11,900	36,500
Total assets		$65,500

Liabilities and Stockholders' Equity

Accounts payable—trade		$10,700
Notes payable (short term)		5,300
Mortgage bonds—due in 19x4		9,500
Common stock—$10 par value,		
4.5 million shares authorized,		
2.5 million shares issued and		
outstanding		25,000
Paid-in capital in excess of par		5,000
Retained earnings		10,000
Total liabilities and stockholders' equity		$65,500

MND CORPORATION
Income Statement
For the Year Ended May 31, 19x1
(in thousands)

Cash sales		$10,000
Credit sales		60,000
Total sales		70,000
Cost of sales:		
Inventory of finished goods 6/1/x0	$ 4,000	
Cost of goods manufactured	50,000	
Cost of goods available	54,000	
Inventory of finished goods 5/31/x1	5,000	49,000
Gross margin on sales		21,000
Operating costs:		
Marketing	3,000	
General and administrative	10,800	13,800
Operating income		7,200
Interest cost		1,200
Income before federal income tax		6,000
Federal income tax		2,400
Net income		$ 3,600

1. MND's current ratio is
   a. 1.81.
   b. 1.25.
   c. 1.14.
   d. 2.71.
   e. Some amount other than those shown above.
2. The average collection period for accounts receivable is
   a. 5.0 days.
   b. 61.7 days.
   c. 72.0 days.
   d. 36.0 days.
   e. Some amount other than those shown above.
3. The inventory turnover for finished goods for the current fiscal year was
   a. 10.9 times.
   b. 10.0 times.
   c. 9.8 times.
   d. 11.1 times.
   e. Some amount other than those shown above.
4. The ratio of total debt to stockholders' equity is
   a. .73:1.
   b. .64:1.
   c. .40:1.
   d. .24:1.
   e. Some amount other than those shown above.
5. MND's earnings per share for the 19x0–x1 fiscal year is
   a. $0.80/share.
   b. $2.40/share.
   c. $1.33/share.
   d. $1.44/share.
   e. Some amount other than those shown above.
6. The return on stockholders' investment is
   a. 15.0%.
   b. 5.5%.
   c. 9.0%.
   d. 9.2%.
   e. Some amount other than those shown above.
7. The times interest earned ratio for MND is
   a. 7.9 times.
   b. 3.0 times.
   c. 5.0 times.
   d. 6.0 times.
   e. Some amount other than those shown above.

(CMA adapted)

17–7 Effects of Transactions on Short-Term Liquidity Ratios

The following data apply to items 1 through 4.

Depoole Company is a manufacturer of industrial products and employs a calendar year for financial reporting purposes. Items 1 through 4 present several of Depoole's transactions during 19x0. Assume that total quick assets exceeded total current liabilities both before and after each transaction described. Further assume that Depoole has positive profits in 19x0 and a credit balance throughout 19x0 in its retained earnings account.

1. Payment of a trade account payable of $64,500 would
   a. Increase the current ratio but the quick ratio would not be affected.
   b. Increase the quick ratio but the current ratio would not be affected.
   c. Increase both the current and quick ratios.
   d. Decrease both the current and quick ratios.
   e. Have no effect on the current and quick ratios.
2. The purchase of raw materials for $85,000 on open account would
   a. Increase the current ratio.
   b. Decrease the current ratio.
   c. Increase net working capital.
   d. Decrease net working capital.
   e. Increase both the current ratio and net working capital.
3. The collection of a current accounts receivable of $29,000 would
   a. Increase the current ratio.
   b. Decrease the current ratio.
   c. Increase the quick ratio.
   d. Decrease the quick ratio.
   e. Not affect the current or quick ratios.
4. Obsolete inventory of $125,000 was written off during 19x0. This would
   a. Decrease the quick ratio.
   b. Increase the quick ratio.
   c. Increase net working capital.
   d. Decrease the current ratio.
   e. Decrease both the current and quick ratios.

(CMA adapted)

17-8   Calculation of Ratios

The following data apply to items 1 through 5.

The 19x9 financial statements for Johanson Company are reproduced below.

JOHANSON COMPANY
Statement of Financial Position
December 31, 19x8, and 19x9
(in thousands)

	19x8	19x9
Assets		
Current assets:		
Cash and temporary investments	$ 380	$ 400
Accounts receivable (net)	1,500	1,700
Inventories	2,120	2,200
Total current assets	4,000	4,300
Long-term assets:		
Land	500	500
Building and equipment (net)	4,000	4,700
Total long-term assets	4,500	5,200
Total assets	$ 8,500	$ 9,500
Liabilities and Equities		
Current liabilities:		
Accounts payable	$ 700	$ 1,400
Current portion long-term debt	500	1,000
Total current liabilities	1,200	2,400
Long-term debt	4,000	3,000
Total liabilities	5,200	5,400
Stockholders' equity:		
Common stock	3,000	3,000
Retained earnings	300	1,100
Total stockholders' equity	3,300	4,100
Total liabilities and equities	$ 8,500	$ 9,500

JOHANSON COMPANY
Statement of Income and Retained Earnings
For the Year Ended December 31, 19x9
(in thousands)

Net sales		$28,800
Less: Cost of goods sold	$15,120	
Marketing costs	7,180	
Administrative costs	4,100	
Interest	400	
Income taxes	800	27,600
Net income		1,200
Retained earnings, January 1		300
Subtotal		1,500
Cash dividends declared and paid		400
Retained earnings, December 31		$ 1,100

1. The acid-test ratio for 19x9 for Johanson Company is
    a.   1.1 to 1.
    b.   .9 to 1.
    c.   1.8 to 1.
    d.   .2 to 1.
    e.   .17 to 1.
2. The average number of days' sales outstanding in 19x9 for Johanson Company is
    a.   18 days.
    b.   360 days.
    c.   20 days.
    d.   4.4 days.
    e.   80 days.
3. The times interest earned ratio in 19x9 for Johanson Company is
    a.   3.0 times.
    b.   1.0 times.
    c.   72.0 times.
    d.   2.0 times.
    e.   6.0 times.
4. The inventory turnover in 19x9 for Johanson Company is
    a.   13.6 times.
    b.   12.5 times.
    c.   .9 times.
    d.   7.0 times.
    e.   51.4 times.
5. The dividend payout ratio in 19x9 for Johanson Company is
    a.   100%.
    b.   36%.
    c.   20%.
    d.   8.8%.
    e.   33.3%.

(CMA adapted)

17–9   Calculation of Ratios

The previous year's financial statements for the Zeta Corporation are given below.

ZETA CORPORATION
Income Statement
For the Year Ended December 31, 19x1

Net sales		$800,000
Cost of goods sold		320,000
Gross margin		480,000
Depreciation	$ 30,000	
Marketing and administrative costs	200,000	230,000
Income before taxes		250,000
Income taxes (48 percent)		120,000
Net income		$130,000

Managerial Accounting

Calvin Engler

Check Figures

Chapter 2

Exercise

2-5	a. Cost of goods manufactured.............	$640,000	
	b. Cost of goods sold	$650,000	
2-9	a. Cost of goods manufactured.............	$647,000	
	b. Cost of goods sold	$662,000	
2-10	a. Cost of goods manufactured.............	$674,000	
	b. Cost of goods sold	$689,000	

Problem

2-11	a. Cost of goods manufactured.............	$699,000	
	b. Operating income	$108,000	
2-13	a. Cost of goods manufactured.............	$914,000	
	b. Operating income	$489,000	
2-14	a. Cost of goods manufactured.............	$978,500	
	b. Operating income	$506,000	
2-17	a. Cost of goods manufactured.............	$804,000	
	b. Operating income	$421,000	
2-23	a. Operating income	$122,000	
	b. Cost of goods manufactured.............	$500,000	

Chapter 3

Exercise

3-7	Cost of goods manufactured	$970,000	
3-8	Cost of goods manufactured	$39,760	
3-9	a. Total cost	$63,500	
	Unit cost	$63.50	
	b. Selling price	$120.65	
3-11	Unit cost	$27.40	
3-12	a. POR	70% DLC	
3-13	a. POR	65% DLC	
3-14	a. POR	115% DLC	
3-16	a. Work in process.............	$3,240	
	Finished goods	$2,160	
	Cost of goods sold	$30,600	
3-18	a. Dept. A POR	$2.00/DLH	
	Dept. B POR	$0.90/MH	
	b. Total cost	$243,500	
	Unit cost	$2.435	

Problem

3-19	c. Cost of goods manufactured at normal	$1,032,000	
	Cost of goods sold at actual	$1,038,400	
3-20	b. Cost of goods manufactured at normal	$992,000	
	Cost of goods sold at actual	$955,400	
3-21	b. Raw materials................	$62,000	
	Work in process.............	$102,000	
	Finished goods	$114,000	
	c. POR	110% DLC	
3-22	b. POR	90% DLC	

Chapter 3 (continued)

Problem

3-23	c. Unit cost—Job 101	$71.504	
	Unit cost—Job 102	$127.00	
	d. Raw materials................	$21,000	
	Work in process..............	$80,700	
	Finished goods	$28,666	
3-24	c. Cost of goods manufactured at normal	$954,600	
	Cost of goods sold at actual	$924,800	
3-25	b. Cost of goods manufactured at normal	$917,600	
	Cost of goods sold at actual	$898,400	
3-26	b. POR	75% DLC	
3-27	c. Unit cost—Job 101	$79.88	
	Unit cost—Job 102	$141.95	
	d. Raw materials................	$23,820	
	Work in process..............	$90,265	
	Finished goods	$32,033	
3-28	b. Cost of goods manufactured at normal	$492,000	
	Cost of goods sold at actual	$488,500	
3-29	a. Work in process.............	$480	
	Finished goods	$960	
	Cost of goods sold	$4,560	

Chapter 4

Problem

4-13	a. Unit costs:		
	Materials	$3.10	
	Labor	$4.20	
	Overhead...................	$4.62	
4-14	a. Cutting Dept. Unit costs:		
	Materials	$2.70	
	Labor	$2.75	
	Overhead...................	$2.20	
	Finishing Dept. Unit costs:		
	Materials	$0.41	
	Labor	$1.45	
	Overhead...................	$1.305	
4-15	a. Unit costs:		
	Materials	$2.76	
	Conversion	$6.762	
4-16	a. Unit costs:		
	Materials	$2.45	
	Labor	$3.60	
	Overhead...................	$2.52	
4-17	a. Unit costs:		
	Materials	$1.62	
	Labor	$2.14	
	Overhead...................	$1.712	
4-18	a. Cutting Dept. Unit costs:		
	Materials	$1.16	
	Labor	$2.40	
	Overhead...................	$1.44	
	Finishing Dept. Unit costs:		
	Materials	$0.59	
	Labor	$2.30	
	Overhead...................	$2.07	
4-19	a. Unit costs:		
	Materials	$2.10	
	Conversion	$4.86	

1

©Richard D. Irwin, Inc., 1987
2 3 4 5 6 7 8 9 MG 4 3 2 1 0 9 8 7
56-1988-01   ISBN 0-256-05429-0

Problem

4-20   a. Cutting Dept. Unit costs:

Materials $3.75
Labor $4.30
Overhead................... $3.87

Finishing Dept. Unit costs:

Materials $4.26
Labor $6.90
Overhead................... $4.83

4-21   a. Mixing Dept. Unit costs:

Materials $2.70
Labor $3.152
Overhead.................. $3.783

Coloring Dept. Unit costs:

Materials $0.56
Labor $6.5321
Overhead.................. $5.2257

4-22   Unit costs:

Materials..................... $10.00
Labor..................... $4.00
Overhead $2.50

4-23   a.2. Unit costs:

Materials................. $1.25
Labor..................... $2.20
Overhead $1.32

4-24   a. Unit costs:

Materials $2.76
Labor $3.40
Overhead................... $3.74

4-25   a. Unit costs:

Materials $2.71
Labor $3,084
Overhead................... $3.70

4-26   a. Unit costs:

Materials $1.20
Labor $2.10
Overhead................... $1.68

4-27   a. Unit costs:

Materials $0.46
Labor $1.20
Overhead................... $1.80

4-28   Unit costs:

Materials..................... $1.1816
Conversion $5.3103

4-29   2. Unit costs:

Materials $5.80
Labor $8.00
Overhead.................. $7.20

Chapter 5

Exercise

5-9   b. Y = $60,540 + $10.215X
5-10   b. Y = $60,540 + $10.215X

Problem

5-13   c. Cost formulas:

Indirect labor—TC = $15,000 + $0.85X
Utilities—TC = $5,000 + $1.50X
Misc.—TC = $80,000 + $2.65X

d. Net income—$260,000

5-14   b. CMR = 70%
c. CMPU = $28/unit
d. $140,000 increase
$210,000 decrease

Problem

5-15   c. Cost formulas:

Overhead—Y = $90,000 + $1.00X
Marketing—Y = $60,000 + $0.40X
Administrative—$80,000 + $0.20X

d. Net income $244,000

5-16   Cost formulas:

Overhead—Y = $200,000 + $0.80X
Administrative—$100,000 + $0.60X
Net income..................... $49,400

5-18   d. 19x7 Net income:

William $60,000
Mary .... $<6,000>

5-19   c. Y = $76,616 + $9.758X
5-20   c. Y = $76,616 + $9.758X
5-21   a. High-Low: Y = $41,500 + $2.30X
b. Least Squares: Y = $39,859 + $2.1549X

5-22   a. Cost formulas:

Overhead—Y = $93,160 + $0.935X
Marketing—Y = $60,016 + $0.406X

b. Net income $187,954

5-23   a. Cost formulas:

Overhead—Y = $93,160 + $0.935X
Marketing—Y = $60,016 + $0.406X

b. Net income $187,954

5-24   c. Y = $31,775 + $8.243X
5-25   c. Y = $31,775 + $8.243X

Chapter 6

Exercise

6-1   a. $3,000,000
b. $750,000
c. $400,000

6-7   a. CMR 40%
CMPU...................... $3.20
b. $80,000
c.1............................. $9.00
and.................... $3.60
2............................. $550,000
and.................... No

6-10   a. 70%
b. $1,900,000
c. $1,330,000
d. $47.50
e. Yes $900,000
f. .... No

6-12   a. $315,000
b. $34,000
c.1. .... $370,588
2. .... $44,000
d. $11.00

6-15   a. $50,000
b. Yes $80,000
c. Increase in net income $35,000
Advertising $50,000

6-16   a. $500,000 and 50,000 units
b. No. $10,000 decrease in income
c.1. .... $10.60
2. .... $11.50

Exercise

6-22	b.	4
	c.	$220,000
6-23	a.	$400,000
	b.	$100,000
	c.	$700,000
6-28	a.	30,000 units
	b.	33,333 units
	c. Continue with the 19x5 strategy	
6-29	a.	275,000 boxes
	b.	$4.50
	c.	$1,920,000

Problem

6-31	a.	$600,000
	and	20,000 units
	b.	$180,000
	c. $36,000 decrease	No
	d.	15,000 units
	and $540,000	No
	e.	$40,000 increase
	f.	$608,000
	and	15,200 units
	g. Present	$300,000
	Proposed.....................	$352,000
6-32	a.	$280,000
	and	7,000 units
	b.	$90,000
	c. $22,000 increase	Yes
	d.	7,500 units
	and	$285,000
	e.	$16,500 decrease
	f.	$320,000
	and	6,400 units
	g. Present	$120,000
	Proposed.....................	$105,000
6-33	a.	$36,000
	b.	No
6-34	c.	20,000 units
	and	$800,000
	d.1. Loss	$160,000
	2. Profit.....................	$160,000
	3. Profit.....................	$320,000
6-35	b.	7
	c.1.	$140,000 increase
	c.2.	$210,000 decrease
6-36	....	$44/ton
6-37	a. Selling Price = $82,000 or a	
	$2.00 increase	
	b.	5,195 units
	c. Present	$112,240
	Proposed.....................	$142,212
6-38	a. Bluejets	30,000 units
	Penjets......................	10,000 units
	b.	$750,000
	Bluejets	22,500 units
	Penjets......................	7,500 units
	c. Yes	$780,000
	Bluejets	19,500 units
	Penjets	9,750 units
	d. New Mix	$110,000
	Present Mix	$130,000
	e.	$1,300,000
	Bluejets	39,000 units
	Penjets......................	13,000 units
6-39	a.	$120,000
	b. $1,000,000, 25,000 units	Yes
	c. $950,000, 23,750 units	Yes, No
6-40	a.	$99,000
	b. 15,000 units, $900,000	
	c. 20,750 units, $1,245,000	

Problem

6-41	a. Tape recorders	40,000
	Calculators	80,000
	b.	$4,050,000
	c. Tape recorders	34,000
	Calculators	102,000

Chapter 7

Exercise

7-2	3,800; 6,400; 12,000	
7-3	b. Req. Purch.—154,000;	
	171,000; 133,500; 203,250	
7-6	a. $150,000, $200,000	
	b. $135,600, $118,880, $133,320	
	c. $71,000	
	d. $4,200	
7-7	$251,680, $272,600, $366,020	
7-13	a. 31,800, 33,300, 32,400	
	b. $9,720, $9,882, $10,476	
7-14	a. Purchases—21,120, 23,280, 22,660	
	Production—20,400, 22,800, 24,400	
	b. April	18,000
	May........................	21,000
7-16	a.	$67,200
	b.	$67,320
	c.	$21,880

Problem

7-17	a. Thingone....................	$4,200,000
	Thingtwo....................	$4,000,000
	b. Thingone....................	65,000
	Thingtwo....................	41,000
	c. A	469,000
	B	256,000
	C	42,000
	d. A	$3,752,000
	B	$1,280,000
	C	$126,000
	e. Thingone....................	$390,000
	Thingtwo....................	$492,000
	f. Thingone....................	$1,300,000
	Thingtwo....................	$684,000
7-19	a. 18,600	
	b.1. $276,000, $252,000, $43,200	
	2. $340,200	
7-20	Ending balances—$91,400, $6,900,	
	$<221,500>	
7-21	a.1. Year........................	$940,000
	2. Year.......................	$113,500
	3. Year—Prest.................	$33,585
	—Sisal	$33,645
	4. Year.......................	$85,200
	5. Year.......................	$159,400
	b. Finished goods	$14,850
	Raw Materials	$2,970
	c.	$221,130
7-22	Ending cash balances by quarter—	
	$46,500, $40,000, $53,635, $133,935	
7-23	Total assets	$243,500
	Accounts payable	$6,000
7-24	Yearly totals:	
	a.1.	$1,618,000
	2.	129,400
	3.	$154,896
	4.	$124,540
	5.	$286,180
	b. Finished goods	$26,250
	Raw materials	$6,240
	c.	$366,544
	d. Ending cash balance	$225,551
	e. Total assets	$515,951

Problem

7-25 Total assets (000 omitted)	$1,978
7-26 a. Year-end balance (000 omitted)	$700
b. January 31, 19x1 balance	
(000 omitted)	$523

Chapter 8

Exercise

8-4	MPV	$1,300F
	MQV...........................	$1,500U
	LRV	$240U
	LEV	$900F
8-5	a.	24,600 ft.
	b.	$1.60
	c.	$39,360
	d.	2,450 DLH
	e.	$9.20
8-6	a.	$0.80
	b.	200,000 ft.
	c.	$0.81/bd. ft.
	d.	$8.00
	e.	6 hrs.
	f.	$8.20
8-9	MPV	$315U
	MQV...........................	$500U
	LRV	$654F
	LEV	$979U
8-10	a. MPV	$23,000F
	MQV	$18,000U
	b. LRV	$11,000F
	LEV	$16,000U
8-11	a.	95,800 ft.
	b.	$1.08/bd. ft.
	c.	$103,464
	d.	6,150 DLH
	e.	$8.10
8-12	a. MPV	$13,600F
	MQV	$8,000U
	b. LRV	$8,500F
	LEV	$20,000U
8-13	Nyclyn—15kg	$19.50
	Salex—121tr	$21.60
	Protet—5kg...................	$12.00
8-14	a. MPV	$540U
	b. MQV	$675F
	c. LRV	$315U
	d. LEV	$900U
8-15	a.1. MPV	$520U
	2. MQV	$600U
	3. LRV	$820U
	4. LEV	$800U
8-18	a. MPV	$4,000U
	MQV	$500U
	LRV........................	$2,040F
	LEV........................	$500U
	b. MPV	$2,025U
8-19	a. MPV	$2,000U
	MQV	$750U
	LRV	$1,100U
	LEV	$1,750U
	b.1............................	40,000 lbs.
	2.............................	26,000 lbs.
	3.............................	25,000 lbs.
	4.............................	$0.80
8-20	a. MPV	$2,000F
	MQV	$400U
	LRV........................	$1,300U
	LEV........................	$600U
	b. MPV	$1,225U

Problem

8-21	a.1. MQV—404.................	$600U
	405..................	$3,400U
	a.2. LRV—404.................	$295U
	405..................	$960F
	a.3. LEV—404.................	$500F
	405..................	$3,000U
	b. MPV—Purchase 1	$8,000U
	Purchase 2	$7,500F
8-22	a.1. MPV	$200U
	2. MQV	$2,000U
	3. LRV	$4,150F
	4. LEV	$1,500U
	b. MPV—Purchase 1	$4,000U
	Purchase 2	$4,200F
8-24	a. Lot 22	$41,100
	Lot 23	$69,870
	Lot 24	$45,792
	b. MPV	$1,900U
	c.1. 100 yds (U), 360 yds (F), 25 yds (U)	
	c.2. 20 hrs (F), 30 hrs (U), 10 hrs (U)	
	c.3. $298 (U), $513 (U), $289 (U)	
8-25	a.1. Lot 201	$250 U
	Lot 202	$7,250U
	2. $630U, $165U	
	3. $1,500U, $1,500F	
	b. Purchase 1	$2,000U
	Purchase 2	$2,000F
8-26	a.	24,000 lbs.
	b.	25,000 lbs.
	c.	4,000 hrs.
	d.	3,800 hrs.
	e.	$4.20
8-27	a.	$50,000F
	b.	$200,000U
	c.	$15,000U
	d.	$35,000U
8-28	a.1.	$0.80/bd. ft.
	2.	$2/50 bd. ft.
	3.	$0.75/bd. ft.
	4.	$6.00 hr.
	5.	5 hrs./set
	6.	$5.95
8-29	a.1.	$0.82/yd.
	2.	50,000 yds.
	3.	1,200 dz.
	4.	36,500
	5.	$6.00/hr.
	6.	$6.10
	7.	3,400 DLH
	8.	3,600 DLH
	b. MPV	$1,000U
	MQV	$400U
	LRV	$340U
	LEV	$1,200F
8-30	MPV	$310U
	MQV...........................	$372U
	Joint Variance..................	$62U

Chapter 9

Exercise

9-2	a.	$72,650
	b. Budget	$69,330
	Actual.......................	$75,850
9-3	a.	$13.46 DLH
9-4	Total overhead—70,000—$61,950	
	80,000—$67,900	
	90,000—$73,850	

4

Exercise

9-5	Total overhead—50,000—$75,500; 55,000—$79,850; 60,000—$84,200	
9-6	Total overhead—Budget	$66,800
	Actual	$66,330
9-7	a. Variable POR	$0.88/DLH
	Fixed POR	$1.34/DLH
	b.	$19.64
9-8	Total overhead—32,000—$50,640; 34,000—$52,780; 36,000—$54,920; 38,000—$57,060	
9-9	Total overhead—32,000—$52,120; 34,000—$53,940; 36,000—$55,760	
9-10	Budget	$49,620
	Actual	$50,200
9-13	a. Spending	$6,000U
	Efficiency	$3,000U
	b. Spending	$2,000U
	Volume	$8,000U
9-14	a.	101,300 hrs.
	b.	101,000 hrs.
	c.	$1.50/hr.
	d.	$153,000
	e.	102,000 hrs.
	f.	$354,550
9-15	a.	$2.75 DLH
	b.	$2.25 DLH
	c.	$337,500
	d.	150,500 hrs.
	e.	160,000 hrs.
	f.	$1,375U
	g.	$442,000
	h.	$27,500U

Problem

9-16	Budget	$8,469
	Actual	$8,565
9-17	a. Variable	$41,580
	Fixed	$51,000
	b. Variable—Spending	$460U
	Efficiency	$660U
	Fixed—Spending	$1,000U
	Volume	$12,600U
9-18	a. MPV	$14,250U
	MQV	$5,500U
	LRV	$28,400U
	LEV	$12,000U
	Variable—Spending	$5,000U
	Efficiency	$5,000U
	Fixed—Spending	$15,000U
	Volume	$20,000U
	b. Budget	$1,778,000
	Actual	$1,883,150
9-19	a. MPV	$50,000F
	b. MQV	$200,000U
	c. LRV	$15,000U
	d. LEV	$35,000U
	e. Variable—Spending	$6,500U
	Efficiency	$30,000U
	Fixed—Spending	$5,000F
	Volume	$35,000U
9-20	b.1. Efficiency	$18,000U
	2. Spending	$1,900U
9-21	a.1. MPV	$1,300U
	MQV	$1,000U
	2. LRV	$1,530U
	LEV	$2,400U
	3. Spending	$459U
	Efficiency	$2,040U

Problem

9-21	(continued)	
	a.4. Spending	$271U
	Volume	$21,000F
	b. Budget	$360,000
	Actual	$348,000
9-22	a.	$2,496U
	b.	10,400 hours
	c.	10,000 hours
	d.	10,000 units
	e.	$2,100U
	f.	$2,000U
	g.	$1,700U
	h.	$800U
	i.	$1,000U
	j.	$10,000U
9-23	a.1. MPV	$598F
	MQV	$60F
	2. LRV	$3,800F
	LEV	$10,000F
	3. Spending	$442F
	Efficiency	$5,100F
	4. Spending	$10,000F
	Volume	$60,000U
	b. Budget	$440,000
	Actual	$470,000
9-24	a. MPV	$1,300U
	MQV	$1,000U
	LRV	$1,530U
	LEV	$2,400U
	Variable Spending	$459U
	Efficiency	$2,040U
	Fixed Spending	$271U
	Volume	$21,000F
9-25	a. MPV	$3,825F
	MQV	$1,500U
	LRV	$3,830U
	LEV	$2,100U
	b. Variable Spending	$1,915U
	Efficiency	$600U
	Fixed Spending	$4,000U
	Volume	$12,000F
9-26	a. Standard cost	$29.80
	Selling price	$44.70
	b. Standard cost	$29.00
	Selling price	$43.50

Chapter 10

Exercise

10-2	a.	$55,000
	b.	$42,500
10-3	a.	10,000 units
	b.	$2.50/unit
	c.	$25,000
	d. Operating income	$15,000
10-4	a. Operating income	$62,000
10-5	a. AC	$8.20
	VC	$7.20
	b. AC Net income	$26,000
	VC Net income	$24,000
10-6	a. VC Net income	$-0-
10-7	a. 19x1	15,000
	19x2	10,000
	b. 19x1	$60,000
	19x2	$60,000
	c. 19x1	$62,000
	19x2	$80,000

Exercise

10-8	a. 19x1	20,000
	19x2	2,000
	b. 19x1	$100,000
	19x2	$17,000
	c. 19x1	$215,000
	19x2	$97,000
10-10	b. 19x2 operating income	$100,000
	19x1 operating income	$60,000
10-11	b. Segment margin—Aspirin	$132,000
	Segment margin—Relaxaid	$250,000
10-12	a.	$23,808
	b.	$11,718
10-13	Segment margin—Auto heater hose	$94,000
	Segment margin—Hose clamps ..	$15,000
10-14	a. Increased contribution margin	
	for Blankets	$25,000
	Increased contribution margin	
	for Pillows..................	$28,000
	b. Increased contribution margin	
	for Blankets	$15,000
	Increased contribution margin	
	for Pillows..................	$11,200
10-15	a. Segment margin—Greeting	
	cards	$215,000
	Segment margin—Posters	$<15,000>
	Segment margin—Stationery	$15,000
	b. Increased contribution margin	$20,000
10-16	a.	No
	b. Product A.................	$20,000 increase
	Product B.................	$60,000 increase
	c. Segment margin—Product A	$100,000
	Segment margin—Product B	$5,000
10-17	Segment margin—Division C	$111,000
	Segment margin—Division D	$103,000
10-18	Segment margin—Product G	$180,000
	Segment margin—Product H	$<50,000>
	b. No. Loss	$22,000

Problem

10-19	a. 19x4 operating income	$369,500
	19x5 operating income	$560,500
	b. 19x4 operating income	$365,000
	19x5 operating income	$565,000
	d. AC............................	$26.90
	VC............................	$26.00
10-20	a. 19x7 AC.....................	$22
	VC............................	$18
	19x8 AC.....................	$21
	VC............................	$18
	b. 19x7 operating income	$2,400
	19x8 operating income	$2,400
	c. 19x8 AC operating income	$5,400
10-21	a. 19x6 operating income	$4,000
	b. 19x6 operating loss	$<1,400>
	c. AC............................	$25,200
	VC............................	$19,800
10-22	a. 19x2 operating income	$20,500
	19x3 operating income	$130,500
10-23	a. 19x5 operating loss	$<50,000>
	19x6 operating income	$130,000
	c. Yes. BES = $460,000	
10-24	a. AC............................	$19
	VC............................	$16
	b. AC operating income	$4,000
	VC operating loss	$<2,600>
	c. Fixed overhead	$6,600
	d. BES = $107,845	

Problem

10-25	a. 19x7 operating income	$85,000
	19x8 operating income	$22,000
	19x9 operating income	$85,000
10-26	a. 19x5 operating income	$64,000
	19x6 operating income	$194,000
10-28	a. Segment margin—European ...	$205,975
	Segment margin—Asian.......	$35,000
	Segment margin—Television	$83,375
	Segment margin—Clock radios	$<7,375>
10-29	a. Segment margin—Northwest	$9,525
	Segment margin—Northeast ...	$28,425
	b.	No
10-30	a. Segment margin—Sewing	
	machines	$<25,350>
	Segment margin—Calculators	$22,500
10-31	a. Segment margin—Local	$310,000
	Segment margin—Regional....	$65,000
	b.	No
	c. Contribution margin—	
	Product A	$185,000
	Product B	$112,000
	Product C	$152,000
10-32	Segment margin—Cereals	$403,000
	Segment margin—Breakfast Bars	$98,000
	Segment margin—Dog Food—	
	$19,000	No
10-33	a. Segment margin—Northeast ...	$25,000
	Segment margin—Southeast ..	$<19,000>
	Segment margin—West	$166,000
	b.	No
	c.	Yes
10-34	a. Segment margin—East	$610,000
	Segment margin—West	$186,500
	b.	No
	c. Contribution margin—	
	Product A	$440,000
	Product B	$305,500
	Product C	$108,000
10-35	a. Segment margin—East	$142,000
	Segment margin—West	$469,000
	b.	No
	c. Contribution margin—	
	Product A	$368,000
	Product B	$378,000
	Product C	$670,000

Chapter 11

Exercise

11-1	a.1.	$920,000
	2.	$1,940,000
	3.	$1,020,000
	b.1.	$820,000
	2.	$940,000
	3. $120,000	Yes
11-2	a.1.	$96,000
	2.	$188,000
	3.	$92,000
	b.1.	$25,000
	2.	$81,000
	3.	$56,000
	c. Yes. Advantage of purchasing is	$36,000
11-3	b. Net cash flow—$467,500	Yes
11-6	a. Incremental profit—$18,000 ...	Yes
11-7	a. Incremental profit—$16,000 ...	Yes
	b. Operating income............	$116,000

Exercise

11-10 a. Advantage of producing—
$30,000 — No
   b.1. .... No
      2. .... Indifferent
      3. .... Yes
11-11 a. Advantage of buying .... $-0-
   b. Yes. Increase in profit $8,000
11-14 a. Process A Profit $15,000
      Process C Profit $5,000
11-15 a. Either $7 or $6
      (Calculus—$6.50)
   b. Start with $9 and then $8, $7,
      and $6 until 7,000,000 units are
      sold
11-16 a. $21.00
   b. 200%
   c. 133 1/3%
11-17 a. Selling price—$75.00 .... 42.18%
   b. 84%
   c. 74.4%
11-18 a. 34%
   b. $33.50
11-19 a.1. .... 145.83%
      2. .... $59.00
   b.1. .... 118.5185%
      2. .... $59.00
11-20 a.1. .... $41.50
      2. .... $36.00
      3. .... $27.75
   b.1. .... 69.38%
      2. .... 63.64%
      3. .... 52.05%
11-21 a. Contribution margin per case:
      B......................... $35.00
      C $20.00
      Contribution margin per hour:
      B......................... $35.00
      C $40.00
   b. B—55,000 hours @ 1 hour =
      55,000 cases, C—25,000 hours
      divided by .5 hours = 50,000
      cases

Problem

11-24 a.1. .... $135,000
      2. .... $680,000
      3. .... $545,000
   b.1. .... $105,000
      2. .... $180,000
      3. .... $75,000
11-25 a. Keep old machine $308,000
      Purchase new machine $349,000
   b. Net cash flow $41,000
11-26 a. $140,000
   b. After-tax ROI = 8% .... No
   c. $800,000
   d. $2,000,000
11-27 a. Dresses..................... $30,000
      Capes $9,120
      Handbags $3,825
11-28 a. $379,500
   b. Incremental profit $130,000
   c.1. Incremental profit $378,000
      2. Incremental profit $30,000
11-29 a.1. .... $21,050
   a.2. .... $32,550
   a.3. .... $3,350
   a.4. .... $2,550
   b. $1,450 cash advantage........ Yes
11-30 a. In favor of purchasing $30,000
   c. In favor of new line $15,000

Problem

11-31 a. In favor of making $60,000
   b. 1. .... $35,000 increase
      2. .... $95,000 increase
      3. Opportunity loss .... $<95,000>
   c. $50,000 .... continue making
      Buy $90,000
11-32 a. Yes, incremental profit from
      processing.................. $.0875/lb.
   b. .... $.0875
   c. $8.60
11-33 a. Process BJ7—Profit .... $.05/lb.
      Process JT8—Profit .... $.10/lb.
   b.1. AX6 .... $30,000
      BJ7....................... $16,500
      JT8....................... $13,500
      2. AX6 .... $30,000
      BJ7....................... $17,750
      JT8....................... $16,500
11-34 a. Either $9 or $10 (Calculus—$9.50)
   b. Start with $14 and then $13, $12,
      and $11 until 16,000,000 units
      are sold
   c. $12 and then $10
11-35 a. $40
   b. 150%
   c. Contribution margin $1,400,000
   d. 300%
   e. 233 1/3%.................... No
11-36 a.1. Increase in income $1,200
      2. .... $13,800
11-37 a. $34,750
   b. $55,906
11-38 a.1. .... 25%
      2. .... $50.00
   b.1. .... 100%
      2. .... $50.00
   c.1. .... 96.07843%
      2. .... $50.00
   d. Incremental profit $100,000
11-39 a. $40,000—$37.00, 50,000—
      $32.00, 80,000—$24.50
   b. 40,000—85%, 50,000—77.8%,
      80,000—63.3%
   c. 40,000—270%, 50,000—220%,
      80,000—145%
   d. 40,000—208%, 50,000—167%
      80,000—104%
11-40 a. Earrings $8.80
      Lockets..................... $36.00
      Pendants $56.80
      Bracelets $130.80
      Rings...................... $99.20
   b. Earrings .... .3 hr.
      Lockets..................... 1 hr.
      Pendants .... .8 hr.
      Bracelets .... 2.8 hrs.
      Rings...................... 2.2 hrs.
   c. Earrings $29.33
      Lockets..................... $36.00
      Pendants $71.00
      Bracelets $46.71
      Rings...................... $45.09
   d. Earrings .... 2,100 hrs.
      Lockets..................... 4,000 hrs.
      Pendants .... 9,600 hrs.
      Bracelets .... 28,000 hrs.
      Rings...................... 33,000 hrs.
   e. Pendants 12,000
      Bracelets 10,000
      Rings...................... 10,181

Exercise

12-1 a. $15,970.28
    b.1. Yes, NPV > 0
      2. NPV = 0
      3. No, NPV < 0
12-3 a. NPV (Zippy) = $81,120.50
      NPV (Speedy) = $<3,476.25>
    b. PI (Zippy) = 1.16
      PI (Speedy) = .99
12-4 a. $-0-
    b.1. Yes. NPV = $1,508.45
      2. NPV = 0
      3. No. NPV = $<1,346.10>

12-5 a. Machine	$25,743.60
List	$23,787.30
b. Machine	$35,317.70
List	$37,653.00

12-6 a. No. NPV = $<3,655>

b.	13.19%
12-7	13.96%
12-8 a.	14%
b.	17%
12-9 a. G	$16,477
H.	$2,822
J.	$10,772
K.	$17,696
Select Project K	
b. G	1.21
H.	1.05
J.	1.15
K.	1.20
Select Project G	
12-11 a. L	2.5 yrs.
M	3.2 yrs.
N.	3.1 yrs.
b. L	$37,630
M	$53,274
N.	$61,596
12-14 A	12%
B	12.2%
C	10%
B = Highest return	
12-15 1. a.	$7,867.60
b.	$7,969.25
c.	$8,023.55
2. a.	$35,859.20
b.	$37,199.19
12-16 1. a.	$5,674
b.	$5,584
c.	$5,537
2. a.	$204,410.70
b.	$206,979.60
12-17 1.	$5,980
2.	$3,704
12-18 1. Yes	$250,000
At the beginning of the year	$65,000
2.	$1,307,152
12-19 a.	$8,478.76
b.	$10,000

Problem

12-20 a. 1.	$984,715
2.	$194,000/yr.
3.	$<112,862>
b. 1.	$894,268
2.	$422,444
3.	$<471,824>

12-21 a. 1.	$215,075
2.	$86,000/yr.
3.	$101,813
b. 1.	$167,127
2.	$169,498
3.	$2,371
12-22 a. 1.	$98,598
2.	$23,500/yr.
3.	$10,415
b. 1.	$43,247
2.	$12,000
3.	$12,419
c. No. NPV of keeping old	
machine	$2,004
12-23 a. 1.	$70,351
2.	$11,500/yr.
b. NPV	$<2,004>
12-24 a. No. NPV of Old	$41,090
NPV of New	$31,904
b. NPV	$<9,186>
12-25 a. No. NPV of Old	$<73,429>
NPV of New	$<48,207>
b. NPV in favor of new machine	$25,222
12-26 a. 1.	$135,000
2.	$136,000/yr.
3.	$302,445
b. 1.	$105,000
2.	$36,000
3.	$5,016
12-27 a. Yes. NPV of Old	$<230,136>
NPV of New	$<183,120>
b. NPV of new machine	$47,016
12-28 Yes. NPV	$51,475
12-29 Yes. NPV	$15,608
12-30 a. Machine X	12.43%
Machine Y	14.47%

12-31 a. N—1.49, O—1.35, P—1.41,
      Q—1.50
    b. 1. Q,N,O,P
      2. N,P,Q,O
      3. Q,N,P,O

12-32 a.	$44,087
b.	$49,254
12-33 a.	$15,319
b.	$14,149
12-34 a. 1.	$240,000
2.	$56,000
b. No. NPV	$<6,318>
c.	13.56%

12-35 a. 1. R—4 yrs., S—5 yrs.
      2. R—$60,806, S—$41,118
      3. R—21.43%, S—18.44%
      4. R—1.30, S—1.23
      5. R—15%, S—13.3%
12-36 a.1. T—4 yrs., V—5.14yrs.
      2. T—$63,886, V—$69,952
      3. T—18.65%, V—17.79%
      4. T—1.16, V—1.19
      5. T—12.5%, V—12.8%

12-37 a.	$200,000
b.	$12,000/yr.
c.	4 yrs.
d.	15%
e.	21.43%
f.	Yes

Problem

12-38	a.	$248,000
	b.	$15,375
	c.	4.03 yrs.
	d.	12.3%
	e.	18.38%
	f.	Yes

Chapter 13

Exercise

13-1 1. No. NPV = $<82>
2. No. NPV = $<1,353>
3. No. NPV = ... $<2,493>

13-2 1. No. NPV = ... $<1,435>
2. No. NPV = ... $<2,583>
3. No. NPV = ... $<3,614>

13-3 a. JCN—NPV = $24,768
C.N.R.—NPV = $<56,716>
b. JCN—1.05
C.N.R.—.92

13-4 a. JCN—NPV = $21,133
C.N.R.—NPV = $<62,168>
b. JCN—1.04
C.N.R.—.92

13-5 a. Machine—NPV = $39,839
Customer list—NPV = $38,188
b. Machine—NPV = $77,747
Customer list—NPV = $92,257

13-6 a. Machine—NPV = $38,597
Customer list—NPV = $51,481
b. Machine—NPV = $81,161
Customer list—NPV = $104,583

13-8	NPV = $5,884	Yes
13-9	NPV = $4,898	Yes
13-10	NPV = $77,186	Yes

Problem

13-11	a. 1.	$983,816
	2. $145,500 per year plus $250,000 of tax shield	
	3.	$<63,757>
	b. 1.	$831,431
	2. $70,500 each year plus $175,000 of tax shield	
	3.	$<341,702>
13-12	a. 1.	$983,816
	2. $145,500 per year plus $250,000 of tax shield	
	3.	$<55,868>
	b. 1.	$831,431
	2. $70,500 each year plus $175,000 of tax shield	
	3.	$<333,811>
13-13	a. 1.	$98,948
	2. $17,625 per year plus $25,000 of tax shield	
	3.	$<288>
	b. 1.	$26,997
	2. $9,000 each year plus $5,000 of tax shield minus $11,250 of machine overhaul	
	3.	$7,145
13-14	1.	$71,951
	2. $8,625 per year plus $20,000 of tax shield plus $11,250 machine overhaul	
	3.	$<7,433>
13-15	a. 1.	3.19 yrs.
	2.	22.7%
	3.	$1,362.57

Problem

13-15 (continued)

	4.	1.08
	5.	17.1%
13-16	a. NPV of old machine	$24,407
	NPV of new machine	$16,135
	b. NPV of purchasing new machine	$<8,273>
13-17	a. NPV of old machine	$<142,425>
	NPV of new machine	$<281,448>
	b. NPV of purchasing new machine	$<139,024>
13-18	a. NPV of old machine	$<176,912>
	NPV of new machine	$<143,144>
	b. NPV of purchasing new machine	$33,768
13-19	a. NPV	$<17,162>
	b.	No
13-20	a. NPV	$<12,429>
	b.	No
13-21	a. NPV	$<31,202>
	b.	No
13-22	a. NPV	$<12,123>
	b.	No
13-23	a. NPV	$32,755
	b. NPV	$35,070
13-24	a. NPV	$11,481
	b. NPV	$10,124

Chapter 14

Exercise

14-1	a. 1. Clothing	18%
	Jewelry	21%
	2. Clothing	2.4
	Jewelry	1.8
	3. Clothing	43.2%
	Jewelry	37.8%
	4. Clothing	$92,800
	Jewelry	$168,111
14-2	a. 1. Blankets	12%
	Pillows....................	10%
	2. Blankets	2.0
	Pillows....................	3.0
	3. Blankets	24%
	Pillows....................	30%
	4. Blankets	$27,000
	Pillows....................	$60,000
14-5	Center A—$126,000, $360,000, 14%, $54,000	
	Center B—$2,000,000, $500,000, 12%, 18%	
	Center C—$1,500,000, 3.33, 46.7%, 21%	
14-6	Center D—$1,536,000, $230,400, 15%, $129,600	
	Center E—$88,000, 2, 22%, 17%	
	Center F—$150,000, $375,000, 3.2, 22%	
14-8	Transfer price .... No	$8.00
	b. Transfer price .... Yes	$3.00
14-9	Transfer price .... No	$14.20/yd
	b. Transfer price .... Yes	$4.00/yd
14-10	a. Margin—Tubing..............	$2,250,000
	Margin—Lamps	$15,000,000
	b. Margin—Tubing..............	$1,750,000
	Margin—Lamps	$15,500,000

Problem

14-12	a. 1.	....	20%
	2.		1.2
	3.	....	24%
	b.	....	$50,000
	c. 1.	....	19.05%
	2.		1.355
	3.		25.8%
	4. $73,200	....	Yes, Yes
14-13	a. 1.	....	12%
	2.	....	1.8
	3.	....	21.6%
	4.	....	$124,444
	b. 1.	....	$120,000
	2.	....	$192,000
	3.	....	$444,444 decrease
	4.	....	$888,888 increase
	5. New values		
	a.	....	18.6%;
	b.	....	1.69
	c.	....	31.4%
	d.	....	$378,889
14-14	a. 1.	....	11%
	2.	....	1.6
	3.	....	17.6%
	4.	....	$81,000
	b. 1.	....	$108,000
	2.	....	$216,000
	3.	....	$800,000 decrease
	4.	....	$720,000 increase
	5. New values		
	a.	....	8.3%
	b.	....	1.62
	c.	....	13.5%
	d.	....	$<12,000>
14-16	a. 1. X	....	11%
	Y	....	10%
	Z	....	12%
	2. X	....	2.2
	Y	....	2.5
	Z	....	2.3
	3. X	....	24.2%
	Y	....	25%
	Z	....	27.6%
	4. X	....	$29,818
	Y	....	$21,600
	Z	....	$25,217

14-17 a. Price—$8/motor, No
$160,000 loss
b. Price—$2/motor, Yes
$1,040,000 savings
c. Price—$7.40/motor, No
$40,000 loss
d. Price—$5/motor, Yes,
$440,000 gain

14-18	a. Income—Chemical	....	$8,000,000
	Fertilizer	....	$2,400,000
	b. Price	....	$9.20/lb.
	Income—Chemical	....	$8,000,000
	Fertilizer	....	$<200,000>
	c. Income—Chemical	....	$4,400,000
	Fertilizer	....	$2,400,000
	d. Price	....	$2.00/lb.
	Income—Chemical	....	$4,400,000
	Fertilizer	....	$3,400,000
14-19	a. 1.	....	$2,800,000
	2.	....	$5,500,000
	3.	....	$8,300,000
	b. 1.	....	Yes
	2.	....	No
	Profit at 4 million = $6,200,000		Yes

Problem

14-20	a. Transfer price—$13.00	....	No
	b. Transfer price—$7.00	....	Yes
14-21	a. 1.	....	9%
	2.	....	1.8
	3.	....	16.2%
	b.	....	$22,400
	c. 1.	....	16.9%
	2.	....	$30,900
	d.	....	$6.00
	e.	....	$11.00/unit
	Purchase externally		
	f.	....	$9.00/unit
	Purchase internally		
	g.	....	$10.80/unit
	Purchase externally		
14-22	a.	....	Yes
	Increase in income of $132,000		
	b.	....	No
	Decrease in income of $35,500		
		....	Yes
	Increase in income of $312,500		

Chapter 15

Exercise

15-1	b. 6X, 7Y	....	$144
15-2	b. 12X, 7Y	....	$2,200
15-3	b. 6S, 1.5T	....	$420
15-4	b. 10X, 8Y	....	$630
15-7	b. 6L, 2M	....	$450
15-8	b. 3X, 6Y	....	$210
15-9	1,414 units/order		
15-10	949 units/order		
15-11	10,000 units/year		
15-12	a.	....	1,732 units
	b.	....	$1,068
15-15		....	1,342 units
15-16	a.	....	120 units
	b.	....	420 units
	c.	....	300 units

Problem

15-18 Contribution margin—X − 10 =
$16.50
Contribution margin—Y − 12 =
$35.00

15-19	a.	....	1,369
	b.	....	11
	c.	....	3,300 units
	35% of the time		
	d. Safety stock	....	600 units
	Reorder point	....	3,900 units
	e.	....	4,500 units
	f.	....	$1,200
15-20	a.	....	1,000 units
	b.	....	$1,875
15-21	a.	....	1,265 units
	c. New EOQ for (a)	....	1,512
15-23	a. $172.80 per order		
	b. $20.00 per windshield		
	c. 432 windshields/order		
	d. $8,640		
	e. 216 windshields		
15-24	a. Order size 1	....	$19,142
	2	....	$18,664
	3	....	$18,546
	4	....	$18,518 (EOQ)
	5	....	$18,526
	6	....	$18,552
	b.	....	560 units

Problem

15-25 Part A.
a.	8,000	25%
	9,000	60%
	10,000	15%
b.	8,000 units	$230,000
	9,000 units	$270,000
	10,000 units	$220,000
c.	....	$248,500

Part B.
a.	8,000 units	$82,000
	9,000 units	$162,000
	10,000 units	$152,000
b.	....	$7,500

15-26
20,000	$80,000
30,000	$170,000
40,000	$160,000
50,000	$110,000
Optimum = 30,000	

15-27
a. 10,000	$2,000
20,000	$3,500
30,000	$4,000
40,000	$2,500
b. Optimum = 30,000	

Chapter 16
Exercise

16-1	Increase in working capital	$59,436
16-2	Increase in working capital	$536,725
16-3	a. Increase in working capital....	$100,000
	Total sources	$317,000
	Total uses	$217,000
16-4	a. Increase in working capital....	$120,000
	Total sources	$390,000
	Total uses	$270,000
16-10	....	$393,000
16-12	a. Increase in working capital....	$480,000
	b. Total sources	$1,260,000
	Total uses	$780,000
16-13	Increase in cash	$100,000
	Total sources	$810,000
	Total uses	$710,000
16-14	Decrease in cash...............	$6,440,000
	Total sources	$16,200,000
	Total uses	$22,640,000
16-15	Decrease in cash...............	$20,000
	Total sources	$370,000
	Total uses	$390,000
16-16	Decrease in cash...............	$20,000
	Total sources	$370,000
	Total uses	$390,000
16-17	Increase in cash	$20,000
	Total sources	$392,000
	Total uses	$372,000
16-18	Increase in cash	$100,000
	Total sources	$810,000
	Total uses	$710,000

Problem

16-19	a. Decrease in working capital ...	$262,000
	Total sources	$1,180,000
	Total uses	$1,442,000
16-20	Decrease in cash...............	$150,000
	Total sources	$1,292,000
	Total uses	$1,442,000
16-21	a. Increase in working capital....	$150,000
	Total sources	$340,000
	Total uses	$190,000
16-22	Increase in cash	$80,000
	Total sources	$340,000
	Total uses	$260,000

Problem

16-23	a. Increase in working capital....	$230,000
	b. Total sources	$985,000
	Total uses	$755,000
16-24	Increase in cash	$260,000
	Total sources	$975,000
	Total uses	$715,000
16-25	a. Decrease in working capital ...	$300,000
	Total sources	$1,600,000
	Total uses	$1,900,000
	b. Decrease in cash	$400,000
	Total sources	$1,500,000
	Total uses	$1,900,000
16-26	Total assets	$725,000
16-27	Increase in cash	$80,000
	Total sources	$340,000
	Total uses	$260,000
16-28	Increase in cash	$260,000
	Total sources	$975,000
	Total uses	$715,000

Chapter 17
Exercise

17-13	Total assets	$150
17-14	Net income 19x2	$54,000
	Net income 19x1	$64,800
17-15	Total assets	$150,000
17-17	a.	16.46%
	b.	22.8%
	c.	Positive
17-18	a.	0.33 to 1
	b.	5.0
	c.	8.3
	d.	0.67 to 1

Problem

17-19	Total assets	$7,600
17-20	a. Re—1.	2.11 to 1
	2.	1.14 to 1
	3.	10.42 times
	4.	35 days
	5.	6.13 times
	Flex—1.	2.15 to 1
	2.	0.99 to 1
	3.	7.95 times
	4.	45.9 days
	5.	3.96 times
	c. Re—1.	10 times
	2.	0.96 to 1
	Flex—	12 times
	....	0.79 to 1
	e. Re—1.	$8.40
	2.	3.5%
	3.	18 times
	4.	59.5%
	5.	18.0%
	6.	30.4%
	Flex—1.	$8.79
	2.	2.9%
	3.	19 times
	4.	56.9%
	5.	15.2%
	6.	24.0%
17-21	a. 1.	3.33 to 1
	2.	1.62 to 1
	3.	50 days
	4.	3.50 to 1
	5.	1.24
	6.	$2.00
	7.	5 to 1
	8.	60%

Problem

17-21 (continued)
    a. (continued)

	9.	6.29 times
	10.	4.0%
	11.	7.7%
	12.	12%
17-22 a. 19X5—1. Working capital.....		$164,200
	2.	1.92 to 1
	3.	1.10 to 1
	4.	12.81 times
	5.	28.10 days
	6.	7.76 times
	7.	46.39 days
	8.	1.46
	9.	7.25 times
19X4—1. Working capital.....		$133,200
	2.	3.06 to 1
	3.	1.46 to 1
	4.	17.86 times
	5.	20.16 days
	6.	10.88 times
	7.	33.09 days
	8.	0.81
	9.	5.93 times
17.23 a. 19X5—1.		12.89%
	2.	24.04%
	3.	$2.05/share
	4.	9.76 times
	5.	24.39%
	6.	2.5%

Problem

17-23 (continued)

19X4—1.		10.19%
	2.	14.41%
	3.	$0.98/share
	4.	18.37 times
	5.	51.02%
	6.	2.8%
17-25 a. Primary EPS		$2.31
Net income		1.87/share
b. Fully diluted EPS		$2.21
Net income		$1.72/share
17-26 a. Primary EPS		$2.63
Net income		$2.13/share
b. Fully diluted EPS		$2.36
Net income		$1.99/share
17-27 a. 1. Net income		
Common stock		$56,000
Preferred stock		$32,000
Bonds payable		$39,200
2. Return on common		
Common stock		14%
Preferred stock		16%
Bonds payable		19.6%
17-28 a. Total assets		$600,000
Net income		$120,000
b. 1.		30%
2.		15 to 1
3.		$5.20/share
4.		$6.00/share
5.		6 2/3%

ZETA CORPORATION
Balance Sheet
As of December 31, 19x1

Assets

Current assets:

Cash	$ 20,000	
Marketable securities	2,000	
Accounts receivable	45,000	
Inventories	60,000	
Total current assets		$127,000
Plant and equipment	580,000	
Less: Accumulated		
depreciation	180,000	400,000
Total assets		$527,000

Liabilities and Equity

Current liabilities:

Accounts payable	$ 44,000	
Notes payable	21,000	
Total current liabilities		$ 65,000
Long-term debt		95,000
Equities:		
Common stock, $10 par	230,000	
Retained earnings	137,000	367,000
Total liabilities and equity		$527,000

The following additional data are available:

1. Balances of selected data at the beginning of the year consist of:

a.	Accounts receivable	$ 40,000
b.	Inventories	50,000
c.	Total assets	480,000
d.	Total stockholders' equity	283,000

2. The interest cost for the year amounted to $11,600 and is included as part of the administrative costs.
3. Dividends paid during the year were $46,000 at the rate of $2 per share.
4. All sales were credit sales.
5. The market value per share was $30.

Required   Compute the following:

a.   Current ratio.
b.   Acid-test ratio.
c.   Accounts receivable turnover.
d.   Collection period of receivables. (Use 360 days.)
e.   Inventory turnover.
f.   Days to sell inventory. (Use 360 days.)
g.   Debt-to-equity ratio.
h.   Times interest earned.

17–10 Calculation of Ratios

Refer to the financial statements and the additional data given in Exercise 17–9.

Required   *a.* Compute the following:
    (1) Return on total assets.
    (2) Return on common stockholders' equity.
    (3) Earnings per share.
    (4) Price-earnings ratio.
    (5) Dividend payout ratio.
    (6) Dividend yield ratio.
    b. Was the financial leverage for the year positive or negative? Explain.

17–11 Interpretation of Ratios

Thorpe Company is a wholesale distributor of professional equipment and supplies. The company's sales have averaged about $900,000 annually for the three-year period 19x3–x5. The firm's total assets at the end of 19x5 amounted to $850,000.

The president of Thorpe Company has asked the controller to prepare a report which summarizes the financial aspects of the company's operations for the past three years. This report will be presented to the board of directors at their next meeting.

In addition to comparative financial statements, the controller has decided to present a number of relevant financial ratios which can assist in the identification and interpretation of trends. At the request of the controller, the accounting staff has calculated the following ratios for the three-year period 19x3–x5:

	19x3	19x4	19x5
Current ratio	2.00	2.13	2.18
Acid-test (quick) ratio	1.20	1.10	0.97
Accounts receivable turnover	9.72	8.57	7.13
Inventory turnover	5.25	4.80	3.80
Percent of total debt to total assets	44	41	38
Percent of long-term debt to total assets	25	22	19
Sales to fixed assets (fixed asset turnover)	1.75	1.88	1.99
Sales as a percent of 19x3 sales	1.00	1.03	1.06
Gross margin percentage	40.0	38.6	38.5
Net income to sales	7.8%	7.8%	8.0%
Return on total assets	8.5%	8.6%	8.7%
Return on stockholders' equity	15.1%	14.6%	14.1%

In the preparation of his report, the controller has decided first to examine the financial ratios independently of any other data to determine if the ratios themselves reveal any significant trends over the three-year period.

Required   Answer the following questions. Indicate in each case which ratio(s) you used in arriving at your conclusion.

    a. The current ratio is increasing while the acid-test (quick) ratio is decreasing.

Using the ratios provided, identify and explain the contributing factor(s) for this apparently divergent trend.

b. In terms of the ratios provided, what conclusion(s) can be drawn regarding the company's use of financial leverage during the 19x3–x5 period?

(CMA adapted)

17–12 Completion of Missing Income Statement Data

Complete the following comparative operating statement of Forward Corporation:

FORWARD CORPORATION
Operating Statement
For Years Ending on December 31
(in thousands of dollars)

	19x4	19x3	19x2	Cumulative Amount	Annual Average Amount
Net sales		2,280	1,998		
Cost of goods sold	1,910				1,920
Gross profit		300			357
Total operating costs					280
Income before taxes	186	25	20		
Net income	93	13	10		

17–13 Completion of Missing Balance Sheet Data through the Use of Ratios

The Rigid Company's balance sheet consists of only the following items:

Cash
Accounts receivable
Inventory $40
Fixed assets (net)
Current liabilities
Common stock   50
Retained earnings

The following additional information is also available:

1. Total assets minus liabilities equals $110.
2. Stockholders' equity equals 2.75 times total debt.
3. Current ratio is 2.25 to 1.
4. Inventory turnover is 14.4 times (based on cost of goods sold and ending inventory).
5. Days' sales in accounts receivable are 15 days (based on a 360-day year).
6. Gross profit is 25 percent of cost of goods sold.

Required Use the given information to complete the balance sheet.

17–14 **Preparation of Income Statements from Selected Information and Interpretation of Results**

The following data are available for the Disco Company for 19x1 and 19x2:

	19x2	19x1
Gross profit percentage	40%	35%
Ending accounts receivable	$150,000	$90,000
Number of days' sales in ending accounts receivable . .	60	45
Income tax rate	50%	40%
Net income as a percent of sales	6%	9%
Maximum credit allowed to creditors	60 days	30 days

Required
a. Prepare income statements in comparative form for the two years.
b. Comment on the trend in sales volume, gross profit percentage, and net income percentage.
c. Compute the ending accounts-receivable-turnover ratios and briefly comment on the trend in view of the changing credit terms. All sales are made on credit.

17–15 **Preparation of a Balance Sheet from Selected Ratios and Other Information**

The Burnt Company had maintained its records in a safe place for many years. However, a fire has destroyed them just before its June 19x8 fiscal year-end, leaving only the following information:

Inventory	$ 40,000
Common stock, no par	50,000
Net assets	110,000
Current ratio	2.25 to 1
Inventory turnover	14.4
Accounts receivable turnover	24
Gross profit	20%
Ratio of debt (all current) to equity	1 to 2.75

Additional balance sheet accounts must be computed. There were no prepaid costs or accumulated depreciation at June 30, 19x8.

Required Prepare a balance sheet in good form. Use a 360-day year in your computations.

17–16 **Effects of Transactions on Ratios**

Give the effect of each of the following transactions or events on working capital, current ratio, and the quick ratio (acid test). Assume a current ratio of 3 to 1 and a quick ratio of 1.4 to 1 before any of the transactions that follow. (Effects: I for increase, D for decrease, and N for no effect.)

	Working Capital	Current Ratio	Acid-Test Ratio
1. Company pays $5,000 short-term notes payable in cash.	_____	_____	_____
2. Company sells equipment for $3,000 cash.	_____	_____	_____
3. Company purchases short-term marketable securities for $4,000.	_____	_____	_____
4. Company purchases building by issuing common stock (par value $20) valued at $40,000.	_____	_____	_____
5. Company purchases equipment for $2,000 cash.	_____	_____	_____
6. Company pays long-term bond payable, $5,000.	_____	_____	_____
7. Company collects $2,000 on a long-term note receivable.	_____	_____	_____
8. Company purchases inventory of $5,000 for $2,000 cash plus long-term note payable of $3,000.	_____	_____	_____
9. Company issues short-term note payable and receives $5,000 cash.	_____	_____	_____
10. Fire destroys $4,000 of inventory (no insurance).	_____	_____	_____
11. Obsolete inventory of $3,000 was found and written off.	_____	_____	_____
12. Accounts payable of $10,000 were paid in cash.	_____	_____	_____
13. Land with a book value of $20,000 was sold for $15,000.	_____	_____	_____
14. Merchandise inventory of $2,000 bought on open trade credit.	_____	_____	_____
15. Automobile sold for $2,000 at loss of $6,000.	_____	_____	_____

17–17 Computation of ROI and Effects of Financial Leverage

The Exeter Company makes the following information available:

	Beginning of 19x3	Ending of 19x3
Current assets	$ 300,000	$ 360,000
Property, plant, and equipment—net . .	890,000	950,000
Total assets	$1,190,000	$1,310,000
Current liabilities	$ 140,000	$ 160,000
Long-term debt	200,000	200,000
Preferred stock, $10 par value,		
12 percent dividend rate	150,000	150,000
Common stock	300,000	300,000
Retained earnings	400,000	500,000
Total liabilities and		
stockholders' equity	$1,190,000	$1,310,000

The company had a net income of $189,000 and its income tax rate for 19x3 was 30 percent. Interest cost for the year amounted to $24,000.

Required
a. Compute the return on total assets.
b. Compute the return on common stockholders' equity.
c. Was the financial leverage for the year positive or negative? Explain.

17–18 Calculation of Short-Term Liquidity Ratios

Given the following for the Rex Corporation for the years 19x1 and 19x2:

REX CORPORATION
Selected Financial Data

	As of December 31	
	19x2	19x1
Cash	$ 10,000	$ 80,000
Accounts receivable (net)	50,000	150,000
Merchandise inventory	90,000	150,000
Short-term marketable securities	30,000	10,000
Land and buildings (net)	340,000	360,000
Mortgage payable (no current portion)	270,000	280,000
Accounts payable (trade)	70,000	110,000
Short-term notes payable	200,000	40,000

	Year Ended December 31	
	19x2	19x1
Cash sales	$1,800,000	$1,600,000
Credit sales	500,000	800,000
Cost of goods sold	1,000,000	1,400,000

Required
Compute the following:

a. Quick (acid-test) ratio as of December 31, 19x2.
b. Receivable turnover for 19x2.
c. Merchandise inventory turnover for 19x2.
d. Current ratio at December 31, 19x2.

PROBLEMS 17–19 Construction of a Balance Sheet from Selected Ratios and Other Data

It is Sunday and you have just opened your briefcase in order to work with Elusive Company's December 31, 19x1, balance sheet. To your dismay, you discover that the computer printouts that your assistant stuffed into your briefcase contained only the sketchy information below:

1. Accounts receivable and inventory were the same at the end of the year as at the beginning.
2. Net income, $600.
3. Times interest earned is 5 (ignore income taxes). The company has outstanding 5 percent bonds issued at par.

4. Net income to sales, 20 percent. Gross margin ratio, 40 percent. Inventory turnover, 6.
5. Accounts receivable turnover, 4.
6. Sales to working capital, 5. Current ratio, 1.6.
7. Acid-test ratio, 1.0 (exclude prepaid costs).
8. Plant and equipment is one-third depreciated.
9. Dividends paid on 8 percent nonparticipating preferred stock was $40. The effective yield in the current year was 10 percent. These shares were issued two years ago at par.
10. Earnings per common share, $2.80.
11. Common stock has a $10 par value and was issued at a 5 percent premium.
12. Retained earnings at January 1, 19x1, was $900.

Required Given the information available, complete the balance sheet as of December 31, 19x1. Also, determine the amount of dividends paid on the common stock in 19x1.

Cash	
Accounts receivable	
Inventory	
Prepaid costs	
Plant and equipment (net) . . .	$6,000
Total assets	
Current liabilities	
Bonds payable	
Stockholders' equity	
Total liabilities and equity . . .	

17-20 Comprehensive Ratio Analysis with Industry Comparisons

Early one morning, even before your coffee break, a senior member of your institution's financial policy committee hurriedly walks into your office and hands you the data that follows. "This afternoon, our committee will consider the relative merits of Re Company and Flex Company which are both in the flexible hose manufacturing business," said he and added: "Please prepare a preliminary ratio analysis and conclusions so as to enable me to give intelligent answers to expected questions."

Balance Sheets
As of December 31, 19x7
(in thousands)

	Re Company	Flex Company
Cash	$ 30	$ 20
Accounts receivable	100	180
Inventory	110	234
Plant and equipment, net	300	480
Total assets	$ 540	$ 914
Current liabilities	$ 114	$ 202
Bonds payable	150	200
Common stock, $10 par	100	140
Retained earnings	176	372
Total liabilities and equity	$ 540	$ 914

Data from Income Statements
For the Year Ending December 31, 19x7
(in thousands)

Sales	$1,000	$1,400
Cost of goods sold	650	910
Interest cost	14	16
Income before taxes	120	176
Net income	84	123
Tax rate	30%	30%

Balances at January 1, 19x7
(in thousands)

Accounts receivable	$ 92	$ 172
Inventory	102	226
Total assets	500	850

Other Selected Data for 19x7

Dividends paid per share	$ 5	$ 5
Market price per share at year-end	144	170

Flexible Hose Manufacturing Industry
Averages for 19x7

Current ratio	2.2 to 1
Acid-test ratio	1.2 to 1
Accounts receivable turnover (average) . . .	10 times
Inventory turnover (average)	5.8 times
Times interest earned	8 times
Debt-to-equity ratio	.8 to 1
Dividend yield	3%
Price-earnings ratio	14
Dividend payout ratio	60%
Return on total assets (average)	9%
Return on common equity	15.5%

Required   To satisfy the senior member's request—

a. Compute the following ratios for each company:
   (1) Current ratio.
   (2) Acid-test ratio.
   (3) Average accounts receivable turnover.
   (4) Average collection period for receivables.
   (5) Average inventory turnover.
b. Using the above ratios as well as industry ratios, indicate which company is the better short-term credit risk and why.

c. Compute the following ratios for each company:
   (1) Times interest earned.
   (2) Total debt-to-equity ratio.
d. Using the above ratios and any other applicable ratios from (1) above, determine which company should be in a better position to take on *additional* long-term debt and why.
e. Compute the following ratios for each company:
   (1) Earnings per share.
   (2) Dividend yield.
   (3) Price-earnings ratio.
   (4) Dividend payout ratio.
   (5) Return on total assets.
   (6) Return on common equity.
f. For each of the companies, indicate whether financial leverage is positive or negative and explain how you reached this conclusion.
g. Using the above ratios, present preliminary conclusions regarding the relative market standing and attractiveness of both companies.

17–21   Computation of Ratios

The Point Company is listed on the New York Stock Exchange. The market value of its common stock was quoted at $10 per share at December 31, 19x5, and 19x4. Point's balance sheet at December 31, 19x5, and 19x4, and statement of income and retained earnings for the years then ended are presented below:

POINT COMPANY
Balance Sheet
December 31, 19x5, and 19x4
(in thousands)

	December 31	
	19x5	19x4
Assets		
Current assets:		
Cash	$ 3,500	$ 3,600
Marketable securities, at cost which approximates market	13,000	11,000
Accounts receivable, net of allowance for doubtful accounts	105,000	95,000
Inventories, lower of cost or market	126,000	154,000
Prepaid costs	2,500	2,400
Total current assets	250,000	266,000
Property, plant, and equipment, net of accumulated depreciation	311,000	308,000
Investments, at equity	2,000	3,000
Long-term receivables	14,000	16,000
Goodwill and patents, net of accumulated amortization	6,000	6,500
Other assets	7,000	8,500
Total assets	$590,000	$608,000

Liabilities and Stockholders' Equity

Current liabilities:

Notes payable	$ 5,000	$ 15,000
Accounts payable	38,000	48,000
Accrued liabilities	24,500	27,000
Income taxes payable	1,000	1,000
Payments due within one year on long-term debt	6,500	7,000
Total current liabilities	75,000	98,000
Long-term debt	169,000	180,000
Estimated product warranty liability	74,000	67,000
Other liabilities	9,000	8,000

Stockholders' equity:

Common stock, par value $1 per share; authorized 20 million shares; issued and outstanding 10 million shares	10,000	10,000
5% cumulative preferred stock, par value $100 per share; $100 liquidating value; authorized 50,000 shares; issued and outstanding 40,000 shares	4,000	4,000
Additional paid-in capital	107,000	107,000
Retained earnings	142,000	134,000
Total stockholders' equity	263,000	255,000
Total liabilities and stockholders' equity	$590,000	$608,000

POINT COMPANY
Statement of Income and Retained Earnings
For the Years Ended December 31, 19x5, and 19x4
(in thousands)

	Year Ended December 31	
	19x5	19x4
Net sales	$600,000	$500,000
Costs:		
Cost of goods sold	490,000	400,000
Marketing and administrative costs	66,000	60,000
Other, net	7,000	6,000
Total costs	563,000	466,000
Income before income taxes	37,000	34,000
Income taxes	16,800	15,800
Net income	20,200	18,200
Retained earnings at beginning of period	134,000	126,000
Dividends on common stock	(12,000)	(10,000)
Dividends on preferred stock	(200)	(200)
Retained earnings at end of period	$142,000	$134,000

Required   *a.*   Based on the above information, compute (for the year 19x5 only) the following:

(1) Current (working capital) ratio.

(2) Quick (acid-test) ratio.

(3) Number of days' sales in average receivables, assuming a business year consisting of 300 days and all sales on account.

(4) Inventory turnover.

(5) Debt-to-equity ratio.

(6) Earnings per share on common stock.

(7) Price-earnings ratio on common stock.

(8) Dividend payout ratio on common stock.

(9) Times interest earned.

(10) Return on total assets.

(11) Return on common stockholders' equity.

(12) Dividend yield ratio.

b.   For 19x5, is the financial leverage positive or negative? Explain your answer.

(AICPA adapted)

17–22   **Comprehensive Problem—Part 1: Short-Term Liquidity and Creditor Ratios**

The Telly Manufacturing Company was organized five years ago and manufactures toys. Its most recent three years' balance sheets and income statements are presented below.

TELLY MANUFACTURING COMPANY
Comparative Condensed Balance Sheets
As of June 30, 19x5, 19x4, and 19x3

	19x5	19x4	19x3
Assets			
Cash	$ 12,000	$ 15,000	$ 16,000
Accounts receivable, net	183,000	80,000	60,000
Inventory	142,000	97,000	52,000
Other current assets	5,000	6,000	4,000
Plant and equipment (net)	160,000	110,000	70,000
Total assets	$ 502,000	$ 308,000	$ 202,000
Liabilities and Equity			
Accounts payable	$ 147,800	$ 50,400	$ 22,000
Federal income tax payable	30,000	14,400	28,000
Long-term liabilities	120,000	73,000	22,400
Common stock, $5 par value	110,000	110,000	80,000
Retained earnings	94,200	60,200	49,600
Total liabilities and equity	$ 502,000	$ 308,000	$ 202,000

TELLY MANUFACTURING COMPANY
Condensed Income Statements
For the Years Ended June 30, 19x5, 19x4, and 19x3

	19x5	19x4	19x3
Net sales (mostly cash)	$1,684,000	$1,250,000	$1,050,000
Cost of goods sold	927,000	810,000	512,000
Gross margin on sales	757,000	440,000	538,000
Marketing and administrative costs	670,000	396,700	467,760
Operating income	87,000	43,300	70,240
Interest cost	12,000	7,300	2,240
Income before federal income tax	75,000	36,000	68,000
Income tax	30,000	14,400	28,000
Net income	$ 45,000	$ 21,600	$ 40,000

A reconciliation of its retained earnings for the years ended June 30, 19x4, and June 30, 19x5, is as follows:

TELLY MANUFACTURING COMPANY
Statement of Retained Earnings
For the Years Ended June 30, 19x5, and 19x4

	19x5	19x4
Balance, beginning	$60,200	$49,600
Add: Net income	45,000	21,600
Subtotal	105,200	71,200
Deduct: Dividends paid	11,000	11,000
Balance, ending	$94,200	$60,200

Additional information:

1. All sales are on account.
2. Long-term liabilities are owed to the firm's bank.
3. The firm's terms of sale are net 30 days.

You are employed as an assistant to a bank loan officer and she has asked you to evaluate the firm's request for an additional long-term loan of $100,000.

In the course of evaluating the loan, you ascertain that the following ratios are typical for toy manufacturers:

Current ratio	2.2:1
Acid-test ratio	1.2:1
Accounts receivable turnover	14 times
Collection period of receivables	26 days
Inventory-turnover ratio	8 times
Days to sell inventory	45 days
Debt-to-equity ratio	.75 to 1
Times interest earned	6 times

Required *a.* Compute the following for 19x4 and 19x5:
   (1)   Working capital.
   (2)   Current ratio.
   (3)   Acid-test ratio.
   (4)   Accounts receivable turnover.
   (5)   Collection period of receivables.
   (6)   Inventory-turnover ratio.
   (7)   Days to sell inventory.
   (8)   Debt-to-equity ratio.
   (9)   Times interest earned.
b. Using 19x3 as the base year, compute an index-number trend series for:
   (1)   Sales.
   (2)   Cost of goods sold.
   (3)   Gross margin.
   (4)   Marketing and administrative costs.
   (5)   Net income.
c. Based on your above analyses, would you advise the bank to grant the loan? Write a brief report giving the reasons for your recommendation.

17–23   Comprehensive Problem—Part 2: Investor Ratios

Refer to the data in Problem 17–23. One of the current shareholders of the Telly Manufacturing Company approaches you with an offer to sell you 4,000 shares of common stock at $20 per share, the current (19x5) market price per share. The market price for 19x4 was $18 per share.

As part of your analysis in evaluating the offer, you are able to ascertain that the following data are typical for investments of this kind:

Return on total assets	10%
Return on common stockholders' equity	18%
Price-earnings ratio	12%
Dividend payout ratio	30%
Dividend yield ratio	5%

Required *a.* Compute the following for the years 19x4 and 19x5:
   (1)   Return on total assets.
   (2)   Return on common stockholders' equity.
   (3)   Earnings per share.
   (4)   Price-earnings ratio.
   (5)   Dividend payout ratio.
   (6)   Dividend yield ratio.
b. Is the financial leverage positive or negative for 19x5? 19x4? Explain each answer.
c. Based on your above analysis, do you plan to accept the offer? Explain.

17–24   Comprehensive Problem—Part 3: Year-to-Year Changes and Common-Size Statements

Refer to the data in Problem 17–23. The president of the Telly Manufacturing Company requests you to assist him in analyzing certain aspects of the firm's 19x4 and 19x5 financial statements.

Required *a.* For 19x4 and 19x5, prepare the balance sheets and income statements showing the year-to-year changes in both dollars and percent. Use 19x4 as the base period.

b. For 19x4 and 19x5, prepare the balance sheets and income statements in common-size format.

c. Write a brief report summarizing any significant information revealed by your analysis.

17–25   Computation of Primary EPS and Fully Diluted EPS

The Preston Company showed the following for 19x8:

Income before extraordinary item	$800,000
Extraordinary item—casualty loss	
(net after taxes)	200,000
Net income for period	$600,000

At January 1, 19x8, there were 210,000 shares of common stock outstanding. On October 1, 19x8, an additional 60,000 shares were sold for cash.

In 19x4, 8 percent bonds were issued at par, $2 million. These are convertible into 40,000 shares of common stock. None have been converted.

In 19x2, 35,000 shares of $8 cumulative preferred stock were issued at par, $100. Each preferred share is convertible into four shares of common stock. None have been converted.

Assume an income tax rate of 40 percent.

Required   a. Calculate primary earnings per share. (Round to the nearest cent.)

b. Calculate fully diluted earnings per share. (Round to the nearest cent.)

17–26   Computation of Primary EPS and Fully Diluted EPS

Foster, Inc., showed the following for 19x6:

Income before extraordinary item	$600,000
Extraordinary item—casualty loss (net after taxes)	100,000
Net income for period	$500,000

At January 1, 19x6, there were 190,000 shares of common stock outstanding. On October 1, 19x6, an additional 40,000 shares were sold for cash.

In 19x4, 6 percent bonds were issued at par, $1 million. These are convertible into 20,000 shares of common stock. None have been converted.

In 19x2, 25,000 shares of $3 cumulative preferred stock were issued at $90 per share. Each preferred share is convertible into two shares of common stock. None have been converted.

Assume an income tax rate of 40 percent.

Required   a. Calculate primary earnings per share.

b. Calculate fully diluted ernings per share.

17–27   Using Financial Leverage

A newly formed corporation, Katonah Company, was formed with an initial issuance of 20,000 shares of common stock with a par value of $10 per share for a total capitalization (in cash) of $200,000.

The firm will require another $200,000 to commence operations. The three principal stockholders each have a different plan for raising the needed $200,000. The plans are:

1. Stockholder R believes that the firm should sell 20,000 shares of stock to a limited group of individuals for $200,000.
2. Stockholder S believes that the firm should sell $200,000 of 12 percent preferred stock.
3. Stockholder T believes that the firm should borrow the $200,000 for 10 years at a 12 percent interest rate.

The firm expects to earn $80,000 annually from operations (before interest cost and income taxes). The firm's income tax rate will be 30 percent.

Required   *a.* For each of the three plans, compute:
(1)   The net income of the firm.
(2)   The return on common stockholders' equity.

b. Write a brief report to the stockholders indicating which plan you believe they should adopt and explain why each plan produces a different return on common stockholders' equity.

17–28   Preparation of Financial Statements from Given Ratios and Selected Miscellaneous Data

Argo Sales Corporation has in recent prior years maintained the following relationships among the data on its financial statements:

1. Gross profit rate on net sales 40%
2. Net profit rate on net sales 10%
3. Rate of marketing costs to net sales 20%
4. Accounts receivable turnover . . . . 8 per year
5. Inventory turnover . . . . 6 per year
6. Acid-test ratio . . . . 2 to 1
7. Current ratio . . . . 3 to 1
8. Quick-asset composition: 8% cash, 32% marketable securities, 60% accounts receivable
9. Asset turnover (sales ÷ total assets) . . . . 2 per year
10. Ratio of total assets to intangible assets . . . . 20 to 1
11. Ratio of accumulated depreciation to cost of fixed assets . . . . . . 1 to 3
12. Ratio of accounts receivable to accounts payable . . . . 1.5 to 1
13. Ratio of working capital to stockholders' equity . . . . 1 to 1.6
14. Ratio of total debt to stockholders' equity . . . . 1 to 2

The corporation had a net income of $120,000 for 19x8 which resulted in earnings of $5.20 per share of common stock. Additional information includes the following:

1. Capital stock authorized, issued (all in 19x0), and outstanding:
Common, $10 per share par value, issued at 10% premium
Preferred, 6% nonparticipating, $100 per share par value, issued at a 10% premium
2. Market value per share of common at December 31, 19x8: $78
3. Preferred dividends paid in 19x8: $3,000
4. Times interest earned in 19x8: 33
5. The amounts of the following were the same at December 31, 19x8, as at January

1, 19x8: inventory, accounts receivable, 5% bonds payable—long term, and total stockholders' equity

6. All purchases and sales were "on account."

Required

a. Prepare in good form the condensed (1) balance sheet and (2) income statement for the year ending December 31, 19x8, presenting the amounts you would expect to appear on Argo's financial statements (ignoring income taxes). Major captions appearing on Argo's balance sheet are: current assets, fixed assets, intangible assets, current liabilities, long-term liabilities, and stockholders' equity. In addition to the accounts divulged in the problem, you should include accounts for prepaid costs, accrued liabilities, and administrative costs.

b. Compute the following for 19x8 (show your computations):

(1) Rate of return on common stockholders' equity.
(2) Price-earnings ratio for common stock.
(3) Dividends paid per share of common stock.
(4) Dividends paid per share of preferred stock.
(5) Dividend yield on common stock.

(AICPA adapted)

INDEX

This book has been set VideoComp in 10 and 9 point Times Roman, leaded 2 points. Part and chapter numbers are 18 point Helvetica Bold and 72 point Helvetica Extra Bold. Part and chapter titles are 20 point Helvetica Bold. The size of the type page is 36 by 48 picas.